D0022863

SECOND EDITION

Fundamentals of Investments

SECOND EDITION

Fundamentals of Investments

Gordon J. Alexander

University of Minnesota

William F. Sharpe

Stanford University

Jeffery V. Bailey

Richards & Tierney, Inc.

Prentice Hall, Englewood Cliffs, New Jersey

Library of Congress Cataloging-in-Publication Data

Alexander, Gordon J.
Fundamentals of investments / by Gordon J. Alexander, William F. Sharpe, Jeffery V. Bailey. — 2nd ed.
p. cm.
Includes bibliographical references and index.
ISBN 0-13-335449-0
1. Investments. I. Sharpe, William F. II. Bailey, Jeffery V. III. Title.
HG4521.A419 1993
332.6–dc20 92-20869
CIP

Acquisition Editor: Leah Jewell
Production Editor: Lisa Kinne
Marketing Manager: Patti Arneson
Copy Editor: Eleanor Walter
Designer: Meryl Poweski
Cover Designer: Meryl Poweski
Prepress Buyer: Trudy Pisciotti
Manufacturing Buyer: Patrice Fraccio
Supplements Editor: David Shea
Editorial Assistant: Eileen Deguzman
Production Assistant: Renee Pelletier
Cover Art: Dome over the feature court at Square One Mall, Mississauga, Ontario, Canada. Owned and operated by Hammerson Canada Inc. Photograph courtesy of Shin Shugino/Taylor & Browning Assoc.

A Paramount Communications Company
Englewood Cliffs, New Jersey 07632

Printed in the United States of America
10 9 8 7 6 5 4

ISBN 0-13-335449-0

Prentice-Hall International (UK) Limited, *London*
Prentice-Hall of Australia Pty., Limited, *Sydney*
Prentice-Hall Canada Inc., *Toronto*
Prentice-Hall Hispanoamericana, S.A., *Mexico*
Prentice-Hall of India, Private Limited, *New Delhi*
Prentice-Hall of Japan, Inc., *Tokyo*
Simon & Schuster Asia Pte. Ltd., *Singapore*
Editora Prentice-Hall do Brasil, Ltda., *Rio de Janeiro*

To my mother and in memory of my father
GJA

To Kathy
WFS

To Ann
JVB

Contents

6 Inflation 115

PART THREE MODERN PORTFOLIO THEORY

7 The Portfolio Selection Problem 137

8 Efficient Sets 153

9 Riskfree Lending and Borrowing 193

10 The Capital Asset Pricing Model 217

11 Factor Models 241

12 Arbitrage Pricing Theory 259

PART FOUR COMMON STOCKS

13 Characteristics of Common Stocks 279

14 Financial Analysis of Common Stocks 335

15 Dividend Discount Models 381

16 Dividends and Earnings 419

17 Investment Management 463

18 Portfolio Performance Evaluation 487

PART FIVE
FIXED-INCOME SECURITIES

Preface

Writing a textbook is never easy. For a subject as diverse as investments, the task is particularly difficult. The undisciplined writer could fill volumes and never finish. How does an author best go about organizing the many topics that constitute the field of investments? We chose to start by establishing a basic set of principles that would guide our development of Fundamentals of Investments.

We sincerely believe that the serious student of investments, even a neophyte undergraduate, should acquire a balanced knowledge of both investment theory and practice. Granted, someone desiring only an introductory exposure to investment practice could get by with a minimal discussion of theory and focus almost exclusively on institutional details and personal finance applications. That approach, however, would leave the student unable to appreciate the many subtle and important issues faced daily by the investment professional.

We have structured Fundamentals to present students taking their first course in investments with the basic building blocks of modern investment thought. While the text is meant to present a thorough discussion of investments, we have constantly tried to remain faithful to three principles:

1. Keep the material practical and relevant.
2. Make the text easy to comprehend.
3. Design the text to permit a modular use by instructors.

First, we have written Fundamentals to give students a working knowledge of the financial instruments available to investors and the ways in which markets for these instruments operate. We have avoided tangential discussions of issues not germane to the primary subject at hand. Second, we want the text to be accessible to students unfamiliar with investments. Therefore, we have tried to write in a clear, concise style, keeping mathematical notation to a minimum, and including numerous examples to explain the concepts presented. Finally, we want instructors to be able to use the text in a modular fashion. While we have organized the text in what we believe to be a logical order, some instructors may wish to change that order or skip over certain sections entirely. The organization of the text accommodates such preferences.

This is the second edition of Fundamentals. As any textbook author will attest, a previous work can always be improved. After the first edition was published, we received many helpful suggestions from instructors and reviewers regarding ways in which we could make Fundamentals better. In response, we have made a number of changes that we believe substantially enhance Fundamentals in terms of our goals of practicality, ease of comprehension, and flexibility. Specifically, the second edition contains the following differences from the first:

- More international content. The globalization of investments is occurring at a rapid pace. It is imperative that students become familiar with an increasingly broad array of international investing concepts. Chapter 26 deals directly with international investing. Moreover, throughout the text, we have considerably expanded the discussions of data and research on international securities and security markets.
- Expanded coverage of options and futures. The use of these types of securities has increased dramatically in just the last few years. Accordingly, Chapters 24 and 25 have been extended in order to more fully present the basic concepts behind them.
- Updated material. Where appropriate, we have updated the text to keep students abreast of the latest developments in investments. We have revised tables and graphs to incorporate current information. Further, we have added discussions of recent important academic research.
- Additional end-of-chapter problems. We have roughly doubled the number of questions and problems at the end of each chapter.
- CFA examination questions. To give students a sense of some of the knowledge required of certified investment professionals, we have added questions from recent Chartered Financial Analyst examinations, where appropriate.
- Answers to selected problems. Students often wish to know if they are working in the right direction when solving end-of-chapter problems. At the end of the text, we have included answers to selected problems.
- Redesigned chapter summaries. To facilitate a quick review of a chapter's highlights, we have rewritten each chapter's summary in a point-by-point format.
- *Money Matters* topical discussions. Students typically want to know how concepts presented in the text are applied in the "real world." In each chapter, we have added a feature entitled *Money Matters* that offers light and stimulating discussions of issues ranging from portfolio optimizers to insider trading.

- Annotated references. For those students interested in further study of subjects presented in the text, at the end of each chapter we have included a detailed set of references organized by topic.
- New co-author. Jeff Bailey, who contributed to the first edition, is now a co-author. Jeff is a full-time practitioner in the field of investments and has brought a wealth of knowledge about how things are done "in the trenches."

Many people ask us how Fundamentals differs from Investments. After all, Investments has been one of the most successful finance textbooks published. Why another version of such a popular text?

Both Fundamentals and Investments are comprehensive, covering the major aspects and theories of investing, while avoiding excessive detail. Further, both books contain similar features, such as a glossary of terms introduced in the text, and both books offer an instructor's manual and investment software.

Investments, however, is written primarily for students who have stronger backgrounds in economics, statistics, and accounting. We felt that most students in their first investments course could benefit from a textbook designed to provide a less theoretical and technical approach to investments. Therefore, while we have not ignored the quantitative nature of modern investment theory and practice, we have considerably reduced the mathematical content from that contained in Investments. Moreover, we have organized Fundamentals in a modular fashion, unlike Investments, where the presentation style is more integrated.

Fundamentals contains a wealth of teaching aids that we believe instructors will find valuable. The terms highlighted within the text and listed at the end of each chapter help emphasize important concepts. The Glossary allows students to quickly reference terms listed earlier in the text, thereby creating a continuity of concepts across chapters. The point-by-point chapter summaries permit students to easily identify essential thoughts developed in each chapter.

We are particularly proud of the *Money Matters* articles presented in each chapter. Specifically written for Fundamentals, these articles are designed to give students a sense of how various investment issues and techniques are approached by practitioners. For example, the *Money Matters* in Chapter 2 shows how short selling is used by hedge fund managers. Chapter 18 discusses custom benchmark portfolios—a sophisticated performance evaluation tool that is gaining increasing attention. Chapter 26 considers the controversial issue of whether to hedge a foreign investment portfolio. We believe that the *Money Matters* articles will provide both interesting reading for the students and a stimulating source of classroom discussion material.

An extended supplements package also accompanies Fundamentals. Included in this package are:

- Instructor's Manual. Solutions to all end-of chapter problems are presented in a thorough and well-explained fashion. Also, a set of course outlines designed to accommodate a variety of teaching approaches is presented.
- Tutorial Software. Robert Ritchey of Texas Tech University has developed software to give students a means of applying various concepts presented in Fundamentals. Students can test the sensitivity of a bond's

price to various yield and term-to-maturity assumptions or apply the Black-Scholes model to option pricing. Selected end-of-chapter problems are also available for analysis. The software operates under Lotus 1-2-3.

- Test Item File and Prentice Hall DataManager. The Test Item File gives an instructor access to hundreds of exam questions (true/false, multiple choice, and problems) and their solutions. The Prentice Hall DataManager facilitates classroom management with a computer-assisted test design system and an electronic gradebook.
- Investment Analysis Software. Investment software systems from both Disclosure Information Service and Value Line give students personal computer access to a wide range of individual company financial and market data. Students can identify stocks using customized selection criteria and can design their own portfolios. They can also create data files compatible with popular spreadsheet programs such as Lotus 1-2-3 and Excel.

Many people have assisted us in preparing the second edition of this book, and we would like to acknowledge them as well as those who helped us with the first edition. We would like to thank Seth Anderson, Ann Bailey, Jeffrey Born, James Conley, Thomas Eyssell, Joseph Finnerty, Robert Jennings, Linda Kramer, Jaroslaw Komarynsky, K.C. Ma, S. Maheswaran, Carl McGowan, Ronald Melicher, Tom Nohel, Thomas O'Brien, Sailesh Ramamurtie, Anthony Sanders, Arlene Spiegel, Leonard Washko, and J. Kenton Zumwalt for their help at various stages in preparing this book for publication. We are also especially grateful for the efforts of five people at Prentice Hall: Acquisition Editor, Leah Jewell; Copy Editor, Eleanor Walter; Production Editor, Lisa Kinne; Designer, Meryl Poweski; and Marketing Manager, Patti Arneson.

We learned much by writing this book, and hope that you will learn much by reading it. While we believe that the book is free of errors of any sort, experience tells us that this might not be the case. Thus, we encourage those with constructive comments to send them to us.

GJA
WFS
JVB

PART I
INTRODUCTION

1 Introduction

THE INVESTMENT ENVIRONMENT
▪ Securities ▪ Security Markets
Money Matters: In Search Of Past Performance
▪ Financial Intermediaries
THE INVESTMENT PROCESS
▪ Investment Policy ▪ Security Analysis ▪ Portfolio Construction
▪ Portfolio Revision ▪ Portfolio Performance Evaluation
Money Matters: Investments As A Career
THE INVESTMENT INDUSTRY
SUMMARY
KEY TERMS
QUESTIONS AND PROBLEMS
REFERENCES

This book is about investing in marketable securities. Accordingly, it focuses on the investment environment and process. The **investment environment** includes the kinds of marketable securities that exist and where and how they are bought and sold. The **investment process** is concerned with how an investor should proceed in making decisions about what marketable securities to invest in, how extensive the investments should be, and when the investments should be made. Before discussing the investment environment and process in more detail, the term **investment** will be described.

investment environment
investment process
investment

Investment, in its broadest sense, means the sacrifice of current dollars for future dollars. Two different attributes are generally involved: time and risk. The sacrifice takes place in the present and is certain. The reward comes later, if at all, and the magnitude is generally uncertain. In some cases the element of time predominates (for example, government bonds). In other cases risk is the dominant attribute (for example, call options on common stocks). In yet others, both time and risk are important (for example, shares of common stock).

A distinction is often made between investment and **savings.** Savings is defined as forgone consumption; investment is restricted to "real" investment of the sort that increases national output in the future. While this definition may prove useful in other contexts, it is not especially helpful here. However, it is useful to make a distinction between real and financial investments.

savings

Real investments generally involve some kind of tangible asset, such as land, machinery, or factories. **Financial investments** involve contracts writ-

real investments
financial investments

ten on pieces of paper, such as common stocks and bonds. In primitive economies most investment is of the real variety. However, in a modern economy, much investment is of the financial variety. Highly developed institutions for financial investment greatly facilitate real investment. By and large, the two forms of investment are complementary, not competitive.

The financing of an apartment house provides a good example. Apartments are sufficiently tangible ("bricks and mortar") to be considered real investment. But where do the resources come from to pay for the land and the construction of the apartments? Some may come from direct investment: for example, a wealthy doctor who wants to build the apartment house may use some of his or her own money to finance the project. The rest of the resources may be provided by a mortgage. In essence, someone loans money to the doctor, with repayment promised in fixed amounts on a specified schedule over many years. In the typical case the "someone" is not a person but an institution acting as a financial intermediary. Thus, the doctor has made a real investment in the apartment house, and the institution has made a financial investment in the doctor.

primary market

secondary market

For a second example, consider what happens when General Motors finds itself in need of money to pay for plant construction. This real investment may be financed by the sale of new common stock in the **primary market** for securities. The common stock itself represents a financial investment to the purchasers, who may subsequently trade these shares in the **secondary market** (for example, on the New York Stock Exchange). While transactions in the secondary market do not generate money for General Motors, the fact that such a market exists makes the common stock more attractive and thus facilitates real investment. Investors would pay less for new shares of common stock if there were no way to subsequently sell them quickly and inexpensively.

These examples have introduced the three main elements of the investment environment—securities (also known as financial investments or financial assets), security markets (also known as financial markets), and financial intermediaries (also known as financial institutions). They will be discussed in more detail next.

THE INVESTMENT ENVIRONMENT

Securities

When someone borrows money from a pawnbroker, he or she must leave some item of value as security. Failure to repay the loan (plus interest) means that the pawnbroker can sell the pawned item to recover the amount of the loan (plus interest) and perhaps make a profit. The terms of the agreement are recorded via pawn tickets. When a college student borrows money to buy a car, the lender usually holds formal title to the car until the loan is repaid. In the event of default, the lender can repossess the car and sell it to recover his or her costs. In this case the official certificate of title, issued by the state, serves as the security for the loan.

When someone borrows money for a vacation, he or she may simply sign a piece of paper promising repayment with interest. The loan is unsecured in the sense that there is no collateral, meaning no specific asset has been promised to the lender in the event of default. In such a situation, the lender would have to take the borrower to court to try to recover the amount of the loan. Only a piece of paper called a promissory note stands as evidence of such a loan.

When a firm borrows money, it may or may not offer collateral. For example, some loans may be secured (backed) with specific pieces of property (buildings, equipment, and so on). Such loans are recorded by means of mortgage bonds, which indicate the terms of repayment and the particular assets pledged to the lender in the event of default. However, it is much more common for a corporation to simply pledge all of its assets, perhaps with some provision for the manner in which the division will take place in the event of default. Such a promise is known as a debenture bond.

Finally, a firm may promise a right to share in the firm's profits in return for an investor's funds. Nothing is pledged, and no irrevocable promises are made. The firm simply pays whatever its directors deem reasonable from time to time. However, to protect against serious malfeasance, the investor is given the right to participate in the determination of who will be members of the board of directors. His or her property right is represented by a share of common stock, which can be sold to someone else who will then be able to exercise that right. The holder of common stock is said to be an *owner* of the corporation and can, in theory, exercise control over its operation through the board of directors.

In general, only a piece of paper represents the investor's rights to certain prospects or property and the conditions under which he or she may exercise those rights. This piece of paper, serving as evidence of property rights, is called a security. It may be transferred to another investor and with it go all its rights and conditions. Thus, everything from a pawn ticket to a share of GM common stock is a security. Hereafter the term **security** will be used to refer to *a legal representation of the right to receive prospective future benefits under stated conditions*. The primary task of security analysis is to identify mispriced securities by determining these prospective future benefits, the conditions under which they will be received, and the likelihood of such conditions.

security

By and large the focus here will be on securities that may be easily and efficiently transferred from one owner to another. Thus, the concern will be with common stocks and bonds rather than with pawn tickets, although much of the material in this book applies to all three types of instruments.

Figure 1-1 and Table 1-1 show the year-by-year results obtained from investing in four types of securities over the sixty-five-year period from 1926 through 1990. In each case the percentage change in a hypothetical investor's wealth from the beginning to the end of the year is shown. This amount, known as the **rate of return** (or simply the *return*), is calculated as follows:

rate of return

$$\text{return} = \frac{\text{end-of-period wealth} - \text{beginning-of-period wealth}}{\text{beginning-of-period wealth}}. \qquad (1.1)$$

In calculating the return on a security, it can be assumed that the investor purchased one unit of the security (for example, one bond or one share of common stock) at the beginning of the period. The cost of such an investment would be the value entered in the denominator of equation (1.1). Then, the value in the numerator is the answer to a simple question—how much better (or worse) off is the investor at the end of the period if, hypothetically speaking, this investment had been made at the beginning of the period?

For example, assume that Widget Corporation's common stock was selling for \$40 per share at the beginning of 1991 and for \$45 at the end of 1991

FIGURE 1-1
Annual Returns, 1926–1990
Source: Ibbotson Associates, Inc., *Stocks, Bonds, Bills, and Inflation 1991 Yearbook* (Chicago: 1991). All rights reserved.

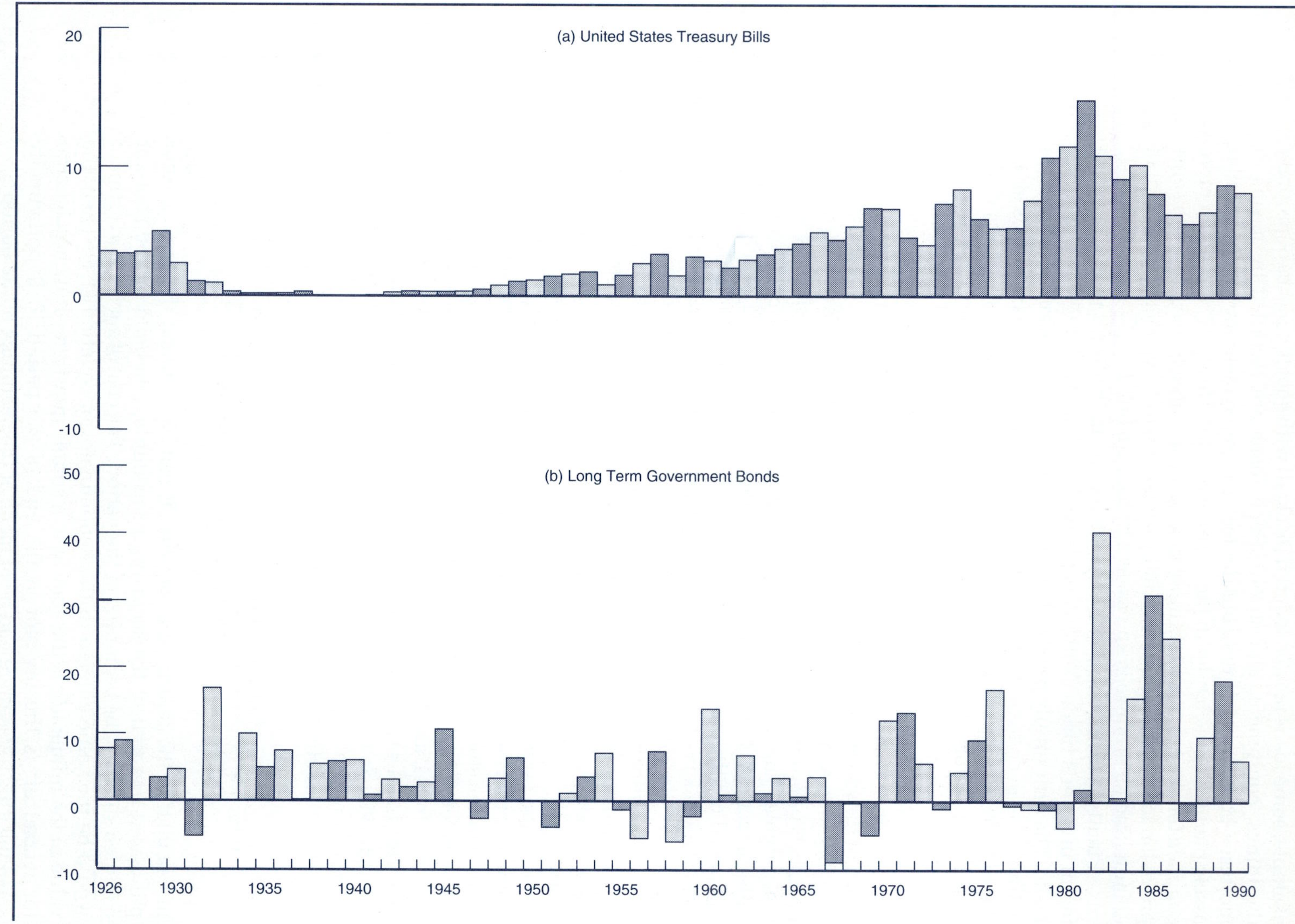

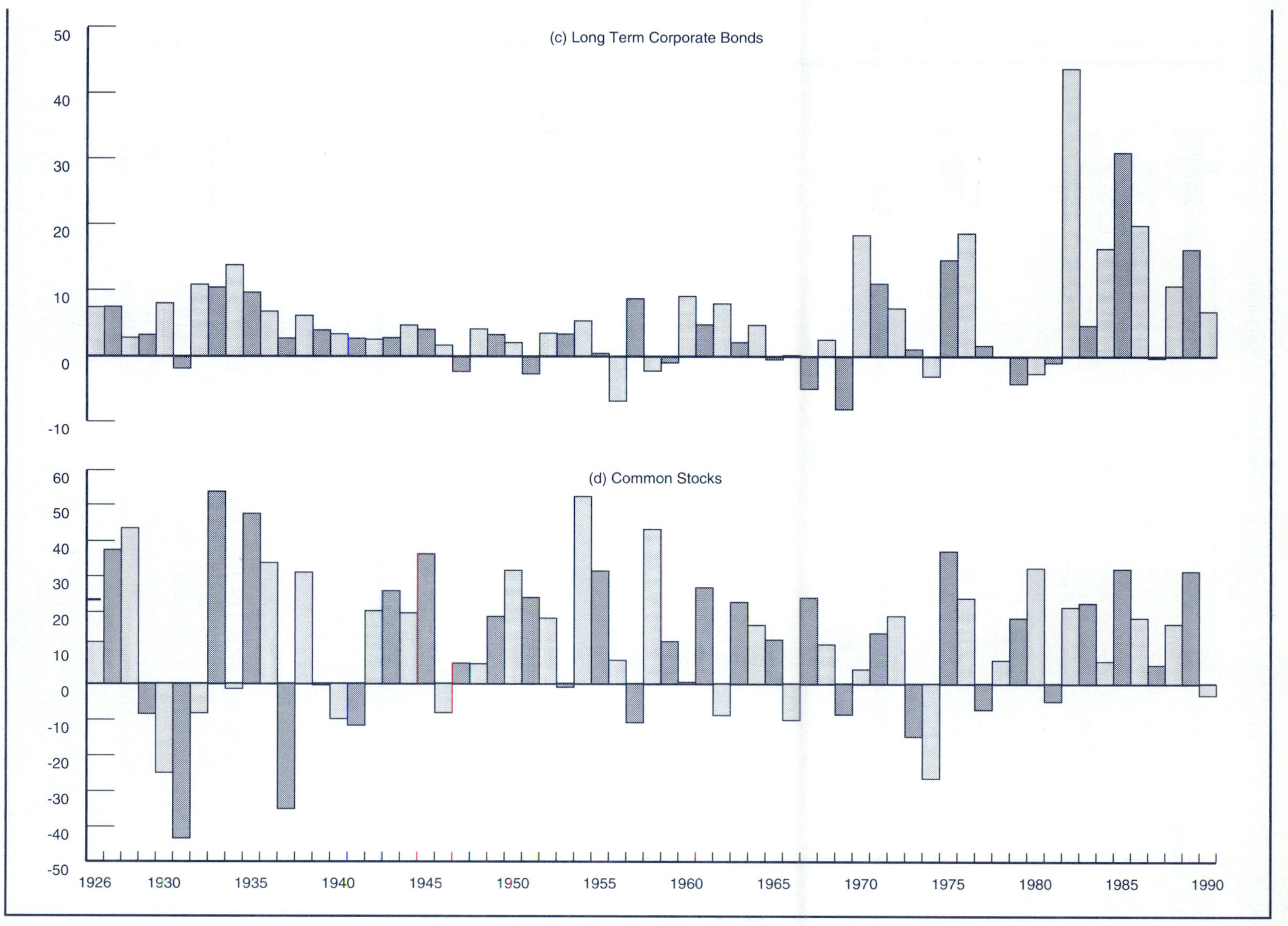
(c) Long Term Corporate Bonds
50
40
30
20
10
0
-10
(d) Common Stocks
60
50
40
30
20
10
0
-10
-20
-30
-40
-50
1926
1930
1935
1940
1945
1950
1955
1960
1965
1970
1975
1980
1985
1990

TABLE 1-1
Annual Returns: Stocks, Bonds, Treasury Bills, and Changes in the Consumer Price Index

TOTAL RETURNS

Year	Treasury Bills	Long-Term Government Bonds	Long-Term Corporate Bonds	Common Stocks	Change in CPI
1926	3.27%	7.77%	7.37%	11.62%	−1.49%
1927	3.12	8.93	7.44	37.49	−2.08
1928	3.24	0.10	2.84	43.61	−0.97
1929	4.75	3.42	3.27	−8.42	0.19
1930	2.41	4.66	7.98	−24.90	−6.03
1931	1.07	−5.31	−1.85	−43.34	−9.52
1932	0.96	16.84	10.82	−8.19	−10.30
1933	0.30	0.08	10.38	53.99	0.51
1934	0.16	10.02	13.84	−1.44	2.03
1935	0.17	4.98	9.61	47.67	2.99
1936	0.18	7.51	6.74	33.92	1.21
1937	0.31	0.23	2.75	−35.03	3.10
1938	−0.02	5.53	6.13	31.12	−2.78
1939	0.02	5.94	3.97	−0.41	−0.48
1940	0.00	6.09	3.39	−9.78	0.96
1941	0.06	0.93	2.73	−11.59	9.72
1942	0.27	3.22	2.60	20.34	9.29
1943	0.35	2.08	2.83	25.90	3.16
1944	0.33	2.81	4.73	19.75	2.11
1945	0.33	10.73	4.08	36.44	2.25
1946	0.35	−0.10	1.72	−8.07	18.17
1947	0.50	−2.63	−2.34	5.71	9.01
1948	0.81	3.40	4.14	5.50	2.71
1949	1.10	6.45	3.31	18.79	−1.80
1950	1.20	0.06	2.12	31.71	5.79
1951	1.49	−3.94	−2.69	24.02	5.87
1952	1.66	1.16	3.52	18.37	0.88
1953	1.82	3.63	3.41	−0.99	0.62
1954	0.86	7.19	5.39	52.62	−0.50
1955	1.57	−1.30	0.48	31.56	0.37
1956	2.46	−5.59	−6.81	6.56	2.86
1957	3.14	7.45	8.71	−10.78	3.02
1958	1.54	−6.10	−2.22	43.36	1.76
1959	2.95	−2.26	−0.97	11.96	1.50
1960	2.66	13.78	9.07	0.47	1.48
1961	2.13	0.97	4.82	26.89	0.67
1962	2.73	6.89	7.95	−8.73	1.22

and paid dividends of $3 per share during the year. The 1991 return on Widget would then be calculated as [($45 + $3) − $40]/$40 = .20 or 20%.[1]

Treasury Bills The first type of security listed in Figure 1-1 involves loaning money on a short-term basis to the U.S. Treasury Department. Such a loan carries little (if any) risk that payment will not be made as promised. Moreover, while the rate of return varies from period to period, at the beginning of any single period it is known with certainty. The return on these

[1]Generally, any cash received during the period is treated as if it were received at the end of the period. However, this treatment typically causes the actual return to be understated. For example, if the dividends on Widget were received at mid-year, the investor could have put them in a bank savings account and earned, say, 5% interest on them for the rest of the year. This interest then would have amounted to .05 × $3.00 = $.15, resulting in the annual return being equal to [($45 + $3 + $.15) − $40]/$40 = .20375 or 20.375%.

TABLE 1-1 Continued

	TOTAL RETURNS				
Year	Treasury Bills	Long-Term Government Bonds	Long-Term Corporate Bonds	Common Stocks	Change in CPI
1963	3.12	1.21	2.19	22.80	1.65
1964	3.54	3.51	4.77	16.48	1.19
1965	3.93	0.71	−0.46	12.45	1.92
1966	4.76	3.65	0.20	−10.06	3.35
1967	4.21	−9.19	−4.95	23.98	3.04
1968	5.21	−0.26	2.57	11.06	4.72
1969	6.58	−5.08	−8.09	−8.50	6.11
1970	6.53	12.10	18.37	4.01	5.49
1971	4.39	13.23	11.01	14.31	3.36
1972	3.84	5.68	7.26	18.98	3.41
1973	6.93	−1.11	1.14	−14.86	8.80
1974	8.00	4.35	−3.06	−26.47	12.20
1975	5.80	9.19	14.64	37.20	7.01
1976	5.08	16.75	18.65	23.84	4.81
1977	5.12	−0.67	1.71	−7.18	6.77
1978	7.18	−1.16	−0.07	6.58	9.03
1979	10.38	−1.22	−4.18	18.44	13.31
1980	11.24	−3.95	−2.62	32.42	12.40
1981	14.71	1.86	−0.96	−4.91	8.94
1982	10.54	40.36	43.79	21.41	3.87
1983	8.80	0.65	4.70	22.51	3.80
1984	9.85	15.48	16.39	6.27	3.95
1985	7.72	30.97	30.90	32.16	3.77
1986	6.16	24.53	19.85	18.47	1.13
1987	5.47	−2.71	−0.27	5.23	4.41
1988	6.35	9.67	10.70	16.81	4.42
1989	8.37	18.11	16.23	31.49	4.65
1990	7.81	6.18	6.78	−3.17	6.11
AVERAGE	3.72%	4.90%	5.51%	12.15%	3.25%
STANDARD DEVIATION	3.38%	8.53%	8.41%	20.80%	4.75%

Source: Ibbotson Associates, Inc., *Stocks, Bonds, Bills, and Inflation 1991 Yearbook* (Chicago: 1991).

investments, known as Treasury bills, ranged from a high of 14.71% per year (in 1981) to a low of virtually zero (in 1940) with an average value of 3.72% during the entire sixty-five-year period.

The second and third types of securities shown in Figure 1-1 involve the purchase of bonds, and thus also involve loaning money. Each type of bond represents a fairly long-term commitment on the part of the issuer (that is, the borrower) to the investor (that is, the lender). This commitment is to make cash payments each year (the coupon amount) up to some point in time (the maturity date) when a single final cash payment (the principal) will also be made. The amount for which such bonds can be bought and sold varies from time to time. Thus, while coupon payments are easily predicted, the end-of-period selling price of the security is quite uncertain at the beginning of the period, making it difficult to predict the return in advance.

Long-Term Bonds The second type of security (long-term government bonds) involves twenty-year loans to the U.S. Treasury Department, and is known as

Treasury bonds. The third type of security (long-term corporate bonds) involves twenty-year loans to high-quality U.S. corporations, and is simply referred to as corporate bonds. To date, both types of bonds had their highest annual return in 1982, reaching 40.35% for government bonds and 43.79% for corporate bonds. However, the lowest annual return was reached in different years. For government bonds, the lowest return occurred in 1967 (−9.19%) while the lowest return for corporate bonds was reached in 1969 (−8.09%). Note that on average, government bonds had a higher return than Treasury bills (4.90% > 3.72%) and corporate bonds had a higher return than government bonds (5.51% > 4.90%). Thus, while the second and third types of securities have considerable variability, on average they provide somewhat larger returns than Treasury bills.

Common Stocks The fourth and final type of security involves the purchase of a group of common stocks, each of which represents a commitment on the part of a corporation to periodically pay whatever its board of directors deems appropriate as a cash dividend. While the amount of cash dividends to be paid during the next year is subject to some uncertainty, it is relatively predictable. However, the amount for which a stock can be bought or sold varies considerably, making the annual return highly unpredictable. Figure 1-1 shows the return from a portfolio of stocks (currently 500 different firms) selected by Standard & Poor's Corporation to represent the average performance of common stocks. Returns ranged from an exhilarating 53.99% in 1933 to a depressing −43.34% in 1931, and averaged 12.15% per year over the entire period. Such investments can provide substantial returns, being even larger on average than the returns provided by corporate bonds. However, they also have substantial variability, being even more volatile than either type of long-term bond.

Table 1-1 provides year-by-year annual returns for the four types of securities shown in Figure 1-1. The table also includes the annual percentage change in the Consumer Price Index (CPI) as an indicator of variations in the cost of living. Average annual returns are shown at the bottom of the table. Below these values are the values of the standard deviations of annual returns, which serve as measures of the variability of the returns on the respective securities.[2] In addition, Table 1-2 provides average returns and standard deviations for Japanese and U.S. securities during the period from 1971 to 1987 (the latest year for which Japanese data are available). The historical record revealed in Figure 1-1, Table 1-1, and Table 1-2 illustrates a general principle: *when sensible investment strategies are compared with one another, risk and return tend to go together.* That is, securities that have higher average returns tend to have greater amounts of risk.

It is important to note that historical variability is not necessarily an indication of prospective risk. The former deals with the record over some past period; the latter has to do with uncertainty about the future. The pattern of returns on Treasury bills provides one example. Although the values have varied from period to period, in any given period the amount to be earned is known in advance and is thus riskless. On the other hand, the annual return on a common stock is very difficult to predict. For such an investment,

---

[2]Standard deviation was calculated as being equal to the square root of $\sum_{t=1}^{65} (r_t - \bar{r})^2/64$, where r_t is the return for year t ($t = 1$ corresponds to 1926, $t = 2$ to 1927, and so on) and $\bar{r}$ is the average return over the sixty-five-year period. A larger standard deviation means a greater amount of dispersion in the sixty-five returns, and hence indicates more risk.

TABLE 1-2
Summary Statistics for Japanese and U.S. Securities, 1971–1987

	AVERAGE RETURN		STANDARD DEVIATION	
	Japan	U.S.	Japan	U.S.
Short-Term Interest Rates	7.10%	7.72%	2.47%	2.89%
Long-Term Government Bonds	8.71	8.95	5.93	12.96
Long-Term Corporate Bonds	9.24	9.35	5.52	13.34
Common Stocks	22.87	12.02	25.80	17.50
Inflation	5.98	6.53	5.77	3.67

Source: Adapted from Ibbotson Associates, Inc., *Stocks, Bonds, Bills, and Inflation 1991 Yearbook* (Chicago: 1991). All rights reserved. Yasushi Hamao, "A Standard Data Base for the Analysis of Japanese Securities Markets," *Journal of Business*, 64, no. 1 (January 1991), p. 101.

variability in the past may provide a fairly good measure of the uncertainty surrounding the future return.[3]

To see how difficult it is to predict common stock returns, cover the portion of Table 1-1 from 1941 on, and then try to guess the return in 1941. Having done this, uncover the value for 1941 and try to guess the return for 1942. Proceed in this manner a year at a time, keeping track of your overall predictive accuracy. Unless you are very clever or very lucky, you will conclude that the past pattern of stock returns provides little help in predicting the next year's return. It will be seen that this is a characteristic of an **efficient market**—that is, a market where security prices reflect information immediately. At this stage, it is enough to indicate that the past variability of stock returns can be taken as a rough approximation of future risk.

efficient market

Is one of these four types of securities obviously "the best"? No. To oversimplify, the right security or combination of securities depends on the ultimate beneficiary's situation and preferences for return relative to his or her distaste for risk. There may be "right" or "wrong" securities for a particular person or purpose. But it would be surprising indeed to find a security that is clearly wrong for everyone and every purpose. Such situations are simply not present in an efficient market.

Security Markets

Security markets exist in order to bring together buyers and sellers of securities, meaning they are mechanisms created to facilitate the exchange of financial assets. There are many ways in which they can be distinguished. One way has already been mentioned—primary and secondary financial markets. Here the key distinction was whether or not the securities were being offered for sale by the issuer. Interestingly, the primary market itself can be subdivided into seasoned and unseasoned new issues. A seasoned new issue refers to the offering of an additional amount of an already existing security, while an unseasoned new issue involves the initial offering of a security to the public. Unseasoned new issues are often referred to as initial public offerings, or ipo's.

Another way of distinguishing security markets involves the life span of financial assets. **Money markets** typically involve financial assets that have a

money markets

[3]Studies have found that (1) stocks have not become more volatile recently, and (2) stocks have tended to be more volatile during recessions (particularly during the Great Depression of 1929 to 1939).

MONEY MATTERS
In Search of Past Performance

"Those who do not remember the past are condemned to repeat it," asserts a famous maxim. From the investor's perspective, those words of wisdom might be rephrased as, "Those who do not remember the past are condemned to invest unwisely."

Developing a basic knowledge of past security markets performance is not simply an exercise in cocktail party conversation trivia. Rather, that knowledge is a critical element in many phases of the investment process. Perhaps most importantly, it permits the investor to recognize and profit from the relationship between risk taking and economic reward inherent in the structure of security markets.

From a theoretical perspective, the existence of this risk-return trade-off is central to models of asset pricing (see Chapters 10 and 12). From a more practical perspective, an investor should understand the nature of the relationship between investment risk and return if he or she is to allocate his or her funds among various asset classes optimally over the long run, consistent with his or her level of risk tolerance (see Chapter 17). Moreover, to effectively evaluate the success of an investment program, an investor must be capable of placing absolute results in the context of the risk-return characteristics of that investment program (see Chapter 18).

Despite the importance of security markets performance data, the availability of comprehensive historical performance information is relatively new. Even today, continuing efforts notwithstanding, the past performance of many asset classes in which investors place large sums of money—such as commodities, real estate, and foreign stocks and bonds—is relatively unknown.

Historical performance data on U.S. security markets became widely available to investors with the work of Ibbotson and Sinquefield (I&S) in the late 1970s. Prior to the I&S research, only a few narrowly focused studies concerning interest rates and stock prices had been conducted in the U.S. and Europe. The I&S research brought together returns on U.S. stocks, bonds, Treasury bills, and inflation. Their study, the results of which are summarized and discussed in this chapter, directly compared the performance of the U.S. security markets and quantified the risk premiums earned by investors in those markets.

The I&S research has had a number of important consequences for the investment profession.

1. The study was widely disseminated, reaching a broad audience of investment practitioners.
2. It permitted investors to attach hard numbers to previously held beliefs about the risk premiums earned in various asset classes and the correlation of returns between those asset classes.
3. It provided a rationale for investors, particularly large institutional investors such as pension funds, to increase their investments in equity assets.
4. It stimulated research into the past performance of nontraditional investments, including gold, real estate, and venture capital.

In the last several years, an increasing number of studies have appeared detailing the performance of foreign security markets. The growing popularity of foreign investing by individuals and institutional investors (see Chapter 26) has spurred the demand for information regarding the past performance of foreign markets. Research has been hampered in many countries by fragmented and nonautomated record-keeping procedures. Nevertheless, in the future investors can expect to have greater access to foreign security markets performance data, a development that will reinforce the trend toward the globalization of investments.

---

capital markets

life span of one year or less, while **capital markets** typically involve financial assets that have a life span of greater than one year. Thus, Treasury bills are traded in a money market and Treasury bonds are traded in a capital market.

Financial Intermediaries

Financial intermediaries, also known as financial institutions, are organizations that issue financial claims against themselves (meaning that they sell financial assets representing claims on themselves in return for cash) and use the proceeds from this issuance to purchase primarily the financial assets of others. Since financial claims simply represent the right-hand side of the balance sheet for an organization, the key distinction between financial intermediaries and other types of organizations involves what is on the left-hand side of the balance sheet.

For example, a typical commercial bank issues financial claims against itself in the form of debt (such as checking and savings accounts) and equity, but then again so does a typical manufacturing firm. However, looking at the assets held by a commercial bank reveals that most of the bank's money is invested in loans to individuals and corporations as well as in U.S. government securities such as Treasury bills, while the typical manufacturing firm has its money invested mostly in land, buildings, machinery, and inventory. Thus, the bank has invested primarily in financial assets, while the manufacturing firm has invested primarily in real assets. Accordingly, banks are classified as financial intermediaries and manufacturing firms are not. Other types of financial intermediaries include savings and loan associations, savings banks, credit unions, life insurance companies, mutual funds, and pension funds.

Financial intermediaries provide an indirect method for corporations to acquire funds. As shown in Figure 1-2(a), corporations can obtain funds directly from the general public by the use of the primary market, as mentioned earlier. Alternatively, they can obtain funds indirectly from the general public by using financial intermediaries, as shown in Figure 1-2(b). Here the corporation gives a security to the intermediary in return for funds; in turn, the intermediary acquires funds by allowing the general public to maintain such investments as checking and savings accounts with them.

Having made this introduction to the investment environment, we now turn to the investment process.

THE INVESTMENT PROCESS

As previously mentioned, the investment process describes how an investor should go about making decisions with regard to what marketable securities to invest in, how extensive the investment should be, and when the investment should be made. A five-step procedure for making these decisions forms the basis of the investment process:

1. Set investment policy,
2. Perform security analysis,

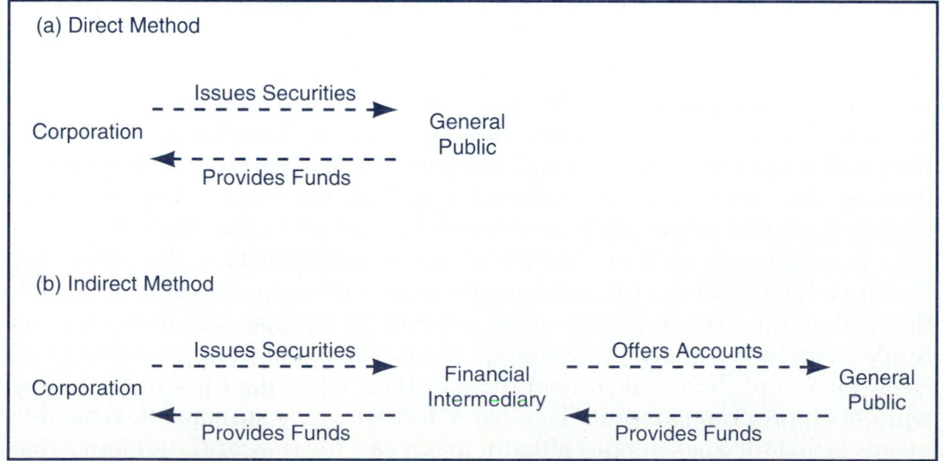

FIGURE 1-2
Corporate Funds Acquisition

3. Construct a portfolio,
4. Revise the portfolio, and
5. Evaluate the performance of the portfolio.

Investment Policy

investment policy

The initial step, setting **investment policy,** involves determining the investor's objectives and the amount of his or her investable wealth. Since there is a positive relationship between risk and return for sensible investment strategies, it is not appropriate for an investor to say that his or her objective is to "make a lot of money." What is appropriate for an investor in this situation is to state that the objective is to attempt to make a lot of money while recognizing there is some chance that large losses may be incurred. Thus, investment objectives should be stated in terms of both risk and return.

This step of the investment process concludes with identification of the potential categories of financial assets for consideration in the ultimate portfolio. This identification will be based on, among other things, the investment objectives, amount of investable wealth, and tax status of the investor. For example, as shall be seen later, usually it does not make sense for individual investors to purchase preferred stock or for tax-exempt investors (such as pension funds) to invest in tax-exempt securities like municipal bonds.

Security Analysis

security analysis

The second step of the investment process, performing **security analysis,** involves examining a number of individual securities (or groups of securities) within the broad categories of financial assets previously identified. One purpose in conducting such examinations is to identify those securities that currently appear to be mispriced. There are many approaches to security analysis. However, most of these approaches fall into one of two classifications. The first classification is known as **technical analysis;** those who utilize this approach to security analysis are known as technical analysts. The second classification is known as **fundamental analysis;** those who utilize it are known as fundamental analysts. In discussing these two approaches to security analysis, the focus at first will be on common stocks. Later they will be discussed in terms of other types of financial assets.

technical analysis

fundamental analysis

In its simplest form, technical analysis involves the study of stock market prices in an attempt to predict future price movements for the common stock of a particular firm. Initially, past prices are examined in order to identify recurring trends or patterns in price movements. Then, more recent stock prices are analyzed in order to identify emerging trends or patterns that are similar to past ones. This matching of emerging trends or patterns with past ones is done in the belief that these trends or patterns repeat themselves; thus, by identifying an emerging trend or pattern, the analyst will (allegedly) be able to predict future price movements for that particular stock.

Fundamental analysis begins with the assertion that the "true" (or "intrinsic") value of any financial asset is equal to the present value of all cash flows that the owner of the asset expects to receive. Accordingly, the fundamental stock analyst will attempt to forecast the timing and size of these cash flows, and then will convert them to their equivalent present value by using an appropriate discount factor and dividend discount model. What this means is that the analyst must attempt to forecast the stream of dividends that a particular stock will provide in the future, which is equivalent to forecasting the firm's earnings per share and payout ratios. Once the true value of the common stock of a particular firm has been determined, it is compared to the current market price of the common stock in order to see if the stock is fairly priced or not. Stocks that have a true value less than their current market price are known as overvalued or overpriced stocks, while those that have a true value greater than their current market price are known as undervalued or underpriced stocks. The magnitude of the difference between the true value and current market price is also important information, since the strength of the analyst's conviction that a given stock is mispriced will depend, in part, on it. Fundamental analysts believe that any notable cases of mispricing will be corrected by the market in the future, meaning that prices of undervalued stocks will show unusual appreciation and prices of overvalued stocks will show unusual depreciation.

Portfolio Construction

portfolio construction

The third step of the investment process, **portfolio construction,** involves identifying those specific assets in which to invest, as well as determining the proportions of the investor's wealth to put in each one. Here the issues of selectivity, timing, and diversification need to be addressed by the investor. **Selectivity,** also known as microforecasting, refers to security analysis and thus focuses on forecasting price movements of individual securities. **Timing,** also known as macroforecasting, involves the forecasting of price movements of common stocks in general relative to fixed-income securities, such as corporate bonds. **Diversification** involves constructing the investor's portfolio in a manner such that risk is minimized, subject to certain restrictions.

selectivity
timing
diversification

Portfolio Revision

portfolio revision

The fourth step of the investment process, **portfolio revision,** concerns the periodic repetition of the previous three steps. That is, over time the investor may change his or her investment objectives which, in turn, means that the currently held portfolio may no longer be optimal. Instead, perhaps a new portfolio should be formed by selling certain securities that are currently held and purchasing certain other ones that are not currently held. Another motivation for revising a given portfolio is that over time the prices of securities change, meaning that some securities that initially were not attractive may become attractive and others that were attractive at one time may no longer be so. Thus, the investor may want to add the former to his or her portfolio, while simultaneously deleting the latter. Such a decision will depend upon, among other things, the size of the transaction costs incurred in making these changes, as well as the magnitude of the perceived improvement in the investment outlook for the revised portfolio.

Portfolio Performance Evaluation

portfolio performance evaluation

The fifth step of the investment process, **portfolio performance evaluation,** involves periodically determining how the portfolio performed in terms of not only the return earned, but also the risk experienced by the investor. Thus, appropriate measures of return and risk, as well as relevant standards (or "benchmarks"), are needed.

MONEY MATTERS
Investments as a Career

From the novice investor to the prospective money manager, the study of investments offers a wealth of interesting and valuable information. In one way or another, investments touch all of our lives. Our contact with investing may be as simple as wanting to understand the investment options available to us in our employer's pension plan. Or we may choose to invest our own personal assets and want to know about buying and selling securities. Or we may be hoping to pursue an investment career and want to acquire a solid grounding in the workings of the security markets.

For those interested in making investments a career, the long-term outlook would appear bright. As shown in Table 1-3, employment in the industry has continued to grow faster than the overall economy. The industrywide downturn of the early 1990s has certainly been discomforting. Nevertheless, demographic factors imply that the investment industry will soon renew its upward trend. As the U.S. population continues to age, one can expect savings rates to rise and the demand for investment services to continue to grow.

Within the investment industry, there exists a wide range of career options. Using the outline of the investment industry shown in Table 1-3 as a starting point, those options are briefly discussed here.

Insurance Grouped together, insurance-related jobs constitute the largest sector within the investment industry. One can view the insurance sector as split into two components: the first part, the agents and brokers, delivers insurance products to individuals and businesses. The other part, the insurance companies, invests the funds generated by the premiums paid on the insurance products. The insurance companies' combined investment portfolios are worth trillions of dollars and are invested across a variety of asset types. The insurance industry employs thousands of security analysts and portfolio managers to invest these funds.

Banking The banking sector provides such traditional services as collecting deposits, providing access to deposited funds through check writing, and lending. Banks also provide custodial services to institutional investors (such as mutual funds and pension funds) and trust services to wealthy individuals. In this latter capacity, banks employ security analysts and portfolio managers to invest their clients' funds in the stock, bond, and money markets. In recent years, banks have moved aggressively to offer investment services such as discount brokerage to individual investors and underwriting services to a restricted clientele. Legal limitations on banks' involvement in the investment industry are being dismantled at an increasing rate. In the future both

THE INVESTMENT INDUSTRY

Government statisticians group a number of related occupations into an industry called "Finance, Insurance, and Real Estate." Table 1-3 shows the number of people employed in such occupations in recent years. As can be seen, the absolute and relative size of the industry has been increasing. In 1988 approximately one out of every sixteen nonagricultural workers dealt with investments, broadly defined. Some provide advice (and are thus known as **investment advisors**), some are in sales, some arrange transfers of property or securities from one investor to another, others manage investors' funds (they are known as **professional money managers**), and still others handle the record keeping in this most abstract and paper-oriented of industries.

investment advisors

professional money managers

money center and regional banks hope to become major participants in many financial services from which they have been excluded in the past. If so, investment-related employment at banks could increase significantly in the years ahead.

Security and Commodity Brokerages and Services The brokerage sector facilitates investors' purchases and sales of securities by providing investment advice, execution and processing of trades, record keeping, and market making. Brokerage firms also provide underwriting services to corporations and governmental organizations as well as portfolio management for institutions and individuals through mutual funds and separately managed accounts. These firms also trade for their own accounts in the domestic and foreign capital markets. Although it is the most lucrative and high-profile sector of the investment industry, the brokerage business is very cyclical and employment has taken wide swings in tandem with the profitability of the business.

Real Estate Persons working in the real estate sector engage in land acquisition, facilitating the financing and construction of residential and commercial properties, property management, and the purchase and sale of properties. The real estate industry exhibited strong growth in the early and mid-1980s. However, a severe downturn began in the late 1980s, caused in large part by the excesses of earlier years. How soon profitability and growth will return is uncertain at this time.

Other Investment Sectors Of particular interest are the investment occupations of pension fund administrators and pension consultants. Pension fund administrators oversee the management of corporate and public pension funds. These administrators set long-term investment policies for their pension funds, directly invest the pension assets or hire external investment managers to do so, and make funds available to the plan beneficiaries. Pension consultants offer specialized research and advice to pension funds on a wide range of pension and investment issues.

What type of training can best prepare one for a career in investments? There is no rigid formula. Most current entrants into the industry have received undergraduate degrees (although not necessarily in business) and many have earned or plan to soon acquire MBA degrees. The Chartered Financial Analyst (CFA) certification (see Chapter 14) has become an increasingly common requirement for advancement in the investment industry.

Despite these common denominators, the background of successful investors is quite varied, ranging from art history majors to nuclear physicists. Investing requires a blend of verbal, writing, math, and cognitive skills. In the last twenty years the investment industry has become more "quantitative" and computer-oriented. However, the need for "qualitative" skills—particularly intuition, insight, and initiative—remains critical.

TABLE 1-3 Number of Employees: Finance, Insurance, and Real Estate

EMPLOYER	NUMBER OF EMPLOYEES (thousands)						
	1960	1965	1970	1975	1980	1985	1988
Banking	673	792	1,044	1,274	1,571	1,706	1,738
Credit agencies, other than banks	261	327	360	432	570	750	898
Security and commodity brokerages and services	114	129	205	170	227	355	449
Insurance carriers	832	893	1,030	1,085	1,224	1,292	1,442
Insurance agents, brokers, and services	196	233	288	339	452	542	640
Real estate	517	569	661	748	981	1,132	1,295
Other finance, insurance, and real estate	76	80	57	117	135	180	216
Total	2,669	3,023	3,645	4,165	5,160	5,957	6,678
Employees in this industry as a percent of total employees in nonagricultural industries	4.92%	4.97%	5.14%	5.41%	5.71%	6.10%	6.32%

Source: U.S. Bureau of the Census, *Statistical Abstract of the United States* (Washington, D.C.), various editions.

SUMMARY

1. Because this book is about investing, it focuses on the investment environment and the investment process.

2. An investment involves the sacrifice of current dollars for future dollars.

3. Investments may be made in real or financial assets (securities) through either primary or secondary markets.

4. The primary task of security analysis is to identify mispriced securities by determining the prospective future benefits of owning those securities, the conditions under which those benefits will be received, and the likelihood of such conditions.

5. The rate of return on an investment measures the percentage change in the investor's wealth due to owning the investment.

6. Studies of the historical rates of return on various types of securities demonstrate that common stocks produce relatively high but variable returns. Bonds generate lower returns with less varibility. Treasury bills provide the lowest returns with the least variability.

7. In an efficient market, security prices reflect information immediately. Security analysis will not enable investors to earn abnormally high returns.

8. Security markets exist in order to bring together buyers and sellers of securities.

9. The investment process describes how an investor makes decisions about what securities in which to invest, how extensive these investments should be, and when they should be made.

10. The investment process involves five steps: set investment policy; perform security analysis; construct a portfolio; revise the portfolio; and evaluate portfolio performance.

11. While the investment industry is of modest importance relative to total employment figures, it has a profound impact on everyone's life.

KEY TERMS

investment environment
investment process
investment
savings
real investments
financial investments
primary market
secondary market
security
rate of return
efficient market
money markets
capital markets
investment policy
security analysis
technical analysis
fundamental analysis
portfolio construction
selectivity
timing
diversification
portfolio revision
portfolio performance evaluation
investment advisors
professional money managers

QUESTIONS AND PROBLEMS

1. Why don't secondary security markets generate capital for the issuers whose securities are traded in those markets?

2. Colfax Glassworks stock currently sells for \$36 per share. One year ago, the stock sold for \$33. The company recently paid a \$3 per share dividend. What was the rate of return for an investor in Colfax stock over the last year?

3. At the end of 1990, Ray Fisher decided to take \$50,000 in savings out of the bank and invest it in a portfolio of stocks and bonds; \$20,000 was placed into common stocks and \$30,000 into corporate bonds. A year later, at the end of 1991, Ray's stock and bond holdings were worth \$25,000 and \$23,000, respectively. \$1,000 in cash dividends was received on the stocks and \$3,000 in coupon interest payments was received on the bonds. (This stock and bond income was not reinvested in the portfolio.)

(a) What was the return on Ray's stock portfolio during 1991?
(b) What was the return on Ray's bond portfolio during 1991?
(c) What was the return on Ray's total portfolio during 1991?

4. Explain why the rate of return on an investment represents the investor's relative increase in wealth from that investment.
5. Why are Treasury bills considered to be a riskfree investment? In what way do investors bear risk when they own Treasury bills?
6. Why are corporate bonds riskier than U.S. government bonds?
7. Compare the distributions of returns for the four asset classes shown in Figure 1-1. Which asset class has offered the most consistent returns? The most variable returns? The greatest chance of gain? The least chance of gain?
8. In 1951, the Treasury Department and the Federal Reserve System came to an agreement known as the "Accord," whereby the Fed was no longer obligated to peg interest rates on Treasury securities. What was the average return and standard deviation on Treasury bills for the ten-year periods from 1942 to 1951 and from 1952 to 1961? From these data, does it appear that the Fed did indeed stop pegging interest rates?
9. Below is a table showing the annual returns on a portfolio of small stocks during the twenty-year period from 1971 to 1990. What is the average return and standard deviation of this portfolio? How do they compare with the 1971–1990 average return and standard deviation of the common stock portfolio whose annual returns are shown in Table 1-1?

1971:	16.50%	1976:	57.38%	1981:	13.88%	1986:	6.85%
1972:	4.43	1977:	25.38	1982:	28.01	1987:	−9.30
1973:	−30.90	1978:	23.46	1983:	39.67	1988:	22.87
1974:	−19.95	1979:	43.46	1984:	−6.67	1989:	10.18
1975:	52.82	1980:	39.88	1985:	24.66	1990:	−21.56

10. Does it seem reasonable that higher-return securities historically have exhibited higher risk? Why?
11. Describe how life insurance companies, mutual funds, and pension plans each act as financial intermediaries.
12. Why does it not make sense to establish an investment objective of "making a lot of money"?
13. What factors might an individual investor take into account in determining his or her investment policy?
14. Distinguish between technical and fundamental security analysis.

REFERENCES

1. A major source of historical returns on U.S. security markets is contained in either one of the two following references:

Robert G. Ibbotson and Rex A. Sinquefield, *Stocks, Bonds, Bills, and Inflation: The Past and the Future* (Charlottesville, Va.: Financial Analysts Research Foundation, 1983). Note that the Financial Analysts

Research Foundation has since been renamed the Research Foundation of the ICFA which can be contacted by calling (804)980-3647.

Ibbotson Associates, Inc., *Stocks, Bonds, Bills, and Inflation 1991 Yearbook* (Chicago: 1991). This annual yearbook of monthly and annual data can be purchased for $85 by calling (312)263-3435.

2. Comparable Japanese data for a more limited time period are presented in:

Yasushi Hamao, "A Standard Data Base for the Analysis of Japanese Security Markets," *Journal of Business*, 64, no. 1 (January 1991): 87–102.

3. The volatility of common stocks is examined in:

G. William Schwert, "Why Does Stock Market Volatility Change Over Time?" *Journal of Finance*, 44, no. 5 (December 1989): 1115–53.

Peter Fortune, "An Assessment of Financial Market Volatility: Bills, Bonds, and Stocks," *New England Economic Review*, (November/December 1989): 13–28.

4. For a discussion and analysis of U.S. common stock indices, see:

G. William Schwert, "Indexes of U.S. Stock Prices from 1802 to 1987," *Journal of Business*, 63, no. 3(July 1990): 399–426.

PART II
THE INVESTMENT ENVIRONMENT

2 Buying and Selling Securities

When a security is sold, many people are likely to be involved. Although it is possible for two investors to trade with each other directly, the usual transaction employs the services provided by brokers, dealers, and markets.

broker

A **broker** acts as an agent for an investor and is compensated via commission. Many individual investors deal with brokers in large retail or "wire" houses—firms with many offices that are connected by private wires with their own headquarters and, through the headquarters, with major markets. The people in these brokerage firms with prime responsibility for individual investors are termed **account executives** or **registered representatives.**

account executives
registered representatives

The institutional investors, such as commercial banks and pension funds, deal with these large retail brokerage firms and also with smaller firms that maintain only one or two offices and specialize in institutional business. Two other types of brokerage firms are **regional brokerage firms** and **discount brokers.** The former concentrate on transactions within a geographic area, meaning that the securities being traded have a special following in that area of the country. This may be because the issuers of the securities are located in that area. Discount brokers provide "bare-bones" services at low cost, meaning that they provide fewer services than "full-service" brokerage firms such as Merrill Lynch and Shearson Lehman Brothers. Investors who simply want to have their orders executed and do not seek advice can substantially reduce the commission they pay by using a discount broker.

regional brokerage firms
discount brokers

MONEY MATTERS
Discount Brokers

Your brother-in-law has his latest stock pick-to-click. Nirvana Corporation, he breathlessly informs you, is a sure double. For some reason, this time you believe him. However, never before having bought a stock, it suddenly dawns on you that you don't have the foggiest idea where to go to purchase this guaranteed jackpot winner. Vague memories of a TV commercial for a brokerage firm with a large bull as a mascot come to mind, but is this any way to make a decision?

While stretching things a bit, this story accurately points out that most amateur investors think only in terms of what to buy or sell. They often fail to recognize that who they trade through can have an important impact on the success of their investments, for commission costs constitute a surprisingly large fraction of their total investments and the commissions charged can vary dramatically among brokers.

We all know that investment returns are inherently uncertain. It only makes sense, therefore, to pay close attention to those aspects of an investment that we can control. Simply put, if a dollar of commissions can be saved, that dollar flows straight to the investor's bottom line.

In a survey conducted by *Fortune* magazine (March 16, 1987), a 200-share trade in a $20 stock (a $4,000 investment) could cost an investor between $25 and $115 in commissions, depending on the broker used. In percentage terms, those dollar costs translate into 0.625% and 2.875% of the investment, respectively. When one considers that professional investors who can consistently outperform the market indices on a risk-adjusted basis (see Chapter 18) by even 1% to 2% a year are rare, these levels of commission costs represent a heavy burden for the small investor.

To add insult to injury, after the May Day deregulation of commissions (discussed later in this chapter), commissions fell sharply for large institutional investors but actually rose for small investors. These costs have continued to climb in recent years. As a result, it definitely pays for the small investor to seek the lowest available commissions.

Brokers can be classified into two groups: full-service and discount. Full-service brokers, as the name implies, offer clients a wide range of financial services: investment research and advice, financial planning, home equity loans, life insurance, and cash management accounts, to mention only a few. Perhaps more importantly, clients receive the personal touch, with individual "account representatives" assigned to their accounts.

Conversely, discount brokers offer a relatively limited number of investment services. Deep-discount brokers focus on only one type of service; for example, simply executing stock trades cheaply and efficiently. Other discount brokers may provide a wider list of services, such as trading a full range of bonds (government, municipal, and corporate); trading options; and selling insurance, limited partnerships, and mutual funds. Customer contact with discount brokers is less personal than with full-service brokers, as salesmen are not assigned to client accounts.

In reality, the brokerage business is a continuum of services, ranging from the deep-discount brokers to the full-service brokers. Investors must weigh service against costs. That is, commission charges tend to vary directly with the level of service provided, with discount brokers of various types charging 20% to 90% less than the full-service brokers on small trades.

All brokers feature a number of common services. All are registered with the SEC and provide SIPC insurance, and most offer margin loans (discussed later in this chapter). Trade execution varies little in quality from one broker to another for small investors. Most small trades are handled automatically through the SuperDOT system (discussed later in this chapter), allowing little leeway for brokerage firms to distinguish themselves in executing these trades.

Which type of broker should you select? The factors to consider are highly personal. If you are the type of investor that knows precisely what securities to buy or sell, does his or her own research, requires no "hand-holding," and buys "plain vanilla" securities, then it makes little sense to pay the heavy commissions charged by a full-service broker. On the other hand, if you trade in uncommon securities—unlisted small stocks or foreign stocks, for example—or if you are an investing novice and want counseling and recommendations from your broker (with all the caveats attached to relying on a broker for investment advice), then it may pay for you to use a full-service broker.

---

commissions

An account executive's compensation is typically determined in large part by the **commissions** paid by his or her customers—an amount that is directly related to the amount of turnover (that is, trading) in an investor's account. This provides some temptation to recommend frequent changes in investors' holdings. Furthermore, since the commission rates on various types of investments differ, there is some temptation to recommend changes in those types of investments with the highest rates. In the long run, account executives who encourage excessive turnover (or "churning") will often lose customers and may even be subjected to lawsuits. Nonetheless, such behavior may be advantageous for them in the short run.

It is a simple matter to open an account with a brokerage firm: simply appear at (or call) the local office. An account executive will be assigned to you and will help you fill out some forms. After the initial forms have been signed, everything else can be done by mail or telephone. Transactions will be posted to your account as they would to a bank account. For example, you can deposit money, purchase securities using money from the account, and add the proceeds from security sales to the account. Brokers exist (and charge fees) to make security transactions as simple as possible. All that the investor has to do is to provide the broker with what is referred to here as **order specifications.**

order specifications

In discussing order specifications, it will be assumed that the investor's order involves common stock. In this situation the investor must specify:

1. The name of the firm,
2. Whether the order is to buy or sell shares,
3. The size of the order,
4. How long the order is to be outstanding, and
5. What type of order is to be used.

The last three specifications will be discussed next in more detail.

ORDER SIZE

In buying or selling common stock, the investor will place an order involving either a round lot, an odd lot, or both. Generally **round lot** means that the order is for 100 shares, or a multiple of 100 shares.[1] **Odd lot** orders generally are for 1 to 99 shares. Orders that are for more than 100 shares but are not a multiple of 100 should be viewed as a mixture of round and odd lots. Thus an order for 259 shares should be viewed as an order for two round lots and an odd lot of 59 shares.

round lot
odd lot

TIME LIMIT

The investor must specify a time limit on his or her order, meaning the time within which the broker should attempt to fill the order. For **day orders,** the broker will attempt to fill the order only during the day in which it was entered. If the order is not filled by the end of the day, then it is cancelled. If a time limit is not specified by the investor, the broker will treat an order as a day order. Week and month orders expire at the end of the respective calendar week and month during which they were entered, provided they have not been filled by then.

day orders

Open orders, also known as **good-till-cancelled** (or GTC) **orders,** remain

open orders
good-till-cancelled orders

[1]Occasionally a round lot is for less than 100 shares. When this happens, it is usually for stocks that are either high-priced or traded infrequently.

in effect until they are either filled or cancelled by the investor. However, during the time period before the order has been filled, the broker may periodically ask the investor to confirm the order. In contrast to GTC orders are **fill-or-kill orders,** also known as FOK orders. These orders are cancelled if the broker is unable to execute them immediately.

fill-or-kill orders
discretionary orders

Discretionary orders allow the broker to set the specifications for the order. The broker may have virtually complete discretion, in which case he or she decides on all the order specifications; or limited discretion, in which case he or she decides only on the price and timing of the order.

TYPES OF ORDERS

Market Orders

market order

By far the most common type of order is the **market order.** Here the broker is instructed to buy or sell a stated number of shares immediately. In this situation the broker is obligated to act on a "best-efforts" basis to get the best possible price (as low as possible for a purchase order, as high as possible for a sell order) at the time the order is placed. Consequently, when placing a market order the investor can be fairly certain that the order will be executed, but is uncertain of the price. However, there is generally fairly good information available beforehand concerning the likely price at which such an order will be executed. Not surprisingly, market orders are day orders.

Limit Orders

limit order
limit price

A second type of order is a **limit order.** Here, a **limit price** is specified by the investor when the order is placed with the broker. If the order is to purchase shares, then the broker is to execute the order only at a price that is less than or equal to the limit price. If the order is to sell shares, then the broker is to execute the order only at a price that is greater than or equal to the limit price. Thus, for limit orders to purchase shares the investor specifies a ceiling on the price and for limit orders to sell shares the investor specifies a floor on the price. In contrast to a market order, an investor using a limit order cannot be certain that the order will be executed.

For example, assume that the common stock of the ABC Corporation is currently selling for $25 a share. An investor placing a limit order to sell 100 shares of ABC with a limit price of $30 per share and a time limit of one day is not likely to have the order executed, since this price is notably above the current price of $25. Only if today's price becomes much more favorable (meaning in this case that the stock price rises by at least $5 per share) will the limit order be executed.

Stop Orders

stop order
stop price

Two special kinds of orders are stop orders (also known as stop-loss orders) and stop limit orders. For a **stop order** the investor must specify what is known as a **stop price.** If it is a sell order, the stop price must be below the market price at the time the order is placed; conversely, if it is a buy order, the stop price must be above the market price at the time the order is placed. If later someone else trades the stock at a price that reaches or passes the stop price, then the stop order becomes, in effect, a market order. Hence, a stop order can be viewed as a conditional market order.

Continuing with the ABC Corporation example, a stop sell order at $20 would not be executed until a trade involving others had taken place at a price of $20 or lower. Conversely, a stop buy order at $30 would not be executed until a trade involving others had taken place at a price of $30 or more. If the price did not fall to $20, then the stop sell order would not be executed. Similarly, if the price did not rise to $30, the stop buy order would not be executed. In contrast, a limit order to sell at $20 or a limit order to buy at $30 would be executed immediately, since the current market price is $25.

One potential use of stop orders is to "lock in" paper profits. For example, assume an investor had purchased ABC stock at $10 per share two years ago, and thus has paper profits of $15 = $25 − $10 per share. Entering a stop sell order at $20 per share means that the investor will be sure of making roughly $10 = $20 − $10 per share if the stock falls in price to $20. If instead of falling the stock price rises, then the investor's stop sell order is ignored and the investor's paper profits will increase in size. Thus, the stop sell order will provide the investor with a degree of profit protection.[2]

One of the dangers of stop orders is that the actual price at which the order is executed may be some distance from the stop price. This can occur if the stock price moves very rapidly in a given direction. For example, ABC may have an industrial accident that results in a spate of lawsuits and causes the stock price to fall very rapidly to $12 per share. In this situation a stop sell order at $20 may be executed at, say, $16 instead of near the stop price of $20.

Stop Limit Orders

stop limit order

The **stop limit order** is a type of order that is designed to overcome the uncertainty of the execution price associated with a stop order. With a stop limit order the investor specifies not one but two prices—a stop price and a limit price. Once someone else trades the stock at a price that reaches or passes the stop price, then a limit order is created at the limit price. Hence, a stop limit order can be viewed as a conditional limit order.

Continuing with the example, the investor could place a stop limit order to sell ABC stock where the stop price is $20 and the limit price is $19. In effect, a limit order to sell ABC stock at a price of $19 or higher would be activated for the investor only if others trade ABC at a price of $20 or less. Conversely, the investor could enter a stop limit order to buy ABC stock where the stop price is $30 and the limit price is $31. This means that a limit order to buy ABC stock at a price of $31 or lower would be activated for the investor only if others trade ABC at a price of $30 or more.

Note that if the stop price is reached, execution is assured for a stop order but not for a stop limit order. Continuing with the ABC example, the industrial accident may cause the stock price to fall to $12 so rapidly that the stop limit order to sell (where the stop price was $20 and the limit price was $19) might not have been executed, whereas the stop order (where the stop price was $20) would have been executed at $16.

MARGIN ACCOUNTS

cash account

A **cash account** with a brokerage firm is like a regular checking account: deposits (cash and the proceeds from selling securities) must cover withdraw-

[2]Stop buy orders can be used to lock in paper profits for what are known as short sales, which will be discussed later in this chapter.

als (cash and the costs of purchasing securities). A **margin account** is like a checking account that has overdraft privileges: within limits, if more money is needed than is in the account, a loan is automatically made by the broker.[3]

margin account
hypothecation agreement

When opening a margin account with a brokerage firm, an investor must sign a **hypothecation agreement,** also known as a customer's agreement. This agreement grants the brokerage firm the right to pledge the investor's securities as collateral for bank loans, provided the securities were purchased using a margin account. Most brokerage firms also expect investors to allow them to lend their securities to others who wish to "sell them short," a procedure that will be described later in this chapter.

street name

In order to facilitate either the pledging or the lending of securities, brokerage firms request that securities purchased through a margin account be held in **street name.**[4] This means that the owner of the security, as far as the original issuer is concerned, is the brokerage firm—that is, the registered owner is the brokerage firm. As a result, in the case of common stock the issuer will send all dividends, financial reports, and voting rights to the brokerage firm, not to the investor. However, the brokerage firm will act merely as a conduit in this situation and simply forward these items to the investor.[5] Accordingly, holding a security in street name will not result in the investor being treated in a substantively different manner from holding the security in his or her own name.[6]

With a margin account, an investor may undertake certain types of transactions that are not allowed with a cash account. These transactions are known as margin purchases and short sales, which will be discussed next.

Margin Purchases

margin purchase
debit balance
call money rate

With a cash account, an investor who purchases a security must pay the entire cost of the purchase with cash. However, with a margin account the investor must come up with cash for only a percentage of the cost and can borrow the rest from the broker.[7] The amount borrowed from the broker as a result of such a **margin purchase** is referred to as the investor's **debit balance.** The interest charged on loans advanced by a broker for a margin purchase is usually calculated by adding a service charge (for example, 1%) to the broker's **call money rate.** In turn, the call money rate is the rate paid by the broker to a bank

[3]There are other types of accounts. It should also be noted that an investor may have more than one type of account with a brokerage firm.

[4]Investors with cash accounts may voluntarily elect to have their securities held in street name. Reasons offered for doing so include reduced risk of theft and improved record keeping (typically the brokerage firm will send monthly statements detailing the investor's holdings).

[5]It is possible that the investor will not receive the voting rights, particularly if the stock has been loaned to a "short seller." This will be discussed later in the chapter.

[6]The investor whose securities are held in street name may be concerned about what would happen if the brokerage firm were to go bankrupt. If this were to happen, the Securities Investor Protection Corporation (SIPC), a government-chartered firm that insures investors' accounts against brokerage firm failure, would step in and cover the investors' losses up to $500,000. Some brokerage firms have gone further and purchased private insurance in addition to the insurance offered by SIPC.

settlement date

[7]With either a cash or a margin account, the investor usually has up to five business days after an order is executed to provide the broker with the necessary cash. Accordingly, the fifth business day after execution is known as the **settlement date.** For margin purchases, the loan value of certain other securities can be used instead of cash as a down payment, in which case these securities must be provided by the settlement date. Sellers of securities must also provide their brokers with their securities by the settlement date. If requested, an investor may be able to get an extension to the settlement date.

that loaned the broker the cash that ultimately went to the investor to pay for part of the purchase.

For example, the bank may loan money to the broker at a rate of 10%, and then the broker may loan this money to the investor at a rate of 11%. Note that the call money rate (10% in this example) can change over time, and with it the interest rate that investors are charged for loans used to finance margin purchases.

The securities purchased by the investor serve as collateral on the loan made by the broker. In turn, the broker uses these securities as collateral on the loan made by the bank. Thus, the broker is, in a sense, acting as a financial intermediary in the lending process by facilitating a loan from the bank to the investor.

initial margin requirement

Initial Margin Requirement The minimum percentage of the purchase price that must come from the investor's own funds is known as the **initial margin requirement.** Regulations T, U, and G, prescribed in accordance with the Securities Exchange Act of 1934, give the Federal Reserve Board the responsibility for setting this percentage when either common stocks or convertible bonds are being purchased.[8] However, the exchanges where the purchase orders are filled are allowed to set a percentage higher than the one set by the Federal Reserve Board, and brokers are allowed to set it even higher. Thus, hypothetically, the Federal Reserve Board could set the initial margin requirement at 50%, the New York Stock Exchange could then make it 55%, and the broker could ultimately make it 60%. As can be seen in Table 2-1, the initial margin requirement since 1934 as set by the Federal Reserve Board has ranged from 40% to 100%. In 1992 it was 50%.[9]

Consider, as an example, an investor who purchases on margin 100 shares of Widget Corporation for \$50 per share. With a margin requirement of 60%, the investor must pay the broker \$3,000 = .6 × 100 shares × \$50 per share. The remainder of the purchase price, \$2,000 = (1 − .6) × 100 shares × \$50 per share, is funded by a loan from the broker to the investor. At this time (that is, when the purchase is made), the investor's balance sheet looks like this:

Assets = 100 shares at \$50 per share	Loan	= \$2,000
= \$5,000	Equity	= \$3,000

Note how the sum of the items on the left-hand side of the balance sheet equals the sum of the items on the right-hand side. This is simply due to the fact that, from basic accounting:

$$\text{equity} = \text{total assets} - \text{total liabilities} \tag{2.1}$$

[8]Regulation T covers credit extended by brokers and dealers, Regulation U covers credit extended by banks, and Regulation G covers credit extended by anyone other than brokers, dealers, or banks. All common stocks and convertible bonds that are listed on a national securities exchange (for example, the New York Stock Exchange, the American Stock Exchange, or the National Market System of NASDAQ) can be purchased on margin. Furthermore, four times a year the Federal Reserve Board publishes a roster of other securities that can purchased on margin. The determination of which firms are put on this roster is based on factors such as the number of shareholders and firm size.

[9]Initial margin requirements on nonconvertible bonds are set in a similar fashion, except that the Federal Reserve Board is not involved. Typically, the investor wishing to purchase nonconvertible bonds on margin will face a much lower initial margin requirement (for example, 10% for purchases of U.S. Treasury securities).

TABLE 2-1
Initial Margin Requirements of the Federal Reserve Board

PERIOD		INITIAL MARGIN REQUIREMENTS		
Beginning Date	**Ending Date**	**Margin Stocks**	**Short Sales**	**Convertible Bonds**
Oct. 1, 1934	Jan. 31, 1936	25–45%	a	b
Feb. 1, 1936	March 31, 1936	25–55	a	b
April 1, 1936	Oct. 31, 1937	55	a	b
Nov. 1, 1937	Feb. 4, 1945	40	50%	b
Feb. 5, 1945	July 4, 1945	50	50	b
July 5, 1945	Jan. 20, 1946	75	75	b
Jan. 21, 1946	Jan. 31, 1947	100	100	b
Feb. 1, 1947	March 29, 1949	75	75	b
March 30, 1949	Jan. 16, 1951	50	50	b
Jan. 17, 1951	Feb. 19, 1953	75	75	b
Feb. 20, 1953	Jan. 3, 1955	50	50	b
Jan. 4, 1955	April 22, 1955	60	60	b
April 23, 1955	Jan. 15, 1958	70	70	b
Jan. 16, 1958	Aug. 4, 1958	50	50	b
Aug. 5, 1958	Oct. 15, 1958	70	70	b
Oct. 16, 1958	July 27, 1960	90	90	b
July 28, 1960	July 9, 1962	70	70	b
July 10, 1962	Nov. 5, 1963	50	50	b
Nov. 6, 1963	March 10, 1968	70	70	b
March 11, 1968	June 7, 1968	70	70	50%
June 8, 1968	May 5, 1970	80	80	60
May 6, 1970	Dec. 5, 1971	65	65	50
Dec. 6, 1971	Nov. 23, 1972	55	55	50
Nov. 24, 1972	Jan. 2, 1974	65	65	50
Jan. 3, 1974	Present	50	50	50

[a]Requirement was the margin "customarily required" by the broker.

[b]Initial margin requirements for convertible bonds were not adopted by the Federal Reserve Board until March 11, 1968.

Source: Federal Reserve Bulletin, various issues.

where total liabilities represents the debit balance (that is, the total dollar amount of loans the investor has currently outstanding). It is important that this simple relationship be remembered, since it will be used time and again in this chapter.

As the price of Widget stock changes day to day, the balance sheet of the investor will change, since the value of the assets on the left-hand side will change accordingly.[10] For example, if Widget stock falls to $25 per share, the investor's balance sheet would then look like this:

Assets = 100 shares at $25 per share	Loan	= $2,000
= $2,500	Equity	= $ 500

Note that the investor's equity has fallen by the amount of the decline in the stock price, $2,500 = ($50 − $25) × 100 shares.

[10]Generally, at the end of each month the interest on the loan will be calculated and added to the amount of the loan appearing on the right-hand side of the investor's balance sheet. For ease of exposition, this fact is ignored in the examples given here.

Actual Margin

actual margin

The **actual margin** in the account of an investor who has purchased stocks can be calculated as:

$$\text{actual margin} = \frac{\text{equity}}{\text{market value of assets}} \tag{2.2a}$$

or, substituting equation (2.1) in the numerator of equation (2.2a), as:

$$\text{actual margin} = \frac{\text{market value of assets} - \text{loan}}{\text{market value of assets}}. \tag{2.2b}$$

In the simple case where the investor has purchased one stock on margin, this equation can be written as:

$$\text{actual margin} = \frac{(n \times mp) - [(1 - im) \times pp \times n]}{n \times mp} \tag{2.2c}$$

where n denotes the number of shares owned by the investor, mp denotes the current market price of the stock, im denotes the initial margin requirement, and pp denotes the purchase price of the stock. Upon examination of equation (2.2c), it can be seen that at the time of the margin purchase, the actual margin and initial margin are the same. However, subsequent to the purchase, the actual margin can be either greater than or less than the initial margin. In this example, when the stock fell to \$25 per share, the actual margin dropped to 20% = \$500/\$2,500.

Keep in mind that the 100 shares of Widget are being kept as collateral on the loan of \$2,000 to the investor. If the price of Widget drops further, the broker may become nervous, since an additional sudden price decline could bring the value of the collateral below the amount of the loan. For example, if the price dropped to \$15 per share, the broker would have collateral worth \$1,500 = \$15 × 100 shares, while the amount of the loan is \$2,000. If the investor skipped town, the broker would still have to make good on the bank loan of \$2,000 but would only have \$1,500 worth of the investor's assets to seize in order to pay off the loan. This means that the broker would have to bear the \$500 difference and hope to track down the investor and recoup this amount at a later date.

Maintenance Margin To prevent such an occurrence, brokers require that investors keep the actual margin in their accounts at or above a certain percentage. This percentage is known as **maintenance margin,** and is set by the exchanges, not the Federal Reserve Board, with the brokers given the right to set it even higher. As of 1992, the New York Stock Exchange had set this percentage for common stock and convertible bond purchases at 25%.

maintenance margin

If an account falls below the maintenance margin requirement, the account is said to be **undermargined.** Accordingly, the broker will issue a **margin call,** requesting the investor to either (1) deposit cash or securities into the account; (2) pay off part of the loan; or (3) sell some securities currently held in the account and use the proceeds to pay off part of the loan. Any of these actions will raise the numerator or lower the denominator on the

undermargined
margin call

right-hand side of equation (2.2b), thereby increasing the actual margin.[11] If the investor does not act (or cannot be reached), then in accordance with the terms of the account, the broker will sell securities from the account to restore the actual margin to (at least) the maintenance margin requirement.

Earlier it was shown that if Widget dropped to $25 per share the actual margin in the account would be 20%. Assuming the maintenance margin requirement had been set at 30%, the account would be undermargined. In response, if the investor gave the broker a deposit of $357 in cash (or in the form of marketable securities), his or her balance sheet would look like this:

Assets: Cash	= $ 357	Loan	= $2,000
Shares	= $2,500	Equity	= $ 857

With this response, the investor's actual margin would now be restored to 30% = $857/($357 + $2,500), the maintenance margin requirement. Alternatively, the investor could respond by paying off $250 of the loan, resulting in the following balance sheet:

Assets: Shares	= $2,500	Loan	= $1,750
		Equity	= $ 750

Note that this response similarly restores the investor's actual margin to 30% = $750/$2,500.

When the investor purchases stock on margin, it is possible to determine what price the stock would have to fall below in order to receive a margin call, assuming there are no other assets held in the account. The procedure for making this calculation involves the use of equation (2.2c), where the market price of the assets (*mp*) is the unknown and the actual margin (*am*) is set at the maintenance margin requirement (*mm*). Rewriting this equation so that *mp* is on the left-hand side results in:

$$mp = \frac{(1 - im) \times pp}{1 - mm}. \tag{2.3}$$

Continuing with the example, the investor will receive a margin call if the market price of Widget stock falls below [(1 − .6) × $50]/(1 − .3) = $29 per share.

If instead of falling the stock price rises, then the investor can take part of the increase in the value of equity out of the account in the form of cash, since the actual margin in the account will have risen above the initial margin requirement.[12] In this situation the account is said to be **unrestricted** or **overmargined.** For example, assume Widget rises to $60 per share shortly after the investor purchased it on margin. At this point, the investor's actual

unrestricted
overmargined

[11]The broker may ask the investor to immediately (in some cases within five business days, in other cases even sooner) bring the actual margin up to a level corresponding to the maintenance margin requirement, or to a level that is even higher, ranging up to the initial margin requirement.

[12]Alternatively, the cash could be used as part of the initial margin requirement on an additional margin purchase by the investor. In fact, if it was large enough, it could be used to meet the entire requirement.

margin will be 67% = \$4,000/\$6,000, and his or her balance sheet will look like this:

Assets	= 100 shares at \$60 per share	Loan	= \$2,000
	= \$6,000	Equity	= \$4,000

Consequently, the investor could withdraw in cash an amount equal to \$400 = change in equity × (1 − *im*) = (\$4,000 − \$3,000) × (1 − .6). Note that this amount corresponds to the increase in the value of the stock times one minus the initial margin requirement, or (\$60 − \$50) × 100 shares × (1 − .6) = \$400. The reason why the investor cannot withdraw the full amount of the increase in the value of the stock is that the amount of the investor's loan rises by the amount of the cash withdrawn, and is thereby subject to the initial margin requirement. After withdrawing the \$400, the investor's balance sheet would look like this:

Assets	= 100 shares at \$60 per share	Loan	= \$2,400
	= \$6,000	Equity	= \$3,600

Note that the actual margin in the account is now 60% = \$3,600/\$6,000, the initial margin requirement.

Having discussed the cases where the stock price of the shares purchased on margin either (1) fell to such a degree that the actual margin was below the maintenance margin requirement, meaning that the account was undermargined; or (2) increased, resulting in the actual margin being above the initial margin requirement and the account being unrestricted, there remains one case left to consider. This case involves the situation where the stock price falls but not by enough to make the actual margin drop below the maintenance margin requirement. That is, the actual margin in the account is below the initial margin requirement but above the maintenance margin requirement. In this situation, no action by the investor is necessary. However, the account will be **restricted,** meaning that any transaction having the effect of decreasing the actual margin further (such as withdrawing cash) will not be allowed.

restricted account

In the previous example, if Widget drops to \$40 per share, the actual margin in the account will be 50% = (\$4,000 − \$2,000)/\$4,000. Since this is above the maintenance margin requirement of 30% but is below the initial margin requirement of 60%, the investor's account will be restricted. More generally, the investor's account will be restricted if Widget falls in price from \$50 to any price above \$29, the price that triggers a margin call. This daily calculation of the actual margin in an investor's account is known as having the account **marked to the market.**

marked to the market

Rate of Return The use of margin purchases allows the investor to engage in **financial leverage.** That is, by using debt to fund part of the purchase price, the investor can increase the expected rate of return of the investment. However, there is a complicating factor in the use of margin, and that is the effect on the risk of the investment.

financial leverage

Consider Widget again. If the investor believes that the stock will rise by \$15 per share over the next year, the expected rate of return on a cash purchase of 100 shares of Widget will be (\$15 × 100 shares)/(\$50 × 100 shares) = 30%, assuming that no cash dividends are paid and the purchase price is \$50 per share. A margin purchase, on the other hand, would have an expected return of [($15 × 100 shares) − (.11 × $2,000)]/$3,000 = ($1,500 − $220)/ $3,000 = 42.7%, where the interest rate on margin loans is 11% and the initial margin requirement is 60%. Thus, the investor has increased the expected rate of return from 30% to 42.7% by the use of margin.

However, what will happen to the rate of return if the stock falls by $10 per share? In this case the investor who made a cash purchase would have a rate of return equal to ($ − 10 × 100 shares)/($50 × 100 shares) = −20%. The margin purchaser, on the other hand, would have a rate of return equal to [($ − 10 × 100) − (.11 × $2,000)]/$3,000 = ($ − 1,000 − $220)/$3,000 = −40.7%. Thus, the margin purchaser will experience a much larger loss than the cash purchaser for a given dollar decline in the price of the stock.

Margin purchases are usually made in the expectation that the stock price will rise in the near future, meaning that the investor thinks that the stock's current price is too low. If an investor thinks that a given stock is not too low but too high, then the investor may engage in what is known as a short sale, which is discussed next.

Short Sales

short sale

An old adage from Wall Street is to "buy low, sell high." Most investors hope to do just that by buying securities first and selling them later.[13] However, with a **short sale** this process is reversed: the investor sells a security first and buys it back later. In this case the old adage about investors' aspirations might be reworded as "sell high, buy low."

Short sales are accomplished by borrowing stock certificates for use in the initial trade, then repaying the loan with certificates obtained in a later trade. Note that the loan here involves certificates, not dollars and cents (although it is true that the certificates at any point in time have a certain monetary value). This means that the borrower must repay the lender by returning certificates, not dollars and cents (although it is true that an equivalent monetary value, determined on the date the loan is repaid, can be remitted instead). It also means that there are no interest payments to be made by the borrower.

Rules Governing Short Sales Any order for a short sale must be identified as such. The Securities and Exchange Commission has ruled that short sales may not be made when the market price for the security is falling, on the assumption that the short-seller could exacerbate the situation, cause a panic, and profit therefrom—an assumption inappropriate for an efficient market with astute, alert traders. The precise rule is that a short sale must be made on an **up-tick** (for a price higher than that of the previous trade), or on a **zero-plus tick** (for a price equal to that of the previous trade but higher than that of the last trade at a different price).[14]

up-tick
zero-plus tick

Within five business days after a short sale has been made, the short-seller's broker must borrow and deliver the appropriate securities to the purchaser. The borrowed securities may come from the inventory of securities owned by the brokerage firm itself or from the inventory of another brokerage

---

[13]After purchasing a security, an investor is said to have established a long position in the security.

[14]The tick rule is not applicable in the over-the-counter market, suggesting that short selling can be done at any time in that market. (This market will be discussed in Chapter 3.)

firm. However, they are more likely to come from the inventory of securities held in street name by the brokerage firm for investors that have margin accounts with the firm. The life of the loan is indefinite, meaning there is no time limit on it.[15] If the lender wants to sell the securities, then the short seller will not have to repay the loan if the brokerage firm can borrow shares elsewhere, thereby transferring the loan from one source to another. However, if the brokerage firm cannot find a place to borrow the shares, then the short seller will have to repay the loan immediately. Interestingly, the identities of the borrower and lender are known only to the brokerage firm—that is, the lender does not know who the borrower is and the borrower does not know who the lender is.

The Transaction An example of a short sale is indicated in Figure 2-1. At the start of the day, Mr. Lane owns 100 shares of the XYZ Company, which are being held for him in street name by Brock, Inc., his broker. During this particular day, Ms. Smith places an order with her broker at Brock to short sell 100 shares of XYZ (Mr. Lane believes that the price of XYZ stock is going to rise in the near future, while Ms. Smith believes that it is going to fall). In this situation, Brock takes the 100 shares of XYZ that they are holding in street name for Mr. Lane and sells them for Ms. Smith to some other investor, in this case Mr. Jones. At this point XYZ will receive notice that the ownership of 100 shares of its stock has changed hands, going from Brock (remember that Mr. Lane held his stock in street name) to Mr. Jones. At some later date, Ms. Smith will tell her broker at Brock to purchase 100 shares of XYZ (perhaps from a Ms. Poole) and use these shares to pay off her debt to Mr. Lane. At this point, XYZ will receive another notice that the ownership of 100 shares has changed hands, going from Ms. Poole to Brock, restoring Brock to their original position.

Cash Dividends What happens when XYZ declares and subsequently pays a cash dividend to its stockholders? *Before the short sale,* Brock would receive a check for cash dividends on 100 shares of stock. After depositing this check in their own account at a bank, Brock would write a check for an identical amount and give it to Mr. Lane. Thus, neither Brock nor Mr. Lane has been worse off by having the shares held in street name. *After the short sale,* XYZ will see that the owner of those 100 shares is not Brock any more, but is now Mr. Jones. Thus, XYZ will now mail the dividend check to Mr. Jones, not Brock. However, Mr. Lane will still be expecting his dividend check from Brock. Indeed, if there was a risk that he would not receive it, he would not have agreed to have his securities held in street name. Brock would like to mail him a check for the same amount of dividends that Mr. Jones received from XYZ—that is, for the amount of dividends that Mr. Lane would have received from XYZ had he held his stock in his own name. If Brock does this, then they will be losing an amount of cash equal to the amount of the dividends paid. In order to prevent themselves from experiencing this loss, what does Brock do? They make Ms. Smith, the short seller, give them a check for an equivalent amount.

[15]The New York Stock Exchange, the American Stock Exchange, and NASDAQ publish monthly lists of the **short interest** in their stocks (short interest refers to the number of shares of a given company that have been sold short where, as of a given date, the loan remains outstanding). To be on the NYSE or AMEX list, either the total short interest must be equal to or greater than 100,000 shares or the change in the short interest from the previous month must be equal to or greater than 50,000 shares. The respective figures for NASDAQ are 50,000 and 25,000.

short interest

FIGURE 2-1
Short Selling of Common Stock

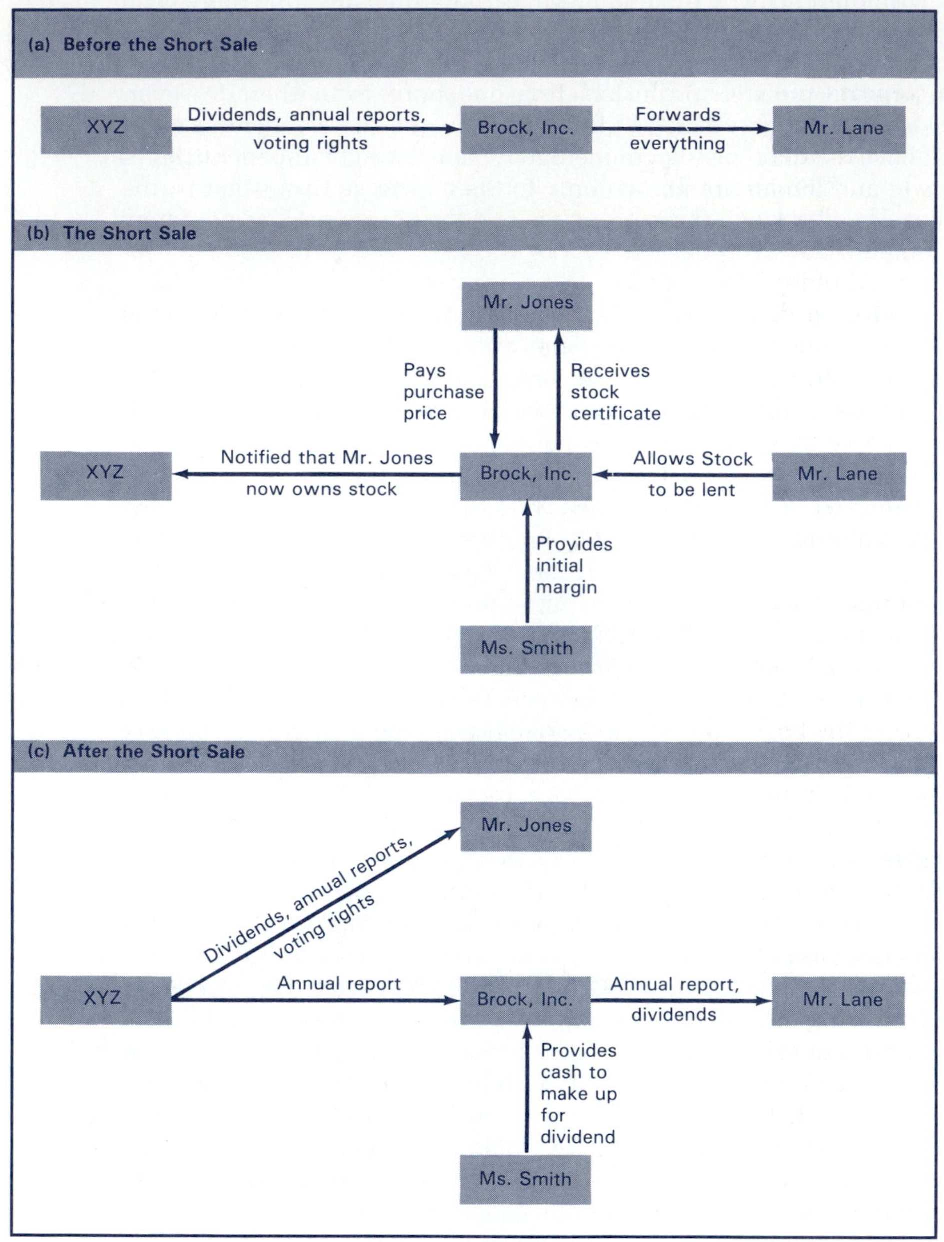

Consider all the parties involved in the short sale now. Mr. Lane is content, since he has received his dividend check from his broker. Brock is content, since their net cash outflow is still zero, just as it was before the short sale. Mr. Jones is content, since he received his dividend check directly from XYZ. What about Ms. Smith? She should not be upset with having to reimburse Brock for the dividend check given by them to Mr. Lane, since the price of XYZ's common stock can be expected to fall by an amount roughly equal to the amount of the cash dividend, thereby reducing the dollar value of her loan from Brock by an equivalent amount.

Financial Reports and Voting Rights What about financial reports and voting rights? Before the short sale these were sent to Brock, who then forwarded them to Mr. Lane. After the short sale, Brock will no longer be receiving them, so what happens? Financial reports are easily procured by brokerage firms free of charge, so Brock will probably get copies of them from XYZ and mail a copy to Mr. Lane. However, voting rights are different. These are limited to the registered stockholders (in this case, Mr. Jones) and cannot be replicated in the manner of cash dividends by Ms. Smith, the short seller. Thus, when voting rights are issued, the brokerage firm (Brock, Inc.) will try to find voting rights to give to Mr. Lane if he asks for them (perhaps Brock owns shares or manages a portfolio that owns shares of XYZ, and will give the voting rights from these shares to Mr. Lane). Unless he is insistent, however, there is a chance Mr. Lane will not get his voting rights once his shares have been borrowed and used in a short sale. In all other matters, he will be treated just as if he were holding the shares of XYZ in his own name.

Initial Margin Requirement As previously mentioned, a short sale involves a loan. Thus, there is a risk that the borrower (in the example, Ms. Smith) will not repay the loan. What would happen in this situation? The brokerage firm would be left without the 100 shares that the short seller, Ms. Smith, owes the firm. Either the brokerage firm, Brock, is going to lose money or else the lender, Mr. Lane, is going to lose money. To prevent this from happening, the cash proceeds from the short sale, paid by Mr. Jones, are not given to the short seller, Ms. Smith. Instead, they are held in her account with Brock until she repays her loan. Will this assure the brokerage firm that the loan will be repaid? No, unfortunately it will not.

In the example, assume the 100 shares of XYZ were sold at a price of $100 per share. In this case, the proceeds from the short sale of $10,000 are held in Ms. Smith's account, but she is prohibited from withdrawing it until the loan is repaid. Now imagine that at some date after the short sale, XYZ stock rises by $20 per share. In this situation, Ms. Smith owes Brock 100 shares of XYZ with a current market value of $12,000 = 100 shares × $120 per share, but only has $10,000 in her account. If she skips town, Brock will have collateral of $10,000 (in cash) but a loan of $12,000, resulting in a loss of $2,000. How will Brock protect itself from experiencing losses from short sellers who do not repay their loans? By the use of margin requirements. In this example, Ms. Smith must not only leave the short sale proceeds with her broker, but she must also give her broker initial margin applied to the amount of the short sale.[16] Assuming the initial margin requirement is 60%, she must give her broker .6 × $10,000 = $6,000 cash. Thus, at the time the short sale is made her balance sheet will look like this:

Assets = ($100 × 100 shares) × (1 + .6)	Liabilities	= $100 × 100 shares
= $16,000 cash		= $10,000 loan
	Equity	= $6,000

[16]Table 2-1 presents the initial margin requirement for short sales; note that it has been set at the same level as for margin purchases of common stocks in the postwar period.

Notice that since equation (2.1) was used to establish the amount in equity, the left-hand side of Ms. Smith's balance sheet equals the total amount on the right-hand side.

Actual and Maintenance Margin In this example, XYZ stock would have to rise in value to a price above $160 per share in order for Brock to be in jeopardy of not being repaid. Thus, initial margin provides the brokerage firm with a certain degree of protection. However, this protection is not complete, since it is not unheard of for stocks to rise in value by more than 60% [= ($160 − $100)/$100]. It is maintenance margin that protects the brokerage firm from losing money in such situations. In order to examine the use of maintenance margin in short sales, the actual margin in a short sale will be defined as:

$$\text{actual margin} = \frac{\text{equity}}{\text{loan}} \tag{2.4a}$$

$$= \frac{\text{market value of assets held} - \text{loan}}{\text{loan}}. \tag{2.4b}$$

The numerator in equations (2.4a) and (2.4b) is identical to the numerator for calculating actual margin for margin purchases as shown in equations (2.2a) and (2.2b). However, the denominator is different. For short sales it is equal to the current dollar value of the loan, whereas for margin purchases it is equal to the current market value of the assets held in the account.

Assuming that only the short sale proceeds and initial margin are held as assets, equation (2.4b) can be rewritten as:

$$am = \frac{[(sp \times n) \times (1 + im)] - (mp \times n)}{mp \times n} \tag{2.5}$$

where am denotes actual margin, sp denotes the shorted price (that is, the price at which the stock was short sold), n denotes the number of shares sold short, im denotes the initial margin requirement, and mp denotes the current market price of the stock.

In this example, if XYZ stock rises to $130 per share, the actual margin in Ms. Smith's account will be {[($100 × 100) × (1 + .6)] − ($130 × 100)}/($130 × 100) =23%. Assuming that the maintenance margin requirement is 30%, the account is undermargined, thereby causing Ms. Smith to receive a margin call. Just like margin calls on margin purchases, she will be asked to put up more margin, meaning that she will be asked to add cash or securities to her account. Thus, if she adds $900 cash to her account, the balance sheet will look like this:

Assets	= $16,000 + $900	Liabilities	= $130 × 100 shares
	= $16,900 cash		= $13,000
		Equity	= $3,900

and, using equation (2.4b), the actual margin will be equal to ($16,900 − $13,000)/$13,000 = 30%.

At the time a short sale is made, it is possible to calculate the market price that the stock of the shorted company would have to rise above in order for the short seller to receive a margin call. Using mm to denote the maintenance margin requirement, all that is necessary is to substitute mm for am in equation (2.5) and solve for mp:

$$mp = \frac{sp \times (1 + im)}{1 + mm}. \tag{2.6}$$

In this example, the market price that would trigger a margin call is [$100 × (1 + .6)]/(1 + .3) = $123. That is, if the market price of the stock of XYZ rises above $123 per share, the account will be undermargined and Ms. Smith can expect to receive a margin call from Brock.

If instead of rising the stock price falls, then the short seller can take a bit more than the increase in equity out of the account in the form of cash, since in this case the actual margin has risen above the initial margin requirement and the account is thus unrestricted.[17] For example, if the market price of XYZ falls to $75 per share, then Ms. Smith's balance sheet will look like this:

Assets = $16,000 cash	Liabilities	=	$75 × 100 shares
		=	$7,500
	Equity	=	$8,500

In this situation, Ms. Smith's actual margin has risen to 113% = ($16,000 − $7,500)/$7,500. A withdrawal of $4,000 in cash from the account will reduce the actual margin to [($16,000 − $4,000) − $7,500]/ $7,500 = 60%, the initial margin requirement. After such a withdrawal is made, Ms. Smith's balance sheet would look like this:

Assets	= $16,000 − $4,000	Liabilities	=	$7,500
	= $12,000 cash	Equity	=	$4,500

Note that in this case the stock fell by $25 per share, causing the equity in her account to rise from $6,000 to $8,500, for a total dollar increase of $2,500. However, Ms. Smith was able to withdraw cash in the amount of $4,000. This is in contrast to margin purchases, where the amount that could be withdrawn was less than the amount of the increase in equity. The reason behind this is that for margin purchases, actual margin is calculated in a manner different from that for short sales, as was mentioned previously.

Having discussed the cases for short sales where the stock price either (1) fell and the account was thereby unrestricted; or (2) went up to such a degree that the maintenance margin requirement was violated and the account was thereby undermargined, there is one more case left to be considered. This is the case where the stock price goes up but not to such a degree that the maintenance margin requirement is violated. In this case, the initial margin requirement has been violated, which means that the account is restricted. Here, "restricted" has a meaning similar to its meaning for margin purchases. That is, any transaction that has the effect of further decreasing the actual margin in the account will be prohibited. In the example with XYZ, Ms.

[17]Alternatively, the short seller could sell short a second security and not have to put up all (or perhaps any) of the initial margin.

Smith's account will be restricted if the market price of the stock rises from \$100 to a price less than \$123, the price that will trigger margin calls. As with margin purchases, the daily calculation of the actual margin in a short seller's account is known as having the account marked to the market.

An interesting question is: what happens to the cash in the short seller's account? When the loan is repaid the short seller will have access to the cash (actually, the cash is typically used to buy the shares that are needed to repay the loan). Before the loan is repaid, however, it may be that the short seller can earn interest on the portion of the cash balance that represents margin (some brokerage firms will accept certain securities, such as Treasury bills, in lieu of cash for meeting margin requirements). In regard to the cash proceeds from the short sale, sometimes the securities may be lent only on the payment of a premium by the short seller, meaning that the short seller not only does not earn interest on the cash proceeds but must pay a fee for the loan. At other times the lender may pay the short seller interest on the cash proceeds. Usually, however, securities are loaned "flat"—the brokerage firm keeps the cash proceeds from the short sale and enjoys the use of this money, and neither the short seller nor the investor who lent the securities receives any direct compensation. In this case, the brokerage firm makes money not only from the commission paid by the short seller, but also on the cash proceeds from the sale (they may, for example, earn interest by purchasing Treasury bills with these proceeds).

Rate of Return The use of short selling results in rates of return to the investor that are of opposite sign to what would be earned if the shares were purchased on margin (assuming that initial margin for the short sale is met by depositing cash and that the short loan is "flat," and ignoring interest on the margin loan). Hence, short sales also involve the use of financial leverage.

Consider XYZ once again, where Ms. Smith short sold its stock at a price of \$100 per share. If she later repays the short loan when the stock is selling for \$75 per share and just after XYZ has paid a \$1 per share cash dividend, then her rate of return would be equal to (\$100 − \$75 − \$1)/(.6 × \$100) = +40%. In contrast, note that the return for someone who had purchased the stock of XYZ on margin would be equal to (\$75 + \$1 − \$100)/(.6 × \$100) = −40%, while the rate of return for someone who had purchased the stock without using margin would be equal to (\$75 + \$1 − \$100)/\$100 = −24%.

However, if Ms. Smith has incorrectly predicted the future price movement of XYZ and it goes up to \$120 per share just after paying a \$1 per share cash dividend, then her rate of return would be equal to (\$100 − \$120 − \$1)/(.6 × \$100) = −35%. Conversely, if the stock had been purchased on margin, her rate of return would have been equal to (\$120 + \$1 − \$100)/(.6 × \$100) = +35%. Without margin, the rate of return on the stock would be equal to (\$120 + \$1 − \$100)/\$100 = +21%.

What happens to these rate of return calculations if interest is earned on both the initial margin and short proceeds? It increases the rate of return to the short seller. Consider the example where XYZ fell to \$75, and assume that the short seller earned 5% on the initial margin deposit and 4% on the short proceeds. In the case, the return to the short seller would be equal to [\$100 − \$75 − \$1 + (.05 × .6 × \$100) + (.04 × \$100)]/(.6 × \$100) = 51.7%, which is notably higher than the 40% previously calculated. Hence, financial leverage is even more apparent when either form of interest is paid to the short seller.

MONEY MATTERS
Hedge Funds

In certain respects, the average investor can be viewed as a wrestler fighting with one hand tied behind his back. Most investors search only for underpriced securities to purchase. But as the text describes, investors can take advantage of overpriced securities by selling them short. Given that there should exist at least as many overpriced situations as underpriced, skillful investors who forgo short selling would appear to be overlooking a significant portion of the mispriced investment opportunities.

Aggressive short selling of individual securities is practiced by relatively few professional investors. Many of these investors operate through obscure, unpublicized businesses known as *hedge funds*.

The classic hedge fund takes both long and short positions in stocks and bonds. The hedge fund manager balances the "longs" and "shorts" so that the fund is largely unaffected by movements in the broad market. In "up" markets, the longs benefit while the shorts lose value. The converse occurs in "down" markets. The portfolio manager thereby "hedges" away market risk (see Chapter 8) in the fund.

How does a hedge fund profit if its long positions are offset by short positions? If the portfolio manager has selected wisely, the long positions are held in securities that will appreciate in value relative to the securities that have been sold short. In the simplest case, assume that the hedge fund manager has information about the stocks of General Motors and Ford that leads him or her to believe that GM will do well in the near term while Ford will perform poorly. He or she will buy GM and sell short an equivalent dollar amount of Ford.

In reality, hedge fund investment strategies may be much more complex, involving the arbitraging (see Chapter 12) of price discrepancies between related financial instruments. Security purchases also may be made on margin (see this chapter). Further, rather than have their short sale proceeds profitlessly held in escrow, professional short sellers typically receive 75% or more of the interest earned by the broker on the escrowed funds.

Despite these complexities, the basic principle of hedge fund investing remains: profits result from the hedge fund manager's ability to simultaneously buy securities that will appreciate in relative value and short sell securities that will decline in relative value. With no significant market risk, the hedge fund's performance will be determined by the portfolio manager's security selection capabilities (the ability to produce a positive "alpha"—see Chapter 18).

Hedge funds are usually organized as private partnerships. They avoid government regulation by limiting the number of partners to no more than 100 and by avoiding all advertising. Consequently, they are not required to disclose performance results, expenses, or portfolio composition as are registered investment companies (see Chapter 23). Informally, returns of up to 120% in a good year and consistent annual returns of 20% have been reported for successful funds, despite a market risk posture similar to Treasury bills.

Interested in investing in hedge funds? Be sure to have substantial assets on hand. Initial investments are typically $500,000 and up. Fees range between 1% and 2% and the typical fund's general partners keep 20% of all fund profits. Withdrawals are usually restricted. Investors may have to commit funds for months or even years and afterward may be limited to quarterly or semiannual withdrawals.

Despite these limitations, many well-heeled investors have invested hundreds of millions of dollars in hedge funds. Successful hedge fund managers, both past and present, are the stuff of Wall Street legend, including Michael Steinhardt, Warren Buffett (in his earlier days), and Julian Robertson, among others. Hedge funds provide an interesting study of the techniques of aggressive investment managers, a perspective one cannot usually find in more traditionally managed equity funds.

Aggregation

An investor with a margin account may purchase several different securities on margin or may short sell several different securities. Alternatively, he or she may purchase some on margin and short sell others. The determination of whether an account is undermargined, restricted, or overmargined depends on the total activity in the account. For example, if one stock is undermargined and another is overmargined, then the overmargined stock can be used to offset the undermargined stock, provided that it is overmargined to a sufficiently large degree. How these multiple transactions are aggregated in one account in order to determine if the account is undermargined, restricted, or overmargined on any given day will be shown next.

Multiple Margin Purchases In the case of multiple margin purchases, aggregation is straightforward. The investor's balance sheet is restated by recalculating the market value of all the stocks held using current market prices. Here the "current market price" of any particular security usually means the price at which the last trade was made in the market involving that security on the previous day. Next, the total amount of the investor's liabilities is carried over from the previous day, since the amounts of the margin loans do not change from day to day. Then, using equation (2.1), the equity in the account can be recalculated. In turn, this allows equation (2.2a) to be used in order to recalculate the actual margin in the account.

Consider, for example, an investor who purchased 100 shares of Widget on margin at $50 per share on July 1 and then on July 15 purchased 100 shares of XYZ on margin at $100 per share. Assuming that the initial margin requirement is 60% and the market prices of Widget and XYZ on July 31 are $60 and $80 per share, respectively, the investor's balance sheet on July 31 will look like this:

Assets:		Liabilities:	
100 shares of Widget at $60 per share =	$ 6,000	loan on Widget purchase 100 × $50 × (1 − .6) =	$ 2,000
100 shares of XYZ at $80 per share =	$ 8,000	loan on XYZ purchase 100 × $100 × (1 − .6) =	$ 4,000
		Equity: ($14,000 − $2,000 − $4,000) =	$ 8,000
Total Assets =	$14,000	Total Liabilities and Equity =	$14,000

Thus, the investor's actual margin is equal to $8,000/$14,000 = 57%. Assuming that the maintenance margin requirement is 30%, note that the investor's actual margin is below the initial margin requirement but is above the maintenance margin requirement. Accordingly, the investor's account would be restricted.

Multiple Short Sales In a similar manner, the actual margin of an investor who has short sold more than one stock can be determined. In this case, however, it is not the assets that are reevaluated every day as the account is marked to the market. Instead, it is the liabilities that are reevaluated based on current market prices, since the short seller's liabilities are shares whose market values are changing every day. Once the dollar values of the liabilities are recalculated, the actual margin in the account can be determined using equation (2.4b).

Consider, for example, an investor who short sold 100 shares of Widget at $50 per share on July 1 and then on July 15 short sold 100 shares of XYZ at $100 per share. As before, assume the initial and maintenance margin requirements are 60% and 30%, respectively. If the market prices of Widget and XYZ on July 31 are $60 and $80 per share, respectively, the short seller's balance sheet on July 31 will look like this:

Assets		Liabilities and Equity	
Assets: proceeds from sale of Widget = 100 × $50 =	$ 5,000	Liabilities: loan of Widget stock = 100 × $60 =	$ 6,000
initial margin on Widget = 100 × $50 × .6 =	$ 3,000	loan of XYZ stock = 100 × $80 =	$ 8,000
proceeds from sale of XYZ = 100 × $100 =	$10,000	Equity: ($24,000 − $6,000 − $8,000) =	$10,000
initial margin on XYZ = 100 × $100 × .6 =	$ 6,000		
Total Assets =	$24,000	Total Liabilities and Equity =	$24,000

Thus, in this situation the short seller's actual margin is ($24,000 − $6,000 − $8,000)/($6,000 + $8,000) = 71%, which means that the account is unrestricted or overmargined. Accordingly, the short seller may withdraw cash from the account if he or she so desires.

Both Martin Purchases and Short Sales The situation where the investor has purchased some stocks, perhaps on margin, and has short sold others is more complicated than either of the situations just described. This is because the equation used to calculate actual margin for margin purchases, equation (2.2a) or (2.2b), and the equation used to calculate actual margin for short sales, equation (2.4a) or (2.4b), are different. This can be seen by simply noting what is in the denominator in each equation. For margin purchases, the market value of the assets appears in the denominator. However, for short sales, the market value of the loan appears in the denominator. If both kind of transactions are appearing in the same account, neither equation can be used to calculate the overall actual margin in the account. However, the account can be analyzed in terms of the dollar amount of assets that are necessary for the account to meet the maintenance margin requirement. This can be illustrated by continuing with the example.

Consider a third investor who short sells 100 shares of Widget on July 1 at $50 per share and purchases 100 shares of XYZ on margin at $100 per share on July 15. Again, assuming that Widget and XYZ are selling for $60 and $80 per share on July 31, this investor's balance sheet on that date will look like this:

Assets		Liabilities and Equity	
Assets: cash proceeds from sale of Widget = 100 × $50 =	$ 5,000	Liabilities: loan of Widget stock = 100 × $60 =	$ 6,000
cash deposit for initial margin on Widget = 100 × $50 × .6 =	$ 3,000	loan for purchase of XYZ = 100 × $100 × (1 − .6) =	$ 4,000
market value of 100 shares of XYZ = 100 × $80 =	$ 8,000	Equity: ($16,000 − $6,000 − $4,000) =	$ 6,000
Total Assets =	$16,000	Total Liabilities and Equity =	$16,000

In this situation, the broker will require the investor to have assets of sufficient value to protect the short sale loan of Widget stock and the cash loan to purchase XYZ on margin. In general, the amount required as collateral against a short sale is equal to the current market value of the shorted stock times the quantity of one plus the maintenance margin requirement. For the short sale loan of Widget stock, this amounts to $6,000 × (1 + .3) = $7,800, where .3 corresponds to the maintenance margin requirement.

The amount required as collateral against a margin purchase is, in general, equal to the dollar value of the margin loan divided by the quantity of one minus the maintenance margin requirement. For the cash loan to purchase XYZ, this amounts to $4,000/(1 − .3) = $5,714.

The total amount required in this example is thus $7,800 + $5,714 = $13,514. Since the assets in the account are currently worth $16,000, the investor will not receive a margin call. To see if the account is restricted, the previous calculations are repeated using the initial margin requirement of 60% instead of the maintenance margin requirement of 30%. For the Widget stock loan, the amount required for the account to be unrestricted is $6,000 × (1 + .6) = $9,600. The corresponding amount for the XYZ loan is $4,000/(1 − .6) = $10,000. Summing these amounts gives a total of $9,600 + $10,000 = $19,600, indicating that this account is restricted.

SUMMARY

1. Investors typically buy or sell securities through brokers who are compensated for their services with commissions.

2. When transacting in a security, investors must specify: the security's name; buy or sell; order size; time limit; and type of order.

3. The four standard types of orders are: market, limit, stop, and stop limit.

4. Investors may purchase securities with cash or may borrow from brokerage firms to buy securities on margin.

5. Investors must make down payments on their margin purchases, maintain minimum equity positions in their margin accounts, and pay interest on margin loans.

6. If an investor's actual margin falls below the maintenance margin, the investor's account is undermargined. The investor will receive a margin call and must put up additional equity.

7. Buying on margin results in financial leverage, thereby magnifying (positively or negatively) the impact of a security's return on the investor's wealth.

8. Short sales involve the sale of securities that are not owned, but rather are borrowed by the sellers. The borrowed securities must ultimately be purchased in the market and returned to the lenders.

9. A short seller must deposit the proceeds of the short sale and initial margin with his or her broker. The short seller must also maintain minimum equity positions in his or her margin account or face a margin call.

10. For investors who purchase on margin or short sell several securities, the determination of whether an account is undermargined, restricted, or overmargined depends on the aggregated activity in their accounts.

KEY TERMS

broker
account executives
registered representatives
regional brokerage firms
discount brokers
commissions
order specifications
round lot
odd lot
day orders
open orders
good-till-cancelled orders
fill-or-kill orders
discretionary orders
market order
limit order
limit price
stop order
stop price
stop limit order
cash account
margin account
hypothecation agreement
street name
margin purchase
debit balance
settlement date
call money rate
initial margin requirement
actual margin
maintenance margin
undermargined
margin call
unrestricted
overmargined
restricted account

marked to the market	short sale	zero-plus tick
financial leverage	up-tick	short interest

QUESTIONS AND PROBLEMS

1. Describe the conflict of interest that typically exists in the investment advisory relationship between a brokerage firm and its clients.
2. How many round lots and what odd lot size are in an order for 511 shares?
3. Discuss the advantages and disadvantages to the investor of the following:
   (a) market order,
   (b) limit order,
   (c) stop order.
4. Why are margin account securities held in street name?
5. Lollypop Killefer purchases on margin 200 shares of Landfall Corporation stock at $75 per share. The initial margin requirement is 55%. Prepare Lollypop's balance sheet for this investment at the time of purchase.
6. Buck Ewing opened a margin account at a local brokerage firm. Buck's initial investment was to purchase 200 shares of Woodbury Corporation on margin at $40 per share. Buck borrowed $3,000 from the broker to complete the purchase.
   (a) At the time of the purchase, what was the actual margin in Buck's account?
   (b) If Woodbury stock subsequently rises in price to $60 per share, what is the actual margin in Buck's account?
   (c) If Woodbury stock subsequently falls in price to $35 per share, what is the actual margin in Buck's account?
7. Distinguish between the initial margin requirement and the maintenance margin requirement.
8. Snooker Arnovich buys on margin 1,000 shares of Rockford Systems stock at $60 per share. The initial margin requirement is 50% and the maintenance margin requirement is 30%. If the Rockford stock falls to $50, will Snooker receive a margin call?
9. Avalon Company's stock is currently selling for $15 per share. The initial margin requirement is 60% and the maintenance margin requirement is 35%. Cap Anson buys 100 shares of Avalon stock on margin. To what price must the stock fall for Cap to receive a margin call?
10. Lizzie Arlington has deposited $20,000 in a margin account with a brokerage firm. If the initial margin requirement is 50%, what is the maximum dollar amount of stock that Lizzie can purchase on margin?
11. Explain the purpose of the maintenance margin requirement.
12. Penny Bailey bought on margin 500 shares of South Beloit Inc. at $35 per share. The initial margin requirement is 45% and the annual interest on margin loans is 12%. Over the next year the stock rises to $40. What is Penny's return on investment?
13. Calculate Buck Ewing's rate of return in parts (b) and (c) of Problem #6 under the assumption that the margin loan was outstanding for one year and carried an interest rate of 10%, and that the prices of $60 and $35

were observed after one year during which the firm did not pay any cash dividends.

14. Ed Delahanty purchased 500 shares of Niagara Falls Corporation stock on margin at the end of 1990 for $30 per share. The initial margin requirement was 55%. Ed paid 13% interest on the margin loan and never faced a margin call. Niagara Falls paid dividends of $1 per share during 1991.

- **(a)** At the end of 1991, if Ed sold the Niagara Falls stock for $40 per share, what was Ed's rate of return for the year?
- **(b)** At the end of 1991, if Ed sold the Niagara Falls stock for $20 per share, what was Ed's rate of return for the year?
- **(c)** Recalculate your answers to parts (a) and (b) assuming that Ed made the Niagara Falls stock purchase for cash instead of on margin.

15. Beauty Bancroft sells short 500 shares of Rockdale Manufacturing at $25 per share. The initial margin requirement is 50%. Prepare Beauty's balance sheet as of the time of the transaction.

16. Through a margin account, Candy Cummings short sells 200 shares of Madison Inc. stock for $50 per share. The initial margin requirement is 45%.

- **(a)** If Madison stock subsequently rises to $58 per share, what is the actual margin in Candy's account?
- **(b)** If Madison stock subsequently falls to $42 per share, what is the actual margin in Candy's account?

17. Dinty Barbare short sells 500 shares of Naperville Products at $45 per share. The initial margin and maintenance margin requirements are 55% and 35% respectively. If Naperville stock rises to $50, will Dinty receive a margin call?

18. Sun Prairie Foods stock currently sells for $50 per share. The initial margin requirement is 50% and the maintenance margin requirement is 40%. If Willie Keeler sells short 300 shares of Sun Prairie stock, to what price can the stock rise before Willie receives a margin call?

19. Eddie Gaedel is an inveterate short seller. Is it true that Eddie's potential losses are infinite? Why? Conversely, is it true that the maximum return that Eddie can earn on an investment is 100%? Why?

20. The stock of DeForest Inc. at the beginning of 1991 sold for $70 per share. At that time, Deerfoot Barclay short sold 1,000 shares of the stock. The initial margin requirement was 50%. DeForest stock has risen to $75 at year-end 1991 and Deerfoot faced no margin calls in the interim. Further, the stock paid a $2 dividend at year-end. What was Deerfoot's 1991 return on this investment?

21. Calculate Candy Cummings's rate of return in parts (a) and (b) of Problem #16 assuming that the short loan was flat but the initial margin deposit earned interest at a rate of 8%, and that the prices of $58 and $42 were observed after one year during which the firm did not pay any dividends.

22. What aspects of short selling do brokerage houses typically find to be especially profitable?

23. Distinguish between an investor receiving a margin call and having his or her margin account restricted.

24. Pooch Barnhart purchases 100 shares of Batavia Lumber Company stock on margin at $50 per share. Simultaneously, Pooch short sells 200 shares of Geneva Shelter stock at $20 per share. With an initial margin requirement of 60%:

(a) What is the initial equity (in dollars) in Pooch's account?

(b) If Batavia and Geneva rise to $55 and $22 per share respectively, what is Pooch's equity position (in dollars)?

25. On May 1, Ivy Olson short sold 100 shares of Minnetonka Minerals stock at $25 per share and bought on margin 200 shares of St. Louis Park Company stock for $40 per share. The initial margin requirement was 50%. On June 30, Minnetonka stock sold for $36 per share and St. Louis Park stock sold for $45 per share.

(a) Prepare a balance sheet showing the aggregate financial position in Ivy's margin account as of June 30.

(b) Calculate whether Ivy's account is restricted as of June 30.

REFERENCES

1. For a discussion of the mechanics of purchasing and selling securities, along with margin purchasing and short selling, see:

DeWitt M. Foster, *The Stockbroker's Manual* (Miami: Pass, Inc., 1990). Copies can be obtained by calling (305) 270-2550.

2. An interesting discussion of margin requirements and their impact on market volatility is contained in:

David A. Hsieh and Merton H. Miller, "Margin Requirements and Market Volatility," *Journal of Finance*, 45, no. 1 (March 1990): 3–29.

3. A recent study that examines levels and changes in short interest is:

Averil Brent, Dale Morse, and E. Kay Stice, "Short Interest: Explanations and Tests," *Journal of Financial and Quantitative Analysis*, 25, no. 2 (June 1990): 273–89.

3

Security Markets

A **security market** can be defined as a mechanism for bringing together buyers and sellers of financial assets in order to facilitate trading. Security markets are **secondary** (as opposed to primary) **markets,** since the financial assets traded on them were issued at some previous point in time. In **call markets,** trading is allowed only at certain specified times. In such a market, when a security is "called," those individuals that are interested in either buying or selling it are physically brought together.[1] Then, there may be an explicit auction in which prices are called out until the quantity demanded is as close as possible to the quantity supplied. Alternatively, orders may be left with a clerk and periodically an official of the exchange sets a price that allows the maximum number of shares from the previously accumulated orders to be traded.

security market

secondary markets

call markets

In **continuous markets,** trades may occur at any time. While only investors are needed for such a market to operate, it generally would not be very effective without intermediaries also being present. In a continuous

continuous markets

[1]Enough time is allowed to elapse between calls (for example, an hour or more) so that a substantial number of orders to buy and sell will accumulate.

market without intermediaries, an investor who wants to buy or sell a security quickly might have to either spend a great deal of money searching for a good offer or run the risk of accepting a poor one. Since orders from investors arrive more or less randomly, prices in such a market would vary considerably, depending on the flow of buy orders relative to the flow of sell orders. However, anyone willing to take temporary positions in securities could potentially make a profit by ironing out these transitory variations in supply and demand. This is the role of intermediaries known as dealers (also known as market-makers) and specialists. In the pursuit of personal gain, they generally reduce fluctuations in security prices that are unrelated to changes in value and in doing so provide **liquidity** for investors. Here, liquidity refers to the ability of investors to convert securities into cash at a price that is similar to the price of the previous trade, assuming that no new information has arrived since the previous trade.

liquidity

Security markets for common stocks (as well as certain other securities) in the U.S. typically involve dealers or specialists. This chapter will provide a detailed description of how these markets function and the role played by dealers and specialists. While the focus will be on markets for common stocks, many of the features of such markets will be applicable to the markets for other types of financial assets (such as bonds). **Organized exchanges,** which are central physical locations where trading is done under a set of rules and regulations, will be discussed first. Examples of such exchanges for common stocks are the New York Stock Exchange, the American Stock Exchange, and various regional exchanges.

organized exchanges

MAJOR MARKETS IN THE UNITED STATES

The New York Stock Exchange

The New York Stock Exchange (NYSE) is a corporation that has 1,366 full members. It has a charter and a set of rules and regulations that govern its operation and the activities of its members. A twenty-six-person board of directors that is elected by the membership supervises the exchange. Twelve of the directors are members and twelve are not members; the latter are known as "public directors." The remaining two directors are full-time employees: a chairman who also functions as the chief executive officer and a vice-chairman who also functions as president.

In order to become a member, a **seat** (comparable to a membership card) must be purchased from a current member.[2] By holding a seat, the member has the privilege of being able to execute trades using the facilities provided by the exchange. Since most trades of common stocks, in both dollar size and number of shares, take place on the NYSE, this privilege is valuable.[3] Not surprisingly, many brokerage firms are members, meaning that either an

seat

[2]The applicant for membership must also pass a written examination, be sponsored by two current members of the exchange, and be approved by the board. Recently the NYSE began allowing members to lease their seats to individuals acceptable to the exchange; as of the end of 1990, there were 583 leased seats. In addition to the 1,366 full memberships, in 1990 there were 42 individuals who held special memberships; in return for an annual fee, these members are granted access to the trading floor.

[3]During 1990, trading volume on the NYSE averaged, on a daily basis, 156.8 million shares, worth in excess of $5 billion. The American Stock Exchange, the second largest organized exchange, had comparable daily values of less than one-tenth these amounts.

officer (if the brokerage firm is a corporation), or a general partner (if the brokerage firm is a partnership), or an employee of the firm is a member. Indeed, many brokerage firms have more than one member. A brokerage firm with one or more NYSE memberships is often referred to as a **member firm** (or member corporation or member organization).

member firm

A stock that is available for trading on the NYSE is known as a **listed security.** In order for a company's stock to be listed the company must apply to the NYSE. The initial application is usually informal and confidential. If approved, the company then makes a formal application that is publicly known. Given an earlier approval on the informal application, approval at this stage is almost certain. The criteria used by the NYSE in approving an application are "(1) the degree of national interest in the company; (2) its relative position and stability in the industry; and (3) whether it is engaged in an expanding industry, with prospects of at least maintaining its relative position."[4] The specific requirements are displayed in Table 3-1. Companies that are approved for listing must agree to pay a nominal annual fee and provide certain information to the public. After listing, if trading interest in a security declines substantially, it may be **delisted** by the Exchange, meaning that it is no longer available for trading on the NYSE. (Delistings also occur when a listed company is acquired by another company or is merged into another company.) At other times there may be a **trading halt,** meaning that there is a temporary suspension of trading in that security. Trading halts typically are issued for a given stock when trading in it is roiled due to unsubstantiated rumors, such as a rumor of a pending takeover attempt or a rumor that the firm will soon announce unexpectedly low quarterly earnings.

listed security

delisted

trading halt

[4]New York Stock Exchange *Fact Book 1991*, p. 26.

TABLE 3-1
New York Stock Exchange Criteria for Listing and Delisting a Security

(a) Initial Listing Requirements of the NYSE[a]
1. Either (a) the pretax income for the most recent year must be at least $2,500,000 and the pretax income over each of the preceding two years must be at least $2,000,000, or (b) the pretax income over the most recent three years must be at least $6,500,000 in total with a minimum of $4,500,000 in the most recent year.
2. Net tangible assets must be worth at least $18,000,000.
3. There must be at least 1,100,000 shares outstanding that are publicly held and these shares must have an aggregate market value of at least $18,000,000 (this amount is subject to periodic adjustment based on market conditions).
4. There must be either (a) at least 2,000 stockholders who each own a minimum of 100 shares, or (b) at least 2,200 stockholders with the monthly trading volume averaging at least 100,000 shares over the most recent six months.

(b) NYSE Conditions for Delisting a Security[b]
1. The number of stockholders that each own at least 100 shares falls below 1,200.
2. The number of shares that are publicly held falls below 600,000.
3. The aggregate market value of publicly held shares falls below $5,000,000 (this amount is subject to periodic adjustment based on market conditions).

[a]Generally, *all* these requirements must be met for initial listing.

[b]Normally a security will be considered for delisting if *any one* of these conditions occur. However, under certain circumstances a security may be delisted even though none of the conditions occur.

Source: Adapted from the New York Stock Exchange *Fact Book 1991*.

Table 3-1 shows various criteria that are used by the NYSE to determine whether or not to list or delist a stock. Companies may apply for listing on more than one exchange, and under certain conditions an exchange may set up "unlisted trading privileges" for transactions in a stock already listed on another exchange.

American Depository Receipts

An interesting example of securities that are listed on two exchanges (dually listed) involves certain foreign companies that are listed on a major exchange in their home country as well as on a U.S. exchange. In some cases the stock itself is traded in the U.S. (most dually listed Canadian stocks are traded in this manner). In other cases, what is traded in the U.S. is not the foreign company's stock but what is known as **American Depository Receipts** (ADRs). ADRs are financial assets that are issued by U.S. banks and represent indirect ownership of a certain number of shares of a specific foreign company that are held on deposit in a bank in the company's home country. The U.S. bank that has created the ADRs sees to it that the U.S. investor receives, in U.S. dollars, all cash dividends that the company pays. In addition, anything else that is received by the bank, such as financial reports, is forwarded to the investor. In return for providing these services, the bank charges the investor a small fee.[5]

New York Stock Exchange Members Members in the NYSE fall into one of four categories, depending on the type of trading activity in which they engage. These categories are commission brokers, floor brokers, floor traders, and specialists. Of the 1,366 members of the NYSE, roughly 700 are commission brokers, 400 are specialists, 225 are floor brokers, and 41 are floor traders. The trading activities of members in these categories are as follows:

commission brokers

1. **Commission brokers.** These members take orders that the public has placed with brokerage firms and see to it that they are executed on the exchange; the brokerage firms that they work for are paid commissions by the customers for their services.

floor brokers

2. **Floor brokers,** also known as two-dollar brokers. These members assist commission brokers when there are too many orders flowing into the market for the commission brokers to handle alone. For their assistance, they receive part of the commission paid by the customer. (Sometimes both floor brokers, as defined here, and commission brokers are lumped together and called floor brokers.)

floor traders

3. **Floor traders.** These members trade solely for themselves and are prohibited by exchange rules from handling public orders; they hope to make money by taking advantage of perceived trading imbalances that result in temporary mispricing, thereby allowing them to "buy low and sell high." These members are also known as registered competitive market-makers, competitive traders, or registered traders.

specialists

limit order book

4. **Specialists.** These members perform two roles. First, any limit order that the commission broker cannot execute immediately because the current market price is not at or better than the specified limit price will be left with the specialist for possible execution in the future. If this order is subsequently executed, the specialist is paid part of the customer's commission. The specialist keeps these orders in what is known as the **limit order book** (or specialist's book). Stop and stop limit orders are also

[5]ADRs are discussed in more detail in Chapter 26.

left with the specialist, who then enters them in the same book. In this capacity, the specialist is acting as a broker (that is, agent) for the customer's broker and can be thought of as a "broker's broker."

dealer

Second, the specialist acts as a **dealer** in certain stocks (in particular, for the same stocks in which he or she acts as a broker). This means that the specialist buys and sells certain stocks for his or her own account, and is allowed to seek a profit in doing so. However, in acting as a dealer, the specialist is required by the NYSE to maintain a "fair and orderly market" in those stocks in which he or she is registered as a specialist. Thus, the NYSE expects the specialist to buy or sell shares from his or her own account when there is a temporary imbalance between the number of buy and sell orders (in doing so, specialists are allowed to short sell their assigned stocks). Even though the NYSE monitors the trading activities of the specialists, this requirement is so ill-defined that it is difficult, if not impossible, to enforce.

trading post

As might be inferred from the preceding discussion, specialists are at the center of the trading activity on the NYSE. Each stock that is listed on the NYSE currently has one specialist assigned to it.[6] (In a few instances in the past two (or more) specialists were assigned to the same stock.) Since there are over 1,700 common stocks listed on the NYSE and only 400 specialists, this suggests that each specialist is assigned more than one stock, and indeed this is the case. All orders involving a given stock must be taken physically to a **trading post,** a spot on the floor of the NYSE where the specialist for that stock stands at all times during the hours the NYSE is open.[7] It is here that an order is either executed or left with the specialist.

bid price
asked price

Placing a Market Order The operation of the New York Stock Exchange is best described by an example. Mr. B asks his broker for the current price of General Motors shares. The broker punches a few buttons on a television-like quotation machine and finds that the current **bid** and **asked prices** on the NYSE are as favorable as the prices available on any other market, being equal to 61 and 61¼, respectively. In addition, the quotation machine indicates that these bid and asked prices are good for orders of at least 100 and 500 shares, respectively. This means that the NYSE specialist is willing to buy at least 100 shares of GM at a price of $61 (the bid price) and is willing to sell at least 500 shares of GM at $61.25 (the asked price).[8] After being given this information, Mr. B instructs his broker to "buy 300 at market," meaning that he wishes to place a market order with his broker for 300 shares of GM.

At this point the broker transmits the order to his or her firm's New York

---

[6]The assignment is made by the board of directors, and also includes any preferred stock or warrants that the company has listed on the exchange. In 1990 there were 1,769 companies listed on the NYSE, with 2,284 issues being traded, meaning there were over 500 different issues of preferred stocks and warrants being traded on the NYSE. Bonds are also listed on the NYSE but are traded in an entirely different manner that does not involve the use of specialists; in 1990 there were 743 issuers that had 2,912 issues of bonds listed on the NYSE.

[7]The NYSE is currently open from 9:30 A.M. until 4:00 P.M. However, the NYSE is considering extending its hours of operation in order to overlap with the London and Tokyo stock markets. The NYSE does allow certain computerized trading to take place after close during its Closing Session I (4:15 P.M. to 5:00 P.M.) and Closing Session II (4:00 P.M. to 5:15 P.M.); such trades are based on 4:00 P.M. closing prices.

[8]As a matter of NYSE policy, only the specialist is allowed to see the contents of the limit order book. Accordingly, these GM orders may represent either orders for the specialist's own account or public orders.

headquarters, where the order is subsequently relayed to the brokerage firm's "booth" on the side of the exchange floor. Upon receiving the order, the firm's commission broker goes to the trading post for GM.

The existence of a standing order to buy at 61 means that no one else is prepared to sell at a lower price and the existence of a standing order to sell at 61¼ means that no higher price need be paid. This leaves only the spread between the two prices for possible negotiation. If Mr. B is lucky, another broker (for example, one with a market order to sell 300 shares for Ms. S) will "take" the order at a price "between the quotes" (here, at 61⅛). Information will be exchanged between the two brokers and the sale made. Figure 3-1 illustrates the procedure used to fill Mr. B's order.

If the gap between the quoted bid and asked prices is wide enough, an auction may occur among various commission brokers, with sales made at one or more prices between the specialist's quoted values. This auction is known as a **double** (or two-way) **auction,** since both buyers and sellers are participating in the bidding process.

double auction

What if no response had been forthcoming from the floor when Mr. B's order arrived? In such a case, the specialist would "take the other side,"

FIGURE 3-1
Order Flow for a NYSE-Listed Security

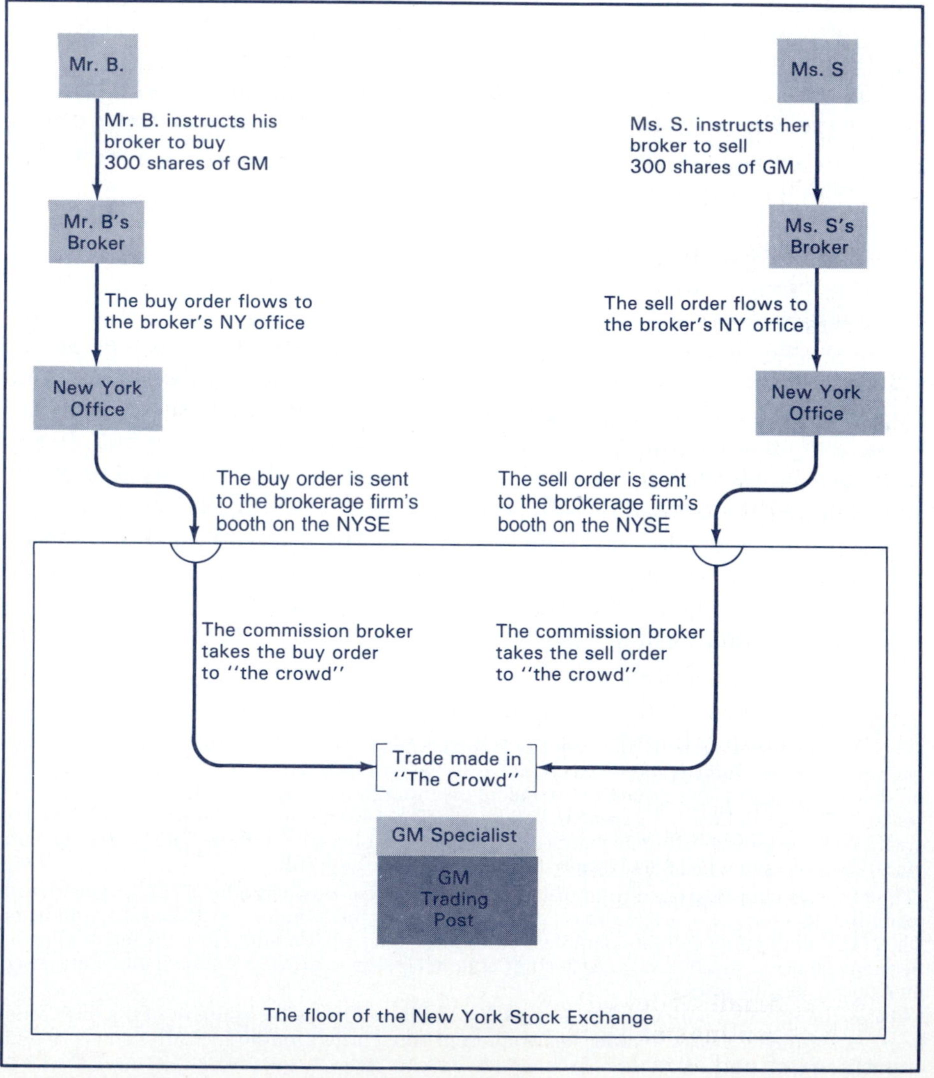

selling 300 shares to Mr. B's broker at a price of $61.25 per share. The actual seller might be the specialist or another investor whose limit order is being executed by the specialist.

If the bid-ask spread on a stock is no larger than the standard unit in which prices are quoted (typically ⅛ of a point, or 12.5 cents), market orders are generally executed directly by the specialist. This is because there is no spread for possible negotiation. In the previous example, if the specialist had quoted bid and asked prices of 61 and 61⅛, then there is no incentive for Mr. B's commission broker to try to obtain a better price for the purchase order than 61⅛, since any seller could obtain a price of 61 from the specialist. That is, to entice someone other than the specialist to sell GM to Mr. B, his commission broker would have to offer a better price than 61, since this is the price the seller could obtain from the specialist. Given that the next highest price is 61⅛, and that the specialist is willing to sell at that price, Mr. B's commission broker will deal with the specialist rather than the "crowd."

Placing a Limit Order So far, the discussion has been concerned with what would happen to a market order that was placed by Mr. B. What if Mr. B had placed a limit order instead of a market order? There are two situations that can occur with a limit order. First, the limit price may be within the bid and asked prices of the specialist. Second, the limit price may be outside these prices.

In the first situation where the specialist is quoting prices of 61 and 61¼, assume Mr. B has placed a limit order with his broker to buy 300 shares of GM at a price of 61⅛ or better. When this order is carried to the trading post, it is possible that it will be executed by the commission broker for the limit price of 61⅛, since someone in the "crowd" may be willing to take the other side of the transaction. After all, anyone with a sell order can transact with the specialist at the specialist's price of 61. To these people, the limit price of 61⅛ looks more attractive, since it represents a higher selling price to them. Thus, they would prefer doing business with Mr. B's commission broker rather than with the specialist.

In the second situation, assume Mr. B has placed a limit order to buy 300 shares of GM with a limit price of 60. When this order is carried to the trading post, the commission broker will not even attempt to fill it, since the limit price is outside the specialist's current bid and asked prices. That is, since anyone with a sell order can deal with the specialist at a price of 61, there is no chance that anyone will want to sell to Mr. B for the lower limit price of 60. Thus, the order will be given to the specialist to be entered in the specialist's book for possible execution in the future. Limit orders in the book are executed in order of price. For example, all purchase orders with limit prices of 60½ will be executed (if at all) before Mr. B's order is executed. If there are several limit orders in the book at the same price, they are executed in order of arrival (that is, first-in-first-out).

It may not be possible to fill an entire order at a single price. For example, a broker with a market order to buy 500 shares might obtain 300 shares at 61⅛ and have to pay 61¼ for the remaining 200. Similarly, a limit order to buy 500 shares at 61⅛ or better might result in the purchase of 300 shares at 61⅛ and the entry of a limit order in the specialist's book for the other 200 shares.

Large and Small Orders The NYSE has developed special procedures to handle both routine small orders and exceptionally large orders. Small orders, generally defined as orders involving 2,099 or fewer shares, can be handled

Super Designated Order Turnaround
block trade

with a procedure known as the **Super Designated Order Turnaround** system (or SuperDOT, known earlier as DOT). In order to use SuperDOT, the member firm must be a participating subscriber. With this system, the New York office of the customer's brokerage firm can send the customer's order directly to the specialist, whereupon it will be executed immediately (if possible) with a confirmation of the execution sent immediately to the brokerage firm.[9]

Exceptionally large orders are generally defined as orders involving 10,000 or more shares and are known as **blocks.** Typically, these orders are placed by institutional customers, and may be handled in a variety of ways. One way of handling a block order is to take it directly to the specialist and negotiate a price for it. However, if the block is large enough, it is quite likely that the specialist will lower the bid price (for sell orders) or raise the asked price (for buy orders) by a substantial amount. This will occur because of the risks involved, since specialists are prohibited by the exchange from soliciting offsetting orders from the public and, thus, do not know how easily they can obtain an offsetting order. Even with these disadvantages, this procedure is used on occasion, generally for relatively small blocks, and is referred to as a **specialist block purchase** or **specialist block sale,** depending on whether the institution is selling or buying shares.[10]

specialist block purchase
specialist block sale
exchange distribution
exchange acquisition

Larger blocks can be handled by use of an **exchange distribution** (for sell orders) or **exchange acquisition** (for buy orders). Here, a brokerage firm attempts to execute the order by finding enough offsetting orders from its customers. The block seller or buyer pays all brokerage costs, and the trade price is within the current bid and asked prices as quoted by the specialist. A similar procedure, known as a **special offering** (for sell orders) or **special bid** (for buy orders), involves letting all brokerage firms solicit offsetting orders from their customers.

special offering
special bid
secondary distribution

Another way of selling blocks is to have a **secondary distribution,** where the shares are sold off the exchange after the close of trading in a manner similar to the sale of new issues of common stock. The exchange must give approval for such distributions, and usually does so if it appears that the block could not be absorbed easily in normal trading on the exchange. Accordingly, secondary distributions generally involve the sale of exceptionally large blocks.

upstairs dealer market
block houses

While all of these ways of handling block orders are used at one time or another, most block orders are handled in what is known as the **upstairs dealer market.** By using **block houses,** which are set up to deal with large orders, institutions have been able to get better prices for their orders. This occurs because the block houses, when informed by an institution that it wants to place a block order, will proceed to line up trading partners (including itself) to take the other side of the order. After this is done the block house will attempt to reach a mutually acceptable price with the original institution. Assuming that such a price is reached (if not, the institution can take the order to a different block house), the order will be "crossed" on the floor of the exchange, meaning that the specialist is given the opportunity to

---

[9]For odd lot orders, the brokerage firm may execute the order internally (meaning it sells shares from its own inventory or adds shares to its inventory, depending on whether the customer is buying or selling) or may use SuperDOT. There are special features of SuperDot that are used to execute opening orders—that is, orders that are received up to the time the NYSE opens in the morning.

[10]One alternative for the institution that is thinking of placing the block order is to sequentially place many small orders. However, institutions generally do not want to do this, since it means that their block order will not be executed with due speed.

fill any limit orders that are in the specialist's book at the block's selling price.[11] However, there is a limit on the number of shares (1,000 shares or 5% of the size of the block, whichever is greater) that can be taken by the specialist to fill these limit orders.

For example, suppose the PF Pension Fund informs a block house that it wishes to sell 20,000 shares of General Motors common stock. The block house then proceeds to find three institutional investors that want to buy, say, 5,000 shares apiece; the block house decides that it too will buy 5,000 shares of GM from PF. Noting that the buyers have said that they would be willing to pay $70 per share, the block house subsequently informs PF that it will buy the 20,000 shares for $69.75 each, less a commission of $8,000. Assuming PF accepts the deal, the block house now becomes the owner of the shares but must first "cross" them on the NYSE, since the block house is a member of the exchange. In this example, assume that when the block is crossed at $69.75, the specialist buys 500 shares at this price for a limit order that is in his or her book. After the cross, the block house gives 5,000 shares to each of the institutional buyers in exchange for $350,000 (= 5,000 shares × $70 per share) and hopes that the remaining 4,500 shares that it now owns can be sold in the near future at a favorable price. Needless to say, the possibility of not being able to sell them at a favorable price is one of the risks involved in being a block house.

Other Exchanges

Table 3-2 shows the total trading volume of securities listed on each of the active stock exchanges in the United States in1990. Not surprisingly, the New York Stock Exchange dominates the list. Second in importance is the American Stock Exchange (AMEX), which lists shares of somewhat smaller companies of national interest (a few of which are also listed on the New York Stock Exchange). All the others are termed **regional exchanges,** since historically each served as the sole location for trading securities primarily of interest to investors in its region. However, the major regional exchanges now depend to a substantial extent on transactions in securities that are also listed on a national exchange. Interestingly, the regional exchanges are currently larger, in aggregate, than the AMEX. Major regional exchanges currently in existence include the Boston, Cincinnati, Midwest, Pacific, and Philadelphia exchanges.

regional exchanges

Other stock exchanges use procedures similar to those of the New York Stock Exchange. The role of specialists and the extent of automation may differ slightly but the approach is basically the same.

Options exchanges and futures exchanges utilize some procedures that differ significantly from those employed by stock exchanges. Futures exchanges often have daily price limits instead of having specialists with directions to maintain "fair and orderly markets." The Chicago Board Options Exchange separates the two functions of the specialist; an "order book official" is charged with the maintenance of the book of limit orders, with one or more registered "market-makers" assigned the role of dealer. These exchanges will be discussed in more detail in Chapters 24 and 25.

[11]The order must be crossed on an exchange where the stock is listed, provided that the block house is a member of that exchange.

TABLE 3-2
Trading Volumes of the Stock Exchanges

(a) 1990 Trading Volume

Market	SHARES[a]		DOLLARS[a]	
	Annual	Daily	Annual	Daily
NYSE	39,665	157	$1,325,332	$5,238
AMEX	3,329	13	37,715	149
Regionals	6,208	25	178,139	704
NASDAQ	33,380	132	452,430	1,788
Third Market	2,589	10	86,494	342

(b) Five-Year Comparisons

Year	NYSE			NASDAQ		
	Companies	Issues	Daily Share Volume[a]	Companies	Issues	Daily Share Volume[a]
1990	1,769	2,284	157	4,132	4,706	132
1989	1,719	2,241	165	4,293	4,963	133
1988	1,681	2,234	161	4,451	5,144	123
1987	1,647	2,244	189	4,706	5,537	150
1986	1,573	2,257	141	4,417	5,189	114

[a]In millions.

Source: Adapted from the New York Stock Exchange *Fact Book 1991* and the NASDAQ *1991 Fact Book & Company Directory.*

The Over-the-Counter Market

In the early days of the United States, banks acted as the primary dealers for stocks and bonds, and investors literally bought and sold securities "over the counter" at the banks. Transactions are more impersonal now, but the designation remains in use for transactions that are not executed on an organized exchange but, instead, involve the use of a dealer. Most bonds are sold over the counter, as are the securities of small (and some not-so-small) companies.

National Association of Securities Dealers
National Association of Securities Dealers Automated Quotations

The over-the-counter (OTC) market for stocks is highly automated. In 1971 the **National Association of Securities Dealers** (NASD), which serves as a self-regulating agency for its members, put into operation the **National Association of Securities Dealers Automated Quotations** system (NASDAQ). This nationwide communications network allows brokers to know instantly the terms offered currently by all major dealers in securities covered by the system.

Dealers who subscribe to Level III of NASDAQ are given terminals with which to enter bid and asked prices for any stock in which they "make a market." Such dealers must be prepared to execute trades for at least one "normal unit of trading" (usually 100 shares) at the prices quoted. As soon as a bid or asked price is entered for a security, it is placed in a central computer file and may be seen by other subscribers (including other dealers) on their own terminals. When new quotations are entered, they replace the dealer's former prices.

When there is competition among dealers, those who are not well-informed either price themselves out of the market by having too wide a bid-ask spread, or go out of business after incurring heavy losses. In the first situation, nobody does business with such a dealer, since there are better prices available with other dealers. The second situation occurs when the dealer accumulates a large inventory at too high a price or disposes of inventory at too low a price; thus, the dealer will be doing the opposite of the familiar Wall Street adage of "buy low, sell high." In general, the interests of investors are best served by a market in which dealers with unlimited access to all sources of information compete with one another, thereby leading to narrow bid-ask spreads around the "intrinsic" value of the security.

Most brokerage firms subscribe to Level II of NASDAQ for their trading rooms, obtaining terminals that can display the current quotations on any security in the system. All bid and asked quotations are displayed, with the dealer offering each quotation being identified so that orders can be routed to the dealer with the best price.[12] Imagine how difficult it would be to get the best price for a customer in the absence of such a terminal (as was the case before NASDAQ existed). A broker would have to contact dealers one by one to try to find the best price; after determining what appears to be the best price, the broker would then proceed to contact that dealer again. However, when this dealer is contacted, it may turn out that the price has gone up or down in the meantime and that the previously quoted price may no longer be the best one.

Level I of NASDAQ is used by individual account executives to get a feel for the market. It shows the **inside quotes,** meaning the highest bid and the lowest asked price for each security, along with last-sale reports.

inside quotes

NASDAQ classifies stocks with larger trading volumes (which also meet certain other requirements) as belonging to the **National Market System** (NASDAQ/NMS). Every transaction made by a dealer for such a stock is reported directly, providing up-to-date detailed trading information to NASDAQ users. Furthermore, any stock included in NASDAQ/NMS is automatically eligible for margin purchases and short sales. For the less active issues, dealers report only the total transactions at the close of each day, and only certain ones are eligible for margin purchases and short sales (the Federal Reserve Board determines which ones are eligible four times a year).

National Market System

As its name indicates, NASDAQ is primarily a quotation system. Actual transactions are often made via direct negotiation over the telephone between broker and dealer.[13] The price paid by a customer buying shares is likely to be higher than the amount paid by the broker to procure the shares, with the difference being known as a **markup.** When selling shares, the customer will receive a price less than that received by the broker, with the difference being known as a **markdown.** (In both cases, the customer may also be charged a commission.) The size of these markups and markdowns is usually less than 5% of the price paid or received; brokers are periodically examined by the Securities and Exchange Commission to see that these markups and markdowns are "reasonable."

markup

markdown

To be included in NASDAQ, a security must have at least two registered market-makers (that is, dealers) and a minimum number of publicly held shares; moreover, the issuing firm must meet stated capital and asset require-

[12]Generally the order will be a market order, since there is no central "limit order book" in the over-the-counter market except for small orders; stop and stop limit orders are not allowed in the OTC market. See footnote 13.

[13]Orders involving up to 1,000 shares of any NASDAQ/NMS security (for non-NMS securities, the limit is 500 shares) are handled by a computer system known as **SOES** (Small Order Execution System). Such orders can be either market or limit orders, since SOES maintains a composite limit order book.

SOES

ments. As shown in Table 3-2, at the end of 1990, 4,706 issues were included in the system.[14] While this total is more than double the total for the NYSE, trading volume is less than that of the NYSE, especially when measured in dollars.

pink sheets

The NASDAQ system covers only a portion of the outstanding OTC stocks, and no bonds. Brokers with orders to buy or sell other OTC securities rely on quotations that are published daily on either NASDAQ's OTC Bulletin Board or on what are known as **pink sheets** (there are also less formal communication networks) in order to obtain "best execution" for their clients.

The Third and Fourth Markets

third market

Until the 1970s, the New York Stock Exchange required its member firms to trade all NYSE-listed stocks at the Exchange and to charge fixed commissions. For large institutions this was expensive. In particular, the existence of a required minimum commission rate created a serious problem, since it exceeded the marginal cost of arranging large trades. Brokerage firms that were not members of the exchange faced no restrictions on the commissions they could charge and thus could compete effectively for large trades in NYSE-listed stocks. Such transactions were said to take place in the **third market.** More generally, the term third market now refers to the trading of any exchange-listed security in the over-the-counter market. The existence of such a market is enhanced today by the fact that their trading hours are not fixed (unlike exchanges), and that they can continue to trade securities even when trading is halted on an exchange. As can be seen in Table 3-2, on average 10 million shares were traded in the third market during each day of 1990.

Until 1976, NYSE member firms were prohibited by Rule 394 from either acting as dealers in the third market or executing orders involving NYSE-listed securities for their customers in the third market. In 1976, Rule 394 was replaced by Rule 390, which permits the execution of these orders in the third market but still prohibits member firms from acting as dealers in the third market. However, the Securities and Exchange Commission has issued a rule that permits member firms to act as dealers in securities that became listed on the NYSE after April 26, 1979. Controversy still exists over Rule 390, as some people argue that it should be abolished completely to spur competition between the NYSE and the over-the-counter market, whereas others argue that having all orders funneled to the NYSE will lead to the most competitive marketplace possible.

fourth market

Instinet

Many institutions have dispensed with brokers and exchanges altogether for transactions in exchange-listed stocks and other securities. Trades of this type, where the buyer and seller deal directly with each other, are sometimes said to take place in the **fourth market.** In the U.S., some of these transactions are facilitated by an automated computer/communications system called **Instinet,** which provides quotations and execution automatically.[15] A subscriber can enter a limit order in the computerized "book," where it can be seen by other subscribers who can, in turn, signal their desire to take it. Whenever two orders are matched, the system automatically records the

[14]Of this total, 256 were foreign securities consisting of 86 ADRs and 170 non-ADRs; 132 of the 170 non-ADRs were Canadian issues.

[15]The use of an intermediary like a computer system makes it difficult to categorize such trades. Some people would refer to the market where trades involving a "matchmaker" take place as the "3.5 market." The term fourth market would then be used only when referring to the market where no matchmaker is involved.

MONEY MATTERS

Crossing Systems: The Evolution of the Fourth Market

Scientists define the evolution of a species as its gradual adoption of features that facilitate its long-term survival. In this context it is fitting to refer to the evolution of the fourth market. From its rudimentary beginnings, the fourth market has evolved into a sophisticated trading mechanism where millions of shares change hands daily. Further, like any successful new species, the fourth market is posing a threat to existing species, in this case the organized security exchanges. How this competition plays out will influence the nature of trading well into the twenty-first century.

The fourth market, where large institutional investors (such as pension funds, mutual funds, and endowment funds) deal directly with one another without the intervention of a market-maker, began as a technological response to the high commission rates charged by brokerage firms. As discussed in the text, the original fourth market trading mechanism, run by Instinet, allows investors to trade with each other through an automated communications system at commissions that are only a small fraction of those charged by brokers.

However, this trading process (which still exists) is rather cumbersome. Investors submit buy or sell limit orders (see Chapter 2) on individual securities at irregular times. If an interested investor on the "other side" of the trade happens to access the system at the right time, the trade may be completed. While the transaction costs of trading on the original fourth market are quite low (about a penny per share), the odds of being able to complete large trades in numerous securities are small. Without improvement, the fourth market would surely have been pushed aside by other trading mechanisms, just as many promising, but ineffective, prehistoric creatures succumbed to competitors.

But the fourth market did evolve. Crossing systems now conduct regular market sessions in which investors may submit large packages of securities for trade. More specifically, current crossing systems work as follows:

1. Periodic trading sessions are established and widely announced.
2. Prior to these trading sessions, investors anonymously submit lists of stocks they wish to buy or sell and the associated quantities.
3. At the scheduled time (usually once or twice a day), the lists of desired trades are compared automatically by computer.
4. Trade prices are based on then current market prices as set on the organized security exchanges.
5. Offsetting buys and sells are matched. When buy orders do not equal sell orders for a security, matches are allocated based on the total dollar value of trades entered by each investor. Thus investors are encouraged to submit large trading volume requests.
6. Investors are notified of the completed trades and the system handles the transfer of stocks.
7. Unmatched trades are returned to the investors for resubmission or execution elsewhere.

The primary users of crossing networks are investors with no urgent need to trade. Index funds (see Chapter 17), for example, trade only to adjust their portfolios so as to most effectively track the performance of a specific market index. Whether they trade this morning or this afternoon usually has little bearing on their results. Therefore, transaction costs are their primary concern. Because crossing systems charge only 1¢ to 2¢ per share (as opposed to the 3¢ to 12¢ charged to large investors by brokerage firms) and avoid the costs associated with the bid-asked spread and price impact (discussed later in this chapter), they are by far the lowest-cost alternative for these patient investors.

Crossing systems can only operate effectively if a sufficient number of investors submit trades, thereby generating a reasonable likelihood of successful matches. Currently, two crossing systems exist: POSIT (run by Jeffries & Company, a brokerage firm, and BARRA, a consulting firm) and the Crossing Network (run by Instinet). When both began operations in 1987, trading volume was minimal. In subsequent years, however, volume has increased. Currently, almost 8 million shares a day change hands through the crossing systems. While this figure translates into less than 5% of the New York Stock Exchange's daily volume, participating investors are typically matching 10% to 20% of their submitted trades and that figure is expected to grow.

Crossing systems are just beginning to conduct global operations. Given that transaction costs on foreign markets are usually many times greater than they are in the U.S., the room for future growth appears enormous. The evolution of the fourth market continues.

transaction and sets up the paperwork for its completion. Subscribers can also use the system to find likely partners for a trade, then conduct negotiations by telephone. Other examples are the Crossing Network and POSIT (Portfolio System for Institutional Trading).

Foreign Markets

The two largest stock markets in the world outside New York are located in London and Tokyo. Both of these markets have recently undergone major changes in their rules and operating procedures. Furthermore, both of them have active markets in foreign securities. In particular, at the end of 1989 the London Stock Exchange listed 680 foreign stocks (in addition to 2,041 U.K. and Irish stocks) while the Tokyo Stock Exchange listed 125 foreign stocks (in addition to 1,627 Japanese stocks).

SEAQ

SEAF

London In October 1986, the "big bang" introduced several major reforms to the London Stock Exchange. Fixed brokerage commissions were eliminated, membership was opened up to corporations, and foreign firms were allowed to purchase existing member firms. Furthermore, an automated dealer quotation system similar to NASDAQ was introduced. This system, known as **SEAQ** (Stock Exchange Automated Quotations), involves competing market-makers whose quotes are displayed over a computer network. Small orders can be executed by using **SEAF** (SEAQ Automated Execution Facility) that functions like NASDAQ's SOES; large orders are handled over the telephone. Limit orders are not centrally handled but instead are handled by individual brokers or dealers who note when prices have moved sufficiently that they can be executed.

NASDAQ International

In an attempt to recapture some of the trading in U.S. securities from the London Stock Exchange, NASD received approval from the SEC for a computer system like NASDAQ that involves trading of many of the stocks listed on either the NYSE, AMEX, or NASDAQ/NMS. This system, known as **NASDAQ International,** opens for trading at 3:30 A.M., which corresponds to the opening time of the London Stock Exchange, and closes at 9:00 A.M., a half-hour before the NYSE opens.

CORES

FORES

Tokyo Similar to the London Stock Exchange, the Tokyo Stock Exchange has recently experienced major reforms. **CORES** (Computer-assisted Order Routing and Execution System), a computer system for trading all but the 150 most active securities, was introduced in 1982. Then in 1986 the exchange began to admit foreign firms as members, and in 1991 **FORES** (Floor Order Routing and Execution System) was introduced as a computer system to facilitate trading in the most active stocks.

Interestingly, the system of trading both the most active and the relatively less active securities is quite different from any system found in either the U.S. or the U.K. It is centered around members known as *saitori* who act, in a sense, as auctioneers in that they are neither dealers nor specialists. Instead they are middlemen who accept orders from member firms and are not allowed to trade in any stocks for their own account.

At the opening of the exchange (since the exchange is open from 9:00 A.M. to 11:00 A.M. and 1:00 P.M. to 3:00 P.M., there are two openings per day) the saitori members follow a method called *itayose,* which operates like a call market in that the saitori seeks to set a single price so that the amount of trading is maximized (subject to certain constraints). This involves constructing supply and demand schedules for the market and limit orders that have been received, and noting where the two schedules intersect (an example of how this is done is described in Chapter 4 and illustrated in Figures 4-1 through 4-4).

After the opening of the exchange, the saitori follows a method known as *zaraba*, where orders are processed continually as they are received. That is, market orders are offset against previously unfilled limit orders. New limit orders are filled, if possible, against previously unfilled limit orders; if these new limit orders cannot be filled, then they are entered in the limit order book for possible future execution. Unlike the limit order book on the NYSE, the limit order book in Tokyo is available for inspection by member firms. Further, unlike the NYSE the Tokyo Stock Exchange prohibits trading at prices outside a given range based on the previous day's closing price. Hence there can be situations where trading in a stock ceases until the next day (when the price range is readjusted) unless two parties decide to trade within the current range.

THE CENTRAL MARKET

The Securities Acts Amendments of 1975 mandated that the U.S. Securities and Exchange Commission should move as rapidly as possible toward the implementation of a truly nationwide competitive central security market:

> The linking of all markets for qualified securities through communication and data processing facilities will foster efficiency, enhance competition, increase the information available to brokers, dealers, and investors, facilitate the offsetting of investors' orders, and contribute to best execution of such orders.[16]

Implementation of these objectives has proceeded in steps. In 1975, a **Consolidated Tape** began to report trades in stocks listed on the New York and American stock exchanges that took place on the two exchanges, on major regional exchanges, in the over-the-counter market using the NASDAQ system, and in the fourth market using the Instinet system. Since 1976, this information has been used to produce the **composite stock price tables** published in the daily press.

Consolidated Tape

composite stock price tables

The second step involved the setting of commissions charged to investors by brokerage firms that are members of the NYSE. Prior to 1975, investors would find the same commission being charged by all NYSE member firms for a given order. This was due to the fact that the NYSE required its members to charge a fixed commission. However, as a result of the Securities Acts Amendments of 1975, this system of fixed commissions was abolished and all brokerage firms were free to set their commissions at whatever level they desired.

The next step involved quotations. To obtain the best possible terms for a client, a broker must know the prices currently available on all major markets. To facilitate this, the Securities and Exchange Commission instructed stock exchanges to make their quotations available for use in a **Consolidated Quotations System** (CQS). With the implementation of this system in 1978, bid and asked prices were made more accessible to those

Consolidated Quotations System

[16]From *Securities Acts Amendments of 1975*, section 11A.

Intermarket Trading System

subscribing to quotation services. Increasingly, a broker is able to rely on electronics to determine the best available terms for a trade, thus avoiding the need for extensive "shopping around."

In 1978, the **Intermarket Trading System** (ITS) was inaugurated. This electronic communications network links seven exchanges (the NYSE, AMEX, Boston, Cincinnati, Midwest, Pacific, and Philadelphia exchanges) and certain over-the-counter security dealers, enabling brokers, dealers, and specialists at various locations to interact with one another. ITS display monitors provide the bid and asked prices quoted by market-makers (these quotes are obtained from CQS) and the system allows the broker to route orders electronically to where the best price exists at that moment. However, the market-maker providing the best price may withdraw it on receipt of an order. Another drawback is that brokers are not required to route orders to the market-maker providing the best price. At the end of 1990, 2,126 exchange-listed stocks were included on the system and daily trading volume averaged 9.4 million shares.

The final step in the process has not been implemented. It involves the establishment of a single centralized limit order book (CLOB), with associated procedures for linking markets electronically and the setting of rules concerning its use and disclosure. In implementing this step, many issues must be settled: Should there be specialists, and if so, how should they operate? What requirements (if any) should be imposed on market-makers? Who should operate the central market system?

There are many long-entrenched and powerful institutions in the securities industry. The eventual nature of the overall set of markets will undoubtedly depend in part on the relative political power of the various vested interests.

CLEARING PROCEDURES

Most stocks are sold the "regular way," which requires delivery of certificates within five business days. On rare occasions, a sale may be made as a "cash" transaction, requiring delivery the same day, or as a "seller's option," giving the seller the choice of any delivery day within a specified period (typically, no more than sixty days). On other occasions, extensions to the five-day time limit are granted.

It would be extremely inefficient if every security transaction had to end with a physical transfer of stock certificates from the seller to the buyer. A brokerage firm might sell 500 shares of American Telephone & Telegraph stock for one client, Mr. A, and later that day buy 500 shares for Ms. B, another client. Mr. A's 500 shares could be delivered to the buyer, and Ms. B's shares could be obtained by accepting delivery from the seller. However, it would be much easier to transfer Mr. A's shares to Ms. B and instruct Ms. B's seller to deliver 500 shares directly to Mr. A's buyer. This would be especially helpful if the brokerage firm's clients, Mr. A and Ms. B, held their securities in street name. Then, the 500 shares would not have to be moved and their ownership would not have to be changed on the books of AT&T.

Clearinghouses

clearinghouse

The process can be facilitated even more by a **clearinghouse,** the members of which are brokerage firms, banks, and other financial institutions. Records of transactions made by members during a day are sent there. At the end of the day, both sides of the trades are verified for consistency, then all transactions are netted out. Each member receives a list of the net amounts of securities to be delivered or received along with the net amount of money to be paid or collected. Every day, each member settles with the clearinghouse instead of with various other firms.

A centralized clearinghouse, operated by the National Securities Clearing Corporation, handles trades made on the New York and American stock exchanges and in the over-the-counter market. Some regional exchanges also maintain clearinghouses. Not all exchange members join such organizations; some choose to use the services of other members. Some banks belong in order to facilitate delivery of securities which, for example, serve as collateral for call loans.

By holding securities in street name and using clearinghouses, brokers can reduce the cost of transfer operations. But even more can be done: certificates can be immobilized almost completely. The **Depository Trust Company** (DTC) accomplishes this by maintaining computerized records of the securities "owned" by its member firms (brokers, banks, and so on). Members' stock certificates are credited to their accounts at the DTC, while the certificates are transferred to the DTC on the books of the issuing corporation and remain registered in its name unless a member subsequently withdraws them. Whenever possible, one member will "deliver" securities to another by initiating a simple bookkeeping entry in which one account is credited and the other debited for the shares involved. Dividends paid on securities held by the DTC are simply credited to members' accounts based on their holdings and may be subsequently withdrawn in cash.

Depository Trust Company

The Securities Acts Amendments of 1975 instructed the Securities and Exchange Commission to develop a central system of this sort to eliminate the movement of stock certificates and possibly eliminate stock certificates entirely. Eventually, when cash dividends are to be paid by a corporation, instead of writing checks, its computers may transfer money directly using other computers that are in touch with still other computers in banks, brokerage firms, and other financial institutions. Moreover, the central market system may be integrated with the central clearing system so that agreement of two parties to the terms of a transaction will automatically bring about the transfer of ownership required to complete the trade.

INSURANCE

In the late 1960s, many brokerage firms were confronted with an unexpectedly large volume of transactions. Unfortunately, at that time computerized systems were unable to handle the workload. This gave rise to back-office problems and resulted in a rash of "**fails to deliver**"—instances in which a seller's broker did not deliver certificates to a buyer's broker on or before the required settlement date.

fails to deliver

Worse yet, several brokerage firms subsequently failed, and some of their clients discovered for the first time that certificates "in their accounts" were not physically available. Such events led to serious concern about the desirability of any procedure that kept certificates out of the hands of the investor. To avoid erosion of investor confidence, member firms of the New York Stock Exchange spent substantial sums to cover the losses of failed firms or to merge them with successful firms. But such remedies were only temporary; insurance provided a more permanent solution.

Securities Investor Protection Corporation (SIPC)

Securities Investor Protection Corporation

The Securities Investor Protection Act of 1970 established the **Securities Investor Protection Corporation** (SIPC), a quasi-governmental agency that insures the accounts of clients of all brokers and members of exchanges registered with the Securities and Exchange Commission against loss due to a brokerage firm's failure. Each account is insured up to a stated amount ($500,000 per customer in 1991). The cost of the insurance is supposed to be borne by the covered brokers and members through premiums; should this amount be insufficient, SIPC can borrow up to $1 billion from the U.S. Treasury.

A number of brokerage firms have gone further, arranging for additional coverage from private insurance companies.

COMMISSIONS

Fixed Commissions

In the 1770s, people interested in buying and selling stocks and bonds met under a buttonwood tree at 68 Wall Street in New York City. In May 1792, a group of brokers pledged "not to buy or sell from this day for any person whatsoever, any kind of public stock at a less rate than one quarter percent commission on the specie value, and that we will give preference to each other in our negotiations."[17] A visitor to the New York Stock Exchange in the early 1990s could see a copy of this "buttonwood agreement" publicly displayed. This was not surprising, since the Exchange is a lineal descendant of the group that met under the buttonwood tree. And, until 1968, the Exchange required its member brokers to charge fixed minimum commissions for stocks, with no "rebates, returns, discounts or allowances in 'any shape or manner,' direct or indirect."[18] The terms had changed, but the principle established 180 years earlier remained in effect.

In the United States, most cartels designed to limit competition by fixing prices are illegal. But this one was exempted from prosecution under the antitrust laws. Before 1934 the Exchange was, in essence, considered a private club for its members. This changed with passage of the Securities Exchange Act of 1934, which required most exchanges to be registered with the Securities and Exchange Commission (SEC). The Commission, in turn, encouraged exchanges to "self-regulate" their activities, including the setting of minimum commissions.

Competitive Commissions

May Day

As mentioned earlier in this chapter, the system of fixed commissions was finally terminated by the Securities Acts Amendments of 1975 (but only after repeated challenges by the NYSE). Since May 1, 1975 (known in the trade as **May Day**), brokers have been free to set commissions at any desired rate or to negotiate with customers concerning the fees charged for particular trades. The former procedure is more commonly employed in "retail" trades exe-

[17]See Wilford J. Eiteman, Charles A. Dice, and David K. Eiteman, *The Stock Market* (New York: McGraw-Hill Book Company, 1969), p. 19.

[18]Eitemen, Dice, and Eiteman, *The Stock Market*, p. 138.

cuted for small investors, while the latter is used more often when handling large trades involving institutional investors and others.

In the era of fixed commissions, brokerage firms did not compete with one another over commissions. However, those brokerage firms that belonged to the New York Stock Exchange competed with one another in a different manner—namely, by offering a panoply of ancillary services to customers. Large institutions were provided with security analysis, performance measurement services, and the like in return for **soft dollars**—brokerage commissions ostensibly paid for having the brokerage firm execute their trades and indirectly designated as payment for services rendered. It appears that for every $3 in commissions received on large trades, brokerage firms were willing to spend up to roughly $2 to provide ancillary services to the customers. Thus, it follows that it cost brokerage firms roughly $1 per $3 of commissions received just to execute a large trade for a customer. Apparently, up to two-thirds of the fixed commission rate ($2 out of $3) on such large orders was pure (marginal) profit.

soft dollars

Experience after May Day provided confirmation. Rates for large trades fell substantially. So did those charged for small trades by firms offering only "bare-bones" brokerage services. On the other hand, broad-line firms that provided extensive services to small investors for no additional fee continued to charge commissions similar to those specified in the earlier fixed schedules. In succeeding years, as costs have risen, charges for smaller transactions have increased, while those for large trades have not.

During the 1960s and 1970s, a number of procedures were used to subvert the fixed commission rates. In particular, the third and fourth markets expanded their operations while regional exchanges invented ways to serve as conduits to return a portion of the fixed commissions to institutional investors.

No legal restriction gave the New York Stock Exchange its monopoly power in the first instance. Instead, the situation has been attributed to the natural monopoly arising from economies of scale in bringing together many people (either physically or via modern communications technology) to trade with one another. The potential profits from such a monopoly are limited by the advantages it confers. The increasing institutionalization of security holdings and progress in communications and computer technology have diminished the advantages associated with a centralized physical exchange. Thus, the removal of legal protection for this particular type of price fixing may have only accelerated a trend already underway.

Increased competition among brokerage firms has resulted in a wide range of alternatives for investors. Following May Day, some firms "unbundled"—meaning that they priced their services separately from their pricing of order execution. Other firms "went discount," meaning that they dropped almost all ancillary services and cut commissions accordingly. Still others "bundled" new services into comprehensive packages. Some of these approaches have not stood the test of time, but just as mail-order firms, discount houses, department stores, and expensive boutiques coexist in the retail clothing trade, many different combinations are viable in the brokerage industry.

Figure 3-2 shows typical commission rates charged by retail brokerage firms for small- to medium-sized trades. These rates are representative of those charged by full-line retail brokers that provide offices with quotation boards, research reports, account executives available for advice and information, and the like. The rates also apply to trades made by customers whose

FIGURE 3-2
Typical Commission Rates for Selected Transactions; Dollar Commission as a Percentage of the Value of the Order

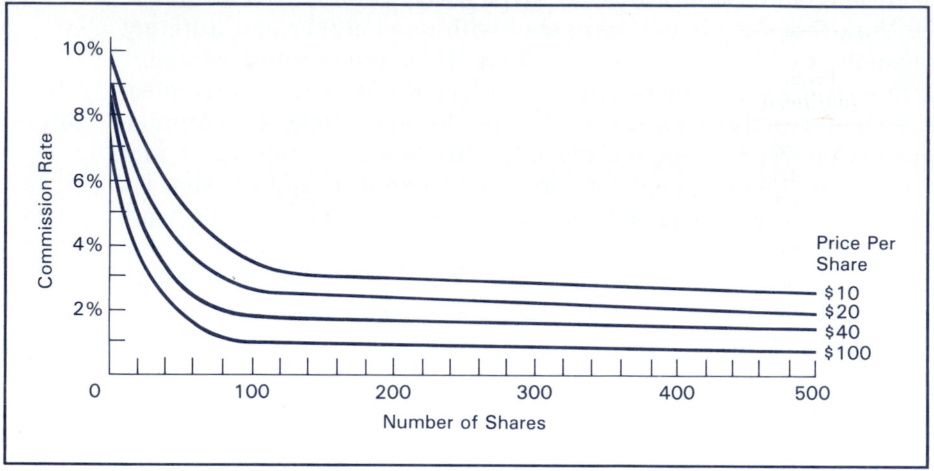

volume of business is small. Discount firms with little but execution capability typically charge 30% to 70% less. As in any other competitive industry, it behooves the customer to decide what is worth paying for and then to shop around to obtain the best possible price.

TRANSACTION COSTS

The Bid-Ask Spread

Commission costs are only a portion of the total cost associated with buying or selling a security. Consider a "round-trip" transaction, in which a stock is purchased and then sold during a period in which no new information causes investors to collectively reassess the value of the stock (more concretely, the bid and asked prices quoted by dealers do not change). The stock will be purchased typically at the dealers' asked price and sold at the bid price, which is lower. The **bid-ask spread** thus constitutes a portion of the round-trip transaction costs.

bid-ask spread

How large is the spread between the bid and asked prices for a typical stock? According to one study, the spread is approximately $.30 per share for the securities of large, actively traded companies. This amounts to less than 1% of the price per share for most stocks of this type—a reasonably small amount to pay for the ability to buy or sell in a hurry.

However, not all securities enjoy this type of liquidity. Shares of smaller firms tend to sell at lower prices but at similar bid-ask spreads. As a result, the percentage transaction cost is considerably larger. This is shown in panel (a) of Table 3-3. Stocks were assigned to sectors based on each firm's **market capitalization,** which is equal to the market value of the firm's outstanding equity. For example, if the total market value of the common stock of a company was less than $10 million, it was considered to be in sector 1 (the

market capitalization

TABLE 3-3 Bid-Ask Spreads and Round-Trip Transaction Costs

(a) Common Stock Bid-Ask Spreads: Small Orders

	CAPITALIZATION						
Sector	From (millions)	To (millions)	Number of Issues	Percent of U.S. Market	Average Price	Average Spread	Spread / Price
1 (small)	$ 0	$ 10	1,009	.36%	$ 4.58	$.30	6.55%
2	10	25	754	.89	10.30	.42	4.07
3	25	50	613	1.59	15.16	.46	3.03
4	50	75	362	1.60	18.27	.34	1.86
5	75	100	202	1.27	21.85	.32	1.46
6	100	500	956	15.65	28.31	.32	1.13
7	500	1,000	238	12.29	35.43	.27	.76
8	1,000	1,500	102	8.87	44.34	.29	.65
9 (large)	1,500	99,999	180	57.48	52.40	.27	.52

(b) Percentage Round-Trip Transaction Costs, Common Stock

	CAPITALIZATION								
	Dollar Value of Block ($ thousands)								
Sector	5	25	250	500	1,000	2,500	5,000	10,000	20,000
1 (small)	17.3%	27.3%	43.8%						
2	8.9	12.0	23.8	33.4%					
3	5.0	7.6	18.8	25.9	30.0%				
4	4.3	5.8	9.6	16.9	25.4	31.5%			
5	2.8	3.9	5.9	8.1	11.5	15.7	25.7%		
6	1.8	2.1	3.2	4.4	5.6	7.9	11.0	16.2%	
7	1.9	2.0	3.1	4.0	5.6	7.7	10.4	14.3	20.0%
8	1.9	1.9	2.7	3.3	4.6	6.2	8.9	13.6	18.1
9 (large)	1.1	1.2	1.3	1.7	2.1	2.8	4.1	5.9	8.0

Source: Thomas F. Loeb, "Trading Cost: The Critical Link Between Investment Information and Results," *Financial Analysts Journal*, 39, no. 3 (May/June 1983), pp. 41–42.

smallest capitalization sector), and if the market value was greater than $1.5 billion, the company was included in sector 9 (the largest capitalization sector). As the table shows, the larger the capitalization, the greater was the average price per share. Note also that the average spread in dollars was actually greater for the smallest capitalization stocks than for the largest. Most importantly, however, the ratio of the average spread to the average price fell continuously from 6.55% for the smallest sector to .52% for the largest sector. This means that the larger the capitalization of the firm, the greater the liquidity will be for that investment.

Another study looked at NYSE stocks, based on their trading activity, and found similar-sized spreads. Specifically, the 20% most active stocks had a spread of .62%. The spreads increased uniformly thereafter, with the 20% least active stocks having the largest spread of 2.06%.[19]

[19]Roger D. Huang and Hans R. Stoll, *Major World Equity Markets: Current Structure and Prospects for Change*, Monograph Series in Finance and Economics 1991–93, New York University Salomon Center, New York City, 1991, p. 11.

Price Impact

price impacts

Brokerage commissions and bid-ask spreads represent transaction costs for small orders (typically 100 shares). For larger-sized orders, the possibility of **price impacts** must also be considered. Consider purchase orders. Due to the law of supply and demand, the larger the size of the order, the more likely the investor's purchase price will be higher. Furthermore, the more rapidly the order is to be completed and the more knowledgeable the individual or organization placing the order, the higher the purchase price charged by the dealer.

Panel (b) of Table 3-3 provides estimates of average costs for transactions in the upstairs dealer market. All three sources of costs are included: bid-ask spreads, brokerage commissions, and price impacts. The figures refer to the total cost for a "round-trip"—a purchase followed by a sale—and reveal that for any capitalization sector, larger block sizes are associated with larger percentage transaction costs. The figures also reveal that for any given dollar-size block, larger capitalization sectors are associated with smaller percentage transaction costs [a similar observation can be made upon examination of panel (a)].

Panel (a) of Figure 3-3 plots the percentage transaction costs for blocks of $25,000 each, which correspond to the values in the third column from the left in panel (b) of Table 3-3. Values range from 27.3% (for small-capitalization stocks) to 1.2% (for large-capitalization stocks).

Panel (b) of Figure 3-3 shows the relationship between order size and transaction cost for each of the three largest capitalization sectors, which correspond to the last three rows of panel (b) of Table 3-3. The figure shows that the impact of a very large order on price can be substantial, and the impact is greater for smaller capitalizations.

INVESTMENT BANKING

primary market

investment bankers

The discussion so far has focused on secondary markets for securities, where securities that were initially issued at some previous point in time are subsequently traded. The focus will now shift to the **primary market** for securities, which is the name given to the markets where the initial issuance itself takes place. Some issuers deal directly with purchasers in this market, but many rely on **investment bankers,** who serve as intermediaries between issuers and the ultimate purchasers of their securities.

private placements

Investment banking services are typically performed by brokerage firms and, to a limited extent, by commercial banks. In some instances, only a few large institutional investors are solicited, and the entire issue is sold to one or more of them. Such **private placements** are frequently used for bond issues. As long as relatively few potential buyers are contacted (say, fewer than twenty-five), requirements for detailed disclosure, public notice, and so on may be waived, considerably reducing the cost of floating an issue. Such placements are often announced after the fact, via advertisements in the financial press.

syndicate
underwrite

When public sale is contemplated, much more must be done. Many firms may serve as intermediaries in the process. One, acting as the "lead" investment banker, will put together a syndicate (or purchase group) and a selling group. The **syndicate** includes firms that purchase the securities from the issuing corporation and are thus said to **underwrite** the offering. The

FIGURE 3-3
Round-Trip Transaction Costs

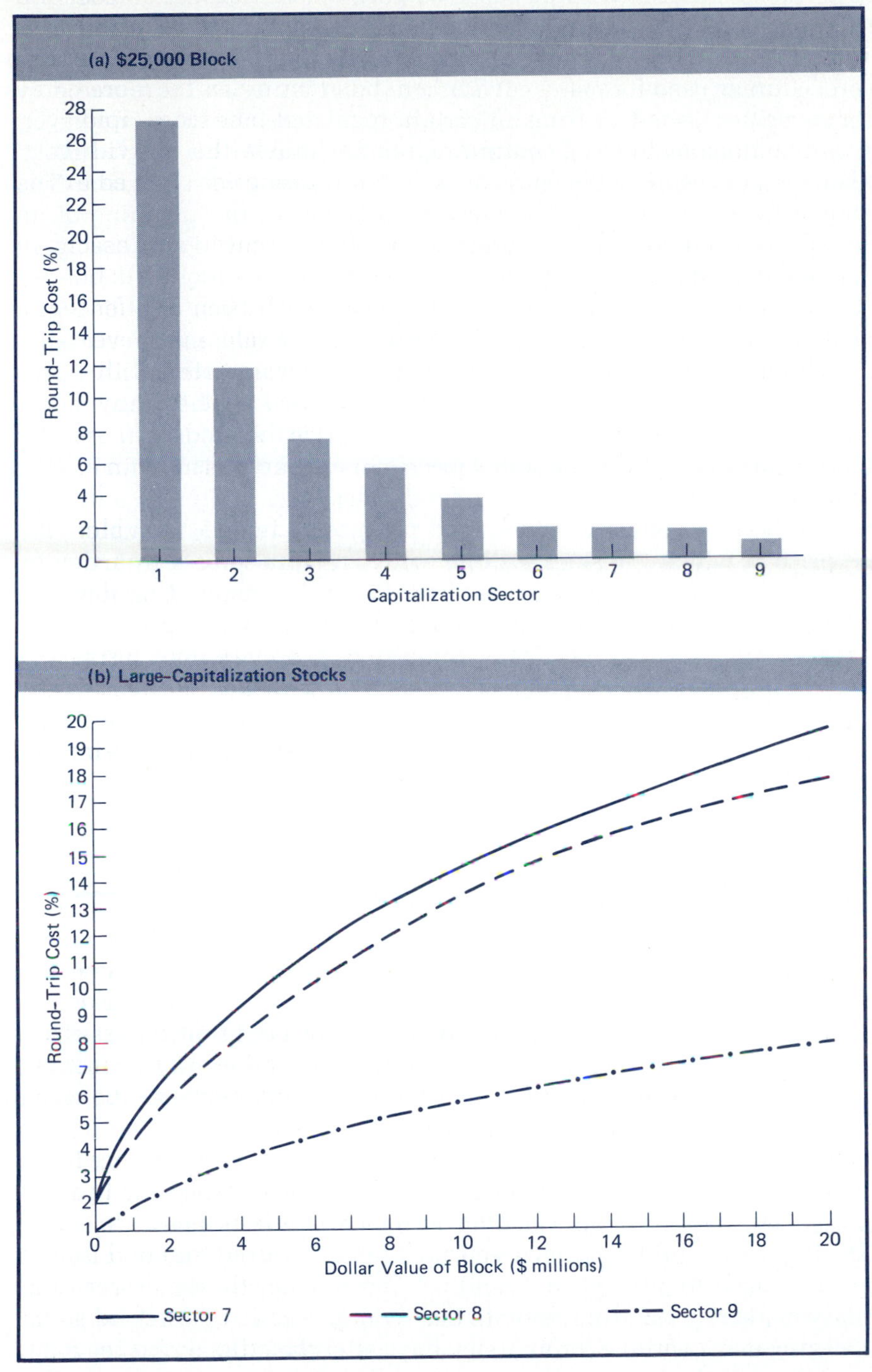

selling group
competitive bidding

selling group includes firms that contact potential buyers and do the actual selling, usually on a commission basis.

The process begins with discussions between the issuing corporation and one or more investment bankers. Some issuers utilize **competitive bidding,** then select the investment banker offering the best overall terms. This procedure is used for many government bond issues and is required by law for securities issued by firms in certain regulated industries. However, many corporations maintain a continuing relationship with a single investment banker and negotiate the terms of each new offering with that firm. The investment banker is likely to be heavily involved in the planning of an offering, the terms involved, the amount to be offered, and so on, serving, in effect, as a financial consultant to the corporation.

registration statement
prospectus
red herring

Once the basic characteristics of an offering have been established, a **registration statement** is filed with the Securities and Exchange Commission and a preliminary **prospectus** disclosing material relevant to the prospective buyer is issued. (This prospectus is often referred to as a **red herring,** since it has a disclaimer printed in red ink across the first page that informs the reader that it is not an offer to sell.) The actual price of the security is not included in the preliminary prospectus, and no final sales may be made until the registration becomes effective and a final prospectus issued, indicating the "offer" price at which the stock will be sold. The final prospectus may be issued as soon as, in the opinion of the Securities and Exchange Commission, there has been adequate disclosure and a reasonable waiting period has passed (usually twenty days). The Commission, however, does not take a position regarding the investment merits of an offering or the reasonableness of the price.

A security issue may be completely underwritten by an investment banker and the other members of the syndicate. If it is, the issuing corporation receives the public offering price less a stated percentage spread (although underwriters will occasionally be compensated with some combination of shares and warrants, perhaps in addition to a smaller spread). The underwriters, in turn, sell the securities at the public offering price (or less) and may buy some of the securities themselves. Underwriters who provide this sort of **firm commitment** bear all the risk, since the public may not be willing to buy the entire issue.

firm commitment

rights offering

standby agreement

best-efforts basis

Not all agreements are of this type. In the case of a **rights offering** (where the current stockholders are given the opportunity to buy the new shares first), an underwriter may agree to purchase at a fixed price all securities not taken by current stockholders. This is termed a **standby agreement.** In the case of a nonrights offering (where the shares are offered to the general public first), members of an investment banking group may serve as agents instead of dealers, agreeing only to handle an offering on a **best-efforts basis.**

pegging

During the period when new securities remain unsold, the investment banker is allowed to attempt to "stabilize" the price of the security in the secondary market by standing ready to make purchases at a particular price. Such **pegging** may continue for up to ten days after the official offering date. There is a limit to the amount that can be purchased in this manner, usually stated in the agreement under which the underwriting syndicate is formed, since the members typically share the cost of such transactions. If there is to be any pegging, a statement to that effect must be included in the prospectus.

In any security transaction, there may be explicit and implicit costs. In a primary distribution, the explicit cost is the underwriting spread and the implicit cost is any difference between the public offering price and the price that might have been obtained otherwise. The spread provides the investment banker with compensation for selling the issue and bearing the risk that the issue may not be completely sold to the public, thereby leaving them with ownership of the unsold shares. The lower the public offering price, the smaller the risk that the issue will not be sold quickly at that price. If an issue is substantially underpriced, the investment banking syndicate can be assured that the securities will sell rapidly, requiring little or no support in the secondary market. Since many corporations deal with only one investment banker and since the larger investment banking firms rely on one another for inclusion in syndicates, it has been alleged that issuers pay too much in spreads, given the prices at which their securities are offered. In other words, the returns to underwriting are alleged to be overly large relative to the risks involved due to ignorance on the part of issuers or the existence of an informal cartel among investment bankers.

initial public offerings

Whether or not this is the case, a number of **initial public offerings** (ipo's) do appear to have been underpriced. Ipo's are the first offerings of shares of a company to the public and are sometimes referred to as **unseasoned offerings.** On average, offerings of these unseasoned securities appear to have been underpriced. Investors able to purchase a cross-section of such shares at their offering prices might thus expect better performance than those holding other securities of equal risk. It is not surprising that such offerings are often rationed by the members of the selling group to "favored" customers. It is "not uncommon for underwriters to receive, prior to the effective date, 'public indication of interest' for five times the number of shares available."[20] Unfavored customers are presumably allowed to buy only the new issues that are not substantially underpriced. And since costs may be incurred in becoming a "favored" customer, it is not clear that even such an investor obtains abnormally large returns overall.

unseasoned offerings

While the return obtained by the purchaser of a new issue may be substantial on average, the amount may be very good or very bad in any particular instance. While the odds may be in the purchaser's favor, a single investment of this type is far from a sure bet.

A relatively recent change in regulations has made it possible for large corporations to foster greater competition among underwriters. Starting in 1982, the Securities and Exchange Commission allowed firms to register securities in advance of issuance under Rule 415. With such **shelf registration,** securities may be sold up to two years later. With securities "on the shelf," the corporation can require investment bankers to bid competitively, simply refusing to sell shares if desirable bids are not forthcoming.

shelf registration

REGULATION OF SECURITY MARKETS

Directly or indirectly, security markets in the U.S. are regulated under both federal and state laws. The Securities Act of 1933 was the first major legislation at the federal level. Sometimes called the "truth in securities" law, it requires registration of new issues and disclosure of relevant information by the issuer. Furthermore, the act prohibits misrepresentation and fraud in

[20]Securities and Exchange Commission, *Report of Special Study on Security Markets*, 1973. Also, see Roger G. Ibbotson, "Price Performance of Common Stock New Issues," *Journal of Financial Economics*, 2, no. 3 (September 1975): 235–72.

security sales. The Securities Exchange Act of 1934 extended the principles of the earlier act to cover secondary markets and required national exchanges, brokers, and dealers to be registered. It also made possible the establishment of self-regulatory organizations (SRO's) to oversee the securities industry.

Securities and Exchange Commission

Since 1934, both acts (and subsequent amendments to them, such as the Securities Acts Amendments of 1975 that were discussed earlier in the chapter), have been administered by the **Securities and Exchange Commission** (SEC), a quasi-judicial agency of the U.S. government.[21] The SEC is run by five commissioners appointed by the president and confirmed by the Senate; each commissioner is appointed for a five-year term. The commissioners are aided by a large permanent staff of lawyers, accountants, economists, and others.

The SEC is the primary administrative agency for a number of other pieces of federal legislation. The Public Utility Holding Company Act of 1935 brought such corporations under the SEC's jurisdiction. The Bankruptcy Act of 1938 specified that the SEC should advise the court in the reorganization of a firm under bankruptcy proceedings whenever there is a substantial public interest in the firm's securities. The Maloney Act of 1938 extended the SEC's jurisdiction to include the over-the-counter market and recognized the National Association of Security Dealers as an SRO. The Trust Indenture Act of 1939 gave the SEC power to ensure that bond indenture trustees (individuals who represent bondholders in dealing with bond issuers) were free from any conflicts of interest. The Investment Company Act of 1940 extended disclosure and registration requirements to investment companies (these are companies that use their funds primarily to purchase securities issued by the U.S. government, state governments, other companies, and so on). It was amended in1970 in order to give certain rights to owners of investment companies who wanted to sell their shares before fulfilling the terms of a contractual purchase plan. The Investment Advisors Act of 1940 required the registration of those individuals who provide others with advice about security transactions; advisors were also required to disclose any potential conflicts of interest. As mentioned earlier, the Securities Investor Protection Act of 1970 provided for the coverage of losses by investors in the event of failure of a brokerage firm by establishing the Securities Investor Protection Corporation. The Insider Trading and Fraud Act of 1988 was established to help define insider (a person who possesses material nonpublic information) trading and establish fines for insider trading violations.

self-regulation

As mentioned earlier, federal securities legislation relies heavily on the principle of **self-regulation.** The SEC has delegated its power to control trading practices for listed securities to the registered exchanges. However, the SEC has retained the power to alter or supplement any of the resulting rules or regulations. The SEC's power to control trading practices in over-the counter securities has been similarly delegated to the National Association of Securities Dealers (NASD), a private association of brokers and dealers in OTC securities. In practice, the SEC staff usually discusses proposed changes with both the NASD and the registered exchanges in advance. Consequently, few rules are formally altered or rejected.

An important piece of legislation that makes security markets in the U.S. different from those in many other countries is the Banking Act of 1933, also

[21]The Commodity Futures Trading Commission (CFTC) was established in 1974 by Congress to regulate futures markets, and the Municipal Securities Rulemaking Board (MSRB) was established in 1975 to regulate trading in municipal securities.

known as the Glass-Steagall Act. This act prohibited commercial banks from engaging in investment banking activities, since it was felt that there was an inherent conflict of interest in allowing banks to engage in both commercial and investment banking activities. Because of this act, banks have not played as prominent a role in security markets in the U.S. as elsewhere. Recently, however, their role has increased, as the federal government has taken action to spur competition among various types of financial institutions. Two key pieces of legislation were the Depository Institutions Deregulation and Monetary Control Act of 1980 and the Depository Institution Act of 1982. Many banks now offer security brokerage services, retirement funds, and the like via subsidiaries of their holding companies. Furthermore, long-standing limitations on rates paid on deposits and checking accounts were removed. As a result, the line between commercial banking and investment banking is becoming more blurred every day.

Initially, security regulation in the U.S. was the province of state governments. Beginning in 1911, state *blue sky laws* were passed to prevent "speculative schemes which have no more basis than so many feet of blue sky."[22] While such statutes vary substantially from state to state, most of them outlaw fraud in security sales and require the registration of certain securities as well as brokers and dealers (and, in some cases, investment advisors). Some order has been created by the passage in many states of all or part of the Uniform Securities Acts proposed by the National Conference of Commissions on Uniform State Laws in 1956.

Securities that are traded across state lines, as well as the brokers, dealers, and exchanges involved in such trading, typically fall under the purview of federal legislation. However, a considerable domain still comes under the exclusive jurisdiction of the states. Moreover, federal legislation only supplements state legislation; it does not supplant it. Some argue that the investor is overprotected as a result. Others suggest that the regulatory agencies (especially those that rely on "self-regulation" by powerful industry organizations) in fact protect the members of the regulated industry against competition, thereby damaging the interests of their customers instead of protecting them. Both positions undoubtedly contain some elements of truth.

SUMMARY

1. Security markets facilitate the trading of securities by providing a means of bringing buyers and sellers of financial assets together.

2. In the U.S., common stocks are traded primarily on organized security exchanges or on the over-the-counter market.

3. Organized security exchanges provide central physical locations where trading is done under a set of rules and regulations.

4. The primary organized security exchange is the New York Stock Exchange. Various regional exchanges also operate.

5. Trading on organized security exchanges is conducted only by members who transact in a specified group of securities.

6. Exchange members fall into one of four categories depending on the type of trading activity in which they engage. Those categories are: commission broker; floor broker; floor trader; and specialist.

7. Specialists are charged with maintaining an orderly market in their assigned stocks. In this capacity they perform two roles. They maintain a limit order book for unexecuted trades and they act as a dealer, trading in their stocks for their own accounts.

[22]See *Hall v.Geiger-Jones Co.*, 242 U.S. 539 (1917).

8. In the OTC market, individuals act as dealers in a manner similar to specialists. However, OTC dealers face competition from other dealers.

9. Much of the trading in the OTC market is done through a computerized system known as NASDAQ.

10. Trading in listed securities may take place outside the various exchanges on the third and fourth markets.

11. Foreign security markets each involve their own particular operating procedures, rules, and customs.

12. Following legislation in 1975, the SEC has mandated procedures designed to create a truly nationwide central security market.

13. Clearinghouses facilitate the transfer of securities and cash between buyers and sellers. Most U.S. security transactions are now cleared electronically.

14. The SIPC is a quasi-governmental agency that insures the accounts of clients of all brokers and members of exchanges registered with the SEC against loss due to a brokerage firm's failure.

15. Following May Day (May 1, 1975), commissions have been negotiated between brokerage firms and their larger clients.

16. Commission rates typically vary inversely with the number of shares traded.

17. Transaction costs are a function of the stock's bid-asked spread, the price impact of the trade, and the commission.

18. The primary market for securities involves the initial issuance of securities.

19. While some issuers deal directly with purchasers, most issuers hire investment bankers to assist them in the sale of the securities.

20. The most prominent security markets regulator is the SEC, a federal agency run by five commissioners. Regulation of the U.S. security markets involves both federal and state law.

21. The SEC has delegated to the various exchanges and NASD the power to control trading practices through a system of "self-regulation."

KEY TERMS

security market
secondary markets
call markets
continuous markets
liquidity
organized exchanges
seat
member firm
listed security
delisted
trading halt
American Depository Receipts
commission brokers
floor brokers
floor traders
specialists
limit order book
dealer
trading post
bid price
asked price
double auction
Super Designated Order Turnaround
block trade
specialist block purchase
specialist block sale
exchange distribution
exchange acquisition
special offering
special bid
secondary distribution
upstairs dealer market
block houses
regional exchanges
National Association of Securities Dealers
National Association of Securities Dealers Automated Quotations
inside quotes
National Market System
SOES
markup
markdown
pink sheets
third market
fourth market
instinct
SEAQ
SEAF
NASDAQ International
CORES
FORES
Consolidated Tape
composite stock price tables
Consolidated Quotations System
Intermarket Trading System
clearinghouse
Depository Trust Company
fails to deliver
Securities Investor Protection Corporation
May Day
soft dollars
bid-ask spread
market capitalization
price impacts
primary market
investment bankers
private placements
syndicate
underwrite
selling group
competitive bidding
registration statement
prospectus

red herring
firm commitment
rights offering
standby agreement
best-efforts basis
pegging
initial public offerings
unseasoned registration
shelf registration
Securities and Exchange Commission
self-regulation

QUESTIONS AND PROBLEMS

1. What are ADRs? Why are they attractive to U.S. investors seeking to make investments in foreign corporations?
2. Discuss the advantages and disadvantages of the NYSE specialist system.
3. Differentiate between the role of a specialist on the NYSE and the role of a dealer in the OTC market.
4. List several reasons why a corporation might desire to have its stock listed on the NYSE.
5. Describe the functions of commission brokers, floor brokers, and floor traders.
6. Pigeon Falls Fertilizer Company is listed on the NYSE. Gabby Hartnett, the specialist handling Pigeon Falls stock, is currently bidding 35⅜ and asking 35⅝. What would be the likely outcomes of the following trading orders?
   (a) Through a broker, Eppa Rixey places a market order to buy 100 shares of Pigeon Falls stock. No other broker from the crowd takes the order.
   (b) Through a broker, Eppa places a limit order to sell 100 shares of Pigeon Falls stock at 36.
   (c) Through a broker, Eppa places a limit order to buy 100 shares of Pigeon Falls stock at 35½. Another broker offers to sell 100 shares at 35½.
7. Because specialists such as Chick Gandil are charged with maintaining a "fair and orderly" market, at times they are required to "sell" when others are "buying" and "buy" when others are "selling." What does this requirement mean in practice? How can Chick earn a profit when required to act in such a manner?
8. Why can't all security trades on the NYSE, no matter how large, be handled through the SuperDOT system?
9. Why is NASDAQ so important to the success of the OTC market?
10. What are some of the major steps that have been taken toward the ultimate emergence of a truly nationwide security market?
11. Define the terms *third market* and *fourth market*.
12. Why was May Day such an important event for the NYSE?
13. What is the purpose of SIPC insurance? Given the recent experiences of the banking and savings and loan deposit insurance programs, under what conditions might SIPC insurance be expected to be effective? Under what conditions might it fail to accomplish its objectives?
14. Transaction costs can be thought of as being derived from three sources. Identify and describe those sources.
15. After May Day, why did commission rates fall so sharply for large investors, but decline so little (or even increase) for small investors?
16. What functions does a clearinghouse perform?

17. Fiddler Basinski is considering an investment in Poynette Lumber Company. Based on an analysis of Poynette's prospects, Fiddler expects the company's stock to rise from $40 to $45 over the next six months. Using data in Table 3-3(b), Poynette stock is in sector 1. Fiddler plans to invest $25,000 in the company and then liquidate the investment six months later. Given Fiddler's price appreciation expectations, is this investment likely to be profitable? Why?
18. Describe the primary conclusions of the results of the Loeb trading cost study presented in Table 3-3.
19. Why are liquid and continuous secondary security markets important to the effective functioning of primary security markets?
20. Describe the role of an underwriting syndicate in a public security offering.
21. Distinguish between a competitive bid underwriting and a negotiated underwriting.
22. Investment bankers frequently attempt to stabilize the price of a newly issued security in the secondary market.
    (a) How is this stabilization accomplished?
    (b) What is the purpose of the stabilization?
    (c) What can go wrong with the stabilization attempts?
23. Why must companies that publicly issue securities file a prospectus with the SEC? What does SEC acceptance of the prospectus imply?
24. Discuss why ipo's appear to generate abnormal returns for investors. Are these returns a "sure thing"? What are the economic implications of these high returns for ipo issuers?

REFERENCES

1. A good reference source for U.S. stock markets is:

   Robert A. Schwartz, *Equity Markets* (New York: Harper & Row, 1988).

2. Other valuable sources are following factbooks, which are updated annually:

   New York Stock Exchange 1991 Fact Book (to order, write: New York Stock Exchange, Publications Department, 11 Wall St., New York, NY 10005).

   American Stock Exchange 1991 Fact Book (to order, write: American Stock Exchange, Publications Department, 86 Trinity Place, New York, NY 10006).

   1991 NASDAQ Fact Book & Company Directory (to order, write: NASD, Book Order Department, P.O. Box 9403, Gaithersburg, MD 20898).

3. For a description of foreign stock markets, see:

   Roger D. Huang and Hans B. Stoll, *Major World Equity Markets: Current Structure and Prospects for Change*, Monograph Series in Finance and Economics 1991-93, New York University Salomon Center, New York City, 1991.

   Guiseppe Tullio and Giorgio P. Szego, eds., "Equity Markets—An International Comparison: Part A," *Journal of Banking and Finance*, 13, nos. 4/5 (September 1989): 479–782.

   Guiseppe Tullio and Giorgio P. Szego, eds., "Equity Markets—An International Comparison: Part B," *Journal of Banking and Finance*, 14, nos. 2/3 (August 1990): 231–672.

4. Other useful sources for information on market microstructure are:

   Peter A. Abken, "Globalization of Stock, Futures, and Options Markets," Federal Reserve Bank of Atlanta *Economic Review*, 76, no. 4 (July/August 1991): 1–22.

   Ian Domowitz, "The Mechanics of Automated Execution Systems," *Journal of Financial Intermediation*, 1, no. 2 (June 1990): 167–94.

   James L. Hamilton, "Off-Board Trading of NYSE-Listed Stocks: The Effects of Deregulation and the National Market System," *Journal of Finance*, 42, no. 5 (December 1987): 1331–45.

   Lawrence E. Harris, *Liquidity, Trading Rules, and Electronic Trading Systems*, Monograph Series in Finance and Economics 1990-94, New York University Salomon Center, New York City, 1990.

5. For a discussion of the effects of listing and delisting on a firm's stock, see:

   John J. McConnell and Gary C. Sanger, "The Puzzle in Post-Listing Common Stock Returns," *Journal of Finance*, 42, no. 1 (March 1987): 119–40.

   Gary C. Sanger and John J. McConnell, "Stock Exchange Listings, Firm Value, and Security Market Efficiency: The Impact of NASDAQ," *Journal of Financial and Quantitative Analysis*, 21, no. 1 (March 1986): 1–25.

   Gary C. Sanger and James D. Peterson, "An Empirical Analysis of Common Stock Delistings," *Journal of Financial and Quantitative Analysis*, 25, no. 2 (June 1990): 261–72.

6. Studies that examine the costs of trading include:

   Robert W. Holthausen, Richard W. Leftwich, and David Mayers, "The Effect of Large Block Transactions on Security Prices," *Journal of Financial Economics*, 19, no. 2 (December 1987): 237–67.

   Robert W. Holthausen, Richard W. Leftwich, and David Mayers, "Large-Block Transactions, the Speed of Response, and Temporary and Permanent Stock-Price Effects," *Journal of Financial Economics*, 26, no. 1 (July 1990): 71–95.

   Thomas F. Loeb, "Trading Cost: The Critical Link Between Investment Information and Results," *Financial Analysts Journal*, 39, no. 3 (May/June 1983): 39–44.

   Wayne H. Mikkelson and M. Megan Partch, "Stock Price Effects and Costs of Secondary Distributions," *Journal of Financial Economics*, 14, no. 2 (June 1985): 165–94.

4

The Determination of Security Prices

Although there are over 1 billion shares of American Telephone & Telegraph common stock outstanding, on an average day fewer than 2 million shares will be traded. What determines the prices at which such trades take place? A simple (and correct) answer is: demand and supply. A more fundamental (and also correct) answer is: investors' estimates of AT&T's future earnings and dividends, for such estimates greatly influence demand and supply. Before dealing with such influences, it is useful to examine the role of demand and supply in the determination of security prices.

DEMAND AND SUPPLY SCHEDULES

As shown in the previous two chapters, securities are traded by many people in many different ways. While the forces that determine prices are similar in all markets, they are slightly more obvious in markets using periodic "calls"; one such market corresponds to the *itayose* method of price determination that is used by the *saitori* at the twice-a-day openings of the Tokyo Stock Exchange, as mentioned in Chapter 3.

The Demand-to-Buy Schedule

At a designed time, all brokers holding orders to buy or sell a given stock for customers gather at a specified location on the floor of the exchange. Some of

demand-to-buy schedule

the orders are market orders. For example, Mr. A may have instructed his broker to buy 100 shares of Minolta at the lowest possible price, whatever it may be. His personal **demand-to-buy schedule** at that time is shown in Figure 4-1(a): he wishes to buy 100 shares no matter what the price. While this schedule captures the contractual nature of Mr. A's market order at a specific point in time, Mr. A undoubtedly has a good idea that his ultimate purchase price will be near the price for which orders were executed just before he placed his order. Thus, his true demand schedule might be sloping downward from the upper-left portion to the lower-right portion of the graph. This is shown by the dashed line in the figure. It indicates his desire to buy more shares if the price is lower. However, to simplify his own tasks as well as his broker's tasks, he has estimated that the price for which his order will be ultimately executed will be in the range at which he would choose to hold 100 shares. In the example shown here, this price is 945 yen per share.

FIGURE 4-1
Individual Investors' Demand-to-Buy Schedules

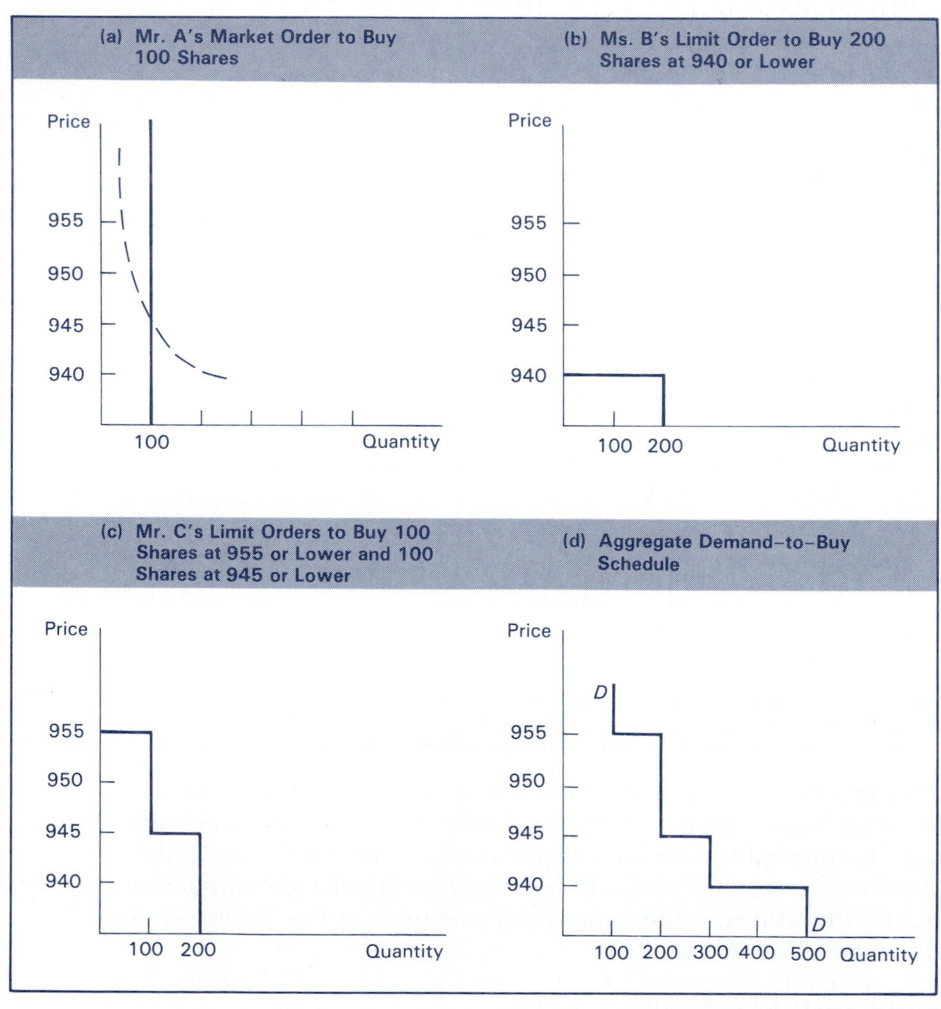

Other customers may place limit orders with their brokers. Thus Ms. B may have instructed her broker to buy 200 shares of Minolta at the lowest possible price if and only if that price is less than or equal to 940 yen per share. Her demand schedule is shown in Figure 4-1(b).

Some customers may give their broker two or more orders for the same security. Thus, Mr. C may wish to buy 100 shares of Minolta at a price of 955 or less, plus an additional 100 shares if the price is at or below 945. To do this, Mr. C places a limit order for 100 shares at 955 and a second limit order for 100 shares at 945. Figure 4-1(c) portrays his demand schedule.

If one could look at all the brokers' books and aggregate all the orders to buy Minolta (both market and limit orders), it would be possible to determine how many shares would be bought at every possible price. Assuming that only Mr. A, Ms. B, and Mr. C have placed buy orders, the resulting aggregate demand-to-buy schedule would look like the line *DD* in Figure 4-1(d). Note that at lower prices more shares would be demanded.

The Supply-to-Sell Schedule

Brokers will also hold market orders to sell shares of Minolta. For example, Ms. X may have placed a market order to sell 100 shares of Minolta at the highest possible price. Figure 4-2(a) displays her **supply-to-sell schedule.** As with market orders to buy, customers generally place such orders on the supposition that the actual price will be in the range in which their true desire would be to sell the stated number of shares. Thus, Ms. X's actual supply schedule might appear more like the dashed line in Figure 4-2(a), indicating her willingness to sell more shares at higher prices.

supply-to-sell schedule

Customers may also place limit orders to sell shares of Minolta. For example, Mr. Y may have placed a limit order to sell 100 shares at a price of 940 or higher, and Ms. Z may have placed a limit order to sell 100 shares at a price of 945 or higher. Panels (b) and (c) of Figure 4-2 illustrate these two supply-to-sell schedules.

Similar to the buy orders, if one could look at all the brokers' books and aggregate all the orders to sell Minolta (both market and limit orders), it would be possible to determine how many shares would be sold at every possible price. Assuming that only Ms. X, Mr. Y, and Ms. Z have placed sell orders, the resulting aggregate supply-to-sell schedule would look like line *SS* in Figure 4-2(d). Note that at higher prices more shares would be supplied.

Interaction of the Schedules

The aggregate demand and supply schedules are shown on one graph in Figure 4-3. Generally, no one would have enough information to draw the actual schedules. However, this in no way diminishes their usefulness as representations of the underlying forces that are interacting to determine the market clearing price of Minolta.

What actually happens when all the brokers gather together with their order books in hand? A clerk of the exchange "calls out" a price—for example, 940 yen per share. The brokers then try to complete transactions with one another at that price. Those with orders to buy at that price signify the number of shares they wish to buy. Those with orders to sell do likewise. Some deals will be tentatively made, but as Figure 4-3 shows, more shares will be demanded at 940 than will be supplied. In particular, 300 shares will be demanded but only 200 shares will be supplied. When trading is completed

FIGURE 4-2
Individual Investors' Supply-to-Sell Schedules

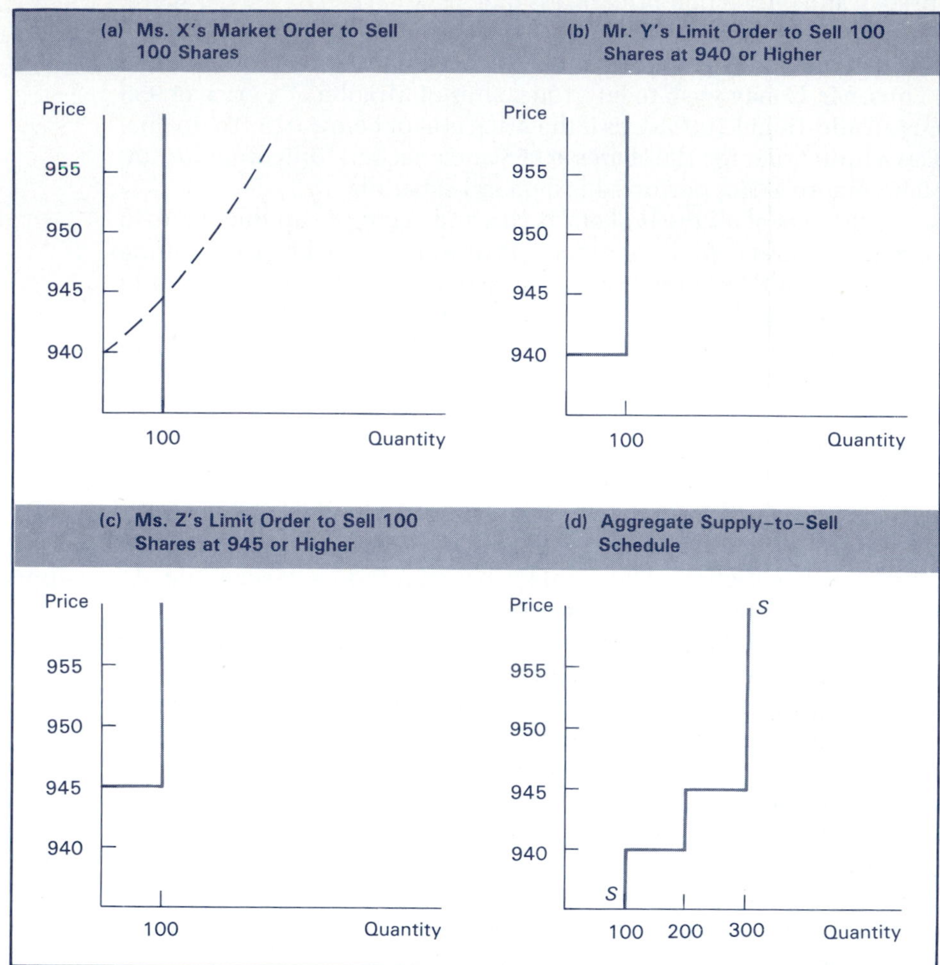

(meaning that all possible tentative deals have been made), there will be a number of brokers calling "buy" but nobody will stand ready to sell to them. The price of 940 was too low.

Seeing this, the clerk will cry out a different price; for example, 950. Since the previous trades are all cancelled at this point, the brokers will consult their order books once again and signify the extent to which they are willing to buy or sell shares at this new price. In this case, as Figure 4-3 shows, when trading is completed, there will be a number of brokers calling "sell" but nobody will stand ready to buy from them. In particular, 300 shares will be supplied but there will be a demand for only 200 shares. The price of 950 was too high.

Undaunted, the clerk will try again. And again, if necessary. Only when there are relatively few unsatisfied brokers will the price (and the associated tentative deals) be declared final. As Figure 4-3 shows, 945 is such a price. At

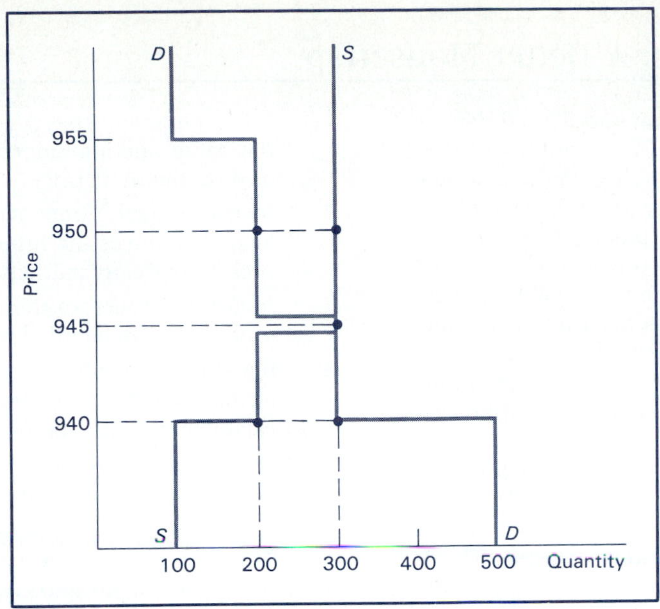

FIGURE 4-3
Determining a Security's Price by the Interaction of the Aggregate Demand-to-Buy and Supply-to-Sell Schedules

945, customers collectively wish to sell 300 shares. Furthermore, there is a collective demand for 300 shares at this price. Thus, quantity demanded equals quantity supplied. The price was "just right."

Another way to view this process is to focus on the quantity that would actually be traded at any given price. For any particular price, this would be the smaller of (1) the quantity people are willing to buy, and (2) the quantity others are willing to sell, as shown in Figure 4-4. At the price where the

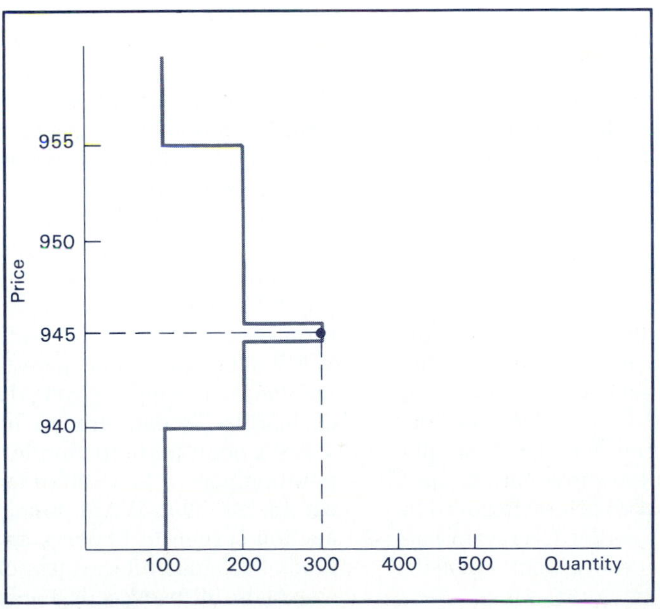

FIGURE 4-4
Aggregate Quantity Traded

MONEY MATTERS

Single Price Auctions: A Better Mousetrap

So you think that supply and demand curves are merely esoteric figments of ivory-tower thinking. Perhaps a valid concept, you say, but they cannot possibly be of any practical use in establishing security prices. Well, don't tell that to Wunsch Auction Systems Inc. (WASI). Since early 1991, that organization has been holding regular security auctions for a broad list of common stocks. Market clearing prices in those auctions are determined by the explicit interaction of investors' supply and demand preferences.

Step back for a moment and recall how prices are set on organized security exchanges or the OTC market (see Chapter 3). Dealers (whether specialists or OTC dealers) "make markets" in particular securities. That is, acting as intermediaries, they buy and sell from other investors for their own accounts. The dealers quote prices (bid-asked) to sellers and buyers on a continuous basis. They adjust prices as they sense supply and demand building and ebbing. It is the competitive efforts of these intermediaries that determine security prices.

WASI has developed a market mechanism quite different from that of the traditional dealer markets. The firm's owners have designed what they refer to as a Single Price Auction (SPA). The concept behind the SPA is simple. Auctions are scheduled on a regular basis (currently twice a day—before the New York Stock Exchange opens and after it closes). Prior to a scheduled auction, investors submit orders to buy or sell specified quantities of a security at specified prices (essentially limit orders—see Chapter 2).

At the time of the auction, the orders of all participating investors are aggregated by computer. That is, the computer calculates supply and demand curves for each security being auctioned. The intersection of these curves determines the market clearing price for a security. At that price, the maximum number of shares of stock will be exchanged. (All bids above and all offers below the equilibrium price are matched, while orders at the equilibrium price are matched on a time priority basis.)

Investors are able to access the auction order information (in graphical or tabular form) up to the time of the auction through an open limit order book. As opposed to a specialist's proprietary closed limit order book, the SPA permits investors to examine the current supply and demand for a stock. This allows investors to raise their bid prices (or lower their asked prices) to adjust to the current market conditions. In order to prevent manipulative behavior, withdrawn orders incur a penalty charge.

The SPA possesses some intriguing advantages over traditional dealer markets:

1. It is simple and fair. All investors have access to the same auction information and all investors trade at the same price.
2. Investors have direct access to the market. This feature removes the inherent conflicts of interest present in dealer markets.
3. Investors' orders are anonymous. Orders and trade executions are handled by computer.
4. It matches "natural" buyers and sellers (those with an explicit desire to transact), thereby perhaps establishing more robust and stable prices.
5. Transaction costs are low (about 1¢ per share versus 10¢ to 20¢ per share in dealer markets).

This last point warrants elaboration. Traditional dealer markets are continuous—trading can occur at any time during the trading day. Continuous trading mechanisms are expensive and require dealers because the "other side" of a trade is not always immediately available. Dealers provide liquidity to investors who wish to transact immediately.

With more frequent large trades being made by institutional investors in the last decade, the ability of dealer markets to provide continuous liquidity has been severely tested. The market crash of October 1987 was an extreme, but not singular, example.

Many (and perhaps most) investors do not require immediate liquidity. They can wait several hours to trade, particularly if by waiting their transaction costs are significantly reduced. In lieu of the continuous intervention of the dealer, the SPA substitutes a periodic call to market (akin to the crossing systems discussed in Chapter 3). Without the expensive overhead of the dealer, the SPA can afford to match buyers and sellers at a small fraction of the cost of the dealer market.

What are the disadvantages of the SPA? Conceptually, there are none to investors who do not require immediate liquidity. However, if you throw a party and no one comes, the party is a failure no matter how elaborate the preparations. Likewise, to be successful, the SPA must convince enough investors to trade through it so as to generate sufficient liquidity. To do so WASI must overcome investor inertia, and at times ignorance, as well as strong opposition from organized exchanges. To date, traders have not beaten a path to WASI's door; participation in the SPA has been disappointingly low. (In an effort to stimulate investor interest, in late 1991 WASI announced plans to move the auction system to Phoenix and rename it the Arizona Stock Exchange.) Regardless of whether the WASI version of the SPA succeeds in its present form, the concept of the SPA is likely to gain much more attention in the years ahead.

quantity that would be traded is maximized, demand will equal supply. As can be seen in the figure, this occurs at a price of 945.

Trading procedures employed in security markets vary from auction markets to dealer markets and from call markets to continuous markets. However, the similarities are more important than the differences. In the U.S., for example, specialists at the New York Stock Exchange and dealers in the over-the-counter market provide some of the functions of the *saitori* at the Tokyo Stock Exchange, and trades can take place at any time. Nevertheless, the basic principles of security price determination still operate. In general, market price equates quantity demanded with quantity supplied.

THE DEMAND-TO-HOLD SECURITIES

For some purposes it is useful to ignore moment-to-moment changes in customers' orders and focus instead on the fundamental forces at work. Instead of asking how many shares an investor wishes to buy or sell at a given price, the number of shares the investor wishes to hold at that price can be determined. There is, of course, a close relationship between the two quantities. If an investor wishes to hold more shares than are currently held, the difference is the investor's demand-to-buy schedule. Conversely, if the investor wishes to hold fewer shares than are currently held, the difference is the investor's supply-to-sell schedule.

The Demand-to-Hold Schedule

demand-to-hold schedule

In Figure 4-5 one investor's **demand-to-hold schedule** for a security is shown by curve *dd*. This simply plots the number of shares that investor wishes to hold at each possible price. In general, lower prices are associated with larger numbers of shares. Of course, the entire schedule is predicated on the investor's current feelings about the security's future prospects. If something makes the investor more optimistic about the security, he or she will generally wish to hold more shares at any given price. In that case, the entire schedule may shift to the right, as shown by curve *d′d′*. Alternatively, if something makes the investor more pessimistic about the security, the entire curve may shift to the left, as shown by curve *d″d″*.

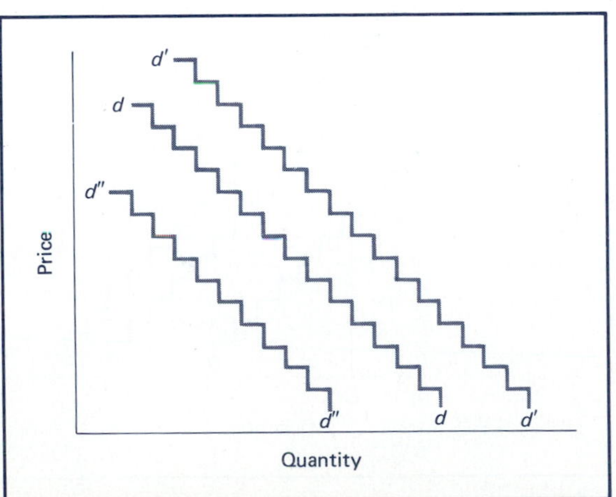

FIGURE 4-5
An Individual Investor's Demand-to-Hold Schedule

A factor that complicates analysis of this type is the tendency for some investors to regard sudden and substantial price changes in a security as indicators of changes in the future prospects of the issuer. In the absence of further information, an investor may interpret such a change as an indication "someone knows something that I don't know." While exploring the situation, the investor may at least temporarily revise his or her own assessment of the issuer's prospects and, in doing so, may alter the demand-to-hold schedule. For this reason, few investors place limit orders at prices substantially different from the current price, for fear that such orders would be executed only if prospects changed significantly, giving recognition to the idea that a careful reevaluation would be in order before buying or selling shares under such conditions.

Despite this complication, it is possible to construct an aggregate schedule indicating the total number of shares of a given firm that investors will wish to hold at various prices, assuming no change in their views of the relative prospects of the firm. This overall demand-to-hold schedule, obtained by adding the individual investors' demand-to-hold schedules, would look like curve *DD* in Figure 4-6. In the short run, at least, the available number of shares is fixed—for example, at Q in the figure. Only one price will equate the aggregate demand to hold with the available number of shares. In Figure 4-6, it is *P*. At any higher price, current holders of the security will collectively wish to hold fewer shares than are outstanding. In their attempts to sell such shares, they will drive the price down until they or others are willing to hold all the shares. Conversely, if the price is below *P*, investors will collectively wish to hold more shares than are available. In their attempts to buy shares, they will drive the price up until they no longer want additional shares. Ultimately, the price will settle at *P*, where aggregate demand equals the available quantity.

The Elasticity of the Schedule

How elastic (that is, flat) will be the aggregate demand-to-hold schedule for a security? The answer depends in part on the extent to which the security is regarded as "unique." Securities are considered more unique when they have

FIGURE 4-6
Aggregate Demand-to-Hold and Available Quantity Schedules

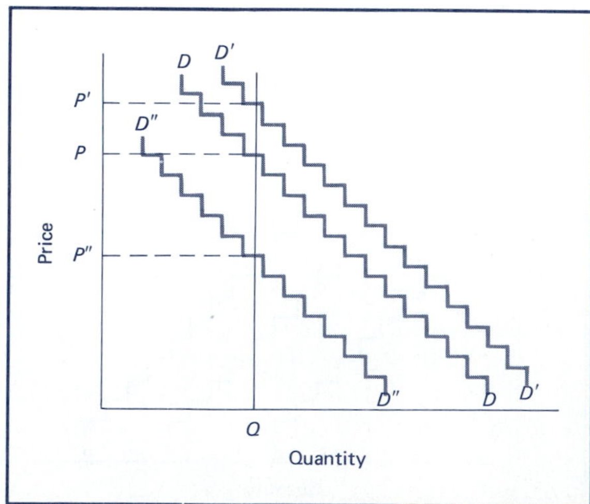

few close substitutes. Securities are considered less unique when they have more close substitutes. This means that the aggregate demand schedule will be more elastic (that is, more flat) for less unique securities. Equivalently, the less unique a security is, the greater will be the increase in the quantity demanded for a given fall in price. This is because these shares will produce a smaller increase in the typical portfolio's risk when substituted for other shares.

Shifts of the Schedule

If one investor becomes more optimistic about the prospects for a security while another investor becomes more pessimistic about the same security, they may very likely trade with one another with no effect on the aggregate demand-to-hold schedule. In this situation there will be no change in the market price for the security. However, if more investors become optimistic rather than pessimistic, the schedule will shift to the right (for example, to $D'D'$ in Figure 4-6), causing an increase in price (to P'). *Correspondingly, if more investors become pessimistic rather than optimistic, the schedule will shift to the left* (for example, to $D''D''$ in Figure 4-6), causing a decrease in price (to P'').

THE EFFECTS OF PROCEDURES FOR SHORT SALES

Thus far, the individual investor's demand-to-hold schedule has been drawn only in the region of positive quantities. But there is more to it: the higher the price, the smaller the quantity the investor will wish to hold. At some price, the desired amount is zero, and at higher prices, the investor may consider short selling the security.

If short sellers received the proceeds from such sales, an individual investor's demand-to-hold schedule for a given security would look like the curve in Figure 4-7(a). This curve can be thought of in either of two ways: as a demand curve (that is, at price A, the investor wishes to hold quantity B) or as a marginal value curve (that is, if quantity B is held, the marginal value of one share more or less will be the amount A).

In fact, however, short sellers generally do not receive the proceeds of such sales. As mentioned in Chapter 2, these proceeds are held by the short seller's brokerage firm as collateral. In many instances, the short seller does not even receive interest on this money and, furthermore, short sellers must meet initial margin requirements on the face amount of the short sale proceeds. This changes the situation from that which is shown in Figure 4-7(a). Selling a security one owns generates cash that can be used for other purposes, but selling a security that one does not own requires an investment of cash. Thus, the decision to go short requires a higher price than it would if the short seller got the full use of the proceeds. The effective demand-to-hold schedule would look like the curve in Figure 4-7(b). To the right of the vertical axis the curve is the same as in Figure 4-7(a), but to the left the curve is higher.

The effect of this is shown in Figure 4-7(c). The solid curve is the effective demand-to-hold schedule. The dashed curve is the portion of the original demand curve in Figure 4-7(a) that is to the left of the vertical axis. If the current price of the security is P^*, this investor will go short only Q_1^* shares, not Q_2^* shares. Thus, his or her pessimism about the security will not have as much impact on the market as it would if short sellers got the full use of the short sale proceeds. In a sense, the investor chooses a holding (Q_1^*) at

FIGURE 4-7
Demand-to-Hold Curves

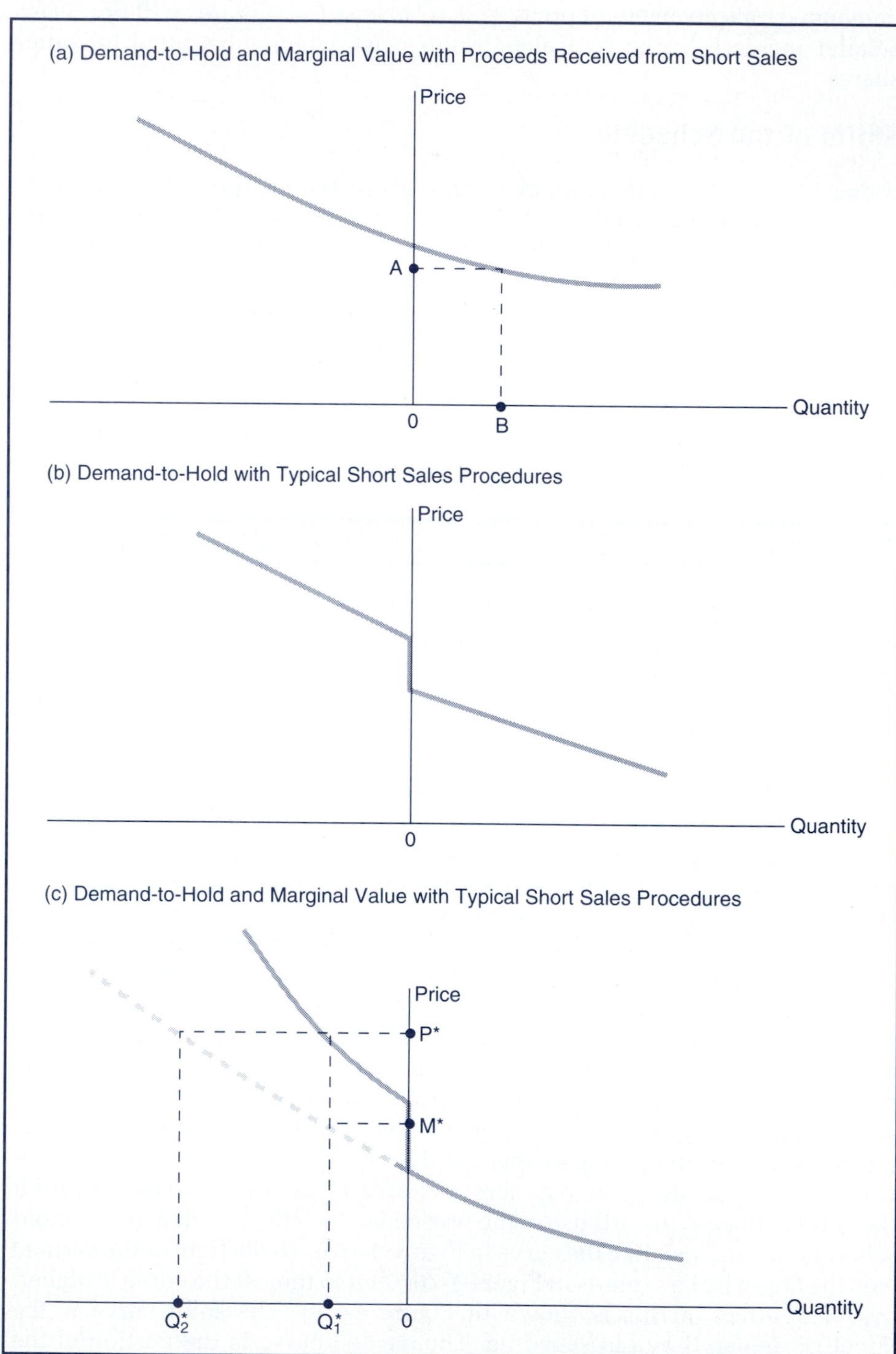

which he or she considers the marginal value (M^*) to be less than the current market price (P^*).

PRICE AS A CONSENSUS

However one chooses to analyze security price determination, it is important to remember that a free market price for a security reflects a kind of consensus. This can be seen in Figure 4-8. Assume that the current market price for this particular security is P^*. Some individuals hold the security. For each of them, the situation is like that shown in Figure 4-8(a), where it can be seen that the investor has adjusted his or her portfolio so that the marginal value of a share (M^*) equals its market price.

A few investors may be short sellers. Their situation is like that shown in Figure 4-8(b). Because of the short sale rules, each short seller will have taken a position at which the marginal value of a share is less than the price. Many investors will choose to hold no shares, and thus their position is neither long nor short. Their situation is shown in Figure 4-8(c). For each of them, the marginal value is equal to or, as in the case shown here, somewhat below the market price.

Were it not for short-selling rules, every investor would adjust his or her portfolio holdings until the marginal value of a security equaled its current market price. Since the market price is the same for everyone, so would be the marginal value for all investors (assuming that all investors pay attention to the market). Price would clearly represent a consensus of investor opinion about value.

Short-selling rules change this situation, but only slightly. Since some investors (primarily pessimists) might choose holdings at which marginal value is below the market price, this market price could be slightly higher than an average of investors' marginal values. Accordingly, securities may be slightly "overpriced."

However, short sale rules are likely to have a small impact on market prices. Even for the short seller, the disparity between market price and marginal value may be small. For those who hold no shares it would be smaller yet (or even zero). And, for those who hold shares it will be zero. Moreover, short positions are typically a small fraction of long positions. For practical purposes, price can reasonably be considered equal to a consensus opinion of investors concerning marginal value. For it to be seriously in error as an estimate of that value, many investors must be poorly informed or poor analysts. Moreover, there must be either (1) a preponderance of such investors with overly optimistic forecasts, or (2) a preponderance of such investors with overly pesssimistic forecasts. Otherwise, the actions of such investors will offset each other, making price a good estimate of the present value of the security's future prospects.

MARKET EFFICIENCY

Imagine a world in which (1) all investors have costless access to currently available information about the future, (2) all investors are good analysts, and (3) all investors pay close attention to market prices and adjust their holdings appropriately. In such a market, a security's price will be a good estimate of its

FIGURE 4-8
Price of a Security as a Consensus

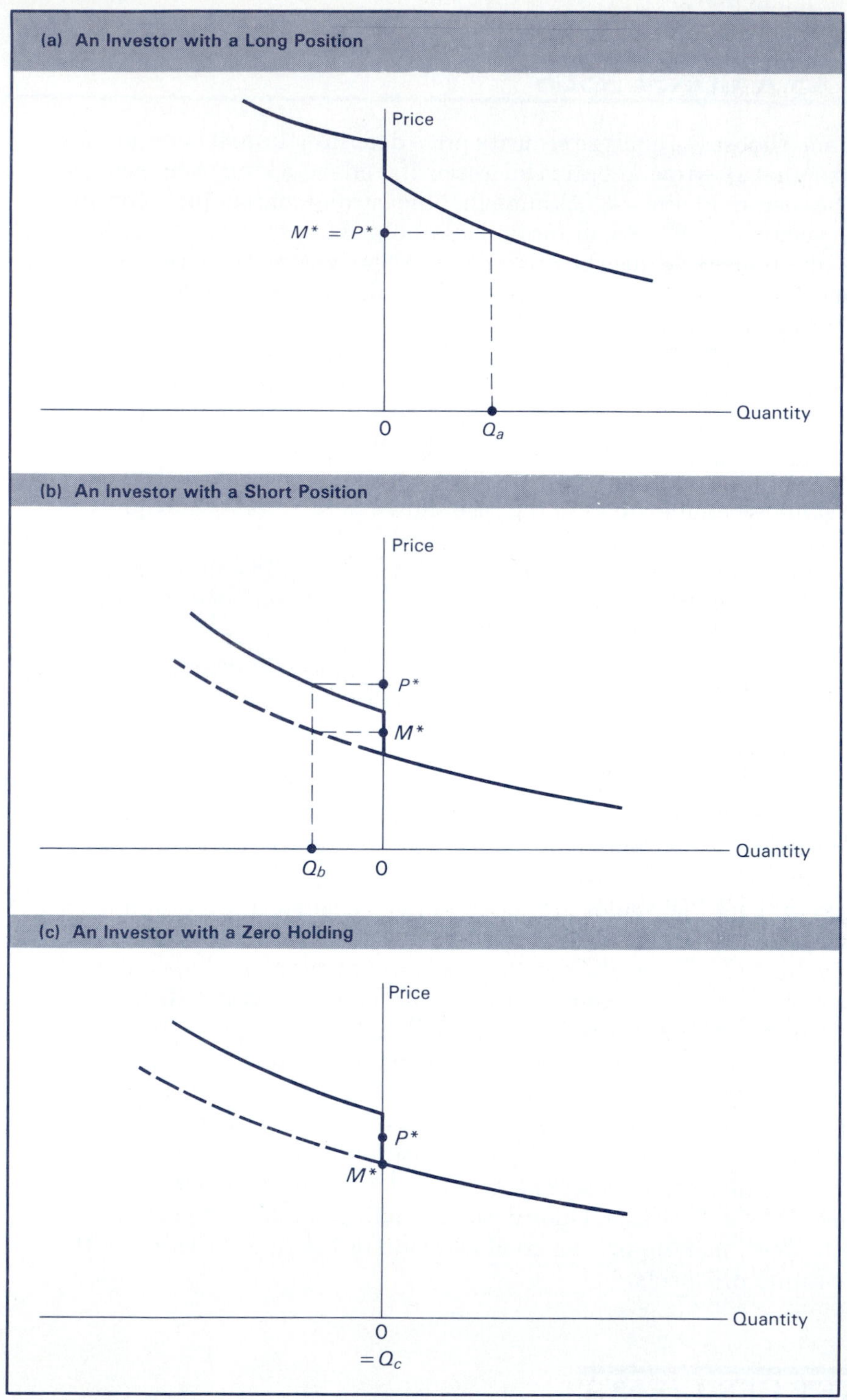

investment value, where investment value is the present value of the security's future prospects as estimated by well-informed and capable analysts.

investment value

An **efficient market** can now be defined:

efficient market

> A (perfectly) efficient market is one in which every security's price equals its investment value at all times.

In an efficient market, a set of information is fully and immediately reflected in market prices. But what information? A popular definition is the following:[1]

FORM OF EFFICIENCY	SET OF INFORMATION REFLECTED IN SECURITY PRICES
Weak	Previous prices of securities
Semistrong	All publicly available information
Strong	All information, both public and private

An equivalent definition of an efficient market is the following:

> A market is efficient with respect to a particular set of information if it is impossible to, on average, make abnormal profits by using this set of information to formulate buying and selling decisions.

For example, a market would be described as having **weak-form efficiency** if it were impossible to make abnormal profits on average by using past prices to make decisions about when to buy and sell securities. The evidence suggests that major security markets in the U.S. are weak-form efficient. However, U.S. markets do not conform so well to the definition of **semistrong-form efficiency** (although the lack of a precise meaning for "publicly available" makes this form of efficiency somewhat ambiguous). They conform even less well to the definition of **strong-form efficiency.**

weak-form market efficiency

semistrong-form market efficiency

strong-form market efficiency

In an efficient market, any new information would be immediately and fully reflected in prices. New information is just that: new, meaning a surprise (anything that is not a surprise is predictable and should have been predicted before the fact). Since happy surprises are about as likely as unhappy ones, price changes in an efficient market are about as likely to be positive as negative. While a security's price might be expected to move upward by an amount that provides a reasonable return on capital (when considered in conjunction with dividend payments), anything above or below this would, in such a market, be unpredictable. In a perfectly efficient market, price changes would be close to random.[2]

Now consider a crazy market, in which prices never bear any particular relationship to investment value. In such a world, price changes might also appear to be random. However, major security markets in the U.S. are

[1]Eugene F. Fama, "Efficient Capital Markets: A Review of Theory and Empirical Work," *Journal of Finance*, 25, no. 5 (May 1970), 383–417.

[2]Some people assert that security prices follow a **random walk,** meaning that security price changes (say, from one day to the next) are independently and identically distributed. That is, the price change from day t to day $t + 1$ is not influenced by the price change from day $t - 1$ to t; and the size of the price change from one day to the next can be viewed as being determined by the spin of a roulette wheel (with the same roulette wheel being used every day).

random walk

certainly not crazy. They may not attain perfect efficiency, but they are certainly much closer to it than to craziness. To understand financial markets, it is important to understand perfectly efficient markets.

As mentioned earlier, in an efficient market, a security's price will be a good estimate of its investment value, where investment value is the present value of the security's future prospects as estimated by well-informed and capable analysts. Any substantial disparity between price and value would reflect market inefficiency. In a well-developed and free market, major inefficiencies are rare. The reason is not hard to find. Major disparities between price and investment value will be noted by alert analysts who will seek to take advantage of their discoveries. Securities priced below value (known as underpriced or undervalued securities) will be purchased, creating pressure for price increases due to the increased demand to buy. Securities priced above value (known as overpriced or overvalued securities) will be sold, creating pressure for price decreases due to the increased supply to sell. As investors seek to take advantage of opportunities created by temporary inefficiencies, they will cause the inefficiencies to be reduced, denying the less alert and the less informed a chance to obtain large abnormal profits.

In the U.S. there are thousands of professional security analysts and even more amateurs. Not surprisingly, due to their actions the major U.S. security markets appear to be much closer to efficiency than to craziness.

SUMMARY

1. The forces of supply and demand interact to determine a security's market price.

2. An investor's demand-to-buy schedule indicates the quantity of a security that the investor wishes to purchase at various prices.

3. An investor's supply-to-sell schedule indicates the quantity of a security that the investor wishes to sell at various prices.

4. The demand and supply schedules for individual investors can be aggregated to create aggregate demand and supply schedules for a security.

5. The intersection of the aggregate demand and supply schedules determines the market clearing price of a security.

6. The market price of a security can be thought of as representing a consensus opinion about the future prospects for the security.

7. In an efficient market, a security's market price will fully reflect all available information relevant to the security's value at that time.

8. The concept of market efficiency can be expressed in three forms: weak, semistrong, and strong.

9. The three forms of market efficiency make different assumptions about the set of information reflected in security prices.

KEY TERMS

demand-to-buy schedule
demand-to-hold schedule
investment value
efficient market
weak-form market efficiency
semistrong-form market efficiency
strong-form market efficiency
random walk

QUESTIONS AND PROBLEMS

1. What is the difference between call security markets and continuous security markets?

2. What is the relationship between the demand-to-hold schedule and the demand-to-buy and supply-to-sell schedules for a particular security?
3. At two separate points in time, year-ends 1990 and 1991, Deerfoot Bay drew up the following personal demand-to-hold schedule for an investment in Lisle Bakery stock. Calculate Deerfoot's demand-to-buy schedule at year-end 1991.

1990		1991	
Price	**Quantity**	**Price**	**Quantity**
$30	1,000	$30	1,100
40	900	40	990
50	800	50	880
60	700	60	770
70	600	70	660

4. Using an aggregate demand-to-hold schedule and associated demand-to-buy or supply-to-sell schedules, explain and illustrate the effect of the following events on the equilibrium price and quantity traded of Fairchild Corporation's stock.
   (a) Fairchild officials announce that next year's earnings are expected to be significantly higher than analysts had previously forecast.
   (b) A wealthy shareholder initiates a large secondary offering of Fairchild stock.
   (c) Another company, quite similar to Fairchild in all respects except for being privately held, decides to offer its outstanding shares for sale to the public.
5. Is it true that in the short-run the supply schedule for a security is perfectly inelastic, while the demand-to-hold schedule is typically elastic? Explain.
6. Short sellers do not receive the proceeds from their short sales, must put up initial margin, and often do not receive interest on these sums held by their brokers. How do these conditions affect the aggregate demand-to-hold schedules for securities?
7. Imp Begley is pondering the statement, "The pattern of security price behavior might appear the same whether markets were efficient or if security prices bore no relationship whatsoever to investment value." Explain the meaning of this statement to Imp.
8. We all know that investors have widely diverse opinions about the future course of the economy and earnings forecasts for various industries and companies. How then is it possible for all these investors to arrive at an equilibrium price for any particular security?
9. Distinguish among the three forms of market efficiency.
10. Would you expect that fundamental security analysis makes security markets more efficient? Why?
11. Would you expect that NYSE specialists should be able to earn an abnormal profit in a semistrong efficient market? Why?
12. Is it true that in a perfectly efficient market no investor would consistently be able to earn a profit?
13. While security markets may not be perfectly efficient, what is the rationale for expecting them to be highly efficient?

14. What are the implications of the three forms of market efficiency for technical and fundamental analysis (discussed in Chapter 1)?
15. How can security markets be efficient if prices appear to behave in a random manner?
16. The years 1986 and 1987 probably will long be remembered for the insider trading scandals that were exposed.
    (a) Is successful insider trading consistent with the three forms of market efficiency? Explain.
    (b) Play the role of devil's advocate and present a case for the benefits to the financial markets of insider trading.

REFERENCES

1. A discussion and examination of the demand curves for stocks is contained in:

   Andrei Shleifer, "Do Demand Curves Slope Down?" *Journal of Finance*, 41, no. 3 (July 1986): 579–90.

   Lawrence Harris and Eitan Gurel, "Price and Volume Effects Associated with Changes in the S&P 500: New Evidence for the Existence of Price Pressures," *Journal of Finance*, 41, no. 4 (September 1986): 815–29.

   Stephen W. Pruitt and K.C. John Wei, "Institutional Ownership and Changes in the S&P 500," *Journal of Finance*, 44, no. 2 (June 1989): 509–13.

2. For an article that presents an argument that securities are "overpriced" due to short sale restrictions, see:

   Edward M. Miller, "Risk, Uncertainty, and Divergence of Opinion," *Journal of Finance*, 32, no. 4 (September 1977): 1151–68.

3. Many people believe that the following articles are the seminal pieces on efficient markets:

   Eugene F. Fama, "Efficient Capital Markets: A Review of Theory and Empirical Work," *Journal of Finance* 25, no. 5 (May 1970): 383–417.

   Eugene F. Fama, "Efficient Capital Markets: II," *Journal of Finance*, 46, no. 5 (December 1991): 1575–1617.

4. For an excellent review on efficient markets, see:

   Stephen F. LeRoy, "Capital Market Efficiency: An Update," Federal Reserve Bank of San Francisco *Economic Review*, no. 2 (Spring 1990): 29–40.

   A more detailed version of this paper can be found in:

   Stephen F. LeRoy, "Efficient Capital Markets and Martingales," *Journal of Economic Literature*, 27, no. 4 (December 1989): 1583–1621.

5. Another interesting survey article on efficient markets is:

   Peter Fortune, "Stock Market Efficiency: An Autopsy?" *New England Economic Review*, (March/April 1991): 17–40.

5

Taxes

Neither taxation nor inflation should be regarded as an unmitigated evil. Each provides benefits to some individuals that may outweigh the associated costs that others have to bear. Regardless of whether the benefits outweigh the costs, both taxes and inflation have an impact on investment decisions and investment results. And, they are sufficiently important in present-day societies to warrant considerable discussion. While the next chapter deals with inflation, this chapter provides an overview of some of the more important aspects of taxation from the viewpoint of the investor.

Federal and state tax laws play a major role in the way securities are priced in the marketplace, since investors are understandably concerned with after-tax returns, not before-tax returns. Accordingly, the investor should determine the tax rate applicable to him or her before making any investment decision. This tax rate is not the same for all securities for a given individual investor: it can be as low as 0% in the case of certain tax-exempt securities issued by states and municipalities, and in excess of 35% for corporate bonds, when both federal and state taxes are considered. After determining the applicable tax rate, the investor can estimate a security's expected after-tax return and risk. Upon doing so, an investment decision can be made wisely.

TAXES IN THE U.S.

This chapter will focus on taxes levied on U.S. citizens and corporations. Many other countries, however, impose taxes similar to those of the U.S., so much of this discussion is at least partly relevant for non–U.S. citizens.

Many of the specific tax rates and provisions in this chapter were enacted with the Tax Reform Act of 1986 and amended by the Omnibus Budget Reconciliation Act of 1990. Changes do occur from year to year, and current regulations should, of course, be consulted when preparing tax returns or considering major investment decisions. However, the material given here can be considered broadly representative of current taxation (primarily federal) in the U.S.

Generally speaking, the most important taxes for investment decision making are personal and corporate income taxes. The essential elements of each will be described, and the manner in which they influence the pricing of securities will be considered.

CORPORATE INCOME TAXES

There are three forms of business organizations in the U.S. and in most other countries—corporations, partnerships, and single proprietorships. The corporate form of organization is the largest in terms of the dollar value of assets owned, even though there are more firms organized as partnerships or single proprietorships. Legally, a corporation is regarded as a separate entity, while a proprietorship or partnership is considered an extension of its owner or owners. Income earned by proprietorships and partnerships is taxed primarily through the personal income tax levied on their owners. Income earned by a corporation may be taxed twice—once when it is earned, via the corporate income tax, and again when it is received as dividends by holders of the firm's securities, via the personal income tax.[1]

This double taxation of corporate income may at first seem inefficient, if not unfair. It also raises questions about the efficiency of the corporate form of organization. Suffice it to say that limited liability and the ability to subdivide ownership and to transfer shares of that ownership appear to be of sufficient value to more than offset the tax law disadvantages. Moreover, without the corporate income tax, personal tax rates would have to be increased if the level of government expenditures were to remain constant without increasing the national debt.

Corporate Tax Rates

marginal tax rate
average tax rate

The corporate income tax is relatively simple in one respect. Usually there are only a few basic rates. For example, in 1991 a tax rate of 15% was applicable to the first $50,000 of taxable annual income, a rate of 25% to the next $25,000, a rate of 34% to the next $25,000, a rate of 39% to the next $235,000, and a rate of 34% to all additional income. Figure 5-1 illustrates what are known as the **marginal tax rate** and **average tax rate** schedules for corporations. A corporation's marginal tax rate is the tax rate it would pay on an additional dollar of income. For example, a corporation earning $85,000 would pay $17,150 in income taxes:

$$
\begin{aligned}
0.15 \times \$50{,}000 &= \$\ 7{,}500 \\
0.25 \times \ 25{,}000 &= \ \ 6{,}250 \\
0.34 \times \ 10{,}000 &= \ \ \underline{3{,}400} \\
\text{Total income tax} &= \$17{,}150.
\end{aligned}
$$

[1]Certain corporations with thirty-five or fewer shareholders may elect to be treated as partnerships for tax purposes. Such firms, often called "Subchapter S corporations" (after the enabling provision of the Internal Revenue Code), constitute an exception to the general rule.

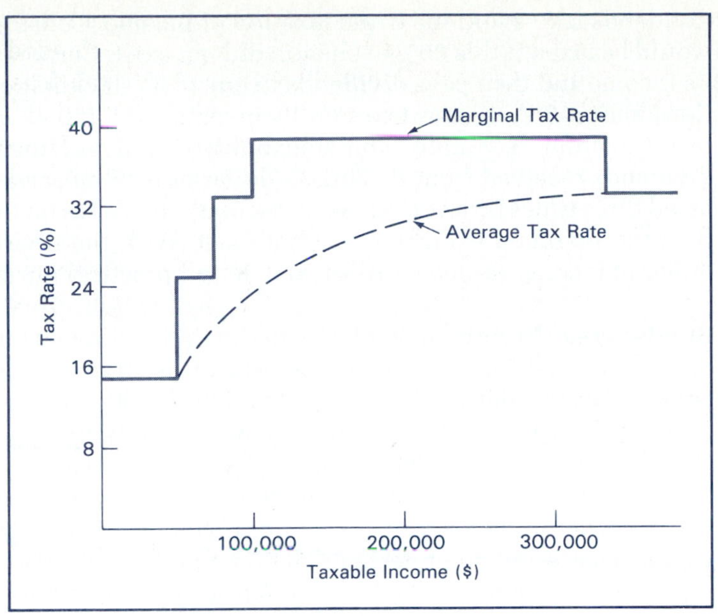

FIGURE 5-1
Marginal and Average Corporate Tax Rates, 1991

For this corporation, the marginal tax rate is 34%, since an additional dollar of income would be taxed at this rate. In other words, if this firm had income of $85,001 instead of $85,000, its tax bill would have been $17,150.34 instead of $17,150. Thus $.34 (= $17,150.34 − $17,150.00) more in taxes would be paid as a result of earning $1 (= $85,001 − $85,000) more in income.

The average tax rate is equal to the total amount of taxes paid divided by the total income subject to tax. The average tax rate for the previous example would thus be 20.18% = $17,150/$85,000. That is, 20.18% of this firm's total income would be taken by the government in the form of corporate income taxes. As can be seen in Figure 5-1, the average rate is equal to the marginal rate for incomes below $50,000 and above $335,000. For incomes between these two figures, the average rate is below the marginal rate.

The average rate measures the overall impact of taxes, but the marginal rate is more relevant for most decisions. For example, if a corporation were considering an investment that would increase its income from $85,000 to $90,000 each year, the increase in income after taxes would be (1 − .34) × $5,000 = $3,300, not (1 − .2018) × $5,000 = $3,991.

As shown in Figure 5-1, the larger a corporation's taxable income, the closer its average tax rate comes to the marginal tax rate until the rates are equal for incomes above $335,000. Most corporations with publicly traded shares have incomes of at least this size, meaning that most corporations pay taxes on their reported income at an average rate that is equal to the marginal rate of 34%.

Corporate Income from Dividends, Interest, and Capital Gains

Congress has provided that 80% of the dividends received by a corporation can be excluded from income when calculating the corporation's income tax liability. The effective tax rate on an additional dollar of dividends received by a corporation with an income in the 34% range is thus (1 − .80) × .34 = .068, or 6.8%. The reason for this special treatment of dividends is to avoid the triple taxation of income. Consider how dividends would be taxed if this 80% exclusion did not exist. Corporation A is taxed on its income and then pays dividends to one of its stockholders, corporation B. Corporation B then pays taxes on its income, which includes the dividends received from A. Finally, the stockholders of B pay income taxes on the dividends received from B. Thus, a dollar of income earned by A would be taxed three times (a tax on A, then a tax on B, then a tax on the stockholders of B) if the dividend exclusion did not exist. With the dividend exclusion, a dollar of income earned by A is taxed, for all practical purposes, only twice.

Bonds versus Preferred Stocks No deduction is allowed for interest received on bonds bought by a corporate investor; it is simply added to income and taxed at the regular rates. This means that the effective tax rate on interest received from bonds is 34%, an amount substantially greater than the 6.8% effective tax rate on common and preferred stocks. This differential tax treatment has an effect on the relative prices that corporate investors are willing to pay for these securities, since their concern is with relative after-tax yields. That is, since preferred stocks are generally viewed as being riskier than bonds, the after-tax yield on preferred stocks needs to be higher in order for investors to be interested in purchasing them. Given the favorable tax treatment on preferred stocks for corporate investors, it is possible for preferred stocks to have a lower before-tax yield than bonds while still enabling the corporate investor who buys the more risky preferred stock to be rewarded by earning, relative to bonds, a higher after-tax yield. Since the noncorporate investor faces the same marginal tax rate for both dividend income from preferred stocks and interest income from bonds, preferred stocks will provide such an investor with a relatively lower after-tax return. It follows that preferred stocks are relatively unattractive investments for noncorporate investors.

Table 5-1 provides an example that illustrates the before-tax and after-tax yields for both a corporate investor with a marginal tax rate of 34% and an individual investor with a marginal personal tax rate of 28%. It can be shown

TABLE 5-1 Comparison of Yields of Preferred Stocks and Corporate Bonds

	INVESTMENT	
	Preferred Stock	**Corporate Bond**
A. Features		
Price	\$10 per share	\$1,000 per bond
Annual dollar yield	\$.70 per share	\$80 per bond
Aggregate investment	100 shares	1 bond
Cost of aggregate investment	\$1,000	\$1,000
Aggregate annual dollar yield	\$70	\$80
Before-tax percentage yield	7% = \$70/\$1,000	8% = \$80/\$1,000
B. Corporate Investor[a]		
After-tax dollar yield	\$65.24 = \$70[1 − (.20 × .34)]	\$52.80 = \$80 (1 − .34)
After-tax percentage yield	6.524% = \$65.24/\$1,000	5.28% = \$52.80/\$1,000
C. Individual Investor[b]		
After-tax dollar yield	\$50.40 = \$70 (1 − .28)	\$57.60 = \$80 (1 − .28)
After-tax percentage yield	5.04% = \$50.40/\$1,000	5.76% = \$57.60/\$1,000

[a]Assuming a marginal corporate income tax rate of 34%.

[b]Assuming a marginal individual income tax rate of 28%.

that the individual investor will be better off purchasing the bond, whereas the corporate investor will be better off purchasing the preferred stock. Careful scrutiny will reveal this to be true for any other marginal tax rate for the individual investor.

Tax-Exempt Organizations

Many organizations are wholly or partly exempt from federal income taxes. Nonprofit religious, charitable, or educational foundations generally qualify. A small tax (2% in 1991) is levied on the net investment income of such a foundation. In addition, the foundation should pay out either all income received by the end of the year following receipt, or a minimum percentage of its assets (5% in 1991), whichever is higher, since failure to do so can result in a confiscatory tax on the difference.

Investment companies, often called mutual funds, may elect to be treated as regulated investment companies for tax purposes. This privilege is granted if certain conditions are met. For example, the funds of the investment company must be invested primarily in securities, without undue concentration in any one. Thus, its income takes the form of dividends and interest received on its investments, as well as capital gains from price appreciation realized when investments are sold at a price that is higher than their purchase price. A regulated investment company pays income tax only on income and capital gains not distributed to its shareholders. As a result of this tax treatment, such companies distribute substantially all income and gains, and in doing so, end up not having to pay any taxes.

Employee pension, profit-sharing, and stock-bonus plans may also qualify for tax-exempt status. Such a plan may entrust its assets, which are usually securities, to a "fiduciary" (for example, a bank). The fiduciary receives new contributions, makes required payments, and manages the investments owned by the plan. A fiduciary under a qualified plan (that is, a plan that meets all the requirements of applicable legislation) pays no taxes on either income or capital gains.

Another example of a tax-exempt entity is the personal trust. Here, funds are provided for the benefit of one or more individuals by another individual or individuals with a fiduciary serving as a trustee. Some trusts are created by wills, others by a contract among living persons. Whatever the origin, trusts generally pay taxes only on income that is not distributed to the designated beneficiaries.

Income and capital gains earned by investment companies, pension funds, and personal trusts do not go untaxed forever. Payments made to investment company shareholders, pension fund beneficiaries, and the beneficiaries of personal trusts are subject to applicable personal income tax rules. The exemptions apply only to taxes that might otherwise be levied at the previous stage.

PERSONAL INCOME TAXES

While the corporate income tax is an important feature of the investment scene, its impact on most individuals is indirect. This is not so for the personal income tax. Few investors avoid dealing with it in detail, at both an economic and an emotional level. Its provisions have major and direct impacts on investment behavior.

Personal Tax Rates

Taxes must be paid on an individual's income, defined as "all wealth which flows to the taxpayer other than as a mere return of capital. It includes gains and profits from any source, including gains from the sale or other disposition of capital assets."[2] Certain items are excluded from the definition of income; others are deducted from it before computing the tax due. Moreover, capital gains and losses are subject to special procedures, which will be described in a later section. Deductions and exclusions of special importance for investment purposes are described in this section as well as in later sections.

Two figures are relevant for tax purposes. Adjusted gross income is obtained by subtracting certain allowed deductions (for example, business expenses and contributions to certain retirement funds) from gross income. This amount, less a number of personal expense deductions, equals taxable income, the figure on which tax liability is based. The amount of tax calculated on this basis must be paid unless the taxpayer is able to claim tax credits, which may be subtracted directly from the tax liability to obtain a final amount due the government.

While the Tax Reform Act of 1986 (as amended by the Omnibus Budget Reconciliation Act of 1990) brought sweeping changes aimed at simplification, many people are still of the opinion that almost nothing about personal income taxes in the U.S. is simple.[3] Four different schedules of tax rates are currently in effect, the appropriate one depending on whether the particular taxpayer is single, married and filing a joint return with his or her spouse, married but filing returns separately, or a head of a household. Table 5-2 shows the tax rates in effect in 1991 for the first two types of taxpayers. (Note that the figures shown here—and elsewhere—are indexed to inflation, and hence will change over time.) The rates are plotted in Figures 5-2(a) and 5-2(b).[4]

The top line in each figure shows the marginal tax rate, which was defined earlier when corporate income taxes were being discussed. A similar definition applies here: the marginal tax rate is the tax rate an individual would pay on an additional dollar of taxable income. While this rate is

[2] *1988 Federal Tax Course* (Englewood Cliffs, N.J.: Prentice Hall, 1987), p. 89.

[3] The Act itself is over 900 pages long.

[4] The appendix shows how two subtle yet complicated changes made in 1990 cause the tax rate schedules to be slightly different from what is shown here.

TABLE 5-2
Personal Income Tax Rates, 1991

TAXABLE INCOME		
At Least	**But Not More Than**	**Amount of Taxes**
Single Taxpayers:		
$ 0	$20,350	$ 0 + 15% of income over $ 0
20,350	49,300	3,052.50 + 28 of income over $20,350
49,300	. . .	11,158.50 + 31 of income over $49,300
Married Taxpayers Filing Jointly:		
$ 0	$34,000	$ 0 + 15% of income over $ 0
34,000	82,150	5,100 + 28 of income over $34,000
82,150	. . .	18,582 + 31 of income over $82,150

FIGURE 5-2
Marginal and Average Personal Tax Rates, 1991

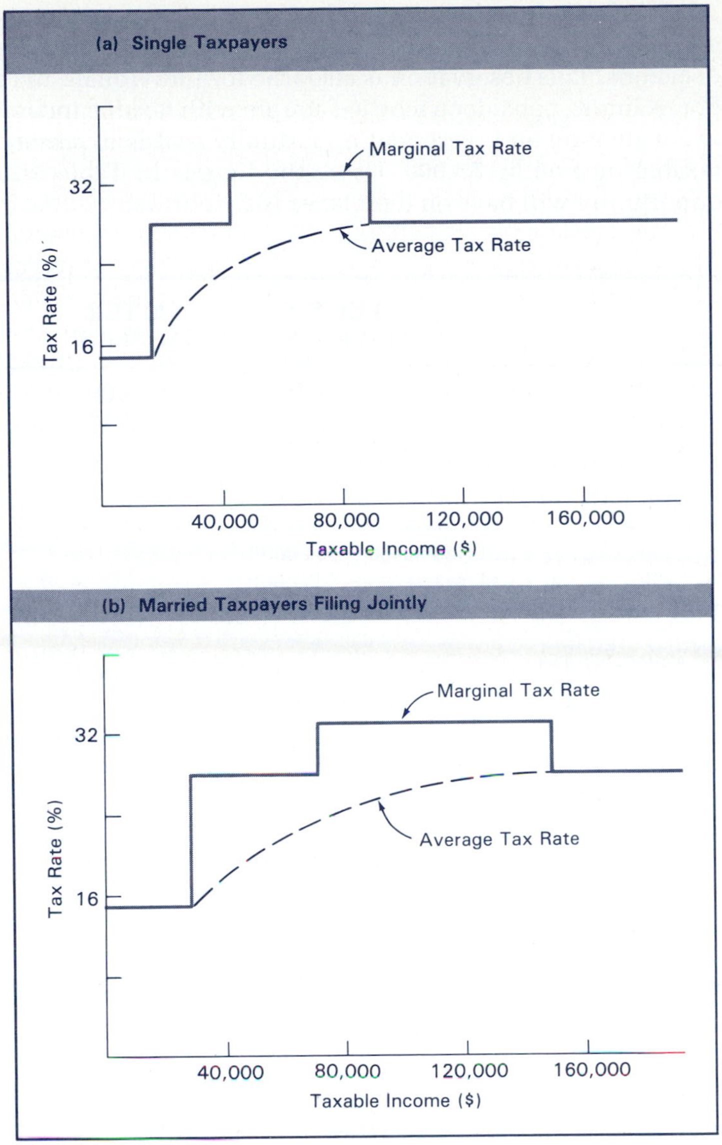

(a) Single Taxpayers

Marginal Tax Rate
Average Tax Rate
Tax Rate (%)
32
16
40,000 80,000 120,000 160,000
Taxable Income ($)

(b) Married Taxpayers Filing Jointly

Marginal Tax Rate
Average Tax Rate
Tax Rate (%)
32
16
40,000 80,000 120,000 160,000
Taxable Income ($)

constant over certain ranges of income, it increases as the taxpayer moves to higher taxable income brackets.

The lower line in both Figure 5-2(a) and 5-2(b) shows the average tax rate, which was also defined earlier when corporate income taxes were being discussed. Again, a similar definition applies here: the average tax rate is the ratio of total tax paid to total taxable income and is generally smaller than the marginal tax rate.[5]

[5]The exception is for taxpayers in the lowest income bracket, where the average and marginal tax rates are equal.

Earlier, it was mentioned that for corporations, the marginal tax rate is generally more relevant than the average tax rate in making certain kinds of decisions. This observation is also true for individuals and married couples. For example, consider a married couple with taxable income of $60,000 who are evaluating an investment opportunity that is expected to increase their taxable income by $3,000. Using the figures in Table 5-2, the impact this opportunity will have on their taxes is as follows:

	BEFORE INCREASE	AFTER INCREASE	DIFFERENCE
Taxable income	$60,000	$63,000	$3,000
Tax	12,380[a]	13,220[b]	840
Spendable income	$47,620	$49,780	$2,160

Marginal tax rate = ($13,220 − $12,380)/$3,000 = $840/$3,000 = 28.00%

[a]$12,380 = $5,100 + [.28 × ($60,000 − $34,000)].
[b]$13,220 = $5,100 + [.28 × ($63,000 − $34,000)].

As shown in this table, the increase of $3,000 in taxable income will result in an increase of $840 in taxes, leaving a net increase in spendable income of $2,160. The calculations for this particular example are simple because the change in taxable income left the taxpayer in the same bracket. Thus, 28% of the additional income will be taxed away, leaving 72% to be spent. The fact that the average tax rate is 20.63% (= $12,380/$60,000) before the increase and 20.98% (= $13,220/$63,000) after the increase is irrelevant to this couple in deciding whether or not to make the investment.

When a decision moves income into a higher bracket, the computations are more complex. For example, assume the opportunity in question would increase income by $30,000. Again using the figures in Table 5-2, the impact on taxes would be:

	BEFORE INCREASE	AFTER INCREASE	DIFFERENCE
Taxable income	$60,000	$90,000	$30,000
Tax	12,380[a]	21,016[b]	8,636
Spendable income	$47,620	$68,984	$21,364

Marginal tax rate = ($21,016 − $12,380)/$30,000 = $8,636/$30,000 = 28.79%

[a]$12,380 = $5,100 + [.28 × ($60,000 − $34,000)].
[b]$21,016 = $18,582 + [.31 × ($90,000 − $82,150)].

As shown in this table, an increase of $30,000 in taxable income will result in an increase of $8,636 in taxes, leaving a net increase in spendable income of $21,364. Thus, 28.79% of the additional income will be taxed away, an amount greater than the 28% figure that was applicable to the previous example. As before, the average tax rate of 20.63% (= $12,380/$60,000) before the increase and 23.35% (= $21,016/$90,000) after the increase is irrelevant to the couple in making their decision.

Tax-Exempt Bonds

tax-exempt bonds

A major consideration for investors with large taxable incomes is the possibility of obtaining tax-exempt income. The simplest way to accomplish this is to purchase **tax-exempt bonds.** These securities exist because the notion of federalism has been interpreted to imply that the federal government should not tax states and municipalities, nor the income produced from their bonds.[6] While the legal basis is complex, the facts are simple. Interest income from most bonds issued by states, municipalities, and their agencies need not be included in taxable income in determining the amount of federal taxes that are owed. The benefit for a high-bracket taxpayer is notable.

Consider again the couple in the previous example. Assume that for the same cost, they can obtain an increase in taxable income of either \$30,000 per year by investing in corporate bonds, or \$24,000 per year by purchasing tax-exempt bonds. As shown earlier, their effective tax rate on an increase of \$30,000 in taxable income would be 28.79%, leaving 71.21% or \$21,364 to be spent. But \$24,000 in tax-exempt income could all be spent—clearly a preferable investment opportunity.

This relationship is no secret. Not surprisingly, tax-exempt bonds offer lower pre-tax rates of interest than others. Thus, they are not attractive for investors with low marginal tax rates. For example, if the couple had a marginal tax rate of 15% instead of 28.79%, they would prefer the corporate bonds. This is because their after-tax return would be \$25,500 [= \$30,000 × (1 − .15)], an amount greater than the \$24,000 provided by the tax-exempt bonds.

If couples with a marginal tax rate of 29.16% find the tax-exempt bonds more attractive, and couples with a marginal tax rate of 15% find the corporate bonds more attractive, then there should be a marginal tax rate in between these two rates that makes couples in that bracket indifferent between the two types of bonds. In this example, if the couple had a marginal tax rate of 20%, they would be indifferent between the corporate bonds and the tax-exempt bonds, since both would provide an after-tax return of \$24,000. However, a 20% marginal tax rate does not currently exist. What this means is that couples with rates equal to or greater than the next highest tax rate (28%) would prefer the tax-exempt bonds; couples with rates equal to or less than the next lowest tax rate (15%) would prefer the corporate bonds.

The 20% marginal tax rate figure was determined by solving the following equation for t:

$$\$30{,}000 \times (1 - t) = \$24{,}000.$$

More generally, the marginal tax rate figure can be arrived at by solving the following equation for t:

$$\text{taxable bond yield} \times (1 - t) = \text{tax-exempt bond yield}$$

or

$$1 - t = \text{tax-exempt bond yield/taxable bond yield}$$

[6]Chapter 19 describes various types of bonds that are available for investment, and gives a more detailed discussion of how they are taxed.

or

$$t = 1 - \text{ratio of tax-exempt to taxable bond yields.}$$

Figure 5-3 shows the ratio, over time, of the yield-to-maturity for a group of tax-exempt bonds issued by municipalities to that of a group of taxable bonds issued by public utilities.[7] On this basis, tax-exempt bonds appear to be competitive with taxable bonds for investors subject to marginal tax rates between 20% (when the ratio of bond yields is 80%) and 40% (when the ratio of bond yields is 60%). For those wealthy enough to be considering investments that provide income in the higher ranges, tax-exempt bonds are well worth investigation. Less wealthy investors are likely to find them unattractive.

Capital Gains and Losses

The provisions of the personal income tax laws that deal with the treatment of capital gains and losses have had a great impact on investor behavior. Only the basic elements of these provisions can be described here. Complete understanding of the details would require an effort sufficient to keep many lawyers, tax accountants, and investment advisors busy.

realized capital gain

unrealized capital gain

Realization A change in the market value of a capital asset is not relevant for tax purposes until it is **realized** as a capital gain (or loss) by sale or exchange. If a security purchased for $50 appreciates to a value of $100 in a year, no tax is due on the **unrealized capital gain.** But if it is sold for $120 two years after purchase, the difference of $70 must be declared as capital gains realized at the time of sale and tax paid at the rate applicable to it.

This rule makes the end of the year an interesting time for stockbrokers. Depending on their situations, taxpayers may be either anxious or reluctant to realize capital gains or losses before a new tax year begins. Consider, for example, a taxpayer who earlier in the year had sold 1,000 shares of stock A for

[7]These yields are also compared in Chapter 19 (see, in particular, Figure 19-7).

FIGURE 5-3
Ratio of Prime Long-Term Municipal Bond Yield to New Aa Long-Term Public Utility Bond Yield, 1970–1990

Source: Adapted from *Analytical Record of Yields and Yield Spreads*, Salomon Brothers Inc., various issues, Part III, Table 4.

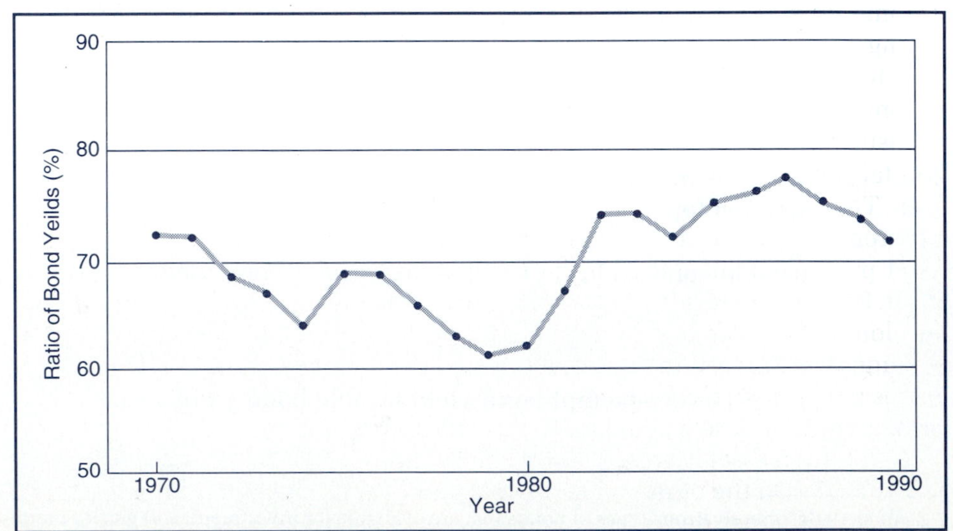

$50 per share, having purchased it three years ago for $20 per share. This investor has a capital gain of $30,000 [= 1,000 × ($50 − $20)], and will have to pay taxes on this gain if nothing is done. However, it is now December and the investor currently owns 1,000 shares of stock B, which is selling for $65 per share. Having purchased it four years ago for $95 per share, the investor has an unrealized loss of $30,000 [= 1,000 × ($65 − $95)] on the investment in B. Nevertheless, the investor believes that stock B will rebound in the near future and, hence, wants to continue owning it. It might seem at first glance that the investor should sell B on December 31 and then buy it back January 1, thereby establishing a capital loss of $30,000 on B to offset the capital gain on A. This would remove the tax liability that the investor had on the gain on A, while essentially maintaining his or her position in B. However, the same stock cannot be bought and sold simultaneously in such tax exchanges. This is because the tax laws preclude a deduction associated with a loss on a **wash sale** where a security is sold and a "substantially identical" one is bought within 30 days.

wash sale

Brokerage firms publish lists pairing similar stocks for those investors who wish to sell a particular stock for tax purposes; by selling a stock and simultaneously purchasing the matching stock, the investor will be able to continually maintain a portfolio with similar investment characteristics. In the previous example, a brokerage firm may have stocks B and C matched together. These two stocks have different issuers, but may be in the same industry and, in the opinion of the brokerage firm, be poised for a similar rebound next year. Accordingly, the investor might sell B and purchase C.

End-of-year sales and purchases motivated by tax considerations are fairly common. At this time, securities that experienced substantial price changes during the year tend to have large numbers of trades as investors sell to realize gains or losses. If buyers recognize that the sellers are motivated by knowledge of the tax laws, and not some previously unrecognized bad news affecting the company in question, such "selling pressure" should not seriously depress the company's stock price.

Capital gains and losses are, of course, those realized on capital assets, but the regulations define capital assets rather narrowly. Capital assets include all kinds of property except that held in conjunction with the taxpayer's trade or business (for example, inventories). Gains or losses on property that is an integral part of a taxpayer's business are considered regular income. Gains on the sale of one's personal residence are capital gains, but, owing to special provisions in the tax law, some gains on property held only to rent to others may be considered income. Pro rata appreciation of a fixed-income security issued at a significant discount (for example, a 90-day Treasury bill) may also be considered income, as it is more like interest than capital gains.

capital gains and losses

The capital gain or loss realized when an asset is sold or exchanged is the difference between the value received and the asset's adjusted basis. For an asset purchased outright, the (initial) basis is equal to the actual cost of the asset. For an asset received as a gift or inheritance, the recipient's basis may be the donor's adjusted basis or the value at the time of receipt, depending on the relationship between the two and the value at the time of the sale. Gains and losses are categorized as short-term if the asset is held for a year or less, and long-term if the asset is held for more than a year.

While an asset is held, improvements may be made and their cost added to the basis. On the other hand, any return of capital must be deducted from the basis, as must depreciation. The basis is adjusted to account for such

MONEY MATTERS
Capital Gains Taxes: Too High?

Should capital gains taxes be reduced? That question has sparked considerable controversy in recent years. The Bush administration made cutting capital gains taxes the centerpiece of its domestic policy agenda. Democrats have used the issue to paint Republicans as the uncaring party of the rich.

Investors have a large stake in the outcome of the capital gains tax debate. Despite all the rhetoric, the true public policy issue is not whether a capital gains tax cut will make investors richer as a group (a likely short-run result). Rather, it is whether a capital gains tax cut will make the economy (and, hence, investors) wealthier in the long run.

We will not attempt to provide a definitive answer to this question. Numerous commentators have argued the case long and hard. We simply want to summarize the arguments on both sides of the debate. You, as an investor and as a voting citizen, will have to draw your own conclusions.

Economists agree that taxing any commodity or activity reduces the output of that commodity or activity. Taxing gains on capital assets, therefore, undoubtedly reduces the amount of capital assets "produced." However, the government must obtain its revenues from some source. Given a certain level of required revenues, if capital gains taxes were lowered, then other taxes would have to be raised (at least in the short run). Here the law of unintended consequences comes into play. If, for example, income taxes were raised to make up for the revenue shortfall, people would cut back on taxable employment, certainly a detrimental consequence from the economy's perspective.

The issue boils down to whether one believes that lower capital gains taxes would stimulate sufficient investment (and the benefits derived therefrom) to compensate for the losses that would result from raising other taxes. (We note that some proponents of lower capital gains taxes contend that cutting capital gains taxes would cause more existing investments to be sold, increasing tax revenues and negating the need for raising other taxes.)

Advocates of lower capital gains taxes typically decry what they perceive as strong disincentives present in our economy to savings and investment. For example, *The Wall Street Journal* (December 19, 1991) reported that U.S. capital gains taxes are the highest in the world. Many countries totally exempt capital gains from taxation (Italy and the Netherlands, for example), while in others effective tax rates are much lower than in the U.S.

The arguments of many proponents hark back to the "supply-side" economics of the early Reagan administration years. They assert that lower capital gains taxes will promote additional investment and encourage savings. As a consequence, the economy will move to a higher long-run growth path. As by-products, stock markets will rise in value, interest rates will decline, and corporate leverage will be reduced.

Proponents also point to a fairness issue. A significant portion of an investor's return is simply compensation for expected inflation. As a result, capital gains taxes effectively tax an investor's principal as well as earnings on that principal. A cut in capital gains taxes would diminish this inequity. (Some countries, such as Australia and the U.K., index capital asset original cost values to inflation in calculating capital gains taxes.)

Opponents of lower capital gains taxes (class warfare demagogues aside) argue that good investments are still amply rewarded in the U.S. Under current federal tax laws, investors retain over two-thirds of their capital gains. Further, investors may defer capital gains taxes for years by not selling their assets (thus reducing the present value of their tax liabilities). They may even completely forgo capital gains taxes by passing on their assets to their heirs. Moreover, contend opponents, why should capital gains taxes be lowered on existing investments, the owners of which would be by far the largest beneficiaries of the reduction? Their assets represent investment decisions that cannot be rescinded no matter what the level of capital gains taxes. Lowering taxes on these assets would do nothing to stimulate future investment and would simply aggravate current budget problems. Some opponents also assert that reducing capital gains taxes would encourage a short-term trading mentality on the part of investors, a development they view as detrimental to what they contend are already short-sighted capital markets. (This line of reasoning has led to proposals for sliding-scale capital gains tax rates whereby the longer the asset is held, the lower would be the tax rate when it is finally sold.)

Is there a simple answer to this debate? Clearly, no. The politics of the issue has become severely entangled with economics. Given the strong ideological stances of the interested parties, the controversy is likely to rage for years. On what side of the capital gains tax debate do you fall?

changes. The accounting required can become rather complicated. For example, if an investor buys 100 shares at $40 each, then buys another 100 at $50, and later sells 100 shares at $60, what is the realized capital gain? If the two round lots had been kept separate and only the shares that cost the higher amount were sold, the gain is $10 per share. This is the preferred alternative, since it minimizes current tax outlays. If, however, adequate identification of the lots is not possible, regulations require first-in-first-out accounting, which would place the basis at $40 per share and the gain at $20 per share.

The ability to control the realization of capital gains and losses has a number of obvious advantages. Most important, tax can be paid at the most opportune time. The clearest case involves the realization of capital gains around the time of retirement. Shortly before retirement is usually a time when the taxpayer's income is relatively high, which in turn means that the taxpayer's marginal tax rate is relatively high. After retirement the taxpayer's income and, in turn, marginal tax rate are usually substantially lower. Accordingly, it is generally advantageous for the taxpayer who is near retirement to wait until after retirement to realize any capital gains.

Treatment The tax treatment of capital gains begins by bringing all short-term capital gains and losses together to obtain either a net short-term capital gain or a loss. Similarly, all long-term gains and losses are brought together to obtain either a net long-term capital gain or a loss. Finally, all gains and losses are brought together to obtain a net capital gain or loss. Having made these calculations, the taxpayer will fall into one of the following categories, and will be taxed as indicated:

1. Net capital gain attributable to net short-term capital gains being greater than net long-term capital losses. This is taxed as ordinary income.
2. Net capital gain attributable to net short-term capital losses being less than net long-term capital gains. This is taxed as ordinary income, subject to a maximum rate of 28%. This means that if the taxpayer is in the 31% tax bracket, the net capital gain will be taxed at only 28%; the remaining income will be taxed at a rate that is determined by ignoring the net capital gains.
3. Net capital gain attributable to having both net short-term capital gains and long-term capital gains. Both the net short-term capital gains and the net long-term capital gains are taxed as ordinary income, but the net long-term capital gains are subject to a maximum rate of 28%.
4. Net capital loss. If the loss is less than or equal to $3,000, then the entire amount may be deducted from the taxpayer's ordinary income this year. Any excess over $3,000 can in future years be deducted from ordinary income or used to offset capital gains.

As an example, assume that Mr. and Mrs. Smith have taxable income of $200,000, which includes $40,000 of net capital gains. Their tax bill can be determined by first noting in Table 5-2 that their marginal tax rate appears to be 31%. Since this is greater than 28%, their tax bill can be calculated by taking advantage of the 28% maximum tax rate on capital gains, provided that at least part of the $40,000 is attributable to net long-term capital gains. There are three cases to consider.

In case 1, the $40,000 was determined by aggregating a net short-term capital gain and a net long-term capital loss (such as $60,000 and $20,000, respectively), causing the full $200,000 to be treated as ordinary income.

Hence, the resulting tax bill is \$55,116 [= \$18,582 + .31 × (\$200,000 − \$82,150)], and the net capital gain is taxed at a rate of 31%.

In case 2, the \$40,000 was determined by aggregating a net short-term capital loss and a net long-term capital gain (such as \$10,000 and \$50,000, respectively). Note from Table 5-2 that their taxable income before net capital gain is equal to \$160,000 (= \$200,000 − \$40,000), and will be subject to taxes amounting to \$42,716 [= \$18,582 + .31 × (\$160,000 − \$82,150)]. The net capital gain will be subject to a rate of 28%, resulting in taxes amounting to \$11,200 (= .28 × \$40,000). Hence the Smiths' total tax bill comes to \$53,916 (= \$42,716 + \$11,200).

In case 3, the \$40,000 was determined by aggregating a net short-term capital gain and a net long-term capital gain (such as \$10,000 and \$30,000, respectively). The Smiths' taxable income before the net long-term capital gain is equal to \$170,000 (= \$200,000 − \$30,000), and will be subject to taxes amounting to \$45,816 [= \$18,582 + .31 × (\$170,000 − \$82,150)]. The net long-term capital gain will be subject to a rate of 28%, resulting in taxes amounting to \$8,400 (= .28 × \$30,000). Hence the Smiths' total tax bill comes to \$54,216 (= \$45,816 + \$8,400).

In summary, note that the tax bill of the Smiths is different for the three cases. It amounts to either \$55,116 or \$53,916 or \$54,216, depending upon how the net capital gain of \$40,000 was determined. The best situation from the Smiths' viewpoint is if it is due entirely to a net long-term capital gain (the tax bill would thus be minimized at \$53,916), while the worst situation is if it is due entirely to a net short-term capital gain (the tax bill would thus be maximized at \$55,116).

Sale of Residence Special provisions apply to capital gains realized from the sale of an individual's main residence. If a new residence is purchased within two years, no tax need be paid, provided that the price of a new home exceeds the proceeds realized from the sale of the old one. In this case, the untaxed gain on the old home will be added to any gain from the new one when it is sold later. Thus, the upwardly mobile individual or couple who would never think of buying a less expensive home can look forward to a life that is free from the payment of capital gains taxes on increases in property values.

An additional provision softens the blow if cheaper housing is desired later in life. A person 55 or older can elect to make a once-in-a-lifetime exclusion of the first \$125,000 of realized gain on the sale of a residence if he or she has lived there for three of the preceding five years.

State Income Taxes

Most states levy personal income taxes, following a format similar to that of the federal government. Although lower, state taxes are also likely to be progressive. The impact of these taxes is not quite as large as might first appear, since income taxes paid to state governments may be deducted from income before computing federal income tax. For example, consider an investor whose marginal rates for state and federal income taxes are 10% and 28%, respectively. Assume in this example that federal taxes are not deductible in computing state taxes. An additional \$100 of income will result in \$10 of state tax. This leaves \$90 subject to federal income tax, thereby increasing the investor's federal income taxes by \$25.20. Overall, \$35.20 will be taxed away, giving an effective combined marginal rate of 35.2%. More generally, the combined marginal tax rate equals $s + [(1 - s)f]$, where s and f denote the marginal state and federal tax rates, respectively.

The situation becomes a bit more complicated if the state allows the taxpayer to deduct the amount of federal taxes paid in determining the amount of taxable income. In this situation there is **cross-deductibility,** since state taxes are deductible for federal tax purposes and federal taxes are deductible for state tax purposes. Now, using the previous \$100 example, \$7.41 = \$100 × [.1 − (.1 × .28)]/[1 − (.1 × .28)] will be paid in state income taxes and \$25.93 = \$100 × [.28 − (.1 × .28)]/[1 − (.1 × .28)] will be paid in federal income taxes, for a combined total of \$33.34. Thus, the effective combined marginal tax rate is 33.34%. More generally, the amount of state tax paid per additional dollar earned equals $[s - (s \times f)]/[1 - (s \times f)]$, and the corresponding amount of federal tax paid equals $[f - (s \times f)]/[1 - (s \times f)]$. The combined marginal tax rate is therefore $[s + f - (2 \times s \times f)]/[1 - (s \times f)]$.

cross-deductibility

Another interesting feature of state taxation is that the interest income from bonds issued by municipalities within a state may be exempt from that state's income tax. Some states extend this exemption to include dividends from certain corporations domiciled within the state. Furthermore, cities that levy personal income taxes typically exempt from taxation the interest income on any municipal bonds they have issued. In this situation, the resident of the city that purchases such a bond escapes taxation on three levels—federal, state, and local.

TAX SHELTERS

Many advertisements implore high-tax-bracket investors to put their money in cattle, oil drilling, real estate, and other investments with purportedly attractive tax characteristics. Such "tax shelters" are devised to take advantage of tax provisions allowing large deductions to create a "tax loss" in the present, followed later by a profit, generally in the form of a capital gain. Since their attractiveness is greater the higher the taxpayer's marginal tax rate, presumably only those in the highest brackets should find such investments interesting. Such enterprises are generally formed as limited partnerships. A promoter, or general partner, puts together the operation, with individual investors as limited partners. The hoped-for results are tidy profits for the promoter and the investors, at the expense of the tax collector.

A little thought should call into question the likely results for such an investment. First of all, many of the key provisions of the tax law have been changed recently, and it is not unrealistic to expect more changes in the future. Second, even if loopholes remain unplugged, economic forces may diminish any opportunities for abnormally high profits. If large gains can be made, why should the promoter share them to any major extent with the investors? But one can go even further. If large profits remain for promoters, why won't more promoters enter the business? The answer is that they will, potentially until the risk and return available from promoting tax shelters is competitive with that in other occupations. Anomalies in the tax laws are more likely to bring abnormally large amounts of investment into cattle feeding programs, oil drilling, and so on, than to provide well-lighted roads to untold riches for high-tax-bracket investors.

This is not to deny that advantages can be gained from the early discovery of some scheme for tax-sheltered investment. Often investors in such deals reduce their taxes, as advertised, but only by taking real and permanent losses. Occasionally, the arrangements appear more like con games in which the professional swindler profits at the expense of the amateur investor, leaving the Internal Revenue Service unscathed.

Having said this, it should be pointed out that there are features of the tax code that virtually everyone should consider when investing their money. Specifically, investors should seriously consider taking advantage of the opportunities available to them to invest their money on a pre-tax basis where, in addition, the income earned on the initial investment grows tax-free. If this is not possible, then they should consider doing just the latter—investing their money in a manner so that the income earned on the initial investment can grow tax-free.

Keogh Plans and Individual Retirement Accounts

Two examples can be used to illustrate the point. First, the tax code allows individuals who are self-employed to set aside as much as 25% of their income each year on a pre-tax basis, subject to a maximum of $30,000, in what is known as a **Keogh plan** (also known as an H.R. 10 plan). This money can be invested according to the investor's desires, and can be withdrawn after the investor reaches an age of 59½ (such withdrawals must begin by the age of 70½; penalties exist if withdrawals do not take place between the ages of 59½ and 70½). The key feature of Keogh plans is that both the amount invested and the income earned on this investment are not subject to taxation until funds are withdrawn from the plan, at which point the funds are taxed as ordinary income.[8] Hence the investor benefits by deferring the payment of income taxes on both the amount invested and the income earned on the investment until a later date.

Keogh plan

The second example is what is known as an **individual retirement account** or IRA, which can be set up by anyone. According to the tax code, an individual who is employed can contribute up to $2,000 per year to an IRA. Hence a married couple where both husband and wife work can set aside $4,000; if only one spouse works, a maximum of $2,250 can be set aside. While the amount contributed to an IRA comes out of after-tax income (except in special circumstances), the earnings on the investment are allowed to grow without the payment of taxes until withdrawn.[9]

individual retirement account

Consider an individual who is thinking about investing $2,000 of gross income for twenty years. This investor is in the 31% marginal tax bracket and anticipates being in it for the rest of his or her life. Bonds currently earn 10% and are anticipated to continue earning this amount indefinitely. If the investor deposits the $2,000 in a Keogh plan which in turn buys the bonds, it will grow to be worth $\$13,455 = \$2,000 \times (1.10)^{20}$ at the end of twenty years. Assuming that the money is withdrawn at that time, the investor will receive $\$9,284 = \$13,455 \times (1 - .31)$ after taxes.

Alternatively, the investor could consider investing in an IRA which, in turn, buys the bonds. However, taxes on the $2,000 amounting to $\$620 = \$2,000 \times .31$ must be paid first. Depositing the remaining $\$1,380 = \$2,000 - \$620$ results in the IRA having a balance of $\$9,284 = \$1,380 \times (1.10)^{20}$ at the end of twenty years. Assuming that the money is withdrawn

[8]Other plans that are treated similarly with respect to taxation are known as 401(k) plans, run by corporations, and 403(b) plans, run by certain nonprofit organizations.

[9]Single premium deferred annuities, available from many insurance companies, are treated similarly for tax purposes.

at that time, the investor will receive $6,815 = $1,320 + [($9,284 − $1,320) × (1 − .31)] after taxes.

As a basis for comparison, consider what would happen if the investor avoids using either a Keogh plan or an IRA and invests directly in bonds. Doing so means that only $1,380 is available for investment, and that each year the investor will get to keep earnings amounting to only 6.9% = 10% × (1 − .31) of the amount invested. Hence, after twenty years the investor will have an amount available after taxes equal to $5,241 = $1,380 × $(1.069)^{20}$.

In summary, the after-tax payoffs for the three alternatives discussed are:

Keogh plan:	$9,284
IRA:	$6,815
direct investment:	$5,241

Note that the Keogh plan and IRA provide the investor with 77% and 30% more money after taxes, respectively, than could be earned by investing directly. Another way to view these payoffs is to note that the direct investment would have to earn 14.5% before taxes in order to provide the same after-tax payoff provided by investing in a Keogh plan that earns 10%. Similarly, the direct investment would have to earn 12% before taxes in order to provide the same after-tax payoff provided by the IRA. It is no surprise that a popular book advises readers that "One of the best ways to obtain extra investment funds is to avoid taxes legally."[10]

SUMMARY

1. Because investors concern themselves with after-tax returns, federal and state tax laws play a major role in the way securities are priced.

2. Corporations pay taxes on their income. These taxes result in corporate owners being double-taxed: once on the corporation's income and once on their income from the corporation.

3. Individuals also pay taxes on their income. Special procedures are used to calculate the taxes assessed on the capital gains income of individuals.

4. In the case of both individuals and corporations, the marginal tax rate is more relevant than the average tax rate for making investment decisions.

5. Tax-exempt bonds generally pay lower interest rates than equivalent-risk taxable bonds. Comparable tax-exempt and taxable bonds should be evaluated on an after-tax basis.

6. Capital assets are defined rather narrowly by the tax code. They include all kinds of property except that held in conjunction with the taxpayer's business.

7. A change in the market value of a capital asset is not relevant for tax purposes until it is realized as a capital gain (or loss) by sale or exchange.

8. The capital gain or loss realized when an asset is sold is the difference between the value received and the asset's adjusted basis.

9. The calculation of capital gains taxes involves: netting all short-term gains and losses; netting all long-term gains and losses; and netting short-term net gains (losses) against long-term net gains (losses). The outcome of these computations determines how an investor's capital gains are taxed.

10. Because state taxes are deductible on a federal level and perhaps vice versa, the combined

[10] Malkiel, Burton G., *A Random Walk Down Wall Street* (New York: W.W. Norton & Company, Inc., 1990), p. 279.

marginal tax rate is not the sum of the state and federal marginal tax rates.

11. Some tax shelters, such as Keogh plans and IRAs, permit the deferment of taxes on the investor's wage income and investment earnings.

12. Other, more speculative tax shelters are devised to take advantage of tax provisions, allowing large deductions to create a "tax loss" in the present followed later by a profit, usually in the form of a capital gain.

KEY TERMS

marginal tax rate
average tax rate
tax-exempt bonds
alternative minimum tax
realized capital gain
unrealized capital gain
wash sale
capital gains and losses
cross-deductibility
Keogh plan
individual retirement account

QUESTIONS AND PROBLEMS

1. Describe how corporate owners are subject to double taxation of their corporate income.

2. Why is the marginal tax rate more relevant to investment decision making than the average tax rate?

3. Given the following income tax schedule, draw a graph illustrating the marginal and average tax rates as a function of income level.

INCOME	TAX RATE
\$0–\$10,000	10%
\$10,001–\$20,000	13%
\$20,001–\$30,000	15%
\$30,001–\$50,000	20%
\$50,001 and above	25%

4. Given that interest payments are tax deductible for a corporation, while dividend payments are not, why don't corporations finance all of their operations with debt?

5. Preferred stocks have several fixed-income characteristics, yet generally provide lower after-tax yields to individual investors than do straight-debt securities. However, corporations seem to find it particularly attractive to hold preferred stocks. Why?

6. Minneapolis Pipelines pays an annual dividend of \$0.80 per share on its preferred stock. The stock currently sells for \$12 per share. Maplewood Chemicals is considering investing idle cash in either Minneapolis' preferred stock or a bond yielding 9.8%. If Maplewood's marginal tax rate is 34%, which investment is more attractive?

7. U.S. federal personal income tax rates are progressive in that the marginal tax rate increases with income (see Figure 5-2). What is the justification for this tax structure? Make a case for or against progressive tax rates.

8. Footsie Belardi earned \$35,000 in 1991. Using the single filer tax schedule in Table 5-2, calculate Footsie's taxes due for the year 1991.

9. Is the following statement true or false? Because tax-exempt municipal bonds provide investors with interest income that is exempt from federal (and possibly state and local) taxes, all investors should prefer tax-exempt municipal bonds to other similar risk debt investments. Explain.

10. Consider a tax-exempt municipal bond yielding 6%. To an investor in the following marginal tax brackets, what is the before-tax interest rate that a taxable bond would have to offer to be considered equivalent to the municipal bond?
    (a) 10%
    (b) 28%
    (c) 33%
11. Spot Bethea must choose between investing in a tax-free municipal bond yielding 5% and a taxable bond yielding 7.5%. Spot's marginal tax rate is 30%. Which bond should Spot choose?
12. Federal tax rates on capital gains have been a controversial issue in recent years. Describe the economic-benefits case for lower capital gains tax rates.
13. What is a wash sale? Why does the IRS prohibit such transactions for tax calculation purposes?
14. Pinky Higgins and spouse have taxable income of $100,000 in 1992, which includes a net capital gain of $80,000. What is their tax bill if the gain is entirely long-term? What is their tax bill if the gain is entirely short-term? What is their tax bill if the gain is half short-term and half long-term?
15. Pinky Higgins and spouse have taxable income of $100,000 in 1992, which includes capital gains of $20,000. What is their tax bill if the gain is entirely long-term? What is their tax bill if the gain is entirely short-term? What is their tax bill if the gain is half short-term and half long-term?
16. Is it true that the combined state and federal personal income tax rate is the sum of the two tax rates? Why?
17. Jean Dubuc lives in a state where the tax schedule lists an 8% marginal tax rate. The federal tax schedule lists a 25% marginal tax rate. Accounting for cross-deductibility, what is Jean's effective combined marginal tax rate?
18. Would you expect that tax shelters would be as attractive to lower-income persons as to higher-income persons? Should lower-income persons invest in tax shelters at all? Why?

APPENDIX A

Additional Tax Changes Made in 1990

There were two additional subtle changes made in 1990 that are not reflected in Table 5-2, Figure 5-2, and the discussion in this chapter. First, the personal exemption of $2,150 per person is phased out when the taxpayer's adjusted gross income is between $100,000 and $225,000, if the taxpayer is single, and between $150,000 and $275,000, if the taxpayer is married and filing a joint return (note that the phaseout takes place over a range of $125,000 of income, and is done in increments of $2,500). Second, $.03 of a taxpayer's itemized deductions will be disallowed for each $1 that the taxpayer's adjusted gross income exceeds $100,000 (subject to a maximum loss of 80% of the taxpayer's itemized deductions).

The net effect of these two changes is to increase a taxpayer's 31% marginal tax rate by as much as .5% [= .31 × ($2,050/$125,000)] per exemption declared and .9% [= .31 × ($.03/$1)] per dollar of deductions lost. Hence a single taxpayer could face a marginal tax rate of as high as 32.4% (= 31% + .5% + .9%) while a family of four could face a marginal tax rate of as high as 33.9% [= 31% + (4 × .5%) + .9%].

However, after a point the marginal tax rate will return to 31%, as 100% of the personal exemptions and 80% of the itemized deductions will have been lost. Just when this happens varies from taxpayer to taxpayer; it almost certainly will happen by the time the taxpayer's adjusted gross income reaches $225,000, if single, or $275,000, if married filing jointly.

As an example, consider a single taxpayer who has an adjusted gross income of $150,000, itemized deductions of $20,000, and a personal exemption of $2,150. Only $18,500 [= $20,000 − .03 × ($150,000 − $100,000)] of deductions will be allowed, and the personal exemption will be reduced to $1,290 [= $2,150 − $2,150 × ($150,000 − $100,000)/$125,000]. Hence the taxpayer's taxable income is $130,210 (= $150,000 − $18,500 − $1,290), resulting in a tax of $36,241 [= $11,158.50 + .31 × ($130,210 − $49,300)].

If this taxpayer made $10,000 in additional income, then only $18,200 [= $20,000 − .03 × ($160,000 − $100,000)] of deductions would be allowed, and the personal exemption would be reduced to $1,118 [= $2,150 − $2,150 × ($160,000 − $100,000)/$125,000]. With a taxable income of

$140,682 (= $160,000 − $18,200 − $1,118), the tax bill would be $39,487 [= $11,158.50 + .31 × ($140,682 − $49,300)]. Since this is $3,246 (= $39,487 − $36,241) more due to the additional $10,000 of income, it can be seen that the marginal tax rate is approximately 32.4%.

REFERENCES

1. A good reference source for reading about the federal tax code is: John L. Kramer and Lawrence C. Phillips, eds., *Prentice Hall's Federal Taxation, 1992* (Englewood Cliffs, N.J.: Prentice Hall, 1991).
2. For a valuable book that provides a framework for analyzing how tax rules affect decision making, see:

   Myron S. Scholes and Mark A. Wolfson, *Taxes and Business Strategy* (Englewood Cliffs, N.J.: Prentice Hall, 1992).

6

Inflation

The story is told of the modern-day Rip Van Winkle, who awoke in the year 2010 and immediately called his broker. (Fortunately, pay phones at the time permitted a call of up to three minutes without charge.) He first asked what had happened to the $10,000 he had instructed the broker to put in short-term Treasury bills, continually reinvesting the proceeds. The broker promptly informed him that due to high interest rates and the power of compounding, his initial $10,000 investment had grown to be worth over $1 million. Stunned, Mr. Van Winkle inquired about his stocks, which were also worth about $10,000 when he dozed off. The broker told him that he was in for an even more pleasant surprise: they were now worth $2.5 million. "In short, Mr. Van Winkle," said the broker, "you are a millionaire 3.5 times over." At this point an operator cut in: "Your three minutes are over, please deposit $100 for an additional three minutes." While this clearly overstates the case, there is no doubt that inflation is a major concern for investors. By and large, people have come to fear significant inflation, particularly when it is unpredictable.

This chapter begins by describing how **inflation** is typically measured. Then the benefits and costs of inflation are discussed, along with who gains and who loses when it is present. The chapter ends by discussing the impact that inflation has had on common stocks. In particular, it will be seen that, in spite of the fact that the historical average rate of return on common stocks has been roughly 8% greater than the average rate of inflation, stocks have not provided investors with protection against inflation in the short term.

inflation

Measuring Inflation

cost-of-living index

There is no completely satisfactory way to summarize the price changes that have occurred over a given time period for the large number of goods and services available in the U.S. Nevertheless, the federal government has attempted to do so by measuring the cost of a specific mix of major items (a "basket of goods") at various points in time. The "overall" price level computed for this representative combination of items is termed a **cost-of-living index.** The percentage change in this index over a given time period can then be viewed as a measure of the inflation (or deflation) that took place from the beginning of the period to the end of the period.

Whether or not this measure of inflation is relevant for a given individual depends to a major extent on the similarity of his or her purchases to the mix of items used to construct the index. Even if an individual finds the mix to be appropriate at the beginning of a period, the rate of increase in the price of the mix over the time period is likely to overstate the increase in the cost of living for the individual. There are two reasons for this. First, improvements in the quality of the items in the mix are seldom taken adequately into account. This means the end-of-period price for a good is not comparable to the beginning-of-period price, since the good is different. For example, a new Toyota may have a 5% higher sticker price than a similar model had the previous year, but the newer model may have better tires on it than the older model. Hence, it would be inaccurate to conclude that the price of this particular model rose by 5% over the year.

Second and perhaps more important, little or no adjustment is made in the mix as relative prices change. The rational customer can reduce the cost of attaining a given standard of living as prices change by substituting relatively less expensive goods for those that have become relatively more expensive. For example, if the price of beef rises 20% over a given year while the price of chicken rises only 10% over the same year, then the customer may start to eat more chicken and less beef. Failure to take into account this change in the mix will result in an overstatement in the rate of inflation. Despite these two drawbacks, cost-of-living indices provide at least rough estimates of changes in prices.

Consumer Price Index

In Chapter 1, Table 1-1 provided some historical perspective on the rate of inflation in the U.S. It showed the annual rate of increase in the **Consumer Price Index** (CPI) from 1926 through 1990.[1] As an aid to interpretation, these rates are plotted on a graph shown in panel (a) of Figure 6-1. As can be seen in the figure, the CPI did not grow at a constant rate over the period of 1926 to 1990. Following the substantial deflation from 1926 to 1933, prices increased in almost every year. Generally speaking, there were four subperiods with different rates of inflation: fairly rapid (but uneven) inflation from 1934 to 1952, mild inflation from 1953 to 1965, and again fairly rapid (but uneven) inflation from 1966 to 1981, followed again by mild inflation for 1982 to 1990.

geometric mean

Table 6-1 shows the average annual rate of growth of the CPI for each of these subperiods, measured by what is known as the **geometric mean** growth rate of the CPI. This growth rate, when compounded over the subperiod and

[1]The Consumer Price Index is based on the retail prices for a basket of goods and services. It is calculated monthly by the Bureau of Labor Statistics of the U.S. Department of Commerce.

FIGURE 6-1
Nominal and Real Returns on Short-Term Default-Free Investments, 12-Month Periods Ending December 1926 to December 1990

Source: Ibbotson Associates, Inc., *Stocks, Bonds, Bills, and Inflation 1991 Yearbook* (Chicago: 1991).

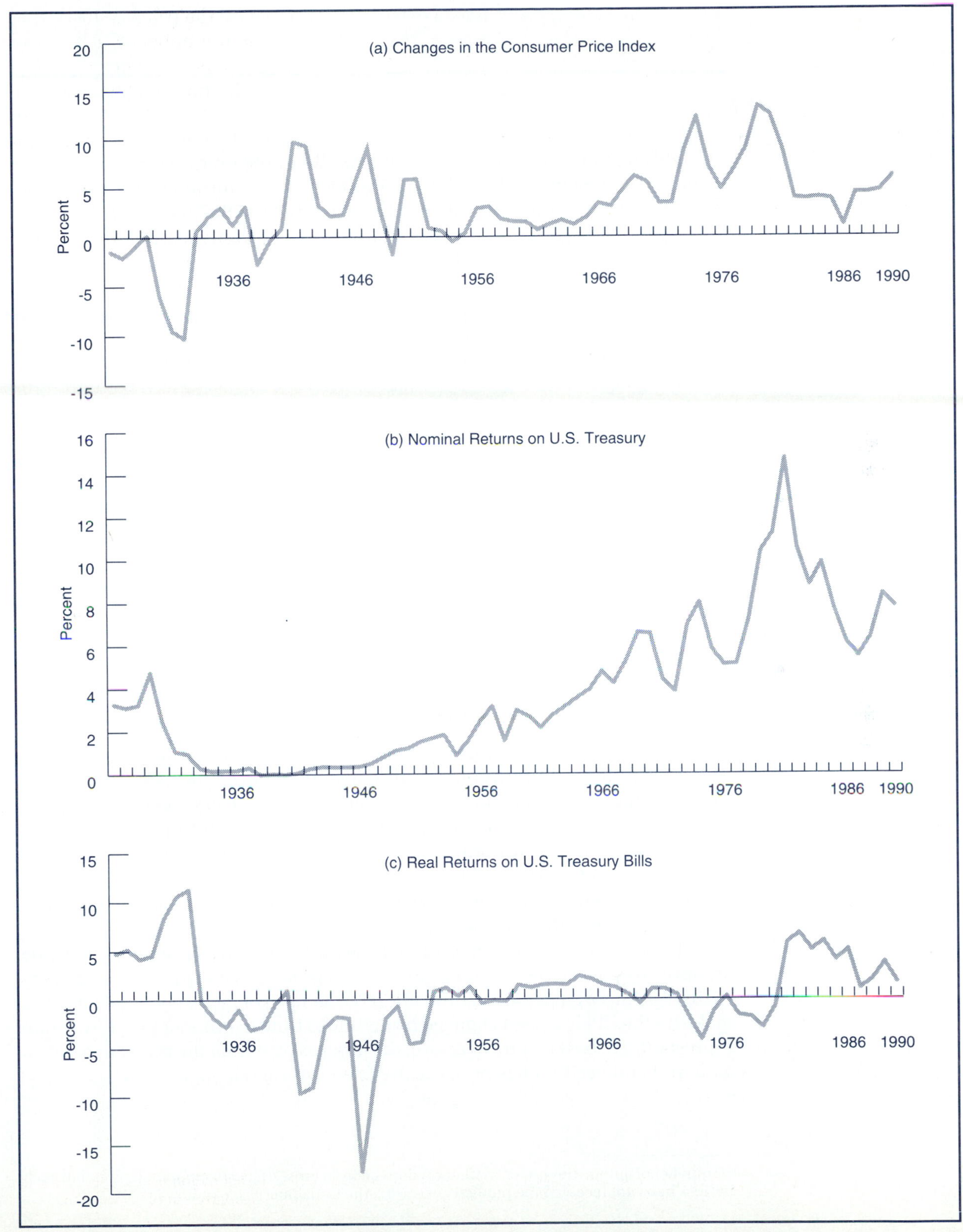

TABLE 6-1
Growth Rates of the U.S. Consumer Price Index

FROM	TO	RATE OF GROWTH (% PER YEAR)
1926	1933	−3.8%
1934	1952	3.8
1953	1965	1.4
1966	1981	7.0
1982	1990	4.0

applied to the beginning index value, results in the ending index value. For example, at the end of 1965, the CPI was 95.5 and at the end of 1981, it was at 281.5 (here the CPI was adjusted so that its value in 1967 was 100). Thus, the geometric mean growth rate was 7.0%, since 95.5, when compounded at this rate over 16 years, equals 281.5:

$$281.5 = 95.5 \times (1 + .070)^{16}$$

More generally, the geometric mean (g) can be calculated by solving the following equation for g:

$$C_e = C_b\,(1 + g)^y \tag{6.1}$$

which results in,

$$g = (C_e/C_b)^{1/y} - 1 \tag{6.2}$$

where y denotes the number of years and C_e and C_b denote the ending and beginning CPI values, respectively.

PRICE INDICES

As mentioned earlier, no price index can prove totally satisfactory as an indicator of the cost of living for all consumers. Most indices are likely to overstate the extent to which the cost of attaining a given level of satisfaction actually increases during any inflationary period, even for the people whose purchases the index was intended to reflect. Although this is fairly well understood, and most governments compute a number of alternative indices to provide a wider choice for analysis, many people tend to focus on one index as an indicator of the price level.

In the U.S. the Consumer Price Index often fills this role, despite some attempts by government officials to discourage such widespread use.[2] Recognizing its importance, the composition of the market basket of goods used to make up the CPI has been changed from time to time in order to provide a more representative basket. Furthermore, the process by which the relevant data are gathered and verified has periodically been improved.

[2]A number of authorities prefer "deflators" derived from gross domestic product figures, but such indices have not received the publicity accorded the Consumer Price Index.

MONEY MATTERS
Inside the Consumer Price Index

No doubt you have seen the evening news report, "Consumer prices grew last month at an annual rate of 4.8%." If you are like most people, you rarely give such pronouncements much thought. Not that you are uninterested in the current rate of inflation, but inflation merely means that what you buy now costs more than it did last year. Have you ever stopped to think about how both the "what you buy" is determined and the "now costs more" is calculated? For answers to these questions, we have to go inside the Consumer Price Index.

The CPI is a measure of the average price paid by urban consumers for a specific "market basket" of goods and services. As an index, the CPI is a relative measure; it compares the price currently paid for the market basket to the price of the market basket in a reference (or base) year. For example, suppose we have identified our market basket. It costs $3 to purchase today, yet ten years ago it would have cost $1. We could express the price difference as a ratio: 3 to 1, or 3.0, with ten years ago serving as our base year. For convenience, we could multiply our index by 100 to give it a value of 300.0.

The Bureau of Labor Statistics (BLS) computes the CPI in precisely the same fashion. At year-end 1991, the CPI had a value of 137.9. The BLS currently uses the average of prices in the three-year period from 1982 to 1984 as the base for its CPI calculations. Thus, at year-end 1991, it cost $1.379 to purchase the market basket that cost $1 in1983 (the mid-point of the period from 1982 to 1984); prices rose 37.9% (4.1% per year) over the intervening eight years. Further, if the CPI increases to 142.7 at the end of 1992, that change would represent a 3.5% increase in the market basket's nominal value. We would then say that 1992 consumer price inflation was 3.5%.

What exactly is this market basket from which the CPI is created? Currently, 184 priced items make up the market basket, ranging from ground beef to college tuition. The BLS categorizes these items into seven broad expenditure groups: food and beverages; housing; apparel; medical care; transportation; entertainment; and other goods and services. Housing represents the largest component of the index with a relative weight (at the time of the latest CPI revision) of 42.6%, followed by transportation at 18.7%, and food and beverages at 17.8%.

Once the BLS determines the composition of the market basket, the composition remains fixed until the next revision. With some algebraic manipulation, one can show that the current weight of an item in the market basket is equal to its relative price change from the base year to present times its original weight in the market basket. The importance of that bit of math trivia lies in the fact that those items in the index that have the largest relative price changes exhibit the largest increase in weight in the CPI.

This result causes certain problems. Consider how you would respond if the price of apples rose relative to the price of oranges. You would tend to buy fewer apples and more oranges, thereby decreasing the relative weight of apples in your own market basket. The CPI would therefore overstate the cost of your market basket, because the relative weight of apples would actually be increased in the CPI market basket. Hence, your inflation rate would not be as great as that reported by the CPI.

In order to recalibrate the CPI, the BLS updates its composition periodically. Roughly every ten years the BLS surveys urban consumers to determine their expenditure patterns. In its survey, the BLS interviews what it refers to as "consumer units"—essentially financially independent households—across various parts of the country. Based on the results of this survey, the BLS assigns goods and services, and their respective weights, to the CPI. The CPI's composition may change from the previous survey due to one or more factors: population shifts, definitional changes, price changes, and demand shifts. The last BLS survey took place from 1982 to 1984 and its results were put into effect in 1987.

Despite (or perhaps because of) the CPI's intricate construction, the BLS must make many estimates and assumptions in collecting price data. Identifying the cost of apples may be simple. But estimating the rent that homeowners would have to pay to live in their houses is a difficult proposition. Consequently, one should always view the CPI numbers with a healthy dose of skepticism. Nevertheless, the CPI represents the government's best estimate of national consumer prices. It serves as the primary source of inflation data for businesses and government alike.

Nominal Returns

Modern economies gain much of their efficiency through the use of money—a generally agreed upon medium of exchange. Instead of trading corn for a stereo to be delivered in one year, as in a barter economy, the citizen of a modern economy can trade his or her corn for money, then trade this "current" money for "future" money by investing it. Later, the "future" money can be used to buy a stereo. The rate at which the citizen can trade "current" money for "future" money depends on the investment he or she makes, and is known as the **nominal return** (also known as the nominal rate).

nominal return

Real Returns

real return

In times of changing prices, the nominal return on an investment may be a poor indicator of the **real return** (also known as the real rate) obtained by the investor.[3] This is because part of the additional dollars received from the investment may be needed to recoup the citizen's lost purchasing power due to inflation that has occurred over the investment period. As a result, adjustments to the nominal return are needed to remove the effect of inflation in order to determine the real return. Frequently, the CPI is used for this purpose.

For example, assume that at the start of a given year the CPI is at a level of 121, and that at the end of the year it is at a level of 124. This means that it costs $124 at the end of the year to buy the same amount of the CPI market basket of goods that at the start of the year could have been purchased for $121. Assuming that the nominal return is 8% for this year, the citizen who started the year with $121 and invested it would have $121 × 1.08 = $130.68 at year-end. At this point, the citizen could purchase ($130.68/$124) − 1 = .0539 = 5.39% more of the CPI market basket of goods than at the beginning of the year. Thus, the real return for this investment was 5.39%, after allowing for inflation.

These calculations can be summarized in the following formula:

$$[C_o \times (1 + NR)/C_1] - 1 = RR \tag{6.3}$$

where:

C_0 = CPI at the beginning of the year,

C_1 = CPI at the end of the year,

NR = the nominal return,

RR = the real return.

Alternatively, the citizen could note that an increase in the CPI from 121 to 124 can be translated into an inflation rate of (124/121) − 1 = .0248 or

[3]Here, real return refers to the increase in purchasing power that the citizen has received as a result of making a particular investment.

2.48%. Denoting this inflation rate as I, the real return can be calculated using the following formula:

$$[(1 + NR)/(1 + I)] - 1 = RR. \tag{6.4}$$

Note that for the example, $RR = (1.08/1.0248) - 1 = .0539$ or 5.39%.

For quick calculation, the real return can be estimated by simply subtracting the inflation rate from the nominal return:

$$NR - I \cong RR \tag{6.5}$$

where $\cong$ means "is approximately equal to." In this example, the "quick method" results in an estimate of the real return of $.08 - .0248 = .0552$ or 5.52%. Thus, the error resulting from use of this method is $.0552 - .0539 = .0013$ or .13%.[4]

The Effect of Investor Expectations

The simplest view of investors' attitudes toward inflation is that they are concerned with real returns, not nominal returns, and that a single price index is adequate to characterize the difference. Looking to the future, investors do not know what the rate of inflation will be, nor do they know what the nominal return on an investment will be. However, in both cases they have expectations about what these figures will be, which are denoted as EI (expected rate of inflation) and ENR (expected nominal return), respectively. Thus, the expected real return on an investment can be approximated by:

$$ERR = ENR - EI. \tag{6.6}$$

If a security is to provide a given expected real return, the expected nominal return must be larger by the expected rate of inflation for the relevant holding period. This can be seen by rearranging the equation (6.6):

$$ENR = ERR + EI. \tag{6.7}$$

For example, if the expected rate of inflation is 4% and a given security is to provide investors with an expected real return of 6%, then the security must be priced in the marketplace so that its expected nominal return is 10%. In summary, if investors are concerned with real returns, all securities will be priced by the actions of the marketplace so that expected nominal returns incorporate the expected rate of inflation.

INTEREST RATES AND INFLATION

At the start of a given investment holding period, nominal interest rates for securities having no risk of default should cover both a requisite expected real return and the expected rate of inflation for the period in question. At the end

[4]This error will be larger for higher rates of inflation. Thus, in those countries with "hyperinflation," the quick method will have a substantial amount of error associated with it. For example, if the nominal return is 110% and the inflation rate is 100%, then the true real return is 5% but the quick method will indicate that it is twice as large, 10%.

of the period, the real return actually received will be the difference between the nominal return and the rate of inflation actually experienced. Only when actual inflation equals expected inflation will the actual real return equal the expected real return on such securities.

As mentioned earlier, panel (a) of Figure 6-1 indicates the annual rate of inflation, as measured by changes in the Consumer Price Index, over the sixty-five-year time period from 1926 to 1990. Panel (b) shows how short-term nominal interest rates varied over this time period; Treasury bill rates, taken from Table 1-1, are used for this purpose. Panel (c), derived by subtracting panel (a) from panel (b), represents real returns.

One cannot help being struck by the fact that those who invested in short-term securities over this period frequently ended up with less purchasing power than they started with, since the real return was negative in twenty-five of the sixty-five years. Perhaps even more surprising, the average real return over the period was close to zero.

While expected real returns may vary from year to year, this variation may be relatively small. If so, investors may have been willing to invest in short-term highly liquid securities even though they expected to earn very little in real terms. If they are currently willing to do so, such securities will be priced to give a very low expected real return.[5]

If this assumption is made, the "market's" predicted rate of inflation over the near future can be estimated by simply subtracting, say 1%, from the nominal interest rate (also known as the yield) on short-term government securities, namely, Treasury bills. In a sense, the resulting figure represents a consensus prediction of inflation—a prediction that an "average" investor in this market would make, and one that is likely to be more accurate than the predictions of any single forecaster.

THE EFFECT OF INFLATION ON BORROWERS AND LENDERS

Although deviations of actual inflation from expected inflation may have relatively little effect on the real return on investments in general, they may have a significant effect on specific investments. In fact, one would expect a direct impact on the real returns associated with investments whose payments are fixed in terms of dollars to be received.

A simple example will illustrate the relationship. Assume that everyone currently expects the rate of inflation to be 5% over the next year, and that a lender has agreed to make loans at a nominal rate of 5% (that is, the lender is content with having an expected real return of zero). Thus, one can borrow \$100 now and pay back one year later \$105 = \$100 × 1.05 for a one-year loan. That is, if actual inflation equals expected inflation, a one-year loan would require a payment equivalent to \$100 in constant (current) dollars a year hence. In this case, the real rate of interest would turn out to be zero.

---

[5]However, there apparently are periods of time when such securities have an expected real return that is positive. For example, in the 1981–1986 period, Treasury bill returns actually exceeded the rate of change in the CPI by over 5%. This suggests that investors probably expected a positive real return over the latter part of the period.

Now, imagine that an individual takes advantage of the lender's offer, borrowing $100 for one year. How will the borrower and lender be affected if the actual rate of inflation differs from the expected rate of inflation?

Assume that in the first year, prices rise by 9% instead of the expected 5%, meaning that unexpected inflation is 4% = 9% − 5%. In this situation, the short-term borrower gains at the expense of the lender. Why? The borrower still must repay $105, but in terms of constant dollars, this is only $96.33 = $105/1.09, a figure that is less than the amount of the loan. As a result, the lender receives a real rate of interest of − 3.67% = ($96.33 − $100)/$100, instead of the anticipated rate of 0%.

What if first-year prices had risen by only 3%, meaning that unexpected inflation is − 2% = 3% − 5%? In this situation, the short-term lender gains at the expense of the borrower. While the borrower must repay $105, in terms of constant dollars this amounts to $101.94 = $105/1.03, a figure that is greater than the amount of the loan. As a result, the lender receives a real rate of interest of 1.94% = ($101.94 − $100)/$100, instead of the anticipated rate of 0%.

These results can be generalized: when the actual rate of inflation exceeds the expected rate of inflation, those with commitments to make payments that are fixed in nominal terms (debtors) gain in real terms at the expense of those to whom payments are to be made (creditors). Conversely, when actual inflation is less than expected inflation, creditors gain and debtors lose.[6] This uncertainty in the real return on fixed-income securities that is due to uncertain inflation is frequently referred to as **purchasing-power risk.**

purchasing-power risk

INDEXATION

The previous section suggests that in a world of uncertain inflation, even default-free bonds are subject to purchasing-power risk. Contractual nominal interest rates can cover expected inflation, but the subsequent real return from any investment with fixed nominal payments will depend on the actual amount of inflation. As long as the two differ, the expected real return will be uncertain. However, there is a way to design a bond so that its expected real return is certain. It involves the use of *indexation*.

If a specified price index can adequately measure purchasing power, there is no reason why a contract cannot be written with specified real payments instead of specified nominal payments. Thus, if the CPI currently stands at C_0, and will be C_1 one year later, C_2 two years later, and so on, in return for a loan of $100, a borrower might promise to pay amounts that are currently unknown but will be equal to $10 × C_1 one year later, $10 × C_2 two years later, . . . , and $110 × C_{10} ten years later. To convert these payments to

[6]More specifically, it can be shown that long-term borrowers are likely to gain somewhat more than short-term borrowers when actual inflation exceeds expected inflation and lose somewhat more when actual inflation falls below expectations. Similarly, long-term lenders are likely to lose somewhat more than short-term lenders when actual inflation exceeds expectations and gain somewhat more when actual inflation falls below expectations.

constant real dollars, each one must be divided by the corresponding price level:

TIME	AMOUNT IN NOMINAL DOLLARS	PRICE LEVEL (CPI)	AMOUNT IN REAL DOLLARS
1	$10 \times C_1$	C_1	10
2	$10 \times C_2$	C_2	10
.	.	.	.
.	.	.	.
.	.	.	.
10	$110 \times C_{10}$	C_{10}	110

The real value of each payment is the amount shown in the final column, regardless of what happens to prices (that is, regardless of the actual values of C_1, C_2, and so on). Thus, the loan is said to be fully indexed, since all amounts are tied to a stated price index on a one-for-one basis. This means that when the price index goes up by 10%, for example, all of the subsequent payments go up by 10%.

In some countries, a great many contracts are tied to standard price indices (two notable examples are Israel and Brazil). Government bonds, returns on savings accounts, wage contracts, pension plans, insurance contracts—all have been indexed at various times and places. In the U.S., social security payments are indexed, as are the wages and pension plans of many employees. Some of these are fully indexed, while others are only partially indexed, meaning that, for example, payments might be increased by 7% when the price index increases by 10%.

The key advantage of indexation is its role in reducing or eliminating purchasing-power risk. Typically, higher expected inflation is accompanied by increased uncertainty about the actual rate of inflation. This increased uncertainty means that the potential gains and losses to both nonindexed borrowers and nonindexed lenders are larger. Since both borrowers and lenders dislike the prospect of losses more than they like the prospect of gains, there will be increased pressure for indexation by both borrowers and lenders when a country moves into periods of high inflationary expectations.

Thus, when uncertainty about inflation is substantial, one would expect indexation to become widespread. However, laws regulating interest rates frequently prevent the issuance of fully indexed debt, since these laws usually place a ceiling on the nominal rate but not the real rate. This leads to predictable inefficiencies when expected inflation increases, since rationing of credit that is subject to such ceilings would be required. Rationing would be necessary because a ceiling on the nominal rate means that the real rate declines as inflationary expectations increase, which in turn makes this type of credit attractive to borrowers.[7]

A notable example occurred in the 1970s in the U.S. At that time, ceilings placed on nominal rates paid by savings and loan companies, coupled with increased inflationary expectations, caused a substantial outflow of funds from such companies and a corresponding reduction in the amount of money made available by them for home mortgages. On the other

[7]Actually, rationing might not occur as lenders may simply refuse to make those kinds of loans that are subject to ceilings when inflationary expectations are high.

side were those issuers of securities that were not subject to rate ceilings and who offered an appropriate nominal rate and, thus, had little difficulty in attracting funds. The term **disintermediation** was invented to describe this pattern of funds flow.

disintermediation

Since inflation is generally harder to predict for longer time periods relative to shorter time periods, uncertainty about inflation often leads to a reduction in the average term-to-maturity of newly issued fixed-income securities. Here term-to-maturity refers to the length of time from the date of issuance of the security until the date that the last payment is promised to be made. For example, the average term-to-maturity of fixed-coupon debt issued in periods of great inflationary uncertainty is usually shorter than in more stable times.

variable rates

Alternatively, debt with long maturities can be written with **variable rates** (also known as floating rates) of interest. Such instruments provide long-term debt at short-term rates. Interest payments are allowed to vary, with each one determined by adding a fixed number of percentage points (say, 2%) to a specified base rate that changes periodically. Two base rates frequently used are the prime rate and the yield on 90-day U.S. Treasury bills. If short-term interest rates anticipate inflation reasonably well, such a variable rate security is a kind of substitute for a fully indexed bond.

TAXATION, INFLATION, AND THE RETURN ON CAPITAL

Certain general features of the U.S. tax system lead to movements of wealth from the private sector to the federal government that increase with the rate of inflation.[8] Thus, one of the potential beneficiaries of inflation in the U.S. is the federal government.[9]

Consider a one-year security with an expected real pretax return of 7% that is held by someone in a 30% marginal tax bracket. In the absence of inflation, the investor would expect to receive a real return of $(1 - .3) \times 7\% = 4.9\%$. Now, assume that expected rate of inflation is 2%, so that the expected pretax nominal return on the security is $[(1.07 \times 1.02) - 1] = 9.14\%$. In this case, the investor's expected after-tax nominal return is $(1 - .3) \times 9.14\% = 6.40\%$, but in real terms this is $[(1.0640/1.02) - 1 = 4.31\%$. Similarly, if expected inflation is 4%, then the expected pretax nominal return will be 11.28%, the investor's expected after-tax nominal return will be 7.90%, and his or her expected after-tax real return will be 3.75%.

Since it is reasonable to assume that, over time, actual inflation rates will approximately equal expected inflation rates, it can be seen that the higher the actual inflation rate, the lower the actual real after-tax return. In this example, the after-tax real return decreased from 4.9% with no inflation to 4.31% with 2% inflation and to 3.75% with 4% inflation. Thus, taxation of interest income can be viewed as being equivalent to having an effective tax rate on real

[8]The effect of inflation on corporate earnings is influenced by the tax system; the appendix to this chapter discusses this issue.

[9]The federal government also benefits from unexpected inflation because it is the largest borrower of funds in the economy and, as shown earlier, borrowers in general benefit when inflation turns out to be higher than expected.

returns that increases with inflation; that is, the higher the inflation rate, the larger the portion of the real pretax return that is allocated to the government. This phenomenon could be avoided by levying taxes on real returns instead of nominal returns.

For the expected after-tax real return of a fixed-income security to be the same with a high expected rate of inflation as with a low expected rate of inflation, its current price must be sufficiently lower with the high inflation rate. This will result in the expected pretax nominal return being sufficiently higher in order to compensate for both the higher inflation rate and the larger effective tax rate. In the previous example, the expected pretax nominal return would have to rise to 10.0% if the expected rate of inflation were 2%, and to 13.0% if it were 4%. If this asset were a bond that pays the investor $1,000 one year later, its current price would have to be $934.58 with no expected inflation, $909.09 with 2% expected inflation, and $884.96 with 4% expected inflation:

Expected rate of inflation	0.0%	2.0%	4.0%
Expected pretax nominal rate of return	7.0%	10.0%	13.0%
Expected after-tax nominal return = (1 − .3) × pretax nominal return	4.9%	7.0%	9.1%
Expected after-tax real return = [(1 + after-tax nominal return) ÷ (1 + rate of inflation)] − 1	4.9%	4.9%	4.9%
Current price of a bond paying $1,000 in one year = $1,000/(1 + expected pretax nominal rate of return)	$934.58	$909.09	$884.96

Unfortunately, this is not the way bond prices and expected pretax nominal returns react to changes in the expected rate of inflation, as will be shown next.

STOCK RETURNS AND INFLATION

Long-Term Relationships It is reasonable to assume that investors are more concerned with real returns than with nominal returns, since real returns reflect how much better off they are after adjusting for inflation. Accordingly, the real returns of securities need to be analyzed. This is done in Table 6-2 for common stocks and Treasury bills for the long-term period of 1802 to 1990 and five relatively long subperiods.

Column (2) of the table shows that, on average, the rate of return on common stocks has substantially exceeded the rate of inflation, providing a real return of nearly 8% for the entire period examined and in excess of 7% in all of the subperiods. In comparison, the rate of return on Treasury bills exceeded the rate of inflation by over 3% in the entire period. However, the subperiods show substantial variation, as the real return ranged from less than .5% over the period from 1926 to 1990 to over 5% in the period from 1802 to 1888. Also of interest is the **equity premium** shown in column (4), which is simply the difference between the real rate of return on stocks and bills. While being less than 2% from 1802 to 1888, it has since then been nearly 7%, an amount that some researchers believe is inexplicably large. In summary, Table 6-2 shows that common stocks have historically returned substantially

equity premium

PERIOD (1)	REAL RETURN ON STOCKS (2)	REAL RETURN ON BILLS (3)	EQUITY PREMIUM (2)-(3) = (4)
1802–1990[1]	**7.81%**	**3.19%**	**4.62%**
1802–1888[1]	7.52%	5.62%	1.90%
1889–1978[1]	7.87	.91	6.96
1979–1990[1]	9.44	2.73	6.71
1926–1990[2]	8.90	.47	8.43
1950–1990[2]	9.01	.94	8.07

[1]*Source:* Andrew B. Abel, "The Equity Premium Puzzle," Federal Reserve Bank of Philadelphia *Business Review* (September–October 1991), p. 8.

[2]*Source:* Table 1-1.

TABLE 6-2
Rates of Return on Bills and the Equity Premium

more than the rate of inflation and Treasury bills. That is, in the long run, common stocks have had a large positive real return.

Short-Term Relationships Another interesting question to investigate is the relationship between the short-term rate of return on stocks and rate of inflation. Conventional wisdom suggests that stock returns should be relatively high when inflation is relatively high and relatively low when inflation is relatively low. Why? Because stocks represent claims on real assets that should increase in value with inflation.

Figure 6-2 displays the relationship between annual stock returns and rates of inflation for the period from 1926 to 1990. The figure shows that there is no discernible relationship between the rate of inflation and stock returns.

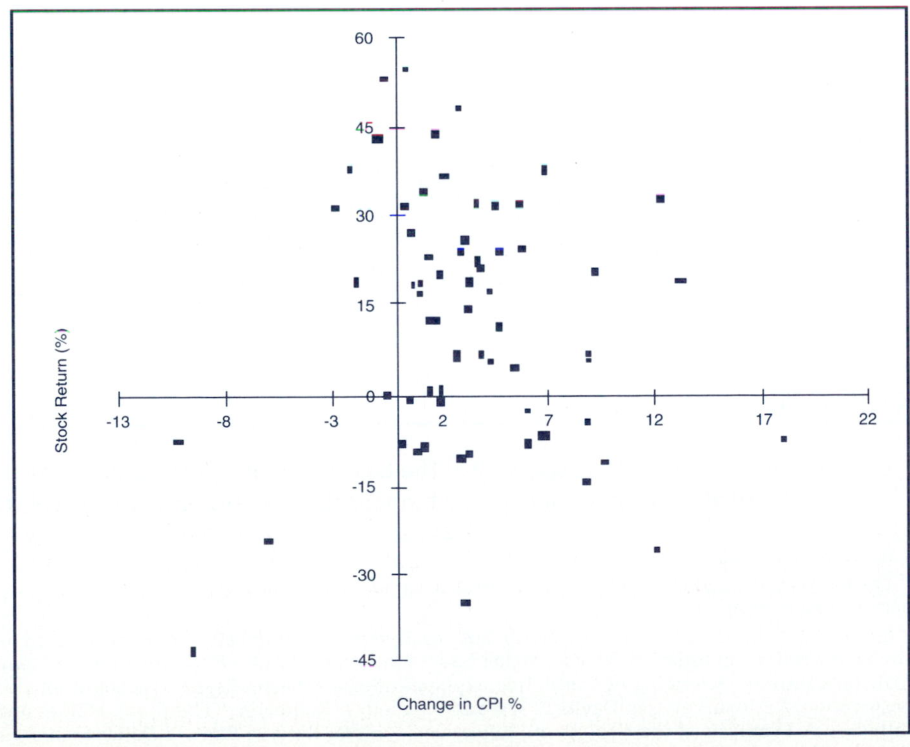

FIGURE 6-2
Annual Stock Returns and Rates of Inflation (1926–1990)
Source: Ibbotson Associates, Inc., *Stocks, Bonds, Bills, and Inflation 1991 Yearbook* (Chicago: 1991).

Indeed, the correlation coefficient between these two variables is −.019, which for all practical purposes is equal to zero and indicates that there is no significant statistical relationship between the rate of inflation and stock returns.[10] That is, when inflation is relatively high, there is no tendency for stock returns to be either relatively high or low. Similarly, when inflation is relatively low, there is no tendency for stock returns to be either relatively high or low.[11] Accordingly, stocks are not good hedges against inflation in the short term.

SUMMARY

1. Inflation measures the percentage change in a specific cost-of-living index at various points in time.

2. Whether a measure of inflation is relevant for a given individual depends to a large extent on the similarity of his or her purchases to the composition of the price index.

3. The Consumer Price Index is the most widely used U.S. price level indicator.

4. An investor's real return is a function of the difference between the investor's nominal return and the inflation rate.

5. Real returns are important to an investor because they represent how much the investor's purchasing power has increased (or decreased) and thus how much better (or worse) off is the investor.

6. If investors are concerned with real returns, securities will be priced so that expected nominal returns incorporate the expected inflation rate.

7. When the actual inflation rate exceeds the expected inflation rate, debtors gain in real terms at the expense of creditors. The opposite is the case when actual inflation is less than expected inflation.

8. Investment returns can be indexed by tying security payments to changes in the price level. Indexation reduces or removes an investment's purchasing-power risk.

9. Over long periods of time, common stocks have generated large, positive real returns. Treasury bills have produced much lower, but still positive, real returns.

10. Over short periods of time, the correlation between stock returns and inflation is not significantly positive.

KEY TERMS

inflation
cost-of-living index
Consumer Price Index
geometric mean
nominal return
real return
purchasing-power risk
disintermediation
variable rates
equity premium
sustainable earnings
replacement cost accounting
inventory valuation adjustment
capital consumption adjustment

QUESTIONS AND PROBLEMS

1. If the price index value was 340 at the beginning of a particular year and it was 370 at the end of that year, what was the inflation rate for the year?

[10] The correlation coefficient for the period from 1950 to 1990 is equal to −.275. Similar results occur when monthly data are used.

[11] Interestingly, there appears to be a significant negative relationship between the real return on stocks and the rate of inflation. That is, higher rates of inflation seem to be accompanied by lower real stock returns. A number of conflicting explanations have been offered to account for this observation; for a survey, see David P. Ely and Kenneth J. Robinson, "The Stock Market and Inflation: A Synthesis of the Theory and Evidence," Federal Reserve Bank of Dallas *Economic Review* (March 1989): 17–29.

2. Given the following beginning and ending values for a particular price index, and the respective number of years between the measurement of the two values, calculate the annual compound (geometric mean) inflation rate.

	PRICE INDEX BEGINNING VALUE	PRICE INDEX ENDING VALUE	YEARS COVERED
(a)	100	120	1
(b)	120	175	3
(c)	175	150	2

3. Calculate the arithmetic (that is, the simple) mean rate of inflation using the data in Table 1-1 for the same time periods given in Table 6-1. What is the relationship between the arithmetic and geometric means?
4. Calculate the average real return on long-term government and corporate bonds from the data given in Table 1-1. How do these real returns compare with the real returns on Treasury bills and common stocks?
5. Why do cost-of-living indices frequently overstate the true economic impact of inflation on typical consumers?
6. Given the following average compound annual inflation rates, how much would $1 be worth in terms of purchasing power five years from today expressed in today's dollars?
   (a) 5%
   (b) 10%
   (c) 15%
7. Bingo Binks' portfolio earned an 8% average compound annual return over the period from 1984 to 1991. The average compound annual inflation rate over this time period was 4%. Bingo's portfolio was worth $15,000 at the beginning of 1984. At the end of 1991, what was the portfolio worth expressed in 1984 dollars?
8. Distinguish between the nominal and the real rate of return on an investment.
9. Kirby Higbe started 1991 with investments valued at $11,500. At the end of 1991 those same investments were worth $13,000. During the same time period the price index rose from 210 to 230. What was Kirby's real rate of return during 1991?
10. How are economywide inflation rates calculated? Are all consumers affected equally by the increase in overall prices measured by the price index? Explain.
11. Assume that your portfolio grows 9% in value per year and annual inflation is 5%. How many years will it take for the nominal value of your portfolio to triple? How many years will it take for the real value of your portfolio to triple?
12. Why is it reasonable to assume that rational investors will build an expected inflation premium into the returns that they require from their investments?
13. In the late 1970s and early 1980s, a period of unexpectedly high inflation, Happy Felsch referred to long-term bonds issued by U.S. corporations and the Treasury as "certificates of confiscation." Why would Happy make such a comment?

14. Why is it often argued that the federal government is one of the greatest beneficiaries of inflation?
15. Despite the uncertain prospects for future U.S. inflation, virtually no inflation-indexed bonds have been issued in this country, by either governments or corporations. Speculate as to why such bonds have not been created.
16. From the perspective of after-tax returns, what is the problem with fully inflation-indexed securities?
17. Explain why the returns on bonds are found to be negatively correlated with unexpected inflation. Why does this relationship become progressively more negative as one considers longer-lived bonds?
18. Common stocks, somewhat surprisingly, do not appear to be effective hedges against either expected or unexpected short-run inflation. Explain why the stocks of some companies might be better hedges against inflation than others.
19. (Appendix Question) In the late 1970s and early 1980s, there was considerable discussion concerning the "quality" of corporate earnings. Straight-line depreciation and the FIFO inventory valuation methods were often cited as the causes of "poor-quality" earnings. Further, it was argued that these accounting methods effectively resulted in tax overpayments. Discuss the reasons for both contentions.
20. (Appendix Question) Wilson Tools produces specialized tools. In 1990, its production process used 50,000 parts at a cost of $40 per part. The firm sold all of its tools in 1990 at a price of $50. In 1991, unit production and sales remained constant, but costs and sales prices increased by 5%. Calculate Wilson's 1991 net adjusted earnings using an inventory valuation adjustment.

APPENDIX

A

The Effect of Inflation on Corporate Earnings

One definition of earnings (that is, profits) holds that if a firm paid out the entire amount of earnings each year, it would neither increase nor decrease in size, measured by the real value of its productive capacity. This notion is often summarized by the term **sustainable earnings.** A firm that pays out more than the total amount of such earnings can be expected to decline, while one that pays out less can be expected to grow.

sustainable earnings

While there may be some objections to the principle of this definition of earnings, there are more problems associated with its implementation. And, these problems are seriously aggravated in an inflationary environment.

INVENTORY VALUATION ADJUSTMENT

Consider a firm that purchases ten units of some semifinished good at the beginning of each year, hires labor to work on it, and then sells the finished product at the end of the year. For simplicity, assume that labor is paid from the proceeds of sales and there is no corporate income tax. In the absence of inflation, the firm's operations might be summarized as follows:

Receipt from sales (10 units at $200 each)		$2,000
Less cost of goods sold:		
Purchase of semifinished goods (10 units at $100 each)	$1,000	
Labor wages	800	
Total cost		1,800
Net earnings		$ 200
Net cash received at year-end ($2,000 − $800)		1,200

Thus, the firm invests $1,000 at the beginning of the year to purchase semifinished goods in order to obtain $1,200 a year later, giving the firm a rate of return of 20%. Viewed somewhat differently; after an initial investment of $1,000, earnings of $200 can be paid out each year, assuming no inflation. This $200 is the magnitude of sustainable earnings.

Now, assume that after the firm purchases the semifinished goods, all prices and wages increase by 10%. The results would then be:

Receipt from sales (10 units at $220 each)		$2,200
Less cost of goods sold:		
Purchase of semifinished goods		
(10 units at $100 each)	$1,000	
Labor wages	880	
Total cost		1,880
Net earnings		$ 320
Net cash received at year-end ($2,200 − $880)		1,320

Thus, an investment of $1,000 produces a net cash inflow of $1,320 one year later, for a return of 32% and earnings of $320. Is this the amount of sustainable earnings? No. Assuming no further inflation, $1,100 will be required to replace the inventory of 10 units at the beginning of the next year. This means that only $220 = $1,320 − $1,100 can be paid out if the firm is to avoid a decline in real productive capacity. Put somewhat differently, the total "earnings" of $320 resulted from an increase in the value of the firm's inventory of $100 plus "adjusted" earnings from normal operations of $220.

replacement cost accounting

To make this distinction, a number of authorities recommend **replacement cost accounting.** In essence, this involves the use of estimated replacement costs (that is, future costs) instead of historic costs (that is, past costs) when calculating profits. In this case such a procedure would give:

Receipt from sales (10 units at $220 each)		$2,200
Less cost of goods sold:		
Purchase of semifinished goods		
(10 units at $110 each)	$1,100	
Labor wages	880	
Total cost		1,980
Net adjusted earnings		$ 220
Net cash received at year-end ($2,200 − $880)		1,320

An equivalent procedure would be to subtract an **inventory valuation adjustment** from reported profit. This adjustment would represent the excess of replacement cost over the reported cost:

inventory valuation adjustment

Receipt from sales (10 units at $220 each)		$2,200
Less cost of goods sold:		
Purchase of semifinished goods		
(10 units at $100 each)	$1,000	
Labor wages	880	
Total cost		1,880
Net earnings		$ 320
Less inventory valuation adjustment:		
Replacement cost (10 units at $110 each)	$1,100	
Reported cost (10 units at $100 each)	1,000	
Amount of adjustment		100
Net adjusted earnings		$ 220

Even after the adjustment, profit is stated in current (that is, year-end) dollars. To compare this amount with that of a previous year, the value must be adjusted for price-level changes. Specifically, the amount in current dollars is $220, while the amount in constant dollars is $200 = $220/1.10, which is the amount that would have been earned in the absence of inflation.

The size of the appropriate inventory valuation adjustment depends on the length of time inventory is held, the extent of the rise in its replacement cost, and the method used to account for such costs when calculating reported earnings. The Last-In First-Out (LIFO) method of inventory accounting comes closest to replacement costs, while the First-In First-Out (FIFO) method lies at the other end of the spectrum.

CAPITAL CONSUMPTION ADJUSTMENT

A similar situation arises with capital assets. Using various depreciation formulas, their historic costs are charged to operations over their assumed productive lives. Accelerated depreciation is generally used for tax purposes, but more gradual procedures may be used for reporting earnings to stockholders. However, assets "used up" in the production process are generally valued at historic, not replacement, costs. Other things being equal, this can cause an understatement of cost and an overstatement of sustainable earnings.

At the beginning of each year, a firm will own certain capital assets. During the year the replacement costs of these assets may change, resulting in associated gains or losses, although such changes may not be realized at that time. The portion of these assets used up in production (and thus depreciated) should be valued at replacement cost in order to estimate sustainable earnings from operations. If historic costs are used instead, the resulting amount should be adjusted by an amount known as the **capital consumption adjustment** in order to account for the difference between replacement and historic costs.

capital consumption adjustment

As an example, assume that a firm has just purchased a computer for $500 and, for simplicity, that corporate income is not taxed. The firm has decided to use straight-line depreciation over five years, when the computer will have zero salvage value. Hence, annual depreciation will amount to $100 (= $500/5). After one year the computer has a replacement value of $350 (that is, a similar computer that is one year old can be bought on the used-computer market for $350). This suggests that the depreciation on the computer for the first year should be $150 instead of $100. Thus, earnings for the first year are overstated by $50.

Note that if an accelerated depreciation method such as the 200% double-declining balance method had been used, it is possible that the book amount of depreciation would be overstated, causing earnings to be understated. In the example, the depreciation in the first year would amount to $200 (= 2 × $500/5). Thus, depreciation would have been overstated by $50 (= $200 − $150), thereby causing earnings to be understated by $50.

INTEREST EXPENSE ADJUSTMENT

So far two adjustments to a firm's financial statements to account for the effects of inflation have been presented. There is a third adjustment that typically receives much less attention but is no less important. Namely, the effect of inflation on a firm's debt causes an overstatement of the interest expense associated with the debt. This overstatement of interest expense in turn means that the firm's earnings are understated.

In order to see why this is so, consider the following simple example where again, for simplicity, it is assumed that corporate income is not taxed. A firm has recently borrowed $1,000 from a bank for one year with the interest rate on the loan being 10%. Hence at the end of the year the firm will pay the bank $1,100, and show $100 as interest expense on its income statement. At year-end the rate of inflation is calculated to have been 7%. This means that in effect the year-end payment of $1,100 to the bank represents a repayment of principal to the bank of $1,070 (= $1,000 × 1.07) and an interest payment of $30 (= $1,100 − $1,070). Now imagine that the firm had earnings before interest of $200, causing it to report net earnings of $100 (= $200 − $100). However, the firm's payment of interest to the bank really amounted to $30 instead of $100, so its net earnings really amounted to $170. Hence, by ignoring the impact of inflation of debt, the firm has understated its earnings by $70.

SURVEY OF CURRENT BUSINESS

The U.S. Department of Commerce in its *Survey of Current Business* reports the aggregate inventory valuation and capital consumption adjustments for U.S. nonfinancial corporations, along with their earnings before and after making these adjustments (unfortunately, the *Survey* does not report an amount for the interest expense adjustment). Table 6-A reflects these figures for the fifteen-year period from 1976 to 1990, along with the corresponding rate of inflation, as measured by the percentage change in the CPI. Not surprisingly, the aggregate adjustment to earnings as reflected in column (6) is generally negative when the rate of inflation is relatively high, with the

TABLE 6-A Earnings Before and After Inventory Valuation and Capital Consumption Adjustments: U.S. Nonfinancial Corporations, 1976–1990

YEAR (1)	EARNINGS BEFORE TAXES[1] (2)	INVENTORY VALUATION ADJUSTMENT[1] (3)	CAPITAL CONSUMPTION ADJUSTMENT[1] (4)	EARNINGS BEFORE TAXES, AFTER ADJUSTMENTS[1] (2)-(3)-(4) = (5)	PERCENTAGE DIFFERENCE [(5)-(2)]/(2) = (6)	PERCENTAGE CHANGE IN THE CONSUMER PRICE INDEX (7)
1976	$130.2	−$14.5	−$14.3	$101.4	−22.1%	4.8%
1977	143.5	−15.2	−11.8	116.5	−18.8	6.8
1978	174.3	−24.3	−12.4	137.6	−21.1	9.0
1979	193.4	−42.6	−14.1	136.7	−29.3	13.3
1980	183.0	−43.0	−17.0	123.0	−32.8	12.4
1981	183.0	−23.6	−9.1	150.3	−17.9	8.9
1982	123.5	−9.5	4.1	118.1	−4.4	3.9
1983	151.5	−10.0	19.0	160.5	5.9	3.8
1984	189.3	−5.5	32.9	216.7	14.5	4.0
1985	175.9	−.7	52.6	227.8	29.5	3.8
1986	172.6	8.3	49.6	230.5	33.5	1.1
1987	197.2	−18.9	46.3	224.6	13.9	4.4
1988	251.1	−27.0	41.8	265.9	5.9	4.4
1989	241.5	−21.7	21.2	241.0	−.2	4.7
1990	229.1	−11.4	1.8	219.5	−4.2	6.1

[1]Measured in billions.

Source: U.S. Department of Commerce, *Survey of Current Business*, various issues.

adjustment being positive for the most part during recent years when inflation has been relatively low.

FASB 33

The Financial Accounting Standards Board's *Statement of Accounting Standards Number 33*, issued in 1980, required firms with either total assets of more than $1 billion or inventories, property, plant, and equipment with a gross value of more than $125 million to provide supplementary inflation-adjusted financial statements to their stockholders. This allowed the stockholders to more accurately estimate the level of the firm's sustainable earnings. However, as inflation ebbed in the 1980s the Board decided in 1987 to no longer require firms to publish such statements, most likely due to the fact that security analysts were apparently not using them because they were confusing and did not reflect interest rate adjustments. Furthermore, it has been argued that the adjustments for inventory, capital consumption, and interest expense roughly offset each other (at least in the aggregate for the stocks in the S&P 500), meaning that nominal earnings give a roughly accurate picture of the firm's true earnings.

REFERENCES

1. The seminal work linking interest rates and inflationary expectations is: Irving Fisher, *The Theory of Interest* (New York: Macmillan, 1930).

2. For a review article on this linkage, see:

Herbert Taylor, "Interest Rates: How Much Does Expected Inflation Matter?" Federal Reserve Bank of Philadelphia *Business Review* (July/August 1982): 3–12.

3. The relationship between real interest rates and inflation is discussed in: George G. Pennachi, "Identifying the Dynamics of Real Interest Rates and Inflation: Evidence Using Survey Data," *Review of Financial Studies*, 4, no. 1 (1991): 53–86.

4. The following papers present an analysis of the effect of inflation on the accounting treatment of inventory, depreciation, and interest:

William H. Beaver, Paul A. Griffin, and Wayne R. Landsman, "How Well Does Replacement Cost Income Explain Stock Return [sic]?" *Financial Analysts Journal* 39, no. 2 (March/April 1983): 26–30, 39;

Charles G. Callard and David C. Kleinman, "Inflation-Adjusted Accounting: Does It Matter?" *Financial Analysts Journal*, 41, no. 3 (May/June 1985): 51–59.

Kenneth R. French, Richard S. Ruback, and G. William Schwert, "Effects of Nominal Contracting on Stock Returns," *Journal of Political Economy*, 91, no. 1 (February 1983): 70–96.

Franco Modigliani and Richard A. Cohn, "Inflation and the Stock Market," *Financial Analysts Journal*, 35, no. 2 (March/April 1979): 24–44.

William C. Nordby, "Applications of Inflation-Adjusted Accounting Data," *Financial Analysts Journal*, 39, no. 2 (March/April 1983): 33–39.

5. For a discussion of the relationship of the inflation rate to the returns on stocks, bonds, and real estate, see:

Eugene F. Fama and G. William Schwert, "Asset Returns and Inflation," *Journal of Financial Economics*, 5, no. 2 (November 1977): 115–46.

6. Other papers dealing with the relationship between inflation and stock returns can be found at the end of the following survey articles:

Andrew B. Abel, "The Equity Premium Puzzle," Federal Reserve Bank of Philadelphia *Business Review* (September/October 1991): 3–14;

David P. Ely and Kenneth J. Robinson, "The Stock Market and Inflation: A Synthesis of the Theory and Evidence," Federal Reserve Bank of Dallas *Economic Review* (March 1989): 17–29.

7. The equity premium has also been reviewed and analyzed in:

Jeremy J. Siegel, "The Equity Premium: Stock and Bond Returns Since 1802," *Financial Analysts Journal*, 48, no. 1 (January/February 1992): 28–38, 46.

8. International evidence on the relationship between stock returns and inflation is provided by:

Bruno Solnik, "The Relation Between Stock Prices and Inflationary Expectations: The International Evidence," *Journal of Finance*, 38, no. 1 (March 1983): 35–48;

N. Bulent Gultekin, "Stock Market Returns and Inflation: Evidence From Other Countries," *Journal of Finance*, 38, no. 1 (March 1983): 49–65.

PART III
MODERN PORTFOLIO THEORY

7 The Portfolio Selection Problem

In 1952, Harry M. Markowitz published a landmark paper that is generally viewed as the origin of the "modern portfolio theory" approach to investing. Markowitz's approach to investing begins by assuming that an investor has a given sum of money to invest at the present time. This money will be invested for a particular length of time known as the investor's **holding period.** At the end of the holding period, the investor will sell the securities that were purchased at the beginning of the period and then either spend the proceeds on consumption or reinvest the proceeds in various securities (or do some of both). Thus, Markowitz's approach can be viewed as a single-period approach, where the beginning of the period is denoted $t = 0$ and the end of the period is denoted $t = 1$. At $t = 0$, the investor must make a decision on what particular securities to purchase and hold until $t = 1$.[1] Since a portfolio is a collection of securities, this decision is equivalent to selecting an optimal portfolio from a set of possible portfolios. Hence it is often referred to as the "portfolio selection problem."

holding period

In making this decision at $t = 0$, the investor should recognize that security returns (and thus portfolio returns) over the forthcoming holding

[1]Markowitz recognized that investing was generally a multiperiod activity, where at the end of each period, part of the investor's wealth was consumed and part was reinvested. Nevertheless, his one-period approach can be shown to be optimal under a variety of reasonable circumstances. See Edwin J. Elton and Martin J. Gruber, *Finance as a Dynamic Process* (Englewood Cliffs, N.J.: Prentice Hall, 1975), particularly Chapter 5.

expected returns

risk

period are unknown. Nevertheless, the investor could estimate the **expected** (or mean) **returns** on the various securities under consideration, and then invest in the one with the highest expected return. (Methods for estimating expected returns will be discussed in Chapter 15.) Markowitz notes that this would generally be an unwise decision because the typical investor, while wanting "returns to be high," also wants "returns to be as certain as possible." This means that the investor, in seeking to both maximize expected return and minimize uncertainty (that is, **risk**), has two conflicting objectives that must be balanced against each other when making the purchase decision at $t = 0$. The Markowitz approach for how the investor should go about making this decision gives full consideration to both of these objectives.

One interesting consequence of having these two conflicting objectives is that the investor should diversify by purchasing not just one security but several. The ensuing discussion of Markowitz's approach to investing begins by defining more specifically what is meant by initial and terminal wealth.

INITIAL AND TERMINAL WEALTH

In Equation (1.1) of Chapter 1 it was noted that the one-period rate of return on a security could be calculated as:

$$\text{return} = \frac{\text{end-of-period wealth} - \text{beginning-of-period wealth}}{\text{beginning-of-period wealth}}$$

where beginning-of-period wealth is the purchase price of one unit of the security at $t = 0$ (for example, one share of a firm's common stock), and end-of-period wealth is the market value of the unit at $t = 1$, along with the value of any cash (and cash equivalents) paid to the owner of the security between $t = 0$ and $t = 1$.

Determining the Rate of Return on a Portfolio

Since a portfolio is a collection of securities, its return r_p can be calculated in a similar manner:

$$r_p = \frac{W_1 - W_0}{W_0}. \tag{7.1}$$

W_0 denotes the aggregate purchase price at $t = 0$ of the securities contained in the portfolio. W_1 denotes the aggregate market value of these securities at $t = 1$, as well as the aggregate cash (and cash equivalents) received between $t = 0$ and $t = 1$ from owning these securities. Equation (7.1) can be manipulated algebraically, resulting in:

$$W_0 (1 + r_p) = W_1. \tag{7.2}$$

initial wealth

terminal wealth

From equation (7.2) it can be seen that beginning-of-period or **initial wealth** (as W_0 is sometimes called), when multiplied by one plus the rate of return on the portfolio, is equal to end-of-period or **terminal wealth** (as W_1 is sometimes called).

Earlier, it was noted that the investor must make a decision on what portfolio to purchase at $t = 0$. In doing so, the investor does not know what the value of W_1 will be for most of the various alternative portfolios under consideration since the investor does not know what the rate of return will be for most of these portfolios.[2] Thus, according to Markowitz, the investor should view the rate of return associated with any one of these portfolios to be what is known in statistics as a **random variable.** Now, it is known from statistics that a random variable can be "described" by what are known as its moments, two of which are its **expected value** (or mean) and **standard deviation.**[3]

random variable
expected value
standard deviation

Markowitz asserts that investors should base their portfolio decisions solely on expected returns and standard deviations. That is, the investor should estimate the expected return and standard deviation of each portfolio and then choose the "best" one based on the relative magnitudes of these two parameters. The intuition behind this is actually quite straightforward. Expected return can be viewed as a measure of the potential reward associated with any portfolio, and standard deviation can be viewed as a measure of the risk associated with any portfolio. Thus, once each portfolio has been examined in terms of its potential rewards and risks, the investor is in a position to identify the one portfolio that appears most desirable to him or her.

Example Consider the two alternative portfolios denoted A and B, shown in Table 7-1. Portfolio A has an expected annual return of 8% and portfolio B has an expected annual return of 12%. Assuming that the investor has initial wealth of $100,000 and a one-year holding period, this means that the expected levels of terminal wealth associated with A and B are $108,000 and $112,000, respectively. It would appear, then, that B is the more desirable portfolio. However, A and B have annual standard deviations of 10% and 20%, respectively. Table 7-1 shows that this means there is a 2% chance that the investor will end up with terminal wealth of $70,000 or less if he or she purchases B, whereas there is virtually no chance that the investor's terminal wealth will be less than $70,000 if A is purchased. Similarly, B has a 5% chance of being worth less than $80,000 while A again has no chance. Continuing, B has a 14% chance of being worth less than $90,000, while A has only a 4% chance. Going on, B has a 27% chance of being worth less than $100,000, while A has only a 21% chance. Since the investor has initial wealth of $100,000, this last observation means there is a greater probability of having a negative return if B (27%) is purchased instead of A (21%). Overall, it can be seen from Table 7-1 that A is less risky than B, meaning that on this dimension A would be more desirable. The ultimate decision in regard to whether to purchase A or B will depend on this particular investor's attitude toward risk and return, as will be shown next.

---

[2]One portfolio that would not have an uncertain rate of return would involve the investor putting all of his or her initial wealth in a government security that matures at $t = 1$. Alternatively, the investor's initial wealth could be put into a passbook savings account at a bank. However, for almost all other portfolios the rate of return would be uncertain.

[3]A random variable's expected value is, in a sense, its "average" value. Thus, the expected value for the return of a portfolio can be thought of as its expected or average return. The standard deviation of a random variable is a measure of the dispersion (or "spread") of possible values the random variable can take on. Accordingly, the standard deviation of a portfolio is a measure of the dispersion of possible returns that could be earned on the portfolio. Sometimes **variance** is used as a measure of the dispersion instead of standard deviation. However, since the variance of a random variable is simply the squared value of the standard deviation of the random variable, this distinction is not of importance here. These concepts will be discussed in more detail in Chapter 8.

variance

TABLE 7-1
A Comparison of Terminal Wealth Levels for Two Hypothetical Portfolios

LEVEL OF TERMINAL WEALTH[a]	PERCENT CHANCE OF BEING BELOW THIS LEVEL OF TERMINAL WEALTH	
	Portfolio A[b]	Portfolio B[c]
$ 70,000	0%	2%
$ 80,000	0%	5%
$ 90,000	4%	14%
$100,000	21%	27%
$110,000	57%	46%
$120,000	88%	66%
$130,000	99%	82%

[a]Initial wealth is assumed to be $100,000, and both portfolios are assumed to have normally distributed returns.

[b]The expected return and standard deviation of A are 8% and 10%, respectively.

[c]The expected return and standard deviation of B are 12% and 20%, respectively.

INDIFFERENCE CURVES

indifference curves

The method that should be used in selecting the most desirable portfolio involves the use of **indifference curves.** These curves represent an investor's preferences for risk and return, and thus can be drawn on a two-dimensional figure where the horizontal axis indicates risk as measured by standard deviation (denoted σ_p) and the vertical axis indicates reward as measured by expected return (denoted $\bar{r}_p$).

Figure 7-1 illustrates a "map" of indifference curves that a hypothetical investor might possess. Each curved line indicates one indifference curve for the investor, and represents all combinations of portfolios that the investor would find equally desirable. For example, the investor with the indifference curves in Figure 7-1 would find portfolios A and B (the same two portfolios that were shown in Table 7-1) equally desirable, even though they have

FIGURE 7-1
Map of Indifference Curves for a Risk-Averse Investor

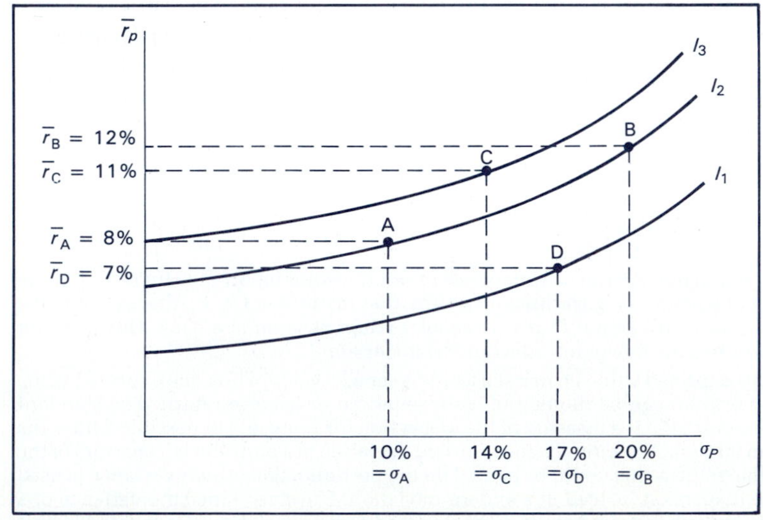

different expected returns and standard deviations, since they both lie on the same indifference curve, I_2. Portfolio B has a higher standard deviation (20%) than portfolio A (10%), and is therefore less desirable on that dimension. However, exactly offsetting this loss in desirability is the gain in desirability provided by the higher expected return of B (12%) relative to A (8%). This example leads to the first important feature of indifference curves: *all portfolios that lie on a given indifference curve are equally desirable to the investor.*

An implication of this feature is that *indifference curves cannot intersect.* To see that this is so, consider two curves that do interesect, such as those that are shown in Figure 7-2. Here the point of intersection is represented by X. Remember that all the portfolios on I_1 are equally desirable. This means they are all as desirable as X, since X is on I_1. Similarly, all the portfolios on I_2 are equally desirable, and are as desirable as X, since X is also on I_2. Given X is on both indifference curves, all the portfolios on I_1 must be as desirable as those on I_2. But this presents a contradiction, since I_1 and I_2 are two curves that are supposed to represent different levels of desirability. Thus, in order for there to be no contradiction, these curves cannot intersect.

While the investor represented in Figure 7-1 would find portfolios A and B equally desirable, he or she would find portfolio C, with an expected return of 11% and a standard deviation of 14%, to be preferable to both of them. This is because portfolio C happens to be on an indifference curve, I_3, that is located to the northwest of I_2. Now, C has a sufficiently larger expected return relative to A to more than offset its higher standard deviation and, on balance, make it more desirable than A. Equivalently, C has a sufficiently smaller standard deviation than B to more than offset its smaller expected return and, on balance, make it more desirable than B. This leads to the second important feature of indifference curves: *an investor will find any portfolio that is lying on an indifference curve that is "further northwest" to be more desirable than any portfolio lying on an indifference curve that is "not as far northwest."*

Lastly, it should be noted that *an investor has an infinite number of indifference curves.* This simply means that whenever there are two indifference curves that have been plotted on a graph, it is possible to plot a third indifference curve that lies between them. As can be seen in Figure 7-3, given

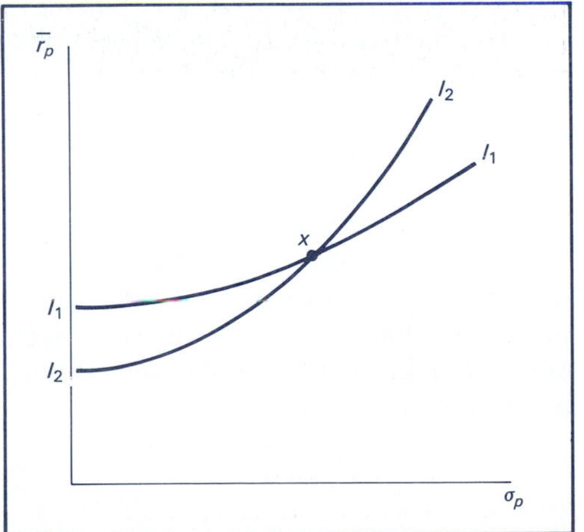

FIGURE 7-2
Intersecting Indifference Curves

FIGURE 7-3
Plotting a Third Indifference Curve Between Two Others

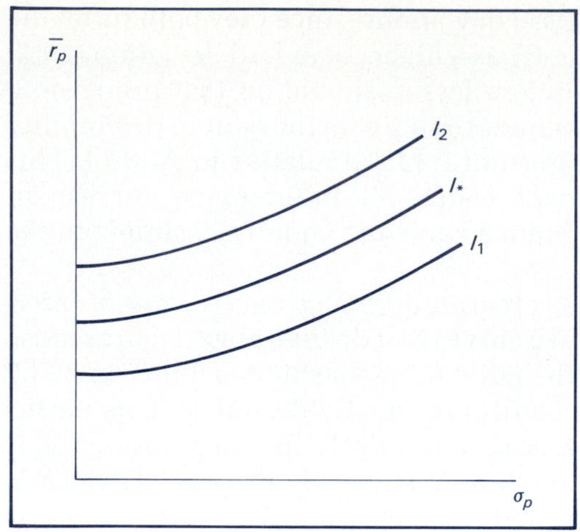

indifference curves I_1 and I_2, it is possible to graph a third curve, I^*, lying between them.

A good question to ask at this point is: how does an investor determine what his or her indifference curves look like? After all, each investor has a map of indifference curves that, while having the previously noted features, is nevertheless unique to that individual. It turns out that one method of explicitly determining the shape and location of an investor's indifference curves involves asking that investor a set of questions about gambles.[4]

For example, an investor might be asked which one of two alternatives he or she would find more desirable. The first alternative would simply involve receiving a certain cash payoff of $5,000. The second alternative involves the flip of a coin where heads means a payoff of $4,000 and tails means a payoff of $10,000. If the investor states that he or she would prefer to coin flip, then the size of the certain payoff is increased to, say, $5,500, and the question is repeated. However, if the certain payoff is preferred, then its payoff is lowered to, say, $4,500, and the question is repeated. This procedure of changing the size of the certain payoff and repeating the question is continued until a payoff is reached where the investor finds both alternatives equally desirable. At this juncture it is possible to tell something about the investor's attitudes toward risk and return. Once the investor is asked about other different-sized gambles, it will be possible to estimate the shape and location of his or her indifference curves.

A second method, as will be shown in Chapter 17, involves presenting the investor with a set of hypothetical portfolios, along with their expected returns and standard deviations. Then he or she would be asked to choose the most desirable one. Given the choice that is made, the shape and location of the investor's indifference curves can be estimated. This is because it is presumed that the investor would have acted as if he or she has indifference curves in making this choice, even though indifference curves would not have been explicitly used.

---

[4]For an example of how this procedure can be utilized, see Ralph O. Swalm, "Utility Theory—Insights into Risk Taking," *Harvard Business Review*, 44, no. 6 (November–December 1966): 123–36. Also see footnote 5.

In summary, every investor has an indifference map representing his or her preferences for expected returns and standard deviations.[5] This means the investor should determine the expected return and standard deviation for each potential portfolio, plot them on a graph such as Figure 7-1, and then select the one portfolio that lies on the indifference curve that is "furthest northwest." As shown in this example, from the set of the four potential portfolios—A, B, C, and D—the investor should select C.

NONSATIATION AND RISK AVERSION

Nonsatiation

Two assumptions are implicit in this discussion of indifference curves. First, it is assumed that investors, when given a choice between two otherwise identical portfolios, will always choose the one with the higher level of expected return. More fundamentally, an assumption of **nonsatiation** is made in utilizing the Markowitz approach, meaning that investors are assumed to always prefer higher levels of terminal wealth to lower levels of terminal wealth. This is because higher levels of terminal wealth allow the investor to spend more on consumption at $t = 1$ (or in the more distant future). Thus, given two portfolios with the same standard deviation, such as A and E in Figure 7-4, the investor will choose the portfolio with the higher expected return. In this case, it is portfolio A.

nonsatiation

[5]At some point the reader may wonder why an investor's preferences are based only on expected returns and standard deviations. For example, it may seem logical that the investor's preferences should be based on expected returns, standard deviations, and the probability that a portfolio will lose money. The assertion that an investor's preferences are not based on anything other than expected returns and standard deviations follows from some specific assumptions coupled with *utility theory*. See Gordon J. Alexander and Jack Clark Francis, *Portfolio Analysis* (Englewood Cliffs, N.J.: Prentice Hall, 1986), particularly chapters 2 and 3, for more details. It should be noted that there is some dispute about the validity of using utility theory to describe people's behavior. The people holding the opposing viewpoints are typically economists and psychologists, and they are often referred to as rationalists and behaviorists, respectively. For a discussion of their views, see the entire second part of the October 1986 issue of the *Journal of Business*.

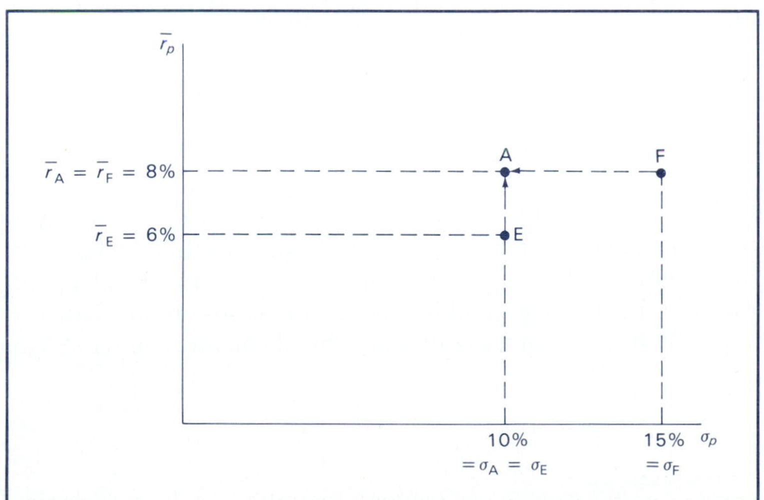

FIGURE 7-4
Nonsatiation, Risk Aversion, and Portfolio Choice

MONEY MATTERS
Investor Irrationality

On a lazy Saturday morning you decide to go to the mall to do some shopping. Although there is no urgency, you plan to buy two items, a small calculator and a vacuum cleaner. Before you left, you made a mental note that the calculator and the vacuum cleaner should cost $10 and $300, respectively.

Upon arriving at the mall, however, you discover that the calculator sells for $20 and the vacuum cleaner costs $310. Assuming that you believe both items can be purchased at a store a few miles away for the initially expected prices, would you buy either item at the mall?

Many people would choose to go to the nearby store to purchase the calculator, but would buy the vacuum cleaner at the mall. These decisions are puzzling, because in both cases the expected savings from traveling to the nearby store is $10. The only difference is that $10 is a large proportion of the calculator's price, but a small proportion of the vacuum cleaner's cost.

In an economic sense these two decisions are contradictory and termed "irrational," even though one can easily imagine normal, intelligent people acting this way. Moreover, this situation is not an isolated aberration; examples of this sort of irrational economic behavior abound.

Much of modern investment theory rests on the assumption that investors behave in a strictly rational manner. Widespread violations of this assumption raise difficult questions. In recent years a school of thought called *cognitive psychology* has begun to address some of these issues.

The manifestations of irrational economic decision making have been studied in a variety of situations. As examples, we consider two interesting cases: risk-seeking behavior on the part of presumably risk-averse investors, and stock market overreaction to new information.

RISK-SEEKING BEHAVIOR

As discussed in this chapter, investment theory assumes that investors are risk-averse. They will undertake risky investments only if the expected rewards exceed those of less risky investments by amounts sufficient to compensate for the additional risk. Contradicting this assumption is the observation that people often act in a risk-seeking manner when faced with choices involving large losses.

Suppose that you are offered two investments. You could place $10,000 in a riskfree bond and earn $800 in interest. Or you can invest $10,000 in a low-quality "junk" bond (see Chapter 21) that promises to make an

---

However, it is not quite so obvious what the investor will do when having to choose between two portfolios having the same level of expected return but different levels of standard deviation, such as A and F. This is where the second assumption enters the discussion.

Risk Aversion

risk-averse investor

Generally, it is assumed that investors are **risk-averse,** which means that the investor will choose the portfolio with the smaller standard deviation, A.[6] What does it mean to say that an investor is risk-averse? It means that the investor, when given the choice, will not want to take fair gambles, where a *fair gamble* is defined to be one that has an expected payoff of zero. For example, consider a gamble that involves an equal chance of winning or losing such as flipping a coin where heads means you win $5 and tails means

risk-seeking investor
risk-neutral investor

[6]Investors that are **risk-seeking** would choose F, and investors that are **risk-neutral** would find A and F to be equally desirable. The appendix to this chapter discusses both risk-neutral and risk-seeking investors.

interest payment of $1,000. You estimate that the probability of the junk bond making its promised interest payment is 85%—there is a 15% chance of receiving no interest at all (without loss of principal). Most people choose the riskfree bond, even though its expected return is lower than that of the junk bond (8% versus 8.5%). This choice is consistent with risk-averse behavior in that a certain outcome is preferred to a risky investment with a more lucrative expected reward.

Now change the context of the problem. You have made a $10,000 investment in a speculative company that is currently in financial trouble. The owners of the company offer you a choice: accept a certain loss of $8,000, with your remaining funds returned to you, or take an 85% chance of a complete loss of your $10,000, with a 15% chance of having all your funds returned to you. Most people select the risky option even though its expected return is lower (–85% versus –80%), indicating risk-seeking preferences.

This contradictory response when dealing with large losses, as opposed to gains, is similar to the inconsistent choice of saving $10 on the purchase of a calculator, but not on a vacuum cleaner purchase. In both cases an individual's behavior is dependent on the way the economic problem is presented or "framed."

INVESTOR OVERREACTION

Investor overreaction refers to the observed tendency for investors to bid up security prices excessively in response to unexpected good news and to bid down stock prices excessively upon receiving unexpected bad news. The key word here is *excessively*—greater than is warranted by changes in the fundamental factors that determine the "fair" value of a security.

Investor overreaction is irrational in that it focuses narrowly on recent information, extrapolating that news into the future. It overstates the quality and relevance of current information.

Research by a number of investigators has discovered evidence of stock market overreaction. In one famous study, Werner DeBondt and Richard Thaler (*Journal of Finance,* July 1985) found that stocks with extremely strong or weak recent relative performance later tended to reverse that relative performance. They hypothesized that the prices of these stocks had been bid up or down excessively by investors, with prices subsequently moving back predictably to fairer valuation levels as the investor overreaction subsided.

The observations of cognitive psychologists come as no surprise to the many professional investors who view security markets as inefficient and driven by the twin emotions of fear and greed. For those people who consider security markets to be highly efficient (see Chapter 4) and populated by rational investors, the arguments of cognitive psychology proponents present interesting challenges.

you lose $5. Since the coin has a 50-50 chance of being heads or tails, the expected payoff is $0 [= (.5 × $5) + (.5 × −$5)]. Accordingly, the risk-averse investor will choose to avoid this gamble. Intuitively, the reason the investor will avoid the gamble is that the potential loss represents an amount of "displeasure" that is greater than the amount of "pleasure" associated with the potential gain.

The two assumptions of nonsatiation and risk aversion cause indifference curves to be positively sloped and convex.[7] While it is assumed that all investors are risk-averse, it is not assumed that they have identical degrees of risk aversion. Some investors may be highly risk-averse, and some might be only slightly so. This means that different investors will have different maps of indifference curves. Panels (a), (b), and (c) of Figure 7-5 display maps for investors that are highly risk-averse, moderately risk-averse, and slightly risk-averse, respectively. As can be seen in these figures, a more risk-averse investor has more steeply sloped indifference curves.

[7]Convexity of indifference curves means that their slopes increase when moving from left to right along any particular one. That is, they "bend upward." The underlying rationale for convexity lies in utility theory; see footnote 5.

FIGURE 7-5
Indifference Curves for Different Types of Risk-Averse Investors

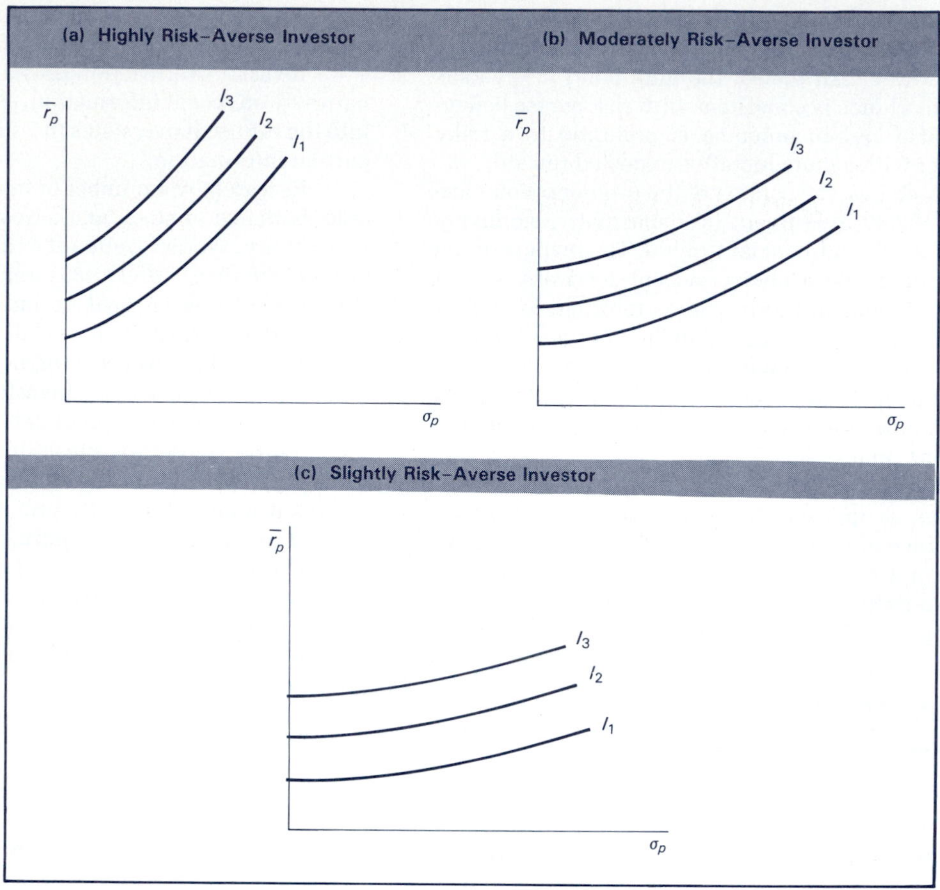

SUMMARY

1. The Markowitz approach to portfolio selection assumes that investors seek both maximum expected return for a given level of risk and minimum uncertainty (risk) for a given level of expected return.

2. Expected return serves as the measure of potential reward associated with a portfolio. Standard deviation is viewed as the measure of a portfolio's risk.

3. An indifference curve represents the various combinations of risk and return that the investor finds equally desirable.

4. Investors are assumed to consider any portfolio lying on an indifference curve further to the "northwest" more desirable than any portfolio lying on an indifference curve that is not as far "northwest."

5. The assumptions of investor nonsatiation and risk aversion cause indifference curves to be positively sloped and convex.

KEY TERMS

holding period
expected returns
risk
initial wealth
terminal wealth
random variable
expected value
standard deviation
variance
indifference curves
nonsatiation
risk-averse investor
risk-seeking investor
risk-neutral investor

QUESTIONS AND PROBLEMS

1. Listed below are twelve portfolios, their expected returns and standard deviations, and the amount of satisfaction (measured in "utils") that they provide Arky Vaughn. Given this information, graph the identifiable indifference curves of Arky.

PORTFOLIO	EXPECTED RETURN	STANDARD DEVIATION	AMOUNT OF SATISFACTION
1	5%	0%	10 utils
2	6	10	10
3	9	20	10
4	14	30	10
5	10	0	20
6	11	10	20
7	14	20	20
8	19	30	20
9	15	0	30
10	16	10	30
11	19	20	30
12	24	30	30

2. Why are the indifference curves of typical investors assumed to slope upward to the right?
3. What does a set of convex indifference curves imply about an investor's trade-off between risk and return as the amount of risk varies?
4. Why are typical investors assumed to prefer portfolios on indifference curves lying to the "northwest"?
5. What is meant by the statement that "risk-averse investors exhibit diminishing marginal utility of income"? Why does diminishing marginal utility cause an investor to refuse to accept a "fair bet"?
6. Explain why an investor's indifference curves cannot intersect.
7. Why are the indifference curves of more risk-averse investors more steeply sloped than those of investors with less risk aversion?
8. Consider the following two sets of indifference curves for Hack Wilson and Kiki Cuyler. Determine whether Hack or Kiki:
   (a) is more risk-averse,
   (b) prefers investment A to investment B,
   (c) prefers investment C to investment D.

   Explain the reasons for your answers.

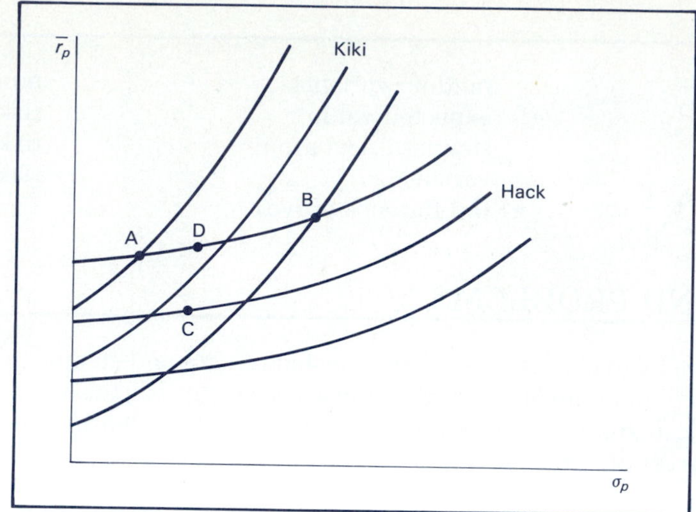

9. Do you agree with the assumptions of nonsatiation and risk aversion? Make a case for or against these assumptions.
10. (Appendix Question) Assume that you must choose between two investments. Investment 1 promises a certain return of $850. Investment 2 provides a 90% chance of a $1,000 return and a 10% chance of earning nothing.
    (a) Based on your initial reaction, which investment do you prefer?
    (b) Is one of the choices inconsistent with risk aversion?
    (c) Sample others to determine their choices.
11. (Appendix Question) Assume that you must choose between two investments. Investment 1 will produce a sure loss of $850. Investment 2 has a 90% chance of a $1,000 loss and a 10% chance of no loss.
    (a) Based on your initial reaction, which investment do you prefer?
    (b) Is one of the choices inconsistent with risk aversion?
    (c) Solicit the reaction of others. Do you find that people tend to behave differently when faced with losses as opposed to gains?

APPENDIX A

Risk-Neutral and Risk-Seeking Investors

Earlier it was mentioned that the Markowitz approach assumes investors are risk-averse. While this is a reasonable assumption to make, it is not necessary to do so. Alternatively, it can be assumed that investors are either risk-neutral or risk-seeking.

Consider the risk-seeking investor first. This investor, when faced with a fair gamble, will want to take the gamble. Furthermore, larger gambles are more desirable than smaller gambles. This is because the "pleasure" derived from winning is greater than the "displeasure" derived from losing. Since there is an equal chance of winning and losing, on balance the risk-seeking investor will want to take the gamble. What this means is that when faced with two portfolios that have the same expected return, this type of investor will choose the one with the higher standard deviation.

For example, in choosing between A and F in Figure 7-4, the risk-seeking investor will choose F. This suggests that the risk-seeking investor will have negatively sloped indifference curves.[8] In addition, risk-seeking investors will prefer to be on the indifference curve furthest from the origin (that is, "furthest northeast"). Figure A-1 illustrates a map of the indifference curves for a hypothetical risk-seeking investor. As shown in the figure, when choosing between A, B, C, and D (the same four portfolios shown in Figure 7-1), this investor will choose B.

The risk-neutral case lies between the risk-seeking and risk-averse cases. While the risk-averse investor does not want to take fair gambles and the risk-seeking investor does want to take such gambles, the risk-neutral investor does not care whether or not the gamble is taken. This means that risk, or more specifically, standard deviation, is unimportant to the risk-neutral investor in evaluating portfolios. Accordingly, the indifference curves for such investors are horizontal lines as shown in Figure A-2. These investors prefer to be on the indifference curve that is "furthest north." When faced with the choice of A, B,

[8]It can also be shown that for a risk-seeking investor, these indifference curves will be concave, meaning that their slopes decrease when moving from left to right along any particular one. The underlying rationale for concavity lies in utility theory; see footnotes 5 and 7.

FIGURE A-1
Map of Indifference Curves for a Risk-Seeking Investor

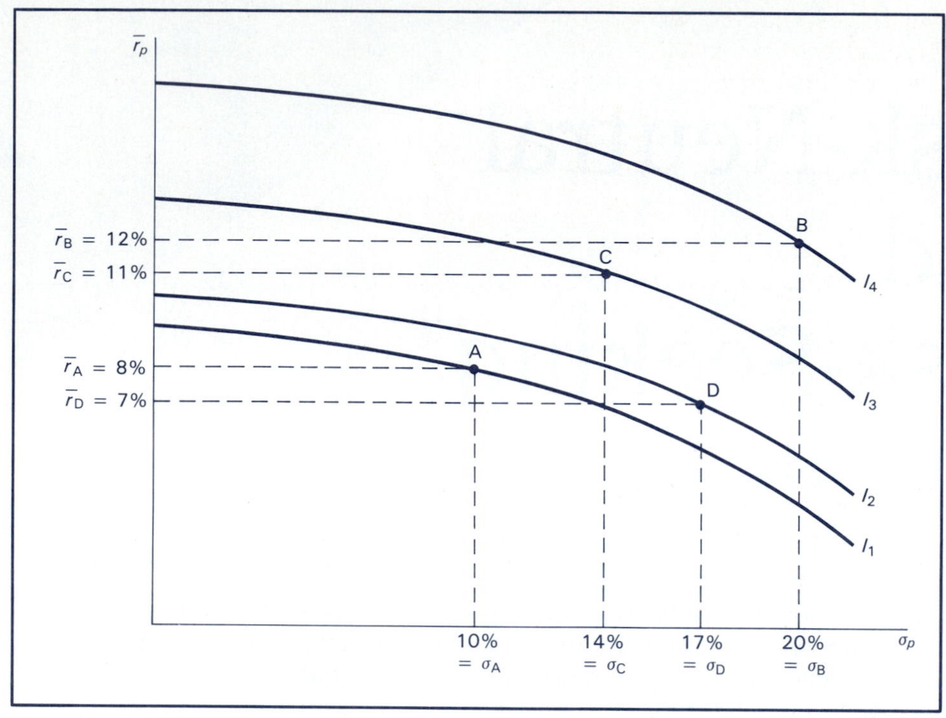

FIGURE A-2
Map of Indifference Curves for a Risk-Neutral Investor

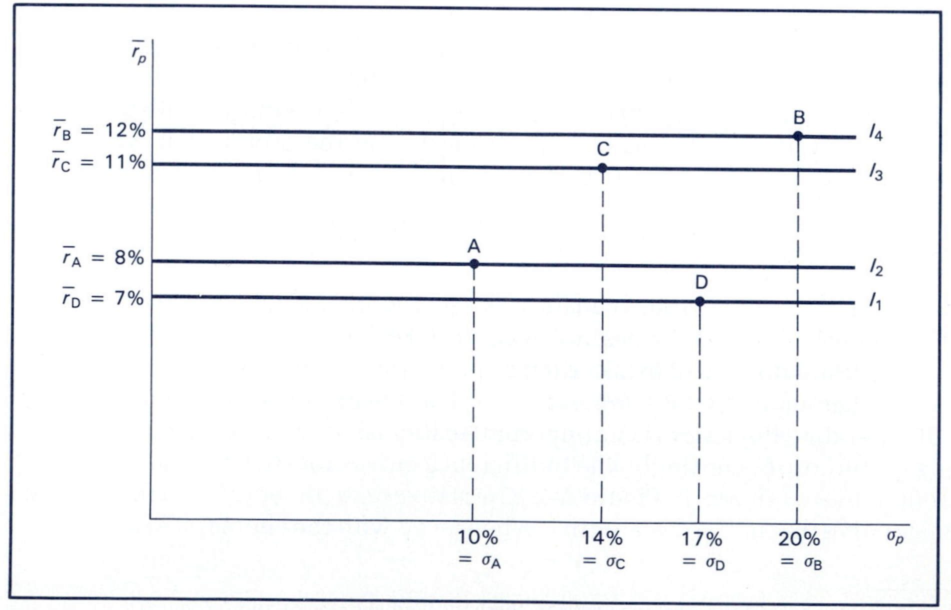

C, and D, such an investor will choose B, since it has the highest expected return.

While investors can be either risk-seeking or risk-neutral, there is evidence to suggest that they are more accurately characterized as being, in general, risk-averse. One piece of evidence is the observation that riskier portfolios have historically had higher average returns, suggesting that investors have had to be induced with higher rewards in order to get them to make riskier purchases. If investors were not risk-averse, they would not have had to be induced in this manner.

REFERENCES

1. The seminal work developing the mean-variance model is credited to Harry Markowitz, who developed his ideas in a paper and later in a book:
   Harry M. Markowitz, "Portfolio Selection," *Journal of Finance*, 7, no. 1 (March 1952): 77–91;
   Harry M. Markowitz, *Portfolio Selection: Efficient Diversification of Investments* (New York: John Wiley & Sons, 1959). (A reprint of this book that also contains some new material is available from Basil Blackwell, Inc., in Cambridge, Mass.; its copyright date is 1991.)
2. While utility theory can be traced back to the work of Daniel Bernoulli in the early part of the eighteenth century, the modern notion of utility theory was developed in:
   John von Neumann and Oskar Morgenstern, *Theory of Games and Economic Behavior* (New York: John Wiley & Sons, 1944);
   Kenneth J. Arrow, *Essays in the Theory of Risk-Bearing* (Chicago: Markham Publishing Company, 1971).
3. Significant other work in utility theory is reviewed in:
   Paul J. H. Schoemaker, "The Expected Utility Model: Its Variants, Purposes, Evidence and Limitations," *Journal of Economic Literature*, 20, no. 2 (June 1982): 529–63.
4. For a discussion of why only expected returns and variances suffice in evaluating portfolios, see:
   Yoram Kroll, Haim Levy, and Harry M. Markowitz, "Mean-Variance versus Direct Utility Maximization," *Journal of Finance*, 39, no. 1 (March 1984): 47–61;
   H. Levy and H. M. Markowitz, "Approximating Expected Utility by a Function of Mean and Variance," *American Economic Review*, 69, no. 3 (June 1979): 308–17.
5. For an introduction to uncertainty and utility theory, see:
   Mark P. Kritzman, ". . . About Uncertainty," *Financial Analysts Journal*, 47, no. 2 (March/April 1991): 17–21;
   Mark Kritzman, ". . . About Utility," *Financial Analysts Journal*, 48, no. 3 (May/June 1992): 17–20.

8

Efficient Sets

The previous chapter introduced the portfolio selection problem that every investor faces. It also introduced the investment approach of Harry Markowitz as a method of solving that problem. With this approach, an investor should evaluate alternative portfolios on the basis of their expected returns and standard deviations by using indifference curves. In the case of a risk-averse investor, the portfolio with the indifference curve that is "furthest northwest" would be the one selected for investment.

However, the previous chapter left certain questions unanswered. In particular, how does the investor calculate the expected return and standard deviation for a portfolio? And, how can Markowitz's approach be used once it is recognized that there are an infinite number of portfolios available for investment? This chapter will provide the answers that Markowitz gave to these questions, beginning with the first one.

CALCULATING EXPECTED RETURNS FOR PORTFOLIOS

With the Markowitz approach to investing, the focus of the investor is on terminal (or end-of-period) wealth, W_1. That is, in deciding which portfolio to purchase with his or her initial (or beginning-of-period) wealth, W_0, the investor should focus on the effect the various portfolios have on W_1. This effect can be measured by the expected return and standard deviation of each portfolio.

As mentioned previously, a portfolio is a collection of securities. Thus, it seems logical that the expected return and standard deviation of a portfolio should depend on the expected return and standard deviation of each security contained in the portfolio. It also seems logical that the amount invested in each security should be important. Indeed, this is the case.

In order to show how the expected return of a portfolio depends on both the expected return of the individual securities and the amount invested in these securities, consider the three-security portfolio shown in Table 8-1(a). Assume that the investor has a one-year holding period, and that for this period he or she has estimated the expected returns on Able, Baker, and Charlie stock to be 16.2%, 24.6%, and 22.8%, respectively. This is equivalent to stating that the investor has estimated the expected end-of-period values of these three stocks to be, respectively, \$46.48 [since (\$46.48 − \$40)/\$40 = 16.2%], \$43.61 [since (\$43.61 − \$35)/\$35 = 24.6%], and \$76.14 [since

TABLE 8-1
Calculating the Expected Return for a Portfolio

(a) Security and Portfolio Values

SECURITY NAME	NUMBER OF SHARES IN PORTFOLIO	INITIAL MARKET PRICE PER SHARE	TOTAL INVESTMENT	PROPORTION OF INITIAL MARKET VALUE OF PORTFOLIO
Able Co.	100	\$40	\$4,000	\$4,000/\$17,200 = .2325
Baker Co.	200	35	7,000	7,000/ 17,200 = .4070
Charlie Co.	100	62	6,200	6,200/ 17,200 = .3605
Initial Market Value of Portfolio = W_o = \$17,200				Sum of Proportions = 1.0000

(b) Calculating the Expected Return for a Portfolio Using End-of-Period Values

SECURITY NAME	NUMBER OF SHARES IN PORTFOLIO	EXPECTED END-OF-PERIOD VALUE PER SHARE	AGGREGATE EXPECTED END-OF-PERIOD VALUE
Able Co.	100	\$46.48	\$46.48 × 100 = \$4,648
Baker Co.	200	43.61	43.61 × 200 = 8,722
Charlie Co.	100	76.14	76.14 × 100 = 7,614

Expected End-of-Period Value of Portfolio = $\overline{W}_1$ = \$20,984
Portfolio Expected Return = $\bar{r}_p$ = (\$20,984 − \$17,200)/\$17,200 = 22.00%

(c) Calculating the Expected Return for a Portfolio Using Security Expected Returns

SECURITY NAME	PROPORTION OF INITIAL MARKET VALUE OF PORTFOLIO	SECURITY EXPECTED RETURNS	CONTRIBUTION TO PORTFOLIO EXPECTED RETURN
Able Co.	.2325	16.2%	.2325 × 16.2% = 3.77%
Baker Co.	.4070	24.6	.4070 × 24.6 = 10.01
Charlie Co.	.3605	22.8	.3605 × 22.8 = 8.22

Portfolio Expected Return = $\bar{r}_p$ = 22.00%

(\$76.14 − \$62)/\$62 = 22.8%].[1] Furthermore, assume that this investor has initial wealth of \$17,200.

Using End-of-Period Values

The expected return on this portfolio can be calculated in several ways, all of which give the same answer. Consider the method shown in Table 8-1(b). This method involves calculating the expected end-of-period value of the portfolio, and then using the formula for calculating the rate of return that was shown in Chapter 1. That is, first the initial portfolio value (W_0) is subtracted from the expected end-of-period value of the portfolio ($\overline{W}_1$), and then this difference is divided by the initial portfolio value (W_0), the result of which is the portfolio's expected return. While the example shown in Table 8-1(b) involves three securities, the procedure can be generalized to any number of securities.

Using Security Expected Returns

An alternative method for calculating the expected return on this portfolio is shown in Table 8-1(c). This procedure involves calculating the expected return of a portfolio as the *weighted average* of the expected returns of its component securities. The relative market values of the securities in the portfolio are used as weights. In symbols, the general rule for calculating the expected return of a portfolio consisting of N securities is:

$$\bar{r}_P = \sum_{i=1}^{N} X_i \bar{r}_i \tag{8.1a}$$

$$= X_1\bar{r}_1 + X_2\bar{r}_2 + \ldots + X_N\bar{r}_N \tag{8.1b}$$

where:

$\bar{r}_P$ = the expected return of the portfolio,
X_i = the proportion of the portfolio's initial value invested in security *i* (hence each X_i is a nonnegative number and the sum of all the X_i's equals one),
$\bar{r}_i$ = the expected return of security *i*, and
N = the number of securities in the portfolio.

expected return vector

Thus, an **expected return vector** can be used to calculate the expected return for any portfolio formed from the N securities. This vector consists of one column of numbers, where the entry in row *i* contains the expected return of security *i*. In the previous example, the expected return vector was estimated by the investor to be:

Row 1	16.2%
Row 2	24.6%
Row 3	22.8%

[1]The figures given for the expected end-of-period values include both the expected prices and the expected dividends for the period. For example, Able has an expected end-of-period value of \$46.48, which could consist of a hypothetical expected cash dividend of \$2 and share price of \$44.48. These expected returns and values are estimated by use of security analysis, which will be discussed in Chapter 15.

where the entries in rows 1, 2, and 3 denote the expected returns for securities 1, 2, and 3, respectively.

Since a portfolio's expected return is a weighted average of the expected returns of its securities, *the contribution of each security to the portfolio's expected return depends on its expected return and its proportionate share of the initial portfolio's market value.* Nothing else is relevant. It follows from equation (8.1a) that an investor who simply wants the greatest possible expected return should hold one security: the one he or she considers to have the greatest expected return. Very few investors do this, and very few investment advisors would counsel such an extreme policy. Instead, investors should diversify, meaning that their portfolios should include more than one security. This is because diversification can reduce risk, as measured by standard deviation.

CALCULATING STANDARD DEVIATIONS FOR PORTFOLIOS

A useful measure of risk should somehow take into account both the probabilities of various possible "bad" outcomes and their associated magnitudes. Instead of measuring the probability of a number of different possible outcomes, the measure of risk should somehow estimate the extent to which the actual outcome is likely to diverge from the expected outcome. Standard deviation is a measure that does this, since it is an estimate of the likely divergence of an *actual* return from an *expected* return.

It may seem that any single measure of risk would provide at best a very crude summary of the "bad" possibilities. But in the more common situation where a portfolio's prospects are being assessed, standard deviation may prove to be a very good measure of the degree of uncertainty. The clearest example arises when the **probability distribution** for a portfolio's returns can be approximated by the familiar bell-shaped curve known as a **normal distribution.** This is often considered a plausible assumption for analyzing returns on diversified portfolios when the holding period being studied is relatively short (say, a quarter or less).

probability distribution
normal distribution

A question about standard deviation as a measure of risk is: why count "happy" surprises (those above the expected return) at all in a measure of risk? Why not just consider the deviations *below* the expected return? Measures that do so have merit. However, the results will be the same if the probability distribution is symmetric, as is the normal distribution. Why? Because the left side of a symmetric distribution is a mirror image of the right side. Thus, a list of portfolios ordered on the basis of "downside risk" will not differ from one ordered on the basis of standard deviation if returns are normally distributed.[2]

[2]If returns are not normally distributed, the use of standard deviation can still be justified in an approximate sense provided there are small probabilities of extremely high and low returns. See H. Levy and H. M. Markowitz, "Approximating Expected Utility by a Function of Mean and Variance," *American Economic Review*, 69, no. 3 (June 1979): 308-17; and Yoram Kroll, Haim Levy, and Harry M. Markowitz, "Mean-Variance versus Direct Utility Maximization," *Journal of Finance*, 39, no. 1 (March 1984): 47–61.

Formula for Standard Deviation

Now, just how is the standard deviation of a portfolio calculated? For the three-security portfolio consisting of Able, Baker, and Charlie, the formula is:

$$\sigma_P = \left[\sum_{i=1}^{3} \sum_{j=1}^{3} X_i X_j \sigma_{ij} \right]^{1/2} \tag{8.2}$$

where σ_{ij} denotes the **covariance** of the returns between security *i* and security *j*.

covariance

Covariance What is covariance? It is a statistical measure of the relationship between two random variables. That is, it is a measure of how two random variables such as the returns on securities *i* and *j* "move together." A positive value for covariance indicates that the securities' returns tend to move together—for example, a better-than-expected return for one is likely to occur along with a better-than-expected return for the other. A negative covariance indicates a tendency for the returns to offset one another—for example, a better-than-expected return for one security is likely to occur along with a worse-than-expected return for the other. A relatively small or zero value for the covariance indicates that there is little or no relationship between the returns for the two securities.

Correlation Closely related to covariance is the statistical measure known as correlation, since it is known that the covariance between two random variables is equal to the correlation between the two random variables times the product of their standard deviations:

$$\sigma_{ij} = \rho_{ij}\sigma_i\sigma_j \tag{8.3}$$

where ρ_{ij} (the Greek letter *rho*) denotes the **correlation coefficient** between the return on security *i* and the return on security *j*. The correlation coefficient rescales the covariance to facilitate comparison with corresponding values for other pairs of random variables. Correlation coefficients always lie between -1 and $+1$. A value of -1 represents perfect negative correlation, and a value of $+1$ represents perfect positive correlation. Most cases lie between these two extreme values.

correlation coefficient

Figure 8-1(a) presents a scatter diagram for the returns on hypothetical securities A and B when the correlation between these two securities is perfectly positive. Note how all the points lie precisely on a straight upward-sloping line. This means that when one of the two securities has a relatively high return, then so will the other. Similarly, when one of the two securities has a relatively low return, then so will the other.

Alternatively, the returns on the two securities will have a perfectly negative correlation when the scatter diagram indicates that the points lie precisely on a straight downward-sloping line, as shown in Figure 8-1(b). In such a case the returns on the two securities can be seen to move opposite each other. That is, when one security has a relatively high return, then the other will have a relatively low return.

A case of special importance arises when the scatter diagram of security returns shows a pattern that cannot be represented even approximately by an upward-sloping or downward-sloping line. In such an instance, the returns

FIGURE 8-1
Returns on Two Securities

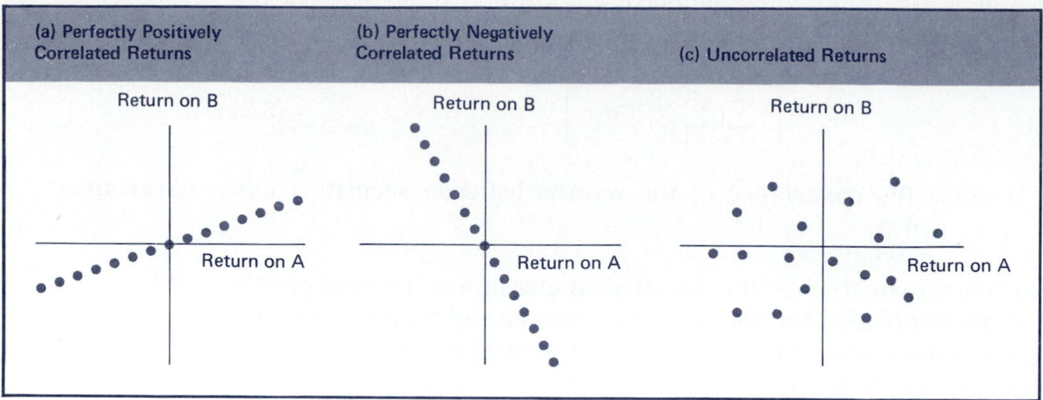

are uncorrelated, meaning that the correlation coefficient is zero. Figure 8-1(c) provides an example. In this situation, when one security has a relatively high return, then the other can have either a relatively high, low, or average return.

Double Summation Given an understanding of covariance and correlation, it is important to understand how the *double summation* indicated in equation (8.2) is performed. While there are many ways of performing double summation, all of which lead to the same answer, one way is perhaps more intuitive than the others. It starts with the first summation and sets i at its initial value of 1. Then the second summation is performed for j going from 1 to 3. At this point, i in the first summation is increased by 1, so that now $i = 2$. Again the second summation is performed by letting j go from 1 to 3, except that now $i = 2$. Continuing, i in the first summation is again increased by 1, so that $i = 3$. Then the second summation is again performed by letting j go from 1 to 3. At this point, note that $i = 3$ and $j = 3$, which are the upper limits for both the first and second summations. This means it is time to stop, as the double summation has been finished. This process can be shown algebraically as follows:

$$\sigma_P = \left[\sum_{j=1}^{3} X_1 X_j \sigma_{1j} + \sum_{j=1}^{3} X_2 X_j \sigma_{2j} + \sum_{j=1}^{3} X_3 X_j \sigma_{3j} \right]^{1/2} \tag{8.4a}$$

$$\begin{aligned} &= [X_1X_1\sigma_{11} + X_1X_2\sigma_{12} + X_1X_3\sigma_{13} \\ &+ X_2X_1\sigma_{21} + X_2X_2\sigma_{22} + X_2X_3\sigma_{23} \\ &+ X_3X_1\sigma_{31} + X_3X_2\sigma_{32} + X_3X_3\sigma_{33}].^{1/2} \end{aligned} \tag{8.4b}$$

Each term in the double sum involves the product of the weights for two securities, X_i and X_j, and the covariance between these two securities. Note how there are nine terms to be added together in order to calculate the standard deviation of a portfolio consisting of three securities. It is no coincidence that the number of terms to be added together (9) equals the number of securities squared (3^2).

In general, calculating the standard deviation for a portfolio consisting of N securities involves performing the double sum indicated in equation (8.2) over N securities, thereby involving the addition of N^2 terms:

$$\sigma_P = \left[\sum_{i=1}^{N} \sum_{j=1}^{N} X_i X_j \sigma_{ij} \right]^{1/2}. \tag{8.5}$$

An interesting feature of the double sum occurs when the subscripts i and j refer to the same security. In equation (8.4b), this occurs in the first ($X_1X_1\sigma_{11}$), fifth ($X_2X_2\sigma_{22}$), and ninth ($X_3X_3\sigma_{33}$) terms. What does it mean to have the subscripts for covariance refer to the same security? For example, consider security one (Able) so that $i = j = 1$. Since σ_{11} denotes the covariance of security one (Able) with security one (Able), equation (8.3) indicates that:

$$\sigma_{11} = \rho_{11}\sigma_1\sigma_1. \tag{8.6}$$

Now the correlation of any security with itself, in this case ρ_{11}, can be shown to be equal to +1.[3] This means that equation (8.6) reduces to:

$$\begin{aligned} \sigma_{11} &= +1 \times \sigma_1 \times \sigma_1 \\ &= \sigma_1^2 \end{aligned} \tag{8.7}$$

which is just the standard deviation of security 1 squared, known as the **variance** of security 1. Thus, the double sum involves both variance and covariance terms.

variance

Variance-Covariance Matrix As an example, consider the following **variance-covariance matrix** for the stocks of Able, Baker, and Charlie:

variance-covariance matrix

	Column 1	Column 2	Column 3
Row 1	146	187	145
Row 2	187	854	104
Row 3	145	104	289

The entry in cell (i,j) denotes the covariance between security i and security j. For example, the entry in (1,3) denotes the covariance between the first and third securities, which in this case is 145. Also, the entry in cell (i,i) denotes the variance of security i. For example, the variance of security 2 appears in cell (2,2), and is equal to 854. Using this variance-covariance matrix along with the formula given in equation (8.4b), the standard deviation of any portfolio that consists of investments in Able, Baker, and Charlie can now be

[3]Remember that correlation refers to how two random variables move together. If the two random variables are the same, then they must move exactly together with each other. This can be visualized by graphing the values of the same random variable on both the X-axis and Y-axis. In such a graph, all points would lie on a straight 45-degree line passing through the origin, thereby implying a correlation of +1.

calculated. For example, consider the portfolio given in Table 8-1 that had proportions $X_1 = .2325$, $X_2 = .4070$, and $X_3 = .3605$:

$$\begin{aligned}\sigma_P = [& X_1X_1\sigma_{11} + X_1X_2\sigma_{12} + X_1X_3\sigma_{13} \\ & + X_2X_1\sigma_{21} + X_2X_2\sigma_{22} + X_2X_3\sigma_{23} \\ & + X_3X_1\sigma_{31} + X_3X_2\sigma_{32} + X_3X_3\sigma_{33}]^{1/2}\end{aligned}$$

$$\begin{aligned}= [& (.2325 \times .2325 \times 146) + (.2325 \times .4070 \times 187) + (.2325 \times .3605 \times 145) \\ & + (.4070 \times .2325 \times 187) + (.4070 \times .4070 \times 854) + (.4070 \times .3605 \times 104) \\ & + (.3605 \times .2325 \times 145) + (.3605 \times .4070 \times 104) + (.3605 \times .3605 \times 289)]^{1/2}\end{aligned}$$

$$= [277.13]^{1/2}$$

$$= 16.65\%.$$

Several interesting features about variance-covariance matrices deserve mention. First, such matrices are square, meaning that the number of columns equals the number of rows, and that the total number of cells for N securities equals N^2. Second, the variances of the securities appear on the diagonal of the matrix, which are the cells that lie on a line going from the upper-left-hand corner to be lower-right-hand corner of the matrix. In the previous example, the variance of security 1, 146, appears in row one of column one. Similarly, the variances of securities 2 and 3 appear in row two of column two (854) and row three of column three (289), respectively. Third, the matrix is symmetric, meaning that the number appearing in row i of column j also appears in row j of column i. That is, the elements in the cells above the diagonal also appear in the corresponding cells below the diagonal. In the previous example, note that the element in row one of column two, 187, also appears in row two of column one. Similarly, 145 appears in both row one of column three and row three of column one, and 104 appears in both row two of column three and row three of column two. The reason for this feature is quite simple—the covariance between two securities does not depend on the order in which the two securities are specified. This means that, for example, the covariance between the first and second securities is the same as the covariance between the second and first securities.[4]

At this point, the formulas for calculating the expected return and standard deviation for a portfolio formed from N securities have been presented. In order to use them, the expected returns for each of the N securities (which can be displayed in what is referred to as the expected return vector) and all the variances and pairwise covariances (which can be displayed in the variance-covariance matrix) are needed. Now, the second question that was raised at the beginning of this chapter can be addressed. Namely, given that an infinite number of portfolios exist, how can the Markowitz approach to investing be used? After all, an investor cannot first calculate the expected return and standard deviation for all portfolios that exist, and then choose the one lying on the indifference curve that is furthest northwest, since this would be a virtually endless task. The answer to this question lies within the efficient set theorem.

---

[4]For any variance-covariance matrix there is an implied correlation matrix that can be determined by using the data in the variance-covariance matrix and equation (8.3). Specifically, this equation can be used to show that the correlation between any two securities i and j is equal to $\sigma_{ij}/\sigma_i\,\sigma_j$; the values for σ_{ij}, σ_i and σ_j can be obtained from the variance-covariance matrix. For example, $\rho_{12} = 187/(\sqrt{146} \times \sqrt{854}) = .53$.

THE EFFICIENT SET THEOREM

As mentioned earlier, an infinite number of portfolios can be formed from a set of N securities. Consider the previous situation where N was equal to 3. The investor could purchase just shares of Able, or just shares of Baker. Alternatively, the investor could purchase a combination of shares of Able and Baker. For example, the investor could put 50% of his or her money in each company, or 25% in one company and 75% in the other, or 33% in one and 67% in the other, or any percent (between 0% and 100%) in one company with the rest going into the other company. Without even considering investing in Charlie, there are already an infinite number of possible portfolios for consideration.[5]

Does the investor need to evaluate all these portfolios? Fortunately, the answer to this question is no. The key to why the investor needs to look at only a subset of the available portfolios lies in the **efficient set theorem,** which states that:

efficient set theorem

> An investor will choose his or her optimal portfolio from the set of portfolios that:
>
> 1. Offer maximum expected return for varying levels of risk, and
> 2. Offer minimum risk for varying levels of expected return.

The set of portfolios meeting these two conditions is known as the **efficient set** or efficient frontier.

efficient set

The Feasible Set

Figure 8-2 provides an illustration of the location of the **feasible set,** also known as the opportunity set, from which the efficient set can be identified. The feasible set simply represents the set of all portfolios that could be formed from a group of N securities. That is, all possible portfolios that could be formed from the N securities lie either on or within the boundary of the feasible set (the points denoted G, E, S, and H in the figure are examples of such portfolios). In general, this set will have an umbrella-type shape similar to the one shown in the figure. Depending on the particular securities involved, it may be more to the right or left, or higher or lower, or fatter or skinnier than indicated here. The point is that its shape will, except in perverse circumstances, look similar to what appears here.

feasible set

The Efficient Set Theorem Applied to the Feasible Set

The efficient set can now be located by applying the efficient set theorem to this feasible set. First, the set of portfolios that meet the first condition of the efficient set theorem must be identified. Looking at Figure 8-2, there is no

[5]This can be seen by noting that there are an infinite number of points on the real number line between 0 and 100. If these numbers are thought of as representing the percentage of the investor's funds going into shares of Able, with 100 minus this number going into Baker, it can be seen that there are an infinite number of portfolios that could be formed from just two different securities. In making this assertion, however, it has been assumed that an investor can buy a fraction of a share if he or she so desires. For example, the investor can buy not only one or two or three shares of Able, but also 1.1 or 1.01 or 1.001 shares.

MONEY MATTERS
The Trouble with Optimizers

Suppose that the captain of a modern luxury liner chose not to use the ship's state-of-the-art navigational system (a system that employs computers to triangulate off geostationary-orbiting satellites, thereby estimating the ship's position accurately to within a few feet). Instead, suppose that the captain chose to rely on the old-fashioned method of navigating by the stars, an antiquated method fraught with problems and imprecision. Most people would view the captain's choice as, at best, eccentric and, at worse, highly dangerous.

When it comes to constructing portfolios, most investment managers make a choice analogous to that of the ship's captain. They reject computer-based portfolio construction methods in favor of traditional approaches. Are their decisions as foolhardy as the captain's? Or is there a method to their apparent madness?

As this chapter discusses, the concepts of the efficient set and the investor's optimal portfolio are central to modern investment theory. But how can investors actually go about estimating the efficient set and selecting their optimal portfolios? Harry Markowitz first described the solution in the early 1950s. Using a mathematical technique called *quadratic programming*, investors can process expected returns, standard deviations, and covariances to calculate the efficient set. Given an estimate of their indifference curves (as reflected in their individual risk tolerances—see Chapter 17), they can then select a portfolio from the efficient set.

Simple, right? Certainly not in the 1950s. Given the data processing facilities available to investors at that time, calculating the efficient set for even a few hundred securities was essentially impossible. However, with the advent of low-cost, high-speed computers in the 1980s and the development of sophisticated risk models (see Chapter 11), an efficient set can be created for thousands of securities in a matter of minutes. The necessary computer hardware and software are available to virtually every money management firm at a relatively low cost. In fact, the process has become so commonplace that it has acquired its own terminology. Using a computer to identify the efficient set and select an optimal portfolio has colloquially come to be known as using an "optimizer." Portfolios are "optimized" and investors are said to apply "optimization techniques."

Despite the technology's widespread availability, few investment managers actually use an optimizer to build portfolios. Instead, they rely on a series of qualitative rules and judgments.

Why do investment managers resist applying optimization techniques to portfolio building? Ignorance is not the answer. Most investment managers are well aware of Markowitz's portfolio selection concepts and the available technology, having graduated from business schools where these ideas are discussed in detail. Instead, the resistance derives from two sources: territorial concerns and implementation inadequacies.

From a territorial perspective, most investment managers are simply not oriented toward a quantitative

portfolio offering less risk than that of portfolio E. This is because if a vertical line were drawn through E, there would be no point in the feasible set that was to the left of the line. Also, there is no portfolio offering more risk than that of portfolio H. This is because if a vertical line were drawn through H, there would be no point in the feasible set to the right of the line. Thus, the set of portfolios offering maximum expected return for varying levels of risk is the set of portfolios lying on the "northern" boundary of the feasible set between points E and H.

Considering the second condition next, there is no portfolio offering an expected return greater than portfolio S, since no point in the feasible set lies above a horizontal line going through S. Similarly, there is no portfolio offering a lower expected return than portfolio G, since no point in the feasible set lies below a horizontal line going through G. Thus, the set of portfolios offering minimum risk for varying levels of expected return is the set of portfolios lying on the "western" boundary of the feasible set between points G and S.

Remembering that both conditions have to be met in order to identify the efficient set, it can be seen that only those portfolios lying on the "northwest" boundary between points E and S do so. Accordingly, these portfolios form

approach to investing. Their decision making emphasizes intuition and complex subjective judgments. The application of optimization techniques to portfolio construction imposes a very systematic and formal structure with which most investment managers are uncomfortable. Security analysts must become responsible for generating quantifiable expected return estimates and risk forecasts. Portfolio managers must implement the decisions of a computer. As a result, the optimizer destroys the "artistry and grace" of investment management.

Further, with the introduction of an optimizer, a new breed of investment professional gains influence—the quantitative analyst (derisively called a "quant")—who coordinates the collection and application of risk and return estimates. Authority gained by quantitative analysts diminishes the influence of the traditional security analysts and portfolio managers, much to their consternation.

From the implementation perspective, optimizers have evidenced serious problems in practice; they tend to produce counterintuitive, uninvestable portfolios. This situation is not so much a problem with the optimizer as it is the fault of the human operators supplying inputs to the optimizer. Here the GIGO (garbage in, garbage out) paradigm rules.

By their design, optimizers are attracted to securities with high expected returns, low standard deviations, and low covariances with other securities. Often this information is derived from historical databases covering thousands of securities. Unless the risk and return data are carefully checked, errors (for example, understating a security's standard deviation) can easily lead the optimizer to recommend purchases of securities for erroneous reasons. Even if the data are "clean," extreme historical values for some securities may lead the optimizer astray.

Unless programmed to take transaction costs into account, optimizers also display a nasty habit of generating high turnover and recommending investments in illiquid securities. *High turnover* refers to significant changes in portfolio composition from one period to the next. High turnover can result in unacceptably large transaction costs (see Chapter 3), thereby hindering portfolio performance. *Liquidity* refers to the ability to actually buy the securities selected by the optimizer. Selected securities may possess desirable risk-return characteristics, but may not trade in sufficient volume to permit purchase without incurring sizable transaction costs.

Solutions to these implementation problems do exist, ranging from careful data checking to placing constraints on maximum turnover or minimum liquidity. Unfortunately, data checking is time-consuming and never foolproof. Moreover, optimization constraints arbitrarily reduce the information processing advantages of optimizers.

The combination of territorial and implementation problems has given investment managers convenient reasons to avoid optimizers and stick to traditional portfolio construction methods. Consequently, despite an increased understanding and application of quantitative investment management techniques, many investment managers will continue to navigate primarily by the stars.

---

the efficient set, and it is from this set of **efficient portfolios** that the investor will find his or her optimal one.[6] All the other feasible portfolios are **inefficient portfolios,** and can be safely ignored.

efficient portfolios

inefficient portfolios

Selection of the Optimal Portfolio

How will the investor select an **optimal portfolio?** As shown in Figure 8-3, the investor should plot his or her indifference curves on the same figure as the efficient set, and then proceed to choose the portfolio that is on the indifference curve that is furthest "northwest." This portfolio will correspond to the point where an indifference curve is just tangent to the efficient set. As can be seen in the figure, this is portfolio O* on indifference curve I_2. While the investor would prefer a portfolio on I_3, no such portfolio exists, and so wanting to be on this indifference curve is just wishful thinking. In regard to

optimal portfolio

[6]In order to determine the compositions of the portfolios on the efficient set, the investor must solve a quadratic programming problem. See Markowitz's book entitled *Portfolio Selection* (cited at the end of the chapter), particularly pp. 176–85.

FIGURE 8-2
Feasible and Efficient Sets

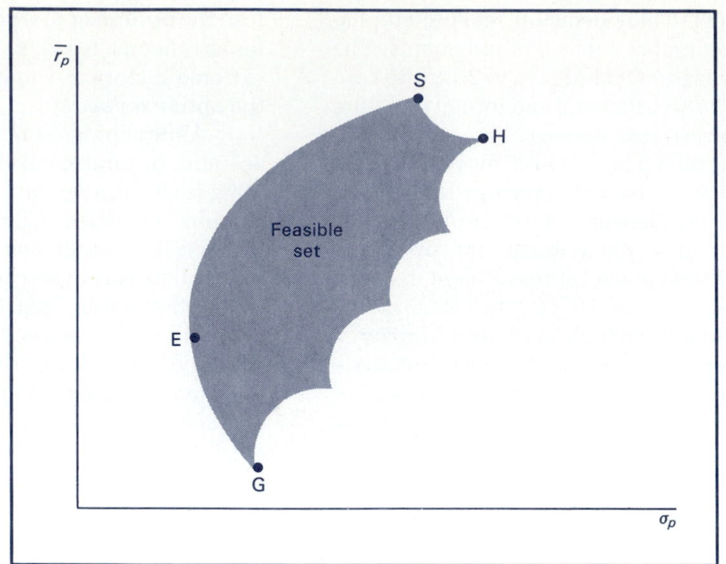

I_1, there are several portfolios that the investor could choose (for example, O). However, the figure shows that portfolio O* dominates such portfolios, since it is on an indifference curve that is "further northwest." Figure 8-4 shows how the highly risk-averse investor will choose a portfolio close to E. Figure 8-5 shows that the investor who is only slightly risk-averse will choose a portfolio close to S.[7]

[7]The risk-neutral investor will choose portfolio S, while the risk-seeking investor will choose either S or H.

FIGURE 8-3
Selecting an Optimal Portfolio

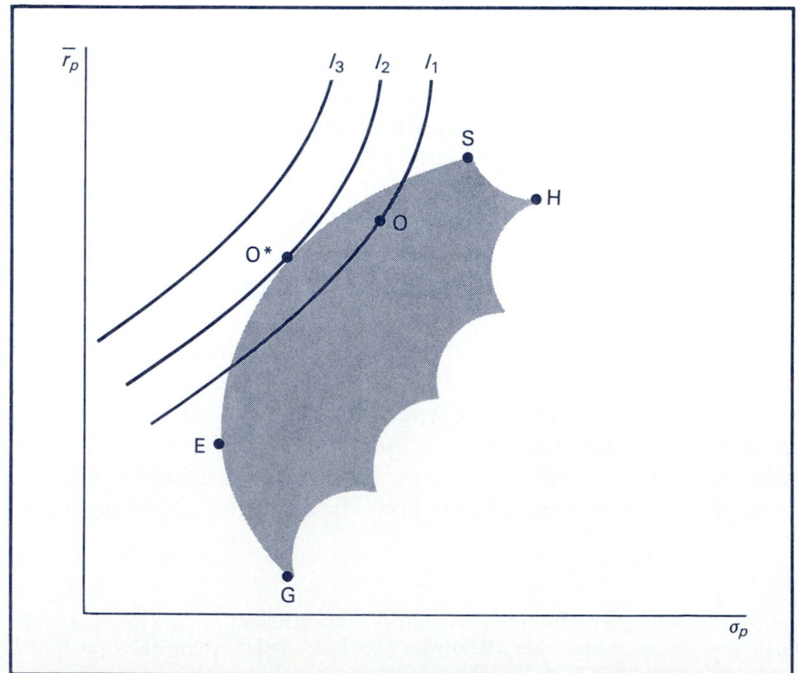

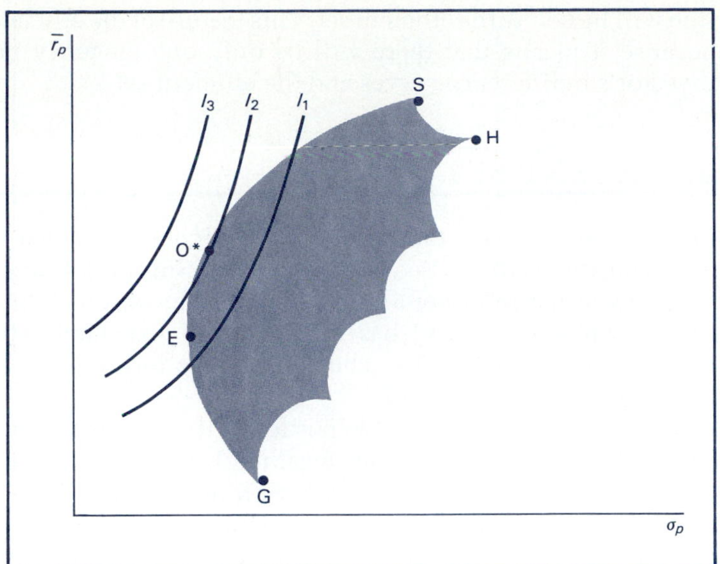

FIGURE 8-4
Portfolio Selection for a Highly Risk-Averse Investor

Upon reflection, the efficient set theorem is quite rational. In Chapter 7, it was shown that the investor should select the portfolio that put him or her on the indifference curve "furthest northwest." The efficient set theorem, stating that the investor need not be concerned with portfolios that do not lie on the northwest boundary of the feasible set, is a logical consequence.

Indifference curves for the risk-averse investor were shown to be positively sloped and convex in Chapter 7. Now it will be shown that the efficient set is generally positively sloped and concave, meaning that if a straight line is drawn between any two points on the efficient set, the straight

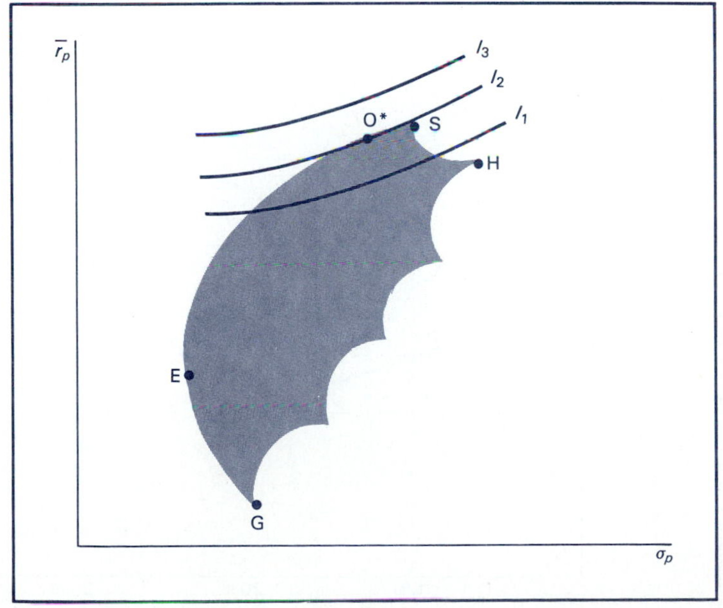

FIGURE 8-5
Portfolio Selection for a Slightly Risk-Averse Investor

line will lie below the efficient set. This feature of the efficient set is important because it means that there will be only one tangency point between the investor's indifference curves and the efficient set.

CONCAVITY OF THE EFFICIENT SET

In order to see why the efficient set is concave, consider the following two-security example. Security 1, the Ark Shipping Company, has an estimated expected return of 5% and standard deviation of 20%. Security 2, the Gold Jewelry Company, has an estimated expected return of 15% and standard deviation of 40%. Their respective locations are indicated by the letters A and G in Figure 8-6.

Now consider all possible portfolios that an investor could purchase by combining these two securities together. Let X_1 denote the proportion of the investor's funds invested in Ark Shipping and $X_2 = 1 - X_1$ denote the proportion invested in Gold Jewelry. Thus, if the investor purchased just Ark Shipping, then $X_1 = 1$ and $X_2 = 0$. Alternatively, if the investor purchased just Gold Jewelry, then $X_1 = 0$ and $X_2 = 1$. A combination of .17 in Ark Shipping and .83 in Gold Jewelry is also possible, as the respective combinations of .33 and .67, and .50 and .50. While there are many other possibilities, only the following seven portfolios will be considered:

	PORTFOLIO A	PORTFOLIO B	PORTFOLIO C	PORTFOLIO D	PORTFOLIO E	PORTFOLIO F	PORTFOLIO G
X_1	1.00	.83	.67	.50	.33	.17	.00
X_2	.00	.17	.33	.50	.67	.83	1.00

FIGURE 8-6
Upper and Lower Bounds to Combinations of Securities A and G

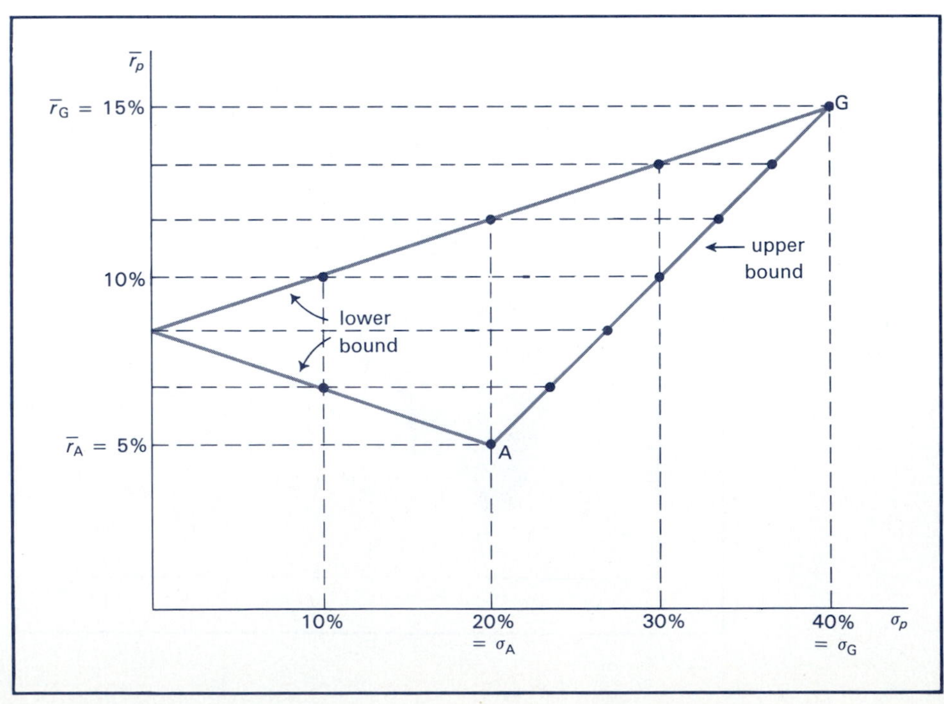

In order to consider these seven portfolios for possible investment, their expected returns and standard deviations must be calculated. All the necessary information to calculate the expected returns for these portfolios is at hand, since all that is needed in order to utilize equation (8.1a) has been provided:

$$\bar{r}_P = \sum_{i=1}^{N} X_i \bar{r}_i \tag{8.1a}$$

$$= \sum_{i=1}^{2} X_i \bar{r}_i$$

$$= X_1 \bar{r}_1 + X_2 \bar{r}_2$$

$$= (X_1 \times 5\%) + (X_2 \times 15\%).$$

For portfolios A and G, this calculation is trivial, since the investor is purchasing shares of just one company. Thus, their expected returns are 5% and 15%, respectively. For portfolios B, C, D, E, and F, the expected returns are, respectively:

$$\bar{r}_B = (.83 \times 5\%) + (.17 \times 15\%) = 6.70\%$$

$$\bar{r}_C = (.67 \times 5\%) + (.33 \times 15\%) = 8.30\%$$

$$\bar{r}_D = (.50 \times 5\%) + (.50 \times 15\%) = 10\%$$

$$\bar{r}_E = (.33 \times 5\%) + (.67 \times 15\%) = 11.70\%$$

$$\bar{r}_F = (.17 \times 5\%) + (.83 \times 15\%) = 13.30\%.$$

In calculating the standard deviation of these seven portfolios, equation (8.5) must be utilized:

$$\sigma_P = \left[\sum_{i=1}^{N} \sum_{j=1}^{N} X_i X_j \sigma_{ij} \right]^{1/2} \tag{8.5}$$

$$= \left[\sum_{i=1}^{2} \sum_{j=1}^{2} X_i X_j \sigma_{ij} \right]^{1/2}$$

$$= [X_1 X_1 \sigma_{11} + X_1 X_2 \sigma_{12} + X_2 X_1 \sigma_{21} + X_2 X_2 \sigma_{22}]^{1/2}$$

$$= [X_1^2 \sigma_1^2 + X_2^2 \sigma_2^2 + 2X_1 X_2 \sigma_{12}]^{1/2}$$

$$= [(X_1^2 \times 20\%^2) + (X_2^2 \times 40\%^2) + 2X_1 X_2 \sigma_{12}]^{1/2}.$$

For portfolios A and G, this calculation is trivial, since the investor is purchasing shares of just one company. Thus, their standard deviations are just 20% and 40%, respectively.

For portfolios B, C, D, E, and F, application of equation (8.5) indicates that the standard deviations depend on the magnitude of the covariance between the two securities. As shown in equation (8.3), this covariance term is equal to the correlation between the two securities multiplied by the product of their standard deviations:

$$\sigma_{12} = \rho_{12} \times \sigma_1 \times \sigma_2$$

$$= \rho_{12} \times 20\% \times 40\%$$

$$= 800\rho_{12}.$$

This means that the standard deviation of any portfolio consisting of Ark Shipping and Gold Jewelry can be expressed as:

$$\sigma_P = [(X_1^2 \times 20\%^2) + (X_2^2 \times 40\%^2) + (2X_1X_2 \times 800\rho_{12})]^{1/2}.$$
$$= [400X_1^2 + 1{,}600X_2^2 + 1{,}600X_1X_2\rho_{12}]^{1/2}. \quad (8.8)$$

Consider portfolio D first. The standard deviation of this portfolio will be somewhere between 10% and 30%, the exact value depending upon the size of the correlation coefficient. How were these bounds of 10% and 30% determined? First, note that for portfolio D, equation (8.8) reduces to:

$$\sigma_D = [(400 \times .25) + (1{,}600 \times .25) + (1{,}600 \times .5 \times .5 \times \rho_{12})]^{1/2}$$
$$= [500 + 400\rho_{12}]^{1/2}. \quad (8.9)$$

Inspection of equation (8.9) indicates that σ_D will be at a minimum when the correlation coefficient, ρ_{12}, is at a minimum. Now remembering that the minimum value for any correlation coefficient is -1, it can be seen that the lower bound on σ_D is:

$$\sigma_D = [500 + (400 \times -1)]^{1/2}$$
$$= [500 - 400]^{1/2}$$
$$= [100]^{1/2}$$
$$= 10\%.$$

Similarly, inspection of equation (8.9) indicates that σ_D will be at a maximum when the correlation coefficient is at a maximum, which is $+1$. Thus, the upper bound on σ_D is:

$$\sigma_D = [500 + (400 \times 1)]^{1/2}$$
$$= [500 + 400]^{1/2}$$
$$= [900]^{1/2}$$
$$= 30\%.$$

In general, it can be seen from equation (8.8) that for any given set of weights X_1 and X_2, the lower and upper bounds will occur when the correlation between the two securities is -1 and $+1$, respectively. Proceeding to apply the same analysis to the other portfolios reveals that their lower and upper bounds are:

	STANDARD DEVIATION OF PORTFOLIO	
Portfolio	**Lower Bound**	**Upper Bound**
A	20%	20.00%
B	10	23.33
C	0	26.67
D	10	30.00
E	20	33.33
F	30	36.67
G	40	40.00

These values are shown in Figure 8-6.

Interestingly, the upper bounds all lie on a straight line connecting points A and G. This means that any portfolio consisting of these two securities cannot have a standard deviation that plots to the right of a straight line connecting the two securities. Instead, the standard deviation must lie on or to the left of the straight line. This observation suggests a motivation for diversifying a portfolio. Namely, *diversification generally leads to risk reduction,* since the standard deviation of a portfolio will generally be less than a weighted average of the standard deviations of the securities in the portfolio.

Also interesting is the observation that the lower bounds all lie on one of two line segments that go from point A to a point on the vertical axis corresponding to 8.30% and then to point G. This means that any portfolio consisting of these two securities cannot have a standard deviation that plots to the left of either of these two line segments. For example, portfolio B must lie on the horizontal line going through the vertical axis at 6.70%, but bounded at the values of 10% and 23.33%.

In sum, any portfolio consisting of these two securities will lie within or on the boundary of the triangle shown in Figure 8-6, with its actual location depending on the magnitude of the correlation coefficient between the two securities.

What if the correlation were zero? In this case, equation (8.8) reduces to:

$$\begin{aligned}\sigma_p &= [(400X_1^2) + (1{,}600X_2^2) + (1{,}600X_1X_2 \times 0)]^{1/2}\\ &= [400X_1^2 + 1{,}600X_2^2]^{1/2}.\end{aligned}$$

Applying the appropriate weights for X_1 and X_2, the standard deviation for portfolios B, C, D, E, and F can therefore be calculated as follows:

$$\begin{aligned}\sigma_B &= [(400 \times .83^2) + (1{,}600 \times .17^2)]^{1/2}\\ &= 17.94\%,\\ \sigma_C &= [(400 \times .67^2) + (1{,}600 \times .33^2)]^{1/2}\\ &= 18.81\%,\\ \sigma_D &= [(400 \times .50^2) + (1{,}600 \times .50^2)]^{1/2}\\ &= 22.36\%,\\ \sigma_E &= [(400 \times .33^2) + (1{,}600 \times .67^2)]^{1/2}\\ &= 27.60\%,\\ \sigma_F &= [(400 \times .17^2) + (1{,}600 \times .83^2)]^{1/2}\\ &= 33.37\%.\end{aligned}$$

Figure 8-7 indicates the location of these portfolios, along with the upper and lower bounds that were shown in Figure 8-6. As can be seen, these portfolios, as well as all other possible portfolios consisting of Ark Shipping and Gold Jewelry, lie on a line that is curved or bowed to the left. While not shown here, if the correlation were less than zero, the line would curve more to the left. If the correlation were greater than zero, it would not curve quite as much to the left. The important point of this figure is that as long as the correlation is less than +1 and greater than −1, the line representing the set of portfolios consisting of various combinations of the two securities will have

FIGURE 8-7
Portfolios Formed by Combining Securities A and G

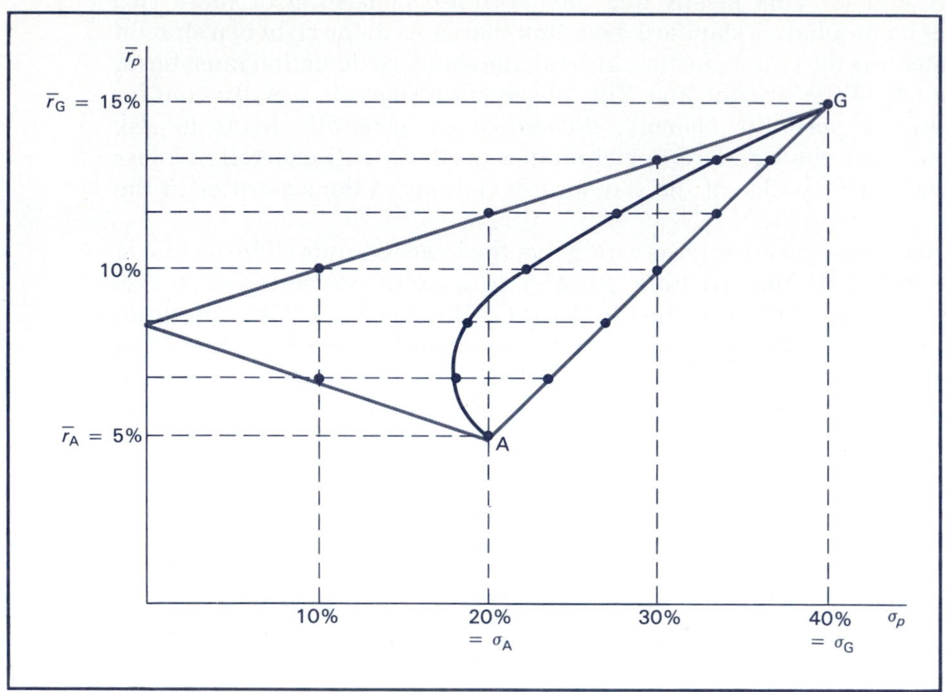

some degree of curvature to the left. Furthermore, the northwest portion will be concave.

Similar analysis can be applied to a situation where there are more than two securities under consideration. When this is done, as long as the correlations are less than +1 and greater than −1, the northwest portion must be concave, just as it is in the two-security example.[8] Thus, in general the efficient set will be concave.

THE MARKET MODEL

Suppose the return on a common stock over a given time period (say, a month) is related to the return over the same period that is earned on a market index such as the widely-cited S&P 500.[9] That is, if the market has gone up then it is likely that the stock has gone up, and if the market has gone down then it is

[8]This "curvature property" can also be used to explain why the right-hand side of the feasible set has the umbrella shape noted in Figure 8-2. A more rigorous demonstration of concavity is contained in Appendix A.

[9]This is an example of a single-factor model where the factor is the return on a market index (see Chapter 11 for more on factor models; see Chapters 10, 14, and 26 for more on market indices). The model is actually more general than indicated here in that the return need not be on a market index. It can be on any variable that is believed to have a major influence on individual stock returns, such as the rate of increase in industrial production or gross domestic product.

likely that the stock has gone down. One way to capture this relationship is with the **market model:**

market model

$$r_i = \alpha_i + \beta_i r_I + \epsilon_i \tag{8.10}$$

where: r_i = return on security i for some given period,
r_I = return on market index I for the same period,
α_i = intercept term,
β_i = slope term, and
ϵ_i = random error term.

Assuming that the slope term β_i is positive, what equation (8.10) means is that the higher the return on the market index, the higher the return on the security is likely to be (note that the expected value of the random error term is zero). Consider stock A, for example, which has $\alpha_i = 2\%$ and $\beta_i = 1.2$. This means that the market model for stock A is:

$$r_A = 2\% + 1.2r_I + \epsilon_A \tag{8.11}$$

so that if the market index has a return of 10%, the return on the security is likely to be 14% = 2% + (1.2 × 10%). Similarly, if the market index's return is –5%, then the return on security A is likely to be –4% = 2% + (1.2 × –5%). The term ϵ_i, known as the **random error term** in equation (8.10), simply shows that the market model does not explain security returns perfectly. That is, when the market index goes up by 10% or down by 5%, the return on security A is not going to be exactly 14% or –4%, respectively. The difference between what the return actually is and what it is expected to be, given the return on the market index, is attributed to the effect of the random error term. Hence, if the security's return was 9% instead of 14%, the 5% difference would be attributed to the random error term (that is, $\epsilon_A = -5\%$; this will be illustrated shortly in Figure 8-10). Similarly, if the security return was –2% instead of –4%, the 2% difference would be attributed to the random error term (that is, $\epsilon_A = +2\%$).

random error term

The random error term can be viewed as a random variable that has a probability distribution with a mean of zero and a standard deviation denoted $\sigma_{\epsilon i}$. That is, it can be viewed as the outcome that results from the spin of a roulette wheel.

For example, security A may be thought of as having a random error term corresponding to a roulette wheel with integer values on it that range from −10% to +10%, with the values evenly spaced.[10] This means that there are 21 possible outcomes, each of which has an equal probability of occurring. Given the range of numbers, it also means that the expected outcome of the random error term is zero:

$$[-10 \times 1/21] + [-9 \times 1/21] + \ldots + [9 \times 1/21] + [10 \times 1/21] = 0.$$

As can be seen, this calculation involves multiplying each outcome by its probability of occurring and then summing up the resulting products. The

[10]Since the range refers to the possible outcomes and the spacing refers to the probabilities of the various outcomes occurring, it can be seen that the roulette wheel is just a convenient way of referring to the random error term's probability distribution. Typically, it is assumed that a random error term has a normal distribution.

standard deviation of this random error term can now be shown to be equal to 6.06%:

$$\{[(-10-0)^2 \times 1/21] + [(-9-0)^2 \times 1/21] + \dots + [(9-0)^2 \times 1/21] + [(10-0)^2 \times 1/21]\}^{1/2} = 6.06\%.$$

This calculation involves subtracting the expected outcome from each possible outcome, then squaring each one of these differences, multiplying each square by the probability of the corresponding outcome occurring, adding the products, and finally taking the square root of the resulting sum.

Figure 8-8 illustrates the roulette wheel corresponding to this random error term. In general, securities will have random error terms whose corresponding roulette wheels have different ranges and different forms of uneven spacing. While all of them will have an expected value of zero, they will typically have different standard deviations. For example, security B may have a random error term whose expected value and standard deviation are equal to zero and 4.76%, respectively.[11]

[11]This would be the case if security B had a random error term whose roulette wheel had integers from −9% to +9% on it, but the spacing for each integer between −5% and +5% was twice as large as the spacing for each integer from −9% to −6% and +6% to +9%. This means that the probability of any specific integer between −5% and +5% occurring is equal to 2/30, while the probability of any specific integer from −9% to −6% and +6% to +9% occurring is equal to 1/30.

FIGURE 8-8
Security A's Random Error Term

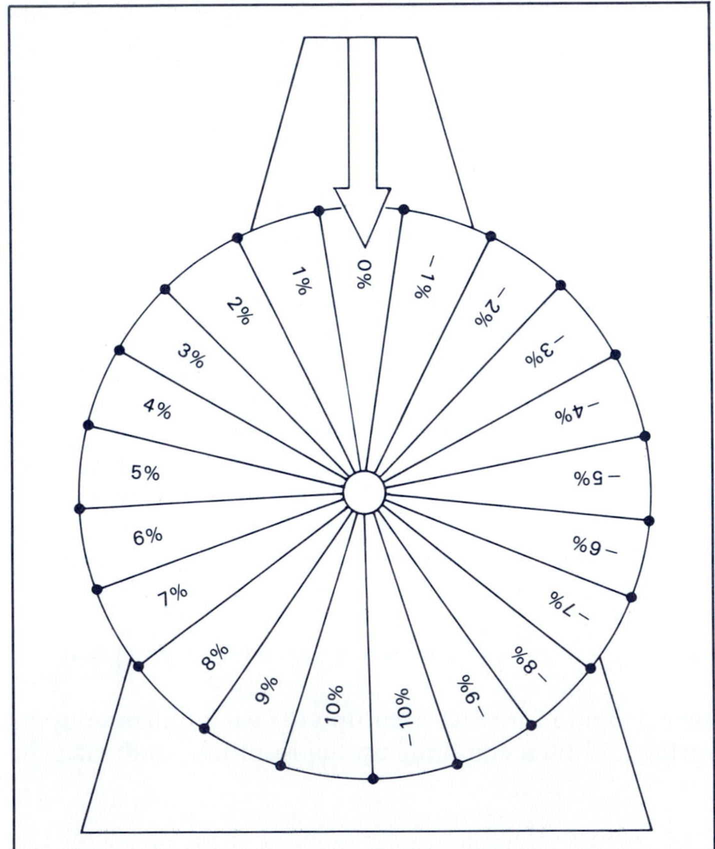

Graphical Representation of the Market Model

The solid line in panel (a) of Figure 8-9 provides a graph of the market model for security A. This line corresponds to equation (8.10), but without the random error term. Accordingly, the line that is graphed for security A is:

$$r_A = 2\% + 1.2r_I. \tag{8.12}$$

Here the vertical axis measures the return on the particular security (r_A) while the horizontal axis measures the return on the market index (r_I). The line goes through the point on the vertical axis corresponding to the value of α_A, which in this case is 2%. In addition, the line has a slope equal to β_A, or 1.2.

Panel (b) of Figure 8-9 presents the graph of the market model for security B. The line can be expressed as the following equation:

$$r_B = -1\% + .8r_I. \tag{8.13}$$

This line goes through the point on the vertical axis corresponding to the value of α_B, −1%. Note that its slope is equal to β_B, or .8.

Beta

At this point it can be seen that the slope in a security's market model measures the sensitivity of the security's returns to the market index's returns. Both lines in Figure 8-9 have positive slopes, indicating that the higher the returns of the market index, the higher the returns of the two securities. However, the two securities have different slopes, indicating that they have different sensitivities to the returns of the market index. Specifically, A has a higher slope than B, indicating that the returns of A are more sensitive than the returns of B to the returns of the market index.

For example, if the market index has a return of 10%, it will have returned 5% more than expected (assuming its expected return was 5%). Panel (a) of Figure 8-9 indicates that security A should have a return that is 6% (= 14% − 8%) greater than initially expected. Similarly, panel (b) indicates that security B should have a return that is 4% (= 7% − 3%) greater than

FIGURE 8-9
Market Model

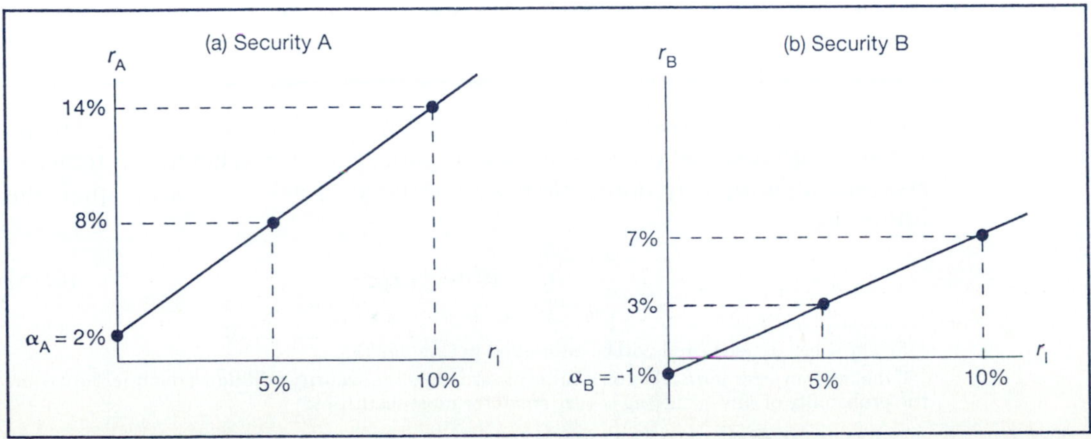

beta

initially expected. The reason for the 2% (= 6% − 4%) difference is that security A has a higher slope than security B—that is, A is more sensitive than B to returns on the market index.

The slope term in the market model is often referred to as **beta,** and is equal to:

$$\beta_i = \sigma_{iI}/\sigma_I^2 \tag{8.14}$$

where σ_{iI} denotes the covariance of the returns on stock i and the market index and σ_I^2 denotes the variance of returns on the market index. A stock that has a return that mirrors the return on the market index will have a beta equal to one (and an intercept of zero, resulting in a market model that is $r_i = r_I + \epsilon_i$). Hence, stocks with betas greater than one (such as A) are more volatile than the market index and are known as **aggressive stocks.** In contrast, stocks with betas less than one (such as B) are less volatile than the market index and are known as **defensive stocks.**[12]

aggressive stocks

defensive stocks

Actual Returns

The random error term suggests that for a given return on the market index, the actual return on a security will usually lie off the line shown by its graph.[13] If the actual returns on securities A and B turn out to be 9% and 11%, respectively, and the market index's actual return turns out to be 10%, then the actual return on A and B could be viewed as having the following three components:

	SECURITY A	SECURITY B
Intercept	2%	−1%
Actual return on the market index × beta	12% = 10% × 1.2	8% = 10% × .8
Random error outcome	−5% = 9% − (2% + 12%)	4% = 11% − (−1% + 8%)
Actual return	9%	11%

In this case, the roulette wheels for A and B can be thought of as having been "spun," resulting in values (that is, random error outcomes) of −5% for A and +4% for B. These values can be viewed as being equal to the vertical distance by which each security's actual return ended up being off its market model line, as shown in Figure 8-10.

DIVERSIFICATION

market risk

unique risk

According to the market model, the total risk of any security i, measured by its variance and denoted σ_i^2, consists of two parts: (1) the **market** (or systematic) **risk;** and (2) **unique** (or nonmarket or unsystematic) **risk.** That is, σ_i^2 equals the following:

$$\sigma_i^2 = \beta_i^2\sigma_I^2 + \sigma_{\epsilon i}^2 \tag{8.15}$$

[12]Just how beta is estimated will be addressed in Chapter 13.

[13]If the random error term takes on a value of zero, then the security will lie *on* the line. However, the probability of this occurring is very small for most securities.

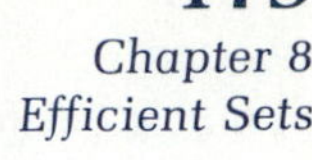

FIGURE 8-10
Market Model and Actual Returns

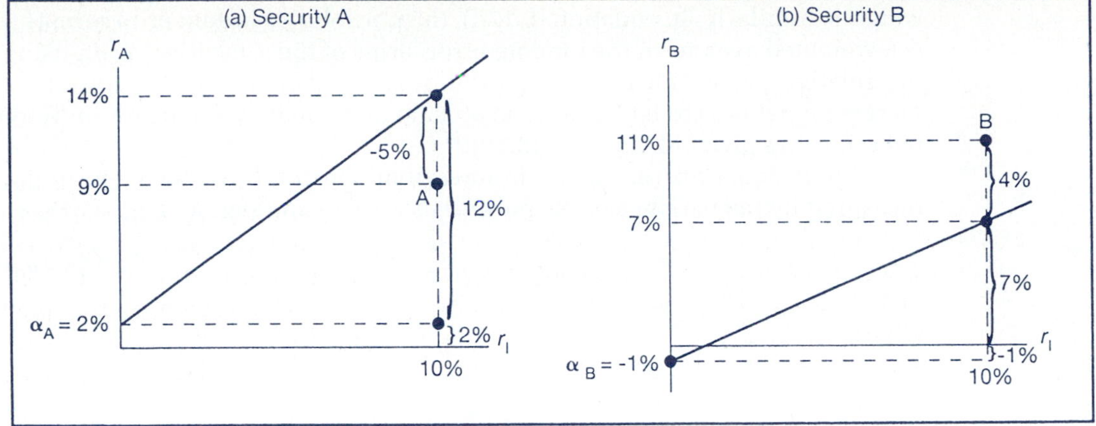

where σ_I^2 denotes the variance of returns on the market index. Thus, $\beta_i^2\sigma_I^2$ denotes the market risk of security i and $\sigma_{\epsilon i}^2$ denotes the unique risk of security i as measured by the variance of the random error term, ϵ_i, appearing in equation (8.10).

Portfolio Total Risk

When the return on every risky *security* is related to the return on the market index as specified by the market model, what can be said about the total risk of a *portfolio*? If the proportion of funds invested in security i for a given portfolio p is denoted X_i, then the return on this portfolio will be:

$$r_p = \sum_{i=1}^{N} X_i r_i. \tag{8.16}$$

Substituting the right-hand side of equation (8.10) for r_i in equation (8.16) results in the following market model for the portfolio:

$$\begin{aligned} r_p &= \sum_{i=1}^{N} X_i(\alpha_i + \beta_i r_I + \epsilon_i) \\ &= \sum_{i=1}^{N} X_i\alpha_i + \left(\sum_{i=1}^{N} X_i\beta_i\right) r_I + \sum_{i=1}^{N} X_i\epsilon_i \\ &= \alpha_p + \beta_p r_I + \epsilon_p \end{aligned} \tag{8.17a}$$

where:

$$\alpha_p = \sum_{i=1}^{N} X_i\alpha_i \tag{8.17b}$$

$$\beta_p = \sum_{i=1}^{N} X_i\beta_i \tag{8.17c}$$

$$\epsilon_p = \sum_{i=1}^{N} X_i\epsilon_i \tag{8.17d}$$

In equations (8.17b) and (8.17c), the portfolio's vertical intercept (α_p) and beta (β_p) are shown to be weighted averages of the intercepts and betas of the securities, respectively, using their relative proportions in the portfolio as weights. Similarly, in equation (8.17d), the portfolio's random error term (ϵ_p) is a weighted average of the random error terms of the securities, again using the relative proportions in the portfolio as weights. Thus, the portfolio's market model is a straightforward extension of the market model for individual securities given in equation (8.10).[14]

From equation (8.17a), it follows that the total risk of a portfolio, measured by the variance of the portfolio's returns and denoted σ_p^2, will be:

$$\sigma_p^2 = \beta_p^2 \sigma_I^2 + \sigma_{\epsilon p}^2 \tag{8.18a}$$

where:

$$\beta_p^2 = \left(\sum_{i=1}^{N} X_i \beta_i \right)^2 \tag{8.18b}$$

and, assuming the random error components of security returns are uncorrelated:

$$\sigma_{\epsilon p}^2 = \sum_{i=1}^{N} X_i^2 \sigma_{\epsilon i}^2. \tag{8.18c}$$

Equation (8.18a) shows that the total risk of any portfolio can be viewed as having two components similar to the two components of the total risk of an individual security. These components are again referred to as market risk ($\beta_p^2 \sigma_I^2$) and unique risk ($\sigma_{\epsilon p}^2$).

diversification

Next, it will be shown that increased **diversification** can lead to the reduction of a portfolio's total risk. This will occur due to a reduction in the size of the portfolio's unique risk, while the portfolio's market risk will remain approximately the same size.

Portfolio Market Risk

Generally, the more diversified a portfolio (that is, the larger the number of securities in the portfolio), the smaller will be each proportion X_i. This will not cause β_p to either decrease or increase significantly unless a deliberate attempt is made to do so by adding either relatively low or high beta securities, respectively, to the portfolio. That is, since a portfolio's beta is an average of the betas of its securities, there is no reason to suspect that increasing the amount of diversification will cause the portfolio beta, and thus the market risk of the portfolio, to change in a particular direction. Accordingly,

Diversification leads to *averaging* of market risk.

This makes sense because when prospects for the economy turn sour (or rosy), most securities will fall (or rise) in price. Regardless of the amount of

[14]Appendix B shows how the market model can be used to estimate expected returns, variances, and covariances for the securities in the feasible set; with these estimates in hand, the efficient set can subsequently be determined. See footnote 6.

diversification, portfolio returns will always be susceptible to such market-wide influences.

Portfolio Unique Risk

The situation is entirely different for unique risk. In a portfolio, some securities will go up as a result of unexpected good news specific to the company that issued the securities (such as an unexpected approval of a patent). Other securities will go down as a result of unexpected company-specific bad news (such as an industrial accident). Looking forward, approximately as many companies can be expected to have good news as bad news, leading to little anticipated net impact on the return of a "well-diversified" portfolio. This means that as a portfolio becomes more diversified, the smaller will be its unique risk and, in turn, its total risk.

This can be quantified precisely if the random error components of security returns are assumed to be uncorrelated, as was done when equation (8.18c) was written. Consider the following situation. If the amount invested in each security is equal, then the proportion X_i will equal $1/N$ and the level of unique risk, as shown in equation (8.18c), will be equal to:

$$\sigma^2_{\epsilon p} = \sum_{i=1}^{N} \left[\frac{1}{N}\right]^2 \sigma^2_{\epsilon i} \tag{8.19a}$$

$$= \frac{1}{N} \left[\frac{(\sigma^2_{\epsilon 1} + \sigma^2_{\epsilon 2} + \ldots + \sigma^2_{\epsilon N})}{N} \right]. \tag{8.19b}$$

The value inside the square brackets in equation (8.19b) is simply the average unique risk of the component securities. But the portfolio's unique risk is only one-Nth as large as this, since the term $1/N$ appears outside the square brackets. Now as the portfolio becomes more diversified, the number of securities in it (that is, N) becomes larger. In turn, this means that $1/N$ becomes smaller, resulting in the portfolio having less unique risk.[15] That is,

Diversification can substantially *reduce* unique risk.

Roughly speaking, a portfolio that has 30 or more securities in it will have a relatively small amount of unique risk. This means that its total risk will be only slightly greater than the amount of market risk that is present. Thus, such portfolios are "well diversified." Figure 8-11 illustrates how diversification results in the reduction of unique risk but the averaging of market risk.

An Example

Consider the two securities, A and B, that were referred to earlier. These two securities had betas of 1.2 and .8, respectively; the standard deviations of their random error terms were, respectively, 6.06% and 4.76%. Thus, given that $\sigma_{\epsilon A} = 6.06\%$ and $\sigma_{\epsilon B} = 4.76\%$, it follows that $\sigma^2_{\epsilon A} = 6.06^2 = 37$ and $\sigma^2_{\epsilon B} = 4.76^2 = 23$. Now, assume that the standard deviation of the market

---

[15] Actually, all that is necessary for this reduction in unique risk to occur is for the maximum amount invested in any one security to continually decrease as N increases.

FIGURE 8-11
Risk and Diversification

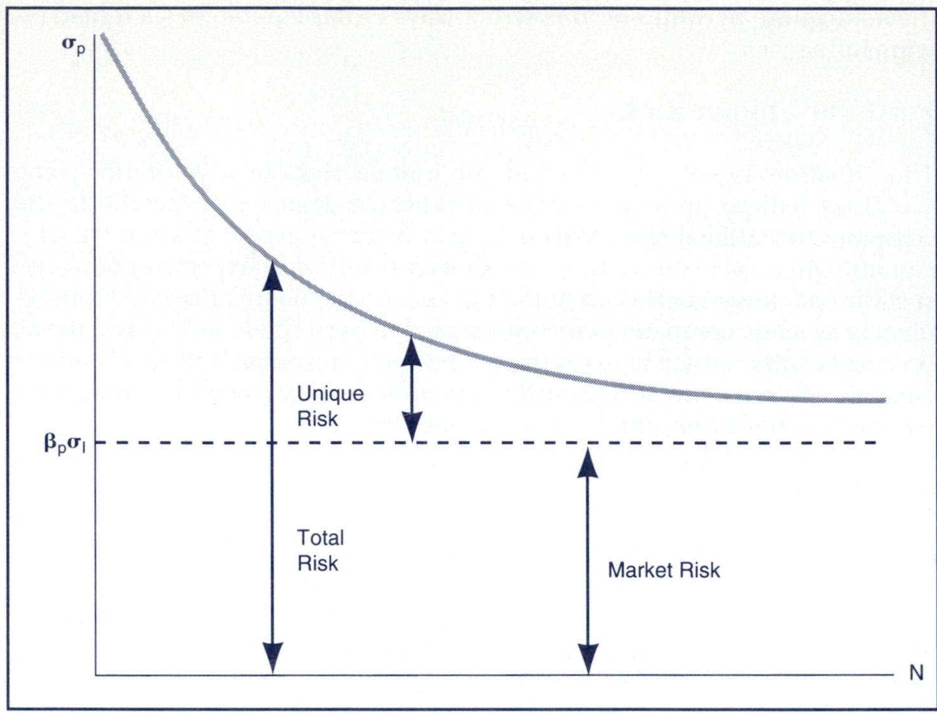

index, $\sigma_{I,}$ is 8%, which implies that the variance of the market index is $8^2 = 64$. Using equation (8.15), this means that the variances of securities A and B are as follows:

$$\begin{aligned}\sigma_A^2 &= (1.2^2 \times 64) + 37 \\ &= 129 \\ \sigma_B^2 &= (.8^2 \times 64) + 23 \\ &= 64.\end{aligned}$$

A Two-Security Portfolio Consider combining securities A and B into a portfolio, with an equal amount of the investor's money going into each security. That is, consider a portfolio that has $X_A = .5$ and $X_B = .5$. Since $\beta_A = 1.2$ and $\beta_B = .8$, the beta of this portfolio can be calculated using equation (8.17c):

$$\begin{aligned}\beta_p &= X_A\beta_A + X_B\beta_B \\ &= (.5 \times 1.2) + (.5 \times .8) \\ &= 1.0.\end{aligned}$$

Using equation (8.18c), the variance of the portfolio's random error term, $\sigma_{\epsilon p,}^2$ will be equal to:

$$\begin{aligned}\sigma_{\epsilon p}^2 &= (.5^2 \times 37) + (.5^2 \times 23) \\ &= 15.\end{aligned}$$

From equation (8.18a), it can be seen that this portfolio will have the following variance:

$$\sigma_p^2 = (1.0^2 \times 64) + 15$$
$$= 79.$$

This represents the total risk of the two-security portfolio.

A Three-Security Portfolio Consider what would happen if a third security (C) was combined with the other two to form a three-security portfolio having $X_A = X_B = X_C = .33$. This third security has a beta of 1.0 and a random error term whose standard deviation ($\sigma_{\epsilon C}$) is 5.50%. Thus, the variance of the random error term is $\sigma_{\epsilon C}^2 = 5.5^2 = 30$, and the security's variance is:

$$\sigma_C^2 = (1.0^2 \times 64) + 30$$
$$= 94$$

First of all, note that the three-security portfolio has the same amount of market risk as the two-security portfolio, since both portfolios have a beta of 1.0:

$$\beta_p = X_A\beta_A + X_B\beta_B + X_C\beta_C$$
$$= (.33 \times 1.2) + (.33 \times .8) + (.33 \times 1.0)$$
$$= 1.0.$$

Thus, increased diversification has not led to a change in the level of market risk. Instead, it has led to an averaging of market risk.

Using equation (8.18c), the variance of the portfolio's random error term will be equal to:

$$\sigma_{\epsilon p}^2 = (.33^2 \times 37) + (.33^2 \times 23) + (.33^2 \times 30)$$
$$= 10.$$

Note that the variance of this three-security portfolio's random error term is less than the variance of the two-security portfolio's random error term (that is, $10 < 15$). Thus, in this example, increased diversification has indeed reduced unique risk.

From equation (8.18a), it can be seen that this three-security portfolio will have the following variance:

$$\sigma_p^2 = (1.0^2 \times 64) + 10$$
$$= 74.$$

This represents the total risk of the portfolio, and is less than the total risk of the two-security portfolio ($74 < 79$). Thus, increased diversification has led to a reduction in total risk.

SUMMARY

1. The expected return on a portfolio is a weighted average of the expected returns of its component securities, with the relative portfolio proportions of the component securities serving as weights.

2. Covariance and correlation measure the extent to which two random variables "move together."

3. The standard deviation of a portfolio depends on the standard deviations and proportions of the component securities as well as their covariances with one another.

4. The efficient set contains those portfolios that offer both maximum expected return for varying levels of risk and minimum risk for varying levels of expected return.

5. Investors are assumed to select their optimal portfolios from among the portfolios lying on the efficient set.

6. An investor's optimal portfolio is identified as the tangency point between the investor's indifference curves and the efficient set.

7. The proposition that the efficient set is concave follows from the definition of portfolio standard deviation and the existence of assets whose returns are not perfectly positively or negatively correlated.

8. Diversification usually leads to risk reduction, because the standard deviation of a portfolio generally will be less than a weighted average of the standard deviations of the component securities.

9. The relationship between the return on a security and the return on a market index is known as the market model.

10. The market index's return does not completely explain the return on a security. The unexplained elements are captured by the random error term of the market model.

11. The slope in a security's market model measures the sensitivity of the security's return to the market index's return. The slope term is known as the security's beta.

12. According to the market model, the total risk of a security consists of market (systematic) risk and unique (nonmarket or unsystematic) risk.

13. A portfolio's vertical intercept, beta, and random error term are weighted averages of the component securities' intercepts, betas, and random error terms, respectively, with the securities' relative proportions in the portfolio serving as weights.

14. Diversification leads to an averaging of market risk.

15. Diversification can substantially reduce unique risk.

KEY TERMS

expected return vector
probability distribution
normal distribution
covariance
correlation coefficient
variance
variance-covariance matrix
efficient set theorem
efficient set
feasible set
efficient portfolios
inefficient portfolios
optimal portfolio
market model
random error term
beta
aggressive stocks
defensive stocks
market risk
unique risk
diversification

QUESTIONS AND PROBLEMS

1. Squeaky Bluege has been considering an investment in Oakdale Merchandising. Squeaky has estimated the following probability distribution of returns for Oakdale stock:

RETURN	PROBABILITY
−10%	.10
0	.25
10	.40
20	.20
30	.05

Based on Squeaky's estimates, calculate the expected return and standard deviation of Oakdale stock.

2. Gibby Brock has estimated the following joint probability distribution of returns for investments in the stock of Lakeland Halfway Homes and Afton Brewery:

LAKELAND	AFTON	PROBABILITY
−10%	15%	.15
5	10	.20
10	5	.30
20	0	.35

Based on Gibby's estimates, calculate the covariance and correlation coefficient between those two investments.

3. Calculate the correlation matrix that corresponds to the variance-covariance matrix given in the text for Able, Baker, and Charlie.

4. At the beginning of 1991, Corns Bradley owned four securities in the following amounts and with the following current and expected end-of-year prices:

SECURITY	SHARE AMOUNT	CURRENT PRICE	EXPECTED YEAR-END PRICE
A	100	$50	$60
B	200	35	40
C	50	25	50
D	100	100	110

What is the expected return on Corns' portfolio in 1991?

5. Given the following information about four stocks comprising a portfolio, calculate each stock's expected return. Then, using these individual security expected returns, calculate the portfolio's expected return.

STOCK	INITIAL INVESTMENT VALUE	EXPECTED END-OF-PERIOD INVESTMENT VALUE	PROPORTION OF PORTFOLIO INITIAL MARKET VALUE
A	$500	$700	19.2%
B	200	300	7.7
C	1,000	1,000	38.5
D	900	1,500	34.6

6. Both the covariance and the correlation coefficient measure the extent to which the returns on securities move together. What is the relationship between the two statistical measures? Why is the correlation coefficient a more convenient measure?

7. Given the following variance-covariance matrix for three securities, as well as the percentage of the portfolio that each security comprises, calculate the portfolio's standard deviation.

	SECURITY A	SECURITY B	SECURITY C
Security A	459	−211	112
Security B	−211	312	215
Security C	112	215	179
	$X_A = .50$	$X_B = .30$	$X_C = .20$

8. Rube Bressler owns three stocks and has estimated the following joint probability distribution of returns:

OUTCOME	STOCK A	STOCK B	STOCK C	PROBABILITY
1	−10	10	0	.30
2	0	10	10	.20
3	10	5	15	.30
4	20	−10	5	.20

Calculate the portfolio's expected return and standard deviation if Rube invests 20% in stock A, 50% in stock B, and 30% in stock C. Assume that each security's return is completely uncorrelated with the returns of the other securities.

9. If a portfolio's expected return is equal to the weighted average of the expected returns of the component securities, why is a portfolio's risk not generally equal to the weighted average of the component securities' standard deviations?

10. When is the standard deviation of a portfolio equal to the weighted average of the standard deviation of the component securities? Show this mathematically for a two-security portfolio. (Hint: Some algebra is necessary to solve this problem. Remember that $\sigma_{ij} = \rho_{ij}\sigma_i\sigma_j$. Try different values of ρ_{ij}.)

11. Listed below are estimates of the standard deviations and correlation coefficients for three stocks.

STOCK	STANDARD DEVIATION	CORRELATION WITH STOCK A	B	C
A	12%	1.00	−1.00	0.20
B	15	−1.00	1.00	−0.20
C	10	0.20	−0.20	1.00

(a) If a portfolio is composed of 20% of stock A and 80% of stock C, what is the portfolio's standard deviation?

(b) If the portfolio is composed of 40% of stock A, 20% of stock B, and 40% of stock C, what is the portfolio's standard deviation?

(c) If you were asked to design a portfolio using only stocks A and B, what percentage investment in each stock would produce a zero standard deviation? (Hint: Some algebra is necessary to solve this problem. Remember that $X_B = (1 - X_A)$.)

12. Why would you expect individual securities to generally lie in the "eastern" portion of the feasible set while only portfolios would lie in the "northwestern" portion?

13. Explain why most investors prefer to hold a diversified portfolio of securities as opposed to placing all of their wealth in a single asset. Use an illustration of the feasible and efficient sets to explain your answer.

14. Why would you expect most U.S. common stocks to have positive covariances? Give an example of two stocks that you would expect to have a very high positive covariance. Give an example of two stocks that you would expect to have a very low positive (or even negative) covariance.

15. Discuss why the concepts of covariance and diversification are closely related.

16. In terms of the Markowitz model, explain, using words and graphs, how an investor goes about identifying his or her optimal portfolio. What specific information does an investor need to identify this portfolio?

17. Dode Brinker owns a portfolio of two securities with the following expected returns, standard deviations, and weights:

SECURITY	EXPECTED RETURN	STANDARD DEVIATION	WEIGHT
A	10%	20%	.35
B	15	25	.65

For varying levels of correlation between the two securities, what is the maximum portfolio standard deviation? What is the minimum?

18. Briefly explain why the efficient set must be concave.

19. How is beta derived from a security's market model? Why are high beta securities termed "aggressive"? Why are low beta securities termed "defensive"?

20. In the following table you are presented with ten years of return data for Glenwood City Properties and for a market index. Plot the returns of Glenwood City and the market on a graph, with the market index's returns on the horizontal axis and Glenwood City's returns on the vertical axis. Draw your best guess of the market model through these points. From this graph only, compute an estimate of the beta of Glenwood's stock.

YEAR	GLENWOOD CITY	MARKET INDEX
1	8.1%	8.0%
2	3.0	0.0
3	5.3	14.9
4	1.0	5.0
5	−3.1	−4.1
6	−3.0	−8.9
7	5.0	10.1
8	3.2	5.0
9	1.2	1.5
10	1.3	2.4

21. Consider the stocks of two companies, Woodville Weasel Farms and New Richmond Furriers.

(a) If you are told that the slope of Woodville's market model is 1.20 and that the slope of New Richmond's market model is 1.00, which stock is likely to be more risky in a portfolio context? Why?

(b) If you are now also told that the standard deviation of the random error term for Woodville stock is 10.0%, while it is 21.5% for New Richmond stock, does your answer change? Explain.

22. Two portfolios, one invested in electric utilities and one invested in gold mining companies, each have the same beta of 0.60. Why would a security analyst be interested to know that the gold portfolio has a much larger standard deviation of the random error term (unique risk) than the utility portfolio?

23. Lyndon Station stock has a beta of 1.20. Over five years the following returns were produced by Lyndon stock and a market index. Assuming a market model intercept term of 0%, calculate the standard deviation of the market model random error term over this period.

YEAR	LYNDON RETURN	MARKET RETURN
1	17.2%	14.0%
2	−3.1	−3.0
3	13.3	10.0
4	28.5	25.0
5	9.8	8.0

24. Why does diversification lead to a reduction in unique risk, but not in market risk? Explain both intuitively and mathematically.

25. Siggy Broskie owns a portfolio composed of three securities with the following characteristics:

SECURITY	BETA	STANDARD DEVIATION RANDOM ERROR TERM	PROPORTION
A	1.20	5%	.30
B	1.05	8	.50
C	.90	2	.20

If the standard deviation of the market index is 18%, what is the total risk of Siggy's portfolio?

26. Consider two portfolios, one composed of four securities and one composed of ten securities. All the securities have a beta of 1.00 and unique risk of 30%. Each portfolio distributes weight equally among its component securities. If the standard deviation of the market index is 20%, calculate the total risk of both portfolios.

27. (Appendix Question) Why is the market model approach a simpler technique than the original Markowitz approach for constructing the efficient set?

28. (Appendix Question) How many parameters must be estimated to analyze the risk-return profile of a fifty-stock portfolio using: (a) the original Markowitz approach, and (b) the market model approach?

APPENDIX A

More on the Concavity of the Efficient Set

Earlier, concavity was discussed by showing what happens when two securities (such as Ark Shipping and Gold Jewelry) are combined to form a portfolio. It is important to recognize that the same principles hold if two portfolios are combined to form a third portfolio. That is, point A in Figure 8-7 could represent a portfolio of securities with an expected return of 5% and a standard deviation of 20%, and point G could represent another portfolio of securities with an expected return of 15% and a standard deviation of 40%. Combining these two portfolios will result in a third portfolio that has an expected return and standard deviation dependent upon the proportions invested in A and G. Assuming that the correlation between A and G is zero, the location of the third portfolio will lie on the curved line connecting A and G.

Recognizing this, it can now be shown why the efficient set is concave. One way to do this is to show that it cannot have any other shape. Consider the efficient set shown in Figure A-1. Note that there is a "dent" in it between points U and V. That is, between U and V there is a region on the efficient set where it is not concave. Can this truly be an efficient set? No, since an investor could put part of his or her funds in the portfolio located at U and the rest of his or her funds in the portfolio located at V. The resulting portfolio, a combination of U and V, would have to lie to the left of the alleged efficient set. Thus, the new portfolio would be "more efficient" than a portfolio with the same expected return that was on the alleged efficient set between U and V.

For example, consider the portfolio on the alleged efficient set that lies halfway between U and V; it is indicated as point W in Figure A-2. If it truly is an efficient portfolio, then it would be impossible to form a portfolio with the same expected return as W but with a lower standard deviation. However, by putting 50% of his or her funds in U and 50% in V, the investor would have a portfolio that dominates W, since it would have the same expected return but a lower standard deviation. Why will it have a lower standard deviation? Remember, if the correlation between U and V were +1, this portfolio would lie on the straight line connecting U and V, and would thus have a lower standard deviation than W. In Figure A-1 Z denotes this point. Since the

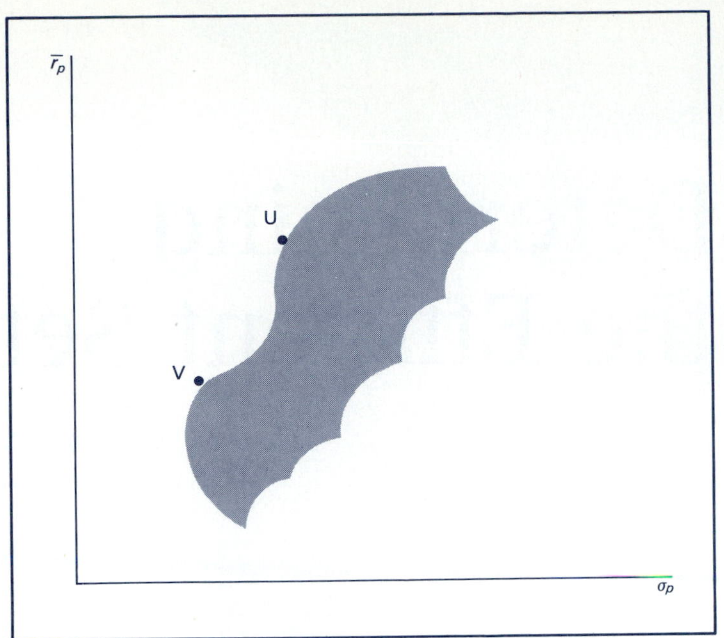

FIGURE A-1
Concavity of the Efficient Set

actual correlation is less than or equal to + 1, it would have a standard deviation as low as or lower than Z's standard deviation. This means that the alleged efficient set was constructed in error, since it is easy to find "more efficient" portfolios in the region where it is not concave.

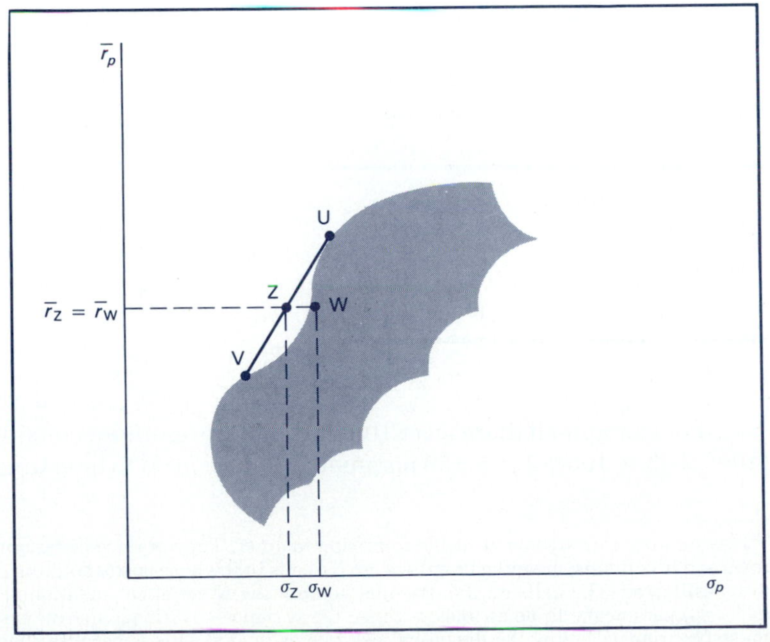

FIGURE A-2
Removing a "Dent" from the Efficient Set

APPENDIX

B Determining the Efficient Set

In order to construct the efficient set, the investor must estimate the expected returns for all the securities under consideration, as well as all of the variances and covariances. Subsequently, the optimal portfolio can be identified by noting where one of the investor's indifference curves is tangent to the efficient set, as shown in Figure 8-3.

Considerable effort is needed to construct this efficient set. First, the expected return for each security must be estimated. Given there are N risky securities, this means that N parameters must be estimated. Second, the variance for each one of these securities must be estimated. Again, since there are N risky securities, this means that another N parameters must be estimated. Third, the covariance between each pair of risky securities must be estimated. There are $(N^2 - N)/2$ of these parameters to be estimated.[16] This means that the total number of parameters that need to be estimated is equal to $(N^2 + 3N)/2$, determined as follows:

Expected returns	N
Variances	N
Covariances	$(N^2 - N)/2$
Total	$(N^2 + 3N)/2$

For example, if there were 100 risky securities under consideration, then $[100^2 + (3 \times 100)]/2 = 5{,}150$ parameters would need to be estimated, consist-

[16]This number was arrived at in the following manner. The variance-covariance matrix has N rows and N columns, meaning that there are N^2 cells in it whose corresponding parameters need to be estimated. The cells on the diagonal contain the N variances mentioned earlier, leaving $(N^2 - N)$ parameters to be estimated. Since the variance-covariance matrix is symmetric, only those covariances below the diagnonal need be estimated (this is because they also appear in corresponding locations above the diagonal), leaving a total of $(N^2 - N)/2$ parameters to be estimated.

ing of 100 expected returns, 100 variances, and 4,950 covariances. These parameters can be estimated one by one, a task that will be quite time-consuming if not, practically speaking, impossible. Alternatively, an approximate approach based on the market model can be used.[17]

With the market model approach, the expected return on the market index must be estimated initially. Then, the vertical intercept and beta for each security must be estimated. At this point, $(1 + 2N)$ parameters have been estimated (1 for $\bar{r}_I$; $2N$ for the vertical intercept and beta for each of the N risky securities). In turn, these figures can be used to estimate the expected return for each security using equation (8.10), restated as follows:

$$\bar{r}_i = \alpha_i + \beta_i\,\bar{r}_I. \tag{8.20}$$

Earlier, the expected return on the market index was estimated to be 5%. Given these figures, the expected return for security A was estimated to be 8%, since the vertical intercept and beta of this security were estimated to be 2% and 1.2, respectively:

$$\begin{aligned}\bar{r}_A &= 2\% + (5\% \times 1.2)\\ &= 8\%.\end{aligned}$$

Similarly, the expected return for security B was estimated to be 3%, since its vertical intercept and beta were estimated to be −1% and .8, respectively:

$$\begin{aligned}\bar{r}_B &= -\,1\% + (5\% \times .8)\\ &= 3\%.\end{aligned}$$

Using the market model approach, the variance of any security i can be estimated by multiplying the squared value of the security's beta by the variance of the market index and then adding the variance of the random error term to the product. The equation for doing this is as follows:

$$\sigma_i^2 = \beta_i^2\sigma_I^2 + \sigma_{\epsilon i}^2 \tag{8.21}$$

where σ_I^2 denotes the variance of the market index and $\sigma_{\epsilon i}^2$ denotes the variance of the random error term for security i.

Assuming the variance on the market index is 49, the variances of security A and B can be estimated as follows:

$$\begin{aligned}\sigma_A^2 &= (1.2^2 \times 49) + 6.06^2\\ &= 107.28,\\ \sigma_B^2 &= (.8^2 \times 49) + 4.76^2\\ &= 54.02,\end{aligned}$$

[17]It is an approximate approach because it makes a number of assumptions, some of which are questionable. For example, this approach assumes that the random error terms for any two securities are uncorrelated [an assumption that was needed in deriving equation (8.18c) and later in (8.22)]. This means that the outcome from a spin of the roulette wheel for one security (such as Mobil) has no bearing on the outcome from a spin of the roulette wheel for any other security (such as Exxon). It has been argued that this is not true for securities within certain industries. See Benjamin F. King, "Market and Industry Factors in Stock Price Behavior," *Journal of Business*, 39, no. 1 (January 1966): 139–70; and James L. Farrell, Jr., "Analyzing Covariation of Returns to Determine Homogeneous Stock Groupings," *Journal of Business*, 47, no. 2 (April 1974): 186–207.

respectively. This means that the standard deviations of these securities are estimated to be equal to $10.38\% = \sqrt{107.28}$ and $7.35\% = \sqrt{54.02}$, respectively.

Lastly, the covariance between any two securities i and j can be estimated by the product of the three numbers: the beta of security i, the beta of security j, and the variance of the market index. That is, the following formula can be used:

$$\sigma_{ij} = \beta_i \beta_j \sigma_I^2 \tag{8.22}$$

Thus, for securities A and B, the estimated covariance would be:

$$\begin{aligned}\sigma_{A,B} &= 1.2 \times .8 \times 49 \\ &= 47.04.\end{aligned}$$

In summary, if the market model approach is used to estimate expected returns, variances, and covariances, then the following parameters must first be estimated:

Expected return on the market index	1
Variance of the market index	1
Vertical intercept for each security	N
Beta for each security	N
Variance of random error term for each security	N
Total	$3N + 2$

Thus, for 100 risky securities, $(3 \times 100) + 2 = 302$ parameters need to be estimated when the market model approach is used to determine the efficient set and tangency portfolio. With this approach, once these 302 parameters have been estimated, then it is a simple matter to use equations (8.21), (8.22), and (8.23) to estimate the expected returns, variances, and covariances for the risky securities. Alternatively, the expected returns, variances, and covariances could be estimated one by one as noted earlier, in which case 5,150 parameters would need to be estimated. As can be seen with this example, the market model approach results in a notable reduction in the number of parameters that need to be estimated.

With the market model approach (or the one-by-one approach), after the expected returns, variances, and covariances have been estimated, a computer can be given these values. Then, using a "quadratic programming algorithm" the computer can proceed to identify the efficient set. At this juncture, the investor's optimal portfolio can be determined by finding the point at which one of the indifference curves is tangent to the efficient set.

REFERENCES

1. As mentioned at the end of Chapter 7, the seminal work developing the mean-variance model is credited to Harry Markowitz, who developed his ideas in a paper and later in a book:

Harry M. Markowitz, "Portfolio Selection," *Journal of Finance*, 7, no. 1 (March 1952): 77–91;

Harry M. Markowitz, *Portfolio Selection: Efficient Diversification of Investments* (New York: John Wiley & Sons, 1959). (A reprint of this book that also contains some new material is available from Basil Blackwell, Inc., in Cambridge, Mass.; its copyright date is 1991.)

2. The technique used for determining the location of the efficient set along with the composition of the "corner portfolios" that lie on it was developed in:

Harry M. Markowitz, "The Optimization of a Quadratic Function Subject to Linear Constraints," *Naval Research Logistics Quarterly*, 3, nos. 1–2 (March–June 1956): 111–33.

3. The market model, initially mentioned by Markowitz in a footnote on p. 100 of his book, was developed in:

William F. Sharpe, "A Simplified Model for Portfolio Analysis," *Management Science*, 9, no. 2 (January 1963): 277–93.

4. An extensive discussion of the market model can be found in chapters 3 and 4 of:

Eugene F. Fama, *Foundations of Finance* (New York: Basic Books, Inc., 1976).

5. For discussions of how diversification reduces market risk, see:

John L. Evans and Stephen H. Archer, "Diversification and the Reduction of Dispersion: An Empirical Analysis," *Journal of Finance*, 23, no. 5 (December 1968): 761–67;

W. H. Wagner and S. C. Lau, "The Effect of Diversification on Risk," *Financial Analysts Journal*, 27, no. 6 (November–December 1971): 48–53;

Meir Statman, "How Many Stocks Make a Diversified Portfolio?" *Journal of Financial and Quantitative Analysis*, 22, no. 3 (September 1987): 353–63.

6. A discussion of some statistical problems that are encountered in partitioning total risk is contained in:

Bert Stine and Dwayne Key, "Reconciling Degrees of Freedom When Partitioning Risk: A Teaching Note," *Journal of Financial Education*, 19 (Fall 1990): 19–22.

9

Riskfree Lending and Borrowing

The previous two chapters focused on how an investor should go about determining what portfolio to select for investment. With Markowitz's approach, the investor is assumed to have a certain amount of initial wealth (W_0) to invest for a given holding period. Of all the portfolios that are available, the optimal one was shown to correspond to the point where one of the investor's indifference curves is tangent to the efficient set. At the end of the holding period, the investor's initial wealth will have either increased or decreased, depending on the portfolio's rate of return. The resulting end-of-period wealth (W_1) could then be either completely reinvested, completely spent on consumption, or partially reinvested and partially consumed.

With the Markowitz approach, it is assumed that the assets being considered for investment are individually risky. That is, each one of the N risky assets has an uncertain return over the investor's holding period. Since none of the assets has a perfectly negative correlation with any other asset, all the portfolios also have uncertain returns over the investor's holding period, and thus are risky. Furthermore, with the Markowitz approach, the investor is not allowed to use borrowed money, along with his or her initial wealth, to purchase a portfolio of assets. This means that the investor is not allowed to use financial leverage, which in Chapter 2 was referred to as margin.

In this chapter, the Markowitz approach to investing is expanded by first allowing the investor to consider investing in not only risky assets but also in a riskfree asset. That is, there will now be N assets available for purchase, consisting of $N - 1$ risky assets and one riskfree asset. Second, the investor will be allowed to borrow money, but will have to pay a given rate of interest on the loan. The next section considers the effect of adding a riskfree asset to the set of risky assets.

DEFINING THE RISKFREE ASSET

riskfree asset

What exactly is a **riskfree asset** in the context of Markowitz's approach? Since this approach involves investing for a single holding period, it means that the return on the riskfree asset is certain. That is, if the investor purchases this asset at the beginning of the holding period, then he or she knows exactly what the value of the asset will be at the end of the holding period. Since there is no uncertainty about the terminal value of the riskfree asset, the standard deviation of the riskfree asset is, by definition, zero.

In turn, this means that the covariance between the rate of return on the riskfree asset and the rate of return on any risky asset is zero. This can be seen by remembering that the covariance between the returns on any two assets i and j is equal to the product of the correlation coefficient between the assets and the standard deviations of the two assets: $\sigma_{ij} = \rho_{ij}\sigma_i\sigma_j$. Given that $\sigma_i = 0$ if i is the riskfree asset, it follows that $\sigma_{ij} = 0$.

Since a riskfree asset has, by definition, a certain return, this type of asset must be some kind of fixed-income security with no possibility of default. Since all corporate securities have some chance of default, the riskfree asset cannot be issued by a corporation. Instead, it must be a security issued by the federal government. However, not just any security issued by the U.S. Treasury qualifies as a riskfree security.

Consider an investor with a three-month holding period who purchases a Treasury security maturing in 20 years. Such a security is risky since the investor does not know what this security will be worth at the end of his or her holding period. That is, interest rates very likely will have changed in an unpredictable manner during the investor's holding period, meaning that the market price of the security will have changed in an unpredictable manner.

interest-rate risk

Since the presence of such **interest-rate risk** makes the value of the Treasury security uncertain, it cannot qualify as a riskfree asset. Indeed, any Treasury security with a maturity date greater than the investor's holding period cannot qualify as a riskfree asset, regardless of whether it matures one day or 19¾ years after the end of the investor's holding period.

Next, consider a Treasury security that matures before the end of the investor's holding period, such as a 30-day Treasury bill in the case of the investor with the three-month holding period. In this situation, the investor does not know at the beginning of the holding period what interest rates will be in 30 days. This means that the investor does not know the interest rate at which the proceeds from the maturing Treasury bill can be reinvested (that is, "rolled over") for the remainder of the holding period. The presence of such

reinvestment-rate risk

reinvestment-rate risk in all Treasury securities of shorter maturity than the investor's holding period means that these securities do not qualify as a riskfree asset.

This leaves only one type of Treasury security to qualify as a riskfree asset—a Treasury security with a maturity that matches the length of the investor's holding period. For example, the investor with the three-month holding period would find that a Treasury bill with a three-month maturity date had a certain return. Since this security matures at the end of the investor's holding period, it provides the investor with an amount of money at the end of the holding period that is known for certain at the beginning of the holding period when an investment decision has to be made.[1]

Investing in the riskfree asset is often referred to as **riskfree lending,** since such an investment involves the purchase of Treasury bills, and thus involves a loan by the investor to the federal government.

riskfree lending

ALLOWING FOR RISKFREE LENDING

With the introduction of a riskfree asset, the investor is now able to put part of his or her money in this asset and the remainder in any of the risky portfolios that are in Markowitz's feasible set. Adding these new opportunities expands the feasible set significantly and, more importantly, changes the location of part of Markowitz's efficient set. The nature of these changes needs to be analyzed, since investors are concerned with selecting a portfolio from the efficient set. In doing so, consideration is given initially to determining the expected return and standard deviation for a portfolio that consists of combining an investment in the riskfree asset with an investment in a single risky security.

Investing in Both the Riskfree Asset and a Risky Asset

In Chapter 8, the companies of Able, Baker, and Charlie were assumed to have expected returns, variances, and covariances as indicated in the following expected return vector and variance-covariance matrix:

$$ER = \begin{bmatrix} 16.2 \\ 24.6 \\ 22.8 \end{bmatrix} \quad VC = \begin{bmatrix} 146 & 187 & 145 \\ 187 & 854 & 104 \\ 145 & 104 & 289 \end{bmatrix}$$

Defining the riskfree asset as security number 4, consider all portfolios that involve investing in just the common stock of Able and the riskfree asset. Let X_1 denote the proportion of the investor's funds invested in Able and $X_4 = 1 - X_1$ denote the proportion invested in the riskfree asset. If the investor put all of his or her money in the riskfree asset, then $X_1 = 0$ and $X_4 = 1$. Alternatively, the investor could put all of his or her money in just Able, in which case $X_1 = 1$ and $X_4 = 0$. A combination of .25 in Able and .75 in the riskfree asset is also possible, as are respective combinations of .50 and

[1]To be truly riskfree, the security must not provide the investor with any coupon payments during the holding period. Instead, it must provide the investor with only one cash inflow, and that inflow must occur at the end of the investor's holding period. Any intervening coupon payments would subject the investor to reinvestment-rate risk, since he or she would not know the rate at which the coupon payments could be invested for the remainder of the holding period. It should also be noted that the discussion has focused on an asset that is riskfree in nominal terms, since the presence of uncertain inflation means that virtually all Treasury securities are risky in real terms.

.50, and .75 and .25. While there are other possibilities, the focus here will be on these five portfolios.

	PORTFOLIO A	PORTFOLIO B	PORTFOLIO C	PORTFOLIO D	PORTFOLIO E
X_1	.00	.25	.50	.75	1.00
X_4	1.00	.75	.50	.25	.00

Assuming that the riskfree asset has a rate of return (often denoted r_f) of 4%, all the necessary information for calculating the expected returns and standard deviations for these five portfolios is at hand. Equation (8.1a) from the previous chapter can be used to calculate the expected returns for these portfolios:

$$\bar{r}_p = \sum_{i=1}^{N} X_i \bar{r}_i \tag{8.1a}$$

$$= \sum_{i=1}^{4} X_i \bar{r}_i .$$

Now, portfolios A, B, C, D, and E do not involve investing in the second and third securities (that is, Baker and Charlie companies), meaning that $X_2 = 0$ and $X_3 = 0$ in these portfolios. Thus, the previous equation reduces to:

$$\bar{r}_p = X_1 \bar{r}_1 + X_4 \bar{r}_4$$

$$= (X_1 \times 16.2\%) + (X_4 \times 4\%)$$

where the riskfree rate is now denoted $\bar{r}_4$.

For portfolios A and E this calculation is trivial, since all the investor's funds are being placed in just one security. Thus, their expected returns are just 4% and 16.2%, respectively. For portfolios B, C, and D, the expected returns are, respectively:

$$\bar{r}_B = (.25 \times 16.2\%) + (.75 \times 4\%)$$

$$= 7.05\%$$

$$\bar{r}_C = (.50 \times 16.2\%) + (.50 \times 4\%)$$

$$= 10.10\%$$

$$\bar{r}_D = (.75 \times 16.2\%) + (.25 \times 4\%)$$

$$= 13.15\%.$$

The standard deviations of portfolios A and E are simply the standard deviations of the riskfree asset and Able, respectively. Thus, $\sigma_A = 0\%$ and $\sigma_E = 12.08\%$. In calculating the standard deviations of portfolios B, C, and D, equation (8.5) from the previous chapter must be utilized:

$$\sigma_p = \left[\sum_{i=1}^{N} \sum_{j=1}^{N} X_i X_j \sigma_{ij} \right]^{1/2} \tag{8.5}$$

$$= \left[\sum_{i=1}^{4} \sum_{j=1}^{4} X_i X_j \sigma_{ij} \right]^{1/2} .$$

Remembering that $X_2 = 0$ and $X_3 = 0$ in these portfolios, this equation reduces to:

$$\begin{aligned}\sigma_p &= [X_1X_1\sigma_{11} + X_1X_4\sigma_{14} \\ &\quad + X_4X_1\sigma_{41} + X_4X_4\sigma_{44}]^{1/2} \\ &= [X_1^2\sigma_1^2 + X_4^2\sigma_4^2 + 2X_1X_4\sigma_{14}]^{1/2}.\end{aligned}$$

This equation can be reduced even further, since security number 4 is the riskfree security that, by definition, has $\sigma_4 = 0$ and $\sigma_{14} = 0$. Accordingly, it reduces to:

$$\begin{aligned}\sigma_p &= [X_1^2\sigma_1^2]^{1/2} \\ &= [X_1^2 \times 146]^{1/2} \\ &= X_1 \times 12.08\%.\end{aligned}$$

Thus, the standard deviations of portfolios B, C, and D are:

$$\begin{aligned}\sigma_B &= .25 \times 12.08\% \\ &= 3.02\%, \\ \sigma_C &= .50 \times 12.08\% \\ &= 6.04\%, \\ \sigma_D &= .75 \times 12.08\% \\ &= 9.06\%.\end{aligned}$$

In summary, the five portfolios have the following expected returns and standard deviations:

PORTFOLIO	X_1	X_4	EXPECTED RETURN	STANDARD DEVIATION
A	.00	1.00	4.00%	0.00%
B	.25	.75	7.05	3.02
C	.50	.50	10.10	6.04
D	.75	.25	13.15	9.06
E	1.00	.00	16.20	12.08

These portfolios are plotted in Figure 9-1. It can be seen that they all lie on a straight line connecting the points representing the location of the riskfree asset and Able. While only five particular combinations of the riskfree asset and Able have been examined here, it can be shown that any combination of the riskfree asset and Able will lie somewhere on the straight line connecting them; the exact location will depend on the relative proportions invested in these two assets. Furthermore, this observation can be generalized to combinations of the riskfree asset and any risky asset. That is, any portfolio that consists of a combination of the riskfree asset and a risky asset will have an expected return and standard deviation such that it plots somewhere on a straight line connecting them.

FIGURE 9-1
Combining Riskfree Lending with Investing in a Risky Asset

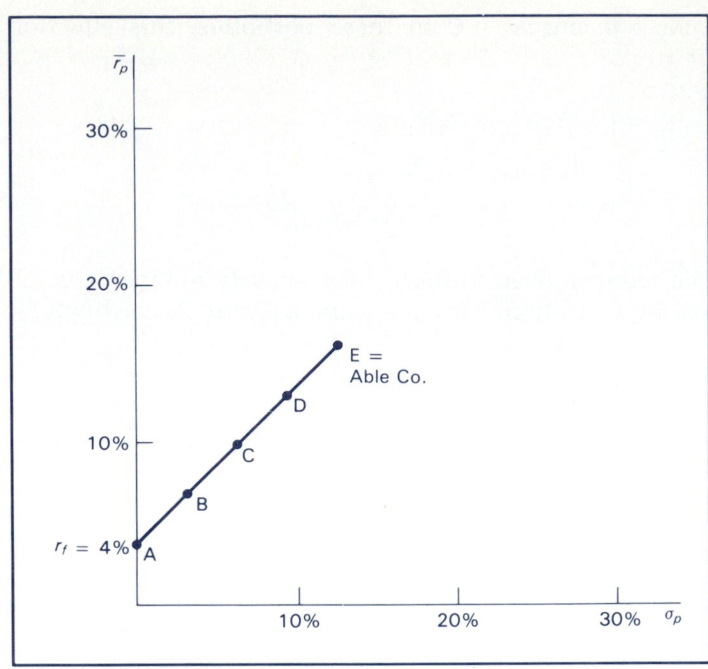

Investing in Both the Riskfree Asset and a Risky Portfolio

Next, consider what happens when a portfolio consisting of more than just one risky security is combined with the riskfree asset. For example, consider the risky portfolio PAC that consists of Able and Charlie in proportions of .80 and .20, respectively. Its expected return (denoted $\bar{r}_{PAC}$) and standard deviation (denoted σ_{PAC}) are equal to:

$$\begin{aligned} \bar{r}_{PAC} &= (.80 \times 16.2\%) + (.20 \times 22.8\%) \\ &= 17.52\%, \\ \sigma_{PAC} &= [(.80 \times .80 \times 146) + (.20 \times .20 \times 289) + (2 \times .80 \times .20 \times 145)]^{1/2} \\ &= 12.30\%. \end{aligned}$$

Any portfolio that consists of an investment in both PAC and the riskfree asset will have an expected return and standard deviation that can be calculated in a manner identical to what was previously shown for combinations of an individual asset and the riskfree asset. That is, a portfolio that has the proportion X_{PAC} invested in the portfolio PAC and the proportion $X_4 = 1 - X_{PAC}$ in the riskfree asset will have an expected return and standard deviation that are equal to, respectively,

$$\bar{r}_p = (X_{PAC} \times 17.52\%) + (X_4 \times 4\%)$$

$$\sigma_p = X_{PAC} \times 12.30\%.$$

For example, consider investing in a portfolio that consists of PAC and the riskfree asset in proportions of .25 and .75, respectively.[2] This portfolio will have an expected return of:

$$\begin{aligned} \bar{r}_p &= (.25 \times 17.52\%) + (.75 \times 4\%) \\ &= 7.38\%, \end{aligned}$$

and a standard deviation of:

$$\begin{aligned} \sigma_p &= .25 \times 12.30\% \\ &= 3.08\%. \end{aligned}$$

Figure 9-2 shows that this portfolio lies on a straight line connecting the riskfree asset and PAC. In particular, it is indicated by the point P on this line. Other portfolios consisting of various combinations of PAC and the riskfree asset will also lie on this line, with their exact locations depending on the relative proportions invested in PAC and the riskfree asset. For example, a portfolio that involves investing a proportion of .50 in the riskfree asset and a proportion of .50 in PAC lies on this line exactly halfway between the two endpoints.

In summary, combining the riskfree asset with any risky portfolio can be viewed as being no different from combining the riskfree asset with an individual risky security. In both cases, the resulting portfolio has an ex-

[2]Note that investing the proportion .25 in portfolio PAC is equivalent to investing the proportion .20 (= .25 × .80) in Able and the proportion .05 (= .25 × .20) in Charlie.

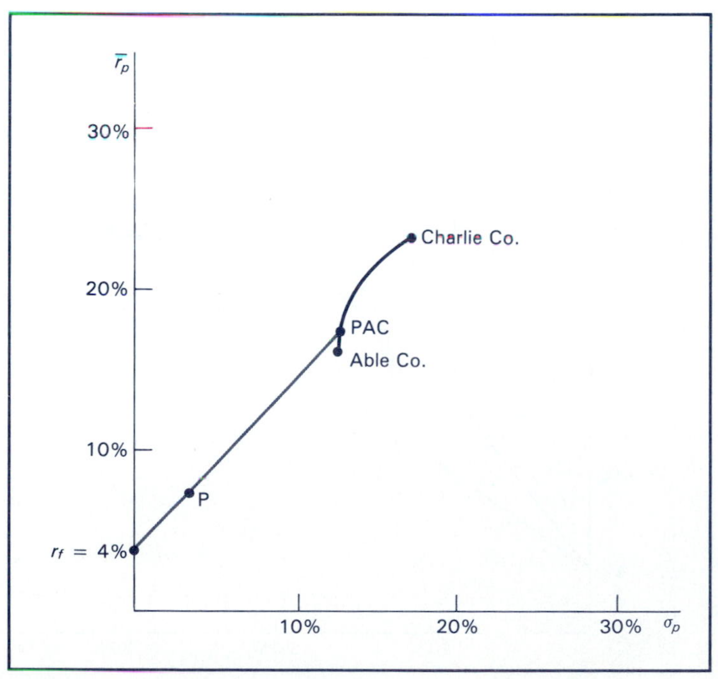

FIGURE 9-2
Combining Riskfree Lending with Investing in a Risky Portfolio

pected return and standard deviation such that it lies somewhere on a straight line connecting the two endpoints.

The Effect of Riskfree Lending on the Efficient Set

As mentioned earlier, the feasible set is changed significantly as a result of the introduction of riskfree lending. Figure 9-3 shows how it changes the feasible set for the example at hand. Here all risky assets and portfolios, not just Able and PAC, are considered in all possible combinations with the riskfree asset. In particular, note that there are two boundaries that are straight lines emanating from the riskfree asset. The bottom line connects the riskfree asset with Baker. Thus, it represents portfolios formed by combining Baker and the riskfree asset.

The other straight line emanating from the riskfree asset represents combinations of the riskfree asset and a particular risky portfolio on the efficient set of the Markowitz model. It is a line that is just tangent to the efficient set of the Markowitz model, with the tangency point being denoted T. This tangency point represents a risky portfolio consisting of Able, Baker, and Charlie in proportions equal to, respectively, .12, .19, and .69. Substituting these proportions into equations (8.1a) and (8.5) indicates that the expected return and standard deviation of T are 22.4% and 15.2%, respectively.

While other risky efficient portfolios from the Markowitz model can also be combined with the riskfree asset, portfolio T deserves special attention. Why? Because there is no other portfolio consisting purely of risky assets that, when connected by a straight line to the riskfree asset, lies northwest of it. In other words, of all the lines that can be drawn emanating from the riskfree asset and connecting with either a risky asset or risky portfolio, none has a greater slope than the line that goes to T.

FIGURE 9-3
Feasible and Efficient Sets When Riskfree Lending Is Introduced

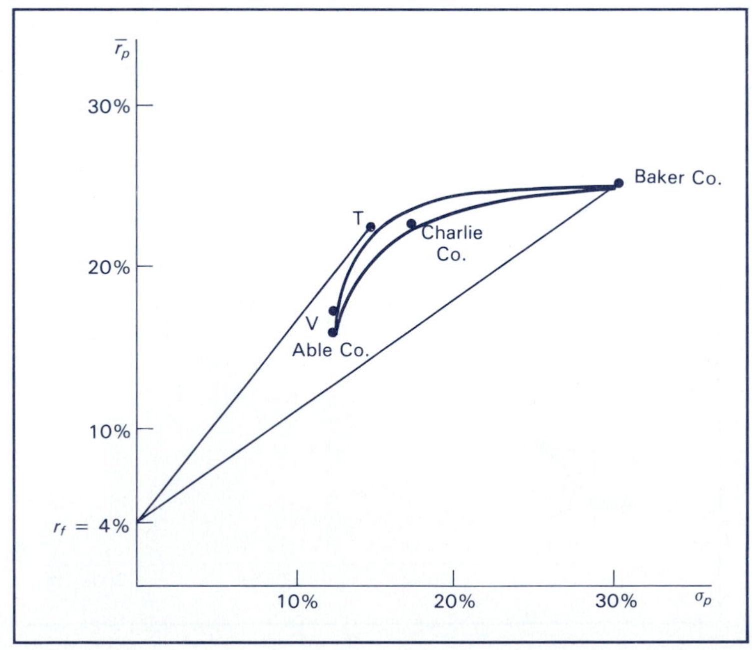

This is important since part of the efficient set of the Markowitz model is dominated by this line. In particular, the portfolios on the Markowitz model efficient set going from the minimum risk portfolio, denoted V, to T are no longer efficient when a riskfree asset is made available for investment. Instead, the efficient set now consists of a straight-line segment and a curved segment. The straight-line segment is the straight line going from the riskfree asset to T, and thus consists of portfolios made up of various combinations of the riskfree asset and T. The curved segment consists of those portfolios to the northeast of T on the Markowitz model efficient set.

The Effect of Riskfree Lending on Portfolio Selection

Figure 9-4 shows how an investor would go about selecting an optimal efficient portfolio when there is a riskfree asset available for investment in addition to a number of risky assets. If the investor's indifference curves look like those shown in panel (a), the investor's optimal portfolio O* will involve investing part of his or her initial wealth in the riskfree asset and the rest in T, since his or her indifference curves are tangent to the efficient set between the riskfree asset and T.[3] Alternatively, if the investor is less risk-averse and has indifference curves that look like those shown in panel (b), then the investor's optimal portfolio O* will not involve any riskfree lending since his or her indifference curves are tangent to the curved segment of the efficient set that lies to the northeast of T.

ALLOWING FOR RISKFREE BORROWING

The analysis that was presented in the previous section can be expanded by allowing the investor to borrow money. This means that the investor is no longer restricted to his or her initial wealth when it comes time to decide how much money to invest in risky assets.[4] However, if the investor borrows money, then interest must be paid on the loan. Since the interest rate is known and there is no uncertainty about repaying the loan, it is often referred to as **riskfree borrowing.**

riskfree borrowing

It will be assumed that the rate of interest charged on the loan is equal to the rate of interest that could be earned from investing in the riskfree asset.[5] Using the earlier example, this means that the investor now has not only the opportunity to invest in a riskfree asset that earns a rate of return of 4%, but also may borrow money, for which the investor must pay a rate of interest equal to 4%.

The effect that the introduction of riskfree borrowing has on the location and shape of the efficient set is as significant as the effect that the introduction of riskfree lending had on it. However, it should be recognized that no investor would want to simultaneously invest in the riskfree asset and incur riskfree

[3] A more risk-averse investor (meaning an investor whose indifference curves have greater slopes) would choose an optimal portfolio that is closer to the riskfree asset on the line that connects the riskfree asset to T. Only if the investor is infinitely risk-averse will the optimal portfolio consist of an investment in just the riskfree asset.

[4] Allowing for borrowing can be viewed as giving the investor the opportunity to engage in margin purchases if he or she so desires. That is, with borrowing the investor is allowed to use financial leverage.

[5] The appendix discusses what happens to the efficient set when the investor is able to borrow but at a rate that is greater than the rate that can be earned by investing in the riskfree asset.

FIGURE 9-4
Portfolio Selection with Riskfree Lending

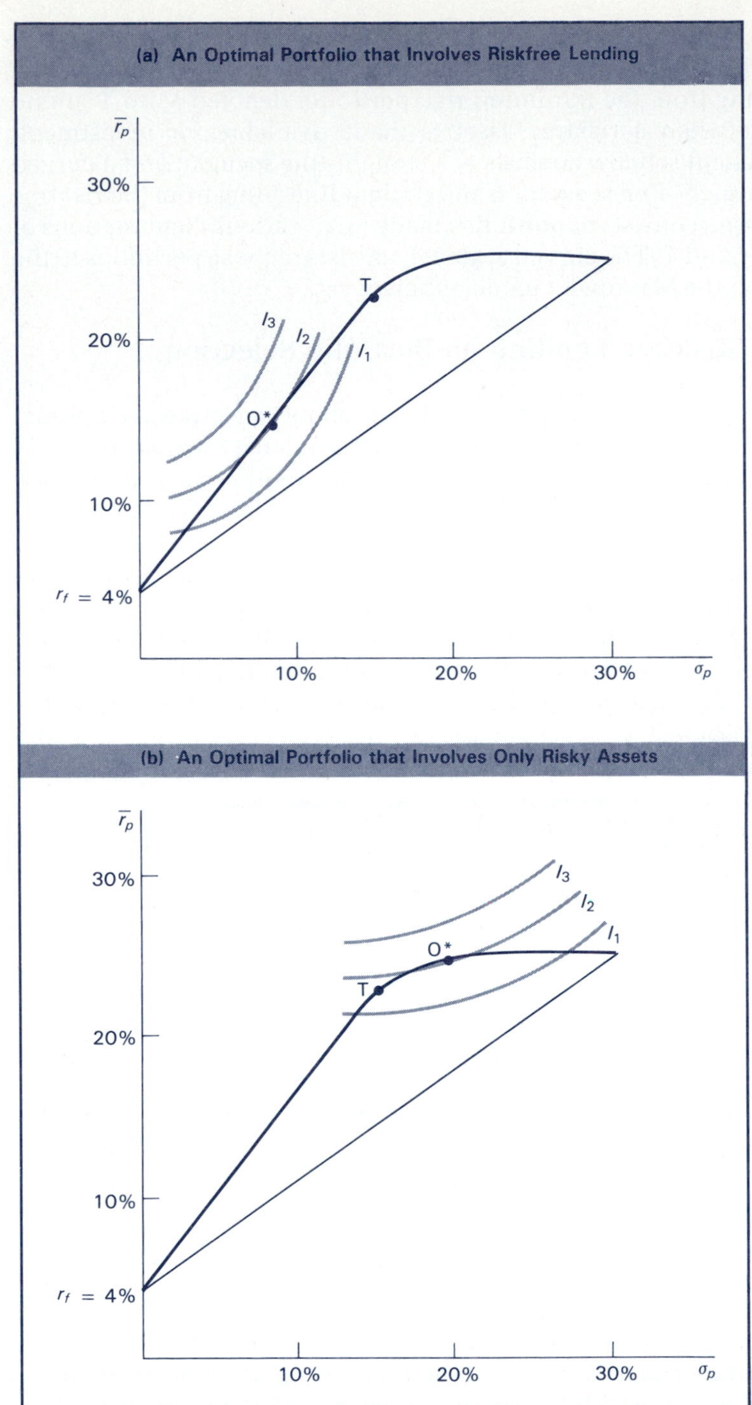

borrowing. Doing so would mean that the investor was engaged in two activities when an identical position could have been established with only one activity.

For example, an investor who is considering investing \$5,000 in the riskfree asset in order to earn 4% while at the same time paying interest at a rate of 4% in order to borrow \$9,300 could equivalently simply borrow \$4,300 (= \$9,300 − \$5,000). Accordingly, the investor can be allowed to lend or borrow at the riskfree rate, but not do both, without any loss of generality in the analysis.

Earlier, the proportion invested in the riskfree asset was denoted X_4 and this proportion was constrained to be a nonnegative number between zero and one. Now, with the opportunity to borrow at the same rate, X_4 will no longer be so constrained. In the earlier example, the investor had initial wealth of \$17,200. If the investor borrows money, then he or she will have in excess of \$17,200 to invest in the risky securities of Able, Baker, and Charlie.

For example, if the investor borrows \$4,300, then he or she will have a total of \$21,500 (= \$17,200 + \$4,300) to invest in these securities. In this situation, X_4 can be viewed as being equal to −.25 (= − \$4,300/\$17,200). However, the sum of the proportions must still equal one. This means that if the investor has borrowed money, the sum of the proportions invested in risky assets would be greater than one. For example, borrowing \$4,300 and investing \$21,500 in Able means that the proportion in Able, X_1, equals 1.25 (= \$21,500/\$17,200). Note how in this case $X_1 + X_4 = 1.25 + (-.25) = 1$.

Borrowing and Investing in a Risky Security

In order to evaluate the effect that the introduction of riskfree borrowing has on the efficient set, the example presented in the previous section will be expanded. In particular, consider portfolios F, G, H, and I, where the investor will invest all the borrowed funds as well as his or her own funds in Able. Thus, the proportions for these portfolios can be summarized as follows:

	PORTFOLIO F	PORTFOLIO G	PORTFOLIO H	PORTFOLIO I
X_1	1.25	1.50	1.75	2.00
X_4	−.25	−.50	−.75	−1.00

The expected returns of these portfolios are calculated in the same manner as was shown in the previous section. That is, equation (8.1a) is still used:

$$\bar{r}_p = \sum_{i=1}^{N} X_i \bar{r}_i \qquad (8.1a)$$

$$= \sum_{i=1}^{4} X_i \bar{r}_i$$

$$= X_1 \bar{r}_1 + X_4 \bar{r}_4$$

$$= (X_1 \times 16.2\%) + (X_4 \times 4\%).$$

Thus, portfolios F, G, H, and I have the following expected returns:

$$\begin{aligned}
\bar{r}_F &= (1.25 \times 16.2\%) + (-.25 \times 4\%) \\
&= 19.25\% \\
\bar{r}_G &= (1.50 \times 16.2\%) + (-\ .50 \times 4\%) \\
&= 22.30\% \\
\bar{r}_H &= (1.75 \times 16.2\%) + (-\ .75 \times 4\%) \\
&= 25.35\% \\
\bar{r}_I &= (2.00 \times 16.2\%) + (-\ 1.00 \times 4\%) \\
&= 28.40\%.
\end{aligned}$$

Similarly, the standard deviations of these portfolios are calculated by using equation (8.5) as was done in the previous section:

$$\begin{aligned}
\sigma_p &= \left[\sum_{i=1}^{N} \sum_{j=1}^{N} X_i X_j \sigma_{ij} \right]^{1/2} \qquad (8.5) \\
&= \left[\sum_{i=1}^{4} \sum_{j=1}^{4} X_i X_j \sigma_{ij} \right]^{1/2}
\end{aligned}$$

which was shown to reduce to:

$$\sigma_p = X_1 \times 12.08\%.$$

Thus, the standard deviations of the four portfolios are:

$$\begin{aligned}
\sigma_F &= 1.25 \times 12.08\% \\
&= 15.10\% \\
\sigma_G &= 1.50 \times 12.08\% \\
&= 18.12\% \\
\sigma_H &= 1.75 \times 12.08\% \\
&= 21.14\% \\
\sigma_I &= 2.00 \times 12.08\% \\
&= 24.16\%.
\end{aligned}$$

In summary, these four portfolios, as well as the five portfolios that involve riskfree lending, have the following expected returns and standard deviations:

PORTFOLIO	X_1	X_4	EXPECTED RETURN	STANDARD DEVIATION
A	.00	1.00	4.00%	0.00%
B	.25	.75	7.05	3.02
C	.50	.50	10.10	6.04
D	.75	.25	13.15	9.06
E	1.00	.00	16.20	12.08
F	1.25	−.25	19.25	15.10
G	1.50	−.50	22.30	18.12
H	1.75	−.75	25.35	21.14
I	2.00	−1.00	28.40	24.16

In Figure 9-5, it can be seen that the four portfolios that involve riskfree borrowing (F, G, H, and I) all lie on the same straight line that goes through the five portfolios that involve riskfree lending (A, B, C, D, and E). Furthermore, the larger the amount of borrowing, the further out on the line the portfolio lies (equivalently, the smaller the value of X_4, the further out on the line the portfolio lies).

While only four particular combinations of borrowing and investing in Able have been examined here, it can be shown that any combination of borrowing and investing in Able will lie somewhere on this line, with the exact location depending on the amount of borrowing. Furthermore, this observation can be generalized to combinations of riskfree borrowing and an

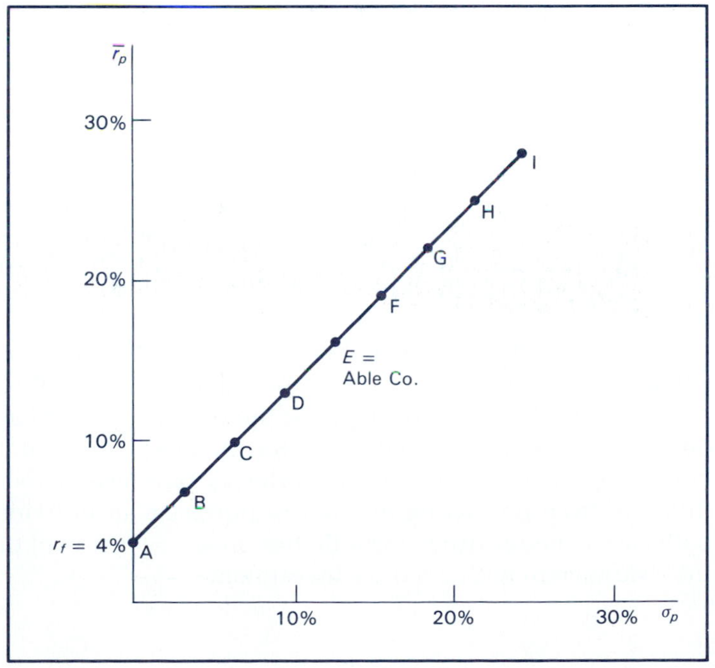

FIGURE 9-5
Combining Riskfree Borrowing and Lending with Investing in a Risky Asset

investment in any particular risky asset. That is, borrowing at the riskfree rate and investing all the borrowed money and the investor's own money in a risky asset will result in a portfolio that has an expected return and standard deviation such that it lies on the extension of the straight line connecting the riskfree rate and the risky asset.

Borrowing and Investing in a Risky Portfolio

Next, consider what happens when a portfolio of more than one risky asset is purchased with both the investor's own funds and borrowed funds. Earlier it was shown that the portfolio having proportions invested in Able and Charlie equal to .80 and .20, respectively, had an expected return of 17.52% and a standard deviation of 12.30%. This portfolio was referred to as PAC. Any portfolio that involves borrowing money at the riskfree rate and then investing these funds and the investor's own funds in PAC will have an expected return and standard deviation that can be calculated in a manner identical to that which was previously shown when borrowing was incurred and Able was purchased. That is, a portfolio that involves borrowing the proportion X_4 and investing these funds and all the investor's own funds in PAC will have an expected return and standard deviation that are equal to, respectively,

$$\bar{r}_p = (X_{PAC} \times 17.52\%) + (X_4 \times 4\%)$$

$$\sigma_p = X_{PAC} \times 12.30\%.$$

For example, consider borrowing an amount of money equal to 25% of the investor's initial wealth, and then investing all the investor's own funds and these borrowed funds in PAC. Thus, $X_{PAC} = 1 - X_4 = 1 - (-.25) = 1.25$.[6] This portfolio will have an expected return of:

$$\bar{r}_p = (1.25 \times 17.52\%) + (-.25 \times 4\%)$$
$$= 20.90\%,$$

and a standard deviation of:

$$\sigma_p = 1.25 \times 12.30\%$$
$$= 15.38\%.$$

In Figure 9-6, it can be seen that this portfolio (denoted P) lies on the extension of the line that connects the riskfree rate with PAC. Other portfolios consisting of PAC and borrowing at the riskfree rate will also lie somewhere on this extension, with their exact location depending on the amount of the borrowing. Thus, borrowing in order to purchase a risky portfolio is no different from borrowing in order to purchase an individual risky asset. In both cases, the resulting portfolio lies on an extension of the line connecting the riskfree rate with the risky investment.

[6]Note that investing the proportion 1.25 in portfolio PAC is equivalent to investing the proportion 1.00 (= 1.25 × .80) in Able and the proportion .25 (= 1.25 × .20) in Charlie.

MONEY MATTERS
The Cost of Short-Term Borrowing

The extension of the Markowitz model to incorporate borrowing and lending assumes that investors can borrow or lend at the riskfree rate. Certainly, every investor has the opportunity to lend at the riskfree rate—he or she can simply purchase U.S. Treasury securities with maturities corresponding to the length of his or her investment holding period.

Borrowing at the riskfree rate is another matter. In reality, only one entity has the option to borrow at the riskfree rate: the U.S. Treasury. Other investors, be they individuals or corporations, must borrow at interest rates exceeding those paid by the Treasury.

Just what level of interest rates do investors pay to borrow? To provide some perspective on this issue, we briefly survey some of the interest rates available in the market for short-term financial assets known as the *money market*.

The standard of comparison for all money market interest rates is the rate paid on short-term U.S. Treasury securities called U.S. Treasury bills (see Chapter 1). The return on Treasury bills is completely certain because the federal government will never default on its obligations. It always has the option to print money or raise taxes to pay off its debts.

Other borrowers, no matter how strong their current financial position, run at least some risk of defaulting on their short-term debts. Largely due to this fact, virtually all non-Treasury borrowers must pay interest rates exceeding those paid by the Treasury. The difference between what the Treasury pays to borrow money and what other borrowers pay is known as the "spread." How large is the spread for non-Treasury borrowers?

If you, as an individual investor, wished to finance your investment in securities, you would typically purchase them on margin from your broker. In such transactions the broker actually borrows money elsewhere in the money market (usually drawing down a line of credit at a bank and pledging securities as collateral). The interest rate paid by the broker is known as the *broker call money* (or broker call loan) *rate* (see Chapter 3). Brokers add anywhere from 1% to 2% to the call money rate to determine the interest rate charged their margin purchase customers.

In 1990, the broker call money rate averaged roughly 9.34%. By comparison, the U.S. Treasury paid an average interest rate on 90-day Treasury bills of 7.87%. Assuming a one percentage point markup over the broker call money rate, margin investors faced an average spread over three-month Treasuries of 2.47 percentage points during 1990.

Large, financially strong corporations usually borrow in the money market through an instrument known as *commercial paper*. Commercial paper represents the negotiable, short-term, unsecured promissory notes of finance, industrial, utility, insurance, and bank holding companies. In 1990, three-month commercial paper interest rates averaged 8.48%, a spread of 0.61 percentage points over similar-maturity Treasury bills.

Corporations without the size and financial strength to borrow in the commercial paper market must obtain their short-term financing from banks. The interest rate officially quoted by banks on short-term unsecured loans to their best customers is known as the *prime rate*. The prime rate is not always an accurate measure of short-term borrowing costs, as banks often discount from it on loans to their financially strong borrowers. Financially weaker clients, on the other hand, may be charged a premium above the prime rate. In 1990, the prime rate averaged 10.01%, a 2.14 percentage point spread over Treasuries.

Banks themselves borrow in the money market through large denomination (usually $1 million or larger) certificates of deposit. While these loans are unsecured and do not carry federal deposit insurance, the strong financial standing of most banks requires them to pay little more than the government for short-term borrowing. In 1990, rates for large, three-month certificates of deposit averaged 8.15%, only 0.28 percentage points above Treasuries.

From this brief money market survey, we can see that the riskfree rate is relevant to investor borrowing only as a base of comparison. Investors actually have to pay more, sometimes much more, to borrow in the money market. But then, of course, such borrowing is not considered riskfree, at least by the lenders.

The Effect of Riskfree Borrowing and Lending on the Efficient Set

Figure 9-7 shows how the feasible set is changed when borrowing and lending at the riskfree rate are allowed. Here, all risky assets and portfolios, not just Able and PAC, are considered. The feasible set is the entire area between the

FIGURE 9-6
Combining Riskfree Borrowing and Lending with Investing in a Risky Portfolio

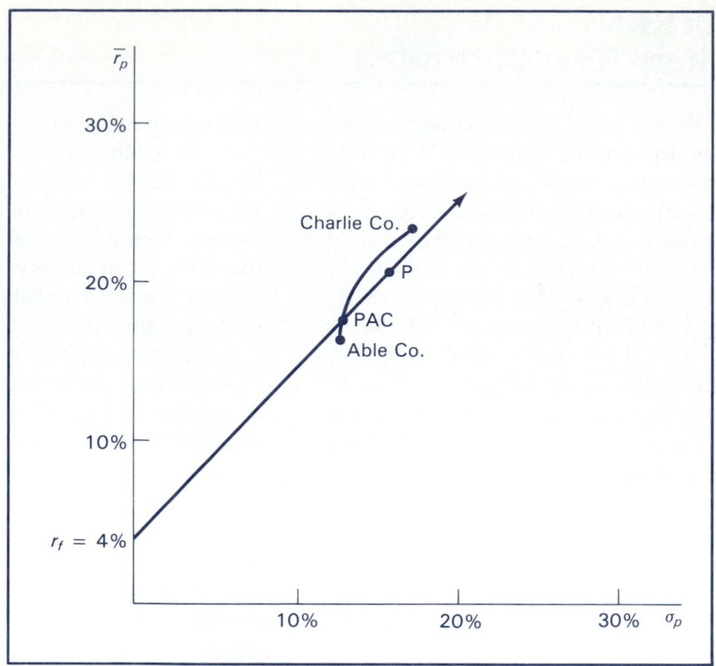

two lines emanating from the riskfree rate that go through the location of Baker and the portfolio denoted T. These two lines extend indefinitely to the right if it is assumed that there is no limit to the amount of borrowing that the investor can incur.

The straight line that goes through portfolio T is of special importance, since it represents the efficient set. That is, it represents the set of portfolios

FIGURE 9-7
Feasible and Efficient Sets When Riskfree Borrowing and Lending Are Introduced

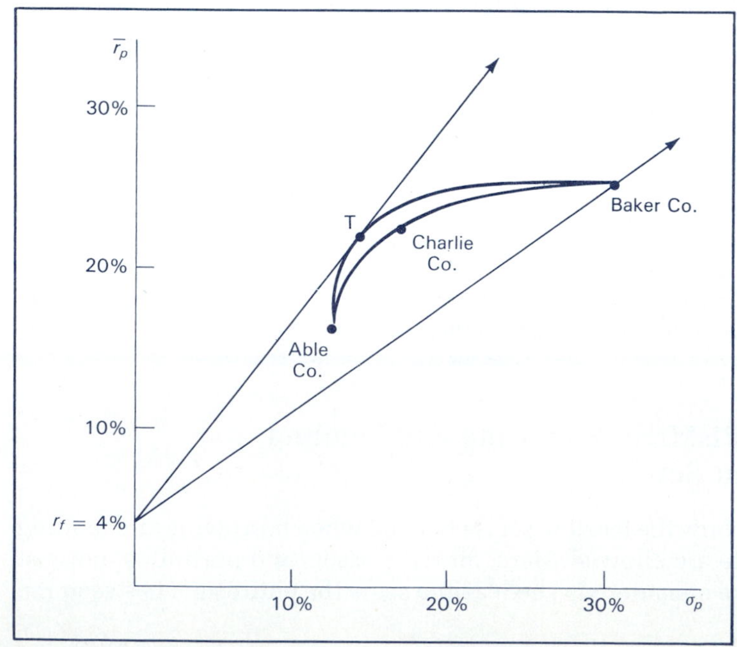

that offer the best opportunities, since it represents the set of feasible portfolios lying furthest northwest. Portfolio T, as was mentioned earlier, consists of investments in Able, Baker, and Charlie in proportions equal to, respectively, .12, .19, and .69.

As before, the line going through T is just tangent to the Markowitz model efficient set. None of the portfolios, except for T, that were on the Markowitz model efficient set are efficient when riskfree borrowing and lending are introduced. This can be seen by noting that every portfolio (except

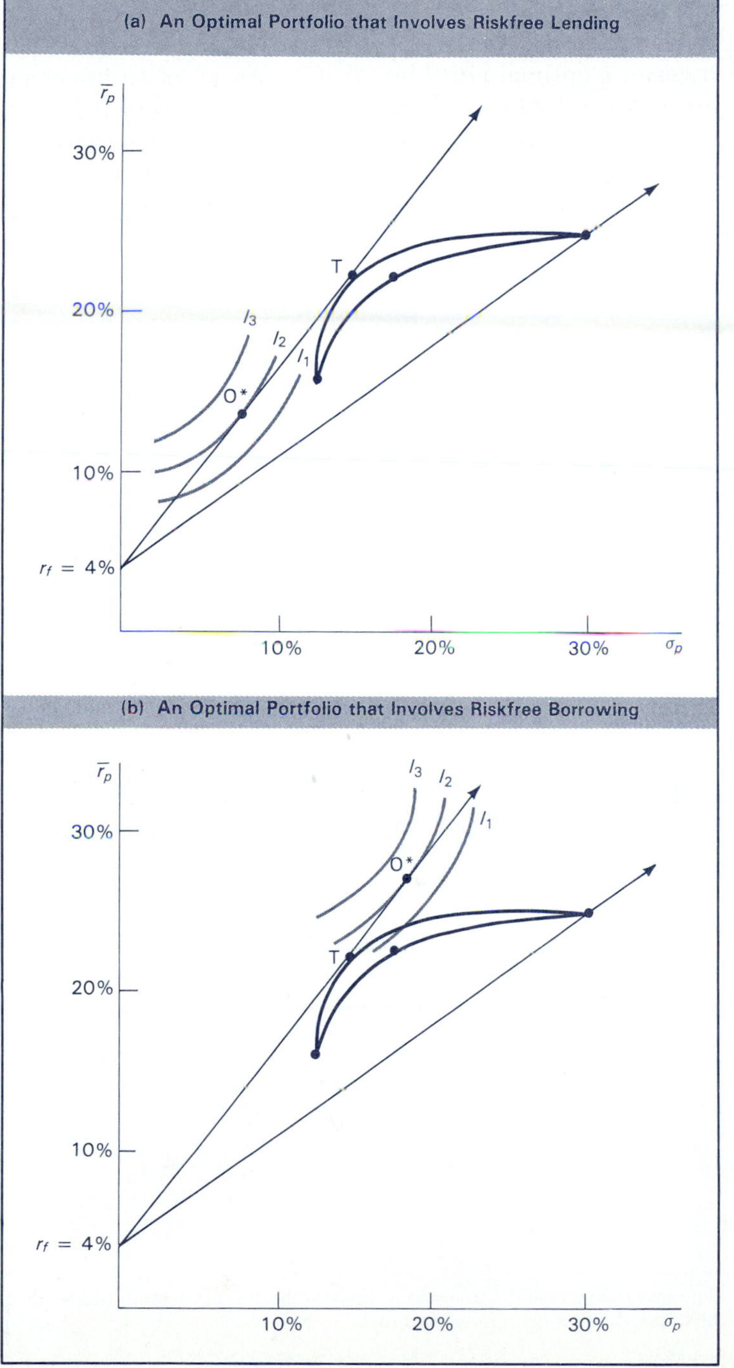

FIGURE 9-8
Portfolio Selection with Riskfree Borrowing and Lending

T) that lies on the Markowitz model efficient set is dominated by a portfolio on this straight line having the same standard deviation along with a higher expected return.

The Effect of Riskfree Borrowing and Lending on Portfolio Selection

Given the opportunity to either borrow or lend at the riskfree rate, an investor would proceed to identify the optimal portfolio by plotting his or her indifference curves on this graph and noting where one of them is tangent to the linear efficient set. Figure 9-8 shows two alternative situations. If the investor's indifference curves look like the ones in panel (a), then the investor's optimal portfolio O* will consist of an investment in the riskfree asset as well as in T. Alternatively, if the investor is less risk-averse and has indifference curves that look like those shown in panel (b), then the investor's optimal portfolio O* will consist of borrowing at the riskfree rate and investing these funds as well as his or her own funds in T.[7]

SUMMARY

1. The return on a riskfree asset is certain. The riskfree asset's standard deviation is zero as is its covariance with other assets.

2. In extending the Markowitz feasible set to include riskfree lending, investors are assumed to allocate their funds among a riskfree asset and a portfolio of risky assets.

3. With riskfree lending, the efficient set becomes a straight line from the riskfree rate to a point tangent to the curved Markowitz efficient set, in addition to the portion of the Markowitz efficient set that lies northeast of this tangency point.

4. Introducing riskfree borrowing permits an investor to engage in leverage. The investor may use all of his or her money, plus money borrowed at the riskfree rate, to purchase a portfolio of risky assets.

5. With riskfree lending and borrowing, the efficient set becomes a straight line from the riskfree rate through a point tangent to the curved Markowitz efficient set.

6. With riskfree lending and borrowing, the efficient set consists of combinations of a single risky portfolio and various proportions of riskfree lending or borrowing.

7. The investor's optimal portfolio is determined by plotting his or her indifference curves against the efficient set.

8. The investor's optimal portfolio will include an investment in the risky portfolio and borrowing or lending at the riskfree rate.

9. Investors with higher levels of risk aversion will engage in less borrowing (or more lending) than investors with less risk aversion.

KEY TERMS

riskfree asset
interest-rate risk
reinvestment-rate risk
riskfree lending
riskfree borrowing

[7]The less risk-averse the investor is, the smaller the proportion invested in the riskfree rate and the larger the proportion invested in T.

QUESTIONS AND PROBLEMS

1. Why is a "pure discount" government security (that is, one that does not make coupon payments, pays interest at maturity, and hence sells at a discount from par) with no risk of default still risky to an investor whose holding period does not coincide with the maturity date of the security?
2. Distinguish between reinvestment-rate risk and interest-rate risk.
3. The covariance between a riskfree asset and a risky asset is zero. Explain why this is the case and demonstrate it mathematically.
4. Lindsay Brown owns a risky portfolio with a 15% expected return. The riskfree return is 5%. What is the expected return on Lindsay's total portfolio if Lindsay invests the following proportions in the risky portfolio and the remainder in the riskfree asset?
   (a) 120%
   (b) 90%
   (c) 75%
5. Consider a risky portfolio with an expected return of 18%. With a riskfree return of 5%, how could you create a portfolio with a 24% expected return?
6. Happy Buker owns a risky portfolio with a 20% standard deviation. If Happy invests the following proportions in the riskfree asset and the remainder in the risky portfolio, what is the standard deviation of Happy's total portfolio?
   (a) −30%
   (b) 10%
   (c) 30%
7. Oyster Burns' portfolio is composed of an investment in a risky portfolio (with a 12% expected return and a 25% standard deviation) and a riskfree asset (with a 7% return). If Oyster's total portfolio has a 20% standard deviation, what is its expected return?
8. Hick Cady argues that buying a risky portfolio with riskfree borrowing is equivalent to a purchase of the risky portfolio on margin. Patsy Cahill contends that such an investment can be viewed as selling the riskfree asset short and using proceeds to invest in the risky portfolio. Who is correct? Explain.
9. How does the efficient set change when riskfree borrowing and lending are introduced into the Markowitz model? Explain with words and graphs.
10. Why does the efficient set, with the Markowitz model extended to include riskfree borrowing and lending, have only one point in common with the efficient set of the Markowitz model without riskfree borrowing and lending? Why are the other points on the "old" efficient set no longer desirable? Explain with words and graphs.
11. Based on the assumptions developed in this chapter, is it true that all investors will hold the same risky portfolio? Explain.
12. How does the feasible set change when riskfree borrowing and lending are introduced into the Markowitz model? Explain with words and graphs.
13. With the Markowitz model extended to include riskfree borrowing and lending, draw the indifference curves, efficient set, and optimal portfo-

lio for an investor with high risk aversion and an investor with low risk aversion.

14. Given the following expected return vector and variance-covariance matrix for three assets

$$ER = \begin{bmatrix} 10.1 \\ 7.8 \\ 5.0 \end{bmatrix} \quad VC = \begin{bmatrix} 210 & 60 & 0 \\ 60 & 90 & 0 \\ 0 & 0 & 0 \end{bmatrix}.$$

and given the fact that Pie Traynor's risky portfolio is split 50-50 between the two risky assets:

(a) Which security of the three must be the riskfree asset? Why?

(b) Calculate the expected return and standard deviation of Pie's portfolio.

(c) If the riskfree asset makes up 25% of Pie's total portfolio, what is the total portfolio's expected return and standard deviation?

15. What does the efficient set look like if riskfree borrowing is permitted but no lending is allowed? Explain with words and graphs.

16. What will be the effect on total portfolio expected return and risk if you borrow money at the riskfree rate and invest it in the optimal risky portfolio?

17. Suppose your level of risk aversion decreased as you grew richer. In a world of riskfree borrowing and lending, how would your optimal portfolio change? Would the types of risky securities that you hold change? Explain with words and graphs.

18. (Appendix Question) How does the efficient set change when the condition of borrowing and lending at the same riskfree rate is changed to borrowing at a rate greater than the rate at which riskfree lending can be conducted? Explain with words and graphs.

APPENDIX

A

Allowing for Different Borrowing and Lending Rates

In this chapter, it was assumed that the investor could borrow funds at the same rate that could be earned on an investment in the riskfree asset. As a result, the feasible set became the area bounded by two straight lines emanating from the riskfree rate. The upper line represented the efficient set, and had one portfolio in common with the curved efficient set of the Markowitz model. This portfolio was located where the straight line from the riskfree rate was tangent to the curved efficient set. Now the concern will be with what happens if it is assumed that the investor can borrow but at a rate that is greater than the rate that can be earned by an investment in the riskfree asset. The rate on the riskfree asset will be denoted r_{fL}, where L indicates lending, since as was mentioned earlier, an investment in the riskfree asset is equivalent to lending money to the government. The rate at which the investor can borrow money will be denoted r_{fB}, and is of a magnitude such that $r_{fB} > r_{fL}$.

One way to understand the effect on the efficient set of assuming that these two rates are different is as follows. First, consider what the efficient set would look like if riskfree borrowing and lending were possible at the same rate, r_{fL}. The resulting efficient set would be the straight line shown in Figure A-1 that goes through the points r_{fL} and T_L.

Second, consider what the efficient set would look like if riskfree borrowing and lending were possible at the higher rate, r_{fB}. The resulting efficient set would be the straight line shown in Figure A-1 that goes through the points r_{fB} and T_B. Note that the portfolio T_B lies on Markowitz's efficient set above the portfolio T_L, since it corresponds to a tangency point associated with a higher riskfree rate.

Third, since the investor cannot borrow at r_{fL}, that part of the line emanating from r_{fL} that extends past T_L is not available to the investor, and can thus be removed from consideration.

Fourth, since the investor cannot lend at the riskfree rate r_{fB}, that part of the line emanating from r_{fB} and going through T_B but lying to the left of T_B is not available to the investor, and can thus be removed from consideration.

FIGURE A-1
Evaluating Different Riskfree Rates

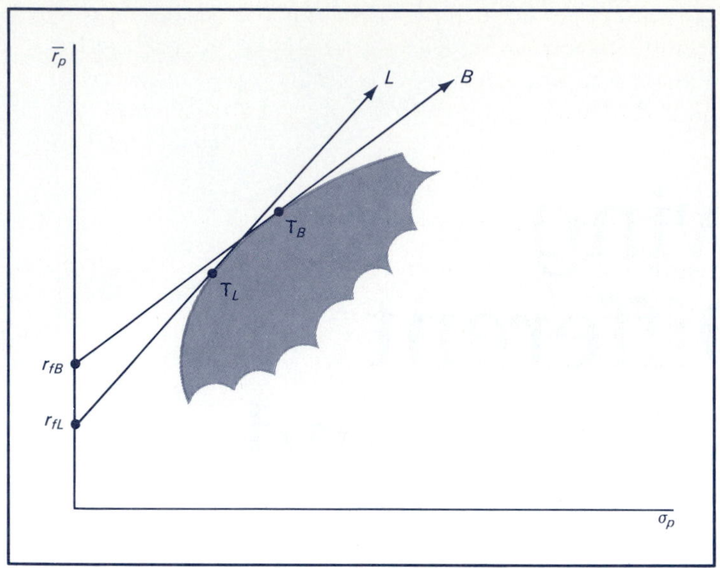

The northwest boundary of what remains, shown in Figure A-2, is the resulting efficient set.

This efficient set consists of three distinct but connected segments. The first segment is the straight line going from r_{fL} to T_L, and represents various amounts of riskfree lending combined with investing in the portfolio of risky assets denoted T_L. The second segment is the curved line going from T_L to T_B, and represents various risky portfolios that were also on Markowitz's curved efficient set. The third segment is the straight line extending outward from T_B, and represents various amounts of borrowing combined with an investment in the risky portfolio denoted T_B.

FIGURE A-2
Efficient Set When the Riskfree Rates Are Different

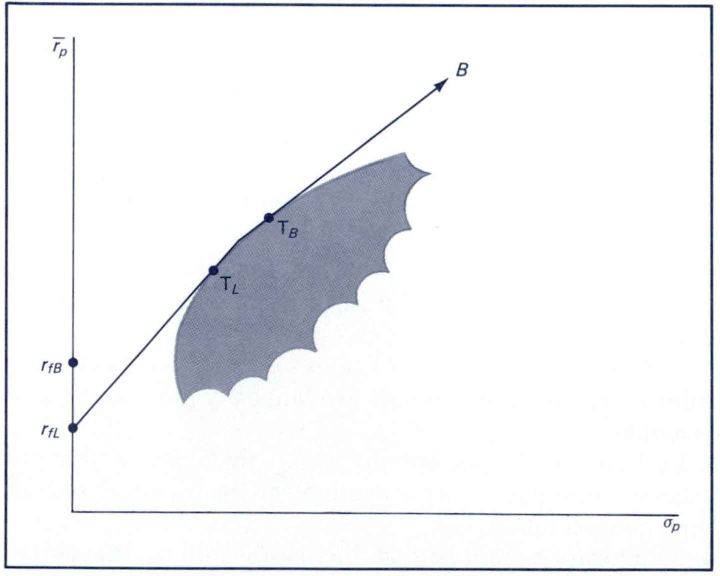

The optimal portfolio for an investor will be, as before, the portfolio that corresponds to the point where an indifference curve is tangent to the efficient set. Depending on the investor's indifference curves, this tangency point could be on any one of the three segments that comprise the efficient set.

REFERENCES

1. Credit for extending Markowitz's model to include riskfree lending and borrowing belongs to:

   James Tobin, "Liquidity Preference as Behavior Towards Risk," *Review of Economic Studies*, 26, no. 1 (February 1958): 65–86;

   James Tobin, "The Theory of Portfolio Selection," in *The Theory of Interest Rates*, ed. F. H. Hahn and F. P. R. Brechling (London: Macmillan and Co., 1965).

2. For a discussion of various mean-variance models that involve different sets of assumptions regarding riskfree lending and borrowing, margin purchasing, and short selling, see:

   Gordon J. Alexander and Jack Clark Francis, *Portfolio Analysis* (Englewood Cliffs, N.J.: Prentice Hall, 1986), Chapter 4;

   Eugene F. Fama, *Foundations of Finance* (New York: Basic Books, Inc., 1976), Chapters 7 and 8.

10

The Capital Asset Pricing Model

Chapters 7, 8, and 9 presented a method for identifying an investor's optimal portfolio. With this method, the investor needs to estimate the expected returns and variances for all securities under consideration. Furthermore, all the covariances among these securities need to be estimated and the riskfree rate needs to be determined. Once this is done the investor can identify the composition of the tangency portfolio, as well as its expected return and standard deviation. At this juncture the investor can proceed to identify the optimal portfolio by noting where one of his or her indifference curves touches but does not intersect the efficient frontier. This portfolio will involve an investment in the tangency portfolio, along with a certain amount of either riskfree borrowing or lending, since the efficient set is linear (that is, a straight line).

Such an approach to investing can be viewed as an exercise in **normative economics**, where investors are told what they should do. Thus, the approach is prescriptive in nature. In this chapter the realm of **positive economics** is entered, where a descriptive model of how assets are priced is presented. The model assumes, among other things, that all investors use the approach to investing given in chapters 7, 8, and 9. The major implication of the model is that the expected return of an asset will be related to a measure of risk for that asset known as *beta*. The exact manner in which expected return and beta are related is specified by the **Capital Asset Pricing Model** (CAPM). This model provides the intellectual basis for a number of the current practices in the investment industry. While many of these practices are based on various

normative economics

positive economics

Capital Asset Pricing Model

extensions and modifications of the CAPM, a sound understanding of the original version is necessary in order to understand them. Accordingly, this chapter presents the original version of the CAPM.

ASSUMPTIONS

In order to see how assets are priced, a model (that is, a theory) must be constructed. This requires simplification, in that the model builder must abstract from the full complexity of the situation and focus only on the most important elements. The way this is achieved is by making certain assumptions about the environment. These assumptions need to be simplistic in order to provide the degree of abstraction that allows for some success in building the model. The "reasonableness" of the assumptions (or lack thereof) is of little concern. Instead, the test of a model is in its ability to help one understand and predict the process being modeled. As Milton Friedman, recipient of the 1976 Nobel Memorial Prize in Economics, has stated in a famous essay:

> [T]he relevant question to ask about the "assumptions" of a theory is not whether they are descriptively "realistic," for they never are, but whether they are sufficiently good approximations for the purpose in hand. And this question can be answered only by seeing whether the theory works, which means whether it yields sufficiently accurate predictions.[1]

Some of the assumptions behind the CAPM are also behind the normative approach to investing that was described in the previous three chapters. These assumptions are as follows:

1. Investors evaluate portfolios by looking at the expected returns and standard deviations of the portfolios over a one–period horizon.
2. Investors are never satiated, so when given a choice between two otherwise identical portfolios, they will choose the one with the higher expected return.
3. Investors are risk-averse, so when given a choice between two otherwise identical portfolios, they will choose the one with the lower standard deviation.
4. Individual assets are infinitely divisible, meaning that an investor can buy a fraction of a share if he or she so desires.
5. There is a riskfree rate at which an investor may either lend (that is, invest) money or borrow money.
6. Taxes and transaction costs are irrelevant.

To these assumptions the following ones are added:

7. All investors have the same one-period horizon.
8. The riskfree rate is the same for all investors.
9. Information is freely and instantly available to all investors.

[1]Milton Friedman, *Essays in the Theory of Positive Economics* (Chicago: University of Chicago Press, 1953), p. 15.

10. Investors have **homogeneous expectations,** meaning that they have the same perceptions in regard to the expected returns, standard deviations, and covariances of securities.

homogeneous expectations

As can be seen by examining these assumptions, the CAPM reduces the situation to an extreme case. Everyone has the same information and agrees about the future prospects for securities. Implicitly, this means that investors analyze and process information in the same way. The markets for securities are **perfect,** meaning that there are no "frictions" to impede investing; potential impediments such as finite divisibility, taxes, transaction costs, and different riskfree borrowing and lending rates have been assumed away. This allows the focus to be changed from how an individual should invest to what would happen to security prices if everyone invested in a similar manner. By examining the collective behavior of all investors in the market-place, the nature of the resulting equilibrium relationship between each security's risk and return can be developed.

perfect markets

THE CAPITAL MARKET LINE

The Separation Theorem

Having made these ten assumptions, the resulting implications can now be examined. First, investors would analyze securities and determine the composition of the tangency portfolio. In doing so, *everyone would obtain in equilibrium the same tangency portfolio.* However, this is not surprising, since there is complete agreement among investors on the estimates of the securities' expected returns, variances, and covariances, as well as on the size of the riskfree rate. This also means that the linear efficient set (described in Chapter 9) is the same for all investors because it simply involves combinations of the agreed-upon tangency portfolio and either riskfree borrowing or lending.

Since all investors face the same efficient set, the only reason they will choose different portfolios is that they have different indifference curves. Thus, different investors will choose different portfolios from the same efficient set because they have different preferences toward risk and return. For example, as was shown in Figure 9-8, the investor in panel (a) will choose a different portfolio than the investor in panel (b). However, while the chosen portfolios will be different, *each investor will choose the same combination of risky securities,* denoted T in Figure 9-8. That is, each investor will spread his or her funds among risky securities in the same relative proportions, adding riskfree borrowing or lending in order to achieve a personally preferred overall combination of risk and return. This feature of the CAPM is often referred to as the **separation theorem:**

separation theorem

> The optimal combination of risky assets for an investor can be determined without any knowledge about the investor's preferences toward risk and return.

In other words, the determination of the optimal combination of risky assets can be made without determining the shape of an investor's indifference curves.

The reasoning behind the separation theorem involves a property of the linear efficient set that was introduced in Chapter 9. There it was shown that all portfolios that were located on the linear efficient set involved an investment in a tangency portfolio combined with varying degrees of riskfree borrowing or lending. With the CAPM, each person faces the same linear efficient set, meaning that each person will be investing in the same tangency portfolio (combined with a certain amount of either riskfree borrowing or lending that depends upon that person's indifference curves). It therefore follows that the risky portion of each person's portfolio will be the same.

In the example from Chapter 9, three securities were considered, corresponding to the stock of Able, Baker, and Charlie companies. With a riskfree rate of return of 4%, the tangency portfolio, T, was shown to consist of investments in Able, Baker, and Charlie in proportions equal to .12, .19, and .69, respectively. If the ten assumptions of the CAPM are made, then the investor shown in panel (a) of Figure 9-8 would invest approximately half of his or her money in the riskfree asset and the remainder in T. The investor shown in panel (b), on the other hand, would borrow an amount of money equal to approximately half of the value of his or her initial wealth and proceed to invest these borrowed funds as well as his or her own funds in T.[2] Thus, the proportions invested in the three stocks for panel (a) and (b) investors would equal:[3]

$$(.5) \times \begin{bmatrix} .12 \\ .19 \\ .69 \end{bmatrix} = \begin{bmatrix} .060 \\ .095 \\ .345 \end{bmatrix} \text{ for the investor in panel (a)}$$

$$(1.5) \times \begin{bmatrix} .12 \\ .19 \\ .69 \end{bmatrix} = \begin{bmatrix} .180 \\ .285 \\ 1.035 \end{bmatrix} \text{ for the investor in panel (b).}$$

While the proportions to be invested in each of these three risky securities for the panel (a) investor (.060, .095, .345) can be seen to be different in size from their values for the panel (b) investor (.180, .285, 1.035), the relative proportions are the same, being equal to .12, .19, and .69, respectively.

The Market Portfolio

Another important feature of the CAPM is that in equilibrium, each security must have a nonzero proportion in the composition of the tangency portfolio.[4] That is, no security could, in equilibrium, have a proportion in T that was zero. The reasoning behind this feature lies in the previously mentioned separation theorem, where it was asserted that the risky portion of every investor's portfolio would be independent of the investor's risk-return preferences. The justification for the theorem was that the risky portion of each investor's portfolio would simply be an investment in T. If every investor is purchasing T, and T does not involve an investment in each security, then nobody is investing in those securities with zero proportions in T. This means that the prices of these zero-proportion securities must fall, thereby causing

[2]If the investor had initial wealth of $40,000, this means that he or she would borrow $20,000 and then invest $60,000 (= $40,000 + $20,000) in T.

[3]Note how the proportions in these three stocks sum to .5 for the panel (a) investor and 1.5 for the panel (b) investor. Since the respective proportions for the riskfree rate are .5 and −.5, the aggregate proportions for the stocks and riskfree rate sum to 1.0 for each investor.

[4]Securities that have zero net amounts outstanding will not appear in the tangency portfolio. Options and futures, discussed in Chapters 24 and 25, are examples of such securities.

the expected returns of these securities to rise, until the resulting tangency portfolio has a nonzero proportion associated with them.

In the previous example, Charlie had a current price of $62 and an expected end-of-period price of $76.14. This meant that the expected return for Charlie was 22.8% = ($76.14 − $62)/$62. Now imagine that the current price of Charlie is $72, not $62, meaning that its expected return is 5.8% = ($76.14 − $72)/$72. If this were the case, the tangency portfolio associated with a riskfree rate of 4% would involve just Able and Baker in proportions of .90 and .10, respectively.[5] Since Charlie has a proportion of zero, nobody would want to hold shares of Charlie. Consequently, orders to sell would be received in substantial quantities, with virtually no offsetting orders to buy being received. As a result, Charlie's price would fall, as brokers would try to find someone to buy the shares. However, as Charlie's price falls, its expected return would rise, since the same end-of-period price of $76.14 is forecasted for Charlie as before and it would now cost less to buy one share. Eventually, as the price falls, investors would change their minds and want to buy shares of Charlie. Ultimately, at a price of $62, investors will want to hold shares of Charlie so that, in aggregate, the number of shares demanded will equal the number of shares outstanding. Thus, in equilibrium, Charlie will have a nonzero proportion in the tangency portfolio.

Another interesting situation could also arise. What if each investor concludes that the tangency portfolio should involve a proportionate investment in the stock of Baker equal to .40, but at the current price of Baker there are not enough shares outstanding to meet the demand? In this situation orders to buy Baker will flood in, and brokers will raise the price in search of sellers. This will cause the expected return of Baker to fall, making it less attractive and thereby reducing its proportion in the tangency portfolio to a level where the number of shares demanded equals the number of shares outstanding.

Ultimately, everything will balance out. When all the price adjusting stops, the market will have been brought into equilibrium. First, each investor will want to hold a certain amount of each risky security. Second, the current market price of each security will be at a level where the number of shares demanded equals the number of shares outstanding.[6] Third, the riskfree rate will be at a level where the total amount of money borrowed equals the total amount of money lent. As a result, in equilibrium the proportions of the tangency portfolio will correspond to the proportions of what is known as the **market portfolio,** defined as follows:

market portfolio

> The market portfolio is a portfolio consisting of all securities where the proportion invested in each security corresponds to its relative market value. The relative market value of a security is simply equal to the aggregate market value of the security divided by the sum of the aggregate market values of all securities.[7]

The reason the market portfolio plays a central role in the CAPM is that the efficient set consists of an investment in the market portfolio, coupled

---

[5]While the expected return of Charlie has been changed, all the variances and covariances as well as the expected returns for Able and Baker are assumed to have the same values that were given in Chapter 9. The singular change in the expected return of Charlie alters not only the composition of the tangency portfolio but, more generally, the location and shape of the efficient set.

[6]In this situation the market for the security is said to have "cleared."

[7]The aggregate market value for the common stock of a company is equal to the current market price of the stock times the number of shares outstanding.

MONEY MATTERS
The Immeasurable Market Portfolio

The market portfolio holds a special place in modern investment theory and practice. It is central to the CAPM, which assumes that the market portfolio lies on the efficient set and that all investors hold the market portfolio in combination with a desired amount of riskfree borrowing and lending. Further, the market portfolio represents the ultimate in diversification. Consequently, passive investors (or index fund managers—see Chapter 17), who do not "bet" on the performance of particular securities but rather desire broad diversification, seek to hold the market portfolio. The market portfolio also serves as a universal performance evaluation standard. Investment managers and their clients often compare the managers' results against the returns on the market portfolio.

Despite its widespread application, the market portfolio is surprisingly ill-defined. In theory, the composition of the market portfolio is simple: all assets weighted in proportion to their respective market values. In reality, actually identifying the "true" market portfolio (or even a close approximation) is beyond the capability of any individual or organization.

Consider how we might go about specifying the market portfolio. The process would involve two steps: enumerating the assets to be included and calculating the market values of those assets.

First, we must list the various types of assets that constitute the market portfolio. Remember, we should think global—that is, include assets held by investors in both the United States and foreign countries. Of course, we want to include all securities representing the assets of businesses. Therefore, we should include common stocks, preferred stocks, and corporate bonds. In that vein we should also consider the value of proprietorships and partnerships. How about government debt? Well, yes, assuming that the debt is backed by real assets such as buildings or paper clips. (Due to deficit spending, much of the government's debt is actually backed by future taxes and thus does not represent current wealth—a technical matter often overlooked.) We should also include real estate, cash holdings, monetary metals (primarily gold), and art. But wait, we are not done yet. We should also include consumer durable assets such as autos, furniture, and major appliances. Last, but certainly not least, we should include the largest asset of all, the training and education in which people have invested vast sums, called human capital.

Simply listing the composition of the market portfolio is a complex undertaking. Measuring its value is even more problematic. Given the sophistication of U.S.

---

with a desired amount of either riskfree borrowing or lending. Thus, it is common practice to refer to the tangency portfolio as the market portfolio, and to denote it as M instead of T. In theory, M consists of not only common stocks but also such other kinds of investments as bonds, preferred stocks, and real estate. However, in practice some people restrict M to just common stocks.

The Efficient Set

In the world of the Capital Asset Pricing Model it is a simple matter to determine the relationship between risk and return for efficient portfolios. Figure 10-1 portrays it graphically. Point M represents the market portfolio and r_f represents the riskfree rate of return. Efficient portfolios plot along the line starting at r_f and going through M, and consist of alternative combinations of risk and return obtainable by combining the market portfolio with riskfree borrowing or lending. This linear efficient set of the CAPM is known as the

Capital Market Line

Capital Market Line (CML). All portfolios other than those employing the market portfolio and riskfree borrowing or lending would lie below the CML, although some might plot very close to it.

The slope of the Capital Market Line is equal to the difference between the expected return of the market portfolio and that of the riskless security,

capital markets, the values of domestic publicly traded assets are relatively easy to collect. (We should be careful, however, to avoid double-counting; for example, when one corporation owns part of another corporation.) Data availability in foreign markets varies from country to country. In some markets, such as those in the United Kingdom and Japan, security data collection systems are just as sophisticated as those in the United States. In other markets, such as those in Third World countries, comprehensive security data is difficult to acquire.

A similar situation exists with respect to nonpublicly traded asset values. In some countries, such as the United States, the government attempts to make accurate estimates of a myriad of asset values, from real estate to consumer durable goods. In other countries, little or no effort is made to compile these data.

Finally, with respect to estimating the value of human capital—well, good luck.

The difficulties involved in determining the composition and value of the "true" market portfolio has led to the use of market portfolio proxies. In dealing with common stocks, for example, most researchers and practitioners arbitrarily define the market portfolio to be a broad stock market index, such as the S&P 500 or the Wilshire 5000.

What are the ramifications of not knowing the market portfolio's true composition? From a theoretical perspective, the potential problems are significant. In two controversial articles (*Journal of Financial Economics*, March 1977, and *Journal of Finance*, September 1978), Richard Roll argued that the ambiguity of the market portfolio leaves the CAPM untestable. He contended that only if one knows the true market portfolio can one test whether it actually lies on the efficient set. Considering that the CAPM linear relationship between expected return and beta depends on the efficiency of the market portfolio, Roll's argument should not be taken lightly. Further, Roll argues that the practice of using proxies for the market portfolio is loaded with problems. Different proxies, even if their returns are highly correlated, could lead to different beta estimates for the same security. Roll's arguments, it should be noted, were strongly contested by prominent CAPM defenders.

From a practical perspective, investors have generally been willing to overlook the market portfolio's ambiguity. Passive managers typically segment the market into various asset classes, such as stocks and bonds. They then define, somewhat arbitrarily, a market portfolio for each of those asset classes and construct their portfolios to track the performance of the respective asset class market portfolios. Similarly, performance evaluators employ market proxies in their CAPM–risk-adjusted return calculations (see Chapter 18), despite Roll's warnings to the contrary.

One can interpret this obliviousness to the market portfolio's ambiguity to mean that the problem is nonexistent or as a sign of serious problems in current investment theory and practice. The jury is still out.

$(\bar{r}_M - r_f)$, divided by the difference in their risks, $(\sigma_M - 0)$, or $(\bar{r}_M - r_f)/\sigma_M$.[8] Since the vertical intercept of the CML is r_f, the straight line characterizing the CML has the following equation:

$$\bar{r}_P = r_f + \left[\frac{\bar{r}_M - r_f}{\sigma_M}\right]\sigma_P \tag{10.1}$$

where $\bar{r}_p$ and σ_p refer to the expected return and standard deviation of an efficient portfolio.[9] In the previous example, the market portfolio associated with a riskfree rate of 4% consisted of Able, Baker, and Charlie (these stocks are assumed to be the only ones that exist) in the proportions of .12, .19, and

[8]The slope of a straight line can be determined if the location of two points on the line are known. It is determined by "rise over run," meaning that it is determined by dividing the vertical distance between the two points by the horizontal distance between the two points. In the case of the CML, two points are known, corresponding to the riskfree rate and the market portfolio, so its slope can be determined in this manner.

[9]The equation of a straight line is of the form: $y = a + bx$, where a is the vertical intercept and b is the slope. Since the vertical intercept and slope of the CML are known, its equation can be written as shown here by making the appropriate substitutions for a and b.

FIGURE 10-1
The Capital Market Line

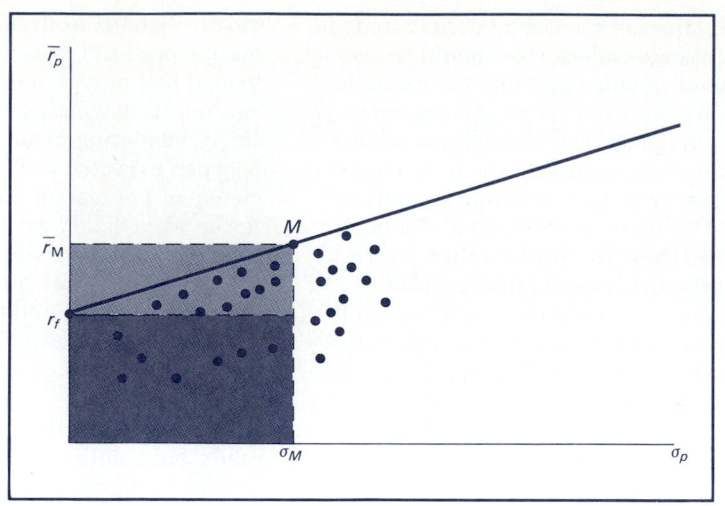

.69, respectively. Since it was shown in Chapter 9 that the expected return and standard deviation for a portfolio with these proportions was 22.4% and 15.2%, respectively, the equation for the resulting CML is:

$$\bar{r}_P = 4 + \left[\frac{22.4 - 4}{15.2}\right]\sigma_P$$
$$= 4 + 1.21\sigma_P.$$

Equilibrium in the security market can be characterized by two key numbers. The first is the vertical intercept of the CML (that is, the riskfree rate), which is often referred to as the reward for waiting. The second is the slope of the CML, which is often referred to as the reward per unit of risk borne. In essence, the security market provides a place where time and risk can be traded with their prices determined by the forces of supply and demand. Thus, the intercept and slope of the CML can be thought of as the price of time and the price of risk, respectively. In the example, they are equal to 4% and 1.21, respectively.

THE SECURITY MARKET LINE

Implications for Individual Risky Assets

The Capital Market Line represents the equilibrium relationship between the expected return and standard deviation for efficient portfolios. Individual risky securities will always plot below the line since a single risky security, when held by itself, is an inefficient portfolio. The Capital Asset Pricing Model does not imply any particular relationship between the expected return and the standard deviation (that is, total risk) of an individual security. To say more about the expected return of an individual security, deeper analysis is necessary.

In Chapter 8 the following equation was given for calculating the standard deviation of any portfolio:

$$\sigma_P = \left[\sum_{i=1}^{N} \sum_{j=1}^{N} X_i X_j \sigma_{ij} \right]^{1/2} \tag{8.5}$$

where X_i and X_j denoted the proportions invested in securities i and j, respectively, and σ_{ij} denoted the covariance of returns between security i and j. Now consider using this equation to calculate the standard deviation of the market portfolio:

$$\sigma_M = \left[\sum_{i=1}^{N} \sum_{j=1}^{N} X_{iM} X_{jM} \sigma_{ij} \right]^{1/2} \tag{10.2}$$

where X_{iM} and X_{jM} denote the proportions invested in securities i and j in forming the market portfolio, respectively. It can be shown that another way to write equation (10.2) is as follows:

$$\begin{aligned} \sigma_M = \Bigg[& X_{1M} \sum_{j=1}^{N} X_{jM}\sigma_{1j} \\ & + X_{2M} \sum_{j=1}^{N} X_{jM}\sigma_{2j} \\ & + X_{3M} \sum_{j=1}^{N} X_{jM}\sigma_{3j} \\ & + \ldots \\ & + X_{NM} \sum_{j=1}^{N} X_{jM}\sigma_{Nj} \Bigg]^{1/2}. \end{aligned} \tag{10.3}$$

At this point a property of covariance can be used: the covariance of security i with the market portfolio (σ_{iM}) can be expressed as the weighted average of every security's covariance with security i:

$$\sum_{j=1}^{N} X_{jM}\sigma_{ij} = \sigma_{iM}. \tag{10.4}$$

This property, when applied to each one of the N risky securities in the market portfolio, results in the following:

$$\begin{aligned} \sigma_M = [\; & X_{1M}\sigma_{1M} \\ & + X_{2M}\sigma_{2M} \\ & + X_{3M}\sigma_{3M} \\ & + \ldots \\ & + X_{NM}\sigma_{NM}]^{1/2} \end{aligned} \tag{10.5}$$

where σ_{1M} denotes the covariance of security 1 with the market portfolio, σ_{2M} denotes the covariance of security 2 with the market portfolio, and so on. Thus, the standard deviation of the market portfolio is equal to the square root of a weighted average of the covariances of all the securities with it, where the weights are equal to the proportions of the respective securities in the market portfolio.

At this juncture an important point can be observed. Under the CAPM, each investor holds the market portfolio and is concerned with its standard deviation, since that will influence the slope of the CML and hence the magnitude of his or her investment in the market portfolio. The contribution of each security to the standard deviation of the market portfolio can be seen in equation (10.5) to depend on the size of its covariance with the market portfolio. Accordingly, each investor will note that *the relevant measure of risk for a security is its covariance with the market portfolio,* σ_{iM}. This means that securities with larger values of σ_{iM} will be viewed by investors as contributing more to the risk of the market portfolio. It also means that securities with larger standard deviations should not be viewed as necessarily being riskier than those securities with smaller standard deviations.

From this analysis it follows that securities with larger values for σ_{iM} will have to provide proportionately larger expected returns in order for investors to be interested in purchasing them. In order to see why, consider what would happen if such securities did not provide investors with proportionately larger levels of expected return. In this situation these securities would contribute to the risk of the market portfolio while not contributing proportionately to the expected return of the market portfolio. This means that deleting such securities from the market portfolio would cause the expected return of the market portfolio, relative to its standard deviation, to rise. Since investors would view this as a favorable change, the market portfolio would no longer be the optimal risky portfolio to hold. Thus, security prices would be out of equilibrium.

The exact form of the equilibrium relationship between risk and return can be written as follows:

$$\bar{r}_i = r_f + \left[\frac{\bar{r}_M - r_f}{\sigma_M^2}\right]\sigma_{iM}. \tag{10.6}$$

As can be seen in panel (a) of Figure 10-2, equation (10.6) represents a straight line having a vertical intercept of r_f and a slope of $[(\bar{r}_M - r_f)/\sigma_M^2]$. Since the slope is positive, the equation indicates that securities with larger covariances with the market (σ_{iM}) will be priced so as to have larger expected returns ($\bar{r}_i$). This relationship between covariance and expected return is known as the **Security Market Line** (SML).[10]

Security Market Line

Interestingly, a risky security with $\sigma_{iM} = 0$ will have an expected return equal to the rate on the riskfree security, r_f. Intuitively, the reason for this is that the risky security, just like the riskfree security, does not contribute to the risk of the market portfolio. This is so even though the risky security has a positive standard deviation while the riskfree security has a standard deviation of zero.

It is even possible for some risky securities (meaning securities with positive standard deviations) to have expected returns less than the riskfree rate. According to the CAPM, this will occur if they have $\sigma_{iM} < 0$, thereby contributing a negative amount of risk to the market portfolio (meaning that they cause the risk of the market portfolio to be lower than it would be if less were invested in them).

---

[10] A more rigorous derivation of the SML is provided in the appendix.

FIGURE 10-2
The Security Market Line

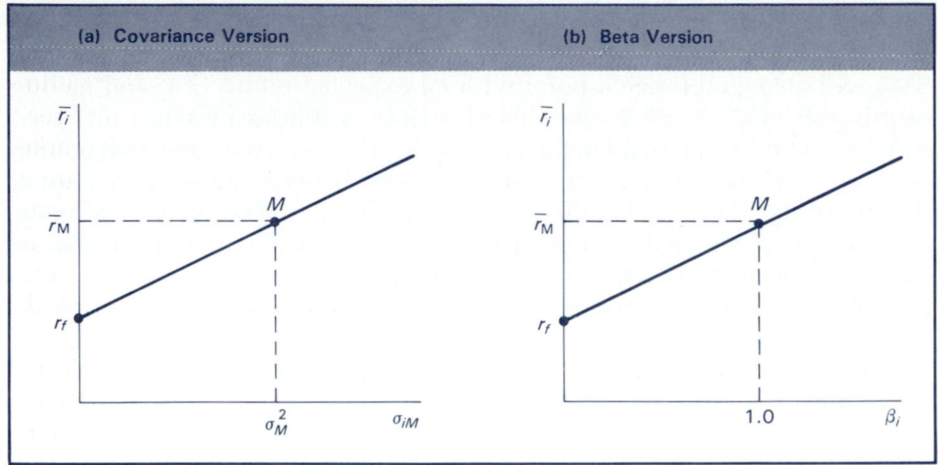

Also of interest is the observation that a risky security with $\sigma_{iM} = \sigma_M^2$ will have an expected return equal to the expected return on the market portfolio, $\bar{r}_M$. This is because such a security contributes an average amount of risk to the market portfolio.

Another way of expressing the SML is as follows:

$$\bar{r}_i = r_f + (\bar{r}_M - r_f)\beta_i \tag{10.7}$$

where the term β_i is defined as:

$$\beta_i = \frac{\sigma_{iM}}{\sigma_M^2}. \tag{10.8}$$

The term β_i is known as the **beta coefficient** (or simply the beta) for security i, and is an alternative way of representing the covariance of a security. Equation (10.7) is a different version of the SML, as can be seen in panel (b) of Figure 10-2. While having the same intercept as the earlier version shown in equation (10.6), r_f, it has a different slope. The slope of this version is $(\bar{r}_M - r_f)$, while the slope of the earlier version was $[(\bar{r}_M - r_f)/\sigma_M^2]$.

beta coefficient

One property of beta is that *the beta of a portfolio is simply a weighted average of the betas of its component securities, where the proportions invested in the securities are the respective weights.* That is, the beta of a portfolio can be calculated as:

$$\beta_P = \sum_{i=1}^{N} X_i\beta_i. \tag{10.9}$$

Earlier it was shown that the expected return of a portfolio is a weighted average of the expected returns of its component securities, where the proportions invested in the securities are the weights. This means that since every security plots on the SML, so will every portfolio. More broadly:

> Not only every security but also every portfolio must plot on an upward-sloping straight line in a diagram with expected return on the vertical axis and beta on the horizontal axis.

This means that efficient portfolios plot on both the CML and the SML, while inefficient portfolios plot on the SML but below the CML.

Also of interest is that the SML must go through the point representing the market portfolio itself. Its beta is one, and its expected return is $\bar{r}_M$, so its coordinates are $(1, \bar{r}_M)$. Since riskfree securities have beta values of zero, the SML will also go through a point with an expected return of r_f and having coordinates of $(0, r_f)$. This means that the SML will have a vertical intercept equal to r_f and a slope equal to the vertical distance between these two points, $(\bar{r}_M - r_f)$, divided by the horizontal distance between these two points, $(1 - 0)$, or $(\bar{r}_M - r_f)/(1 - 0) = (\bar{r}_M - r_f)$. Thus, these two points suffice to fix the location of the SML, indicating the "appropriate" expected returns for securities and portfolios with different beta values.

The equilibrium relationship shown by the SML comes to exist through the combined effects of investors' adjustments in holdings and the resulting pressures on security prices (as shown in Chapter 4). Given a set of security prices, investors calculate expected returns and covariances, then determine their optimal portfolios. If the number of shares of a security collectively desired differs from the number available, there will be upward or downward pressure on its price. Given a new set of prices, investors will reassess their desires for the various securities. The process will continue until the number of shares collectively desired for each security equals the number available.

For the individual investor, security prices and prospects are fixed while the quantities held can be altered. For the market as a whole, however, these quantities are fixed (at least in the short run) and prices are variable. As in any competitive market, equilibrium requires the adjustment of each security's price until there is consistency between the quantity desired and the quantity available.

It may seem logical to examine historical returns on securities in order to determine whether or not securities have been priced in equilibrium as suggested by the CAPM. However, the issue of whether or not such testing of the CAPM can be done in a meaningful manner is controversial. For at least some purposes affirmative test results may not be necessary in order to make practical use of the CAPM.

An Example

In the example that was used earlier, Able, Baker, and Charlie were shown to form the market portfolio in proportions equal to .12, .19, and .69, respectively. Given these proportions, the market portfolio was shown to have an expected return of 22.4% and a standard deviation of 15.2%. The riskfree rate in the example was 4%. Thus, for this example the SML as indicated in equation (10.6) is:

$$\bar{r}_i = r_f + \left[\frac{\bar{r}_M - r_f}{\sigma_M^2}\right]\sigma_{iM} \qquad (10.6)$$

$$= 4 + \left[\frac{22.4 - 4}{(15.2)^2}\right]\sigma_{iM}$$

$$= 4 + .08\sigma_{iM}. \qquad (10.10)$$

The following expected return vector and variance-covariance matrix were used in the examples shown in Chapter 8 and Chapter 9, and are also used here:

$$ER = \begin{bmatrix} 16.2 \\ 24.6 \\ 22.8 \end{bmatrix} \quad VC = \begin{bmatrix} 146 & 187 & 145 \\ 187 & 854 & 104 \\ 145 & 104 & 289 \end{bmatrix}.$$

At this point, the covariances of each security with the market portfolio can be calculated by using equation (10.4). More specifically, the covariances with the market portfolio for Able, Baker, and Charlie are equal to:

$$\begin{aligned}\sigma_{1M} &= \sum_{j=1}^{3} X_{jM}\sigma_{1j} \\ &= (.12 \times 146) + (.19 \times 187) + (.69 \times 145) \\ &= 153,\end{aligned}$$

$$\begin{aligned}\sigma_{2M} &= \sum_{j=1}^{3} X_{jM}\sigma_{2j} \\ &= (.12 \times 187) + (.19 \times 854) + (.69 \times 104) \\ &= 257,\end{aligned}$$

$$\begin{aligned}\sigma_{3M} &= \sum_{j=1}^{3} X_{jM}\sigma_{3j} \\ &= (.12 \times 145) + (.19 \times 104) + (.69 \times 289) \\ &= 236.\end{aligned}$$

Note how the SML as given in equation (10.10) states that the expected return for Able should be equal to $4 + (.08 \times 153) = 16.2\%$. Similarly, the expected return for Baker should be $4 + (.08 \times 257) = 24.6\%$ and the expected return for Charlie should be $4 + (.08 \times 236) = 22.8\%$. Each one of these expected returns corresponds to the respective value given in the expected return vector.

Alternatively, equation (10.8) can be used to calculate the betas for the three companies. More specifically, the betas for Able, Baker, and Charlie are equal to:

$$\begin{aligned}\beta_1 &= \frac{\sigma_{1M}}{\sigma_M^2} \\ &= \frac{153}{(15.2)^2} \\ &= .66,\end{aligned}$$

$$\begin{aligned}\beta_2 &= \frac{\sigma_{2M}}{\sigma_M^2} \\ &= \frac{257}{(15.2)^2} \\ &= 1.11,\end{aligned}$$

$$\begin{aligned}\beta_3 &= \frac{\sigma_{3M}}{\sigma_M^2} \\ &= \frac{236}{(15.2)^2} \\ &= 1.02.\end{aligned}$$

Now equation (10.7) indicated that the SML could be expressed in a form where the measure of risk for an asset was its beta. For the example under consideration, this reduces to:

$$\begin{aligned} \bar{r}_i &= r_f + (\bar{r}_M - r_f)\beta_i \\ &= 4 + (22.4 - 4)\beta_i \\ &= 4 + 18.4\beta_i. \end{aligned} \qquad (10.11)$$

Note how the SML as given in this equation states that the expected return for Able should be equal to 4 + (18.4 × .66) = 16.2%. Similarly, the expected return for Baker should be 4 + (18.4 × 1.11) = 24.6% and the expected return for Charlie should be 4 + (18.4 × 1.02) = 22.8%. Each one of these expected returns correspond to the respective value given in the expected return vector.

It is important to realize that if any other portfolio is assumed to be the market portfolio, meaning that if any set of proportions other than .12, .19, and .69 is used, then such an equilibrium relationship between expected returns and betas (or covariances) will not hold. Consider a hypothetical market portfolio with equal proportions (that is, .333) invested in Able, Baker, and Charlie. Since this portfolio has an expected return of 21.2% and a standard deviation of 15.5%, the hypothetical SML would be as follows:

$$\begin{aligned} \bar{r}_i &= r_f + \left[\frac{\bar{r}_M - r_f}{\sigma_M^2}\right]\sigma_{iM} \\ &= 4 + \left[\frac{21.2 - 4}{(15.5)^2}\right]\sigma_{iM} \\ &= 4 + .07\sigma_{iM}. \end{aligned}$$

Able has a covariance with this portfolio of:

$$\begin{aligned} \sigma_{1M} &= \sum_{j=1}^{3} X_{jM}\sigma_{1j} \\ &= (.333 \times 146) + (.333 \times 187) + (.333 \times 145) \\ &= 159 \end{aligned}$$

which means that Able's expected return according to the hypothetical SML should be equal to 15.1% = 4 + (.07 × 159). However, since this does not correspond to the 16.2% figure that appears in the expected return vector, a portfolio with equal proportions invested in Able, Baker, and Charlie cannot be the market portfolio.[11]

[11]Baker and Charlie have covariances of 382 and 179, respectively, which means that their expected returns should be equal to 30.74% = 4 + (.07 × 382) and 16.53% = 4 + (.07 × 179). However, these figures do not correspond to the respective ones (24.6% and 22.8%) appearing in the expected return vector, indicating that there are discrepancies for all three securities. While this example has used the covariance version of the SML, the analysis is similar for the beta version of SML that is shown in equation (10.7).

THE MARKET MODEL

Chapter 8 introduced the market model, where the return on a common stock was assumed to be related to the return on a market index in the following manner:

$$r_i = \alpha_i + \beta_i r_I + \epsilon_i \tag{8.10}$$

where: r_i = return on security i for some given period,
r_I = return on market index for the same period,
α_i = intercept term,
β_i = slope term, and
ϵ_i = random error term.

It is natural to think about the relationship between the market model and the Capital Asset Pricing Model. After all, both models have a beta term (β_i) in them and both models somehow involve the market.

First of all, the market model is a *factor model,* or to be more specific, a single-factor model where the factor is a market index. Unlike the CAPM, however, it is not an *equilibrium model* that describes how prices are set for securities.

Second, the market model utilizes a *market index* such as the S&P 500, whereas the CAPM involves the *market portfolio*. There is a subtle yet important distinction here. The market portfolio is a collection of all the securities in the marketplace, whereas a market index is based on a sample of those securities (500 in the case of the S&P 500). This means that conceptually the beta of a stock based on the market model differs from the beta of the stock according to the CAPM. This is because the market model beta is measured relative to a market index while the CAPM beta is measured relative to the market portfolio. In practice, however, the composition of the market portfolio is not precisely known, so a market index is used. Thus, while conceptually different, betas determined with the use of a market index are treated as if they were determined with the use of the market portfolio.

In the example, only three securities were in existence—the common stocks of Able, Baker, and Charlie. Subsequent analysis indicated that the CAPM market portfolio consisted of these stocks in the proportions of .12, .19, and .69, respectively. It is against this portfolio that the betas of the securities should be measured. However, in practice they are likely to be measured against a market index (for example, one that is based on just the stocks of Able and Charlie in proportions of .20 and .80, respectively).

Market Indices

Since the performance of the market portfolio is not reported in the daily press, the betas based on it can never be precisely determined. Instead, betas are measured based on indices that measure the performance of some of the major components of the market portfolio. Hence, the distinction between the market portfolio and a market index is one that exists conceptually but not in practice. That is, each security's beta estimated from the market model using a market index is treated as if it were the security's beta based on the market portfolio.

One of the most widely known indices is the Standard & Poor's Stock Price Index (referred to earlier as the S&P 500), a value-weighted average price of 500 large stocks. Complete coverage of the stocks listed on the New York Stock Exchange is provided by the NYSE Composite Index, which is broader than the S&P 500 in that it considers more stocks. The American Stock Exchange computes a similar index for the stocks it lists, and the National Association of Security Dealers provides an index of over-the-counter stocks traded on the NASDAQ system. The Wilshire 5000 stock index is the most comprehensive index of common stock prices that is published regularly in the United States and is thus closer than the others to representing the overall performance of American stocks.[12]

Without question the most widely quoted market index is the Dow Jones Industrial Average (DJIA). Although based on the performance of only thirty stocks and utilizing a less satisfactory averaging procedure, the DJIA provides at least a fair idea of what is happening to stock prices.[13] Table 10-1 provides a listing of the thirty stocks whose prices are reflected in the DJIA.

Market and Unique Risk

In Chapter 8 it was shown that the total risk of a security σ_i^2 could be partitioned in two components as follows:

$$\sigma_i^2 = \beta_i^2\sigma_I^2 + \sigma_{\epsilon i}^2 \tag{8.15}$$

where the components are:

$$\beta_i^2\sigma_I^2 = \text{market risk, and}$$

$$\sigma_{\epsilon i}^2 = \text{unique risk.}$$

Since beta (or covariance) is the relevant measure of risk for a security according to the CAPM, it is only appropriate to explore the relationship between it and the total risk of the security. It turns out that the relationship is identical to that given in equation (8.15) *except that the market portfolio is involved instead of a market index:*

$$\sigma_i^2 = \beta_i^2\sigma_M^2 + \sigma_{\epsilon i}^2 \tag{10.12}$$

market risk

As with the market model, the total risk of security *i*, measured by its variance and denoted σ_i^2, is shown to consist of two parts. The first component is the portion related to moves of the market portfolio. It is equal to the product of the square of the beta of the stock and the variance of the market portfolio, and is often referred to as the **market** (or systematic) **risk** of the security. The second component is the portion not related to moves of the market portfolio.

[12]Other indices of common stocks are commonly reported in the daily press. Many of these are components of the major indices mentioned here. For example, *The Wall Street Journal* reports on a daily basis not only the level of the S&P 500 but also the levels of the Standard & Poor's Industrials, Transportations, Utilities, and Financials. These last four indices reflect the performance of particular sectors of the stock market. Their components, 500 stocks in total, make up the S&P 500 (Standard & Poor's also reports the level of a 400 MidCap index based on the stock prices of middle-sized companies). See Chapters 14 and 26 for a more thorough discussion of stock market indices.

[13]Charles Dow started this index in 1884 by simply adding the prices of eleven companies and then dividing the sum by eleven. In 1928, securities were added to bring the total number up to thirty. Since then the composition of these thirty has been changed periodically. Due to things like stock dividends and splits, the divisor is no longer simply equal to the number of stocks in the index.

TABLE 10-1
Stocks in the Dow Jones Industrial Average at Year-End 1991

Allied-Signal
Alcoa
American Express
American Telephone & Telegraph
Bethlehem Steel
Boeing
Caterpillar
Chevron
Coca-Cola
Walt Disney
DuPont
Eastman Kodak
Exxon
General Electric
General Motors
Goodyear Tire
IBM
International Paper
McDonald's
Merck
Minnesota Mining & Manufacturing (3M)
J.P. Morgan
Philip Morris
Proctor & Gamble
Sears, Roebuck
Texaco
Union Carbide
United Technologies
Westinghouse
Woolworth

Source: Reprinted by permission of *The Wall Street Journal*,

It is denoted $\sigma^2_{\epsilon i}$ and is often referred to as the **unique** (or unsystematic) **risk** of the security.

unique risk

An Example

From the earlier example, the betas of Able, Baker, and Charlie were calculated to be .66, 1.11, and 1.02, respectively. Since the standard deviation of the market portfolio was equal to 15.2%, this means that the market risk of the three firms is equal to $(.66^2 \times 15.2^2) = 100$, $(1.11^2 \times 15.2^2) = 285$, and $(1.02^2 \times 15.2^2) = 240$, respectively.

The unique risk of any security can be calculated by solving equation (10.12) for $\sigma^2_{\epsilon f}$:

$$\sigma^2_{\epsilon i} = \sigma^2_i - \beta^2_i \sigma^2_M \tag{10.13}$$

Thus, equation (10.13) can be used to calculate the unique risk of Able, Baker, and Charlie, respectively:

$$\begin{aligned}\sigma^2_{\epsilon 1} &= 146 - 100 \\ &= 46, \\ \sigma^2_{\epsilon 2} &= 854 - 285 \\ &= 569,\end{aligned}$$

$$\sigma^2_{\epsilon 3} = 289 - 240$$
$$= 49.$$

Unique risk is sometimes expressed as a standard deviation. This is calculated by taking the square root of $\sigma^2_{\epsilon i}$, and would be equal to $\sqrt{46} = 6.8\%$ for Able, $\sqrt{569} = 23.9\%$ for Baker, and $\sqrt{49} = 7\%$ for Charlie.

Motivation for the Partitioning of Risk

At this point one may wonder: why partition total risk into two parts? For the investor, it would seem that risk is risk—whatever its source. The answer lies in the domain of expected returns.

Market risk is related to the risk of the market portfolio and to the beta of the security in question. Securities with larger betas will have larger amounts of market risk. In the world of the CAPM, securities with larger betas will have larger expected returns. These two relationships together imply that securities with larger market risks should have larger expected returns.

Unique risk is not related to beta. This means that there is no reason why securities with larger amounts of unique risks should have larger expected returns. Thus, according to the CAPM, investors are rewarded for bearing market risk but not for bearing unique risk.

SUMMARY

1. The Capital Assets Pricing Model (CAPM) is based on a specific set of assumptions about investor behavior and the existence of perfect security markets.

2. Based on these assumptions, all investors will hold the same efficient portfolio of risky assets.

3. Investors will differ only in the amounts of riskfree borrowing or lending they undertake.

4. The risky portfolio held by all investors is known as the market portfolio.

5. The market portfolio consists of all securities, each weighted in proportion to its market value relative to the market value of all securities.

6. The linear efficient set of the CAPM is known as the Capital Market Line (CML). The CML represents the equilibrium relationship between the expected return and standard deviation of efficient portfolios.

7. Under the CAPM, the relevant measure of risk for a security is its covariance with the market portfolio.

8. The linear relationship between market covariance and expected return is known as the Security Market Line (SML).

9. The beta of a security is an alternative way of measuring the risk of a security in the market portfolio. Beta is a measure of covariance relative to the market portfolio's variance.

10. The beta from the CAPM is similar in concept to the beta from the market model. However, the market model is not an equilibrium model of security prices as is the CAPM. Further, the market model uses a market index, which likely is a subset of the CAPM's market portfolio.

11. As with the market model, under the CAPM, the total risk of a security can be separated into market (systematic) risk and unique (unsystematic) risk.

KEY TERMS

normative economics
positive economics
Capital Asset Pricing Model
homogeneous expectations
perfect markets
separation theorem
market portfolio
Capital Market Line
Security Market Line
beta coefficient
market risk
unique risk

QUESTIONS AND PROBLEMS

1. Describe the key assumptions underlying the CAPM.
2. Many of the underlying assumptions of the CAPM are violated to some degree in the "real world." Does that fact invalidate the model's conclusions? Explain.
3. What is the separation theorem? What implications does it have for the optimal portfolio of risky assets held by investors?
4. What constitutes the "market portfolio"? What problems does one confront in specifying the composition of the true market portfolio? How have researchers and practitioners circumvented these problems?
5. In the equilibrium world of the CAPM, is it possible for a security not to be part of the market portfolio? Explain.
6. Describe the price adjustment process that equilibrates the market's supply and demand for securities. What conditions will prevail under such an equilibrium?
7. Will an investor who owns the market portfolio have to buy and sell units of the component securities every time the relative prices of those securities change? Why?
8. Given an expected return of 12% for the market portfolio, a riskfree rate of 6%, and a market portfolio standard deviation of 20%, draw the Capital Market Line.
9. Explain the significance of the Capital Market Line.
10. Assume that two securities constitute the market portfolio. Those securities have the following expected returns, standard deviations, and proportions:

SECURITY	EXPECTED RETURN	STANDARD DEVIATION	PROPORTION
A	10%	20%	.40
B	15	28	.60

    Based on this information and given a correlation of .30 between the two securities and a riskfree rate of 5%, specify the equation for the Capital Market Line.

11. Distinguish between the Capital Market Line and the Security Market Line.
12. The market portfolio is assumed to be composed of four securities. Their covariances with the market and their proportions are shown below:

SECURITY	COVARIANCE WITH MARKET	PROPORTION
A	242	.20
B	360	.30
C	155	.20
D	210	.30

    Given these data, calculate the market portfolio's standard deviation.

13. Explain the significance of the slope of the SML. How might the slope of the SML change over time?
14. Why should the expected return for a security be directly related to the security's covariance with the market portfolio?
15. The risk of a well-diversified portfolio to an investor is measured by the standard deviation of the portfolio's returns. Why shouldn't the risk of an individual security be calculated in the same manner?
16. A security with a high standard deviation is not necessarily highly risky to the investor. Why might you suspect that securities with above-average standard deviations tend to have above-average betas?
17. Kitty Bransfield owns a portfolio composed of three securities. The betas of those securities and their proportions in Kitty's portfolio are shown below. What is the beta of Kitty's portfolio?

SECURITY	BETA	PROPORTION
A	.90	.30
B	1.30	.10
C	1.05	.60

18. Assume that the expected return on the market portfolio is 15% and its standard deviation is 21%. The riskfree rate is 7%. What is the standard deviation of a well-diversified (no unique risk) portfolio with an expected return of 16.6%?
19. Given that the expected return on the market portfolio is 10%, the riskfree rate of return is 6%, the beta of stock A is .85, and the beta of stock B is 1.20:
    (a) Draw the SML.
    (b) What is the equation for the SML?
    (c) What are the equilibrium expected returns for stocks A and B?
    (d) Plot the two risky securities on the SML.
20. You are given the following information on two securities, the market portfolio, and the riskfree rate:

	EXPECTED RETURN	CORRELATION WITH MARKET PORTFOLIO	STANDARD DEVIATION
Security 1	15.5%	0.90	20.0%
Security 2	9.2	0.80	9.0
Market portfolio	12.0	1.00	12.0
Riskfree rate	5.0	0.00	0.0

    (a) Draw the SML.
    (b) What are the betas of the two securities?
    (c) Plot the two securities on the SML.
21. Assume that two securities, A and B, constitute the market portfolio. Their proportions and variances are .39, 160, and .61, 340, respectively.

The covariance of the two securities is 190. Calculate the betas of the two securities.

22. The CAPM permits the standard deviation of a security to be segmented into market and unique risk. Distinguish between the two types of risk.

23. Is an investor who owns any portfolio of risky assets other than the market portfolio exposed to some unique risk? Explain.

APPENDIX

A

A Derivation of the Security Market Line

Figure A-1 shows the location of the feasible set of the Markowitz model, along with the riskfree rate and the associated efficient set that represents the Capital Market Line. Within the feasible set of the Markowitz model lies every individual risky security. An arbitrarily chosen risky security, denoted i, has been selected for analysis and is shown on the figure.

Consider any portfolio, denoted p, that consists of the proportion X_i

FIGURE A-1
Deriving the Security Market Line

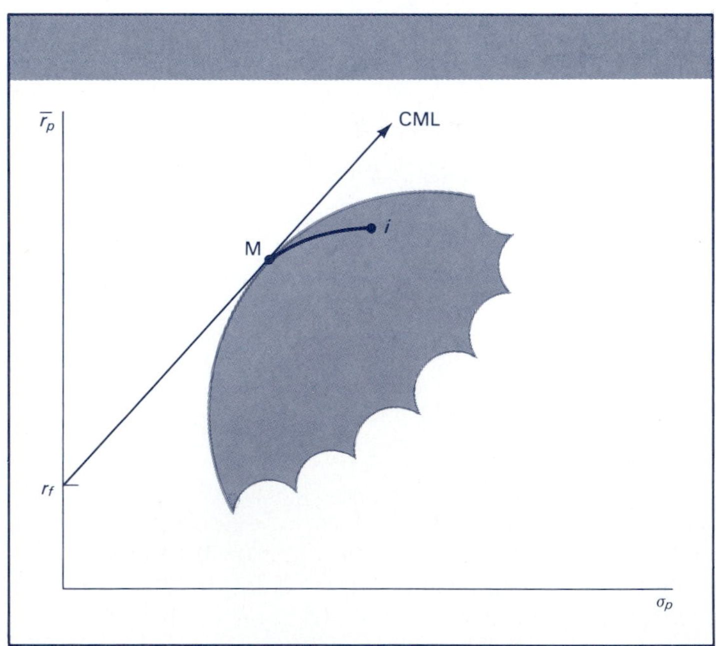

invested in security i and the proportion $(1 - X_i)$ invested in the market portfolio M. Such a portfolio will have an expected return equal to:

$$\bar{r}_p = X_i\bar{r}_i + (1 - X_i)\bar{r}_M \tag{10.14}$$

and a standard deviation equal to:

$$\sigma_p = [X_i^2\sigma_i^2 + (1 - X_i)^2\sigma_M^2 + 2X_i(1 - X_i)\sigma_{iM}]^{1/2}. \tag{10.15}$$

All such portfolios will lie on a curved line connecting i and M such as the one shown in Figure A-1.

Of concern is the slope of this curved line. Since it is a curved line, its slope is not a constant. However, its slope can be determined with the use of calculus. First, using equation (10.14), the derivative of $\bar{r}_p$ with respect to X_i is taken:

$$\frac{d\bar{r}_P}{dX_i} = \bar{r}_i - \bar{r}_M. \tag{10.16}$$

Second, using equation (10.15), the derivative of σ_p with respect to X_i is taken:

$$\frac{d\sigma_P}{dX_i} = \frac{X_i\sigma_i^2 - \sigma_M^2 + X_i\sigma_M^2 + \sigma_{iM} - 2X_i\sigma_{iM}}{[X_i^2\sigma_i^2 + (1 - X_i)^2\sigma_M^2 + 2X_i(1 - X_i)\sigma_{iM}]^{1/2}}. \tag{10.17}$$

Third, it can be noted the slope of the curved line iM, $d\bar{r}_p/d\sigma_p$, can be written as:

$$\frac{d\bar{r}_P}{d\sigma_P} = \frac{d\bar{r}_P/dX_i}{d\sigma_P/dX_i}. \tag{10.18}$$

This means that the slope of iM can be calculated by substituting equations (10.16) and (10.17) into the numerator and denominator of equation (10.18), respectively:

$$\frac{d\bar{r}_P}{d\sigma_P} = \frac{[\bar{r}_i - \bar{r}_M][X_i^2\sigma_i^2 + (1 - X_i)^2\sigma_M^2 + 2X_i(1 - X_i)\sigma_{iM}]^{1/2}}{X_i\sigma_i^2 - \sigma_M^2 + X_i\sigma_M^2 + \sigma_{iM} - 2X_i\sigma_{iM}}. \tag{10.19}$$

Of interest is the slope of the curved line iM at the endpoint M. Since the proportion X_i is zero at this point, the slope of iM can be calculated by substituting zero for X_i in equation (10.19). After doing so, many terms drop out, leaving:

$$\frac{d\bar{r}_P}{d\sigma_P} = \frac{[\bar{r}_i - \bar{r}_M][\sigma_M]}{\sigma_{iM} - \sigma_M^2}. \tag{10.20}$$

At M the slope of the CML, $(\bar{r}_M - r_f)/\sigma_M$, must equal the slope of the curved line iM. This is because the slope of the curved line iM increases when moving from the endpoint i, converging to the slope of the CML at the endpoint M. Accordingly, the slope of the curve iM at M, as shown on the right-hand side of equation (10.20), is set equal to the slope of the CML:

$$\frac{[\bar{r}_i - \bar{r}_M][\sigma_M]}{\sigma_{iM} - \sigma_M^2} = \frac{(\bar{r}_M - r_f)}{\sigma_M}. \tag{10.21}$$

Solving equation (10.21) for $\bar{r}_i$ results in the covariance version of the SML:

$$\bar{r}_i = r_f + \left[\frac{\bar{r}_M - r_f}{\sigma_M^2}\right]\sigma_{iM}. \tag{10.6}$$

The beta version of the SML is derived by substituting β_i for σ_{iM}/σ_M^2 in equation (10.6).

REFERENCES

1. Credit for the initial development of the CAPM is usually given to:

   William F. Sharpe, "Capital Asset Prices: A Theory of Market Equilibrium Under Conditions of Risk," *Journal of Finance*, 19, no. 3 (September 1964): 425–42;

   John Lintner, "The Valuation of Risk Assets and the Selection of Risky Investments in Stock Portfolios and Capital Budgets," *Review of Economics and Statistics*, 47, no. 1 (February 1965): 13–37, and "Security Prices, Risk, and Maximal Gains from Diversification," *Journal of Finance*, 20, no. 4 (December 1965): 587–615;

   Jan Mossin, "Equilibrium in a Capital Asset Market," *Econometrica*, 34, no. 4 (October 1966): 768–83.

2. The Sharpe and Lintner papers were compared in:

   Eugene F. Fama, "Risk, Return, and Equilibrium: Some Clarifying Comments," *Journal of Finance*, 23, no. 1 (March 1968): 29–40.

3. Some extended versions of the CAPM can be found in:

   Gordon J. Alexander and Jack Clark Francis, *Portfolio Analysis* (Englewood Cliffs, N.J.: Prentice Hall, 1986), Chapter 8;

   Edwin J. Elton and Martin J. Gruber, *Modern Portfolio Theory and Investment Analysis* (New York: John Wiley, 1991), Chapter 12.

4. For a comparison of the market model and CAPM betas, see:

   Harry M. Markowitz, "The 'Two Beta' Trap," *Journal of Portfolio Management*, 11, no. 1 (Fall 1984): 12–20.

5. For a discussion of why the CAPM is difficult to meaningfully test, see:

   Richard Roll, "A Critique of the Asset Pricing Theory's Tests; Part I. On Past and Potential Testability of the Theory," *Journal of Financial Economics*, 4, no. 2 (March 1977): 129–76.

6. Several tests of the CAPM, along with Roll's critique of them, are summarized in Chapter 10 of:

   Gordon J. Alexander and Jack Clark Francis, *Portfolio Analysis* (Englewood Cliffs, N.J.: Prentice Hall, 1986).

7. For an assertion that the use of modern portfolio theory does not depend upon successful testing of the CAPM, see:

   Harry M. Markowitz, "Nonnegative or Not Nonnegative: A Question about CAPMs," *Journal of Finance*, 38, no. 2 (May 1983): 283–95.

8. A discussion of some of the statistical difficulties encountered in using modern portfolio theory (specifically, how to cope with *estimation risk*) is contained in Chapter 6 of:

   Gordon J. Alexander and Jack Clark Francis, *Portfolio Analysis* (Englewood Cliffs, N.J.: Prentice Hall, 1986).

Factor Models

11

The objective of modern portfolio theory is to provide a means by which the investor can identify his or her optimal portfolio when there is an infinite number of possibilities. Using a framework involving expected returns and standard deviations, it was shown that the investor needs to estimate the expected return and standard deviation for each security under consideration for inclusion in the portfolio, along with all the covariances between securities. With these estimates, the investor can derive the curved efficient set of Markowitz. Then, for a given riskfree rate, the investor can identify the tangency portfolio and determine the location of the linear efficient set. Finally, the investor can proceed to invest in this tangency portfolio and borrow or lend at the riskfree rate, with the amount of borrowing or lending depending on the investor's risk-return preferences.

FACTOR MODELS AND RETURN-GENERATING PROCESSES

The task of identifying the curved Markowitz efficient set can be greatly simplified by introducing a **return-generating process.** A return-generating process is a statistical model that describes how the return on a security is produced. Chapter 8 presented a type of return-generating process known as the market model. The market model states that a security's return is a

return-generating process

function of the return on a market index. However, there are many other types of return-generating processes for securities.

Factor Models

factor models

These types of processes are often called **factor models** (or index models) because they assert that the return on a security is sensitive to the movements of various factors (or indices). In attempting to accurately estimate expected returns, variances, and covariances for securities, these models are potentially more useful than the market model. They have this potential because it appears that actual security returns are sensitive to more than movements in a market index. That is, within the economy there seems to be more than one pervasive factor that affects security returns.

As a return-generating process, a factor model represents the behavior of security prices: it attempts to capture the major economic forces that systematically move the prices of all securities. Implicit in the construction of a factor model is the assumption that the returns on two securities will be correlated (that is, move together) only through common reactions to one or more of the factors specified in the model. Any aspect of a security's return unexplained by the factor model is assumed to be unique (or specific) to the security and therefore uncorrelated with the unique elements of returns on other securities. As a result, a factor model is a powerful tool for portfolio management. It can supply the information needed to calculate expected returns, variances, and covariances for every security, a necessary condition to estimate the curved Markowitz efficient set.

Application

As a practical matter, all investors employ factor models, whether they do so explicitly or implicitly. It is impossible to consider separately the interrelationship of every security with every other. Numerically, the problem of calculating covariances among securities rises exponentially as the number of securities analyzed increases.[1]

Conceptually, thinking about the tangled web of security variances and covariances becomes mind-boggling as the number of securities increases beyond just a few securities, let alone hundreds or thousands. Even the vast data-processing capabilities of high-speed computers are strained when they are called upon to construct efficient sets from a large number of securities.

Abstraction is therefore an essential step in identifying the curved Markowitz efficient set. Factor models supply the necessary level of abstraction. They provide investment managers with a framework to identify important factors in the economy and the marketplace and assess the extent to which different securities will respond to changes in these factors.

Given the belief that one or more factors influence security returns, a primary goal of security analysis is to determine these factors and the sensitivities of security returns to movements in these factors. A formal statement of such a relationship is termed a *factor model of security returns*. The discussion begins with the simplest form of such a model, a one-factor model.

[1]See Appendix B to Chapter 8.

ONE-FACTOR MODELS

Some investors argue that the return-generating process for securities involves a single factor. For example, they might contend that the returns on securities respond to the growth rate in gross domestic product (GDP).[2] Table 11-1 and Figure 11-1 illustrate one way of providing substance for such statements.

An Example

On the horizontal axis of Figure 11-1 is the growth rate in GDP, while the vertical axis measures the return on Widget's stock. Each point in the graph represents the combination of Widget's return and GDP growth rate for a particular year as reported in Table 11-1. A line has been statistically fitted to the data.[3] This line has a positive slope of 2.0, indicating that there exists a positive relationship between GDP growth rates and Widget's returns; higher rates of GDP growth are associated with higher returns.

In equation form, the relationship between GDP growth and Widget's return can be expressed as follows:

$$r_t = a + b\text{GDP}_t + e_t \tag{11.1}$$

where: r_t = the return on Widget in period t,
GDP_t = the rate of growth in GDP in period t,
e_t = the unique (or "specific") return on Widget in period t,
b = **sensitivity** of Widget to GDP growth,[4] and
a = the "zero" factor for GDP.

sensitivity

[2]GDP is similar to gross national product (GNP) in that it is a measure of a country's total output of goods and services. However, GDP treats imports and exports slightly differently than GNP and, as a result, requires fewer revisions after it is initially reported. Furthermore, international comparisons are straightforward with GDP, since most countries report GDP instead of GNP. Consequently, only GDP is currently reported by the U.S. government.

[3]Only six data points are shown in the figure for ease of exposition. The standard statistical procedure used to fit a line to a group of data is referred to as simple linear regression. This procedure is discussed in Chapter 13 and in Mark Kritzman ". . . About Regression," *Financial Analysts Journal*, 47, no. 3 (May/June 1991), 12-15; it can be found in most statistics books, such as James T. McClave and P. George Benson, *Statistics for Business and Economics* (San Francisco: Dellen Publishing Company, 1991), Chapter 11.

[4]Sometimes b is referred to as the **factor loading** (or attribute) of the security.

factor loading

TABLE 11-1
Factor Model Data

YEAR	GROWTH RATE IN GDP[1]	RATE OF INFLATION[2]	RETURN ON WIDGET STOCK
1986	5.7%	1.1%	14.3%
1987	6.4	4.4	19.2
1988	7.9	4.4	23.4
1989	7.0	4.6	15.6
1990	5.1	6.1	9.2
1991	2.9	3.1	13.0

[1]Source: *Economic Report of the President* (Washington, D.C.: U.S. Government Printing Office, 1992), p. 304.

[2]Source: *Economic Report of the President* (Washington, D.C.: U.S. Government Printing Office, 1992), p. 365.

FIGURE 11-1
A One-Factor Model

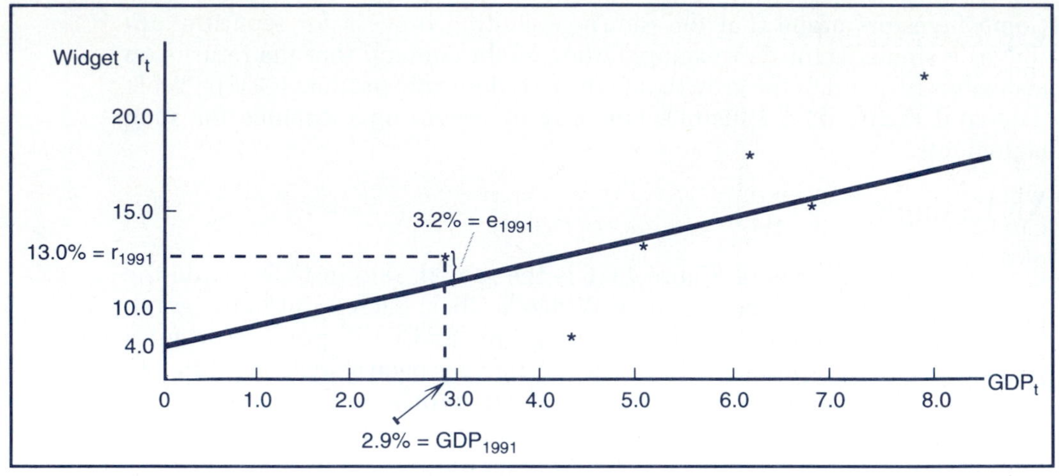

In Figure 11-1 the "zero" factor is 4.0% per period. This is the return that would be expected for Widget if GDP growth equaled zero. The sensitivity of Widget to GDP growth, b, is 2.0, and is the same as the slope of the line in Figure 11-1. This value indicates that, in general, higher growth in GDP is associated with higher returns for Widget. If GDP growth equaled 5%, Widget should generate a return of 14% [= 4% + (2.0 × 5%)]. If GDP growth were 1% higher (that is, 6%), Widget's return should be 2.0% higher, or 16.0%.

In this example, in 1991 GDP growth was 2.9% and Widget actually returned 13.0%. Therefore, Widget's unique return (given by e_t) in this particular year was +3.2%. This was determined by subtracting from Widget's actual return of 13.0% an amount that represents Widget's expected return, given that GDP went up by 2.9%. In this case, Widget would have an expected return of 9.8% [= 4.0 + (2.0 × 2.9)], thereby resulting in a unique return of +3.2% (= 13.0% − 9.8%).

In effect, the one-factor model presented in Figure 11-1 and equation (11.1) attributes Widget's return in any particular period to three elements:

1. An effect common in any period (the term a),
2. An effect that differs across periods depending on the growth rate of GDP (the term $bGDP_t$), and
3. An effect specific to the particular period observed (the term e_t).

Generalizing the Example

This example of a one-factor model can be generalized in equation form for any security i in period t:

$$r_{it} = a_i + b_i F_t + e_{it} \tag{11.2}$$

where F is the value of the factor in period t and b_i is the sensitivity of security i to this factor. If the value of the factor were zero, the return on the security would equal $a_i + e_{it}$. Note that e_{it} is a random error term, just like the random error term that was discussed in Chapter 8. That is, it is a random variable with an expected value of zero and a standard deviation σ_{ei}, and can be thought of as the outcome occurring from a spin of a roulette wheel.

Expected Return The expected return on security i in period t, according to the one-factor model, can be written as:

$$\bar{r}_{it} = a_i + b_i\overline{F}_t \qquad (11.3)$$

where $\overline{F}_t$ denotes the expected value of the factor in period t. Thus, the term a_i can be seen to represent the expected return on security i if the expected value of the factor is zero.

Alternatively, if the expected value of the factor is some nonzero value (as is typically the case), then equation (11.3) can be used to estimate the expected return on the security. For example, if the expected growth rate in GDP is 3%, then the expected return for Widget would equal 10% [= 4% + (2 × 3%)].

Variance With the one-factor model, it can also be shown that the variance of any security i is equal to:

$$\sigma_i^2 = b_i^2\sigma_F^2 + \sigma_{ei}^2 \qquad (11.4)$$

where σ_F^2 is the variance of the factor F and σ_{ei}^2 is the variance of the random error term e_i. Thus, if the variance of the factor σ_F^2 equals 3.0 and the residual variance σ_{ei}^2 equals 15.2, then according to this equation Widget's variance would equal:

$$\begin{aligned} \sigma_i^2 &= (2^2 \times 3.0) + (15.2) \\ &= 27.2. \end{aligned}$$

Covariance With a one-factor model the covariance between any two securities i and j can be shown to equal:

$$\sigma_{ij} = b_i b_j \sigma_F^2. \qquad (11.5)$$

In the example of Widget, equation (11.5) can be used to estimate the covariance between Widget and another hypothetical security such as the stock of Whatever Company. Assuming the factor sensitivity of Whatever is 4.0, the covariance between Widget and Whatever would equal:

$$\begin{aligned} \sigma_{ij} &= 2.0 \times 4.0 \times 3.0 \\ &= 24.0. \end{aligned}$$

Assumptions Equations (11.4) and (11.5) are based on two critical assumptions. The first assumption is that the random error term and the factor are uncorrelated, meaning that the outcome of the factor has no bearing on the outcome of the random error term.

The second assumption is that the random error terms of any two securities are uncorrelated, meaning that the outcome of the random error term of one security has no bearing on the outcome of the random error term of any other security. In other words, the returns of two securities will be correlated (that is, move together) only through common responses to the factor. If either of these two assumptions is invalid, then the model is an approximation, and a different factor model (perhaps one with more factors) will theoretically be a more accurate model of the return-generating process.

The Market Model

The market model can now be shown to be a specific example of a one-factor model where the factor is the return on a market index. In Chapter 8, the market model appeared as:

$$r_i = \alpha_i + \beta_i r_I + \epsilon_i. \tag{8.10}$$

Comparing equation (8.10) with the general form of the one-factor model in equation (11.2), the similarity between the two equations is readily apparent. The intercept term, α_i, from the market model equation corresponds to the "zero" factor term, a_i, from equation (11.2). Further, the slope term, β_i, from the market model equates to the sensitivity term, b_i, from the generalized one-factor model. Each equation has a random error term, e_{it} in the factor model and ϵ_{it} in the market model.[5] Finally, the market index return plays the role of the single factor.

However, as mentioned earlier, the concept of a one-factor model does not restrict the investor to using a market index as the factor. Many other factors are plausible, such as GDP or industrial production or inflation.

Two Important Features of One-Factor Models

Two features of one-factor models are of particular interest.

The Tangency Portfolio First, the assumption that the returns on all securities respond to a single common factor greatly simplifies the task of identifying the tangency portfolio. In order to determine the composition of the tangency portfolio, the investor needs to estimate all the expected returns, variances, and covariances. This can be done with a one-factor model by estimating a_i, b_i, and σ_{ei} for each of the N risky securities.[6]

Also needed are the expected value of the factor, $\overline{F}_t$, and its standard deviation, σ_F. With these estimates, equations (11.3), (11.4), and (11.5) can subsequently be used to calculate expected returns, variances, and covariances for the securities. Using these values, the curved efficient set of Markowitz can then be derived, from which the tangency portfolio can be determined for a given riskfree rate.

The common responsiveness of securities to the factor eliminates the need to estimate directly the covariances between the securities. Those covariances are captured by the securities' sensitivities to the factor and the factor's variance.

Diversification The second interesting feature of one-factor models has to do with diversification. Earlier it was shown that diversification leads to an averaging of market risk and a reduction in unique risk. This feature is also true of any one-factor model, except now instead of market and unique risk, the words factor and nonfactor risk are used. That is, in equation (11.4) the

---

[5]The time subscript t was deleted from the random error term of the market model shown in equation (8.10) simply for ease of exposition.

[6]This is shown in more detail in Appendix B to Chapter 8.

first term on the right-hand side is known as the **factor risk** of the security and the second term is known as the **nonfactor** (or idiosyncratic) **risk** of the security.

factor risk

nonfactor risk

With a one-factor model, the variance of a portfolio is given by:

$$\sigma_p^2 = b_p^2 \sigma_F^2 + \sigma_{ep}^2 \tag{11.6a}$$

where:

$$b_p = \sum_{i=1}^{N} X_i b_i \tag{11.6b}$$

$$\sigma_{ep}^2 = \sum_{i=1}^{N} X_i^2 \sigma_{ei}^2. \tag{11.6c}$$

Equation (11.6a) shows that the total risk of any portfolio can be viewed as having two components similar to the two components of the total risk of an individual security shown in equation (11.4). In particular, the first and second terms on the right-hand side of equation (11.6a) are the factor risk and nonfactor risk of the portfolio, respectively.

As a portfolio becomes more diversified (meaning it contains more securities), each proportion X_i will become smaller. However, this will not cause b_p to either decrease or increase significantly unless a deliberate attempt is made to do so by adding securities with values of b_i that are either relatively low or high, respectively. This is because, as equation (11.6b) shows, b_p is simply a weighted average of the sensitivities of the securities, b_i, with the values of X_i serving as the weights. Thus, *diversification leads to an averaging of factor risk.*

However, as a portfolio becomes more diversified, there is reason to expect σ_{ep}^2, the nonfactor risk, to decrease. This can be shown by examining equation (11.6c). Assuming the amount invested in each security is equal, then this equation can be rewritten by substituting $1/N$ for X_i:

$$\sigma_{ep}^2 = \sum_{i=1}^{N} \left[\frac{1}{N}\right] \sigma_{ei}^2$$

$$= \frac{1}{N} \left[\frac{\sigma_{e1}^2 + \sigma_{e2}^2 + \ldots + \sigma_{eN}^2}{N}\right].$$

The value inside the brackets is the average nonfactor risk for the component securities. But the portfolio's nonfactor risk is only one-Nth as large as this, since the term $1/N$ appears outside the brackets. As the portfolio becomes more diversified, the number of securities in it, N, becomes larger. This means that $1/N$ becomes smaller, which in turn reduces the nonfactor risk of the portfolio. Simply stated, *diversification reduces nonfactor risk.*[7]

[7]Actually, all that is necessary for this reduction in nonfactor risk to occur is for the maximum amount invested in any one security to continually decrease as N increases. An example based on the market model is given in Chapter 8.

The health of the economy affects most firms, and thus changes in expectations concerning the future of the economy can be expected to have profound effects on the returns of most securities. However, the economy is not a simple, monolithic entity. Several common influences with pervasive effects might be identified. For example:

1. The growth rate of gross domestic product,
2. The level of interest rates,
3. The inflation rate, or
4. The level of oil prices.

Two-Factor Models

Instead of a one-factor model, a multiple-factor model for security returns that considers these various influences may be more accurate. As an example of a multiple-factor model, consider a two-factor model. That is, assume that the return-generating process contains two factors.

In equation form, the two-factor model is as follows:

$$r_i = a_i + b_{i1}F_1 + b_{i2}F_2 + e_i \tag{11.7}$$

where F_1 and F_2 are the two factors that are pervasive influences on security returns and b_{i1} and b_{i2} are the sensitivities of security i to these two factors. As with the one-factor model, e_i is a random error term and a_i is the expected return on security i if each factor has a value of zero.

Figure 11-2 provides an illustration of Widget Company's stock, whose returns are affected by both the growth rate in GDP and the rate of inflation. As was the case in the one-factor example, each point in the figure corresponds to a particular year. This time, however, each point is a combination of Widget's return, the rate of inflation, and the growth in GDP in that year as given in Table 11-1. To this scatter of points is fit a two-dimensional plane, which is described by the following adaptation of equation (11.7):

$$r_t = a + b_1\text{GDP}_t + b_2\text{INF}_t + e_t.$$

The slope of the plane in the GDP growth rate direction (the term b_1) represents Widget's sensitivity to changes in GDP growth. The slope of the plane in the inflation rate direction (the term b_2) is Widget's sensitivity to changes in the inflation rate. Note that the sensitivities b_1 and b_2 in this example are positive and negative, respectively, having corresponding values of 2.2 and −.7.[8] This indicates that as GDP growth or inflation rises, Widget's return should increase or decrease, respectively.

The intercept term (the zero factor) in Figure 11-2 of 5.8% indicates Widget's expected return if both GDP growth and inflation were zero. Finally, in a given year the distance from Widget's actual point to the plane indicates its unique return (e_t), the portion of Widget's return not attributed to either

[8]These values were arrived at by applying multiple regression (see McClave and Benson, *Statistics*, Chapter 12) to the data given in Table 11-1.

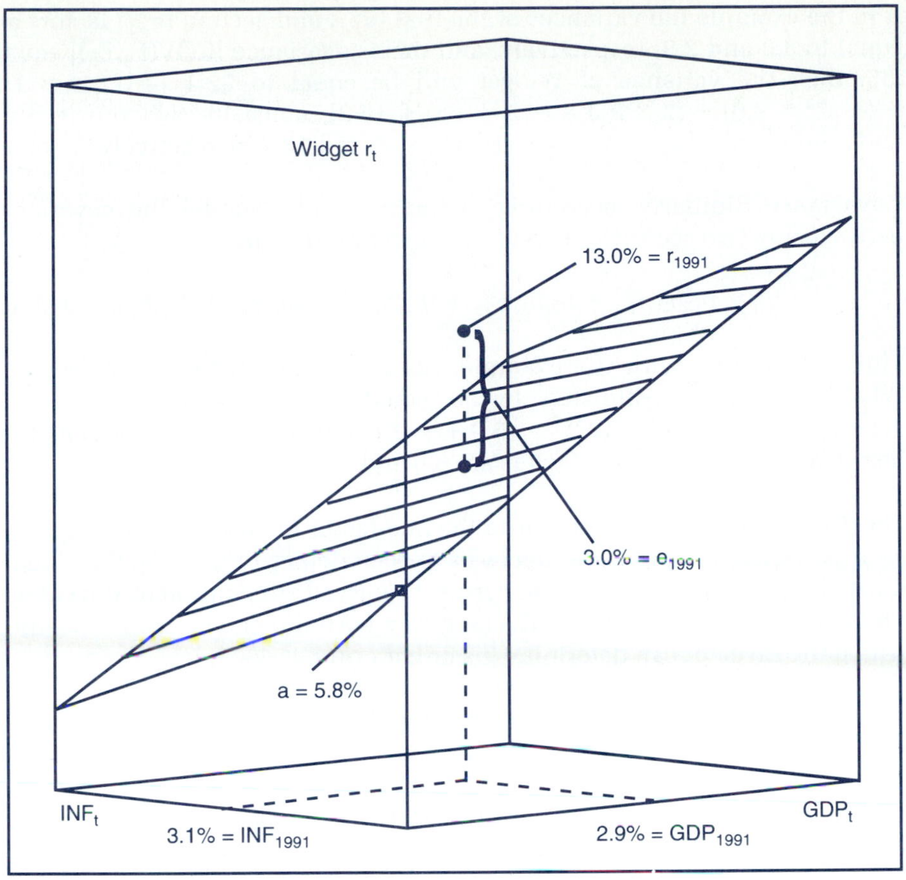

FIGURE 11-2
A Two-Factor Model

GDP growth or inflation. For example, Widget's expected return in 1991, given that GDP grew by 2.9% and inflation was 3.1%, equals 10.0% [= 5.8 + (2.2 × 2.9) − (.7 × 3.1)]. Hence, its unique return for 1991 is equal to +3.0% (= 13.0% − 10.0%).

Four parameters need to be estimated for each security with the two-factor model. They are a_i, b_{i1}, b_{i2}, and the standard deviation of the random error term, denoted σ_{ei}. For each of the factors, two parameters need to be estimated. These parameters are the expected value of each factor ($\bar{F}_1$ and $\bar{F}_2$) and the variance of each factor (σ^2_{F1} and σ^2_{F2}). Finally, the covariance between the factors, $COV(F_1,F_2)$, needs to be estimated.

Expected Return With these estimates, the expected return for any security i can be determined by using the following formula:

$$\bar{r}_i = a_i + b_{i1}\bar{F}_1 + b_{i2}\bar{F}_2. \tag{11.8}$$

In the example, the expected return for Widget would be equal to 8.9% [= 5.8 + (2.2 × 3.0) − (.7 × 5.0)], provided that the expected increases in GDP and inflation were 3% and 5%, respectively.

Variance According to the two-factor model, the variance for any security i will be:

$$\sigma^2_i = b^2_{i1}\sigma^2_{F1} + b^2_{i2}\sigma^2_{F2} + 2b_{i1}b_{i2}COV(F_1,F_2) + \sigma^2_{ei}. \tag{11.9}$$

If in the example the variances of the first (σ^2_{F1}) and second (σ^2_{F2}) factors are equal to 3.0 and 2.9, respectively, and their covariance [$COV(F_1,F_2)$] equals .65, then the variance of Widget will be equal to 32.1 [= $(2.2^2 \times 3.0) + (-.7^2 \times 2.9) + (2 \times 2.2 \times -.7 \times .65) + 18.2$], since its two sensitivities and random error term variance are 2.2, −.7, and 18.2, respectively.

Covariance Similarly, according to the two-factor model the covariance between any two securities i and j can be determined by:

$$\sigma_{ij} = b_{i1}b_{j1}\sigma^2_{F1} + b_{i2}b_{j2}\sigma^2_{F2} + (b_{i1}b_{j2} + b_{i2}b_{j1})COV(F_1,F_2). \tag{11.10}$$

Thus, continuing with the example, the covariance between Widget and Whatever can be estimated to be equal to 39.9 [= $(2.2 \times 6.0 \times 3.0) + (-.7 \times -5.0 \times 2.9) + (2.2 \times -5.0 + -.7 \times 6.0) \times .65$], since the sensitivities of Whatever to the two factors are 6.0 and −5.0, respectively.

The Tangency Portfolio Similar to the one-factor model, once the expected returns, variances, and covariances have been determined using these equations, the investor can proceed to derive the curved efficient set of Markowitz. Then, for a given riskfree rate, the tangency portfolio can be identified, after which the investor can determine his or her optimal portfolio.

Diversification Everything said earlier regarding one-factor models and the effects of diversification apply here as well. In particular:

1. Diversification leads to an averaging of factor risk,
2. Diversification can substantially reduce nonfactor risk, and
3. For a "well-diversified portfolio," nonfactor risk will be insignificant.

As with a one-factor model, the sensitivity of a portfolio to a particular factor in a multiple-factor model is a weighted average of the sensitivities of the securities, where the weights are equal to the proportion invested in each security. This can be seen by remembering that the return on a portfolio is a weighted average of the returns of its component securities:

$$r_p = \sum_{i=1}^{N} X_i r_i. \tag{11.11}$$

Substituting the right-hand side of equation (11.7) for r_i on the right-hand side of equation (11.11) results in:

$$\begin{aligned} r_p &= \sum_{i=1}^{N} X_i(a_i + b_{i1}F_1 + b_{i2}F_2 + e_i) \\ &= \left[\sum_{i=1}^{N} X_i a_i\right] + \left[\sum_{i=1}^{N} X_i b_{i1} F_1\right] + \left[\sum_{i=1}^{N} X_i b_{i2} F_2\right] + \left[\sum_{i=1}^{N} X_i e_i\right] \\ &= a_p + b_{p1}F_1 + b_{p2}F_2 + e_p \end{aligned} \tag{11.12}$$

where:

$$a_p = \sum_{i=1}^{N} X_i a_i$$

$$b_{p1} = \sum_{i=1}^{N} X_i b_{i1}$$

$$b_{p2} = \sum_{i=1}^{N} X_i b_{i2}$$

$$e_p = \sum_{i=1}^{N} X_i e_i.$$

Note that the portfolio sensitivities, b_{p1} and b_{p2}, are weighted averages of the respective individual sensitivities b_{i1} and b_{i2}.

Extending the Model

To extend the discussion to more than two factors requires the abandonment of diagrams, as the analysis must move beyond three dimensions. Nevertheless, the concepts are the same. If there are *k* factors, the multiple-factor model can be written as:

$$r_i = a_i + b_{i1}F_1 + b_{i2}F_2 + \ldots + b_{ik}F_k + e_i$$

where each security has *k* sensitivities, one for each of the *k* factors.

ESTIMATING FACTOR MODELS

While many methods of estimating factor models are used, these methods can be grouped into three primary approaches:

1. Time-series approaches,
2. Cross-sectional approaches, and
3. Factor analysis approaches.

Time-Series Approaches

Time-series approaches are perhaps the most intuitive to investors.[9] The model builder begins with the assumption that he or she knows in advance the factors that influence security returns. Identification of the relevant factors typically proceeds from an analysis of the economics of the firms involved. Aspects of macroeconomics, microeconomics, industrial organization, and fundamental security analysis will play a major role in the process. For example, as discussed earlier, certain macroeconomic variables might be expected to have a pervasive impact on security returns, including such things as growth in GDP, inflation, interest rates, and so on. With these factors specified, the model builder collects historical information concerning the values of the factors and security returns from period to period. Using this data, the model builder can calculate the sensitivities of the securities' returns to the factors, the securities' zero factors and unique returns, and the standard deviations of the factors and their correlations. In this approach, accurate measurement of factor values is crucial. In practice, this can be quite difficult.

[9]The examples given earlier in the chapter are examples of this approach.

MONEY MATTERS
Working with Multiple-Factor Models

No one knows exactly which variables affect security prices, let alone how those variables interact. Nevertheless, factor models provide valuable, if incomplete, explanations of the complex workings of security markets.

A factor model expresses the return and risk of a security in terms of one or more financial or economic characteristics. It presumes that these characteristics (or factors) affect all securities to some degree. Further, a factor model implies that securities with the same sensitivities to these factors should behave in the same way.

In Chapter 8, we studied the most widely recognized factor model, the market model. The market model is the essence of simplicity. It relates a security's return and risk to a single factor, the return on a market index.

Simplicity is said to be a virtue. That a security's return should depend heavily on how the market performs and that a security's risk should be related to the sensitivity of its returns to movements in the market are intuitively appealing concepts.

Investment researchers and practitioners, however, have often been frustrated by the shallowness of the market model. Few doubt that the relationships underlying security price movements are much more complex than those implied by the market model. For example, stocks within an entire industry sometimes move in the opposite direction of the stock market. When Iraq invaded Kuwait in August 1990, the U.S. stock market declined sharply. Oil company stocks, conversely, surged ahead. The market model could not account for this event.

The conviction that security prices are related to factors other than the market's return has led to the development of multiple-factor models. These factor models relate a security's return to more than one common economic variable or financial characteristic. The market's return may be one of these factors, but then again, it may not.

The process of constructing multiple-factor models is far from an exact science. No firm rules exist to guide the model builder in selecting factors for inclusion. While certain statistical tests can be applied to gauge the explanatory power of a particular factor model, the model builder retains wide latitude to include or exclude potential factors.

Three primary criteria influence the choice of factors. Most importantly, selected factors should exhibit a demonstrably significant impact on many securities. For example, the growth in GDP affects almost all security prices. Conversely, while the growth in defense expenditures may have a meaningful impact on the stocks of defense contractors, few other stocks are likely to be affected by this factor.

Second, selected factors should possess theoretical justification. Including factors based solely on past statistical relationships with security prices is a dangerous game. These relationships may be simply coincidences and may not persist in the future. For example, economic theory strongly supports the observation that the level of real interest rates affects many security prices. On the other hand, there is no theoretical justifi-

Security prices reflect investors' estimates of the present values of firms' future prospects. At any given time the price of Widget stock is likely to depend on the projected growth rate of GDP, the projected rate of inflation, and so on. If investors' projections of such fundamental economic conditions change, so too will the price of Widget. Since the return on a stock is influenced heavily by changes in its price, stock returns would be expected to be more highly correlated with changes in expected future values of fundamental economic variables than with the actual changes that occur contemporaneously. For example, a large increase in inflation that was fully anticipated might have no effect on the stock price of a company whose earnings are highly sensitive to inflation.

For this reason, whenever possible it is desirable to select factors that measure changes in expectations rather than realizations, since the latter typically include both changes that were anticipated and those that were not. One way to accomplish this goal is to rely on variables that involve changes in market prices. Thus, the difference in the returns on two portfolios—one consisting of stocks thought to be unaffected by inflation and the other consisting of stocks thought to be affected by inflation—could be used as a measure of revisions in inflation expectations. Those who construct factor

cation for the observed relationship between an original National Football League team winning the Super Bowl and the stock market subsequently performing well.

Finally, factors should be selected for which timely, accurate data are readily available. For example, the spread between high- and low-quality bond yields (a measure of investor risk aversion and default risk) is widely and accurately reported. Conversely, even though one might believe that changes in the personal savings rate have a significant impact on security prices, such information is notoriously inaccurate and undergoes significant revisions.

How do investors use multiple-factor models? There are four principal uses, conducted primarily at the portfolio level:

1. Risk forecasts.
2. Return forecasts.
3. Portfolio construction.
4. Performance attribution.

Regarding risk forecasts, if we know our portfolio's sensitivities to the model's factors, the variances of the factors, the covariances among the factors, and the unique risk of the portfolio (all of this information can be estimated from historical return data), we can estimate the expected variability of our portfolio's returns using the multiple-factor model. Moreover, we can identify the forecasted contributions of the factors to our portfolio's expected variability.

With respect to return forecasting, if we are bold enough to estimate the future values of the factors, we can use the model to estimate the return on a portfolio with particular factor sensitivities. More importantly, we can "tilt" our portfolio toward those factors that are expected to realize high values and away from those factors expected to realize unfavorable values.

In the case of portfolio construction, we might wish to build a portfolio that has factor sensitivities similar to those of a reference (or benchmark) portfolio. For example, we may want to construct a forty-stock portfolio with factor sensitivities similar to a broad market index. A multiple-factor model allows us to quantify the market index's factor sensitivities. Using computer-based optimization techniques discussed in Chapter 8, we can build a portfolio that has sensitivities (and, hence, the risk and expected return) similar to those of the market index.

Finally, with respect to performance attribution, multiple-factor models allow investors to analyze the sources of return earned on a portfolio (see the Appendix to Chapter 18). Suppose we know our portfolio's return over the past year, the portfolio's sensitivities to the model's factors during the year, and the realized values of those factors. A factor model allows us to draw conclusions about what portion of our portfolio's return was due to particular factors and what portion was due to unique elements unexplained by the factor model. If we have pursued a strategy of emphasizing certain factors relative to a benchmark portfolio, our performance attribution analysis will show how those factors contributed to our portfolio's return relative to the benchmark. Or, if we have concentrated on picking individual securities, with no significant factor "bets" relative to the benchmark, our performance attribution analysis will show the contribution (either positive or negative) to the portfolio's return from the unique return portion of the factor model.

models using the time-series approach often rely on market-based surrogates for changes in forecasts of fundamental economic variables in this manner.

Cross-Sectional Approaches

Cross-sectional approaches are less intuitive than time-series approaches but can often be just as powerful a tool. The model builder begins with estimates of securities' sensitivities to certain factors. Then, in a particular time period, the values of the factors are estimated based on securities' returns and their sensitivities to the factors. This process is repeated over multiple time periods, thereby providing an estimate of the factors' standard deviations and their correlations.[10]

[10]This procedure can also be used where the factor sensitivities are easily measured quantities like size, historic beta, and dividend yield. In such cases the factors that are identified can be thought of as a size factor, a market factor, and a dividend yield factor, respectively. See William F. Sharpe, "Factors in New York Stock Exchange Security Returns, 1931–1979," *Journal of Portfolio Management*, 8, no. 4 (Summer 1982): 5–19. An application is presented in Blake R. Grossman and William F. Sharpe, "Financial Implications of South African Divestment," *Financial Analysts Journal*, 42, no. 4 (July–August 1986): 15–29.

For example, if an investor had estimated the sensitivities of a group of stocks to inflation, in a given month he or she could estimate the inflation rate in that month by statistically comparing the returns on the securities in that month to their inflation factor sensitivities. Suppose under a one-factor model that Gotcha Company stock has a sensitivity to inflation of 1.10 and a zero factor of 0.5% per month. If Gotcha returned 2% in a particular month, by implication the inflation rate that month was 1.36% [= (2% − .5%)/1.10]. If this calculation was performed over many stocks, a statistically valid estimate of the predicted inflation rate for that month could be derived.

Note that this approach works entirely differently from the time-series approach. With the latter approach, the values of the factors are known and the sensitivities are estimated. With the former the sensitivities are known and the values of the factors are estimated.

Factor Analysis Approaches

Finally, with factor analysis approaches the model builder knows neither the factor values nor the securities' sensitivities to those factors. A statistical technique called factor analysis is used to extract the number of factors and securities' sensitivities based simply on a set of securities' past returns. Factor analysis takes the returns on a sample of securities and attempts to identify one or more statistically significant factors that could have generated the covariances of returns observed within the sample. In essence, the return data "tells" the model builder about the structure of the factor model. Unfortunately, factor analysis does not specify what economic variables the factors represent.

Limitations

There is no reason to assume that a good factor model for one period will be a good one for the next period; key factors change—remember the effect of energy prices on security markets in the 1970s and more recently during the war in the Persian Gulf. The risks and returns associated with various factors and the sensitivities of securities to factors can change over time.

It would be convenient if neither the relevant factors nor the values of the relevant magnitudes were to change from period to period. If this were so, mechanical procedures could be applied to security returns over an extended past period and the factor model inferred, along with all the needed magnitudes. As it is, statistical estimation methods should be tempered with the judgment of the model builder to account for the dynamic nature of the investment environment.

FACTOR MODELS AND EQUILIBRIUM

It should be kept in mind that a factor model is not an equilibrium model of asset pricing. However, if equilibrium exists, then there will be certain relationships between the parameters of the factor model and those of the equilibrium asset pricing model.

For example, if actual returns can be viewed as being generated by a one-factor model where the factor is the return on the market portfolio, r_M, then according to equation (11.3), expected returns will be equal to $a_i + b_i\bar{r}_M$, since $\overline{F} = \bar{r}_M$. But if equilibrium exists according to the Capital Asset Pricing Model, then equation (10.7) states that expected returns will also be equal to:

$$\bar{r}_i = r_f + (\bar{r}_M - r_f)\beta_i, \tag{10.7}$$

which can be rewritten as:

$$\begin{aligned} \bar{r}_i &= r_f - r_f\beta_i + \bar{r}_M\beta_i \\ &= (1 - \beta_i)r_f + \bar{r}_M\beta_i. \end{aligned}$$

This means that the parameters of the one-factor model and the CAPM must have the following relationships:

$$\begin{aligned} a_i &= (1 - \beta_i)r_f \\ b_i &= \beta_i. \end{aligned}$$

That is, if expected returns are determined according to the CAPM and actual returns are generated by the one-factor market model, then a_i and b_i must be equal to $(1 - \beta_i)r_f$ and β_i, respectively.[11]

SUMMARY

1. A factor model is a return-generating process that relates returns on securities to the movement in one or more common factors.

2. Any aspect of a security's return unexplained by the factor model is assumed to be unique to the security and therefore uncorrelated with the unique element of returns on other securities.

3. The market model is a specific example of a factor model where the factor is the return on a market index.

4. The assumption that the returns on securities respond to common factors greatly simplifies the task of calculating the curved Markowitz efficient set.

5. The sensitivity of a portfolio to a factor is the weighted average of the sensitivities of the component securities, with the securities' proportions of the portfolio serving as weights.

6. The total risk of a security is composed of factor risk and nonfactor risk.

7. Diversification leads to an averaging of factor risk.

8. Diversification reduces nonfactor risk.

9. Three basic methods are used to estimate factor models: the time-series approach; the cross-sectional approach; and the factor analysis approach.

10. A factor model is not an equilibrium model of asset prices as is the CAPM. However, if equilibrium exists, certain relationships will hold between the factor model and the equilibrium asset pricing model.

KEY TERMS

return-generating process
factor models
sensitivity
factor loading (attribute)
factor risk
nonfactor risk

[11]If the factor in a one-factor world is the return on the market portfolio (as shown here), then technically the random error term for any security cannot be completely uncorrelated with the factor. This is because the market portfolio consists of all securities and hence is influenced by the nonfactor return of each security.

QUESTIONS AND PROBLEMS

1. Included among the factors that might be expected to be pervasive are expectations regarding growth in real GNP, real interest rates, inflation, and oil prices. For each factor, provide an example of an industry that is expected to have a high (either positive or negative) sensitivity to the factor.
2. Why do factor models greatly simplify the process of deriving the curved Markowitz efficient set?
3. Many investment management firms assign each of their security analysts to research a particular group of stocks. (Usually these assignments are organized by industry.) How are these assignments an implicit recognition of the validity of factor model relationships?
4. What are two critical assumptions underlying any factor model? Cite hypothetical examples of violations of those assumptions.
5. Cupid Childs, a wise investment statistician, once said with respect to factor models, "Similar stocks should display similar returns." What did Cupid mean by this statement?
6. Based on a one-factor model, consider a security with a zero-factor value of 4% and a sensitivity to the factor of 0.50. The factor takes on a value of 10%. The security generates a return of 11%. What portion of the security's return is related to the factor and what portion is related to nonfactor elements?
7. Based on a one-factor model, consider a portfolio of two securities with the following characteristics:

SECURITY	FACTOR SENSITIVITY	NONFACTOR RISK (σ^2_{ei})	PROPORTION
A	.20	49	.40
B	3.50	100	.60

   (a) If the standard deviation of the factor is 15%, what is the factor risk of the portfolio?
   (b) What is the nonfactor risk of the portfolio?
   (c) What is the portfolio's standard deviation?
8. Based on a one-factor model, security A has a sensitivity of −0.50, while security B has a sensitivity of 1.25. If the covariance between the two securities is −312.50, what is the standard deviation of the factor?
9. Based on a one-factor model, for two securities A and B:

$$r_A = 5\% + .8F + e_A$$

$$r_B = 7\% + 1.2F + e_B$$

$$\sigma_F = 18\%$$

$$\sigma_{eA} = 25\%$$

$$\sigma_{eB} = 15\%.$$

   Calculate the standard deviation of each security.
10. Based on a one-factor model, if the average nonfactor risk (σ^2_{ei}) of all

securities is 225, what is the nonfactor risk of a portfolio with equal weights assigned to its 10 securities? 100 securities? 1,000 securities?

11. Based on the discussion of factor and nonfactor risk and given a set of securities that can be combined into various portfolios, what might be a useful measure of the relative diversification of each of the alternative portfolios?

12. With a five-factor model (assuming uncorrelated factors) and a thirty-stock portfolio, how many parameters must be estimated to calculate the expected return and standard deviation of the portfolio? How many additional parameter estimates are required if the factors are correlated?

13. Beyond the factors discussed in the text, speculate as to other factors that could reasonably be expected to pervasively affect security returns.

14. Based on a three-factor model, consider a portfolio composed of three securities with the following characteristics:

SECURITY	FACTOR 1 SENSITIVITY	FACTOR 2 SENSITIVITY	FACTOR 3 SENSITIVITY	PRO-PORTION
A	−.20	3.60	.05	.60
B	.50	10.00	.75	.20
C	1.50	2.20	.30	.20

What are the sensitivities of the portfolio to factors 1, 2, and 3?

15. Dode Cicero owns a portfolio of two securities. Based on a two-factor model, the two securities have the following characteristics:

SECURITY	ZERO FACTOR	FACTOR 1 SENSITIVITY	FACTOR 2 SENSITIVITY	NON-FACTOR RISK (σ^2_{ei})	PRO-PORTION
A	2%	.30	2.0	196	.70
B	3	.50	1.8	100	.30

The factors are uncorrelated. Factor 1 has an expected value of 15% and a standard deviation of 20%. Factor 2 has an expected value of 4% and a standard deviation of 5%. Calculate the expected return and standard deviation of Dode's portfolio. [Hint: Think about how equation (11.6a) could be extended to a two-factor model by considering equation (11.9).]

16. Based on a two-factor model, consider two securities with the following characteristics:

	SECURITY A	SECURITY B
Factor 1 sensitivity	1.5	0.7
Factor 2 sensitivity	2.6	1.2
Nonfactor risk (σ^2_{ei})	25.0	16.0

The standard deviations of factor 1 and factor 2 are 20% and 15%, respectively, and the factors have a covariance of 225. What are the standard deviations of securities A and B? What is their covariance?

17. Are factor models consistent with the CAPM? If returns are determined by a one-factor model (where that factor is the return on the market portfolio) and the CAPM holds, what relationships must exist between the two models?

REFERENCES

1. General discussions of factor models can be found in:

   William F. Sharpe, "Factors in New York Stock Exchange Security Returns, 1931–1979," *Journal of Portfolio Management*, 8, no. 4 (Summer 1982): 5–19; and "Factor Models, CAPMs, and the ABT (sic)," *Journal of Portfolio Management*, 11, no. 1 (Fall 1984): 21–25.

2. Empirical papers that attempt to identify relevant factors and estimate the magnitudes of the associated values include:

   Robert D. Arnott, "Cluster Analysis and Stock Price Movement," *Financial Analysts Journal*, 36, no. 6 (November/December 1980): 56–62;

   Nai-fu Chen, Richard Roll, and Stephen A. Ross, "Economic Forces and the Stock Market," *Journal of Business*, 59, no. 3 (July 1986): 383–403;

   Robert D. Arnott, Charles M. Kelso, Jr., Stephen Kiscadden, and Rosemary Macedo, "Forecasting Factor Returns: An Intriguing Possibility," *Journal of Portfolio Management*, 16, no. 1 (Fall 1989): 28-35.

   Edwin J. Elton and Martin J. Gruber, "Estimating the Dependence Structure of Share Prices—Implications for Portfolio Selection," *Journal of Finance*, 28, no. 5 (December 1973): 1203–32;

   Tony Estep, Nick Hanson, and Cal Johnson, "Sources of Value and Risk in Common Stocks," *Journal of Portfolio Management*, 9, no. 4 (Summer 1983): 5–13;

   James J. Farrell, Jr., "Analyzing Covariation of Returns to Determine Homogeneous Stock Groupings," *Journal of Business*, 47, no. 2 (April 1974): 186–207;

   George J. Feeney and Donald D. Hester, "Stock Market Indices: A Principal Components Analysis," in Donald D. Hester and James Tobin, eds., *Risk Aversion and Portfolio Choice* (New York: John Wiley & Sons, 1967);

   Benjamin F. King, "Market and Industry Factors in Stock Price Behavior," *Journal of Business*, 39, no. 1 (January 1966): 139–70;

   Barr Rosenberg and Vinay Marathe, "The Prediction of Investment Risk: Systematic and Residual Risk," in *Proceedings of the Seminar on the Analysis of Security Prices* (Center for Research in Security Prices, Graduate School of Business, The University of Chicago, November 1975).

3. For an analysis of the Super Bowl-stock market relationship, see: Edward A. Dyl and John D. Schatzberg, "Did Joe Montana Save the Stock Market?" *Financial Analysts Journal*, 45, no. 5 (September–October 1989): 4–5; Thomas M. Kruger and William F. Kennedy, "An Examination of the Super Bowl Stock Market Predictor," *Journal of Finance*, 45, no. 2 (June 1990): 691–97.

12 Arbitrage Pricing Theory

The Capital Asset Pricing Model is an equilibrium model that describes why different securities have different expected returns. In particular, this positive economic model of asset pricing asserts that securities have different expected returns because they have different betas. However, there exists an alternative model of asset pricing that was developed by Stephen Ross. It is known as **Arbitrage Pricing Theory** (APT), and in some ways it is less complicated than the CAPM.

Arbitrage Pricing Theory

The CAPM requires a large number of assumptions, including those initially made by Harry Markowitz when he developed the mean-variance model. For example, each investor is assumed to choose his or her optimal portfolio by the use of indifference curves that are based on portfolio expected returns and standard deviations. In contrast, APT makes fewer assumptions. One primary APT assumption is that each investor, when given the opportunity to increase the return of his or her portfolio without increasing its risk, will proceed to do so. The mechanism for doing so involves the use of arbitrage portfolios.

FACTOR MODELS

APT starts out by making the innocuous assumption that security returns are related to an unknown number of unknown factors.[1] For ease of exposition,

[1]Factor models are discussed in detail in Chapter 11.

imagine that there is only one factor and that factor is the rate of increase in industrial production. Hence, security returns are related to the following one-factor model:

$$r_i = a_i + b_i F_1 + e_i \tag{12.1}$$

where: r_i = rate of return on security i,
F_1 = the value of the factor, which in this case is the rate of growth in industrial production, and
e_i = random error term.

sensitivity

In this equation, b_i is known as the **sensitivity** of security i to the factor or the factor loading for security i.[2]

Imagine that an investor currently owns three stocks where the current market value of his or her holdings in each one is \$4,000,000. Hence, the investor's current investable wealth W_0 is equal to \$12,000,000. Everyone believes that these three stocks have the following expected returns and sensitivities:

i	$\bar{r}_i$	b_i
1	15%	.9
2	21	3.0
3	12	1.8

Do these expected returns and factor sensitivities represent an equilibrium situation? If not, what will happen to stock prices and hence expected returns to restore equilibrium?

Arbitrage Portfolios

arbitrage portfolio

According to APT, the investor will explore the possibility of forming an **arbitrage portfolio** in order to increase the expected return of his or her current portfolio without increasing its risk. Just what is an arbitrage portfolio? First of all, it is a portfolio that does not require any additional funds from the investor. If X_i denotes the change in the investor's holdings of security i (and hence the weight of security i in the arbitrage portfolio), this requirement of an arbitrage portfolio can be written as:

$$X_1 + X_2 + X_3 = 0. \tag{12.2}$$

Second, an arbitrage portfolio has no sensitivity to any factor. Since the sensitivity of a portfolio to a factor is just a weighted average of the sensitivities of the securities in the portfolio to that factor, this requirement of an arbitrage portfolio can be written as:

$$b_1X_1 + b_2X_2 + b_3X_3 = 0 \tag{12.3a}$$

[2]There are other ways to write the equation for a factor model. Note that from equation (12.1) it follows that $\bar{r}_i = a_i + b_i\bar{F}_1$, where $\bar{r}_i$ and $\bar{F}_1$ are the expected return for security i and the expected value of the factor, respectively. Substituting $\bar{r}_i - b_i\bar{F}_1$ for a_i in equation (12.1) results in the following alternative formulation of a one-factor model: $r_i = \bar{r}_i + b_i(F_1 - \bar{F}_1) + e_i$. Letting $f_1 = F_1 - \bar{F}_1$, a third formulation of a one-factor model is: $r_i = \bar{r}_i + b_i f_1 + e_i$ where f_1 can be interpreted as the unexpected change in the value of the factor.

or, in this example:

$$.9X_1 + 3.0X_2 + 1.8X_3 = 0. \qquad (12.3b)$$

Thus, in this example an arbitrage portfolio will have no sensitivity to industrial production.

At this point many potential arbitrage portfolios can be identified. These candidates are simply portfolios that meet the conditions given in equations (12.2) and (12.3b). Note that there are three unknowns (X_1, X_2, and X_3) and two equations in this situation, which means that there is an infinite number of combinations of values for X_1, X_2, and X_3 that satisfy these two equations.[3] As a way of finding one combination, consider arbitrarily assigning a value of .1 to X_1. Doing so results in two equations and two unknowns:

$$.1 + X_2 + X_3 = 0 \qquad (12.4a)$$

$$.09 + 3.0X_2 + 1.8X_3 = 0. \qquad (12.4b)$$

The solution to equations (12.4a) and (12.4b) is $X_2 = .075$ and $X_3 = -.175$. Hence a potential arbitrage portfolio is one with these weights.

In order to see if this candidate is indeed an arbitrage portfolio, its expected return must be determined. If it is positive, then an arbitrage portfolio will have been identified.[4] Mathematically, this third and last requirement for an arbitrage portfolio is:

$$X_1\bar{r}_1 + X_2\bar{r}_2 + X_3\bar{r}_3 > 0 \qquad (12.5a)$$

or, for this example,

$$15X_1 + 21X_2 + 12X_3 > 0. \qquad (12.5b)$$

Using the solution for the candidate, it can be seen that its expected return is $(15 \times .1) + (21 \times .075) + (12 \times -.175) = .975\%$. Since this is a positive number, an arbitrage portfolio has indeed been identified.

The arbitrage portfolio just identified involves buying \$1,200,000 of stock 1 and \$900,000 of stock 2. How were these dollar figures arrived at? By taking the current market value of the portfolio (W_0 = \$12,000,000) and multiplying it by the weights for the arbitrage portfolio of $X_1 = .1$ and $X_2 = .075$. Where does the money come from to make these purchases? From selling \$2,100,000 of stock 3 (note that $X_3W_0 = -.175 \times \$12,000,000 = -\$2,100,000$).

The Investor's Position

At this juncture the investor can evaluate his or her position from either of two equivalent viewpoints: as holding both the old portfolio and the arbitrage

[3]There will always be an infinite number of solutions whenever there are more unknowns than equations. For example, consider a situation where there is one equation with two unknowns: $Y = 3X$. Note that there is an infinite number of paired values of X and Y that solve this equation, such as (1,3), (2,6), and (3,9).

[4]If its expected return is negative, then simply changing the signs of the weights will cause the expected return to become positive. Note that the new weights will also sum to zero and will still represent a portfolio that has zero sensitivity to the factor. Thus, the new weights will represent an arbitrage portfolio.

portfolio or as holding a new portfolio. Consider, for example, the weight in stock 1. The old portfolio weight was .33 and the arbitrage portfolio weight was .10, with the sum of these two weights being equal to .43. Note that the value of the holdings of stock 1 in the new portfolio amount to $5,200,000 (= $4,000,000 + $1,200,000), so its weight is .43 (= $5,200,000/$12,000,000), equivalent to the sum of the old and arbitrage portfolio weights.

Similarly, the portfolio's expected return is equal to the sum of the expected returns of the old and arbitrage portfolios, or 16.975% (= 16% + .975%). Equivalently, the new portfolio's expected return can be calculated using the new portfolio's weights and the expected returns of the stocks, or 16.975% [= (.43 × 15%) + (.41 × 21%) + (.16 × 12%)].

Continuing, the sensitivity of the new portfolio is 1.9 [= (.43 × .9) + (.41 × 3.0) + (.16 × 1.8)]. This is the same as the sum of the sensitivities of the old and arbitrage portfolios (= 1.9 + 0.0).

What about the risk of the new portfolio? Assume that the standard deviation of the old portfolio was 11%. The variance of the arbitrage portfolio will be small, since its only source of risk is nonfactor risk. Similarly, the variance of the new portfolio will differ from that of the old only as a result of changes in its nonfactor risk. Thus, it can be concluded that the risk of the new portfolio will be approximately 11%.[5] Table 12-1 summarizes these observations.

PRICING EFFECTS

What are the consequences of buying stocks 1 and 2 and selling stock 3? Since everyone will be doing so, their market prices will be affected and, accordingly, their expected returns will adjust. Specifically, the prices of stocks 1 and 2 will rise because of increased buying pressure. In turn, this will cause their expected returns to fall. Conversely, the selling pressure put on stock 3 will cause its stock price to fall and its expected return to rise.

This buying and selling activity will continue until all arbitrage possibilities are eliminated. At this point there will exist a linear relationship between expected returns and sensitivities of the following sort:

$$\bar{r}_i = \lambda_0 + \lambda_1 b_i \tag{12.6}$$

[5]Formally, the APT assumes that the arbitrage portfolio has no nonfactor risk, meaning that it is assumed that $\sigma^2_{ep} = 0$. Since the total risk of a portfolio σ^2_p is equal to $b^2_p\sigma^2_F + \sigma^2_{ep}$ according to the one-factor model [see equation (11.6a) in the previous chapter] and given that the arbitrage portfolio has no factor risk by design, meaning $b^2_p\sigma^2_F = 0$ because $b_p = 0$, this means that the arbitrage portfolio has zero total risk.

TABLE 12-1
How an Arbitrage Portfolio Affects an Investor's Position

	OLD PORTFOLIO	+	ARBITRAGE PORTFOLIO	=	NEW PORTFOLIO
Weights:					
X_1	.333		.100		.433
X_2	.333		.075		.408
X_3	.333		−.175		.158
Properties:					
$\bar{r}_p$	16.000%		.975%		16.975%
b_p	1.900		.000		1.900
σ_p	11.000%		small		approx. 11.000%

where λ_0 and λ_1 are constants. This equation is the asset pricing equation of the APT when returns are generated by one factor.[6] Note that it is the equation of a straight line, and hence it says that in equilibrium there will be a linear relationship between expected returns and sensitivities.

In the example, one possible equilibrium setting could have $\lambda_0 = 8$ and $\lambda_1 = 4$.[7] Consequently, the pricing equation would be:

$$\bar{r}_i = 8 + 4b_i. \tag{12.7}$$

This would result in the following equilibrium levels of expected returns for stocks 1, 2, and 3:

$$\bar{r}_1 = 8 + (4 \times .9) = 11.6\%$$

$$\bar{r}_2 = 8 + (4 \times 3.0) = 20.0\%$$

$$\bar{r}_3 = 8 + (4 \times 1.8) = 15.2\%.$$

As a result, the expected returns for stocks 1 and 2 will have fallen from 15% and 21%, respectively, to 11.6% and 20% because of increased buying pressure. Conversely, increased selling pressure will have caused the expected return on stock 3 to rise from 12% to 15.2%.

A Graphical Illustration Figure 12-1 illustrates the asset pricing equation of equation (12.6). Any security that has a factor sensitivity and expected return such that it lies off the line will be mispriced according to the APT, and will present investors with the opportunity of forming arbitrage portfolios. Security B is an example. If an investor buys security B and sells security S in equal dollar amounts, then the investor will have formed an arbitrage portfolio.[8] How can this be?

First of all, by selling an amount of S to pay for the long position in B the investor will not have committed any new funds. Second, since B and S have the same sensitivity to the factor, the selling of S and buying of B will constitute a portfolio with no sensitivity to the factor. Finally, the arbitrage portfolio will have a positive expected return since the expected return of B is greater than the expected return of S.[9] As a result of investors buying B its price will rise and, in turn, its expected return will fall until it is located on the APT asset pricing line.[10]

---

[6]Technically, this pricing equation is only approximately true unless certain additional assumptions are made in order to be certain that the arbitrage portfolio has no risk associated with it. See footnote 5.

[7]Why 8 and 4 for λ_0 and λ_1, respectively? The magnitudes that these two parameters assume in equilibrium will depend on many things, such as the relative degrees of risk aversion held by investors and how much wealth investors have.

[8]If B were to plot below the APT asset pricing line, then investors would do just the opposite of what is described here. Namely, they would buy S and sell B.

[9]A simpler way of viewing this transaction is as a stock swap where S is being swapped for B. Since it is a swap, no new funds are needed. Furthermore, since both B and S have the same factor sensitivity, the swap will not alter the sensitivity of the currently held portfolio. Finally, the replacement of S with B will increase the currently held portfolio's expected return since B has a higher level of expected return than S.

[10]Technically, the APT asset pricing line would shift upward a bit due to the selling of S.

FIGURE 12-1
APT Asset Pricing Line

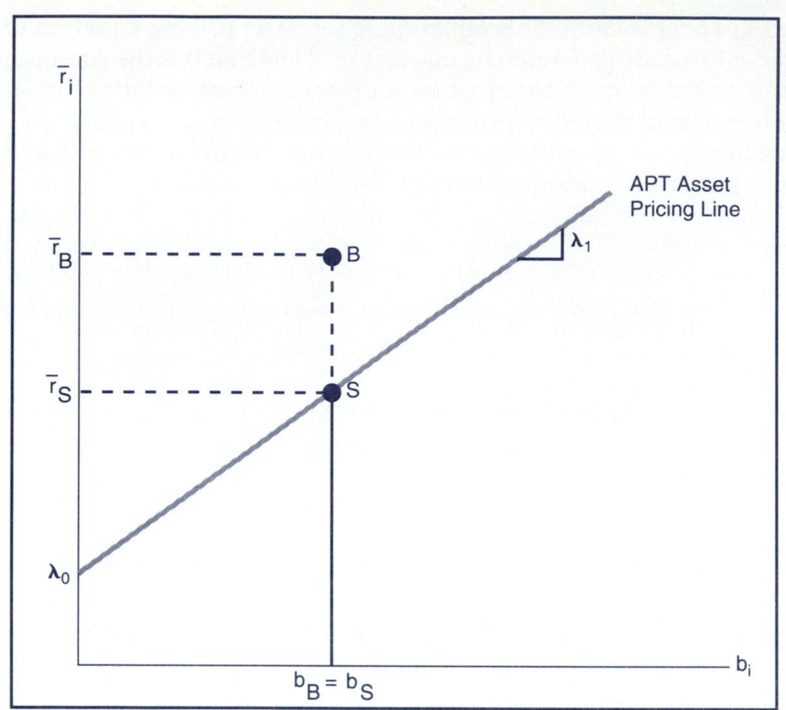

Interpreting the APT Pricing Equation

How can the constants λ_0 and λ_1 that appear in the APT pricing equation (12.6) be interpreted? Assuming that there is a riskfree asset in existence, such an asset will have a rate of return that is a constant. Therefore, this asset will have no sensitivity to the factor. From equation (12.6) it can be seen that $\bar{r}_i = \lambda_0$ for any asset with $b_i = 0$. In the case of the riskfree asset it is also known that $\bar{r}_i = r_f$, implying that $\lambda_0 = r_f$. Hence the value of λ_0 in equation (12.6) must be r_f, allowing this equation to be rewritten as:

$$\bar{r}_i = r_f + \lambda_1 b_i. \tag{12.8}$$

pure factor portfolio

In terms of λ_1, its value can be seen by considering a **pure factor portfolio** (or pure factor play) denoted p^* that has unit sensitivity to the factor, meaning $b_{p^*} = 1.0$. (If there were other factors, such a portfolio would have no sensitivity to them.) According to equation (12.8), such a portfolio will have the following expected return:

$$\bar{r}_{p^*} = r_f + \lambda_1. \tag{12.9a}$$

Note that this equation can be rewritten as:

$$\bar{r}_{p^*} - r_f = \lambda_1. \tag{12.9b}$$

factor risk premium

Thus, λ_1 is the expected excess return (meaning the expected return over and above the riskfree rate) on a portfolio that has unit sensitivity to the factor. Accordingly, it is known as a **factor risk premium** (or factor expected return

MONEY MATTERS
Applying APT

Since its inception in the mid-1970s, Arbitrage Pricing Theory (APT) has provided researchers and practitioners with an intuitive and flexible framework by which to address important investment management issues. As opposed to the Capital Asset Pricing Model (CAPM), with its specific assumptions concerning investor preferences as well as the critical role played by the market portfolio, APT operates under relatively weaker assumptions. With its emphasis on multiple sources of systematic risk, APT has attracted considerable interest as a tool for better explaining investment results and more effectively controlling portfolio risk.

Despite its attractive features, APT has not been widely applied by the investment community. The reason lies largely with APT's most significant drawback: the lack of specificity regarding both the multiple factors that systematically affect security returns and the long-term return associated with each of the factors. Rightly or wrongly, the CAPM unambiguously states that a security's covariance with the market portfolio is the single systematic source of its investment risk within a well-diversified portfolio. APT, conversely, is conspicuously silent regarding the particular systematic factors affecting security risk and return. Investors must fend for themselves in determining those factors.

Assuming that one has determined a set of APT factors and has estimated securities' sensitivities to those factors, how might one go about applying APT to investment management? We consider two potential uses: strategic investment planning and active portfolio management.

Strategic Investment Planning All investors, be they individuals or organizations, have unique financial circumstances and risk tolerances that determine the level of systematic risk to which they desire to be exposed. Suppose that you were employed in the energy industry. Obviously, your financial well-being will be strongly affected by the profitability of both the energy industry in general and your company in particular. In good times, your chances for promotions or pay raises are enhanced. In bad times, raises are less likely and you might even find yourself unemployed.

Given your financial dependence on the energy industry, you should have a strong interest in how your personal investment portfolio is exposed to a systematic factor such as energy prices. In an APT context, you would prefer a portfolio with a negative sensitivity to changes in energy prices. When energy prices (and presumably the profits of the energy industry) rise relative to other consumer prices, your portfolio (other things remaining the same) will decline in relative value. This result should not be of much concern—it is likely that both you and your employer will be doing well financially. However, when energy prices decline and your company's earnings suffer, thereby putting you in a potentially precarious financial situation, your portfolio will be performing relatively well.

This negative portfolio exposure to changes in energy prices is a long-term strategy on your part to protect yourself against the vagaries of the energy market. Other investors will likely focus on other systematic factors to which they wish to be positively or negatively exposed. APT provides a framework through which to address these issues in a disciplined, logical fashion.

Active Portfolio Management In a similar manner, portfolio managers may desire that their portfolios be positively or negatively exposed to certain APT factors. However, they have different motivations for implementing these exposures. While the strategic planner is making long-term decisions unique to his or her financial circumstances, the active portfolio manager is making tactical (short-term) adjustments to his or her portfolios, seeking to outperform a particular benchmark portfolio. Emphasizing or de-emphasizing a portfolio's relative exposures to certain APT factors is one means to achieve this differential (and, hopefully, superior) performance.

Many money management firms develop economic forecasts as part of their standard investment processes (see Chapter 17). These forecasts can be readily related to APT factors. For example, a money management firm might be anticipating unexpectedly strong growth in the economy. By creating portfolios that exhibit a positive sensitivity (greater than that of the benchmark) to unexpected changes in industrial production, the portfolio manager can translate his or her firm's economic forecast into his or her portfolios. If indeed the economy performs as the portfolio manager anticipates (other things remaining the same), his or her portfolios will benefit relative to their benchmarks.

premium). Letting $\delta_1 = \bar{r}_{p*}$ denote the expected return on a portfolio that has unit sensitivity to the factor, equation (12.9b) can be rewritten as:

$$\delta_1 - r_f = \lambda_1. \tag{12.9c}$$

Inserting the left-hand side of equation (12.9c) for λ_1 in equation (12.8) results in a second version of the APT pricing equation:

$$\bar{r}_i = r_f + (\delta_1 - r_f)b_i. \tag{12.10}$$

In the example, since $r_f = 8\%$ and $\lambda_1 = \delta_1 - r_f = 4\%$, it follows that $\delta_1 = 12\%$. That is, the expected return on a portfolio that has unit sensitivity to the first factor is 12%.

MULTIPLE FACTORS

What happens to the APT pricing equations (12.6) and (12.10) when returns are generated by a multiple-factor model instead of a one-factor model? It turns out that these equations are extended in a relatively straightforward manner to accommodate the additional factors.[11]

In the case of k factors $(F_1, F_2, \ldots, F_k)$ each security will have k sensitivities $(b_{i1}, b_{i2}, \ldots, b_{ik})$ in the following k-factor model:

$$r_i = a_i + b_{i1}F_1 + b_{i2}F_2 + \ldots + b_{ik}F_k + e_i. \tag{12.11}$$

In turn, this suggests that securities will be priced by the following equation, which is similar to equation (12.6):

$$\bar{r}_i = \lambda_0 + \lambda_1 b_{i1} + \lambda_2 b_{i2} + \ldots + \lambda_k b_{ik}. \tag{12.12}$$

As before, this is a linear equation, except now it is in $k + 1$ dimensions, with the dimensions being r_i, b_{i1}, b_{i2}, . . . , and b_{ik}.

Extending the APT pricing equation (12.10) to this situation is relatively uncomplicated. As before, λ_0 is equal to the riskfree rate. Each value of δ_i represents the expected return on a portfolio of stocks that has unit sensitivity to factor i and zero sensitivity to all the other factors. As a result, equation (12.10) can be expanded as follows:

$$\bar{r}_i = r_f + (\delta_1 - r_f)b_{i1} + (\delta_2 - r_f)b_{i2} + \ldots + (\delta_k - r_f)b_{ik}. \tag{12.13}$$

A SYNTHESIS OF THE APT AND THE CAPM

Unlike the APT, the CAPM does not assume that returns are generated by a factor model. However, this does not mean that the CAPM is inconsistent with a world in which returns are generated by a factor model. Indeed, it is possible to have a world where returns are generated by a factor model, where the remaining assumptions of the APT hold, and where all the assumptions of the CAPM hold. This situation will now be examined.

[11]The Appendix shows this in more detail by considering a two-factor model.

market portfolio

Consider what would happen if returns are generated by a one-factor model and that factor is the **market portfolio.** In such a situation δ_1 will correspond to the expected return on the market portfolio and b_i will represent the beta of stock i measured relative to the market portfolio. Hence, the CAPM will hold.

What if returns are generated by a one-factor model and that factor is *not* the market portfolio? Now δ_1 will correspond to the expected return on a portfolio with unit sensitivity to the factor portfolio and b_i will represent the sensitivity of stock i measured relative to the factor.[12] However, if the CAPM also holds, then expected returns will be related to both securities' betas and sensitivities:

$$\bar{r}_i = r_f + (\bar{r}_M - r_f)\beta_i \tag{12.14}$$

$$\bar{r}_i = r_f + (\delta_1 - r_f)b_i. \tag{12.15}$$

Beta Coefficients and Factor Sensitivities How can expected returns be linearly related to both betas and sensitivities? This will happen because betas and sensitivities themselves will be related to each other in the following manner:

$$\beta_i = \frac{COV(F_1, r_M)}{\sigma_M^2} b_i \tag{12.16}$$

where $COV(F_1, r_M)$ denotes the covariance between the factor and the market portfolio and σ_M^2 denotes the variance of the return on the market portfolio.[13] Since the quantity $COV(F_1, r_M)/\sigma_M^2$ is a constant and does not change from one security to another, equation (12.16) is equivalent to saying that β_i will be equal to a constant times b_i when equations (12.14) and (12.15) both hold.

Factor Risk Premiums Continuing with this situation, note what happens if the right-hand side of equation (12.16) is substituted for β_i on the right-hand side of equation (12.14):

$$\bar{r}_i = r_f + (\bar{r}_M - r_f)\frac{COV(F_1, r_M)}{\sigma_M^2} b_i. \tag{12.17}$$

Comparing this equation with equation (12.8) reveals that if the assumptions of both APT (with one factor) and the CAPM hold, then the following relationship must hold:

$$\lambda_1 = (\bar{r}_M - r_f)\frac{COV(F_1, r_M)}{\sigma_M^2}. \tag{12.18}$$

[12]If the factor is a market index (instead of the market portfolio) such as the S&P 500, then δ_1 will correspond to the expected return on the index and b_i will represent the beta of stock i measured relative to the index.

[13]This can be seen by noting that $COV(r_i, r_M) = COV(a_i + b_iF_1 + e_i, r_M)$, which simplifies to $COV(r_i, r_M) = b_iCOV(F_1, r_M) + COV(e_i, r_M)$. Since the last term is approximately zero, this equation reduces to $COV(r_i, r_M) = b_iCOV(F_1, r_M)$. Dividing both sides by σ_M^2 and recognizing from Chapter 10 that $COV(r_i, r_M)/\sigma_M^2 = \beta_i$ produces equation (12.16).

Hence λ_1 will have a positive value if the factor is positively correlated with the returns on the market portfolio.[14] However, if the factor is negatively correlated with the returns on the market portfolio, then the value of λ_1 will be negative.

By itself, APT says nothing about the size of the factor risk premium λ_1. However, if the CAPM also holds, it can provide some guidance. This guidance is given in equation (12.18), which has been shown to hold if the assumptions of both APT and the CAPM are taken as given.

Imagine that the factor moves with the market portfolio, meaning that it is positively correlated with the market portfolio and that $\mathrm{COV}(F_1, r_M)$ is positive.[15] Since σ_M^2 and $(\bar{r}_M - r_f)$ are both positive, it follows that the right-hand side of equation (12.18) is positive and hence λ_1 is positive. Furthermore, since λ_1 is positive, it can be seen in equation (12.8) that the higher the value of b_i, the higher will be the expected return of the security.[16] To generalize, if a factor is positively correlated with the market portfolio, then a security's expected return will be a *positive* linear function of the security's sensitivity to that factor.

Using the same kind of argument, if the factor moves against the market portfolio, meaning that F_1 is negatively correlated with r_M, then λ_1 will be negative. This means that the higher the value of b_i, the lower will be the expected return on the security. Generalizing, if a factor is negatively correlated with the market portfolio, then a security's expected return will be a *negative* linear function of the security's sensitivity to that factor.

IDENTIFYING THE FACTORS

Left unanswered by APT are the number and identity of the factors. Several researchers have investigated stock returns and estimated that there are anywhere from three to five factors. Subsequently, various people attempted to identify these factors. In one paper by Chen, Roll, and Ross, the following factors were identified:

1. Growth rate in industrial production,
2. Rate of inflation (both expected and unexpected),
3. Spread between long-term and short-term interest rates, and
4. Spread between low-grade and high-grade bonds.[17]

Another paper by Berry, Burmeister, and McElroy identifies five factors. Of these five factors, three correspond closely to the last three identified by Chen, Roll, and Ross. The other two are the growth rate in aggregate sales in the economy and the rate of return on the S&P 500.[18]

---

[14]In such a situation, the covariance term in equation (12.18) will be positive. Since $(\bar{r}_M - r_f)$ and σ_M^2 are also positive, it follows that λ_1 will be positive.

[15]$\mathrm{COV}(F_1, r_M)$ will be positive if the correlation is positive since it is equal to the product of the correlation and the standard deviations of F_1 and r_M.

[16]The greater the extent to which the factor moves with the market portfolio, meaning the higher the correlation between F_1 and r_M, the greater will be the associated expected return premium λ_1.

[17]Note that the third factor can be interpreted as a measure of the term structure of interest rates, and the fourth factor can be interpreted as a measure of the default risk premium that investors demand for holding risky corporate bonds instead of Treasury bonds.

[18]Technically, they used the rate of return on the S&P 500 that could not be attributed to the other four factors.

Finally, consider the five factors used by Salomon Brothers in what they refer to as their Fundamental Factor Model. Only one factor, inflation, is in common with the factors identified by the others. The remaining factors are as follows:

1. Growth rate in gross national product,
2. Rate of interest,
3. Rate of change in oil prices, and
4. Rate of growth in defense spending.[19]

In summary, it is interesting to note that the three sets of factors have some common characteristics. First, they contain some indication of aggregate economic activity (industrial production, aggregate sales, GNP). Second, they contain inflation. Third, they contain some type of interest rate factor (either spreads or a rate itself). Considering the fact that stock prices can be thought of as being equal to the discounted value of future dividends, the factors make intuitive sense.[20] Future dividends will be related to aggregate economic activity, and the discount rate used to determine present value will be related to inflation and interest rates.

SUMMARY

1. Arbitrage Pricing Theory (APT) is an equilibrium model of security prices, as is the Capital Asset Pricing Model (CAPM).
2. APT makes fewer assumptions about investor preferences than does the CAPM.
3. APT assumes that security returns are generated by a factor model but does not identify the factors.
4. An arbitrage portfolio includes long and short positions in securities. It must have a net market value of zero, no sensitivity to any factor, and a positive expected return.
5. Investors will invest in arbitrage portfolios, driving up the prices of the securities held in long positions and driving down the prices of securities held in short positions until all arbitrage possibilities are eliminated.
6. When all arbitrage possibilities are eliminated, the equilibrium expected return on a security will be a linear function of its sensitivities to the factors.
7. A factor risk premium is the equilibrium return over the riskfree rate expected to be generated by a portfolio with a unit sensitivity to the factor and no sensitivity to any other factor.
8. The APT and the CAPM are not necessarily inconsistent with each other. If security returns are generated by a factor model and the CAPM holds, then a security's beta will depend on the security's sensitivity to the factors and the covariances between the factors and the market portfolio.
9. APT does not specify the number or identity of the factors. Most research into APT factors focuses on indicators of aggregate economic activity, inflation, and interest rates.

KEY TERMS

Arbitrage Pricing Theory
sensitivity
arbitrage portfolio
pure factor portfolio
market portfolio

[19]Technically, they use inflation-adjusted figures for all the variables except the rate of interest.

[20]Dividend discount models will be discussed in depth in Chapter 15.

QUESTIONS AND PROBLEMS

1. In what significant ways does APT differ from the CAPM?
2. Why would an investor wish to form an arbitrage portfolio?
3. What three conditions define an arbitrage portfolio?
4. Socks Seybold owns a portfolio with the following characteristics (assume that returns are generated by a single-factor model):

SECURITY	SENSITIVITY	PROPORTION	EXPECTED RETURN
A	2.0	.20	20%
B	3.5	.40	10
C	0.5	.40	5

   Socks decides to create an arbitrage portfolio by increasing the holdings of security A by .20. (Hint: Remember, X_B must equal $-X_C - X_A$.)
   (a) What must be the weights of the other two securities in Socks' arbitrage portfolio?
   (b) What is the expected return on the arbitrage portfolio?
   (c) If everyone follows Socks' buy and sell decisions, what will be the effects on the prices of the three securities?
5. Assume that security returns are generated by a single-factor model. Hap Morse holds a portfolio whose component securities have the following characteristics:

SECURITY	SENSITIVITY	PROPORTION	EXPECTED RETURN
A	.60	.40	12%
B	.30	.30	15
C	1.20	.30	8

   Specify an arbitrage portfolio in which Hap might invest. (Remember, there is an infinite number of possibilities—choose one.) Demonstrate that this portfolio satisfies the conditions of an arbitrage portfolio.
6. Why must the variance of a well-diversified arbitrage portfolio be small?
7. Why is the concept of arbitrage central to the asset pricing mechanism of APT?
8. Based on a single-factor model, Wyeville Labs' stock has a factor sensitivity of 3.0. Given a riskfree rate of 5% and a factor risk premium of 7%, what is the equilibrium expected return on Wyeville stock?
9. According to APT, why must the relationship between a security's equilibrium expected return and its factor sensitivities be linear?
10. Based on a single-factor model, assume that the riskfree rate is 6% and the expected return on a portfolio with unit sensitivity to the factor is 8.5%. Consider a portfolio of two securities with the following characteristics:

SECURITY	SENSITIVITY	PROPORTION
A	4.0	.30
B	2.6	.70

According to APT, what is the portfolio's equilibrium expected return?

11. Is it true that if one believes that APT is the correct theory of asset pricing, then the risk-return relationship derived from the CAPM is necessarily incorrect? Why?

12. Assume that the CAPM holds and that returns on securities are generated by a single-factor model. Given the following information:

$\sigma_M^2 = 400 \qquad b_A = 0.70 \qquad b_B = 1.10 \qquad COV(F, r_M) = 370$

(a) Calculate the beta coefficients of securities A and B.

(b) If the riskfree rate is 6% and the expected return on the market portfolio is 12%, what is the equilibrium expected return on securities A and B?

13. If the CAPM and APT both hold, why must it be the case that the factor risk premium is negative for a factor that is negatively correlated with the market portfolio? Explain both mathematically and intuitively.

14. Although APT does not specify the identity of the relevant factors, most empirical APT research has focused on certain types of factors. What are some of the common characteristics of those factors?

15. (Appendix Question) Dandelion Pfeffer owns a portfolio with the following characteristics:

SECURITY	FACTOR 1 SENSITIVITY	FACTOR 2 SENSITIVITY	PROPORTION	EXPECTED RETURN
A	2.50	1.40	.30	13%
B	1.60	0.90	.30	18
C	0.80	1.00	.20	10
D	2.00	1.30	.20	12

Assume that returns are generated by a two-factor model. Dandelion decides to create an arbitrage portfolio by increasing the holding of security B by .05.

(a) What must be the weights of the other three securities in Dandelion's portfolio?

(b) What is the expected return on the arbitrage portfolio?

16. (Appendix Question) Assume that the CAPM holds and that returns are generated by a two-factor model. Given the following information:

$\sigma_M^2 = 324 \qquad b_{A1} = 0.80 \qquad b_{B1} = 1.00$
$COV(F_1, r_M) = 156 \qquad b_{A2} = 1.10 \qquad b_{B2} = 0.70$
$COV(F_2, r_M) = 500$

calculate the beta coefficients of securities A and B.

CFA Exam Questions

17. As the manager of a large, broadly diversified portfolio of stocks and bonds, you realize that changes in certain macroeconomic variables may directly affect the performance of your portfolio. You are considering using an arbitrage pricing theory (APT) approach to strategic portfolio planning and want to analyze the possible impacts of the following four factors:

- industrial production;
- inflation;
- risk premia or quality spreads; and
- yield curve shifts.

(a) Indicate how each of these four factors influences the cash flows and/or the discount rates in the traditional discounted cash flow valuation model. Explain how unanticipated changes in each of these four factors could affect portfolio returns.

(b) You now use a constant-proportion allocation strategy of 60% stock and 40% bonds, which you rebalance monthly.

Compare and contrast an active portfolio approach that incorporates macroeconomic factors, such as the four factors listed above, to the constant-proportion strategy currently in use.

APPENDIX A

Multiple-factor Models and APT

The example in the chapter used a one-factor model to derive the asset pricing equation of APT. While the multiple-factor version of this pricing equation was given, its derivation was not shown. The purpose of this appendix is to illustrate its derivation by considering a two-factor model.

TWO-FACTOR MODELS

In the case of two factors, denoted F_1 and F_2, each security will have two sensitivities, b_{i1} and b_{i2}, in the following factor model:

$$r_i = a_i + b_{i1}F_1 + b_{i2}F_2 + e_i. \qquad \text{(A.1)}$$

For example, consider a situation where there are four securities that have the following expected returns and sensitivities:

i	$\bar{r}_i$	b_{i1}	b_{i2}
1	15%	.9	2.0
2	21	3.0	1.5
3	12	1.8	.7
4	8	2.0	3.2

In addition, there is an investor who has \$5,000,000 invested in each of the securities (note that this means that the investor has initial wealth W_0 of \$20,000,000). How are these securities priced in equilibrium?

ARBITRAGE PORTFOLIOS

In order to answer this question, the possibility of forming an arbitrage portfolio must be explored. First of all, an arbitrage portfolio must have weights that satisfy the following equations:

$$X_1 + X_2 + X_3 + X_4 = 0 \tag{A.2}$$

$$.9X_1 + 3X_2 + 1.8X_3 + 2X_4 = 0 \tag{A.3}$$

$$2X_1 + 1.5X_2 + .7X_3 + 3.2X_4 = 0. \tag{A.4}$$

That is, the arbitrage portfolio must not involve an additional commitment of funds by the investor and must have zero sensitivity to each factor.

Note that there are three equations that need to be satisfied, and that each equation involves four unknowns. Since there are more unknowns than equations, there are an infinite number of solutions. One solution can be found by setting X_1 equal to .1 (an arbitrarily chosen amount) and then solving for the remaining weights. Doing so results in the following weights: $X_2 = .088$, $X_3 = -.108$, and $X_4 = -.08$.

These weights represent a potential arbitrage portfolio. What remains to be done is to see if this portfolio has a positive expected return. Calculating the expected return of the portfolio reveals that it is equal to $1.41\% = (.1 \times 15\%) + (.088 \times 21\%) + (-.108 \times 12\%) + (-.08 \times .08)$. Hence, an arbitrage portfolio has been identified.

This arbitrage portfolio involves the purchase of stocks 1 and 2, funded by selling stocks 3 and 4. Consequently, the buying and selling pressures will drive the prices of stocks 1 and 2 up and stocks 3 and 4 down. In turn, this means that the expected returns of stocks 1 and 2 will fall and stocks 3 and 4 will rise until equilibrium is reached. That is, equilibrium will have been attained when any portfolio that satisfies the conditions given by equations (A.2), (A.3), and (A.4) will have an expected return of zero. This will occur when the following linear relationship between expected returns and sensitivities exists:

$$\bar{r}_i = \lambda_0 + \lambda_1 b_{i1} + \lambda_2 b_{i2}. \tag{A.5}$$

As before in equation (12.6), this is a linear equation, except now it is in three dimensions, $\bar{r}_i$, b_{i1}, and b_{i2}. Hence, it corresponds to the equation of a plane.

In the example, one possible equilibrium setting would be where $\lambda_0 = 8$, $\lambda_1 = 4$, and $\lambda_2 = -2$. Thus, the pricing equation would be:

$$\bar{r}_i = 8 + 4b_{i1} - 2b_{i2}. \tag{A.6}$$

As a result, the four stocks would have the following equilibrium levels of expected returns:

$$\bar{r}_1 = 8 + (4 \times .9) - (2 \times 2) = 7.6\%$$

$$\bar{r}_2 = 8 + (4 \times 3) - (2 \times 1.5) = 17.0\%$$

$$\bar{r}_3 = 8 + (4 \times 1.8) - (2 \times .7) = 13.8\%$$

$$\bar{r}_4 = 8 + (4 \times 2) - (2 \times 3.2) = 9.6\%.$$

Thus, the expected returns of stocks 1 and 2 have fallen from 15% and 21%, respectively, while the expected returns of stocks 3 and 4 have risen from 12% and 8%, respectively. Given the buying and selling pressures generated by investing in arbitrage portfolios, these changes are in the predicted direction.

PRICING EFFECTS

Extending the APT pricing equation (12.10) to this situation is relatively uncomplicated. As before, λ_0 is equal to the riskfree rate. This is because the riskfree asset has no sensitivity to either factor, meaning that its values of b_{i1} and b_{i2} are both zero. Hence, since $\bar{r}_i = r_f$ and $\bar{r}_i = \lambda_0$, it follows that $\lambda_0 = r_f$. Thus, equation (A.5) can be rewritten as:

$$\bar{r}_i = r_f + \lambda_1 b_{i1} + \lambda_2 b_{i2}. \tag{A.7}$$

In the example, it can be seen that $r_f = 8\%$.

Next, consider a portfolio that has unit sensitivity to the first factor and zero sensitivity to the second factor. As mentioned earlier, a portfolio such as this one, which has unit sensitivity to one factor and no sensitivity to any other factor and in addition has zero nonfactor risk, is known as a pure factor portfolio or pure factor play. Specifically, it has $b_1 = 1$ and $b_2 = 0$. It can be seen from equation (A.7) that the expected return on this portfolio, denoted δ_1, will be equal to $r_f + \lambda_1$. Since it follows that $\delta_1 - r_f = \lambda_1$, equation (A.7) can be rewritten as:

$$\bar{r}_i = r_f + (\delta_1 - r_f)b_{i1} + \lambda_2 b_{i2}. \tag{A.8}$$

In the example, it can be seen that $\delta_1 - r_f = 4$. This means that $\delta_1 = 12$ since $r_f = 8$.

Last, consider a portfolio that has zero sensitivity to the first factor and unit sensitivity to the second factor, meaning that it has $b_1 = 0$ and $b_2 = 1$. It can be seen from equation (A.7) that the expected return on this portfolio, denoted δ_2, will be equal to $r_f + \lambda_2$. Accordingly, $\delta_2 - r_f = \lambda_2$, thereby allowing equation (A.8) to be rewritten as:

$$\bar{r}_i = r_f + (\delta_1 - r_f)b_{i1} + (\delta_2 - r_f)b_{i2}. \tag{A.9}$$

In the example, it can be seen that $\delta_2 - r_f = -2$. This means that $\delta_2 = 6$ since $r_f = 8$.

THREE FACTORS

With a three-factor model, equation (A.7) would have an additional term, $\lambda_3 b_{i3}$, added to the right-hand side, while equation (A.9) would have $(\delta_3 - r_f)b_{i3}$ added to its right-hand side. Extensions to larger factor models follow similarly.

OBSERVATIONS

Consider what happens if the CAPM holds even though returns are generated by a multiple-factor model such as a two-factor model. Again, expected returns will be related to securities' betas and sensitivities:

$$\bar{r}_i = r_f + (\bar{r}_M - r_f)\beta_i \tag{A.10}$$

$$\bar{r}_i = r_f + (\delta_1 - r_f)b_{i1} + (\delta_2 - r_f)b_{i2}. \tag{A.11}$$

In an extension of equation (12.16), expected returns will be linearly related to both betas and sensitivities if they are related to each other in the following manner:

$$\beta_i = \frac{COV(F_1,r_M)}{\sigma_M^2} b_{i1} + \frac{COV(F_2,r_M)}{\sigma_M^2} b_{i2} \tag{A.12}$$

where $COV(F_1,r_M)$ and $COV(F_2, r_M)$ denote the covariance between the first factor and the returns on the market portfolio and covariance between the second factor and the returns on the market portfolio, respectively. Since the quantities $COV(F_1,r_M)/\sigma_M^2$ and $COV(F_2,r_M)/\sigma_M^2$ are constants, it can be seen from equation (A.12) that β_i will be a function of b_{i1} and b_{i2} when equations (A.10) and (A.11) hold.

Note what happens if the right-hand side of equation (A.12) is substituted for β_i on the right-hand side of equation (A.10):

$$\bar{r}_i = r_f + (\bar{r}_M - r_f) \left[\frac{COV(F_1,r_M)}{\sigma_M^2} b_{i1} + \frac{COV(F_2,r_M)}{\sigma_M^2} b_{i2} \right] \tag{A.13a}$$

which can be rewritten as:

$$\bar{r}_i = r_f + (\bar{r}_M - r_f) \left[\frac{COV(F_1,r_M)}{\sigma_M^2} b_{i1} \right] + (\bar{r}_M - r_f) \left[\frac{COV(F_2,r_M)}{\sigma_M^2} b_{i2} \right]. \tag{A.13b}$$

Comparing this equation with equation (A.7) reveals that if the assumptions of both APT (with two factors) and the CAPM hold, then the following relationships must hold:

$$\lambda_1 = (\bar{r}_M - r_f) \frac{COV(F_1,r_M)}{\sigma_M^2} \tag{A.14a}$$

$$\lambda_2 = (\bar{r}_M - r_f) \frac{COV(F_2,r_M)}{\sigma_M^2}. \tag{A.14b}$$

Hence λ_1 and λ_2 will have positive values if the factors are positively correlated with the returns on the market portfolio.[21] However, if either factor is negatively correlated with the returns on the market portfolio, then the corresponding value of λ will be negative (as was the case with λ_2 in the example).

REFERENCES

1. Credit for the initial development of APT belongs to:

   Stephen A. Ross, "The Arbitrage Theory of Capital Asset Pricing," *Journal of Economic Theory*, 13, no. 3 (December 1976): 341–60, and "Risk, Return, and Arbitrage," in *Risk and Return in Finance*, Vol. I, ed. Irwin Friend and James L. Bicksler (Cambridge, Mass.: Ballinger Publishing Company, 1977), Section 9.

[21]For the reasoning behind this assertion, see footnote 14.

2. The fundamental asset pricing equation of Ross' APT is only approximately correct unless additional assumptions are made. The following papers address this issue:

Nai-fu Chen and Jonathan E. Ingersoll, Jr., "Exact Pricing in Linear Factor Models with Finitely Many Assets: A Note," *Journal of Finance*, 38, no. 3 (June 1983): 985–88;

Philip H. Dybvig, "An Explicit Bound on Individual Assets' Deviations from APT Pricing in a Finite Economy," *Journal of Financial Economics*, 12, no. 4 (December 1983): 483–96;

Mark Grinblatt and Sheridan Titman, "Factor Pricing in a Finite Economy," *Journal of Financial Economics*, 12, no. 4 (December 1983): 497–507;

Gregory Connor, "A Unified Beta Pricing Theory," *Journal of Economic Theory*, 34, no. 1 (October 1984): 13–31.

3. Nontechnical descriptions of APT can be found in:

Richard W. Roll and Stephen A. Ross, "Regulation, the Capital Asset Pricing Model, and the Arbitrage Pricing Theory," *Public Utilities Fortnightly*, 111, no. 11 (May 26, 1983): 22–28;

Richard Roll and Stephen A. Ross, "The Arbitrage Pricing Theory Approach to Strategic Portfolio Planning," *Financial Analysts Journal*, 40, no. 3 (May–June 1984): 14–26;

Dorothy H. Bower, Richard S. Bower, and Dennis E. Logue, "A Primer on Arbitrage Pricing Theory," *Midland Corporate Finance Journal*, 2, no. 3 (Fall 1984): 31–40.

4. Factors have been identified in the following papers:

Nai-fu Chen, Richard Roll, and Stephen A. Ross, "Economic Forces and the Stock Market," *Journal of Business*, 59, no. 3 (July 1986): 383–403;

Michael A. Berry, Edwin Burmeister, and Marjorie B. McElroy, "Sorting Out Risks Using Known APT Factors," *Financial Analysts Journal*, 44, no. 2 (March–April 1988): 29–42;

Tony Estep, Nick Hansen, and Cal Johnson, "Sources of Value and Risk in Common Stocks," *Journal of Portfolio Management*, 9, no. 4 (Summer 1983): 5–13.

5. For a discussion of the relationships between the APT and the CAPM, see:

K. C. John Wei, "An Asset-Pricing Theory Unifying the CAPM and APT," *Journal of Finance*, 43, no. 4 (September 1988): 881–92.

PART IV
COMMON STOCKS

13

Characteristics of Common Stocks

Common stocks are easier to describe than fixed-income securities such as bonds, but are harder to analyze. Fixed-income securities almost always have a limited life and an upper dollar limit on cash payments to investors. Common stocks have neither. Although the basic principles of valuation apply to both, the role of uncertainty is larger for common stocks, so much that it often dominates all other elements in their valuation.

common stock

Common stock represents equity, or an ownership position in a corporation. It is a residual claim, in the sense that creditors and preferred stockholders must be paid as scheduled before common stockholders can receive any payments. In bankruptcy, common stockholders are in principle entitled to any value remaining after all other claimants have been satisfied. (However, in practice, courts sometimes violate this principle.)

limited liability

The great advantage of the corporate form of organization is the **limited liability** of its owners. Common stocks are generally "full-paid and nonassessable," meaning that common stockholders may lose their initial investment, but no more. That is, if the corporation fails to meet its obligations, the stockholders cannot be forced to give the corporation the funds that are needed to pay off the obligations. However, as a result of such a failure, it is possible that the value of a corporation's shares will be negligible. This will result in the stockholders' having lost an amount equal to the price previously paid to buy the shares.

THE CORPORATE FORM

charter

A corporation exists only when it has been granted a **charter** (or certificate of incorporation) by a state. This document specifies the rights and obligations of stockholders. It may be amended with the approval of the stockholders, perhaps by a majority or two-thirds vote, where each share of stock generally entitles its owner to one vote. Both the initial terms of the charter and the terms of any amendment must also be approved by the state in which the corporation is chartered. The state of Delaware has captured a disproportionate number of corporate charters because it is particularly hospitable in this respect as well as in levying corporate taxes.

Stock Certificates

The ownership of a firm's stock has typically been represented by a single certificate, with the number of shares held by the particular investor noted on it. Such a stock certificate is usually registered, with the name, address, and holdings of the investor included on the corporation's books. Dividend payments, voting material, annual and quarterly reports, and other mailings are then sent directly to the investor, taking into account the size of his or her holdings.

transfer agent
registrar

Shares of stock held by an investor may be transferred to a new owner with the assistance of either the issuing corporation or, more commonly, its designated **transfer agent.** This agent will cancel the old stock certificate and issue a new one in its place, made out to the new owner. Frequently a **registrar** will make sure that this canceling and issuing of certificates has been done properly. Usually banks and trust companies act as transfer agents and registrars. Many stockholders have chosen to avoid these rather cumbersome procedures. Instead, depository arrangements (discussed in Chapter 3) are used that substitute computerized records for embossed certificates.

Voting

proxy

Since an owner of a share of common stock is one of the owners of a corporation, he or she is entitled to vote on matters brought up at the corporation's annual meeting, and to vote for the corporation's directors. Any owner may attend and vote in person, but most choose instead to vote by **proxy.** That is, the incumbent directors and senior management will typically solicit all the stockholders, asking each one to sign a proxy statement. Such a statement is a power of attorney authorizing the designated party listed on the statement to cast all of the investor's votes on any matter brought up at the meeting. Occasionally, desired positions on specific issues may be solicited on the proxy statement. However, most of the time the positions held by the incumbents are made known with the proxy solicitation. Since the majority of votes are generally controlled by the incumbents via proxy statements, the actual voting turns out to be perfunctory, leaving little if any controversy or excitement.

Proxy Fight Once in a while, however, a **proxy fight** develops. Insurgents from outside the corporation solicit proxies to vote against the incumbents, often in order to effect a takeover of some sort. Stockholders are deluged with literature and appeals for their proxies. The incumbents often win, but the possibility of a loss in such a skirmish tends to curb activities clearly not in the stockholders' best interests.

proxy fight

When proposals are to be voted on, the number of votes given an investor equals the number of shares held. Thus, when a yes or no vote is called for, anyone controlling a majority of the shares will be able to make sure that the outcome he or she favors will receive a majority of the votes. When directors are to be elected, however, there are two types of voting systems that can be used, one of which does not give a majority owner complete control of the outcome. This type of voting system is known as a **cumulative voting system,** while the other type of voting system that does allow a majority owner to completely control the outcome is known as a **majority voting system** (or straight voting system).

cumulative voting system

majority voting system

Under both systems, the winners of the election are those candidates who have received the highest vote totals. Thus, if six candidates were running for the three directorships, the three receiving the largest number of votes would be elected.

Majority Voting System With both voting systems, a stockholder receives a total number of votes that is equal to the number of directors to be elected times the number of shares owned. However, with the majority voting system, the stockholder may only give any one candidate, as a maximum, a number of votes equal to the number of shares owned. This means that in a situation where three directors are to be elected, a stockholder with 400 shares would have 1,200 votes but could give no more than 400 of these votes to any one candidate. Note that if there are a total of 1,000 shares outstanding and one stockholder owns (or has proxies for) 501 shares, then he or she can give 501 votes to each of the three candidates he or she favors. In doing so, this stockholder will be certain they are elected, regardless of how the remaining 499 shares are voted. The majority shareholder's candidates would each have 501 votes, while the most any other candidate could receive is 499 votes. Thus, with a majority voting system, a stockholder owning (or controlling with proxies) one share more than 50% can be certain of electing all the candidates that he or she favors.

Cumulative Voting System The cumulative voting system differs from the majority voting system in that a stockholder can cast his or her votes in any manner. As a result, a minority stockholder can be certain of having some representation on the board of directors, provided that the number of shares owned is sufficiently large. In the previous example, the minority owner of the 400 shares could cast all of his or her 1,200 votes for one candidate. Imagine that this owner wanted director A to be elected, but the majority owner of 501 shares wanted candidates B, C, and D to be elected. In this situation, the minority stockholder could give all 1,200 votes to A and be certain that A would be one of the three directors elected, regardless of what the majority stockholder did. Why? If the majority owner held the remaining 600 shares, he or she would have 1,800 votes. There is no way that candidate

A, favored by the minority stockholder, can come in lower than second place in the vote totals. This is because A will receive 1,200 votes, and there is no way that the 1,800 votes of the majority stockholder can be cast to give more than one of his or her favored candidates a vote total in excess of 1,200. Thus, the minority stockholder can be certain that A will be elected, while the majority stockholder can be certain that only two of his or her favorites will be elected.

How many shares, as a minimum, must a stockholder own in order to be able to elect a certain number of candidates under a cumulative voting system? In general, the formula for making such a determination is:

$$n = \left(\frac{ds}{D + 1}\right) + 1 \tag{13.1}$$

where: n = the minimum number of shares that must be owned,
d = the number of directors the stockholder wants to be certain of electing,
s = the number of shares outstanding, and
D = the number of directors to be elected.

Thus, the minimum number of shares a stockholder needs in order to be certain of electing one director when three are to be elected and there are 1,000 shares outstanding is $251 = [(1 \times 1{,}000)/(3 + 1)] + 1$. Since in the example the minority stockholder owned 400 shares, it can be seen from the formula that he or she is certain of being able to elect one director. Note that the minimum number of shares that must be owned in order to be certain of electing two directors is $501 = [(2 \times 1{,}000)/(3 + 1)] + 1$. The minimum number owned to be certain of electing all three directors is $751 = [(3 \times 1{,}000)/(3 + 1)] + 1$.

In summary, the cumulative voting system gives minority stockholders the right to have some representation on the board of directors, provided that the number of shares owned is sufficiently large. In contrast, the majority voting system does not give minority stockholders the right to such representation, even if 49.9% of the shares are owned by the minority stockholder.

The voting system that a corporation decides to use depends not only on the desires of the corporate founders but also the state in which the firm is incorporated. Some states require cumulative voting systems. In Delaware, however, there is no cumulative voting unless it is specifically stated in the corporate charter.

Takeovers

takeover
tender offer
bidder
target firm

Periodically, a firm or a wealthy individual who is convinced that the management of a corporation is not fully exploiting its opportunities will attempt a **takeover.** This is frequently done with a **tender offer** being made by a **bidder** to a **target firm.**[1] Before this offer is announced, some of the target

merger
management buyout
leveraged buyout

[1]Another form of a takeover is a **merger.** A merger occurs when two firms combine their operations, the result being that only one firm exists. Mergers usually are negotiated by the management of the two firms. Tender offers differ in that management of the bidder makes a direct appeal to the stockholders of the target firm for their shares. Tender offers also differ in that afterwards both firms will still exist, since most tender offers are not for all the shares of the target. **Management buyouts** are a special kind of tender offer where the current management of the firm uses borrowed funds to buy the company (hence they are also called **leveraged buyouts,** or LBOs).

firm's shares are usually acquired by the bidder in the open market through the use of brokers (once 5% of the stock is so acquired, the bidder has ten days to report the acquisition to the SEC on a 13d form). Then, in its quest to acquire a substantial number of the target's shares, the bid is announced to the public. Advertisements to purchase shares are placed in the financial press, and material describing the bid is mailed to the target's stockholders. The bidder generally offers to buy at a stated price some or all shares offered ("tendered") by the current stockholders of the target. This buying offer is usually contingent on the tender of a minimum number of shares by the target's stockholders by a fixed date. When the buying offer is first made, the offered price ("tender price") is generally set considerably above the current market price, although the offer itself usually leads to a subsequent price increase.

Management of the target firm frequently responds to tender offers with advertisements, mailings, and the like, urging its stockholders to reject the bidder's offer. Sometimes a **white knight** will be sought, meaning that another firm that is favorably inclined toward current management will be invited to make a better offer to the target's stockholders. Another type of response by management is to pay **greenmail** to the bidder, meaning that any shares held by the bidder will be bought by the target firm at an above-market price. Still another type of response is for management of the target firm to issue a tender offer of its own, known as a **repurchase offer,** where the firm offers to buy back some of its own stock. (Occasionally repurchase offers are made by firms that have not received tender offers from outside bidders.) Other types of corporate defenses include the **Pac-Man defense,** where the initial target turns around and makes a tender offer for the initial acquirer; the **crown jewel defense,** where the target sells its most attractive assets to make the firm less attractive; and the use of **poison pills,** where the target gives its shareholders certain rights that can be exercised only in the event of a subsequent takeover and that, once exercised, will be extremely onerous to the acquirer.

white knight

greenmail

repurchase offer

Pac-Man defense

crown jewel defense

poison pill defense

Ownership versus Control

Much has been written about the effect of the separation of ownership and control of the modern corporation.[2] This separation gives rise to what is known as a principal-agent problem. In particular, stockholders can be viewed as principals who hire management to act as their agent. The agent is to make decisions that maximize shareholder wealth as reflected in the firm's stock price. No problem would exist if stockholders could monitor the managers costlessly, since the stockholders would then be capable of determining for certain whether or not management had acted in their best interests. However, monitoring is not costless, and complete monitoring of every decision is, practically speaking, impossible.[3] As a result, some, but not complete, monitoring is done. This gives management a certain degree of

[2]See, for example, Michael C. Jensen and William H. Meckling, "Theory of the Firm: Managerial Behavior, Agency Costs and Ownership Structure," *Journal of Financial Economics,* 3, no. 4 (October 1976): 305–60; Eugene F. Fama, "Agency Problems and the Theory of the Firm," *Journal of Political Economy,* 88, no. 2 (April 1980): 288–307; Eugene F. Fama and Michael C. Jensen, "Separation of Ownership and Control," *Journal of Law and Economics,* 26 (June 1983): 301–25; Eugene F. Fama and Michael C. Jensen, "Agency Problems and Residual Claims," *Journal of Law and Economics,* 26 (June 1983): 327–49; the entire issues of vol. 11 (April 1983) and vol. 20 (January/March 1988) of the *Journal of Financial Economics;* and Michael C. Jensen, "Eclipse of the Public Corporation," *Harvard Business Review,* 89, no. 5 (September–October 1989): 61–74.

[3]An example of monitoring is having the firm's financial statements independently audited.

latitude in making decisions, and leaves open the possibility that some decisions will be made that are not in the stockholders' best interests.[4] However, the possibility of a proxy fight or tender offer provides at least some check on such decisions.

To align the interests of management with their own, stockholders frequently offer certain incentives to management. An example is the use of stock options. These options are given to certain high-level managers and allow them to purchase a specified number of shares at a stated price (often above the market price when the options are initially issued) by a stated date. Thus, they motivate these managers to make decisions that will increase the stock price of the firm as much as possible. Furthermore, given their relatively long initial lifespan (in comparison with listed options, discussed in Chapter 24), stock options implicitly exert pressure on management to take a long-term view in making decisions.

Stockholders' Equity

par value of common stock

Par Value When a corporation is first chartered, it is authorized to issue up to a stated number of shares of common stock, each of which will often carry a specified **par value.** Legally, a corporation may be precluded from making payments to common stockholders if doing so would reduce the balance-sheet value of stockholders' equity below the amount represented by the par value of outstanding stock. For this reason the par value is typically low relative to the price for which the stock is initially sold. Some corporations issue no-par stock (if so, a stated value must be recorded in place of the par value).

When stock is initially sold for more than its par value, the difference may be carried separately on the corporation's books under stockholders' equity. Frequently, the entry is for "capital contributed in excess of par value" or "paid-in capital." The par value of the stock is carried in a separate account, generally simply entitled "common stock," with an amount that is equal to the number of shares outstanding times the par value per share (for no-par stock, the stated value).

book value of the equity
book value per share

Book Value With the passage of time, a corporation will generate income, much of which is paid out to creditors (as interest) and stockholders (as dividends). Any remainder is added to the amount shown as cumulative retained earnings on the corporation's books. The sum of the cumulative retained earnings and other entries (such as "common stock" and "capital contributed in excess of par value") under stockholders' equity is the **book value of the equity.** The **book value per share** is obtained by dividing the book value of the equity by the number of shares outstanding.

Reserved and Treasury Stock Typically, a corporation will issue only part of its authorized stock. Some of the remainder may be specifically reserved for outstanding options, convertible securities, and so on. However, if a corporation wishes to issue new stock in excess of the amount originally authorized,

---

[4]For example, management may decide to have lavishly furnished offices and an executive jet when the conduct of business suggests that these are not merited. Furthermore, management may invest in negative net present value investment projects when the firm has "free cash flow" instead of paying it to the shareholders. See Michael C. Jensen, "Agency Costs of Free Cash Flow, Corporate Finance and Takeovers," *American Economic Review*, 76, no. 2 (May 1986): 323–29.

the charter must be amended. This requires approval by both the state and the stockholders.

Sometimes a corporation will repurchase some of its outstanding stock, either in the open market through the services of a broker or with a tender offer. Afterwards, this stock may be "held in the treasury." Such **treasury stock** is not entitled to vote or receive dividends and is equivalent economically (though not legally) to unissued stock.

treasury stock

A major study of over 1,300 stock repurchases found that nearly 90% of the repurchases analyzed were executed in the open market, with the remainder being "self-tender offers."[5] Furthermore, there were two types of self-tender offers that occurred with approximately equal frequency. The first type is a "fixed-price" self-tender offer, where the corporation makes an offer to repurchase a stated number of shares at a set, predetermined price. The second type is a "Dutch-auction" self-tender offer, where the corporation again makes an offer to repurchase a stated number of shares but at a price that is determined by inviting existing shareholders to submit offers to sell. The ultimate repurchase price is the lowest offered price at which the previously stated number of shares can be repurchased from those shareholders that have submitted offers.[6]

Figure 13-1 shows the average stock price behavior surrounding the announcement date for the three types of stock repurchases just mentioned. For each repurchase, the stock's "abnormal" return was determined by relating daily returns on the stock to the corresponding returns in the stock

[5]Robert Comment and Gregg A. Jarrell, "The Relative Signalling Power of Dutch-Auction and Fixed-Price Self-Tender Offers and Open-Market Share Repurchases," *Journal of Finance*, 46, no. 4 (September 1991): 1243–71.

[6]It should be noted that while there were similar numbers of fixed-price and Dutch-auction tender offers, the Dutch-auction method is becoming increasingly popular, particularly among larger corporations.

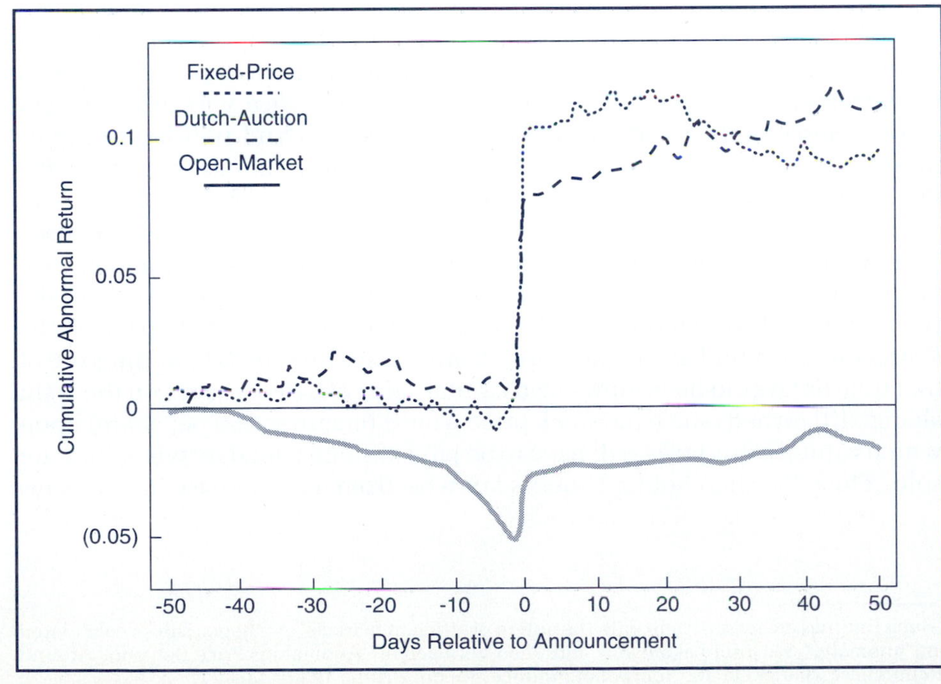

FIGURE 13-1
Abnormal Stock Price Behavior Around Repurchase Announcements

Source: Robert Comment and Gregg A. Jarrell, "The Relative Signalling Power of Dutch-Auction and Fixed-Price Self-Tender Offers and Open-Market Share Repurchases," *Journal of Finance*, 46, no. 4 (September 1991): 1254.

market index. This was done for the 50-day period immediately prior to the repurchase announcement and the 50-day period immediately following it. These abnormal returns were averaged across firms for each day relative to the announcement and then cumulated across time. The figure shows that open market repurchases are typically made after the stock price has had an abnormal decline. However, fixed-price and Dutch-auction repurchases are made after a period of fairly normal returns. Also of interest is the observation that the stock price jumped upward on the announcement of the repurchase offer for all three types (the average size of the abnormal return on the announcement date was 11% for fixed-price, 8% for Dutch-auction, and 2% for open-market). Finally, after the repurchase offer the stock price did not tend to fall back to its pre-announcement level.

Interestingly, another study found that investors could form profitable investment strategies to take advantage of the observed abnormal return associated with the announcement of a stock repurchase.[7] Specifically, the strategy involves fixed-price self-tender offers where the stock is purchased by the investor in the open market shortly before the offer's expiration date if it is selling at least 3% below the repurchase price. Then the investor tenders the stock to the firm on the expiration date; if the repurchase is oversubscribed (meaning that more shares are submitted for repurchase than the corporation has indicated it will buy), then the number of shares that the corporation does not buy are sold in the marketplace shortly after the expiration date. The result is that for an investment of less than a week, this strategy will generate an abnormal return of more than 9%.

Why do firms repurchase their stock? Previously it was mentioned that one motive was to repel a takeover attempt. Two other explanations have been offered. First, management may be attempting to send a signal to their shareholders (and the public) that the corporation's stock is undervalued in the marketplace. Second, it may be beneficial tax-wise to the current shareholders to use excess cash for repurchasing stock instead of using it to pay a cash dividend.

For example, consider a shareholder who bought 10 shares of stock at $40 per share that are now worth $50 per share, resulting in an unrealized capital gain of $10 per share or $100 in total. Furthermore, the shareholder could receive a $10 per share cash dividend from the firm as part of a general disbursement of excess cash. As a result, the stock price will drop $10 per share, removing the capital gain, but all of this dividend will be treated as taxable income to the shareholder. Alternatively, the corporation could spend the same amount to repurchase its stock. If the shareholder tenders his or her pro rata share, then the investor will receive $100 for two shares of stock (= $100 cash dividend/$50 share price, assuming perfect markets) and have to pay capital gains on only the amount of the $100 that exceeds the cost of the two shares that were repurchased, which is $80 (2 shares × $40). Hence, the shareholder would have to pay capital gains taxes on only $20 of the $100 at that time but would have unrealized capital gains of $10 per share on the eight shares still owned (since the stock price would remain at $50 per share) upon which capital gains taxes will have to be paid at some later date when they are sold. Thus, the shareholder benefits tax-wise from a repurchase in two ways

---

[7]Such findings are inconsistent with the notion of efficient markets, and hence can be considered an "anomaly." See Josef Lakonishok and Theo Vermaelen, "Anomalous Price Behavior Around Repurchase Tender Offers," *Journal of Finance*, 45, no. 2 (June 1990): 455–77.

in that a *smaller* amount is taxed at that time at a capital gains tax rate, which is potentially a *lower* rate than the ordinary income tax rate.

Classified Stock Some corporations issue two or more classes of common stock. For example, Class A stock might have a preferred position in regard to dividends but might not have any voting rights. In contrast, Class B stock might have full voting rights but a lower position in regard to dividends. Often this is equivalent to an issue of preferred stock, along with a normal issue of common stock.

An interesting example involves the three classes of General Motors common stock. These classes are referred to as $1⅔ par value, Class E, and Class H stock. A share in each class has 1, ¼, and ½ vote, respectively. In terms of dividends, the Class E and Class H stocks are allowed to receive an amount that does not exceed the "adjusted earnings" of GM's Electronic Data Systems and Hughes Electronics subsidiaries, respectively; the $1⅔ par value stock is allowed to receive dividends that do not exceed the remainder of GM's earnings.

Another example involves Canadian corporations. Because of the Canada Income Tax Act of 1971, Canadian firms are allowed to have Class A and Class B shares. The only difference between the two classes is that Class A shares receive cash dividends whereas Class B shares receive stock dividends. Furthermore, owners of either class can swap their shares one-for-one for shares of the other class at any time.

Americus Trust Securities An unusual type of security somewhat like classified stock involves Americus Trust securities. These securities are issued by the Americus Shareowner Service Corporation, and are listed on the American Stock Exchange. They can be described most easily with an example.

Americus buys some of the outstanding shares of Exxon, and then issues two kinds of trust securities, *Exxon primes* and *Exxon scores*. An investor can subsequently buy either of these securities through a broker, and can find them listed on the American Stock Exchange as "A-xonpr" and "A-xonsc," respectively. Note that Exxon itself has nothing to do with either the creation or subsequent trading of the primes and scores.

The owner of an Exxon prime is entitled to all cash dividends that Exxon pays to Americus, and any price appreciation in Exxon up to a set limit (the "termination claim") at the expiration of the trust security. The owner of an Exxon score is entitled to all of the remaining (if any) price appreciation on Exxon. Given a price limit of $60 and a five-year expiration date, this means that if Exxon is selling for $50 on the expiration date, the prime owner will receive $50 and the score owner will receive nothing. However, if Exxon is selling for $100, then the prime owner will receive $60 and the score owner will receive $40. Currently, there are in excess of twenty companies that have some of their shares divided into primes and scores by Americus.

Letter or Restricted Stock In the United States, security regulations require that most stock be registered with the SEC before it may be sold in a public offering. Under some conditions, unregistered stock may be sold directly to a purchaser, but its subsequent sale is **restricted**, usually by a letter from the buyer stating that the stock is to be held as an investment. Such **letter stock** must be held for at least two years and cannot be sold even at that time unless ample information on the company is available and the amount sold is a relatively small percentage of the total amount outstanding.

restricted
letter stock

CASH DIVIDENDS

dividends

date of record

Payments made in cash to stockholders are termed **dividends.** These are typically declared quarterly by the board of directors and paid to the stockholders of record at a date specified by the board known as the **date of record.** The dividends may be of almost any size, subject to certain restrictions such as those contained in the charter or in documents given to creditors. Thus, even though this is unusual, dividends may even be larger than the current earnings of the corporation. (If so, they are usually paid out of past earnings.)

ex-dividend date

Compiling a list of stockholders to receive the dividend is not as simple as it may initially seem, since for many firms the list changes almost constantly as shares are bought and sold. The way of identifying those stockholders who are to receive the dividend is by use of an **ex-dividend date.** Because of the time required to record the transfer of ownership of common stock, major stock exchanges specify an ex-dividend date that is four business days before the date of record. Investors purchasing shares before an ex-dividend date are entitled to receive the dividend in question; those purchasing on or after the ex-dividend date are not entitled to the dividend.

For example, a dividend may be declared on April 15 with a date of record of Friday, May 15. In this situation Monday, May 11, would become the ex-dividend date. If an investor bought shares on Friday, May 8, he or she would subsequently receive the cash dividend (unless the shares were sold later in the day on the 8th). However, if the shares were bought on Monday, May 11, the investor would not receive the cash dividend. Besides a declaration date (April 15), an ex-dividend date (May 11), and a date of record (May 15), there is also a fourth date, the "payment date." On this date (perhaps May 25) the checks for the cash dividends are put in the mail.

STOCK DIVIDENDS AND STOCK SPLITS

stock dividend

Occasionally, the board of directors decides to forgo a cash dividend and "pays" a **stock dividend** instead. For example, if a 5% stock dividend is declared, the owner of 100 shares receives 5 additional shares that are issued for this occasion. The accounting treatment of a stock dividend is to increase the "common stock" and "capital contributed in excess of par" accounts by an amount equal to the market value of the stock at the time of the dividend times the number of new shares issued (the "common stock" account would increase by an amount equal to the par value times the number of new shares; the remainder of the increase would go into the "capital contributed in excess of par" account). In order to keep the total book value of stockholders' equity the same, the "retained earnings" account is reduced by an equivalent amount.

stock split

A **stock split** is similar to a stock dividend in that the stockholder owns more shares afterwards. However, it is different in both magnitude and accounting treatment. With a stock split, all the old shares are destroyed and new ones are issued with a new par value; afterwards, the number of new shares outstanding is usually larger than the previous number of old shares by 25% or more, with the exact amount depending on the size of the split. In contrast, a stock dividend usually results in an increase of less than 25%. While a stock dividend results in adjustments to the dollar figures in certain stockholders' equity accounts, no adjustments are made for a split. For example, if a $1-par value stock is split "2-for-1," the holder of 200 old shares will receive 400 new $.50-par value shares, and none of the dollar figures in stockholders' equity would change.

A **reverse stock split** reduces the number of shares and increases the par value per share. For example, in a reverse 2-for-1 split, the holder of 200 $1-par shares would exchange them for 100 $2-par shares. Again, there would not be any change in the dollar figures in stockholders' equity.

reverse stock split

Stock dividends and splits must be taken into account when following the price of a company's shares. For example, a fall in price per share may be due solely to a large stock dividend. To reduce confusion, most financial services provide data adjusted for at least some of these changes. Thus, if a stock split 2-for-1 on January 30, 1988, prices prior to that date might be divided by two to facilitate comparison.

Reasons for Stock Dividends and Splits

Why do corporations issue stock dividends and split their stocks? Nothing of importance would appear to be changed, since such actions do not increase revenues or reduce expenses. All that happens is that there is a change in the size of the units in which ownership may be bought and sold. Moreover, since the process involves administrative effort, and costs something to execute, one wonders why it is done.

It is sometimes argued that stockholders respond positively to "tangible" evidence of the growth of their corporation. Another view holds that splits and stock dividends, by decreasing the price per share, may bring the stock's price into a more desirable trading range and hence increase the total value of the amount outstanding.[8]

Figure 13-2 presents the average behavior of stock returns for 219 stock

[8]Some evidence in support of this view is provided by Josef Lakonishok and Baruch Lev, "Stock Splits and Stock Dividends: Why, Who, and When," *Journal of Finance*, 42, no. 4 (September 1987): 913–32.

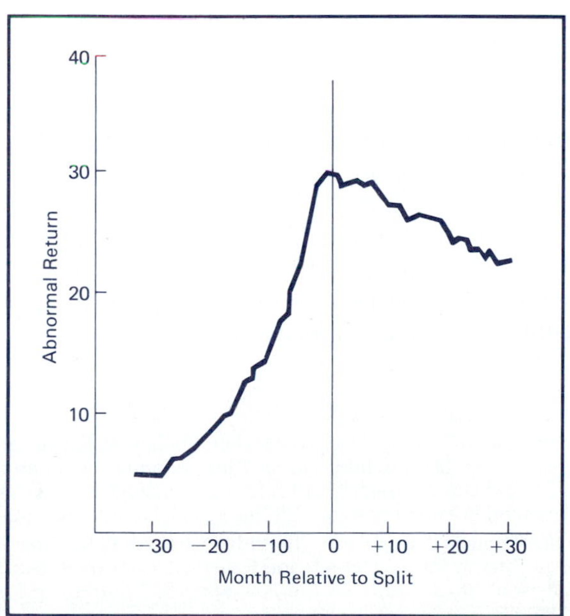

FIGURE 13-2
Abnormal Stock Returns Before and After Stock Splits
Source: Sasson Bar-Yosef and Lawrence D. Brown, "A Re-examination of Stock Splits Using Moving Betas," *Journal of Finance*, 32, no. 4 (September 1977): 1074.

splits that occurred between 1945 and 1965. For each split, the stock's "abnormal" return was determined by relating monthly returns on the stock to the corresponding returns in the stock market. This was done month by month for the 54-month period immediately prior to the split and the 54-month period immediately following it. These abnormal returns were averaged across firms for each month relative to the firm's split and then cumulated across time.

As the figure shows, the stocks tended to have a positive abnormal return of about 30% during the 54 months prior to splitting. Was this due to anticipation of the coming split? Not likely, since these splits are not announced until roughly two months before the effective date (denoted as "0" in the figure). The causal relationship could well be just the reverse: stocks split after unusual price increases. That is, unexpected positive developments (such as unexpected large increases in earnings) caused abnormal increases in the stock prices of these firms, after which the firms decided to split their stock. The behavior of the postsplit prices indicates that afterwards investors did not continue to receive positive abnormal returns. In the study shown in Figure 13-1, investors actually lost some ground. Other studies, using different stocks and time periods, found either no abnormal returns or slightly positive abnormal returns after the split.[9]

The evidence also suggests that rather than *decreasing* transaction costs, stock splits actually *increased* them. A study of presplit and postsplit behavior showed that after splits, trading volume rose less than proportionately, and both commission costs and bid-ask spreads, expressed as a percentage of value, increased—hardly reactions that are favorable to stockholders.[10] For example, after a 2-for-1 stock split, there will be twice as many shares outstanding, so it is reasonable to expect the daily number of shares that are traded to double. It is also reasonable to expect the commission for buying 200 shares after the split to be the same as the commission for buying 100 shares before the split. Instead, it was found that after the split the number of shares traded daily was less than twice as large and the commission was larger.

Another study of stock splits and stock dividends uncovered an apparent market inefficiency.[11] This study examined the performance of stocks around the ex dates associated with their stock splits and dividends (the *ex date* is the date by which an investor has to buy the shares in order to receive the newly issued shares; ex dates typically occur a few weeks after the announcement of the stock split or stock dividend). If an investor bought shares of a firm the day before its ex date and sold it the day after the ex date, then on average the investor would make an abnormal return of roughly 2% for stock dividends and 1% for stock splits. Such an observance appears to violate the notion of efficient markets because it suggests that an investor can make abnormal returns by trading stocks using a simple strategy based on publicly available information.

---

[9]See Eugene F. Fama, Lawrence Fisher, Michael C. Jensen, and Richard Roll, "The Adjustment of Stock Prices to New Information," *International Economic Review*, 10, no. 1 (February 1969): 1–21; and Guy Charest, "Split Information, Stock Returns and Market Efficiency—I," *Journal of Financial Economics*, 6, no. 2/3 (June/September 1978): 265–96.

[10]See Thomas E. Copeland, "Liquidity Changes Following Stock Splits," *Journal of Finance*, 34, no. 1 (March 1979): 115–41, and Robert M. Conroy, Robert S. Harris, and Bruce A. Benet, "The Effects of Stock Splits on Bid-Ask Spreads," *Journal of Finance*, 45, no. 4 (September 1990): 1285–95.

[11]Mark S. Grinblatt, Ronald W. Masulis, and Sheridan Titman, "The Valuation Effects of Stock Splits and Stock Dividends," *Journal of Financial Economics*, 13, no. 4 (December 1984): 461–90.

PREEMPTIVE RIGHTS

Under common law (and most state laws), a stockholder has an inherent right to maintain his or her proportionate ownership of the corporation. The existence of these **preemptive rights** means that when new shares are to be sold, the current stockholders must be given the right of first refusal in regard to the purchase of the new shares.[12] This is accomplished by issuing a certificate to each stockholder that indicates the number of new shares he or she is authorized to purchase. This number will be proportional to the number of existing shares currently owned by the stockholder. Usually, the new shares will be priced below the current market price of the stock, making such **rights** valuable. The stockholder can exercise the rights by purchasing his or her allotted amount of new shares, thereby maintaining his or her proportional ownership in the firm, but at the cost of providing additional capital. Alternatively, the rights can be sold to someone else.[13]

preemptive rights

rights

For example, if a firm needs $10,000,000 for new equipment, it may decide to sell new shares in order to raise the capital. Given that the current market price of the stock is $60 per share, a **rights offering** may be used to raise the capital where the **subscription price** is set at $50 per share.[14] Accordingly, $10,000,000/$50 = 200,000 new shares are to be sold. Assuming that the firm has 4,000,000 shares outstanding, this means that the owner of one share will receive the right to buy 200,000/4,000,000 = 1/20 of a new share. Since the number of rights received is equal to the number of shares owned, it can be seen that 20 shares must be owned in order to be able to buy one new share. Thus, if a stockholder owns 100 shares, he or she will receive 100 rights allowing him or her to buy (1/20) × 100 = 5 new shares. These rights are valuable because the owner of them can buy stock at $50 a share when the market price is significantly higher. The current owner of 100 shares can either use the 100 rights by coming up with cash equal to 5 × $50 = $250, or sell the 100 rights to someone else. But this raises a question: what is a fair price for the rights?

rights offering
subscription price

Rights are distributed in a manner similar to cash dividends. That is, there is a date of record and, four business days earlier, an **ex-rights date.** Before the ex-rights date, the value of a right can be calculated by using the following equation:

ex-rights date

$$C_o - (RN + S) = R \qquad (13.2)$$

where: C_o is the "rights-on" market price of the stock,
R is the value of a right,
N is the number of rights needed to buy one share, and
S is the subscription price.

[12]Current stockholders may not be given this right if there is a provision in the charter denying it, or if it is denied by the stockholders at the annual meeting.

[13]The investor could simply let the rights expire, causing that investor's proportion in the corporation to decline as others are given ownership in the expanded firm in return for the provision of new capital. Sometimes there is an **oversubscription privilege** given to the subscribing stockholders. This means that those stockholders who have exercised their rights will be given an opportunity to buy the shares that were not purchased; this opportunity can become important if the rights are not transferable.

oversubscription privilege

[14]The subscription price is usually set at roughly 80% of the current market price of the stock.

The equation can be interpreted in the following manner. If an investor purchases one share before the ex-rights date, by definition he or she pays the market price of C_o, shown on the left-hand side of the equation. Alternatively, the investor could purchase the number of rights necessary to buy one share of the new stock at a cost of RN and set aside an amount of money equal to the subscription price S. The total cost of doing this is $(RN + S)$. The only difference between the two alternatives is that the first one gives the investor not only one share of stock but also one right. Thus, the difference in the cost of the two alternatives, $C_o - (RN + S)$, must equal the value of a right, R, as shown in equation (13.2).

Equation (13.2) can be rewritten as:

$$R = \frac{C_o - S}{N + 1}. \tag{13.3}$$

Thus, in the previous example, the value of a right when the stock is selling for \$60 would be equal to approximately (\$60 − \$50)/(20 + 1) = \$.48.

On or after the ex-rights date, the value of a right can be calculated by using the following equation:

$$C_e - (RN + S) = 0 \tag{13.4}$$

where C_e is the ex-rights market price of the stock. The reasoning behind this equation is similar to the reasoning behind equation (13.2). That is, an investor can purchase one share by either buying it in the open market at a cost of C_e or purchasing the requisite number of rights and setting aside the subscription price, for a total cost of $RN + S$. Since the purchase of one share ex-rights means that the investor does not receive a right, the two alternatives provide the investor with the same item. Thus, the cost of these two alternatives should be equivalent, so the difference in their cost should be zero.

Equation (13.4) can be rewritten as:

$$R = \frac{C_e - S}{N}. \tag{13.5}$$

In the previous example, if the stock is selling for \$56 after the ex-rights date, then the value of a right at that time would be approximately (\$56 − \$50)/20 = \$.30.

STOCK QUOTATIONS

Figures 13-3 through 13-6 provide examples of quotations summarizing a day's transactions in stocks traded over the counter and on various stock exchanges.

Active stocks traded with the aid of the National Association of Securities Dealers' Automated Quotation system (NASDAQ) are summarized in the forms shown in Figures 13-3 (a), (b), and (c). Transactions in securities designated National Market Issues are summarized in detail, as shown in Figure 13-3 (a). High and low prices for trades over the preceding 52 weeks are given, along with the annual per-share amount of dividends, in dollars, based on the latest declared amount (letters refer to footnotes providing details

FIGURE 13-3
Summary of Stocks Traded with the Aid of the NASDAQ System
Source: Reprinted by permission of *The Wall Street Journal,* © Dow Jones & Company, Inc., March 30, 1992, pp. C6, C8. All rights reserved.

(a) National Market Issues

52 Weeks Hi	Lo	Stock	Sym	Div	Yld %	PE	Vol 100s	Hi	Lo	Close	Net Chg
		-A-A-A-									
40½	26½	A&W Brands	SODA	.44	1.2	24	884	37	35¼	36	−1
15½	5¾	ABS Ind	ABSI	.32	2.2	32	25	15¼	14½	14½	− ½
17½	9¼	ACC	ACCC	.16	1.0	73	3	16¾	16¾	16¾	− ¼
43¼	20½	ADC Tel	ADCT		...	25	550	26	25¼	26	+ ¼
9¼	4¼	AEL Ind A	AELNA		...	34	41	7½	7½	7½	...
14½	9¼	AEP Ind	AEPI		...	15	2	12	12	12	...
37½	19¼	AES Cp	AESC	.20i	.5	...	1192	37½	36¾	36¾	− ⅝
9¼	**6¾**	**ARI Netwk**	**ARIS**		...	...	**25**	**7½**	**7**	**7½**	**+ ½**
20	7⅛	ASK Cptr	ASKI		...	...	831	15½	15⅛	15⅛	− ¼
32¾	14½	AST Rsrch	ASTA		...	8	3828	18¾	17½	17¾	− ¾
11¾	8	AamesFnl	AAMS	.03e	.3	...	280	10⅝	10⅜	10½	− ½
14½	7½	AaronRents	ARON	.10	.7	19	157	13½	13	13½	+ ½
17½	**7¾**	**Abaxis**	**ABAX**		...	...	**203**	**8¼**	**7¾**	**7¾**	**− ½**
14½	12⅜	AbbeyHlthcr	ABBY		...	...	618	13	12¾	13	+ ⅛
6½	**2⅝**	**AbingtnBcp**	**ABBK**		...	...	**3**	**6½**	**6½**	**6½**	**+1**
13	**6⅜**	**Accelint**	**ACLE**	**.28**	**3.6**	**34**	**5**	**7¾**	**7¾**	**7¾**	**+ ½**
7½	5¾	AccessHlth	ACCS		...	...	55	6	6	6	...
8¼	2⅞	AcclmEntn	AKLM		...	...	1243	8⅛	7⅞	7⅞	− ⅛
13⅝	9	Acmat	ACMT		...	17	10	10	10	10	− ¼
8	5	Acmat A	ACMTA		...	10	10	6¼	6¼	6¼	...
18¾	12	AcmeSteel	ACME	.02e	.1	...	104	17¼	16⅝	16¾	+ ½
2	**½**	**ActnAutRnt**	**AXXN**		...	...	**253**	**19/32**	**17/32**	**19/32**	**+ 3/32**
22	10	Acxiom	ACXM		...	62	43	15¾	15½	15½	− ½
4⅞	1⅛	AdacLabs	ADAC	.04e	1.0	98	5131	4 1/16	3 13/16	3 15/16	− 1/16
s 11¼	5	Adage	ADGE		...	32	68	6	5¾	5¾	− ¼
35⅜	10	Adaptec	ADPT		...	31	1090	32½	30¾	31¼	−1½
11½	6	AddintnRes	ADDR		...	...	520	9½	8⅞	9¼	+ ¼
25¾	14	AdiaSvcs	ADIA	.16	1.1	21	373	15	14⅛	14⅛	− ⅛
68½	41¼	AdobeSys	ADBE	.32	.6	23	4959	55	52	53¼	−1½
3¾	1⅜	Adtec	JAIL		...	...	9	3½	3½	3½	...
16¼	12¼	AdvaCare	AVCR		...	...	1001	12⅝	12½	12⅝	+ ⅛
▲ 19⅜	**14¾**	**AdvntgHlth**	**ADHC**		...	...	**1251**	**20¼**	**18**	**18**	**−1⅜**
12	8½	AdvRoss	AROS		...	2	13	10¼	9¾	9¾	...
10¼	6¼	AdvCircuit	ADVC		...	10	118	9⅝	9½	9⅝	− ¼
21	8½	AdvIntrvnt	LAIS		...	...	1121	9¼	8½	9¼	+ ¼
20¾	6½	AdvLogicRsrch	AALR		...	6	87	7½	7	7	− ¼
6¾	1⅝	AdvMktg	ADMS		...	45	124	6⅛	5¾	5⅞	− ⅛
16⅛	3	AdvPolymer	APOS		...	...	562	11	10⅜	11	...
9¼	5⅛	AdvPromoTch	APTV		...	...	1153	7¼	6¾	7	+ ⅛
4½	**2¼**	**AdvSemi**	**ASMIF**		...	...	**28**	**3**	**3**	**3**	**− ¼**
24¼	14¾	AdvTelecom	ATEL		...	17	444	20¼	19½	20¼	+ ¼
19¼	**5¾**	**AdvTissue**	**ATISA**		...	...	**873**	**13⅝**	**12⅝**	**12⅝**	**−1**
50¼	12½	Advanta	ADVN	.24	.6	18	1334	43⅞	42½	43¼	− ⅜
14¼	12¾	AdvntgBcp	AADV		...	...	313	14⅛	13¾	13⅞	+ ⅛
27⅞	16¼	Advo	ADVO		...	18	263	19¾	18⅞	19¼	− ¾
3¾	1 5/16	Aequitron	AQTN		...	15	216	2¾	2½	2½	− ⅛
⅝	5/32	AeroSysInc	AESM		...	...	149	11/32	9/32	9/32	...
8⅛	4	Aerovox	ARVX		...	242	367	7⅝	7⅛	7¼	− ⅛
34½	13¼	AffIBkshCO	AFBK	.40	1.2	20	50	32½	32⅜	32⅜	− ¼
41¾	22⅛	Affymax	AFMXF		...	...	489	26	24¾	25	− ½
12⅜	7⅜	AgSvcAm	AGSV		...	9	82	12⅜	12	12	− ⅜

(b) Other Active Issues

Stock & Div		Sales 100s	Bid	Asked	Net Chg.
		-A-A-A-			
A&A Fd g		45	3⅞	4⅛	+ ⅛
ACOI		50	1	1⅜	...
ACTV		62	2¼	2½	...
ACTV wt		60	13/16	15/16	− 1/16
AFN		274	1 11/16	1 13/16	...
AGBag		55	3⅜	3⅝	...
ANB	1.20	7	35	37	...
APA		24	5	6	...
ASA		255	1 11/16	1⅞	...
ATC Env		46	3⅛	3⅜	...
AW A h		192	7⅜	7⅝	− ⅜
Accuhlt		5	4½	5	...
ActnPr		5	1¾	2	+ ⅛
ActnSt pf		10	¼	¾	...
Adelph h		18	16¾	17¼	+ ¼
Admar s		164	2⅜	2⅝	...
AdvEnv		769	2⅜	2 7/16	+ ⅛
AdvMed		27	4	4¼	...
AdNMR		487	3⅝	3¾	− ⅛
A NMR wt		65	3¾	4	− ⅜
AdNMR wtB		20	1½	2⅛	− ⅜
AdvLfe		321	1 9/16	1 11/16	...
Aerody		6	8⅜	8½	...
Aero wtA		9	2¼	2½	...
Aeroson		140	2¼	2½	...
AirMeth		509	1 5/16	1⅜	− 1/16
AirMt wt		30	3/16	¼	...
AirCure		65	9	9½	...
ArCur wt		79	3½	3¾	...
AirInt		644	1 11/16	1¾	...
Ajay		205	1⅜	1 7/16	+ 1/32
Alcde pf		z7	2	2½	...
Alcoln s		293	6⅜	6⅝	− ⅜
AllACm s		16	9	10	+ ¼
AldCAdv		10	2⅞	3⅜	...
AldWste		136	4½	4⅞	...
Alpha1		308	10	10¾	− ¼
Alph1 wtB		23	5¼	6	− ¼
Alphr un		29	6¼	7¼	...
Alpnet		695	15/16	1 1/16	+ ⅛
AltrSl s		3	7¼	7⅝	...
AmbMd		3	5¼	6	...
Amribc	.20	z29	25½	26¼	...
vjAWAirl		763	⅜	7/16	...
AAcft		1275	¾	27/32	− 1/16
AmAset		55	1¾	2	+ ¼
AmBio		543	3 3/16	3 5/16	...
AmBiogn		426	8⅛	8⅜	− ⅜
AmBiom		61	10⅝	11	...
AmBio wt		47	2⅞	3¼	...
ABsCpt		1015	2 1/16	2¼	− 3/16
AmDrg		352	2½	2 9/16	...
AmEduc		72	3¾	4½	− ½
AmFB		20	4½	5¼	...
AIM 84	.60e	237	4⅝	5	...
AIM 85	1.21e	15	10½	11	...
AMdAlt		135	2 1/16	2 3/16	...
AmMdTc		115	3 9/16	3 13/16	− 1/16
ANtPt		3	3⅜	3⅝	...
APacBk		185	3	3¼	...
ASvFL		1107	11/16	13/16	...
Amrhst		100	4⅝	5⅛	− ⅛
Ampal pf	.32	19	14½	15½	− ¼
AnlySur		34	3⅜	3⅝	...
Angecn		529	4⅛	4⅜	+ ⅛
Anuhco		204	2¾	3	+ 1/16
Apco	1.52e	20	19¾	22¾	...
Aphton		9	20¾	22	...
ApogeTc		23	4¼	4¾	...
AplRecy		281	10¾	12	− ½
ApdMicr		9	4⅜	4⅝	...

(c) Less Active Issues

Stock	Bid	Asked
AAON	¼	⅜
ADM Tr	11/32	⅜
AFP	15/32	⅝
API	⅝	25/32
ATC wtB	⅜	¾
ATC wtC	11/32	21/32
ATNN	7/32	9/32
Abatix	1⅞	2¼
Acap	¼	⅞
AcqCa	1⅜	1¾
ActP wtA	5/32	11/32
ActP wtB	3/32	3/16
ActnSt h	1/32	1/16
AdvEn wt	⅞	15/16
AdGrav	2	2⅛
AdvTob	⅛	3/16
Aero wtB	1½	1⅝
Agristr	1 3/16	1 5/16
AirMt un	1⅜	2
AirTrn	5/16	7/16
AirIn wtA	⅜	13/32
AirIn wtB	9/32	5/16
Ajay wt	19/32	13/16
Alanco	5/16	11/32
AlskAp	5/32	3/16
Alcide	1	1⅛
AlfaInt	3/32	5/32
AlliWell	1/16	3/32
AlphaSo	5/16	11/32
Altex	3/32	⅛
Amacan	5/32	9/32
AmbFd	⅝	⅞
Ameral	1/16	3/32
AAst wtA	1¼	1½
AAst wtB	½	1
AAst wtC	½	⅞
AmBcpNV	6¼	9¼
AmCyto	⅜	¾
ADrg wt	1	1 1/16
AmElct	3/32	9/32
AmEnt	1 1/16	1¼
AmFbre	7/16	½
AFn pfD	10	10¾
AmFran	¼	½
AMetl	⅜	½
AmNwk	¼	5/16
ASafty	17/32	9/16
AmScr	1/32	1/16
AScr pf	⅛	⅜
Ametech	1½	1⅝
An-Con	3/16	¼
AngSwis	1/32	1/16
Aplan h	15/32	½
Ap DNA	1	1 3/32
ApldLsr	3¼	3½
ApLsr wtA	1½	1⅝
ApdL wtB	½	¾
ApdLsr un	10	10¼
ApdM wt	1 7/16	1⅝
AquaS	15/32	17/32
Arman wt	5/32	7/32
Armeno	5/32	3/16
Artagph	11/16	13/16
Artech s	1¼	2
ASDR	1/32	1/16
AspenE	3/16	7/32
AspnWd	11/16	¾
Astrcm	9/32	⅜
AtrixInt	1¾	1 15/16
Atrxl wt	¼	9/32
Atrxl un	1⅞	2⅛
AudKng	2½	2⅞

concerning extra or special dividends and yields; the footnotes also explain the sporadic entries in the extreme left column and why certain rows are either emboldened or underlined). This dollar amount is divided by the **closing price** (the price at which the last trade of the day was made) to obtain the figure shown for **dividend yield.** The price-earnings ratio (the closing price divided by the last twelve months' earnings per share) is given next. The remaining entries summarize the day's transactions in the major markets in which the stock is traded. Sales, in hundreds of shares, are indicated,

closing price
dividend yield

followed by the highest and lowest prices at which trades were completed during the day. The next entry is the closing price, and the final entry shows the difference between the day's closing price and that of the preceding day.

Information on over-the-counter stocks with somewhat less activity is shown in Figure 13-3 (b). Volume traded through NASDAQ during the day is shown (in hundreds of shares) along with the highest bid price and lowest ask price by dealers as of 4 P.M. Eastern time. The net change in the bid price from the previous day is also shown. Investors pay the ask price to purchase shares and receive the bid price when they sell shares. In addition, markdowns or markups and commissions may be added by the investor's retail broker.[15]

Information on over-the-counter stocks with relatively little activity is shown in Figure 13-3 (c). Only bid and ask price quotations (as of 4 P.M. Eastern time) are given.

Activity in stocks traded on U.S. stock exchanges is shown in Figure 13-4. Stocks listed on the New York Stock Exchange are shown in the upper-left side of the figure. Those listed on the American Stock Exchange are shown in the upper-right side of the figure. The information provided for both of these exchanges is identical in format to the information provided for NASDAQ/NMS that was shown in panel (a) of Figure 13-3.

The bottom panel of Figure 13-4 describes the activity in various regional stock exchanges in the United States. However, any trading that involves securities that are also listed on either the NYSE or AMEX ("dually listed securities") is excluded, since these trades are reflected in either panel (a) or (b). Less information is provided for trading on the regional exchanges than on organized exchanges, as all that is reported is the daily sales and the high, low, and closing prices, along with the change in the close from the previous day.

Figure 13-5 displays trading activity in the "Emerging Company Marketplace" on the American Stock Exchange. Such trading began on March 18, 1992, and involves smaller start-up companies that do not meet the AMEX's regular listing requirements. Previously these stocks were traded on NASDAQ but were not National Market System issues. The information provided in the figure is identical in format to the information presented for the regularly listed AMEX stocks shown in Figure 13-4 (b).

Figure 13-6 displays the trading activity in various foreign stock markets. The top part of the figure shows the trading activity in the two major markets in Canada—Toronto and Montreal; the bottom part of the figure shows some of the trading activity in a few other foreign markets. In both parts of the figure the prices given are stated in the local currency of the country in which the exchange is located. More information is provided for the Canadian markets, presumably because of the greater interest among Americans in the securities traded in these markets.

INSIDER TRADING

The Securities and Exchange Commission requires the officers and directors of a corporation whose securities are traded on an organized exchange to report any transactions they have made in the firm's shares. Such a report,

[15]American Depository Receipts (ADRs) for foreign stocks that are traded on NASDAQ are shown separately under a heading of "ADRs." Exchange-listed ADRs are not shown separately. Instead, they are integrated into the tables with listed U.S. securities.

FIGURE 13-4
Summary of Activity in Stocks Traded on U.S. Exchanges

Source: Reprinted by permission of *The Wall Street Journal*, © Dow Jones & Company, Inc., March 30, 1992, pp. C3, C10. All rights reserved worldwide.

(a) Stocks Listed on the New York Stock Exchange

	52 Weeks Hi	Lo	Stock	Sym	Div	Yld %	PE	Vol 100s	Hi	Lo	Close	Net Chg
						-A-A-A-						
	16⅞	10⅝	AAR	AIR	.48	3.4	17	419	14⅝	14⅛	14¼	− ¼
	11⅝	10⅜	ACM Gvt Fd	ACG	.96	9.3	...	679	10½	10⅜	10⅜	− ⅛
	10⅜	8⅞	ACM OppFd	AOF	.80e	8.5	...	325	9⅜	9¼	9⅜	...
	11¼	9⅜	ACM SecFd	GSF	.96	9.4	...	944	10⅜	10⅛	10¼	...
	9½	8⅜	ACM SpctmFd	SI	.79	9.0	...	760	8¾	8⅝	8¾	...
	9⅜	7⅞	ACM MgdIncFd	AMF	.95	10.9	...	1030	8⅞	8⅝	8¾	...
	12⅞	10⅞	ACM MgdMultFd	MMF	1.08	9.6	...	174	11¼	11⅛	11¼	+ ⅛
n	9½	5	ADT	ADT		...	...	1634	9	8⅞	9	...
	32⅞	20¼	AFLAC	AFL	.40	1.5	15	1867	28	27½	27½	− ¼
	26	15	AL Labs A	BMD	.18	.8	76	153	23⅜	22¾	22⅞	− ⅜
	2⅛	**¾**	**AM Int**	**AM**		...	...	**1165**	**1½**	**1⅜**	**1⅜**	**− ⅛**
	12	4⅛	AM Int pf		1.50j	...	...	68	5¾	5⅝	5⅝	− ¼
	11¾	9¾	AMEV Sec	AMV	1.05	9.4	...	155	11¼	11⅛	11⅛	− ¼
	80¼	54½	AMR	AMR		...	...	3223	75⅛	73¾	74	...
	28	25	ANR pf		2.67	10.4	...	6	25⅝	25⅝	25⅝	− ⅝
	44¼	34½	ARCO Chm	RCM	2.50	6.4	20	159	39¼	38⅞	39	− ¼
	2⅝	**1**	**ARX**	**ARX**		...	...	**318**	**1⅞**	**1¾**	**1⅞**	**+ ⅛**
	56	43⅝	ASA	ASA	2.00	4.4	...	179	45	44⅝	45	+ ¼
	6½	**3¼**	**ATT Cap yen wt**			...	...	**591**	**3¾**	**3½**	**3¾**	**− ¼**
	69½	46¾	AbbotLab	ABT	1.20	2.0	24	3656	61½	60½	60¾	− ⅝
	14⅝	12⅛	Abitibi g	ABY	.50	...	...	20	13	12⅞	12⅞	− ¼
	6¼	3⅜	AcmeElec	ACE		...	31	4	5⅝	5⅝	5⅝	− ⅛
	11¾	5½	AcmeCleve	AMT	.40	4.1	...	222	10⅛	9¾	9⅞	− ¼
	40	18⅞	Acuson	ACN		...	13	2472	20¾	20⅛	20⅜	− ¼
	20¼	16⅜	AdamsExp	ADX	1.63e	8.6	...	68	19	18⅞	18⅞	− ⅛
	9	3⅞	AdobeRes	ADB		...	...	220	5	5	5	− ⅛
	20⅛	12⅞	AdobeRes pfB			...	...	21	14⅜	14⅜	14⅜	− ⅛
	18	10¾	AdobeRes pfA			...	...	5	12½	12½	12½	...
	21½	**8⅜**	**AdvMicro**	**AMD**		...	**11**	**17275**	**19⅛**	**17½**	**17½**	**−1⅝**
	49⅛	29½	AdvMicro pf		3.00	6.9	...	207	45¼	43¼	43½	−2
	9⅛	2⅞	Advest	ADV		...	...	337	7¼	6⅞	7	− ⅛
	71¾	54¾	Aegon	AEG	3.72r	5.2	7	6	70⅞	70½	70⅞	+ ½
	49⅛	31⅞	AetnaLife	AET	2.76	6.6	9	1970	43	41½	41⅞	−1⅛
	12⅛	7½	AffilPub	AFP	.24	2.4	21	476	10⅛	9⅞	10	+ ⅛
n	25¾	21½	AgriMinl	AMC	.18e	.7	...	167	24¼	24	24⅛	...
	20⅞	12⅝	Ahmanson	AHM	.88	5.7	7	2662	15⅝	15⅛	15⅜	− ⅜
	26½	24	Ahmanson pf		2.40	9.2	...	76	26⅛	26	26⅛	+ ¼
	22½	4	Aileen	AEE		...	15	103	18⅛	17⅞	18	− ⅛
s	46⅝	30½	AirProduct	APD	.80	1.9	19	2558	44⅜	43	43	−1⅜
	30	19¼	AirbornFrght	ABF	.30	1.2	18	437	24⅞	24½	24⅝	...
	26	14	Airgas	ARG		...	25	71	24½	24	24	− ¾
	14	8⅛	Airlease	FLY	1.68	14.3	7	113	11¾	11½	11¾	+ ⅛

(b) Stocks Listed on the American Stock Exchange

	52 Weeks Hi	Lo	Stock	Sym	Div	Yld %	PE	Vol 100s	Hi	Lo	Close	Net Chg
						-A-A-A-						
	9¼	7⅞	AIM StratFd	AST	.63	7 4	...	35	8⅝	8½	8½	...
	7	3¾	ALCComm	ALC		...	...	19	6¼	6⅛	6⅛	− ⅛
	6⅞	3⅞	AMC Entn	AEN		...	40	9	4⅜	4⅜	4⅜	...
	⅞	**⅛**	**AOI Coal**	**AOI**		...	...	**29**	**½**	**⅜**	**½**	**+ 1/16**
	1½	**¼**	**ARC Int**	**ATV**		...	...	**245**	**1⅛**	**1**	**1⅛**	**− ⅛**
n	10⅝	4⅛	ARM Fnl	RXM		...	...	109	8⅝	8¼	8¼	...
	57	48¾	AT&T Fund	ATF	2.61e	5.0	...	99	52⅜	51¾	52⅛	− ⅛
	5½	2⅛	ATI Med	ATI		...	...	147	3¾	3⅝	3⅝	...
	22¾	6⅛	Abiomed	ABD		...	...	70	14½	14¼	14¼	...
	8⅜	4¼	AcmeUtd	ACU	.20	3.0	16	110	6⅞	6¾	6¾	− ⅛
	7⅛	4½	ActionInd	ACX		...	27	220	7	6⅞	7	+ ⅛
	6¾	**3½**	**ActonCp**	**ATN**		...	...	**28**	**6¾**	**6⅜**	**6¾**	**+ ⅜**
▲	21⅝	15½	Acton pf		3.75	16.9	...	11	22½	21½	22¼	+ ¾
n	4¼	2½	AdamsRes	AE		...	8	30	3½	3½	3½	− ⅛
s	31¼	12	AdvMagnet	AVM		...	...	260	18¾	18½	18½	− ½
	19¼	9½	AdvMed	AMA		...	...	345	12⅞	12	12⅜	− ¼
	9⅞	7½	AdvMed pf		1.00	10.7	...	13	9⅜	9¼	9⅜	...
	24⅛	15⅞	AirWaterTech	AWT		...	...	385	17⅛	16¾	17	− ⅛
s	31¾	11¾	AirExprss	AEX	.16	.6	16	198	29⅛	28⅞	28⅞	...
	2⅞	**¾**	**AircoaHotel**	**AHT**		...	...	**10**	**1½**	**1⅜**	**1⅜**	**− ¼**
n	19⅜	12¼	AlafstBcsh	AFB	.80	4.5	8	9	17¾	17⅝	17¾	+ ⅛
	8¾	5	AlbaWaldn	AWS		...	10	20	8⅛	7⅞	7⅞	− ⅜
	3⅛	**5/16**	**Alfin**	**AFN**		...	...	**106**	**2**	**1⅝**	**1⅝**	**− ⅜**
	9⅛	2⅝	AllouHlth	ALU		...	15	68	7¾	7½	7½	− ¼
	5⅝	¼	AllouHlth wt			...	...	5	4¾	4¾	4¾	...
	15/16	¼	AllstarIns	SAI		...	...	50	11/16	11/16	11/16	...
	4	1⅝	AlphaInd	AHA		...	24	37	2⅜	2¼	2⅜	...
	14⅞	**3**	**AlpineGp**	**AGI**		...	...	**795**	**11½**	**10½**	**10⅞**	**− ¾**
s	55¾	27⅝	Alza	AZA		...	81	1629	44⅞	42⅞	43⅛	−1⅝
s	41¼	17	Alza wt			...	...	57	30⅛	28⅝	28⅞	−1½
	2⅛	**1**	**AmaxGold wt**			...	...	**7**	**1 9/16**	**1½**	**1 9/16**	**+ ⅛**
	20⅝	11⅝	Amdahl	AMH	.10	.6	19	2802	17½	16¾	16¾	− ¼
	3½	5/16	Amerhlth	AHH		...	...	108	2⅛	2	2⅛	...
	16⅜	13	AmFPrepFd2	PF	1.65	10.5	...	5	15¾	15¾	15¾	...
	20¼	14⅜	AmBkCT	BKC	1.32	6.7	10	7	19⅝	19½	19⅝	...
	21⅝	12¼	AmBiltrite	ABL	.15	.7	12	14	20⅜	20¼	20¼	− ¼
	4½	2⅛	AmExplor	AX		...	...	181	2⅜	2¼	2⅜	...
	2	**⅜**	**AmExplor wt**			...	...	**10**	**7/16**	**7/16**	**7/16**	**− 1/16**
	26	18¾	AmFructse A	AFCA	.48	2.1	10	80	24⅛	23⅜	23⅜	− ½
	26	18¼	AmFructse B	AFCB	.48	2.0	10	2	23½	23½	23½	− ⅛
	6	1¼	AmHlthCare	AHI		...	10	485	4⅝	4⅜	4½	− ⅛

(c) Stocks Listed on Regional Exchanges

PACIFIC

Sales	Stock	High	Low	Close	Chg.
1300	AdNMR	4	3⅝	3⅝	− ⅛
8300	AFn pfF	15	15	15	− ¼
1600	AmPac	34½	33¼	33½	−2
2400	BetaPhse	1⅛	1	1⅛	+ ⅛
1000	BrockCp	1¼	1¼	1¼	.....
9400	CanSoPt g	3½	3¼	3½	+3-16
17300	MagelPt	1	15-16	1	.....
29000	NVF	7-64	3-32	7-64	+1-64
129100	OKC LP un	14¼	12¾	13⅜	− ¼
29600	PhnxRs	2⅜	2¼	2¼	+ ⅛
200	PopeRs	40½	40½	40½	+ ½
100	RckwdN	3-32	3-32	3-32	.....
8400	SoetPS	5½	5	5⅜	.....
1100	SCGspfA	17	17	17	− ¼
200	VanGld	3-16	3-16	3-16	−1-16
7	Minstr 00t	93	93	93	+½
10	NVF 10s03	37	37	37	+1
13	RapAm 10s06	⅝	⅝	⅝	...
52	TWA 15s94f	54½	54¼	54¼	+1¼
36	TWA 12s01f	9⅛	9⅛	9⅛	−⅛
40	TWA 12s08f	9⅛	9⅛	9⅛	+⅛

Total sales .... 6,955,000 shares.

PHILADELPHIA

Sales	Stock	High	Low	Close	Chg.
120	BltGE pfH	95	93½	95	− ½
1000	ExecTel	4⅞	4⅞	4⅞	− ⅛
24300	Exten	11-16	⅝	⅝	.....
10000	PopeEvRob	7-64	7-64	7-64	+1-128
100	RelIns pfA	24⅜	24⅜	24⅜	+ ¼

Total sales 2,939,000 shares.

BOSTON

Sales	Stock	High	Low	Close	Chg.
1000	Bailey	3⅜	3⅜	3⅜	− ⅛
4500	CstlCarib	21-32	⅝	21-32	+1-32
1000	LoJack	2¾	2¾	2¾	+ ¼
10000	MegoA	1 7-16	1 7-16	1 7-16	−1-16
5000	MegoB	1 7-16	1 7-16	1 7-16	−1-16
100	PrcOpt	5⅜	5⅜	5⅜	− ⅛
33200	Thoratc	¾	⅝	¾	+ ⅛
300	VSI Ent	5¼	5¼	5¼	.....

Total sales 3,315,000 shares.

MIDWEST

Sales	Stock	High	Low	Close	Chg.
300	GreifBr	38⅞	38¾	38⅞	+ ⅜

Total stocks sales 11,660,000

FIGURE 13-5
Emerging Company Marketplace on the AMEX

Source: Reprinted by permission of *The Wall Street Journal,* © Dow Jones & Company, Inc., March 30, 1992, p. C10.

	52 Weeks Hi	52 Weeks Lo	Stock	Sym	Div	Yld %	PE	Vol 100s	Hi	Lo	Close	Net Chg
	9 1/2	3 3/4	AdvPhotonix	APIA		...	...	29	7 5/8	7 1/2	7 1/2	− 1/8
	1 7/16	1	AltaEngy	ALE		...	6	71	1 3/16	1 3/16	1 3/16	...
	3 1/8	3/16	AmPacMint	DLS		...	300	1	3	3	3	...
	6 1/2	5/16	AudreRecog	ARS		...	...	324	4 7/16	4 1/16	4 1/8	− 3/16
	5 5/8	1 3/8	CancerTrt	CTH		...	63	12	4 3/8	4 3/8	4 3/8	...
	2 1/2	**1/2**	**ColonlData**	**CDT**		...	...	**82**	**1 3/4**	**1 5/8**	**1 5/8**	**− 1/8**
n	3 3/8	2 1/2	DigitranSys	DGT		...	24	64	3 1/4	3 1/8	3 1/8	− 1/8
	4 9/16	2 5/8	Epigen	EPN		...	...	115	3 5/8	3 1/2	3 5/8	+ 1/8
	3 1/8	1/4	Epigen wtA			...	...	9	2 1/4	2 1/8	2 1/8	...
	1 1/4	**1/8**	**Epigen wtB**			...	...	**33**	**7/8**	**11/16**	**11/16**	**− 3/16**
	15 1/4	**6 1/2**	**Epigen un**			...	...	**35**	**11 3/4**	**11 1/2**	**11 1/2**	**−1**
n	2 1/4	1 11/16	IntertelComm	ITR		...	...	322	1 13/16	1 13/16	1 13/16	...
	3 3/8	**1**	**IonLaserTch**	**ILT**		...	**16**	**237**	**2 5/8**	**2 3/8**	**2 3/8**	**− 1/4**
	7 1/2	5/8	MediaLogic	TST		...	13	111	6 7/8	6 1/2	6 3/4	− 1/4
	4 3/16	1/8	Medphone	MPO		...	...	555	1 11/16	1 1/2	1 9/16	...
	1/2	1/8	Medphone wt			...	...	30	7/16	3/8	3/8	...
s	3 1/4	1/4	NoCoastEngy	NCE		...	...	21	3	2 13/16	3	...
n			NoInstr	NIZ		...	14	76	2 7/8	2 1/2	2 7/8	...
	10 1/8	4 1/2	OceanOptiq	OPQ		...	23	234	9 1/2	8 7/8	9 1/4	− 1/8
n▼	9 5/8	9	PNF Ind	PNI		...	..	70	9 1/8	8 3/4	8 3/4	− 1/4
n	14	7 7/8	Printron wi			...	...	38	9 7/8	9 1/2	9 5/8	− 1/8
n	4 3/8	3 5/8	ProfDental	PRO		...	...	12	3 15/16	3 15/16	3 15/16	− 1/16
	2 7/16	**1 1/8**	**RandersGp**	**RGI**		...	**169**	**91**	**1 3/4**	**1 11/16**	**1 11/16**	**− 3/16**
	3 3/4	1 1/8	ThreeFive	TFS		...	46	2	2 3/4	2 3/4	2 3/4	+ 1/8
	4 9/16	**9/16**	**TopSource**	**TPS**		...	...	**437**	**3 5/8**	**3 1/8**	**3 5/8**	**+ 1/4**
n	6 1/4	3 1/8	Topox	TPO		...	...	284	3 5/8	3 3/8	3 3/8	− 1/8
	3 1/8	2 1/8	UniqueMobil	UQM		...	...	31	3	2 3/4	2 15/16	

insiders

known as form 4, must be filed within ten days following the month in which the transaction takes place. This reporting requirement is also applicable to any stockholder who owns 10% or more of the firm's shares.[16] Such stockholders, officers, and directors are often referred to as **insiders.** The information they provide about their trading is subsequently reported in the Securities and Exchange Commission's monthly *Official Summary of Securities Transactions and Holdings.*[17] For example, the summary of trades made in January (and reported by early February) is published early in March. Thus, up to two months may elapse before knowledge of such trades becomes widespread.

The Securities and Exchange Acts require corporate insiders to return all short-term profits from security transactions in their own stocks to the corporation. For this purpose, "short term" is defined as less than six months, meaning that the shares were both bought and sold within a six-month time

[16]This reporting requirement should not be confused with SEC Rule 13d, which requires investors to disclose their holding in a company once it is equal to 5% or more of the company's stock. Unlike form 4 investors, Rule 13d investors are not viewed as insiders by the SEC, and do not have to report every transaction they subsequently make.

[17]The *Value Line Investment Survey* (published by Value Line, Inc., New York, N.Y.) reports an "index of insider decisions" for each stock covered in its weekly service. In essence, this is a cumulative index of the net number of purchasers (including those who exercise options) and sellers. The *Weekly Insider Report* (published by Vickers Stock Research Corp., Brookside, N.J.) reports a ratio of total insider buying to total insider selling. For an article about what constitutes insider trading, see Gary L. Tidwell, "Here's a Tip—Know the Rules of Insider Trading," *Sloan Management Review*, 28, no. 4 (Summer 1987): 93–98.

FIGURE 13-6

Summary of Trading Activity on Selected Foreign Exchanges

Source: Reprinted by permission of *The Wall Street Journal*, © Dow Jones & Company, Inc., March 30, 1992, p. C11. All rights reserved worldwide.

(a) CANADIAN MARKETS

TORONTO

Quotations in Canadian Funds
Quotations in cents unless marked $
Friday, March 27, 1992

Sales	Stock	High	Low	Close	Chg.
36985	Abti Prce	$15⅝	15¼	15¼	- ⅝
6345	Agnico E	470	460	470	
43060	Air Canada	$6⅝	6⅜	6⅜	- ¼
23428	Alt Energy	$11	10⅝	10¾	- ⅛
2200	Alta Nat	$14¼	14⅛	14¼	+ ¼
129775	A Barick	$29½	29⅛	29⅜	
8400	Atco I f	$11½	11½	11½	+ ⅛
104445	Aur Res o	239	235	235	- 2
159403	BCE Inc	$46⅞	46½	46½	- ½
5127	BC Gas	$17½	17⅜	17½	
605000	BF Realty	7	6	6	- 1
844	BP Canada	$11⅝	11⅝	11⅝	- ⅛
4200	BtBk Nk ii	$9½	9½	9½	+ ¼
46500	BtBk nk iv	$11¾	11⅜	11¾	+ ½
221139	Bank N S	$20¾	20⅜	20⅜	- ⅜
3052	BCE Mobl	$28½	28	28½	
51850	Bramalea	400	380	390	
12104	BC Tele	$22	21⅝	21⅝	- ⅛
051750	CAE	$6¼	6⅛	6⅛	- ¼
6375	CCL B f	$8¾	8⅝	8¾	+ ⅛
1300	Cambridg	$19¼	19⅛	19⅛	+ ⅜
7096	Camdev	$9¼	8	9¼	+ 1½
130770	CI Bk Com	$30¼	29¾	29⅞	- ½
17100	CP Forest	$25	24¾	24⅞	+ ⅛
311341	CP Ltd	$16¾	16½	16½	- ¼
42321	CTire A f	$18¾	18½	18½	- ⅛
21760	Cdn Turbo	365	360	365	+ 5
300	C Util B	$19½	19½	19½	
11750	Canfor	$27¾	27½	27¾	+ ¼
1590	Cara	$5⅝	5½	5⅝	
300	Celanes 1 p	$31½	31½	31½	
405	Cntrl Cap	27	27	27	
15200	Cineplex	380	370	375	
31700	Co Steel f	$18¼	18	18¼	+ ⅛
5800	CocaCBev	$7¾	7⅝	7¾	
200	Conwest A	$9	9	9	+ ½
15600	Crownx A f	138	135	138	
117526	Corel Sys	$22	19¾	20	- 1
40000	Denison A p	28	28	28	+ 3
20000	Denison B f	17	16	16	- 1
7100	Derlan	$6¼	6⅛	6¼	
608	Dicknsn A f	425	425	425	
22112	Dofasco	$16¾	16¼	16¼	- ½
28350	Du Pont A	$47	46¾	47	+ ¼
1700	Dylex A f	425	420	425	
315050	Encor Inc	24½	20	21	- 2
21400	Equty Svr A	100	100	100	+ 6
3700	Euro Nev	$15⅜	15¼	15⅜	
100	FPI Ltd	450	450	450	-10
34600	Fahnstk A f	$11	10⅜	10¾	- ⅛
7396	Fed Ind A	$7½	7¼	7⅜	
11600	Finning L	$12¾	12¾	12¾	
8172	Flet CCan A	$16⅜	15¾	15¾	- ¼
7450	Flet Clnv 2	$25⅜	25	25	- ⅛
3100	FSesn Hl f	$20¾	20¼	20¾	- ½
850	Franco	$24¾	24¼	24¾	+ ½
6100	Gendis A	$20⅝	20⅝	20⅝	+ ⅛
2900	Goldcorp f	305	300	300	- 5
1000	Graft G	110	110	110	+15
500	Hayes D	$12¼	12¼	12¼	
46825	Hees Intl	$15⅝	15⅛	15⅝	+ ⅜
82600	Hemlo Gld	$8½	8⅜	8⅜	- ⅛
26642	Harrows A	50	50	50	- 1
75465	Horsham f	$9¼	9⅛	9¼	- ⅛
3885	H Bay Co	$31⅞	31¾	31⅞	+ ⅛
223631	I Corona	490	480	480	- 5
5855	Imasco L	$35⅜	35⅜	35⅜	- ⅛
9136	Intrprov P	$25⅛	25	25	- ⅛
3170	Ipsco	$19⅞	19¾	19¾	- ⅛
4749	ISG Tech	$14	13¼	13¼	- ⅞
3000	Ivaco A f	305	305	305	
1900	Jannock	$17¼	17	17¼	+ ½
59150	Labatt	$25⅞	25⅝	25¾	- ⅛
24950	Loblaw Co	$18¼	18⅛	18⅛	- ⅛
56573	Mackenzie	$6⅝	6⅜	6½	
3804	Madelin o	340	330	335	- 5
132420	Magna A f	$30⅞	29⅜	29⅜	- 1¼
17445	M L Foods	$17¼	17⅛	17⅛	- ⅛
34000	MDS H A	$20⅜	19⅞	20	+ ¼
260205	Maclean H	$11⅞	11¾	11¾	- ⅛
6664	Maritime f	$21½	21⅛	21¼	- ⅛
1202	Mark Res	$5	5	5	
25100	Minnova	$17¼	17	17¼	
7250	Molson A f	$35	34¾	35	+ ¼
257	Molson B	$34⅝	34½	34⅝	+ ⅜
21100	Noma A f	$6⅛	6	6⅛	+ ⅛
15220	Noranda F	$8¼	8⅛	8¼	
33175	Noranda I	$17⅝	17⅛	17⅜	- ⅜
10722	Norcen	$20⅛	20⅛	20⅛	+ ⅛
150451	Nova Cor f	$8½	8¼	8¼	- ¼
700	Nowsco W	$8	7⅞	8	
25512	Onex C f	$7⅛	7	7⅛	+ ⅛
19300	Oshawa A f	$19	18¾	19	
112525	PWA Corp	$5	490	490	
6162	Pgurin A f	470	460	465	+ 5
39094	Petro Cdn	$8⅝	8⅛	8⅜	- ⅛
70870	Placer Dm	$11⅜	11⅛	11¼	
45777	Poco Pete	$5	490	490	-10
2000	Que Sturg o	18	18	18	+ 1
1200	Rayrock f	$5½	5½	5½	+ ⅛
203641	Renisanc	$13	12¾	12⅞	
500	Rogers A	$14⅜	14⅜	14⅜	- ⅛
51179	Rogers B f	$12⅝	12⅜	12⅜	- ⅛
427949	Royal Bnk	$24¾	24¼	24¼	- ⅜
117238	Ry Trco	$8¼	8⅛	8¼	+ ⅛
59249	Saskoil	460	430	435	-20
18862	Sceptre R	100	93	95	+ 2
1300	Scotts f	$14⅞	14⅞	14⅞	
24200	Sears Can	$9⅝	9⅝	9⅝	
121350	SHL Systm	$15½	15¼	15¼	- ¼
16957	Shell Can	$44⅞	44½	44½	- ¼
38367	Sherritt	$8⅞	8⅝	8¾	- ⅛
5591	Southam	$19¼	19⅛	19⅛	- ⅛
23276	Spar Aero f	$20	19⅝	20	+ ½
43490	Stelco A	$5⅜	5⅛	5¼	+ ⅛
400	Teck Cor A	$17	16½	16½	- ¼
283280	Teck B f	$17⅜	17⅛	17¼	
19739	Telus Cor	$14⅝	14½	14½	- ⅛
135883	ThomCor	$16½	16⅜	16⅜	- ⅛
545505	Tor Dm Bk	$16¾	16⅜	16⅜	- ⅜
179842	TIPS	1865	1845	1845	-20
2233	Torstar B f	$23	22¾	22¾	
152917	TrnAlta U	$12⅜	12¼	12¼	- ⅛
151575	TrCan PL	$16½	16¼	16¼	- ⅛
15315	Trilon A	$9⅜	9⅛	9¼	- ⅛
5810	Trimac	$8⅛	8	8⅛	
169590	Trizec A f	$8¼	8	8¼	+ ¼
7998	Unicorp A f	193	180	185	+ 5
35000	U Energy	$15¼	15	15¼	
11100	Westmin	$5⅛	495	5⅛	+22
500	Weston	$37	37	37	

Total sales 27,958,844 shares

f-No voting rights or restricted voting rights.

MONTREAL

Sales	Stock	High	Low	Close	Chg.
23936	Bank Mont	$43⅝	43	43⅛	- ½
6320	BombrdrA	$16¼	16¼	16¼	- ⅛
44056	BombrdrB	$16⅜	16¼	16¼	
13350	Cambior	$07⅜	07¼	07⅜	
10360	Cascades	$07⅝	07½	07½	- ¼
5306	DomTxtA	$08⅞	08¾	08⅞	
275	Donohue	$15⅝	15	15	- ¾
43025	Bio Pha	$34¾	33⅞	33⅞	- ¾
47655	NatBk Cda	$10¾	10½	10⅝	- ⅛
4217	Power Corp	$14¾	14⅝	14⅝	- ⅛
1200	Provigo	$08⅞	08¾	08¾	- ⅛
1048	Quebecr A	$13¼	13¼	13¼	+ ¼
5600	Quebecr B	$13⅛	12⅞	13	+ ⅛
30928	Teleglobe	$12¼	12¼	12¼	
57950	Videotron	$16½	16	16⅜	- ⅜

Total Sales 6,690,652 shares; as of 4:00 pm.

(b) OTHER FOREIGN MARKETS

Friday, March 27, 1992

TOKYO

(in yen)

	Close	Prev. Close
ANA	1120	1120
Aiwa	1230	1240
Ajinomoto	1360	1370
Alps Elec	929	930
Amada Co	1050	1070
Ando Elec	1080	1120
Anritsu	890	891
Asahi Chem	628	619
Asahi Glass	1120	1130
Bank of Tokyo	1140	1200
Bk of Yokohama	1000	1050
Banyu Pharm	1120	1160
Bridgestone	1110	1100
Brother Ind	446	446
C. Itoh	470	475
CSK	2800	2790
Canon Inc	1290	1290
Canon Sales	2120	2210
Casio Computer	1080	1110
Chubu Pwr	2700	2730
Chugai Pharm	1160	1200
Citizen Watch	759	750
Dai Nippon Print	1500	1480
Dai-ichi Kangyo	1840	1890
Daiei	899	919
Daiichi Seiyaku	1580	1610
Dainippon Pharm	1450	1530
Daiwa House	1810	1840
Daiwa Securities	785	785
Eisai	1480	1490
Ezaki Glico	1310	1340
Fanuc	4130	4080
Fuji Bank	1930	1980
Fuji Hi	311	317
Fuji Photo Film	2740	2770
Fujisawa Pharm	1190	1190
Fujitsu	664	670
Furukawa Elec	475	476
Green Cross	1000	1020
Haseko	658	657
Hirose Elec	3120	3090
Hitachi Cable	635	643
Mitsubishi Real	995	1020
Mitsubishi Hi	590	601
Mitsubishi Kasei	456	463
Mitsubishi Matl	471	472
Mitsubishi Trust	1200	1200
Mitsubishi Whse	1360	1330
Mitsui Mar&Fire	725	766
Mitsui Real	1080	1140
Mitsui TaiyoKobe	1120	1150
Mitsui Trust	1250	1260
Mitsui & Co	628	640
Mitsukoshi	1070	1100
Mochida Pharm	3160	3650
NCR Japan	925	925
NEC	955	966
NGK Spark	800	805
NIFCO	1280	1270
NKK	288	288
NSK	539	545
NTN	493	480
NTT	640000	640000
Nihon Unisys Ltd	1420	1480
Nikko Securities	651	669
Nikon Corp	680	680
Nintendo	9610	9750
Nippon Chemi-con	725	744
Nippon Columbia	545	540
Nippon El Glass	1500	1540
Nippon Express	646	651
Nippon Hodo	2730	2760
Nippon Meat	1700	1720
Nippon Oil	714	720
Nippon Sanso	535	545
Nippon Shinpan	783	799
Nippon Steel	315	320
Nissan Motor	610	600
Nissin Food	2220	2300
Nitsuko	655	650
Nomura Securities	1240	1250
OKK	630	649
Obayashi Corp	685	696
Odakyu Railway	853	862
Oji Paper	856	863
Oki Elec Ind	445	453
Okuma Corp	1040	1020
Toyo Seikan	3680	3730
Toyobo	425	430
Toyoda Mach	740	750
Toyota Motor	1370	1360
Tsugami	660	684
Uny	1230	1200
Ushio	610	621
Wacoal	852	870
Yamaha	1320	1350
Yamaichi Sec	585	585
Yamanouchi Phm	2730	2740
Yamatake-Hnywl	1300	1330
Yamato Transport	1060	1090
Yamazaki Baking	1910	1920
Yasuda Fire	700	700
Yokogawa Elec	861	879

LONDON

(in pence)

	Close	Prev. Close
Albert Fisher	67	67
Allied-Lyons	614	621
Argyll Group	317	318
Arjo Wiggins	229	230
Assoc Brit Fds	422	420
BAA PLC	555	560
Barclays	322	335
Bass	535	536
BAT Indus	667	670
Blue Circle	254	254
BOC Group	640	643
Body Shop	330	324
Boots	423	430
Borland	3125	3350
Bowater Indus	738	785
BPB Indus	158	160
British Aero	298	299
British Airwys	252	256
British Gas	250.5	252
British Pete	255	254
Sears	97	100
Sedgwick Grp	203	202
Shell Trnspt	441	443
Siebe PLC	636	627
Smithkln Bchm	845	858
Smith&Nephew	148	147
Std Chartrd	440	442
Storehouse	115	118
Sun Alliance	270	271
Tarmac	131	131
Tate & Lyle	414	422
Tesco	257.5	256
Thorn EMI	730	740
Trafalgar Hse	127	119
TSB Group	128	130
Utd Biscuits	400	400
Unilever	906	913
Vodafone	332	342
Warburg	491	493
Wellcome	1020	1014
WPP Group	68	70

South African Mines (in U.S. dollars)

	Close	Prev. Close
Bracken	0.38	0.33
Deelkraal	1.75	1.75
Doornfontein	0.35	0.35
Durban Deep	4.75	4.75
E. Rand Gold	1.33	1.38
E. Rand Prop	2.38	2.38
Elandsrand	5.81	5.91
Elsburg	0.67	0.67
Grootvlei	1.20	1.20
Harmony	5.35	5.45
Hartebstftn	3.88	3.93
Impala Pltm	11.00	11.09
Kinross	10.12	10.38
Leslie	0.58	0.58
Libanon	0.60	0.60
Loraine	0.83	0.83
Randfontein	4.12	4.12
Rustenburg	19.69	19.69
Southvaal	18.25	18.25
Stilfontein	0.80	0.80

MILAN

(in lire)

	Close	Prev. Close
Banca Com	3550	3545
Benetton	13180	13100
Ciga	1660	1660
CIR	1590	1596
FIAT Com	4774	4710
FIAT Pref	3158	3160
Generali	28490	28500
Mediobanca	13410	13420
Montedison	1346	1338
Olivetti Com	2790	2814
Olivetti NC	1875	1870
Pirelli Co	4295	4270
Pirelli SpA	1265	1215
Rinascente	6470	6643
RAS	19050	19050
Saipem	1515	1601
SIP	1390	1368
Snia	1145	1130

PARIS

(in French francs)

	Close	Prev. Close
Accor	780	772
Air Liquide	753	751
Alcatel Alstm	599	604
BSN-Gervais	1097	1103
Carrefour	2580	2540
Club Med	526	531
Dassault Avitn	345.2	346
Elf Aquitaine	357	358
Elf Sanofi	1177	1189
Euro Disneyld	147.5	149.7
Generale Eaux	2289	2290
Hachette	165	171.3
Havas	494	495
Imetal	320	323
Lafarge Coppe	357.5	354
LVMH	4417	4420
Machines Bull	35	35
Matra	170.5	172.6
Michelin	166	166
L'Oreal	789	793

	Close	Prev. Close
AMEV	55.30	55.50
Buhrmn-Tett	46	46.60
DSM	105.80	105.40
Elsevier	112	114
Fokker	33.60	33.70
Gist-Brocades	35.70	35.90
Heineken	186.70	187.90
Hoogovens	50.80	51.10
Intl Ndrlndn Gr	52	52.50
KLM	35.70	36.50
KNP	43.20	43.80
Nedlloyd	59.40	59.80
Oce-van Grntn	78.70	78.60
Pakhoed Hldg	45.90	46.30
Philips	36.10	36.30
Robeco	98.20	98.30
Rodamco	51.20	51.40
Rolinco	96.80	96.70
Rorento	71.50	71.50
Royal Dutch	141.70	142.30
Unilever	182.50	184.50
VOC	42.90	43.30
VNU	82.50	82.50
VRG-Group	49.80	49.50
Wessanen	89.90	89.60
Wolters Kluwer	69.80	69.90

HONG KONG

(in Hong Kong dollars)

	Close	Prev. Close
Bank E Asia	23.80	23.60
Cathay Pacific	11.80	12
Cheung Kong	22.20	22.90
China L & P	30.75	30.75
Dairy Farm	11.60	11.40
Hang Seng Bk	45.75	46
HK Electric	16.30	16.20
HK Land	10.20	10.20
HK Telecom	8.50	8.60
HSBC Hldgs	40.25	40.25
Hutchsn Whmp	15.70	16.10
Jardine Mathsn	48	47.75
Sun Hung Kai	27.20	27.40
Swire Pacific	28.50	28
Wharf Holdings	13.50	13.50

period.[18] As a result of this requirement, few insiders buy and sell within a six-month time period. Instead, most prefer to spread their buy-and-sell orders over a longer time period so that they do not have to return their profits.

In the United States, it is illegal for anyone to enter into a security transaction if they have taken advantage of "inside" information about the corporation that is unavailable to other people involved in the transaction. This proscription includes not only insiders but also those to whom they give such secret information (the recipient of such a "tip" is termed the "tippee").

Legally, there are two types of nonpublic information: that which is "private" (that is, legal) and that which is "inside" (that is, possibly illegal). Unfortunately, the distinction between the two types is highly ambiguous, causing continuing problems for security analysts.

Legal issues aside, two questions of relevance to outside investors may be posed: (1) Do insiders make unusual profits on transactions in their own stocks? and (2) If they do, can others profit by following their example as soon as it becomes public knowledge?

Insiders trade their stock for many reasons. For example, some purchases result from the exercise of options and some sales result from the need for cash. Moreover, it is not unusual to find some insiders purchasing a stock during a month in which other insiders are selling it. However, when a major piece of inside information suggests that a stock's value differs significantly from its current market price, it would be reasonable to expect a preponderance of insider trades on one side of the market (that is, either purchases or sales).

One way to search for such situations is to examine the *Official Summary* and count the number of days during a month that each insider traded his or her firm's stock (excluding the exercise of options). If the days on which purchases were made exceeds those on which sales were made, the individual can be counted as a net purchaser during that month; and if the converse holds, the individual would be a net seller. Next, the number of net purchasers and sellers for the firm's stock can be considered. If there were at least, say, three more net purchasers than net sellers, it might be inferred that, on balance, favorable insider information motivated the insider trades during the month. Conversely, if there are at least three more net sellers than net purchasers, it might be inferred that, on balance, unfavorable insider information motivated the insider trades.

Different cutoff levels could be used in this process to reflect the intensity of insider trading. A cutoff of 1 would require a simple majority of trades of one type, whereas a cutoff of 5 would require a "supermajority" of trades of one type.

Such a procedure was used in a detailed study of insider transactions during the 1950s and 1960s.[19] Table 13-1 summarizes the key results. The two columns on the right-hand side of the table indicate the "abnormal" returns over an eight-month period on securities that exceeded the cutoff level for insider trading. For example, during the 1960s, if an investor purchased every stock in the sample for which there were three or more net purchasers, and sold every stock for which there were three or more net sellers during a month,

---

[18] If the insider bought the stock by exercising an option that was given to him or her as part of his or her compensation, then the six-month period is measured from the day the option was granted.

[19] Jeffrey F. Jaffe, "Special Information and Insider Trading," *Journal of Business*, 47, no. 3 (July 1974): 410–28. See also Joseph E. Finnerty, "Insiders and Market Efficiency," *Journal of Finance*, 31, no. 4 (September 1976): 1141–48.

TABLE 13-1
Abnormal Returns Associated with Insider Trading

SAMPLE			AVERAGE ABNORMAL RETURN (%) OVER EIGHT MONTHS FOLLOWING	
Cutoff (No. of Net Purchasers or Sellers)	No. of Cases	Period	Month of Transaction	Month Information Became Publicly Available
1	362	1960s	1.36	.70
3	861	1960s	5.07	4.94
4	293	1950s	5.14	4.12
5	157	1950s	4.48	4.08

Source: Jeffrey F. Jaffe, "Special Information and Insider Trading," *Journal of Business*, 47, no. 3 (July 1974): 421, 426. © 1974, The University of Chicago.

more or less coincident with the transactions of the insiders themselves, then the investor would have earned, on average, an abnormal return of 5.07% over the subsequent eight months. If the transactions had been made instead at roughly the time the information was published in the *Official Summary*, an average abnormal return of 4.94% would have been earned over the next eight months.

As the first row in the table shows, a bare majority of insider trades does not appear to isolate possible effects of insider information. But a majority of 3, 4, or 5 does seem to do so. The figures shown are gross of any transaction costs, but even so, it appears that insiders can and do make money from their special knowledge of their companies. This is not surprising, since if anyone can know the true value of a firm, it should be the insiders. Since the information these insiders presumably are using is nonpublic in nature, these findings suggest that markets are not strong–form efficient. (The notion of market efficiency was introduced in Chapter 4.)

On the other hand, the abnormal returns associated with transactions that could have been made by outsiders, using only publicly available information on insider trading, are quite surprising. Moreover, those associated with cutoffs of 3, 4, or 5 pass statistical tests designed to see if they might result simply from chance. After transaction costs, trades designed to capitalize on such information appear to still produce abnormal returns (although not highly so), suggesting that markets are not even semistrong–form efficient. However, more recent studies have found that outsiders cannot use the publicly available information about insider trading to make abnormal profits, and thus support the notion that markets are semistrong–form efficient.[20] With such conflicting evidence, it would appear that whether or not insider trading information can be profitably used by outsiders is an open question.

[20]See Herbert S. Kerr, "The Battle of Insider Trading and Market Efficiency," *Journal of Portfolio Management*, 6, no. 4 (Summer 1980): 47–58; Wayne Y. Lee and Michael E. Solt, "Insider Trading: A Poor Guide to Market Timing," *Journal of Portfolio Management*, 12, no. 4 (Summer 1986): 65–71; H. Nejat Seyhun, "Insiders' Profits, Costs of Trading, and Market Efficiency," *Journal of Financial Economics*, 16, no. 2 (June 1986): 189–212; Michael S. Rozeff and Mir A. Zaman, "Market Efficiency and Insider Trading: New Evidence," *Journal of Business*, 61, no. 1 (January 1988): 25–44; and Ji-Chai Lin and John S. Howe, "Insider Trading in the OTC Market," *Journal of Finance*, 45, no. 4 (September 1990): 1273–84.

MONEY MATTERS: Inside Information

In 1990, Michael Milken pleaded guilty to six felony charges. He was fined $600 million and sentenced to ten years in prison. Milken's conviction brought to a close a saga involving criminal behavior by a number of highly influential individuals and organizations on Wall Street. The common thread tying together all of the defendants: rampant trading on inside information.

Insider trading has always been a controversial subject. The concept itself is rife with paradox. At the heart of our prosperous capital markets is the proposition that certain participants should not possess significant, unfair advantages over others. If you believe that the game is rigged against you, that the people with whom you trade consistently have ready access to valuable inside information, then you will soon take your investments to a fairer playing field.

Conversely, without inside information there would be little rationale for trading to occur. Unless you believe that you know something others do not, why would you trade (aside from portfolio adjustments necessitated by a changing financial situation)? Further, how would information relevant to security values be transmitted to stock prices unless someone who knew more than others traded on that information?

Thus an overdose or a dearth of trading on inside information would seem to be detrimental to security markets. But how much inside information trading is optimal? While no one knows the answer, to better understand the issues involved we have to be more specific about what we mean by "inside information."

Justice Potter Stewart once wrote about pornography: "I can't define it. But I know what it is when I see it." A similar attitude must be taken in defining inside information. The Association for Investment Management and Research (AIMR), the representative organization for investment professionals, defines inside information (or, more formally, material nonpublic information) as

> ". . . any information about a company, or the market for the company's securities, that has not been generally disclosed to the marketplace, the dissemination of which is likely to affect significantly the market price of the company's securities or is likely to be considered important by reasonable investors in determining whether to trade in such securities." (*AIMR Standards of Practice Handbook*, 5th ed.)

While this definition provides a useful starting point, it involves several vague concepts. Does "generally disclosed" mean that everyone knows the information or that it is available simply by contacting the company? Similarly, how large a price impact is implied

EX ANTE AND EX POST VALUES

ex ante
ex post

Equilibrium theories such as the Capital Asset Pricing Model and the Arbitrage Pricing Theory imply that in the opinion of well-informed investors, securities with certain attributes will, other things being equal, have large expected returns, while those with other attributes will have small expected returns. Thus, the focus of these theories is on future or **ex ante** (Latin for "before the fact") expected returns. However, only historical or **ex post** (Latin for "after the fact") actual returns are subsequently observed. These historical returns are undoubtedly different from the expected returns, making it extremely difficult to tell whether security attributes and expected returns do in fact go together in the manner implied by either the CAPM or the APT. Moreover, such theories are relatively silent concerning simple ways in which a security's future or ex ante attributes and expected return might be estimated by examining historical or ex post returns.

To bridge this gap, a number of investigators have used the average historical return of a security as an estimate of its expected return. This requires an assumption that the expected return did not change over some arbitrary time period and that this time period contains a sufficient number of historical returns to make a reasonably accurate estimate of the expected

by the term "affect significantly"? Further, who are the "reasonable investors" who determine the importance of the information? Unfortunately, neither Congress, the courts, nor the Securities Exchange Commission has been able or willing to operationally define inside information. The issue has been handled on a case-by-case basis, à la Justice Stewart.

If defining inside information has proved troublesome, enforcing the laws against trading on inside information has been much more difficult, even in some flagrant cases. As the concept has evolved in the courts, for an "insider" to have violated insider trading laws through the disclosure of inside information, that person must:

1. Be in possession of inside information.
2. Be in a position of trust and confidence.
3. Stand to gain from the disclosure; for example, monetarily or through an exchange with someone or as a "gift" to another person.

An individual receiving and trading on inside information (the "tippee") may also violate the law if: (1) the "tipper" had a fiduciary duty to a client; (2) the tipper breached that duty through the disclosure; and (3) the tippee had knowledge of that breach. Proving all three points makes it difficult to prosecute many tippees, especially those who have received inside information third- or fourth-hand.

Security analysts are placed in a precarious position with respect to inside information. One can view their jobs as the creation of inside information. Security analysts examine the prospects for companies and their securities, attempting to identify mispriced securities. If they are successful, their information is unique, nonpublic, and material—clearly inside information. The courts have generally recognized the legality of trading on inside information derived in this manner. But security analysts have frequent contact with corporate insiders as part of their jobs. This contact potentially exposes them to inside information of the illegal, if unintentional, kind. Most investment firms and the AIMR have guidelines for dealing with these situations. Nevertheless, the ambiguity of the situation can cause confusion and may be difficult to control.

The interrelated nature of many large investment firms makes the dissemination of inside information a potentially serious problem. For example, investment banking firms typically operate divisions that trade for the firms' own accounts. Investment bankers have access to valuable inside information concerning corporate mergers and acquisitions. If traders at an investment banking firm acquired this information, they would be in a position to profit handsomely. To prevent such conflicts, investment firms establish "Chinese Walls"; that is, regulations against information transfers, rules against trading on inside information, and policies against personnel serving in multiple capacities in various departments. Unfortunately, these precautions are not always effective. The insider trading scandals of the 1980s were largely a result of the ample opportunities for inside information abuse existing at investment banking firms.

return. However, an objection may be made in that expectations almost certainly would have changed over the time period needed to obtain a reasonably useful estimate of the expected return for any given security.[21] Despite this objection, it is worthwhile to examine historical returns to see how they can be used to come up with meaningful predictions about the future.[22] The next section explores the prediction of a firm's beta. It begins by discussing the estimation of the firm's historical beta by use of the market model.

[21]It has been argued that roughly 300 months (25 years) of historical returns are needed in order for a simple averaging technique to produce reasonably useful estimates of expected returns, provided that the "true" but unobserved expected return is constant during this entire period. See J. D. Jobson and Bob Korkie, "Estimation for Markowitz Efficient Portfolios," *Journal of the American Statistical Association*, 75, no. 371 (September 1980): 544–54; and "Putting Markowitz Theory to Work," *Journal of Portfolio Management*, 7, no. 4 (Summer 1981): 70–74.

[22]In doing so, a number of researchers have uncovered certain "empirical regularities" in common stocks; the appendix discusses a number of them. For a more detailed summary, see Donald B. Keim, "The CAPM and Equity Return Regularities," *Financial Analysts Journal*, 42, no. 3 (May/June 1986): 19–34; Douglas K. Pearce, "Challenges to the Concept of Market Efficiency," Federal Reserve Bank of Kansas City *Economic Review*, 72, no. 8 (September/October 1987): 16–33; and Robert A. Haugen and Josef Lakonishok, *The Incredible January Effect* (Homewood, Ill.: Dow Jones-Irwin, 1988).

COMMON STOCKS BETAS

For purposes of portfolio management, the relevant risk of a security concerns its impact on the risk of a well-diversified portfolio. In the world of the CAPM, such portfolios would be subject primarily to market risk. This suggests the importance of a security's beta, which measures its sensitivity to future market movements. To estimate beta, in principle the possible sources of such movements should be considered. Then, the reaction of the security's price to each of these sources should be estimated, along with the probability of each reaction. In the process, the economics of the relevant industry and firm, the impact of both operating and financial leverage on the firm, and other fundamental factors should be taken into account.

But what about investigating the extent to which the security's price moved with the market in the past? Such an approach ignores myriad possible differences between the past and the future. However, it is easily done and provides a useful starting point.

historical beta

simple linear regression

As shown in Chapter 8, a security's beta can be regarded as the slope of the market model. If this line were constant over time, meaning that it was not changing from period to period, then the **historical beta** for a security could be estimated by examining the historical relationship between the returns on the security and on a market index. The statistical procedure used for making such estimates of ex post betas is **simple linear regression**, also known as ordinary least squares (OLS).[23]

As an example, consider estimating the ex post beta for Minnesota Mining and Manufacturing (3M) using the Standard & Poor's 500 index as a surrogate for the market portfolio. Part A of Table 13-2 presents the data necessary to calculate the returns on a quarterly basis over the four-year period from 1988 to 1991 for both 3M and the S&P 500; part B presents the returns on both 3M and the S&P 500, and the calculations necessary to

[23]For an introduction to regression, see Chapter 11 of James T. McClave and P. George Benson, *Statistics for Business and Economics* (San Francisco: Dellen Publishing Company, 1991), and Mark P. Kritzman, "... About Regressions," *Financial Analysts Journal*, 47, no. 3 (May/June 1991): 12–15.

TABLE 13-2
The Market Model for 3M, 1988–1991

A. QUARTERLY DATA

Quarter		3m			S&P 500		
		Price at Start	Price at End	Div.	Index at Start	Index at End	Div.
1988	1	$66.125	$56.750	$0.53	255.94	260.14	2.25
	2	56.750	65.750	0.53	260.14	271.78	2.54
	3	65.750	64.125	0.53	271.78	271.38	2.46
	4	64.125	61.375	0.53	271.38	275.31	2.48
1989	1	61.375	67.000	0.65	275.31	296.39	2.50
	2	67.000	71.125	0.65	296.39	319.23	2.86
	3	71.125	75.250	0.65	319.23	350.87	2.83
	4	75.250	80.500	0.65	350.87	359.69	2.86
1990	1	80.500	81.500	0.73	359.69	338.70	2.77
	2	81.500	87.250	0.73	338.70	359.54	3.21
	3	87.250	79.500	0.73	359.54	314.94	3.00
	4	79.500	84.875	0.73	314.94	326.45	3.12
1991	1	84.875	88.125	0.78	326.45	371.30	2.79
	2	88.125	94.000	0.78	371.30	377.92	3.24
	3	94.000	91.000	0.78	377.92	389.20	3.13
	4	91.000	94.750	0.78	389.20	417.26	3.04

TABLE 13-2
Continued

B. CALCULATIONS[a]

Quarter		3M Returns = Y (1)	S&P 500 Returns = X (2)	Y^2 (3)	X^2 (4)	$Y \times X$ (5)
1988	1	−13.38%	2.52%	178.92	6.35	−33.71
	2	16.79	5.45	282.00	29.71	91.54
	3	−1.67	0.76	2.77	0.57	−1.26
	4	−3.46	2.36	11.99	5.58	−8.18
1989	1	10.22	8.56	104.53	73.36	87.57
	2	7.13	8.67	50.79	75.19	61.80
	3	6.71	10.80	45.07	116.59	72.49
	4	7.84	3.33	61.47	11.08	26.10
1990	1	2.15	−5.07	4.62	25.66	−10.89
	2	7.95	7.10	63.22	50.42	56.46
	3	−8.05	−11.57	64.74	133.87	93.09
	4	7.68	4.65	58.97	21.58	35.67
1991	1	4.75	14.59	22.55	212.97	69.29
	2	7.55	2.66	57.03	7.05	20.05
	3	−2.36	3.81	5.58	14.54	−9.01
	4	4.98	7.99	24.78	63.85	39.78
Sum (Σ) =		54.84 $= \Sigma Y$	66.62 $= \Sigma X$	1039.03 $= \Sigma Y^2$	848.38 $= \Sigma X^2$	590.80 $= \Sigma XY$

1. Beta:

$$\frac{(T \times \Sigma XY) - (\Sigma Y \times \Sigma X)}{(T \times \Sigma X^2) - (\Sigma X)^2} = \frac{(16 \times 590.80) - (54.84 \times 66.62)}{(16 \times 848.38) - (66.62)^2} = .63$$

2. Alpha:

$$[\Sigma Y/T] - [\text{Beta} \times (\Sigma X/T)] = [54.84/16] - [.63 \times (66.62/16)] = .79\%$$

3. Standard Deviation of Random Error Term:

$$\{[\Sigma Y^2 - (\text{Alpha} \times \Sigma Y) - (\text{Beta} \times \Sigma XY)]/[T - 2]\}^{1/2}$$
$$= \{[1039.03 - (.79 \times 54.84) - (.63 \times 590.80)]/[16 - 2]\}^{1/2} = 6.67\%$$

4. Standard Error of Beta:

$$\text{Standard Deviation of Random Error Term}/\{\Sigma X^2 - [(\Sigma X)^2/T]\}^{1/2}$$
$$= 6.67/\{848.38 - [(66.62)^2/16]\}^{1/2} = .28$$

5. Standard Error of Alpha:

$$\text{Standard Deviation of Random Error Term}/\{T - [(\Sigma X)^2/\Sigma X^2]\}^{1/2}$$
$$= 6.67/\{16 - [(66.62)^2/848.38]\}^{1/2} = 2.03$$

6. Correlation Coefficient:

$$\frac{(T \times \Sigma XY) - (\Sigma Y \times \Sigma X)}{\{[(T \times \Sigma Y^2) - (\Sigma Y)^2] \times [(T \times \Sigma X^2) - (\Sigma X)^2]\}^{1/2}}$$
$$= \frac{(16 \times 590.80) - (54.84 \times 66.62)}{\{[(16 \times 1039.03) - (54.84)^2] \times [(16 \times 848.38) - (66.62)^2]\}^{1/2}} = .52$$

7. Coefficient of Determination:

$$(\text{Correlation Coefficient})^2 = (.52)^2 = .27$$

8. Coefficient of Nondetermination:

$$1 - \text{Coefficient of Determination} = 1 - .27 = .73$$

[a]All summations are to be carried out over t, where t goes from 1 to T (in this example, t = 1, 2, . . . , 16).

determine 3M's ex post beta and alpha, as well as certain other statistical parameters. As can be seen, 3M's beta and alpha were equal to .63 and .79%, respectively, over this period.[24]

Given these values for alpha and beta, the market model for 3M is:

$$r_{3M} = .79\% + .63r_I + \epsilon_{3M}. \tag{13.6}$$

Figure 13-7 presents a scatter diagram of the returns on 3M (r_{3M}) and the S&P 500 index (r_I). Also shown in the figure is a graph of the market model except that the random error term is deleted. That is, the figure has a graph of the following line:

$$r_{3M} = .79\% + .63r_I. \tag{13.7}$$

The vertical distance of each point in the scatter diagram from this line represents an estimate of the size of the random error term for the corresponding quarter. The exact distance can be found by rewriting equation (13.6) as:

$$r_{3M} - (.79\% + .63r_I) = \epsilon_{3M}. \tag{13.8}$$

For example, looking at part B of Table 13-2, in the second quarter of 1991 the return on 3M and the S&P 500 were 7.55% and 2.66%, respectively. The value of ϵ_{3M} for that quarter can be calculated by using equation (13.8) as follows:

$$7.55\% - [.79\% + (.63 \times 2.66\%)] = 5.08\%.$$

The values of ϵ_{3M} can be similarly calculated for the other 15 quarters of the estimation period. The standard deviation of the resulting set of 16 numbers is

[24]3M's beta and alpha would have been equal to .63 and .17%, respectively, if excess returns (that is, returns less the riskfree rate) had been used in the calculations instead of returns. Using returns or excess returns (as well as including or ignoring dividends in calculating returns) appears to make little difference in the estimated size of beta. However, there is a substantive difference in the estimated size of alpha. See William F. Sharpe and Guy M. Cooper, "Risk-Return Classes of New York Stock Exchange Common Stocks, 1931–1967," *Financial Analysts Journal*, 28, no. 2 (March/April 1972): 46–54.

FIGURE 13-7
Market Model for 3M

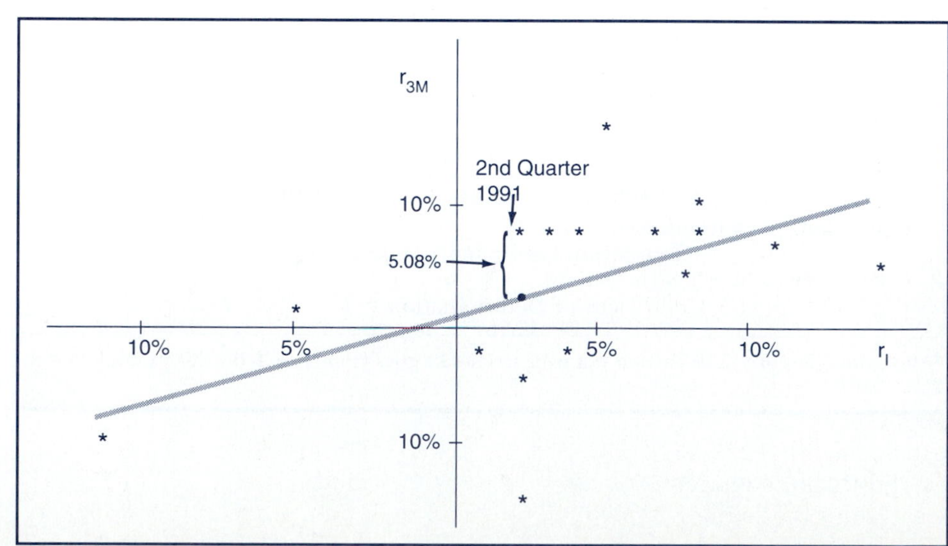

an estimate of the **standard deviation of the random error term** (or residual standard deviation), and is shown in part B of Table 13-2 to be equal to 6.67%. This number can be viewed as an estimate of the historical unique risk of 3M.

standard deviation of the random error term

The market model for 3M that is shown in Figure 13-7 corresponds to the regression line for the scatter diagram. Recalling that a straight line is defined by its intercept and slope, it can be shown that there are no other values for alpha and beta that will define a straight line that fits the scatter diagram any better than the regression line. This means that there is no line that could be drawn that would result in a smaller standard deviation of the random error term. Thus, the regression line is often referred to as the line of "best fit."

Equivalently, the line of best fit is the line that has the smallest sum of squared values of the random error terms. That is, the 16 random error terms associated with the regression line can each be squared and then summed. This sum ("sum of squared errors") is smaller for the line of best fit than the sum associated with any other line.

For example, if alpha was set equal to 1.5% and beta equal to .8 in equation (13.8), then the random error term value of ϵ_{3M} could be calculated for each of the 16 quarters. With these 16 values, the standard deviation of the random error term could be calculated by squaring each value, summing up the squared values, and dividing the sum by 14 = (16 − 2); the standard deviation of the random error term would then be the square root of this number. However, it would be larger than 6.67%, which is the standard deviation of the random error term associated with the line of best fit (that is, the line with an alpha of .79% and a beta of .63).

It should be remembered that a security's "true" historical beta cannot be observed. All that can be done is to estimate its value. Thus, even if a security's "true" beta remained the same forever, its estimated value, obtained in the manner shown in Table 13-2, would still change from time to time because of mistakes (known as sampling errors) in estimating it. For example, if the 16 quarters from 1984 to 1987 were examined, the resulting estimated beta for 3M would almost certainly be different from .63, the estimated value for 1988 to 1991. The **standard error of beta** shown in part B of Table 13-2 attempts to indicate the extent of such estimation errors. Given a number of necessary assumptions (for example, the "true" beta did not change during the estimation period of 1988 to 1991), the chances are roughly two out of three that the "true" beta is within a standard error, plus or minus, of the estimated beta. Thus, 3M's "true" beta is likely to be between the values of .35 (= .63 − .28) and .91 (= .63 + .28). Similarly, the **standard error of alpha** provides an indication of the magnitude of the possible sampling error that has been made in estimating alpha.

standard error of beta

standard error of alpha

The **correlation coefficient** (part B of Table 13-2) provides an indication of how closely the returns on 3M were associated with the returns on the S&P 500. Since its range is between −1 and +1, the value for 3M of .52 indicates a mildly strong positive relationship between 3M and the S&P 500. That is, larger returns for 3M seem to be associated with larger returns on the S&P 500.

correlation coefficient

The **coefficient of determination** represents the proportion of variation in the return on 3M that is related to the variation in the return on the S&P 500. That is, it shows how much of the movements in 3M's returns can be explained by movements in the returns on the S&P 500. With a value of .27, it can be seen that 27% of the movements in the return on 3M from 1988 to 1991 can be attributed to movements in the return on the S&P 500.

coefficient of determination

Since the **coefficient of nondetermination** is one minus the coefficient of determination, it represents the proportion of movements in the return on 3M

coefficient of nondetermination

that is not due to movements in the return on the S&P 500. Thus, 73% of the movements in 3M cannot be attributed to movements in the S&P 500.

Figure 13-8 shows a page from the Security Risk Evaluation report prepared by Merrill Lynch, Pierce, Fenner & Smith Inc. Percentage price changes for many stocks, calculated for each of 60 months (when available), were compared using the corresponding percentage changes in the Standard & Poor's 500 using the market model as in Table 13-2. Seven of the resulting values from this analysis are of interest for each stock.

The values shown for *Beta* and *Alpha* indicate the slope and intercept, respectively, of the straight line that is the "best fit" for the scatter diagram of the percentage price changes for the stock and index. For example, during the 60-month period covered, the stock of Ask Computer had a beta and alpha of 1.65 and −.06%, respectively.

FIGURE 13-8
Sample Page from Security Risk Evaluation by Merrill Lynch, Pierce, Fenner & Smith Inc.

Ticker Symbol	Security Name	92/04 Close Price	Beta	Alpha	R-Sqr	Resid Std Dev-n	---Std. Err.--- of Beta	of Alpha	Adjusted Beta	Number of Observ
AOI	AOI COAL CO	0.500	1.11	−1.79	0.07	19.23	0.49	2.51	1.07	60
APAT	APA OPTICS INC	4.875	0.60	0.80	0.08	9.66	0.25	1.26	0.73	60
APIE	API ENTERPRISES INC	0.688	1.00	2.51	0.02	26.90	0.69	3.51	1.00	60
ASKI	ASK COMPUTER SYS INC	14.875	1.65	−0.06	0.37	10.82	0.28	1.41	1.43	60
ATV	ARC INTL CORP	0.813	1.22	−1.38	0.07	20.71	0.53	2.70	1.15	60
ASTA	AST RESEARCH INC	16.750	1.47	1.66	0.16	16.75	0.43	2.19	1.31	60
ARX	ARX INC	1.875	1.02	−1.90	0.07	17.02	0.43	2.22	1.01	60
ASAA	ASA INTL LTD	1.875	0.79	−1.03	0.01	23.55	0.60	3.07	0.86	60
RCH	ARCO CHEM CO	45.375	1.33	0.03	0.47	7.35	0.19	1.00	1.22	55
ANBC	ANB CORP	36.375	−0.02	1.80	0.10	1.90	0.13	0.56	0.32	12
ATCE	ATC ENVIRONMENTAL INC	2.813	−0.02	0.68	0.02	21.22	0.75	3.22	0.32	46
ATI	ATI MED INC	3.750	0.26	0.07	0.01	19.11	0.49	2.49	0.51	60
ATCIC	ATC INC	1.750	0.61	0.38	0.00	26.63	0.68	3.47	0.74	60
ATNN	ATNN INC	0.219	1.38	1.51	0.00	50.89	1.30	6.64	1.25	60
ATTNF	ATTN AVECA ENTERTAIN-MENT COR	1.750	2.81	0.39	0.05	42.49	1.59	6.97	2.20	39
AVSY	AVTR SYS INC	0.203	−0.54	6.23	0.06	55.49	3.33	14.41	−0.02	18
AWCSA	AW COMPUTER SYS INC CLASS A	5.875	1.23	7.08	0.01	71.41	1.85	9.29	1.15	60
ARON	AARON RENTS INC	13.125	0.92	−0.23	0.16	10.30	0.26	1.34	0.95	60
ABIX	ABATIX ENVIRONMENTAL CORP	1.750	0.00	0.36	0.03	17.54	0.67	2.96	0.34	37
ABT	ABBOTT LABS	66.000	0.87	0.87	0.51	4.31	0.11	0.56	0.92	60
ABERF	ABER RES LTD	0.969	1.53	3.52	0.02	29.18	1.11	4.93	1.35	37
AANB	ABIGAIL ADAMS NATL BANCORP I	11.000	−1.50	1.81	0.14	12.61	0.70	2.80	−0.66	24
ABBK	ABINGTON BANCORP INC	5.875	1.37	−0.15	0.09	20.09	0.51	2.62	1.24	60
ABD	ABIOMED INC	13.000	1.08	1.04	0.07	18.21	0.47	2.43	1.05	57
ABY	ABITIBI PRICE INC	12.625	0.65	−1.42	0.23	6.00	0.15	0.80	0.77	57
ABRI	ABRAMS INDS INC	4.313	1.28	1.90	0.07	20.91	0.53	2.73	1.18	60
ACAP	ACAP CORP	0.500	0.05	0.88	0.02	13.80	0.35	1.80	0.37	60
ACLE	ACCEL INTL CORP	6.750	1.12	−0.66	0.20	11.10	0.28	1.45	1.08	60
AKLM	ACCLAIM ENTHT INC	6.375	1.29	0.02	0.03	23.62	0.84	3.58	1.19	46
ACCU	ACCUHEALTH INC	5.438	0.53	0.60	0.00	13.47	0.49	2.17	0.69	41

Based on S&P 500 Index, Using Straight Regression — Page 3

Source: Reprinted by permission. Copyright © 1992 Merrill Lynch, Pierce, Fenner & Smith Incorporated.

The value of *R-Sqr*, short for **R-squared,** is equivalent to the coefficient of determination shown in Table 13-2.[25] Having a value of .37 means that 37% of the variation in Ask Computer's price changes could be attributed to changes in the market index over the 60-month period.

R-squared

The value for *Resid Std Dev-n* (**residual standard deviation**) corresponds to the standard deviation of the random error term in Table 13-2. Ask Computer can be seen to have a residual standard deviation of 10.82%.

residual standard deviation

Std. Err. of Beta (standard error of beta) indicates that there is roughly a two out of three chance that the "true" beta for Ask Computer is between the values of 1.37 (= 1.65 − .28) and 1.93 (= 1.65 + .28). Similarly, the value under *Std. Err. of Alpha* indicates that there is roughly a two out of three chance that the "true" alpha for Ask Computer lies between −1.47 (= −.06 − 1.41) and 1.35 (= −.06 + 1.41).

The seventh value in Figure 13-8 that is of particular interest is the *Adjusted Beta* value, which is discussed next.

Adjusting Beta

Without any information at all, it would be reasonable to estimate the beta of a stock to be equal to 1.0, the average size of beta. Given a chance to see how the stock moved relative to the market over some time period, a modification of this prior estimate would seem appropriate. Such a modification would sensibly produce a final estimate of beta that would lie between the value of 1.0 and its initially estimated value based purely on historical price changes.

Formal procedures for making such modifications have been adopted by most investment firms that estimate betas. The specific adjustments made typically differ from time to time and, in some cases, from stock to stock. In Figure 13-5, the **adjusted beta** values were obtained by giving approximately 34% weight to the average marketwide beta of 1.0 and approximately 66% weight to the historical estimate of beta for each stock. Thus, the adjusted beta for Ask Computer is 1.43 = (.34 × 1.0) + (.66 × 1.65). More generally,

adjusted beta

$$\beta_a = (.34 \times 1.0) + (.66 \times \beta_h) \tag{13.9}$$

where β_a and β_h are the adjusted and historical betas, respectively.[26] Examination of equation (13.9) indicates that this procedure takes the historical beta for a security and adjusts it by giving it a value closer to 1.0. Thus, historical betas less than 1.0 are made larger, but will still be less than 1.0, and historical betas greater than 1.0 are made smaller, but will still be greater than 1.0. The adjustments are in this direction because the weights (.66 and .34) are positive and add up to 1.0, indicating that the adjustment procedure is an averaging technique.

Table 13-3 shows the extent to which such a procedure anticipates differences between historical and future betas. The second column lists the

---

[25]R is used here to denote the correlation coefficient; sometimes (as in Chapter 8) the Greek letter rho (ρ) is used instead. Thus R-squared is equivalent to rho-squared, or the square of the correlation coefficient.

[26]Adjusted betas are also published in the *Value Line Investment Survey;* their adjusted beta is equal to $(.35 \times 1.0) + (.67 \times \beta_b)$. Thus, the adjustment procedures of Value Line and Merrill Lynch are quite similar. See Meir Statman, "Betas Compared: Merrill Lynch vs. Value Line," *Journal of Portfolio Management*, 7, no. 2 (Winter 1981): 41–44 and Frank K. Reilly and David J. Wright, "A Comparison of Published Betas," *Journal of Portfolio Management*, 14, no. 3 (Spring 1988): 64–69.

TABLE 13-3
Ex Ante and Ex Post Beta Values for Portfolios of 100 Securities

PORTFOLIO (1)	JULY 1947–JUNE 1954 Unadjusted (2)	Adjusted (3)	JULY 1954–JUNE 1961 (4)	JULY 1961–JUNE 1968 (5)
1	.36	.48	.57	.72
2	.61	.68	.71	.79
3	.78	.82	.88	.88
4	.91	.93	.96	.92
5	1.01	1.01	1.03	1.04
6	1.13	1.10	1.13	1.02
7	1.26	1.21	1.24	1.08
8	1.47	1.39	1.32	1.15

Source: Marshall E. Blume, "Betas and Their Regression Tendencies," *Journal of Finance*, 30, no. 3 (June 1975): 792.

unadjusted historical betas for eight portfolios of 100 securities each, based on monthly price changes from July 1947 through June 1954 (the portfolios were designed to have significantly different betas during this period). The third column of the table shows the values obtained when an adjustment of the type used by Merrill Lynch was applied. The betas in the fourth column are based on price changes over the subsequent seven years. For a majority of the portfolios, the adjusted betas are closer in magnitude to the subsequent historical betas than are the unadjusted betas. This suggests that the adjusted historical beta is a more accurate estimate of the future beta than the unadjusted historical beta.

The fifth column of Table 13-3 shows the historical betas estimated using data from a third seven-year period. Comparing the unadjusted betas in columns 2, 4, and 5, it can be seen that there is a continuing tendency for betas to shrink toward the mean value of 1.0 over time. Thus, adjustment procedures seem to have some usefulness when it comes to estimating betas for a future time period.

It seems plausible that "true" betas not only vary over time but have a tendency to move back toward average levels, since extreme values are likely to be moderated over time. A firm whose operations or financing make the risk of its equity considerably different from that of other firms is more likely to move back toward the average than away from it over time. Such changes in betas are due to real economic phenomena, not simply an artifact of overly simple statistical procedures. There is, however, no reason to expect every stock's "true" beta to move to the same average in the same manner at the same speed. In this regard, some fundamental analysis of the firm may prove more useful than the adoption of more sophisticated statistical methods for processing past price changes in estimating beta.

While at the portfolio level, historical betas can provide useful information about future betas, historical betas for individual securities are subject to great error and should be treated accordingly. This can be seen by noting the magnitude of the standard errors of the betas shown earlier in Figure 13-5.

Table 13-4 provides another view. Every stock listed on the New York Stock Exchange was assigned to one of ten classes in each year from 1931 through 1967, based on the magnitude of its historical beta calculated using data from the preceding five years. The stocks in the top 10% of each January's ranking were assigned to class 10, the next 10% to class 9, and so on. The table shows the percent of the stocks that were in the same class (column 1) and

TABLE 13-4
Movement of Stocks Among Beta Classes

RISK CLASS	PERCENT OF STOCKS IN THE SAME BETA CLASS FIVE YEARS LATER		PERCENT OF STOCKS IN THE SAME BETA CLASS OR WITHIN ONE RISK CLASS FIVE YEARS LATER	
	Actual (1)	Expected If There Were No Relationship (2)	Actual (3)	Expected If There Were No Relationship (4)
10 (highest beta values)	35.2%	10%	69.3%	20%
9	18.4	10	53.7	30
8	16.4	10	45.3	30
7	13.3	10	40.9	30
6	13.9	10	39.3	30
5	13.6	10	41.7	30
4	13.2	10	40.2	30
3	15.9	10	44.6	30
2	21.5	10	60.9	30
1 (lowest beta values)	40.5	10	62.3	20

Source: William F. Sharpe and Guy M. Cooper, "Risk-Return Classes of New York Stock Exchange Common Stocks, 1931–1967," *Financial Analysts Journal*, 28, no. 2 (March/April 1972): 53.

within one risk class (column 3) five years later. Also shown are the entries that would be expected if there were no relationship between such past and future beta classes. Examination of the table reveals that individual security betas have some but not a great deal of predictive value.

Figure 13-9 shows that the predictive ability of historical portfolio betas improves with the amount of diversification in a portfolio. The vertical axis plots the percentage of the differences in (measured) portfolio betas (based on weekly price changes) in one year that can be attributed to differences in their (measured) betas in the prior year. The horizontal axis indicates the number of securities in each portfolio. It can be seen in the figure that the historical betas for portfolios containing roughly ten to twenty securities or more have a high degree of predictive ability. Thus, individual security betas are worth estimating even though they are rather inaccurate when viewed by themselves. This is because their individual inaccuracies seem to cancel out one another when the beta of a diversified portfolio is calculated, resulting in quite an accurate estimate of the portfolio's beta.

Leverage and Beta

The beta of a *firm* represents the sensitivity of the aggregate value of the firm to changes in the value of the market portfolio. It depends on both the demand for the firm's products and the firm's operating costs. However, most firms have both debt and equity outstanding. This means that the beta of a firm's *equity* (that is, stock) depends on the beta of the firm and the firm's financial leverage. For example, imagine that there are two firms that are identical in every way except that firm A has debt while firm B is free of debt. This means that even though they have the same earnings before interest and taxes (EBIT), they will have different earnings after taxes (EAT) because A, unlike B, has to make interest payments. In this situation, the firm betas for A and B are the same, but the stock beta for A will be greater than the stock beta for B. The difference in the debt is the reason for the difference in the stock betas. This is because the debt makes the earnings available to common stockholders more

FIGURE 13-9
Percent of Differences in Beta Values Attributable to Differences in Prior Year's Betas
Source: Robert A. Levy, "On the Short-Term Stationarity of Beta Coefficients," *Financial Analysts Journal*, 27, no. 6 (November/December 1971): 57.

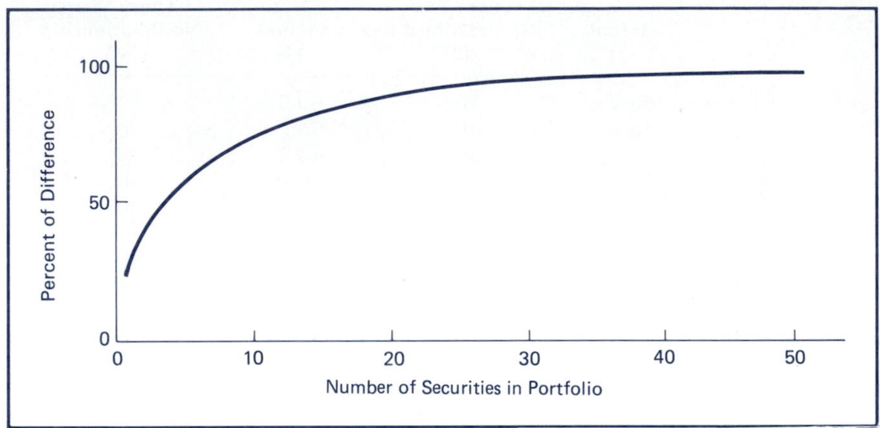

variable for A than B. Thus, the stock beta for A could be viewed as being equal to the stock beta it would have if it had no debt (that is, the beta of B) plus an adjustment for the amount of debt it actually has outstanding.

One method that has been suggested for determining the influence of debt on the beta of the stock of a firm involves a four-step procedure.[27] First, the current market value of the firm's outstanding debt (D) and equity (E) must be determined. Once this is done, the current market value of the levered firm V_L can be determined:

$$V_L = D + E. \tag{13.10}$$

Second, the market value of the firm *if it were unlevered* must be determined. This can be done by using the following formula:

$$V_u = V_L - \tau D \tag{13.11}$$

where: V_u = market value of the firm if it was unlevered,
τ = average corporate tax rate for the firm, and
D = market value of the firm's debt.

Third, the beta of the firm can be calculated after estimating the beta of the firm's debt (β_{debt}) and equity (β_{equity}) by using the following formula:

$$\beta_{firm} = \beta_{debt} \frac{(1 - \tau)D}{V_u} + \beta_{equity} \frac{E}{V_u}. \tag{13.12}$$

[27]The method is developed more fully in Richard A. Brealey and Stewart C. Myers, *Principles of Corporate Finance* (New York: McGraw-Hill, 1991), 191–92, 468–69, and Thomas E. Copeland and J. Fred Weston, *Financial Theory and Corporate Policy* (Reading, Mass.: Addison-Wesley, 1988), Chapter 13.

Fourth, having used equation(13.12) to estimate the beta of the firm, the effect of any degree of leverage on the equity beta of the firm can be determined by restating this equation. Specifically, solving equation (13.12) for β_{equity} results in:[28]

$$\beta_{equity} = \beta_{firm} + (\beta_{firm} - \beta_{debt})\left(\frac{D}{E}\right)(1 - \tau). \tag{13.13}$$

In evaluating equation (13.13), it should be noted that the value of β_{firm} does not change as the firm's debt-equity ratio (*D/E*) is changed. Assuming that the value of β_{debt} also does not change, it can be seen that increasing the firm's debt-equity ratio will increase the beta of the firm's equity. Intuitively this makes sense, since a higher debt-equity ratio will make a firm's EAT more volatile. Conversely, lowering a firm's debt-equity ratio should lower the firm's equity beta since it makes EAT less volatile.

This property of beta can be useful in estimating the beta of a firm's equity if the firm has recently altered its debt-equity ratio (or is contemplating increasing the ratio). For example, imagine that Widget had until last month \$60 million of equity and \$40 million of debt outstanding for a total firm value of \$100 million; its tax rate is 30%. Using the market model as shown in Table 13-2, but applied to data before the recent equity issuance, it is determined that the equity beta and debt beta of Widget are 1.40 and .20, respectively. However, Widget has just issued \$20 million of equity and used the proceeds to retire some of the debt so that the current values of Widget's debt and equity are \$74 million and \$20 million, respectively. (The \$74 million value of equity represents the sum of \$20 million in new equity and \$54 million in old equity, which has decreased in value by \$6 million due to the loss of tax shields resulting from the \$20 million reduction in Widget's debt.) What is the equity beta of Widget likely to be in the immediate future?

The previously described four-step procedure can be used to answer this question. First, it is noted from equation (13.10) that the value of Widget before the new equity issuance was \$100 million. Second, it is noted from equation (13.11) that the value of Widget if the firm was unlevered would be equal to \$100 million − (.3 × \$40 million) = \$88 million. Third, the beta of the firm can be estimated using equation (13.12):

$$\beta_{firm} = .20\left[\frac{(1 - .3)\$40 \text{ million}}{\$88 \text{ million}}\right] + 1.40\left[\frac{\$60 \text{ million}}{\$88 \text{ million}}\right]$$
$$= 1.02.$$

Lastly, the current equity beta (that is, the equity beta after the recent issuance of \$20 million of equity) can be estimated by using equation (13.13):

$$\beta_{equity} = 1.02 + (1.02 - .20)\left(\frac{\$20 \text{ million}}{\$74 \text{ million}}\right)(1 - .3)$$
$$= 1.17.$$

[28]To derive equation (13.13), note that equation (13.11) can be written as $V_u = D + E - \tau D$ since $V_L = D + E$. Hence, the quantity $D + E - \tau D$ can be substituted for V_u in equation (13.12), and then the altered equation can be solved for β_{equity} and simplified, resulting in equation (13.13).

Hence the reduction in the amount of debt that Widget has outstanding has reduced the beta of the equity from 1.40 to 1.17.[29]

Industry Beta Values

Firms in industries having highly cyclical demand or large fixed costs might be expected to have higher firm betas than those in industries with more stable demand or greater variable costs, since they will have greater variability in EBIT. Differences in financial leverage could wholly offset such factors, leaving few, if any, differences among the equity betas of firms in different industries. However, this does not seem to be the case. Firms in certain industries do tend to have higher equity betas than those in other industries, and, by and large, the classifications agree with prior expectations.

Table 13-5 shows the average equity betas for stocks in various industry classifications. Stock prices of firms whose products are termed "necessities" tend to respond less than the stock prices of most other firms when expectations about the future health of the economy are revised. That is, firms in necessities (such as utilities or food) tend to have low betas because they tend to have more stable earnings. On the other hand, stock prices of firms that manufacture "luxuries" tend to respond more than most others when expectations about the future health of the economy are revised. That is, firms in luxuries (such as travel or electronics) tend to have high betas because they tend to have more cyclical earnings.

[29]It is assumed here that Widget's bond beta and average tax rate were unaffected by the new issuance of equity. More complex analyses are sometimes utilized to take into account the possible impact of capital structure changes upon them.

TABLE 13-5
Average Values of Beta for Stocks in Selected Industries, 1966–1974

INDUSTRY	BETA VALUE	INDUSTRY	BETA VALUE
Air transport	1.80	Energy, raw materials	1.22
Real property	1.70	Tires, rubber goods	1.21
Travel, outdoor recreation	1.66	Railroads, shipping	1.19
Electronics	1.60	Forest products, paper	1.16
Miscellaneous finance	1.60	Miscellaneous, conglomerate	1.14
Nondurables, entertainment	1.47	Drugs, medicine	1.14
Consumer durables	1.44	Domestic oil	1.12
Business machines	1.43	Soaps, cosmetics	1.09
Retail, general	1.43	Steel	1.02
Media	1.39	Containers	1.01
Insurance	1.34	Nonferrous metals	.99
Trucking, freight	1.31	Agriculture, food	.99
Producer goods	1.30	Liquor	.89
Aerospace	1.30	International oil	.85
Business services	1.28	Banks	.81
Apparel	1.27	Tobacco	.80
Construction	1.27	Telephone	.75
Motor vehicles	1.27	Energy, utilities	.60
Photographic, optical	1.24	Gold	.36
Chemicals	1.22		

Source: Barr Rosenberg and James Guy, "Prediction of Beta from Investment Fundamentals," *Financial Analysts Journal*, 32, no. 4 (July/August 1976): 66.

Forecasting Beta Information of the type shown in Table 13-5 can be used to adjust historical equity betas. For example, the knowledge that a corporation is in the air transport industry suggests that a reasonable prior estimate of its equity beta is 1.8. Thus, it makes more sense to adjust its historical equity beta toward a value of 1.8 than 1.0, the average for all stocks, as was suggested in equation (13.9).

The procedure used to adjust historical betas involves an implicit prediction equation for future betas. Equation (13.9) can be written more generally as:

$$\beta_a = a + b\beta_h \tag{13.14}$$

where a and b are constants. One way to consider the differences in industry betas is to alter equation (13.14) as follows:

$$\beta_a = a\beta_{ind} + b\beta_h \tag{13.15}$$

where β_{ind} denotes the average equity beta of the industry to which the stock belongs.

For example, consider the values of .33 and .67 for a and b, respectively. Air Express is an air transport firm whose historical beta is 2.0. What is its adjusted beta? Noting that the average equity beta for stocks in the air transport industry is 1.8, its adjusted beta can be calculated by using equation (13.15) as follows:

$$\begin{aligned}\beta_a &= (.33 \times 1.8) + (.67 \times 2.0)\\ &= 1.93.\end{aligned}$$

Thus, Air Express has an adjusted beta of 1.93 that lies between its historical beta of 2.0 and the average equity beta in its industry of 1.8. Indeed, this is what equation (13.15) accomplishes: it alters a historical beta to give an adjusted beta lying between β_h and β_{ind}.

Multiple-Industry Firms What should be done if the firm has divisions that are in different industries? In a situation where there are two industries involved, equation (13.15) could be modified as follows:

$$\beta_a = a(E_{ind1}\beta_{ind1} + E_{ind2}\beta_{ind2}) + b\beta_h \tag{13.16}$$

where E_{ind1} and E_{ind2} denote the percentage of the firm's earnings that are from industry number 1 and 2, respectively, and β_{ind1} and β_{ind2} are the betas for industries 1 and 2, respectively.[30]

As an example, consider Electrospace, a firm that has half of its earnings coming from a division that is in the electronics industry and half of its earnings coming from a division that is in the aerospace industry. Assuming that a and b are equal to .33 and .67, respectively, and that the historical beta for Electrospace is 1.2, its adjusted beta can be calculated in two steps.

First, the value of $E_{ind1}\beta_{ind1} + E_{ind2}\beta_{ind2}$ needs to be calculated. Doing so produces a value of $(.5 \times 1.6) + (.5 \times 1.3) = 1.45$. This can be interpreted as

[30]The term $(E_{ind1}\beta_{ind1} + E_{ind2}\beta_{ind2})$ would simply be expanded if more than two industries were involved.

the average equity beta for any stock whose firm has equal business interests in the electronics and aerospace industries.

Second, the adjusted beta of Electrospace can be calculated using equation (13.16) as (.33 × 1.45) + (.67 × 1.20) = 1.28. Note that this value lies between the firm's historical beta of 1.20 and its "industry" beta of 1.45.

Adjustments Based on Financial Characteristics Various financial characteristics can also be used to estimate an adjusted beta. For example, stocks with high-dividend yields might have lower betas because more of their value is associated with near-term than far-term dividends. Equation (13.16) could thus be augmented to:

$$\beta_a = a(E_{ind1}\beta_{ind1} + E_{ind2}\beta_{ind2}) + b\beta_h + cY \qquad (13.17)$$

where c is a constant and Y is the dividend yield of the firm's stock.

Table 13-6 shows a beta prediction equation of this form, using historic data from 1928 through 1982.[31] To estimate the beta of a security using this prediction equation, start with a constant based on the industry (referred to as the "sector") in which the security is classified. Then add to this constant an amount equal to the security's historical beta times 0.576 [note that this is similar to the adjustment to historical beta shown in equation (13.9)]. Finally, add (1) the security's dividend yield times −.019; and (2) the security's "size attribute" times −.105.[32] Algebraically, the model is:

$$\beta_a = a_s + (.576 \times \beta_h) + (-.019 \times Y) + (-.105 \times S) \qquad (13.18)$$

where a_s denotes the constant associated with the sector to which the stock belongs, β_h is the historical beta, Y is the dividend yield, and S is the size of the firm. With this formula, securities having higher yields are predicted to have lower betas, as are those with larger market values of equity outstanding.

An Example As an example, consider a stock that is classified as belonging to the "basic industry." It has a historical beta of 1.2, a dividend yield over the previous twelve months of 4%, and an aggregate market value of $7 billion (that is, the firm has 100 million shares outstanding and the stock is selling for $70 per share). Using equation (13.18), its adjusted beta is:

$$\begin{aligned}\beta_a &= .455 + (.576 \times 1.2) + (-.019 \times 4) + [-.105 \times (\log 7)] \\ &= .455 + .69 - .08 - .09 \\ &= .98.\end{aligned}$$

Such prediction equations, based on multifactor models, fit historical data considerably better than those that use only historical betas. One study

[31]In this method, both historical and adjusted betas are calculated relative to a value-weighted index of the returns on all stocks listed on the New York Stock Exchange. All attributes were calculated using data available a full month prior to the beginning of the month in which stock returns are measured. This avoids statistical problems and provides results that can be used for actual portfolio management.

[32]The dividend yield is measured in percent per year. The "size attribute" is calculated by taking the logarithm (to the base 10) of the total market value of equity outstanding (that is, price per share times shares outstanding), expressed in billions of dollars.

TABLE 13-6
A Beta Prediction Equation Derived from a Factor Model

CONSTANT TERM	
Sector	**Value**
Basic industry	.455
Capital goods	.425
Consumer staple	.307
Consumer cyclical	.443
Credit cyclical	.429
Energy	.394
Finance	.398
Transportation	.255
Utilities	.340
VARIABLE TERMS	
Attribute	**Coefficient**
Beta	.576
Yield	−.019
Size	−.105

Source: Blake Grossman and William F. Sharpe, "Factors in Security Returns," paper presented at the Center for the Study of Banking and Financial Markets, University of Washington, March 1984.

reported an improvement of 86% over the more simple "adjusted beta" approach.[33] However, such figures describe only the extent to which the equations fit a given set of data. Since the true test of a prediction equation is its ability to *predict*, only extensive experience with such approaches can, in the final analysis, determine how well various factor models can predict beta values.

Beta Services

Services providing betas on a regular basis in published form are available in several countries. Many use only past price changes to form estimates. Some derive their estimates from more general factor models. One service uses weekly data for two years; another, monthly data for five years. One estimates betas for U.S. securities relative to Standard & Poor's 500; another, relative to the New York Stock Exchange Composite Index; and so on. In each case, estimates for individual securities are subject to error. Thus, it is hardly surprising that estimated values for a given security obtained by different services using different procedures are not the same. This does not indicate that some are useless, only that they should be used appropriately and with caution.

[33]Barr Rosenberg and Vinay Marathe, "The Prediction of Investment Risk: Systematic and Residual Risk," *Proceedings of the Seminar on the Analysis of Security Prices,* University of Chicago, November 1975. Also see Barr Rosenberg, "Prediction of Common Stock Investment Risk," *Journal of Portfolio Management,* 11, no. 1 (Fall 1984): 44–53; and "Prediction of Common Stock Betas," *Journal of Portfolio Management,* 11, no. 2 (Winter 1985): 5–14.

SUMMARY

1. Common stock represents an ownership position in a corporation. Common stockholders possess a residual claim on the corporation's earnings and assets. Further, their liability for the corporation's obligations is limited.

2. Common stockholders elect the corporation's directors through either a majority or a cumulative voting system.

3. Corporations may at times repurchase some of their outstanding stock either in the open market or through a tender offer. Such actions may involve an attempt to repel a takeover, a signal to shareholders that the stock is undervalued, or a tax-wise distribution of cash to shareholders.

4. Stock dividends and splits involve the issuance of additional shares of common stock to current stockholders, proportional to their ownership positions. No change in the total value of the corporation is caused by a stock dividend or split.

5. Preemptive rights give existing stockholders the right of first refusal to purchase new shares. Such shares are purchased in a rights offering.

6. Daily information regarding transactions in publicly traded stocks can be found in business newspapers and the business sections of most local newspapers.

7. In the United States, trading on inside information is illegal in public security markets. However, defining inside information is difficult.

8. A security's beta can be estimated using historical return data for the security and a market index. The beta is the slope of the security's market model, calculated through a simple linear regression.

9. Beta estimates based on historical return data are sometimes adjusted to account for a tendency of betas to drift toward an average value of 1.0 over time.

10. Estimates of betas are generally more accurate when dealing with diversified portfolios than with individual securities.

11. Forecasts of a security's beta can be improved by accounting for certain characteristics of the corporation such as the industry (or industries) in which it operates, its financial leverage, or its market capitalization.

KEY TERMS

common stock
limited liability
charter
transfer agent
registrar
proxy
proxy fight
cumulative voting system
majority voting system
takeover
tender offer
bidder
target firm
white knight
greenmail
repurchase offer
merger
management buyout
leveraged buyout
Pac-Man defense
crown jewel defense
poison pill defense
par value of common stock
book value of the equity
book value per share
treasury stock
restricted
letter stock
dividends
date of record
ex-dividend date
stock dividend
stock split
reverse stock split
preemptive rights
rights
rights offering
subscription price
ex-rights date
oversubscription privilege
closing price
dividend yield
insiders
ex ante
ex post
historical beta
simple linear regression
standard deviation of the random error term
standard error of beta
standard error of alpha
correlation coefficient
coefficient of determination
coefficient of nondetermination
R-squared
residual standard deviation
adjusted beta
empirical regularities
anomalies
size effect
January effect
day-of-the-week effect
turn-of-the-month effect
holiday effect

QUESTIONS AND PROBLEMS

1. What is the significant advantage of the corporate form of business organization? Why would you expect that this advantage would be important to the success of a capitalist economy?
2. Fall Creek Company is conducting annual elections for its five-member board of directors. The firm has 1,500,000 shares of voting common stock outstanding.
   (a) Under a majority voting system, how many shares must a stockholder own to ensure being able to elect his or her choices to each of the five director seats?
   (b) Under a cumulative voting system, how many shares must a stockholder own to ensure being able to elect his or her choices to two of the director seats?
   (c) Arlie Latham holds 20% of Fall Creek's outstanding stock. How many directors can Arlie elect under a cumulative voting system?
3. As takeover and merger activity has increased in recent years, the issue of corporate ownership versus control has become more controversial. Discuss the principal-agent problem as it relates to shareholder-management relations. Specifically, why is there a potential conflict between the two groups? What steps can be taken to mitigate this problem?
4. When a bidder makes a tender offer for a target firm, what types of defenses are often applied to fend off the bidder? Do these defenses generally seem to be in the best interests of the target firm's shareholders? Why?
5. Why might a corporation wish to issue more than one class of common stock?
6. With respect to the payment of corporate dividends, distinguish between declaration date, ex-dividend date, and date of record.
7. Theoretical arguments and empirical research generally support the case that stock dividends and splits do not enhance shareholder wealth. However, corporations continue to declare stock dividends and splits. Summarize the arguments for and against stock dividends and splits from the perspective of the shareholder.
8. Menomonie Publishing stock currently sells for $40 per share. The company has 1,200,000 shares outstanding. What would be the effect on the number of shares outstanding and on the stock price of the following:
   (a) 15% stock dividend
   (b) 4-3 stock split
   (c) Reverse 3-1 stock split
9. St. Paul Corp. is planning to raise $35,000,000 through the sale of new common stock under a rights offering. The subscription price is $70 per share, while the stock currently sells for $80 per share, rights on. Total outstanding shares equal 10,000,000. Of this amount, Addie Joss owns 100,000 shares.
   (a) How many shares of stock will each right permit its owner to purchase?
   (b) What will be the total value of Addie's rights a day before the ex-rights date, assuming that the market price of St. Paul stock remains at $80 per share?
   (c) After the ex-rights date, if the market value of each St. Paul Corp.

right equals $0.20, what must be the ex-rights market price of St. Paul's stock?

10. Pep Clark owns stock in DeKalb Dairy. DeKalb is planning a rights offering in which seven shares must be owned to buy one additional share at a price of $15. DeKalb stock currently sells for $63 per share.
   (a) What is the value of a DeKalb right?
   (b) At the time of the offering announcement, Pep's assets consisted of $1,500 in cash and 490 shares of DeKalb. List and show the value of Pep's assets prior to the ex-rights date.
   (c) List and show the value of Pep's assets on the ex-rights date if DeKalb stock sells for $60 per share on that date.
   (d) List and show the value of Pep's assets if Pep sells the DeKalb rights on the ex-rights date.

11. Using a recent *Wall Street Journal* as a data source, select an NYSE-listed stock whose name begins with the same letter as the first letter of your last name. For this stock, calculate its rate of return for that day of the week. What was the stock's trading volume that day?

12. From the perspective of an efficient markets proponent, why is it surprising that trades based on insider trading data found in the SEC's *Official Summary of Securities Transactions and Holdings* appear to produce significant abnormal profits?

13. Tomah Electronics' stock price at the end of several quarters, along with the market index value for the same periods, is shown below. Tomah pays no dividends. Calculate the beta of Tomah's stock over the eight quarters.

QUARTER	QUARTER-END TOMAH STOCK PRICE	QUARTER-END MARKET INDEX VALUE
0	60.000	210.00
1	62.500	220.50
2	64.375	229.87
3	59.875	206.88
4	56.875	190.33
5	61.500	209.36
6	66.500	238.67
7	69.750	257.76
8	68.375	262.92

14. Shown here are ten quarters of return data for Baraboo Associates' stock, as well as return data over the same period for a broad stock market index. Using this information, calculate the following statistics for Baraboo Associates stock:
   (a) beta,
   (b) alpha,
   (c) standard deviation of random error term, and
   (d) coefficient of determination.

QUARTER	BARABOO RETURN	MARKET RETURN
1	3.8%	2.7%
2	5.3	3.1
3	−7.2	−4.9
4	10.1	9.9
5	1.0	2.7
6	2.5	1.2
7	6.4	3.8
8	4.8	4.0
9	6.0	5.5
10	2.2	2.0

15. What is the rationale for calculating "adjusted" betas as described in the text?

16. The market value of Oswego Computers' total debt outstanding is $10 million. Further, the unlevered market value of Oswego is $40 million. The firm's average corporate tax rate is 35%.

(a) If the beta of the firm's debt is .40 and the beta of its equity is 1.20, what is the firm's beta?

(b) If the firm borrows another $10 million and uses the proceeds to purchase an equivalent amount of its own equity, what will be the effect on the beta of its equity?

17. Why would one expect that the betas of companies within industries should be more similar than the betas of companies across industries?

18. Necedah Power is an electric utility company. Its historical beta is .70. Its stock offers a dividend yield of 7.6%. The market value of its outstanding equity is currently $140 million. Based on the data from Table 13-6, calculate Necedah's beta.

19. Explain the primary differences between multiple-factor models of beta and historical models of beta. In particular, why might you expect that the multiple-factor models would do a better job of forecasting actual betas than do the historical models?

20. (Appendix Question) Boileryard Clarke, an astute investment observer, wrote, "Testing for empirical regularities is conceptually difficult because it is really a two-hypothesis test: one test relates to the validity of the underlying asset pricing model and the other test relates to the existence of the empirical regularity." What does Boileryard mean by this statement?

21. (Appendix Question) The empirical regularities cited in this chapter have potentially troubling implications for the Capital Asset Pricing Model and/or the concept of highly efficient markets. Discuss some of these implications.

CFA Exam Questions

22. You ask John Statdud, your research assistant, to analyze the relationship between the return on Coca-Cola Enterprises (CCE) common stock and the return on the market using the Standard & Poor's 500 Stock Index as a proxy for the market. The data include monthly returns for both CCE and the S&P 500 over a recent five-year period. The results of the regression are indicated below:

$$R_{CCE,t} = .59 + .94\ (R_{S\&P,t}) + e_{CCE,t}$$
$$(.81)\quad(3.10)$$

where $R_{CCE,t}$ = return on CCE common stock in month t,
$R_{S\&P,t}$ = return on the S&P 500 Stock Index in month t, and
$e_{CCE,t}$ = residual error in month t.

The numbers in parentheses are the t-statistics (the .01 critical value is 2.66). The coefficient of determination (R^2) for the regression is .215.

Statdud wrote the following summary of the regression results:

1. The regression statistics indicate that during the five-year period under study, when the annual return on the S&P 500 was zero, CCE had an average annual return of 0.59%.
2. The alpha value of .59 is a measure of the variability of the return on the market.
3. The coefficient of .94 indicates CCE's sensitivity to the return on the S&P 500 and suggests that the return on CCE's common stock is less sensitive to market movements than the average stock.
4. The t-statistic of 3.10 for the slope coefficient indicates that the coefficient is not statistically significant at the .01 level.
5. The R^2 for the regression of .215 indicates that the average estimate deviates from the actual observation by an average of 21.5%.
6. There is no concern that the slope coefficient lacks statistical significance since beta values tend to be less stable (and therefore less useful) than alpha values.
7. The regression should be rerun using ten years of data. This would improve the reliability of the estimated coefficients while not sacrificing anything.

Identify which of the seven statements made by Statdud are incorrect and justify your answer(s).

23. You are a portfolio manager meeting a client. During the conversation that followed your formal review of her account, your client asked the following question: "My granddaughter, who is studying investments, tells me that one of the best ways to make money in the stock market is to buy the stocks of small-capitalization firms on a Monday morning late in December and to sell the stocks one month later. What is she talking about?"

(a) Identify the apparent market anomalies [empirical regularities] that would justify the proposed strategy.

(b) Explain why you believe such a strategy might or might not work in the future.

APPENDIX

A

Empirical Regularities in the Stock Market

Researchers have recently uncovered certain **empirical regularities** in common stocks. That is, certain cross-sectional differences among stock returns have been found to occur with regularity. Some regularities should occur according to certain asset pricing models. For example, the CAPM asserts that different stocks should have different returns because different stocks have different betas. What makes the regularities that are about to be discussed of special interest is that they are not predicted by any of the traditional asset pricing models. Accordingly, they are sometimes also referred to as **anomalies.**

empirical regularities

anomalies

THE SIZE EFFECT

size effect

One measure of the size of a firm at a particular point in time is the aggregate market value of its common stock. That is, the size of a firm can be measured by multiplying the market price of its common stock at a particular point in time by the number of shares it has outstanding.[34] A simple test for seeing if firms that are of smaller size have had different returns than firms of larger size

[34]Some studies have used other measures of size, such as the price-to-earnings ratio (or its inverse, the earnings-to-price ratio) and the ratio of book value of equity per share to market value per share, with similar findings. See S. Basu, "Investment Performance of Common Stocks in Relation to Their Price-Earnings Ratios: A Test of the Efficient Market Hypothesis," *Journal of Finance,* 32, no. 3 (June 1977): 663–82; and "The Relationship Between Earnings' Yield, Market Value and Return for NYSE Common Stocks: Further Evidence," *Journal of Financial Economics,* 12, no. 1 (June 1983): 129–56; and Barr Rosenberg, Kenneth Reid, and Ronald Lanstein, "Persuasive Evidence of Market Inefficiency," *Journal of Portfolio Management,* 11, no. 3 (Spring 1985): 9–16. Although the use of price-earnings ratios to identify small firms generates results similar to those using market values, there appears to be some question about the ratio's usefulness. See Marc R. Reinganum, "Misspecification of Capital Asset Pricing: Empirical Anomalies Based on Earnings' Yields and Market Values," *Journal of Financial Economics,* 9, no. 1 (March 1981): 19–46; Rolf W. Banz and William J. Breen, "Sample Dependent Results Using Accounting and Market Data: Some Evidence," *Journal of Finance,* 41, no. 4 (September 1986): 779–93; and Jeffrey Jaffe, Donald B. Keim, and Randolph Westerfield, "Earnings Yields, Market Values, and Stock Returns," *Journal of Finance,* 44, no. 1 (March 1989): 135–38.

can be conducted using data prepared by Ibbotson Associates.[35] All stocks on the New York Stock Exchange were ranked by market value outstanding on December 31, 1925. A portfolio was then formed using the stocks in the bottom quintile (that is, the smallest 20%). Within the portfolio, stocks were purchased in proportion to their market value (that is, the portfolio was value-weighted). This portfolio was "held" for five years. On December 31, 1930, all the stocks on the NYSE were again ranked on size and a new value-weighted portfolio formed from the bottom quintile. This portfolio was "held" for the next five years, when another similar revision was made; such revising continued through 1980, with a slightly modified procedure being used after 1980.

Returns for the "small-firm portfolio" were then calculated for every month from 1926 through 1990. Table 13-7 contrasts the performance of this portfolio with that of Standard & Poor's 500. Since the S&P 500 consists of stocks with large market capitalizations, this can be viewed as a comparison of small stocks with large ones.

On average, the small-firm portfolio outperformed the S&P 500 by 0.41% per month, or approximately 4.96% per year. Although the small-firm portfolio outperformed the S&P 500 only 50.1% of the time, the average difference was positive and statistically significant. This does not imply that a small-firm investment strategy dominated investing in the S&P 500. Table 13-7 indicates that the small-firm portfolio's returns varied much more, having a standard deviation of 35.39% while that of the S&P 500 was 20.80%.

SEASONALITY IN STOCK RETURNS

The desire of individuals for liquidity may be thought to change from day to day and from month to month. If so, there may be seasonal patterns in stock returns. One might presume that such patterns would be relatively unimportant. Indeed, according to the notion of efficient markets, such patterns should be quite minor (if they exist at all), since they are not suggested by traditional asset pricing models. However, the evidence indicates that at least two are significant: the "January effect" and the "day-of-the-week effect."

[35]More elaborate studies of the size effect include Rolf Banz, "The Relationship Between Return and Market Value of Common Stocks," *Journal of Financial Economics*, 9, no. 1 (March 1981): 3–18; and Marc R. Reinganum, "Misspecification of Capital Asset Pricing."

TABLE 13-7
Small- and Large-Stock Performance, 1926–1990

	SMALL STOCKS	SP500	SMALL STOCKS − SP500
Average annual return	17.11%	12.15%	4.96%
Standard deviation	35.39%	20.80%	22.07%
Number of months with positive values	455	460	391
Percent of months with positive values	58.3%	59.0%	50.1%

Source: Based on data in Ibbotson Associates, Inc., *Stocks, Bonds, Bills and Inflation, 1991 Yearbook* (Chicago: 1991).

The January Effect

January effect

There is no obvious reason to expect stock returns to be higher in certain months than in others. However, in a study that looked at average monthly returns on NYSE-listed common stocks, significant seasonalities were found.[36] In particular, the average return in January was higher than the average return in any other month. Table 13-8 indicates the average stock return in January and the other eleven months for various time periods. While the difference in returns was minor in the early part of the century, more recently it appears that the average return in January has been approximately 3% higher than the average monthly return in February through December.[37]

The Day-of-the-Week Effect

day-of-the-week effect

It is often assumed that the expected daily returns on stocks are the same for all days of the week. That is, the expected return on a given stock is the same for Monday as it is for Tuesday as it is for Wednesday as it is for Thursday as it is for Friday. However, a number of studies have uncovered evidence that refutes this belief. Two early studies looked at the average daily return on NYSE-listed securities and found that the return on Monday was quite different.[38] In particular, the average return on Monday was found to be much lower than the average return on any other day of the week. Furthermore, the average return on Monday was negative, while the other days of the week had positive average returns. Table 13-9 displays these findings.

The rate of return on a stock for a given day of the week is typically calculated by subtracting the closing price on the previous trading day from the closing price on that day, adding any dividends for that day to the

[36]Michael S. Rozeff and William R. Kinney, Jr., "Capital Market Seasonality: The Case of Stock Returns," *Journal of Financial Economics*, 3, no. 4 (October 1976): 379–402. For an argument that the market does not have a January effect, see Jay R. Ritter and Navin Chopra, "Portfolio Rebalancing and the Turn-of-the-Year Effect," *Journal of Finance*, 44, no. 1 (March 1989): 149–66.

[37]Interestingly, it appears that returns over the first half of any month (defined to include the last day of the previous month) are significantly higher than the returns over the second half of the month. See Robert A. Ariel, "A Monthly Effect in Stock Returns," *Journal of Financial Economics*, 18, no. 1 (March 1987): 161–74. Another study found this effect to be concentrated in the first three trading days (plus the last trading day of the previous month), and labeled it the **turn-of-the-month effect.** See Josef Lakonishok and Seymour Smidt, "Are Seasonal Anomalies Real? A Ninety-Year Perspective," *Review of Financial Studies*, 1, no. 4 (Winter 1988): 403–25.

turn-of-the-month effect

[38]Kenneth R. French, "Stock Returns and the Weekend Effect," *Journal of Financial Economics*, 8, no. 1 (March 1980): 55–69; and Michael R. Gibbons and Patrick Hess, "Day of the Week Effects and Asset Returns," *Journal of Business*, 54, no. 4 (October 1981): 579–96.

TABLE 13-8
Seasonality in Stock Returns

TIME PERIOD	AVERAGE STOCK RETURN IN JANUARY	AVERAGE STOCK RETURN IN OTHER MONTHS	DIFFERENCE IN RETURNS
1904–1928	1.30%	.44%	.86%
1929–1940	6.63	−.60	7.23
1941–1974	3.91	.70	3.21
1904–1974	3.48	.42	3.06

Source: Michael S. Rozeff and William R. Kinney, Jr., "Capital Market Seasonality: The Case of Stock Returns," *Journal of Financial Economics*, 3, no. 4 (October 1976): 388.

TABLE 13-9 Analysis of Daily Returns

	MONDAY	TUESDAY	WEDNESDAY	THURSDAY	FRIDAY
A. French Study					
January 1953–December 1977	−.17%	.02%	.10%	.04%	.09%
B. Gibbons & Hess Study					
July 1962–December 1978	−.13%	.00%	.10%	.03%	.08%

Source: Kenneth R. French, "Stock Returns and the Weekend Effect," *Journal of Financial Economics*, 8, no. 1 (March 1980): 58; and Michael R. Gibbons and Patrick Hess, "Day of the Week Effects and Asset Returns," *Journal of Business*, 54, no. 4 (October 1981): 582–83.

difference, and then dividing the resulting number by the closing price as of the previous trading day:

$$r_t = \frac{(P_t - P_{t-1}) + D_t}{P_{t-1}} \tag{13.19}$$

where P_t and P_{t-1} are the closing prices on day t and $t - 1$, and D_t is the value of any dividends paid on day t. This means that the return for Monday uses the closing price on Monday as P_t and the closing price on Friday as P_{t-1}. Thus, the change in the price of a stock for Monday $(P_t - P_{t-1})$ actually represents the change in price *over the weekend*, as well as during Monday. This observation has caused some people to refer to the "day-of-the-week" effect as the "weekend" effect, and has led to further examination of daily returns.

holiday effect

Somewhat related to the day-of-the-week effect is the **holiday effect.** A study of this effect found that average stock returns on trading days immediately before federal holidays (when the market is closed; there are eight per year) are 9 to 14 times higher than the average daily return during the rest of the year.[39] Furthermore, this abnormally high return is spread out from the closing price two days before the holiday to the opening price on the day after the holiday. Tests indicate that it is unrelated to the size, January, or day-of-the-week effects.

INTERRELATIONSHIPS

Given the presence of three regularities (the size, January, and day-of-the-week effects), researchers have attempted to see if there are any interrelationships between them. For example, is the January effect more pronounced for small firms? A brief discussion of this interrelationship follows.[40]

Size and January Effects

Having observed that small firms have higher returns than large firms, and that returns in January are higher than in any other month of the year, it is

[39]Robert A. Ariel, "High Stock Returns Before Holidays: Existence and Evidence on Possible Causes," *Journal of Finance*, 45, no. 5 (December 1990): 1611–26.

[40]Other interrelationships are discussed in William F. Sharpe and Gordon J. Alexander, *Investments* (Englewood Cliffs, N.J.: Prentice Hall, 1990), 451–57.

interesting to ponder whether or not these two effects are somehow interrelated. One study that examined this issue found that the two effects were strongly interrelated.[41] All NYSE-listed and AMEX-listed stocks over the seventeen-year period of 1963 to 1979 were examined in this study. At the end of each year, each firm was ranked by the size of the aggregate market value of its equity (that is, the year-end market price per share times the number of shares outstanding). Ten portfolios were then formed based on size with portfolio number one containing the smallest 10% of the firms, portfolio number two containing the next smallest 10%, and so on.

Abnormal returns were calculated subsequently for each portfolio on a monthly basis over the seventeen-year period, and averaged for each month. Figure 13-10 displays the results.

It can be seen from this figure that the size effect was most pronounced in January, since the line for this month slopes down sharply from left to right. The other eleven months of the year appear to be quite similar to each other. Generally, each one of these months displays a slight downward slope, indicating that the size effect also existed for these months, but only to a minor degree. Also of interest is the observation that large firms had a negative abnormal return in January. Thus, the January effect has been due primarily to the behavior of small firms, and the size effect has been concentrated mainly in the month of January.

Further examination of this interrelationship between the size effect and the January effect has revealed that it is concentrated in the first five trading

[41] Donald B. Keim, "Size-related Anomalies and Stock Return Seasonality: Further Empirical Evidence," *Journal of Financial Economics*, 12, no. 1 (June 1983): 13–32.

FIGURE 13-10
Interrelationship Between the Size Effect and the January Effect
Source: Donald B. Keim, "Size-related Anomalies and Stock Return Seasonality: Further Empirical Evidence," *Journal of Financial Economics*, 12, no. 1 (June 1983): 21.

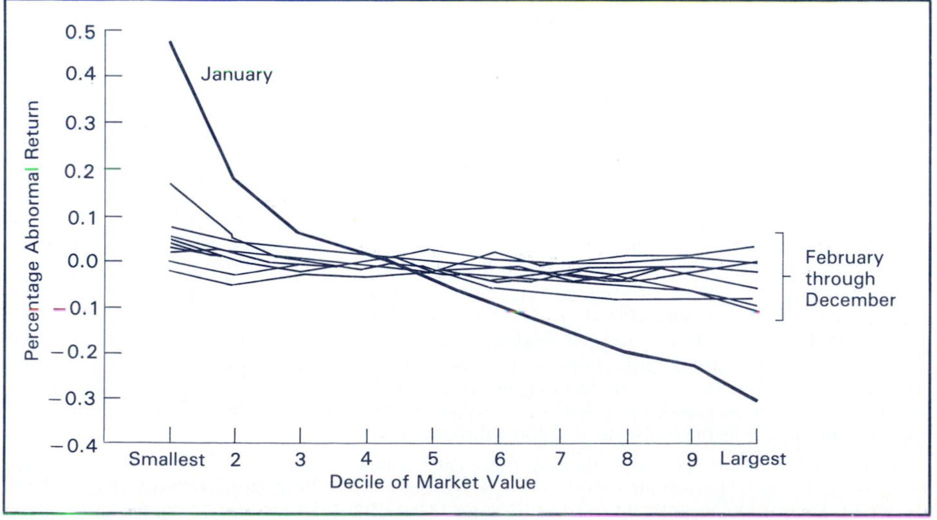

days of January.[42] In particular, the difference in returns between the smallest-firm portfolio and the largest-firm portfolio over these five days was 8.0%, while over the entire year it was 30.4%. Thus, 26.3% (8.0%/30.4%) of the annual size effect occurred during these five days (if the size effect had been spread evenly over the year, then .4% of it would have been attributed to these five days).

Attempts have been made to explain this interrelationship between the January effect and the size effect. One explanation that appears to have some merit has to do with "tax selling." This explanation begins by arguing that stocks that have declined during the year have downward pressure on their prices near year-end as investors sell them to realize capital losses in order to minimize tax payments. After the end of the year, this pressure is removed and the prices jump back to their "fair" values. A related argument asserts that some professional money managers wish to sell those stocks that have performed poorly during the past year in order to avoid their appearance on year-end reports. Such activity is often referred to as "window dressing." Note that these arguments fly in the face of the notion of efficient markets (the notion of efficient markets would suggest that this cannot be true, because if investors sensed that stocks were becoming undervalued at year-end, they would flood the market with buy orders, thereby preventing any substantive undervaluation from occurring). Nevertheless, it does appear to have some merit in that those stocks that declined during the previous year had the largest appreciation in January.[43] However, this association between January returns and previous year stock-price declines does not appear to be attributable solely to such downward tax-selling price pressure. This is because the biggest "losers" during a year appear to subsequently have abnormally high returns for as long as five Januaries thereafter. This contradicts such arguments, since according to them the abnormal price rebound should occur in only the first subsequent January.[44]

Contradictory evidence is also provided by noting that the January effect exists in Japan (as will be shown later), yet Japan has no capital gains tax and

---

[42]Rogalski also finds that the anomalous price behavior of stocks in January mostly occurs in the first five trading days. Roll has observed that the largest daily differences in the returns between small firms and large firms occurs over the last trading day of the year and the first four trading days of the year; furthermore, eight of the subsequent ten trading days also have notably large differences in returns. See Richard Rogalski, "New Findings Regarding Day-of-the-Week Returns Over Trading and Non-Trading Periods: A Note," *Journal of Finance,* 39, no. 5 (December 1984): 1603–14; and Richard Roll, "Vas ist das?" *Journal of Portfolio Management,* 9, no. 2 (Winter 1983): 18–28.

[43]See Roll, "Vas ist das?"; Edward A. Dyl, "Capital Gains Taxation and Year-End Stock Market Behavior," *Journal of Finance,* 32, no. 1 (March 1977): 165–75; Ben Branch, "A Tax Loss Trading Rule," *Journal of Business,* 50, no. 2 (April 1977): 198–207; Dan Givoly and Arie Ovadia, "Year-End Tax-Induced Sales and Stock Market Seasonality," *Journal of Finance,* 38, no. 1 (March 1983): 171–85; Marc R. Reinganum, "The Anomalous Stock Market Behavior of Small Firms in January: Empirical Tests for Tax-Loss Selling Effects," *Journal of Financial Economics,* 12, no. 1 (June 1983): 89–104; Josef Lakonishok and Seymour Smidt, "Capital Gain Taxation and Volume of Trading," *Journal of Finance,* 41, no. 4 (September 1986): 951–74; Jay R. Ritter, "The Buying and Selling Behavior of Individual Investors at the Turn of the Year," *Journal of Finance,* 43, no. 3 (July 1988): 701–17; Joseph P. Ogden, "Turn-of-Month Evaluations of Liquid Profits and Stock Returns: A Common Explanation for the Monthly and January Effects," *Journal of Finance,* 45, no. 4 (September 1990): 1259–72; Greggory A. Brauer and Eric C. Chang, "Return Seasonality in Stocks and Their Underlying Assets: Tax-Loss Selling versus Information Explanations," *Review of Financial Studies,* 3, no. 2 (1990): 255–80.

[44]See K. C. Chan, "Can Tax-Loss Selling Explain the January Seasonal in Stock Returns?" *Journal of Finance,* 41, no. 5 (December 1986): 1115–28; Werner F. M. DeBondt and Richard Thaler, "Does the Stock Market Overreact?" *Journal of Finance,* 40, no. 3 (July 1985), 793–805; and "Further Evidence on Investor Over-reaction and Stock Market Seasonality," *Journal of Finance,* 42, no. 3 (July 1987), 557–81.

disallows any deduction for capital losses.[45] Rebutting this evidence is the observation that the January effect apparently did not exist prior to the imposition of income taxes in the United States.[46]

A second possible explanation is that small stocks may be relatively riskier in January than during the rest of the year. If this is true, then they should have a relatively higher average return in January. A study, finding that the betas of small stocks tend to increase at the beginning of the year, lends support to this explanation.[47]

International Evidence

Several people have investigated foreign stock markets in order to see if similar anomalies exist outside the United States. Since the Tokyo Stock Exchange is the largest non-U.S. exchange, evidence concerning anomalies there will be discussed next. Overall, the anomalies that have been observed in the United States also appear, for the most part, in Japan.

Size Effect Table 13-10 presents evidence that suggests that the size effect also exists in Japan.[48] The data used in panel (A) were based on all stocks in the First Section of the Tokyo Stock Exchange (the Tokyo Stock Exchange has two "sections"; the second is less than 10% of the size, measured by the market value of the securities traded on it, of the first). Two indices were prepared and examined over the period from 1952 to 1980; they include the same stocks but are compiled differently. The EW index weights all the stocks equally and the VW index weights the stocks by market value.[49] Hence the EW index is

[45]A similar observation has been made regarding Canada. See Angel Berges, John J. McConnell, and Gary G. Schlarbaum, "The Turn-of-the-Year in Canada," *Journal of Finance*, 39, no. 1 (March 1984): 185–92.

[46]See Steven L. Jones, Winson Lee, and Rudolf Apenbrink, "New Evidence on the January Effect Before Personal Income Taxes," *Journal of Finance*, 46, no. 5 (December 1991): 1909–24.

[47]Richard J. Rogalski and Seha M. Tinic, "The January Size Effect: Anomaly or Risk Mismeasurement?" *Financial Analysts Journal*, 42, no. 6 (November–December 1986): 63–70. See also Avner Arbel, "Generic Stocks: An Old Product in a New Package," *Journal of Portfolio Management*, 11, no. 4 (Summer 1985): 4–13; and K. C. Chan and Nai-fu Chen, "Structural and Return Characteristics of Small and Large Firms," *Journal of Finance*, 46, no. 4 (September 1991): 1467–84.

[48]See Kiyoshi Kato and James S. Schallheim, "Seasonal and Size Anomalies in the Japanese Stock Market," *Journal of Financial and Quantitative Analysis*, 20, no. 2 (June 1985): 243–60; and Yasushi Hamao, "Fifteen-Year Performance of Japanese Capital Markets," in *Japanese Capital Markets*, Edwin J. Elton and Martin J. Gruber, eds. (New York: Ballinger, 1990), 3–26.

[49]The construction of market indices is discussed in more detail in Chapter 14.

TABLE 13-10
The Size Effect on the Tokyo Stock Exchange

	SMALL STOCKS	LARGE STOCKS	DIFFERENCE
A. 1952–1980: EW vs. VW[a]	22.7%	17.6%	5.1%
B. 1973–1987: TSEsmall vs. TOPIX[b]	21.7	13.3	8.4
TSE2 vs. TOPIX[b]	16.7	13.3	3.4

[a]Adapted from Kiyoshi Kato and James S. Schallheim, "Seasonal and Size Anomalies in the Japanese Stock Market," *Journal of Financial and Quantitative Analysis*, 20, no. 2 (June 1985): 248.

[b]Adapted from Yasushi Hamao, "Fifteen-Year Performance of Japanese Capital Markets," in *Japanese Capital Markets*, Edwin J. Elton and Martin J. Gruber, eds. (New York: Ballinger, 1990), 10.

influenced much more by the performance of small stocks. As the table indicates, the EW index returned 5.1% more, suggesting the presence of a size effect.

Panel (B) of Table 13-10 also indicates the presence of a size effect between 3.4% and 8.4% for the period from 1973 to 1987. Here the performance of small firms is measured with two indices [large stocks are measured by the TOPIX index, which is computed in a manner similar to the VW index in panel (A)]. First, the smallest quintile of stocks in the First Section is formed into a value-weighted index denoted TSEsmall. Second, the stocks in the Second Section are formed into a value-weighted index denoted TSE2. Interestingly, over the same time period the difference in the returns on the S&P 500 (a large stock value-weighted index) and the returns on the smallest quintile of NYSE-listed stocks was 7.8%, comparable to the differences in Tokyo.

January Effect Table 13-11 shows the presence of a January effect in the Tokyo Stock Exchange.[50] The first two rows involve the same indices used in panel (A) of Table 13-10; panel (C) uses a value-weighted index prepared by *Capital International Perspective*. In all three panels the average return in January is clearly higher than the average monthly return in the remaining eleven months. Interestingly, June also has an unusually high average return, but not nearly as dramatic as January's.

Day-of-the-Week Effect Evidence regarding the day-of-the-week effect is provided in Table 13-12.[51] It should be noted that the Tokyo Stock Exchange was open on Saturday mornings during the periods examined; hence there is an average return reported for Saturday as well as Monday through Friday. Two indices are involved. The first is the TOPIX index, which is a value-weighted index based on all stocks listed in the First Section; the second is the Nikkei Dow, which is based on 225 large, well-established companies on the

[50]See Kato and Schallheim, "Seasonal and Size Anomalies"; and Mustafa N. Gultekin and N. Bulent Gultekin, "Stock Market Seasonality: International Evidence," *Journal of Financial Economics*, 12, no. 4 (December 1983): 469–81.

[51]See Jeffrey Jaffe and Randolph Westerfield, "Patterns in Japanese Common Stock Returns: Day of the Week and Turn of the Year Effects," *Journal of Financial and Quantitative Analysis*, 20, no. 2 (June 1985): 261–72, and "The Weekend Effect in Common Stock Returns: The International Evidence," *Journal of Finance*, 40, no. 2 (June 1985): 433–54; Kiyoshi Kato, Sandra L. Schwartz, and William T. Ziemba, "Day of the Week Effects in Japanese Stocks," in *Japanese Capital Markets*, 249–81.

TABLE 13-11 The January Effect on the Tokyo Stock Exchange

	JAN.	FEB.–DEC.	DIFFERENCE	JUNE	FEB.–MAY AND JULY–DEC.	DIFFERENCE
A. 1952–1980: EW[a]	7.1%	1.4%	6.7%	2.8%	1.3%	1.5%
B. 1952–1980: VW[a]	4.5	1.2	3.3	2.5	1.1	2.4
C. 1959–1979: VW[b]	3.5	.7	2.8	2.1	.5	1.6

[a]Adapted from Kiyoshi Kato and James S. Schallheim, "Seasonal and Size Anomalies in the Japanese Stock Market," *Journal of Financial and Quantitative Analysis*, 20, no. 2 (June 1985): 248.

[b]Adapted from Mustafa N. Gultekin and N. Bulent Gultekin, "Stock Market Seasonality: International Evidence," *Journal of Financial Economics*, 12, no. 4 (December 1983): 475.

TABLE 13-12 The Day-of-the-Week Effect on the Tokyo Stock Exchange

	MONDAY	TUESDAY	WEDNESDAY	THURSDAY	FRIDAY	SATURDAY
A. 1970–1983: Nikkei Dow[a]	−.02%	−.09%	.15%	.03%	.06%	.12%
B. 1970–1983: Topix[a]	−.01	−.06	.12	.03	.06	.10
C. 1978–1987: Topix[b]	.00	−.09	.14	.06	.10	.14

[a]Adapted from Jeffrey Jaffe and Randolph Westerfield, "Patterns in Japanese Common Stock Returns: Day of the Week and Turn of the Year Effects," *Journal of Financial and Quantitative Analysis*, 20, no. 2 (June 1985): 263.

[b]Kiyoshi Kato, Sandra L. Schwartz, and William T. Ziemba, "Day of the Week Effects in Japanese Stocks," in *Japanese Capital Markets*, Edwin J. Elton and Martin J. Gruber, eds. (New York: Ballinger, 1990), 253.

Tokyo Stock Exchange and is a price-weighted index like the Dow Jones Industrial Average.

The table indicates that Monday returns are, in general, negative, just as in the United States (see Table 13-9 for comparisons). Furthermore, Wednesday returns are the largest, again similar to the United States. Second largest is Saturday, the last trading day of the week in Japan. This is similar to the United States in that the last trading day of the week is the second largest. What is surprising is that Tuesday is negative, and even more so than Monday. Otherwise, the day-of-the-week effect in Japan is similar to that observed in the United States.[52]

Size and January Effects Examination of Table 13-11 reveals that the size effect occurs for the most part in January. Hence these two effects are interconnected in a manner similar to that in the United States, as can be seen by examining the average returns indicated in panels (A) and (B).

These panels show that there is a pronounced difference in the average returns between the equal-weighted and value-weighted indices of 2.6% (=7.1% − 4.5%) in January, but a relatively small difference of .2% (=1.4% − 1.2%) during the other eleven months of the year. This is notable because the EW index gives much larger weights to small stocks than the VW index, suggesting that the difference between the two indices can be attributed to the performance of the small stocks. In summary, it would appear that in Japan the size effect is primarily a January effect.

SUMMARY OF EMPIRICAL REGULARITIES

On balance, what do these regularities suggest the investor should do? First, investors who want to buy stocks should avoid doing so late on Friday or early

[52]Additional patterns have been discovered. Imagine splitting the set of Mondays in two where one set corresponds to Mondays that follow a week where the market declined and the second set corresponds to Mondays that follow a week where the market rose. Interestingly, in both the United States and Japan, the average return for the first set of Mondays is significantly negative (−.39% in the United States and −.18% in Japan) while the average return for the second set of Mondays is slightly positive (.06% in the United States and .11% in Japan). See Jeffrey F. Jaffe, Randolph Westerfield, and Christopher Ma, "A Twist on the Monday Effect in Stock Prices: Evidence from the U.S. and Foreign Stock Markets," *Journal of Banking and Finance*, 13, no. 4/5 (September 1989): 641–50.

on Monday. Conversely, investors who want to sell stocks should try to sell late on Friday or early on Monday. Second, if small firms are to be purchased, they should be purchased in late December or somewhat earlier; if small firms are to be sold, they should be sold in mid-January or somewhat later. Third, if large firms are to be purchased, they should be purchased in early February or somewhat later; if large firms are to be sold, they should be sold in late December or somewhat earlier.

Two words of caution are in order here. First, none of these empirical regularities is of a sufficient magnitude to suggest that riches are to be made by exploiting them. Indeed, transaction costs would devour most if not all of any profits that might be made.[53] All that they suggest is that if, for whatever reason, a buy or sell order is to be placed, there are some times when it may be more advantageous to do so. Second, while these regularities have been found to exist in the past, and in some instances for long periods of time and in several foreign markets, there is no guarantee that they will continue to exist in the future.[54] It may be the case that as more investors become aware of them and time their trades accordingly, such regularities will cease to exist.

REFERENCES

1. For a discussion of the motivations for takeovers and the associated consequences, see:

Michael C. Jensen and Richard S. Ruback, "The Market for Corporate Control: The Scientific Evidence," *Journal of Financial Economics*, 11, nos. 1–4 (April 1983): 5–50;

Richard Roll, "The Hubris Hypothesis of Corporate Takeovers," *Journal of Business*, 59, no. 1, pt. 2 (April 1986): 197–216;

J. Fred Weston, Kwang S. Chung, and Susan E. Hoag, *Mergers, Restructuring, and Corporate Control* (Englewood Cliffs, N.J.: Prentice Hall, 1990);

Andrei Shleifer and Robert W. Vishny, "The Takeover Wave of the 1980s," *Journal of Applied Corporate Finance*, 4, no. 3 (Fall 1991): 49–56;

Michael C. Jensen, "Corporate Control and the Politics of Finance," *Journal of Applied Corporate Finance*, 4, no. 2 (Summer 1991): 13–33.

2. For a study of how risk arbitrageurs (investors who buy and sell stocks of firms involved in takeovers and divestitures) are able to earn substantial returns, see:

David F. Larcker and Thomas Lys, "An Empirical Analysis of the Incentives to Engage in Costly Information Acquisition: The Case of Risk Arbitrage," *Journal of Financial Economics*, 18, no. 1 (March 1987): 111–26.

3. Three interesting studies of stock repurchases are:

Josef Lakonishok and Theo Vermaelen, "Anomalous Price Behavior Around Repurchase Tender Offers," *Journal of Finance*, 45, no. 2 (June 1990): 455–77;

---

[53]See Donald B. Keim, "Trading Patterns, Bid-Ask Spreads, and Estimated Security Returns: The Case of Common Stocks at Calendar Turning Points," *Journal of Financial Economics*, 25, no. 1 (November 1989): 75–97.

[54]The appendix to Chapter 22 discusses regularities in the bond market.

Robert Comment and Gregg A. Jarrell, "The Relative Signalling Power of Dutch-Auction and Fixed-Price Self-Tender Offers and Open-Market Share Repurchases," *Journal of Finance*, 46, no. 4 (September 1991): 1243–71;

Laurie Simon Bagwell, "Dutch Auction Repurchases: An Analysis of Shareholder Heterogeneity," *Journal of Finance*, 47, no. 1 (March 1992); 71–105.

4. Stock splits and stock dividends are examined in:

Eugene F. Fama, Lawrence Fisher, Michael C. Jensen, and Richard Roll, "The Adjustment of Stock Prices to New Information," *International Economic Review*, 10, no. 1 (February 1969): 1–21;

Sasson Bar-Yosef and Lawrence D. Brown, "A Re-examination of Stock Splits Using Moving Betas," *Journal of Finance*, 32, no. 4 (September 1977): 1069–80;

Guy Charest, "Split Information, Stock Returns, and Market Efficiency-I," *Journal of Financial Economics*, 6, no. 2/3 (June/September 1978): 265–96;

J. Randall Woolridge, "Ex-Date Stock Price Adjustment to Stock Dividends: A Note," *Journal of Finance*, 38, no. 1 (March 1983): 247–55;

Thomas E. Copeland, "Liquidity Changes Following Stock Splits," *Journal of Finance*, 34, no. 1 (March 1979): 115–41;

Mark S. Grinblatt, Ronald W. Masulis, and Sheridan Titman, "The Valuation Effects of Stock Splits and Stock Dividends," *Journal of Financial Economics*, 13, no. 4 (December 1984): 461–90;

Josef Lakonishok and Baruch Lev, "Stock Splits and Stock Dividends: Why, Who, and When," *Journal of Finance*, 42, no. 4 (September 1987): 913–32;

Robert S. Conroy, Robert S. Harris, and Bruce A. Benet, "The Effects of Stock Splits on Bid-Ask Spreads," *Journal of Finance*, 45, no. 4 (September 1990): 1285–95;

David A. Dubofsky, "Volatility Increases Subsequent to NYSE and AMEX Stock Splits," *Journal of Finance*, 46, no. 1 (March 1991): 421–31.

5. Insider trading has been examined in a number of studies. Some of the major ones are:

Jeffrey F. Jaffe, "Special Information and Insider Trading," *Journal of Business*, 47, no. 3 (July 1974): 410–28;

Joseph E. Finnerty, "Insiders and Market Efficiency," *Journal of Finance*, 31, no. 4 (September 1976): 1141–48;

Herbert S. Kerr, "The Battle of Insider Trading and Market Efficiency," *Journal of Portfolio Management*, 6, no. 4 (Summer 1980): 47–58;

Wayne Y. Lee and Michael Solt, "Insider Trading: A Poor Guide to Market Timing," *Journal of Portfolio Management*, 12, no. 4 (Summer 1986): 65–71;

H. Nejat Seyhun, "Insiders' Profits, Costs of Trading, and Market Efficiency," *Journal of Financial Economics*, 16, no. 2 (June 1986): 189–212;

Michael S. Rozeff and Mir A. Zaman, "Market Efficiency and Insider Trading: New Evidence," *Journal of Business*, 61, no. 1 (January 1988): 25–44;

Ji-Chai Lin and John S. Howe, "Insider Trading in the OTC Market," *Journal of Finance*, 45, no. 4 (September 1990): 1273–84.

6. The behavior of beta coefficients has been extensively studied. See, for example:

   Marshall Blume, "On the Assessment of Risk," *Journal of Finance*, 26, no. 1 (March 1971): 1–10;

   Robert A. Levy, "On the Short-Term Stationarity of Beta Coefficients," *Financial Analysts Journal*, 27, no. 6 (November/December 1971): 55–62;

   William F. Sharpe and Guy M. Cooper, "Risk-Return Classes of New York Stock Exchange Common Stocks, 1931–1967," *Financial Analysts Journal*, 28, no. 2 (March–April 1972): 46–54;

   Robert S. Hamada, "The Effect of the Firm's Capital Structure on the Systematic Risk of Common Stocks," *Journal of Finance*, 27, no. 2 (May 1972): 435–52;

   Marshall Blume, "Betas and Their Regression Tendencies," *Journal of Finance*, 30, no. 3 (June 1975): 785–95;

   Barr Rosenberg and Vinay Marathe, "The Prediction of Investment Risk: Systematic and Residual Risk," *Proceedings of the Seminar on the Analysis of Security Prices*, Center for Research in Security Prices, Graduate School of Business, University of Chicago, November 1975;

   Barr Rosenberg and James Guy, "Prediction of Beta from Investment Fundamentals," *Financial Analysts Journal*, 32, no. 3 (May–June 1976): 60–72, and no. 4 (July–August 1976): 62–70;

   Meir Statman, "Betas Compared: Merrill Lynch vs. Value Line," *Journal of Portfolio Management*, 7, no. 2 (Winter 1981): 41–44;

   Barr Rosenberg, "Prediction of Common Stock Investment Risk," *Journal of Portfolio Management*, 11, no. 1 (Fall 1984): 44–53;

   Barr Rosenberg, "Prediction of Common Stock Betas," *Journal of Portfolio Management*, 11, no. 2 (Winter 1985): 5–14;

   George Foster, *Financial Statement Analysis* (Englewood Cliffs, N.J.: Prentice Hall, 1986), chapter 10;

   Frank K. Reilly and David J. Wright, "A Comparison of Published Betas," *Journal of Portfolio Management*, 14, no. 3 (Spring 1988): 64–69;

   Thomas E. Copeland and J. Fred Weston, *Financial Theory and Corporate Policy* (Reading, Mass.: Addison-Wesley, 1988), chapter 13;

   Richard A. Brealey and Stewart C. Myers, *Principles of Corporate Finance* (New York: McGraw-Hill, 1991), 191–92, 468–69.

7. Many of the studies conducted concerning various empirical regularities are cited in the appendix; others are discussed in:

   Donald B. Keim, "The CAPM and Equity Return Regularities," *Financial Analysts Journal*, 42, no. 3 (May/June 1986): 19–34;

   Lawrence Harris, "How to Profit from Intradaily Stock Returns," *Journal of Portfolio Management*, 12, no. 2 (Winter 1986): 61–64, and "A Transaction Data Study of Weekly and Intradaily Patterns in Stock Returns," *Journal of Financial Economics*, 16, no. 1 (May 1986): 99–117;

   Michael Smirlock and Laura Starks, "Day-of-the-Week and Intraday Effects in Stock Returns," *Journal of Financial Economics*, 17, no. 1 (September 1986): 197–210;

   Richard H. Thaler, "Anomalies: The January Effect," *Journal of Economic Perspectives*, 1, no. 1 (Summer 1987): 197–201, and "Anomalies: Seasonal Movements in Security Prices II—Weekend, Holiday, Turn of the Month, and Intraday Effects," *Journal of Economic Perspectives*, 1, no. 2 (Fall 1987): 169–77;

Douglas K. Pearce, "Challenges to the Concept of Market Efficiency," Federal Reserve Bank of Kansas City *Economic Review*, 72, no. 8 (September/October 1987): 16–33;

Elroy Dimson, ed., *Stock Market Anomalies* (Cambridge, England: Cambridge University Press, 1988);

Robert A. Haugen and Josef Lakonishok, *The Incredible January Effect* (Homewood, Ill.: Dow Jones-Irwin, 1988);

Josef Lakonishok and Seymour Smidt, "Are Seasonal Anomalies Real? A Ninety-Year Perspective," *Review of Financial Studies*, 1, no. 4 (Winter 1988): 403–25;

Donald B. Keim, "Trading Patterns, Bid-Ask Spreads, and Estimated Security Returns: The Case of Common Stocks at Calendar Turning Points," *Journal of Financial Economics*, 25, no. 1 (November 1989): 75–97;

Burton G. Malkiel, *A Random Walk Down Wall Street* (New York: W. W. Norton & Company, 1990), chapter 8;

Eugene F. Fama, "Efficient Capital Markets: II," *Journal of Finance*, 46, no. 5 (December 1991): 1575–1617.

8. For a tongue-in-check article on anomalies that shows that market returns are influenced by superstition since returns on Friday the 13th are, on average, abnormally low, see:

Robert W. Kolb and Ricardo J. Rodriguez, "Friday the Thirteenth: 'Part VII'—A Note," *Journal of Finance*, 42, no. 5 (December 1987): 1385–87.

14

Financial Analysis of Common Stocks

In a broad sense, financial analysis involves determining the levels of risk and expected return of individual financial assets as well as groups of financial assets. For example, financial analysis involves both individual common stocks, such as IBM; groups of common stocks, such as the computer industry; or, on an even larger basis, the stock market itself. In this case, financial analysis would result in a decision of how to split the investor's money between the stock and bond markets, as well as a decision of whether to buy or sell computer stocks in general and IBM in particular.

An alternative definition of financial analysis is more pragmatic: finan-

MONEY MATTERS: The Chartered Financial Analysts Program

The investment profession encompasses a wide range of activities. Investment bankers, brokers, portfolio managers, traders, security analysts, salespeople, consultants, and pension fund administrators all fall under the rubric of investment professionals. These individuals, and the organizations for which they work, directly or indirectly affect the financial well-being of millions of people.

The Chartered Financial Analyst (CFA) program was born of a need to bring a common set of investment management concepts and standards of professional conduct to the diverse membership of the investment industry. From its modest beginnings in 1963, when 268 professionals were effectively "grandfathered" as chartered members, the CFA program has grown to a worldwide organization, with over 15,000 CFA charters awarded and more than 14,000 candidates currently enrolled. While the CFA charter is far from a prerequisite for employment in the investment industry, many organizations are encouraging or even requiring new employees to participate in the CFA program.

From its inception, the Institute of Chartered Financial Analysts (ICFA), which administers the CFA program, has pursued three explicit objectives:

1. To compile a comprehensive set of currently accepted concepts and techniques relevant to the investment decision-making process (the CFA "Body of Knowledge").
2. To establish a uniform set of ethical standards to guide the activities of investment professionals.
3. To ensure that CFA charterholders have demonstrated satisfactory understanding of the Body of Knowledge and that they adhere to the established ethical standards.

Of course, like any other professional certification organization, the ICFA has multiple motives for promoting the CFA designation. By setting difficult hurdles for prospective members to clear, the CFA certification process enhances the monetary value of the charter to existing holders. Further, by demonstrating a responsible and comprehensive education and ethics program, the ICFA helps the investment industry ward off onerous government regulation and provides the industry with wider latitude to police itself.

To enroll in the CFA program, persons must hold a bachelor's degree (or equivalent work experience), provide three acceptable character references, and pay the required registration fee. Once accepted into the program, to earn the CFA designation, candidates must pass three exams, possess three years of investment-related work experience, be a member of (or have applied to) a constituent Financial Analyst Federation society, demonstrate a high level of professional conduct, and abide

financial analyst

cial analysis is what financial analysts do. The *Financial Analyst's Handbook*[1] defines the term **financial analyst** as synonymous with security analyst or investment analyst—"one who analyzes securities and makes recommendations thereon."[2] Using this definition, financial analysis can be viewed as the activity of providing inputs to the portfolio management process. This chapter (as well as chapters 15 and 16) takes such a view in discussing the financial analysis of common stocks. Chapter 17 subsequently discusses how financial analysis can be used by people known as **portfolio managers** or investment managers.

portfolio managers

PROFESSIONAL ORGANIZATIONS

In the United States, those who belong to a local society of financial analysts automatically belong to a national organization known as the Association for Investment Management and Research (AIMR). Among other things, member-

[1]Sumner N. Levine, ed., *Financial Analyst's Handbook I* (Homewood, Ill.: Dow Jones-Irwin, 1975).

[2]William C. Norby, "Overview of Financial Analysis," in Levine, *Financial Analyst's Handbook I*, p. 3.

by the Code of Ethics and Standards of Practice of the Association for Investment Management and Research.

The CFA course of study and examinations are the cornerstone of the CFA certification process. Candidates must pass three six-hour exams. The ICFA administers these exams once a year in June at over 100 locations, primarily in the United States and Canada. As candidates may take only one exam per year, a minimum of three years is required to complete the examination sequence.

The ICFA specifies a set of review materials and assigned readings for candidates to use in preparation for the exams. The study program has evolved over the years as new concepts have been introduced into the exams. The ICFA estimates that candidates average over 160 hours per exam in individual study time. Many candidates also participate in independently sponsored study groups.

The CFA examinations are designed in a progressive format. Each exam level becomes increasingly comprehensive, building on previous levels. As shown in Figure 14-1, in 1991 the exams were divided into seven major subject areas:

1. Ethical and professional standards,
2. Financial accounting,
3. Quantitative analysis,
4. Economics,
5. Fixed-income securities analysis,
6. Equity securities analysis, and
7. Portfolio management.

The CFA exams are rigorous and difficult. A high percentage of the candidates fails at least one exam, although exams can be retaken. In 1991, 9,868 candidates sat for the exams. Only 62%, 54%, and 75% of the Level I, II, and III candidates, respectively, passed.

The CFA program experienced tremendous growth in the 1980s. The number of candidates sitting for the exams grew from 1,985 in 1980 to 8,760 in 1990. Given this past success, where does the CFA program go from here?

Clearly, the ICFA desires to continue to enhance the prestige and uniqueness of its CFA certification. In recent years, however, the ICFA has also begun to strongly emphasize the continuing education aspect of its mission. Technological obsolescence is a serious problem in the rapidly changing investment industry. (For example, organized financial futures markets—see Chapter 25—did not even exist in 1980.) Many professionals who received the CFA designation just a decade ago might find it difficult to pass a 1992 exam. Current charterholders are encouraged (although not yet required) to participate in a self-administered continuing education program.

The ICFA also sees a role for itself globally. With the investment industry becoming increasingly international in scope, the ICFA has moved to administer its program abroad. (Twenty percent of the current CFA candidates reside outside of the United States.) It has also begun to join forces with analyst societies in other countries to develop means of jointly recognizing each others' certification programs.

---

ship brings with it a subscription to the *Financial Analysts Journal*, a major source of information on basic research done by other analysts and by members of the academic community. In 1991, there were over 19,000 members in AIMR.

In 1962, The Institute of Chartered Financial Analysts was formed by the Financial Analysts Federation (the precursor to AIMR) to award the professional designation of Chartered Financial Analyst (CFA). During the next twenty-nine years, over 15,000 analysts were designated CFAs. To become a CFA, one must have several years of practical experience and pass a series of three examinations.[3] Figure 14-1, which shows the subjects covered in each of the examinations, provides a good summary of the types of knowledge the successful financial analyst needs.

Societies of financial analysts have been formed around the world. For example, the European Federation of Financial Analysts draws its membership from ten European countries. Other societies are located in countries such as Canada, Australia, Japan, and Brazil.

[3]To obtain more information about becoming a CFA, contact The Institute of Chartered Financial Analysts. Their mailing address is P.O. Box 3668, Charlottesville, VA 22903, and their telephone number is (804) 977-6600. A useful annual publication of the Institute is *The CFA Candidate Study and Examination Program Review*.

FIGURE 14-1

General Topic Outline, CFA Candidate Study and Examination Program

Reprinted, with permission, from the *1992 CFA Candidate Study and Examination Program Review*. Copyright 1991, Association for Investment Management and Research, Charlottesville, Va.

Candidate Level

Ethical and Professional Standards, Securities Law and Regulations

I II III

Applicable Laws and Regulations
Nature and applicability of fiduciary standards
Pertinent laws and regulations
Organization and purpose of governing regulatory bodies

Professional Code and Standards
Code of Ethics
Standards of Professional Conduct
ICFA Bylaws, Article IX
AIMR Bylaws, Article X
AIMR Rules of Procedure

Ethical Standards and Professional Obligations
Relationships with:
(a) clients, customers, public;
(b) corporate managements;
(c) employers, associates, other analysts
Insider information
Supervisory responsibilities
Research reports and investment recommendations
Compensation
Conflicts of interest
Fiduciary duties
Professional misconduct
Investment suitability

Identification of Issues and Administration of Ethical Conduct
Fiduciary responsibility
Insider trading
Corporate governance and the institutional investor
The Prudent Man Rule
Competency and proper care
Conflicts of interest in setting and receiving compensation
General business ethical values and obligations
Ethical organization cultures

Financial Accounting

I II III

Role and Function of Basic Accounting Statements
Income statement
Balance sheet
Statement of cash flows

Using and Interpreting Accounting Statements
Revenue recognition
Inventory costing
Depreciation methods
Investments in marketable securities
Off-balance sheet financing
Troubled debt restructuring
Leases
Postemployment benefits
Income taxes
Prior period adjustments
Earnings per share
Analysis of liquidity cash flow
Foreign currency translation
Intercorporate investments
Business combinations

Candidate Level

Financial Accounting (Continued)

I II III

Special Topics
Goals of financial statement analysis
Implications of efficient market hypothesis
The setting of accounting standards
Adjustments to financial statements
International accounting
Price level adjustments
Current accounting issues

Quantitative Analysis

I II III

Introduction to quantitative methods
Mathematics of compound interest, present and future values
Basic statistics and regression analysis
Measures of risk
Introduction to derivative securities
Advanced regression analysis
Basic options and futures pricing
Advanced options and futures pricing

Economics

I II III

Focus on Macroeconomics
Concept and measurement of GNP
Business fluctuations and economic forecasting
Inflationary process
Aggregate supply and demand
Macro schools of thought

International Economics
Comparative advantage
International payments
Foreign exchange

Focus on Microeconomics and Analysis
Consumer behavior and business decision making
Costs and supply of goods
Product life cycle
Business structure and regulation

Economic Forecasting
Forecasting tools
Relative success
Determinants of interest rates

Applications to Security Analysis and Portfolio Management
Economic factor returns
Currency hedging

Current Economic Issues
U.S.
Global

FIGURE 14-1 (continued)

Candidate Level

I II III

Techniques of Analysis — Fixed-Income Securities

Introduction
Features of fixed-income securities
International fixed-income market

Mathematical Properties
Price/yield relationship
Duration and convexity

Credit Evaluation
Bond ratings
Earnings and cash flow analysis
Asset protection
Contractural covenants

Market Analysis
Yield curves
Forecasting interest rates
International
Derivative securities

Portfolio Strategies
Active
Passive
Index
Immunization/dedication

I II III

Techniques of Analysis — Equity Securities

Introduction
Investment environment
Securities markets
Mechanics of securities transactions
History of stock market — rate of return comparisons
Global investing

Financial Analysis
Ratios
Decomposition of ROE
Analysis of financial statements
Capital structure

Valuation Approaches
Earnings
Dividend discount
Cash flow
Asset valuations
Technical analysis
Other
Anomalies

Company Analysis and Evaluation
Fundamental analysis
Industry and economy context
Outline for analysis
Forecasting
Competitive environment
Corporate planning and strategy
Qualitative Factors
Example of research report

Investment Strategies
Trends
Market inefficiencies
Psychological influences

Corporate Restructuring
Leveraged buyouts
Takeovers

Venture Capital and Closely Held Companies
Analysis
Valuation

Candidate Level

I II III

Objective of Analysis — Portfolio Management

Principles of Financial Asset Management
Definition of portfolio management, basic concepts—return, risk, diversification, portfolio efficiency
Evolution of portfolio management—traditional and recent developments

Investor Objectives, Constraints and Policies
Liquidity requirement
Return requirement
Risk tolerance
Time horizon
Tax considerations
Regulatory and legal considerations
Unique needs, circumstances and preferences
Determination of portfolio policies

Asset Allocation
Expected return and risk
Estimation issues
The optimal portfolio
Dynamic strategies

Derivative Security Analysis
Boundaries and basic properties of option values
Arbitrage and option valuation
Option pricing models
Empirical analysis of options
Option pricing theory applied to other assets
Financial futures

Expectational Factors
Social, political and economic
Capital markets
Individual financial assets

Integration of Portfolio Policies and Expectational Factors
Portfolio construction—asset allocation, active/passive strategies
Monitoring portfolio and responding to change—objectives, constraints and policies, expectational factors
Execution—timing, commission costs, price effects

Portfolio Performance Appraisal
Performance criteria—absolute performance, relative to portfolio objectives and risk level, relative to other portfolios with similar objectives
Measurement of performance—valuation of assets, accounting for income, rates of return and volatility
Evaluation of results—relationship to performance criteria, sources of results
Universe comparisons
Risk adjustment
Benchmark error
Ambiguity between skill and chance
Performance attribution
Normal portfolio
Non-parametric performance measurement
Incentive fees
Gaming performance measurement

REASONS FOR FINANCIAL ANALYSIS

There are two primary reasons for engaging in financial analysis. The first is to try to determine certain characteristics of securities; the second is to attempt to identify mispriced securities.[4] These reasons are discussed next.

Determining Security Characteristics

According to modern portfolio theory, a financial analyst will want to estimate a security's future beta and unique risk, since these are needed to determine the risk (measured by standard deviation) of a portfolio. Perhaps the analyst may also want to estimate the dividend yield of a security over the next year in order to determine its suitability for portfolios in which dividend yield is relevant (owing to, say, legal restrictions). Careful analysis of such things as a company's dividend policy and likely future cash flows may lead to better estimates than can be obtained by simply extrapolating last year's dividend yield.

In many cases it may be desirable to know something about the sources of a security's risk and return. If a portfolio is being managed for a person who is in the oil business, one might want to minimize the sensitivity of the portfolio's return to changes in oil prices. This is because it is likely that if oil prices are in a decline, then the person's income from the oil business will also be in a decline. If the portfolio were sensitive to oil prices (which would be the case if it contained a substantial investment in oil stocks), then it too would be in a decline in value, thereby reinforcing the deterioration of the person's financial position.[5]

Attempting to Identify Mispriced Securities

fundamental analysis

A search for a mispriced security typically involves the use of **fundamental analysis.** In essence, this entails searching for a security in which the financial analyst's estimates of such things as the firm's future earnings and dividends:

1. differ substantially from consensus (that is, average) estimates of others;
2. are viewed as being closer to the correct values than the consensus estimates; and
3. are not currently reflected in the security's market price, but eventually will be reflected in its market price.

Two rather different approaches may be taken in the search for mispriced securities using fundamental analysis. The first approach involves valuation, where an attempt is made to determine the appropriate "intrinsic" or "true" value for a security. After making this determination, the intrinsic value is compared with the security's current market price. If the market price

[4]There is actually a third reason for conducting financial analysis: monitoring the firm's management in order to prevent managers from consuming an excessive amount of perquisites and failing to make appropriate decisions to the detriment of the firm's shareholders. See Michael C. Jensen and William H. Meckling, "Theory of the Firm: Managerial Behavior, Agency Costs and Ownership Structure," *Journal of Financial Economics*, 3, no. 4 (October 1976): 305–60.

[5]For a discussion regarding portfolio selection by an investor who has earned income (for example, from wages or from running a business), see Edward M. Miller, "Portfolio Selection in a Fluctuating Economy," *Financial Analysts Journal*, 34, no. 3 (May/June 1978): 77–83.

is substantially greater than the intrinsic value, the security is said to be overpriced, or overvalued. If the market price is substantially less than the intrinsic value, the security is said to be underpriced, or undervalued. Instead of comparing price with value, the analyst sometimes estimates a security's expected return over a specified period, given its current market price and intrinsic value. This estimate is then compared with the "appropriate" return for securities with similar attributes.

Determining a security's intrinsic value may be done in great detail, using estimates of all major factors that influence security returns (for example, gross domestic product of the economy, industry sales, firm sales and expenses, and capitalization rates). Alternatively, a shortcut may be taken where, for example, an estimate of earnings per share may be multiplied by a "justified" or "normal" price-earnings ratio to determine the intrinsic value of a share of common stock. (To avoid complications arising when seeking the intrinsic value of a stock that has negative earnings per share, some analysts estimate sales per share and multiply this figure by a "normal" price-sales ratio.)

A second approach has the analyst estimate only one or two financial variables and then compare these estimates directly with consensus estimates. For example, next year's earnings per share for a stock may be estimated. If the analyst's estimate substantially exceeds the consensus of other analysts' estimates, the stock may be considered an attractive investment. This is because the analyst expects the actual earnings to provide a happy surprise for the market when announced. In turn, there will be an increase in the stock's price at that time, resulting in the investor receiving a greater-than-normal return. Conversely, when an analyst's estimate of earnings per share is substantially below that of the other analysts, then the analyst expects that the market will receive an unhappy surprise. The resulting decrease in the stock's price will lead to a smaller-than-normal return.

At an aggregate level, an analyst may be more optimistic about the economy than the consensus of other analysts. This would suggest that a larger-than-normal investment in stocks be taken, offset perhaps by a smaller-than-normal investment in fixed-income securities. Conversely, a relatively pessimistic view would suggest a smaller-than-normal investment in stocks, offset perhaps by a larger-than-normal investment in fixed-income securities.

Alternatively, the analyst might agree with the consensus view on both the economy and the individual characteristics of specific securities, but feel that the consensus view of the prospects for a certain group of securities in a particular industry is in error. In such a case, a larger-than-normal investment may be made in stocks from an industry having prospects about which the analyst feels relatively optimistic. Conversely, a smaller-than-normal investment would be made in stocks from an industry about which the analyst feels relatively pessimistic.

Fundamental analysis of common stocks will be discussed in more detail later in this chapter. At that time the method of technical analysis will be introduced and compared with fundamental analysis. The next two chapters will also discuss fundamental analysis of common stocks, while such analysis of fixed-income securities will come later.

Beating the Market

Many books and articles have been written that allegedly show how financial analysis can be used to "beat the market," meaning that they purport to show

how to make abnormally high returns by investing in the stock market. In order to evaluate such systems, an understanding of what "the market" is and how to measure its performance is in order.

market index

Market Indices What did the market do yesterday? How much would an unmanaged common stock portfolio have returned last year? Such questions are often answered by examining the performance of a **market index.** Figure 14-2 displays many indices that are commonly discussed. These indices differ from one another with respect to (1) the securities included in the index, and (2) the method employed in calculating the value of the index.

In order to understand how some of the most popular indices are computed, consider a simple example where the market index is based on two stocks, referred to as A and B. At the end of day t, their closing prices are, respectively, \$10 and \$20 per share. Furthermore, at this time A has 1,500 shares outstanding and B has 2,000 shares outstanding.

price-weighted market index

There are three weighting methods that are often used in computing a market index. The first method, involving **price weighting,** begins by summing the prices of the stocks that are included in the index, and ends by dividing this sum by a constant (the "divisor"). If the index includes only stocks A and B and was started on day t, the divisor would be equal to the number of stocks in the average, 2. Thus, on day t the index would have a value of $(10 + 20)/2 = 15$. The divisor is adjusted thereafter whenever there is a stock split in order to avoid giving misleading indications of the "market's" direction.[6]

For example, assume that on day $t + 1$, B splits 2-for-1 and closes at \$11 per share, while A closes at \$13. In this situation, it is clear that the "market" has risen, since both stocks have a higher price than on day t after adjusting B for the split. If nothing were done in computing the index, its value on day $t + 1$ would be $12 = (13 + 11)/2$, a drop of 20% $[=(12 - 15)/15]$ from day t that falsely suggests that the market went down on day $t + 1$. In reality, the market went up to $17.5 = [13 + (11 \times 2)]/2$, a gain of 16.67% $[=(17.5 - 15)/15]$.

A stock split is accounted for in a price-weighted index by adjusting the divisor whenever a split takes place. In the example, the divisor is adjusted by examining the index on day $t + 1$, the day of the split. More specifically, the following equation would be solved for the unknown divisor d:

$$\frac{13 + 11}{d} = 17.5. \tag{14.1}$$

The value of d that solves this equation is 1.37. The new divisor will continue in use after day $t + 1$ until there is another split, when it will again be recalculated.

The *Dow Jones Industrial Average,* one of the most widely followed indices, is calculated in this manner; it involves the prices of thirty stocks that generally represent large-size firms. Two other Dow Jones Averages, one of which uses twenty transportation stocks, the other fifteen utility stocks, are similarly calculated. Levels of these Dow Jones Averages are reported in almost every daily newspaper. Historical data on the Averages, including

[6]The divisor is also adjusted whenever the composition of the stocks in the index changes (meaning whenever one stock is substituted for another).

FIGURE 14-2
Stock Market Indices Published Daily in *The Wall Street Journal*

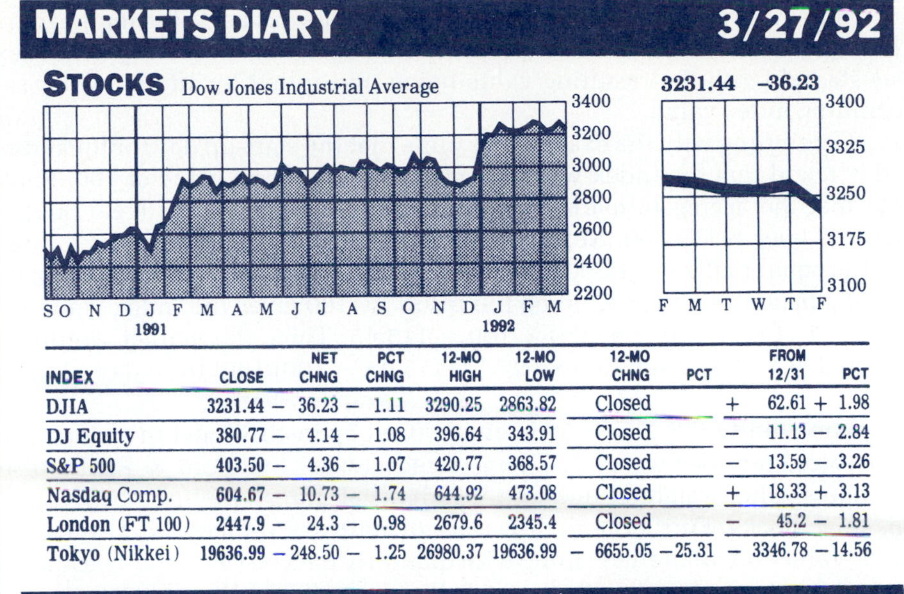

INDEX	CLOSE	NET CHNG	PCT CHNG	12-MO HIGH	12-MO LOW	12-MO CHNG	PCT	FROM 12/31	PCT
DJIA	3231.44	– 36.23	– 1.11	3290.25	2863.82	Closed		+ 62.61	+ 1.98
DJ Equity	380.77	– 4.14	– 1.08	396.64	343.91	Closed		– 11.13	– 2.84
S&P 500	403.50	– 4.36	– 1.07	420.77	368.57	Closed		– 13.59	– 3.26
Nasdaq Comp.	604.67	– 10.73	– 1.74	644.92	473.08	Closed		+ 18.33	+ 3.13
London (FT 100)	2447.9	– 24.3	– 0.98	2679.6	2345.4	Closed		– 45.2	– 1.81
Tokyo (Nikkei)	19636.99	– 248.50	– 1.25	26980.37	19636.99	– 6655.05	– 25.31	– 3346.78	– 14.56

STOCK MARKET DATA BANK 3/27/92

MAJOR INDEXES

HIGH	LOW (†365 DAY)		CLOSE	NET CHG	% CHG	†365 DAY CHG	% CHG	FROM 12/31	% CHG
DOW JONES AVERAGES									
3290.25	2863.82	30 Industrials	3231.44	– 36.23	– 1.11	Closed	....	+ 62.61	+ 1.98
1467.68	1101.55	20 Transportation	1379.67	– 12.33	– 0.89	Closed	....	+ 21.67	+ 1.60
226.15	195.17	15 Utilities	203.24	– 0.69	– 0.34	Closed	....	– 22.91	– 10.13
1192.83	1023.95	65 Composite	1158.20	– 11.04	– 0.94	Closed	....	+ 1.38	+ 0.12
396.64	343.91	Equity Mkt. Index	380.77	– 4.14	– 1.08	Closed	....	– 11.13	– 2.84
NEW YORK STOCK EXCHANGE									
231.84	202.10	Composite	223.31	– 2.18	– 0.97	Closed	....	– 6.13	– 2.67
290.02	253.72	Industrials	279.94	– 2.92	– 1.03	Closed	....	– 5.88	– 2.06
102.27	87.76	Utilities	93.27	– 0.72	– 0.77	Closed	....	– 8.86	– 8.68
212.02	162.80	Transportation	200.38	– 1.92	– 0.95	Closed	....	– 1.49	– 0.74
177.72	147.12	Finance	172.59	– 1.39	– 0.80	Closed	....	– 0.09	– 0.05
STANDARD & POOR'S INDEXES									
420.77	368.57	500 Index	403.50	– 4.36	– 1.07	Closed	....	– 13.59	– 3.26
499.27	438.51	Industrials	480.33	– 5.22	– 1.08	Closed	....	– 12.39	– 2.51
362.50	263.44	Transportation	341.12	– 2.66	– 0.77	Closed	....	– 0.34	– 0.10
155.70	133.52	Utilities	137.72	– 1.24	– 0.89	Closed	....	– 17.44	– 11.24
35.14	28.77	Financials	34.08	– 0.45	– 1.30	Closed	....	– 0.02	– 0.06
154.74	119.18	400 MidCap	145.58	– 1.70	– 1.15	Closed	....	– 1.01	– 0.69
NASDAQ									
644.92	473.08	Composite	604.67	– 10.73	– 1.74	Closed	....	+ 18.33	+ 3.13
741.92	523.54	Industrials	679.11	– 15.56	– 2.24	Closed	....	+ 10.16	+ 1.52
632.09	522.07	Insurance	611.33	– 4.16	– 0.68	Closed	....	+ 10.24	+ 1.70
396.93	309.34	Banks	393.90	+ 0.66	+ 0.17	Closed	....	+ 43.34	+ 12.36
285.08	208.31	Nat. Mkt. Comp.	266.81	– 4.84	– 1.78	Closed	....	+ 7.07	+ 2.72
296.32	207.84	Nat. Mkt. Indus.	270.77	– 6.33	– 2.28	Closed	....	+ 2.98	+ 1.11
OTHERS									
418.99	356.79	Amex	394.36	– 4.50	– 1.13	Closed	....	– 0.69	– 0.17
266.85	228.21	Value-Line (geom.)	257.39	– 2.64	– 1.02	Closed	....	+ 8.05	+ 3.23
212.61	167.00	Russell 2000	203.84	– 2.40	– 1.16	Closed	....	+ 13.91	+ 7.32
4121.28	3529.97	Wilshire 5000	3963.95	– 44.67	– 1.11	Closed	....	– 77.16	– 1.91

†-Based on comparable trading day in preceding year.

value-weighted market index

quarterly dividends and earnings figures, are published from time to time in *Barron's* and other periodicals.[7]

A second weighting method is known as **value weighting** or capitalization weighting. With this method, the prices of the stocks in the index are multiplied by their respective number of shares outstanding and then added up in order to arrive at a figure equal to the aggregate market value for that day. This figure is then divided by the corresponding figure for the day the index was started, with the resulting value being multiplied by an arbitrarily set beginning index value.

Continuing with the example, assume that the start-up day for the index is day t, and that the index will be assigned a beginning value of 100. First, note that the aggregate market value on day t is equal to (\$10 × 1,500) + (\$20 × 2,000) = \$55,000. Next, note that the aggregate market value on day $t + 1$ is equal to (\$13 × 1,500) + (\$11 × 4,000) = \$63,500. Dividing \$63,500 by \$55,000 and then multiplying the result by 100 gives the index value for day $t + 1$ of (\$63,500/\$55,000) × 100 = 115.45. Thus, the market would be reported as having risen by 15.45% [=(115.45 − 100)/100] from day t to day $t + 1$.

The *Standard & Poor's 500,* widely used by institutional investors, is a value-weighted average of 500 large-sized stocks. Standard & Poor's also computes value-weighted indices for industrial, transportation, utility, and financial stocks. Furthermore, a variety of industry indices are also calculated. Values for all indices, along with quarterly data on dividends, earnings, and sales, may be found in Standard & Poor's *Analysts' Handbook* (annual), *Trade and Securities Statistics* (annual), and *Analysts' Handbook Supplement* (monthly).

More comprehensive value-weighted indices for U.S. stocks are computed by other organizations. The New York Stock Exchange publishes a composite index of all stocks listed on that exchange, as well as four subindices (industrials, utilities, transportation, and finance). The American Stock Exchange computes an index of its stocks. The National Association of Securities Dealers (NASD), using its automated quotation service (NASDAQ), computes indices based on the market value of approximately 5,000 over-the-counter stocks; in addition to a composite index, NASD calculates indices for six categories representing industrials, banks, insurance, other finance, transportation, and utilities. NASD also publishes four indices that are based on just those stocks in their National Market System (the previously mentioned NASD indices are based on both NMS and non-NMS stocks). The broadest value-weighted index is calculated by Wilshire Associates. Their index, known as the *Wilshire 5000 Equity Index,* is based on all stocks listed on the New York and American Stock Exchanges plus those "actively traded over-the-counter."[8] Levels of all these indices are published weekly in *Barron's*, with *The Wall Street Journal* providing daily values for several of them.

---

[7]Some bond market indices are calculated in this manner. For example, the *Dow Jones 20-Bond Index* is computed by averaging the prices of ten utility and ten industrial bonds. Bond indices using different procedures are published by Merrill Lynch, Salomon Brothers, Shearson Lehman Brothers, Standard & Poor's, and others. See Chapter 22 (Figure 22-5, for example) for more on bond indices.

[8]The *Russell 1000, 2000, and 3000* are also broad value-weighted indices, covering roughly the largest 1,000 stocks; the next 2,000; and the sum of the two. In terms of international indices, *Morgan Stanley Capital International Perspective* publishes value-weighted indices using various combinations of over 1,000 stocks from many different countries, resulting in a "world market index." These, and other international indices, are discussed in Chapter 26 (see Figure 26-2).

equal-weighted market index

The third method of weighting is known as **equal weighting.** With this method equal dollar-size investments are made in the securities in the index. In the case of A and B, on day t the equal-weighted index would involve one share of A and ½ share of B, resulting in a value of $[10 \times 1] + [20 \times (1/2)] = 20$. On day $t + 1$, the index would adjust for the split of B by multiplying its price by 1 (instead of ½, as was previously done), resulting in an index value of $[13 \times 1] + [11 \times 1] = 24$, an increase of 20% $[=(24 - 20)/20]$. An example is the index calculated by the *Indicator Digest*, involving common stocks listed on the New York Stock Exchange.

price relatives

One popular index that does not involve price weighting, value weighting, or equal weighting is the *Value Line Composite Average*. This index is computed daily by multiplying the previous day's index by the geometric mean of the daily **price relatives** (today's price divided by yesterday's price) of the relevant stocks in the index.[9] For example, the value of the index consisting of A and B on day $t + 1$ would be calculated by first determining the price relatives to be equal to $(13/10) = 1.3$ for A and $(11 \times 2)/20 = 1.1$ for B. Then the geometric mean would be calculated as:

$$[1.3 \times 1.1]^{1/2} = 1.1958.$$

If the value of the index on day t was 120, then the value on day $t + 1$ would be reported as $120 \times 1.1958 = 143.496$, an increase of $1.1958 - 1 = 19.58\%$. In the case of the Value Line index, the initial value was set at 100 on June 30, 1961, and has been updated ever since then in this manner.[10]

In summary, four types of indices have been presented; various people use these indices when they refer to how "the market" has done. However, the indices can give notably different answers. In the example shown here, the market was calculated to have risen by either 16.67%, 15.45%, 20%, or 19.58%, depending on the index used. In practice, most professional money managers investing in NYSE-listed stocks use the S&P 500 as the barometer of the stock market since it is fairly widely based and weights larger companies more heavily than smaller companies.

Conveying Advice on Beating the Market It is interesting to ponder whether or not advice on how to beat the market will remain useful after becoming public. It seems logical that any such prescription that has been in print for long is not likely to allow the investor to continue to "beat the market" without fail. Just because someone asserts that an approach has worked in the past does not mean that it, in fact, has worked. Moreover, even if it did work in the past, as more and more investors apply it, prices will be driven to levels at which the approach will not work in the future. Any system designed to beat the market, once known to more than a few people, carries the seeds of its own destruction.

There are two reasons for not including advice on "guaranteed" ways to beat the market in this book. First, to do so would make a successful system public and hence unsuccessful. Second, the authors know of no such system. Some apparent anomalies and possible inefficiencies have been described

---

[9]In order to determine the geometric mean for N stocks, multiply their price relatives and then take the Nth root of the resulting product.

[10]Value Line also publishes a composite index based on the arithmetic mean [which in this example equals $1.2 = (1.3 + 1.1)/2$] in place of the geometric mean. Value Line also has indices for industrials, rails, and utilities that are similarly computed and updated.

previously. But any book that purports to open the door to the *certainty* of making abnormally high returns for those who follow its advice should be regarded with the greatest skepticism.

This does not mean that financial analysis is useless. While individuals should be skeptical when others tell them how to use financial analysis to beat the market, individuals can try to understand the market with the use of financial analysis.

Financial Analysis and Market Efficiency

The concept of an efficient market (discussed in Chapter 4) may appear to be based on a paradox. Financial analysts carefully analyze the prospects for companies, industries, and the economy in the search for mispriced securities. If, say, an undervalued security is found, then it will be purchased. However, the act of purchasing the security will tend to push its price upward toward its intrinsic value, thereby making it no longer undervalued. That is, financial analysis tends to result in security prices that reflect intrinsic values, which is equivalent to saying that financial analysis tends to make markets efficient. But if this is the case, why would anyone perform financial analysis in an attempt to identify mispriced securities?

There are two responses to this question. First, there are costs associated with performing financial analysis. This means that financial analysis may not be conducted on all securities all the time. As a result, the prices of all securities will not reflect intrinsic values all the time. Pockets of opportunity may arise from time to time, thereby opening the possibility for added benefits from financial analysis. This suggests that people should engage in financial analysis only to the point at which the added benefits cover the added costs.[11] Ultimately, in a highly competitive market, prices would be close enough to intrinsic values to make it worthwhile for only the most skillful analysts to search for mispriced securities. Thus, the market would be nearly, but not perfectly, efficient.[12]

The other response to the question focuses on the first reason given earlier for engaging in financial analysis: to determine certain characteristics of securities. This reason is appropriate even in a perfectly efficient market. Since investors differ in their circumstances (consider the person in the oil business, discussed earlier), portfolios should be tailored to accommodate such differences. Successful performance of this task generally requires estimation of certain characteristics of securities, thereby justifying the use of financial analysis.

Needed Skills

To understand and estimate the risk and return of individual securities as well as groups of securities (such as industries), financial markets and the princi-

[11]If the added benefits exceeded the added costs, then it would be profitable to perform more financial analysis, because the incremental benefits from doing so would cover the associated costs. If, on the other hand, the added costs exceeded the added benefits, then it would be profitable to cut back on the amount of financial analysis, because costs would be reduced by an amount greater than benefits.

[12]For an interesting argument on why the existence of trading costs results in some investors performing financial analysis in an efficient market, see Bradford Cornell and Richard Roll, "Strategies for Pairwise Competitions in Markets and Organizations," *Bell Journal of Economics*, 12, no. 1 (Spring 1981): 201–13.

ples of valuation must be understood. Much of the material required for such an understanding can be found in this book. But, as Figure 14-1 indicates, even more is required. Future prospects must be estimated and interrelationships assessed. This requires the skills of an economist and an understanding of industrial organization. To process relevant historical data, some command of quantitative methods is needed, along with an understanding of the nuances of accounting.

This book cannot provide all the material one needs to become a successful financial analyst. Books on accounting, economics, industrial organization, and quantitative methods are required. Instead, some techniques used by financial analysts will be discussed, along with some of the pitfalls involved. In addition, sources of investment information will be presented.

EVALUATING INVESTMENT SYSTEMS

Many statements have been made in the past asserting that some mechanical investment system, using only available historical data and a set of objective analytical procedures, can provide results superior to those obtained with a passive investment system. (A **passive investment system** involves simply buying and holding a well-diversified portfolio of stocks over a performance evaluation period; the return on a market index is often used to estimate the return on such a portfolio.) Some mechanical systems simply provide predictions of how "the market" will behave; others prescribe a complete set of instructions for investing in individual securities. Almost all of them present impressive statistics based on tests using data from some past evaluation period.

passive investment system

Consider as examples the following four statements:

1. ". . . switch from bonds to stocks after the growth rate of the money supply has risen for two months; switch from stocks to bonds after the growth rate of the money supply has been below its most recent peak for 15 months. Historically, such a policy would have produced over twice the return obtained by simply holding stocks."
2. ". . . this simple formula predicted over 95% of the quarterly variation in Standard & Poor's 500-stock index over the period studied."
3. ". . . A portfolio of the 25 stocks with the greatest historical relative strength would have outperformed a portfolio of the 25 stocks with the smallest relative strength in 8 months out of 12."
4. ". . . This completely objective stock selection procedure, which can be performed without error on a microcomputer, would have outperformed 80% of the professionally managed portfolios during the period in question."

Statements such as these four have been made in the past and will undoubtedly continue to be made in the future. Advocates of such mechanical investment systems may sincerely believe they have found the path to instant affluence. However, their proofs often rest on shaky ground. When evaluating any system, it is imperative that several possible errors be avoided.

Failure to Adjust for Risk

According to the Capital Asset Pricing Model, any investment system that results in the selection of high-beta stocks is likely to produce above-average returns in bull markets and below-average returns in bear markets. Since the stock market over the long term has trended upward, on balance such a system will tend to produce above-average returns over the long run. Therefore, an evaluation of the performance of any investment system should involve not only measuring the resulting average return but also determining the amount of risk incurred. Then the average return from a passive investment system of similar risk can be computed for comparison. Techniques for making such comparisons will be presented in Chapter 18.

Failure to Consider Transaction Costs

Systems that rely on constant trading may produce *gross* returns that exceed those of a passive investment strategy of comparable risk. But this is not an accurate evaluation of a system's performance, because transaction costs should be considered in measuring returns. *Net* returns are calculated by adding transaction costs to the purchase price of an investment, and deducting them from the investment's selling price.

For example, if 100 shares of a stock are purchased at \$19 per share with a transaction cost of \$100, then the cost of the investment is $(100 \times \$19) + \$100 = \$2{,}000$. If the stock is subsequently sold for \$23 per share, with another \$100 transaction cost, then the proceeds from the sale are $(100 \times \$23) - \$100 = \$2{,}200$. As a result, the net return is $(\$2{,}200 - \$2{,}000)/\$2{,}000 = 10\%$, while the gross return is $(\$2{,}300 - \$1{,}900)/\$1{,}900 = 21.05\%$, a substantial difference.

Failure to Consider Dividends

When the performance of a mechanical system is compared with that of a passive investment system, dividends (and interest payments) are often ignored. This may seriously bias the results. For example, a system may be advocated that, in effect, selects low-yield stocks. The prices of such stocks should increase at a faster rate than those of high-yield stocks with the same amount of risk. This is because a stock's return consists of both dividends and capital appreciation. If two stocks have the same risk, they should have the same return, meaning that the stock with a smaller yield will have a larger capital appreciation. Thus, if just capital appreciation is examined, a system that selects low-yield stocks would tend to show a more rapid rate of capital appreciation than a passive investment strategy involving a well-diversified portfolio consisting of both low- and high-yield stocks. Consequently, when yields of systems differ significantly from average yields, it is important to examine total returns, not just the rate of capital appreciation.

Nonoperational Systems

Although obvious, it still must be mentioned: to be useful, a system must not require information about the future. For example, many systems require action after some time series of values (such as a stock's price) has reached a "peak" or "trough." But it is rarely apparent until well afterwards that in fact a peak or trough has been reached. Hence, such a system is nonoperational.

A similar situation arises when an equation is estimated from a set of data. For example, a system might assume that there is a relationship between the money supply at time $t - 1$ and stock prices at time t. The general relationship might be:

$$\overline{SP}_t = a + bM_{t-1} \tag{14.2}$$

where $\overline{SP}_t$ is the predicted level of the S&P 500 at time t, M_{t-1} is the level of the money supply at time $t - 1$, and a and b are constants. In this system, the level of the S&P 500 one period from now can be predicted from the current level of the money supply.

To make such a system operational, specific numerical values for a and b are needed. These numbers might be estimated by examining monthly data over a ten-year period from 1982 through 1991, which means that these numbers would only be known after 1991. However, some people might test the predictive ability of the equation over the same ten-year period of 1982 to 1991 using these numbers. In doing so, they fail to realize that the system would not have been operational with these numbers for this test period, since the numbers were determined after the test period. A true test of the predictive ability of this or any system must involve an estimation period that is earlier than the test period. That is, the test period must use out-of-sample data, as will be discussed shortly.

Spurious Fits

Using a set of data from a past period, it is not too difficult to discover a system that works quite well when tested on the same data. In spite of the previously mentioned criticism that such a system would not have been operational during the test period, some investors might still be tempted to use it in the future if it worked well enough in retrospect. However, there is another criticism that can be made about such a system.

Imagine that equation (14.2) did not appear to work well. If so, then the following equation could be tried:

$$\overline{SP}_t = a + bM_{t-1} + cM_{t-2} \tag{14.3}$$

where M_{t-2} is the level of the money supply at time $t - 2$ and c is a constant. If equation (14.3) does not seem to work well, more variables and constants could be tried. Ultimately an equation could be found that appears to work quite well. However, this does not mean that it would be useful to the investor. If 100 seemingly irrelevant systems are tried with a set of data, due to the laws of probability one of them is likely to give results that are "statistically significant at the 1% level." This should not cause undue excitement, since it would not have any notable predictive power in the future.

For example, stock prices in the United States have been shown to be correlated with both sunspot activity and with the length of skirts. Few would associate causal relationships in these instances. Instead, these correlations are likely to have been "spurious," meaning that they probably were coincidental. Without solid reasons to believe that a relationship is due to underlying forces, it would be unwise to predict its continuation in the future.

Comparisons with Easily Beaten Systems

Often an investment system is said to "explain" a large part of the variation in some stock index. Figure 14-3 shows the quarterly level of the S&P 500 over a

FIGURE 14-3
Actual and Predicted Levels, Standard & Poor's 500-Stock Index, Second Quarter 1960 Through Fourth Quarter 1969

Source: Kenneth E. Homa and Dwight M. Jaffee, "The Supply of Money and Common Stock Prices," *Journal of Finance*, 26, no. 5 (December 1971): 1052.

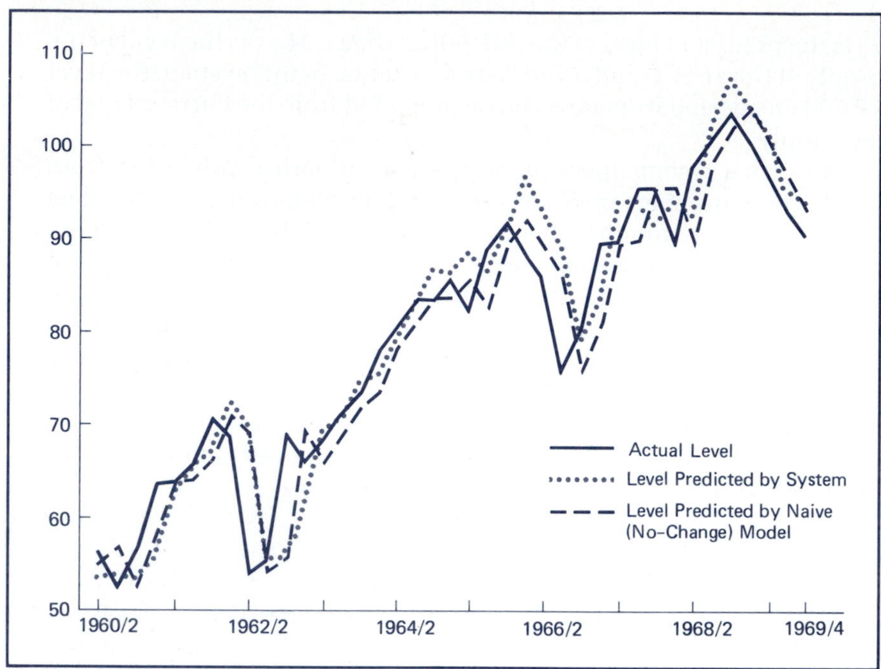

ten-year period (the solid curve), and the levels predicted by a system based on historic levels of the money supply (the dotted curve). The two sets of values appear to be quite similar.

Impressive? Not very. An extremely simple set of predictions, shown by the dashed curve in Figure 14-3, is even better. This procedure predicts that each quarter's index will equal that of the preceding quarter:

$$\overline{SP}_t = SP_{t-1}. \tag{14.4}$$

Any system that is purported to be able to beat the market must predict percentage price changes (or returns), not price levels, because such changes (or returns) determine profits and losses. Thus, a good test is the extent to which predicted changes conform to actual changes. Figure 14-4 shows the percentage price change predicted by the system analyzed in Figure 14-3, along with the corresponding actual change for each quarter. The relationship is, at best, tenuous.

Reliance on Misleading Visual Comparisons

Occasionally the proponent of a system will produce a graph that plots both the level of an indicator intended to predict market moves and the levels of the market itself. Visual comparison of the two curves may suggest that the indicator does indeed predict changes in the market. However, the eye cannot

FIGURE 14-4
Predicted and Actual Quarterly Percentage Changes, Standard & Poor's 500-Stock Index, Second Quarter 1960 Through Fourth Quarter 1969

Source: Kenneth E. Homa and Dwight M. Jaffe, "The Supply of Money and Common Stock Prices," *Journal of Finance*, 26, no. 5 (December 1971): 1052.

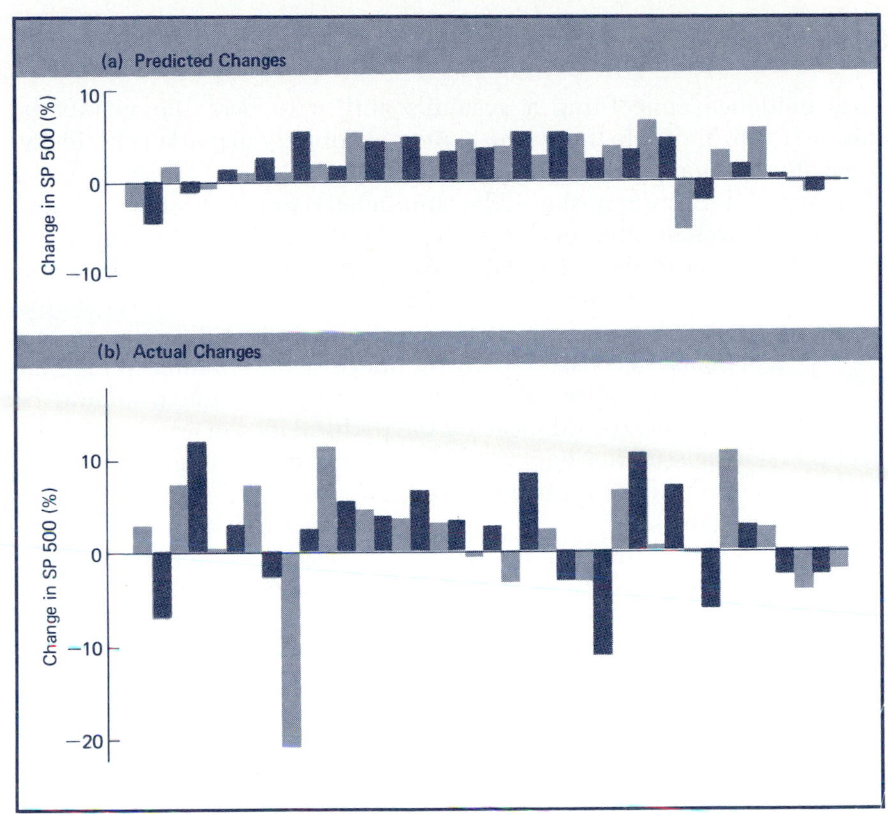

easily differentiate between a situation in which changes in a market "predictor" *lead* the market and one in which the changes *lag* behind the market. This is a crucial distinction because only a leading indicator can bring superior investment performance.

Ex Post Selection Bias

Many studies describe a stock selection system that outperformed standard stock market indices. Some of these systems avoid the errors considered thus far, but another error may be involved. To facilitate computer-based analysis, a standard set of data might have been employed. For example, an investigator might use a database prepared in 1992 with stock price data relating to the period from 1981 through 1991. The stocks included in the database may have been chosen because they existed and were important in 1992 (for example, they may have been considered important because they were listed on the NYSE in 1992). Discovering a superior investment system from analysis of this database is subject to the criticism of **ex post selection bias** (or survivor-

ex post selection bias

ship bias). That is, the system discovered in 1992 was based on an analysis of those stocks that were certain to be alive, well, and important in 1992. Accordingly, it should have done well over the period of 1981 to 1992. However, studies of this type implicitly commit an error described earlier—they require some information not available in advance. In particular, they require knowledge before 1992 of which stocks will be around in 1992.

Failure to Use Out-of-Sample Data

Can any evidence concerning a system's ability to beat the market be persuasive? Probably not to those who believe absolutely in market efficiency. But there are appropriate tests that can be undertaken.

out-of-sample data

The search for a system should be conducted using one set of data, and the test of the system's predictive ability should be performed using an entirely different set of data. The latter set of data is sometimes known as **out-of-sample data** or a holdout sample. To be complete, such a test should involve the (simulated) management of a portfolio and be designed so that each investment decision is based solely on information available at the time the decision is made. Finally, the performance of the system should be measured in the way one would measure the performance of any investment manager (to be discussed in Chapter 18). This involves, among other things, attempting to determine the probability that the investment results were due to chance rather than skill.

Figure 14-5 shows the performance of one system using out-of-sample data. Values forecast by three predictive systems for quarterly percentage changes in the S&P 500 are shown, along with the subsequent actual changes. Each of the predictive systems worked extremely well with past data. The same cannot be said for their predictions using out-of-sample data. The next section describes one system in more detail.

FUNDAMENTAL VERSUS TECHNICAL ANALYSIS

technical analysis

One of the major divisions in the ranks of financial analysts is between those using fundamental analysis (known as fundamental analysts or fundamentalists) and those using **technical analysis** (known as technical analysts or technicians). The fundamentalist tends to look forward; the technician backward. The fundamentalist is concerned with such things as future earnings and dividends, while the technician thinks little (if at all) about such things.

> Technical analysis is the study of the internal stock exchange information as such. The word "technical" implies a study of the market itself and not of those external factors which are reflected in the market. . . . [A]ll the relevant factors, whatever they may be, can be reduced to the volume of the stock exchange transactions and the level of share prices; or more generally, to the sum of the statistical information produced by the market.[13]

[13]Felix Rosenfeld, ed., *The Evaluation of Ordinary Shares*, a summary of the proceedings of the Eighth Congress of the European Federation of Financial Analysts Societies (Paris: Dunod, 1975), p. 297.

FIGURE 14-5
Predicted and Actual Quarterly Percentage Changes, Standard & Poor's 500-Stock Index, Third Quarter 1970 Through Second Quarter 1972
Source: James E. Pesando, "The Supply of Money and Common Stock Prices: Further Observations on the Econometric Evidence," *Journal of Finance*, 29, no. 3 (June 1974): 916.

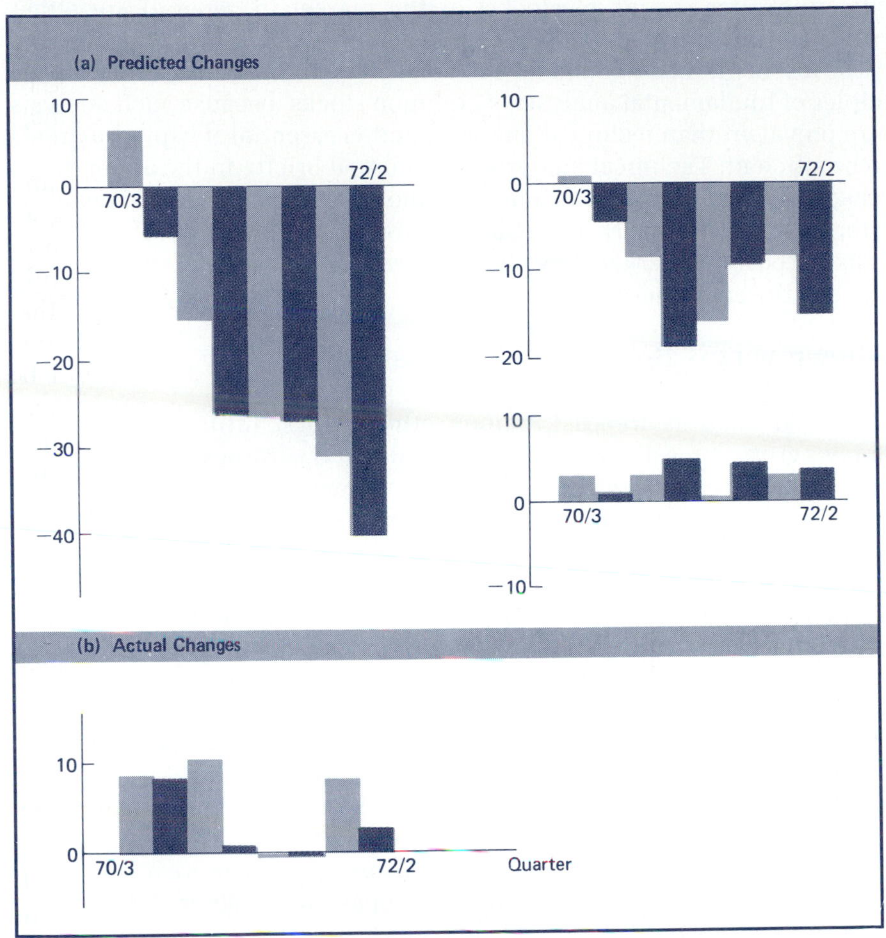

The technician usually attempts to predict short-term price movements and thus makes recommendations concerning the *timing* of purchases and sales of either specific stocks or groups of stocks (such as industries) or stocks in general. It is sometimes said that fundamental analysis is designed to answer the question "What?" and technical analysis to answer the question "When?"

The concept of technical analysis is completely at odds with the notion of efficient markets:

> . . . the methodology of technical analysis . . . rests upon the assumption that history tends to repeat itself in the stock exchange. If a certain pattern of activity

> has in the past produced certain results nine times out of ten, one can assume a strong likelihood of the same outcome whenever this pattern appears in the future. *It should be emphasized, however, that a large part of the methodology of technical analysis lacks a strictly logical explanation.*[14] [Italics added.]

Thus, technicians assert that the study of past patterns of things such as prices and volumes will allow the investor to accurately identify times when certain specific stocks (or groups of stocks, or the market in general) are either overpriced or underpriced.

The rest of this chapter and the next two chapters are concerned with the principles of fundamental analysis of common stocks, because such analysis is more prevalent than technical analysis, and is essential if capital markets are to be efficient. Technical analysis is discussed briefly in the appendix to this chapter, since there is little evidence showing it to be useful in enabling investors to "beat the market."[15] Many "proofs" of the ability of technical analysis to "beat the market" have been offered, but most have committed at least one of the errors described earlier.

Top-Down versus Bottom-Up Forecasting

Fundamental analysts forecast, among other things, future levels of the economy's gross domestic product, future sales and earnings for a number of industries, and future sales and earnings for an even larger number of firms. Eventually such forecasts are converted to estimates of expected returns of specific stocks and, perhaps, certain industries and the stock market itself. In some cases the conversion is made explicitly. For example, an estimate of next year's earnings per share for a firm may be multiplied by a projected price-earnings ratio in order to estimate the expected price of the firm's stock a year hence, thereby allowing a forecast of the expected return to be made. In other cases the conversion is implicit. For example, stocks with projected earnings exceeding consensus estimates may be placed on an "approved" list.

top-down forecasting

Some investment organizations that employ financial analysts follow a sequential **top-down** approach to forecasting. With this approach, the financial analysts are first involved in making forecasts for the economy, then for industries, and finally for companies. The industry forecasts are based on the forecasts for the economy and, in turn, the company forecasts are based on the forecasts for both its industry and the economy.

bottom-up forecasting

Other investment organizations begin with estimates of the prospects for companies and then build to estimates of the prospects for industries and ultimately the economy. Such a **bottom-up** approach may unknowingly involve inconsistent assumptions. For example, one analyst may use one forecast of foreign exchange rates in projecting the foreign sales of company A, while another analyst may use a different forecast in projecting the foreign sales of company B. Top-down systems are less susceptible to this danger, since all the analysts in the organization would use the same forecast of exchange rates.

In practice, a combination of the two approaches is often employed. For example, forecasts are made for the economy in a top-down manner. These

---

[14]Rosenfeld, *The Evaluation of Ordinary Shares*, pp. 297–98.

[15]See, for example, Robert A. Levy, "The Predictive Significance of Five-Point Chart Patterns," *Journal of Business*, 44, no. 3 (July 1971): 316–23; and Eugene F. Fama, "Efficient Capital Markets: A Review of Theory and Empirical Work," *Journal of Finance*, 25, no. 2 (May 1970): 383–417.

forecasts then provide a setting within which financial analysts make bottom-up forecasts for individual companies. The sum of the individual forecasts should be consistent with the original economywide forecast.[16] If not, the process is repeated (perhaps with additional controls) to ensure consistency.

Probabilistic Forecasting

probabilistic forecasting

Explicit **probabilistic forecasting** often focuses on economywide forecasts, since uncertainty at this level is of the greatest importance in determining the risk and expected return of a well-diversified portfolio. A few alternative economic scenarios may be forecast, along with their respective probability of occurrence. Then accompanying projections are made of the prospects for industries, companies, and stock prices. Such an exercise provides an idea of the likely sensitivities of different stocks to surprises concerning the economy and hence is sometimes referred to as "what-if" analysis. By assigning probabilities to the different scenarios, risks may also be estimated.

Econometric Models

econometric model
endogenous variables
exogenous variables

An **econometric model** is a statistical model that provides a means of forecasting the levels of certain variables, known as **endogenous variables.** In order to make these forecasts, the model relies on assumptions that have been made in regard to the levels of certain other variables, known as **exogenous variables.** The model may be extremely complex or it may be a simple formula that can be used with a calculator. In any event, it should involve a blend of economics and statistics, where economics is used to suggest the forms of relevant relationships and statistical procedures are applied to historical data to estimate the exact nature of the relationships involved.

Some investment organizations use large-scale econometric models to translate predictions about such factors as the federal budget, expected consumer spending, and planned business investment into predictions of future levels of gross domestic product, inflation, and unemployment. Several firms and nonprofit organizations maintain such models, selling either the forecasts or the computer program itself to investment organizations, corporate planners, public agencies, and others.

The developers of such large-scale models usually provide several "standard" predictions, based on different sets of assumptions about the exogenous variables; some also assign probabilities to the alternative predictions. In some cases, users can substitute their own set of assumptions and subsequently examine the resulting predictions.

Large-scale econometric models of this type employ many equations that describe many important relationships. While estimates of the magnitudes of such relationships are obtained from historical data, these estimates may or may not enable the model to work well in the future. When predictions turn out to be poor, it is sometimes said that there has been a structural change in the underlying economic relationships. However, the failure may result from the influence of factors omitted from the model. In any event, such a

---

[16]Input-output analysis is sometimes used to ensure consistency between various industries and the economy in aggregate. This type of analysis is based on the notion that the output of certain industries (for example, the steel industry) is the input for certain other industries (for example, the household appliance industry).

situation necessitates changes in either the size of the estimates or the basic form of the econometric model, or even both. Rare indeed is the user who does not "fine-tune" (or completely overhaul) such a model from time to time as further experience is accumulated.

Financial Statement Analysis

For some, the image of a typical financial analyst is that of a gnome, fully equipped with green eyeshade, poring over financial statements in a back room. While the physical description is rarely accurate, it is true that many analysts do study financial statements in an attempt to predict the future.

A company's financial statements can be regarded as the output of a model of the firm—a model designed by management, the company's accountants, and (indirectly) the tax authorities. Different companies use different models, meaning that they treat similar events in different ways. One reason this is possible is because generally accepted accounting principles (GAAP), as established by the Financial Accounting Standards Board (FASB), allow a certain degree of latitude in how to account for various events. Examples include the method of depreciating assets (straight line or accelerated) and the method of valuing inventory (FIFO or LIFO).

To fully understand a company and to compare it with others that use different accounting procedures, the financial analyst must be a financial detective, looking for clues in footnotes and the accompanying text that discuss how the financial statements were prepared. Those who take bottom-line figures such as earnings per share on faith may be more surprised by future developments than those who try to look behind the accounting veil.

The ultimate goal of the fundamental analyst is to determine the values of the outstanding claims on a firm's income (claimants include the firm's bondholders and stockholders). The firm's income must first be projected, then the possible distributions of that income among the claimants must be considered, with relevant probabilities assessed.

In practice, shortcut procedures are often used. Many analysts focus on reported accounting figures, even though such numbers may not adequately reflect true economic values. In addition, simple measures are often used to assess complex relationships. For example, some analysts attempt to estimate the probability that short-term creditors will be paid in full and on time by examining the ratio of liquid assets to the amount of short-term debt. Similarly, the probability that interest will be paid to bondholders in a timely fashion is often estimated by examining the ratio of earnings before interest and taxes to the periodic amount of such interest payments. Often the prospects for a firm's common stock are estimated by examining the ratio of earnings after taxes to the book value of equity.

Ratio Analysis The use of ratios such as these to facilitate predicting the future is widespread. Some ratios use items from the same financial statement (either a particular balance sheet or income statement), while others use items from two different statements. Still other ratios use items from two or more statements of the same type but of different years (for example, this year's balance sheet and last year's balance sheet), or incorporate data on market values.

Ratios may be used in several ways. Some analysts apply absolute standards, on the grounds that a substandard ratio indicates a potential weakness that merits further analysis. Other analysts compare a company's ratios to those of the "average" firm in the same industry in order to detect differences that may need further consideration. Yet others analyze trends in a company's ratios over time, hoping that it will help them predict future changes. Still others combine ratios with technical analysis in order to arrive at investment decisions.

One example of how ratios can be used for investing involves the use of price-earnings (P/E) ratios. This method is based on a belief that stocks with low P/E ratios are out of favor in the investment community.[17] Accordingly, this version of a contrarian investment strategy involves simply finding low P/E stocks and then investing in them (another type of contrarian investment strategy will be discussed shortly). Stocks with high P/E ratios would be shunned with this strategy, since they would generally represent stocks that are viewed favorably in the investment community. Since small firms typically have had higher returns than large firms, even after adjusting for differences in risk, and given that small firms typically have had low P/E ratios, it is not surprising that such a strategy has been successful in the past.[18] Whether the success will continue in the future is another matter.

Another use of ratios is illustrated in Figure 14-6. In this figure, each ratio is equal to the product of the two ratios on its right-hand side, with one exception. The exception is the turnover ratio (sales/assets), whose reciprocal (assets/sales) equals the sum of the reciprocals of the four ratios on its right-hand side. Given the interrelationships among the ratios, it can be seen that once the future values of these ratios are forecasted, then an implied forecast for the price of the firm's stock can be computed. The difficulty with such an approach, however, is in accurately predicting the future values of the ratios.

Ratio analysis can be very sophisticated, but it can also be overly simplistic. Routine extrapolation of a present ratio (or its recent trend) may produce a poor estimate of its future value. (For example, there is no reason for a firm to maintain a constant ratio of inventory to sales.) Moreover, a series of simple projections may produce inconsistent financial statements. For example, projections of ratios imply predictions of the levels of various balance sheet items. However, it may be that when these levels are looked at altogether, the resulting balance sheet does not balance.

Spreadsheets To project future financial statements, one should build a model that includes the relationships among the items on such statements and outside factors. Traditional ratio analysis does this, but somewhat crudely. A much better procedure uses personal computers and spreadsheet software.[19]

Basically, a spreadsheet is an arrangement of information in rows and columns. Each cell on a traditional (paper) spreadsheet typically contains a number or a label. Some of the numbers (for example, sales) are entered directly, others (for example, earnings before interest and taxes) are computed from the numbers in other cells.

---

[17]David Dremen, *Contrarian Investment Strategy* (New York: Random House, Inc., 1979).

[18]The observation that small firms typically have had abnormally high returns is an empirical regularity known as the size effect. It was discussed in the appendix to Chapter 13.

[19]Lotus Development Corporation, Microsoft Corporation, and Borland International Corporation have been leading developers of such software. Their products, Lotus 1–2–3, Excel, and Quattro Pro, respectively, have been top-sellers.

FIGURE 14-6
The Use of Predicted Ratios to Compute Predicted Price
Source: Samuel S. Stewart, Jr., "Corporate Forecasting," in Sumner N. Levine, ed., *Financial Analyst's Handbook I* (Homewood, Ill.: Dow Jones-Irwin, Inc., 1975), p. 912.

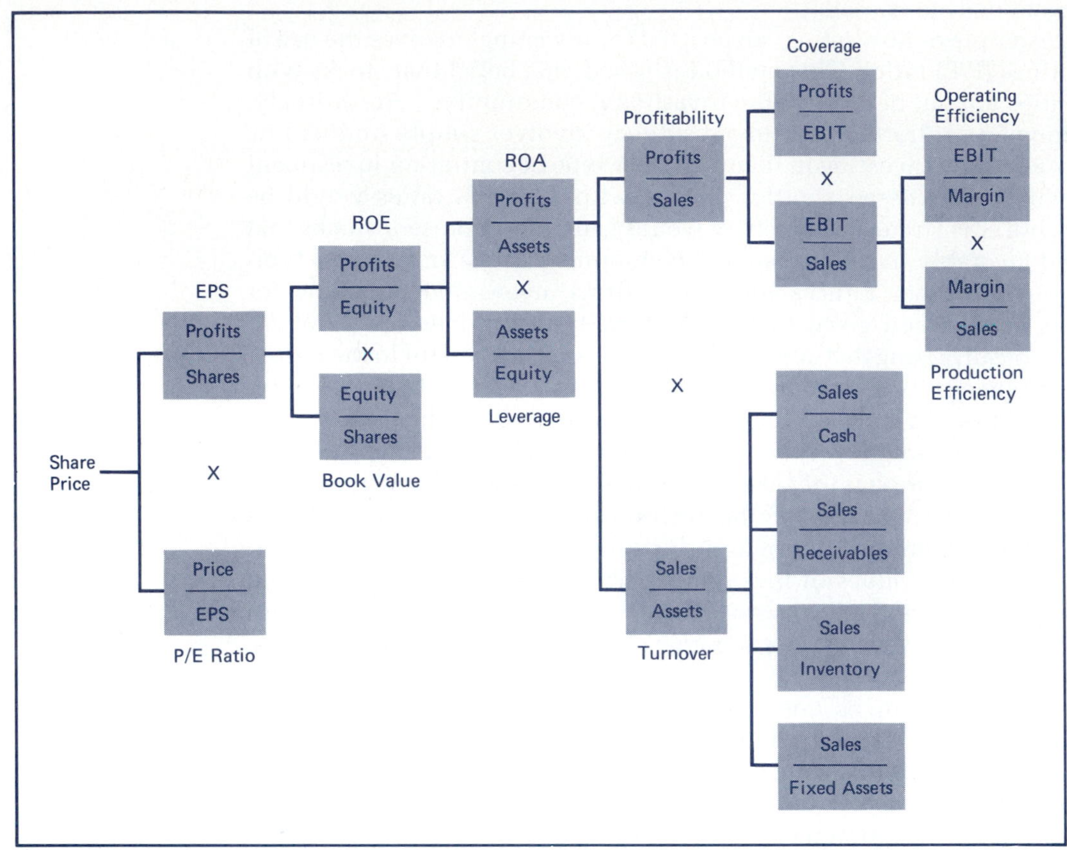

An electronic spreadsheet simulates a traditional spreadsheet on a computer screen. There are, however, notable differences. Most importantly, cells can contain formulas. For example, the cell for earnings before interest and taxes (EBIT) could contain the formula for calculating the value as well as the value produced by the formula. Normally, only the value would be displayed, giving an outward appearance similar to that of a traditional spreadsheet. However, any change in the number in the cell for sales would immediately change the value of EBIT, since the formula for EBIT would contain the value for sales as an input. This feature of electronic spreadsheets allows the user to rapidly explore the implications of changes in key assumptions (such as prices, quantities, and costs) on various balance sheet and income statement items. Accordingly, exploration of this sort is often known as sensitivity analysis or what-if analysis.

In summary, financial statement analysis can help an analyst understand what a company is, where it may be going, what factors affect it, and how these factors affect it. If others are doing such analysis and doing it well, it will be difficult to find mispriced securities in this manner. But it should be possible to more accurately identify firms likely to go bankrupt, firms with higher or lower betas, firms with greater or lesser sensitivities to major factors, and so forth. Increased understanding of such aspects may well provide ample reward for the effort entailed.

CONTRARIAN INVESTMENT STRATEGIES AND STOCK REVERSALS

contrarians

Investors who call themselves **contrarians** like to do the opposite of what most other investors are doing in the market. That is, they buy stocks that others have shunned and think of as losers. Furthermore, they sell stocks that others have feverishly pursued and think of as winners. They do so in the belief that investors tend to overreact to news. That is, stocks that have plunged in price because of some recent piece of bad news (such as recently announced weak earnings) are thought to have fallen too far in price. Hence, such stocks are viewed as being ready for a price rebound as investors realize that they have overreacted to the bad news associated with the stock and subsequently drive the price upward toward the stock's fundamental value.

Similarly, stocks that have been risen rapidly in price due to some recent piece of good news (such as recently announced strong earnings) are thought to have risen too far in price. Hence, such stocks are viewed as being ready for a price drop as investors realize that they have overreacted to the good news associated with the stock and subsequently drive the price downward toward the stock's fundamental value.

Consider the following contrarian strategy that is designed to capitalize on perceived overreactions in the marketplace.

1. Identify those stocks that have been listed on the NYSE over the past seven years (this focuses the contrarians' attention on established stocks).
2. Rank these stocks based on the size of their average monthly return over the past thirty-six months (the portfolio "formation period").
3. Buy those thirty-five stocks that have the lowest average return (the "loser" portfolio) and sell those thirty-five stocks that have the highest average return (the "winner" portfolio), since these stocks are likely to have been most subject to investor overreaction.
4. Hold this position for the next three years (the portfolio "test period") to benefit from the price reversals as investors correct for their overreactions.
5. Repeat the analysis all over again, starting with step 1.

Table 14-1 shows the investment results that this contrarian strategy would have earned over the period from 1933 to 1985. That is, starting in December 1932, only those stocks that had been listed from January 1926 through December 1932 were evaluated. Their average monthly returns from January 1930 through December 1932 were calculated and used to form the "winner" and "loser" portfolios. These two portfolios were then tracked from January 1933 through December 1935. At this point, the whole process was repeated, beginning with the identification of those stocks that had been listed from January 1929 through December 1935 and the formation of the associated winner and loser portfolios.

TABLE 14-1
Testing a Contrarian Investment Strategy

	LOSER PORTFOLIO	WINNER PORTFOLIO	DIFFERENCE
A. 3-year formation period, 3-year test period, 35 stocks per portfolio[a]	6.5%	−1.7%	8.2%
B. 5-year formation period, 5-year test period, 50 stocks per portfolio[b]	7.2%	−2.4%	9.6%

[a]Adapted from Werner F. M. De Bondt and Richard Thaler, "Does the Stock Market Overreact?" *Journal of Finance*, 40, no. 3 (July 1985): 799.

[b]Adapted from Werner F. M. De Bondt and Richard H. Thaler, "Further Evidence on Investor Overreaction and Stock Market Seasonality," *Journal of Finance*, 42, no. 3 (July 1987): 561.

The average annual abnormal (risk-adjusted) return over the period from January 1933 through December 1985 on the "loser" portfolio as shown in panel (A) is +6.5%. Conversely, the average abnormal return on the "winner" portfolio is −1.7%. Thus, there does appear to be some merit to the contrarian strategy. Note, however, that the correction for the overreaction is asymmetric. That is, the losers rebound by a much larger percentage than the winners fall.

Panel (B) indicates the performance when stocks are ranked based on their average return over the previous sixty months and then the winners and losers are held for the subsequent sixty months.[20] As the table shows, the average annual abnormal return for the losers was +7.2%, while the average for the winners was −2.4%. Again, this evidence supports the use of the contrarian strategy.[21]

This evidence should not be viewed as conclusive. Indeed, it is far from the last word on the usefulness of contrarian investment strategies. Other studies have approached this issue from different perspectives and have been unable to confirm the usefulness of such strategies.[22]

What is the bottom line? The usefulness of contrarian investment strategies remains an open question subject to much debate. If one method of analysis is used, they appear to be profitable, even after considering transaction costs. However, with another method, they appear to be incapable of generating abnormal profits. Hence, evaluating investment systems will not

[20]There are other subtle differences in how the portfolios in panels (A) and (B) were formed.

[21]Oddly, 5% of the 7.6% abnormal return for the losers was earned during the Januaries that occurred during the test period. Conversely, −.8% of the −2.4% abnormal return for the winners was earned during Januaries. See the appendix to Chapter 13 for a discussion of the January effect.

[22]Doubt is raised in four studies. In one, it is shown that a different method for estimating beta (which is needed to calculate abnormal returns) results in significantly lower returns for the loser portfolio. In another, it is shown that analysts neither underpredict earnings on losers nor overpredict earnings on winners. The third study shows that the size effect (discussed in the appendix to Chapter 13) is largely responsible for the results since losers tend to be smaller than winners. Lastly, incorrect prices were used when the costs of buying and selling stocks were determined in arriving at the results reflected in Table 14-1. See K. C. Chan, "On the Contrarian Investment Strategy," *Journal of Business*, 61, no. 2 (April 1988): 147–63, April Klein, "A Direct Test of the Cognitive Bias Theory of Share Price Reversals," *Journal of Accounting and Economics*, 13, no. 2 (July 1990): 155–66, Paul Zarowin, "Size, Seasonality, and Stock Market Overreaction," *Journal of Financial and Quantitative Analysis*, 25, no. 1 (March 1990): 113–25, and Jennifer Conrad and Gautam Kaul, "Long-Term Overreaction or Biases in Computed Returns?" unpublished paper, the University of Michigan, 1991, respectively.

always provide unambiguous answers on their potential usefulness.[23] In any event, it has been speculated that the commonplace usage of computerized trading programs designed to implement contrarian strategies will ultimately eliminate any potential such strategies have for generating abnormal profits.[24]

ANALYSTS' RECOMMENDATIONS AND STOCK PRICES

When a security analyst decides that a stock is mispriced and informs certain clients of this, some of the clients may act on the information. As they do so, the price of the security may be affected. As news of the analyst's recommendation spreads, more investors may act, and the price may react even more. At some point, the analyst's information will be "fully reflected" in the stock price.

If the analyst decides a stock is underpriced and clients subsequently purchase it, the stock's price will tend to rise. Conversely, if the analyst decides a stock is overpriced and clients subsequently sell it, the stock's price will tend to decline. If the analyst's views were well founded, no subsequent counterreaction in the stock's price would be expected. Otherwise, the price is likely to return to its prerecommendation level at some later time.

An interesting example of the impact of analysts' recommendations is provided by the behavior of prices of stocks mentioned in the "Heard on the Street" column of *The Wall Street Journal,* which periodically summarizes recent stock recommendations. An analyst's opinion is typically published in "Heard on the Street" after it is first given to clients. The analyst's view is thus "somewhat public" for several days before publication, but when the column appears the opinion becomes "very public," since it then reaches a substantially larger audience.

Panel (a) of Figure 14-7 summarizes the price reactions of about 597 stocks that received positive opinions in "Heard on the Street" during 1970 and 1971. Panel (b) summarizes the reactions of about 188 stocks that received negative opinions during the same time period. In each panel, the vertical axis plots the average cumulative abnormal return—that is, the average return, adjusted for normal reactions to overall market moves. The horizontal axes indicate trading days relative to the date of publication of the recommendation, going from twenty days before to twenty days after publication.

As shown in the two panels, the publication of such a recommendation typically affects the stock's price.[25] After adjusting for market moves, on the

---

[23]Confusing the issue even more is a study that involved weekly data. This contrarian strategy involved forming portfolios based on security returns in the previous week (buying losers and selling winners) and then holding the portfolio for one week, at which point it is revised. Apparently significant returns can be earned from this strategy if transaction costs are small (such as for large institutional investors). However, larger transaction costs result in negative net returns. See Bruce N. Lehmann, "Fads, Martingales, and Market Efficiency," *Quarterly Journal of Economics*, 105, no. 1 (February 1990): 1–28. For an argument that Lehmann has underestimated the size of transaction costs, see Jennifer Conrad, Mustafa N. Gultekin, and Gautam Kaul, "Profitability of Short-Term Contrarian Portfolio Strategies," unpublished paper, the University of Michigan, 1991.

[24]Lehmann, "Fads, Martingales, and Market Efficiency," 26.

[25]Similar observations have been made in regard to the recommendations made by major brokerage houses. See John C. Groth, Wilbur G. Lewellen, Gary G. Schlarbaum, and Ronald C. Lease, "An Analysis of Brokerage House Securities Recommendations," *Financial Analysts Journal*, 35, no. 1 (January/February 1979): 32–40, and James H. Bjerring, Josef Lakonishok, and Theo Vermaelen, "Stock Prices and Financial Analysts' Recommendations," *Journal of Finance*, 38, no. 1 (March 1983): 187–204. For a comment on the first study, see the Letter to the Editor in the May/June 1980 issue by Clinton M. Bidwell, with a responding Letter to the Editor in the July/August 1980 issue by Wilbur G. Lewellen. Also see the first footnote in Chapter 17.

FIGURE 14-7
Effect on Stock Prices of Stock Recommendations in "Heard on the Street": 1970 and 1971

Source: Peter Lloyd-Davies and Michael Canes, "Stock Prices and the Publication of Second-Hand Information," *Journal of Business*, 51, no. 1 (January 1978): 52. © 1978, The University of Chicago.

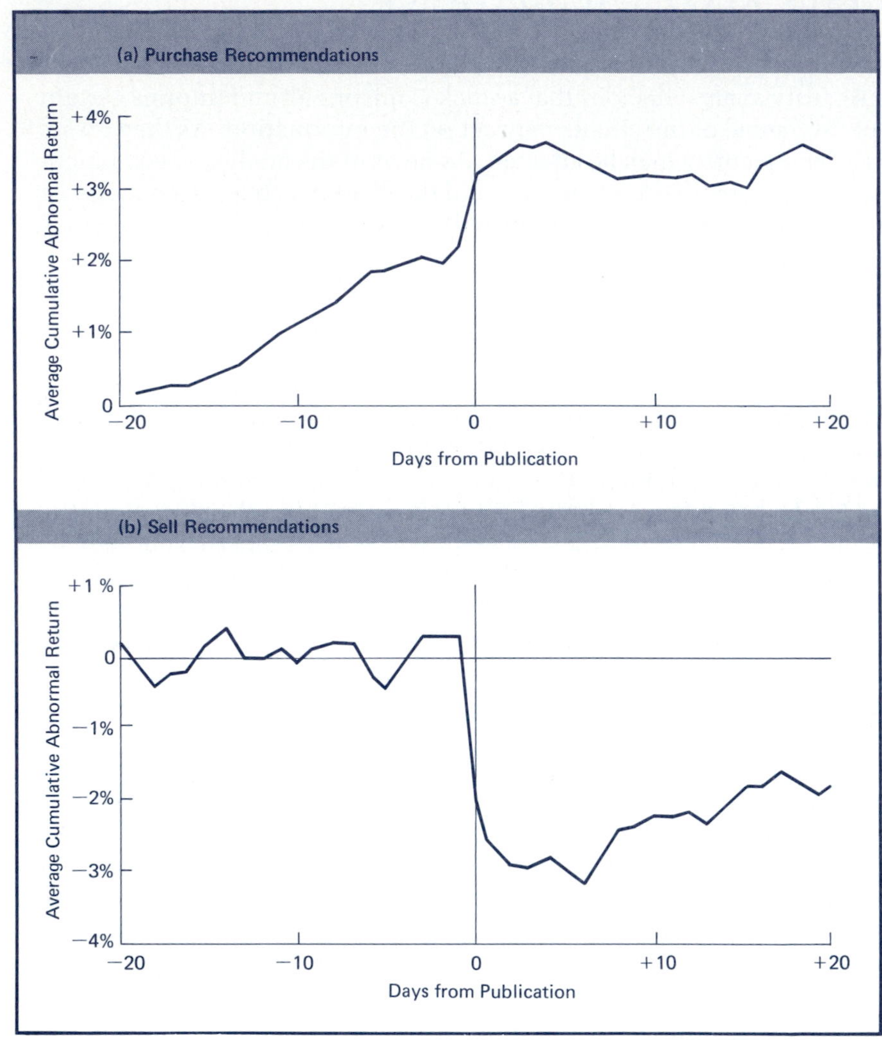

publication date the stocks recommended for purchase rose .923%, while the stocks recommended for sale fell 2.374%. Furthermore, after making such adjustments, 70% of the 597 stocks recommended for purchase rose on the date of publication, and 90% of the 188 stocks recommended for sale fell on the date of publication.

The roughly horizontal lines after day 0 in both panels show that both types of recommendations appeared to contain information. This is because the horizontal lines indicate that there was no significant counterreaction in the twenty days after either a buy or sell recommendation was made.

The upward moves in panel (a) prior to day 0 suggest that prior purchases of the stocks have been made by clients of the analysts. An alternative explanation is that analysts simply recommended purchases of stocks that had recently risen in price. Note, however, that panel (b) is quite different: there is no distinct pattern prior to the date of publication of a sell recommendation. This suggests that the analysts did not tend to recommend the sale of securities that had recently fallen in price.[26]

ANALYST FOLLOWING AND STOCK RETURNS

An interesting issue involves the relationship between the amount of attention devoted by analysts to individual stocks and the price behavior of those stocks. Do stocks that are intensively followed have significantly different returns than those stocks that are relatively neglected by analysts? One study examined all stocks in the S&P 500 for the period from 1970 to 1979 in order to answer such a question. Table 14-2 summarizes the results.

Column (1) shows that the stocks followed by the largest number of analysts had the lowest average returns. However, the stocks followed by the fewest analysts had the highest average return, thereby suggesting the presence of a **neglected firm effect.**

neglected firm effect

It is possible that this effect is simply a reflection of the size effect, since the average return on small-sized firms has been shown to be larger than the average return on larger firms.[27] The reason for this possibility is that the number of analysts following a stock is generally related to the size of the underlying firm. However, columns (2), (3), and (4) show that this is not simply another manifestation of the size effect.[28] It can be seen that the

[26]Two more recent studies made similar observations; both also noted unusually high returns for two days prior to a buy recommendation and unusually low returns for two days prior to a sell recommendation. According to one of the studies, trading volume was unusually high prior to both types of recommendations, leaving open the possibility that some investors traded on advance notice of the contents of the column. See Pu Liu, Stanley D. Smith, and Azmat A. Syed, "Stock Price Reactions to *The Wall Street Journal*'s Securities Recommendations," *Journal of Financial and Quantitative Analysis*, 25, no. 3 (September 1990): 399–410, and Messod D. Beneish, "Stock Prices and the Dissemination of Analysts' Recommendations," *Journal of Business*, 64, no. 3 (July 1991): 393–416. Interestingly, a former author of the "Heard on the Street" column, R. Foster Winans, was convicted of fraud and theft in 1985 for leaking the contents of his column to four brokers and subsequently sharing in the associated profits.

[27]See the appendix to Chapter 13 for a discussion of the size effect.

[28]The presence of the size effect can be seen by noting that the average return for small firms of 13.5% is much larger than the average return for medium and large firms of 10.7% and 9.8%, respectively.

TABLE 14-2
Analyst Following and Stock Returns

AMOUNT OF FOLLOWING	ALL STOCKS (1)	SMALL FIRMS (2)	MEDIUM FIRMS (3)	LARGE FIRMS (4)
High	7.5%	5.0%	7.4%	8.4%
Moderate	11.8	13.2	11.0	10.2
Low	15.4	15.8	13.9	15.3
Low–high	7.9%	10.8%	6.5%	6.9%
Average return	11.0	13.5	10.7	9.8

Source: Adapted from Avner Arbel and Paul Strebel, "Pay Attention to Neglected Firms!" *Journal of Portfolio Management*, 9, no. 2 (Winter 1983): 39.

neglected firm effect exists for all firm sizes. Furthermore, it is most pronounced for small firms—note that the difference between the high and low categories is largest in column (2).

What are the implications of the neglected firm effect? First, it could be that the higher average return associated with neglected firms is a reward for investing in securities that have less available information. Second, since the neglected firm effect exists across all sizes of firms, large institutional investors that are prohibited from investing in small firms can still take advantage of this effect, as it also exists for medium and large firms (although it is notably less significant). Finally, whether or not such a simple rule will be useful in the future is open to debate. Why? If investors increase their purchases of neglected firms, then such firms will no longer be neglected and hence will no longer provide abnormally high returns.

SOURCES OF INVESTMENT INFORMATION

Since information affects the values of investments, the serious financial analyst must be well informed. There is a staggering array of such "investment information," some of it published on paper ("hard copy") and some of it appearing in computer-readable form.

Publications

Space precludes a detailed listing here of publications relating to various industries. An excellent bibliography of such sources, compiled by the New York Society of Security Analysts, can be found in the *Financial Analyst's Handbook*.[29] Periodical literature of interest to the financial analyst is indexed by industries, products, and companies in the *Predicasts F&S Index*.

Anyone planning to invest in anything should read *The Wall Street Journal*. It provides extensive statistical data, financial news, and even a bit of humor. An alternative is the financial section of *The New York Times* or the *Investors Business Daily*. Most other daily newspapers contain financial information, but much less than the *Journal* or the *Times*. A weekly publication with a wealth of statistical data (particularly in the Market Laboratory section) is *Barron's*. Another weekly publication that contains reports prepared by security analysts at various brokerage firms is the *Wall Street Transcript*.

A useful source of daily stock price and volume figures is the *Daily Stock Price Record*, published by Standard & Poor's Corporation. Each issue covers one calendar quarter, and all values for a given stock are listed in a single column. Standard & Poor's also publishes forecasts of company earnings in the weekly *Earnings Forecaster*, and dividend information in the *Dividend Record*. Furthermore, some brokerage houses provide their major clients with copies of Standard & Poor's monthly *Stock Guide* and *Bond Guide*, which are illustrated in Figures 14-8 and 14-9.

Standard & Poor's *Corporation Records* are a major reference source for the financial history of and data on individual companies. They consist of six alphabetical volumes and are periodically updated. A second major reference source is provided by Moody's Investor Services, Inc. Their *Manuals* are

[29]See Levine, *Financial Analyst's Handbook I*, pp. 883–926.

FIGURE 14-8
Standard & Poor's *Stock Guide*, April 1992

6 A&W-ADV

Standard & Poor's Corporation

¶ S&P 500 · # MidCap 400 · • Options

Index	Ticker Symbol	Name of Issue (Call Price of Pfd. Stocks)	Market	Com. Rank. & Pfd. Rating	Par Val.	Inst. Hold Cos	Inst. Hold Shs. (000)	Principal Business	1971-90 High	1971-90 Low	1991 High	1991 Low	1992 High	1992 Low	Mar. Sales in 100s	March, 1992 Last Sale Or Bid High	Low	Last	%Div Yield	P-E Ratio
#1	SODA	A & W Brands	OTC	NR	1¢	115	7013	Mfr soft drink concentrate	34¾	6¼	39¾	26½	40½	35	11238	39	35	35½B	1.2	23
2	AAMS	Aames Financial	OTC	NR	.001	9	566	Mortgage brokerage, California	....	....	10	8	11¾	8½	2719	11¼	8½	8½B	1.4	6
3•[1]	AIR	AAR Corp	NY,M,Ph	A	1	98	8543	Mkts aviation parts/service	37½	1¼	16⅞	9¼	15⅞	12¾	6349	15¾	13⅞	14⅛	3.4	17
4	ABAX	Abaxis Inc	OTC	NR	No	..	...	Dvlp stge:blood analyzer sys	....	....	....	....	17½	6	13193	10¼	6	7B	...	d
5	ABBY	Abbey Healthcare Grp	OTC	NR	0.001	..	...	Home hlth care svcs/products	....	....	....	....	14¼	12⅜	30729	14½	12⅜	12⅞B	...	20
¶6•[2]	ABT	Abbott Laboratories	NY,B,C,M,P,Ph	A+	No	934	226219	Diversified health care prod	46⅝	15/16	69¾	39¼	68⅝	58¾	115429	63¾	58¾	61	2.0	24
7	ABD	Abiomed Inc	AS	NR	1¢	16	354	Medical equip/cardiac sys	16⅞	4¾	22¾	5¼	18⅝	12¼	2307	16	13⅛	13⅞	...	d
8•[3]	ABY	Abitibi-Price[51]	NY,Mo,To,P,Vc	B−	No	31	2016	Newsprint,paper prods	28⅝	2 5/16	14⅝	9⅞	13⅞	12⅛	537	13⅞	12¾	13	♦3.2	d
9	ABRI	Abrams Industries	OTC	B	1	8	451	Construct'n/mfg. real estate	5⅝	¾	4¼	2¾	4¾	4	678	4½	4	4⅜B	4.6	10
☆10	ACCC	ACC Corp	OTC	B	0.015	26	1905	Full-svc telecommun'n co	14⅞	1⅛	15	7¼	17½	12¼	3011	17½	15¼	16¾B	1.0	73
11	ACLE	Accel Int'l	OTC	B	10¢	18	868	Insurance:credit life/disab	14¾	1 11/16	13	6⅝	10	7	1223	8½	7¼	7½B	3.7	33
12	AKLM	Acclaim Entertainment	OTC	NR	2¢	36	3545	Dvlp video game cartridges	16	3⅛	6⅝	2⅞	8¼	4½	40546	8⅛	7	8B	...	d
13	ACET	Aceto Corp	OTC	B+	1¢	34	1318	Mfrs & dstr chemicals	13⅝	7/16	12¼	9⅝	16½	11¼	1401	14¾	13½	14⅜B	1.9	12
14	AK	Ackerley Communications	AS	NR	1¢	14	1023	Brdcstg:pro basketball:adv	12	2⅜	4½	1¼	2⅝	1⅜	1484	2⅜	1⅞	2⅛	...	d
15	ACG	ACM Govt Income Fund	NY,M	NR	1¢	25	448	Closed-end investment co	12⅛	8¾	11⅝	10⅜	11⅝	10⅜	16494	10¾	10⅜	10½	9.1	..
16	AOF	ACM Gvt Opportunity Fd	NY	NR	1¢	4	37	Closed-end investment co	10⅛	7¾	9¾	8¾	10⅜	9⅛	6882	9½	9¼	9¼	⊙8.6	..
17	GSF	ACM Gvt Securities	NY,P	NR	1¢	25	481	Closed-end investment co	12⅛	8⅝	11	9⅝	11¼	10	27029	10½	10⅛	10¼	9.4	..
18	SI	ACM Gvt Spectrum Fund	NY,M	NR	1¢	10	149	Closed-end investment co	10⅛	7¼	9½	8¼	9½	8⅜	12629	8⅞	8½	8½	9.4	..
19	AMF	ACM Managed Income Fund	NY,M	NR	1¢	8	274	Closed-end investment co	10⅛	6½	9⅛	7⅝	9⅝	8⅝	11403	9¼	8⅝	8¾	10.9	..
20	MMF	ACM Managed Multi-Mkt	NY,M,Ph	NR	1¢	3	3	Closed-end investment co	12⅛	10	12⅞	11½	12⅞	10⅞	4762	11⅜	11⅛	11¼	9.6	..
¶21	AMT	Acme-Cleveland	NY,M,Ph	B−	1	88	3467	Mfr indus & telecom prod	35⅝	4½	7½	4¾	11¾	7	5795	11¾	9⅝	10¼	3.9	d
22	ACE	Acme Electric	NY	B−	1	19	1240	Pwr conv eq: transformers	10¾	⅜	6	3⅜	6¼	4½	1281	6¼	4⅞	5¾	...	d
23	ACME	Acme Steel[56]	OTC	NR	1	38	2472	Producer steel/steel prod	26½	8	15¾	10¾	18¾	13¼	2101	17¾	16	17½B	...	d
24	ACU	Acme United	AS,M	B−	2½	13	1234	Medic eq:shears,scissors	19½	1⅜	7⅜	4¼	8⅝	5⅞	1423	7	5⅞	6⅝	3.0	16
25	ACOI	ACOI Inc	OTC	NR	3¢	3	7	Retail non-standard auto insur	9½	1	2½	¾	1¼	1	685	1⅛	1	1B	...	d
26	AXXN	Action Auto Rental	OTC	NR	1¢	23	1787	Insur replacem't auto rental	22¼	1 3/16	2	½	13/16	½	4223	¾	½	5/8B	...	d
27	ACX	Action Indus	AS,B	C	10¢	20	1859	Merchandising programs	18¼	½	7⅛	2⅝	7	5⅝	1287	7	5¾	6⅝	...	9
28	ATN	Acton Corp	AS,B,M,Ph	C	33⅓¢	9	167	RE mgmt,devlp:prop,csity ins	94¾	1 7/16	6¾	3½	6¾	4⅛	291	6¾	4¾	5⅞	...	d
#29•[4]	ACN	Acuson Corp	NY	B	.01¢	205	21283	Medical ultrasound imaging	32¾	5	40	22¾	33⅜	18⅞	64666	21¾	18⅞	20⅛	...	13
30	ACXM	Acxiom Corp	OTC	B−	10¢	34	2232	Computer-based mkting svcs	24	8	22	10	18¼	15	1880	17	15½	15¾B	...	63
31	ADAC	ADAC Laboratories	OTC	B−	No	35	9046	Nuclear medicine comput sys	27⅜	½	2⅝	1	4⅞	1 11/16	232162	4⅞	3	3⅞B	4.1	97
32	ADX	Adams Express	NY,B,M,P,Ph	NR	1	36	289	Closed-end investment co	23⅞	7	20¼	14¼	19½	18½	3019	19½	18¾	18¾	2.8	..
33	AE	Adams Res & Energy	AS,B,M	B−	10¢	6	233	Oil&gas explor,dev,prod'n	70½	1¾	4	2¼	4¼	3	488	3⅞	3	3⅝	...	8
34•[5]	ADPT	Adaptec Inc	OTC	NR	0.001¢	69	6782	Mfr computer data flow sys	24⅛	4⅜	19⅜	8½	35⅜	17⅛	50979	35⅜	29½	30¾B	...	30
#35•[4]	ADCT	ADC Telecommunications	OTC	B	20¢	86	10661	Telecommunications equip	26	⅛	43¼	20½	31	22¾	11604	28¾	24¼	28½B	...	27
36	ADDR	Addington Resources	OTC	NR	1	31	4051	Mining,mkt bituminous coal	23	7	13⅝	6	11¼	8¼	4996	10⅛	8⅝	9¾B	...	d
37	ADIA	Adia Services	OTC	NR	25¢	35	2049	Temporary personnel service	32¼	6¼	25¾	17¾	22¾	14	4035	22	14	14¼B	1.1	21
38	ADB	Adobe Resources[60]	NY,P	NR	1¢	60	9258	Oil & gas explor,devel,prod'n	15⅝	4⅝	9¼	3⅞	5½	4⅜	6901	5⅛	4⅞	5	...	d
39	P⁻A	$1.84cm Cv Pfd([61]20.99)[62]	NY	C	20	10	803	natural gas transmission	20½	13¾	18	10¾	13¼	11⅛	1401	13	12⅛	12½	...	..
#40•[4]	ADBE	Adobe Systems	OTC,M	NR	No	197	20795	Print,graphic software sys	50¾	2⅞	67¾	26¾	68½	49½	140284	58¾	49½	51¼B	0.6	23
41•[7]	ADT	ADT Limited	NY,M,Ph	NR	10¢	86	34612	Security svcs/auctions	....	....	9½	5	9½	6	60528	9½	8⅛	8⅝	...	4
42	AVCR	AdvaCare Inc	OTC	NR	1¢	..	...	Provides medical mgmt svcs	....	....	....	....	16½	11½	12030	14¾	11½	11⅞B	...	d
43	ADVC	Advance Circuits	OTC	B−	10¢	24	1545	Mfr printed circuit boards	11⅛	1/16	10¼	4⅜	10	7½	11528	10	8½	9½B	...	10
44	AROS	Advance Ross	OTC	B	10¢	10	224	Metal fabric'n,envirmt'l use	15½	⅝	12	8¼	10½	8¾	2344	10½	9	9½B	...	2
45	LAIS	Advanced Interventional Sys	OTC	NR	No	30	1787	Excimer laser angioplasty sys	....	....	19¼	11¼	21	8⅝	18496	14¾	8⅝	9B	...	d
46	AALR	Advanced Logic Research	OTC	NR	1¢	29	1948	Mfr/mkt microcomputer sys	19	4½	20¾	8¼	10	6½	20177	8	6½	7½B	...	7
47	AVM	Advanced Magnetics	AS	NR	1¢	15	546	Mfr medical diagnostic prd	11⅝	2⅞	24¾	9	31¼	17½	3895	21⅜	17½	19	...	d

Uniform Footnote Explanations-See Page 1. Other: [1]Ph:Cycle 1. [2]Ph:Cycle 2. [3]To:Cycle 1. [4]P:Cycle 1. [5]ASE:Cycle 1. [6]P:Cycle 2. [7]CBOPE,NY:Cycle 3. [51]1986 & prior prices in Canadian. [52]®$1.16,'91. [53]©$0.04,'92. [54]Pfd in $M. [55]Vote May 5 form Acme Metals. [56]Redemption of stk purch rt. [57]Fiscal Sep'87 earned $0.60. [58]$1.27 in cash or stk:©$1.09,'91. [59]Accum on Pfd. [60]Vote Mar31 Santa Fe Energy Resources acq.0.6com. [61]To 11-1-92,scale to $20 in'97. [62]Santa Fe EnerRes plan acq.0.5974com,0.5065pfd. [63]Incl $1.0672 non-taxable,'91. [64]®$2.15,'90.
[65]Stk dstr of Helo/38 Systems.

☆ See Directory of Company Investor Contacts on page 254.

FIGURE 14-8 (continued)

Common and Convertible Preferred Stocks

A&W-ADV 7

Splits ◆ Index	Cash Divs. Ea. Yr. Since	Dividends: Latest Payment Period $	Date	Ex. Div.	Total $ So Far 1992	Ind. Rate	Paid 1991	Financial Position Mil-$ Cash& Equiv.	Curr. Assets	Curr. Liab.	Balance Sheet Date	Capitalization Lg Trm Debt Mil-$	Shs. 000 Pfd.	Com.	Earnings $ Per Shr. Years End	1987	1988	1989	1990	1991	Last 12 Mos.	Interim Earnings Period	$ per Shr. 1990	1991	Index
1	1991	Q0.11	4-15-92	3-26	0.21	0.44	0.30	2.02	20.5	18.5	9-30-91	10.0	...	9188	Dc	0.20	0.81	□1.14	□1.39	P1.53	1.53				1
2	1992	0.03	2-24-92	2-10	0.03	0.12	....	Equity per shr $3.28			12-31-91	1.08	...	3304	Je	...	...	...	....	p0.98	1.37	6 Mo Dec	p0.24	p0.63	2
3◆	1973	Q0.12	3-4-92	1-28	0.12	0.48	0.48	3.80	284	90.1	11-30-91	67.6	...	15896	My	1.00	1.34	1.56	1.60	0.93	0.82	9 Mo Feb△	0.68	0.57	3
4	....	None Since Public			...	Nil	....	3.42	3.51	0.76	9-30-91	0.31	p...	★5808	Mr	...	...	...	d0.91	....	d1.28	6 Mo Sep	d0.47	d0.84	4
5	....	None Since Public			...	Nil	....	1.87	71.5	52.3	12-28-91	p36.9	p...	★6960	Dc	...	...	...	....	p0.64	p0.64				5
6◆	1926	Q0.30	5-15-92	4-9	0.55	1.20	0.96	146	2891	2229	12-31-91	125	...	425265	Dc	1.39	1.66	1.92	2.22	△□2.55	2.55				6
7	....	None Since Public			...	Nil	....	19.2	20.8	0.84	12-28-91	8.18	...	±6413	Mr	d0.14	d0.48	d0.36	d1.08	....	d0.75	9 Mo Dec	±d0.89	±d0.56	7
8	1949	gQ0.12½	4-30-92	4-9	g0.25	0.50	g0.50	....	541	420	j12-31-91	371	1831	69267	Dc	1.70	△2.60	0.70	d0.68	d1.12	d1.12				8
9◆	1960	Q0.05	3-31-92	3-9	0.10	0.20	0.20	3.46	19.6	15.2	10-31-91	40.4	...	2978	Ap	0.33	0.36	0.48	0.51	0.34	0.42	9 Mo Jan△	0.24	0.32	9
10	**1989**	**Q0.04**	**5-6-92**	**3-31**	**0.08**	**0.16**	**0.16**	**0.79**	**11.5**	**9.31**	**9-30-91**	**1.82**	...	**4409**	**Dc**	**0.11**	**0.10**	**0.43**	**0.53**	**P0.23**	**0.23**				**10**
11◆	1990	Q0.07	5-1-92	3-26	0.13	0.28	0.23	Equity per shr $11.81			12-31-91	23.3	.1	4437	Dc	*1.02	*0.93	*1.02	1.50	0.23	0.23				11
12◆	....	None Since Public			...	Nil	....	6.22	60.0	40.7	11-30-91	1.93	...	p23252	Au	...	0.29	0.54	0.77	d0.31	d0.21	3 Mo Nov	0.02	0.12	12
13◆	1985	S0.127	1-2-92	12-9	0.127	0.28	0.254	18.6	62.0	17.1	12-31-91	3.25	420	4078	Je	0.73	0.99	1.06	1.08	[62]1.17	1.23	6 Mo Dec	0.40	0.46	13
14◆	....	None Paid			...	Nil	....	6.38	50.2	46.0	9-30-91	247	...	±15419	Dc	±□d0.39	±d0.16	±d0.48	±d0.94	....	d1.09	9 Mo Sep	±d0.81	±d0.96	14
15	1987	0.08	4-24-92	4-6	0.34½	0.96	1.26	Net Asset Val $10.13			3-27-92	....	...	48084	Dc	§11.23	§10.55	§10.66	§10.15	§10.59	....				15
16	1988	0.066	4-24-92	4-6	[53]0.322	0.80	1.058	Net Asset Val $9.30			3-27-92	....	...	11742	Jl	...	§9.19	§9.59	§9.01	§9.02	....				16
17	1988	0.08	4-10-92	3-23	0.37	0.96	1.27½	Net Asset Val $10.08			3-27-92	....	...	67037	Dc	...	§10.48	§10.60	§10.16	....	....				17
18	1988	0.066	4-16-92	3-30	0.302	0.80	1.014	Net Asset Val $8.67			3-27-92	....	...	31531	Dc	...	§8.93	§9.13	§8.76	....	....				18
19	1988	0.079	4-24-92	4-6	0.321	0.95	1.008	Net Asset Val $8.74			3-27-92	....	[64]95	p17673	Au	...	...	§9.40	§7.93	§8.39	....				19
20	1990	0.09	4-24-92	4-6	0.382	1.08	1.50	Net Asset Val $10.90			3-27-92	....	...	9903	Nv	...	...	...	§11.53	§11.22	....				20
21	1936	Q0.10	2-21-92	2-3	0.10	0.40	0.40	22.7	78.3	41.7	12-31-91	4.56	161	6291	Sp	*0.71	d5.12	△0.78	△0.44	d0.52	d0.44	3 Mo Dec	*0.11	*0.19	21
22◆	....	0.08	12-3-90	11-5	...	Nil	....	2.60	34.2	29.7	12-27-91	2.38	...	4805	Je	0.15	0.17	△0.75	0.78	d1.60	d1.32	6 Mo Dec	d0.14	0.14	22
23	1992	[60]0.02	4-6-92	3-10	[60]0.02	Nil	....	29.9	129	49.6	9-29-91	59.5	...	5355	Dc	*1.19	*3.22	3.00	1.05	Pd0.43	d0.43				23
24	1990	Q0.05	3-5-92	2-4	0.05	0.20	0.17	1.24	30.3	7.31	9-28-91	11.4	...	p3338	Dc	0.16	0.01	△d0.46	0.40	P0.41	0.41				24
25	....	None Since Public			...	Nil	....	Equity per shr $0.32			6-30-91	p2.20	...	10430	Dc	...	...	d0.10	d0.09	....	d0.05	9 Mo Sep	0.01	0.05	25
26◆	....	5%Stk	5-29-89	5-9	...	Nil	....	Equity per shr $1.81			9-30-91	90.5	...	9972	Dc	0.34	0.64	0.55	d1.35	Pd3.08	d3.08				26
27	....	0.06	6-15-87	5-26	...	Nil	....	0.81	61.3	35.2	12-28-91	0.12	...	5534	Je	d1.37	△0.66	0.33	d3.08	0.44	0.74	6 Mo Dec	0.40	0.70	27
28◆	....	5%Stk	7-15-82	6-25	...	Nil	....	Equity per shr $3.69			12-31-90	p72.7	p991	±p1429	Dc	△*5.66	d1.08	△3.77	d5.10	Pd8.16	d8.16				28
29◆	....	None Since Public			...	Nil	....	143	268	58.8	9-28-91	....	...	35445	Dc	0.49	0.78	1.07	1.33	P1.59	1.59				29
30	....	None Since Public			...	Nil	....	4.82	31.0	12.3	12-31-91	24.1	...	4766	Mr	[67]0.82	0.85	1.16	0.79	....	0.25	9 Mo Dec	0.78	0.24	30
31	1992	0.04	4-6-92	3-23	0.04	0.16	....	4.35	49.8	22.1	12-29-91	....	...	43049	Sp	*0.06	0.27	0.39	0.08	0.02	0.04	3 Mo Dec	0.03	0.05	31
32	1936	[53]0.12	3-1-92	2-11	[53]0.12	○0.53	[58]1.63	Net Asset Val $19.63			3-27-92	....	...	32747	Dc	§15.92	§16.11	§18.35	§16.82	§20.21	....				32
33◆	....	0.20	8-15-78	7-10	...	[60]Nil	....	0.85	9.99	8.19	9-30-91	3.69	...	4161	Dc	0.56	0.56	0.44	0.46	P0.45	0.45				33
34◆	....	None Since Public			...	Nil	....	63.5	108	15.0	12-27-91	0.57	...	9924	Mr	0.50	0.19	1.50	1.19	....	1.01	9 Mo Dec	1.01	0.83	34
35◆	....	None Since Public			...	Nil	....	30.1	120	40.5	10-31-91	43.6	...	13474	Oc	1.18	1.30	1.25	1.73	1.65	1.06	3 Mo Jan△	0.50	d0.09	35
36◆	....	None Since Public			...	Nil	....	19.1	81.4	65.8	9-30-91	135	...	15232	Dc	p1.06	□p1.19	0.67	0.93	P□d0.41	d0.41				36
37	1984	Q0.04	3-13-92	2-24	0.04	0.16	0.16	47.2	138	53.6	9-30-91	6.04	...	±12542	Dc	±1.10	±1.50	±△1.63	±1.41	P±0.67	0.67				37
38	....	None Since Public			...	Nil	....	4.11	36.9	28.6	9-30-91	145	9015	30658	Dc	*d0.15	*d0.17	*d1.07	d0.70	....	d0.20	9 Mo Sep	d1.16	d0.66	38
39	1986	0.46	11-15-91	10-21	...	Nil	[63]1.84	Cv into 1.064 com				....	4159	...	Dc	b0.82	b0.76	bd0.41	b0.38	....	....	Accum $0.46 to 2-15-92			39
40◆	1988	Q0.08	4-9-92	3-23	0.16	0.32	0.30	116	162	36.9	11-29-91	....	...	22133	Nv	0.42	0.98	1.55	1.83	2.25	2.27	3 Mo Feb△	0.55	0.57	40
41◆	....	Plan semi annual div			...	....	....	190	770	524	6-30-91	822	p436	p109648	Dc	△2.51	3.07	3.32	△[64]2.17	....	2.17				41
42	....	None Since Public			...	Nil	....	Equity per shr $2.71			12-31-91	p19.4	p...	★11096	Sp	0.03	0.02	d0.15	Nil	d2.55	d2.44	3 Mo Dec	d0.11	Nil	42
43◆	....	h[65]....	6-17-88	6-20	...	Nil	....	2.30	19.1	9.42	11-30-91	....	...	5436	Au	△d0.14	d1.54	0.90	1.49	1.01	0.96	6 Mo Feb△	0.36	0.31	43
44	....	h....	11-27-64		...	Nil	....	22.8	24.5	2.87	12-31-91	....	20	1827	Dc	1.27	d0.04	0.26	1.37	3.94	3.94				44
45	....	None Since Public			...	Nil	....	1.99	7.78	1.90	9-30-91	0.39	...	★8856	Dc	d0.94	d1.18	d0.73	d0.71	Pd0.91	d0.91				45
46	....	None Since Public			...	Nil	....	33.9	124	31.5	12-31-91	9.00	...	11233	Sp	0.11	0.36	0.41	1.38	1.40	1.13	3 Mo Dec	0.31	0.04	46
47◆	....	None Since Public			...	Nil	....	18.2	20.5	0.99	12-31-91	....	...	★6717	Sp	0.23	0.22	0.23	0.09	d0.70	d0.68	3 Mo Dec	0.01	*0.03	47

◆**Stock Splits & Divs By Line Reference Index** [3]3-for-2,'87. [6]2-for-1,'90 To split 2-for-1,ex Jun 1. [9]5-for-4,'88:4-for-3,'89. [11]Adj to 5%,'90. [12]3-for-5 REVERSE,'88:1-for-2 REVERSE,'89. [13]Adj to 4%,Jun,'90:10%,'91. [14]2-for-1 in Cl'B','87. [22]Adj for 5%,'88. [26]3-for-2,'88:Adj to 5%,'89. [28]1-for-5 REVERSE,'87. [29]3-for-2,'90. [33]1-for-2 REVERSE,'92. [34]To split 2-for-1,ex Apr 6. [35]3-for-2,'87. [36]2-for-1,'89. [40]2-for-1,'87,'88. [41]1-for-10 REVERSE,'91. [43]5-for-4,'90. [47]3-for-2,'91.

FIGURE 14-9
Standard & Poor's *Bond Guide*, April 1992

22 **AAR-ALA** Standard & Poor's Corporation

Company rows (italic): Title-Industry Code & Co. Finances (in Italics) | Ind | Fixed Charge Coverage 1988 | 1989 | 1990 | Year End | Million $: Cash & Equiv. | Curr. Assets | Curr. Liab. | Balance Sheet Date | L. Term Debt (Mil $) | Capitalization (Mil $) | Total Debt % Capital

Exchange / Individual Issue Statistics	Interest Dates	S&P Debt Rating	Date of Last Rating Change	Prior Rating	Eligible	Bond Form	Redemption Provisions: Regular Price	Regular (Begins) Thru	Sinking Fund Price	Sinking Fund (Begins) Thru	Refund/Other Restriction Price	Refund/Other Restriction (Begins) Thru	Outst'g (Mil $)	Underwriting Firm	Underwriting Year	Price Range 1992 High	Price Range 1992 Low	Mo. End Price Sale(s) or Bid	Curr. Yield	Yield to Mat.
AAR Corp	***3a***	*△5.87*	*△4.82*	*△3.45*		*My*	*2.94*	*268.0*	*75.20*	*8-31-91*	*68.30*		*285.0*	*31.5*						
Nts[1] 9½s 2001	mN	BBB			X	R	NC	....	....	....	....	....	65.0	G2	'89	107⅞	101¾	102½	9.27	9.10
Abbott Laboratories	***21a***	*△17.05*	*△15.77*	*△25.19*		*Dc*	*146.0*	*2891*	*2229*	*12-31-91*	*125.0*		*3872*	*17.3*						
• SF Deb 6¼s '93	Jj15	AA +	4/84	AA	X	R	100	....	100	....	....	....	1.04	G1	'68	100½	100	99⅞	6.26	6.40
• SF Deb 7⅝s '96	Ms	AA +	4/84	AA	X	R	100	....	100	....	....	....	11.1	L3	'71	No Sale		99⅛	7.69	7.89
• SF Deb 9.20s '99	aO15	CALL	2/92	AA +		R			Called 4-15-92 at 101.38				17.4	G2	'74	104⅜	100½	101⅜	9.08	Call
ACF Indus	***56***	*0.64*	*2.26*	*0.33*		*Dc*	*722.0*	*775.0*	*375.0*	*9-30-91*	*975.0*		*1551*	*77.1*						
Eq Tr Ctf 14⅞s '92	fA	B +	4/86	BBB	Y	R	NC	....	100	....	....	....	12.0	B1	'82	102	100⅞	100⅞	14.75	11.85
Eq Tr Ctf 14½s '96	jD	B +	4/86	BBB	Y	R	NC	....	100	....	....	....	15.0	B1	'81	101	95	95	15.26	16.04
Eq Tr Ctf 11.60s 2000	Mn15	B +	4/86	BBB	Y	R	NC	....	100	....	....	....	22.5	B1	'80	78	78	78	14.87	16.62
SF Deb 15¼s '96	jD15	B	4/86	BBB −	Y	R	104.20	12-14-92	*100	....	....	....	414	D8	'84	100	92⅝	95⅜	15.99	16.68
Action Industries	***60***	*△1.52*	*△0.24*	*△1.64*		*Je*	*0.81*	*61.30*	*35.20*	*12-28-91*	*0.12*		*46.60*	*40.2*						
◆Sr SF Deb[2] 11¼s '92	mS15	NR	6/87	BB −	Y	R	100	....	100	....	....	....	1.20	D9	'77	No Sale		97	11.60	18.29
Addington Resources, Inc	***45a***	*2.24*	*1.55*	*1.25*		*Dc*	*19.10*	*81.40*	*65.80*	*9-30-91*	*135.0*		*283.0*	*51.6*						
Sr Sec Nts 12s '95	jJ	BB +			Y	R	103.43	(7-1-93)	....	....	....	....	125	D7	'88	104	102½	102½	11.71	11.05
Adelphia Communications	***12a***	*d0.11*	*0.12*	*0.51*		*Mr*	*26.20*			*12-31-91*	*1575*		*881.0*	*179.0*						
Sr Disc[3]Nts 16½s '99	Ms15	CCC +	10/90	B −	Y	R	104	3-14-93	....	....	....	....	250	S1	'88	104½	96	104½	15.79	15.42
Sr Sub Nts 13s '96	fA15	CCC +	12/88	CCC	Y	R	103.71	8-14-92	....	....	....	....	100	P1	'86	102	93	102	12.75	12.38
[4]Adience Equities, Inc	***42***	*2.46*	*2.08*	*1.84*		*Dc*		*79.40*	*42.30*	*6-30-91*	*68.50*		*86.30*	*94.2*						
• Sr Sub[5]Reset Nts 15s '99	Jd15	CC	2/92	CCC +	Y	R	103	(6-15-94)	100	(6-15-97)	....	....	66.0	D8	'89	83⅞	64	s72½	....	Flat
Aetna Life & Casual	***35d***	*△8.39*	*△7.33*	*△4.91*		*Dc*	*3137*			*12-31-91*	*1021*		*8587*	*12.0*						
• Deb 8⅛s 2007	aO15	AA	10/91	AA +	X	R	103.36	10-14-92	100	....	....	....	205	M6	'77	101¾	98	s98⅞	8.22	8.25
Deb 8s 2017	Jj15	AA	10/91	AA +	X	R	104	(1-15-97)	100	(1-15-97)	....	....	200	M2	'87	93⅜	88¼	88¾	9.01	9.15
Nts 8⅝s '98	Ms	AA	10/91	AA +	X	R	NC	....	....	....	....	....	100	M6	'88	103⅞	99⅜	100	8.63	8.62
Affiliated Bankshrs Colo	***10***	*0.44*	*0.49*	*1.72*		*Dc*				*6-30-91*	*54.90*		*256.0*	*21.4*						
Nts 11⅝s '93	Ao	CALL	3/92	BB +		R			Called 5-4-92 at 100				10.0	M6	'83	99¾	99⅝	99¾	11.65	Call
Nts 10½s '97	mS	BB +	9/91	BB	Y	R	100	(9-1-93)	....	....	....	....	15.0		'90	92	92	92	11.41	12.58
Air Products & Chemicals	***14b***	*△4.39*	*△3.94*	*△3.93*		*Sp*	*158.0*	*1006*	*837.0*	*12-31-91*	*950.0*		*3181*	*38.9*						
Deb 8½s 2006	Ao	A +			X	R	100	(4-1-04)	....	....	....	....	100	G2	'86	104¾	98¼	98¾	8.61	8.66
• Deb 8¾s 2021	Ao15	A +			X	R	NC	....	....	....	....	....	100	S5	'91	No Sale		98	8.93	8.94
• Nts 11½s '95	Mn	A +			X	R	NC	....	....	....	....	....	100	G2	'85	113⅞	113⅞	111⅜	10.33	7.31
Nts 8⅞s 2001	fA	A +			X	R	NC	....	....	....	....	....	100	S5	'89	106⅞	100⅞	104⅜	8.50	8.19
Alabama Bancorporation	***10***	*Now AmSouth Bancorp, see*																		
• [6]F/R[7]Nts 4.85s '99	mS	A	8/90	A +	X	R	100	....	....	....	....	....	9.61	F2	'74	98¾	98⅛	98¾	4.91	....
Alabama Gas Corp[8]	***73b***	*3.30*	*2.87*	*2.65*		*Sp*	*1.91*	*57.70*	*86.80*	*12-31-91*	*65.10*		*162.0*	*44.7*						
1st F[9] 8s '94	Fa	A +	9/91	A	X	R	100.43	1-31-93	100	....	....	....	5.24	W6	'69	100¼	100¼	100¼	7.98	7.84
1st G[10] 9½s '96	Jj	A +	9/91	A	X	R	101.73	12-31-92	100	....	....	....	9.90	W6	'71	101⅜	101⅜	101⅜	9.37	9.05
Deb[11] 8¾s 2012	Mn	A	9/91	A −	X	R	105	(5-1-92)	....	....	....	....	9.16	E2	'87	99¼	94⅜	95	9.21	9.30
Deb[12] 9s 2014	mN	A	9/91	A −	X	R	105	(11-1-94)	....	....	....	....	30.0	J2	'89	105⅛	99⅝	100⅛	8.99	8.99
Alabama Power Co.[13]	***72a***	*2.51*	*2.96*	*3.02*		*Dc*	*15.70*	*836.0*	*727.0*	*9-30-91*	*★2610*		*5466*	*47.7*						
1st 4⅜s '92	Jd	A	10/85	A −	X	CR	100	....	100	....	....	....	14.4	B8	'62	99¾	99¾	99¾	4.39	5.80
1st 4⅜s '93	Mn	A	10/85	A −	X	CR	100.16	4-30-92	100.01	4-30-92	....	....	13.8	L3	'63	99½	98¼	99	4.42	5.33
1st 4⅝s '94	Mn	A	10/85	A −	X	CR	100.41	4-30-92	100.21	4-30-92	....	....	24.1	F2	'64	97¾	96⅛	96⅝	4.79	6.38
1st 4⅞s '95	mS	A	10/85	A −	X	CR	100.59	8-31-92	100.20	8-31-92	....	....	33.3	B8	'65	95¾	93½	94	5.19	6.87

Uniform Footnote Explanations-See Page 1. Other: [1] (HRO)For Trigger Event at 100. [2] Int incr fr 11% 5-15-82. [3] Int accrues at 16.5% fr 3-15-92. [4] Now Adience, Inc. [5] Int(min 15%,max 17%)reset on 6-15-92 [6] (HRO)On int dates at 100. [7] Int thru 8-31-92,adj semi-anly aft. [8] Subsid of Energen Corp. [9] Incr fr 7.25% 8-1-82. [10] Incr fr 8.75%,1-1-83. [11] (HRO)Ea May 1 at 100,limited as defined [12] (HRO)Ea Nov 1, at 100,limited as defined. [13] Subsid of Southern Co.

published annually, with periodic updates, and cover various fields: *Bank & Finance, Industrial, International, Municipal & Government, OTC Industrial, OTC Unlisted, Public Utility,* and *Transportation* are the titles of various volumes. In addition, both Standard & Poor's and Moody's also provide a number of other publications to subscribers.

Historical data and analyses for approximately 1,700 stocks and most major industries can be found in the *Value Line Investment Survey*. Adjusted betas are also shown for the individual stocks in the *Survey*. The *Value Line Options* and *Convertibles* manuals, along with the *Survey*, offer estimates of the relative attractiveness of these investments.[30]

Publications of major security analysts' societies include the *Financial Analysts Journal* (United States); *Analyse Financière* (France); and *The Investment Analyst* (United Kingdom). Academic journals that emphasize various aspects of investing include the *Journal of Business*, the *Journal of Finance*, the *Journal of Financial and Quantitative Analysis*, the *Journal of Financial Economics*, and the *Review of Financial Studies*.

Anyone interested in the management of money for institutional or corporate investors (especially pension funds) should read the *Journal of Portfolio Management* and the *Journal of Fixed Income*, which publish the views of both practitioners and academicians. A biweekly periodical widely read by institutional investors and money managers is *Pensions and Investment Age*. *Institutional Investor*, a periodical full of "inside information" on the investment industry, is published monthly. Individual investors will find the articles in the monthly issues of the *AAII Journal*, published by the American Association of Individual Investors, to be informative. Also of interest is *Business Week* (a weekly publication) and two biweeklies, *Forbes* and *Fortune*.

Data on mutual funds is published in a number of places. Examples include publications put out by Lipper Analytical Services, Computer Directions Advisors (CDA), William E. Donoghue, American Association of Individual Investors, Morningstar, and Wiesenberger Financial Services.

While a company's annual and quarterly reports provide useful information, the annual and quarterly business and financial reports (10-K and 10-Q, respectively) filed with the Securities and Exchange Commission usually include more details. While the annual reports are audited, it should be noted that quarterly reports are unaudited.

A source of macroeconomic data such as monetary aggregates (like the money supply) and other monetary items is the *Federal Reserve Bulletin*, a monthly publication by the Board of Governors of the Federal Reserve System. The Department of the Treasury publishes quarterly the *Treasury Bulletin*, which contains data on government debt and interest rates. Data on national income and production is published monthly by the U.S. Department of Commerce in the *Survey of Current Business*. The Department of Commerce also publishes on a monthly basis the *Business Conditions Digest*, where various economic indicators can be found. (These indicators include **leading indicators** that have been found to signal future changes in the economy; **lagging indicators** that change after the economy has done so; and **coincident indicators** that change simultaneously with the economy.)

leading indicators
lagging indicators
coincident indicators

[30]Such estimates for common stocks appear to be useful in helping the investor "beat the market." See the appendix to Chapter 16.

Computer-Readable Data

The rapid increase in the use of microcomputers by those who invest money for others, as well as by those who invest for themselves, has led to a major expansion in the availability of computer-readable investment data.

Large amounts of financial and economic data, such as common stock prices and financial statements, are provided on magnetic tapes that are made available to investors for a fee by Standard & Poor's Compustat Services and Value Line, Inc. These databases are also available on a dial-up basis via time-shared computer services, and on disks for use in microcomputers.

Dial-up services are also provided by *Compuserve, Dow Jones News/Retrieval, Interactive Data Corporation,* and others. Each service is designed so that users of microcomputers can "download" prices and other data into their own machines easily and inexpensively. Often the data is in spreadsheet format so that it is readily available for analysis using, for example, Lotus 1–2–3.

Databases containing prices, fundamental information, and predictions made by brokerage houses and others are provided on compact discs by the Lotus Development Corporation, Standard & Poor's Corporation, and others.

SUMMARY

1. Financial analysts are investment professionals who evaluate securities and then make investment recommendations. Those recommendations may be used by professional money managers (portfolio managers) or by certain clients of the analysts.
2. There are two primary reasons for engaging in financial analysis: to determine certain characteristics of securities and to attempt to identify mispriced securities.
3. To understand and estimate the risk and return of individual securities as well as groups of securities, financial markets and the principles of security valuation must be understood.
4. Market indices are portfolios of securities designed to represent the performance of an entire asset class (for example, stocks or bonds) or a specific segment of an asset class.
5. Market indices are typically computed on the basis of either price-weighting, value-weighting, or equal-weighting the prices of the component securities.
6. Many investors have claimed to have identified investment systems that can outperform a passive investment system. Frequently, however, the investors testing these systems commit fundamental errors that invalidate their results.
7. Technical analysis involves short-term predictions of security price movements based on past patterns of prices and trading volumes. Fundamental analysis concerns estimates of the basic determinants of security values, such as future sales, expenses, and earnings for firms.
8. Many financial analysts focus their research efforts on analyzing company financial statements. This research permits the analyst to better understand a company's business operations, its plans for future growth, what factors affect its profitability, and how those factors affect its profitability.

KEY TERMS

financial analyst
portfolio managers
fundamental analysis
market index
price-weighted market index
value-weighted market index
equal-weighted market index
price relatives
passive investment system
ex post selection bias
out-of-sample data
technical analysis
top-down forecasting
bottom-up forecasting
probabilistic forecasting

econometric model	contrarians	lagging indicators
endogenous variables	neglected firm effect	coincident indicators
exogenous variables	leading indicators	chartists

QUESTIONS AND PROBLEMS

1. Using a recent *Wall Street Journal*, find the closing value of the Dow Jones Industrial Average. On the same date, find the closing prices of the DJIA's component stocks. (The names of those stocks are usually listed on page 3 of the *Journal*'s third section.) Calculate the value of the DJIA's divisor.
2. Consider a price-weighted market index composed of two securities, A and B, with prices of $16 and $30, respectively. The index divisor is currently 2.0. Calculate the value of the divisor when:
   (a) Stock A provides a 5% stock dividend.
   (b) Stock B undergoes a 3-1 stock split.
   (c) Stock A undergoes a 4-1 stock split.
3. It is often argued that the S&P 500 is a better indicator than the Dow Jones Industrial Average of the performance of the entire U.S. stock market. Explain the reasoning behind this contention.
4. Assume that the market is composed of the following three securities:

SECURITY	CURRENT PRICE	SHARES OUTSTANDING
A	$20	20,000
B	35	40,000
C	30	40,000

   (a) What is the aggregate value of the market?
   (b) If security C's price increases by 20%, what is the percentage change in the market's aggregate value?
   (c) If security B splits 2-1, what is the percentage change in the market's aggregate value?
5. Consider three stocks with the following closing prices on two particular dates:

STOCK	DATE 1	DATE 2
X	$16	$22
Y	5	4
Z	24	30

On date 1 there are 100 shares of stock X, 200 shares of stock Y, and 100 shares of stock Z outstanding.
   (a) Construct a price-weighted market index using X, Y, and Z. What is the index's value on date 1?
   (b) What is the price-weighted index's value on date 2?
   (c) Assume that on date 2, stock X splits 4-for-1. What is the price-weighted index's value on that date?

(d) Construct a value-weighted index using the three stocks. Assign the value-weighted index a value of 100 on date 1. What is the index's value on date 2?

6. According to Ferris Fain, "The success of a stock market index depends on its ability to measure the performance of stocks not included in the index." Explain what Ferris means.

7. Consider an equal-weighted market index composed of three securities. The market prices of those securities on three dates are shown below.

SECURITY	DATE 1	MARKET PRICES DATE 2	DATE 3
A	$50	$55	$60
B	30	28	30
C	70	75	73

(a) What is the return on the index from date 1 to date 2?
(b) What is the return on the index from date 2 to date 3?

8. Consider a market index based on these three securities and their associated prices on three dates:

SECURITY	DATE 1	MARKET PRICES DATE 2	DATE 3
L	$20	$23	$30
M	27	30	31
N	40	35	29

If the index's value is 200 on date 1, calculate its value on date 2 and date 3 if the index return is computed on a geometric mean basis.

9. What types of stocks or industries will an equal-weighted market index emphasize relative to a value-weighted market index?

10. List and describe several possible uses of security market indices.

11. If security markets are highly efficient, what role is there for financial analysts?

12. Listed next are several test results from studies of mechanical investment systems. For each test result, identify the primary research error committed and comment as to why the error is applicable to the study.
(a) A portfolio managed using a filter rule (that is, buying a stock after it has appreciated by x%, holding the stock until its price has depreciated by x%, then selling the stock) outperforms a broad market index when the filter is very small (that is, when x is small).
(b) A system estimated over the time period from 1970 to 1980 indicates that the system outperformed a broad market index in the latter half of that period.
(c) A portfolio composed of stocks of highly cyclical industrial companies outperforms a broad market index.
(d) Buying and selling U.S. stocks based on a measure of liberal and conservative voting patterns in Great Britain produces returns that outperform a broad U.S. market index.

(e) The price performance of a portfolio of ipo (initial public offering) high-technology stocks outperforms a broad market index.

13. Despite the arguments and evidence of efficient markets proponents, many investors pay attention to technical analysis in some form. Speculate as to why these investors use this kind of investment research.

14. Distinguish between top-down and bottom-up approaches to financial forecasting. What are the primary advantages and disadvantages of each approach?

15. In 1991, both Hudson Homes and Baldwin Construction earned $1,000,000 in net income. Both companies have assets of $10,000,000. However, Hudson generated a return on equity of 11.1% while Baldwin produced a return on equity of 20.0%. What can explain the differences in return on equity between the two companies?

16. Is it true that when comparing the reported earnings of corporations, "a dollar is a dollar"?

17. (Appendix Question) Technical analysis is predicated on stock prices moving in repetitive patterns. What would one have to believe about the timing of the receipt of information by financial market participants in order to believe in the existence of such patterns?

18. (Appendix Question) The closing, high, and low prices for Fort McCoy Packaging stock over a ten-day interval are shown here. Construct a bar chart for Fort McCoy Packaging stock over this period of time.

DAY	FORT McCOY PACKAGING CLOSING PRICE	HIGH	LOW
1	20	21	19
2	20¼	20¼	18
3	21	22	20½
4	21⅛	22⅞	21⅛
5	21	23¼	20
6	21¾	22	20¾
7	22	23½	20⅛
8	20⅛	22	19¼
9	19⅛	21½	19
10	18¼	21⅞	17⅛

19. (Appendix Question) Calculate the relative strength of Fort McCoy Packaging stock versus the S&P 500 over the ten-day period referred to in problem 18, given the following closing prices for the S&P 500:

DAY	S & P 500	DAY	S & P 500
1	300	6	315
2	302	7	330
3	306	8	325
4	310	9	325
5	320	10	330

CFA Exam Question

20. The duPont formula defines the net return on shareholders' equity as a function of the following components:

- operating margin,
- asset turnover,
- interest burden,
- financial leverage, and
- income tax rate.

Using only the data in the table shown below:

(a) Calculate each of the five components listed above for 1985 and 1989, and calculate the return on equity (ROE) for 1985 and 1989, using all of the five components. Show calculations.

(b) Briefly discuss the impact of the changes in asset turnover and financial leverage on the change in ROE from 1985 to 1989.

	1985	1989
Income Statement Data		
Revenues	$542	$979
Operating income	38	76
Depreciation and amortization	3	9
Interest expense	3	0
Pretax income	32	67
Income taxes	13	37
Net income after tax	19	30
Balance Sheet Data		
Fixed assets	$41	$70
Total assets	245	291
Working capital	123	157
Total debt	16	0
Total shareholders' equity	159	220

APPENDIX A Technical Analysis

Most (but not all) technical analysts rely on charts of stock prices and trading volumes. Virtually all employ colorful, and sometimes even mystical, terminology. For example, a significant price rise on relatively large trading volume might be described as an accumulation, where the stock is allegedly moving from "weak hands" to "strong hands." This is because a rising stock price on large trading volume is viewed as a situation where demand is stronger than supply. In contrast, a significant price decline on relatively large trading volume may be described as a distribution, where the stock is allegedly moving from "strong hands" to "weak hands." This is because a declining stock price on large trading volume is viewed as a situation where supply is stronger than demand. In both situations, relatively large trading volume might be considered a sign of a sustainable change in the stock's price, while relatively small trading volume indicates a transitory change.

What if there is a period when a stock's price does not move significantly? If the stock's price movements are within a narrow band, the stock is said to be in a consolidation phase. A price level that a stock has difficulty rising above is known as a resistance level, and a price level that a stock does not seem to fall below is known as a support level.

Such statements may sound meaningful, but they fail to pass the tests of simple logic. First, changes in a stock's price occur when the consensus opinion concerning its value changes. This means that large volume associated with a price change only reflects a substantial difference of opinion concerning the impact of new information on the stock's value; small volume reflects smaller differences of opinion. Second, if price or volume data could be used to predict future short-term price movements, investors would rush to exploit such information, moving prices rapidly enough to make the information useless.

CHARTS

chartists

Chartists (technicians who rely on chart formations) nonetheless believe that certain patterns carry great significance, although they often disagree among themselves on the significance of a pattern or even on the existence of a pattern. Before displaying some hypothetical examples of patterns, it should be noted that there are three basic types of charts used. They are known as bar charts, line charts, and point and figure charts.

For a *bar chart* the horizontal axis is a time line, with the vertical axis measuring a particular stock's price. More specifically, corresponding to a given day on the horizontal axis will be a vertical line, the top and bottom of which represent the high and low price for that stock on that day. Somewhere on this vertical line will be a small horizontal line representing the closing price for the day. As an example, consider the following hypothetical stock, whose trading background over the last five days is as follows:

DAY	HIGH PRICE	LOW PRICE	CLOSING PRICE	VOLUME
$t - 5$	11	9	10	200
$t - 4$	12	9	11	300
$t - 3$	13	12	12	400
$t - 2$	11	10	11	200
$t - 1$	14	11	12	500

Panel (a) of Figure 14-10 presents a bar chart for this stock, while panel (b) indicates how such a bar chart of prices can be augmented by adding trading volume at the bottom.

Figure 14-11 (a) shows a type of bar chart that is known as "head and shoulders." As time passed, the stock's price initially rose, hit a peak at *A*, and then fell to a bottom at *B*. Recovering from this fall, it went up to an even higher peak at *C*, but then fell again to a bottom at *D*. Next, it rose to a peak at *E* that was not as high as the previous peak, *C*, and then started to fall. As soon as the price went down past its previous low, *D*, immediately a forecast was made that the stock was going to plunge much lower (if the stock had not reached a level equal to *D*, no such forecast would have been made). Figure 14-11 (b) shows a type of bar chart known as "inverted head and shoulders," which results in a forecast that the stock is going to quickly rise by a substantial amount.[31]

For a *line chart*, the axes are the same as with a bar chart. However, only closing prices are presented, and they are connected to each other successively with straight lines, as illustrated in panel (c) of Figure 14-10. While not shown, line charts are also frequently augmented with volume data in a manner identical to bar charts.

Details of construction of *point and figure charts* vary, but the idea is to plot closing prices that form a trend in a single column, moving to the next column only when the trend is reversed. For example, closing prices might be rounded to the nearest dollar and the chart begun by plotting a beginning rounded price on a certain day. As long as the (rounded) price does not change, nothing is done. When a different price is recorded, it is plotted on the chart. A price higher than the initial price is indicated with an *X*, with any gaps between the prices also marked with an *X*. A price below the initial price is marked with an *O* in a similar fashion. Then when a price that is different

[31]For details on many kinds of patterns, see Alan R. Shaw, "Technical Analysis," in Sumner N. Levine, ed., *Financial Analyst's Handbook I* (Homewood, Ill.: Dow Jones-Irwin, Inc., 1975), pp. 944–88; and Chapter 8 in Jerome B. Cohen, Edward D. Zinbarg, and Arthur Zeikel, *Investment Analysis and Portfolio Management* (Homewood, Ill.: Richard D. Irwin, Inc., 1987).

FIGURE 14-10
Types of Charts

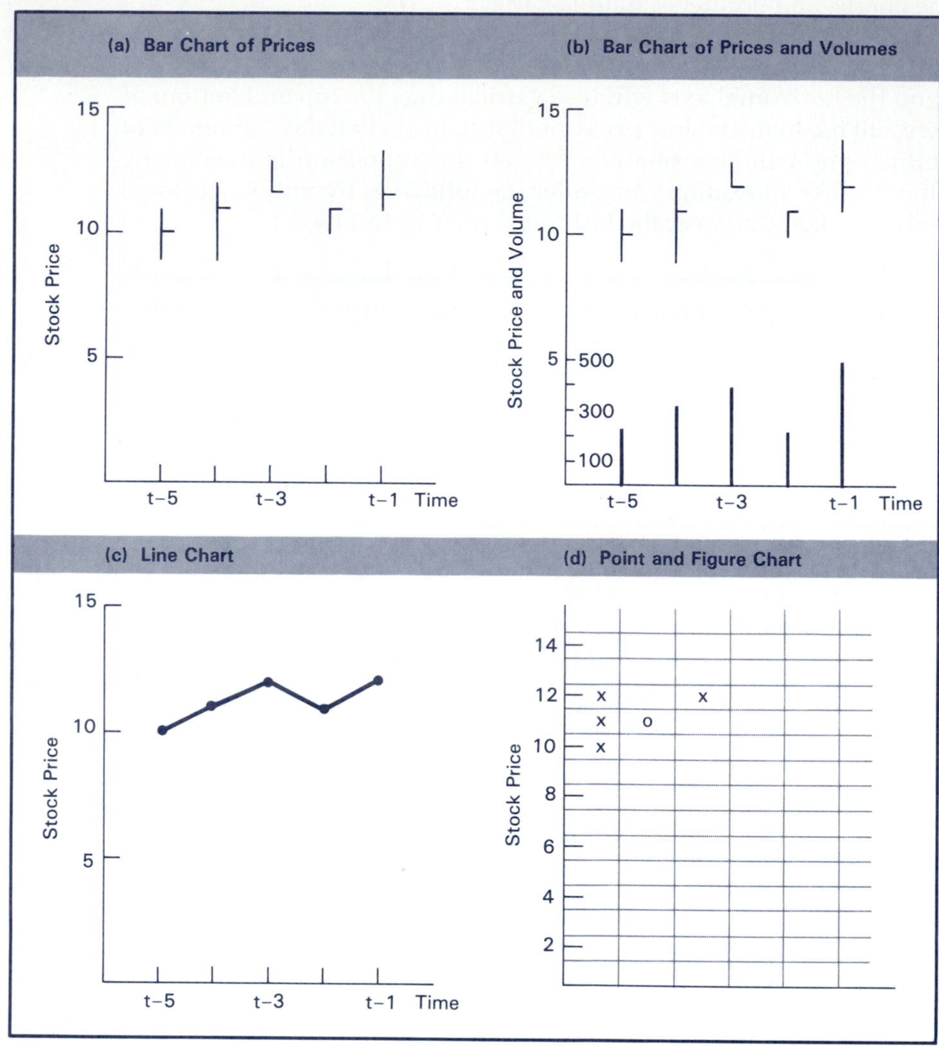

from the last one is recorded, it is plotted in the same column if it is in the same direction.

For example, if the first different price is above the beginning price, this price is plotted above the beginning one. Then, if a price is recorded that is above the second one, it is plotted in the same column, but if it is below the second one, then it is plotted in a new column to the right of the first column. Continuing, as long as new prices are in the same direction, they are plotted in the same column. Whenever there is a reversal, a new column is started. Panel (d) of Figure 14-10 presents a point and figure chart for the same hypothetical stock used in the other panels.

Point and figure enthusiasts look for all sorts of patterns in their charts. As with all chartist techniques, the idea is to recognize a pattern early enough

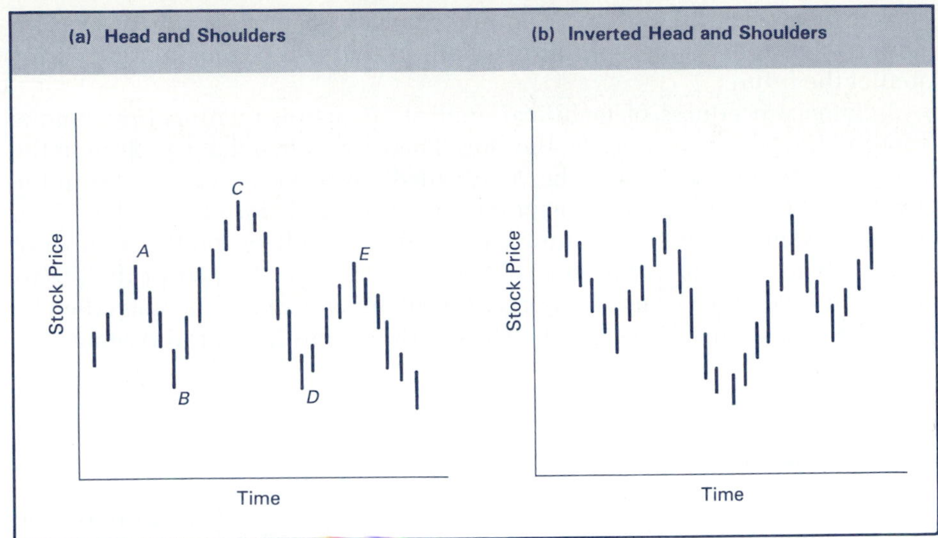

FIGURE 14-11
Bar Chart Patterns

to profit from one's ability to foresee the future course of prices—a neat trick, if one can do it.

MOVING AVERAGES

Many other procedures are used by technicians. Some construct moving averages to try to detect "intermediate" and "long-term" trends. Here a set number of the most recent closing prices on a security are averaged each day. (For example, daily closing prices over the previous 200 days may be used.) This means that each day, the oldest price is replaced with the most recent price in the set of closing prices that will be averaged. Frequently a line chart of these moving averages is plotted along with a line chart of daily closing prices. Each day the charts are updated and then examined for trends to see if there is a buy or sell signal present somewhere.

Alternatively, a long-term moving average may be compared with a short-term moving average (the distinction between the two averages is that the long-term average uses a substantially larger set of closing prices in its calculations than the short-term average). When the short-term average crosses the long-term average, a "signal" is said to have been given. The action recommended will depend on such things as whether the averages have been rising or falling, as well as the direction from which the short-term average crossed the long-term average (it may have been below and now is above, or it may have been above and now is below).

RELATIVE STRENGTH MEASURES

Another procedure used by technicians involves measuring what they call relative strength. For example, a stock's price may be divided by a price index of its industry each day to indicate the stock's movement relative to its industry. Similarly, an industry index may be divided by a market index to indicate the industry's movement relative to the market, or a stock's price may be divided by a market index to indicate a stock's movement relative to the market. The idea here is to examine changes in these relative strength measures with the hope of finding a pattern that can be used to accurately predict the future.

Some procedures of technical analysts focus on relationships among different indexes. For example, the Dow Theory requires that a pattern in the Dow Jones Industrial Average be "confirmed" by a certain movement in the Dow Jones Railroad (now Transportation) Average before action be taken. Another example involves computing the difference between the number of issues advancing and the number declining each day. A chart of the differences cumulated over time, known as the advance-decline line, may then be compared with a market index such as the Dow Jones Industrial Average.

CONTRARY OPINION

Many technical procedures are based on the idea of contrary opinion. The idea here is to determine the consensus opinion and then do the opposite. Two examples that were discussed earlier involved (1) buying stocks that had recently dropped in price and selling stocks that had recently risen in price, and (2) buying stocks with low P/E ratios and selling stocks with high P/E ratios. For a third example, one might see whether the "odd-lotters" (those who buy and sell in lots of less than 100 shares each) are buying, and then sell any holdings of these stocks. If "the little investor is usually wrong," this will be a procedure that is usually right. However, the basic premise about the little investor has yet to be factually established.

The widespread availability of personal computers and "dial-up" services with data on stock prices and volumes has made it possible for individual investors to engage in technical analysis in the privacy of their own homes. Producers of software have been quick to provide programs to perform such analysis, complete with multicolored graphs. Nevertheless, the number of investors that use fundamental analysis is much larger than the number using technical analysis.

REFERENCES

1. For a discussion of contrarian investment strategies, see:

David Dremen, *Contrarian Investment Strategies* (New York: Random House, Inc., 1979);

Werner F. M. De Bondt and Richard Thaler, "Does the Stock Market Overreact?" *Journal of Finance*, 40, no. 3 (July 1985): 793–805;

Werner F. M. De Bondt and Richard H. Thaler, "Further Evidence on Investor Overreaction and Stock Market Seasonality," *Journal of Finance*, 42, no. 3 (July 1987): 557–81;

K. C. Chan, "On the Contrarian Investment Strategy," *Journal of Business*, 61, no. 2 (April 1988): 147–63;

Paul Zarowin, "Short-Run Market Overreaction: Size and Seasonality Effects," *Journal of Portfolio Management*, 15, no. 3 (Spring 1989): 26–29;

Paul Zarowin, "Does the Stock Market Overreact to Corporate Earnings Information?" *Journal of Finance*, 44, no. 5 (December 1989): 1385–99;

Bruce N. Lehmann, "Fads, Martingales, and Market Efficiency," *Quarterly Journal of Economics*, 105, no. 1 (February 1990): 1–28;

Paul Zarowin, "Size, Seasonality, and Stock Market Overreaction," *Journal of Financial and Quantitative Analysis*, 25, no. 1 (March 1990): 113–25;

April Klein, "A Direct Test of the Cognitive Bias Theory of Share Price Reversals," *Journal of Accounting and Economics*, 13, no. 2 (July 1990): 155–66;

Jennifer Conrad and Gautam Kaul, "Long-Term Overreaction or Biases in Computed Returns?" unpublished paper, the University of Michigan, 1991;

Jennifer Conrad, Mustafa N. Gultekin, and Gautam Kaul, "Profitability of Short-Term Contrarian Portfolio Strategies," unpublished paper, the University of Michigan, 1991;

Navin Chopra, Josef Lakonishok, and Jay R. Ritter, "Measuring Abnormal Performances: Do Stocks Overreact?," *Journal of Financial Economics*, 31, no. 2 (April 1992): 235–68.

2. Closely related to the issue of contrarian investment strategies is the issue of how stock price levels in one period are related to stock price levels in a subsequent period. This issue, like the usefulness of contrarian strategies, has been open to debate; two of the earliest papers and two recent ones that contradict them are:

Eugene F. Fama and Kenneth R. French, "Permanent and Temporary Components of Stock Prices," *Journal of Political Economy*, 96, no. 2 (April 1988): 246–73;

James M. Poterba and Lawrence H. Summers, "Mean Reversion in Stock Prices: Evidence and Implications," *Journal of Financial Economics*, 22, no. 1 (October 1988): 27–59;

Myung Jig Kim, Charles R. Nelson, and Richard Startz, "Mean Reversion in Stock Prices? A Reappraisal of the Empirical Evidence," *Review of Economic Studies*, 58, no. 3 (May 1991): 515–28;

Grant McQueen, "Long-Horizon Mean-Reverting Stock Prices Revisited," *Journal of Financial and Quantitative Analysis*, 27, no. 1 (March 1992): 1–18.

3. The reaction of stock prices to the publication of analysts' recommendations is discussed in:

John C. Groth, Wilbur G. Lewellen, Gary G. Schlarbaum, and Ronald C. Lease, "An Analysis of Brokerage House Securities Recommendations," *Financial Analysts Journal*, 35, no. 1 (January/February 1979): 32–40;

James H. Bjerring, Josef Lakonishok, and Theo Vermaelen, "Stock Prices and Financial Analysts' Recommendations," *Journal of Finance*, 38, no. 1 (March 1983): 187–204.

4. The reactions of stock prices to recommendations published in the "Heard on the Street" column in *The Wall Street Journal* are discussed in:

Peter Lloyd-Davies and Michael Canes, "Stock Prices and the Publication of Second-Hand Information," *Journal of Business*, 51, no. 1 (January 1978): 43–56;

Pu Liu, Stanley D. Smith, and Azmat A. Syed, "Stock Price Reactions to *The Wall Street Journal*'s Securities Recommendations," *Journal of*

Financial and Quantitative Analysis, 25, no. 3 (September 1990): 399–410;

Messod Beneish, "Stock Prices and the Dissemination of Analysts' Recommendations," *Journal of Business*, 64, no. 3 (July 1991): 393–416.

The "Heard on the Street" column also sometimes discusses takeover rumors. For an analysis of the effects these rumors have on stock prices, see John Pound and Richard Zeckhauser, "Clearly Heard on the Street: The Effect of Takeover Rumors on Stock Prices," *Journal of Business*, 63, no. 3 (July 1990): 291–308.

5. For a discussion of the neglected firm effect, see:

Avner Arbel and Paul Strebel, "Pay Attention to Neglected Firms!" *Journal of Portfolio Management*, 9, no. 2 (Winter 1983): 37–42.

Avner Arbel, Steven Carvel, and Paul Strebel, "Giraffes, Institutions, and Neglected Firms," *Financial Analysts Journal*, 39, no. 3 (May/June 1983): 57–63.

6. Leading books on financial statement analysis, fundamental analysis, and technical analysis are, respectively:

George Foster, *Financial Statement Analysis* (Englewood Cliffs, N.J.: Prentice Hall, 1986);

Sidney Cottle, Roger Murray, and Frank Block, *Graham and Dodd's Security Analysis* (New York: McGraw-Hill, 1988);

Robert D. Edwards and John Magee, *Technical Analysis of Stock Trends* (Boston: John Magee, Inc., 1966).

15 Dividend Discount Models

In Chapter 14, it was noted that one purpose of financial analysis is to identify mispriced securities. Fundamental analysis was mentioned as one approach for conducting a search for such securities. With this approach, the security analyst makes estimates of such things as the firm's future earnings and dividends. If these estimates are substantially different from the average estimates of other analysts but are felt to be more accurate, then from the viewpoint of the security analyst, a mispriced security will have been identified. If it is also felt that the market price of the security will adjust to reflect these more accurate estimates, then the security will be expected to have an abnormal rate of return. Accordingly, the analyst will issue either a buy or sell recommendation, depending upon the direction of the anticipated price adjustment. Based upon the capitalization of income method of valuation, dividend discount models (DDMs) have been frequently used by fundamental analysts as a means of identifying mispriced stocks. This chapter will discuss DDMs and how they can be related to models based on price-earnings ratios.

CAPITALIZATION OF INCOME METHOD OF VALUATION

capitalization of income method of valuation

discount rate

There are many ways to implement the fundamental analysis approach to identifying mispriced securities. A number of them are either directly or indirectly related to what is sometimes referred to as the **capitalization of income method of valuation.**[1] This method states that the "true" or "intrinsic" value of any asset is based on the cash flows that the investor expects to receive in the future from owning the asset. Since these cash flows are expected in the future, they are discounted to reflect the time value of money, with the **discount rate** reflecting not only the time value of money but also the riskiness of the cash flows.

Algebraically, the intrinsic value of the asset (V) is equal to the sum of the present values of the expected cash flows:

$$V = \frac{C_1}{(1+k)^1} + \frac{C_2}{(1+k)^2} + \frac{C_3}{(1+k)^3} + \ldots$$

$$= \sum_{t=1}^{\infty} \frac{C_t}{(1+k)^t} \tag{15.1}$$

where C_t denotes the expected cash flow associated with the asset at time t and k is the appropriate discount rate for cash flows of this degree of risk. In this equation, the discount rate is assumed to be the same for all periods. Since the symbol "∞" above the summation sign in the equation denotes infinity, all expected cash flows, from immediately after making the investment until infinity, will be discounted at the same rate in determining V.[2]

Net Present Value

net present value

For the sake of convenience, let the current moment in time be denoted as zero, or $t = 0$. If the cost of purchasing an asset at $t = 0$ is P, then its **net present value** (NPV) is equal to the difference between its intrinsic value and cost, or:

$$\text{NPV} = V - P$$

$$= \left[\sum_{t=1}^{\infty} \frac{C_t}{(1+k)^t}\right] - P. \tag{15.2}$$

[1]The appendix describes a model used by some fundamental analysts for identifying winners (that is, underpriced common stocks) that is not directly related to the capitalization of income method of valuation. For a description of the typical financial characteristics of stock market winners, see Marc R. Reinganum, "The Anatomy of Stock Market Winners," *Financial Analysts Journal*, 44, no. 2 (March/April 1988): 16–28.

[2]Sometimes the expected cash flows after some time period will be equal to zero, meaning that the summation only needs to be carried out to that point. Even if they are never equal to zero, in many cases the denominator in equation (15.1) will become so large as t gets large (for example, if t is 40 or more for a discount rate of 15%) that the present value of all expected cash flows past an arbitrary time in the future will be roughly zero, and can be safely ignored.

The net present value calculation shown here is conceptually the same as the net present value calculation made for capital budgeting decisions that has long been advocated in introductory finance textbooks. Capital budgeting decisions involve deciding whether or not a given investment project should be undertaken (for example, should a new machine be purchased?). In making this decision, the focal point is the NPV of the project. Specifically, an investment project would be viewed favorably if its NPV is positive, and unfavorably if its NPV is negative. For a simple project involving a cash outflow now (at $t = 0$) and expected cash inflows in the future, a positive NPV means that the present value of all the expected cash inflows is greater than the cost of making the investment. Conversely, a negative NPV means that the present value of all the expected cash inflows is less than the cost of making the investment.

The same views about NPV apply when financial assets (like a share of common stock), instead of real assets (like a new machine), are being considered for purchase. That is, a financial asset is viewed favorably and said to be underpriced or undervalued if NPV > 0. Conversely, a financial asset is viewed unfavorably and said to be overpriced or overvalued if NPV < 0. From equation (15.2), this is equivalent to stating that a financial asset is underpriced if $V > P$:

$$\left[\sum_{t=1}^{\infty} \frac{C_t}{(1+k)^t}\right] > P. \tag{15.3}$$

Conversely, the asset is overvalued if $V < P$:

$$\left[\sum_{t=1}^{\infty} \frac{C_t}{(1+k)^t}\right] < P. \tag{15.4}$$

Internal Rate of Return

internal rate of return

Another way of making capital budgeting decisions in a manner that is similar to NPV involves calculating the **internal rate of return** (IRR) associated with the investment project. With IRR, NPV in equation (15.2) is set equal to zero and the discount rate becomes the unknown that must be calculated. That is, the IRR for a given investment is the discount rate that makes the net present value of the investment equal to zero. Algebraically, the procedure involves solving the following equation for the internal rate of return, denoted k^*:

$$0 = \left[\sum_{t=1}^{\infty} \frac{C_t}{(1+k^*)^t}\right] - P \tag{15.5}$$

where k^* is the IRR of the investment. Equivalently, equation (15.5) can be rewritten as:

$$P = \left[\sum_{t=1}^{\infty} \frac{C_t}{(1+k^*)^t}\right]. \tag{15.6}$$

The decision rule for IRR involves comparing the project's IRR, denoted k^*, with the required rate of return for an investment of similar risk, denoted k. Specifically, the investment would be viewed favorably if $k^* > k$, and unfavorably if $k^* < k$. As with NPV, the same decision rule applies if either a real asset or a financial asset is being considered for possible investment.[3]

An Application to Common Stocks

dividend discount models

This chapter is concerned with using the capitalization of income method to determine the intrinsic value of common stocks. Since the cash flows associated with an investment in any particular common stock are the dividends that are expected to be paid throughout the future on the shares purchased, the models suggested by this method of valuation are often known as **dividend discount models** (DDMs).[4] Accordingly, D_t will be used instead of C_t to denote the expected cash flow in period t associated with a particular common stock, resulting in the following restatement of equation (15.1):

$$V = \frac{D_1}{(1+k)^1} + \frac{D_2}{(1+k)^2} + \frac{D_3}{(1+k)^3} + \ldots$$

$$= \sum_{t=1}^{\infty} \frac{D_t}{(1+k)^t}. \tag{15.7}$$

Usually the focus of DDMs is on determining the "true" or "intrinsic" value of one share of a particular company's common stock, even if larger-size purchases are being contemplated. This is because it is usually assumed that larger-size purchases can be made at a cost that is a simple multiple of the cost of one share (for example, the cost of 1,000 shares is usually assumed to be 1,000 times the cost of one share). Thus, the numerator in DDMs is the cash dividends per share that are expected in the future.

However, there is a complication in using equation (15.7) to determine the intrinsic value of a share of common stock. In particular, in order to use this equation the investor must forecast *all* future dividends. Since common stock does not have a fixed lifetime, this suggests that an infinitely long stream of dividends must be forecast. While this may seem to be an impossible task, with the addition of certain assumptions, the equation can be made tractable (that is, usable).

These assumptions center around dividend growth rates. That is, the dividend per share at any time t can be viewed as being equal to the dividend per share at time $t-1$ times a dividend growth rate of g_t:

$$D_t = D_{t-1}(1 + g_t) \tag{15.8}$$

---

[3]With complex cash flows (such as a mix of positive and negative cash flows), the IRR method can be misleading. However, this is not a problem for securities such as stocks and bonds. For a discussion of potential problems in other contexts, see Richard A. Brealey and Stewart C. Myers, *Principles of Corporate Finance* (New York: McGraw-Hill, Inc., 1991), Chapter 5.

[4]Since the focus of DDMs is on predicting dividends, there is a particular situation where using DDMs to value common stocks is exceptionally difficult. This is the situation where the firm has not paid dividends on its stock in the recent past, which results in a complete lack of historical record on which to base a prediction of dividends. Examples include valuing the stock of a firm being sold to the public for the first time (known as an initial public offering or ipo), valuing the stock of a firm that has not paid dividends recently (perhaps the firm has never paid dividends, or perhaps it has suspended paying them), and valuing the stock of closely held firms. A more extensive discussion of DDMs is contained in the entire November–December 1985 issue of the *Financial Analysts Journal*. For articles that describe some of the current applications of DDMs, see Barbara Donnelly, "The Dividend Discount Model Comes into Its Own," *Institutional Investor*, 19, no. 3 (March 1985): 77–82, and Kent Hickman and Glen H. Petry, "A Comparison of Stock Price Predictions Using Court Accepted Formulas, Dividend Discount, and P/E Models," *Financial Management*, 19, no. 2 (Summer 1990): 76–87.

or, equivalently:

$$(D_t - D_{t-1})/D_{t-1} = g_t. \tag{15.9}$$

For example, if the dividend per share expected at $t = 2$ is \$4 and the dividend per share expected at $t = 3$ is \$4.20, then $g_3 = (\$4.20 - \$4)/\$4 = 5\%$. The different types of tractable DDMs reflect different sets of assumptions about dividend growth rates, and are presented next. The discussion begins with the simplest case, the zero growth model.

THE ZERO GROWTH MODEL

One assumption that could be made about future dividends is that they will remain at a fixed dollar amount. That is, the dollar amount of dividends per share that were paid over the past year (D_0) will also be paid over the next year (D_1), and the year after that (D_2), and the year after that (D_3), and so on. That is,

$$D_0 = D_1 = D_2 = D_3 = \ldots$$

This is equivalent to assuming that all the dividend growth rates are zero, since if $g_t = 0$, then $D_t = D_{t-1}$ in equation (15.8). Accordingly, this model is often referred to as the **zero growth** (or no growth) **model.**

zero growth model

The impact of this assumption on equation (15.7) can be analyzed by noting what happens when D_t is replaced by D_0 in the numerator:

$$V = \sum_{t=1}^{\infty} \frac{D_0}{(1+k)^t}. \tag{15.10}$$

Fortunately, equation (15.10) can be simplified by noting that D_0 is a fixed dollar amount, which means that it can be written outside the summation sign:

$$V = D_0\left[\sum_{t=1}^{\infty} \frac{1}{(1+k)^t}\right]. \tag{15.11}$$

The next step involves using a property of infinite series from mathematics. If $k > 0$, then it can be shown that:

$$\sum_{t=1}^{\infty} \frac{1}{(1+k)^t} = \frac{1}{k}. \tag{15.12}$$

Applying this property to equation (15.11) results in the following formula for the zero growth model:

$$V = D_0/k. \tag{15.13}$$

Since $D_0 = D_1$, equation (15.13) is written sometimes as:

$$V = D_1/k. \tag{15.14}$$

As an example of how this DDM can be used, assume that the Zinc Company is expected to pay cash dividends amounting to \$8 per share into the indefinite future and has a required rate of return of 10%. Using either equation (15.13) or equation (15.14), it can be seen that the value of a share of Zinc stock is equal to $8/.10 = $80. With a current stock price of $65 per share, equation (15.2) would suggest that the NPV per share is $80 − $65 = $15. Equivalently, since $V = \$80 > P = \$65$, the stock is underpriced by $15 per share, and would be a candidate for purchase.

Internal Rate of Return

Equation (15.13) can be reformulated to solve for the internal rate of return on an investment in a zero growth security. First, the current price of the security is substituted for V and second, k^* is substituted for k. Doing so results in:

$$P = D_0/k^*$$

which can be rewritten as:

$$k^* = D_0/P \qquad (15.15a)$$

$$= D_1/P. \qquad (15.15b)$$

Applying this formula to the stock of Zinc indicates that $k^* = \$8/\$65 = 12.3\%$. Since the IRR from an investment in Zinc exceeds the required rate of return on Zinc (12.3% > 10%), this method also indicates that Zinc is underpriced.[5]

An Application

The zero growth model may seem quite restrictive. After all, it does not seem reasonable to assume that a given stock will pay a fixed dollar–size dividend forever. While such a criticism has validity for common stock valuation, there is one particular situation where this model is quite useful. Specifically, whenever the intrinsic value of a share of preferred stock is to be determined, this DDM will often be appropriate. This is because most preferred stock is nonparticipating, meaning that it pays a fixed dollar–size dividend that will not be changed as earnings per share changes. Furthermore, it can be expected to be paid forever, since preferred stock does not have a fixed lifetime.

THE CONSTANT GROWTH MODEL

constant growth model

The next type of DDM to be considered is one that assumes that dividends will grow from period to period at the same rate forever, and is therefore known as the **constant growth model.**[6] Specifically, the dividends per share that were paid over the previous year (D_0) are expected to grow at a given g, so that the

[5]A share of common stock has a positive NPV if and only if it has an IRR greater than its required rate of return. Thus, there can never be inconsistent signals given by the two approaches. That is, there will never be a situation where one approach indicates that a stock is underpriced and the other approach indicates that it is overpriced. This is true not only for the zero growth model, but for all DDMs.

[6]For an extension of this model that introduces capital gains taxes, see Raymond Chiang and Ricardo J. Rodriguez, "Personal Taxes, Holding Period, and the Valuation of Growth Stocks," *Journal of Economics and Business*, 42, no. 4 (November 1990): 303–9.

dividends expected over the next year (D_1) are expected to be equal to $D_0 (1 + g)$. Dividends the year after that are again expected to grow by the rate g, meaning that $D_2 = D_1 (1 + g)$. Since $D_1 = D_0 (1 + g)$, this is equivalent to assuming that $D_2 = D_0 (1 + g)^2$ and, in general:

$$D_t = D_{t-1} (1 + g) \qquad (15.16a)$$

$$= D_0 (1 + g)^t. \qquad (15.16b)$$

The impact of this assumption on equation (15.7) can be analyzed by noting what happens when D_t is replaced by $D_0 (1 + g)^t$ in the numerator:

$$V = \sum_{t=1}^{\infty} \frac{D_0 (1 + g)^t}{(1 + k)^t}. \qquad (15.17)$$

Fortunately, equation (15.17) can be simplified by noting that D_0 is a given dollar amount, which means that it can be written outside the summation sign:

$$V = D_0 \left[\sum_{t=1}^{\infty} \frac{(1 + g)^t}{(1 + k)^t} \right]. \qquad (15.18)$$

The next step involves using a property of infinite series from mathematics. If $k > g$, then it can be shown that:

$$\sum_{t=1}^{\infty} \frac{(1 + g)^t}{(1 + k)^t} = \frac{1 + g}{k - g}. \qquad (15.19)$$

Substituting equation (15.19) into equation (15.18) results in the valuation formula for the constant growth model:

$$V = D_0 \left[\frac{1 + g}{k - g} \right]. \qquad (15.20)$$

Sometimes equation (15.20) is rewritten as:

$$V = D_1/(k - g) \qquad (15.21)$$

since $D_1 = D_0 (1 + g)$.

As an example of how this DDM can be used, assume that during the past year the Copper Company paid dividends amounting to \$1.80 per share. The forecast is that dividends on Copper stock will increase by 5% per year into the indefinite future. Thus, dividends over the next year are expected to equal \$1.80(1 + .05) = \$1.89. Using equation (15.20) and assuming the required rate of return of 11%, it can be seen that the value of a share of Copper stock is equal to \$1.80[(1 + .05)/(.11 − .05)] = \$1.89/(.11 − .05) = \$31.50. With a current stock price of \$40 per share, equation (15.2) would suggest that the NPV per share is \$31.50 − \$40 = −\$8.50. Equivalently, since $V =$ \$31.50 $< P =$ \$40, the stock is overpriced by \$8.50 per share, and would be a candidate for sale if currently owned.

Internal Rate of Return

Equation (15.20) can be reformulated to solve for the internal rate of return on an investment in a constant growth security. First, the current price of the security is substituted for V and then k^* is substituted for k. Doing so results in:

$$P = D_0\left[\frac{1 + g}{k^* - g}\right] \tag{15.22}$$

which can be rewritten as:

$$k^* = \frac{D_0(1 + g)}{P} + g \tag{15.23a}$$

$$= \frac{D_1}{P} + g. \tag{15.23b}$$

Applying this formula to the stock of Copper indicates that $k^* =$ [\$1.80(1 + .05)/\$40] + .05 = [\$1.89/\$40] + .05 = 9.72%. Since the required rate of return on Copper exceeds the IRR from an investment in Copper (11% > 9.72%), this method also indicates that Copper is overpriced.

Relationship to the Zero Growth Model

The zero growth model of the previous section can be shown to be a special case of the constant growth model. In particular, if the growth rate g is assumed to be equal to zero, then dividends will be a fixed dollar amount forever, which is the same as saying that there will be zero growth. Letting $g = 0$ in equations (15.20) and (15.23a) results in two equations that are identical to (15.13) and (15.15a), respectively.

While assuming constant growth may seem less restrictive than assuming no growth, it may still be viewed as unrealistic in many cases. However, as will be shown next, the constant growth model is important because it is embedded in the multiple growth model.

THE MULTIPLE GROWTH MODEL

multiple growth model

A more general DDM for valuing common stocks is the **multiple growth model.** With this model, the focus is on a time in the future after which dividends are expected to grow at a constant rate g. While the investor is still concerned with forecasting dividends, these dividends do not need to have any specific pattern until this time, after which they will be assumed to have the specific pattern of constant growth. If this time is denoted T, then dividends $D_1, D_2, D_3, \ldots, D_T$ will be forecasted separately by the investor (the investor also forecasts when this time T will occur). Thereafter, dividends are assumed to grow by a constant rate g that the investor must also forecast, meaning that

$$D_{T+1} = D_T\,(1 + g)$$

$$D_{T+2} = D_{T+1}\,(1 + g) = D_T\,(1 + g)^2$$

$$D_{T+3} = D_{T+2}\,(1 + g) = D_T\,(1 + g)^3$$

and so on. Figure 15-1 presents a time line of dividends and growth rates associated with the multiple growth model.

In determining the value of a share of common stock with the multiple growth model, the present value of the forecasted stream of dividends must be determined. This can be done by dividing the stream into two parts, finding the present value of each part, and then adding these two present values together.

The first part consists of finding the present value of all the forecasted dividends up to and including T. Denoting this present value as V_{T-}, it is equal to:

$$V_{T-} = \sum_{t=1}^{T} \frac{D_t}{(1+k)^t}. \tag{15.24}$$

The second part consists of finding the present value of all the forecasted dividends after T, and involves the application of the constant growth model. The application begins by imagining that the investor is not at time zero ($t = 0$) but is at time T ($t = T$), and has not changed his or her forecast of dividends for the stock. This means that next period's dividend, D_{T+1}, and all those thereafter are expected to grow at the rate g. Thus, the investor would be viewing the stock as having a constant growth rate, and its value *at time T* (V_T) could be determined with the constant growth model of equation (15.21):

$$V_T = D_{T+1}\left[\frac{1}{k-g}\right]. \tag{15.25}$$

One way to view V_T is that it represents a lump sum that is just as desirable as the stream of dividends after T. That is, an investor would find a lump sum of cash equal to V_T, to be received at T, to be equally desirable as the stream of dividends $D_{T+1}, D_{T+2}, D_{T+3}$, and so on. Now, given that the investor is at time zero ($t = 0$), not at T, the present value at $t = 0$ of the lump sum V_T must be determined. This is done simply by discounting it for T periods at the

FIGURE 15-1
Time Line for Multiple Growth Model

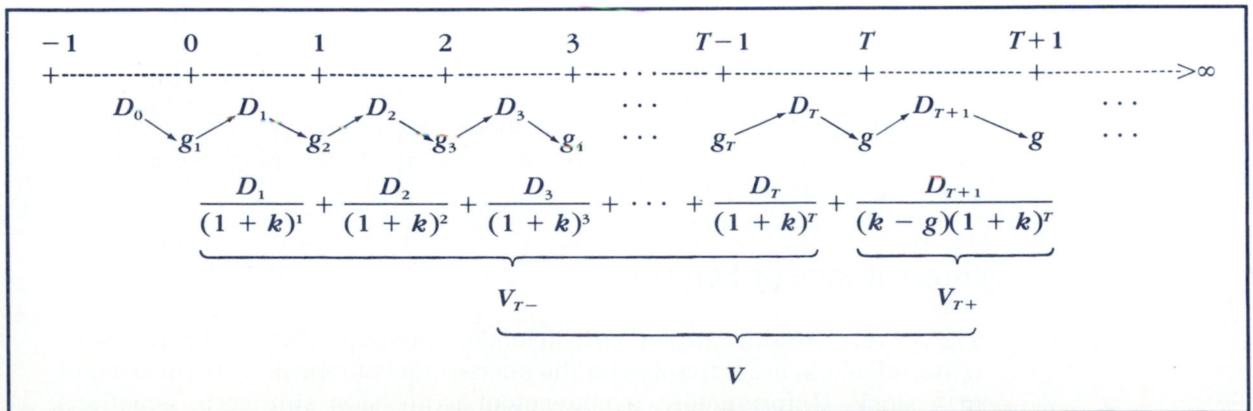

rate k, resulting in the following formula for finding the present value at time zero for all dividends after T, denoted V_{T+}:

$$V_{T+} = V_T\left[\frac{1}{(1+k)^T}\right]$$
$$= \left[\frac{D_{T+1}}{(k-g)(1+k)^T}\right]. \tag{15.26}$$

Having found the present value of all dividends up to and including T with equation (15.24), and the present value of all dividends after T with equation (15.26), the value of the stock can be determined by summing up these two amounts:

$$V = V_{T-} + V_{T+}$$
$$= \left[\sum_{t=1}^{T}\frac{D_t}{(1+k)^t}\right] + \left[\frac{D_{T+1}}{(k-g)(1+k)^T}\right]. \tag{15.27}$$

Figure 15-1 illustrates the valuation procedure for the multiple growth DDM that is given in equation (15.27).

An Example As an example of how this DDM can be used, assume that during the past year the Magnesium Company paid dividends amounting to $.75 per share. Over the next year, Magnesium is expected to pay dividends of $2 per share. Thus, $g_1 = (D_1 - D_0)/D_0 = (\$2 - \$.75)/\$.75 = 167\%$. The year after that, dividends are expected to amount to $3 per share, indicating that $g_2 = (D_2 - D_1)/D_1 = (\$3 - \$2)/\$2 = 50\%$. At this time, the forecast is that dividends will grow by 10% per year into the indefinite future, indicating that $T = 2$ and $g = 10\%$. Consequently, $D_{T+1} = D_3 = \$3(1 + .10) = \$3.30$. Given a required rate of return on Magnesium shares of 15%, the value of V_{T-} and V_{T+} can be calculated, respectively, as follows:

$$V_{T-} = \frac{\$2}{(1+.15)^1} + \frac{\$3}{(1+.15)^2}$$
$$= \$4.01$$

$$V_{T+} = \frac{\$3.30}{(.15-.10)(1+.15)^2}$$
$$= \$49.91.$$

Summing V_{T-} and V_{T+} results in a value for V of $\$4.01 + \$49.91 = \$53.92$. With a current stock price of $55 per share, Magnesium appears to be fairly priced. That is, since V and P are nearly of equal size, Magnesium is not significantly mispriced.

Internal Rate of Return

The zero growth and constant growth models have equations for V that can be reformulated in order to solve for the internal rate of return on an investment in a stock. Unfortunately, a convenient expression similar to equations (15.15a), (15.15b), (15.23a), and (15.23b) is not available for the multiple growth model. This can be seen by noting that the expression for IRR is derived by substituting P for V, and k^* for k in equation (15.27):

$$P = \left[\sum_{t=1}^{T} \frac{D_t}{(1 + k^*)^t}\right] + \left[\frac{D_{T+1}}{(k^* - g)(1 + k^*)^T}\right]. \tag{15.28}$$

This equation cannot be rewritten with k^* isolated on the left-hand side, meaning that a closed-form expression for IRR does not exist for the multiple growth model.

However, all is not lost. It is still possible to calculate the IRR for an investment in a stock conforming to the multiple growth model by using an "educated" trial-and-error method. That is, after setting up equation (15.28), an estimate for k^* could be tried. If the resulting value on the right-hand side was larger than P, then a larger k^* would be tried. Conversely, if the resulting value was smaller than P, then a smaller k^* would be tried. Continuing this search process, the investor could hone in on the value of k^*.[7]

Applying equation (15.28) to the Magnesium Company results in:

$$\$55 = \frac{\$2}{(1 + k^*)^1} + \frac{\$3}{(1 + k^*)^2} + \frac{\$3.30}{(k^* - .10)(1 + k^*)^2}. \tag{15.29}$$

Initially a rate of 14% may be used in attempting to solve this equation for k^*. Inserting 14% for k^* in the right-hand side of equation (15.29) results in a value of \$67.54. Earlier 15% was used in determining V and resulted in a value of \$53.92. This means that k^* must have a value between 14% and 15%, since \$55 is between \$67.54 and \$53.92. If 14.5% is tried next, the resulting value is \$59.97, suggesting that a higher rate should be tried. If 14.8% and14.9% are subsequently tried, the respective resulting values are \$56.18 and \$55.03. Since \$55.03 is the closest to P, the IRR associated with an investment in Magnesium is 14.9%. Given a required return of 15% and an IRR of approximately that amount, the stock of Magnesium appears to be fairly priced.

Relationship to the Constant Growth Model

The constant growth model can be shown to be a special case of the multiple growth model. In particular, if the time when constant growth is assumed to begin is set equal to zero, then:

$$V_{T-} = \sum_{t=1}^{T} \frac{D_t}{(1 + k)^t} = 0$$

and

$$V_{T+} = \left[\frac{D_{T+1}}{(k - g)(1 + k)^T}\right] = \left[\frac{D_1}{k - g}\right]$$

since $T = 0$ and $(1 + k)^0 = 1$. Given that the multiple growth model states that $V = V_{T-} + V_{T+}$, it can be seen that setting $T = 0$ results in $V = D_1/(k - g)$, a formula that is equivalent to the formula for the constant growth model.

---

[7]It is a relatively simple matter to program a computer to conduct the search for k^* in equation (15.28). Most spreadsheets include a function that does so automatically.

Two-Phase and Three-Phase Models

Two dividend discount models that are sometimes used are the two-phase model and the three-phase model.[8] The two-phase model assumes that a constant growth rate (g_1) exists only until some time T, when a different growth rate (g_2) is assumed to begin and continue thereafter. The three-phase method assumes that a constant growth rate (g_1) exists only until some time T_1, when a second growth rate is assumed to begin and last until a later time T_2, when a third growth rate is assumed to begin and last thereafter. By letting V_{T+} denote the present value of all dividends after the last growth rate has begun, and V_{T-} denote the present value of all the preceding dividends, it can be seen that these models are just special cases of the multiple growth models.

In applying the capitalization of income method of valuation to common stocks, it might seem appropriate to assume that the stock will be sold at some point in the future. In this case, the expected cash flows would consist of the dividends up to that point as well as the expected selling price. Since dividends after the selling date would be ignored, the use of a dividend discount model may seem to be improper. However, as will be shown next, this is not so.

VALUATION BASED ON A FINITE HOLDING PERIOD

The capitalization of income method of valuation involves discounting all dividends that are expected throughout the future. Since the simplified models of zero growth, constant growth, and multiple growth are based on this method, they too involve a future stream of dividends. Upon reflection, it may seem that such models are relevant only for an investor who plans to hold a stock forever, since such an investor would expect to receive this stream of future dividends.

But what about an investor who plans to sell the stock in a year?[9] In such a situation, the cash flows that the investor expects to receive from purchasing a share of the stock are equal to the dividend expected one year from now (for ease of exposition, it is assumed that common stocks pay dividends annually) and the expected selling price of the stock. Thus, it would seem appropriate to determine the intrinsic value of the stock to the investor by discounting these two cash flows at the required rate of return as follows:

$$V = \frac{D_1 + P_1}{1 + k}$$

$$= \left[\frac{D_1}{1 + k}\right] + \left[\frac{P_1}{1 + k}\right] \tag{15.30}$$

[8]For a discussion of these models, see Russell J. Fuller and Chi-Cheng Hsia, "A Simplified Common Stock Valuation Model," *Financial Analysts Journal*, 40, no. 5 (September/October 1984): 49–56; Eric H. Sorensen and David A. Williamson, "Some Evidence on the Value of Dividend Discount Models," *Financial Analysts Journal*, 41, no. 6 (November/December 1985): 60–69; and Richard W. Taylor, "A Three-Phase Quarterly Dividend Discount Model," *Financial Analysts Journal*, 44, no. 5 (September/October 1988): 79–80, and "A Three-Phase Quarterly Earnings Model," *Financial Analysts Journal*, 45, no. 5 (September/October 1989): 79.

[9]The analysis is similar if it is assumed that the investor plans to sell the stock after some other length of time, such as six months or two years.

where D_1 and P_1 are the expected dividend and selling price at $t = 1$, respectively.

In order to use equation (15.30), the expected price of the stock at $t = 1$ must be estimated. The simplest approach assumes that the selling price will be based on the dividends that are expected to be paid after the selling date. Thus, the expected selling price at $t = 1$ is:

$$P_1 = \frac{D_2}{(1+k)^1} + \frac{D_3}{(1+k)^2} + \frac{D_4}{(1+k)^3} + \cdots$$

$$= \sum_{t=2}^{\infty} \frac{D_t}{(1+k)^{t-1}}. \tag{15.31}$$

Substituting equation (15.31) for P_1 in the right-hand side of equation (15.30) results in:

$$V = \left[\frac{D_1}{1+k}\right] + \left[\frac{D_2}{(1+k)^1} + \frac{D_3}{(1+k)^2} + \frac{D_4}{(1+k)^3} + \cdots\right]\left[\frac{1}{1+k}\right]$$

$$= \left[\frac{D_1}{(1+k)^1}\right] + \left[\frac{D_2}{(1+k)^2} + \frac{D_3}{(1+k)^3} + \frac{D_4}{(1+k)^4} + \cdots\right]$$

$$= \sum_{t=1}^{\infty} \frac{D_t}{(1+k)^t}$$

which is exactly the same as equation (15.7). Thus, valuing a share of common stock by discounting its dividends up to some point in the future and its expected selling price at that time is equivalent to valuing stock by discounting all future dividends. Simply stated, the two are equivalent because the expected selling price is itself based on dividends to be paid after the selling date. Thus, equation (15.7), as well as the zero growth, constant growth, and multiple growth models that are based on it, is appropriate for determining the intrinsic value of a share of common stock regardless of the length of the investor's planned holding period.

An Example As an example, reconsider the common stock of the Copper Company. Over the past year it was noted that Copper paid dividends of \$1.80 per share, with the forecast that the dividends would grow by 5% per year forever. This means that dividends over the next two years (D_1 and D_2) are forecasted to be \$1.80(1 + .05) = \$1.89 and \$1.89(1 + .05) = \$1.985, respectively. If the investor plans to sell the stock after one year, the selling price could be estimated by noting that at $t = 1$, the forecast of dividends for the forthcoming year would be D_2, or \$1.985. Thus, the anticipated selling price at $t = 1$, denoted P_1, would be equal to \$1.985/(.11 − .05) = \$33.08. Accordingly, the intrinsic value of Copper to such an investor would be equal to the present value of the expected cash flows, which are $D_1 = \$1.89$ and $P_1 = \$33.08$. Using equation (15.30) and assuming a required rate of 11%, this value is equal to (\$1.89 + \$33.08)/(1 + .11) = \$31.50. Note that this is the same amount that was calculated earlier when all the dividends from now to infinity were discounted using the constant growth model: $V = D_1/(k - g) = \$1.89/(.11 - .05) = \$31.50$.

MODELS BASED ON PRICE-EARNINGS RATIOS

Despite the inherent sensibility of dividend discount models, many security analysts use a much simpler procedure to value common stocks. First, a stock's earnings per share over the forthcoming year (E_1) will be estimated and then the analyst (or someone else) will estimate a "normal" **price-earnings ratio** for the stock. The product of these two numbers gives the estimated future price (P_1). Together with estimated dividends to be paid during the period (D_1) and current price (P), the estimated return on the stock over the period can be determined:

price-earnings ratio

$$\text{expected return} = \frac{(P_1 - P) + D_1}{P}. \tag{15.32}$$

Some security analysts expand this procedure, estimating earnings per share and price-earnings ratios for optimistic, most likely, and pessimistic scenarios to produce a rudimentary probability distribution of a security's return. Other analysts determine whether a stock is underpriced or overpriced by comparing the stock's actual price-earnings ratio with its "normal" price-earnings ratio, as will be shown next.[10]

In order to make this comparison, equation (15.7) must be rearranged and some new variables must be introduced. To begin, it should be noted that earnings per share (E_t) are related to dividends per share (D_t) by the firm's **payout ratio** (p_t):

payout ratio

$$D_t = p_t E_t. \tag{15.33}$$

Note that if an analyst has forecasted earnings-per-share and payout ratios, then he or she has implicitly forecasted dividends.

Equation (15.33) can be used to restate the various DDMs where the focus is on estimating what the stock's price-earnings ratio should be instead of on estimating the intrinsic value of the stock. In order to do so, $p_t E_t$ is substituted for D_t in the right-hand side of equation (15.7), resulting in a general formula for determining a stock's intrinsic value that involves discounting earnings:

$$\begin{aligned} V &= \frac{D_1}{(1+k)^1} + \frac{D_2}{(1+k)^2} + \frac{D_3}{(1+k)^3} + \dots \\ &= \frac{p_1 E_1}{(1+k)^1} + \frac{p_2 E_2}{(1+k)^2} + \frac{p_3 E_3}{(1+k)^3} + \dots \\ &= \sum_{t=1}^{\infty} \frac{p_t E_t}{(1+k)^t}. \end{aligned} \tag{15.34}$$

Earlier, it was noted that dividends in adjacent time periods could be viewed as being "linked" to each other by a dividend growth rate, g_t.

earnings-price ratio

[10] Alternatively, some analysts focus on the **earnings-price ratio**, which is the reciprocal of the price-earnings ratio. Accordingly, the formulas for a stock's "normal" earnings-price ratio can be found by simply taking the reciprocal of the forthcoming formulas for determining a stock's "normal" price-earnings ratio. In cases where earnings are close to zero, the earnings-price ratio is computationally preferred by analysts to the price-earnings ratio. This is because it approaches zero in such a situation, while the price-earnings ratio approaches infinity.

Similarly, earnings per share in any year t can be "linked" to earnings per share in the previous year $t - 1$ by a growth rate in earnings per share, g_{et}:

$$E_t = E_{t-1} (1 + g_{et}). \tag{15.35}$$

This implies that:

$$E_1 = E_0 (1 + g_{e1})$$
$$E_2 = E_1 (1 + g_{e2}) = E_0 (1 + g_{e1}) (1 + g_{e2})$$
$$E_3 = E_2 (1 + g_{e3}) = E_0 (1 + g_{e1}) (1 + g_{e2}) (1 + g_{e3})$$

and so on, where E_0 is the actual level of earnings per share over the past year, E_1 is the expected level of earnings per share over the forthcoming year, E_2 is the expected level of earnings per share for the year after E_1, and E_3 is the expected level of earnings per share for the year after E_2.

These equations relating expected future earnings per share to E_0 can be substituted into equation (15.34), resulting in:

$$V = \frac{p_1[E_0(1 + g_{e1})]}{(1 + k)^1} + \frac{p_2[E_0(1 + g_{e1})(1 + g_{e2})]}{(1 + k)^2} + \frac{p_3[E_0(1 + g_{e1})(1 + g_{e2})(1 + g_{e3})]}{(1 + k)^3} + \ldots \tag{15.36}$$

Since V is the intrinsic value of a share of stock, it represents what the stock should be selling for if it were fairly priced. It follows that V/E_0 represents what the price-earnings ratio should be if the stock were fairly priced, and is sometimes referred to as the stock's "normal" price-earnings ratio. Dividing both sides of equation (15.36) by E_0 and simplifying results in the formula for determining the "normal" price-earnings ratio:

$$\frac{V}{E_0} = \frac{p_1(1 + g_{e1})}{(1 + k)^1} + \frac{p_2(1 + g_{e1})(1 + g_{e2})}{(1 + k)^2} + \frac{p_3(1 + g_{e1})(1 + g_{e2})(1 + g_{e3})}{(1 + k)^3} + \ldots \tag{15.37}$$

This shows that, other things being equal, a stock's "normal" price-earnings ratio will be *higher:*

the *greater* the expected payout ratios ($p_1, p_2, p_3, \ldots$),
the *greater* the expected growth rates in earnings per share ($g_{e1}, g_{e2}, g_{e3}, \ldots$), and
the *smaller* the required rate of return (k).

The qualifying phrase "other things being equal" should not be overlooked. For example, a firm cannot increase the value of its shares by simply planning on having greater payouts. This will increase $p_1, p_2, p_3, \ldots$, but will decrease the expected growth rates in earnings per share $g_{e1}, g_{e2}, g_{e3}, \ldots$. Assuming that the firm's investment policy is not altered, the effects of the reduced growth in earnings per share will just offset the effects of the increased payouts, leaving value per share unchanged.

Earlier, it was noted that a stock was viewed as being underpriced if

$V > P$ and overpriced if $V < P$. Since dividing both sides of an inequality by a positive constant will not change the direction of the inequality, such a division can be done here to the two inequalities involving V and P, where the positive constant is E_0. The result is that a stock can be viewed as being underpriced if $V/E_0 > P/E_0$ and overpriced if $V/E_0 < P/E_0$. Thus, a stock will be underpriced if its "normal" price-earnings ratio is greater than its actual price-earnings ratio, and overpriced if its "normal" price-earnings ratio is less than its actual price-earnings ratio.

Unfortunately, equation (15.37) is intractable, meaning that it cannot be used to estimate the "normal" price-earnings ratio for any stock. However, simplifying assumptions can be made that result in tractable formulas for estimating "normal" price-earnings ratios. These assumptions, along with the formulas, parallel those made previously regarding dividends and, with one exception, are discussed next.[11]

The Zero Growth Model

The zero growth model assumed that dividends per share remained at a fixed dollar amount forever. This is most likely if earnings per share remain at a fixed dollar amount forever, with the firm maintaining a 100% payout ratio. Why 100%? Because if a lesser amount were assumed to be paid out, it would mean that the firm was retaining part of its earnings. These retained earnings would be put to some use, and would thus be expected to increase future earnings and hence dividends per share.

Accordingly, the zero growth model can be interpreted as assuming $p_t = 1$ for all time periods and $E_0 = E_1 = E_2 = E_3$ and so on. This means that $D_0 = E_0 = D_1 = E_1 = D_2 = E_2$ and so on, allowing valuation equation (15.13) to be restated as:

$$V = E_0/k. \tag{15.38}$$

Dividing equation (15.38) by E_0 results in the formula for the "normal" price-earnings ratio for a stock having zero growth:

$$V/E_0 = 1/k. \tag{15.39}$$

An Example Earlier, it was assumed that the Zinc Company was a zero growth firm paying dividends of \$8 per share, selling for \$65 a share, and having a required rate of return of 10%. Since Zinc is a zero growth company, it will be assumed that it has a 100% payout ratio which, in turn, means that $E_0 = \$8$. At this point, equation (15.38) can be used to note that a "normal" price-earnings ratio for Zinc is $1/.10 = 10$. Since Zinc has an actual price-earnings ratio of $\$65/\$8 = 8.1$, and since $V/E_0 = 10 > P/E_0 = 8.1$, it can be seen that Zinc stock is underpriced.

The Constant Growth Model

Earlier, it was noted that dividends in adjacent time periods could be viewed as being connected to each other by a dividend growth rate, g_t. Similarly, it was noted that earnings per share can be connected by an earnings growth rate, g_{et}. The constant growth model assumes that the growth rate in dividends

[11]The exception is the multiple growth case.

per share will be the same throughout the future. An equivalent assumption is that earnings per share will grow at a constant rate (g_e) throughout the future, with the payout ratio remaining at a constant level (p). This means that:

$$E_1 = E_0(1 + g_e)$$
$$E_2 = E_1(1 + g_e) = E_0(1 + g_e)(1 + g_e)$$
$$E_3 = E_2(1 + g_e) = E_0(1 + g_e)(1 + g_e)(1 + g_e)$$

and so on. In general, earnings in year t can be connected to E_0 as follows:

$$E_t = E_0(1 + g_e)^t. \tag{15.40}$$

Substituting equation (15.40) into the numerator of equation (15.34) and recognizing that $p_t = p$ results in the following:

$$V = \sum_{t=1}^{\infty} \frac{pE_0(1 + g_e)^t}{(1 + k)^t}$$
$$= pE_0\left[\sum_{t=1}^{\infty} \frac{(1 + g_e)^t}{(1 + k)^t}\right]. \tag{15.41}$$

The same mathematical property of infinite series given in equation (15.19) can be applied to equation (15.41), resulting in:

$$V = pE_0\left[\frac{1 + g_e}{k - g_e}\right]. \tag{15.42}$$

It can be noted that the earnings-based constant growth model has a numerator that is identical to the numerator of the dividend-based constant growth model, since $pE_0 = D_0$. Furthermore, the denominators of the two models are identical. Both assertions require the growth rates in earnings and dividends be the same (that is, $g_e = g$). Examination of the assumptions of the models reveals that these growth rates must be equal. This can be seen by recalling that constant earnings growth means:

$$E_t = E_{t-1}(1 + g_e).$$

Now, when both sides of this equation are multiplied by the constant payout ratio, the result is:

$$pE_t = pE_{t-1}(1 + g_e).$$

Since $pE_t = D_t$ and $pE_{t-1} = D_{t-1}$, this equation reduces to:

$$D_t = D_{t-1}(1 + g_e)$$

which indicates that dividends in any period $t - 1$ will grow by the earnings growth rate, g_e. Since the dividend-based constant growth model assumed that dividends in any period $t - 1$ would grow by the dividend growth rate g, it can be seen that the two growth rates must be equal for the two models to be equivalent.

Equation (15.42) can be restated by dividing each side by E_0, resulting in the following formula for determining the "normal" price-earnings ratio for a stock with constant growth:

$$\frac{V}{E_0} = p\left[\frac{1 + g_e}{k - g_e}\right]. \tag{15.43}$$

An Example Earlier, it was assumed that the Copper Company had paid dividends of \$1.80 per share over the past year, with a forecast that dividends would grow by 5% per year forever. Furthermore, it was assumed that the required rate of return on Copper was 11%, and the current stock price was \$40 per share. Now, assuming that E_0 was \$2.70, it can be seen that the payout ratio was equal to \$1.80/\$2.70 = 66⅔%. This means that the "normal" price-earnings ratio for Copper, according to equation (15.43), is equal to .6667 [(1 + .05)/(.11 − .05)] = 11.67. Since this is less than Copper's actual price-earnings ratio of \$40/\$2.70 = 14.81, it follows that the stock of Copper Company is overpriced.

SOURCES OF EARNINGS GROWTH

So far, no explanation has been given as to why earnings or dividends will be expected to grow in the future. One way of providing such an explanation uses the constant growth model. Assuming that no new capital is obtained externally and no shares are repurchased (meaning that the number of shares outstanding does not increase or decrease), the portion of earnings not paid to stockholders as dividends will be used to pay for the firm's new investments. Given that p_t denotes the payout ratio in year t, then $(1 - p_t)$ will be equal to the portion of earnings not paid out, known as the **retention ratio.** Furthermore, the firm's new investments, stated on a per-share basis and denoted I_t, will be:

retention ratio

$$I_t = (1 - p_t)E_t. \tag{15.44}$$

If these new investments have an average return on equity of r_t in period t and every year thereafter, they will add r_tI_t to earnings per share in year $t + 1$ and every year thereafter. If all previous investments also produce perpetual earnings at a constant rate of return, next year's earnings will equal this year's earnings plus the new earnings resulting from this year's new investments:

$$\begin{aligned} E_{t+1} &= E_t + r_tI_t \\ &= E_t + r_t(1 - p_t)E_t \\ &= E_t[1 + r_t(1 - p_t)]. \end{aligned} \tag{15.45}$$

Since the growth rate in earnings per share, as defined earlier, is:

$$E_{t+1} = E_t[1 + g_{et+1}] \tag{15.46}$$

a comparison of equations (15.45) and (15.46) indicates that:

$$g_{et+1} = r_t(1 - p_t). \tag{15.47}$$

If the growth rate in earnings per share (g_{et+1}) is to be constant over time, then the average return on equity for new investments (r_t) and payout ratio (p_t) must also be constant over time. In this situation, equation (15.47) can be simplified by removing the time subscripts:

$$g_e = r(1 - p). \tag{15.48a}$$

Since the growth rate in dividends per share (g) is equal to the growth rate in earnings per share (g_e), this equation can be rewritten as:

$$g = r(1 - p). \tag{15.48b}$$

From this equation it can be seen that the growth rate g depends on (1) the proportion of earnings that is retained (1 − p), and (2) the average return on equity for the earnings that are retained (r).

The constant-growth valuation formula given in equation (15.20) can be modified by replacing g with the expression on the right-hand side of equation (15.48b), resulting in:

$$\begin{aligned} V &= D_0\left[\frac{1+g}{k-g}\right] \\ &= D_0\left[\frac{1+r(1-p)}{k-r(1-p)}\right]. \end{aligned} \tag{15.49}$$

In terms of price-earnings ratios, the formula in equation (15.43) becomes:

$$\begin{aligned} \frac{V}{E_0} &= p\left[\frac{1+g_e}{k-g_e}\right] \\ &= p\left[\frac{1+r(1-p)}{k-r(1-p)}\right]. \end{aligned} \tag{15.50}$$

Under these assumptions, a stock's price-earnings ratio should be greater, the greater its average return on equity for new investments, other things being equal.

An Example

Continuing with the Copper Company, recall that E_0 = \$2.70 and p = 66⅔%.This means that 33⅓% of earnings per share over the past year were retained and reinvested, an amount equal to .3333 × \$2.70 = \$.90. The earnings per share in the forthcoming year (E_1) are expected to be \$2.70(1 + .05) = \$2.835, since the growth rate (g) for Copper is 5%. The source of the increase in earnings per share of \$2.835 − \$2.70 = \$.135 is the \$.90 per share that was reinvested at t = 0. The average return on equity for new investments (r) is 15%, since \$.135/\$.90 = 15%. That is, the reinvested earnings of \$.90 per share can be viewed as having generated an annual increase in earnings per share of \$.135. This increase will occur not only at t = 1, but also at t = 2, t = 3, and so on. Equivalently, a \$.90 investment at t = 0 will generate a perpetual annual cash inflow of \$.135 beginning at t = 1.

Expected dividends at t = 1 can be calculated by multiplying the expected payout ratio (p) of 66⅔% times the expected earnings per share (E_1)

of \$2.835, or .6667 × \$2.835 = \$1.89. It can also be calculated by multiplying one plus the growth rate (g) of 5% times the past amount of dividends per share (D_0) of \$1.80, or 1.05 × \$1.80 = \$1.89. It can be seen that the growth rate in dividends per share of 5% is equal to the product of the retention rate (33⅓%) and the average return on equity for new investments (15%), an amount equal to .3333 × .15 = 5%.

Two years from now ($t = 2$), earnings per share are anticipated to be \$2.835 × (1 + .05) = \$2.977, a further increase of \$2.977 − \$2.835 = \$.142 that is due to the retention and reinvestment of .3333 × \$2.835 = \$.945 per share at $t = 1$. This expected increase in earnings per share of \$.142 is the result of earning 15% on the reinvestment \$.945, since .15 × \$.945 = \$.142. In summary, the expected earnings per share at $t = 2$ have three components. The first is the earnings attributable to the assets held at $t = 0$, an amount equal to \$2.70. The second is the earnings attributable to the reinvestment of \$.90 at $t = 0$, earning \$.135. The third is the earnings attributable to the reinvestment of \$.945 at $t = 1$, earning \$.142. These three components, when summed, can be seen to be equal to E_2 = \$2.70 + \$.135 + \$.142 = \$2.977. Dividends at $t = 2$ are expected to be 5% larger than at $t = 1$, or 1.05 × \$1.89 = \$1.985 per share. This amount corresponds to the amount calculated by multiplying the payout ratio times the expected earnings per share at $t = 2$, or .6667 × \$2.977 = \$1.985. Figure 15-2 summarizes the example.

A THREE-STAGE DDM

As this chapter's "Money Matters" discusses, the three-stage DDM is the most widely applied form of the general multiple growth DDM. Consider analyzing the ABC Company on April 30, 1990. Over the past year, ABC has had earnings per share of \$1.67 and dividends per share of \$.40. After carefully studying ABC, the security analyst has made the following forecasts of earnings per share and dividends per share for the next five years:

E_1 = \$2.67	E_2 = \$4.00	E_3 = \$6.00	E_4 = \$8.00	E_5 = \$10.00
D_1 = \$ .60	D_2 = \$1.60	D_3 = \$2.40	D_4 = \$3.20	D_5 = \$ 5.00

FIGURE 15-2
Growth in Earnings for Copper Company

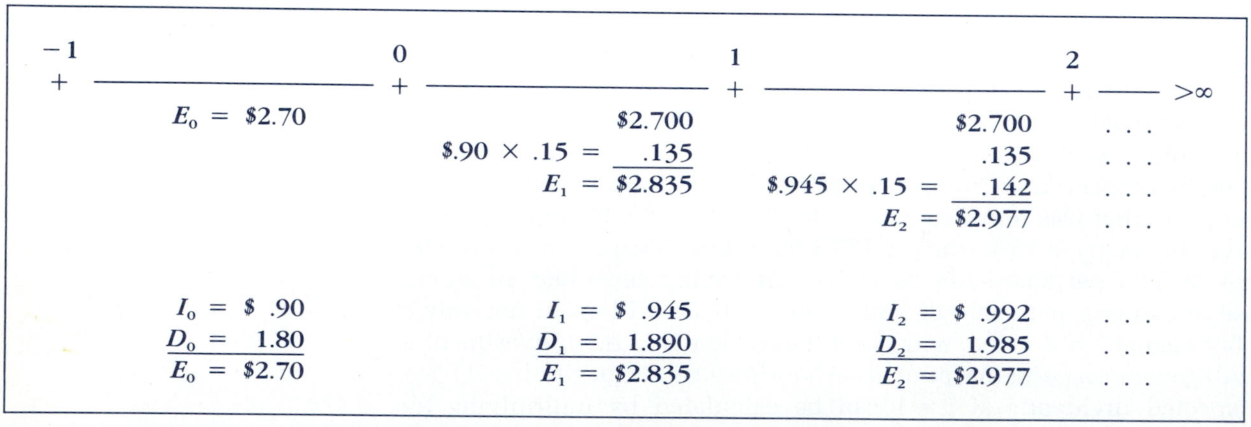

−1		0		1		2 → ∞
	E_0 = \$2.70		\$2.700		\$2.700	. . .
			\$.90 × .15 = .135		.135	. . .
			E_1 = \$2.835		\$.945 × .15 = .142	. . .
					E_2 = \$2.977	. . .
	I_0 = \$ .90		I_1 = \$ .945		I_2 = \$ .992	. . .
	D_0 = 1.80		D_1 = 1.890		D_2 = 1.985	. . .
	E_0 = \$2.70		E_1 = \$2.835		E_2 = \$2.977	. . .

These forecasts imply the following payout ratios and earnings-per-share growth rates:

$$p_1 = 22\% \quad p_2 = 40\% \quad p_3 = 40\% \quad p_4 = 40\% \quad p_5 = 50\%$$
$$g_{e1} = 60\% \quad g_{e2} = 50\% \quad g_{e3} = 50\% \quad g_{e4} = 33\% \quad g_{e5} = 25\%$$

Furthermore, the analyst believes that ABC will enter the transition stage at the end of the fifth year (that is, the sixth year will be the first year of the transition stage), and that the transition stage will last three years. Earnings per share and the payout ratio for year six are forecasted to be $E_6 = \$11.90$ and $p_6 = 55\%$ [thus $g_{e6} = (\$11.90 - \$10.00)/\$10.00 = 19\%$ and $D_6 = .55 \times \$11.90 = \$6.55$].

The maturity stage is forecasted to have an earnings-per-share growth rate of 4% and a payout ratio of 70%. Now, it was shown in equation (15.48b) that with the constant growth model, $g = r(1 - p)$, where r is the average return on equity for new investment and p is the payout ratio. Since the maturity stage has constant growth, this equation can be reformulated and used to determine r:

$$r = g/(1 - p).$$

Thus, r for ABC has an implied value of $4\%/(100\% - 70\%) = 13.33\%$, which is assumed to be satisfactory.

At this point, there are only two missing pieces of information that are needed to determine the value of ABC—the earnings-per-share growth rates and the payout ratios for the transition stage. Taking earnings per share first, it has been forecasted that $g_{e6} = 19\%$ and that $g_{e9} = 4\%$. One method of determining how 19% will "decay" to 4% is to note that there are three years between the sixth and ninth years, and 15% between 19% and 4%. A "linear decay" rate would be determined by noting that 15%/3 years = 5% per year. This rate of 5% would be deducted from 19% to get g_{e7}, resulting in $19\% - 5\% = 14\%$. Then, it would be deducted from 14% to get g_{e8}, resulting in $14\% - 5\% = 9\%$. Finally, as a check, it can be noted that $9\% - 5\% = 4\%$, the value that was forecasted for g_{e9}.

A similar procedure can be used to determine how the payout ratio of 55% in year six will grow to 70% in year nine. The "linear growth" rate will be $(70\% - 55\%)/3$ years = 15%/3 years = 5% per year, indicated $p_7 = 55\% + 5\% = 60\%$ and $p_8 = 60\% + 5\% = 65\%$. Again, a check indicates that $65\% + 5\% = 70\%$, the value that was forecasted for p_9.

With these forecasts of earnings-per-share growth rates and payout ratios in hand, forecasts of dividends per share can now be made:

$$\begin{aligned} D_7 &= p_7 E_7 \\ &= p_7 E_6(1 + g_{e7}) \\ &= .60 \times \$11.90 \times (1 + .14) \\ &= .60 \times \$13.57 \\ &= \$8.14 \end{aligned}$$

MONEY MATTERS
Applying Dividend Discount Models

Over the last thirty years, dividend discount models (DDMs) have achieved wide acceptance among professional common stock investors. While few investment managers rely solely on DDMs to select stocks, many have integrated DDMs into their security valuation procedures.

The reasons for the popularity of DDMs are twofold. First, DDMs are based on a simple, widely understood concept: the fair value of any security should equal the discounted value of the cash flows expected to be produced by that security. Second, the basic inputs for DDMs are standard outputs for many large investment management firms. That is, these firms employ security analysts who are responsible for projecting corporate earnings.

Valuing common stocks with a DDM technically requires an estimate of future dividends over an infinite time horizon. Given that accurately forecasting dividends three years from today, let alone twenty years in the future, is a difficult proposition, how do investment firms actually go about implementing DDMs?

One approach is to use a one- or two-stage dividend growth model, as described in the text. However, while such models are relatively easy to apply, investors typically view the assumed dividend growth assumptions as overly simplistic. Instead, investors have generally preferred three-stage models, believing that they provide the best combination of realism and ease of application.

While many variations of the three-stage DDM exist, in general the model is based on the assumption that companies evolve through three phases during their lifetimes. (Figure 15-3 portrays these stages.)

1. *Growth stage*. Characterized by rapidly expanding sales, high profit margins, and abnormally high growth in earnings per share. Because of highly profitable expected investment opportunities, the payout ratio is low. Competitors are attracted by the unusually high earnings, leading to a decline in the growth rate.
2. *Transition stage*. In later years, increased competition reduces profit margins and earnings growth slows. With fewer new investment opportunities, the company begins to pay out a larger percentage of earnings.
3. *Maturity (steady-state) stage*. Eventually, the company reaches a position where its new investment opportunities offer, on average, only slightly attractive returns on equity. At that time, its earnings growth rate, payout ratio, and return on equity stabilize for the remainder of its life.

The forecasting process of the three-stage DDM involves specifying earnings and dividend growth rates in each of the three stages. While one cannot expect a security analyst to be omniscient in his or her growth forecast for a particular company, one can hope that the forecasted pattern of growth—in terms of magnitude and duration—resembles that actually realized by the company, particularly in the short run.

Investment firms attempt to structure their DDMs to make maximum use of their analysts' forecasting capabilities. Thus, the models emphasize specific forecasts in the near term when it is realistic to expect security analysts to more accurately project earnings and dividends. Conversely, the models emphasize more general forecasts over the longer term when the distinction between companies' growth rates become less discernible. Typically, analysts are required to supply the following information for their assigned companies:

$$\begin{aligned}D_8 &= p_8E_8\\ &= p_8E_6(1+g_{e7})(1+g_{e8})\\ &= .65\times\$11.90\times(1+.14)\times(1+.09)\\ &= .65\times\$14.79\\ &= \$9.61\end{aligned}$$

$$\begin{aligned}D_9 &= p_9E_9\\ &= p_9E_6(1+g_{e7})(1+g_{e8})(1+g_{e9})\\ &= .70\times\$11.90\times(1+.14)\times(1+.09)\times(1+.04)\\ &= .70\times\$15.38\\ &= \$10.76.\end{aligned}$$

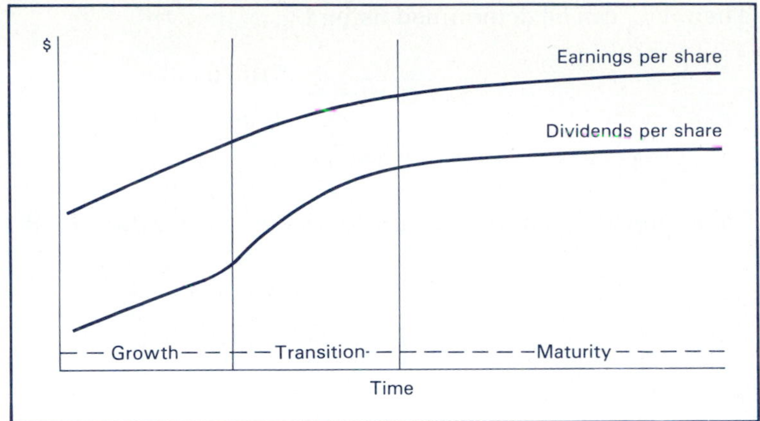

FIGURE 15-3
The Three Stages of the Multiple Growth Model
Source: Adapted from Carmine J. Grigoli, "Demystifying Dividend Discount Models," Merrill Lynch Quantitative Research, April 1982.

1. Expected annual earnings and dividends for the next several years.
2. After these specific annual forecasts end, earnings growth and the payout ratio forecasts until the end of the growth stage.
3. The number of years until the transition stage is reached.
4. The duration (in years) of the transition stage. That is, once abnormally high growth ends, the number of years until the maturity stage is reached.

Most three-stage DDMs assume that during the transition stage, earnings growth declines and payout ratios rise linearly to the maturity stage steady-state levels. (For example, if the transition stage is ten years long, earnings growth at the maturity stage is 5% per year, and earnings growth at the end of the growth stage is 25%, then earnings growth will decline 2% in each year of the transition stage.) Finally, most three-stage DDMs make standard assumptions about companies in the maturity stage—that all such companies have the same growth rates, payout ratios, and return on equity.

With analysts' DDM inputs, plus an appropriate required rate of return for each security, all the necessary information for the three-stage DDM is available. The last step involves merely calculating the discounted value of the estimated dividends to determine the stock's "fair" value.

The seeming simplicity of the three-stage DDM should not lead one to believe that it is without its implementation problems. Investment firms must strive to achieve consistency across their analysts' forecasts. The long-term nature of the estimates involved, the substantial training required to accurately make even short-term earnings forecasts, and the coordination of a number of analysts covering many companies severely complicate the problem. Considerable discipline is required if the DDM valuations generated by a firm's analysts are to be sufficiently comparable and reliable to guide investment decisions. Despite these complexities, if successfully implemented, DDMs can combine the creative insights of security analysts with the rigor and discipline of quantitative investment techniques.

Given a required rate of return on ABC of 12.4%, all the necessary inputs for the multiple growth model have been determined. To begin, it can be seen that $T = 8$, indicating that V_{T-} involves determining the present value of D_1 through D_8:

$$
\begin{aligned}
V_{T-} = &\left[\frac{\$.60}{(1+.124)^1}\right] + \left[\frac{\$1.60}{(1+.124)^2}\right] + \left[\frac{\$2.40}{(1+.124)^3}\right] \\
&+ \left[\frac{\$3.20}{(1+.124)^4}\right] + \left[\frac{\$5.00}{(1+.124)^5}\right] + \left[\frac{\$6.55}{(1+.124)^6}\right] \\
&+ \left[\frac{\$8.14}{(1+.124)^7}\right] + \left[\frac{\$9.61}{(1+.124)^8}\right] \\
= &\ \$18.89.
\end{aligned}
$$

Then, V_{T+} can be determined using D_9:

$$V_{T+} = \frac{\$10.76}{(.124 - .04)(1 + .124)^8}$$
$$= \$50.28.$$

Combining, V_{T-} and V_{T+} results in the intrinsic value of ABC:

$$V = V_{T-} + V_{T+}$$
$$= \$18.89 + \$50.28$$
$$= \$69.17.$$

Given a current market price for ABC of \$50, it can be seen that its stock is underpriced by \$69.17 − \$50 = \$19.17 per share. Equivalently, it can be noted that the actual price-earnings ratio for ABC is \$50/\$1.67 = 29.9 but that a "normal" price-earnings ratio would be higher, equal to \$69.17/ \$1.67 = 41.4, again indicating that ABC is underpriced.

Implied Returns

As shown with the previous example, once the analyst has made certain forecasts, it is relatively straightforward to determine a company's expected dividends for each year up through the first year of the maturity stage. Then, the present value of these predicted dividends can be calculated for a given required rate of return. However, many investment firms use a computerized trial-and-error procedure to determine the discount rate that equates the present value of the stock's expected dividends with its current price. Sometimes this long-run internal rate of return is referred to as the security's **implied return.** In the case of ABC, its implied return at the end of April 1990 is 14.8%.

implied return

The Security Market Line

After implied returns have been estimated for a number of stocks, the associated beta for each stock can be estimated. Then, for all the stocks analyzed, this information can be plotted on a graph that has implied returns on the vertical axis and betas on the horizontal axis.

At this point, there are alternative methods for estimating the Security Market Line (SML).[12] One method involves determining a line of "best fit" for this graph by using a statistical procedure known as "simple regression" (as discussed in Chapter 13). That is, the values of an intercept term and a slope term are determined from the data, thereby indicating the location of the straight line that best describes the relationship between implied returns and betas.[13]

Figure 15-4 provides an example of the estimated SML at the end of April 1990. In this case, the SML has been determined to have an intercept of 8% and a slope of 4%, indicating that, in general, securities with higher betas are

[12]There are numerous methods besides those described here. Some of them are based on more complicated versions of the CAPM, while others are based on the APT (discussed in Chapter 12).

[13]There are ways of forcing the intercept of the line to go through the riskfree rate in order to accord with the implications of the traditional CAPM.

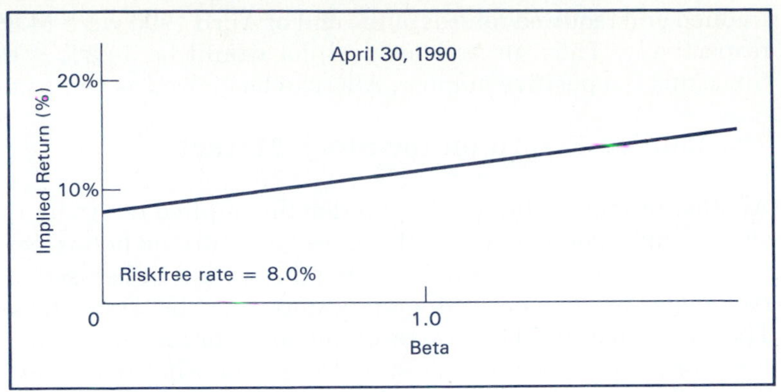

FIGURE 15-4
A Security Market Line Estimated from Implied Returns

expected to have higher implied returns in the forthcoming period. Depending on the sizes of the implied returns, such lines can have steeper or flatter slopes, or even negative slopes.

The second method of estimating the SML involves calculating the implied return for a portfolio of common stocks. This is done by taking a value-weighted average of the implied returns of the stocks in the portfolio, with the resulting return being an estimate of the implied return on the market portfolio. Given this return and a beta of one, the "market" portfolio can be plotted on a graph having implied returns on the vertical axis and betas on the horizontal axis. Next, the riskfree rate, having a beta of zero, can be plotted on the same graph. Finally, the SML is determined by simply connecting these two points with a straight line.

Either of these SMLs can be used to determine the required return on a stock. However, they will most likely result in different numbers, since the two lines will most likely have different intercepts and slopes. For example, note that in the first method the SML may not go through the riskfree rate, while the second method forces the SML to go through this rate.

Required Returns and Alphas

Once a security's beta has been estimated, its required return can be determined from the estimated SML. For example, the equation for the Security Market Line on April 30, 1990 (shown in Figure 15-4), is:

$$k_i = 8 + 4\beta_i.$$

Thus, if ABC has an estimated beta of 1.1 at the end of April 1990, then it would have a required return equal to 8 + (4 × 1.1) = 12.4%.

Once the required return on a stock has been determined, the difference between the stock's implied return (from the dividend discount model) and this required return can be calculated. This difference can then be viewed as an estimate of the stock's *alpha*, and represents ". . . the degree to which a stock is mispriced. Positive alphas indicate undervalued securities and negative alphas indicate overvalued securities."[14] In the case of ABC, its

[14]Carmine J. Grigoli, "Common Stock Valuation," Merrill Lynch Quantitative Analysis, May/June 1984. A subsequent procedure divides the estimated alpha by an estimate of the security's unique risk (that is, nonmarket or unsystematic risk) to obtain a standardized alpha. Then, based on the magnitude of the standardized alpha, the security is classified into one of ten "standardized alpha deciles." Also see Marshall E. Blume, "The Use of 'Alphas' to Improve Performance," *Journal of Portfolio Management*, 11, no. 1 (Fall 1984): 86–92.

implied and required returns at the end of April 1990 were 14.8% and 12.4%, respectively. Thus, its estimated alpha would be 14.8% − 12.4% = 2.4%. Since this is a positive number, ABC can be viewed as being underpriced.

The Implied Return on the Stock Market

Another product of this analysis is that the implied return for the portfolio of stocks can be compared with the expected return on bonds. Specifically, the difference between the stock and bond returns can be used as an input for recommendations concerning asset allocation between stocks and bonds. That is, it can be used to form recommendations regarding what percent of an investor's money should go into stocks and what percent should go into bonds. For example, the greater the implied return on stocks relative to bonds, the larger the percentage of the investor's money that should be placed in common stocks.

DIVIDEND DISCOUNT MODELS AND EXPECTED RETURNS

The procedures described here are similar to those employed by a number of brokerage firms and portfolio managers.[15] A security's implied return, obtained from a dividend discount model, is often treated as an expected return, which in turn can be divided into two components—the security's required return and alpha.

However, the expected return on a stock over a given holding period may differ from its DDM-based implied rate, k^*. A simple set of examples will indicate why this difference can exist.

Assume that a security analyst predicts that a stock will pay a dividend of $1.10 per year forever. On the other hand, the consensus opinion of "the market" (most other investors) is that the dividend will equal $1.00 per year forever. This suggests that the analyst's prediction is a deviant or nonconsensus one.

Assume that both the analyst and other investors agree that the required rate of return for a stock of this type is 10%. Using the formula for the zero-growth model, the value of the stock is $D_1/.10 = 10D_1$, meaning that the stock should sell for ten times its expected dividend. Since other investors expect to receive $1.00 per year, the stock has a current price (P) of $10 per share. The analyst feels that the stock has a value of $1.10/.10 = $11, and thus feels that it is underpriced by $11 − $10 = $1 per share.

Rate of Convergence of Investors' Predictions In this situation, the implied return according to the analyst is $1.10/$10 = 11%. If the analyst buys a share now with a plan to sell it a year later, what rate of return might the analyst expect to earn? The answer depends on what assumption is made regarding the *rate of convergence of investors' predictions*—that is, the answer depends on the expected market reaction to the mispricing that the analyst believes currently exists.

[15]An example of a similar procedure formerly used by Wells Fargo Investment Advisors is described by George Foster in *Financial Statement Analysis* (Englewood Cliffs, N.J.: Prentice Hall, 1986), pp. 428–30.

The cases shown in Table 15-1 are based on an assumption that the analyst is confident that his or her forecast of future dividends is correct. That is, in all of the cases, the analyst expects that at the end of the year, the stock will in fact pay the predicted dividend of $1.10.

No Convergence In column A, it is assumed that other investors will regard the higher dividend as a fluke and steadfastly refuse to alter their projections of subsequent dividends from their initial estimate of $1.00. As a result, the security's price at $t = 1$ can be expected to remain at $10 (= $1.00/.10). In this case, the analyst's total return is expected to be 11% (= $1.10/$10), which will be attributed entirely to dividends since no capital gains are expected.

The 11% expected return can also be viewed as consisting of the required return of 10% plus an alpha of 1% that is equal to the portion of the dividend unanticipated by other investors, $.10/$10. Accordingly, if it is assumed that there will be no convergence of predictions, the expected return would be set at the implied rate, 11%, and the alpha would be set at 1%.

Complete Convergence Column B shows a very different situation. Here, it is assumed that the other investors will see the error of their ways and completely revise their predictions. At the end of the year, it is expected that they too will predict future dividends of $1.10 per year thereafter; thus, the stock is expected to be selling for $11 (= $1.10/.10) at $t = 1$. Under these conditions, the analyst can expect to achieve a total return of 21% by selling the stock at the end of the year for $11, obtaining 11% (= $1.10/$10) in dividend yield and 10% (= $1/$10) in capital gains.

The 10% expected capital gains result directly from the expected repricing of the security because of the complete convergence of predictions. In this case, the fruits of the analyst's superior prediction are expected to be obtained all in one year. Instead of 1% "extra" per year forever, as in column A, the analyst expects to obtain 1% (= $.10/$10) in extra dividend yield plus 10% (= $1/$10) in capital gains this year. By continuing to hold the stock in subsequent years, the analyst would expect to earn only the required return of 10% over those years. Accordingly, if it is assumed that there is complete

TABLE 15-1
Alpha and the Convergence of Predictions

	EXPECTED AMOUNT OF CONVERGENCE		
	0% (A)	100% (B)	50% (C)
Dividend predictions D_2			
Consensus of other investors	1.00	1.10	1.05
Analyst	1.10	1.10	1.10
Expected stock price P_1	10.00	11.00	10.50
Expected return:			
Dividence yield D_1/P	11%	11%	11%
Capital gain $(P_1 - P)/P$	0	10	5
Total expected return	11%	21%	16%
Less required return	10	10	10
Alpha	1%	11%	6%

P_1 is equal to the consensus dividend prediction at $t = 1$ divided by the required return of 10%. The example assumes that the current stock price P is $10, and dividends are forecasted by the consensus at $t = 0$ to remain constant at $1.00 per share, whereas the analyst forecasts the dividends at $t = 0$ to remain constant at $1.10 per share.

convergence of predictions, the expected return would be set at 21% and the alpha would be set at 11%.

Partial Convergence Column C shows an intermediate case. Here, the predictions of the other investors are expected to converge only halfway toward those of the analyst (that is, from $1.00 to $1.05 instead of to $1.10). Total return in the first year is expected to be 16%, consisting of 11% (= $1.10/$10) in dividend yield plus 5% (= $.50/$10) in capital gains.

Since the stock is expected to be selling for $10.50 (= $1.05/.10) at $t = 1$, the analyst will still feel that it is underpriced at $t = 1$ because it will have a value of $11 (= $1.10/.10) at that time. To obtain the remainder of the "extra return" owing to this underpricing, the stock would have to be held past $t = 1$. Accordingly, if it is assumed that there is halfway convergence of predictions, the expected return would be set at 16% and the alpha would be set at 6%.

In general, the expected return and alpha will be larger, the faster the assumed rate of convergence of predictions.[16] Many investors assume no convergence, since they use the implied rate (that is, the internal rate of return, k^*) as a surrogate for a relatively short-term (for example, one year) expected return, as in column A. However, setting the expected return equal to the implied return may instead reflect a belief that (1) deviant predictions are less than perfectly accurate, and (2) other investors will revise their predictions in the corresponding direction by a large enough amount to provide capital gains that will offset any shortfall from the predicted dividend yield.

Predicted versus Actual Returns

An alternative approach does not simply use outputs from a model "as is," but *adjusts* them, based on relationships between previous predictions and actual outcomes. Panels (a) and (b) of Figure 15-5 provide examples.

Each point in Figure 15-5 (a) plots a *predicted* return on the stock market as a whole (on the horizontal axis) and the subsequent *actual* return for that period (on the vertical axis). The line of "best fit" (determined by simple regression) through the points indicates the general relationship between prediction and outcome. If the current prediction is 14%, history suggests that an estimate of 15% would be superior.

Each point in Figure 15-5 (b) plots a predicted alpha value for a security (on the horizontal axis) and the subsequent "abnormal return" for that period (on the vertical axis). Such a diagram can be made for a given security, or for all the securities that a particular analyst makes predictions about, or for all the securities that the investment firm makes predictions about. Again, a line of best fit can be drawn through the points. In this case, if the current prediction of a security's alpha is +1%, this relationship suggests that an "adjusted" estimate of +2.5% would be superior.

information coefficient

An important byproduct of this type of analysis is the measure of correlation between predicted and actual outcomes, indicating the nearness of the points to the line. This **information coefficient** (IC) can serve as a measure of predictive accuracy. If it is too small to be significantly different

[16]In a perfectly efficient market (in the semistrong-form sense), these analysts would sometimes be right and sometimes be wrong, so that on balance their predictions would be of no value. In such a situation, the expected return for any security would be set at its required return and the alpha would be set at zero.

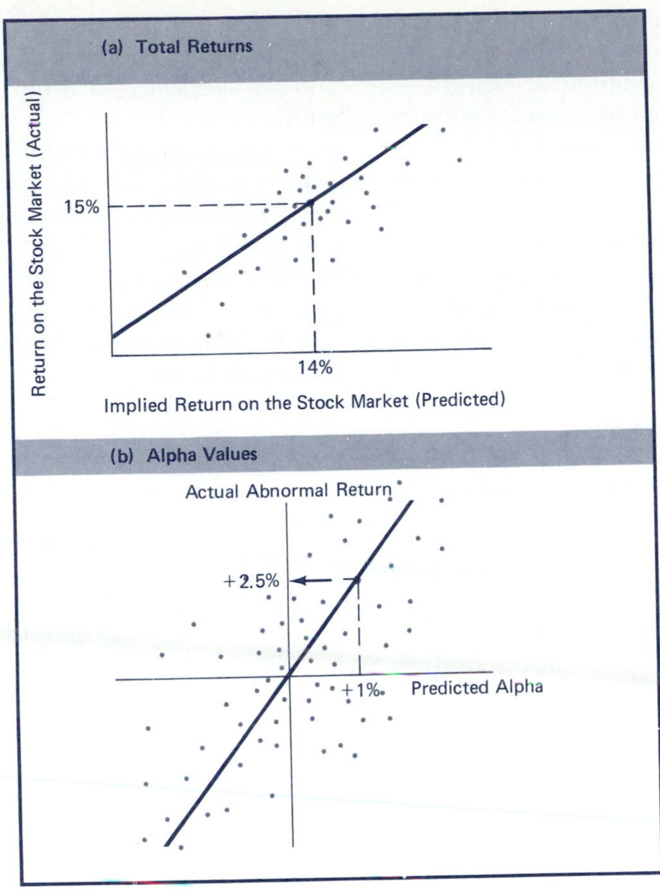

FIGURE 15-5
Adjusting Predictions

from zero in a statistical sense, the value of the predictions is subject to considerable question.[17]

SUMMARY

1. The capitalization of income method of valuation states that the intrinsic value of any asset is equal to the discounted cash flows investors expect to receive from that asset.

2. Dividend discount models (DDMs) are a specific application of the capitalization of income method of valuation to common stocks.

3. To use a DDM, the investor must implicitly or explicitly supply a forecast of all future dividends expected to be generated by a security.

[17]It has been argued that a value of .15 for an IC is indicative of good performance with regard to stock forecasting, and that several different forecasters have recorded ICs of this magnitude (a value of zero would be expected in a perfectly efficient market). See Keith P. Ambachtsheer, "Profit Potential in an 'Almost Efficient' Market," *Journal of Portfolio Management*, 1, no. 1 (Fall 1974): 84–87, and "Where are the Customers' Alphas?" *Journal of Portfolio Management*, 4, no. 1 (Fall 1977): 52–56; Keith P. Ambachtsheer and James L. Farrell, Jr., "Can Active Management Add Value?" *Financial Analysts Journal*, 35, no. 6 (November–December 1979): 39–47; and S. D. Hodges and R. A. Brealey, "Portfolio Selection in a Dynamic and Uncertain World," *Financial Analysts Journal*, 29, no. 2 (March–April 1973): 50–65.

4. Investors typically make certain simplifying assumptions about the growth of common stock dividends. For example, a common stock's dividends may be assumed to exhibit zero growth or growth at a constant rate. More complex assumptions may allow for multiple growth rates over time.

5. Instead of applying DDMs, many security analysts use a simpler method of security valuation that involves estimating a stock's "normal" price-earnings ratio and comparing it with the stock's actual price-earnings ratio.

6. The growth rate in a firm's earnings and dividends depends on its earnings retention rate and its average return on equity for new investments.

7. Determining whether a security is mispriced using a DDM can be done in one of two ways. First, the discounted value of expected dividends can be compared with the stock's current price. Second, the discount rate that equates the stock's current price to the present value of forecasted dividends can be compared with the required return for stocks of similar risk.

KEY TERMS

capitalization of income method of valuation
discount rate
net present value
internal rate of return
dividend discount models
zero growth model
constant growth model
multiple growth model
price-earnings ratio
payout ratio
earnings-price ratio
retention ratio
implied return
information coefficient

QUESTIONS AND PROBLEMS

1. Consider five annual cash flows (the first occurring one year from today):

YEAR	CASH FLOW
1	$5
2	$6
3	$7
4	$8
5	$9

Given a discount rate of 10%, what is the present value of this stream of cash flows?

2. Alta Cohen is considering buying a machine to produce baseballs. The machine costs $10,000. With the machine, Alta expects to produce and sell 1,000 baseballs per year, for $3 per baseball, net of all costs. The machine's life is five years (with no salvage value). Based on these assumptions, and an 8% discount rate, what is the net present value of Alta's investment?

3. Hub Collins has invested in a project that promised to pay $100, $200, $300, respectively, at the end of the next three years. If Hub paid $513.04 for this investment, what is the project's internal rate of return?

4. Afton Products currently pays a dividend of $4.00 per share on its common stock.
   (a) If Afton Products plans to increase its dividend at a rate of 5% per year indefinitely, what will be the dividend per share in ten years?
   (b) If Afton Products' dividend per share is expected to be $5.87 per share at the end of five years, at what annual rate is the dividend expected to grow?

5. Hammond Pipes has issued a preferred stock that pays $12 per share. The dividend is fixed and the stock has no expiration date. What is the intrinsic value of Hammond preferred stock, assuming a discount rate of 15%?

6. Milton Information Services currently pays a dividend of $4.00 per share on its common stock. The dividend is expected to grow at 4% per year forever. Stocks with similar risk currently are priced to provide a 12% expected return. What is the intrinsic value of Milton stock?

7. Spring Valley Bedding stock currently sells for $53 per share. The stock's dividend is expected to grow at 6% per year indefinitely. Spring Valley just paid a dividend of $3.00 per share. Given this information, calculate the stock's internal rate of return.

8. Select a stock whose name begins with the first letter of your last name. From the *Value Line Investment Survey*, find the average annual compounded growth rate in the stock's dividend over the last five years. Assume that this growth rate will continue indefinitely. Also from the *Value Line Investment Survey*, find the beta of the stock. Assuming a riskfree rate of return of 6% and a market expected return of 12%, calculate the SML and the required return on the stock. Finally, using the dividend growth rate and required return, calculate the intrinsic value of the stock. (*Note:* If the data for your stock is incompatible with the constant growth DDM, select another stock.) Compare this intrinsic value to the latest closing price for the stock. Is the stock underpriced or overpriced? What potential problems are involved with this approach to making investment decisions?

9. The constant growth model is an overly simplistic means of valuing most corporations' stocks. However, many market analysts believe that it is a useful means of estimating a fair value for the stock market as a whole. Why might the constant growth DDM be a more reasonable valuation tool for the market in aggregate as opposed to individual stocks?

10. This year Monona Air Cleaners Inc. will pay a dividend on its stock of $6 per share. The following year the dividend is expected to be the same and then increase to $7 the year after. From that point on, the dividend is expected to grow at 4% per year indefinitely. Stocks with similar risk are currently priced to provide a 10% expected return. What is the intrinsic value of Monona's stock?

11. Knapp Carpet recently paid an annual dividend on its stock of $2 per share. The dividend is expected to grow at $1 per share for the next four years. Thereafter, the dividend is expected to grow at 5% per year indefinitely. The required return on stocks with similar risk is 12%. What is the intrinsic value of Knapp stock?

12. Chief Medical Inc. is a little-known producer of cardiac pacemakers. The earnings and dividend growth prospects of the company are disputed by analysts. Albert Bender is forecasting 5% growth in dividends indefinitely. However, his brother John is predicting 20% growth in dividends, but only for the next three years, after which the growth rate is expected to decline to 4% for the indefinite future. Chief dividends per share are currently $3.00. Stocks with similar risk are currently priced to provide a 14% expected return.
    - **(a)** What is the intrinsic value of Chief stock according to Albert?
    - **(b)** What is the intrinsic value of Chief stock according to John?

(c) Assume that Chief stock now sells for $39¾ per share. If the stock is fairly priced at the present time, what is the implied perpetual dividend growth rate? What is the implied P/E (price-earnings ratio) on next year's earnings, based on this perpetual dividend growth assumption and assuming a 25% payout ratio?

13. Elk Mound Candy Company currently pays a dividend of $3.00 per share. That dividend is expected to grow at a 6% rate indefinitely. Stocks with similar risk provide a 10% expected return. Calculate the intrinsic value of Elk Mound stock using an interim computation based on the sale of the stock three years from now.

14. Osseo Operations recently paid an annual dividend of $4.00 per share. Earnings for the same year were $8.00 per share. The required return on stocks with similar risk is 11%. Dividends are expected to grow 6% per year indefinitely. Calculate Osseo's "normal" price-earnings ratio.

15. Rochelle Corp. is expected to pay out 40% of its earnings and to earn an average of 15% per year on its incremental reinvested earnings forever. Stocks with similar risk are currently priced to provide a 12% expected return. By what percentage can Rochelle's earnings be expected to grow each year? What is an appropriate price-earnings multiple for the stock? What portion of the return on Rochelle stock is expected to come from capital gains?

16. What explanations can you offer for the fact that the Security Market Line shown in Figure 15-4 is so flat?

17. Fay Thomas, a financial analyst, once remarked: "Even if your dividend estimates and discount rate assumption are correct, dividend discount models identify stocks that will produce positive alphas only if other investors eventually come to agree with the DDM's valuation conclusions." Is this statement correct? Why or why not?

18. Some people assert that a "true" growth stock is one whose dividends grow at a rate greater than its required rate of return. Why is the constant growth DDM incapable of valuing such a "true" growth company?

CFA Exam Questions

19. The constant growth dividend discount model can be used for both the valuation of companies and the estimation of the long-term total return of a stock.

Assume: $20 = the price of a stock today,
8% = the expected growth rate of dividends, and
$0.60 = the annual dividend one year forward.

(a) Using only the above data, compute the expected long-term total return on the stock using the constant growth dividend discount model. Show calculations.

(b) Briefly discuss three disadvantages of the constant growth dividend discount model in its application to investment analysis.

20. As a firm operating in a mature industry, Arbot Industries is expected to maintain a constant dividend payout ratio and constant growth rate of earnings for the foreseeable future. Earnings were $4.50 per share in the recently completed fiscal year. The dividend payout ratio has been a constant 55% in recent years and is expected to remain so. Arbot's return on equity (ROE) is expected to remain at 10% in the future, and you require an 11% return on the stock.

(a) Using the constant growth dividend discount model, calculate the current value of Arbot common stock. Show your calculations.

After an aggressive acquisition and marketing program, it now appears that Arbot's earnings per share and ROE will grow rapidly over the next two years. You are aware that the dividend discount model can be useful in estimating the value of common stock even when the assumption of constant growth does not apply.

(b) Calculate the current value of Arbot's common stock, using the dividend discount model, assuming that Arbot's dividend will grow at a 15% rate for the next two years, returning in the third year to the historical growth rate and continuing to grow at the historical rate for the foreseeable future. Show your calculations.

APPENDIX A

The Graham-Rea Model

In 1934, a book that was to become the cornerstone of fundamental analysis was published by Benjamin Graham and David L. Dodd. This book, entitled *Security Analysis*, argued that the future earnings power of the firm was the most important determinant of a stock's value.[18] However, in 1974 Graham himself repudiated the book and the principles contained in it.[19] Instead of following his old approach, Graham, along with James Rea, developed a new approach to identifying underpriced common stocks.[20] The reason for his change in attitude was his belief that the stock market was becoming more and more efficient, and that only smaller and smaller pockets of inefficiencies were in existence. Since Graham and Rea believed that these inefficiencies tended to be present in the stocks of certain identifiable firms, they developed a set of criteria to spot such stocks.

The Graham-Rea approach can be applied mechanically, since it involves examining the current financial statements of the firm under consideration and relating certain items from these statements to the firm's current stock price and the current yield on triple-A bonds. Ten questions that can be answered with a simple "yes" or "no" are involved. Table 15-2 lists them, indicating that the first five questions deal with "rewards" and the second five

[18]Graham and Dodd also argued that each dollar of dividends is worth four times as much as each dollar of retained earnings. Subsequent examination of market data indicates that their argument has no support. See J. Ronald Hoffmeister and Edward A. Dyl, "Dividends and Share Value: Graham and Dodd Revisited," *Financial Analysts Journal*, 41, no. 3 (May/June 1985): 77–78; and Lewis D. Johnson, "Dividends and Share Value: Graham and Dodd Revisited, Again," *Financial Analysts Journal*, 41, no. 5 (September/October 1985): 79–80. For the most recent edition of the book, see Sidney Cottle, Roger F. Murray, and Frank E. Block, *Graham and Dodd's Security Analysis*, 5th ed. (New York: McGraw-Hill, Inc., 1988). For a brief discussion of their approach to investing, see Roger F. Murray, "Graham and Dodd: A Durable Discipline," *Financial Analysts Journal*, 40, no. 5 (September/October 1984): 18–23.

[19]See "A Conversation with Benjamin Graham," *Financial Analysts Journal*, 32, no. 5 (September/October 1976): 20–23.

[20]For a description of this approach, see Paul Blustein, "Ben Graham's Last Will and Testament," *Forbes*, August 1, 1977: 43–45; and James B. Rea, "Remembering Benjamin Graham—Teacher and Friend," *Journal of Portfolio Management*, 3, no. 4 (Summer 1977): 66–72.

TABLE 15-2
Graham-Rea Stock Selection Questions

A. REWARDS

1. Is the price-earnings ratio less than one-half the reciprocal of the triple-A bond yield? (For example, if the current triple-A rate is 12%, then the reciprocal is 1/.12 = 8⅓, and half of that is 4⅙. Thus, for a stock to provide a "yes" answer to this question, its price-earnings ratio must be less than 4⅙.)
2. Is the price-earnings ratio less than 40% of the highest "average" price-earnings ratio of the last five years? (Here, the "average" price-earnings ratio for a stock for a given year is the average stock price for the year divided by by the earnings per share for that year.)
3. Is the dividend yield at least ⅔ the triple-A bond yield?
4. Is the stock price below ⅔ of the tangible book value per share? (Here tangible book value per share is simply total assets less total debt, with the difference divided by the number of shares outstanding.)
5. Is the stock price below ⅔ of the net current asset value per share? (Here net current asset value per share is current assets less total debt, with the difference divided by the number of shares outstanding.)

B. RISKS

6. Is the debt-to-equity ratio less than one? (Here the debt-to-equity ratio is simply total debt divided by total equity as shown on the balance sheet.)
7. Is the current ratio greater than two? (Here the current ratio is current assets divided by current liabilities.)
8. Is total debt less than twice the net current asset value? (Here net current asset value is current assets less total debt.)
9. Has the earnings-per-share growth rate of the last ten years averaged at least 7% per year? (If the earnings per share over the last year is denoted E_0 and the earnings per share over the year ending ten years ago is denoted E_{-10}, then the growth rate is the value of g that solves the equation $E_0 = E_{-10}(1 + g)^{10}$. To provide a "yes" answer to this question, g must be at least 7%.)
10. Over the time period examined in question 9, have eight or more of the annual growth rates in earnings per share been equal to −5% or more? (Here the ten annual growth rates in earnings per share would be calculated and then examined to see that no more than two of them were less than −5%.)

Source: Adapted from Paul Blustein, "Ben Graham's Last Will and Testament," *Forbes*, August 1, 1977: 43–45; and James B. Rea, "Remembering Benjamin Graham—Teacher and Friend," *Journal of Portfolio Management*, 3, no. 4 (Summer 1977): 66–72.

questions deal with "risks." The idea behind these questions is to identify stocks that have the highest reward-to-risk ratio. In order for a stock to be recommended for purchase by Graham and Rea, it need not provide a "yes" answer to all of the questions.

The simplest way to use the questions is to first remove all stocks that do not provide a "yes" answer to question 6. Then, of the remaining stocks, remove those that do not provide a "yes" answer to either question 1 or question 3 or question 5. The stocks that are left are candidates for purchase.

In determining when to sell, the Graham-Rea approach says that the investor should sell as soon as the stock has risen 50% or two years have passed since the stock was purchased, whichever occurs first. However, if neither of these two sell signals has occurred and the stock either stops paying dividends or no longer generates the appropriate "yes" answers to the questions, then it should be sold immediately.

How well has the Graham-Rea approach to investing worked? In a recent study of this approach that focused on New York Stock Exchange and American Stock Exchange securities, three observations were particularly interesting.[21] First, since the approach was publicized it was found that the

[21]Henry R. Oppenheimer, "A Test of Ben Graham's Stock Selection Criteria," *Financial Analysts Journal*, 40, no. 5 (September/October 1984): 68–74.

number of stocks that provided the appropriate "yes" answers declined dramatically (for example, by 1980 only five securities had "yes" answers to questions 1 and 6). Second, the historical record suggests that positive abnormal returns would have been earned had this approach been used subsequent to its publication. Third, since many of the firms recommended for purchase were small firms, it is possible that all that this approach does is capture the size effect (that is, the small-firm effect that was discussed in the appendix to Chapter 13). However, the study found that even after adjusting for the size effect, the approach would still have earned positive abnormal returns since its publication.[22]

In closing, it should be noted that a number of professional portfolio managers currently follow the Graham-Rea approach to investing. Examples include the Rea-Graham Fund, LMH Fund, Sequoia Fund, and Pacific Partners Fund.

REFERENCES

1. The foundation for dividend discount models was laid out in:

   John Burr Williams, *The Theory of Investment Value* (Amsterdam: North-Holland Publishing Co., 1964). The original edition was published in 1938.

2. The constant growth and multiple growth models were subsequently developed by, respectively:

   M. J. Gordon, "Dividends, Earnings, and Stock Prices," *Review of Economics and Statistics*, 41, no. 2 (May 1959): 99–105;

   Nicholas Molodovsky, Catherine May, and Sherman Chottiner, "Common Stock Valuation: Principles, Tables and Application," *Financial Analysts Journal*, 21, no. 2 (March/April 1965): 104–23.

3. Some of the biases involved in using dividend discount models are discussed in:

   Adam K. Gehr, Jr., "A Bias in Dividend Discount Models," *Financial Analysts Journal*, 48, no. 1 (January/February 1992): 75–80.

4. For an interesting note on why Japanese P/E ratios appear to be overstated, see:

   Harold Bierman, Jr., "Price/Earnings Ratios Restructured for Japan," *Financial Analysts Journal*, 47, No. 2 (March/April 1991): 91–92.

5. The issue of market volatility has been studied by utilizing dividend discount models. In essence, these studies compare the actual levels of various stock market indices with their intrinsic values, calculated by determining the present value of rational forecasts of subsequent dividends paid on the stocks in the indices. The main observation is that the actual levels fluctuate far more over time than the intrinsic values. A conclusion that some people draw from these studies is that there is excess volatility in stock prices and hence markets are not efficient. This hotly debated topic was introduced in:

[22]A subsequent study focused on only one of the ten Graham-Rea questions, number 5 in Table 15-2. It found that portfolios consisting of securities that had "yes" answers to this question would have earned above-market returns. See Henry R. Oppenheimer, "Ben Graham's Net Current Asset Values: A Performance Update," *Financial Analysts Journal*, 42, no. 6 (November/December 1986): 40–47.

Stephen F. LeRoy and Richard D. Porter, "The Present-Value Relation: Tests Based on Implied Variance Bounds," *Econometrica*, 49, no. 3 (May 1981): 555–74;

Robert J. Shiller, "Do Stock Prices Move Too Much to Be Justified by Subsequent Changes in Dividends?" *American Economic Review*, 71, no. 3 (June 1981): 421–36.

6. For more on market volatility (the last paper discusses and cites some of the critical research), see:

Robert J. Shiller, "Theories of Aggregate Stock Price Movements," *Journal of Portfolio Management*, 10, no. 2 (Winter 1984): 23–37;

Robert J. Shiller, *Market Volatility* (Cambridge, Mass.: The MIT Press, 1989);

Stephen F. LeRoy, "Capital Market Efficiency: An Update," Federal Reserve Bank of San Francisco *Economic Review* (Spring 1990): 29–40;

Stephen F. LeRoy, "Efficient Capital Markets and Martingales," *Journal of Economic Literature*, 27, no. 4 (December 1989): 1583–1621.

16

Dividends and Earnings

Chapter 15 discussed how the intrinsic value of a share of common stock could be determined by discounting expected dividends per share at a rate of return that was appropriate for a security of similar risk. Alternatively, the implied return on a share of common stock could be determined by finding the discount rate that makes the present value of all the expected dividends equal to the current market price of the stock. In either case, a forecast of dividends per share is necessary. Since dividends per share are equal to earnings per share times a payout ratio, dividends can be forecasted by forecasting earnings per share and payout ratios. Currently there are numerous methods that are used by security analysts for forecasting either earnings or dividends. This chapter presents a discussion of some of the important features of dividends and earnings that the analyst should be aware of in making such forecasts. It begins with a discussion of the relationship between earnings, dividends, and investment.

STOCK VALUATION BASED ON EARNINGS

A continual controversy in the investment community concerns the relevance of dividends versus earnings as the underlying source of value of a share of common stock. Clearly, earnings are important to stockholders because earnings provide the cash flow necessary for paying dividends. However, dividends are also important because dividends are what stockholders actually receive from the firm, and are the focus of the dividend discount models discussed in Chapter 15. Indeed, it would seem that if management increased the proportion of earnings per share paid out as dividends, they could make their stockholders wealthier, suggesting that the **dividend decision** (deciding on the amount of dividends to pay) is a very important one.

dividend decision

Ultimately, this controversy was resolved in 1961 when Merton Miller and Franco Modigliani published a seminal paper showing that the underlying source of value of a share of common stock was earnings, not dividends. An implication of this conclusion is that the dividend decision is relatively unimportant to the stockholders, since it will not affect the value of their investment in the firm.

In the course of a year, a firm generates revenues and incurs costs. With cash accounting, the difference between revenues and costs would be termed *cash flow*. With accrual accounting, used by almost all firms, both revenues and costs are likely to include estimates made by accountants of the values of noncash items. Items such as depreciation charges are deducted from cash flow to obtain earnings. Moreover, each year some amount is invested in the business. Of the total (gross) investment, a portion will be equal in value to the estimated depreciation of various real assets (like machines and buildings); the rest is new (net) investment.

The dollar amount of new investment each year should be based on the investment opportunities that are available to the firm, and should be unaffected by the dollar amount of dividends that are to be paid out. In particular, any investment opportunity whose net present value (NPV) is positive should be undertaken. This means that the future prospects of the firm can be described by a stream of expected earnings ($E_1, E_2, E_3, \ldots$) and the expected net investment required to produce such earnings (I_1, I_2, $I_3, \ldots$). Taking these two streams as given, it can be shown that management can set the total dollar amount of current dividends (D_0) at any level without making the current stockholders either better or worse off.[1] This will be done next, with the focus on earnings and how they can be used to pay for new investments and dividends.

Earnings, Dividends, and Investment

Figure 16-1(a) shows one way that the firm can use total earnings for the current year (E_0). In this situation, new investment (I_0) is financed out of earnings and the firm uses the remainder of the earnings to pay dividends (D_0) to its stockholders. For example, if the Plum Company has just earned \$5,000 and has new investments it would like to make that cost \$3,000, then Plum

[1]Here, the quantities of earnings (E_t), new investment (I_t), and dividends (D_t) are measured for the firm on an aggregate basis, not a per-share basis. Note that dividends cannot be set at an arbitrarily high value relative to earnings (for example, earnings of \$10 million and dividends of \$100 million), since the firm would then be unable to get the necessary funds to pay the dividends.

FIGURE 16-1
Earnings, Dividends, and Investment

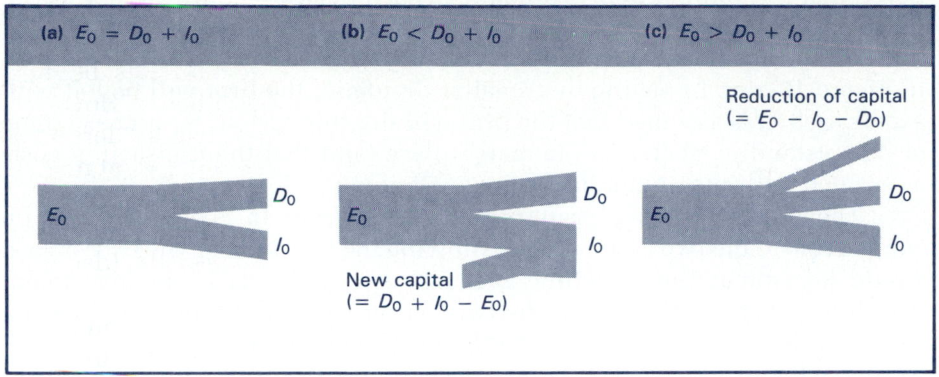

could pay for these investments out of earnings and declare a dividend of $2,000.

Issuing Stock While earnings are exactly equal to dividends and investment ($E_0 = D_0 + I_0$), as in Figure 16-1(a), this need not be the case. In the situation shown in Figure 16-1(b), earnings are less than dividends and investment ($E_0 < D_0 + I_0$). Since the amount of investment has been determined by the number of positive NPV projects that the firm has, the reason for this inequality is that the firm has decided to pay its current stockholders a higher dividend than was given in Figure 16-1(a). However, in order for higher dividends to be paid, additional funds must be obtained from outside the firm. This is accomplished by a new sale of common stock (it is assumed that the flotation costs associated with a new sale of common stock are negligible).

The reason the funds are obtained through a new sale of common stock instead of through a new sale of debt is because of a desire to avoid the confounding effects of a change in the firm's debt-equity ratio. That is, if debt financing is to be allowed, then two things would be changing at the same time—the amount of the dividend and the debt-equity ratio for the firm. As a result, if stockholders appear to be made better off by a change in the amount of the dividend, their betterment may actually be due to a change in the debt-equity ratio. By prohibiting debt financing, the debt-equity ratio will remain constant and only the amount of the dividend will be allowed to change. That is, each additional dollar in equity funds raised by issuing new stock is offset by a dollar in dividend payments. Thus, if stockholders appear to be better off, it has to be due to the change in the amount of the dividend, since everything else (specifically, the amount of investment and the debt-equity ratio) has remained fixed.

Note that if investment is financed out of earnings, as in Figure 16-1(a), then it has been financed with equity, obtained internally. In Figure 16-1(b), investment has also been financed with equity, but here some of the equity has been obtained externally. As a result, the debt-equity ratio for the firm is the same in both situations.

In the case of Plum, instead of paying dividends amounting to $2,000, the firm could decide to pay dividends amounting to $3,000. Since investment is equal to $3,000, Plum will have a cash outflow of $3,000 + $3,000 = $6,000 with earnings amounting to only $5,000. This means that Plum will have to sell $6,000 − $5,000 = $1,000 of new common stock.

Repurchasing Stock In Figure 16-1(c), the situation is reversed from 16-1(b) since earnings are now greater than dividends and investment ($E_0 > D_0 + I_0$). Given that the amount of investment has been determined by the number of positive NPV projects that the firm has, the reason for this inequality is that the firm has decided to pay its stockholders a lower dividend than was given in Figure 16-1(a). In paying this smaller dividend, the firm will be left with excess cash. It is assumed that the firm will use this cash to repurchase some of its outstanding shares in the marketplace (and that the transaction costs associated with such repurchases are negligible).

The reason for this assumption is the desire to keep the situation comparable to the two earlier ones. Allowing the firm to keep the excess cash would be tantamount to letting the firm invest the cash, an investment decision that was not made in the two earlier cases and therefore does not have a positive NPV (remember that I_0 consists of all positive NPV projects). Allowing the firm to keep the excess cash would also mean that the firm has made a decision to lower its debt-equity ratio. This is because retention of the excess cash would increase the amount of equity for the firm, thereby decreasing the amount of debt outstanding relative to the amount of equity.

Continuing with the Plum Company, dividends could be set at \$1,000 instead of \$2,000 or \$3,000. In this case, the firm would have a cash outflow for dividends and investment amounting to \$1,000 + \$3,000 = \$4,000. With earnings of \$5,000, this means that there will be \$5,000 − \$4,000 = \$1,000 of cash left for the firm to use to repurchase its own stock.

The Dividend Decision Thus, the firm has a decision to make regarding the size of its current dividends. The amount of current earnings E_0 and the amount of new investment I_0 have been determined. What is left to be decided is the amount of dividends, D_0. They can be set equal to earnings less investment [as in Figure 16-1(a)], or greater than this amount [as in Figure 16-1(b)], or less than this amount [as in Figure 16-1(c)]. The question that remains to be answered is this: Will one of these three levels of dividends make the current stockholders be better off than the other two? That is, which level of dividends—\$1,000, \$2,000, or \$3,000—will make the current stockholders better off?

The simplest way to answer this question is to consider a stockholder who presently holds 1% of the common stock of the firm, and is determined to maintain this percentage ownership in the future.[2] If the firm follows a dividend policy as shown in Figure 16-1(a), the stockholder's current dividends will equal $.01D_0$ or, equivalently, $.01(E_0 - I_0)$. Similarly, the stockholder's future dividends will be equal to $.01D_t$ or, equivalently, $.01(E_t - I_t)$.

If the firm follows a dividend policy as shown in Figure 16-1(b), however, the stockholder must invest additional funds in the firm's common stock in order to avoid a diminished proportional ownership position in the firm. Why? Because in this situation the firm must raise funds by selling additional shares in order to pay for the larger cash dividends. Since $E_0 < D_0 + I_0$, the total amount of funds that the firm needs to raise is the amount F_0 such that:

$$E_0 + F_0 = D_0 + I_0 \tag{16.1}$$

[2]The use of such a stockholder is for ease of exposition; the same answer would be obtained if other types of stockholders (such as those who are not interested in maintaining a proportional ownership position in the firm in the future) are considered.

or

$$F_0 = D_0 + I_0 - E_0. \tag{16.2}$$

The amount of the additional investment that the stockholder needs to make in order to maintain a 1% position in the firm is $.01F_0$, which from equation (16.2) is equal to $.01(D_0 + I_0 - E_0)$. Since the stockholder receives 1% of the dividends, the net amount the stockholder receives at time zero is equal to $.01D_0 - .01F_0$, or:

$$.01D_0 - .01(D_0 + I_0 - E_0) = .01E_0 - .01I_0. \tag{16.3}$$

Interestingly, the net amount the stockholder receives, $.01E_0 - .01I_0$, is the same as in the first situation. This is because the amount of the extra cash dividend received is exactly offset by the amount the stockholder needs to spend to maintain his or her position of ownership in the firm.

If the firm follows a dividend policy as shown in Figure 16-1(c), then the firm will be repurchasing shares. Accordingly, the stockholder must sell some shares back to the firm in order to avoid having an increased ownership position in the firm. Since $E_0 > D_0 + I_0$, the total amount of funds that the firm will spend on repurchasing its own shares is the amount R_0 such that:

$$E_0 = D_0 + I_0 + R_0 \tag{16.4}$$

or

$$R_0 = E_0 - D_0 - I_0. \tag{16.5}$$

The amount of stock that the stockholder needs to sell back to the firm to maintain a 1% position in the firm is $.01R_0$, which from equation (16.5) is equal to $.01(E_0 - D_0 - I_0)$. Since the stockholder receives 1% of the dividends, the total amount the stockholder receives at time zero is equal to $.01D_0 + .01R_0$, or:

$$.01D_0 + .01(E_0 - D_0 - I_0) = .01E_0 - .01I_0. \tag{16.6}$$

Again, this amount, $.01E_0 - .01I_0$, is the same as in the first situation. That is, in the third situation, the smaller amount of the cash dividend received by the stockholder is exactly made up for by the amount of cash received from the repurchase of shares by the firm.

Thus, no matter what the firm's dividend policy, a stockholder choosing to maintain a constant proportional ownership will be able to spend the same amount of money on consumption at time zero. This amount will be equal to the proportion times the quantity $E_0 - I_0$. Furthermore, this will also be true in the future. That is, in any year t the stockholder will be able to spend on consumption an amount that is equal to the proportion times the quantity $E_t - I_t$.

Earnings Determine Market Value

In determining the value of 1% of the current shares outstanding, remember that the firm is about to declare and pay current dividends. Regardless of the magnitude of these dividends, the stockholder will only be able to spend on consumption an amount equal to $.01(E_0 - I_0)$. Furthermore, the stockholder will be able to spend on consumption an amount equal to $.01(E_t - I_t)$ in any future year t. Discounting these expected amounts by a (constant) rate k reveals that the value of 1% of the current shares outstanding will be:

$$.01V = \frac{.01(E_0 - I_0)}{(1 + k)^0} + \frac{.01(E_1 - I_1)}{(1 + k)^1} + \frac{.01(E_2 - I_2)}{(1 + k)^2} + \ldots$$

Multiplying both sides of this equation by 100 results in the following expression for the total market value of all shares outstanding:

$$V = \frac{(E_0 - I_0)}{(1 + k)^0} + \frac{(E_1 - I_1)}{(1 + k)^1} + \frac{(E_2 - I_2)}{(1 + k)^2} + \ldots \tag{16.7}$$

Equation (16.7) shows that the aggregate market value of equity is equal to the present value of expected earnings net of investment. Note how the size of the dividends does not enter into the formula. This indicates that the market value of the stock is independent of the dividend decision made by the firm. Instead, the market value of the firm is related to the earnings prospects of the firm, along with the required amounts of new investment needed to produce those earnings.[3]

Dividend Discount Models There is nothing inconsistent between the dividend discount models presented in Chapter 15 and the irrelevancy of the dividend decision. The dividend discount models indicated that the value of one share of common stock was equal to the present value of all the dividends expected in the future. The dividend irrelevancy argument suggests that if the firm decides to increase its current dividend, then new shares will need to be sold. This, in turn, suggests that future dividends will be smaller since the aggregate amount of dividends will have to be divided among an increased number of shares outstanding. Ultimately, the current stockholders will be neither better off nor worse off, since the increased current dividend will be exactly offset by the decreased future dividends. Conversely, if the firm decides to decrease its current dividend, then shares will be repurchased and future dividends will be increased due to the fewer shares outstanding. Ultimately, the decreased current dividend will be exactly offset by the increased future dividends, again leaving current stockholders neither better off nor worse off.

An Example All this can be illustrated with the earlier example of the Plum Company. Since Plum currently has reported earnings of $5,000 and investments totaling $3,000, if dividends amounting to $2,000 were paid, then the

[3]It has been argued that if the tax rate on dividends is greater than the tax rate on capital gains, then stockholders will earn more on an after-tax basis if the firm has a relatively low payout ratio. An additional benefit to stockholders if the firm has a low payout ratio is that capital gains taxes are paid only when the stock is sold, and can therefore be deferred. Thus, it appears that stockholders will be better off if the firm has a relatively low payout ratio. However, currently the tax rate on dividends is equal to or only slightly higher than the tax rate on capital gains, diminishing the validity of the argument. For a more detailed discussion of the issue, along with the relevant citations, see pp. 128–35 of Gordon J. Alexander and Jack Clark Francis, *Portfolio Analysis* (Englewood Cliffs, N.J.: Prentice Hall, 1986). Also see James S. Ang, David W. Blackwell, and William L. Megginson, "The Effect of Taxes on the Relative Valuation of Dividends and Capital Gains: Evidence from Dual-Class British Investment Trusts," *Journal of Finance*, 46, no. 1 (March 1991):383–99.

stockholder owning 1% of the firm would receive cash amounting to .01 × $2,000 = $20.

Alternatively, if dividends amounting to $3,000 were paid, then Plum would have to raise $1,000 from the sale of new common stock. The stockholder would receive .01 × $3,000 = $30 in dividends, but would have to pay .01 × $1,000 = $10 to purchase 1% of the new stock, thereby maintaining his or her 1% position of ownership. Consequently, the net cash flow to the stockholder would be $30 − $10 = $20, the same amount as in the previous situation.

Lastly, if dividends amounting to $1,000 were paid, then Plum would have cash amounting to $1,000 to use to repurchase common stock. The stockholder, desirous of maintaining a 1% position, would thus sell shares amounting to .01 × $1,000 = $10. As a result, the stockholder would have a cash inflow totaling $10 + $10 = $20, again the same amount as in the two previous situations.

Under all three situations, the 1% stockholder would receive the same cash flow at the present time ($20), and have the same claim on the future earnings of Plum. That is, in all three cases, the stockholder would still own 1% of Plum and would therefore receive the same amount of dividends in the future. Accordingly, the 1% stockholder (and all the others) will be neither better off nor worse off if Plum pays a dividend amounting to $1,000, $2,000, or $3,000. In summary, the dividend decision is a nonevent—whatever the level of dividends, current stockholders will be neither better off nor worse off. This result is sometimes referred to as the "dividend irrelevancy theorem."

DETERMINANTS OF DIVIDENDS

Few firms attempt to maintain a constant ratio of dividends to current earnings, since doing so would result in a fluctuating dollar amount of dividends. The reason the dividends would fluctuate is that earnings on a year-to-year basis are likely to be quite variable. Instead, firms attempt to maintain a desired ratio of dividends to earnings over some relatively long period, meaning that there is a target payout ratio of dividends to long-run or sustainable earnings. As a result, dividends are usually kept at a constant dollar amount and are increased only when management is confident that it will be relatively easy to keep paying this increased amount in the future.[4] Nonetheless, larger earnings are likely to be accompanied by some sort of increase in dividends, as Table 16-1 shows.

The first two lines of Table 16-1 indicate that of the firms examined, 59.3% of the time their earnings rose and the remainder of the time (40.7% = 100% − 59.3%) their earnings fell. The majority of the time when current earnings rose, firms increased their current dividends. However, whenever current earnings fell, firms would increase their current dividends as frequently as they would decrease their current dividends (note that, roughly speaking, 42.8% ≈ 39.5%).

The next two lines of the table suggest that firms are more likely to increase current dividends if they have had two consecutive years of ris-

[4]In addition to a regular dividend, sometimes a firm will declare a "special" or "extra" dividend, usually at year-end. By calling it a special dividend, the firm is conveying a message to its stockholders that such a dividend is a one-time event.

TABLE 16-1
Dividend and Earnings Changes for 392 Major Industrial Firms, 1946–1964

EARNINGS CHANGES			PERCENT OF CASES IN WHICH FIRMS		
Current Year	Previous Year	Percent of Cases	Increased Dividends	Did Not Change Dividends	Decreased Dividends
+		59.3%	65.8%	13.9%	20.3%
−		40.7	42.8	17.9	39.5
+	+	33.4	74.8	11.4	13.8
+	−	25.9	54.1	17.2	28.7
−	+	24.7	49.7	16.9	33.4
−	−	16.0	31.8	19.4	48.8

Source: Eugene F. Fama and Harvey Babiak, "Dividend Policy: An Empirical Analysis," *Journal of the American Statistical Association*, 63, no. 324 (December 1968): p. 1134.

ing earnings than if they have had falling and then rising earnings (74.8% > 54.1%). The last two lines of the table suggest that firms are more likely to decrease current dividends if they have had two consecutive years of falling earnings than if they have had rising and then falling earnings (48.8% > 33.4%). Overall, the table shows that firms in general are more likely to increase dividends than to decrease them.

The Lintner Model A formal representation of the kind of behavior implied by a constant long-run target payout ratio begins by assuming that the goal of the firm is to pay out p^* (for example, $p^* = 60\%$) of long-run earnings. If this target ratio were maintained every year, total dividends paid in year t would be:

$$D_t^* = p^* E_t \tag{16.8}$$

where D_t^* denotes the target amount for dividends to be paid in year t and E_t is the amount of earnings in year t. The difference between target dividends in year t and the previous year's actual dividends is determined by subtracting D_{t-1} from both sides of equation (16.8), resulting in:

$$D_t^* - D_{t-1} = p^* E_t - D_{t-1}. \tag{16.9}$$

While firms would like to change their dividends from D_{t-1} to D_t^*, few (if any) firms would actually change their dividends by this amount. Instead, the actual change in dividends will be a proportion of the desired change:

$$D_t - D_{t-1} = a(D_t^* - D_{t-1}) \tag{16.10}$$

where a is a "speed of adjustment" coefficient, a number between zero and one.

For example, if a firm has just earned \$5 million (E_t = \$5 million) and has a target payout ratio of 60%, then it would like to pay dividends amounting to .6 × \$5 million = \$3 million. Assuming it paid dividends of \$2 million last year, this represents an increase of \$3 million − \$2 million = \$1 million. However, if $a = 50\%$, then the firm will actually increase the dividends by .5 × \$1 million = \$500,000. Thus, actual dividends will be equal to \$2.5 million = \$2 million + \$500,000, an amount equal to last year's dividends plus the change in dividends from last year to this year.

This model can be summarized by substituting p^*E_t for D_t^* in equation (16.10) and then solving the resulting expression for D_t:

$$D_t = ap^*E_t + (1 - a)D_{t-1}. \tag{16.11}$$

Equation (16.11) indicates that the amount of current dividends is based on the amount of current earnings and the amount of the previous year's dividends.[5] In the previous example, $a = 50\%$, $p^* = 60\%$, $E_t = \$5$ million, and $D_{t-1} = \$2$ million. Thus, actual dividends D_t would be equal to $[.5 \times .6 \times \$5 \text{ million}] + [(1 - .5) \times \$2 \text{ million}] = \$2.5$ million.

By subtracting D_{t-1} from both sides of equation (16.11), it can be seen that the change in dividends is equal to:

$$D_t - D_{t-1} = ap^*E_t - aD_{t-1}. \tag{16.12}$$

When written in this form, the model suggests that the size of the *change* in dividends will be positively related to the current amount of earnings (since ap^* is a positive number) and negatively related to the amount of the previous period's dividends (since $-aD_{t-1}$ is a negative number). Thus, the larger current earnings are, the larger the change in dividends, but the larger the previous period's dividends, the smaller the change in dividends.

Test Results Statistical analysis has been used to see how well this model describes the way a sample of firms set the amount of their dividends. Table 16-2 summarizes some of the values obtained in one such study. The average

[5]Looking backwards in time, it can be shown that current dividends D_t are a linear function of past earnings E_{t-1}, E_{t-2}, E_{t-3}, and so on. More specifically, it can be shown that:

$$D_t = ap^*[(1 - a)^0E_t + (1 - a)^1E_{t-1} + (1 - a)^2E_{t-2} + (1 - a)^3E_{t-3} + \ldots].$$

Since the quantity $(1 - a)$ is a positive fraction (for example, 1/3), when it is raised to a power it becomes smaller in value, with larger powers resulting in values closer to zero. Thus, current dividends depend more on recent past earnings than on distant past earnings, and the equation can be approximated by using an arbitrary number of past earnings (the accuracy of the approximation depends on the number used).

TABLE 16-2 Target Payout Ratios and Speed of Dividend Adjustment Factors for 298 Firms, 1946–1968

SPEED OF ADJUSTMENT COEFFICIENT		TARGET PAYOUT RATIO		PERCENT OF VARIANCE EXPLAINED	
Value	Percent of Firms with Smaller Value	Value	Percent of Firms with Smaller Value	Value	Percent of Firms with Smaller Value
.104	10%	.401	10%	11%	10%
.182	30	.525	30	32	30
.251	50	.584	50	42	50
.339	70	.660	70	54	70
.470	90	.779	90	72	90
average .269		average .591		average 42	

Source: Eugene F. Fama, "The Empirical Relationship Between the Dividend and Investment Decisions of Firms," *American Economic Review*, 64, no. 3 (June 1974): p. 310.

firm had a target payout ratio of 59.1% and adjusted dividends by 26.9% of the way toward its target each year. However, most firms' dividends varied substantially from the pattern implied by their targets and adjustment factors. Somewhat less than half (42%) of the annual variance in the typical firm's dividends could be explained in this manner. This means that the model, while having explained a portion of the changes in dividends that have occurred, has left a substantial portion unexplained.

THE INFORMATION CONTENT OF DIVIDENDS

asymmetric information

It is reasonable to believe that management has more information about the future earnings of the firm than does the public (which includes its own stockholders). This situation of **asymmetric information** suggests that management will seek to convey their information to the public if they have an incentive to do so. Assuming that they have such an incentive, one way of doing so is by announcing a change in the amount of the firm's dividends. When used in this manner, dividend announcements are said to be a signaling device.[6]

Signaling

A relatively simple view of dividend changes is that an announced increase in dividends is a signal that management has increased its assessment of the future earnings for the firm. The announced increase in dividends is therefore "good news" and will, in turn, cause investors to raise their expectations regarding the future earnings of the firm. Conversely, an announced decrease in dividends is a signal that management has decreased its assessment of the future earnings for the firm. The announced decrease in dividends is therefore "bad news" and will, in turn, cause investors to lower their expectations regarding the future earnings of the firm. An implication is that an announced increase in dividends will cause the firm's stock price to rise, and an announced decreased will cause it to fall.

This simple model of dividend changes can be thought of as a special case of the model given in equation (16.12), where the speed of adjustment, a, is zero. With this model, the expected change in dividends, $D_t - D_{t-1}$, is zero, suggesting that a simple increase in dividends will be viewed as good news. Conversely, a simple decrease in dividends will be viewed as bad news.

One way of testing to see if dividend changes do indeed convey information to the public is to see how stock prices react to announcements of changes in dividends. However, care must be exercised in conducting such a study because the firm's announcement of dividends is often made at the same time that the firm announces its earnings. Thus, if such announcements are made at the same time, any price change in the firm's common stock may be attributable to either (or both) announcements. One study attempted to avoid this problem of contamination by only looking at cases where the

[6]Other signaling devices include changes in the firm's capital structure (for example, announcing an issuance of debt with the proceeds being used to repurchase stock). It has been argued that in order for the signal to be useful to the public, (1) management must have an incentive to send a truthful signal; (2) the signal cannot be imitated by competitors in different financial positions; and (3) there cannot be a cheaper means of conveying the same information. See Stephen A. Ross, "The Determination of Financial Structure: The Incentive Signalling Approach," *Bell Journal of Economics*, 8, no. 1 (Spring 1977): 23–40.

FIGURE 16-2
Cumulative Abnormal Returns Starting Ten Days Before a Dividend Announcement
Source: Joseph Aharony and Itzhak Swary, "Quarterly Dividend and Earnings Announcements and Stockholders' Returns: An Empirical Analysis," *Journal of Finance*, 35, no. 1 (March 1980): p. 8.

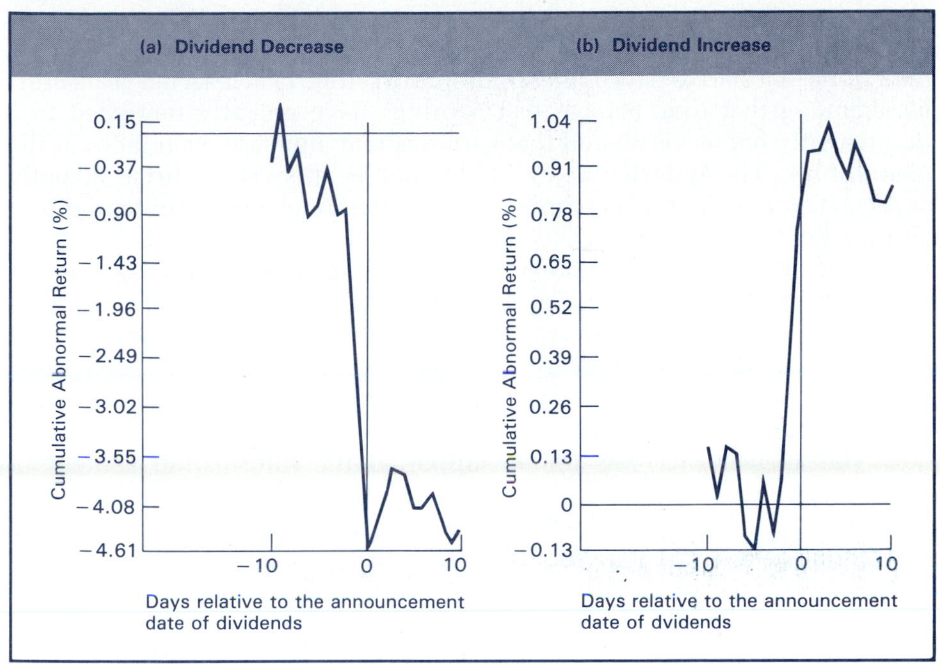

announcement of earnings was at least eleven trading days apart from the announcement of dividends. Figure 16-2 provides an illustration of the average abnormal return associated with a firm's dividend announcement for those firms that announced their dividends eleven or more days after they announced their earnings (similar results were obtained when the authors examined those cases where dividend announcements preceded earnings announcements).

In those cases where firms announced an increase in their dividends, there is a significant positive reaction in their stock prices. Conversely, in those cases where firms announced a decrease in their dividends, there is a significant negative reaction in their stock prices. These findings strongly support the **information content of dividends hypothesis,** where dividend announcements are asserted to contain inside information about the firm's future prospects.

information content of dividends hypothesis

It should be noted that there is nothing inconsistent with dividends being used as a signal and with the dividend irrelevancy argument of Miller and Modigliani that was made earlier. In particular, stockholders will be neither better nor worse off if the *level* of dividends, relative to earnings, is high or low. *Changes* in dividends may, however, be important because they convey information to the public about the future earnings prospects for the firm.

Dividend Initiations and Omissions

One study looked at the relationship between dividend changes and past, current, and future changes in earnings.[7] Specifically, it focused on the most dramatic dividend announcements possible—dividend initiations and omissions—since the information being conveyed in these announcements is clearly unambiguous.

That is, if the information content of dividends hypothesis is correct, then firms that start to pay dividends for the first time in at least ten years must be signaling that they believe that earnings have recently increased to a permanently higher level, and that earnings may increase even more in the near future. The question to be addressed is this: Have firms actually experienced notably higher earnings around the time of such initiations and afterwards?

Conversely, firms that have paid dividends for at least ten years and that suddenly stop paying any dividends must believe that their earnings have recently decreased to a permanently lower level, and that earnings may decrease even more in the future. For them the question is this: Have firms actually experienced notably lower earnings around the time of such omissions and afterwards?

The answer that was found supported the information content of dividends hypothesis. Specifically, the study found that earnings tended to increase for at least one year leading up to dividend initiations and to decrease for up to two years leading up to dividend omissions. Furthermore, earnings continued to increase for at least one year after initiations and to decrease for one year after omissions, and such changes appear to be permanent. Interestingly, the larger the change in the firm's stock price when the dividend initiation or omission is announced, the larger the change in the firm's earnings in both the year of the announcement and the year thereafter. Thus, it seems that dividends do indeed convey information about earnings.

ACCOUNTING EARNINGS VERSUS ECONOMIC EARNINGS

Since the prediction of earnings is of critical importance in security analysis and investment research, a review of what is known about earnings and the relationship between earnings and security prices is essential. At a fundamental level, consideration of the concept of "earnings" itself is needed. Specifically, just what is meant by "earnings" to those who produce the figures, and how does this affect the valuation process?

Accounting Earnings

accounting earnings

A firm's accountants operate under constraints and guidelines imposed by regulatory authorities and professional organizations such as the Securities and Exchange Commission (SEC) and the Financial Accounting Standards Board (FASB). In cooperation with management, the accountants produce, on a quarterly basis, a set of financial statements for the firm that ends with a figure for the firm's **accounting earnings** (also known as the firm's reported

[7]Paul M. Healy and Krishna G. Palepu, "Earnings Information Conveyed by Dividend Initiations and Omissions," *Journal of Financial Economics*, 21, no. 2 (September 1988): 149–75.

earnings). In a broad sense, such earnings represent the difference between revenues and costs, including the costs associated with nonequity sources of funds (such as debt). This difference, the "total earnings available for common stock," is divided by the number of shares outstanding to calculate **earnings per share** (EPS). It may also be divided by the book value per share to calculate the **return on equity** (ROE).

earnings per share

return on equity

A basic principle of accounting makes the book value of a firm's equity at the end of a period (such as a quarter or year) equal to (1) its value at the end of the previous period plus (2) the portion of accounting earnings for the period that is retained by the firm (here it is assumed that there has been no change in the number of shares outstanding during the period). Letting B_t denote the book value of the equity of the firm at the end of period t, E_t^a denote the accounting earnings for period t, and D_t denote the dividends paid during period t, this relationship can be expressed algebraically as:

$$B_t = B_{t-1} + E_t^a - D_t. \tag{16.13}$$

From equation (16.13), it can be seen that accounting earnings equals the change in book value of equity plus dividends paid:

$$E_t^a = B_t - B_{t-1} + D_t. \tag{16.14}$$

Economic Earnings

Economic earnings (E_t^e) may be defined as the amount that would be obtained in equation (16.14) if the change in the book value of the firm equaled the change in the **economic value of the firm:**

economic earnings

economic value of the firm

$$E_t^e = V_t - V_{t-1} + D_t. \tag{16.15}$$

Here the change in the economic value of the firm during period t, $V_t - V_{t-1}$, is defined as the change in the market value of the firm's common stock (assuming that there is no change in the market value of the other securities of the firm).[8]

It is easy to show that reported book values and market values (that is, economic values) of stocks are often considerably different. Figure 16-3 shows the ratio of (1) the year-end market price per share for Standard & Poor's Industrial Stock Index, to (2) the corresponding year-end book value per share. It can be seen that the ratio is typically greater than 1.0 and has fluctuated considerably from year to year.

Figure 16-4 plots book values (horizontal axis) and market values (vertical axis) for the stocks in the Dow Jones Industrial Average. If investors viewed market and book values as nearly equivalent, the points would plot along a 45-degree line (that is, a line with a slope of one) that emanates from the origin. However, as the extensive scatter of the points indicates, market values diverge from book values by different amounts for different stocks.

[8]Sir John R. Hicks, winner in 1972 of the Nobel Award in Economics, defined the weekly economic income of an individual as "the maximum value which he can consume during a week and still be as well off at the end of the week as he was at the beginning" (*Value and Capital*, London: Oxford University Press, 1946, p. 172). The definition of the economic earnings of a firm that is given in equation (16.15) can be viewed as an extension of Hicks' definition for an individual.

FIGURE 16-3
Ratio of Price to Book Value: Standard & Poor's Industrial Stock Index, 1946–1990
Source: Standard & Poor's *Statistical Service*, various issues.

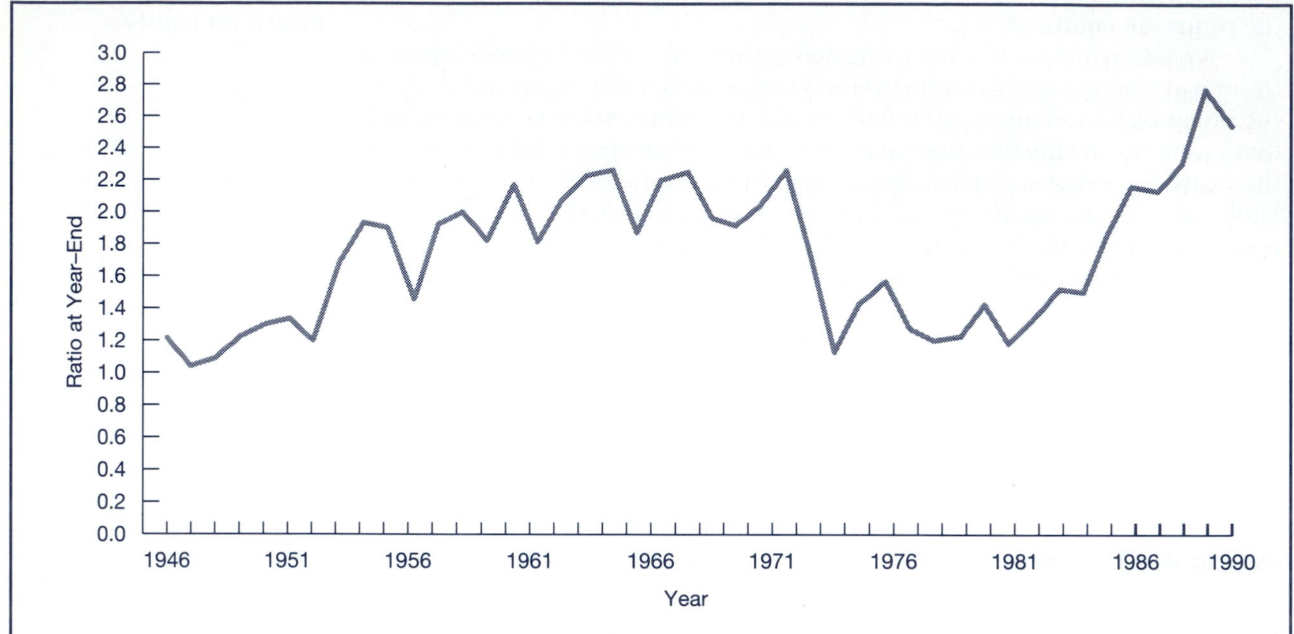

FIGURE 16-4
Market and Book Values, Stocks in Dow Jones Industrial Average, Year-end 1990

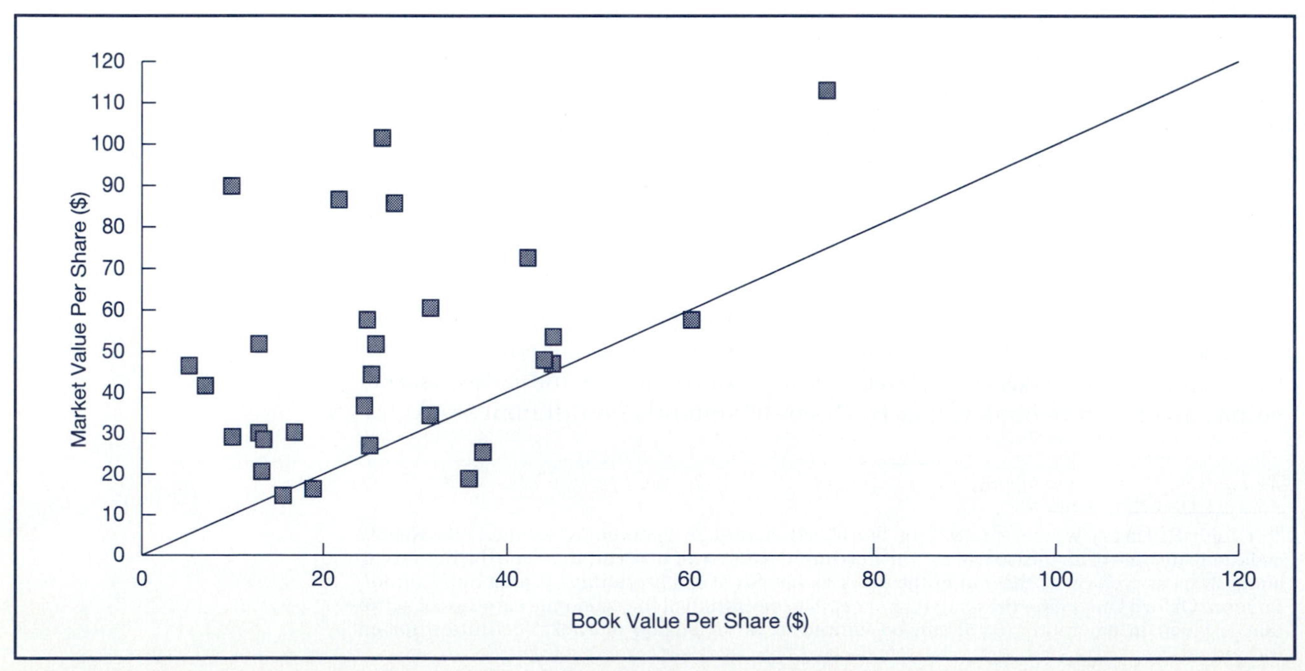

Both Figure 16-3 and Figure 16-4 indicate that there can be sizable differences between market and book values. Since equations (16.14) and (16.15) show that accounting and economic earnings will be equal only if market and book values are equal, the evidence thus suggests that accounting and economic earnings differ by varying amounts for different firms.

The trouble with accounting earnings is the belief held by certain accountants that investors consider current and recent accounting earnings when estimating the value of a security.[9] This tempts management to try to "manage" such earnings in order to make a firm appear more valuable than it is, thereby fooling investors, at least temporarily. This is permissible since the **generally accepted accounting principles** (GAAP) set by the regulatory authorities (such as FASB) allow a large amount of discretion in how certain items are accounted for (examples include methods for depreciation and inventory valuation). As a result, management may pressure accountants to use those principles that maximize the level of reported earnings, or that result in a high growth rate of reported earnings, or that "smooth" earnings by reducing the year-to-year variability of earnings around a growth rate.[10] Some of these activities can be continued only for a limited number of years; others can go on indefinitely.

generally accepted accounting principles

To obtain a truly independent estimate of value, analysts must dissect reported earnings. In doing so, they should not be fooled by any accounting illusions, meaning that they should not be fooled by any manipulations that may have been made by the accountants at management's request.[11] Anyone who estimates value by applying a formula (no matter how complex) to reported earnings is not producing an estimate that is completely free from all possible manipulations by management. This is not to say that reported earnings are irrelevant for security valuation. Instead, they should be viewed as one source of information about the future prospects of a firm.

PRICE-EARNINGS RATIOS

Chapter 15 discussed how dividend discount models could be used to determine if stocks were either underpriced or overpriced. One means of making this determination was to compare the actual price-earnings ratio for a firm with what the security analyst had determined it should be. In view of this use of price-earnings ratios, some evidence on the behavior of overall earnings, prices, and price-earnings ratios will now be presented.

Panel (a) of Figure 16-5 presents a plot of the year-end price-earnings ratios for the Standard & Poor's 500. It can be seen from this that the variation in the ratio on a year-to-year basis is considerable, suggesting that investors do

[9]Two assertions that have been made in regard to what investors look at when valuing stocks are known as the *mechanistic hypothesis* and the *myopic hypothesis*. The former asserts that investors only look at reported earnings and the latter asserts that investors only look at the short-term future. Both these assertions seem to be invalid when data are analyzed. For an in-depth discussion, see George Foster, *Financial Statement Analysis* (Englewood Cliffs, N.J.: Prentice Hall, 1986), pp. 443–45.

[10]For a discussion of a number of related issues, see Ross Watts, "Does It Pay to Manipulate EPS?" in *Issues in Corporate Finance* (New York: Stern Stewart Putnam & Macklis, Ltd., 1983).

[11]There is evidence that investors in publicly-held firms are not fooled by such manipulations; see, for example, John R. M. Hand and Patricia Hughes, "The Motives and Consequences of Debt-Equity Swaps and Defeasances: More Evidence That It Does Not Pay to Manipulate Earnings," *Journal of Applied Corporate Finance*, 3, no. 3 (Fall 1990): 77–81.

FIGURE 16-5
Price, Earnings, and Price-Earnings Ratios, Standard & Poor's 500, Year-end, 1951–1990
Source: Standard & Poor's *Statistical Service*, various issues.

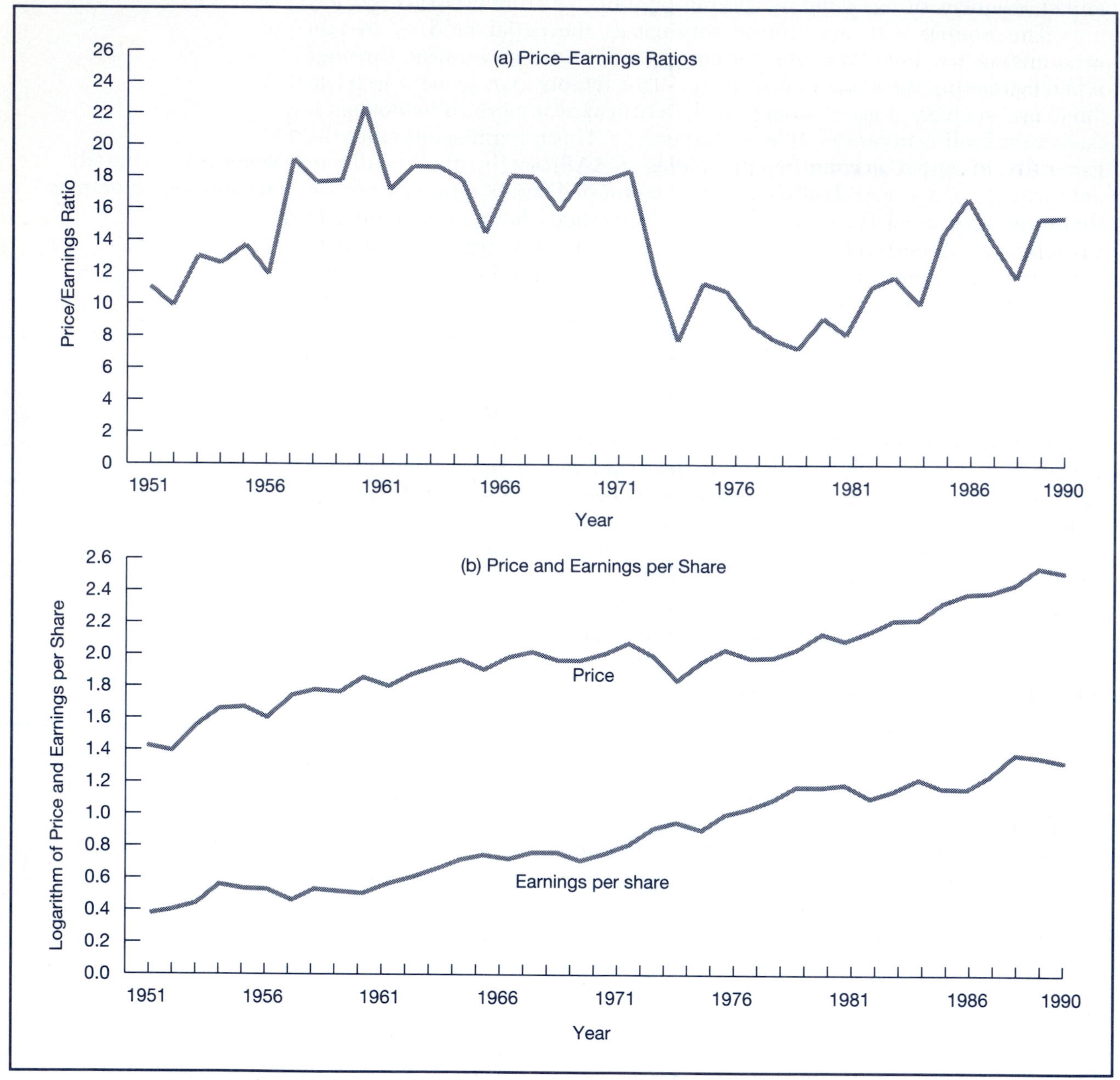

not simply apply a standard multiple to earnings in order to determine an appropriate value.

Panel (b) of Figure 16-5 presents a plot of earnings per share (the lower jagged line) and price (the upper jagged line) for the Standard & Poor's 500.[12] Both lines generally move upward to the right, showing a general trend for both earnings per share and prices to increase over time. However, the two lines are not parallel. This means that earnings per share and prices do not move together in a lockstep manner, an observation that is also apparent in panel (a).

Permanent and Transitory Components of Earnings

When individual common stocks are analyzed, they too show considerable variation in their price-earnings ratios over time. Furthermore, their ratios are quite different from each other at any point in time. One possible explanation notes that reported earnings can be viewed as having two components. The *permanent* component is the component that is likely to be repeated in the future, whereas the *transitory* component is not likely to be repeated.

Earlier, it was argued that the intrinsic value of a stock depends on the firm's future earnings prospects. This suggests that changes in a stock's intrinsic value, and in turn its price, will be correlated with changes in the permanent component of its earnings but not with changes in the transitory component. If the transitory component is positive, then the price-earnings ratio would be relatively low due to a relatively large number in the denominator. Conversely, if the transitory component is negative, then the price-earnings ratio would be relatively high due to a relatively small number in the denominator.

As an example, consider a firm whose current stock price is $30 per share. Its permanent component of earnings per share over the past year is $4, and its transitory component is $1, resulting in reported earnings of $4 + $1 = $5 and a price-earnings ratio of $30/$5 = 6. Remember that this stock's current price is based on its future prospects, which are in turn based on the permanent component of earnings per share over the past year. Thus, if the firm had the same permanent component of $4 but had a transitory component of −$1 instead of +$1, the stock would still have a current price of $30 per share. However, its reported earnings would have been $4 − $1 = $3 and its price-earnings ratio would have been $30/$3 = 10.

The permanent component of earnings will change over time, causing investors to revise their forecasts. This will lead to a change in a firm's stock price and, in turn, its price-earnings ratio. However, changes in the transitory component will have an even greater effect on the price-earnings ratio because this component will sometimes be positive and sometimes be negative. As a result, a firm's price-earnings ratio will be variable over time, as was shown in Figure 16-5(a) for the S&P 500. This also means that at any point in time, the transitory component of earnings for a group of firms will have varying sizes, some being positive and some being negative. As a result, at any point in time, firms will have a range of different price-earnings ratios.

[12]The vertical axis of this figure actually measures the logarithm of earnings per share and of the price index. In this type of diagram, a given vertical distance represents the same percentage change, no matter where it appears, making it easier to compare relative changes. If, for example, prices changed by the same percentage every year, then the plot in such a diagram would be a straight line sloping upward to the right. If logarithms were not used, the plot would curve upward to the right.

If this were a complete explanation for the considerable variation in price-earnings ratios over time and across firms, then most of the variation in a firm's price-earnings ratio would itself be transitory. That is, the ratio would vary over time around some average value. However, the evidence suggests that this is not the case. Figure 16-6 shows the behavior over time of such ratios for two groups of stocks. The first group includes stocks with high price-earnings ratios at the beginning of the period (that is, during a portfolio formation period). The other group includes stocks with low price-earnings ratios at the beginning of the period.

Over time, the price-earnings ratios tend to revert to an average ratio for the market as a whole. The changes are substantial in the first two years, owing undoubtedly to the influence of transitory components of earnings. That is, those stocks in the high price-earnings ratio group apparently had, on average, a negative transitory component in their earnings in the portfolio formation period. (Remember that such a component would tend to give a stock a high ratio.) Conversely, those stocks in the low price-earnings ratio group apparently had, on average, a positive transitory component. (Remember that such a component would tend to give a stock a low ratio.) Over future periods, each group of stocks would tend to have an equal number of stocks with positive

FIGURE 16-6
Price-Earnings Ratios Over Time for Two Groups of Stocks
Source: William Beaver and Dale Morse, "What Determines Price-Earnings Ratios?" *Financial Analysts Journal*, 34, no. 4 (July–August 1978): p. 68.

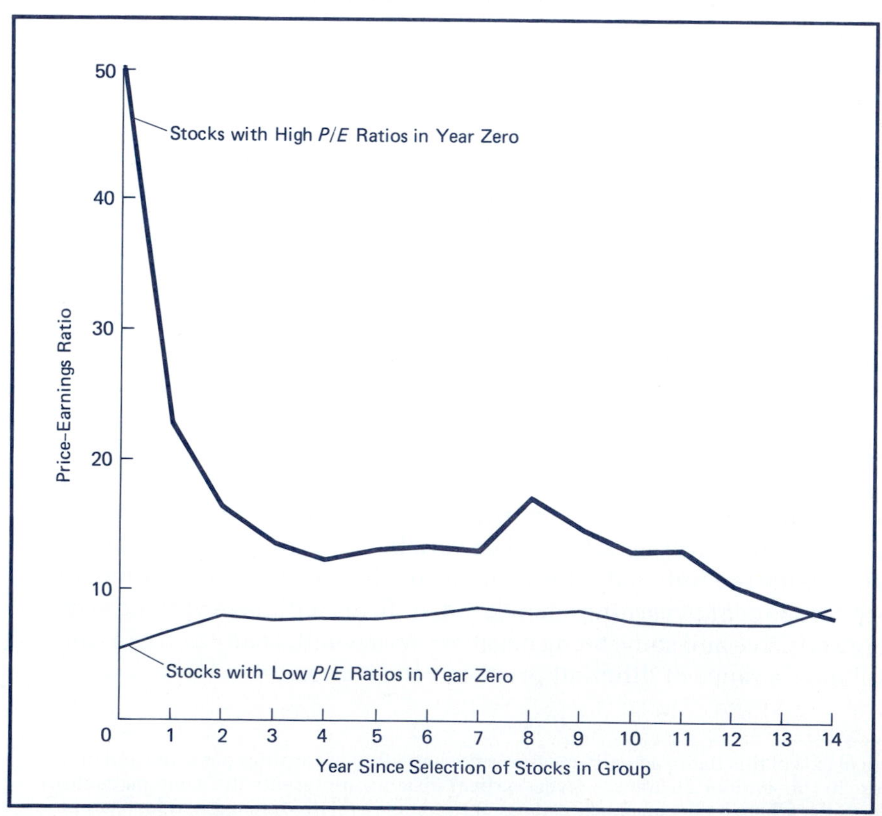

and negative transitory components, resulting in an average transitory component for each group of roughly zero.

However, Figure 16-6 shows that the two groups of stocks have different price-earnings ratios for many years after the portfolio formation period. Three explanations can be offered for this persistent difference. First, appropriate discount rates (that is, required returns) differ because of differences in security attributes. This means that there is no reason to expect different firms to have the same ratio. Second, there may be permanent differences between economic and reported earnings due to the use of different accounting methods. As mentioned earlier, there is evidence that the market sees through such differences in reported earnings. Third, there may be persistent differences in the forecasts of long-term permanent earnings growth rates by security analysts. That is, firms with high price-earnings ratios may have high forecasted long-term permanent earnings growth rates and hence relatively high prices. Conversely, firms with low price-earnings ratios may have low forecasted long-term permanent earnings growth rates and hence relatively low prices.[13] If such forecasts persist over time, then firms with high price-earnings ratios would tend to continue having high ratios over time, while firms with low ratios would tend to continue having low ratios over time. Evidence suggests that indeed this is the case.

RELATIVE GROWTH RATES OF FIRMS' EARNINGS

Since security analysis typically involves forecasting earnings per share, it is useful to examine the historical record to see how earnings per share have changed over time. An interesting question about growth rates in firm earnings over time focuses on "growth stocks." The very idea of a growth stock suggests that growth in some firms' earnings will exceed the average growth of all firms' earnings in most years, while other firms' earnings will grow less than the average.

The results of a study of the earnings growth rates for 610 industrial companies from 1950 and 1964 are shown in Table 16-3. In every year, each firm's earnings were compared with its earnings in the previous year and the percentage change calculated. The year was counted as "good" for the firm if its percentage change was in the top half of the changes for all firms that year, and "bad" if it was in the bottom half. If some firms tend to experience above-average earnings growth rates, then fairly long runs of good years should occur for these firms. Conversely, if some firms tend to experience below-average earnings growth rates, then they should have fairly long runs of bad years.

The middle two columns of Table 16-3 indicate the actual number of runs of various lengths. The right-hand column shows the number that would be expected if there were a 50-50 chance of either a good year or a bad year. The three columns are remarkably similar. Above-average earnings growth in the past does not appear to indicate above-average growth in the future; and below-average growth in the past does not appear to indicate below-average growth in the future. Flipping a coin seems to be as reliable a predictor of future growth as looking at past growth rates.

[13]This suggests that firms will have high price-earnings ratios if they have either negative transitory current earnings or high forecasted long-term permanent earnings, or both. The converse holds for firms with low price-earnings ratios.

TABLE 16-3
Earnings Growth Rates, 610 Firms, 1950–1964

LENGTH OF RUN	ACTUAL NUMBER OF GOOD RUNS	ACTUAL NUMBER OF BAD RUNS	NUMBER OF GOOD OR BAD RUNS EXPECTED IF THE ODDS EACH YEAR WERE 50-50, REGARDLESS OF PAST PERFORMANCE
1	1,152	1,102	1,068
2	562	590	534
3	266	300	267
4	114	120	133
5	55	63	67
6	24	20	33
7	23	12	17
8	5	6	8
9	3	3	4
10	6	0	2
11	2	0	1
12	1	0	1
13	0	0	0
14	0	1	0

Source: Richard A. Brealy, *An Introduction to Risk and Return from Common Stocks* (Cambridge, Mass.: The MIT Press, 1983): p. 89.

A study using longer time periods for measuring growth reached generally similar conclusions.[14] For each of 323 companies with positive earnings in each year from 1946 through 1965, average growth rates were computed for (1) the period from 1946 through 1955 and (2) the period from 1956 through 1965. Differences among firms' earnings growth rates in the first period accounted for less than 1% of the variation in the differences among their earnings growth rates in the second period.

Annual Earnings

random walk model

The results of these studies, as well as certain other studies, suggest that *annual* reported earnings follow what is known in statistics as a **random walk model.** That is, annual earnings for the forthcoming year (E_t) can be thought of as being equal to annual earnings over the past year (E_{t-1}) plus a random error term. (Remember that a random error term can be thought of as a roulette wheel where the numbers on the wheel are distributed around zero.) Accordingly,

$$E_t = E_{t-1} + \epsilon_t \tag{16.16}$$

where ϵ_t is the random error term. With this model, the estimate of next year's earnings is simply the past year's earnings, E_{t-1}. Another way of viewing a

[14]John Lintner and Robert Glauber, "Higgledy Piggledy Growth in America," in James Lorie and Richard Brealey, eds., *Modern Developments in Investment Management* (Hinsdale, Ill., The Dryden Press, 1978). However, a more recent study came to a different conclusion concerning the predictability of earnings changes. This study divided a large number of companies into five groups based on their earnings-to-price (E/P) ratios, and found that lower E/P stock groups exhibited consistently higher long-term earnings growth rates. See Russell J. Fuller, Lex C. Huberts, and Michael Levinson, "It's Not Higgledy-Piggledy Growth!" *Journal of Portfolio Management*, 18, no. 2 (Winter 1992): 38–45.

random walk model for earnings is that the change in earnings is independent and identically distributed:

$$E_t - E_{t-1} = \epsilon_t. \tag{16.17}$$

This means that the change in earnings, $E_t - E_{t-1}$, is unrelated to past changes in earnings and can be thought of as a spin from a roulette wheel that is perhaps unique to the firm but, more importantly, is used year after year. Since the expected outcome from a spin of the roulette wheel is zero, the expected change in earnings is zero. This implies that the expected level of earnings is equal to the past year's earnings, as was suggested earlier.

Quarterly Earnings

In terms of *quarterly* earnings, consideration must be given to the fact that there is typically a seasonal component to a firm's earnings (for example, many firms have high earnings during the quarter that includes Christmas). As a result, a slightly different model appears to be best for forecasting purposes. This model forecasts the growth in earnings for the forthcoming quarter relative to the same quarter one year ago, a quantity denoted $QE_t - QE_{t-4}$. It does so by relating this growth to the growth during the most recent quarter relative to the comparable quarter one year before it, $QE_{t-1} - QE_{t-5}$. Formally, the model for the "seasonally differenced series" of quarterly earnings is known as an *autoregressive model of order one*, and is as follows:

$$QE_t - QE_{t-4} = a(QE_{t-1} - QE_{t-5}) + b + e_t \tag{16.18}$$

where a and b are constants and e_t is a random error term.

Alternatively, the model can be rewritten by moving the term QE_{t-4} to the right-hand side:

$$QE_t = QE_{t-4} + a(QE_{t-1} - QE_{t-5}) + b + e_t. \tag{16.19}$$

By estimating the constants a and b, this model can be used for forecasting quarterly earnings.[15]

For example, assuming estimates for a and b of .4 and .05, respectively, the forecast of a firm's earnings for the next quarter would be equal to $QE_{t-4} + .4(QE_{t-1} - QE_{t-5}) + .05$. Thus, if a firm had earnings per share for the last quarter $(t - 1)$ of \$3, for four quarters before now $(t - 4)$ of \$2, and for five quarters before now $(t - 5)$ of \$2.60, then its forecasted earnings for the forthcoming quarter would be equal to \$2 + .4(\$3 − \$2.60) + \$.05 = \$2.21. Note how the forecast consists of three components—a component equal to last quarter's earnings [\$2]; a component that considers the year-to-year

[15]This model can also be used to forecast annual earnings by working forward one quarter at a time and then adding up the forecasts for the forthcoming four quarters. Doing so would result in a forecast of annual earnings (E_t) equal to $E_{t-1} + c(QE_{t-1} - QE_{t-5}) + d$, where $c = a^1 + a^2 + a^3 + a^4$ and $d = 4b + 3ab + 2a^2b + a^3b$. Note that the random walk model is a special case where a and b are equal to zero.

quarterly growth in earnings [.4($3 − $2.60) = $.16]; and a component that is a constant [$.05].[16]

COMOVEMENT OF EARNINGS

Past changes in security prices are of limited value for the prediction of future changes. And past changes in the overall level of the market are of limited help in the prediction of future market moves. However, security price changes are related to concurrent changes in the prices of the market portfolio and, to a lesser extent, an "industry" portfolio.[17] While the strength of these relationships differs among securities, historical data can generally be utilized to help estimate the relative future strengths of the relationships for different securities. For example, the relationship between a security's returns and market returns has been referred to as the security's beta, and can be estimated by examining historical returns. Similarly, the industry that a security belongs to can be determined and a portfolio of stocks in that industry constructed. Then the historical returns on the security can be compared to this portfolio and an industry beta can be estimated.

It has been argued that security prices are determined by economic earnings, and that security price movements are related to movements in market and industry prices. Thus, an interesting issue is whether or not movements in the economic earnings of a firm are related to movements in the economic earnings of the market and industry portfolios. Such an issue has been explored by looking at accounting earnings and assuming that they are correlated with economic earnings.

Table 16-4 shows that such relationships do exist, at least to some extent. Earnings reported by 217 corporations from 1948 through 1966 were compared first with the earnings for Standard & Poor's 425-stock index (which served as a surrogate for marketwide earnings) and then with the average earnings of all firms in the same industry. The proportion of each firm's earnings variations that could be attributed to each of these factors was determined. The results shown in the table are the average proportions for all the firms in each industry.

The results differ notably from one industry to another, with the marketwide factor ranging between 5% and 48% and the industry factor ranging from 5% to 49%. The bottom row of the table shows the values obtained by averaging over all 217 corporations. Changes in marketwide earnings accounted for 21% of the variation in the earnings of the typical firm, and changes in the earnings of firms in its industry accounted for another 21%.

[16]It has been argued that a slight improvement can be made in this model by replacing the constant term component with what is known as a "moving average" component that is based on the size of the random error term that occurred four quarters before now (e_{t-4}). See Lawrence D. Brown and Michael S. Rozeff, "Univariate Time-Series Models of Quarterly Accounting Earnings per Share: A Proposed Model," *Journal of Accounting Research*, 17, no. 1 (Spring 1979): 179–89; and Allen W. Bathke, Jr. and Kenneth S. Lorek, "The Relationship Between Time Series Models and the Security Market's Expectations of Quarterly Earnings," *Accounting Review*, 59, no. 2 (April 1984): 163–76.

[17]While the definition of what constitutes an "industry" differs from one study to another, various authors have found that security price movements can be attributed not only to market price movements but also to industry price movements. See Alexander and Francis, *Portfolio Analysis*, pp. 195–96, for a description of these studies and the relevant citations.

TABLE 16-4
The Proportion of the Variation of a Firm's Earnings Attributable to Marketwide and Industry Earnings Changes

Industry	PROPORTION ATTRIBUTABLE TO: Marketwide Earnings Changes	Additional Influence of Changes in Industry Earnings
Aircraft	11%	5%
Autos	48	11
Beer	11	7
Cement	6	32
Chemicals	41	8
Cosmetics	5	6
Department stores	30	37
Drugs	14	7
Electricals	24	8
Food	10	10
Machinery	19	16
Nonferrous metals	26	25
Office machinery	14	6
Oil	13	49
Paper	27	28
Rubber	26	48
Steel	32	21
Supermarkets	6	33
Textiles and clothing	25	29
Tobacco	8	19
All firms	21	21

Source: Richard Brealey, "Some Implications of the Comovement of American Company Earnings," *Applied Economics*, 3, no. 3 (September 1971): p. 187.

Earlier, it was mentioned that a security's beta (sometimes known as its **market beta**) is a measure of how the price of the security will covary with the price of the market portfolio. Similarly, a security's **accounting beta** is a measure of how the accounting earnings of the security will covary with the accounting earnings of the market portfolio. If security prices are related to earnings, then it seems reasonable to expect market betas to be related to accounting betas. Studies that have examined this issue have found that market and accounting betas are significantly correlated, with accounting betas explaining between 20% and 40% of the variation that is observed in market betas.

market beta
accounting beta

EARNINGS ANNOUNCEMENTS AND PRICE CHANGES

A number of studies have shown substantial price changes for stocks of companies that report earnings that differ substantially from consensus expectations. One study looked at three groups of fifty stocks.[18] The first group consisted of the fifty stocks listed on the New York Stock Exchange (NYSE) that experienced the greatest price rise during 1970. The second group consisted of fifty stocks chosen randomly from all those listed on the NYSE during 1970. The third group consisted of the fifty stocks listed on the NYSE

[18]Victor Niederhoffer and Patrick J. Regan, "Earnings Changes, Analysts' Forecasts, and Stock Prices," *Financial Analysts Journal*, 28, no. 3 (May–June 1972): 65–71.

that experienced the greatest price decline during 1970. As shown in Figure 16-7, the median changes in the prices of the stocks in the top, random, and bottom groups were 48.4%, −3.2%, and −56.7%, respectively.

Next, the study looked at the actual change in earnings per share from 1969 to 1970 for each stock in each group. As shown in Figure 16-7, the median changes in earnings per share for the top, random, and bottom groups were 21.4%, −10.5%, and −83.0%, respectively.

Lastly, the study determined the forecasted change in earnings per share at the beginning of 1970 for each stock in each group. This was done by using the predictions contained in Standard & Poor's *Earnings Forecaster*, where estimates made by a number of investment research organizations are reported. The median forecasted changes in earnings per share for the top, random, and bottom groups are shown in Figure 16-7 to be 7.7%, 5.8%, and 15.3%, respectively.

Interestingly, the forecasts of earnings per share hardly correspond to the price movements of the stocks. In fact, the earnings of the stocks in the bottom group were expected to increase more than the earnings of the stocks in the top group (15.3%, compared with 7.7%). However, the prediction for the bottom group was disastrously wrong, with a median earnings per share decline of 83.0%. And, as Figure 16-7 shows, prices definitely followed suit. Overall, it appears that unexpected changes in earnings do indeed affect security prices.[19]

[19]Another study using data from 1980 and 1981 reached similar conclusions. That is, the top fifty stocks had forecasted and actual earnings growth rates of 14.3% and 31.3%, respectively; for the bottom fifty stocks the respective rates were 17.4% and −10.3%. See Gary A. Benesh and Pamela P. Peterson, "On the Relation Between Earnings Changes, Analysts' Forecasts and Stock Price Fluctuations," *Financial Analysts Journal*, 42, no. 6 (November/December 1986): 29–39, 55.

FIGURE 16-7
Earnings and Price Changes: Selected Stocks Listed on the New York Stock Exchange During 1970

Source: Victor Niederhoffer and Patrick J. Regan, "Earnings Changes, Analysts' Forecasts, and Stock Prices," *Financial Analysts Journal*, 28, no. 3 (May/June 1972): p. 67.

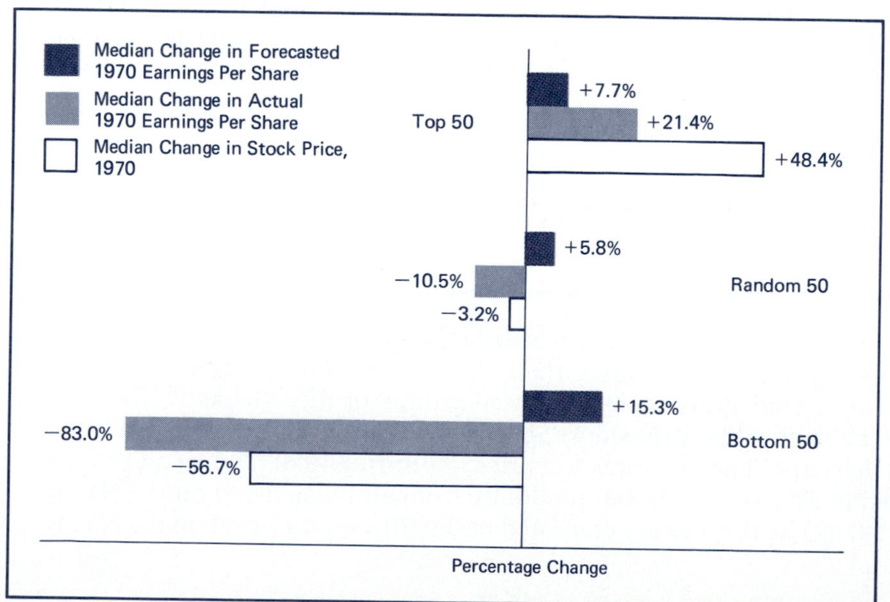

MONEY MATTERS
Earnings Growth and Stock Prices

Your broker approaches you with some intriguing investment advice. "Our analyst tells us that Gonzo Corporation's earnings will grow 25% next year," she says. "With the market's earnings expected to rise only 8% over the same period, Gonzo's stock is a sure winner. Even if our analyst's earnings growth estimate is off by a percent or two, how can you lose?" The analysts in your broker's firm have a reputation for accurate earnings forecasts. Assuming that this particular forecast turns out to be near the mark, is Gonzo stock truly a "sure winner"? The answer is an unequivocable, "It depends."

With all the hype put out by brokerage firms concerning the attractiveness of "growth" companies, it would seem natural to assume that the stock of a company with well-above-average expected earnings growth should perform well. Research, however, demonstrates that the correlation between expected earnings growth and relative stock price performance is at best zero and perhaps slightly negative. That is, above-average forecasted earnings growth does not by itself guarantee superior returns, even if those forecasts subsequently prove correct. (For example, see "Expectations and Share Prices" by Edwin Elton, Martin Gruber, and Mustafa Gultekin, *Management Science*, September 1981.)

Let us be clear as to what we mean by forecasted earnings growth. The typical large U.S. company has many security analysts continuously examining the prospects for its sales, financial condition, management, and, most important, earnings. Each of these analysts arrives at an estimate of the company's expected earnings growth. Averaged, the analysts' various earnings estimates are termed "consensus" earnings forecasts.

Research indicates that the market efficiently impounds consensus earnings expectations into stock prices. To the extent that a particular investor's earnings growth forecast for a company is well above the expected growth in earnings for the market, but merely reflects *consensus* earnings growth expectations for the company, then the investor is unlikely to earn abnormal profits trading on the forecast. The information is already reflected in the stock's price.

In fact, some observers argue that a stock with a considerably above-market consensus earnings forecast represents a high-risk investment. If the company's realized earnings match the consensus' earnings expectation, the stock receives no boost; the stock's price has already incorporated those expectations. Conversely, if the company's realized earnings fail to meet the consensus' lofty expectation, the stock's price is likely to fall sharply. In essence, the argument goes, this type of stock has nowhere to go but down.

How, then, can an investor profit by accurately forecasting corporate earnings? The answer lies in identifying growth opportunities (or disappointments) not yet reflected in market prices. That is, the trick is to both be correct and bet against the consensus.

Research indicates that companies whose actual earnings considerably exceed consensus forecasts produce extremely large risk-adjusted stock returns. (For example, see Figure 16-7 and "Earnings Expectations and Security Prices" by Eugene Hawkins, Stanley Chamberlain, and Wayne Daniel, *Financial Analysts Journal*, September/October 1984.) Interestingly, these large returns may be earned by companies whose actual earnings growth falls well below that of the market. But if the consensus is expecting even lower earnings growth than actually occurs, the positive "earnings surprise" often results in the stock performing relatively well.

Of course, consistently identifying situations in which earnings growth will differ from consensus forecasts requires a unique set of skills. Most competent security analysts have little trouble identifying high-growth or low-growth companies. However, only the rare analyst possesses the insights necessary to identify companies whose earnings will surprise the market.

But do earnings surprises affect prices before or after their announcement? In a completely efficient market, such information would be reflected in prices as soon as it had been disseminated to a few major market participants. The reaction of security prices around the time of earnings announcements has been examined by a number of authors, and will be discussed next.

Deviations from Time-Series Models of Earnings

A comprehensive study involving 2,053 firms from 1974 through 1981 provided evidence concerning the speed of response of security prices to earnings announcements.[20] For each company, an expected earnings figure was computed for each quarter by using the model of the time-series behavior of earnings shown in equation (16.19). With this model, the expected earnings for a firm during period t was equal to $QE_{t-4} + a(QE_{t-1} - QE_{t-5}) + b$. For example, the earnings expected for the firm in the second quarter of 1993 would equal (1) the firm's earnings in the second quarter of 1992 plus (2) the change in earnings from the first quarter of 1992 to the first quarter of 1993 times the parameter a, plus (3) the parameter b. The values of a and b would be determined by analysis of the behavior of earnings prior to the second quarter of 1993.

Given actual earnings and an estimate of expected earnings, a forecast error (FE_t) can be computed for the firm:

$$FE_t = QE_t - \overline{QE}_t \tag{16.20}$$

where QE_t is the actual earnings for quarter t and $\overline{QE}_t$ is the expected earnings for quarter t, forecast at time $t - 1$. Simply stated, equation (16.20) indicates that the forecast error for a quarter is the difference between actual earnings for that quarter and the expected earnings.

The forecast error provides a measure of the "surprise" in the quarterly earnings announcement, but it fails to differentiate between stocks for which large forecast errors are routine and those for which they are rare. The important surprises are those associated with forecast errors that are large by historical standards. To account for this, a forecast error can be related to previous errors to obtain a measure of **standardized unexpected earnings** (SUE):

standardized unexpected earnings

$$SUE_t = \frac{FE_t}{\sigma_{FEt}} \tag{16.21}$$

where σ_{FEt} is the standard deviation of forecast errors over the twenty quarterly earnings of the firm prior to t. (That is, forecast errors were determined for each one of the twenty quarters before t, then the standard deviation for this set of twenty errors was estimated.)

For example, a firm with a forecast of earnings per share of \$3 that subsequently reports actual earnings of \$5 will have a forecast error of \$5 − \$3 = \$2. That is, the earnings announcement will "surprise" people by \$2. Now if the standard deviation of past errors is \$.80, this surprise will be notable, since the standardized unexpected earnings (SUE) will equal \$2/\$.80 = 2.50. However, if the standard deviation is \$4, then this surprise will be minor, since SUE will equal \$2/\$4 = .50. Thus, a large positive value for SUE would indicate that the earnings announcement contained significant "good news," whereas a large negative SUE would indicate that the earnings announcement contained significant "bad news."

In the study, the SUEs associated with all the earnings announcements for all the sampled firms were ranked from smallest to largest. Then they were divided into ten equal-sized groups based on the ranking. Group 1 consisted of those announcements resulting in the most negative SUEs, and group 10

[20]George Foster, Chris Olsen, and Terry Shevlin, "Earnings Releases, Anomalies, and the Behavior of Security Returns," *Accounting Review*, 59, no. 4 (October 1984): 574–603. For a related paper, see Roger Kormendi and Robert Lipe, "Earnings Innovations, Earnings Persistence, and Stock Returns," *Journal of Business*, 60, no. 3 (July 1987): 323–45.

consisted of those with the most positive *SUEs*. After forming these ten groups, the stock returns for each firm in each group were measured for the period from 60 days before its earnings announcement through 60 days after its announcement. Figure 16-8 shows the **abnormal return** for the average firm in each of the ten groups for three different time periods.

abnormal return

Panel (a) shows the average abnormal return for the period from 60 days before the earnings announcement through the day the announcement appeared in *The Wall Street Journal*. This period is denoted (−60, 0).

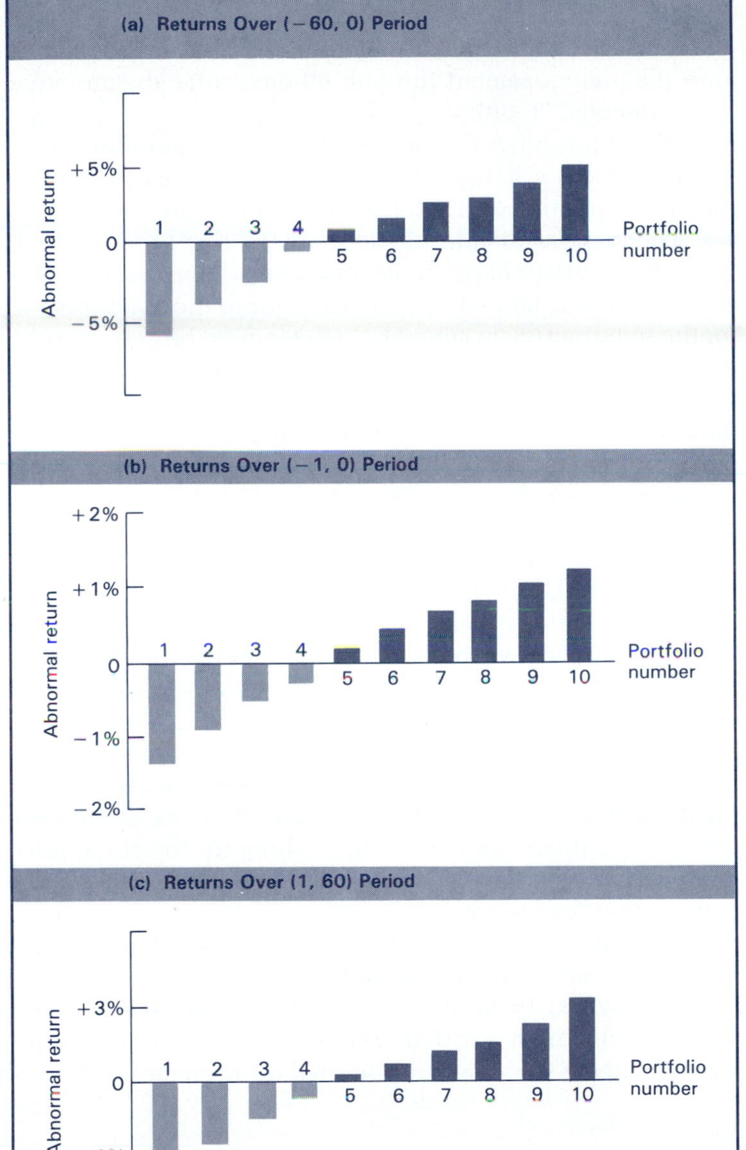

FIGURE 16-8
Security Returns in Period Surrounding Earnings Announcements

Source: George Foster, Chris Olsen, and Terry Shevlin, "Earnings Releases, Anomalies, and the Behavior of Security Returns," *Accounting Review*, 59, no. 4 (October 1984): p. 587.

Panel (b) shows the average abnormal return for the two-day period consisting of the day before the announcement appeared in *The Wall Street Journal* and the day the announcement appeared, a period that is denoted (−1, 0). Since day 0 is the day the announcement appeared in *The Wall Street Journal*, day −1 is the day the announcement was made to the public. If this announcement was made after trading hours on day −1, investors would not have been able to buy or sell the stock until the next day, day 0. If the announcement was made during trading hours on day −1, then investors could have acted on that day. Due to the inability to pinpoint the hour of the announcement, the return over the two-day period was examined to see the immediate impact of the announcement on the price of the security.

Panel (c) shows the average abnormal return for the period from the day after the announcement through 60 days after the announcement, a period that is denoted (1, 60).

Panel (a) shows that prices of firms that announced unexpectedly high earnings (such as *SUE* group 10) tended to increase *prior* to the announcement (day 0), suggesting that information relevant to the earnings announcement was becoming available to the market prior to the actual announcement. Conversely, prices of firms that announced unexpectedly low earnings (such as *SUE* group 1) tended to decrease *prior* to the announcement, undoubtedly for the same reason. In general, there seems to be a strong positive correspondence between the size of the unexpected earnings and the size of the abnormal return. Note that if an investor knew what the earnings were going to be 60 days before the announcement, then this information could be exploited by either buying the stock if the firm was going to announce unexpected large earnings, or short selling the stock if the firm was going to announce unexpected low earnings. However, since investors typically do not have prior access to earnings, such exploitation is generally impossible. Thus, the existence of abnormal returns prior to the announcement date does not necessarily indicate some sort of market inefficiency.

Panel (b) shows that the larger the size of the unexpected earnings, the larger the price movement during the two-day period surrounding the announcement. For example, firms in *SUE* group 1 had an abnormal return of −1.34%, while those in *SUE* group 10 had an abnormal return of 1.26%. As in panel (a), there is a positive relationship between the size of the unexpected earnings and the abnormal stock return.[21] Thus, it appears that the market reacted in a predictable fashion, pushing up the stock prices of those firms announcing "good news" and pushing down the stock prices of those firms announcing "bad news."

As shown in panel (c), the changes in stock prices after the announcement dates are quite remarkable in that they appear to suggest that an inefficiency exists in the market. Prices of stocks of firms announcing unexpectedly high earnings tended to increase for many days *after* the announcement (the average abnormal return over the 60-day period after the

[21]Studies have shown that earnings announcements containing "good news" are often made earlier than expected, while those containing "bad news" are often made later than expected. These studies also show that the "timeliness" (defined as the difference between the actual announcement date and the expected announcement date) affects the size of the abnormal return. Interestingly, around the time of earnings announcements there appears to be both increased trading volume and increased variability in security returns. See George Foster, *Financial Statement Analysis* (Englewood Cliffs, N.J.: Prentice Hall, 1986): pp. 377–86; and V. V. Chari, Ravi Jagannathan, and Aharon Ofer, "Seasonalities in Security Returns: The Case of Earnings Announcements," *Journal of Financial Economics*, 21, no. 1 (May 1988): 101–21.

announcement was 3.23% for *SUE* group 10). Conversely, the prices of firms announcing unexpectedly low earnings tended to decrease for many days *after* the announcement (the average abnormal return over the 60-day period subsequent to the announcement was −3.08% for *SUE* group 1).

As was noted in the two previous panels, there seems to be a strong positive correspondence between the size of the unexpected earnings and the size of the abnormal return. This observation suggests that an investor could make abnormal returns by simply looking at quarterly earnings announcements and, based on the magnitude and sign of the unexpected component, acting appropriately. That is, if the firm announced earnings that were notably above expectations, the investor should subsequently purchase some of the firm's stock. In contrast, if the announced earnings were notably below expectations, the investor should subsequently sell any holdings and perhaps even short-sell the firm's stock. Announcements of earnings that were reasonably close to expectations would not motivate either a buy or sell order. Accordingly, the "post-earnings-announcement drift" can be viewed as an empirical anomaly that is inconsistent with the notion of semi-strong efficient markets.[22]

Unexpected Earnings and Abnormal Returns

One plausible explanation for the abnormal returns associated with large SUEs concerns the cost of information transfer. "New news" must reach a large number of investors before the appropriate new equilibrium price can be completely established. While large institutional investors can obtain news quickly, it may take some time before it reaches smaller institutional investors and individuals. Thus, after an earnings announcement there can be a period of abnormal price movement that is related in sign and magnitude to the nature of the announcement.

Alternatively, perhaps the measurement of "abnormal" returns has been in error. In making such a measurement, a determination of what is a "normal" return must be made. Such a determination is not straightforward, but instead is fraught with difficulty. This means that the estimated abnormal returns could actually be due to measurement errors, leaving open the possibility that a more accurate measure of "normal return" would have resulted in no significant abnormal returns.

Nevertheless, there appear to be striking differences in subsequent stock returns for firms with different *SUE*s. Such differences cannot be wholly explained by different levels of beta. While the magnitudes of the return differences may be too small to warrant extensive trading, they do suggest the consideration of such things as *SUE* values and forecast revisions when money must be invested or a portion of an existing portfolio liquidated.

Security Analysts' Forecasts of Future Earnings

In using only the historical record of past earnings to forecast future earnings, it was mentioned earlier that an autoregressive model of order one, as shown in equation (16.19), seemed to work about as well as any other model.

---

[22]One article argues that it should be listed with the set of empirical regularities described in the appendix to Chapter 13; see Charles P. Jones and Bruce Bublitz, "The CAPM and Equity Return Regularities: An Extension," *Financial Analysts Journal*, 43, no. 3 (May/June 1987): 77–79.

However, security analysts do not restrict themselves to just past earnings when developing their forecasts. Instead, they look at many different pieces of information. This raises several interesting questions. How well can analysts forecast earnings? And do their forecasts incorporate information other than that contained in past earnings? The results of two studies that provide some answers to these questions are shown in Tables 16-5 and 16-6.

In one study, two sets of forecasts were examined for the quarterly earnings of fifty firms over the period from 1971 through 1975.[23] The first set was obtained by applying sophisticated mechanical models to each firm's previous earnings history [such as the autoregressive model of equation (16.19)]. The second set was obtained from the earnings forecasts of security analysts as reported in the *Value Line Investment Survey*.[24] The results suggest that the analysts outperformed the mechanical model. For example, 63.5% of the analysts' forecasts were within 25% of the actual earnings values, while only 54.4% of the forecasts made via mechanical models came as close. Analysts appear to base their forecasts on both past earnings and other information; and the latter appears to help.

In another study, forecasts of annual earnings made by security analysts approximately 240, 180, 120, and 60 days before the announcement date of actual earnings were examined.[25] Typically these days correspond to dates in each of the year's fiscal quarters before the announcement date. Hence, 240 days falls roughly between last year's earnings announcement and this year's first quarter earnings announcement, 180 days falls roughly between the first quarter and second quarter earnings announcement, and so on. These forecasts, made over the period from 1975 to 1982 by analysts at between fifty and 130 brokerage firms, were obtained from the Institutional Brokers Estimate Service (IBES) database developed by the brokerage firm of Lynch, Jones, & Ryan. This database consists of the individual forecasts (although the identity of the forecaster is kept secret) and summary data for each firm (such as the average forecast) and is sold mainly to institutional investors on a monthly basis.

[23]Lawrence D. Brown and Michael S. Rozeff, "The Superiority of Analyst Forecasts as Measures of Expectations: Evidence from Earnings," *Journal of Finance*, 33, no. 1 (March 1978): 1–16.

[24]Value Line also ranks stocks in terms of their relative attractiveness as investments. For a discussion of the usefulness of the Value Line rankings, see the appendix.

[25]Patricia C. O'Brien, "Analysts' Forecasts as Earnings Expectations," *Journal of Accounting and Economics*, 10, no. 1 (January 1988): 53–83.

TABLE 16-5
Accuracy of Mechanical and Judgmental Earnings Forecasts

EARNINGS FORECAST ERROR AS A PERCENT OF ACTUAL EARNINGS	PERCENT OF FORECASTS WITH A SMALLER ERROR	
	Mechanical Model	**Analysts' Forecasts**
5%	15.0%	18.0%
10	26.5	32.0
25	54.5	63.5
50	81.0	86.5
75	87.5	90.5
100	89.5	92.0

Source: Lawrence D. Brown and Michael S. Rozeff, "The Superiority of Analyst Forecasts as Measures of Expectations: Evidence from Earnings," *Journal of Finance*, 33, no. 1 (March 1978), pp. 7–8.

TABLE 16-6
Forecast Accuracy of Time-Series Models and Security Analysts

MODEL	DAYS BEFORE ANNUAL ANNOUNCEMENT DATE			
	240	180	120	60
Random walk	$.963	$.781	$.620	$.363
Autoregressive	.975	.780	.592	.350
Average analyst	.747	.645	.516	.395
Current analyst	.742	.610	.468	.342

Source: Adapted from Patricia C. O'Brien, "Analysts' Forecasts as Earnings Expectations," *Journal of Accounting and Economics*, 10, no.1 (January 1988): Table 4.

Table 16-6 presents a comparison of the accuracy of four forecasts. The first forecast, denoted *RW*, is the annual forecast generated by using a model like the random walk model of equation (16.16). The second, denoted *AR*, is the annual forecast produced by using an autoregressive model like the one shown in equation (16.19). The third is the average forecast published by IBES, and the fourth is the single most current individual forecast published by IBES. Forecast accuracy for a particular model and firm is measured by absolute forecast error, or:

$$FE = |A - F| \tag{16.22}$$

where F denotes the forecast and A denotes the subsequent actual earnings of the firm.

There are several interesting observations to be made from Table 16-6. First, as the announcement date gets closer, all of the forecasting models become more accurate. This is hardly surprising, since more information is available as the announcement date gets closer. Second, for long horizons both the average and most current forecast are more accurate than either of the time-series models. Third, the current forecast is more accurate than any of the other models. However, subsequent examination of the forecasts indicated that the average forecast was more accurate than the most current forecast, provided that none of the individual forecasts used to determine the average was "stale" (that is, more than roughly a week old). This is because such averaging reduces the forecast error by having individual forecast errors offset each other (that is, positive errors will offset negative errors, resulting in a smaller error for the average forecast).

Another interesting observation that has been uncovered about security analysts' forecasts is that they tend to be too optimistic (hence most of the typical analysts' revisions are downward).[26] One interpretation of this observation is that many of the analysts work for brokerage firms and thus find it in their employer's best interest (and their own) to encourage trading and avoid antagonizing any corporation that is or might become an investment banking client.

Management Forecasts of Future Earnings

Often, management itself will make a forecast of next year's earnings for the firm. Generally, the forecasts of security analysts are not as accurate as the forecasts of management when both sets of forecasts are made about the same

[26]Werner F. De Bondt and Richard H. Thaler, "Do Security Analysts Overreact?" *American Economic Review*, 80, no. 2 (May 1990): 52–57.

TABLE 16-7
Security Analyst and Management Forecast Errors

WEEK	AVERAGE ANALYST FORECAST ERROR	AVERAGE ANALYST FORECAST ERROR − AVERAGE MANAGEMENT FORECAST ERROR*
−12	.224	.074
−11	.222	.072
−10	.221	.071
−9	.221	.071
−8	.214	.064
−7	.221	.071
−6	.222	.072
−5	.216	.066
−4	.210	.060
−3	.208	.058
−2	.211	.061
−1	.209	.059
0	.195	.045
+1	.186	.036
+2	.177	.027
+3	.174	.024
+4	.171	.021
+5	.166	.016
+6	.160	.010
+7	.153	.003
+8	.150	.000
+9	.141	−.009
+10	.133	−.017
+11	.129	−.021
+12	.124	−.026

*The size of the average management forecast error was .150.

Source: Adapted from John M. Hassell and Robert H. Jennings, "Relative Forecast Accuracy and the Timing of Earnings Forecast Announcements," *Accounting Review*, 61, no. 1 (January 1986): Tables 2 and 3.

time, as shown in Table 16-7.[27] Here average security analysts' forecasts, as reported weekly by Zach's Investment Company's Icarus Service, were compared with corresponding management forecasts.[28] The objective was to see who was the more accurate forecaster. To do this, forecast errors (FE) were calculated for both sets of forecasts as:

$$FE = |(F - A)/A| \tag{16.23}$$

where F is the earnings forecast and A is the actual earnings subsequently reported by the firm. Hence an earnings forecast of \$3 per share that subsequently turned out to be \$4 would have $FE = |(\$3 - \$4)/\$4| = .25$ or 25%.

Letting $t = 0$ denote the date that the management forecast is released, analysts' forecasts were collected weekly from 12 weeks before to 12 weeks after $t = 0$. As the table shows at the bottom, the average forecast error for management was .150. Analyst forecast errors ranged from .224 at week −12 (meaning 12 weeks prior to the date of the management forecast) to .124 at week +12. Hence, as was shown in Table 16-6, analysts' forecasts became

[27]John M. Hassell and Robert H. Jennings, "Relative Forecast Accuracy and the Timing of Earnings Forecast Announcements," *Accounting Review*, 61, no. 1 (January 1986): 58–75.

[28]Similar to IBES, Zach's Icarus Service provides weekly summaries of earnings forecasts for over 2,000 firms that are provided by analysts at roughly fifty brokerage firms.

more accurate the closer they were to the date the actual earnings were announced, since the size of the average forecast error decreases fairly steadily from $t = 12$ to $t = +12$.

Most important, however, is the observation that management forecasts were more accurate than analyst forecasts from $t = -12$ to $t = +8$ (the difference was found to be statistically significant through $t = +4$). That is, forecasts issued by analysts before, coincident to, or up to four months after management's forecast were less accurate. This observation is not surprising up to $t = 0$, since management has private information about the firm that is not available to the analysts. However, it is surprising that management forecasts are superior from $t = 1$ through $t = 4$ because it suggests that analysts could improve their accuracy simply by using management's previously released forecast. After $t = +4$, the analysts' forecasts were more accurate (the difference was statistically significant beginning nine weeks after the release date of the management forecast—a finding that is not surprising, since the analysts probably had access to more timely information upon which to base their forecasts).

Sources of Errors in Forecasting

Since security analysts' forecasts are not perfect, it is interesting to consider the major source of their errors. One study examined the IBES database and attempted to break down the forecast errors into three components: (1) errors that could be traced to misjudgments about the economy; (2) errors that could be traced to misjudgments about the firm's particular industry; and (3) errors that were purely due to misjudgments about the firm.[29]

The results indicated the following: less than 3% of the typical error was due to a misjudgment about the economy; roughly 30% of the typical error was due to a misjudgment about the industry; and over 65% of the typical error was due to a misjudgment about the firm.

SUMMARY

1. Assuming that a firm undertakes positive NPV projects and maintains a constant debt-equity ratio, shareholders will be indifferent to the level of dividends.

2. If dividends and new investment are greater than earnings, the firm may issue new equity. If dividends and new investment are less than earnings, the firm may repurchase equity. In either case, a stockholder maintaining constant proportional ownership will be able to spend the same amount on consumption, regardless of the level of dividends.

3. Earnings, not dividends, are the source of a firm's value.

4. Few firms attempt to maintain a constant ratio of dividends to current earnings. It is often assumed that firms establish a long-run payout ratio and adjust current actual dividends based on the difference between current target dividends and the last period's actual dividends.

5. Corporate management often uses dividend changes as a signaling device, raising or lowering dividends based on its assessment of the firm's future earnings.

6. A firm has considerable discretion in calculating its accounting earnings. These accounting earnings may differ substantially from the firm's economic earnings. Similarly, a firm's book value may differ considerably from its market value.

---

[29]Edwin J. Elton, Martin J. Gruber, and Mustafa N. Gultekin, "Professional Expectations: Accuracy and Diagnosis of Errors," *Journal of Financial and Quantitative Analysis*, 19, no. 4 (December 1984): 351–63.

7. Earnings can be divided into permanent and transitory components. A firm's intrinsic value will be based on the permanent component of earnings. The transitory component is a significant factor in short-run changes in a firm's price-earnings ratio.

8. There is a positive relationship between accounting betas and market betas. Firms whose earnings covary more with marketwide earnings are likely to have higher market betas.

9. Stocks with the highest returns typically have earnings that are substantially greater than expected, while those with the lowest returns have earnings substantially below expectations.

10. Analysts appear to forecast earnings better than sophisticated mechanical models. Management earnings forecasts are generally more accurate than analysts' forecasts.

KEY TERMS

dividend decision
asymmetric information
information content of dividends hypothesis
accounting earnings
earnings per share
return on equity
economic earnings
economic value of the firm
generally accepted accounting principles
random walk model
market beta
accounting beta
standardized unexpected earnings
abnormal return

QUESTIONS AND PROBLEMS

1. For a given level of earnings (E), net new investment (I), and dividends (D), explain why a firm must issue new stock if $E < D + I$ and it desires to maintain a constant debt-equity ratio. Similarly, why must it repurchase shares if $E > D + I$ and it desires to maintain a constant debt-equity ratio?
2. Merrillan Motors had earnings of $8 million in1991. It made $5 million of investments in projects with positive net present values. Pat Collins owns 20% of the firm's common stock. Assume that Pat desires no change in proportional ownership of Merrillan and the firm wishes to maintain a constant debt-equity ratio. What will be Pat's action in response to:
   (a) Merrillan paying out dividends of $5 million?
   (b) Merrillan paying out dividends of $1 million?
   (c) Merrillan paying out dividends of $3 million?
3. Why is an individual stockholder indifferent between the firm retaining $1 of earnings or paying out the $1 of earnings as a dividend, assuming that the firm and the stockholder maintain a constant debt-equity ratio and a constant proportional ownership position, respectively.
4. If the dividend decision is irrelevant to the valuation of a firm, then are not dividend discount models irrelevant to valuing a share of common stock? Why?
5. Scoops Cooney, a confused investment student, commented, "I understand the irrelevance of the dividend decision to the value of a firm. As a result, I calculate the value of a firm's stock based on the present value of the firm's expected earnings per share." Is Scoops correct? Why?
6. Why do most corporations not maintain a constant payout ratio? What payout strategy do most firms pursue?
7. Hixton Farms has a target payout ratio of 50%. Dividends paid last year amounted to $10 million. Its earnings were $20 million. Hixton's "speed of adjustment" factor for dividends is 60%. What will be its dividend

payments over the next five years if its earnings display the following path:

YEAR	EARNINGS
1	$30 million
2	35 million
3	30 million
4	25 million
5	30 million

Draw a graph of Hixton's actual dividends paid versus the desired dividend payments over this five-year period.

8. How are dividends used as a signaling device by corporate management? To the extent that dividends are a signaling device, how are dividend changes related to stock prices?

9. Discuss why there generally does not exist a one-to-one relationship between corporations' book values and their market values.

10. Why might a steady trend in a firm's reported earnings from year to year suggest that the figures do not represent the firm's economic earnings?

11. Reported earnings typically differ, sometimes considerably, from economic earnings. Nevertheless, it is often argued that reported earnings are intended simply to provide a "source of information" to investors about the value of the firm. If so, might there not be many alternative accounting procedures of equal use to investors? How might one go about evaluating the usefulness of such procedures?

12. Distinguish between permanent and transitory earnings. Would you expect companies across industries to differ in terms of the relative importance of transitory earnings to total earnings? Explain.

13. Price-earnings ratios for individual companies vary over time and across firms. Discuss some of the possible reasons for the variability.

14. Why would you expect a security's market beta to be highly correlated with its accounting beta?

15. Harlond Clift once wrote this in a market newsletter: "I focus my research on consensus earnings forecasts. Those companies that the consensus believes will produce the largest earnings increases next year are most likely to produce the best returns." Is Harlond's opinion consistent with empirical evidence? Explain why or why not.

16. Oakdale Orchards has produced the following earnings over the last nine quarters:

QUARTER	EARNINGS PER SHARE
1	$2.00
2	1.95
3	2.05
4	2.10
5	2.40
6	2.24
7	2.67
8	2.84
9	2.64

The expected earnings for the current quarter are based on the equation $QE_t = QE_{t-4} + .75\ (QE_{t-1} - QE_{t-5})$. Calculate the standardized unexpected earnings in each of the last four quarters given a standard deviation of $0.35.

17. Why might the price of a stock react only partially to an "earnings surprise" on the first day or two after the earnings announcement?

18. (Appendix Question) The Value Line ranking system has long shown a consistent ability to produce positive risk-adjusted returns. These results have been particularly disconcerting for efficient markets proponents. Why?

APPENDIX

A

Value Line Rankings

It has been observed that investors can use the information contained in either a quarterly earnings announcement or a revision of an earnings forecast by security analysts to make abnormal returns. Another source of information that may be useful to investors is the *Value Line Investment Survey* (published weekly by Value Line, Inc., New York for $525 per year), which is reputed to be the largest investment advisory service in the United States.

Each week, every one of approximately 1,700 stocks is assigned one of five possible ranks by Value Line. By design, the categories include the same number of stocks each week, as follows:

RANK	NUMBER OF STOCKS
1 (highest)	100
2 (above average)	300
3 (average)	900
4 (below average)	300
5 (lowest)	100

Many factors go into the ranking procedure. Not surprisingly, the exact details have not been revealed. However, the key elements are all based on publicly available information:[30]

1. The most recent year's earnings and average stock price, relative to the comparable values for the previous ten years, and the stock's average price over the preceding ten weeks relative to that of the preceding fifty-two weeks.

[30]For details, see Arnold Bernhard, "Investing in Common Stocks with the Aid of the Value Line Rankings and other Criteria of Stock Value," Arnold Bernhard and Co., Inc., New York, 1975.

2. A price momentum element that is based on the stock's current price-earnings ratio relative to that of the market, compared with the average of the corresponding figures over the last five years.
3. An earnings momentum element that is based on the most recent quarter's earnings relative to the amount reported four quarters earlier.
4. An earnings "surprise" element where the most recent quarter's earnings are compared with the amount forecasted by Value Line's security analysts.

A test of the resulting rankings showed them to be of some value.[31] Beginning in November 26, 1965, five portfolios were formed (on paper). The first included all stocks ranked "1" at that time, in equal dollar values; the second included all stocks ranked "2," and so on. After six months each portfolio was altered as necessary to again include equal dollar values of all stocks with the appropriate ranks at that time. The procedure was continued until February 3, 1978, when the last set of portfolios was formed. Then, each portfolio's actual rate of return was measured and adjustments for risk were made to determine "abnormal" returns. The results, shown in Table 16-8, indicate that both the actual and abnormal returns are perfectly ordered with the rankings of the securities in the portfolios. More in-depth analysis indicated that most of the abnormal returns occurred in the thirteen-week period subsequent to the formation date. Interestingly, this study shows that the only notable abnormal return is for the securities with a ranking of 5. This suggests that an investor should sell (or even short-sell) any securities that have such a ranking.

This study also looked at those securities whose rank had been changed by Value Line. Roughly seventy to eighty securities change ranks each week, evenly split between those being upgraded and those being downgraded. Almost all the changes are of one rank (seldom does a security jump two ranks—for example, from 1 to 3 or vice versa). Focusing the analysis around the time of the change in rank, it was determined that, on average, securities whose rank had been upgraded earned an abnormal return of .77% in the subsequent thirteen weeks. Conversely, those securities whose rank had been downgraded earned an abnormal return of −1.42% in the subsequent thirteen weeks. Overall, most of the adjustment in the stock prices of these securities

[31]Thomas E. Copeland and David Mayers, "The Value Line Enigma (1965–1978): A Case Study of Performance Evaluation Issues," *Journal of Financial Economics*, 10, no. 3 (November 1982): 289–321.

TABLE 16-8
Performance of Portfolios Formed on the Basis of Value Line Rankings

	RANKING				
	1	2	3	4	5
Actual return over subsequent 26 weeks	7.38%	6.51%	4.10%	2.70%	.37%
Abnormal return over subsequent 26 weeks	.33%	.35%	−.57%	−1.12%	−3.05%

Source: Thomas E. Copeland and David Mayers, "The Value Line Enigma (1965–1978): A Case Study of Performance Evaluation Issues," *Journal of Financial Economics*, 10, no. 3 (November 1982): pp. 298, 301. North-Holland Publishing Company.

was found to be concentrated in the two-week period subsequent to the publication of the change in rank.[32]

These results do not suggest that Value Line provides a guaranteed formula for outstanding portfolio performance. No transaction costs were charged in the calculations, and turnover was high.[33] But the results do suggest that in choosing among stocks, Value Line rankings may prove useful.[34] It can be conjectured that Value Line rankings "work" primarily because they use quarterly earnings in both the earnings momentum and surprise elements that go into the Value Line ranking procedure.[35] After all, it has been noted that there are abnormal price movements subsequent to the announcement of quarterly earnings.

To summarize, the results suggest that there is a two-part puzzle associated with Value Line ranks. First, Value Line appears to have superior forecasting ability that is based on public information. Second, the market takes time to adjust to the Value Line rankings. Both of these observations are puzzling because they are inconsistent with the notion of efficient markets.[36] To further complicate matters, one study found that most rank changes occur shortly after earnings announcements are made. Further investigation revealed that Value Line's superior performance was attributable to the "post-earnings announcement drift." Hence the two anomalies appear to be related.[37]

REFERENCES

1. The seminal paper on dividend policy that established both the "dividend irrelevancy theorem" and the notion that earnings are the basis for the market value of the firm was written by two Nobel laureates in economics:

Merton H. Miller and Franco Modigliani, "Dividend Policy, Growth, and the Valuation of Shares," *Journal of Business*, 34, no. 4 (October 1961): 411–33.

---

[32]A later study found that most of the adjustment actually was in the three-day period after the change. The most notable price movement was associated with those stocks being upgraded from 2 to 1. Other notable but less sizable price movements were associated with upgrades from3 to 2 and downgrades from 1 to 2 and 2 to 3. See Scott E. Stickel, "The Effect of Value Line Investment Survey Rank Changes on Common Stock Prices," *Journal of Financial Economics*, 14, no. 1 (March 1985): 121–43.

[33]A discussion of transaction costs is contained in Copeland and Mayers, "The Value Line Enigma," pp. 319–20; and Clark Holloway, "A Note on Testing an Aggressive Investment Strategy Using Value Line Ranks," *Journal of Finance*, 36, no. 3 (June 1981): 711–19.

[34]Value Line also provides a measure of the risk of individual securities that is known as Safety Rank. This risk measure was found to be more highly correlated with subsequent returns than either beta or standard deviation, suggesting that it is a more useful measure of risk. See Russell J. Fuller and G. Wenchi Wong, "Traditional versus Theoretical Risk Measures," *Financial Analysts Journal*, 44, no. 2 (March/April 1988): 52–57, 67.

[35]One speculation is that the rankings are simply capturing the size effect by giving higher ranks to smaller firms (the size effect is discussed in the appendix to Chapter 13). However, tests suggest that this is not true. See Gur Huberman and Shmuel Kandel, "Value Line Rank and Firm Size," *Journal of Business*, 60, no. 4 (October 1987): 577–89.

[36]For an argument on why these observations do not violate market efficiency, see Gur Huberman and Shmuel Kandel, "Market Efficiency and Value Line's Record," *Journal of Business*, 63, no. 2 (April 1990): 187–216.

[37]See John Affleck-Graves and Richard R. Mendenhall, "The Relation Between the Value Line Enigma and Post-Earnings-Announcement Drift," *Journal of Financial Economics*, 31, no. 1 (February 1992): 75–96.

2. The Lintner Model of dividend behavior and some studies that empirically tested it are:

   John Lintner, "Distribution of Incomes of Corporations Among Dividends, Retained Earnings, and Taxes," *American Economic Review*, 46, no. 2 (May 1956): 97–113;

   John A. Brittain, *Corporate Dividend Policy* (Washington, D.C.: The Brookings Institution, 1966);

   Eugene F. Fama and Harvey Babiak, "Dividend Policy: An Empirical Analysis," *Journal of the American Statistical Association*, 63, no. 324 (December 1968): 1132–61;

   Eugene F. Fama, "The Empirical Relationship Between the Dividend and Investment Decisions of Firms," *American Economic Review*, 64, no. 3 (June 1974): 304–18;

   Terry A. Marsh and Robert C. Merton, "Dividend Behavior for the Aggregate Stock Market," *Journal of Business*, 60, no. 1 (January 1987): 1–40.

3. The determinants of recent dividend behavior appear to be similar to those in the Lintner Model from the 1950s, according to:

   H. Kent Baker, Gail E. Farrelly, and Richard B. Edelman, "A Survey of Management Views on Dividend Policy," *Financial Management*, 14, no. 3 (Autumn 1985): 78–84.

4. A summary of the literature on signaling can be found in:

   Thomas E. Copeland and J. Fred Weston, *Financial Theory and Corporate Policy* (Reading, Mass.: Addison-Wesley Publishing Co., 1988), pp. 501–7, 584–88.

5. The information content of dividends hypothesis, closely linked to the signaling literature, has been the subject of much research. Some of the more important papers are:

   Joseph Aharony and Itzak Swary, "Quarterly Dividend and Earnings Announcements and Stockholders' Returns: An Empirical Analysis," *Journal of Finance*, 35, no. 1 (March 1980): 1–12;

   Clarence C. Y. Kwan, "Efficient Market Tests of the Informational Content of Dividend Announcements: Critique and Extension," *Journal of Financial and Quantitative Analysis*, 16, no. 2 (June 1981): 193–206;

   Paul Asquith and David W. Mullins, Jr., "The Impact of Initiating Dividend Payments on Shareholders' Wealth," *Journal of Business*, 56, no. 1 (January 1983): 77–96;

   Terry E. Dielman and Henry R. Oppenheimer, "An Examination of Investor Behavior During Periods of Large Dividend Changes," *Journal of Financial and Quantitative Analysis*, 19, no. 2 (June 1984): 197–216;

   Paul M. Healy and Krishna G. Palepu, "Earnings Information Conveyed by Dividend Initiations and Omissions," *Journal of Financial Economics*, 21, no. 2 (September 1988): 149–75.

6. The relationship between economic and accounting earnings is discussed in:

   Fischer Black, "The Magic in Earnings: Economic Earnings versus Accounting Earnings," *Financial Analysts Journal*, 36, no. 6 (November/December 1980): 19–24.

7. For a study on the timing of dividend announcements as well as a listing of other studies concerning dividend announcements, see:

Avner Kalay and Uri Loewenstein, "The Informational Content of the Timing of Dividend Announcements," *Journal of Financial Economics*, 16, no. 3 (July 1986): 373–88;

Aharon R. Ofer and Daniel R. Siegel, "Corporate Financial Policy, Information, and Market Expectations: An Empirical Investigation of Dividends," *Journal of Finance*, 42, no. 4 (September 1987): 889–911.

8. For a review of the literature dealing with dividends, see:

James S. Ang, "Do Dividends Matter? A Review of Corporate Dividend Theories and Evidence," Monograph Series in Finance and Economics #1987-2, New York University Salomon Center, Leonard N. Stern School of Business.

9. For a discussion of price-earnings ratios, see:

William H. Beaver, *Financial Reporting: An Accounting Revolution* (Englewood Cliffs, N.J.: Prentice Hall, 1981), Chapters 4 and 5;

William Beaver and Dale Morse, "What Determines Price-Earnings Ratios?" *Financial Analysts Journal*, 34, no. 4 (July–August 1978): 65–76;

George Foster, *Financial Statement Analysis* (Englewood Cliffs, N.J.: Prentice Hall, 1986), pp. 437–42;

Paul Zarowin, "What Determines Earnings-Price Ratios: Revisited," *Journal of Accounting, Auditing, and Finance*, 5, no. 3 (Summer 1990): 439–54.

10. Time-series models of annual and quarterly earnings per share are discussed in:

George Foster, "Quarterly Accounting Data: Time-Series Properties and Predictive-Ability Results," *Accounting Review*, 52, no. 1 (January 1977): 1–21;

Ross L. Watts and Jerold L. Zimmerman, *Positive Accounting Theory* (Englewood Cliffs, N.J.: Prentice Hall, 1986), Chapter 6;

George Foster, *Financial Statement Analysis* (Englewood Cliffs, N.J.: Prentice Hall, 1986), Chapter 7.

11. The relationship between market betas and accounting betas has been explored by:

Ray Ball and Philip Brown, "Portfolio Theory and Accounting," *Journal of Accounting Research*, 7, no. 2 (Autumn 1969): 300–323;

William Beaver and James Manegold, "The Association Between Market-Determined and Accounting-Determined Measures of Systematic Risk: Some Further Evidence," *Journal of Financial and Quantitative Analysis*, 10, no. 2 (June 1975): 231–84.

12. The relationship between unexpected earnings and stock prices has been documented in many studies. See the following as well as their citations:

Leonard Zacks, "EPS Forecasts—Accuracy Is Not Enough," *Financial Analysts Journal*, 35, no. 2 (March/April 1979): 53–55;

Richard J. Rendleman, Jr., Charles P. Jones, and Henry A. Latane, "Empirical Anomalies Based on Unexpected Earnings and the Importance of Risk Adjustments," *Journal of Financial Economics*, 10, no. 3 (November 1982): 269–87;

George Foster, Chris Olsen, and Terry Shevlin, "Earnings Releases, Anomalies, and the Behavior of Security Returns," *Accounting Review*, 59, no. 4 (October 1984): 574–603.

13. Some of the studies that have offered possible explanations for the "post–earnings announcement drift" in stock prices are:

Richard J. Rendleman, Jr., Charles P. Jones, and Henry A. Latane, "Further Insight into the Standardized Unexpected Earnings Anomaly: Size and Serial Correlation Effects," *Financial Review*, 22, no. 1 (February 1987): 131–44;

Victor L. Bernard and Jacob K. Thomas, "Post-Earnings-Announcement Drift: Delayed Price Response or Risk Premium?" *Journal of Accounting Research*, 27, Supplement 1989: 1–36;

Robert N. Freeman and Senyo Tse, "The Multiperiod Information Content of Accounting Earnings: Confirmations and Contradictions of Previous Earnings Reports," *Journal of Accounting Research*, 27, Supplement 1989: 49–79;

Victor L. Bernard and Jacob K. Thomas, "Evidence That Stock Prices Do Not Fully Reflect the Implications of Current Earnings for Future Earnings," *Journal of Accounting and Economics*, 13, no. 4 (December 1990): 305–40;

Richard R. Mendenhall, "Evidence on the Possible Underweighting of Earnings-Related Information," *Journal of Accounting Research*, 29, no. 1 (Spring 1991): 170–79.

14. There have been a large number of studies concerning the earnings forecasts made by security analysts and management. Some of the studies are:

Lawrence D. Brown and Michael S. Rozeff, "The Superiority of Analyst Forecasts as Measures of Expectations: Evidence from Earnings," *Journal of Finance*, 33, no. 1 (March 1978): 1–16;

Lawrence D. Brown and Michael S. Rozeff, "Analysts Can Forecast Accurately!" *Journal of Portfolio Management*, 6, no. 3 (Spring 1980): 31–34;

John G. Cragg and Burton G. Malkiel, *Expectations and the Structure of Share Prices* (Chicago: The University of Chicago Press, 1982), particularly pp. 85–86 and 165;

Dan Givoly and Josef Lakonishok, "Properties of Analysts' Forecasts of Earnings: A Review and Analysis of the Research," *Journal of Accounting Literature*, 3 (Spring 1984): 117–52;

Dan Givoly and Josef Lakonishok, "The Quality of Analysts Forecasts of Earnings," *Financial Analysts Journal*, 40, no. 5 (September–October 1984): 40–47;

Philip Brown, George Foster, and Eric Noreen, *Security Analyst Multi-Year Earnings Forecasts and the Capital Markets* (Sarasota, Fla.: American Accounting Association, 1985);

John M. Hassell and Robert H. Jennings, "Relative Forecast Accuracy and the Timing of Earnings Forecast Announcements," *Accounting Review*, 61, no. 1 (January 1986): 58–75;

Gary A. Benesh and Pamela P. Peterson, "On the Relation Between Earnings Changes, Analysts' Forecasts and Stock Price Fluctuations," *Financial Analysts Journal*, 42, no. 6 (November/December 1986): 29–39, 55;

Lawrence D. Brown, Robert L. Hagerman, Paul A. Griffin, and Mark Zmijewski, "Security Analyst Superiority Relative to Univariate Time-Series Models in Forecasting Quarterly Earnings," *Journal of Accounting and Economics,* 9, no. 1 (April 1987): 61–87;

Robert Conroy and Robert Harris, "Consensus Forecasts of Corporate Earnings: Analysts' Forecasts and Time-Series Methods," *Management Science,* 33, no. 6 (June 1987): 725–38;

Patricia C. O'Brien, "Analysts' Forecasts as Earnings Expectations," *Journal of Accounting and Economics,* 10, no. 1 (January 1988): 53–83;

Werner F. De Bondt and Richard H. Thaler, "Do Security Analysts Overreact?" *American Economic Review,* 80, no. 2 (May 1990): 52–57;

Lawrence D. Brown and Kwon-Jung Kim, "Timely Aggregate Analyst Forecasts as Better Proxies for Market Earnings Expectations," *Journal of Accounting Research,* 29, no. 2 (Autumn 1991): 382–85.

15. For a description of the analyst forecasts published by Value Line and IBES, see:

Donna R. Philbrick and William E. Ricks, "Using Value Line and IBES Analyst Forecasts in Accounting Research," *Journal of Accounting Research,* 29, no. 2 (Autumn 1991): 397–417.

16. As the footnotes to the appendix show, the Value Line Investment Survey has been intensively scrutinized. Those who would like to learn more about Value Line can purchase the following software manual (directly from Value Line or in a shrink-wrap package with this textbook through Prentice Hall) and user's guide:

Value Line, Inc., *VALUE/SCREEN Plus* (Englewood Cliffs, N.J.: Prentice Hall, 1990);

Gerald P. Madden, *Investment Analysis with VALUE/SCREEN Plus* (Englewood Cliffs, N.J.: Prentice Hall, 1991).

17

Investment Management

Investment management, also known as portfolio management, is the process by which money is managed. It may (1) be active or passive; (2) use explicit or implicit procedures; and (3) be relatively controlled or uncontrolled. The trend is toward highly controlled operations consistent with the notion that capital markets are relatively efficient. However, approaches vary, and many different investment "styles" can be found. This chapter will discuss investment management, and in doing so will present various types of investment styles.

TRADITIONAL INVESTMENT MANAGEMENT ORGANIZATIONS

Few people or organizations like to be called "traditional." However, many investment management organizations follow procedures that have changed little from those that were popular decades ago and thus deserve the title. Figure 17-1 shows the major characteristics of a typical investment management organization.

Projections concerning the economy, security and money markets, and so on are made by economists, technicians, fundamentalists, or other market experts within or outside the organization. The projected economic environment is communicated via briefings and written reports—usually in a rather implicit and qualitative manner—to the organization's **security analysts.** Each analyst is responsible for a group of securities, often those in one or more industries (in some organizations, analysts are called industry specialists). Often a group of analysts report to a senior analyst responsible for a sector of the economy or market.

security analyst

The analysts, often drawing heavily on reports of others (for example, "street analysts" in brokerage houses), make predictions about the securities for which they are responsible. In a sense, such predictions are conditional on the assumed economic and market environments, although the relationship is typically quite loose.

Analysts' predictions seldom specify an expected rate of return or the time over which predicted performance will take place. Instead, an analyst's feelings about a security are often summarized by assigning it one of five codes, where a 1 represents a buy and a 5 represents a sell, as indicated in Figure 17-1.[1] (Some organizations reverse the numbers, so that a 5 is a buy and a 1 is a sell; some European organizations favor five codes that are denoted +, 0+, 0, 0−, and −; some organizations have long-term lists as well as short-term lists.)

investment committee

These security codings constitute the information formally transmitted to an **investment committee,** which typically includes the senior management of the organization. In addition, analysts occasionally brief the investment committee on their feelings about various securities. The investment committee's major formal output is often an **approved** (or authorized) **list,** which consists of the securities deemed worthy of accumulation in a given portfolio. The rules of the organization typically specify that any security on the list may be bought, while those not on the list should be either held or sold, barring special circumstances.

approved list

The presence or absence of a security on the approved list constitutes the major information transmitted explicitly from the investment committee to a **portfolio manager**. In some organizations, senior management supervises a "showcase portfolio" (for example, a bank's major commingled equity fund), the composition of which indicates to portfolio managers the relative intensity of senior management's feelings regarding different securities.

portfolio manager

In many ways, this description is a caricature of an investment organization—even one run along traditional lines. Nevertheless, most of these attributes can be observed in practice in one form or another.

In recent years, specialty investment firms have gained considerable popularity. As opposed to traditional investment firms that invest in a broad spectrum of securities, these organizations concentrate their investment efforts on a particular asset class, such as stocks or bonds. They often specialize even further, focusing on a narrow segment of a particular asset class, such as the stocks of small start-up companies.

While these specialty investment firms may follow many of the security analysis procedures of the traditional investment organizations, they usually employ few security analysts; often the portfolio managers serve jointly as analysts. Furthermore, their decision-making processes are typically more

[1]One study found that a firm's stock price tended to move upward when analysts upgraded its coding, and downward when analysts downgraded its coding. Edwin J. Elton, Martin J. Gruber, and Seth Grossman, "Discrete Expectational Data and Portfolio Performance," *Journal of Finance*, 41, no. 3 (July 1986): 699–713, and footnote 25 to Chapter 14.

FIGURE 17-1
A Traditional Investment Management Organization

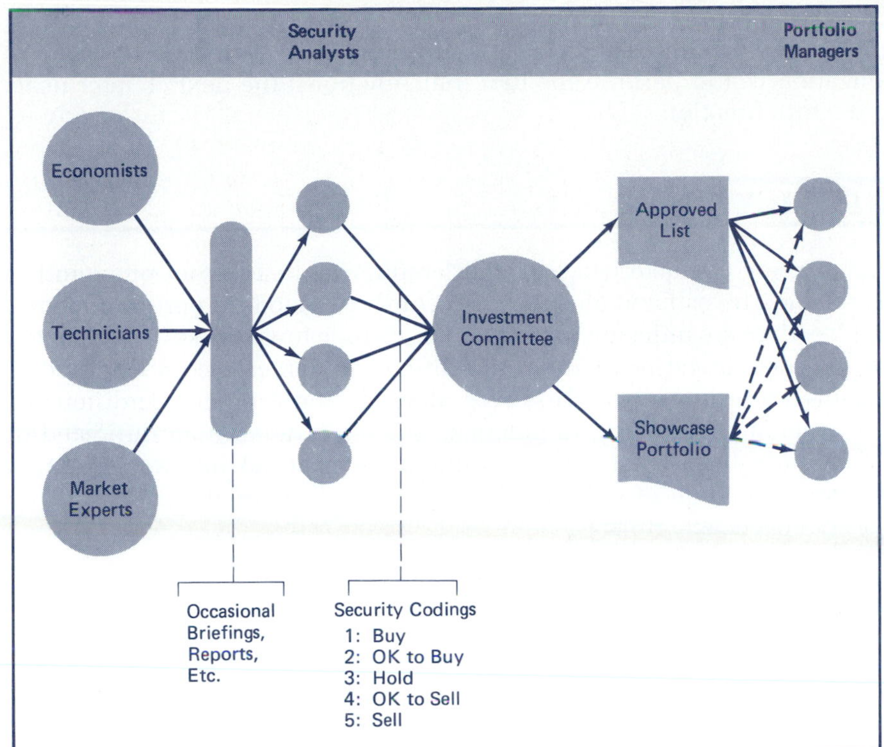

streamlined, often avoiding investment committee structures entirely, thereby permitting portfolio managers considerable discretion to research securities and construct portfolios. Whether this less hierarchical approach to investing actually produces superior results is open to question.

INVESTMENT MANAGEMENT FUNCTIONS

In Chapter 1, a five-step procedure was outlined for making investment decisions. These steps can all be viewed as functions of investment management, and must be undertaken for each client whose money is being managed. They are as follows:

1. *Set investment policy*—determine how much investable wealth the client has, as well as pinpointing his or her investment objectives.
2. *Perform security analysis*—scrutinize individual securities or groups of securities in order to identify mispriced situations.
3. *Construct a portfolio*—identify specific securities to invest in, along with the proportion of investable wealth to be put in each security.
4. *Revise the portfolio*—determine which securities in the current portfolio are to be sold and which securities are to be purchased to replace them.

5. *Evaluate the performance of the portfolio*—determine the actual performance of a portfolio in terms of risk and return, and compare the performance with that of an appropriate "benchmark" portfolio.

The remainder of this chapter deals with how an investment management organization would perform the first four functions; the next chapter deals with the fifth function.

SETTING INVESTMENT POLICY

risk tolerance

One of the key characteristics that differentiates clients from one another concerns their investment objectives. According to modern portfolio theory, these objectives are reflected in the client's attitude toward risk and expected return. As mentioned in Chapter 7, indifference curves are one method of describing these objectives. However, determining a client's indifference curves is not a simple task. In practice, it is often done in an indirect and approximate fashion by estimating the client's level of **risk tolerance,** defined as the largest amount of risk that the client is willing to accept for a given increase in expected return.

Estimating Risk Tolerance

The starting point in making such an estimation is to provide the client with a set of estimates of the risks and expected returns for different combinations of two hypothetical portfolios. For example, imagine the client is told that the expected return on a stock portfolio is 12%, while the return on a riskfree portfolio consisting of Treasury bills is 7.5% (that is, $\bar{r}_S = 12\%$ and $r_F = 7.5\%$). Similarly, the client is told that the standard deviation on the stock portfolio is 15%, while the standard deviation on the riskfree portfolio is, by definition, 0.0% (that is, $\sigma_S = 15\%$ and $\sigma_F = 0.0\%$).[2] Additionally, the client is told that all combinations of these two portfolios lie on a straight line that connects them (this is because the correlation between these two portfolios is 0.0, meaning that $\sigma_{SF} = 0.0$). Some combinations of these two portfolios are shown in Table 17-1.

Note that the investor is being presented with the efficient set that arises when there is a set of stocks and a riskfree borrowing and lending rate. As shown in Chapter 9, this efficient set is linear, meaning that it is a straight line that emanates at the riskfree rate and goes through a tangency portfolio that consists of a certain combination of common stocks. Hence, negative percentages in Treasury bills (shown at the bottom of Table 17-1) represent riskfree borrowing in order to purchase greater amounts of stocks.

At this point, the client is asked to identify the combination that appears to be most desirable, in terms of expected return and standard deviation. Note that asking the investor to identify the most desirable combination is equivalent to asking the investor to locate where his or her indifference curves are tangent to the linear efficient set, since this point will represent the most desirable portfolio.[3]

---

[2]These figures are estimated from post–World War II data; see William F. Sharpe, *Asset Allocation Tools* (Redwood City, Calif.: The Scientific Press, 1987), p. 38.

[3]If such a decision is made on behalf of the client (for example, by a trustee for one or more beneficiaries), the task is much more difficult, but a decision is still required.

TABLE 17-1
Combinations of Stock and Riskfree Treasury Bill Portfolios

PROPORTION IN Stocks	Bills	EXPECTED RETURN	STANDARD DEVIATION	IMPLIED LEVEL OF RISK TOLERANCE
0%	100%	7.50%	0.0%	00
10	90	7.95	1.5	10
20	80	8.40	3.0	20
30	70	8.85	4.5	30
40	60	9.30	6.0	40
50	50	9.75	7.5	50
60	40	10.20	9.0	60
70	30	10.65	10.5	70
80	20	11.10	12.0	80
90	10	11.55	13.5	90
100	0	12.00	15.0	100
110	−10	12.45	16.5	110
120	−20	12.90	18.0	120
130	−30	13.35	19.5	130
140	−40	13.80	21.0	140
150	−50	14.25	22.5	150
.	.	.	.	.
.	.	.	.	.
.	.	.	.	.

After the client has selected the best stock/bond mix, what can be said about his or her risk tolerance? One would, of course, like to identify all the indifference curves that represent a client's attitude toward risk and expected return. However, in practice a more modest goal is usually adopted—to obtain a reasonable representation of the shape of such curves in the likely region of risk and expected return within which the client's optimal choices will most likely fall.

The points in Figure 17-2 plot the alternative mixes presented to the client that were given in Table 17-1. Curve *FCS* shows the risk-return characteristics of all possible mixes and point *C* identifies the attributes of the mix chosen by the client. Note that in this figure expected return is measured on the vertical axis and *variance* on the horizontal axis. While the combinations available to the client plot on a straight line when standard deviation is measured on the horizontal axis, the combinations plot on a concave curve when variance is used (as in this figure).

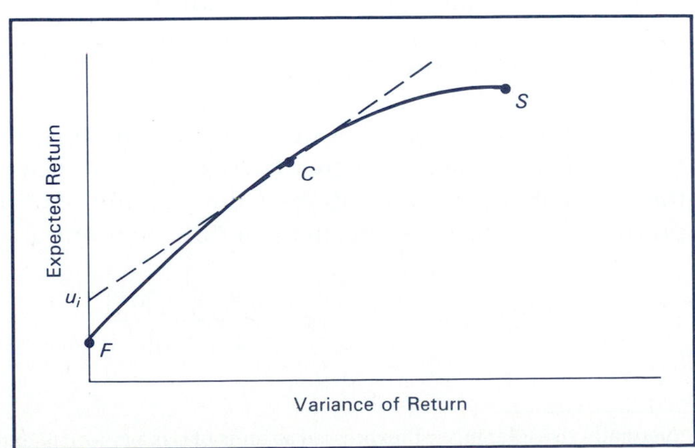

FIGURE 17-2
Inferring Client Risk Tolerance

Assuming that all the possible mixes had been presented to the client and point C had been chosen, it could be inferred that the slope of the client's indifference curve going through C is precisely equal to that of curve FCS at this point. As mentioned earlier, this follows from the observation that the portfolio on the efficient set that a client identifies as being the "best" one corresponds to the one where the client's indifference curves are just tangent to the efficient set.

Constant Risk Tolerance

In principle, the choice of a mix provides information about the slope of an indifference curve at only one point. To go beyond this, an assumption must be made about the general shape of the client's indifference curves. An assumption commonly made is that the client has constant risk tolerance over a range of alternative portfolios in the neighborhood of the point originally chosen. Figure 17-3 shows the nature of this assumption. As indicated in panel (a), indifference curves in a diagram with *variance* on the horizontal axis are *linear* when it is assumed that the client has constant risk tolerance. This means that the equation for an indifference curve of such an investor is equivalent to the equation for a straight line where the variable on the horizontal axis is variance (σ_p^2) and the variable on the vertical axis is expected return ($\bar{r}_p$). Given that the equation of a straight line takes the form of $Y = a + bX$, where a is the vertical intercept and b is the slope, the equation for an indifference curve can be written as:

$$\bar{r}_p = a + b\sigma_p^2$$

or:

$$\bar{r}_p = u_i + \frac{1}{\tau}\sigma_p^2 \qquad (17.1)$$

where u_i is the vertical intercept for indifference curve i and the slope of the indifference curve is $1/\tau$.[4] Note how any two indifference curves for a client differ from one another by the value of the vertical intercept. This is because the indifference curves are parallel, meaning that they have the same slope, $1/\tau$.

Figure 17-3(b) plots the same indifference curves in a more familiar manner—with *standard deviation* on the horizontal axis. Note that the curves have the conventional shape—they indicate that the investor requires more return to compensate for an additional unit of standard deviation as the risk of the portfolio increases. That is, the curves are *convex* when standard deviation is measured on the horizontal axis.

In order to estimate the client's level of risk tolerance τ, it was mentioned that the slope of the indifference curves, $1/\tau$, would be set equal to the slope of the efficient set at the location of the portfolio that was selected, denoted portfolio C. Doing so results in the following formula for estimating τ:

$$\tau = \frac{2[\bar{r}_C - r_F)\sigma_S^2]}{(\bar{r}_S - r_F)^2} \qquad (17.2)$$

---

[4]Normally risk tolerance τ is expressed as units of risk per unit of expected return. However, the reciprocal of risk tolerance $1/\tau$ appears in equation (17.1). This is necessitated by having risk (σ_P^2) on the horizontal axis in Figure 17-3.

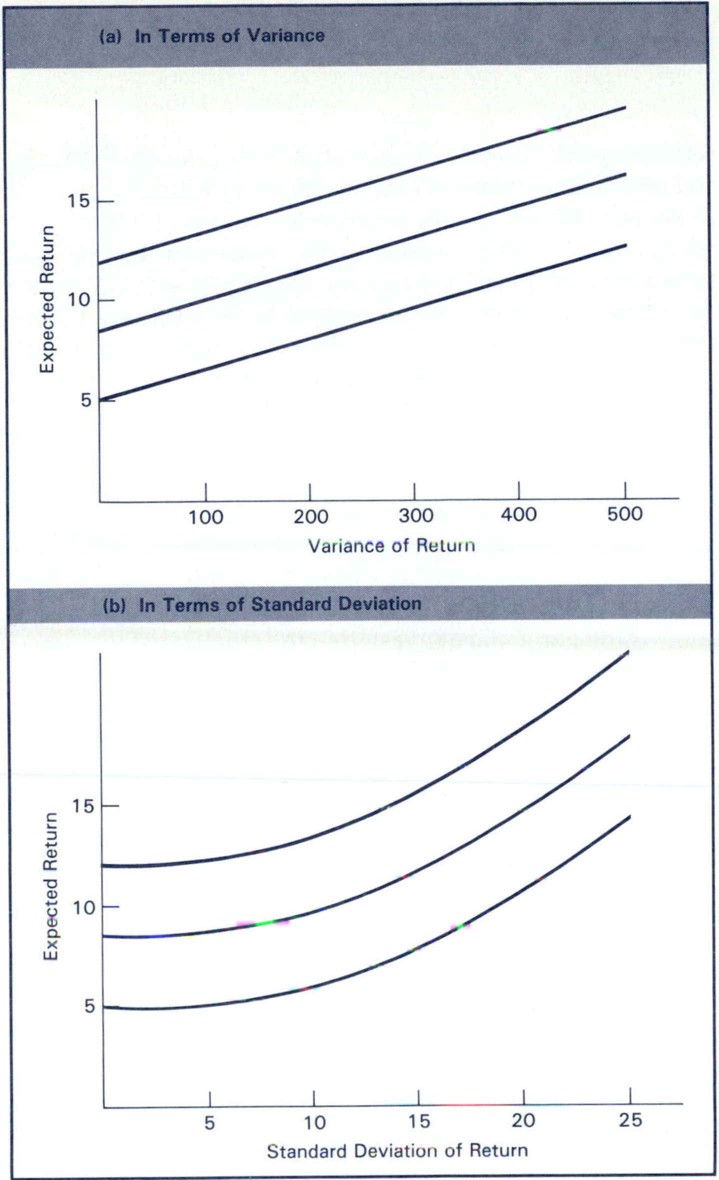

FIGURE 17-3
Constant Risk Tolerance

where $\bar{r}_C$ denotes the expected return of the portfolio that the client selected, $\bar{r}_S$ and r_F denote the expected return of the stock portfolios and riskfree rate, respectively, and σ_S^2 denotes the variance of the stock portfolios. (A detailed presentation of how this formula was derived is presented in the appendix.)

In the example, the client was given a choice between S, F, and various combinations of S and F where $\bar{r}_S = 12\%$, $r_F = 7.5\%$, and $\sigma_S^2 = (15)^2 = 225$. Now, by using equation (17.2), the level of risk tolerance τ inferred from the choice of portfolio C can be determined to be equal to:

$$\tau = \frac{2[(\bar{r}_C - 7.5)225]}{(12 - 7.5)^2}$$

$$= 22.22\bar{r}_C - 166.67. \qquad (17.3)$$

Assuming the choice of a portfolio consisting of a 50% investment in stocks and a 50% investment in riskfree Treasury bills, the client in this example has chosen a portfolio C with an expected return of 9.75%. Accordingly, equation (17.3) can be used to determine the value of τ for this client, resulting in an estimated level of risk tolerance τ equal to $50 = (22.22 \times 9.75) - 166.67$. This means that the client will accept up to an additional 50 units of variance in order to receive an extra 1% in expected return. Thus, the client's indifference curves are estimated to have the form of:

$$\bar{r}_P = u_i + \frac{1}{50}\sigma_P^2. \qquad (17.4)$$

Table 17-1 shows the inferred level of risk tolerance τ if a different portfolio had been chosen by the client (these levels were determined by substituting the appropriate values for $\bar{r}_C$ into the right-hand side of equation (17.3) and then solving for τ). First, note that the level of risk tolerance is the same as the percentage invested in the stock portfolio associated with C. That is, equation (17.3) can be rewritten as $\tau = 100X_S$, where X_S is the proportion invested in the stock portfolio associated with C. It can be shown that this will always be the case when $\bar{r}_S - r_F = 4.5\%$ and $\sigma_S = 15\%$, figures that correspond roughly to the postwar experience in the United States.

Second, note how the level of risk tolerance is lower if the selected portfolio is more conservative (that is, when the level of expected return and standard deviation is lower). Thus, more conservative risk-averse clients will have lower levels of risk tolerance than less conservative risk-averse clients.

Having estimated the client's indifference curves, recall from Chapter 7 that the objective of investment management is to identify the portfolio that lies on the indifference curve furthest to the northwest, because such a portfolio will offer the investor the level of expected return and risk that is preferable to all the other portfolios. This is equivalent to identifying the portfolio that lies on the indifference curve that has the highest vertical intercept, u_i. This can be seen graphically in Figure 17-3(a) and 17-3(b), where the indifference curves have been extended to the vertical axis.

Certainty Equivalent Return

certainty equivalent return

The term u_i thought of as the **certainty equivalent return** for any portfolio that lies on indifference curve i.[5] Thus, portfolio C in Figure 17-2 is as desirable for this particular client as a hypothetical portfolio with an expected return of u_i and no risk—that is, one providing a return of u_i with certainty. When viewed in this manner, the job of the portfolio manager is to identify the portfolio with the highest certainty equivalent return.

Equation (17.1) can be rewritten so that the certainty equivalent return u_i appears on the left-hand side. Doing so results in:

$$u_i = \bar{r}_P - \frac{1}{\tau}\sigma_P^2. \qquad (17.5)$$

[5]The term u_i is also known as the expected utility of indifference curve i; it represents the level of satisfaction associated with all portfolios plotting on indifference curve i.

This equation shows that the certainty equivalent return can be thought of as a risk-adjusted expected return, since a risk penalty that depends on the portfolio's variance and the client's risk tolerance is subtracted from the portfolio's expected return in determining u_i.

In the example, the investor selected the portfolio with $\bar{r}_P = 9.75\%$ and $\sigma_P^2 = 7.5^2 = 56.25$. Thus, the certainty equivalent return for this portfolio is $8.625\% = 9.75 - (56.25/50)$. Equivalently, the risk penalty for the portfolio that was selected was $1.125\% = 56.25/50$. If the certainty equivalent return for any other portfolio shown in Table 17-1 is calculated, it will have a lower value [for example, the 80/20 portfolio has a certainty equivalent return of $8.22\% = 11.1 - (144/50)$]. Thus, the goal of investment management can be thought of as identifying the portfolio that has the maximum value of $\bar{r}_P - (\sigma_P^2/\tau)$, since it will provide the client with the maximum certainty equivalent return.

SECURITY ANALYSIS AND PORTFOLIO CONSTRUCTION

Passive and Active Management

passive management

active management

index funds

Within the investment industry, a distinction is often made between **passive management**—holding securities for relatively long periods with small and infrequent changes—and **active management.** Passive managers generally act as if the security markets are relatively efficient. Put somewhat differently, their decisions are consistent with the acceptance of consensus estimates of risk and return. The portfolios they hold may be surrogates for the market portfolio that are known as **index funds,** or they may be portfolios that are tailored to suit clients with characteristics that differ from those of the average investor.[6] In either case, passive portfolio managers do not try to beat the market.

For example, a passive manager might only have to choose the appropriate mixture of Treasury bills and an index fund that is a surrogate for the market portfolio. The best mixture would depend on the shape and location of the client's indifference curves. Figure 17-4 provides an illustration.

Point *F* plots the riskfree return offered by Treasury bills, and point *M* plots the risk and expected return of the surrogate market portfolio, using consensus estimates. Mixtures of the two investments plot along line *FM*. The client's attitude toward risk and return is shown by the set of indifference curves, and the optimal mixture lies at the point (O^*) where an indifference curve is tangent to line *FM*. In this example, the best mixture uses both Treasury bills and the surrogate market portfolio. In other situations, the surrogate market portfolio might be "levered up" by borrowing (that is, money might be borrowed and added to the client's own investable funds, with the total being used to purchase the surrogate market portfolio).

When management is passive, the overall mixture is altered only when (1) the client's preferences change; or (2) the riskfree rate changes; or (3) the consensus opinion about the risk and return of the surrogate market portfolio

[6]An example of a tailored portfolio would be one consisting of stocks with high dividend yields. Such a portfolio might be purchased for a corporate investor, since 80% of all dividends received by a corporate investor are exempt from corporate income tax.

FIGURE 17-4
Passive Investment Management

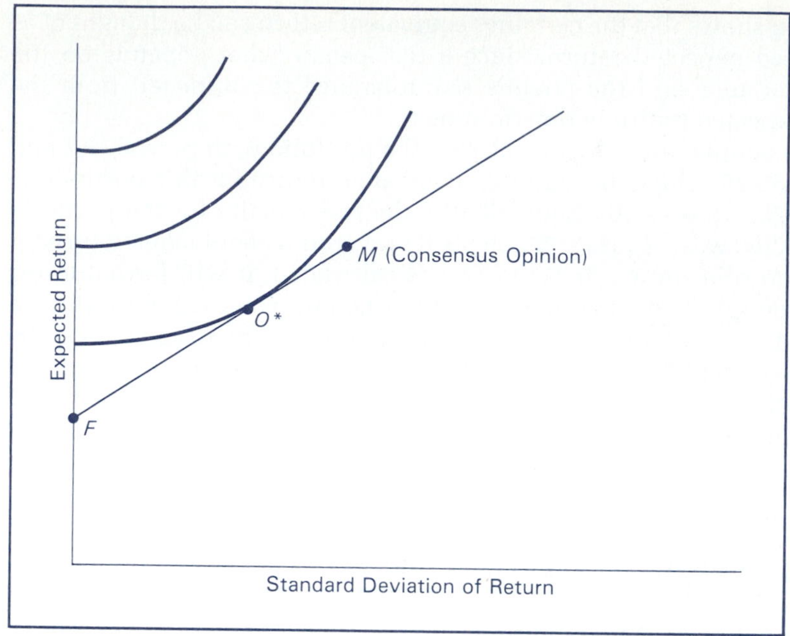

changes. The manager must continue to monitor the last two variables and keep in touch with the client concerning the first one. But no additional activity is required.

Active managers believe that from time to time there are mispriced securities or groups of securities. They do not act as if they believe that security markets are efficient. Put somewhat differently, they use deviant predictions; that is, their estimates of risks and expected returns differ from consensus opinions. While some managers may be more bullish than average about a security, others may be more bearish. The former will hold "more-than-normal" proportions of the security, while the latter will hold "less-than-normal" proportions.

Assuming that there is no tailoring, it is useful to think of a portfolio as having two components: (1) a market portfolio (actually, a surrogate for it); and (2) deviations designed to take advantage of security mispricing. For example, a portfolio can be broken down as follows:

NAME OF SECURITY (COL. 1)	PROPORTION IN ACTUAL PORTFOLIO (COL. 2)	PROPORTION IN MARKET PORTFOLIO (COL. 3)	ACTIVE POSITION (COL. 4)
S1	.30	.45	−.15
S2	.20	.25	−.05
S3	.50	.30	+.20
	1.00	1.00	.00

active positions

The second column shows the actual proportions in the actively managed portfolio. The third column indicates the percentages in a hypothetical surrogate market portfolio—the holdings that might be best for an average client in a perfectly efficient market. The **active positions** can be represented by the differences between the proportions in the actual and market portfolios. Such differences arise because active managers disagree with the consensus about expected returns or risks. When expressed as differences of this sort,

FIGURE 17-5
Investment Styles

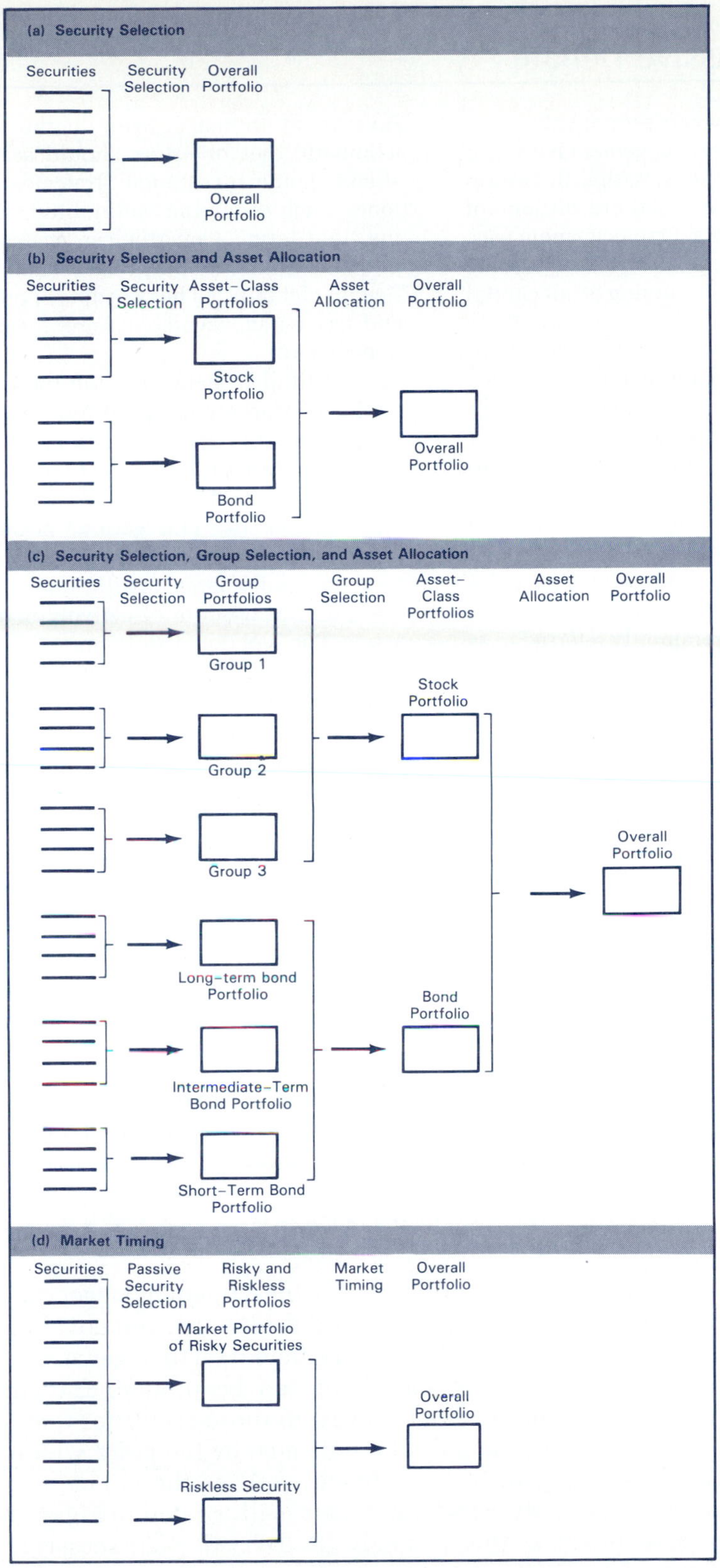

(a) Security Selection

Securities | Security Selection | Overall Portfolio

Overall Portfolio

(b) Security Selection and Asset Allocation

Securities | Security Selection | Asset-Class Portfolios | Asset Allocation | Overall Portfolio

Stock Portfolio

Bond Portfolio

Overall Portfolio

(c) Security Selection, Group Selection, and Asset Allocation

Securities | Security Selection | Group Portfolios | Group Selection | Asset-Class Portfolios | Asset Allocation | Overall Portfolio

Group 1

Group 2

Group 3

Long-term bond Portfolio

Intermediate-Term Bond Portfolio

Short-Term Bond Portfolio

Stock Portfolio

Bond Portfolio

Overall Portfolio

(d) Market Timing

Securities | Passive Security Selection | Risky and Riskless Portfolios | Market Timing | Overall Portfolio

Market Portfolio of Risky Securities

Riskless Security

Overall Portfolio

MONEY MATTERS
The Active Versus Passive Debate

The debate between proponents of active and passive management has raged for over two decades, with little resolution in sight. At stake are billions of dollars in investment management fees, professional reputations, and, some would argue, even the efficient functioning of our capital markets.

As the text describes, passive management involves a long-term, buy-and-hold approach to investing. The investor selects an appropriate target and buys a portfolio designed to closely track the performance of that target. Once the portfolio is purchased, little additional trading occurs, beyond reinvesting income or minor rebalancings necessary to accurately track the target. Because the selected target is usually (although not necessarily) a broad, diversified market index (for example, the Wilshire 5000 for domestic common stocks), passive management is commonly referred to as "indexation" and the passive portfolios are called "index funds."

Active management involves a systematic effort to exceed the performance of a selected target. A wide array of active management investment approaches exists, far too many to summarize in this space. Nevertheless, all active management entails the search for mispriced securities, or mispriced groups of securities. Accurately identifying and adroitly purchasing or selling these mispriced securities provides the active investor with the potential to outperform the passive investor.

Passive management is a relative newcomer to the investment industry. Prior to the mid-1960s, it was axiomatic that investors should search for mispriced stocks. Some investment strategies had passive overtones, such as buying "solid, blue-chip" companies for the "long term." Nevertheless, even these strategies implied an attempt to outperform some nebulously specified market target. The concepts of broad diversification and passive management were, for practical purposes, nonexistent.

Attitudes changed in the 1960s with the popularization of Markowitz's portfolio selection concepts (see Chapter 8), the introduction of the efficient market hypothesis (see Chapter 4), the emphasis on "the market portfolio" derived from the Capital Asset Pricing Model (see Chapter 10), and various academic studies proclaiming the futility of active management. Many investors, especially large institutional investors, began to question the wisdom of actively managing all of their assets. The first domestic common stock index fund was introduced in 1971. By the end of the decade, roughly $100 million was being invested in index funds. Today, hundreds of billions of dollars are invested in domestic and international stock and bond index funds. Even individual investors have become enamored with index funds. Passively managed portfolios are some of the fastest growing products offered by many large mutual fund organizations.

Proponents of active management argue that capital markets are sufficiently inefficient to justify the search for mispriced securities. They may disagree on the degree of the markets' inefficiencies. Technical ana-

---

the actual portfolio can be viewed as an investment in the market portfolio with a series of *bets* being placed on certain securities (such as S3) and against certain other securities (such as S1 and S2).

Security Selection, Asset Allocation, and Market Timing

security selection

Security Selection In principle, the investment manager should make predictions of expected returns, standard deviations, and covariances for all available securities. This will allow an efficient set to be generated, upon which the indifference curves of the client can be plotted. Having done this, the investment manager should invest in those securities that form the optimal portfolio (that is, the portfolio indicated by the point where the indifference curves are tangent to the efficient set) for the client in question. Such a one-stage **security selection** process is illustrated in Figure 17-5(a).

In practice, this is rarely (if ever) done. Excessive costs would be incurred to obtain detailed predictions of the expected returns, standard deviations, and covariances for all the individual securities under consideration. Instead, the decision of which securities to purchase is made in two or more stages.

lysts (see Chapter 14), for example, tend to view markets as dominated by emotionally driven and predictable investors, thereby creating numerous profit opportunities for the creative and disciplined investor. Conversely, managers who use highly quantitative investment tools often view profit opportunities as smaller and less persistent. Nevertheless, all active managers possess a fundamental belief in the existence of consistently exploitable security mispricings. As evidence they frequently point to the stellar track records of certain successful managers and various studies identifying market inefficiencies (see the appendix to Chapter 13 that discusses empirical regularities).

Some active management proponents also introduce into the active-passive debate what amounts to a moralistic appeal. They contend that investors have virtually an obligation to seek out mispriced securities, because their actions help remove these mispricings and thereby lead to a more efficient allocation of capital. Moreover, some proponents derisively contend that passive management implies settling for mediocre, or average, performance.

Proponents of passive management do not deny that exploitable profit opportunities exist or that some managers have established impressive performance results. Rather, they contend that the capital markets are sufficiently efficient to prevent all but those with inside information from consistently being able to earn abnormal profits. They point out that examples of past successes are more likely the result of luck rather than skill. If a thousand people flip a coin ten times, the odds are one of them will flip all heads. In the investment industry, this person is crowned a brilliant money manager.

Passive management proponents also argue that the expected returns from active management are actually less than those for passive management. The fees charged by active managers are typically much higher than those levied by passive managers. (The difference averages anywhere from 0.30% to 1.00% of the managers' assets under management.) Further, passively managed portfolios usually experience very small transaction costs while, depending on the amount of trading involved, active management transaction costs can be quite high. Thus, if active managers, on average, have no information advantage over passive managers, the latter will outperform active managers because of cost differences. Passive management thus entails settling for superior, as opposed to mediocre, results.

The active-passive debate will never be totally resolved. The random "noise" inherent in investment performance tends to drown out any systematic evidence of investment management skill on the part of active managers. Subjective issues therefore dominate the discussion and as a result neither side can convince the other of the correctness of their viewpoints.

Despite the rapid growth in passively managed assets, most domestic and international stock and bond portfolios remain actively managed. Many large institutional investors, such as pension funds, have taken a middle ground on the issue, hiring both passive and active managers. In a crude way, this strategy may be a reasonable response to the unresolved active-passive debate. Clearly, all assets cannot be passively managed—who would be left to maintain security prices at "fair" value levels? On the other hand, investors with above-average investment skill are clearly in the minority of the group currently offering their services to investors.

Figure 17-5(b) illustrates a two-stage procedure where the investment manager has decided to consider investing in a number of common stocks and corporate bonds for a client. In this case, the expected returns, standard deviations, and covariances are estimated for all common stocks under consideration. Then, based on just these common stocks, the efficient set is formed and the optimal stock portfolio identified. Next, the same analysis is performed for all corporate bonds under consideration, resulting in the identification of the optimal bond portfolio. The security selection process used in each of these two **asset classes** can be described as being myopic. That is, covariances between the individual common stocks and corporate bonds have not been considered in the identification of the two optimal portfolios.

asset classes

Asset Allocation The second stage of the process allocates the client's funds among two asset class portfolios, and is known as **asset allocation.**[7] In this

asset allocation

[7]For evidence suggesting that asset allocation is the most important decision an investor has to make, see Gary P. Brinson, L. Randolph Hood, and Gilbert L. Beebower, "Determinants of Portfolio Performance," *Financial Analysts Journal*, 42, no. 4 (July/August 1986): 39–44.

stage, estimates of the expected return and standard deviation are needed for both the optimal stock portfolio and the optimal bond portfolio, along with the covariance between the two portfolios. This will allow the expected return and standard deviation to be determined for all combinations of these two portfolios. Finally, after generating the efficient set from these combinations, the indifference curves of the client can be used to determine which portfolio should be chosen.

For example, the first stage might have indicated that the investor should hold the proportions of stocks S1, S2, and S3 given earlier (that is, the optimal stock portfolio has proportions of .30, .20, and .50, respectively). Similarly, the first stage might have indicated that the investor should hold a proportion of .35 in bond B1 and .65 in bond B2. Then the second stage might indicate that the client's funds should be split so that 60% goes into stocks and 40% into bonds. This translates into individual investments of the following magnitudes:

Stocks:

S1	.60 × .30 =	.18
S2	.60 × .20 =	.12
S3	.60 × .50 =	.30

Bonds:

B1	.40 × .35 =	.14
B2	.40 × .65 =	.26
		1.00

The two-stage process just discussed can be extended by introducing groups. Figure 17-5(c) illustrates a three-stage process. In the first stage, known as security selection, the investment manager would exercise discretion in identifying groups of securities in each asset class. Then, having identified a group, the investment manager would determine the optimal portfolio associated with it. For example, within the asset class of common stocks, it could be that the investment manager has identified all industrial stocks as the first group, all utility stocks as the second group, and all transportation stocks as the third group. Within the asset class of bonds, groups of long-term, intermediate-term, and short-term bonds have been identified. Then, the investment manager would proceed to identify six optimal portfolios, one for each group of securities.

group selection

In the second stage, known as **group selection,** the investment manager determines the appropriate combination of the groups within each asset class. For example, the manager may have decided that the appropriate combination is 70% industrials, 10% utilities, and 20% transportation stocks. Similarly, the manager may have decided that the appropriate combination of bonds is 100% in long-term, with nothing in either intermediate-term or short-term bonds. Thus, in this stage the manager will determine the composition of an optimal stock portfolio and an optimal bond portfolio, but will not know how much to allocate to each one.

The third and final stage makes this allocation and, as noted previously, is referred to as *asset allocation*. It is performed in a manner that is identical to the second stage of the two-stage procedure illustrated in Figure 17-5(b).

Active or passive management may be used in any stage. For example, "active bets" might be placed on individual securities, with funds allocated across security classes based on consensus expected returns for such classes. That is, the investment manager may decide to start every period with 75% in stocks and 25% in bonds. However, the choice of which individual stocks and bonds to invest in will change with time, based on the manager's forecasts.

Alternatively, passive portfolios of individual securities might be constructed, with deviant predictions of asset classes used to allocate funds actively among the classes. For example, the investment manager may decide to always hold common stocks in the same relative proportions they have in the S&P 500, which is often used as a surrogate for the market portfolio. However, the proportion of funds invested in the S&P 500 will change at the start of every period, based on the overall prognosis for the stock and bond markets. Thus, during one period the manager may have as much as 100% of the client's funds in stocks, on the strong belief that the stock market is going to rise rapidly in the near future. Conversely, during another period the manager may have as much as 100% of the client's funds in bonds on the strong belief that the stock market will soon crash dramatically.

Market Timing Figure 17-5(d) portrays a manager following an investment style that is known as **market timing.** The only active decision concerns the appropriate allocation of funds between a surrogate market portfolio and a riskfree asset, such as Treasury bills. An investment organization following this style changes its mixture of risky and riskfree assets based on its own predictions of the risk and expected return of "the market" relative to the riskfree rate, even if there is no change in consensus predictions or the client's attitude toward risk and return.

market timing

Investment organizations that engage in the type of management where "active bets" are placed on individual securities are said to have a security selection style. Those that engage in the type of management where "active bets" are placed on asset classes are said to have an asset allocation style, with market timing being one specific example. Lastly, investment organizations that place "active bets" on certain groups of securities are said to employ a group rotation style. Some organizations use relatively pure **investment styles,** meaning that they use basically just one of the three styles previously mentioned. Others employ various combinations, making it difficult to classify them into neat categories.

investment styles

While these styles have been described in terms of modern portfolio theory, it should be pointed out that other procedures could be used to implement them. For example, with modern portfolio theory an "optimal stock portfolio" [as in Figure 17-5(b)] is to be identified by use of expected returns, standard deviations, and covariances in conjunction with indifference curves. Once it is identified, the portfolio manager will have determined the appropriate relative investments in individual common stocks. However, such an identification could be made using some other procedure. Often it is done on a much less formal and quantitative basis.

International Investing

An interesting extension of the previous discussion of investment styles involves international investing. Consider security selection first. This style, when applied internationally, would involve determining the efficient set associated with a number of stocks found around the world. Alternatively, a security selection with asset allocation style could be used. Here, for example, the portfolio manager could first determine the optimal portfolios associated with just Japanese stocks, just American stocks, and just German stocks. Then, using these optimal portfolios, the manager would decide how much to allocate to each one of the three countries.

Imagine that the optimal Japanese portfolio consisted of two stocks, J_1 and J_2, in proportions of 70% and 30%, respectively, and half of the portfolio's funds were to be devoted to Japanese stocks; then 35% (= .50 × 70%) and 15% (= .50 × 30%) of the portfolio would be invested in J_1 and J_2. Similar calculations could be done for the sets of American and German stocks.

Analogous procedures to those previously described could be followed for the security selection, group rotation, asset allocation, and market timing styles in an international setting. However, the issue of foreign currency risk adds a confounding element to this comparison.[8]

PORTFOLIO REVISION

With the passage of time, a previously purchased portfolio that is currently held will often be viewed as suboptimal by the investment manager, meaning that the portfolio is no longer viewed as the best one for the client. This is because either the client's attitude toward risk and return are thought to have changed or, more likely, the manager's forecasts have changed. In response, the manager could identify a new optimal portfolio and then hope to be able to make the necessary revisions to the current portfolio so that subsequently the new optimal portfolio will be held. However, this is not as straightforward as it might seem at first because transaction costs will have to be paid when any revisions are made.

Such costs were discussed in Chapter 3; they include brokerage commissions and bid-ask spreads. Because of these costs, a security would have to increase in value by a certain amount just to pay these costs and leave the investor neither better nor worse off. This necessary increase in value may exceed 1% for many securities and can range as high as 5% to 10% or more for others.

The existence of transaction costs greatly complicates the life of any investment manager, and the more active the manager, the greater the complications. The hoped-for advantage of any revision must be weighed against the cost of making that revision. That is, a revision can be viewed as bringing certain kinds of benefits—either it will increase the expected return of the portfolio, or it will reduce the standard deviation of the portfolio, or it will do both. To be weighed against these benefits are the transaction costs that will be incurred if the revision is made. As a result, some of the revisions in the holdings of individual securities that the manager may initially want to make will be dropped from consideration because of the transaction costs involved. The goal of the manager is to identify the set of individual revisions that collectively maximize the improvement, after transaction costs, in the risk-return characteristics of the current portfolio.

In order to identify the set of individual revisions, sophisticated procedures (for example, quadratic programming) are required to compare the relevant costs and benefits. Fortunately, improvements in procedures and dramatic decreases in computing costs have made such approaches economically feasible for many investment managers. Asset allocation programs capable of quickly analyzing dozens of asset classes on an inexpensive microcomputer are widely available within the professional investment community.

[8]Foreign currency risk is discussed in Chapter 26.

MANAGER-CLIENT RELATIONS

The larger the amount of money managed, the more communication there is likely to be between investment manager and client. Not surprisingly, corporate, union, and government officials responsible for pension funds spend a great deal of time with those who manage their money. Such officials also concern themselves with a number of prior questions: Who should manage the money, how should it be managed, and how should the managers be instructed and constrained?

Many of the aspects of manager-client relations can be characterized as responses to a difference of opinion concerning the manager's abilities to make "good bets." Often, clients will divide their funds among two or more managers. This type of **split-funding** is used by most pension funds. Two reasons are given. First, it allows the employment of managers with different skills or different styles. Second, the impact of erroneous "bets" can be reduced by diversifying across different managers, since the managers are the "bettors." However, if a client were to broadly diversify across managers without regard to the managers' investment abilities, the overall portfolio would likely produce results similar to those of the market portfolio. Thus, excessive use of split-funding is like explicitly investing in a passive fund, but at considerably greater cost to the client, owing to the expenses associated with transaction costs and fees charged by the investment managers.

split-funding

Whether or not split-funding is used, a client who feels that a manager is "betting" too much would like to simply reduce the size of the "bets." For example, the client might ask a manager to diverge only half as much as he or she normally would from passive proportions of individual securities. Thus, if the manager decides that the optimal proportion in stock S1 is 30% and the market proportion is 45%, this would mean that the manager would ultimately only invest a proportion equal to 37.5% = (30% + 45%)/2. However, there is no simple way to monitor compliance. In the example, the manager could buy 30% of S1 and state that he or she originally wanted to invest 15% in it but settled for 30%, even though truthfully he or she originally wanted 30%. Instead, another approach is often employed: limits are placed on the holdings in any single security.[9]

Institutional investors (for example, pension and endowment funds) often use more than one investment manager and provide each with a set of objectives and a set of constraints on allowed divergences from specified target positions.[10] Individual investors who employ investment managers tend to give such instructions implicitly, if at all. This may reflect less sophistication, a less formal relationship with the manager, or the fact that the management fee for a small account is not large enough to cover the cost of dealing with a series of client-specific objectives and constraints.

SUMMARY

1. Investment decisions are made through a five-step procedure: (1) set investment policy; (2) perform security analysis; (3) construct a portfolio; (4) revise the portfolio; and (5) evaluate the performance of the portfolio.

[9]There are other kinds of limits frequently imposed on the manager, such as limits on the holdings of bonds versus stocks, or on the amount invested in a single industry.

[10]Sometimes these objectives and constraints are stated vaguely; in other cases they are specified precisely.

2. To set investment policy, an investor should specify his or her risk tolerance; that is, the maximum amount of additional risk that the investor will accept for a given increase in expected return.

3. One means of establishing an investor's risk tolerance is for the investor to identify the most desirable portfolio from a set of portfolios. Once this identification has been made, the slope of the investor's indifference curve, and hence the investor's attitude toward risk and expected return, can be established.

4. Passive management rests on the belief that markets are efficient and typically involves investing in an index fund. Active management, conversely, involves a belief that mispriced situations occur and can be identified with a reasonable consistency.

5. There are many forms of active management. They can involve security selection, group selection, asset allocation, and market timing.

6. Portfolio revision involves both realizing that the currently held portfolio is not optimal and specifying another portfolio to hold with superior risk-return characteristics. The investor must balance the costs of moving to the new portfolio against the benefits of the revision.

KEY TERMS

security analyst
investment committee
approved list
portfolio manager
risk tolerance
certainty equivalent return
passive management
active management
index funds
active positions
security selection
asset classes
asset allocation
group selection
market timing
investment styles
split-funding

QUESTIONS AND PROBLEMS

1. Describe the functioning of a "traditional" investment management organization. Much of the decision-making in these organizations is "qualitative" in nature. What types of "quantitative" decision-making techniques might be introduced?

2. Technological changes have decreased the cost and increased the speed of information dissemination in security markets. Why might one suspect that firms following a "traditional" approach to investment management would find it increasingly difficult to generate "positive alphas" in this environment?

3. Consider Table 17-1. If your investment advisor presented you with these data, which stock-bill combination would you choose? Describe your thought process in making this choice.

4. Why is it difficult to specify the risk-return preferences of investment management clients? Why are these problems particularly acute in the case of institutional clients (for example, pension and endowment funds)?

5. Consider a portfolio whose asset mix can vary between stocks and Treasury bills. Given the historical returns of these two assets that is provided in Chapter 1, describe the distribution of possible portfolio returns as the proportion of the portfolio invested in stocks increases and that invested in Treasury bills decreases. What causes the distribution to change as the asset mix changes?

6. Explain the meaning of the slope of an indifference curve at any particular point. For a "typical" risk-averse investor, describe how the investor's risk-return trade-off changes at different points along one of his or her indifference curves.

7. Studies that stimulate the value of an investment portfolio under alternative mixes of stocks and bonds invariably demonstrate that higher stock allocations produce higher returns, particularly as the holding period increases. If you as an investor have a time horizon that is reasonably long, say over ten years, and you have no current income needs, how could you justify holding any bonds in your portfolio?
8. Assume a riskfree return of 7%, an expected stock return of 18%, and a standard deviation of 21%. Under these conditions, if Birdie Cree chooses a 40% stock, 60% riskfree portfolio, what is Birdie's risk tolerance? In words, describe what this value means.
9. Dee Cousineau can earn a riskfree return of 6%. Dee expects the stock market to return 15% and exhibit a standard deviation of 20%. If Dee chooses a portfolio of 60% stocks and 40% riskfree asset, calculate Dee's certainty equivalent return.
10. The portfolio manager's job can be defined as identifying the portfolio with the highest certainty equivalent return. Explain.
11. Despite its obvious simplicity and potential benefits, common stock passive management is a relatively "new" investment tool. Yet in the last twenty years, assets under passive management have grown from essentially zero to over several hundreds of billions of dollars. What are several possible reasons for the tremendous growth in passive management?
12. It is often argued (especially by active managers) that passive management implies settling for "mediocre" performance. Is this statement necessarily true? Why?
13. Gavvy Cravath, an astute investor, once commented, "With the stock market composed of about 6,000 actively traded securities, I view my portfolio as about 5,950 short positions and 50 long positions." Explain what Gavvy means.
14. Should an overpriced stock definitely be excluded from an investor's portfolio? Why?
15. Why is the "one-stage" approach to security selection theoretically superior to the "two-stage" approach? Why is the "two-stage" approach preferred by most investment managers?
16. Why should investment portfolios, even those that are passively managed, be periodically revised? What factors weigh against making such revisions?
17. Many investment management clients split their assets among a number of managers. The rationale for this approach has been described as "diversification of judgment" and "diversification of style." Explain the meaning of these two terms.

CFA Exam Questions

18. Advisor 1: "Long-term asset allocation should be determined using an efficient frontier. Returns, risks (standard deviations), and correlations can be determined for each asset class from historical data. After calculating the efficient frontier for various allocations, you should select the asset mix on the efficient frontier that best meets your fund's risk tolerance."

    Advisor 2: "History gives no guide to the future. For example, everybody agrees that bond risk has increased above historical levels as a result of financial deregulation. A far better approach to long-term asset allocation is to use your best judgment about expected returns on the various asset classes, based on current market conditions. You should rely on your experience to determine the best asset mix and avoid being influenced by computer printouts."

Advisor 1 Rebuttal: "Current market conditions are not likely to persist into the future and are not appropriate for long-term asset allocation decisions. Moreover, your use of judgment and experience can be influenced by biases and emotions and is not as rigorous a method as my efficient frontier approach."

Evaluate the strengths and weaknesses of each of the two approaches presented above. Recommend and justify an alternative process for asset allocation that draws from the strengths of each approach and corrects their weaknesses.

19. Colinos Associates is an investment management firm utilizing a very rigorous and disciplined asset allocation methodology as a key element of its investment approach. Twice a year, three or four economic scenarios are developed, based on the judgment of Colinos' most senior people. Probabilities are then assigned to the scenarios; return forecasts for U.S. stocks, bonds, and cash equivalents (the only asset types used by the firm) are generated; and expected values are computed for each asset category. These expected values are then combined with historical standard deviations and covariances to produce forecasts of results from various combinations of the three asset classes.

From this range of possible outcomes, senior staff selects what it regards as the best asset combinations, defined as those combinations promising the highest three-year returns with a 90% probability of achieving a pre-set minimum annual return requirement. These optimal allocations (sample output in the following table) are then presented to all clients for discussion and implementation. The process is repeated in roughly six months' time, when new allocations are developed.

MINIMUM ANNUAL REQUIRED RETURN (90% PROBABILITY)	ANTICIPATED 3-YEAR COMPOUND ANNUAL RETURN	RECOMMENDED ASSET ALLOCATION		
		Cash	Bonds	Stocks
−6%	12.0%	10%	30%	60%
−4	11.0	20	40	40
−2	10.0	30	40	30
0	9.0	50	30	20
2	8.5	60	30	10
4	8.0	70	20	10
6	7.5	80	15	5

(a) Discuss the strengths and weaknesses of Colinos' asset allocation approach.

(b) Recommend and justify an alternative asset allocation approach for wealthy individuals.

APPENDIX

A

Determining the Risk Tolerance of an Investor

The purpose of this appendix is to derive in some detail the formula for determining the risk tolerance τ of an investor. As mentioned earlier, the equation for an indifference curve of an investor having constant risk tolerance is of the form:

$$\bar{r}_P = u_i + \frac{1}{\tau}\sigma_P^2 \tag{17.1}$$

where u_i and $1/\tau$ are the vertical intercept and slope for indifference curve i, where variance is measured on the horizontal axis. As the equation shows, an indifference curve will be a straight line since u_i and $1/\tau$ are constants (thus, the equation is of the general form $Y = a + bX$, and is a straight line). Furthermore, any two indifference curves for an investor will have the same slope ($1/\tau$), but will have different vertical intercepts (u_i).

In order to estimate the investor's level of risk tolerance τ, it was mentioned that the slope of the indifference curve, $1/\tau$, would be set equal to the slope of the efficient set at the location of the portfolio that was selected, denoted portfolio C. This is because the indifference curve is tangent to the efficient set at this point, so the two must have the same slope. Thus, the slope of the efficient set at point C must be determined in order to estimate τ.

Let X_S denote the proportion invested in the stock portfolio S and $(1 - X_S)$ denote the proportion invested in a riskfree Treasury bill portfolio F. Now the expected return of any portfolio consisting of S and F is simply:

$$\bar{r}_P = X_S\bar{r}_S + (1 - X_S)r_F \tag{17.6}$$

where $\bar{r}_S$ and r_F are the expected return of the stock portfolio and the riskfree rate, respectively. This equation can be solved for X_S, resulting in:

$$X_S = \frac{\bar{r}_P - r_F}{\bar{r}_S - r_F}. \tag{17.7}$$

The equation for the variance of portfolio p is equal to:

$$\sigma_P^2 = X_S^2\sigma_S^2 + (1 - X_S)^2\sigma_F^2 + 2X_S(1 - X_S)\sigma_{SF} \tag{17.8}$$

where σ_S^2 and σ_F^2 are the variances of the stock and riskfree bill portfolios, respectively, and σ_{SF} is the covariance between these two portfolios. However, since F is the riskfree bill portfolio, by definition, σ_F^2 and σ_{SF} are equal to zero. Thus, equation (17.8) reduces to

$$\sigma_P^2 = X_S^2\sigma_S^2. \tag{17.9}$$

Next, the right-hand side of equation (17.7) can be substituted for X_S in equation (17.9), resulting in:

$$\sigma_P^2 = \frac{(\bar{r}_P - r_F)^2}{(\bar{r}_S - r_F)^2}\sigma_S^2. \tag{17.10}$$

This equation can be viewed as describing the functional relationship between the expected return and variance of any portfolio p that can be formed by combining the stock portfolio S and the riskfree bill portfolio F. That is, for a particular S and F, it gives the variance for a portfolio consisting of S and F with expected return $\bar{r}_P$. Equivalently, it represents the slope of the curved line in Figure 17-2 that connects S and F.

Using calculus, the slope of this line can be shown to be equal to:[11]

$$\text{Slope} = \frac{(\bar{r}_S - r_F)^2}{2[(\bar{r}_P - r_F)\sigma_S^2]}\,. \tag{17.11}$$

The next step in estimating the slope of the client's indifference curves is to note that the portfolio on the curve connecting S and F that is of concern is the tangency portfolio C. Thus, the slope of the curve at C is determined by substituting $\bar{r}_C$ for $\bar{r}_P$ in equation (17.11) and equating this value with the slope of the indifference curves, $1/\tau$. Doing this results in the following equation:

$$\frac{1}{\tau} = \frac{(\bar{r}_S - r_F)^2}{2[(\bar{r}_C - r_F)\sigma_S^2]}\,. \tag{17.12}$$

Finally, equation (17.12) can be solved for τ:

$$\tau = \frac{2[(\bar{r}_C - r_F)\sigma_S^2]}{(\bar{r}_S - r_F)^2}\,. \tag{17.13}$$

Note that this is the same formula that was given earlier in equation (17.2) for estimating τ, given the client's choice of portfolio C.[12]

---

[11]Note that the slope of this line, $d\bar{r}_P/d\sigma_P^2$, is equal to $1/[d\sigma_P^2/d\bar{r}_P]$. Thus, the slope can be determined by taking the derivative of σ_P^2 with respect to $\bar{r}_P$ in equation (17.10) and then inverting the resulting expression.

[12]Risk tolerance, along with a computer program for estimating the value of τ, is presented in William F. Sharpe, *Asset Allocation Tools* (Redwood City, Calif.: The Scientific Press, 1987): pp. 33–39.

Note that after substituting $\bar{r}_C$ for $\bar{r}_P$, equation (17.7) can be rewritten as:

$$(\bar{r}_S - r_F)X_S = \bar{r}_C - r_F. \tag{17.14}$$

Thus, $(\bar{r}_S - r_F)X_S$ can be substituted for $\bar{r}_C - r_F$ in the numerator of equation (17.13). Doing so and simplifying results in:

$$\tau = \frac{2[X_S\sigma_S^2]}{(\bar{r}_S - r_F)} \cdot \tag{17.15}$$

In the example given earlier in the chapter, $\sigma_S = 15\%$ and $\bar{r}_S - r_F = 4.5\%$. Substituting these values into equation (17.15) and simplifying results in:

$$\tau = \frac{2[X_S \times 15^2]}{4.5}$$

$$= 100X_S \tag{17.16}$$

as was previously mentioned and illustrated in Table 17-1.

REFERENCES

1. Investment management is discussed in:

William F. Sharpe, "Decentralized Investment Management," *Journal of Finance,* 36, no. 2 (May 1981): 217–34;

Jeffery V. Bailey and Robert D. Arnott, "Cluster Analysis and Manager Selection," *Financial Analysts Journal,* 42, no. 6 (November/December 1986): 20–28;

Richard A. Brealey, "Portfolio Theory versus Portfolio Practice," *Journal of Portfolio Management,* 16, no. 4 (Summer 1990): 6–10;

William F. Sharpe, "The Arithmetic of Active Management," *Financial Analysts Journal,* 47, no. 1 (January/February 1991): 7–9;

Robert H. Jeffery, "Do Clients Need So Many Portfolio Managers?" *Journal of Portfolio Management,* 18, no. 1 (Fall 1991): 13–19;

C. B. Garcia and F. J. Gould, "Some Observations on Active Manager Performance and Passive Indexing," *Financial Analysts Journal,* 47, no. 6 (November/December 1991): 11–13.

2. Investment management for an individual investor is discussed in:

Burton G. Malkiel, *A Random Walk Down Wall Street* (New York: W. W. Norton, 1990), particularly Chapter 11.

3. The discussion of risk tolerance is expanded upon in:

William F. Sharpe, *Asset Allocation Tools* (Redwood City, Calif.: The Scientific Press, 1987): Chapter 2;

William F. Sharpe, "Integrated Asset Allocation," *Financial Analysts Journal,* 43, no. 5 (September/October 1987): 25–32.

4. Investment styles are discussed in:

Keith P. Ambachtsheer, "Portfolio Theory and the Security Analyst," *Financial Analysts Journal,* 28, no. 6 (November–December 1972): 53–57;

William F. Sharpe, "Major Investment Styles," *Journal of Portfolio Management*, 4, no. 2 (Winter 1978): 68–74;

Keith P. Ambachtsheer and James L. Farrell, Jr., "Can Active Management Add Value?" *Financial Analysts Journal*, 35, no. 6 (November–December 1979): 39–47;

Robert D. Arnott and James N. von Germeten, "Systematic Asset Allocation," *Financial Analysts Journal*, 39, no. 6 (November–December 1983): 31–38;

David E. Tierney and Kenneth Winston, "Using Generic Benchmarks to Present Manager Styles," *Journal of Portfolio Management*, 17, no. 4 (Summer 1991): 33–36;

William F. Sharpe, "Asset Allocation: Management Style and Performance Measurement," *Journal of Portfolio Management*, 18, no. 2 (Winter 1992): 7–19.

5. Investing in an international context is discussed in:

Bruno Solnik, *International Investments* (Reading, Mass.: Addison-Wesley Publishing Co., 1991), particularly Chapter 5;

Robert D. Arnott and Roy D. Henriksson, "A Disciplined Approach to Global Asset Allocation," *Financial Analysts Journal*, 45, no. 2 (March/April 1989): 17–28.

6. For a discussion of portfolio revision procedures, see:

Gordon J. Alexander and Jack Clark Francis, *Portfolio Analysis* (Englewood Cliffs, N.J.: Prentice Hall, 1986), pp. 221–28;

William F. Sharpe, *Asset Allocation Tools* (Redwood City, Calif.: The Scientific Press, 1987), pp. 65–68.

18

Portfolio Performance Evaluation

An investor who has been paying someone to actively manage his or her portfolio has every right to insist on knowing what sort of performance was obtained. Such information can be used to alter either the constraints placed on the manager, the investment objectives given to the manager, or the amount of money allocated to the manager. Perhaps more importantly, by evaluating performance in specified ways, a client can forcefully communicate his or her interests to the investment manager and, in all likelihood, affect the way in which his or her portfolio is managed. Moreover, an investment manager, by evaluating his or her own performance, can identify sources of strength or weakness. Thus, while the previous chapter indicated that portfolio performance evaluation was the last stage of the investment management process, it can also be viewed as simply part of a continuing operation. More specifically, it can be viewed as a feedback and control mechanism that can make the investment management process more effective.

Superior performance in the past may have resulted from good luck, in which case such performance should not be expected to continue in the future. On the other hand, superior performance in the past may have resulted from the actions of a highly skilled investment manager (and support staff). Conversely, inferior performance in the past may have been the result of bad luck, but it may also have resulted from excessive turnover, high management fees, or other costs associated with an unskilled investment manager. This suggests that the first task in performance evaluation is to try to determine whether past performance was superior or inferior. Once this task is done, the second task is to try to determine whether such performance was due to skill or luck. Unfortunately, there are difficulties associated with carrying out both of these tasks. Accordingly, this chapter will present not only certain methods that have been advocated and used for evaluating portfolio performance, but also a discussion of the difficulties encountered with their use.

MEASURES OF RETURN

Frequently portfolio performance is evaluated over a time interval of at least four years, with returns measured for a number of periods within the interval—typically monthly or quarterly. This provides a fairly adequate sample size for statistical evaluation (for example, if returns are measured quarterly for four years, there will be sixteen observations). Sometimes, however, a shorter time interval must be used in order to avoid examining an investment management firm's returns that were earned by a different investment manager. The examples to follow will involve 16 quarterly observations for tractability. In practice, one would prefer monthly observations if only four years were to be analyzed.

In the simplest situation where the client neither deposits nor withdraws money from the portfolio during a time period, calculation of the portfolio's return is straightforward. All that is required is that the market value of the portfolio be known at two points in time—the beginning and the end of the period.

In general, the market value of a portfolio at a point in time is determined by adding the market values of all the securities held at that particular time. For example, the value of a common stock portfolio at the beginning of a period is calculated by (1) noting the market price per share of each stock held in the portfolio at that time; (2) multiplying each of these stock prices by the corresponding number of shares held; and (3) adding up the resulting products. This sum will equal the market value of the portfolio at the beginning of the period.

With the beginning and ending portfolio values in hand, the return on the portfolio can be calculated by subtracting the beginning value (V_b) from the ending value (V_e), and then dividing the difference by the beginning value:

$$r_p = \frac{V_e - V_b}{V_b} . \tag{18.1}$$

For example, if a portfolio has a market value of $40 million at the beginning of a quarter and a market value of $46 million at the end of the quarter, then the return on this portfolio for the quarter would be 15% = ($46 million − $40 million)/$40 million.

Measurement of portfolio returns is complicated by the fact that the client may either add or withdraw money from the portfolio. This means that the percentage change in the market value of the portfolio during a period may not be an accurate measurement of the portfolio's return during that period.

For example, consider a portfolio that at the beginning of a quarter has a market value of $100 million. Just before the end of the quarter the client deposits $5 million with the investment manager, and subsequently at the end of the quarter the market value of the portfolio is $103 million. If the quarterly return was measured without consideration of the $5 million deposit, the reported return would be 3% = ($103 million − $100 million)/$100 million. However, this would be incorrect, since $5 million of the ending $103 million market value did not result from the investment actions of the manager. Consideration of the deposit would suggest that a more accurate measure of the quarterly return would be −2% = [($103 million − $5 million) − $100 million]/$100 million.

Identification of exactly *when* any deposits or withdrawals occur is important in accurately measuring portfolio returns. If a deposit or withdrawal occurs just *before* the end of the period, then the return on the portfolio should be calculated by adjusting the ending market value of the portfolio. In the case of a deposit, the ending value should be reduced by the dollar amount (as was done in the previous example); in the case of a withdrawal, the ending value should be increased by the dollar amount.

If a deposit or withdrawal occurs just *after* the start of the period, then the return on the portfolio should be calculated by adjusting the beginning market value of the portfolio. In the case of a deposit, the beginning value should be increased by the dollar amount; in the case of a withdrawal, the beginning value should be decreased by the dollar amount. For example, if the $5 million deposit in the earlier example had been received just after the start of the quarter, the return for the quarter should be calculated as −1.90% = [$103 million − ($100 million + $5 million)]/($100 million + $5 million).

Dollar-Weighted Returns

Difficulties are encountered, however, when deposits or withdrawals occur sometime *between* the beginning and end of the period. One method that has been used for calculating a portfolio's return in this situation results in the portfolio's **dollar-weighted return** (or internal rate of return). For example, if the $5 million deposit in the earlier example was made in the middle of the quarter, the dollar-weighted return would be calculated by solving the following equation for *r*:

dollar-weighted return

$$\$100 \text{ million} = \frac{-\$5 \text{ million}}{(1+r)} + \frac{\$103 \text{ million}}{(1+r)^2}. \tag{18.2}$$

The solution to this equation, $r = -.98\%$, is a semiquarterly rate of return. It can be converted into a quarterly rate of return by adding 1 to it, squaring this value, and then subtracting 1 from the square, resulting in a quarterly return of $[1 + (-.0098)]^2 - 1 = -1.95\%$.[1]

Time-Weighted Returns

Alternatively, the **time-weighted return** on a portfolio can be calculated when there are cash flows occurring between the beginning and end of the period.

time-weighted return

[1]This procedure provides a quarterly return with "quarterly compounding." Alternatively, the semiquarterly return could be doubled, resulting in a quarterly return with "semiquarterly compounding" of −1.96% = − .98% × 2.

This method involves using the market value of the portfolio just before each cash flow occurs. In the earlier example, assume that in the middle of the quarter the portfolio had a market value of \$96 million, so that right after the \$5 million deposit the market value was \$101 million = \$96 million + \$5 million. In this case, the return for the first half of the quarter would be −4% = (\$96 million − \$100 million)/\$100 million; the return for the second half of the quarter would be 1.98% = (\$103 million − \$101 million)/\$101 million. Next, these two semiquarterly returns can be converted into a quarterly return by adding 1 to each return, multiplying the sums, and then subtracting 1 from the product. In the example, this procedure results in a quarterly return of −2.1% = [(1 − .04) (1 + .0198)] − 1.

Comparing Dollar-Weighted and Time-Weighted Returns

Which method is preferable for calculating the return on a portfolio? In the example given here, the dollar-weighted return was −1.95%, while the time-weighted return was −2.1%, suggesting that the difference between the two methods may not be very important. While this may be true in certain situations, examples can be given to show that such differences can be quite large, and that the time-weighted return method is preferable.

Consider a hypothetical portfolio that starts a quarter with a market value of \$50 million. In the middle of the quarter, it has fallen to a market value of \$25 million, at which point the client deposits \$25 million with the investment manager. At the end of the quarter the portfolio has a market value of \$100 million. The semiquarterly dollar-weighted return for this portfolio is equal to the value of r in the following equation:

$$\$50 \text{ million} = \frac{-\$25 \text{ million}}{(1 + r)} + \frac{\$100 \text{ million}}{(1 + r)^2}.$$

Solving this equation for r results in a value of 18.6%, which in turn equals a quarterly dollar-weighted return of 40.66% = $(1.186)^2 - 1$. However, its quarterly time-weighted return is 0%, since its return for the first half of the quarter was −50% and its return for the second half of the quarter was 100% [note that (1 − .5) (1 + 1) − 1 = 0%].

Comparing these two returns—40.66% and 0%—indicates that a sizable difference exists. However, the time-weighted return figure of 0% is more meaningful for performance evaluation than the dollar-weighted return figure of 40.66%. The reason for this can be seen by considering the return over the entire quarter on each dollar that was in the portfolio at the start of the quarter. Each dollar lost half of its value over the first half of the quarter, but then the remaining half-dollar doubled its value over the second half. Consequently, a dollar at the beginning was worth a dollar at the end, suggesting that a return of 0% on the portfolio is a more accurate measure of the investment manager's performance than the 40.66% figure.

In general, the dollar-weighted return method of measuring a portfolio's return for purposes of evaluation is regarded as inappropriate. The reason behind this view is that the return is strongly influenced by the size and timing of the cash flows (namely, deposits and withdrawals) over which the investment manager typically has no control. In the example, the dollar-weighted return was 40.66% because the client fortuitously made a big deposit just before the portfolio appreciated rapidly in value. Thus, the 40.66% return figure results at least partly from the actions of the client, not the manager.

Annualizing Returns

The previous discussion has focused on calculating quarterly returns. Such returns may be added or multiplied to obtain an annual measure of return. For example, if the return in the first, second, third, and fourth quarters of a given year are denoted r_1, r_2, r_3, and r_4, respectively, then the annual return could be calculated by adding the four figures:

$$\text{annual return} = r_1 + r_2 + r_3 + r_4. \qquad (18.3)$$

Alternatively, the annual return could be calculated by adding 1 to each quarterly return, then multiplying the four figures, and finally subtracting 1 from the resulting product:

$$\text{annual return} = [(1 + r_1)(1 + r_2)(1 + r_3)(1 + r_4)] - 1. \qquad (18.4)$$

This return is more accurate because it reflects the value that one dollar would have at the end of the year if it were invested at the beginning of the year and grew *with compounding* at the rate of r_1 for the first quarter, r_2 for the second quarter, r_3 for the third quarter, and r_4 for the fourth quarter. That is, it assumes reinvestment of both the dollar and any earnings at the end of each quarter.

MAKING RELEVANT COMPARISONS

The essential idea behind performance evaluation is to compare the returns obtained by the investment manager through active management with the returns that could have been obtained for the client if one or more appropriate alternative portfolios had been chosen for investment. The reason for this comparison is straightforward—performance should be evaluated on a relative basis, not on an absolute basis.

As an example, consider a client who is told that his or her portfolio, invested broadly in common stocks and of average risk, had a return of 20% last year. Does this suggest superior or inferior performance? If a broad stock market index (like the Wilshire 5000) went up by 10% last year, then it suggests superior performance and is good news. However, if the index went up by 30% last year, then it suggests inferior performance and is bad news. In order to infer whether the manager's performance is superior or inferior, the returns on "similar" portfolios that are either actively or passively managed are needed for comparison.

benchmark portfolios

Such comparison portfolios are often referred to as **benchmark portfolios.** In selecting them, the client should be certain that they are relevant and feasible, meaning that they should represent alternative portfolios that could have been chosen for investment instead of the portfolio being evaluated. That is, the benchmark should reflect the objectives of the client. Hence, if the objective is to earn superior returns by investing in small stocks, then the S&P 500 would be an inappropriate benchmark. Instead, an index like the Russell 2000 would be suitable. *Return* is a key aspect of performance, of course, but some way must be found to account for the portfolio's exposure to *risk*. The choice of benchmark portfolios may be restricted to portfolios perceived to have similar levels of risk, thereby permitting a direct comparison of returns.

Figure 18-1 illustrates such a comparison for a hypothetical common stock (or "equity") portfolio referred to as Fund 07632. In this figure, Fund 07632's performance for each year is represented by a diamond. The hypo-

FIGURE 18-1
Comparing Returns of Equity Portfolios
Source: Adapted from SEI, *Funds Evaluation Service.*

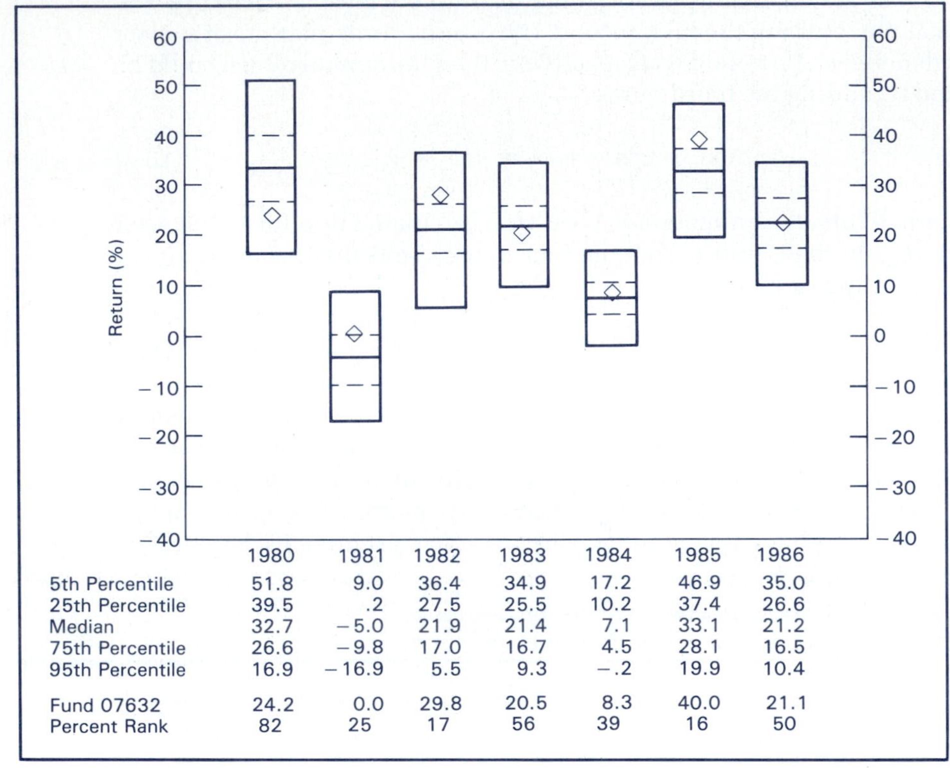

	1980	1981	1982	1983	1984	1985	1986
5th Percentile	51.8	9.0	36.4	34.9	17.2	46.9	35.0
25th Percentile	39.5	.2	27.5	25.5	10.2	37.4	26.6
Median	32.7	−5.0	21.9	21.4	7.1	33.1	21.2
75th Percentile	26.6	−9.8	17.0	16.7	4.5	28.1	16.5
95th Percentile	16.9	−16.9	5.5	9.3	−.2	19.9	10.4
Fund 07632	24.2	0.0	29.8	20.5	8.3	40.0	21.1
Percent Rank	82	25	17	56	39	16	50

thetical comparison portfolios are a set of other common stock portfolios that are represented by the box surrounding the diamond (hence, such a representation is known as a "box plot" or a "floating bar chart"). The top and bottom lines of the box indicate the returns of the 5th and 95th percentile comparison portfolios, respectively. Similarly, the top and bottom dashed lines represent the 25th and 75th percentiles, respectively. The solid line in the middle represents the median (that is, the 50th percentile) portfolio. Note that this particular evaluation technique presumes that the comparison portfolios exhibit risk similar to Fund 07632 and that they represent feasible alternatives for Fund 07632's owner. Failing to meet these conditions will generally invalidate the performance evaluation.

Alternatively, risk may be explicitly measured so that a single measure of performance taking both return and risk into account can be employed. This will allow benchmark portfolios of varying degrees of risk to be compared with the portfolio being evaluated.

RISK-ADJUSTED MEASURES OF PERFORMANCE

Having measured the periodic returns for a portfolio during an evaluation interval (say, quarterly returns for a four-year evaluation interval), the next step is to determine if these returns represent superior or inferior perform-

MONEY MATTERS
Custom Benchmark Portfolios

Investment management has become increasingly specialized in recent years. Managers have chosen not only to concentrate on specific asset classes (for example, stocks or bonds), but within those asset classes they have further focused their efforts on certain types of securities. This specialization has been particularly prevalent among domestic common stock managers. For example, some managers specialize in small, emerging growth company stocks. Others select only from certain industries, such as health care. These specializations have come to be known as "investment styles." Investment styles have significant ramifications for the evaluation of investment manager performance.

We might think about investment management as a fishing contest. Each angler has his or her own fishing hole (investment style). No one fishing hole is assumed to be any better than another, although from year to year the sizes and quantity of fish fluctuate independently in each hole. The anglers attempt to catch the largest fish from their fishing holes. How should we go about evaluating the proficiency of these anglers based on their catches? It would make little sense to directly compare the angler's respective catches. If Angler A's fishing hole was extremely well-stocked this year and Angler B's was not, Angler B would be at a tremendous disadvantage. More appropriately, we would like to compare what each angler caught against the opportunities available in their respective fishing holes. In other words, we want to take into account the impact of managers' investment styles on their performance.

Investment styles tend to dominate the performance of investment managers within a particular asset class. For example, suppose we split the domestic common stock market along two dimensions: market capitalization (share price times shares outstanding) and growth prospects. In 1991, the best-performing group was large, high-growth stocks, which returned 45.0%. Conversely, small, low-growth stocks returned 19.0%, a difference of 26 percentage points. Differences between investment styles of similar magnitudes can be found in other years. These differences are typically large enough so that no investment manager can hope to consistently overcome the performance effect of his or her investment style. Therefore, if we wish to evaluate a manager's investment skill we should take into account how the manager has performed relative to his or her investment style.

One means of dealing with this issue is to develop a comparison portfolio that specifically represents the manager's investment style. This comparison portfolio is referred to as a *custom benchmark portfolio*. The custom benchmark contains the types of securities from which the manager typically selects. Further, these securities are weighted in the custom benchmark in a manner similar to weights typically assigned by the manager. Moreover, the custom benchmark displays portfolio characteristics (for example, price-earnings ratios, earnings growth rates, and market capitalizations) consistent with the manager's actual portfolio.

Consider a manager whose investment style entails investing in large-capitalization, high-dividend-yield stocks. In building portfolios, the manager follows certain rules, some explicitly, others implicitly. For example, the manager does not buy stocks with less than $500 million in market capitalization. All stocks in the manager's portfolio must display at least a 6% dividend yield. The manager assigns each stock an equal weight in the portfolio. Further, to avoid overconcentrations, no industry may constitute more than 10% of the portfolio's market value.

A custom benchmark can be designed to reflect these characteristics of the manager's investment style. The custom benchmark might be composed of 300 stocks, as opposed to the manager's portfolio, which might contain only thirty stocks. The manager, in effect, has searched through his or her fishing hole and selected the thirty stocks that he or she thinks will perform the best. Our evaluation of the manager's performance will be based over time on how these thirty stocks perform relative to the 300 stocks.

This performance evaluation process takes advantage of a powerful paired-comparison test. Given a group of stocks, can the manager consistently identify the best-performing issues? The question is simple and the results easy to interpret. No special risk-adjusted performance measures are required. If the custom benchmark has been properly constructed, it exhibits a risk level consistent with that exhibited on average by the manager.

The primary drawback of custom benchmarks is the effort required to design them. Each manager's investment style has unique aspects, and not all of them are as explicit as those of the large-capitalization, high-yield manager discussed above. Typically, identifying those unique aspects involves examining past portfolios and engaging in lengthy discussions with the manager.

This effort, however, when effectively applied, can produce an effective performance evaluation tool. Moreover, custom benchmarks have uses outside of performance evaluation. For example, clients who hire more than one investment manager use custom benchmarks to examine how various investment styles fit together into an aggregate portfolio. This type of analysis permits a client to better understand and control the investment risks present in the client's total portfolio.

ance. In order to do this, an estimate of the portfolio's risk level during the evaluation interval is needed. Two kinds of risk can be estimated—the portfolio's market (or systematic) risk, measured by its beta, and the portfolio's total risk, measured by its standard deviation.

It is important to analyze risk appropriately. The key issue here is determining the impact of the portfolio on the client's overall level of risk. If the client has many other assets, then the market risk of the portfolio provides the relevant measure of the portfolio's impact on the client's overall level of risk. If, however, the portfolio provides the client's sole support, then its total risk is the relevant measure of risk. Risk-adjusted performance evaluation is generally based on one of these two viewpoints, taking either market risk or total risk into consideration.

Assume that there are T time periods in the evaluation interval (for example, $T = 16$ when there are four years of quarterly data) and let r_{pt} denote the return on the portfolio during period t. The average return on the portfolio, denoted ar_p, is simply:

$$ar_p = \frac{\sum_{t=1}^{T} r_{pt}}{T}. \tag{18.5}$$

Having calculated ar_p, the ex post (that is, "after the fact" or historical) standard deviation can be calculated as:

$$\sigma_p = \left[\frac{\sum_{t=1}^{T} (r_{pt} - ar_p)^2}{T - 1} \right]^{1/2}. \tag{18.6}$$

This estimate of the portfolio's standard deviation can be used as an indication of the amount of total risk that the portfolio had during the evaluation interval.[2] It can be compared directly with the standard deviations of other portfolios, as illustrated in Figure 18-2. (This figure is to be interpreted in the same manner as Figure 18-1).

The returns of a portfolio may also be compared with those of a substitute for the market portfolio, such as Standard & Poor's 500, in order to determine the portfolio's ex post beta during the evaluation interval. Denoting the excess return on the portfolio during period t as $er_{pt} = r_{pt} - r_{ft}$, the return on the S&P 500 (or some other market substitute) during period t as r_{Mt}, and the excess return on the S&P 500 during period t as $er_{Mt} = r_{Mt} - r_{ft}$, this beta can be estimated as follows:

$$\beta_p = \frac{\left(T \sum_{t=1}^{T} er_{Mt}\, er_{pt}\right) - \left(\sum_{t=1}^{T} er_{pt} \sum_{t=1}^{T} er_{Mt}\right)}{\left(T \sum_{t=1}^{T} er_{Mt}^2\right) - \left(\sum_{t=1}^{T} er_{Mt}\right)^2}. \tag{18.7}$$

[2]Sometimes the excess return for a portfolio, which is equal to its return minus the riskfree rate ($= r_{pt} - r_{ft}$), is used instead of r_{pt} in equation (18.5) to determine the average excess return (denoted aer_p). Then, the summation in the numerator of equation (18.6) is carried out using $[(r_{pt} - r_{ft}) - aer_p]^2$ instead of $(r_{pt} - ar_p)^2$. The resulting number is the standard deviation of excess returns, which is sometimes used as an estimate of the total risk of the portfolio. Typically, the two standard deviations are quite similar in numerical value.

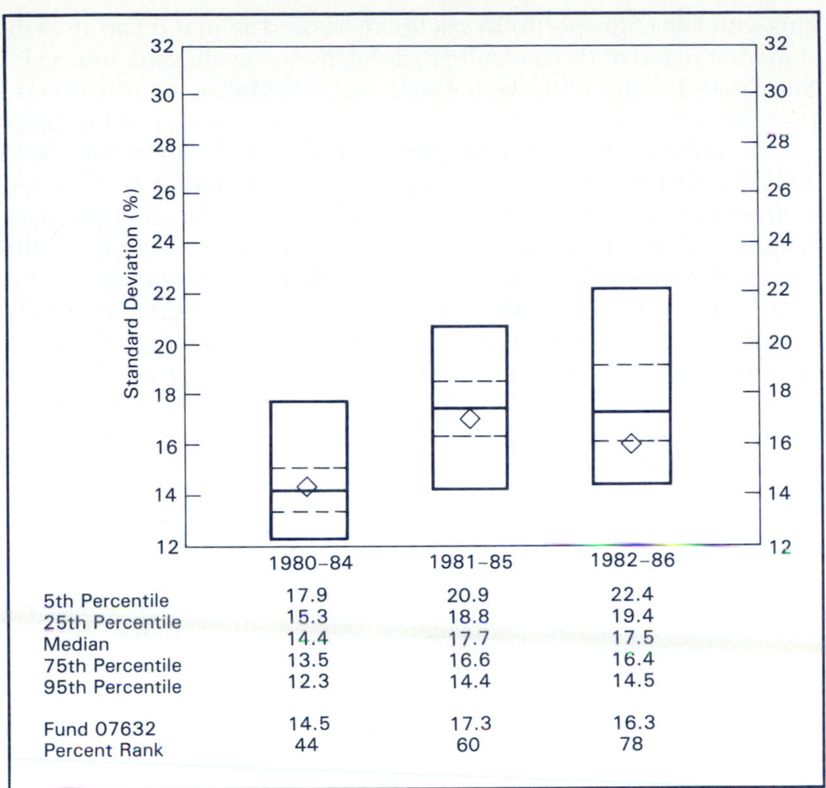

	1980–84	1981–85	1982–86
5th Percentile	17.9	20.9	22.4
25th Percentile	15.3	18.8	19.4
Median	14.4	17.7	17.5
75th Percentile	13.5	16.6	16.4
95th Percentile	12.3	14.4	14.5
Fund 07632	14.5	17.3	16.3
Percent Rank	44	60	78

FIGURE 18-2
Comparing Standard Deviations of Equity Portfolios

Source: Adapted from SEI, *Funds Evaluation Service.*

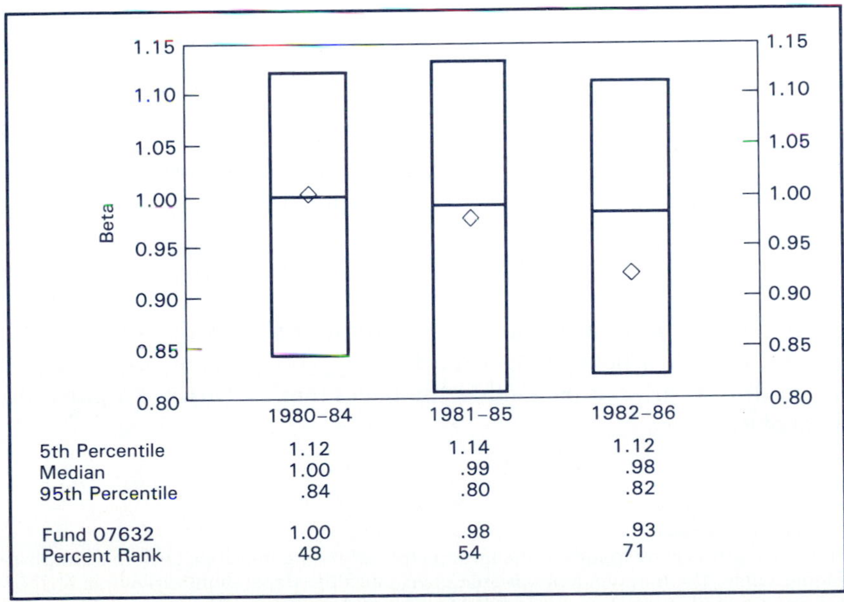

	1980–84	1981–85	1982–86
5th Percentile	1.12	1.14	1.12
Median	1.00	.99	.98
95th Percentile	.84	.80	.82
Fund 07632	1.00	.98	.93
Percent Rank	48	54	71

FIGURE 18-3
Comparing Betas of Equity Portfolios

This estimate of the portfolio's beta can be used as an indication of the amount of market risk that the portfolio had during the evaluation interval.[3] It can be compared directly with the betas of other portfolios, as illustrated in Figure 18-3 (this figure is to be interpreted in the same manner as Figure 18-1).

While a portfolio's return and a measure of its risk can be compared individually with those of other portfolios, as in Figures 18-1 through 18-3, it is often not clear how the portfolio performed on a risk-adjusted basis relative to these other portfolios. For the fund shown in the figures, the average percent rank for the portfolio's return over the five years ending in 1986 is 36% = (17 + 56 + 39 + 16 +50)/5. Over the same period, its standard deviation put it in the 78th percent rank. Assuming that the client is concerned with total risk, how does he or she interpret these percent ranks? In the case of the return, the portfolio was slightly above average; in terms of standard deviation, it was less risky than approximately 3/4 of the other portfolios. Overall, this suggests that the portfolio did better on a risk-adjusted basis than the others, but it does not give the client a clear and precise sense of how much better.

Such a sense can be conveyed by certain CAPM-based measures of portfolio performance. Each one of these measures provides an estimate of a portfolio's risk-adjusted performance, thereby allowing the client to see how the portfolio performed relative to other portfolios and relative to the market. They will be presented next.

Ex Post Characteristic Lines

Over an evaluation interval, an ex post Security Market Line (SML) can be estimated by determining the average riskfree rate and market return:

$$ar_f = \frac{\sum_{t=1}^{T} r_{ft}}{T} \tag{18.8}$$

$$ar_M = \frac{\sum_{t=1}^{T} r_{Mt}}{T}. \tag{18.9}$$

Once these averages have been calculated, the ex post SML is simply the equation of the line going through the points (0, ar_f) and (1, ar_M):

$$ar_p^e = ar_f + (ar_M - ar_f)\beta_p. \tag{18.10}$$

Equivalently, the equilibrium average return during this interval of time for a portfolio with a beta of β_p would simply be equal to $ar_f + (ar_M - ar_f)\beta_p$. Accordingly, ar_p^e can be used as the benchmark return for a portfolio with a beta of β_p.

---

[3]Equation (18.7) corresponds to the formula for estimating the slope term in a simple regression model where the independent variable is er_{Mt} and the dependent variable is er_{pt}. Sometimes returns are used in equation (18.7), where er_{Mt} is replaced by r_{Mt} and er_{pt} is replaced by r_{pt}. In this situation, the beta corresponds to the slope term in the *market model* for the portfolio (as discussed in Chapter 8). Typically, the two betas are quite similar in numerical value.

Panel A of Table 18-1 presents an example by using the quarterly returns for the S&P 500 over the interval 1982 to 1985, along with corresponding returns on 90-day Treasury bills. Using equations (18.8) and (18.9), the average riskfree return and market return were, respectively, 2.23% and 4.88%. Inserting these values into equation (18.10), the ex post SML for this time interval was:

$$\begin{aligned} ar_p^e &= 2.23 + (4.88 - 2.23)\beta_p \\ &= 2.23 + 2.65\beta_p. \end{aligned} \tag{18.11}$$

Thus, after estimating a portfolio's ex post beta and entering this value on the right-hand side of equation (18.11), a benchmark return for the portfolio can be determined. For example, a portfolio with a beta of .8 during 1982 to 1985 would have a benchmark return of 4.35% = 2.23 + (2.65 × .8). Figure 18-4 presents a graph of the ex post SML given by equation (18.11).

If the average return on a portfolio was ar_p, calculated as shown in equation (18.5), then one measure of its risk-adjusted performance would be the difference between its average return and its corresponding equilibrium or benchmark return. This difference is generally referred to as the portfolio's **ex post alpha** (or differential return), and is denoted α_p:

ex post alpha

$$\alpha_p = ar_p - ar_p^e. \tag{18.12}$$

A positive value of α_p for a portfolio would indicate that the portfolio had an average return greater than the benchmark return, suggesting that its performance was superior. On the other hand, a negative value of α_p would indicate that the portfolio had an average return less than the benchmark return, suggesting that its performance was inferior.[4]

By substituting the right-hand side of equation (18.10) for ar_p^e in equation (18.12), it can be seen that a portfolio's ex post alpha is equal to:

$$\alpha_p = ar_p - [ar_f + (ar_M - ar_f)\beta_p]. \tag{18.13}$$

After determining the values for α_p and β_p for a portfolio, the ex post **characteristic line** for the portfolio can be written as:

characteristic line

$$r_p - r_f = \alpha_p + \beta_p(r_M - r_f). \tag{18.14}$$

The characteristic line is similar to the market model except that the portfolio's returns and the market index's returns are expressed in excess of the riskfree return. Graphically, the characteristic line formulation is the equation of a straight line where $(r_M - r_f)$ is measured on the horizontal axis and $(r_p - r_f)$ is measured on the vertical axis. Furthermore, the line has a vertical intercept of α_p and a slope of β_p.

As an example, consider the performance of the hypothetical portfolio "First Fund," indicated in panel A of Table 18-1, for the evaluation interval of 1982 to 1985. During this interval, the First Fund had an average quarterly return of 3.93%. Using equation (18.7), it can be shown that First Fund had a

[4]This measure of performance is sometimes known as the "Jensen coefficient" because it was developed by Michael C. Jensen in "The Performance of Mutual Funds in the Period 1945–1964," *Journal of Finance*, 23, no. 2 (May 1968): 389–416.

TABLE 18-1
The Ex Post Characteristic Line for the First Fund, 1982–1985

A. RETURN DATA

Quarter		Treasury Bill Return	First Fund Return	First Fund Excess Return	S&P 500 Return	S&P 500 Excess Return
1982	1	2.97%	−8.77%	−11.74%	−5.86%	−8.83%
	2	3.06	−6.03	−9.09	−2.94	−6.00
	3	2.85	14.14	11.29	13.77	10.92
	4	1.88	24.96	23.08	14.82	12.94
1983	1	1.90	3.71	1.81	11.91	10.01
	2	2.00	10.65	8.65	11.55	9.55
	3	2.22	−.22	−2.44	−.78	−3.00
	4	2.11	.27	−1.84	.02	−2.09
1984	1	2.16	−3.08	−5.24	−2.52	−4.68
	2	2.34	−6.72	−9.06	−1.85	−4.19
	3	2.44	8.58	6.29	8.73	6.29
	4	2.40	1.15	−1.25	1.63	−.77
1985	1	1.89	7.87	5.98	10.82	8.93
	2	1.94	5.92	3.98	7.24	5.30
	3	1.72	−3.10	−4.82	−2.78	−4.50
	4	1.75	13.61	11.86	14.36	12.61

B. CALCULATIONS[a]

Quarter		First Fund Excess Returns = Y (1)	S&P 500 Excess Returns = X (2)	Y^2 (3)	X^2 (4)	$Y \times X$ (5)
1982	1	−11.74%	−8.83%	137.83	77.93	103.66
	2	−9.09	−6.00	82.63	36.05	54.54
	3	11.29	10.92	127.46	119.26	123.29
	4	23.08	12.94	532.69	167.53	298.66
1983	1	1.81	10.01	3.28	100.11	18.12
	2	8.65	9.55	74.82	91.28	82.61
	3	−2.44	−3.00	5.95	8.97	7.32
	4	−1.84	−2.09	3.39	4.35	3.85
1984	1	−5.24	−4.68	27.46	21.94	24.52
	2	−9.06	−4.19	82.08	17.54	37.96
	3	6.14	6.29	37.70	39.53	38.62
	4	−1.25	−.77	1.56	.60	.96
1985	1	5.98	8.93	35.76	79.82	53.40
	2	3.98	5.30	15.84	28.07	21.09
	3	−4.82	−4.50	23.23	20.25	21.69
	4	11.86	12.61	140.66	158.93	149.56
Sum (Σ) =		27.31 = ΣY	42.49 = ΣX	1,332.34 = ΣY^2	972.16 = ΣX^2	1,039.85 = ΣXY

beta of 1.13. Having an average beta over the sixteen quarters that is greater than the market portfolio's beta of 1 indicates that First Fund was relatively aggressive (if it were less than 1, it would have been relatively defensive).

Given these values for its beta and average return, the location of First Fund in Figure 18-4 is represented by the point having coordinates (1.13, 3.93), denoted FF. The exact vertical distance from FF to the ex post SML can be calculated by using equation (18.13):

$$\begin{aligned}\alpha_p &= ar_p - [ar_f + (ar_M - ar_f)\beta_p] \\ &= 3.93 - [2.23 + (4.88 - 2.23)1.13] \\ &= -1.29\%.\end{aligned}$$

TABLE 18-1
Continued

1. Beta:

$$\frac{(T \times \Sigma XY) - (\Sigma Y \times \Sigma X)}{(T \times \Sigma X^2) - (\Sigma X)^2} = \frac{(16 \times 1{,}039.85) - (27.31 \times 42.49)}{(16 \times 972.16) - (42.49)^2} = 1.13$$

2. Alpha:

$$[\Sigma Y/T] - [\text{Beta} \times (\Sigma X/T)] = [27.31/16] - [1.13 \times (42.49/16)] = -1.29$$

3. Standard Deviation of Random Error Term:

$$\{[\Sigma Y^2 - (\text{Alpha} \times \Sigma Y) - (\text{Beta} \times \Sigma XY)]/[T-2]\}^{1/2}$$
$$= \{[1{,}332.34 - (-1.29 \times 42.49) - (1.13 \times 1{,}039.85)]/[16-2]\}^{1/2} = 3.75$$

4. Standard Error of Beta:

$$\text{Standard Deviation of Random Error Term}/\{\Sigma X^2 - [(\Sigma X)^2/T]\}^{1/2}$$
$$= 3.75/\{972.16 - [(42.49)^2/16]\}^{1/2} = .13$$

5. Standard Error of Alpha:

$$\text{Standard Deviation of Random Error Term}/\{T - [(\Sigma X)^2/\Sigma X^2]\}^{1/2}$$
$$= 3.75/\{16 - [(42.49)^2/972.16]\}^{1/2} = 1.00$$

6. Correlation Coefficient:

$$\frac{(T \times \Sigma XY) - (\Sigma Y \times \Sigma X)}{\{[(T \times \Sigma Y^2) - (\Sigma Y)^2] \times [(T \times \Sigma X^2) - (\Sigma X)^2]\}^{1/2}}$$
$$= \frac{(16 \times 1{,}039.85) - (27.31 \times 42.49)}{\{[(16 \times 1{,}332.34) - (27.31)^2] \times [(16 \times 972.16) - (42.49)^2]\}^{1/2}} = .92$$

7. Coefficient of Determination:

$$(\text{Correlation Coefficient})^2 = (.92)^2 = .85$$

8. Coefficient of Nondetermination:

$$1 - \text{Coefficient of Determination} = 1 - .85 = .15$$

[a]All summations are to be carried out over t, where t goes from 1 to T (in this example, $t = 1, \ldots, 16$).

Since FF lies below the ex post SML, its ex post alpha is negative and its performance would be viewed as inferior.[5] Using equation (18.14), the ex post characteristic line for First Fund would be:

$$r_p - r_f = -1.29 + 1.13(r_M - r_f).$$

Figure 18-5 provides an illustration of this line.[6]

The method for determining a portfolio's ex post alpha, beta, and characteristic line suggests the use of a four-step procedure. First, having gathered the necessary return data, the average market return and riskfree rate

[5]Alternatively, if FF's average return had been 6%, then its coordinates would have been (1.13, 6.00), placing it above the ex post SML. In this situation, FF's ex post alpha would have been .78%, and its performance would have been viewed as superior.

[6]An alternative measure of performance involves dividing the ex post alpha by an estimate of the ex post unique (or unsystematic) risk of the portfolio. This measure, known as the *appraisal ratio*, would be equal to $-1.29/3.75 = -.34$ for First Fund. Comparisons can be made with the value of the appraisal ratio for the market portfolio (its value is defined to be 0) and other portfolios. Note that a positive value indicates superior performance, and that the larger the value, the better the performance. See Jack L. Treynor and Fischer Black, "How to Use Security Analysis to Improve Portfolio Selection," *Journal of Business*, 46, no. 1 (January 1973): 66–86.

FIGURE 18-4
Performance Evaluation Using the Ex Post SML

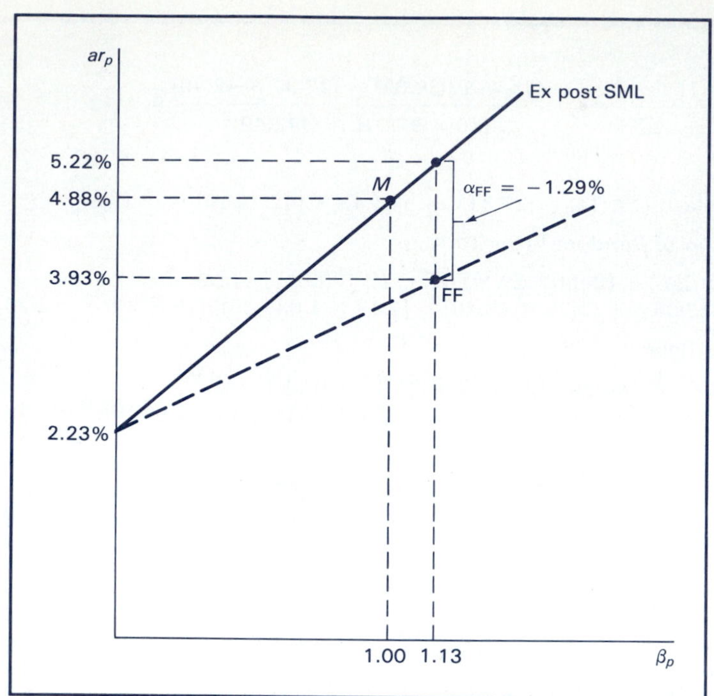

FIGURE 18-5
Ex Post Characteristic Line for First Fund

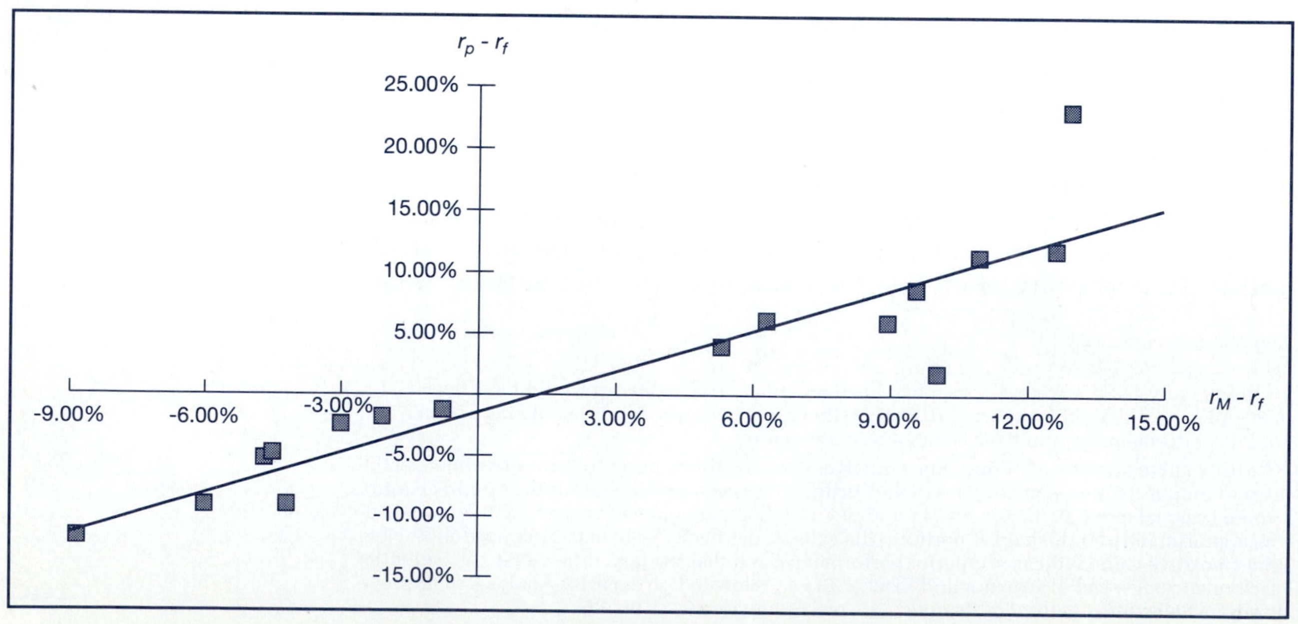

can be determined with equations (18.8) and (18.9). Second, the portfolio's ex post beta can be determined by using the formula in equation (18.7). Third, the portfolio's ex post alpha can be determined by using the formula given in equation (18.13). Fourth, these values for alpha and beta can be inserted in equation (18.14) in order to determine the portfolio's ex post characteristic line. However, there is a simpler method for determining a portfolio's ex post alpha, beta, and characteristic line that also provides a number of other pieces of information relating to the portfolio's performance. This method involves the use of **simple linear regression,** and corresponds to the method presented in Chapters 8 and 13 for estimating the market model for an individual security.

simple linear regression

With this method, the excess return on portfolio p in a given period t is viewed as having three components. The first component is the portfolio's alpha, the second component is a risk premium equal to the excess return on the market times the portfolio's beta, and the third component is a random error team.[7] These three components can be seen on the right-hand side of the following equation:

$$r_{pt} - r_{ft} = \alpha_p + \beta_p(r_{Mt} - r_{ft}) + \epsilon_{pt}. \tag{18.15}$$

Since α_p and β_p are assumed to be constant during the evaluation interval, equation (18.15) can be viewed as a regression equation. Accordingly, there are certain standard formulas for estimating α_p, β_p, and a number of other statistical parameters associated with the regression equation.

Panel B of Table 18-1 presents these formulas, with First Fund being used as an example. As can be seen, the formulas indicate that First Fund's ex post alpha and beta were equal to −1.29 and 1.13, respectively, over the 1982 to 1985 time interval. These values are the same as those arising when equations (18.7) and (18.13) were used earlier. Indeed, they will always result in the same values.

Figure 18-5 presents a scatter diagram of the excess returns on First Fund and the S&P 500. Based on equation (18.15), the regression equation for First Fund is:

$$r_{FF} - r_f = -1.29 + 1.13(r_M - r_f) + \epsilon_{FF} \tag{18.16}$$

where −1.29 and 1.13 are the estimated ex post alpha and beta for First Fund over the 1982 to 1985 time interval. As mentioned earlier, also shown in the figure is the ex post characteristic line for First Fund, a line that is derived by the use of simple linear regression:

$$r_{FF} - r_f = -1.29 + 1.13(r_M - r_f). \tag{18.17}$$

The vertical distance between each point in the scatter diagram and the regression line represents an estimate of the size of the random error term for the corresponding quarter. The exact distance can be found by rewriting equation (18.16) as:

$$\epsilon_{FF} = (r_{FF} - r_f) - [-1.29 + 1.13(r_M - r_f)]. \tag{18.18}$$

[7]The random error term can be viewed as a number that arises from a spin of a roulette wheel, where the numbers on the wheel are symmetrically distributed around zero. That is, the expected outcome from a spin of the roulette wheel is zero; the standard deviation associated with the wheel is denoted $\sigma_{\epsilon p}$.

For example, in the third quarter of 1984 the excess return on First Fund and the S&P 500 were 6.14% and 6.29%, respectively. The value of ϵ_{FF} for that quarter can be calculated by using equation (18.18) as follows:

$$\begin{aligned}\epsilon_{FF} &= (6.14) - [-1.29 + 1.13(6.29)] \\ &= .32\%.\end{aligned}$$

The value of ϵ_{FF} can be calculated similarly for the other fifteen quarters of the evaluation interval. The standard deviation of the resulting set of sixteen numbers is an estimate of the standard deviation of the random error term (also known as the residual standard deviation), and is shown in panel B of Table 18-1 to be equal to 3.75%. This number can be viewed as an estimate of the ex post unique (or unsystematic or nonmarket) risk of First Fund.

The regression line for First Fund that is shown in Figure 18-5 is the line of best fit for the scatter diagram. What is meant by "best fit"? Given that a straight line is defined by its intercept and slope, it means that there are no other values for alpha and beta that fits the scatter diagram any better than this one. In simple regression, this means that there is no line that could be drawn such that the resulting standard deviation of the random error term is smaller than the one of best fit.

It should be pointed out that a portfolio's "true" ex post beta cannot be observed. All that can be done is to estimate its value. Thus, even if a portfolio's "true" beta remained the same forever, its estimated value, obtained in the manner illustrated in Table 18-1 and Figure 18-5, would still change from time to time because of errors (known as sampling errors) in estimating it. For example, if the sixteen quarters for 1983 to 1986 were examined, the resulting estimated beta for First Fund would almost certainly be different from 1.13, the estimated value for 1982 to 1985.

The Standard Error of Beta shown in Table 18-1 attempts to indicate the extent of such estimation errors. Given a number of necessary assumptions (for example, the "true" beta did not change during the estimation period of 1982 to 1985), the chances are roughly two out of three that the "true" beta is within one standard error, plus or minus, of the estimated beta. Thus, First Fund's "true" beta is likely to be between the values of 1.00 = 1.13 − .13 and 1.26 = 1.13 + .13. Similarly, the value under Standard Error of Alpha provides an indication of the magnitude of the possible sampling error that has been made in estimating it.

The value under Correlation Coefficient provides an indication of how closely the excess returns on First Fund were associated with the excess returns on the S&P 500. Since its range is between −1 and +1, the value for First Fund of .92 indicates a strong positive relationship between First Fund and the S&P 500. That is, larger excess returns for First Fund seem to have been closely associated with larger excess returns for the S&P 500.

The Coefficient of Determination represents the proportion of variation in the excess return on First Fund that is related to the variation in the excess return on the S&P 500. That is, it shows how much of the movement in First Fund's excess returns can be explained by movements in the excess returns on the S&P 500. With a value of .85, it can be seen that 85% of the movement in the excess return on First Fund over 1982 to 1985 can be attributed to movement in the excess return on the S&P 500.

Since the Coefficient of Nondetermination is 1 minus the coefficient of determination, it represents the proportion of movement in the excess return on First Fund that does not result from movement in the excess return on the

S&P 500. Thus, 15% of the movement in First Fund cannot be attributed to movement in the S&P 500.

While Table 18-1 shows the formulas for calculating all these values, it should be pointed out that there are many different software packages that can quickly carry out these calculations. The only substantive effort involves gathering all the return data shown in panel A of Table 18-1 and then entering them into a computer.

The Reward-to-Volatility Ratio

reward-to-volatility ratio

Closely related to the differential return measure of portfolio performance is a measure known as the **reward-to-volatility ratio.**[8] This measure, denoted $RVOL_p$, also uses the ex post Security Market Line to form a benchmark for performance evaluation, but in a somewhat different manner. The calculation of the reward-to-volatility ratio for a portfolio involves dividing its average excess return by its market risk as follows:

$$RVOL_p = \frac{ar_p - ar_f}{\beta_p}. \qquad (18.19)$$

Here, the beta of the portfolio can be determined using the formula in equation (18.7).

Continuing with the example of First Fund, it had been noted earlier that its average return for the evaluation interval of 1982 to 1985 was 3.93%. Furthermore, it had been noted that the average Treasury bill rate was 2.23%. Thus, the average excess return for First Fund was 1.70% = 3.93% − 2.23% and, given a beta of 1.13, its reward-to-volatility ratio was 1.50% = 1.70%/1.13.

The reward-to-volatility ratio corresponds to the slope of a line orginating at the average riskfree rate and going through the point (β_p, ar_p). This can be seen by noting that the slope of a line is easily determined if two points on the line are known—it is simply the vertical distance between the two points ("rise") divided by the horizontal distance between the two points ("run"). In this case, the vertical distance is $ar_p - ar_f$ and the horizontal distance is $\beta_p - 0 = \beta_p$, so the slope is $(ar_p - ar_f)/\beta_p$ and thus corresponds to the formula for $RVOL_p$ given in equation (18.19). Note that the value being measured on the horizontal axis is β_p and the value being measured on the vertical axis is ar_p, suggesting that the line can be drawn on the same diagram as the ex post SML.

In the First Fund example, remember that the ex post SML for 1982 to 1985 was shown by the solid line in Figure 18-4. Also appearing in this figure was the point denoted FF, corresponding to (β_p, ar_p) = (1.13, 3.93%) for First Fund. The dashed line in this figure originates from the point $(0, ar_f)$ = (0, 2.23%), goes through FF, and has a slope of (3.93% − 2.23%)/1.13 = 1.50% that corresponds to the value noted earlier for $RVOL_p$.

The benchmark for comparison with this measure of performance is the slope of the ex post SML. Since this line goes through the points $(0, ar_f)$ and $(1, ar_M)$, its slope is simply $(ar_M - ar_f)/(1 - 0) = (ar_M - ar_f)$. If $RVOL_p$ is greater than this value, the portfolio lies above the ex post SML, indicating that it has

[8]This measure of performance is sometimes known as the "Treynor ratio" because it was developed by Jack L. Treynor in "How to Rate Management of Investment Funds," *Harvard Business Review*, 43, no. 1 (January–February 1965): 63–75.

outperformed the market. Alternatively, if $RVOL_p$ is less than this value, the portfolio lies below the ex post SML, indicating that it has not performed as well as the market.

In the case of First Fund, the benchmark is $(ar_M - ar_f)$ = (4.88% − 2.23%) = 2.65%. Since $RVOL_p$ for First Fund is less than the benchmark (1.50% < 2.65%), according to this measure of portfolio performance, First Fund did not perform as well as the market.

In comparing the two measures of performance that are based on the ex post SML, α_p and $RVOL_p$, it should be noted that they will *always* give the same assessment of a portfolio's performance relative to the market portfolio. That is, if one measure indicates that the portfolio outperformed the market, so will the other. Similarly, if one measure indicates that the portfolio did not perform as well as the market, the other measure will show the same thing. This can be seen by noting that any portfolio with a positive ex post alpha (an indication of superior performance) lies *above* the ex post SML and thus must have a slope *greater* than the slope of the ex post SML (also an indication of superior performance). Similarly, any portfolio with a negative ex post alpha (an indication of inferior performance) lies *below* the ex post SML and thus must have a slope *less* than the slope of the ex post SML (also an indication of inferior performance).

However, it should also be noted that it is possible for the two measures to *rank* portfolios differently on the basis of performance simply because the calculations are different. For example, if Second Fund had a beta of 1.5 and an average return of 4.86%, its ex post alpha would be −1.34% = 4.86% − [2.23 + (4.88 − 2.23)1.5]. Thus, its performance appears to be worse than First Fund since it has a smaller ex post alpha (−1.34% < −1.29%). However, its reward-to-volatility ratio of 1.75% = (4.86% − 2.23%)/1.5 is larger than the reward-to-volatility of 1.50% for First Fund, suggesting that its performance was better than First Fund.

The Reward-to-Variability Ratio

Both measures of risk-adjusted performance described so far, ex post alpha (that is, differential return) and the reward-to-volatility ratio, use benchmarks that are based on the ex post Security Market Line (SML). Accordingly, they measure returns relative to the market risk of the portfolio. In contrast, the **reward-to-variability ratio** is a measure of risk-adjusted performance that uses a benchmark based on the ex post Capital Market Line (CML).[9] This means that it measures returns relative to the total risk of the portfolio, where total risk is the standard deviation of portfolio returns.

reward-to-variability ratio

In order to use the reward-to-variability ratio ($RVAR_p$), the location of the ex post CML must be determined. This line goes through two points on a graph where average return is measured on the vertical axis and standard deviation is measured on the horizontal axis. The first point is the vertical intercept of the line, and corresponds to the average riskfree rate during the evaluation interval. The second point corresponds to the location of the market portfolio, meaning that its coordinates are the average return and standard deviation of return for the market portfolio during the evaluation

[9]This measure of performance is sometimes known as the "Sharpe ratio" because it was developed by William F. Sharpe in "Mutual Fund Performance," *Journal of Business*, 39, no. 1 (January 1966): 119–38.

interval, or (σ_M, ar_M). Since the ex post CML goes through these two points, its slope can readily be calculated as the vertical distance between the two points divided by the horizontal distance between the two points, or $(ar_M - ar_f)/(\sigma_M - 0) = (ar_M - ar_f)/\sigma_M$. Given a vertical intercept of ar_f, the equation of this line is:

$$ar_p^e = ar_f + \frac{ar_M - ar_f}{\sigma_M}\sigma_p. \tag{18.20}$$

In the example shown in Table 18-1, the average return and standard deviation for the S&P 500, calculated using equations (18.5) and (18.6), were 4.88% and 7.39%, respectively. Since the average return on Treasury bills was 2.23%, the ex post CML for 1982 to 1985 was:

$$\begin{aligned} ar_p^e &= 2.23 + \frac{4.88 - 2.23}{7.39}\sigma_p \\ &= 2.23 + .36\sigma_p. \end{aligned} \tag{18.21}$$

Figure 18-6 presents a graph of this line.

Having determined the location of the ex post CML, the average return and standard deviation of the portfolio being evaluated can be determined next by using equations (18.5) and (18.6). With these values in hand, the portfolio can be located on the same graph as the ex post CML. In the case of First Fund, its average return and standard deviation were 3.93% and 9.08%, respectively. Thus, in Figure 18-6 its location corresponds to the point having coordinates (9.08%, 3.93%), which is denoted FF.

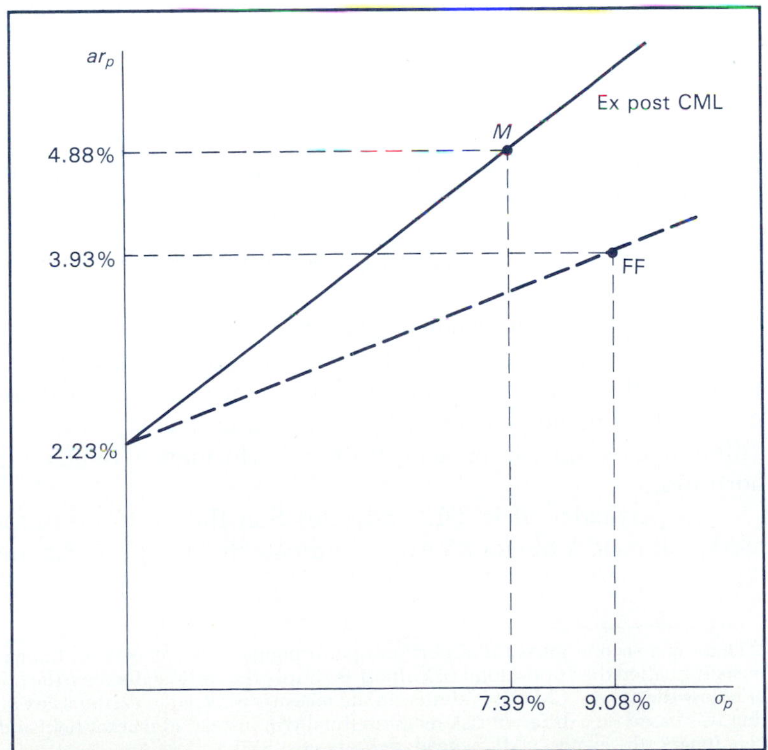

FIGURE 18-6
Performance Evaluation Using the Ex Post CML

The calculation of the reward-to-variability ratio ($RVAR_p$) is analogous to the calculation of the reward-to-volatility ratio ($RVOL_p$) described earlier. Specifically, $RVOL_p$ involves dividing the portfolio's average excess return by its beta, while $RVAR_p$ involves dividing the portfolio's average excess return by its standard deviation:

$$RVAR_p = \frac{ar_p - ar_f}{\sigma_p}. \tag{18.22}$$

Note that $RVAR_p$ corresponds to the slope of a line originating at the average riskfree rate and going through a point having coordinates of (σ_p, ar_p). This can be seen by noting that the slope of this line is simply the vertical distance between the two points divided by the horizontal distance between the two points, or $(ar_p - ar_f)/(\sigma_p - 0) = (ar_p - ar_f)/\sigma_p$, which corresponds to the formula for $RVAR_p$ given in equation (18.22). Since the value being measured on the horizontal axis is σ_p and the value being measured on the vertical axis is ar_p, the line can be drawn on the same diagram as the ex post CML.

In the First Fund example, recall that the ex post CML for 1982 to 1985 was shown by the solid line in Figure 18-6. Also appearing in this figure was the point denoted FF, corresponding to $(\sigma_p, ar_p) = (9.08\%, 3.93\%)$ for First Fund. The dashed line in this figure originates from the point $(0, ar_f) = (0, 2.23\%)$ and goes through FF; the slope of this line is simply $(3.93 - 2.23)/9.08 = .19$.

Since the ex post CML represents various combinations of riskfree lending or borrowing with investing in the market portfolio, it can be used to provide a benchmark for the reward-to-variability ratio in a manner similar to the SML-based benchmark for the reward-to-volatility ratio. As noted earlier, the slope of the ex post CML is $(ar_M - ar_f)/\sigma_M$. If $RVAR_p$ is greater than this value, the portfolio lies above the ex post CML, indicating that it has outperformed the market. Alternatively, if $RVAR_p$ is less than this value, the portfolio lies below the ex post CML, indicating that it has not performed as well as the market.[10]

In the case of First Fund, the benchmark is $(4.88 - 2.23)/7.39 = .36$. Since $RVAR_p$ is less than the benchmark $(.19 < .36)$, First Fund did not perform as well as the market, according to this risk-adjusted measure of portfolio performance.

Comparing the Risk-Adjusted Measures of Performance

The measures of performance that are based on the ex post SML, α_p and $RVOL_p$, can be compared with the measure of performance that is based on the ex post CML, $RVAR_p$. Focusing on $RVOL_p$ (the comparison also applies to α_p), it should be noted that in certain situations, $RVOL_p$ and $RVAR_p$ can give different assessments of a portfolio's performance relative to the market portfolio.

In particular, if $RVOL_p$ indicates that the portfolio outperformed the market, it is possible for $RVAR_p$ to indicate that the portfolio did not perform

[10]There is a second measure of portfolio performance that is based on the ex post CML. This measure, called the *ex post total risk alpha*, is simply the vertical distance the portfolio lies above or below the ex post CML. It is similar to the measure referred to earlier as ex post alpha, except that it is based on a different risk measure (total risk instead of market risk) and uses a different benchmark (the ex post CML instead of the ex post SML).

as well as the market. The reason for this is that the portfolio may have a relatively large amount of *unique* risk. Such risk would not be a factor in determining the value of $RVOL_p$ for the portfolio, since only *market* risk is in the denominator. However, such risk would be included in the denominator of $RVAR_p$ for the portfolio, since this measure is based on *total* risk (that is, both market and unique risk). Thus, a portfolio with a low amount of market risk could have a high amount of total risk, resulting in a relatively high $RVOL_p$ (due to the low amount of market risk) and a low $RVAR_p$ (due to the high amount of total risk). Accordingly, $RVOL_p$ could indicate that the portfolio outperformed the market while at the same time $RVAR_p$ indicates that it did not perform as well as the market.[11]

As an example, consider Third Fund, which had an average return of 4.5%, a beta of .8, and a standard deviation of 18%. Accordingly, $RVOL_{TF} = (4.5\% - 2.23\%)/.8 = 2.71\%$, indicating that Third Fund outperformed the market portfolio since the benchmark is $(4.88\% - 2.23\%)/1.0 = 2.65\%$. However, $RVAR_{TF} = (4.5\% - 2.23\%)/18\% = .12$, indicating that Third Fund did not perform as well as the market portfolio since the benchmark is $(4.88\% - 2.23\%)/7.39\% = .36$. The reason for the difference can be seen by noting Third Fund's low beta relative to the market $(.8 < 1.0)$ but high standard deviation relative to the market $(18\% > 7.39\%)$. This suggests that Third Fund had a relatively high level of unique risk.

It also follows that it is possible for $RVOL_p$ and $RVAR_p$ to rank two or more portfolios differently on the basis of their performance. This is because these two measures of risk-adjusted performance utilize different types of risk.

Continuing with the example, recall that earlier it was shown that First Fund had an average return of 3.93%, a beta of 1.13, and a standard deviation of 9.08%. Thus, $RVOL_{FF} = (3.93\% - 2.23\%)/1.13 = 1.50\%$, which is less than $RVOL_{TF} = 2.65\%$, thereby indicating that First Fund ranked lower than Third Fund. However, $RVAR_{FF} = (3.93\% - 2.23\%)/9.08\% = .13$, which is greater than $RVAR_{TF} = .12$, thereby indicating that First Fund ranked higher than Third Fund.

Did Third Fund do better or worse than the market on a risk-adjusted basis? And did Third Fund perform better or worse than First Fund? The answer to these two questions lies in identifying the appropriate measure of risk for the client. If the client has many other assets, then beta is the relevant measure of risk and performance should be based on $RVOL_p$. To such a client, Third Fund should be viewed as a superior performer relative to both the market and First Fund. However, if the client has few other assets, then standard deviation is the relevant measure of risk and performance should be based on $RVAR_{p.}$ To such a client, Third Fund should be viewed as an inferior performer relative to both the market and First Fund.

MARKET TIMING

A successful market timer positions a portfolio to have a relatively high beta during a market rise and a relatively low beta during a market decline. Why?

[11]Since the market portfolio does not have any unique risk, it can be shown that if $RVOL_p$ indicates that a portfolio did not perform as well as the market, then $RVAR_p$ must also indicate that the portfolio did not perform as well as the market. This is because a portfolio with a relatively high amount of market risk will also have a relatively high amount of total risk.

Because, as noted earlier, the expected return on a portfolio is a linear function of its beta:

$$\bar{r}_p = \alpha_p + r_f + (\bar{r}_M - r_f)\beta_p. \tag{18.23}$$

This means that a high-beta portfolio will have a relatively high expected return if a market rise (that is, $\bar{r}_M > r_f$) is anticipated. Similarly, a low-beta portfolio will have a relatively high expected return if a market decline (that is, $\bar{r}_m < r_f$) is anticipated. Accordingly, the portfolio of a successful timer will outperform a benchmark portfolio that has a constant beta equal to the average beta of the timer's portfolio.

For example, if the market timer successfully set the portfolio beta at zero when $\bar{r}_M < r_f$ and at two when $\bar{r}_M > r_f$, the return on the portfolio would be higher than the return on a portfolio having a beta constantly equal to one. Unfortunately, if the market timer alters the portfolio's beta in ways unrelated to subsequent market moves (for example, sometimes setting the beta equal to zero when $\bar{r}_M > r_f$ and equal to two when $\bar{r}_M < r_f$), then the timer's portfolio will not perform as well as a constant beta portfolio.

To "time the market," either the average beta of the stocks held in the portfolio can be changed or the relative amounts invested in the riskfree asset and stocks can be altered. For example, to increase the beta of a portfolio, low-beta stocks could be sold, with the proceeds used to purchase high-beta stocks. Alternatively, Treasury bills in the portfolio could be sold (or the amount of borrowing increased), with the resulting proceeds invested in stocks.

In Figure 18-7, the excess returns of two hypothetical portfolios are measured on the vertical axis while those of a market index are on the horizontal axis. Straight lines, fit via standard regression methods, reveal positive ex post alpha values in each case. However, the scatter diagrams tell a different story.

The scatter diagram for the portfolio shown in panel (a) seems to indicate that the relationship between the portfolio's excess returns and the market's

FIGURE 18-7
Superior Fund Performance

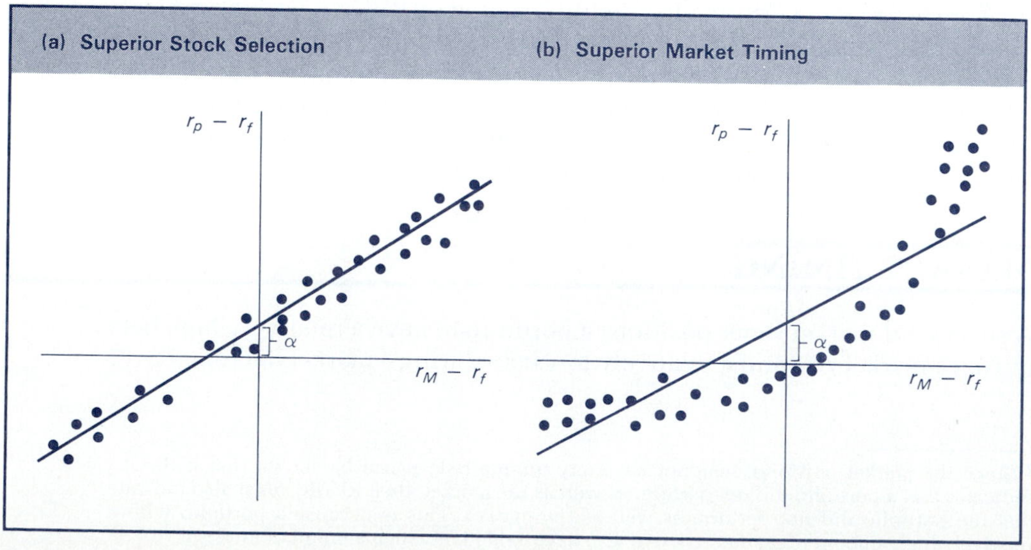

excess returns was linear, since the points cluster close to the regression line. This suggests that the portfolio consisted of securities in a manner such that the beta of the portfolio was roughly the same at all times. Since the ex post alpha was positive, it appears that the investment manager successfully identified and invested in some underpriced securities.

The scatter diagram for the portfolio shown in panel (b) seems to indicate that the relationship between this portfolio's excess returns and the market's excess returns was not linear, since the points in the middle lie below the regression line and those at the ends lie above the regresssion line. This suggests that the portfolio consisted of high-beta securities during periods when the market return was high and low-beta securities during periods when the market return was low. Upon examination, it appears that the portfolio has a positive ex post alpha because of successful market timing by the investment manager.

Quadratic Regression

To measure the ability of an investment manager to successfully time the market, something more complex than a straight line can be "fit" to scatter diagrams such as those shown in Figure 18-7. One procedure fits a curve, where statistical methods are used to estimate the parameters a, b, and c in the following quadratic regression equation:

$$r_{pt} - r_{ft} = a + b(r_{Mt} - r_{ft}) + c[(r_{Mt} - r_{ft})^2] + \epsilon_{pt} \tag{18.24}$$

where ϵ_{pt} is the random error term.

The ex post characteristic *curve* shown in Figure 18-8(a) is simply the following quadratic function, where the values of a, b, and c for the portfolio have been estimated by standard regression methods:

$$r_{pt} - r_{ft} = a + b(r_{Mt} - r_{ft}) + c[(r_{Mt} - r_{ft})^2]. \tag{18.25}$$

FIGURE 18-8
Ex Post Characteristic Curve and Lines

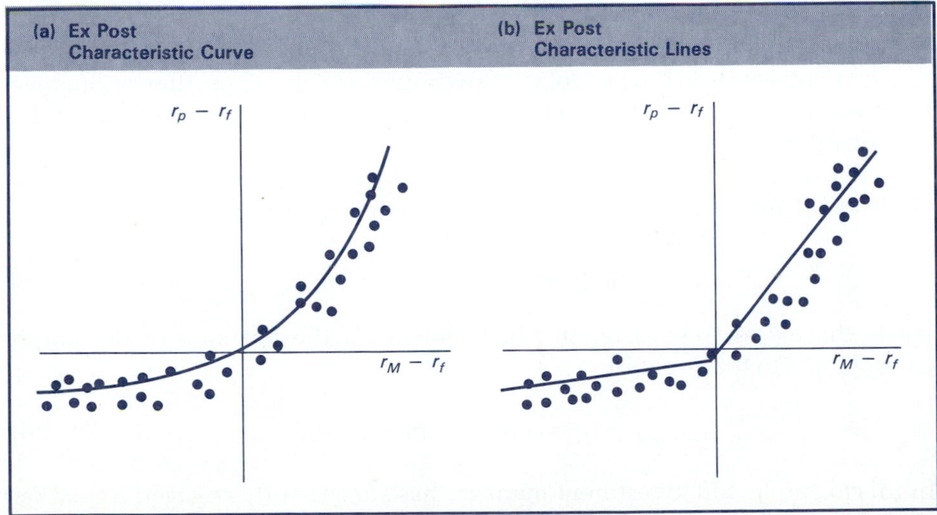

If the estimated value of c is positive [as it is for the portfolio depicted in Figure 18-8(a)], the curve would become less steep as one moves to the left. This would indicate that the portfolio manager successfully timed the market. Note how this equation corresponds to the equation for the ex post characteristic line if c is equal to zero; in such a situation, a and b would correspond to the portfolio's ex post alpha and beta, respectively.

Dummy Variable Regression

An alternative procedure fits *two* ex post characteristic lines to the scatter diagram, as shown in Figure 18-8(b). Periods when risky securities outperform riskfree securities (that is, when $r_{Mt} > r_{ft}$) can be termed *up markets*. Periods when risky securities do not perform as well as riskfree securities (that is, when $r_{Mt} < r_{ft}$) can be termed *down markets*. A successful market timer would select a high up-market beta and a low down-market beta. Graphically, the slope of the ex post characteristic line for positive excess market returns is greater than the slope of the ex post characteristic line for negative excess market returns.

To estimate such a relationship, standard regression methods can be used to estimate the parameters a, b, and c in the following "dummy variable" regression equation:

$$r_{pt} - r_{ft} = a + b(r_{Mt} - r_{ft}) + c[D_t(r_{Mt} - r_{ft})] + \epsilon_{pt}. \tag{18.26}$$

Here, ϵ_{pt} is the random error term and D_t is a "dummy variable" that is assigned a value of 0 for any time period t when $r_{Mt} > r_{ft}$ and a value of -1 for any time period t when $r_{Mt} < r_{ft}$. To see how this works, consider the effective equations for different values of $r_{Mt} - r_{ft}$.

VALUE OF $\mathbf{r_{Mt} - r_{ft}}$	EQUATION
>0	$r_{pt} - r_{ft} = a + b(r_{Mt} - r_{ft}) + \epsilon_{pt}$
$=0$	$r_{pt} - r_{ft} = a + \epsilon_{pt}$
<0	$r_{pt} - r_{ft} = a + (b - c)(r_{Mt} - r_{ft}) + \epsilon_{pt}$

Note that the parameter b corresponds to the portfolio's up-market beta, while $(b - c)$ corresponds to the portfolio's down-market beta. Thus, the parameter c indicates the difference between the two betas, and will be positive for the successful market timer.

For the portfolio shown in Figure 18-8(b), the ex post characteristic line on the right side of the graph corresponds to the equation:

$$r_{pt} - r_{ft} = a + b(r_{Mt} - r_{ft}) \tag{18.27a}$$

while the ex post characteristic line shown on the left side of the graph corresponds to the equation:

$$r_{pt} - r_{ft} = a + (b - c)(r_{Mt} - r_{ft}). \tag{18.27b}$$

In this example, the investment manager has successfully engaged in market timing, since the slope of the line on the right side (that is, b) is greater than the slope of the line on the left side (that is, $b - c$).

In either regression equation (18.24) or (18.26), the value of the parameter a provides an estimate of the investment manager's ability to identify mispriced securities (that is, security selection ability), and the value of the parameter c provides an estimate of the manager's market timing ability. The difference between the two equations is that the quadratic equation indicates that the portfolio's beta fluctuated over many values, depending on the size of the market's excess returns. This can be seen graphically by noting that the slope of the quadratic curve is continually increasing when moving from left to right in Figure 18-8(a). On the other hand, the dummy variable equation indicates that the portfolio's beta fluctuates between just two values, depending on whether r_M is less or greater than r_f. This can be seen graphically by noting that the slope of the equation increases from one value (that is, $b - c$) to a second value (that is, b) when moving from left to right in Figure 18-8(b).

As an example, consider First Fund from earlier. Table 18-2 presents the results from applying regression equations (18.24) and (18.26) to this portfolio for the sixteen quarters in the interval from 1982 to 1985, along with the ex post characteristic line results. The table does not provide any evidence of either selectivity or market timing ability by the portfolio manager. This can be seen by noting that the parameter a is negative while the parameter c is near zero.[12] Further evidence is provided in regard to the lack of market timing ability by noting that the correlation is higher for the ex post characteristic line than for either of the other equations.

CRITICISMS OF RISK-ADJUSTED PERFORMANCE MEASURES

The previously mentioned risk-adjusted measures of portfolio performance have been criticized on several grounds. Some of the major criticisms are described in this section.

[12]The size of parameter c (as well as the parameters a and b) should be judged relative to its standard error; in both of the equations shown here, it is quite small relative to both zero and the respective standard errors. Most standard statistical textbooks have an introductory discussion of the regression procedures that are utilized here. See, for example, Chapters 11 and 12 in James T. McClave and P. George Benson, *Statistics for Business and Economics* 5th ed. (San Francisco: Dellen Publishing Company, 1991).

TABLE 18-2
Market Timing Test Results for First Fund

PARAMETER BEING ESTIMATED[a]	EX POST CHARACTERISTIC LINE	QUADRATIC EQUATION	DUMMY VARIABLE EQUATION
a	−1.29%	−2.12%	−1.33%
	(1.00)	(1.65)	(2.54)
b	1.13	1.03	1.13
	(.13)	(.20)	(.28)
c	—	.02	.02
	—	(.03)	(.78)
Correlation[b]	.92	.91	.91

[a]Standard errors are shown in parentheses below the respective parameters.

[b]The correlation coefficient for the quadratic and dummy variable equations has been adjusted for the number of independent variables.

Use of a Market Surrogate

All of the measures other than the reward-to-variability ratio require the identification of a market portfolio. This means that whatever surrogate is used, it can be criticized as being inadequate. Indeed, it has been shown that by making slight changes in the surrogate, the performance rankings of a set of portfolios can be completely reversed (that is, the top-ranked portfolio with one surrogate could be the bottom-ranked portfolio if a slightly different surrogate was used). However, it has been noted that when commonly used NYSE-based surrogates are involved, such as the Dow Jones Industrial Average, the S&P 500, and an index comparable to the New York Stock Exchange Composite, the performance rankings of common stock portfolios appear to be quite similar.[13]

Distinguishing Skill from Luck

A very long evaluation interval is needed in order to be able to obtain a measure of performance that can distinguish skill from luck on the part of the investment manager. That is, it would be useful to know if an apparently successful manager was skilled or just lucky, since skill can be expected to have a favorable impact on the portfolio's performance in the future, whereas luck cannot be expected to continue. Unfortunately, too many years' worth of data are generally needed to make such a determination.[14]

Measuring the Riskfree Rate

The use of Treasury bills for measuring the riskfree rate in determining benchmark portfolios based on either the ex post SML or CML can be criticized. Consider a benchmark portfolio that involves an investment in both Treasury bills and the market portfolio. Such a benchmark portfolio can be criticized for having too low a rate of return, making it easy for a portfolio to show superior performance. This is because Treasury bills may provide excessively low returns to compensate for their high degree of liquidity. If a higher riskfree rate (such as the commercial paper rate) is used, then any benchmark portfolio that lies between this riskfree rate and the market portfolio on either the ex post SML or CML will have a higher rate of return, and thus represent a higher but more appropriate standard.

Next, consider a benchmark portfolio that involves levering a positive investment in the market portfolio by borrowing at the riskfree rate. Use of the Treasury bill rate can be criticized because realistic borrowing alternatives typically involve a higher rate, and are thus less attractive. Accordingly, benchmarks that involve borrowing at the Treasury bill rate have too high a rate of return, making it difficult for a portfolio to show superior performance. If a higher riskfree borrowing rate (such as the call money rate plus a small premium) is used, then any benchmark portfolio involving riskfree borrowing

---

[13]See Richard Roll, "Ambiguity When Performance Is Measured by the Security Market Line," *Journal of Finance*, 33, no. 4 (September 1978): 1051–69, David Peterson and Michael L. Rice, "A Note on Ambiguity in Portfolio Performance Measures," *Journal of Finance*, 35, no. 5 (December 1980): 1251–56; and Heinz Zimmermann and Claudia Zogg-Wetter, "On Detecting Selection and Timing Ability: The Case of Stock Market Indexes," *Financial Analysts Journal*, 48, no. 1 (January/February 1992): 80–83.

[14]See Dan W. French and Glenn V. Henderson, Jr., "How Well Does Performance Evaluation Perform?" *Journal of Portfolio Management*, 11, no. 2 (Winter 1985): 15–18.

will have a lower rate of return, and thus represent a lower but more appropriate standard.

In summary, measures of portfolio performance based on either the ex post SML or CML and utilizing Treasury bills to determine the riskfree rate are alleged to discriminate in favor of conservative portfolios and against aggressive ones.[15]

Validity of the CAPM

The measures of portfolio performance that involve beta (namely, the ex post alpha and reward-to-volatility measures) are based on the CAPM, yet the CAPM may not be the correct asset pricing model. That is, perhaps assets are priced according to some other model. If so, the use of beta-based performance measures will be inappropriate.

Interestingly, a measure analogous to ex post alpha has been shown to be a meaningful gauge of performance if the Arbitrage Pricing Theory's (APT) model of asset pricing is believed to be more appropriate.[16] Furthermore, the reward-to-variability ratio is immune to this criticism, since it uses standard deviation as a measure of risk and does not rely on the validity of the CAPM or the identification of a market portfolio.

Performance Attribution

The previously mentioned risk-adjusted measures of performance concentrate on the question of *how* a portfolio did relative to both a benchmark and a set of other portfolios. The use of quadratic and dummy variable regression is an attempt to evaluate separately the manager's ability at selectivity and timing. However, the client might want to know more about *why* the portfolio had a certain return over a particular time period. **Performance attribution** using a "factor model" is one method that has been used to try to make such a determination; an example is presented in the appendix.

performance attribution

SUMMARY

1. Performance measurement is an integral part of the investment management process. It is a feedback and control mechanism that can make the investment management process more effective.

2. In evaluating performance, there are two major tasks: determine whether the performance is superior or inferior, and determine whether the performance results from luck or skill.

3. Without intraperiod contributions or withdrawals, measurement of portfolio returns is simple: the difference between ending and beginning portfolio values divided by beginning portfolio value.

4. Intraperiod cash flows complicate the calculation of portfolio returns. Two methods have been developed to calculate returns when these cash

[15]Some people argue that the use of a market surrogate like the S&P 500 will also result in an unfair standard since investing in a market surrogate is not as simple as it may seem. With the existence of index funds and index futures (discussed in Chapter 25), this criticism does not appear to have much force.

[16]Under APT (discussed in Chapter 12), there is another measure of portfolio performance that has even more theoretical justification than the APT-based ex post alpha. This measure is analogous to the CAPM-based "appraisal ratio" mentioned in footnote 6, and involves dividing the APT-based ex post alpha by the ex post standard deviation of the APT-based random error term.

flows occur: dollar-weighted and time-weighted returns.

5. The dollar-weighted return is influenced by the size and timing of cash flows, while the time-weighted return is not. As a result, the time-weighted return is generally the preferred method of measuring portfolio performance.

6. The essential idea behind performance evaluation is to compare an actively managed portfolio's returns against the returns of an alternative benchmark portfolio. An appropriate benchmark should be relevant and feasible and should exhibit risk similar to that of the actively managed portfolio.

7. Risk-adjusted performance measures involve both a portfolio's ex post return and its ex post risk.

8. Ex post alpha (differential return) and the reward-to-volatility ratio compare a portfolio's excess return to the portfolio's systematic risk. The reward-to-variability ratio compares a portfolio's excess return to the portfolio's total risk.

9. Successful market timers will hold a portfolio with a relatively high beta during a market rise and a relatively low beta during a market decline. Quadratic regression and dummy variable regression are two methods designed to measure market timing performance.

10. Risk-adjusted measures of performance have been criticized for: using a market surrogate instead of the "true" market portfolio; being unable to statistically distinguish luck from skill except over very long periods of time; using an inappropriate riskfree rate; and relying on the validity of the CAPM.

KEY TERMS

dollar-weighted return
time-weighted return
benchmark portfolios
ex post alpha
characteristic line
simple linear regression
reward-to-volatility ratio
reward-to-variability ratio
performance attribution
comparative performance attribution

QUESTIONS AND PROBLEMS

1. Crungy Patrick owns a portfolio of three stocks. Crungy's holdings and the prices of the stocks at the end of 1990 and 1991 are shown below. Assuming no contributions, withdrawals, or dividends paid, what is the return on Crungy's portfolio in 1991?

STOCK	SHARES OWNED	1990 PRICE	1991 PRICE
A	100	$10	$15
B	300	5	4
C	250	12	14

2. Why do cash inflows and outflows between the beginning and end of a performance evaluation period complicate the measurement of portfolio returns?

3. At the beginning of 1991, Lave Cross' portfolio was worth $39,000. At year-end, Lave received a gift of $4,000, which was invested in the portfolio. The portfolio's value at year-end was $42,000. What was the return on Lave's portfolio in 1991?

4. New Lisbon Laundry's pension fund was worth $30 million on December 31, 1991. On January 1, 1992 the firm made a $2 million contribution to the fund. At the end of 1992, the pension fund was valued at $38 million. What was the return on the New Lisbon pension fund in 1992?

5. At the beginning of 1991, Con Daily's portfolio was worth $9,000. At the end of each of the next four quarters, Con received a gift of $500, which was invested in the portfolio. At the end of each quarter, Con's portfolio was worth, respectively, $9,800, $10,800, $11,200, and $12,000. What was the time-weighted rate of return on Con's portfolio in 1991?
6. Dell Darling's portfolio is worth $12,000 at the beginning of a thirty-day month. On day 10 of the month, Dell received a contribution to the portfolio of $800. At the end of the month, Dell's portfolio is worth $13,977.71. What was the dollar-weighted return on Dell's portfolio for the month?
7. Ginger Beaumont began the year 1991 with a portfolio valued at $10,000, and made a contribution and a withdrawal from this portfolio over the next three months. Information regarding amounts and dates of these cash flows and the portfolio's market value at various dates is shown next.

DATE	CONTRIBUTION (+) OR WITHDRAWAL (−)	PORTFOLIO VALUE
12/31/90	$ 0	$10,000
1/31/91	+956	9,000
2/28/91	−659	12,000
3/31/91	0	13,000

(a) Calculate the dollar-weighted return for the three-month period.
(b) Calculate the time-weighted return for the three-month period.
(c) Why is the time-weighted return for the quarter less than the dollar-weighted return in this particular problem?

8. Distinguish between time-weighted and dollar-weighted rates of return. Under what performance measurement circumstances might the dollar-weighted return be preferred to the time-weighted?
9. Oats DeMaestri's portfolio is valued at $22,000 at the beginning of a thirty-one-day month. During the month, Oats withdrew $1,500 from the portfolio on day 12 and contributed $600 on day 21. At month-end, the portfolio was worth $21,769.60. What was Oats' dollar-weighted return for the month?
10. At the beginning of a thirty-day month, Buttercup Dickerson owned a portfolio valued at $5,000. On day 10, Buttercup's portfolio was worth $7,300 after a $2,000 contribution had been made on that day. At the end of the month, the portfolio was worth $9,690.18. Calculate both the time-weighted and dollar-weighted returns on Buttercup's portfolio for the month. Why do the two returns differ so substantially?
11. Why does performance evaluation require an appropriate benchmark in order to be meaningful? How would you define the term *appropriate* in this context?
12. It is common practice for performance evaluation services to compare the returns on a common stock portfolio to a distribution of returns obtained from a large sample of other common stock portfolios. What potential problems are involved in this sort of analysis?
13. Pickles Dillhoefer owns a portfolio that over the last five years has produced a 16.8% annual return. During that time the portfolio pro-

duced a 1.10 beta. Further, the riskfree return and market return averaged 7.4% and 15.2% per year. What was the ex post alpha on Pickles' portfolio over this time period? Draw the ex post SML and the position of Pickles portfolio.

14. The performance of the Venus Fund, a common stock mutual fund, compared with that of the S&P 500 over a ten-year period, is as follows:

	VENUS FUND	S&P 500
Average quarterly excess return	0.6%	0.5%
Standard deviation of quarterly excess returns	9.9%	6.6%
Beta	1.10	1.00

Dazzy Vance is considering investing in either the Venus Fund or another mutual fund whose objective is to track the performance of the S&P 500. Which fund would you recommend that Dazzy select, assuming that your decision is based solely on past performance? Justify your answer using various measures of risk-adjusted performance.

15. Why is the reward-to-variability ratio a more appropriate measure of performance than the ex post alpha if the portfolio being assessed represents the entire wealth of the portfolio's owner?

16. Can the ex post alpha, the reward-to-volatility ratio, and the reward-to-variability ratio give conflicting answers to the question of whether a particular portfolio has outperformed the market portfolio on a risk-adjusted basis? If so, which of these measures can conflict with the others, and why can this conflict occur?

17. Does a portfolio's ex post alpha measure gains and losses resulting from security selection, market timing, or both? Explain.

18. Assume that broad stock market indices, such as the S&P 500, are not good surrogates for the "true" market portfolio. What potential problems does this cause for performance evaluation using the ex post alpha measure?

19. You are given the following historical performance information on the capital markets and the Jupiter Fund, a common stock mutual fund.

YEAR	JUPITER FUND BETA	RETURN ON JUPITER FUND	RETURN ON MARKET INDEX	RETURN ON TREASURY BILLS
1	0.90	−2.99%	−8.50%	6.58%
2	0.95	0.63	4.01	6.53
3	0.95	22.01	14.31	4.39
4	1.00	24.08	18.98	3.84
5	1.00	−22.46	−14.66	6.93
6	0.90	−25.12	−26.47	8.00
7	0.80	29.72	37.20	5.80
8	0.75	22.15	23.84	5.08
9	0.80	0.48	−7.18	5.12
10	0.85	6.85	6.56	7.18

(a) Compute Jupiter Fund's average beta over the ten-year period. What percentage investments in the market index and Treasury bills are required in order to produce a beta equal to the fund's average beta?

(b) Compute the year-by-year returns that would have been earned on a portfolio invested in the market index and Treasury bills in the proportions calculated in part a.

(c) Compute the year-by-year returns that would have been earned on a portfolio invested in the market index and Treasury bills in the proportions needed to match Jupiter's beta year-by-year. (Note: These proportions will change yearly as the fund's beta changes.)

(d) One measure of a fund manager's market timing ability is the average difference between (1) what the fund would have earned annually by investing in the market index and Treasury bills so that the year-by-year beta equals the fund's actual year-by-year beta and (2) what the fund would have earned annually by investing in the market index and Treasury bills so that the year-by-year beta equals the fund's average beta. Given your previous calculations, evaluate the market timing ability of Jupiter's manager.

(e) One measure of a fund manager's security selection ability is the average difference between (1) the fund's annual returns and (2) what the fund would have earned annually by investing in the market index and Treasury bills so that the year-by-year beta equals the fund's actual year-by-year beta. Calculate Jupiter's average return and then, using your previous calculations, evaluate the security selection ability of Jupiter's manager.

20. Consider the following annual returns produced by a MiniFund, a mutual fund investing in small stocks:

1971	16.50%	1976	57.38%	1981	13.88%	1986	6.85%
1972	4.43	1977	25.38	1982	28.01	1987	−9.30
1973	−30.90	1978	23.46	1983	39.67	1988	22.87
1974	−19.95	1979	43.46	1984	−6.67	1989	10.18
1975	52.82	1980	39.88	1985	24.66	1990	−21.56

Refering to Table 1-1, use the Treasury bill returns as the riskfree return and the common stock returns as the market return, calculate the following risk-adjusted return measures for the small stock mutual fund.

(a) Ex post alpha

(b) Reward-to-volatility ratio

(c) Reward-to-variability ratio

Comment on the mutual fund's risk-adjusted performance. What problems are associated with using a large capitalization index such as the S&P 500 (the source of the common stock returns) as the benchmark in evaluating this small company mutual fund?

21. In an article in the *Journal of Finance* (March 1983), Jess Chua and Richard Woodward investigated the investment skill of the legendary economist John Maynard Keynes. A portfolio managed by Keynes had the following returns:

	KEYNES' RETURN	MARKET RETURN	RISKFREE RETURN
1928	−3.4%	7.9%	4.2
1929	0.8	6.6	5.3
1930	−32.4	−20.3	2.5
1931	−24.6	−25.0	3.6
1932	44.8	−5.8	1.6
1933	35.1	21.5	0.6
1934	33.1	−0.7	0.7
1935	44.3	5.3	0.6
1936	56.0	10.2	0.6
1937	8.5	−0.5	0.6
1938	−40.1	−16.1	0.6
1939	12.9	−7.2	1.3
1940	−15.6	−12.9	1.0
1941	33.5	12.5	1.0
1942	−0.9	0.8	1.0
1943	53.9	15.6	1.0
1944	14.5	5.4	1.0
1945	14.6	0.8	1.0

Chua and Woodward concluded that Keynes demonstrated superior investment abilities. They did not, however, distinguish between his market timing and security selection skills. Using the quadratic regression and dummy variable techniques, evaluate Keynes' market timing skills. (Hint: use of a regression package found in a standard microcomputer spreadsheet program is highly recommended.)

22. (Appendix Question) What is the purpose of performance attribution? What types of problems can hinder performance attribution?

23. (Appendix Question) Assume that security returns are explained by a four-attribute sector-factor model. Eugene Stephens, a novice pension fund consultant, has been asked to develop a performance attribution report analyzing the returns on Baraboo Corporation's pension fund versus those of the market for the year 1991. Eugene has collected the following information:

	BARABOO PENSION FUND	MARKET PORTFOLIO	SECTOR/ FACTOR VALUES
1991 Return	12.50%	5.5%	—
Beta	1.10	1.00	−0.50
Size	1.30	6.00	−0.60
% Industrial	40%	80%	8.00
% Nonindustrial	60%	20%	16.00

Unfortunately, Eugene is confused by the subject of performance attribution. Carry out the analysis for him.

24. As a corporate treasurer, you are responsible for evaluating prospective investment managers for your company's pension fund. You have interviewed three managers, examined their reported investment performances, and identified clear-cut differences in their investment approaches.

Manager A has developed a very appealing and apparently successful investment process based on extensive research and back-testing, but she has not yet managed money using this process.

Manager B has been investing relatively small amounts of money over only the past two years, producing what appears to be extraordinary investment performance. His process is based on exploiting what he believes to be a market inefficiency (or anomaly) to produce superior returns.

Manager C is a global investment counselor who emphasizes active selection of stocks and bonds across the major world markets. He has a long track record and uses a well-established and widely accepted process for selecting securities.

(a) Discuss the usefulness of historical investment performance in evaluating investment managers.

(b) For each of the three managers, identify and discuss the two most important factors that you would consider in assessing the manager's performance.

APPENDIX A Performance Attribution

With performance attribution, an attempt is made to ascertain why a portfolio had a given return over a particular time period. One procedure for making such a determination involves assuming that security returns are related to a number of prespecified factors as well as to "sector factors."[17] For example, there may be a beta factor, a size factor, and two sector factors that indicate whether or not a stock is issued by an industrial company. With such a model, the returns for a set of stocks during a given time period are related to these factors and sector factors in the following manner:

$$r_i = \beta_i F_1 + s_i F_2 + c_{i1} SF_1 + c_{i2} SF_2 + \epsilon_i. \tag{18.28}$$

Here each stock has four attributes—β_i, s_i, c_{i1}, and c_{i2}. The attributes β_i and s_i are, respectively, the beta and firm size of stock *i* in a given time period; and c_{i1} and c_{i2} are sector factor attributes that have values of one and zero, respectively, if stock *i* is an industrial firm, and values of zero and one if stock *i* is not an industrial firm. (For example, it may be a utility or transportation company such as Northern States Power or Delta Air Lines.)

The factors and sector factors F_1, F_2, SF_1, and SF_2 are parameters that can be estimated using a statistical technique known as multiple regression. For example, the annual returns for 500 firms for 1991 could be calculated. Then, the betas for each stock could be estimated using sixteen quarters of returns ending with the last quarter of 1990 (by using the characteristic line equation given earlier). The firm size for each stock could be measured by taking the market price per share as of December 31, 1990, multiplying it by the number of shares outstanding at that time, and then taking the logarithm of the product (expressed in billions). Lastly, each firm can be classified as either an industrial or nonindustrial, resulting in a zero or one value assigned to c_{i1} and

[17]For a discussion of factor models, see Chapter 11 and William F. Sharpe, "Factors in New York Stock Exchange Security Returns, 1931–1979," *Journal of Portfolio Management*, 8, no. 4 (Summer 1982): 5–18.

c_{i2}. This will result in four columns of 500 numbers representing security attributes—one column with the betas for each stock, one column for the firm sizes of each stock, and two columns of zeros and ones corresponding to whether the firms are industrials or nonindustrials—upon which will be "regressed" the column of annual returns for the 500 stocks during 1991.

Suppose the resulting regression produced estimated values for F_1, F_2, SF_1, and SF_2 of 1.20, −.40, 10.00, and 9.00, respectively. Thus, equation (18.28) for 1991 would be:

$$r_i = 1.20\beta_i - .40s_i + 10.00c_{i1} + 9.00c_{i2} + \epsilon_i. \qquad (18.29)$$

Since the estimated value of F_1 (1.20) is positive, the year of 1991 was one where high-beta stocks tended to outperform low-beta stocks. Furthermore, since the estimated value of F_2 (−.40) is negative, the year 1991 was one where the stocks of small firms tended to outperform the stocks of large firms. With an estimated value for SF_1 that is greater than the estimated value of SF_2 ($10.00 > 9.00$), 1991 also appears to have been a year when industrials tended to outperform nonindustrials.

Equation (18.29) can be used to analyze the 1991 return on a stock. Consider, for example, a hypothetical industrial stock that had a return of 12.13%, a beta of .8, and a size of 4.00 [its market value was $54.6 billion, so s_i = natural logarithm of 54.6 = ln (54.6) = 4.00]. According to equation (18.29), the "normal" return on such a stock is $(1.20 \times .8) - (.40 \times 4.00) + (10.00 \times 1) + (9.00 \times 0) = 9.36\%$. Thus, for this stock, its "nonfactor return" (ϵ_i) for 1991 was $12.13\% - 9.36\% = 2.77\%$, suggesting that this particular stock did relatively well in comparison with other stocks having comparable attributes.

Similar analysis can be conducted on a portfolio's return for 1991. Consider a hypothetical portfolio that had a return of 10.03% in 1991. Upon close examination, it has been determined that this portfolio had an average beta of 1.3 and an average size of 3.2 (that is, the average value of s_i for all the stocks held was 3.2). Furthermore, 67% of the stocks in the portfolio were industrials and 33% were nonindustrials. According to equation (18.29), the "normal" return on such a portfolio is $(1.20 \times 1.30) - (.40 \times 3.20) + (10.00 \times .67) + (9.00 \times .33) = 9.95\%$. Since the nonfactor return on this portfolio was $10.03\% - 9.95\% = .08\%$, this portfolio shows little evidence of successful security selection.

Such absolute performance evaluation with a factor model is interesting, but in many cases comparative performance is more relevant. A manager may do poorly in a bad market. But if he or she provides a higher return than would have been obtained otherwise, the client is clearly better off. With comparative performance, the overall return of a portfolio is compared with that of one or more other benchmark portfolios in order to determine the *differences* in the returns. Then the *sources* of the differences can be determined with **comparative performance attribution.**

Assume that the i in equation (18.28) refers to the portfolio under evaluation. Letting j refer to the return on a benchmark portfolio to which it is to be compared, the difference in their returns is simply $r_i - r_j$. Using equation (18.28), this difference can be expressed as:

$$\begin{aligned} r_i - r_j = {} & (\beta_i F_1 + s_i F_2 + c_{i1}SF_1 + c_{i2}SF_2 + \epsilon_i) \\ & - (\beta_j F_1 + s_j F_2 + c_{j1}SF_1 + c_{j2}SF_2 + \epsilon_j). \qquad (18.30) \end{aligned}$$

Gathering similar terms, this equation can be rewritten as:

$$r_i - r_j = F_1(\beta_i - \beta_j) + F_2(s_i - s_j) + SF_1(c_{i1} - c_{j1}) + SF_2(c_{i2} - c_{j2}) + (\epsilon_i - \epsilon_j). \quad (18.31)$$

Each of the first four terms represents a differential effect equal to the product of (1) the difference in the attributes of the two portfolios and (2) the actual value of the related factor. The last term in the equation indicates the difference in the nonfactor returns of the two portfolios.

Table 18-3 provides an example where portfolio i is the one mentioned earlier that had a return in 1991 of 10.03%. It is being compared with a benchmark portfolio that had a return in 1991 of 11.21%. This benchmark portfolio had a beta of 1.50 and the average size of the firms whose stocks it held was 1.40. Furthermore, 80% of the portfolio's funds were invested in industrials with the remaining 20% being invested in nonindustrials. Using equation (18.29), the "normal" return on such a portfolio in 1991 was $(1.20 \times 1.50) - (.40 \times 1.40) + (10.00 \times .80) + (9.00 \times .20) = 11.04\%$, indicating that the portfolio had a nonfactor return of $11.21\% - 11.04\% = .17\%$.

A direct comparison of the two portfolios reveals a difference in returns of $r_i - r_j = 10.03\% - 11.21\% = -1.18\%$. That is, portfolio i performed worse than portfolio j by 1.18%. Security selection played a small role, since the nonfactor returns were both quite low (.08% for portfolio i and .17% for portfolio j). On balance, sector selection lowered returns for portfolio i relative to portfolio j slightly—the sum of the values in the last column for the two sector-factors was −0.13%. In portfolio i, industrials were underweighted relative to portfolio j, while nonindustrials were overweighted. A successful "sector picker" would have placed bets on (that is, overweighted) the sector with a relatively high factor value (industrials) and placed bets against (that is,

TABLE 18-3 Comparative Performance Attribution

	ATTRIBUTE				
	Portfolio i (a)	Portfolio j (b)	Difference (c) = (a) − (b)	Factor (d)	Differential Effect (e) = (c) × (d)
A. Factors:					
Common Factors					
Beta	1.30	1.50	−.20	1.20	−.24%
Size	3.20	1.40	1.80	−.40	−.72%
Sector Factors					
Industrials	.67	.80	−.13	10.00	−1.30%
Nonindustrials	.33	.20	.13	9.00	1.17%
					−1.09%

	RETURNS		
	Portfolio i (a)	Portfolio j (b)	Difference (c) = (a) − (b)
B. Returns:			
Factor Return	9.95%	11.04%	−1.09%
Nonfactor Return	.08%	.17%	−.09%
Total Return	10.03%	11.21%	−1.18%

underweighted) the sector with a relatively low factor value (nonindustrials), leading to a net positive "sector bet effect." In 1991, the investment manager for portfolio *i* was not as successful a sector picker relative to benchmark portfolio *j*.

The major sources of the relatively lower performance of portfolio *i* were those associated with common factors. The manager had lower-beta stocks than those in benchmark portfolio *j* during a period when high-beta stocks tended to do better than low-beta stocks. That is, the manager placed a bet against high-beta stocks in favor of low-beta stocks, and lost. He or she also had invested in stocks that were larger than those in benchmark portfolio *j* during a period when larger stocks tended to do poorly. That is, the manager placed a bet against smaller firms in favor of larger firms, and lost. Both differences lowered returns relative to the benchmark portfolio, with the "size bet" being more detrimental than the "beta bet."

REFERENCES

1. The use of portfolio benchmarks for performance evaluation is discussed in:

Richard Roll, "Performance Evaluation and Benchmark Errors (I)," *Journal of Portfolio Management*, 6, no. 4 (Summer 1980): 5–12;

Richard Roll, "Performance Evaluation and Benchmark Errors (II)," *Journal of Portfolio Management*, 7, no. 2 (Winter 1981): 17–22;

Gary P. Brinson, Jeffrey J. Diermeier, and Gary G. Schlarbaum, "A Composite Portfolio Benchmark for Pension Plans," *Financial Analysts Journal*, 42, no. 2 (March/April 1986): 15–24;

Mark P. Kritzman, "How to Build a Normal Portfolio in Three Easy Steps," *Journal of Portfolio Management*, 13, no. 4 (Summer 1987) 21–23;

Jeffery V. Bailey, Thomas M. Richards, and David E. Tierney, "Benchmark Portfolios and the Manager/Plan Sponsor Relationship," *Journal of Corporate Finance*, 4, no. 4 (Winter 1988): 25–32;

Arjun Divecha and Richard C. Grinold, "Normal Portfolios: Issues for Sponsors, Managers, and Consultants," *Financial Analysts Journal*, 45, no. 2 (March/April 1989): 7–13;

Edward P. Rennie and Thomas J. Cowhey, "The Successful Use of Benchmark Portfolios: A Case Study," *Financial Analysts Journal*, 46, no. 5 (September/October 1990): 18–26;

Jeffery V. Bailey, "Are Manager Universes Acceptable Performance Benchmarks?" *Journal of Portfolio Management*, 18, no. 3 (Spring 1992): 9–13;

Jeffery V. Bailey, "Evaluating Benchmark Quality," *Financial Analysts Journal*, 48, no. 3 (May/June 1992): 33–39.

2. The three measures of risk-adjusted performance were initially developed in:

Michael C. Jensen, "The Performance of Mutual Funds in the Period 1945–1964," *Journal of Finance*, 23, no. 2 (May 1968): 389–416;

Michael C. Jensen, "Risk, the Pricing of Capital Assets, and the Evaluation of Investment Portfolios," *Journal of Business*, 42, no. 2 (April 1969): 167–85;

Jack L. Treynor, "How to Rate Management of Investment Funds," *Harvard Business Review*, 43, no. 1 (January–February 1965): 63–75;

William F. Sharpe, "Mutual Fund Performance," *Journal of Business*, 39, no. 1 (January 1966): 119–38.

3. More sophisticated measures of portfolio performance that also measured market timing ability were initially developed by:

Jack L. Treynor and Kay K. Mazuy, "Can Mutual Funds Outguess the Market?" *Harvard Business Review*, 44, no. 4 (July–August 1966): 131–36;

Robert C. Merton, "On Market Timing and Investment Performance I. An Equilibrium Theory of Value for Market Forecasts," *Journal of Business*, 54, no. 3 (July 1981): 363–406;

Roy D. Henriksson and Robert C. Merton, "On Market Timing and Investment Performance II. Statistical Procedures for Evaluating Forecasting Skill," *Journal of Business*, 54, no. 4 (October 1981): 513–33.

4. There have been many critcisms leveled at the various measures of portfolio performance that are presented in this chapter. One of the most formidable critiques was:

Richard Roll, "Ambiguity When Performance Is Measured by the Security Market Line," *Journal of Finance*, 33, no. 4 (September 1978): 1051–69.

5. APT-based measures of portfolio performance have been developed by:

Gregory Connor and Robert Korajczyk, "Performance Measurement with the Arbitrage Pricing Theory: A New Framework for Analysis," *Journal of Financial Economics*, 15, no. 3 (March 1986): 373–94;

Bruce N. Lehmann and David M. Modest, "Mutual Fund Performance Evaluation: A Comparison of Benchmarks and Benchmark Comparisons," *Journal of Finance*, 42, no. 2 (June 1987): 233–65;

Nai-Fu Chen, Thomas E. Copeland, and David Mayers, "A Comparison of Single and Multifactor Portfolio Performance Methodologies," *Journal of Financial and Quantitative Analysis*, 22, no. 4 (December 1987): 401–17.

6. Some recent developments in measuring portfolio performance are discussed in:

Stanley J. Kon, "The Market-Timing Performance of Mutual Fund Managers," *Journal of Business*, 56, no. 3 (July 1983): 323–47;

Anat R. Admati and Stephen A. Ross, "Measuring Investment Performance in a Rational Expectations Equilibrium Model," *Journal of Business*, 58, no. 1 (January 1985): 1–26;

Philip H. Dybrig and Stephen A. Ross, "Differential Information and Performance Measurement Using a Security Market Line," *Journal of Finance*, 40, no. 2 (June 1985): 383–99;

Philip H. Dybrig and Stephen A. Ross, "The Analytics of Performance Measurement Using a Security Market Line," *Journal of Finance*, 40, no. 2 (June 1985): 401–16;

Mark Kritzman, "How to Detect Skill in Management Performance," *Journal of Portfolio Management*, 12, no. 2 (Winter 1986): 16–20;

Ravi Jagannathan and Robert A. Korajczyk, "Assessing the Market Timing Performance of Managed Portfolios," *Journal of Business*, 59, no. 2, pt. 1 (April 1986): 217–35;

Anat R. Admati, Sudipto Bhattacharya, Paul Pfleiderer, and Stephen A. Ross, "On Timing and Selectivity," *Journal of Finance*, 41, no. 3 (July 1986): 715–30;

Gary P. Brinson, L. Randolph Hood, and Gilbert L. Beebower, "Determinants of Portfolio Performance," *Financial Analysts Journal*, 42, no. 4 (July/August 1986): 39–44;

William Breen, Ravi Jagannathan, and Aharon R. Ofer, "Correcting for Heteroscedasticity in Tests for Market Timing Ability," *Journal of Business*, 59, no. 4, pt. 1 (October 1986): 585–98;

Robert E. Cumby and David M. Modest, "Testing for Market Timing Ability: A Framework for Forecast Evaluation," *Journal of Financial Economics*, 19, no. 1 (September 1987): 169–89;

Larry J. Lockwood and K. Rao Kadiyala, "Measuring Investment Performance with a Stochastic Parameter Regression Model," *Journal of Banking and Finance*, 12, no. 3 (September 1988): 457–67;

Alex Kane and Gary Marks, "Performance Evaluation of Market Timers: Theory and Evidence," *Journal of Financial and Quantitative Analysis*, 23, no. 4 (December 1988): 425–35;

Mark Grinblatt and Sheridan Titman, "Portfolio Performance Evaluation: Old Issues and New Insights," *Review of Financial Studies*, 2, no. 3 (1989): 393–421;

Cheng-few Lee and Shafiqur Rahman, "Market Timing, Selectivity, and Mutual Fund Performance: An Empirical Investigation," *Journal of Business*, 63, no. 2 (April 1990): 261–78;

Gary P. Brinson, Brian D. Singer, and Gilbert L. Beebower, "Determinants of Portfolio Performance II: An Update," *Financial Analysts Journal*, 47, no. 3 (May/June 1991): 40–48;

Chris R. Hensel, D. Don Ezra, and John H. Ilkiw, "The Importance of the Asset Allocation Decision," *Financial Analysts Journal*, 47, no. 4 (July/August 1991): 65–72;

Eric J. Weigel, "The Performance of Tactical Asset Allocation," *Financial Analysts Journal*, 47, no. 5 (September/October 1991): 63–70;

G. L. Beebower and A. P. Varikooty, "Measuring Market Timing Strategies," *Financial Analysts Journal*, 47, no. 6 (November/December 1991): 78–84, 92.

7. An alternative approach to portfolio performance evaluation that is called style analysis is described in:

William F. Sharpe, "Determining a Fund's Effective Asset Mix," *Investment Management Review*, (December 1988): 59–69;

William F. Sharpe, "Asset Allocation: Management Style and Performance Measurement," *Journal of Portfolio Management*, 18, no. 2 (Winter 1992): 7–19.

8. Other major articles on portfolio performance evaluation are listed in:

Gordon J. Alexander and Jack Clark Francis, *Portfolio Analysis* (Englewood Cliffs, N.J.: Prentice Hall, 1986), Chapter 13.

9. Performance attribution was initially developed and then expanded in:

Eugene F. Fama, "Components of Investment Performance," *Journal of Finance*, 27, no. 3 (June 1972): 551–67;

Ernest M. Ankrim, "Risk-Adjusted Performance Attribution," *Financial Analysts Journal* 48, no. 2 (March/April 1991): 74–82.

PART V
FIXED-INCOME SECURITIES

19

Types of Fixed-Income Securities

This chapter surveys the major types of fixed-income securities, with an emphasis on those currently popular in the United States. Such a survey cannot be exhaustive. A security is, after all, a contract giving the investor certain rights to the future prospects of the issuer. Because the rights given to the investor can differ from one security to another, and because the future prospects of issuers can differ substantially, the number of different types of fixed-income securities is quite large, making a complete survey virtually impossible.

The term *fixed-income* is commonly used to cover the types of securities discussed in this chapter, but is a bit misleading. Typically, these securities promise the investor that he or she will receive certain specified cash flows at certain specified times in the future. It may be one cash flow, in which case the security is known as a **pure-discount security.** Alternatively, it may involve multiple cash flows. If all of these cash flows (except for the last one) are of the same size, they are generally referred to as **coupon payments.** The specified date beyond which the investor will no longer receive cash flows is known as the **maturity date.** On this date, the investor receives the **principal** (also known as the par value or face value) associated with the security, along with the last coupon payment. However, all the cash flows are *promised,* and thus may not be received. That is, in many cases there is at least some risk that a promised payment will not be made in full and on time.

pure-discount security

coupon payments

maturity date

principal

SAVINGS DEPOSITS

Perhaps the most familiar type of fixed-income investment is the personal savings account at a bank, savings and loan company, or credit union. Such an account provides substantial (if not complete) safety of principal, low probability of failure to receive interest, high liquidity, and a relatively low return.

Commercial Banks

Many people maintain a checking account in a commercial bank. Formally, these accounts are termed **demand deposits,** since money can be withdrawn on demand by the depositors. While the bookkeeping required to keep track of withdrawals and deposits is costly to the bank, the balance in such an account is available to support interest-earning loans made by the bank. Within bounds set by regulations, banks offer terms for checking accounts that reflect these aspects. Customers with small balances who write many checks pay the bank, while those with large balances who write few checks are paid by the bank. Often, the two elements are identified separately, with service charges assessed for check writing and interest paid on average balances. In some cases the amount of interest paid increases substantially if a larger minimum balance is maintained.

demand deposits

An alternative to a checking account is a standard savings account. Although a written request for a withdrawal may be required up to thirty days in advance, in practice, requests for withdrawals are almost always honored immediately. Almost any amount may be invested in a savings account. No security is issued; instead, the current balance plus interest earned is posted to the bank's records and (if desired) to the depositor's "passbook."

Almost all banks also offer money market accounts and negotiable order of withdrawal (NOW) accounts, which pay interest and on which checks may be written. Credit unions offer services similar to these accounts, via share draft accounts, and many investment companies (described in Chapter 23) provide at least limited check-writing services.

The standard ("passbook") savings account is only one of many types of **time deposits.** A single-maturity deposit may be withdrawn at a stated maturity date (for example, one year after the initial deposit). A multiple-maturity deposit may be withdrawn at a stated date or left for one or more

time deposits

periods of equal length (thus, a ninety-day multiple-maturity deposit can be withdrawn roughly every three months after the date of the initial deposit). In practice, most single-maturity and multiple-maturity deposits can be withdrawn at any time. However, a penalty must be paid when this is done prior to maturity. Often, the penalty takes the form of recomputing the interest earned using a lower rate. Sometimes, an additional penalty may be deducted from the recomputed account balance.

Some types of time deposits may be made in almost any amount, while others may be made only in units of, say, $1,000 each. The latter may be represented by **certificates of deposit** (CDs), which clearly qualify to be called securities. Large-denomination CDs (generally $100,000 or more and known as "jumbos") may be negotiable—that is, the original depositor may sell the certificate to someone else before maturity. In most cases all interest is paid, along with the principal, at maturity. The top part of Figure 19-1 shows average yields of CDs with various maturities, issued by major banks in certain big states, as published each Thursday in *The Wall Street Journal*.

certificates of deposit

Most bank accounts in the United States are insured by the Federal Deposit Insurance Corporation (FDIC), a government agency that guarantees the payment of principal on any account up to a stated limit ($100,000 in 1992) if the bank is closed and liquidated. The FDIC, created in 1933, levies insurance premiums on its member banks and is authorized to borrow funds from the U.S. Treasury, if needed, although it has never done so. By opening certain kinds of multiple accounts, each under the limit, an investor can have a considerable amount covered by deposit insurance.

Savings and Loan Companies and Mutual Savings Banks

Savings and loan companies and mutual savings banks accept relatively short-term deposits, then use the money primarily to make relatively long-term loans, often for home mortgages. All mutual savings banks and mutual savings and loan companies are nominally owned by their members, while stock savings and loan companies are owned by stockholders (like commercial banks) who may or may not deposit funds or obtain loans there.

In the United States, most accounts in savings companies are insured by the same government agency that insures most bank accounts, the Federal Deposit Insurance Corporation (FDIC). The principal of each account is insured up to the same limit used for bank accounts but here, too, judicious use of multiple accounts makes it possible to have even more covered by deposit insurance.

The terms for deposits offered by institutions of this type are generally similar to those offered by commercial banks. The bottom part of Figure 19-1 presents the highest yields on CDs of various maturities that are issued by federally insured "thrift institutions," as reported weekly in *The Wall Street Journal*.

Credit Unions

A credit union accepts deposits from members of the credit union (membership is limited to individuals sharing some kind of "common bond," often a common employer) and then loans these funds to other members. Typically, loans are relatively small and relatively short-term (for example, to finance

FIGURE 19-1
Yields on Certificates of Deposits

Source: Reprinted by permission of *The Wall Street Journal*, © Dow Jones & Company, Inc., June 19, 1992, p. C17. All rights reserved worldwide.

BANXQUOTE® MONEY MARKETS

Survey ended Thursday, June 18, 1992

AVERAGE YIELDS OF MAJOR BANKS

	MMI*	One Month	Two Months	Three Months	Six Months	One Year	Two Years	Five Years
NEW YORK								
Savings	3.08%	z	z	3.17%	3.23%	3.69%	4.71%	6.22%
Jumbos	3.72%	3.33%	3.40%	3.48%	3.63%	4.03%	4.53%	5.46%
CALIFORNIA								
Savings	3.35%	z	z	3.27%	3.35%	3.72%	4.65%	6.34%
Jumbos	3.52%	3.25%	3.28%	3.37%	3.48%	3.90%	4.83%	6.62%
PENNSYLVANIA								
Savings	3.41%	z	z	3.45%	3.60%	4.06%	4.23%	5.88%
Jumbos	3.83%	3.32%	3.34%	3.42%	3.53%	3.85%	4.51%	5.58%
ILLINOIS								
Savings	3.33%	z	z	3.44%	3.56%	4.02%	4.68%	6.24%
Jumbos	3.51%	3.49%	3.52%	3.57%	3.71%	4.20%	4.91%	6.46%
TEXAS								
Savings	3.26%	z	z	3.38%	3.57%	3.96%	4.77%	6.09%
Jumbos	3.26%	3.45%	3.48%	3.52%	3.68%	4.07%	4.77%	6.16%
FLORIDA								
Savings	3.15%	z	z	2.99%	3.32%	3.63%	4.67%	5.75%
Jumbos	3.26%	2.99%	2.99%	3.17%	3.37%	3.70%	4.73%	5.97%
BANK AVERAGE								
Savings	3.26%	z	z	3.28%	3.44%	3.85%	4.61%	6.08%
Jumbos	3.52%	3.30%	3.33%	3.42%	3.56%	3.96%	4.72%	6.11%
WEEKLY CHANGE (in percentage point)								
Savings	−0.01	z	z	−0.03	−0.02	−0.01	−0.03	−0.05
Jumbos	+0.01	−0.01	−0.02	−0.02	−0.03	−0.02	−0.03	−0.03

SAVINGS CD YIELDS OFFERED THROUGH LEADING BROKERS

	Three Months	Six Months	One Year	Two Years	Five Years
BROKER AVERAGE	3.30%	3.45%	3.95%	4.45%	6.20%
WEEKLY CHANGE	−0.05	....	−0.10	−0.10	−0.18

*Money Market Investments include MMDA, NOW, savings deposits, passbook and other liquid accounts.

Each depositor is insured by the Federal Deposit Insurance Corp. (FDIC) up to $100,000 per issuing institution.

COMPOUND METHODS: c-Continuously. d-Daily. w-Weekly. m-Monthly. q-Quarterly. s-Semi-annually. a Annually. si-Simple interest.

F-Floating rate. P-Prime CD. T-T-Bill CD.

YIELD BASIS: A-365/365. B-360/360. C-365/360.

The information included in this table has been obtained directly from broker-dealers, banks and savings institutions, but the accuracy and validity cannot be guaranteed. Rates are subject to change. Yields, terms and capital adequacy should be verified before investing. Only well capitalized or adequately capitalized depository institutions are quoted.

z-Unavailable.

HIGH YIELD SAVINGS

Small minimum balance, generally $500 to $25,000

Money Market Investments*	Rate		Yield
JC Penney NB, Harrington De	4.41%	dA	4.51%
Columbia First, Arlington Va	4.25%	dC	4.40%
Metropolitan Bank, Arlington Va	4.30%	mA	4.39%
Key Bank USA, Albany NY	4.25%	mA	4.33%
New South FSB, Birmingham Al	4.15%	qA	4.22%

One Month CDs	Rate		Yield
Pioneer Svgs, Newport Beach Ca	3.90%	dA	3.98%
Bank of India, New York NY	3.85%	siC	3.90%
Standard Pac, Newport Beach Ca	3.65%	dC	3.77%
Loyola Federal, Baltimore Md	3.75%	siA	3.75%
New South FSB, Birmingham Al	3.75%	siA	3.75%

Two Months CDs	Rate		Yield
Pioneer Svgs, Newport Beach Ca	4.00%	dA	4.08%
Standard Pac, Newport Beach Ca	3.70%	dC	3.82%
New South FSB, Birmingham Al	3.75%	siA	3.75%
First Bank, Beverly Hills Ca	3.70%	siA	3.70%
Safra National, New York NY	3.60%	dA	3.67%

Three Months CDs	Rate		Yield
AFBA Industrial, Colordo Sps Co	4.16%	dA	4.25%
Pioneer Svgs, Newport Beach Ca	4.10%	dA	4.18%
Eastern Savings, Baltimore Md	3.92%	dA	4.00%
Lasalle Bank, Chicago Il	3.90%	FT	3.96%
New South FSB, Birmingham Al	3.95%	siA	3.95%

Six Months CDs	Rate		Yield
JC Penney NB, Harrington De	4.41%	dA	4.51%
Colonial National, Wilmington De	4.31%	dA	4.40%
AFBA Industrial, Colordo Sps Co	4.31%	dA	4.40%
Pioneer Svgs, Newport Beach Ca	4.30%	dA	4.39%
First Bank, Beverly Hills Ca	4.20%	siA	4.20%

One Year CDs	Rate		Yield
AFBA Industrial, Colordo Sps Co	4.78%	dA	4.90%
JC Penney NB, Harrington De	4.65%	dA	4.76%
Colonial National, Wilmington De	4.55%	dA	4.65%
First Deposit, Tilton NH	4.53%	dA	4.63%
Pioneer Svgs, Newport Beach Ca	4.50%	dA	4.60%

Two Years CDs	Rate		Yield
JC Penney NB, Harrington De	5.41%	dA	5.56%
Key Bank USA, Albany NY	5.30%	mA	5.43%
The Massachusetts Co, Boston Ma	5.25%	mA	5.38%
Home Federal, Washington DC	5.15%	dA	5.28%
New South FSB, Birmingham Al	5.17%	qA	5.27%

Five Years CDs	Rate		Yield
Astoria Federal, Lake Success NY	6.70%	dC	7.03%
Metropolitan Bank, Arlington Va	6.65%	qA	6.82%
Domestic Bank, Cranston RI	6.61%	mA	6.81%
New South FSB, Birmingham Al	6.60%	qA	6.77%
MBNA America, Newark De	6.50%	dA	6.72%

HIGH YIELD JUMBOS

Large minimum balance, generally $95,000 to $100,000

Money Market Investments*	Rate		Yield
JC Penney NB, Harrington De	4.41%	dA	4.51%
Columbia First, Arlington Va	4.25%	dC	4.40%
Metropolitan Bank, Arlington Va	4.30%	mA	4.39%
First Signature, Portsmouth NH	4.27%	dA	4.36%
Key Bank USA, Albany NY	4.25%	mA	4.33%

One Month Jumbo CDs	Rate		Yield
Astoria Federal, Lake Success NY	4.05%	siC	4.11%
Loyola Federal, Baltimore Md	4.00%	siA	4.00%
Colonial National, Wilmington De	3.90%	siA	3.90%
Bank of India, New York NY	3.85%	siC	3.90%
Fidelity Federal, Glendale Ca	3.85%	siA	3.85%

Two Months Jumbo CDs	Rate		Yield
Astoria Federal, Lake Success NY	4.05%	siC	4.11%
Colonial National, Wilmington De	3.95%	siA	3.95%
Fidelity Federal, Glendale Ca	3.90%	siA	3.90%
Pioneer Svgs, Newport Beach Ca	3.85%	siA	3.85%
Standard Pac, Newport Beach Ca	3.85%	siA	3.85%

Three Months Jumbo CDs	Rate		Yield
AFBA Industrial, Colordo Sps Co	4.16%	dA	4.25%
Astoria Federal, Lake Success NY	4.10%	siC	4.16%
Fidelity Federal, Glendale Ca	4.05%	siA	4.05%
Colonial National, Wilmington De	4.00%	siA	4.00%
Decatur Federal, Decatur Ga	4.00%	siA	4.00%

Six Months Jumbo CDs	Rate		Yield
AFBA Industrial, Colordo Sps Co	4.31%	dA	4.40%
First Deposit NCCB, Concord NH	4.31%	dA	4.40%
OBA Federal, Gaithersburg Md	4.25%	siC	4.31%
JC Penney NB, Harrington De	4.30%	siA	4.30%
Citibank SD, Sioux Falls SD	4.11%	dC	4.25%

One Year Jumbo CDs	Rate		Yield
AFBA Industrial, Colordo Sps Co	4.78%	dA	4.90%
First Deposit NCCB, Concord NH	4.74%	dA	4.85%
First Deposit, Tilton NH	4.60%	dA	4.71%
JC Penney NB, Harrington De	4.65%	siA	4.65%
Astoria Federal, Lake Success NY	4.55%	siC	4.61%

Two Years Jumbo CDs	Rate		Yield
Key Bank USA, Albany NY	5.30%	mA	5.43%
The Massachusetts Co, Boston Ma	5.25%	mA	5.38%
First Deposit NCCB, Concord NH	5.21%	dA	5.35%
Standard Pac, Newport Beach Ca	5.30%	siA	5.30%
AFBA Industrial, Colordo Sps Co	5.12%	dA	5.25%

Five Years Jumbo CDs	Rate		Yield
MBNA America, Newark De	6.60%	dA	6.82%
Domestic Bank, Cranston RI	6.61%	mA	6.81%
Metropolitan Bank, Arlington Va	6.61%	mA	6.81%
New South FSB, Birmingham Al	6.75%	siA	6.75%
Continental Bank, Chicago Il	6.50%	mA	6.70%

For more information call MASTERFUND at (800) 325-3242. MASTERFUND is registered with the FDIC as a deposit broker.

Source: BANXQUOTE, Wilmington, De. BANXQUOTE is a registered trademark and service mark of MASTERFUND INC.

the purchase of an automobile). Excess funds are invested in highly liquid short-term assets.

Each credit union is owned by its members, who elect a board of directors. Deposits are generally similar to passbook accounts in a bank or savings and loan company, and also earn "dividends" instead of interest. Many credit unions also offer CDs and checking accounts to their members.

Deposits in all federally chartered credit unions are insured by the National Credit Union Administration (NCUA), a U.S. government agency that serves the same function as the Federal Deposit Insurance Corporation. The amount and type of insurance coverage provided by both of these agencies is essentially identical.

Other Types of Personal Savings Accounts

A number of institutions similar to those just described can be found. For example, there are companies chartered to accept deposits and use the proceeds to make consumer loans. In some countries, the government-run post office accepts savings deposits. Certain kinds of life insurance policies include a savings component, since payments often exceed the amount strictly required to pay for just the insurance involved. The "cash value" of such a policy may be obtained by cancellation; alternatively, some or all of it may be "borrowed" without canceling the policy. The implicit rate of return on the cash value of an insurance policy is typically quite low, reflecting the extremely low risk to the policyholder and the length of the insurance company's commitment.

MONEY MARKET INSTRUMENTS

Certain types of short-term (meaning, arbitrarily, one year or less), highly marketable loans play a major role in the investment and borrowing activities of both financial and nonfinancial corporations. Individual investors with substantial funds may invest in such money market instruments directly, but most do so indirectly via money market accounts at various financial institutions.[1]

Some money market instruments are negotiable and are traded in active secondary dealer markets; others are not. Some may be purchased by anyone with adequate funds, others only by particular types of institutions. Many are sold on a discount basis—for example, a ninety-day note with a face value of $100,000 might be sold for $98,000, where the face value of $100,000 is to be paid to the investor at maturity and the difference of $2,000 represents interest income.

Interest rates on such money market instruments are often reported on what is known as a **bank discount basis**. In the example, this means that the note will be described in the media as having a discount of 2% per quarter, or 8% per year. However, the discount does not represent the true interest rate on the note. In such a situation, the true interest rate is higher—in this case, it equals $2,000/$98,000 = 2.04% per quarter, or the equivalent of 8.16% per year (with quarterly compounding, it would equal $8.41\% = 1.0204^4 - 1$).

bank discount basis

[1]Short-term obligations of the U.S. government and its agencies are also considered money market instruments; they will be described in the next section.

FIGURE 19-2
Interest Rates on Money Market Instruments

Source: Reprinted by permission of *The Wall Street Journal*, , June 19, 1992, p. C15.

MONEY RATES

Thursday, June 18, 1992

The key U.S. and foreign annual interest rates below are a guide to general levels but don't always represent actual transactions.

PRIME RATE: 6½%. The base rate on corporate loans posted by at least 75% of the nation's 30 largest banks.

FEDERAL FUNDS: 3 11/16% high, 3½% low, 3½% near closing bid, 3⅝% offered. Reserves traded among commercial banks for overnight use in amounts of $1 million or more. Source: Babcock Fulton Prebon (U.S.A.) Inc.

DISCOUNT RATE: 3½%. The charge on loans to depository institutions by the Federal Reserve Banks.

CALL MONEY: 5¾% to 6%. The charge on loans to brokers on stock exchange collateral.

COMMERCIAL PAPER placed directly by General Electric Capital Corp.: 3.80% 30 to 119 days; 3.82% 120 to 149 days; 3.85% 150 to 209 days; 3.97% 210 to 270 days. Commercial Paper placed directly by General Motors Acceptance Corp.: 3.80% 30 to 119 days; 3.825% 120 to 149 days; 3.875% 150 to 179 days; 3.925% 180 to 270 days.

COMMERCIAL PAPER: High-grade unsecured notes sold through dealers by major corporations in multiples of $1,000: 3.88% 30 days; 3.88% 60 days; 3.90% 90 days.

CERTIFICATES OF DEPOSIT: 3.28% one month; 3.35% two months; 3.41% three months; 3.51% six months; 3.71% one year. Average of top rates paid by major New York banks on primary new issues of negotiable C.D.s, usually on amounts of $1 million and more. The minimum unit is $100,000. Typical rates in the secondary market: 3.80% one month; 3.85% three months; 3.95% six months.

BANKERS ACCEPTANCES: 3.72% 30 days; 3.72% 60 days; 3.72% 90 days; 3.75% 120 days; 3.80% 150 days; 3.80% 180 days. Negotiable, bank-backed business credit instruments typically financing an import order.

LONDON LATE EURODOLLARS: 3⅞% - 3¾% one month; 3 15/16% - 3 13/16% two months; 3 15/16% - 3 13/16% three months; 4% - 3⅞% four months; 4 1/16% - 3 15/16% five months; 4 1/16% - 3 15/16% six months.

LONDON INTERBANK OFFERED RATES (LIBOR): 3⅞% one month; 3 15/16% three months; 4 1/16% six months; 4½% one year. The average of interbank offered rates for dollar deposits in the London market based on quotations at five major banks. Effective rate for contracts entered into two days from date appearing at top of this column.

FOREIGN PRIME RATES: Canada 7%; Germany 11%; Japan 5.25%; Switzerland 11.63%; Britain 10%. These rate indications aren't directly comparable; lending practices vary widely by location.

TREASURY BILLS: Results of the Monday, June 15, 1992, auction of short-term U.S. government bills, sold at a discount from face value in units of $10,000 to $1 million: 3.66% 13 weeks; 3.75% 26 weeks.

FEDERAL HOME LOAN MORTGAGE CORP. (Freddie Mac): Posted yields on 30-year mortgage commitments. Delivery within 30 days 8.23%, 60 days 8.30%, standard conventional fixed-rate mortgages; 5.75%, 2% rate capped one-year adjustable rate mortgages. Source: Telerate Systems Inc.

FEDERAL NATIONAL MORTGAGE ASSOCIATION (Fannie Mae): Posted yields on 30 year mortgage commitments (priced at par) for delivery within 30 days 8.21%, 60 days 8.30%, standard conventional fixed rate-mortgages; 5.80%, 6/2 rate capped one-year adjustable rate mortgages. Source: Telerate Systems Inc.

MERRILL LYNCH READY ASSETS TRUST: 3.44%. Annualized average rate of return after expenses for the past 30 days not a forecast of future ret rns.

The Wall Street Journal publishes on a daily basis a list of the current interest rates on a number of money market instruments. Figure 19-2 presents such a list. Some of the types of money market instruments mentioned on this list are described next.

Commercial Paper

commercial paper

Commercial paper is an unsecured short-term promissory note issued by both financial and nonfinancial companies. The dollar amount of commercial paper outstanding exceeds the amount of any other type of money market instrument except for Treasury bills, with the majority being issued by financial companies such as bank holding companies as well as companies involved in sales and personal finance, insurance, and leasing. Such notes are often issued by large firms that have unused lines of credit at banks, making it highly likely that the loan will be paid off when it becomes due. As a result, the interest rates on commercial paper reflect this, being relatively low in comparison with other corporate fixed-income securities.

Commercial paper is usually issued in denominations of $1,000 or more, with maturities of up to 270 days (the maximum allowed by the Securities and Exchange Commission without registration). Such paper is generally not negotiable, but the issuer may be willing to prepay the note (perhaps by issuing another) if necessary.

Certificates of Deposit

These are certificates representing time deposits at commercial banks or savings and loan associations that were mentioned earlier. Large- (or jumbo-) denomination CDs are issued in amounts of $100,000 or more, have a specified maturity, and generally are negotiable, meaning that they can be sold by one investor to another. Such certificates are insured by the FDIC or NCUA, but only for $100,000 (in 1992).

Interestingly, foreign banks that have branches in the United States also offer dollar-denominated CDs to investors. Such CDs have been dubbed Yankee CDs by the media.

Bankers' Acceptances

Historically, these instruments were created to finance goods in transit; currently they are generally used to finance foreign trade. For example, the buyer of the goods may issue a promise in writing to the seller to pay a given sum within a short period of time (for example, 180 days or less). A bank then "accepts" this promise, obligating itself to pay the amount when requested, and obtains in return a claim on the goods as collateral. The written promise becomes a liability of both the bank and the buyer of the goods and is known as a **bankers' acceptance.**

bankers' acceptance

The seller of the goods, having received the written promise from the buyer that the bank has "accepted," need not wait until the promise is due in order to receive payment. Instead, the acceptance can be sold to someone else at a price that is less than the amount of the promised payment to be made in the future. Thus, such instruments are pure discount securities.

Eurodollars

In the world of international finance, large short-term CDs denominated in dollars and issued by banks outside the United States (most often in London) are known as **Eurodollar CDs** (or simply Euro CDs). Also available for investment are dollar-denominated time deposits in banks outside the United States, known as **Eurodollar deposits.** A key distinction between Euro CDs and Eurodollar deposits is that Euro CDs are negotiable, meaning that they can be traded, whereas Eurodollar deposits are nonnegotiable, meaning that they cannot be traded.

Eurodollar CDs

Eurodollar deposits

The demand and supply conditions for such instruments may differ from the conditions for other U.S. money market instruments, owing to restrictions imposed (or likely to be imposed) by the United States and other governments. However, enough commonality exists to keep interest rates from diverging too much from rates available on domestic alternatives. One difference from CDs issued by U.S. banks is that the Euro CDs do not have federal deposit insurance.

Repurchase Agreements

repurchase agreement

repo rate

Often one investor (often a financial institution) will sell another investor (often another financial institution) a money market instrument, and agree to repurchase it for an agreed-upon price at a later date. For example, investor A might sell investor B a number of Treasury bills that mature in 180 days for a price of $10 million. As part of the sale, investor A has signed a **repurchase agreement** (or "repo") with investor B (from the perspective of the purchaser, investor B, the agreement is referred to as a "reverse repo"). This agreement specifies that after thirty days, investor A will repurchase these Treasury bills for $10.1 million. Thus, investor A will have paid investor B $100,000 in interest for thirty days' use of $10 million, meaning that investor B has, in essence, purchased a money market instrument that matures in thirty days. The annualized interest rate is known as the **repo rate,** which in this case is equal to 12% [($100,000/$10,000,000) × (360/30)].

U.S. GOVERNMENT SECURITIES

debt refunding

It should come as no surprise that the U.S. government relies heavily on debt financing. Since the 1960s, revenues have seldom covered expenses, and the differences have been financed primarily by issuing debt instruments. Moreover, new debt must be issued in order to get the necessary funds to pay off old debt that comes due. Such **debt refunding** sometimes allows the holders of the maturing debt to exchange it directly for new debt, and in the process receive beneficial treatment for tax purposes.

Some idea of the magnitude and the ownership of U.S. Treasury debt can be gained by examining Table 19-1. Through the U.S. Treasury, federal agencies, and various trust funds, the federal government itself is a large holder, as is the Federal Reserve System. However, a large amount is held by state and local governments as well as private investors of one sort or another. For example, these securities are a major factor in the portfolios of commercial

TABLE 19-1 Ownership of Outstanding Public Debt of U.S. Treasury, End of 1991

HELD BY	DOLLAR AMOUNT (IN BILLIONS)	PERCENT OF TOTAL AMOUNT
Commercial banks	$ 222.0	5.8%
Individuals	263.9	6.9
Insurance companies	168.0	4.4
Money market funds	80.0	2.1
Corporations[1]	150.8	4.0
State and local governments	490.0	12.9
Foreign and international investors	457.7	12.0
Other investors	730.8	19.2
Total of privately-held public debt	$2,563.2	67.3%
U.S. Treasury, federal agencies, and trust funds	968.7	25.5
Federal Reserve Banks	288.4	7.6
Total gross public debt[2]	$3,801.9	100%

[1]Excluding commercial banks and insurance companies.

[2]According to the *Federal Reserve Bulletin*, the components do not sum to the total shown because of rounding.

Source: Federal Reserve Bulletin, June 1992, p. A28.

banks and other financial institutions. To a lesser extent, business corporations also invest in them, primarily as outlets for relatively short-term excess working capital. The amount held by individual households is also substantial, with over half of their investment in U.S. government securities being in savings bonds and notes. Lastly, foreign holdings have become quite large in recent years.

About two-thirds of the public debt is marketable, meaning that it is represented by securities that can be sold at any time by the original purchaser through government security dealers. The major nonmarketable issues are held by U.S. government agencies, foreign governments, state and local governments, and individuals (the latter in the form of U.S. Savings Bonds). Marketable issues include Treasury bills, notes, and bonds. Table 19-2 shows the amounts of interest-bearing U.S. public debt in each category at the end of 1991 (there was an additional $2.8 billion of non-interest-bearing U.S. public debt outstanding at that time, so total U.S public debt amounted to $3,801.9 billion).

term-to-maturity

The relative maturity dates for U.S. government debt are influenced by a number of factors. As time passes, of course, the **term-to-maturity** (that is, the remaining time until maturity) of an outstanding issue will decrease. Moreover, the Treasury has considerable latitude in selecting maturities for new issues and can also engage in refunding operations. From time to time, congressional limits on amounts issued or interest paid on certain types of instruments may force reliance on other types of instruments. Debt operations may also be employed as a conscious instrument of governmental economic policy in an attempt to influence the current interest rates for securities of various maturities.

Table 19-3 shows the maturity structure of marketable, interest-bearing debt in June 1991. Over 30% was short-term debt, maturing in less than one year, and about 70% had a maturity date within five years.

Many types of debt have been issued by the U.S. government as well as by U.S. government agencies and organizations sponsored by the federal government. Figure 19-3 shows a typical list of price quotations for certain types of debt securities that have been issued by the U.S. government. These securities will be discussed next.

TABLE 19-2
Interest-Bearing U.S. Public Debt, End of 1991

CATEGORY		AMOUNT (IN BILLIONS)
Nonmarketable:		
Government account series	$ 959.2	
U.S. Savings Bonds	135.9	
Foreign series	41.9	
State and local government series	159.7	
Total Nonmarketable Debt		$1,327.2
Marketable:		
Bills	$ 590.4	
Notes	1,430.8	
Bonds	435.5	
Total Marketable Debt		2,471.6
Total Debt[1]		$3,798.9

[1]According to the *Federal Reserve Bulletin*, the components do not sum to the total shown because of rounding.

Source: Federal Reserve Bulletin, June 1992, p. A28.

TABLE 19-3
Maturity Structure of Marketable, Interest-Bearing U.S. Public Debt Held by Private Investors, June 1991

MATURITY	AMOUNT (IN BILLIONS)	PERCENT OF TOTAL AMOUNT
Within 1 year	$ 673.2	33.6%
1–5 years	717.1	35.8
5–10 years	264.3	13.2
10–20 years	87.2	4.4
20 years and over	261.3	13.0
Total	$2,003.1	100.0%

Source: *Treasury Bulletin*, Summer Issue, September 1991, p. 38.

U.S. Treasury Bills

Treasury bills are issued on a discount basis, with maturities of up to fifty-two weeks and in denominations of $10,000 or more (although at times denominations as small as $1,000 have been offered). All are issued in book-entry form, where the buyer receives a receipt at time of purchase and the bill's face value at maturity. Although Treasury bills are sold at discount, their dollar yield (that is, the difference between the purchase price and face value if the bill is held to maturity) is treated as interest income for tax purposes.

Offerings of thirteen-week and twenty-six-week bills are usually made once each week; fifty-two-week bills are usually offered every fourth week. All are sold by auction. Bids may be entered on either a competitive or a noncompetitive basis. With a competitive bid, the investor states a price he or she is willing to pay (which can be converted to the interest rate that would be earned if the bid is accepted). For example, an investor might enter a bid for a stated number of thirteen-week bills at a price of 98.512. If the bid is accepted, the investor will pay $9,851.20 for each $10,000 of face value, meaning that an investment of $9,851.20 will generate a receipt of $10,000 if held to maturity thirteen weeks later. With a noncompetitive bid, the investor agrees to pay the average price of all bids that will be accepted by the Treasury.

Before each auction, the Treasury announces the total face value and the maturities of all bills that it plans to issue. At the auction itself, having received the bids, the Treasury proceeds to accept all noncompetitive bids. For example, if $6 billion of thirteen-week bills are to be issued, perhaps $2 billion of noncompetitive bids will have been received by the time of the auction. Since all of these bids will be accepted, the Treasury will accept only $4 billion of competitive bids, taking the highest prices offered by competitive-bidding investors. The average price on the accepted competitive bids will be the price charged to the noncompetitive bidders.

Each Tuesday *The Wall Street Journal* publishes the results of the auction that took place on the previous day. Figure 19-4 presents the results of the auction that took place on June 15, 1992.

Individuals may purchase new issues of Treasury bills directly from one of the twelve Federal Reserve Banks, or indirectly via a bank or broker. Government security dealers maintain an active secondary market in bills, and it is a simple matter to buy or sell one prior to maturity (especially if the original purchase was through a bank or broker). Terms offered by government security dealers are reported daily in the financial press, stated on a "bank discount" basis. To determine the actual dollar prices, an investor needs to "undo" the bank discount computation.

For example, a bill with 120 days left to maturity might be listed as

TREASURY BONDS, NOTES & BILLS

Thursday, June 18, 1992

Representative Over-the-Counter quotations based on transactions of $1 million or more.

Treasury bond, note and bill quotes are as of mid-afternoon. Colons in bid-and-asked quotes represent 32nds; 101:01 means 101 1/32. Net changes in 32nds. n-Treasury note. Treasury bill quotes in hundredths, quoted on terms of a rate of discount. Days to maturity calculated from settlement date. All yields are to maturity and based on the asked quote. Latest 13-week and 26-week bills are boldfaced. For bonds callable prior to maturity, yields are computed to the earliest call date for issues quoted above par and to the maturity date for issues below par. *-When issued.

Source: Federal Reserve Bank of New York.

U.S. Treasury strips as of 3 p.m. Eastern time, also based on transactions of $1 million or more. Colons in bid-and-asked quotes represent 32nds; 101:01 means 101 1/32. Net changes in 32nds. Yields calculated on the asked quotation. ci-stripped coupon interest. bp-Treasury bond, stripped principal. np-Treasury note, stripped principal. For bonds callable prior to maturity, yields are computed to the earliest call date for issues quoted above par and to the maturity date for issues below par.

Source: Bear, Stearns & Co. via Street Software Technology Inc.

GOVT. BONDS & NOTES

Rate	Maturity Mo/Yr	Bid	Asked	Chg.	Ask Yld.
8 1/4	Jun 92n	100:06	100:08	....	0.00
8 3/8	Jun 92n	100:05	100:07	− 1	-1.51
10 3/8	Jul 92n	100:16	100:18	....	1.40
8	Jul 92n	100:16	100:18	....	2.65
4 1/4	Aug 87-92	98:09	98:25	....	12.43
7 1/4	Aug 92	100:17	100:19	....	3.15
7 7/8	Aug 92n	100:20	100:22	....	3.13
8 1/4	Aug 92n	100:22	100:24	....	3.08
8 1/8	Aug 92n	100:27	100:29	....	3.25
8 1/8	Sep 92n	101:06	101:08	....	3.44
8 3/4	Sep 92n	101:12	101:14	....	3.37
9 3/4	Oct 92n	101:28	101:30	− 1	3.45
7 3/4	Oct 92n	101:12	101:14	....	3.62
7 3/4	Nov 92n	101:17	101:19	....	3.65
8 3/8	Nov 92n	101:25	101:27	....	3.63
10 1/2	Nov 92n	102:20	102:22	....	3.59
7 3/8	Nov 92n	101:17	101:19	....	3.68

Rate	Maturity Mo/Yr	Bid	Asked	Chg.	Ask Yld.
8 1/8	Feb 98n	107:06	107:08	+ 6	6.57
7 7/8	Apr 98n	106:01	106:03	+ 7	6.60
7	May 93-98	100:31	101:07	....	5.59
9	May 98n	111:13	111:15	+ 6	6.62
8 1/4	Jul 98n	107:25	107:27	+ 6	6.66
9 1/4	Aug 98n	112:22	112:24	+ 6	6.69
7 1/8	Oct 98n	102:06	102:08	+ 6	6.68
3 1/2	Nov 98	95:00	96:00	+38	4.22
8 7/8	Nov 98n	110:28	110:30	+ 7	6.74
6 3/8	Jan 99n	97:31	98:01	+ 6	6.75
8 7/8	Feb 99n	110:29	110:31	+ 7	6.80
7	Apr 99n	101:05	101:07	+ 8	6.77
8 1/2	May 94-99	105:20	105:28	+ 9	5.21
9 1/8	May 99n	112:09	112:11	+ 6	6.85
8	Aug 99n	106:06	106:08	+ 6	6.88
7 7/8	Nov 99n	105:15	105:17	+ 7	6.91
7 7/8	Feb 95-00	103:28	104:00	+ 1	6.21
8 1/2	Feb 00n	108:28	108:30	+ 7	6.97

Mat.	Type	Bid	Asked	Chg.	Ask Yld.
Feb 00	np	57:27	57:31	+ 6	7.26
May 00	ci	56:12	56:16	+ 7	7.36
May 00	np	56:18	56:22	+ 6	7.32
Aug 00	ci	55:06	55:10	+ 7	7.40
Aug 00	np	55:17	55:21	+ 5	7.32
Nov 00	ci	54:06	54:10	+ 7	7.40
Nov 00	np	54:13	54:18	+ 5	7.35
Feb 01	ci	52:26	52:30	+ 7	7.49
Feb 01	np	53:10	53:14	+ 6	7.38
May 01	ci	51:22	51:26	+ 6	7.53
May 01	np	52:07	52:11	+ 6	7.41
Aug 01	ci	50:20	50:24	+ 6	7.55
Aug 01	np	51:05	51:10	+ 5	7.43
Nov 01	ci	49:17	49:21	+ 6	7.59
Nov 01	np	50:04	50:08	+ 6	7.46
Feb 02	ci	48:05	48:09	+ 6	7.69
May 02	ci	47:07	47:11	+ 6	7.70
Aug 02	ci	46:09	46:13	+ 6	7.71
Nov 02	ci	45:10	45:14	+ 6	7.73
Feb 03	ci	44:03	44:07	+ 4	7.81
May 03	ci	43:07	43:11	+ 5	7.82
Aug 03	ci	42:08	42:12	+ 3	7.85
Nov 03	ci	41:13	41:17	+ 3	7.86
Feb 04	ci	40:11	40:15	+ 3	7.92
May 04	ci	39:16	39:21	+ 3	7.93
Aug 04	ci	38:21	38:25	+ 3	7.95
Nov 04	ci	37:23	37:28	+ 3	7.99
Nov 04	bp	38:03	38:07	+ 3	7.91
Feb 05	ci	36:30	37:02	+ 3	8.00
May 05	ci	36:06	36:10	+ 3	8.01
May 05	bp	36:17	36:22	+ 3	7.93
Aug 05	ci	35:14	35:18	+ 3	8.02
Aug 05	bp	35:25	35:30	+ 3	7.94
Nov 05	ci	34:24	34:28	+ 3	8.02
Feb 06	ci	33:25	33:30	+ 3	8.08
Feb 06	bp	34:12	34:16	+ 3	7.95
May 06	ci	33:03	33:07	+ 3	8.09
Aug 06	ci	32:14	32:18	+ 3	8.09
Nov 06	ci	31:24	31:28	+ 3	8.10
Feb 07	ci	30:29	31:01	+ 3	8.15

Rate	Maturity Mo/Yr	Bid	Asked	Chg.	Ask Yld.
11 5/8	Nov 94n	114:10	114:12	+ 4	5.17
7 5/8	Dec 94n	105:19	105:21	+ 4	5.20
8 5/8	Jan 95n	107:27	107:29	+ 5	5.29
3	Feb 95	94:31	95:31	+ 2	4.63
5 1/2	Feb 95n	100:12	100:14	+ 4	5.32
7 3/4	Feb 95n	105:28	105:30	+ 3	5.32
10 1/2	Feb 95	112:18	112:20	+ 4	5.33
11 1/4	Feb 95n	114:11	114:13	+ 3	5.35
8 3/8	Apr 95n	107:17	107:19	+ 4	5.43
5 7/8	May 95n	101:04	101:06	+ 5	5.43
8 1/2	May 95n	107:31	108:01	+ 4	5.47
10 3/8	May 95	112:30	113:00	+ 4	5.46
11 1/4	May 95n	115:06	115:08	+ 5	5.49
12 5/8	May 95	119:07	119:11	+ 4	5.33
8 7/8	Jul 95n	109:05	109:07	+ 4	5.56
8 1/2	Aug 95n	108:06	108:08	+ 5	5.61
10 1/2	Aug 95n	113:26	113:28	+ 4	5.63
8 5/8	Oct 95n	108:19	108:21	+ 4	5.72
8 1/2	Nov 95n	108:09	108:11	+ 4	5.76
9 1/2	Nov 95n	111:11	111:13	+ 5	5.76
11 1/2	Nov 95	117:14	117:18	+ 5	5.74
9 1/4	Jan 96n	110:22	110:24	+ 5	5.86
7 1/2	Jan 96n	105:05	105:07	+ 4	5.87
7 7/8	Feb 96n	106:10	106:12	+ 4	5.91
8 7/8	Feb 96n	109:17	109:19	+ 5	5.91
7 1/2	Feb 96n	105:03	105:05	+ 5	5.92
7 3/4	Mar 96n	105:27	105:29	+ 4	5.98
9 3/8	Apr 96n	111:10	111:12	+ 5	6.00
7 5/8	Apr 96n	105:15	105:17	+ 6	6.00
7 3/8	May 96n	104:19	104:21	+ 7	6.02
7 5/8	May 96n	105:15	105:17	+ 6	6.03
7 7/8	Jun 96n	106:09	106:11	+ 5	6.07
7 7/8	Jul 96n	106:09	106:11	+ 5	6.09
7 7/8	Jul 96n	106:08	106:10	+ 5	6.11
7 1/4	Aug 96n	103:30	104:00	+ 4	6.15
7	Sep 96n	103:02	103:04	+ 6	6.16
8	Oct 96n	106:23	106:25	+ 4	6.19
6 7/8	Oct 96n	102:17	102:19	+ 4	6.19
7 1/4	Nov 96n	103:28	103:30	+ 5	6.21
6 1/2	Nov 96n	101:05	101:07	+ 5	6.18
6 1/8	Dec 96n	99:22	99:24	+ 5	6.19
8	Jan 97n	106:25	106:27	+ 6	6.25
6 1/4	Jan 97n	99:30	100:00	+ 7	6.25
6 3/4	Feb 97n	101:26	101:28	+ 7	6.28
6 7/8	Mar 97n	102:06	102:08	+ 7	6.32
8 1/2	Apr 97n	108:24	108:26	+ 6	6.35
6 7/8	Apr 97n	102:05	102:07	+ 7	6.34
8 1/2	May 97n	108:25	108:27	+ 6	6.37
6 3/4	May 97n	101:19	101:21	+ 8	6.35
8 1/2	Jul 97n	108:27	108:29	+ 6	6.41
8 5/8	Aug 97n	109:13	109:15	+ 5	6.44
8 3/4	Oct 97n	110:00	110:02	+ 5	6.48
8 7/8	Nov 97n	110:20	110:22	+ 5	6.50
7 7/8	Jan 98n	106:02	106:04	+ 5	6.54

U.S. TREASURY STRIPS

Mat.	Type	Bid	Asked	Chg.	Ask Yld.
Aug 92	ci	99:15	99:15	....	3.63
Nov 92	ci	98:15	98:16	....	3.86
Feb 93	ci	97:17	97:17	+ 1	3.87
May 93	ci	96:16	96:17	....	3.97
Aug 93	ci	95:09	95:10	+ 1	4.22
Nov 93	ci	93:30	93:31	+ 3	4.51
Feb 94	ci	92:22	92:24	+ 3	4.62
May 94	ci	91:09	91:11	+ 4	4.84
Aug 94	ci	89:24	89:26	+ 4	5.06
Nov 94	ci	88:06	88:08	+ 4	5.28
Nov 94	np	88:04	88:06	+ 4	5.32
Feb 95	ci	86:23	86:25	+ 4	5.42
Feb 95	np	86:20	86:22	+ 5	5.47
May 95	ci	85:08	85:11	+ 4	5.55
May 95	np	85:04	85:06	+ 5	5.61
Aug 95	ci	83:25	83:28	+ 5	5.67
Aug 95	np	83:18	83:21	+ 4	5.75
Nov 95	ci	82:11	82:14	+ 5	5.77
Nov 95	np	82:02	82:05	+ 5	5.87
Feb 96	ci	80:13	80:16	+ 5	6.04
Feb 96	np	80:07	80:10	+ 4	6.10
May 96	ci	78:27	78:30	+ 4	6.16
May 96	np	78:22	78:25	+ 5	6.22
Aug 96	ci	77:12	77:15	+ 5	6.25
Nov 96	ci	76:05	76:08	+ 5	6.26
Nov 96	np	75:29	76:00	+ 5	6.34
Feb 97	ci	74:15	74:19	+ 5	6.41
May 97	ci	72:31	73:02	+ 3	6.51
May 97	np	72:26	72:29	+ 5	6.56
Aug 97	ci	71:16	71:20	+ 6	6.59
Aug 97	np	71:20	71:23	+ 5	6.56
Nov 97	ci	70:08	70:12	+ 5	6.62
Nov 97	np	70:02	70:06	+ 4	6.67
Feb 98	ci	68:16	68:20	+ 7	6.78
Feb 98	np	68:13	68:16	+ 5	6.81
May 98	ci	67:06	67:10	+ 7	6.83
May 98	np	67:06	67:10	+ 5	6.83
Aug 98	ci	65:27	65:31	+ 5	6.88
Aug 98	np	66:02	66:05	+ 5	6.83
Nov 98	ci	64:20	64:24	+ 5	6.91
Nov 98	np	64:01	64:05	+ 5	7.06
Feb 99	ci	62:26	62:30	+ 7	7.09
Feb 99	np	62:14	62:18	+ 5	7.18
May 99	ci	61:17	61:21	+ 7	7.14
May 99	np	61:10	61:14	+ 5	7.19
Aug 99	ci	60:07	60:11	+ 6	7.19
Aug 99	np	59:30	60:02	+ 5	7.26
Nov 99	ci	58:31	59:03	+ 7	7.24
Nov 99	np	58:28	59:00	+ 5	7.26
Feb 00	ci	57:18	57:23	+ 6	7.32

Mat.	Type	Bid	Asked	Chg.	Ask Yld.
Feb 20	bp	11:02	11:05	+ 2	8.09
May 20	ci	10:20	10:23	+ 2	8.17
May 20	bp	10:28	10:31	+ 2	8.08
Aug 20	ci	10:14	10:17	+ 2	8.16
Aug 20	bp	10:24	10:27	+ 2	8.05
Nov 20	ci	10:08	10:11	+ 1	8.15
Feb 21	ci	10:03	10:05	+ 2	8.14
Feb 21	bp	10:16	10:19	+ 1	7.99
May 21	ci	9:29	10:00	+ 1	8.13
May 21	bp	10:08	10:11	− 2	8.01
Aug 21	ci	9:24	9:26	+ 2	8.12
Aug 21	bp	10:08	10:11	+ 2	7.94
Nov 21	ci	10:03	10:05	+ 2	7.93
Nov 21	bp	10:09	10:12	+ 2	7.86

TREASURY BILLS

Maturity	Days to Mat.	Bid	Asked	Chg.	Ask Yld.
Jun 25 '92	3	3.09	2.99	−0.07	3.04
Jul 02 '92	10	3.38	3.28	−0.02	3.34
Jul 09 '92	17	3.37	3.27	−0.03	3.33
Jul 16 '92	24	3.39	3.29	+0.03	3.35
Jul 23 '92	31	3.40	3.36	+0.01	3.43
Jul 30 '92	38	3.43	3.39	−0.02	3.46
Aug 06 '92	45	3.49	3.45	....	3.52
Aug 13 '92	52	3.49	3.45	−0.02	3.53
Aug 20 '92	59	3.50	3.48	−0.03	3.56
Aug 27 '92	66	3.54	3.52	−0.02	3.60
Sep 03 '92	73	3.56	3.54	−0.03	3.62
Sep 10 '92	80	3.58	3.56	−0.02	3.64
Sep 17 '92	**87**	**3.61**	**3.59**	**−0.01**	**3.67**
Sep 24 '92	94	3.63	3.61	−0.01	3.71
Oct 01 '92	101	3.64	3.62	−0.01	3.71
Oct 08 '92	108	3.64	3.62	−0.02	3.71
Oct 15 '92	115	3.65	3.63	−0.02	3.72
Oct 22 '92	122	3.66	3.64	−0.01	3.75
Oct 29 '92	129	3.66	3.64	−0.03	3.74
Nov 05 '92	136	3.68	3.66	−0.01	3.76
Nov 12 '92	143	3.68	3.66	−0.03	3.77
Nov 19 '92	150	3.68	3.66	−0.02	3.78
Nov 27 '92	158	3.69	3.67	−0.01	3.78
Dec 03 '92	164	3.70	3.68	−0.02	3.79
Dec 10 '92	171	3.69	3.67	−0.02	3.79
Dec 17 '92	**178**	**3.70**	**3.68**	**−0.01**	**3.81**
Jan 14 '93	206	3.71	3.69	−0.02	3.82
Feb 11 '93	234	3.77	3.75	−0.01	3.89
Mar 11 '93	262	3.80	3.78	−0.01	3.92
Apr 08 '93	290	3.84	3.82	−0.03	3.97
May 06 '93	318	3.88	3.86	−0.02	4.02
Jun 03 '93	346	3.89	3.87	−0.02	4.04

FIGURE 19-3
Price Quotations for U.S. Treasury Securities

Source: Reprinted by permission of *The Wall Street Journal*, © Dow Jones & Company, Inc., June 19, 1992, p. C14. All rights reserved worldwide.

FIGURE 19-4
Treasury Bill Auction Results for June 15, 1992

Source: Reprinted by permission of *The Wall Street Journal*, © Dow Jones & Company, Inc., June 16, 1992, p. C19. All rights reserved worldwide.

Here are the details of yesterday's auction by the Treasury of 13-week and 26-week bills:

Rates are determined by the difference between the purchase price and face value. Thus, higher bidding narrows the investor's return while lower bidding widens it. The percentage rates are calculated on a 360-day year, while the coupon-equivalent yield is based on a 365-day year.

	13-Week	26-Week
Applications	$44,261,740,000	$39,209,700,000
Accepted bids	$11,740,995,000	$11,667,885,000
Accepted at low price	1%	13%
Accepted noncompet'ly ...	$1,220,670,000	$901,140,000
Average price (Rate)	99.075 (3.66%)	98.104 (3.75%)
High price (Rate)	99.077 (3.65%)	98.114 (3.73%)
Low price (Rate)	99.072 (3.67%)	98.099 (3.76%)
Coupon equivalent	3.74%	3.88%
CUSIP number	912794ZL1	912794ZB3

Both issues are dated June 18. The 13-week bills mature Sept. 17, 1992, and the 26-week bills mature Dec. 17, 1992.

"7.48% bid, 7.19% ask." Both of these discounts were obtained by multiplying the actual discount by 360/120 (the inverse of the portion of a 360-day year involved). Thus, to find the actual discount associated with the 7.48% bid, multiply 7.48% by 120/360, resulting in a figure of 2.493%. This means that the dealer is bidding 100% − 2.493% = 97.507% of face value, meaning the dealer is willing to pay $9,750.70 for this $10,000 Treasury bill.

Similarly, the dealer is offering to sell such a bill at a discount of 100% − [7.19% × (120/360)] = 2.397%, meaning the dealer is willing to sell such a bill for $9,760.30 = $10,000 × (100% − 2.397%). The difference between the prices—$9.60 = $9,760.30 − $9,750.70—is known as the **dealer's spread,** and serves as compensation for carrying inventories of bills, taking associated risks, and bearing the clerical and other costs associated with being a market-maker.

dealer's spread

In addition to the bid and asked discounts, *The Wall Street Journal* and other media provide an **equivalent yield** that is based on the asked price. In the example, the equivalent yield would be calculated by determining the dollar discount on the security ($10,000 − $9,760.30 = $239.70) and then dividing this figure by the purchase price ($239.70/$9,760.30 = 2.455%) in order to arrive at the rate of return associated with purchasing the security. Then, this rate of return is annualized by multiplying it by 365, and then dividing the product by the number of days until maturity. The resulting figure is the equivalent yield. In the example, the equivalent yield is 7.47% = 2.455% × (365/120).

equivalent yield

U.S. Treasury Notes

Treasury notes are issued with maturities from one to ten years and generally make coupon payments semiannually. Some, issued prior to 1983, are in **bearer** form, with coupons attached; the owner simply submits each coupon on its specified date to receive payment for the stated amount. Beginning in 1983, the Treasury ceased the issuance of bearer notes (and bonds). All issues since then are in **registered** form; the current owner is registered with the Treasury, which sends him or her each coupon payment when due and the principal value at maturity. When a registered note is sold, the new owner's name and address are substituted for those of the old owner on the Treasury's books.

bearer bond

registered bond

Treasury notes are issued in denominations of $1,000 or more. Coupon payments are set at an amount so the notes will initially sell close to par value. In most cases an auction is held, with both competitive and noncompetitive bids being submitted.

Treasury notes are traded in an active secondary market made by dealers in U.S. government securities. For example, as shown in Figure 19-3, *The Wall Street Journal* carried the following quotation from June 18, 1992:

RATE	MAT. DATE	BID	ASKED	CHG.	ASK YIELD
9	May 98 n	111:13	111:15	+6	6.62

This indicated that a note (n), maturing in May 1998, carried a coupon rate of 9%. It could be sold to a dealer for 111 13⁄32% of par value, which is equivalent to $1,114.0625 per $1,000 of par value. Alternatively, it could be purchased from a dealer for 111 15⁄32% of par value, which is equivalent to $1,114.6875 per $1,000 of par value (thus, the dealer's spread was equal to $.625 = $1,114.6875 − $1,114.0625). On June 18, 1992, the bid price was 6⁄32 more than it had been on the previous trading day, June 17, 1992, resulting in a reported "Chg." of +6 (note how numbers are expressed in 32nds, reflecting an old tradition). The effective yield-to-maturity at the time, based on the asked price, was approximately 6.62% per year.[2]

In practice, the situation facing a potential buyer (or seller) is a little more complicated. The buyer is generally expected to pay the dealer not only the stated price ($1,114.6875), but also any **accrued interest.** For example, if 122 days have elapsed since the last coupon payment and sixty-one days remain, then an amount equal to 122/(122 + 61) = 2⁄3 of the semiannual coupon (2⁄3 × $45 = $30) is added to the stated purchase price to determine the total amount required (in this case, $30 + $1,114.6875 = $1,144.6875). Similarly, if an investor was to sell a note to the dealer, the dealer would pay the investor the stated bid price plus accrued interest (in this case, $1,114.0625 + $30 = $1,144.0625). This procedure is commonly followed with both government and corporate bonds.[3]

accrued interest

U.S. Treasury Bonds

Treasury bonds have maturities greater than ten years at the time of issuance. Those issued prior to 1983 may be in either bearer or registered form; more recent issues will be in registered form. Denominations range from $1,000 upward. Unlike Treasury notes, some Treasury bond issues have **call provisions** that allow them to be "called" during a specified period (usually the period begins five to ten years prior to maturity, and ends at the maturity date). This means that at any scheduled coupon payment date during this period, the Treasury has the right to force the investor to sell the bonds back to the government at par value.

call provisions

[2]The yield-to-maturity on a bond is the discount rate that makes the present value of the future coupon payments and par value equal to its current market price (which in this case is the asked price). Chapter 20 will discuss yields more fully.

[3]The procedure for calculating accrued interest on corporate bonds is different in that it is based on an assumption that there are thirty days in each month and 180 days in each semiannual period. Specifically, (1) the number of complete months left until the next coupon payment is determined and multiplied by 30; (2) the number of days left in the current month is determined and added to the previous figure; (3) the resulting figure is subtracted from 180, thereby giving the number of days that have elapsed since the last coupon payment; (4) this figure is divided by 180, giving the fraction of the period that has elapsed; and (5) this fraction is multiplied by the semiannual coupon, resulting in the amount of accrued interest.

MONEY MATTERS
The Salomon Short Squeeze

The strategy is as old as organized security trading: First, corner the market in a security by controlling most or all of its outstanding shares; second, wait for the arrival of investors who must buy the security. (These will be primarily investors who have sold the security short—see Chapter 2—for various reasons and now must buy it back to cover their short positions.) When investors realize that the supply of the security is tight, they will bid its price up, resulting in handsome profits to the market manipulator. The strategy is known as a "short squeeze."

Salomon Brothers, the giant New York–based bond house, played the short squeeze almost to perfection in 1991. Their only mistake: The firm was caught violating U.S. Treasury security auction rules. The discovery of Salomon's misdeeds and the firm's subsequent punishment rocked Wall Street and has led regulators to consider an overhaul of the process by which Treasury securities are issued.

The market for U.S. Treasury securities is the largest in the world. On average, well over $100 billion in Treasury securities change hands every day. By comparison, less than $10 billion in U.S. common stocks are traded daily. How could a bond dealer, even one as large as Salomon Brothers, hope to corner the Treasury security market? To understand, we must briefly consider how new Treasury issues are brought to market.

The Treasury sells new bills, notes, and bonds through a competitive bidding process. The system is designed to produce the highest price for the Treasury's new debt issues while simultaneously generating a level of investor participation in the auctions that is both large and broad.

Prior to a new security's issuance, the Treasury announces the amount of the security to be sold. Interested investors can submit either noncompetitive or competitive bids. All noncompetitive bids are accepted; the remainder of the issue goes to the competitive bidders. The competitive bidders, however, determine the security's price. The highest bid prices (lowest yields) for the remaining amount of the security are accepted. The noncompetitive bidders pay the quantity-weighted average of the competitive bids.

To facilitate a smooth reception for its frequent and large debt issues, the Treasury employs a network of bond dealers known as *primary dealers*. Effectively, bids for new Treasury securities must be submitted through primary dealers or commercial banks. In exchange for this preferred position (conferred by the Federal Reserve Bank of New York), primary dealers (in 1992 forty in number) are required to bid in all Treasury auctions and to make an active market in all Treasury securities. The designation of primary dealer status is highly prized among bond dealers, both for its prestige and for the monopolistic market position it offers.

The Treasury prohibits any investor from bidding for, or otherwise controlling, more than 35% of any new

Callable issues can be identified in Figure 19-3 by noting which issues have a range of years given as the maturity date (this "range of years" indicates the call period). For example, the 8½ of May 94–99 mature in 1999 but may be called beginning in 1994 (the "8½" indicates that the bonds have a coupon rate of 8½%, paid semiannually).

For callable issues, the yield-to-maturity is calculated using the asked price. If this price is greater than par, then the yield-to-maturity is based on an assumption that the bond will be called at the earliest allowable date. Otherwise, Treasury bonds are comparable to Treasury notes, with dealers' bid and asked quotations being stated in the same form.

U.S. Savings Bonds

These nonmarketable bonds are offered only to individuals and selected organizations. No more than a specified amount (currently $15,000 of issue price) may be purchased by any person in a single year. Two types are available. Series EE bonds are essentially pure discount bonds, meaning that no interest is paid on them prior to maturity. The term-to-maturity at the date of issuance has varied from time to time; for bonds issued in 1992, it was twelve years (however, they may be held as long as an additional eighteen years before they must be redeemed or exchanged for an HH bond). Series HH

Treasury issue. This regulation is designed to prevent market manipulation, and it was this regulation that Salomon Brothers strove to circumvent in the May 22, 1991, auction of a two-year Treasury note.

The Treasury had announced plans to issue $12.3 billion of a note due in May 1993. Salomon had already purchased $590 million of the note in the when-issued market. (An investor can buy a security from another investor several days before it is actually issued by the Treasury. The seller is obligated to obtain and deliver the security to the purchaser once it is issued.) Salomon also aggressively bid for $4.2 billion of the note for its own account (the 35% limit on the note was $4.3 billion). Further, it bid for roughly $6.5 billion of the note for various customers who had agreed to work with Salomon to manipulate the market. (These customers, it turns out, had only ordered $6 billion of the note, leaving Salomon to surreptitiously acquire an additional $500 million for its own account.) In sum, then, Salomon sought to control directly, or through accounts of its customers, 94% of the auctioned security. Effectively, Salomon had illegally cornered the market in the May 1993 two-year note.

The short squeeze occurred next. Short selling is much more prevalent in the U.S. Treasury market than in the common stock market. Given the minuscule amount of security-specific risk (see Chapter 8) associated with Treasury securities, short sellers are able to efficiently hedge their risks through the options and futures markets (see Chapters 24 and 25). Bond dealers will often short Treasury securities to quickly facilitate their customers' needs, fully expecting that the Treasury market's liquidity will permit them to readily acquire the shorted bonds when needed. The Salomon market corner removed this liquidity. By withholding the note from the market, Salomon was able to force short sellers to bid up the note's price, providing the firm with substantial profits when it chose to sell.

The short squeeze did not go unnoticed. Complaints from disadvantaged bond dealers led the Treasury and the Securities and Exchange Commission to conduct investigations. Eventually, Salomon confessed to its misdeeds. Further, it volunteered that it had attempted market corners in other Treasury auctions.

In the wake of the scandal the firm's chairman resigned. Several senior bond traders and other members of management also resigned or were fired. Further, Salomon was fined $290 million. Even more stringent penalties were considered, such as felony prosecutions or stripping Salomon of its primary dealer designation. However, the government stopped short of these steps for fear of destabilizing the Treasury security market.

Charges of rampant collusion among large bond dealers and their customers at Treasury auctions surfaced after the Salomon short squeeze became public knowledge. Critics argue that the current auction system is open to manipulation and favors large, well-placed investors. These critics have called for more open and automated electronic auctions that would encourage more competitive investor participation. Investors would be allowed to submit competitive bids directly, thus bypassing the primary dealers if they so choose. Entrenched institutions die hard, however, and it remains to be seen whether the Salomon short squeeze will bring changes to a well-established, profitable system.

---

bonds mature in twenty years and pay interest semiannually. Both types are registered. Series EE bonds are available in small denominations (the smallest one has an issue price of $50) and may be purchased from commercial banks and many other financial institutions. Some employers even allow employees to obtain them through payroll savings plans. Series HH bonds are available only in exchange for eligible Series EE bonds (that is, a Series EE bond must be purchased first and then held for the minimum time period of six months before it can be exchanged) and can only be obtained from the Treasury Department or one of the twelve Federal Reserve Banks.

Series EE bonds issued in 1992 utilize a floating rate with a minimum floor. If a bond is held for five or more years, interest is paid at a rate equal to (1) 85% of the average market return on Treasury bonds and notes with five years remaining to maturity or (2) 6% per year, whichever is larger. The applicable rate is computed and compounded every six months (in May and November). Should the bond be held for less than five years, a lower rate is used to determine the redemption value of the bond. Series HH bonds issued in 1992 provide a fixed annual rate of 6%, and can be redeemed at any time for par value.

Unlike most other discount bonds, no taxes are paid on the interest as it accumulates semiannually on the Series EE bonds. Only when these bonds are redeemed is the interest subject to federal income tax; no state or local income taxes are involved.[4] Thus, a $15,000 investment that grows to $30,000 in twelve years will only create a tax obligation at the end of the twelfth year. Furthermore, should a Series EE bond be exchanged for a Series HH bond, this tax obligation on the interest earned on the Series EE bond can be deferred until the Series HH bond is redeemed. However, the HH bond interest is subject to federal income tax annually. Hence, the tax obligation on the $30,000 would be deferred if the EE bond is exchanged for an HH bond, but the $1,800 (= .06 × $30,000) annual HH interest would be taxable.

The terms on which Savings Bonds are offered have been revised from time to time. In some cases, improved terms have been offered to holders of outstanding bonds. Terms have sometimes been inferior to those available on less well-known or less accessible instruments with similar characteristics. At such times, the Treasury Department sells Savings Bonds by appealing more to patriotism than to the desire for high return.

Zero-Coupon Treasury Security Receipts

A noncallable Treasury note or bond is, in effect, a portfolio of pure-discount bonds (or, equivalently, a portfolio of zero-coupon bonds). That is, each coupon payment, as well as the principal, can be viewed as a bond unto itself; the investor who owns the bond can therefore be viewed as holding a number of individual pure-discount bonds. In 1982, a number of brokerage firms began separating these components, using a process known as **coupon stripping.**

coupon stripping

With this process, Treasury bonds of a given issue are purchased and placed in trust with a custodian (for example, a bank). Sets of *receipts* are then issued, one set for each coupon date. For example, an August 15, 1997 receipt might entitle its holder to receive $1,000 on that date (and nothing on any other date). The amount required to meet the payments on all the August 15, 1997 receipts would exactly equal the total amount received on that date from coupon payments on the Treasury securities held in the trust account.

In addition to issuing a set of receipts corresponding to coupon dates, another set of receipts would be issued that mature on the date the principal of the securities held in trust is due. Thus, holders of these receipts share in the principal payment.[5]

Three early examples were Lehman Brothers' Lehman Investment Opportunity Notes (LIONs), Merrill Lynch's Treasury Investment Growth Receipts (TIGRs), and Salomon Brothers' Certificates of Accrual on Treasury Securities (CATS). Not surprisingly, such securities are known in the trade as "animals."

Noting the favorable market reaction to the offering of these stripped securities, in 1985 the Treasury Department introduced a program for investors called Separate Trading of Registered Interest and Principal Securities (STRIPS). This program allows purchasers of certain coupon-bearing Treasury securities to keep whatever cash payments they want and to sell the rest.

---

[4]If the bonds are used to pay for certain educational expenses the interest may be completely taxfree.

[5]If the underlying Treasury security is callable, this set of receipts would provide the holders with all coupon payments received after the date of first call as well as the principal.

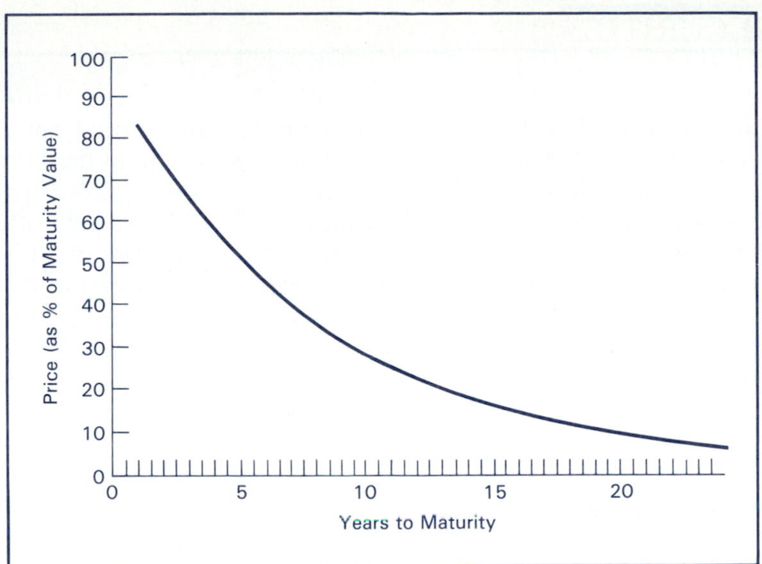

FIGURE 19-5
Typical Market Prices for a Set of Stripped Treasury Securities

The prices at which such pure discount securities sold for on June 18, 1992 are shown in Figure 19-3.

Figure 19-5 shows typical market prices for a set of stripped Treasury securities (such as LIONs, TIGRs, CATS, and STRIPS), where price is expressed as a percent of maturity value. As the figure shows, the longer the investor has to wait until maturity, the lower the price of the security.

The Internal Revenue Service requires that taxes be paid annually on the accrued interest earned on such securities. That is, such securities are treated for tax purposes as **original issue discount** (OID) **securities,** which are securities originally sold at a discount from par owing to their relatively small coupon payments (such tax treatment is also generally applicable to OID securities issued by corporations).

original issue discount securities

For example, a TIGR that matures in two years for $1,000 might be purchased currently for $900. Thus, the investor would earn $100 in interest over two years, realizing it when the TIGR matures. However, the IRS would make the investor pay taxes on a portion of the $100 each year. The amount to be recognized must be calculated on an "economic accrual" basis. This means that the investor cannot report $50 ($100/2) per year as interest income. Instead, first the yield needs to be calculated, which in this case is $5.4\% = (\$1{,}000/\$900)^{1/2} - 1$. This means that the implied value of the TIGR at the end of the first year would be $\$900 \times 1.054 = \$948.60$; thus, the amount of interest income to be recognized then is $\$48.60 = \$948.60 - \$900$. The amount of interest income to be recognized in the second year, assuming that the TIGR is held to maturity, will be $\$51.40 = \$1{,}000 - \$948.60$ (note that $\$1{,}000 = \$948.60 \times 1.054$). Consequently, the taxable investor has a cash outflow not only when purchasing the TIGR, but also every year until it matures; only at that time does the investor experience a cash inflow. As a result, such securities are attractive primarily for tax-exempt investors and for investors in low tax brackets (for example, some people purchase them as investments that are held in the names of their children).

While much of the federal government's activity is financed directly, via taxes and debt issued by the Treasury Department, a substantial amount is financed in other ways. In some situations, various government departments provide explicit or implicit backing for the securities of quasi-governmental agencies. In other situations, the federal government has guaranteed both the principal and coupon payments on bonds issued by certain private organizations. In both cases, some of the arrangements are so convoluted that cynics suggest that the original legislative intent was to obscure the nature and extent of government backing. In any event, a wide range of bonds with different degrees of government backing has been created in this manner. Many of the bonds are considered second in safety only to the debt obligations of the U.S. government itself.

Table 19-4 lists the issuers of these securities and the amounts outstanding in January 1992. A partial list of typical price quotations is shown in Figure 19-6; these quotations can be interpreted in a manner similar to Treasury security quotations.

Bonds of Federal Agencies

Bonds issued by federal agencies provide funds for support of things such as housing (through either direct loans or the purchase of existing mortgages); export and import activities (via loans, credit guarantees, and insurance); the postal service; and the activities of the Tennessee Valley Authority. Many issues are guaranteed by the full faith and credit of the U.S. government, but some (for example, those of the Tennessee Valley Authority) are not.

TABLE 19-4
Debt Outstanding of Federal and Federally Sponsored Agencies, January 1992

DEBT OF FEDERAL AGENCIES	AMOUNT (IN MILLIONS)
Defense Department: Family Housing and Homeowner's Assistance	$ 7
Export-Import Bank	9,809
Federal Housing Administration	335
Postal Service	8,421
Tennessee Valley Authority	24,300
Total	$ 42,872
DEBT OF FEDERALLY SPONSORED AGENCIES	**AMOUNT (IN MILLIONS)**
Federal Home Loan Banks	$104,607
Federal National Mortgage Association	133,988
Federal Home Loan Mortgage Corporation	29,332
Student Loan Marketing Association	38,419
Farm Credit Banks	51,673
Financing Corporation	8,170
Farm Credit Financial Assistance Corporation	1,261
Resolution Funding Corporation	29,996
Total	$397,446

Source: *Federal Reserve Bulletin*, June 1992, p. A31.

FIGURE 19-6
Price Quotations for Government Agency Issues (Excerpts)
Source: Reprinted by permission of *The Wall Street Journal*, © Dow Jones & Company, Inc., June 19, 1992, p. C14. All rights reserved worldwide.

GOVERNMENT AGENCY & SIMILAR ISSUES

Thursday, June 18, 1992

Over-the-Counter mid-afternoon quotations based on large transactions, usually $1 million or more. Colons in bid-and-asked quotes represent 32nds; 101:01 means 101 1/32.

All yields are calculated to maturity, and based on the asked quote. * – Callable issue, maturity date shown. For issues callable prior to maturity, yields are computed to the earliest call date for issues quoted above par, or 100, and to the maturity date for issues below par.

Source: Bear, Stearns & Co. via Street Software Technology Inc.

FNMA Issues

Rate	Mat.	Bid	Asked	Yld.
8.45	7-92	100:08	100:12	0.91
7.75	8-92	100:16	100:20	2.96
9.15	9-92	101:04	101:08	3.26
10.60	10-92	102:02	102:06	3.30
8.20	11-92	101:19	101:23	3.62
9.88	12-92	102:22	102:26	3.73
10.90	1-93	103:25	103:29	3.65
7.95	2-93	102:12	102:20	3.69
7.90	3-93	102:21	102:29	3.73
10.95	3-93	104:26	105:02	3.69
7.55	4-93	102:23	102:31	3.76
10.88	4-93	105:11	105:19	3.73
10.75	5-93	105:18	105:26	3.96
8.80	6-93	104:06	104:14	4.06
8.45	7-93	104:05	104:13	4.13
7.75	11-93	104:07	104:15	4.38
7.38	12-93	103:24	104:00	4.52
7.55	1-94	104:09	104:13	4.57
9.45	1-94	107:02	107:10	4.51
7.65	4-94	104:23	104:31	4.74
9.60	4-94	108:02	108:10	4.73
9.30	5-94	107:25	107:29	4.85
8.60	6-94	106:19	106:27	4.90
7.45	7-94*	104:15	104:19	5.06
8.65	7-94*	100:03	100:11	2.05
8.55	8-94*	100:27	101:03	0.33
8.90	8-94	107:02	107:10	5.23
10.10	10-94	110:03	110:11	5.26
9.25	11-94	108:05	108:13	5.44
8.30	12-94*	102:14	102:22	2.54
5.50	12-94	100:08	100:12	5.34
9.00	1-95	108:09	108:17	5.37
11.95	1-95	115:07	115:19	5.32
8.90	2-95*	102:24	103:00	4.02
11.50	2-95	114:23	115:03	5.28
8.85	3-95	108:13	108:21	5.38
11.70	5-95	116:03	116:15	5.45
8.85	6-95*	105:10	105:18	2.99
11.15	6-95	115:01	115:13	5.46
10.50	9-95	113:07	113:19	5.80
8.40	11-95*	105:14	105:18	4.21
8.80	11-95	108:19	108:27	5.88
10.60	11-95	113:30	114:06	5.91
9.20	1-96	110:00	110:08	5.95
7.00	2-96	103:02	103:10	5.97
7.70	2-96*	103:23	103:27	5.22
9.35	2-96	110:22	110:30	5.96
8.00	4-96*	104:24	104:28	5.12
8.05	6-96*	104:31	105:03	5.29
8.50	6-96	108:01	108:09	6.12
8.75	6-96	108:29	109:05	6.11
8.00	7-96	106:13	106:21	6.12
8.45	7-96*	105:01	105:09	3.35
8.50	8-96*	105:12	105:20	3.29
7.90	8-96	105:13	105:21	6.32
8.15	8-96	106:17	106:25	6.26
8.20	8-96*	106:06	106:10	5.04
7.70	9-96	105:05	105:09	6.25
8.63	9-96	108:17	108:25	6.22
8.75	9-96*	105:06	105:14	4.21
7.05	10-96	102:17	102:21	6.33
8.45	10-96	107:25	108:01	6.30
6.90	11-96*	100:10	100:14	6.69
7.70	12-96	105:11	105:19	6.24
8.20	12-96	107:11	107:19	6.24
6.20	1-97*	98:20	98:28	6.49
7.60	1-97	104:26	105:02	6.30
7.05	3-97*	101:27	101:31	6.24
10.35	12-15	123:16	124:00	8.06
8.20	3-16	101:08	101:16	8.06
8.95	2-18	107:12	107:20	8.23
8.10	8-19	99:06	99:14	8.15
0.00	10-19	10:16	10:24	8.34
9.65	8-20*	110:25	111:01	7.59
9.50	11-20*	109:08	109:16	7.99

Federal Home Loan Bank

Rate	Mat.	Bid	Asked	Yld.
8.40	6-92	100:00	100:04	0.00
8.45	6-92	100:02	100:06	0.00
8.25	7-92	100:15	100:19	2.06
8.38	7-92	100:14	100:18	2.49
5.63	8-92	100:09	100:11	3.58
8.60	8-92	100:26	100:30	3.13
10.35	8-92	101:04	101:10	2.72
5.68	9-92	100:14	100:16	3.68
8.25	9-92	101:04	101:10	3.07
5.55	10-92	100:17	100:19	3.77
8.00	10-92	101:12	101:16	3.55
8.15	10-92	101:14	101:18	3.51
10.85	10-92	102:12	102:16	3.45
7.65	11-92	101:18	101:22	3.60
8.00	11-92	101:22	101:26	3.65
8.80	11-92	102:01	102:05	3.62
11.10	11-92	103:00	103:06	3.46
7.38	12-92	101:23	101:27	3.72
7.95	12-92	102:02	102:08	3.50
9.05	12-92	102:19	102:25	3.55
9.40	12-92	102:24	102:30	3.59
8.30	1-93	102:15	102:21	3.70
9.35	1-93	103:03	103:09	3.67
9.50	1-93	103:06	103:12	3.66
10.70	1-93	103:28	104:02	3.67
4.38	2-93	100:04	100:06	4.09
8.05	2-93	102:20	102:26	3.77
4.83	3-93	100:17	100:21	3.93
8.10	3-93	102:31	103:05	3.82
10.80	3-93	105:00	105:06	3.77
7.55	4-93	102:27	103:01	3.85
8.13	5-93	103:18	103:24	3.95
8.90	5-93	104:03	104:09	4.13
9.13	5-93	104:10	104:16	4.11
10.75	5-93	105:26	106:00	4.06
7.08	6-93	102:20	102:24	4.26
7.00	7-93	102:22	102:24	4.39
7.75	7-93	103:16	103:22	4.26
9.00	7-93	104:26	105:00	4.27
11.70	7-93	107:22	107:30	4.19
6.22	8-93	101:30	102:00	4.45
7.45	8-93	103:11	103:17	4.33
8.18	8-93	104:05	104:13	4.28
11.95	8-93	108:15	108:21	4.30
6.21	9-93	102:02	102:04	4.45
7.95	9-93	104:04	104:10	4.39
8.30	9-93	104:21	104:25	4.36
6.09	10-93	101:31	102:01	4.51
7.88	10-93	104:09	104:15	4.40
8.80	10-93	105:15	105:21	4.40
9.13	11-93	106:08	106:14	4.42
7.38	12-93	104:00	104:06	4.48
7.50	12-93	104:05	104:09	4.54
12.15	12-93	110:27	111:01	4.53
5.00	1-94	100:15	100:19	4.61
7.30	1-94	104:00	104:06	4.54
7.55	1-94	104:12	104:14	4.62
7.45	2-94	104:14	104:20	4.55
9.60	2-94	107:28	108:02	4.54
9.50	2-04	114:14	114:30	7.55

Federal Farm Credit Bank

Rate	Mat.	Bid	Asked	Yld.
4.23	7-92	100:00	100:02	1.71
4.38	7-92	100:01	100:03	0.61
6.55	7-92	100:03	100:05	0.29
13.75	7-92	100:26	100:30	1.59
8.40	7-92	100:13	100:17	2.14
3.85	8-92	100:00	100:02	3.28
4.05	8-92	100:00	100:02	3.44
6.40	8-92	100:09	100:11	3.29
3.85	9-92	100:00	100:04	3.19
4.27	9-92	100:02	100:06	3.24
5.80	9-92	100:11	100:13	3.60
8.25	9-92	100:27	100:29	3.40
8.60	9-92	100:29	101:03	2.79
4.40	10-92	100:04	100:06	3.67
5.63	10-92	100:15	100:17	3.63
4.03	11-92	100:01	100:03	3.75
5.50	11-92	100:17	100:19	3.80
4.00	12-92	100:01	100:03	3.78
4.90	12-92	100:12	100:14	3.88
7.63	12-92	101:18	101:22	3.72
4.48	1-93	100:08	100:10	3.88
8.13	1-93	102:10	102:16	3.70
10.65	1-93	103:24	103:30	3.68
4.15	2-93	100:00	100:02	4.04
4.53	3-93	100:10	100:14	3.87
4.70	4-93	100:14	100:18	3.95
4.35	5-93	100:06	100:10	3.97
4.32	6-93	100:03	100:07	4.08
6.77	6-93	102:11	102:13	4.13
6.88	8-93	102:17	102:19	4.45
6.48	9-93	102:09	102:13	4.38
6.16	10-93	101:31	102:01	4.49
11.80	10-93	109:08	109:14	4.39
7.38	12-93	104:00	104:02	4.57
7.19	2-94	103:28	104:00	4.61
12.35	3-94	112:10	112:22	4.47
5.80	4-94	101:26	101:30	4.65
14.25	4-94	116:04	116:16	4.71
7.45	7-94*	100:00	100:04	2.36
7.38	8-94*	100:19	100:21	1.27
6.90	9-94*	100:21	100:25	2.74
8.63	9-94	106:19	106:25	5.30
13.00	9-94	115:00	115:12	5.45
6.40	11-94*	101:04	101:08	5.82
11.45	12-94	113:25	114:01	5.25
5.60	1-95*	99:30	100:04	5.55
8.30	1-95	106:20	106:28	5.40
6.05	3-95*	101:01	101:05	4.32
6.38	4-95	102:08	102:12	5.44
6.10	5-95*	100:13	100:17	5.45
6.65	5-96	101:25	101:29	6.09
6.60	2-97*	99:12	99:20	6.69
7.00	3-97*	100:21	100:25	5.82
11.90	10-97	122:21	123:01	6.69
8.65	10-99	108:25	109:01	7.04
8.88	12-00*	104:25	105:01	5.20
7.95	4-02*	102:14	102:18	7.30

Student Loan Marketing

Rate	Mat.	Bid	Asked	Yld.
8.25	6-92	100:04	100:08	0.00
8.15	9-92	101:00	101:04	3.33
8.80	12-92	102:04	102:08	3.67
10.50	4-93	105:07	105:13	3.83
7.35	5-93	102:18	102:24	4.07
8.20	5-93	103:13	103:21	4.04
6.87	6-93	102:15	102:19	4.21
8.50	7-93	104:04	104:08	4.26
12.00	12-93	110:11	110:15	4.60
11.88	12-93	110:11	110:15	4.53
7.38	1-94	104:00	104:08	4.51
16.00	2-94	117:25	118:05	4.41
7.43	4-94	104:11	104:19	4.73
7.35	5-94	104:11	104:15	4.87
7.30	5-94	104:09	104:13	4.86
8.50	7-94	106:15	106:19	5.05
7.50	7-94	104:18	104:22	5.06
0.00	10-22	8:15	8:23	8.22

World Bank Bonds

Rate	Mat.	Bid	Asked	Yld.
13.63	9-92	101:28	102:00	3.00
10.90	3-93	104:26	104:30	3.94
10.38	5-93	105:06	105:10	4.26
11.63	12-94	114:05	114:09	5.39
8.63	10-95	108:21	108:25	5.64
7.25	10-96	102:25	103:01	6.42
8.75	3-97	109:00	109:08	6.43
9.88	10-97	114:04	114:12	6.60
8.38	10-99	107:12	107:20	7.02
8.13	3-01	105:11	105:13	7.27
8.85	7-01	102:30	103:06	8.34
6.75	1-02	96:22	96:26	7.22
8.25	5-02	102:16	102:24	7.84
12.38	10-02	132:19	132:27	7.70
8.25	9-16	100:26	101:02	8.15
8.63	10-16	104:23	104:31	8.15
9.25	7-17	111:13	111:21	8.15
8.88	3-26	107:16	107:24	8.19

Financing Corporation

Rate	Mat.	Bid	Asked	Yld.
10.70	10-17	124:08	124:20	8.35
9.80	11-17	114:22	115:02	8.36
9.40	2-18	111:13	111:25	8.28
9.80	4-18	115:00	115:12	8.34
10.00	5-18	117:02	117:18	8.33
10.35	8-18	120:22	121:02	8.35
9.65	11-18	113:09	113:21	8.36
9.90	12-18	116:00	116:16	8.34
9.60	12-18	112:25	113:09	8.35
9.65	3-19	113:22	114:06	8.32
9.70	4-19	114:07	114:19	8.33
9.00	6-19	106:26	107:10	8.31
8.60	9-19	103:00	103:16	8.27

Inter-Amer. Devel. Bank

Rate	Mat.	Bid	Asked	Yld.
14.63	8-92	101:06	101:10	2.34
12.13	10-93	108:26	108:30	4.80
13.25	8-94	115:27	115:31	5.28
11.63	12-94	113:26	113:30	5.45
11.38	5-95	114:11	114:15	5.80
7.50	12-96	104:06	104:14	6.35
9.50	10-97	111:28	112:04	6.74
8.50	5-01	106:01	106:09	7.51
8.38	6-02	103:05	103:13	7.87
12.25	12-08	139:12	139:20	7.91
8.40	9-09*	107:16	107:24	7.01
8.50	3-11	103:19	103:27	8.10

GNMA Mtge. Issues a-Bond

Rate	Mat.	Bid	Asked	Yld.
7.00	30Yr	95:22	95:30	7.78
7.50	30Yr	98:16	98:24	7.82
8.00	30Yr	101:06	101:14	7.87
8.50	30Yr	104:03	104:11	7.83
9.00	30Yr	106:16	106:24	7.78
9.50	30Yr	108:00	108:08	7.72
10.00	30Yr	109:11	109:19	7.42
10.50	30Yr	110:06	110:14	7.25
11.00	30Yr	111:28	112:04	6.82
11.50	30Yr	114:15	114:23	7.03
12.00	30Yr	116:06	116:14	7.17
12.50	30Yr	116:28	117:04	6.34

Tennessee Valley Authority

Rate	Mat.	Bid	Asked	Yld.
8.25	10-94	105:29	106:01	5.39
8.25	11-96	107:02	107:06	6.35
6.00	1-97*	97:25	98:01	6.50
6.50	1-99*	97:12	97:20	6.96
8.38	10-99	107:02	107:06	7.09
7.45	10-01*	100:22	100:26	7.33
6.88	1-02*	96:22	96:30	7.32
8.75	10-19*	104:00	104:08	6.70
8.63	11-29*	102:28	103:04	8.05
8.25	4-42*	99:23	99:31	8.25

Bonds of Federally Sponsored Agencies

federally sponsored agencies

Federally sponsored agencies are privately owned agencies that issue securities and use the proceeds to support the granting of certain types of loans to farmers, homeowners, and the like. A common procedure involves the creation of a series of governmental "banks" that buy securities issued by private organizations that grant the loans in the first instance. Some or all of the initial capital for these "banks" may be provided by the government, but subsequent amounts typically come from bonds issued by the "banks."

While the debts of agencies of this type are usually not guaranteed by the federal government, governmental control is designed to insure that each debt issue is backed by extremely safe assets (for example, mortgages insured by another quasi-governmental agency). Moreover, it is generally presumed that governmental assistance of one sort or another would be provided if there were any danger of default on such debt.

As shown in Table 19-4, there are eight federally sponsored agencies. Federal Home Loan Banks make loans to thrift institutions (primarily savings and loan associations). The Federal National Mortgage Association (FNMA, also known as "Fannie Mae") purchases and sells real estate mortgages—not only those insured by the Federal Housing Administration or guaranteed by the Veterans Administration, but also conventional mortgages. The Federal Home Loan Mortgage Corporation (known as "Freddie Mac") deals only in conventional mortgages. The Student Loan Marketing Association (known as "Sallie Mae") purchases federally guaranteed loans made to students by other lenders (for example, commercial banks) and may make direct student loans under special circumstances. The Farm Credit Banks lend to farmers as well as farm associations and cooperatives, while the Farm Credit Financial Assistance Corporation was created in 1987 to help the Farm Credit Bank System. The Financing Corporation was established in August 1987 to recapitalize the Federal Savings and Loan Insurance Corporation (FSLIC). Lastly, the Resolution Funding Corporation was created in 1989 to assist in the recovery of the thrift industry, mainly by assisting bankrupt or near-bankrupt savings and loans.

Participation Certificates

participation certificates

To support credit for home purchases, the government has authorized the issuance of **participation certificates.** A group of assets (for example, mortgages) is placed in a pool, and certificates representing ownership of those assets are issued to pay for them. The holders of the certificates receive the interest and principal payments as they are made, minus a small service charge. The most important certificates of this type are those issued by the Government National Mortgage Association (GNMA, or "Ginnie Mae"), and are known as GNMA Modified Pass-Through Securities. These securities are guaranteed by GNMA and backed by the full faith and credit of the U.S. government.

GNMA pass-through securities are created by certain private organizations (such as savings and loans and mortgage bankers) that bundle a package of similar (in terms of maturity date and interest rate) mortgages together. These mortgages must be individually guaranteed by either the Federal Housing Administration or the Veterans Administration (thus making them free from default risk) and have, in aggregate, a principal amount of at least $1 million. After these mortgages have been bundled together, an application is made to GNMA for a guarantee on the pass-through securities that each represent $25,000 worth of principal. Once the guarantee is received, the securities are sold to the public through brokers. The interest rate paid on the securities is .5% less than the interest rate paid on the mortgages, with GNMA keeping .1% and the creator .4%.

Unlike most bonds, GNMA pass-through securities pay investors on a monthly basis an amount of money that represents both a pro rata return of principal and interest on the underlying mortgages. For example, a holder of a $25,000 certificate from a $1 million pool would indirectly "own" 2½% of each mortgage in the pool. Each month the homeowners make mortgage payments that consist of part principal and part interest. In turn, each month the investor receives 2½% of the aggregate amount paid by the homeowners. Because the mortgages are free from default risk, there is no default risk on the pass-through securities (if homeowner payments are late, GNMA will either use excess cash or borrow money from the Treasury to make sure that the investors are paid in a timely fashion).

There is one particular risk to investors, however, that arises because homeowners are allowed to prepay their mortgages. This prepayment allowance means that the pass-through securities, although initially having a stated life of thirty years, may actually have a much shorter life. This can cause losses if the investor buys an existing pass-through that is selling at a premium, a situation that can happen if interest rates have fallen since the time the pass-through security was created. In such a situation, homeowners may start to prepay their mortgages, meaning that the investor will receive par value on the security shortly after paying a premium for it, thereby causing the investor to incur a loss.

Consider a pass-through security of $25,000, initially issued with a stated interest rate of 12%. Suppose that interest rates subsequently fall so that new pass-throughs carry a stated rate of 10%. At this time, the older pass-through security has $20,000 of principal outstanding, but as a consequence of the fall in interest rates it is selling at a premium, perhaps for $22,000. Now suppose that interest rates fall further to 8%. At this point, many homeowners prepay their mortgages in order to refinance them at the current rate of 8%. As a result, an investor who purchased the older pass-through security for $22,000 ends up shortly thereafter receiving $20,000, thereby losing $2,000.

Nevertheless, the interest the public has shown in GNMA pass-through securities has caused a number of similar securities to be created. One, issued in denominations of $100,000 or more, is the "guaranteed mortgage certificate" sold by the Federal Home Loan Mortgage Corporation ("Freddie Mac"), a federally sponsored agency that was mentioned earlier. A number of banks have offered similar pass-through mortgage certificates backed by private insurance companies. Some of them have repackaged the cash flows that are paid by the homeowners so that investors can receive something other than a pro rata share of them. Examples include collateralized mortgage obligations (CMOs) and real estate mortgage investment conduits (REMICs).

STATE AND LOCAL GOVERNMENT SECURITIES

The 1987 Census of Governments showed that there were 83,236 governmental units in the United States, in addition to the federal government itself:[6]

---

[6] *1991 Statistical Abstract of the United States*, Table 464, p. 278.

MONEY MATTERS
Collateralized Mortgage Obligations

Twenty years ago the market for securities backed by residential mortgages was a fledgling. Today it stands as a behemoth, dwarfing the corporate bond market in terms of outstanding market value and daily trading volume. Moreover, the market has considerable growth capacity left. Only about one-third of the roughly $2 trillion in single-family mortgages has been converted into tradable securities. Further, the trillion-dollar market for commercial and multi-family residential mortgages remains largely untapped.

The key to the mortgage-backed security market's success has been the creation of financial instruments that appeal to investors who would not or could not invest directly in mortgages. (The process of packaging the cash flows from mortgages into various financial securities is referred to as the "securitization" of mortgages.) The mainstay of the mortgage-backed security market has always been the traditional pass-through security. However, mortgage-backed securities also take other forms, and the pace of innovation is increasing.

Originally designed to help liquify the home mortgage market and thereby increase the availability and lower the cost of home financing, pass-through securities have succeeded beyond anyone's wildest imagination. Investors have been attracted by the higher yields available relative to Treasury securities, combined with the pass-through securities' safety and liquidity.

However, one aspect of traditional pass-through securities has always proven particularly troublesome to investors: The cash flows produced by these securities are uncertain. As the text describes, homeowners have the option to prepay their mortgages. These prepayments may occur because the homeowner decides to sell his or her house. More disconcerting to the pass-through securityholder, however, is that homeowners are more likely to refinance their mortgages as interest rates decline. The pass-through securityholder thus may receive sizable principal repayments at the most inopportune time—when interest rates decline significantly. (This phenomenon was witnessed on a large scale in late 1991 and early 1992, when long-term interest rates tumbled.)

In an effort to overcome this undesirable feature of traditional pass-through securities, many organizations have repackaged these securities into a different form of mortgage-backed security: collateralized mortgage obligations (CMOs).

There are many different variations of CMOs, but the underlying concept behind all of them is relatively simple. Mortgages generate two types of payments: interest and principal. If you own a traditional pass-through security, you receive a pro rata share of the interest and principal payments made on the various mortgages that have been pooled together. On a monthly basis, your investment declines in size as you receive regularly scheduled principal payments. Moreover, if a mortgage in the pool prepays, you receive a pro rata portion of the prepaid principal and no more interest from that mortgage. The pool is now smaller by the amount of the

50	states
3,042	counties
19,200	municipalities
16,691	townships and towns
29,532	special districts
14,721	school districts
83,236	total governmental units

municipal bonds

A great many of these units borrow money, with their securities called **municipal bonds** or simply "municipals" or "muni's" (only the securities of the U.S. government are referred to as "governments"). Table 19-5 provides estimates of the amounts of various types of fixed-income securities outstanding at the end of 1991. With approximately $1,082.1 billion in value, municipals clearly warrant attention.

Issuing Agencies

Table 19-6 shows the dollar values of municipal bonds issued in 1991 by various agencies, while Table 19-7 shows the purposes for the issuance of

paid-off mortgage. Your interest payments from the pool decline and you must find an alternative investment for your prepaid principal.

CMOs are simply a means to allocate principal and interest payments among investors in a mortgage pool. A CMO originator (or sponsor) transforms a traditional mortgage pool into a set of securities, called CMO *tranches* (French for "slice"), that have different priority claims on the interest and principal paid by the mortgages underlying the CMO.

While there is no "typical" form of CMO, we can consider a common CMO structure that is divided into four tranches—*A*, *B*, *C*, and *Z*. Each tranche is initially allocated a specific proportion of the underlying mortgage pool's outstanding principal value. Interest payments, as with any bond, are paid as a percentage of the outstanding principal corresponding to each tranche.

The tranches differ in terms of how they are retired (that is, how principal payments are allocated among them). The *A* tranche receives all principal payments made by the pool until it is retired. The *B* and *C* tranches receive only interest payments as long as the *A* tranche has not been fully paid off. Once it has, the *B* tranche receives all principal payments until it is retired; afterwards, principal payments go to the *C* tranche.

The last tranche, the *Z* (or accrual) tranche, receives neither principal nor interest payments until the other three tranches have been extinguished. Its earned interest goes to retire the principal of the other tranches. Thus the *Z* tranche's principal actually grows over time at a compound rate in a manner similar to the way interest accrues on pure-discount bonds. When the other three tranches have finally been retired, it receives all remaining interest and principal payments.

The primary purpose of dividing a mortgage pass-through pool's principal and income flows into various tranches is to create a set of securities with varying levels of interest rate and prepayment risk. Investors can match their risk preferences with the appropriate securities. The CMO originator expects that investors will pay a premium for this flexibility, with the sum of the parts being worth more than the whole. Investors desiring short-maturity bonds with very predictable cash flows invest in the *A* tranche, while investors seeking intermediate-maturity bonds with less predictable cash flows look to the *B* and *C* tranches. Finally, investors willing to bear the interest-rate risk of long-maturity deep-discount bonds purchase the *Z* tranche. Of course, the market sets prices of the various tranches accordingly, with the *A* tranche exhibiting the lowest yields while the *Z* tranche sells at the highest yields. (The higher-yield tranches of certain CMOs have been popular among investors in recent years as interest rates have fallen. Some observers contend that this popularity results from a misunderstanding of the true risks of these securities.)

The risk of principal prepayments can be allocated across various tranches, but in the final analysis it cannot be reduced. Thus, while holders of the slower-pay tranches may be less exposed to prepayment risk, if interest rates drop sharply they may still receive unexpectedly early prepayments, which can adversely affect the values of their investments. Evaluating this risk can prove extremely difficult, especially for some of the more complex CMO structures. Despite this caveat, CMOs represent an excellent example of how the financial markets respond to the needs of suppliers and users of funds by creating flexible new securities.

---

such debt. States generally issue debt to finance capital expenditures, primarily for highways, housing, and education.[7] The concept behind the issuance of such debt is that the revenue generated by the resulting facilities will be used to make the required debt payments. In some cases, the link is direct (for example, tolls may be used to pay for a bridge); in other cases, somewhat indirect (for example, gasoline taxes may be used to pay for highway construction) or very indirect (for example, state sales taxes or income taxes may be used to pay for the construction of new government buildings).

States cannot be sued without their consent. Thus, bondholders may have no legal recourse in the event of default. This means that state-issued bonds that are dependent on particular revenues from some capital project may involve considerable risk. However, bonds backed by the "full faith and credit" of a state government are generally considered quite safe in spite of the inability of the bondholders to sue. This is because it is anticipated that state

[7]In some cases, no capital expenditure is involved (for example, the proceeds from the debt issue may be used for the payment of a veterans' bonus).

TABLE 19-5
Estimated Amounts of Various Fixed-Income Securities Outstanding, End of 1991

TYPE OF SECURITY	AMOUNT (IN BILLIONS)
U.S. government securities	$ 4,346.8
Corporate and foreign obligations	1,758.0
State and local obligations	1,082.1
Mortgages	4,048.8
Consumer credit	792.5
Other	2,153.6
Total	$14,181.7

Source: Federal Reserve Bulletin, June 1992, p. A42.

TABLE 19-6
New Security Issues of State and Local Governments in 1991, Classified by Issuer

ISSUER	AMOUNT (IN BILLIONS)
States	$ 24.9
Special districts and statutory authorities	80.6
Municipalities, counties, and townships	48.9
Total	$154.4

Source: Federal Reserve Bulletin, June 1992, p. A32.

TABLE 19-7
New Security Issues of State and Local Governments in 1991, Classified by Purpose

PURPOSE	AMOUNT (IN BILLIONS)
Education	$ 21.7
Transportation	13.4
Utilities and conservation	21.4
Social welfare	26.1
Industrial aid	8.5
Other	63.3
Total	$154.4

Source: Federal Reserve Bulletin, June 1992, p. A32.

legislatures will do whatever is necessary to see that such bonds are paid off in a timely manner.

Unlike state governments, local governments can be sued against their will, making it possible for bondholders to force officials to collect whatever amount is needed in order to meet required debt payments. In many cases, only revenues from specific projects may be used (for example, the tolls collected on a particular highway). In other cases, collections from a particular tax may be used, although possibly only up to some statutory limit.

Some local governments (for example, Cleveland in 1978–1979) have defaulted on their debts, and others (for example, New York City in 1975) have "restructured" their debt, giving holders new certificates offering lower or deferred interest and longer maturities in exchange for currently outstanding certificates.

Counties and municipalities are familiar to most people, but other forms of local government also exist. Examples include school districts as well as other districts and authorities that have been created to finance and operate seaports, airports, and the like. All are created by state charter and may be granted monopoly powers as well as rights to collect certain types of taxes. However, limits are often placed on the amount of taxes collected, the tax rate charged, and the amount (or type) of debt issued.

The primary source of funding for such agencies is the property tax. Since a given property may be liable for taxes levied by several agencies (such as a city, a county, a school district, a port authority, and a sewer district), the risk of an agency's bonds may depend on both the value of property subject to its taxes and the amount of other debt dependent on the same property.

Types of Municipal Bonds

In 1991, new municipal bonds with a par value of $154.4 billion were issued. Of this total, $55.1 billion were general obligation bonds (G.O.s) and $99.3 billion were revenue bonds.[8]

general obligation bonds

General obligation bonds are backed by the full faith and credit (and thus the full taxing power) of the issuing agency. Most are issued by agencies with unlimited taxing power, although in a minority of cases the issuer is subject to limits on the amount of taxes or the tax rate (or both).

revenue bonds

Revenue bonds are backed by revenues from a designated project, authority, or agency or by the proceeds from a specific tax. In many cases, such bonds are issued by agencies that hope to sell their services, pay the required expenses, and have enough left over to meet required payments on outstanding debt. Except for the possible granting of monopoly powers, the authorizing state and local government may provide no further assistance to the issuer. Such bonds are only as creditworthy as the enterprise associated with the issuer.

industrial development bonds

Many revenue bonds are issued to finance capital expenditures for publicly owned utilities (for example, water, electricity, or gas). Others are issued to finance quasi-utility operations (for example, public transportation). Some are financed by special assessments levied on properties benefiting from the original expenditure (for example, those connected to a new sewer system). **Industrial development bonds** (IDBs) are used to finance the purchase or construction of industrial facilities that are to be leased to firms on a favorable basis. In effect, such bonds provide cheap financing to businesses choosing to locate in the geographical area of the issuer.

While most municipal financing involves the issuance of long-term securities, there are a number of different types of short-term securities that have been issued in order to meet short-term demands for cash. Traditionally used types include tax anticipation notes (TANs), revenue anticipation notes (RANs), grant anticipation notes (GANs), and tax and revenue anticipation notes (TRANs). In each case, the name of the security refers to the source of repayment. Thus, some can be classified as general obligation securities and others as revenue securities.

More recently, municipalities have started to issue two other kinds of short-term securities. Tax-exempt commercial paper is similar to corporate commercial paper, having a fixed interest rate and a maturity typically within 270 days. Variable-rate demand obligations have an interest rate that changes periodically (perhaps weekly) as some prespecified market interest rate changes. Furthermore, they can be redeemed at the desire of the investor within a prespecified number of days after giving notice to the issuer (for example, seven days after notification of intent).

---

[8]*Federal Reserve Bulletin*, June 1992, p. A32.

Tax Treatment

Through a reciprocal arrangement with the federal government, coupon payments on state and local government securities are exempt from federal taxation, and coupon payments on Treasury and agency (except FNMA) securities are exempt from state and local taxation. Similar tax treatment is accorded to short-term and long-term issues that are pure-discount securities.

However, a different tax treatment is generally given to coupon-bearing securities that were issued at par value but were subsequently bought at a discount in the marketplace. Such securities provide the investor with income not only from the coupons but also from the difference between the purchase price and the par value. Unlike the coupons, which are tax-exempt, this difference is treated as taxable interest income. The taxpayer must recognize a portion of the difference as income each year that the security is held (the portion must be based on the "economic accrual" method that was mentioned earlier in the discussion of stripped securities) and pay ordinary income taxes on that amount.

Another interesting tax feature of municipals is that if the investor resides in the state of the issuer, then he or she is generally exempt not only from paying federal taxes on the coupon payments, but also from paying state taxes. Furthermore, if the investor resides in a city with an income tax and purchases municipals issued by the city, then usually he or she is exempt from paying city taxes on the coupon payments. Thus, a resident of New York City who purchases a municipal security issued by the city (or one of its political subdivisions) will not have to pay federal, state, or city income taxes on the coupon payments. However, if the NYC resident were to purchase a California municipal, then both New York State and New York City income taxes would have to be paid on the coupon payments. While state and city income tax rates are at much lower rates than those of the federal government, this feature nevertheless tends to make local issues more advantageous from an after-tax return viewpoint (an advantage that is offset to a certain degree by the resulting lack of diversification).

The avoidance of federal income tax on interest earned on a municipal bond makes such a security attractive to wealthy individual investors as well as corporate investors. As shown in Figure 19-7, this has resulted in municipal securities having yields that are considerably lower than those on taxable securities.[9] Consequently, this has lowered the cost of financing to the municipal issuer and suggests that a federal subsidy has been provided to the issuer.

Over the years, this subsidy has been used to support activities deemed worthy of encouragement (even though the encouragement is somewhat hidden). For example, private universities may issue tax-exempt bonds to finance certain types of improvements and private firms may do so to finance certain pollution-reducing activities. Such bonds are generally backed only by the resources of the issuer, with government involvement limited to the granting of favorable tax treatment. The Tax Reform Act of 1986 has greatly restricted the granting of such tax treatment, leading to the emergence of **taxable municipals,** which typically are issued to finance things that are not viewed as essential under the tax law.

taxable municipals

[9]As noted in Chapter 5 (see Figure 5.3 and the related discussion), the yields on municipal bonds have historically been 20% to 40% below the yields of similar taxable bonds.

FIGURE 19-7
Average Yields of Long-Term Fixed-Income Securities (Monthly Averages)
Source: Treasury Bulletin, Summer Issue, September 1991, p. 69.

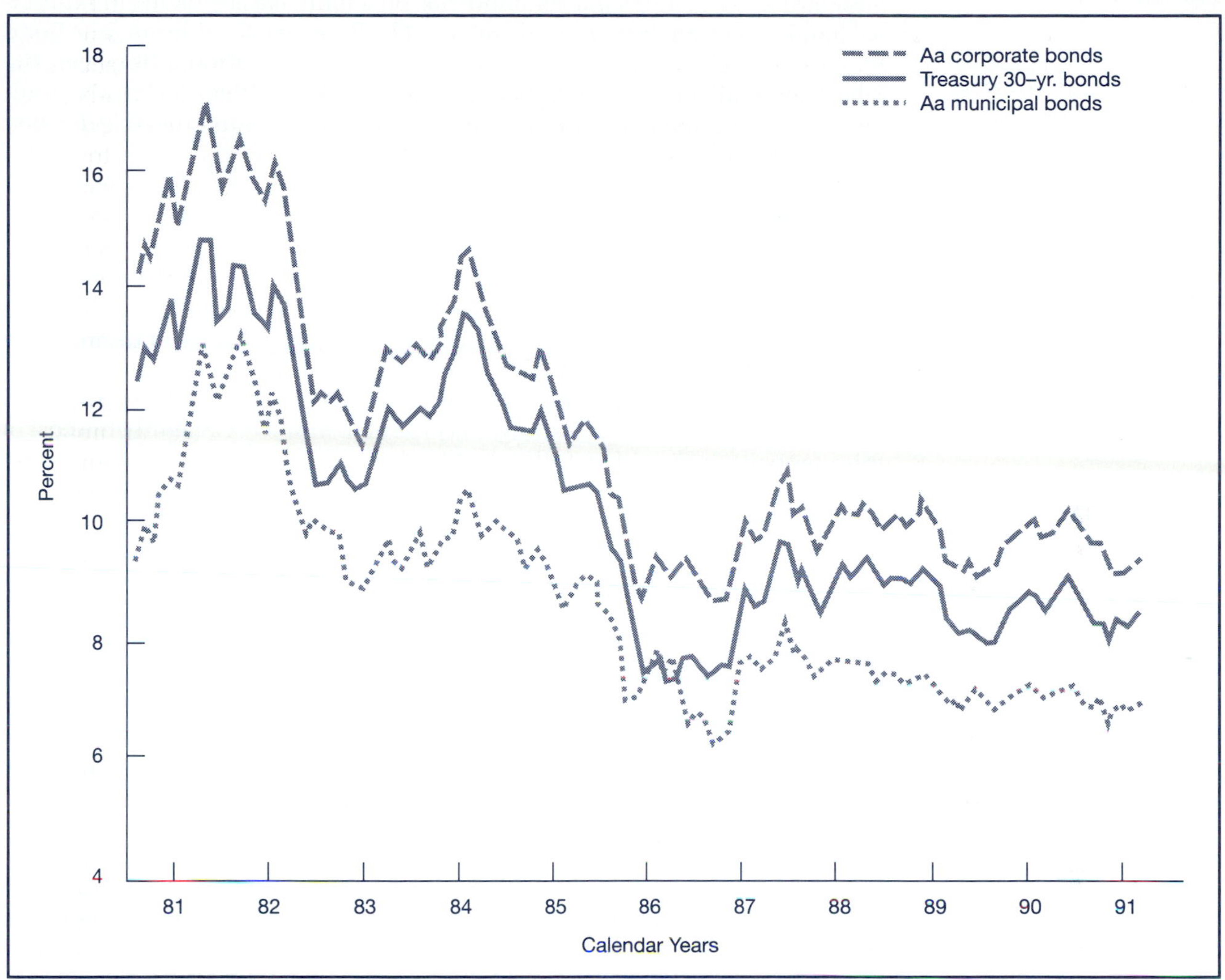

The Market for Municipal Bonds

Municipals are usually issued as **serial bonds**, where one prespecified group matures a year after issue, another two years after issue, another three years after, and so on. Alternatively, **term bonds** (that is, bonds that all mature on the same date) or a mixture of serial and term bonds may be issued. The overall package is generally offered by the issuer on a competitive basis to various underwriters. The winning bidder then reoffers the individual bonds to investors at a higher price.

serial bonds

term bonds

Unlike corporate bonds, municipal bonds do not need to be registered with the SEC before public issuance. Indeed, the federal government leaves most regulation in this market to state and local authorities.

Municipal bonds may be callable at specified dates and prices. Occasionally, the issuing authority is obligated to make designated payments into

sinking fund

a **sinking fund**, which is used to buy similar bonds (or perhaps even its own bonds). As the issuing authority's bonds mature, the money for paying them off will come from having the sinking fund sell some of its holdings.

A secondary market in municipal bonds is made by various dealers. Standard & Poor's Corporation publishes on a daily basis a listing of municipal bond quotations by various dealers in *The Blue List*. In addition, *The Bond Buyer* has a teletype system that provides dealer quotations. However, the relatively small amounts of particular issues and maturities outstanding limit the size of the market. Many individuals who invest in municipals simply buy new issues and hold them to maturity.

Municipal Bond Insurance

An investor concerned about possible default of a municipal bond can purchase an insurance policy to cover any losses that would be incurred if coupons or principal are not paid in full and on time. That is, an investor can contract with a company to have a specific portfolio of bonds insured. Alternatively, the issuer of the bonds can purchase such insurance from one of the firms that specialize in issuing this type of insurance. Generally the cost of this insurance is more than fully offset by the lower interest rate that the issuer has to pay as a result of insuring its bonds. In either case, the cost of the insurance will depend on the bonds included and their ratings.

CORPORATE BONDS

Corporate bonds are similar to other kinds of fixed-income securities in that they promise to make specified payments at specified times and provide legal remedies in the event of default. Restrictions are often placed on the activities of the issuing corporation in order to provide additional protection for bondholders (for example, there may be restrictions on the amount of additional bonds that can be issued in the future).

Corporate bonds that are pure-discount securities, meaning that they do not provide the investor with coupon payments, generally have the discount taxed as ordinary income by the federal government. The method of taxation is the same as the method for stripped Treasury bonds that was mentioned earlier—namely, a portion of the discount must be recognized as income each year that the security is held, thereby causing the investor to have to pay taxes on that amount.

Corporate bonds carrying coupon payments have the coupon taxed as income each year. Furthermore, if the bond was originally sold at par but later bought at a discount in the marketplace, then the investor generally will have to pay ordinary income taxes on both the coupon payments and the discount. Using the "economic accrual" method that was discussed earlier, the investor must recognize a portion of the discount as income each year that the bond is held, and pay taxes on it.[10]

From the viewpoint of the issuing corporation, debt differs from equity in two crucial respects. First, principal and interest payments are obligatory.

[10]The taxation of securities in general and bonds in particular is a complex matter, with many exceptions and alternative procedures. Any investor would be well advised to check carefully beforehand to be certain of the method of taxation involved for any security being considered for purchase.

Failure to make any payment in full and on time can expose the issuer to expensive, time-consuming, and potentially disruptive legal actions. Second, unlike dividend payments, interest payments are considered expenses to the corporation, and hence can be deducted from earnings before calculating the corporation's income tax liability. As a result, each dollar paid in interest reduces earnings before taxes by a dollar, thereby reducing corporate taxes by 34 cents for a firm in the 34% marginal tax bracket. This leads to less than a dollar decline in earnings after taxes (in the 34% tax bracket example, the decline in earnings is 66 cents).

The Indenture

An issue of bonds is generally covered by an **indenture,** in which the issuing corporation promises a specified **trustee** that it will comply with a number of stated provisions. Chief among these is the timely payment of required coupons and principal on the issue. Other terms are often included to control the sale of pledged property, the issuance of other bonds, and the like.

indenture
trustee

The trustee for a bond issue, usually a bank or trust company, acts on behalf of the bondholders. Some actions may be required by the indenture, while others may be done at the trustee's discretion, such as acting in response to a request from some specific bondholders.

If the corporation defaults on an interest payment, after a relatively short period of time (perhaps one to six months) the entire principal typically becomes due and payable—a procedure designed to enhance the bondholders' status in any forthcoming bankruptcy or related legal proceedings.

Types of Bonds

An exhaustive list of the names used to describe bonds would be intolerably long. Different names are often used for the same type of bond, and occasionally the same name will be used for two quite different bonds. A few major types do predominate, however, with relatively standard nomenclature.

Mortgage Bonds Bonds of this type represent debt that is secured by the pledge of specific property. In the event of default, the bondholders are entitled to obtain the property in question and sell it to satisfy their claims on the firm. In addition to the property itself, the holders of mortgage bonds have an unsecured claim on the corporation.

mortgage bonds

Mortgage bondholders are usually protected by a number of terms included in the bond indenture. The corporation may be constrained from pledging property for other bonds (or such bonds, if issued, must be "junior" or "second" mortgages, with a claim on the property only after the first mortgage is satisfied). Certain property acquired by the corporation after the bonds were issued may also be pledged to support the bonds.

Collateral Trust Bonds These bonds are backed by other securities that are usually held by the trustee. A common situation of this sort arises when the securities of a subsidiary firm are pledged as collateral by the parent firm.

collateral trust bonds

Equipment Obligations Known also as equipment trust certificates, these securities are backed by specific pieces of equipment (for example, railroad cars and commercial aircraft). If necessary, the equipment can be readily sold and delivered to a new owner. The legal arrangements used to facilitate the

equipment obligations

issuance of such bonds can be very complex. The most popular procedure uses the "Philadelphia Plan," in which the trustee initially holds the equipment and issues obligations, and then leases the equipment to a corporation. Money received from the lessee is subsequently used to make interest and principal payments to the holders of the obligations; ultimately, if all payments are made on schedule, the leasing corporation takes title to the equipment.

debentures

Debentures These are general obligations of the issuing corporation and thus represent unsecured credit. To protect the holders of such bonds, the indenture will usually limit the future issuance of secured debt as well as any additional unsecured debt.

subordinated debentures

Subordinated Debentures When more than one issue of debenture is outstanding, a hierarchy may be specified. For example, subordinated debentures are junior to unsubordinated debentures, meaning that in the event of bankruptcy, junior claims are to be considered only after senior claims have been fully satisfied.

Other Types of Bonds Income bonds are more like preferred stock (described in a later section) than bonds. Payment of interest in full and on schedule is not absolutely required, and failure to do so need not send the corporation into bankruptcy. Interest on **income bonds** may or may not qualify as a tax-deductible expense for the issuing corporation. This type of bond is rarely used, except in reorganizations of bankrupt railroads.

income bonds

guaranteed bonds
participating bonds
voting bonds
serial bonds

Guaranteed bonds are issued by one corporation but backed in some way by another (for example, by a parent firm). **Participating bonds** require stated interest payments and provide additional amounts if earnings exceed some stated level. **Voting bonds,** unlike regular bonds, give the holders some voice in management. **Serial bonds,** with different portions of the issue maturing at different dates, are sometimes used by corporations for equipment financing (as mentioned earlier, they are also used by municipalities).

convertible bonds

Convertible bonds may, at the holder's option, be exchanged for other securities, often common stock. Such bonds, which have become very popular in recent years, are discussed in more detail in the appendix to Chapter 24.

Call Provisions

Management would like to have the right to pay off the corporation's bonds at par at any time prior to maturity. This would provide them with flexibility, since debt could be reduced or its maturity altered via refunding. Most important, expensive high-coupon debt that was issued during a time of high interest rates could be replaced with cheaper low-coupon debt if rates decline.

Not surprisingly, investors hold quite a different opinion on the matter. The issuer's ability to redeem an issue at par at any time virtually precludes a rise in price over par and robs the holder of potential gains from price appreciation associated with declining interest rates; moreover, it introduces a new form of uncertainty. A bond with such a feature will almost certainly sell for less than one without it.

call provisions

Despite the cost of obtaining this sort of flexibility, many corporations include **call provisions** in their bond indentures that give the corporation the option to call some or all of the bonds from their holders at stated prices during specified periods prior to maturity. In a sense, the firm sells a bond and simultaneously buys an option from the holders. The net price of the bond is thus the difference between the value of the bond and the option. (Interestingly, some recent corporate issues have given the investor the option of forcing the issuer to call the security.)

Investors are usually given some call protection: During the first few years after being issued, a bond may not be callable. Later, when the bond is callable, a **call premium** may be specified in the call provision. Such a premium indicates that if the issue is called, the issuer must pay the bondholders a **call price** that is a stated amount above par. Often, the amount above par becomes smaller as time passes and the maturity date approaches.

call premium

call price

An entire issue may be called, or only specific bonds that are chosen randomly by the trustee may be called. In either case, a notice of redemption will appear in advance in the financial press.

Sinking Funds

A bond indenture will often require the issuing corporation to make annual payments into a **sinking fund.** The idea is to pay part of the principal of the debt (as well as the interest) each year, thereby reducing the amount outstanding at maturity.

sinking fund

Sinking funds operate by having the corporation transmit cash to the trustee, who can then purchase bonds in the open market. Alternatively, the corporation may obtain the bonds itself, by either purchase or call, and deposit them with the trustee. Call prices for sinking fund purchases may differ from those specified for when the entire issue is to be repaid prior to maturity.

Required contributions to a sinking fund may or may not be the same each year. In some cases, the required amount may depend on earnings, output, and so on; in others, the goal is to make the total paid for interest and principal the same each year.

Private Placements

Bonds intended for eventual public sale are usually issued in denominations of $1,000 each. Both bearer and registered forms may be utilized. Often, however, a single investor (or a small group of investors) will buy an entire issue. Such **private placements** are typically purchased by large financial institutions.

private placements

Bankruptcy

When a corporation fails to make a scheduled coupon or principal payment on a bond, the corporation is said to be in default on that obligation. If the payment is not made within a relatively short period, some sort of litigation almost inevitably follows.

A corporation unable to meet its obligatory debt payments is said to be technically insolvent (or insolvent in the equity sense). If the value of the firm's assets falls below its liabilities, it is said to be insolvent (or insolvent in the bankruptcy sense).

Behind these definitions lie much legislation, many court cases, and varied legal opinions. While the details differ, the usual situation begins with a default on one or more required coupon payments. If voluntary agreements with creditors cannot be obtained, this usually leads to a filing of bankruptcy—usually "voluntary"—by the corporation itself. Subsequent developments involve courts, court-appointed officials, representatives of the firm's creditors, and the management of the firm, among others.

Liquidation A question that arises in most bankruptcy cases is whether or not the firm's assets should be liquidated (that is, sold) and the proceeds divided among the creditors. Such an action is taken only if the court feels that the resulting value would exceed that likely to be obtained if the firm continued in operation (perhaps after substantial reorganization).

If the firm's assets are liquidated in a "straight bankruptcy," secured creditors receive either the property pledged for their loans or the proceeds from the sale of the secured property. If this amount falls short of their claims, the difference is considered an unsecured debt of the firm; on the other hand, any excess is made available for other creditors. Next, assets are used to pay the claims of priority creditors to the extent possible. These include claims for such items as administrative expenses, wages (up to a stated limit per person), uninsured pension claims, taxes, and rents. Anything left over is used to pay unsecured creditors in proportion to their claims on the firm.

Reorganization If the value of a firm's assets when employed as part of a "going concern" appears to exceed their value in liquidation, a reorganization of the firm and its liabilities may be undertaken. Such proceedings, conducted under the provisions of the Federal Bankruptcy Act, may be voluntary (initiated by the firm) or involuntary (initiated by three or more creditors). A number of parties must concur in the proposed reorganization, including the holders of two-thirds of the value in each general class of creditor that is affected by the reorganization.

Among the goals of reorganization are "fair and equitable" treatment of various classes of securities, and the elimination of "burdensome" debt obligations. Typically, creditors are given new claims on the reorganized firm, with the amounts of the new claims intended to be at least equal in value to the amounts that the creditors would have received in liquidation. For example, holders of debentures might receive bonds of longer maturity, holders of subordinated debentures might become stockholders, and stockholders might be left without any claims on the firm.

Arrangements A third procedure is available to financially distressed corporations. The Federal Bankruptcy Act authorizes arrangements, in which debts may be extended (to longer maturities) or reduced.

Some Financial Aspects of Bankruptcy While the subject is far too complex for detailed treatment here, two aspects of bankruptcy deserve some discussion.

First, the choice between continuation of a firm and liquidation of its assets should be unrelated to considerations of bankruptcy. If an asset can be sold for more than the present value of its future earnings, it should be. Management may have to be taken to court to be forced to do this, but the issue is not really one of solvency or lack thereof.

Second, the definition of insolvency is rather vague. Assume, for the sake of argument, that assets can be adequately valued at the larger of liquidating or going-concern value. A firm is said to be insolvent if this value is less than that of the firm's liabilities. But how should the liabilities be valued? Their current market value will inevitably be less than the value of the assets, while their book value can be greater than the value of the assets.

Trading in Corporate Bonds

While most of the trading in corporate bonds takes place utilizing dealers in the over-the-counter market, many corporate bonds are listed on the New York Stock Exchange (a notably smaller number are listed on the American Stock Exchange). However, trading in corporate bonds on the NYSE takes place at a location that is different from the location where common stocks are traded. Furthermore, no specialists are involved in the trading of corporate bonds on the NYSE. Instead, orders for "active" issues are traded in a "ring" in the Bond Room. Here, the member announces a bid or asked price, depending on whether the member is buying or selling. This invites other members to make counteroffers or to accept the announced price.

"Inactive" issues of bonds that are listed on the NYSE are traded through a computer system known as the **Automated Bond System** (ABS). With this system, members enter their bid or asked prices, along with the quantities, into computer terminals located on the floor of the Bond Room. Other members can see these orders by looking at display terminals, and can respond by entering an order at a terminal.

Automated Bond System

Since some corporate bonds are traded on the New York Stock Exchange, the prices at which such trades are made can be found in the financial press. Figure 19-8 provides an example. Consider the following entry in this figure:

BONDS	CURRENT YIELD	VOLUME	CLOSE	NET CHANGE
ATT 7s01	7.2	273	97⅜	. . .

This entry indicates that American Telephone and Telegraph bonds carrying a 7% coupon (paid semiannually) and maturing in 2001 last traded on June 22, 1992, at 97⅜. Since these bonds have a par value of $1,000, this means that the last trade was at $973.75. The **current yield,** meaning the annual coupon rate divided by the current closing price, was approximately 7.2% = $70/$973.75. In all, 273 bonds traded hands on the exchange during the day, and the closing price was unchanged from that of the previous day.

current yield

In a sense, the New York Stock Exchange is the "odd-lot" market for bonds, even though at the end of 1991 it had nearly 2,800 bonds available for trading (with 1,773 of them being U.S. corporate debt issues with an aggregate par value of $281.7 billion).[11] That is, major trades of bonds are generally negotiated elsewhere by dealers and institutional investors, either directly or through brokers. Thus, reported prices on the NYSE may be poor guides to values associated with large transactions.

FOREIGN BONDS

The foreign bond market refers to bonds issued and denominated in the currency of a country other than the one in which the issuer is primarily

[11]New York Stock Exchange *Fact Book 1991*, pp. 48, 50.

FIGURE 19-8

Price Quotations for Corporate Bonds (Excerpts)

Source: Reprinted by permission of *The Wall Street Journal,* © Dow Jones & Company, Inc., June 23, 1992, p. C16. All rights reserved worldwide.

NEW YORK EXCHANGE BONDS

Quotations as of 4 p.m. Eastern Time
Monday, June 22, 1992

Volume $37,420,000

	Domestic Mon.	Domestic Fri.	All Issues Mon.	All Issues Fri.
Issues traded	531	511	535	512
Advances	188	173	191	173
Declines	203	190	204	191
Unchanged	140	148	140	148
New highs	30	22	31	22
New lows	8	4	8	4

SALES SINCE JANUARY 1
(000 omitted)

1992	1991	1990
$6,050,038	$6,786,128	$5,208,186

Dow Jones Bond Averages

–1991– High	–1991– Low	–1992– High	–1992– Low		–1992– Close	–1992– Chg.	–1992– %Yld	–1991– Close	–1991– Chg.
98.93	91.30	100.17	98.41	20 Bonds	99.88	– 0.27	7.98	94.23	– 0.08
100.81	93.44	101.17	98.45	10 Utilities	99.85	– 0.11	7.96	95.19	– 0.14
97.15	89.06	100.55	97.26	10 Industrials	99.91	– 0.43	8.00	93.28	– 0.01

CORPORATION BONDS
Volume, $37,250,000

Bonds	Cur Yld	Vol	Close	Net Chg
AForP 5s30	8.9	10	56¼	...
AMR 9s16	9.1	438	98⅝	...
AMR zr06	...	52	44	+ 1
Advst 9s08	cv	27	91	...
AetnLf 8⅛07	8.1	30	100½	+ ½
AirbF 6¾01	cv	155	81½	– ¼
AlaP 9s2000	8.7	29	103⅛	...
AlaP 8⅞s03	8.6	10	103½	+ ½
AlaP 8¼s03	8.1	1	102	+ 1¼
AlaP 9½08	9.0	3	106	+ 1
AlskAr zr06	...	7	34	+ ½
AlldC zr92	...	48	98⅝	– 1/32
AlldC zr96	...	5	78	– ⅛
AlldC zr95	...	10	81⅛	+ ⅛
AlldC zr03	...	15	40⅜	– 1⅝
AlldC zr09	...	15	23	+ ½
Allwst 7¼14	cv	10	85½	– ½
AAirl 4¼92	4.3	1	99½	...
AmBrnd 7½99	7.5	10	100⅜	+ ⅛
ACyan 8⅜06	8.2	40	102	+ ¾
AmStor 01	cv	58	100	– 1⅞
ATT 5⅝95	5.7	32	99⅜	– ⅛
ATT 5½97	5.7	25	96	+ ⅛
ATT 6s00	6.5	35	92	+ ¼
ATT 5⅛01	6.0	78	85¼	+ ¼
ATT 7s01	7.2	273	97⅜	...
ATT 7⅛03	7.3	83	97¾	– ¼
ATT 8⅝26	8.5	369	101⅜	...
ATT 8⅝31	8.5	17	101½	...
ATT 7⅛02	7.3	433	98	+ ¼
ATT 8⅛22	8.2	397	98½	...
vjAmes 7½14f	cv	204	3¼	+ ½
Amoco 6s98	6.2	395	97	+ ⅛
Amoco 7⅞07	7.8	25	100¾	+ ½
Amoco 8⅝16	8.3	20	104¼	...
AmocoCda 7⅜13	6.6	21	112	...
Andarko 6¼14	6.4	5	97½	– 1½
Anhr 8s96	7.8	50	102¼	– ¼
Anhr 8⅝16	8.5	40	101¾	...
Arml 9.2s00	9.9	16	92½	+ 1⅝
Arml 8½01	9.8	56	86¾	+ 3¼
Arml 13½94	12.7	24	106⅛	– ¼
AshO 6¾14	cv	4	84¼	+ ¼
Atchsn 4s95	4.4	1	91⅝	– ⅝
ARich 7.7s00	7.6	7	101¼	...
ARch 10½95	10.2	49	102½	+ ¼
ARch 9½96	9.2	12	103¼	...
ARch 9¼93	9.0	30	103	+ ¼
AubrnHl 16⅞20f	...	58	125	– ¼
AutDt zr12	...	1	35½	– ¼
Avnet 6s12	cv	35	88¾	– 2¼
BRE 9½08	cv	10	105½	– ½
Bally 10s06f	cv	37	95⅛	– 1⅜
BalGE 8⅜06	8.3	2	101	...
BncFla 9s03	cv	27	81	...
Banka 8⅞05	8.7	100	102	+ ⅜
Banka 8¾01	8.5	25	102¾	– ⅛
Bkam 8.35s07	8.3	6	100¼	– ⅛
Bkam zr92	...	23	98 1/16	...
Bkam zr93	...	83	94¾	...
BnkTr 8⅛99	8.1	5	100½	...
Barnt 8½99	8.2	47	103½	...
BellPa 8⅝06	8.4	35	102⅝	– ½
BellPa 7⅛12	7.7	10	92⅜	– ½
BellPa 7½13	7.9	20	95½	+ ¼
BellPa 9⅝14	9.1	76	105¼	– ¼
BellPa 8¾15	8.5	3	102⅞	+ ⅛
BellPa 9¼19	8.8	5	105	...
BrkHa zr04	...	90	51¼	...
BethSt 6⅞99	8.1	20	84½	– ⅛
BethSt 9s00	9.3	6	96¾	+ ⅛
BethSt 8.45s05	9.4	116	90	+ ⅛
BethSt 8⅜01	9.3	10	89¾	...
Bevrly 7⅝03	cv	20	84¾	...
BlkD 8⅜97	8.3	5	101	– ⅛
Boeing 8⅜96	7.9	10	106½	+ ⅛
BoisC 7s16	cv	40	85	...
BwnSh 9¼05	cv	15	93¼	– ¼
BwnFer 6¼12	cv	74	85¾	– 1
BurNo 8½96	8.4	1	101½	– ½
BurNo 9⅝96	9.2	5	104¼	...

Bonds	Cur Yld	Vol	Close	Net Chg
CmwE 8¾05	8.6	16	102⅛	+ ¼
CmwE 9⅜04	9.0	81	104	...
CmwE 8⅛07J	8.2	243	99⅝	+ ⅛
CmwE 8¼07	8.3	7	100	+ ⅛
ConrPer 6¾01	cv	151	89½	...
ConrPer 6½02	cv	40	101½	+ ⅞
Consec 12¾97	12.0	36	105⅞	+ ⅜
ConNG 7¼15	cv	21	103	– 1½
CnPw 8⅝00	8.4	25	102⅜	+ ⅝
CnPw 7½02J	7.7	4	97½	...
CnPw 7½02O	7.7	8	97⅝	+ ⅛
CnPw 8⅝03	8.5	14	101⅜	+ ⅛
CnPw 8⅞07	8.8	5	101⅛	– ⅜
CnPw 8⅝07	8.5	5	102	+ 1⅛
CtlOil 7½99	7.5	28	99⅜	– ⅝
vjCtlInf 9s06f	cv	100	8	+ 1
Crane 7s94	7.0	1	100	...
CrayRs 6⅛11	cv	74	73½	– 1½
Crestr 7¾97	7.9	8	98⅛	– ⅛
CumE zr05	...	57	37	– ½
Dana dc5⅞06	cv	25	90¾	– ¼
DataDes 8½08	cv	5	50	+ 3
DatGen 8⅜02	10.1	56	83	...
DataGn 01	cv	73	82	– 1
Datpnt 8⅞06	cv	45	58	– 1¼
DetEd 6s96	6.2	20	96½	– ¼
DetEd 9s99	8.9	67	101½	+ ⅛
DetEd 8.15s00	8.1	10	101⅛	– ⅛
DetEd 8⅛01	8.1	16	100¾	– ⅜
Disney zr05	...	519	47	...
Dow 6.70s98	6.9	50	96½	+ ½
Dow 7.4s02	7.5	2	98½	+ 2½
Dow 8⅝08	8.4	2	102¾	– ⅛
duPnt 8.45s04	8.3	91	101⅞	– ⅛
duPnt 8½16	8.3	30	101⅞	+ ¼
DukeP 7⅜01	7.4	17	99½	+ ⅛
DukeP 7¾02	7.7	20	100½	– ⅛
DukeP 7⅜02	7.5	21	98½	+ 1½
DukeP 8⅛03	7.9	55	103	+ 1⅛
DukeP 8⅜06	8.1	22	103	+ ½
DukeP 8⅛07	8.0	25	101	– ⅞
DuqL 8¾00	8.6	5	101¾	– ¾
EKod 8⅝16	8.6	269	100	...
EKod zr11	...	21	28⅛	...
EmbSuit 10½94	10.3	2	101¾	– ¾
EmbsySuit 10⅞02	10.5	4	103½	+ ¼
EBP 6¾06	cv	125	68	– ½
Enron 10¾98	9.8	4	110	...
Ens 7.65s98	8.0	5	95½	+ ¼
Ens 10s01	cv	30	103	– ¼
EqutR 9s96	9.0	14	100⅜	– 2½
Exxon 6s97	6.2	180	97⅛	– ½
Exxon 6½98	6.6	273	98⅝	...
ExxP 5⅝97	5.9	65	95¾	+ 2⅝
FairCp 12s01	14.0	104	85½	+ ⅛
vjFairfd 13¼92	...	35	44	+ 1
FdHL zr19	...	10	9	– ⅝
FedDS 9scld	...	4	99 31/32	– 1/32
FedDS 10s00	10.1	179	99	– ⅛
Fldcst 6s12	cv	50	71	– 2
FtSec 5.10s99t	5.2	6	99	...
FUnRE 10¼09	cv	3	99	...
FrdC 7⅞cld	...	40	100	...
FrdC 8⅜01	8.3	26	101½	...
FrpMCG zr11	...	12	31	– 2
FreptM 10⅞01	10.2	14	106⅜	+ ⅜
Frpt dc6.55s01	cv	15	90	– 1½
FreptM zr06	...	65	29⅝	– ¼
Fuqua 9½98	9.9	50	95½	+ ½
GMA 7.85s98	7.7	3	101¾	+ 1¼
GMA 8¾s00	8.7	32	101⅛	– ⅝
GMA 8cld	...	235	100 19/32	+ 1/16
GMA 8s02	8.0	35	100⅜	+ ⅜
GMA 8¼06	8.2	46	100⅛	...
GMA dc6s11	7.9	127	76¼	...
GMA zr12	...	3	158	– 1
GMA zr15	...	12	127¼	– ⅛
GMA 10⅜95	10.2	44	101¼	...
GMA 8⅞96	8.6	29	102⅝	+ ⅛
GMA 8¼16	8.6	576	96	– ⅛
GMA 8s93J	7.8	10	102¼	– ¾
GMA 8s93O	7.7	30	103¼	– ⅛
GMA 8s94	7.7	124	104	...
GMA 7⅞97	7.7	101	102⅜	+ ⅛

Bonds	Cur Yld	Vol	Close	Net Chg.
vjJonsLl 6½88f	...	66	4⅝	– 1⅜
vjJoneL 6¾94f	...	2	5⅞	...
K mart 8⅜17	8.5	311	98⅝	...
KerrMc 7¼12	cv	3	104¼	– 2¼
Keycrp 7¾02	8.1	10	96	+ 1
Kolmrg 8¾09	cv	30	78	...
Kraft 8⅜04	8.2	7	102⅜	+ 1⅛
vjLTV 5s88mf	...	98	5	– ¾
vjLTV 9¼97f	...	25	12¼	...
vjLTV 13⅞02f	...	1	11¼	...
vjLTV 14s04f	...	75	11¾	– ¼
vjLTV 11½97f	...	44	5¼	– ⅛
vjLTV 8¾98f	...	72	4¾	– ¾
vjLTV 15s00f	...	25	12½	+ ½
vjLTV Int 5s88f	cv	6	9¼	– 1¾
LaQuin 10s02	cv	10	104	...
LaFrg 7s13	cv	7	93¼	– 1
Leucadia 10⅜02	10.3	192	100⅞	– ⅛
LoewCp zr04	...	86	47¼	...
LomNM 10½93f	...	20	58½	– 1½
LglsLt 11.7s93	11.3	4	104	– 3¼
LglsLt 11¾94	10.6	2	110¾	...
LglsLt 11⅜19	9.5	10	116¾	+ ½
LouN 2 03r	4.6	1	63	+ ½
LouLE 8½00	cv	30	99½	+ ⅛
vjLykes 7½94N f	...	51	2¾	– 1⅛
MACOM 9¼06	cv	55	91¾	– ¼
MGM Grd 11¾99	11.5	218	102	...
MGM Grd 12s02	11.7	297	102¾	– ¾
MGMUA 13s96f	...	220	74⅝	– ⅜
MfrH 8⅛04	8.4	77	97⅛	– 1⅜
MfrH 8⅛07	8.4	1	97	– ⅜
Manvl zr03	...	90	81⅞	– ⅛
MarO 8.5s06	8.5	17	100⅛	+ ⅛
MarO 9½94	9.1	157	104⅞	+ ⅛
Marriott zr06	...	15	32⅜	– ⅜
Masco 5¼12	cv	17	84½	– 2
vjMcCro 7½s94f	...	12	15⅝	+ ½
McDnl zr94	...	25	91⅞	...
McDnl 8⅞19	8.7	1	102½	– ⅛
McDnl 8 11	8.3	30	106½	...
McDnlDg 7⅞97	8.2	104	96⅜	– ⅛
MeYk 7⅝02	7.9	10	96	...
Mead 6¾12	cv	125	93½	– ½
Melln 7¼99	7.3	15	100	...
MesaCap na96	...	15	81	– ⅝
MesaCap 13½99	15.9	88	84⅞	– ⅜
MichB 7¾11	8.0	30	96⅞	...
MichB 8⅛15	8.0	10	101⅛	...
Mickl dc11½98	11.5	5	100	...
MidlBk 11.35s93	11.1	30	101 13/16	+ 9/32
MPac 4¼05	6.1	2	70	– 2½
MPac 4¾20f	...	6	54⅝	– 1⅜
MPac 4¾30f	...	1	52⅝	– 1⅛

Bonds	Cur Yld	Vol	Close	Net Chg.
PacTT 8⅜17	8.4	352	99⅞	...
PacTT 9s18	8.7	50	103¾	...
PacTT 9⅝18	9.0	12	106½	+ ⅛
PacTT 9⅞16	9.3	15	106¼	– ⅜
PacTT 9¾19	9.2	20	105½	– ¼
PGE 8⅞s02	8.6	29	103	+ ⅛
PGE 7½s03	7.7	20	97¼	– 1¼
PGE 7½s04	7.7	5	97	– ⅞
PGE 9⅛s06	8.8	5	103⅝	– ⅛
PGE 8½09	8.3	5	102½	+ ⅛
ParCm 7s03A	7.6	37	92	+ ⅜
ParCm 7s03B	7.6	46	92¼	+ ⅞
PennC 11s97	10.9	124	101⅜	– ⅛
Pennzl 8⅜96	8.3	5	100½	– 1
Pennzl 8⅝96	8.5	12	102	+ ¼
Pepsic 7⅝98	7.5	20	102⅛	– ⅝
Petrie 8s10	cv	76	108	– 1
PhilEl 7¾00	7.8	10	99¾	– ⅛
PhilEl 7½98	7.5	5	100¼	– ½
PhilEl 9⅛06	8.8	38	104	...
PhilEl 8⅝03	8.5	29	102	+ ¾
PhilEl 9⅜17	8.9	58	105	– 1
PhilP 12¼12	11.3	10	108¾	+ ⅜
PhilP 11¼13	10.5	5	106⅞	+ ⅛
PierOn dc11½03	11.4	30	101	– ⅛
Pier1 6⅞02	cv	85	89	– 2
Pittstn 9.2s04	cv	20	100½	– ½
PotEl 7¾s07	7.8	10	99	– ½
PotEl 8⅜09	8.2	20	102¼	...
PotEl 8¼17	8.3	5	99⅞	...
PotEl 7s18	cv	1	99¾	...
ProcG 8¼05	8.1	21	101⅝	– ⅞
PSInd 7s02	7.5	3	92¾	+ ½
PSEG 8s37	8.6	15	93⅛	+ ⅛
PSEG 8¾16	8.6	21	101⅝	+ 1½
PSEG 9⅛93	8.7	20	104½	+ 2⅜
PSEG 7⅝00	cv	15	102	+ 1⅞
RJRNb 10½98	9.4	41	111⅛	...
RJR Nb 8.3s99	8.2	60	101½	...
RJR Nb 13½01	11.8	100	114⅝	...
RJR Nb na15s01	...	818	119⅝	– ⅛
RJR Nb zr01	...	3492	91⅞	– ⅛
RJR Nb 8¾04	8.6	35	101½	...
RJR NbH 17⅜09	9.6	393	181¾	+ ⅛
RalsP 9½16	9.1	40	104¼	+ ⅛
RalsP 9s96	8.4	25	107	...
RalsP 9⅜16	9.0	10	104	+ ⅛
RapA72 7s94f	...	10	1¼	+ ¼
vjRapA 10¾03f	...	5	1	– ⅛
RelFncl 11⅜08	12.0	30	94⅝	+ 1⅛
RelGp 9⅞98	10.2	100	96¾	– 1¾
RelGp 14s96	13.7	448	102	...
RelGp 11s96	12.2	232	90½	– ¼
RelGp 11½01	13.1	100	87⅝	+ ⅝

Bonds	Cur Yld	Vol	Close	Net Chg
StrTch 8s15	cv	43	110	– 8
SunCo 7⅛02	7.5	10	95	...
vjSunsh 9½94f	...	5	31	– 1
vjSunsS 8½95f	...	1	28¾	– ½
TCFox 13¼00	12.7	11	104	– ½
Tandy 10s94	9.6	5	104¼	+ 1¾
Teledy 7s99	7.4	9	94½	– ½
Teledy 10s04A	9.8	27	101¾	...
Teledy 10s04C	9.8	7	101⅝	– ⅛
TencCr 8⅜97	8.3	10	100½	– 1½
TencCr 9¾94	9.4	2	103½	– ¾
TencoCr 9s95	8.5	10	105⅞	+ 1¾
TennGas dc6s11	8.3	23	72	– ⅜
TennGas 11⅛13	10.5	51	105¾	...
TennGas 9⅜17	9.3	30	100¾	– ½
TennGas 13.7s92	13.6	10	100 23/32	– 17/32
Terra 8½12	cv	7	93½	– ½
Tesor dc12¾01	15.0	70	85¼	+ ⅛
Texco 9s96	8.4	10	107⅝	– ¼
Texco 8.65s98	8.2	20	105⅝	– ⅞
Texco 8½03	8.1	10	105⅛	...
Texco 8⅞05	8.6	9	103	...
TxInd 9s08	cv	5	96⅝	+ ⅛
Tidwtr 7s10	cv	10	90	+ 1
Time 9⅞09	9.7	25	102	...
Time 8¾17	8.8	83	100	+ 3⅞
Trvlr 8.7s95	8.6	30	100¾	+ ¼
Trvlr 7⅝97	7.6	201	100⅜	+ ⅜
Trvlr 8.32s15	cv	168	92¼	...
TucEP 8⅛01	8.8	30	92⅜	+ 1⅜
UCCEL 7¼95	cv	25	95⅜	+ 1¼
UNC 7½06	cv	14	80	...
US West zr11	...	33	26⅜	– ⅛
USAir 12⅞00	13.1	604	98	+ ⅛
USG na16s08	...	1530	14¾	– ¼
USLICO 8s11	cv	1	89	...
USX 4⅝96	4.9	73	93½	– ⅛
USX 7s17	cv	55	92⅜	+ ⅛
UnAL 4¼92	4.3	1	99⅝	...
UTelO 7.6s02	7.7	15	98⅛	+ 1⅝
UCarb 15s06	13.7	13	109¼	– ¾
UCarb 7½12	cv	135	91½	– 1¾
UnEl 8⅝07	8.4	15	103⅛	+ 1⅞
UPac 11⅞10	11.1	15	106⅞	+ 1⅞
Unisys 13⅞92	13.7	3	101⅝	– ⅛
Unisys 10¾95	10.7	80	100½	...
Unisys 8.2s96	8.6	18	95	– 1
Unisy na15s97	...	394	109	– ¼
Unisys 8¼00	cv	436	102¼	– ½
Utilicp 6⅝11	cv	3	100	...
VerY 10⅛07	9.5	1	106¾	+ 2¾
WarC 9⅛96	9.1	101	100¼	+ ⅛
WarC 11½13	10.7	15	107¾	+ 1¾
WasteM 01s	...	12	127¼	+ 1¼
WasteM zr12	...	25	34	– ¼
Weingrt 8s09	cv	5	104	...
Wendys 7¼10	cv	25	99½	...
Wendys 7s06	cv	5	109¼	– 1¾
WstCNA 7¼15	cv	41	58½	+ 1
WstDig 9s14	cv	94	66½	– 1¼
WstC 7.6s97	7.6	10	99⅜	– ⅛
WstgE 9s09	cv	40	125	...
Weyh 7.65s94	7.6	3	101⅛	...
Weyh 5¼17	cv	50	87½	– 1
Whirl zr11	...	26	29⅝	+ ⅛
WilcxGb 7s14	cv	15	70½	– ½
WisBl 7¼07	7.7	5	94	– 1½
WisBl 8s14	7.9	7	101½	+ ½
WisBl 8¼16	8.0	20	102½	+ 2¼
Witco 5½12	cv	35	93	...
WUTl 9¼97f	...	10	17½	...
Xerox 6s95	cv	25	100½	+ ½
Xerox 8⅝99	8.5	40	101¾	...
vjYngtS 4½90r	...	32	115⅛	– ¼
Zenith 6¼11	cv	43	57¾	– ¼

FOREIGN BONDS
Volume, $140,000

Bonds	Cur Yld	Vol	Close	Net Chg
Austla 11⅜93	10.9	10	104¼	+ ¼
Austla 12⅛08	11.2	5	108	+ ⅝
EurIn 12⅝99	11.5	100	110	– ⅞
ToyotaMC 7.1s94	6.9	5	102⅜	+ ⅛

located. For example, Toyota has issued bonds that are denominated in U.S. dollars, mature in 1994, and carry a 7.1% coupon rate. A brief listing of some of these bonds is contained daily at the end of the "New York Exchange Bonds" quotations section in *The Wall Street Journal*, as shown in Figure 19-8. Interestingly, foreign bonds that are issued in the United States and are denominated in U.S. dollars are referred to as Yankee bonds, while foreign (that is, non-Japanese) bonds that are issued in Japan are referred to as Samurai bonds.

In issuing foreign bonds, the issuer must abide by the rules and regulations imposed by the government of the country in which the bonds are issued. This may be relatively easy or difficult, depending on the country involved.

One of the main advantages of purchasing foreign bonds is the opportunity to obtain international diversification of a bond portfolio while not having to be concerned about foreign exchange fluctuations. For example, one might be able to buy a Toyota bond in Japan that is denominated in yen, but in doing so one would have to worry about the yen-dollar exchange rate. This is because the coupon payments and ultimately the principal would be paid to the U.S. purchaser in yen, which would then have to be converted into dollars at an exchange rate that currently is unknown. However, the buyer could avoid such worries by purchasing a Toyota bond that is denominated in U.S. dollars.

EUROBONDS

Owing in part to government restrictions on investment in foreign securities, a number of borrowers have found it advantageous to sell securities in other countries. The term **Eurobond** is loosely applied to bonds that are offered outside the country of the borrower and outside the country in whose currency the securities are denominated.[12] Thus, a bond issued by a U.S. corporation that is denominated in Japanese yen (or U.S. dollars) and sold in Germany would be referred to as a Eurobond.

Eurobond

Since the Eurobond market is neither regulated nor taxed, it offers substantial advantages for many issuers and buyers of bonds. For example, a foreign subsidiary of a U.S. corporation may issue a Eurobond in "bearer" form. No tax will be withheld by the corporation, and the tax (if any) paid by the purchaser will depend on his or her country of residence. For tax reasons, interest rates on Eurobonds tend to be somewhat lower than those of domestic bonds denominated in the same currency.

PREFERRED STOCK

In some respects, **preferred stock** is like a perpetual bond. A given dollar amount is to be paid each year by the issuer to the investor. This amount may be stated as a percent of the stock's par value (for example, 8% of $100, meaning $8 per year) or directly as a dollar figure (for example, $2.75 per year). Since the security is a "stock," such payments are called dividends

preferred stock

[12]There are also fixed-income securities of this nature that have shorter lives; they are sometimes referred to as Euronotes or Euro-commercial paper. The market where they (and Eurobonds) are issued and traded is known as the Eurocredit market.

instead of interest and hence do not qualify as a tax-deductible expense for the issuing corporation. Furthermore, failure to make such payments does not constitute grounds for bankruptcy proceedings.

A recent innovation is adjustable rate preferred stock (ARPS), where the dividend is reset periodically in terms of an applicable rate. For example, the annualized "percent of par" for the dividend might be reset every three months to be equal to the largest of the rates on (1) three-month Treasury bills; (2) ten-year Treasury bonds; and (3) twenty-year Treasury bonds. Related to ARPS are dutch auction rate preferred stock (DARPS), where the dividend is reset periodically (more often than for ARPS) at a level that results from bidding by current and potential owners.[13]

cumulative dividends

Preferred stock is generally preferred as to dividends. Specified payments must be made on the preferred stock before any dividends may be paid to holders of the firm's common stock. Failure to pay a preferred dividend in full does not constitute default, but unpaid dividends are usually **cumulative.** This means that all previously unpaid preferred stock dividends must be paid (but seldom with interest) before any dividends may be paid on the common stock.

No indenture is provided with a preferred stock issue. However, various provisions protecting the preferred stockholders against potentially harmful actions may be written into the corporation's charter. For example, one provision may limit the dollar amount of senior securities that can be issued in the future. While preferred stockholders typically do not have voting rights, there may be another provision that gives them voting rights when the corporation is in arrears on its preferred dividends.

Many issues of preferred stock are callable, often at a premium; such stock is sometimes said to be redeemable at a stated redemption price. Participating preferred stock entitles the holder to receive extra dividends when earnings permit. Convertible preferred stock may, at the option of the holder, be converted into another security (usually the firm's common stock) on stated terms. Some firms issue more than one class of preferred stock, with preference accorded the various classes in a specified order.

In the event of a dissolution of the firm, preferred stock is often preferred as to assets. Generally this means that preferred stockholders are entitled to receive the stock's par value before any payment is made to common stockholders.

Since preferred stock has many features of a bond without the substantial tax advantage that bonds give to the issuer, it is used less often than debt. In 1991, $17.4 billion of preferred stock was issued, compared with $287.0 billion of publicly offered corporate debt.[14]

As indicated in Chapter 5, interest income from bonds held by a corporate investor is subject to the corporate income tax, but 80% of any dividend income received is exempt from taxation. For a corporate investor this makes the effective tax rate on dividends from preferred stock approximately 6.8% (= .34 × .20), compared with 34% for interest received on bonds. For this reason, preferred stocks tend to sell at prices that give lower before-tax returns than long-term bonds, even though the latter may be considerably

---

[13]For a discussion of ARPS and DARPS, see Michael J. Alderson, Keith C. Brown, and Scott L. Lummer, "Dutch Auction Rate Preferred Stock," *Financial Management*, 16, no. 2 (Summer 1987), 68–73.

[14]*Federal Reserve Bulletin*, June 1992, p. A32.

lower in risk. As a result, preferred stocks are generally unattractive holdings for noncorporate investors, such as individuals and tax-exempt investors.

Many preferred stocks are traded on major exchanges in a manner similar to common stocks. Typically, they are assigned to the same specialist that is responsible for the firm's common stock. Trading prices are reported in the financial press in the same format used for common stocks.

SUMMARY

1. The most familiar types of fixed-income securities are personal savings deposits. These include demand deposits, time deposits, and certificates of deposit issued by commercial banks, savings and loan companies, mutual savings banks, and credit unions.

2. Highly marketable, short-term securities are referred to as money market instruments. These securities include commercial paper, large-denomination certificates of deposits, bankers' acceptances, repurchase agreements, and Eurodollar CDs.

3. The U.S. Treasury issues debt securities to finance the government's borrowing needs. These securities are issued in various maturities—short-term (Treasury bills), intermediate-term (Treasury notes), and long-term (Treasury bonds). The Treasury also issues savings bonds to individual investors.

4. Treasury notes or bonds can be converted into a set of pure-discount bonds by issuing marketable receipts entitling the holder to a specific coupon payment or the bond's principal payment. Separating a bond into its component payments is known as coupon stripping.

5. Federal agencies also issue securities to finance their operations. In some cases this debt may be explicitly backed by the U.S. Treasury. In other cases the government guarantee may be implicit.

6. Participation certificates represent ownership of a pool of securities. The holders receive cash flows from the pool's securities in proportion to their ownership in the pool.

7. State and local governments issue a wide variety of fixed-income securities. These securities may be backed solely by the full faith and credit of the issuer or by a specific revenue source.

8. Because municipal securities are generally exempt from federal taxation, those securities usually offer lower yields than taxable securities.

9. Corporate bonds, such as mortgage bonds or equipment obligations, may be backed by specific assets. Alternatively, corporate bonds, such as debentures, may represent general obligations of the issuing corporations.

10. Corporate bonds (and some government bonds) may contain call provisions, giving the issuer the right to redeem the security prior to maturity under specified terms.

11. Corporations entering bankruptcy may undergo liquidation, reorganization, or arrangement.

12. Preferred stock dividends are generally fixed, but do not represent legal obligations of issuers. Most preferred stock dividends are cumulative, requiring payment of all unpaid preferred dividends before common stock dividends can be paid.

KEY TERMS

pure-discount security
coupon payments
maturity date
principal
demand deposits
time deposits
certificates of deposit
bank discount basis
bankers' acceptance
Eurodollar CDs
Eurodollar deposits
repurchase agreement
repo rate
debt refunding
term-to-maturity
accrued interest
call provisions
federally sponsored agencies
participation certificates
municipal bonds
general obligation bonds
revenue bonds
industrial development bonds
taxable municipals
serial bonds
term bonds
sinking fund
indenture
trustee
mortgage bonds

collateral trust bonds
equipment obligations
debentures
subordinated debentures
income bonds
guaranteed bonds
participating bonds
voting bonds
convertible bonds
call premium
call price
private placements
Automated Bond System
current yield
Eurobond
preferred stock
cumulative dividends

QUESTIONS AND PROBLEMS

1. What is the annual equivalent yield on a thirteen-week Treasury bill selling at a price of 96?
2. Consider a thirteen-week Treasury bill, issued today, that is selling for $9,675.00. (Its face value is $10,000.00.)
   (a) What is the annual discount based on the selling price of the security?
   (b) What is the annual equivalent yield of the security?
3. Rank the various money market instruments discussed in the text in terms of default risk. Explain the reasoning behind your rankings. Find the latest interest rates for these securities. Do they correspond with your default-risk rankings?
4. The U.S. Treasury once issued notes and bonds only in bearer form. Now its notes and bonds are issued only in registered form. Given the characteristics of bearer and registered bonds, speculate as to what reasons might have prompted the Treasury to change the form of issuance.
5. Using *The Wall Street Journal* as a data source, identify a particular Treasury note or bond. What is its coupon rate? What is its maturity date? What is the latest bid-ask spread for the security? What is the security's yield-to-maturity?
6. Describe the standard practice by which sellers of government and corporate bonds are compensated for accrued interest.
7. What is the rationale for a bond issuer including a call provision in the terms of its bond issue? How do bond investors typically respond to the inclusion of a call provision?
8. How do zero coupon fixed-income securities provide returns to investors?
9. Why does the IRS treat the difference between the price of a bond purchased at a discount and its face value as ordinary income to the investor, as opposed to treating it as a capital gain?
10. Bonds issued by federal agencies have an explicit or implicit promise that the federal government will ensure payment of interest and principal. Why then are these securities usually priced by the market to offer yields above Treasury securities?
11. What is a mortgage participation certificate? What is the primary risk that such securities present investors?
12. Cozy Dolan, an amateur investor, commented, "I prefer investing in GNMA pass-through securities. Their government guarantee gives me a riskfree return." Comment on Cozy's comment.
13. Distinguish between a general obligation municipal bond and a revenue bond.

14. Eurobonds have become a very popular form of financing in recent years. What features of the Eurobond market make Eurobonds attractive to issuers and bondholders?
15. Pigeon Falls Airlines was in difficult financial shape owing to ongoing recession and labor problems. To this point the firm had issued no debt but believed that borrowing in the bond market was the only way to get through the tough times. Because of its poor financial condition, Pigeon Falls' investment bankers advised it that a debenture issue would not be well received. What other bond issuance options might Pigeon Falls pursue?
16. A callable bond is sometimes described as a combination of a noncallable bond and an option. Explain why this description is appropriate. Further, explain how these two features affect the price of a callable bond.
17. Is it true that most corporations that default on their debt eventually enter bankruptcy and see their assets liquidated to repay creditors? Explain.
18. In trying to explain the concept of preferred stock to a novice investor, Patsy Donovan referred to it as a "hybrid" security. What did Patsy mean by this term?
19. What is the purpose of the cumulative dividends restriction of most preferred stock?

REFERENCES

1. A concise summary description of the various types of money market instruments is contained in:

   Timothy Q. Cook and Timothy D. Rowe, *Instruments of the Money Market* (Federal Reserve Bank of Richmond, 1986).

2. The following contains thorough descriptions of the various types of fixed-income securities discussed in this chapter:

   Frank J. Fabozzi and Franco Modigliani, *Capital Markets: Institutions and Instruments* (Englewood Cliffs, N.J.: Prentice Hall, 1992), Chapters 13–18.

3. For a discussion of coupon stripping, see:

   Miles Livingston and Deborah Wright Gregory, "The Stripping of U.S. Treasury Securities," Monograph Series in Finance and Economics #1989-1, New York University Salomon Center, Leonard N. Stern School of Business;

   Deborah W. Gregory and Miles Livingston, "Development of the Market for U.S. Treasury STRIPS," *Financial Analysts Journal*, 48, no. 2 (March/April 1992): 68–74.

4. For a discussion of the market for securities issued by the U.S. Treasury, see:

   Peter Wann, *Inside the U$ Treasury Market* (New York: Quorum Books, 1989).

5. For a discussion of mortgage-backed securities, see:

   Earl Baldwin and Saundra Stotts, *Mortgage-Backed Securities: A Reference Guide for Lenders & Issuers* (Chicago: Probus Publishing, 1990);

Sean Becketti and Charles S. Morris, "The Prepayment Experience of FNMA Mortgage-Backed Securities," Monograph Series in Finance and Economics #1990-3, New York University Salomon Center, Leonard N. Stern School of Business;

Frank J. Fabozzi and Franco Modigliani, *Mortgage & Mortgage-Backed Securities Markets* (Boston: Harvard Business School Press, 1992);

Eduardo S. Schwartz and Walter N. Torous, "Prepayment, Default, and the Valuation of Mortgage Pass-through Securities," *Journal of Business*, 65, no. 2 (April 1992): 221–239.

Andrew Carron, "Understanding CMOs, REMICs, and Other Mortgage Derivatives," *Journal of Fixed Income*, 2, no. 1 (June 1992): 25–43.

6. For a discussion municipal bonds, see:

Peter Fortune, "The Municipal Bond Market, Part I: Politics, Taxes, and Yields," Federal Reserve Bank of Boston *New England Economic Review*, (September/October 1991): 13–36;

Peter Fortune, "The Municipal Bond Market, Part II: Problems and Policies," Federal Reserve Bank of Boston *New England Economic Review*, (May/June 1992): 47–64.

7. For a discussion of the foreign bond and Eurobond markets, see:

Bruno Solnik, *International Investments* (Reading, Mass.: Addison-Wesley, 1991), Chapters 6–7.

8. For a discussion of the Eurocredit market, see:

Arie L. Melnik and Steven E. Plaut, "The Short-Term Eurocredit Market," Monograph Series in Finance and Economics #1991-1, New York University Salomon Center, Leonard N. Stern School of Business.

9. For a discussion of how government bond markets function in the United Kingdom, Japan, and Germany, see:

Thomas J. Urich, "U.K., German and Japanese Government Bond Markets," Monograph Series in Finance and Economics #1991-2, New York University Salomon Center, Leonard N. Stern School of Business.

10. The accuracy of reported prices for corporate bonds is analyzed in:

Kenneth P. Nunn, Jr., Joanne Hill, and Thomas Schneeweis, "Corporate Bond Price Data Sources and Risk/Return Measurement," *Journal of Financial and Quantitative Analysis*, 21, no. 2 (June 1986): 197–208;

Oded Sarig and Arthur Warga, "Bond Price Data and Bond Market Liquidity," *Journal of Financial and Quantitative Analysis*, 24, no. 3 (September 1989): 367–78;

Arthur D. Warga, "Corporate Bond Price Discrepancies in the Dealer and Exchange Markets," *Journal of Fixed Income*, 1, no. 3 (December 1991): 7–16.

20

Fundamentals of Bond Valuation

A useful first step in understanding bond valuation is to consider those fixed-income securities that are certain of making their promised payments in full and on time. The obvious candidates are the securities representing the debt of the U.S. government. Since the government can print money whenever it chooses, the promised payments on such securities are virtually certain to be made on schedule. However, there is a degree of uncertainty as to the purchasing power of the promised payments. While U.S. government bonds may be riskless in terms of their nominal payments, they may be quite risky in terms of their real (or inflation-adjusted) payments.

Despite this concern with inflation risk, it will be assumed hereafter that there are fixed-income securities whose nominal and real payments are certain. Specifically, to the extent that inflation exists, it will be assumed that its magnitude can be accurately predicted. Such an assumption makes it possible to focus on the impact of *time* on bond valuation. Having accomplished this, the influence of other attributes on bond valuation can be considered.

YIELD-TO-MATURITY

There are many interest rates, not just one. Furthermore, there are many ways that interest rates can be calculated. One such method results in an interest rate that is known as the yield-to-maturity; another results in an interest rate known as the spot rate, which will be discussed in the next section.

In describing yields-to-maturity and spot rates, three hypothetical Treasury securities that are available to the public for investment will be considered. Such securities are widely believed to be free from default risk, meaning that investors have no doubts about being paid fully and on time. Thus, the impact of differing degrees of default risk on yields-to-maturity and spot rates will have been removed by considering these securities.

The three Treasury securities to be considered will be referred to as bonds A, B, and C. Bond A matures in a year, at which time the investor will receive \$1,000. Similarly, bond B matures in two years, at which time the investor will receive \$1,000. Bond C is a coupon bond that pays the investor \$50 one year from now and matures two years from now, paying the investor \$1,050 at that time. The prices at which these bonds are currently being sold in the market are:

Bond A (the one-year pure-discount bond):	\$934.58
Bond B (the two-year pure-discount bond):	\$857.34
Bond C (the two-year coupon bond):	\$946.93

yield-to-maturity

The **yield-to-maturity** on any fixed-income security is the single interest rate (with interest compounded at some specified interval) that, if paid by a bank on the amount invested, would enable the investor to obtain all the payments made by the security in question. It is a simple matter to determine the yield-to-maturity on the one-year security, bond A. Since an investment of \$934.58 will pay \$1,000 one year later, the yield-to-maturity on this bond is the rate r_A that a bank would have to pay on a deposit of \$934.58 in order for the account to have a balance of \$1,000 after one year. Thus, the yield-to-maturity on bond A is the rate r_A that solves the following equation:

$$(1 + r_A) \times \$934.58 = \$1{,}000 \qquad (20.1)$$

which is 7%.

In the case of bond B, assuming annual compounding at a rate r_B, an account with \$857.34 invested initially (the cost of B) would grow to $(1 + r_B) \times \$857.34$ in one year. Leaving this total intact, the account would growto $(1 + r_B) \times [(1 + r_B) \times \$857.34]$ by the end of the second year. The yield-to-maturity is the rate r_B that makes this amount equal to \$1,000. In other words, the yield-to-maturity on bond B is the rate r_B that solves the following equation:

$$(1 + r_B) \times [(1 + r_B) \times \$857.34] = \$1{,}000 \qquad (20.2)$$

which is 8%.

For bond C, consider investing \$946.93 in an account. At the end of one year, the account would grow in value to $(1 + r_C) \times \$946.93$. Then the investor would remove \$50, leaving a balance of $\{[(1 + r_C) \times \$946.93] - \$50\}$. At the end of the second year this balance would have grown to an amount equal to $(1 + r_C) \times \{[(1 + r_C) \times \$946.93] - \$50\}$. The yield-to-maturity on bond C is the rate r_C that makes this amount equal to \$1,050:

$$(1 + r_C) \times \{[(1 + r_C) \times \$946.93] - \$50\} = \$1{,}050 \qquad (20.3)$$

which is 7.975%.

Equivalently, yield-to-maturity is the discount rate that makes the present value of the promised future cash flows equal to the current market price of the bond.[1] When viewed in this manner, yield-to-maturity is analogous to internal rate of return, a concept used for making capital budgeting decisions that is often described in introductory finance textbooks. This can be seen for bond A by dividing both sides of equation (20.1) by $(1 + r_A)$, resulting in:

$$\$934.58 = \frac{\$1{,}000}{(1 + r_A)} . \tag{20.4}$$

Similarly, for bond B both sides of equation (20.2) can be divided by $(1 + r_B)^2$, resulting in:

$$\$857.34 = \frac{\$1{,}000}{(1 + r_B)^2} \tag{20.5}$$

while for bond C both sides of equation (20.3) can be divided by $(1 + r_C)^2$:

$$\$946.93 - \frac{\$50}{(1 + r_C)} = \frac{\$1{,}050}{(1 + r_C)^2}$$

or:

$$\$946.93 = \frac{\$50}{(1 + r_C)} + \frac{\$1{,}050}{(1 + r_C)^2} . \tag{20.6}$$

Since equations (20.4), (20.5), and (20.6) are equivalent to equations (20.1), (20.2), and (20.3), respectively, the solutions must be the same as before, with $r_A = 7\%$, $r_B = 8\%$, and $r_C = 7.975\%$.

For coupon-bearing bonds, the procedure for determining yield-to-maturity involves trial and error. In the case of bond C, a discount rate of 10% could be tried initially, resulting in a value for the right-hand side of equation (20.6) of $913.22, a value that is too low. This indicates that the number in the denominator is too high, so a lower discount rate is used next—say 6%. In this case, the value on the right-hand side is $981.67, which is too high and indicates that 6% is too low. This means that the solution is between 6% and 10%, and the search could continue until the answer, 7.975%, is found.

Fortunately, computers are good at trial-and-error calculations. One can describe a very complex series of cash flows to a computer and get an answer concerning yield-to-maturity in short order. In fact, some hand-held calculators come with built-in programs to find yield-to-maturity, where one simply enters the number of days to maturity, the annual coupon payments, and the current market price, then presses the key that indicates yield-to-maturity.

Yield-to-maturity is the most commonly used measure of a bond's "interest rate" or "return." It can be computed for any bond and it facilitates comparisons among different investments. However, it has some serious drawbacks. In order to understand these drawbacks, the concept of spot rates must be introduced.

---

[1]This calculation assumes that the bond will not be called prior to maturity. If it is assumed that the bond will be called as soon as possible, then the discount rate that makes the present value of the corresponding cash flows equal to the current market price of the bond is known as the bond's *yield-to-call*.

MONEY MATTERS
Fixed-Income Investing Based on the Yield-to-Maturity

Fixed-income investing used to be so simple. Interest rates were low and dramatic fluctuations in rates were rare. Only the highest-quality companies issued bonds. For the bond investor, decisions were few—one simply bought and held long-term bonds. Bonds were considered a safe investment, suitable for "widows and orphans."

That comfortable environment was demolished in the late 1970s and early 1980s. Rampant inflation, expanding federal budget deficits, and a host of other economic ills led to escalating U.S. interest rates and a corresponding sharp depreciation in long-term bond values. Perhaps even more troubling to bond investors was that during this period interest rate volatility increased substantially. Owners of long-term bonds found their portfolios subject to large, unpredictable swings in value. Interest rates on thirty-year bonds, which were below 8% in 1977, leapt to 14% in 1982 and declined to under 8% again by 1986.

This increase in interest rate volatility had many ramifications for fixed-income portfolio management. It created a huge demand for financial instruments to control interest-rate risk, from options and futures to floating rate notes to "puttable" bonds. It turned staid bond houses into high-powered trading firms and created fortunes for successful bond traders.

While a discussion of these developments could fill volumes, our focus will be on a narrower subject: the distortions that interest-rate volatility has brought to the yield-to-maturity (YTM) as a measure of fixed-income promised return.

As the text describes, a bond's YTM is that interest rate that equates the price of the bond to the sum of the bond's discounted promised cash flows. Equivalently, if the bond investor took all of the bond's promised cash flows and invested them at the YTM, he or she would be just as well off at the end of the bond's life as if he or she had initially placed the dollar amount of the bond's price in a savings account paying an interest rate equal to the YTM.

We can define a bond's promised return as the wealth that we anticipate accumulating from the bond's promised cash flows and the reinvested income on those cash flows over a certain period, relative to the price that we paid for the bond. Consequently, under specific assumptions, a bond's YTM is appropriately viewed as its promised return.

Fixed-income investors have traditionally used the YTM as a means of comparing the promised returns to maturity offered by competing fixed-income investments. All other things being equal, a higher-YTM bond is preferred to a lower-YTM bond. Even when competing bonds differ in terms of such fundamental factors as risk

SPOT RATES

spot rate

A **spot rate** is measured at a given point in time as the yield-to-maturity on a pure-discount security, and can be thought of as the interest rate associated with a spot contract. Such a contract, when signed, involves the immediate loaning of money from one party to another. The loan, along with interest, is to be repaid in its entirety at a specific time in the future. The interest rate that is specified in the contract is the spot rate.

Bonds A and B in the previous example were pure-discount securities, meaning that an investor who purchased either one would expect to receive only one cash payment from the issuer. Accordingly, in this example the one-year spot rate is 7% and the two-year spot rate is 8%. In general, the t-year spot rate s_t is the solution to the following equation:

$$P_t = \frac{M_t}{(1 + s_t)^t} \qquad (20.7)$$

where P_t is the current market price of a pure-discount bond that matures in t years and has a maturity value of M_t. For example, the values of P_t and M_t for bond B would be \$857.34 and \$1,000, respectively, with $t = 2$.

Spot rates can also be determined in another manner if only coupon-

of default, the YTM provides a base from which to conduct further security analysis.

This use of the YTM is predicated on several assumptions, the most critical of which is that interest income generated by a fixed-income security is reinvested (compounded) at the YTM. If this assumption is true, then the YTM correctly states the return over the bond's life that the buy-and-hold investor will realize on his or her bond investment. If the assumption is false, then the realized return will differ, perhaps significantly, from the YTM.

The realized return on a bond held to maturity is a function of the bond's stated coupon rate, its market price, and its reinvestment rate. The reinvestment rate can represent a surprisingly large portion of the realized return, roughly 50% to 70% for a "typical" long-term coupon-bearing fixed-income security. (Note that the reinvestment rate issue does not exist for a pure-discount security.)

The presumption that all interest income can be reinvested at the YTM in essence implies a flat, unchanging yield curve. That is, the interest rates offered by similar-quality bonds of any maturity are assumed to be equal; ninety-day Treasury bill yields equal those of thirty-year Treasury bonds. Moreover, this interest rate is assumed not to change over time. While these assumptions may seem preposterous today (in 1992, Treasury bond yields exceeded Treasury bill yields by over 4 percentage points), in the 1950s and 1960s, when Treasury bills yielded about 1% to 3% and Treasury bonds yielded 3% to 5%, with relatively little volatility, they did not seem as inappropriate.

However, once the assumption of a flat, unchanging yield curve is dropped, the YTM no longer necessarily represents an adequate estimate of promised long-term return. The bond investor must determine at what interest rates the bond's interest income will be invested. Suppose, for example, that you buy at par a ten-year $1,000 face value bond with an annual interest payment of $80. The bond's YTM is therefore 8%. If you are able to reinvest all of your interest income at 8%, your realized return over the bond's life will also be 8%. That is, you will be as rich at the end of the bond's life as you would have been had you invested in a savings account paying 8% a year. However, if your reinvestment rate rises to 12%, your realized annual return over ten years will be 9.17%. On the other hand, if your reinvestment rate falls to 4%, your realized annual return will be only 6.96%.

In a world of sloping yield curves and sharply fluctuating interest rates, calculating the promised return on a fixed-income security becomes problematic. The YTM approach to bond valuation may no longer be an adequate representation of a bond's long-run promised return. Instead, a bond's cash flows should be individually discounted at the various interest rates associated with the maturities of those cash flows; that is, the spot rates applicable to those maturities. Unfortunately, estimating the appropriate spot rates is more complicated than calculating a single YTM. Ah, but then again, fixed-income investing used to be so simple.

---

bearing Treasury bonds are available for longer maturities. Generally the one-year spot rate (s_1) will be known, since there generally will be a one-year pure-discount Treasury security available for making this calculation. However, it may be the situation that no two-year pure-discount Treasury security exists. Instead, only a two-year coupon-bearing bond may be available for investment, having a current market price of P_2, a maturity value of M_2, and a coupon payment one year from now equal to C_1. In this situation, the two-year spot rate (s_2) is the solution to the following equation:

$$P_2 = \frac{C_1}{(1 + s_1)^1} + \frac{M_2}{(1 + s_2)^2}. \tag{20.8}$$

For example, assume that only bonds A and C exist. In this situation it is known that the one-year spot rate, s_1, is 7%. Now, equation (20.8) can be used to determine the two-year spot rate, s_2, where $P_2 = \$946.93$, $C_1 = \$50$, and $M_2 = \$1{,}050$:

$$\$946.93 = \frac{\$50}{(1 + .07)^1} + \frac{\$1{,}050}{(1 + s_2)^2}.$$

The solution to this equation is $s_2 = .08 = 8\%$. Thus, the two-year spot rate is determined to be the same in this example, regardless of whether it is determined directly by analyzing pure-discount bond B or indirectly by analyzing coupon-bearing bond C in conjunction with bond A. While this will not always be the case, often the differences are insignificant.

DISCOUNT FACTORS

discount factors

Having determined a set of spot rates, it is a straightforward matter to determine the corresponding set of **discount factors.** A discount factor d_t is equivalent to the present value of \$1 to be received t years in the future from a Treasury security, and is equal to:

$$d_t = \frac{1}{(1 + s_t)^t}. \tag{20.9}$$

market discount function

The set of these factors is sometimes referred to as the **market discount function,** and changes day to day as spot rates change. In the example, $d_1 = 1/(1 + .07)^1 = .9346$; and $d_2 = 1/(1 + .08)^2 = .8573$.

Once the market discount function has been determined, it is fairly straightforward to find the present value of any Treasury security (or, for that matter, any default-free security). Let C_t denote the cash payment to be made to the investor at year t on the security being evaluated. The multiplication of C_t by d_t is termed **discounting:** converting the given future value into an equivalent present value. The latter is equivalent in the sense that P present dollars can be converted into C_t dollars in year t via available investment instruments, given the currently prevailing spot rates. An investment paying C_t dollars in year t with certainty should sell for $P = d_tC_t$ dollars today. If it sells for more, it is overpriced; if it sells for less, it is underpriced. These statements rest solely on comparisons with equivalent opportunities in the marketplace. Valuation of default-free investments thus requires no assessment of individual preferences, only careful analysis of available opportunities in the marketplace.

discounting

The simplest and, in a sense, most fundamental characterization of the structure of the market for default-free bonds is given by the current set of discount factors, referred to earlier as the market discount function. With this set of factors, it is a simple matter to evaluate a default-free bond that provides more than one payment, for it is, in effect, a package of bonds, each of which provides only one payment. Each amount is simply multiplied by the appropriate discount factor and the resultant present values summed.

For example, assume that the Treasury is preparing to offer for sale a two-year coupon-bearing security that will pay \$70 in one year and \$1,070 in two years. What is a fair price for such a security? It is simply the present value of \$70 and \$1,070. How can this be determined? By multiplying the \$70 and \$1,070 by the one-year and two-year discount factors, respectively. Doing so results in (\$70 × .9346) + (\$1,070 × .8573), which equals \$982.73.

No matter how complex the pattern of payments, this procedure can be used to determine the value of any default-free bond of this type. The general formula for a bond's present value (PV) is:

$$PV = \sum_{t=1}^{n} d_tC_t \tag{20.10}$$

where the bond has promised cash payments C_t for each year t through year n.

At this point, it has been shown how spot rates and, in turn, discount factors can be calculated. However, no link between different spot rates (or different discount factors) has been established. For example, it has yet to be shown how the one-year spot rate of 7% is related to the two-year spot rate of 8%. The concept of forward rates makes the link.

FORWARD RATES

In the example, the one-year spot rate was determined to be 7%. This means that the market has determined that the present value of \$1 to be paid by the Treasury department in one year is \$1/1.07, or \$.9346. That is, the relevant discount rate for converting a cash flow one year from now to its present value is 7%. Since it was also noted that the two-year spot rate was 8%, the present value of \$1 to be paid by the Treasury department in two years is $\$1/1.08^2$, or \$.8573.

An alternative view of \$1 to be paid in two years is that it can be discounted in two steps. The first step determines its equivalent one-year value. That is, \$1 to be received in two years is equivalent to $\$1/(1 + f_{1,2})$ to be received in one year. The second step determines the present value of this equivalent one-year amount by discounting it at the one-year spot rate of 7%. Thus, its current value is:

$$\frac{\$1/(1 + f_{1,2})}{(1 + .07)}.$$

However, this value must be equal to \$.8573, since it was mentioned earlier that according to the two-year spot rate, \$.8573 is the present value of \$1 to be paid in two years. That is,

$$\frac{\$1/(1 + f_{1,2})}{(1 + .07)} = \$.8573 \tag{20.11}$$

which has a solution for $f_{1,2}$ of 9.01%.

The discount rate $f_{1,2}$ is known as the **forward rate** from year one to year two. That is, it is the discount rate for determining the equivalent value of a dollar one year from now if it is to be received two years from now. In the example, \$1 to be received two years from now is equivalent in value to \$1/(1.0901) = \$.9174 to be received one year from now (in turn, note that the present value of \$.9174 is \$.9174/1.07 = \$.8573).

forward rate

Symbolically, the link between the one-year spot rate, two-year spot rate, and one-year forward rate is:

$$\frac{\$1/(1 + f_{1,2})}{(1 + s_1)} = \frac{\$1}{(1 + s_2)^2} \tag{20.12}$$

which can be rewritten as:

$$f_{1,2} = \frac{(1 + s_2)^2}{(1 + s_1)} - 1 \tag{20.13}$$

or:

$$(1 + s_1)(1 + f_{1,2}) = (1 + s_2)(1 + s_2). \tag{20.14}$$

Figure 20-1 illustrates this by referring to the example and then generalizing from it.

More generally, for year $t - 1$ and year t spot rates, the link to the forward rate between years $t - 1$ and t is:

$$f_{t-1,t} = \frac{(1 + s_t)^t}{(1 + s_{t-1})^{t-1}} - 1 \tag{20.15}$$

or:

$$(1 + s_{t-1})^{t-1} \times (1 + f_{t-1,t}) = (1 + s_t)^t. \tag{20.16}$$

There is another interpretation that can be given to forward rates. Consider a contract made now where money will be loaned a year from now and paid back two years from now. Such a contract is known as a forward contract; the interest rate on the one-year loan that is specified in it (note that the interest will be paid when the loan matures in two years) is known as the forward rate.

It is important to distinguish this rate from the rate for one-year loans that will prevail for deals made a year from now (the spot rate at that time). A forward rate applies to contracts made now but relating to a period "forward" in time. By the nature of the contract, the terms are certain now, even though the actual transaction will occur later. If instead one were to wait until next year and sign a contract to borrow money in the spot market at that time, the terms might turn out to be better or worse than today's forward rate, since the future spot rate is not perfectly predictable.

In the example, the marketplace has priced Treasury securities such that a representative investor making a two-year loan to the government would demand an interest rate equal to the two-year spot rate, 8%. Equivalently, the investor would be willing to simultaneously (1) make a one-year loan to the

FIGURE 20-1
Spot and Forward Rates

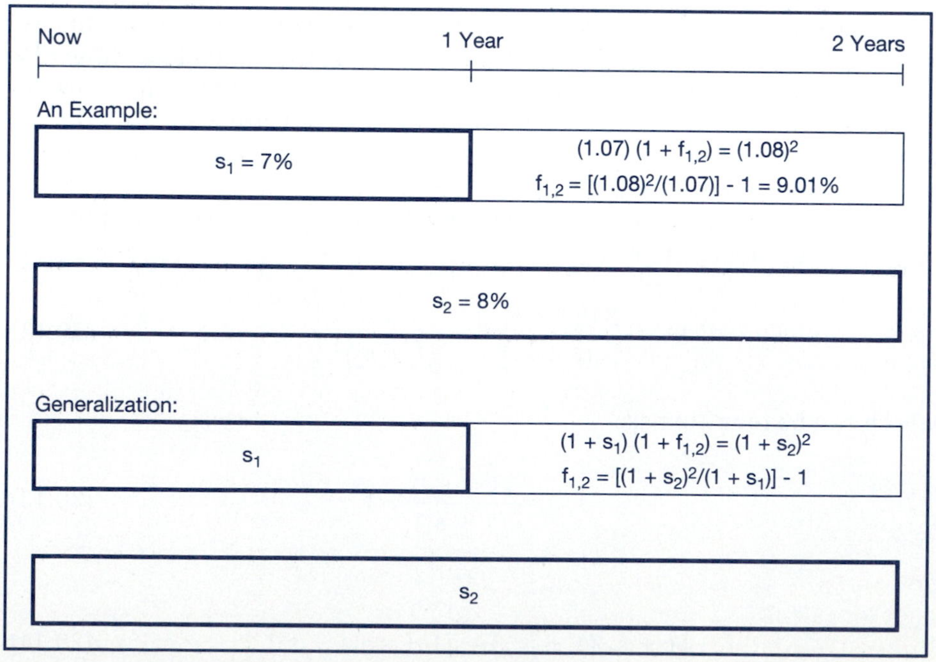

government at an interest rate equal to the one-year spot rate, 7%; and (2) sign a forward contract with the government to loan the government money one year from now, being repaid two years from now where the interest rate to be paid is the forward rate, 9.01%.

When viewed in this manner, forward contracts are implicit. However, forward contracts are sometimes made explicitly. For example, a contractor might obtain a commitment from a bank for a one-year construction loan a year hence at a fixed rate of interest. Financial futures markets (discussed in Chapter 25) provide standardized forward contracts of this type. For example, in June 1992 one could contract to pay $966.56 in September 1992 to purchase a ninety-day Treasury bill that would pay $1,000 in December 1992.

FORWARD RATES AND DISCOUNT FACTORS

In equation (20.9) it was shown that a discount factor for t years could be calculated by adding one to the spot rate for t years, raising this sum to the power t, and then taking the reciprocal of the result. For example, it was shown that the two-year discount factor associated with the two-year spot rate of 8% was equal to $1/(1 + .08)^2 = .8573$.

Equation (20.14) suggests an equivalent method for calculating discount factors. In the case of the two-year factor, this method involves multiplying the one-year spot rate by the forward rate and taking the reciprocal of the result:

$$d_2 = \frac{1}{(1 + s_1) \times (1 + f_{1,2})} \tag{20.17}$$

which in the example is:

$$d_2 = \frac{1}{(1 + .07) \times (1 + .0901)}$$
$$= .8573.$$

More generally, the discount factor for year t that is shown in equation (20.9) can be restated as follows:

$$d_t = \frac{1}{(1 + s_{t-1})^{t-1} \times (1 + f_{t-1,t})}. \tag{20.18}$$

Thus, given a set of spot rates, it is possible to determine the market discount function in either of two ways, both of which will provide the same figures. First, the spot rates can be used in equation (20.9) to arrive at a set of discount factors. Alternatively, the spot rates can be used to determine a set of forward rates and then the spot rates and forward rates can be used in equation (20.18) to arrive at a set of discount factors.

COMPOUNDING

Thus far, the discussion has concentrated on annual interest rates by assuming that cash flows are compounded (or discounted) annually. This is often appropriate, but for more precise calculations a shorter period may be more desirable. Moreover, some lenders explicitly compound funds more often than once each year.

compounding

Compounding is the payment of "interest on interest." At the end of each compounding interval, interest is computed and added to principal. This sum becomes the principal on which interest is computed at the end of the next interval. The process continues until the end of the final compounding interval is reached.

No problem is involved in adapting the previously stated formulas to compounding intervals other than a year. The simplest procedure is to count in units of the chosen interval. For example, yield-to-maturity can be calculated using any chosen compounding interval. If payment of P dollars now will result in the receipt of F dollars ten years from now, the yield-to-maturity can be calculated using annual compounding by finding a value r_a that satisfies the equation:

$$P(1 + r_a)^{10} = F \tag{20.19}$$

since F will be received ten annual periods from now. The result, r_a, will be expressed as an annual rate with annual compounding.

Alternatively, yield-to-maturity can be calculated using semiannual compounding by finding a value r_s that satisfies the equation:

$$P(1 + r_s)^{20} = F \tag{20.20}$$

since F will be received twenty semiannual periods from now. The result, r_s, will be expressed as a semiannual rate with semiannual compounding. It can be doubled to give an annual rate with semiannual compounding; alternatively, the annual rate with annual compounding can be computed for a given value of r_s by using the following equation:

$$1 + r_a = (1 + r_s)^2. \tag{20.21}$$

For example, consider an investment costing $2,315.97 that will pay $5,000 ten years later. Applying equations (20.19) and (20.20) to this security results in, respectively:

$$\$2{,}315.97(1 + r_a)^{10} = \$5{,}000$$

and:

$$\$2{,}315.97(1 + r_s)^{20} = \$5{,}000,$$

where the solutions are $r_a = 8\%$ and $r_s = 3.923\%$. Thus, this security can be described as having an annual rate with annual compounding of 8%, a semiannual rate with semiannual compounding of 3.923%, and an annual rate with semiannual compounding of 7.846% = 2 × 3.923%.[2]

annual percentage rate

To reduce the massive confusion caused by the many different methods that can be used to express interest rates, the Federal Truth-in-Lending Act requires every lender to compute and disclose the **annual percentage rate**

[2]Note how, using equation (20.21), $r_a = (1.03923)^2 - 1 = 8\%$, a solution that is the same as the one provided by equation (20.19).

(APR) implied by the terms of a loan. This is simply the annualized yield-to-maturity, computed by (1) determining the periodic yield-to-maturity based on a compounding interval that is equal to the most frequent time between payments on the loan, and (2) multiplying the resulting periodic yield by the number of compounding intervals in a year. While some complications arise when payments are required at irregular intervals, the use of APRs has clearly simplified the task of comparing lenders' terms.

Semiannual compounding is commonly used to determine the yield-to-maturity for bonds, since coupon payments are usually made twice each year. Most preprogrammed calculators and computers use this approach.[3]

YIELD CURVES

At any point in time, Treasury securities will be priced approximately in accord with the existing set of spot rates and the associated discount factors. While there have been times when all the spots rates are roughly equal in size, generally they have different values. Often the one-year spot rate is less than the two-year spot rate, which in turn is less than the three-year spot rate, and so on (that is, s_t increases as t increases). At other times, the one-year spot rate is greater than the two-year spot rate, which in turn is greater than the three-year spot rate, and so on (that is, s_t decreases as t increases). It is wise for the security analyst to know which case currently prevails, as this is a useful starting point in valuing fixed-income securities.

Unfortunately, this is easier said than done. Only the bonds of the U.S. government are clearly free from default risk. However, such bonds differ in tax treatment, as well as in callability and other features. Despite these problems, a summary of the approximate relationship between yields-to-maturity on Treasury securities of various terms-to-maturity is presented in each issue of the *Treasury Bulletin*. This summary is given in the form of a graph illustrating the current yield curve. Figure 20-2 provides an example.

A **yield curve** is a graph that shows the yields-to-maturity (on the vertical axis) for Treasury securities of various maturities (on the horizontal axis) as of

yield curve

[3]Consider what would happen if the number of compounding intervals in a year becomes arbitrarily large so that each interval is very small. In the limit there will be an infinite number of infinitely small intervals; such a situation involves *continuous compounding*, and is discussed in the appendix.

FIGURE 20-2
Typical Yield Curve Shapes

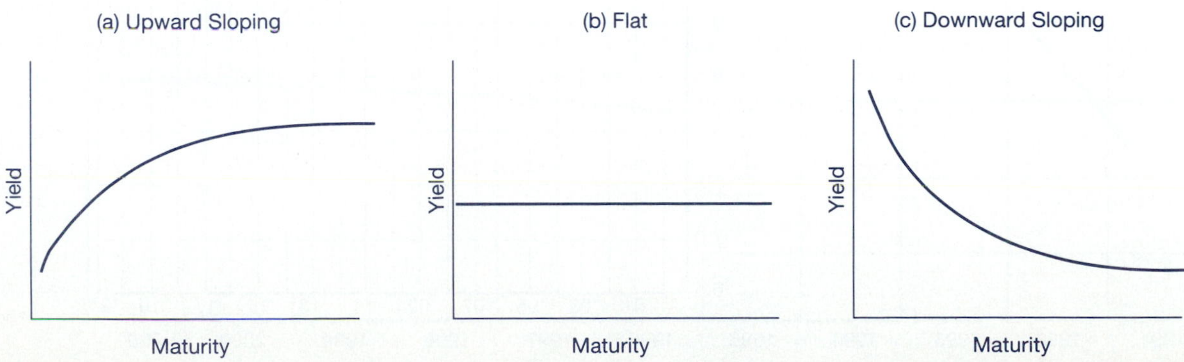

term structure

a particular date. This provides an estimate of the current **term structure** of interest rates, and will change daily as yields-to-maturity change. Figure 20-2 illustrates some of the commonly observed shapes that the yield curve has taken in the past.[4]

While not shown in Figure 20-3, this relationship between yields and maturities is less than perfect. That is, not all Treasury securities lie exactly on the yield curve. Part of this is because of the previously mentioned differences in tax treatment, callability, and the like. Part is because of the fact that the yield-to-maturity on a coupon-bearing security is not clearly linked to the set of spot rates currently in existence. Since the set of spot rates is a fundamental determinant of the price of any Treasury security, there is no reason to expect yields to lie exactly on the curve. Indeed, a more meaningful graph would be one where spot rates are measured on the vertical axis instead of yields-to-maturity. With this in mind, an interesting question to ponder is this: Why are

[4]Occasionally, the yield curve will be "humped," where it rises for a short while and then declines, perhaps leveling off for intermediate to long-term maturities.

FIGURE 20-3
Yield Curve of Treasury Securities, June 28, 1991 (based on closing bid quotations)
Source: Treasury Bulletin, Summer Issue, September 1991, p. 66.

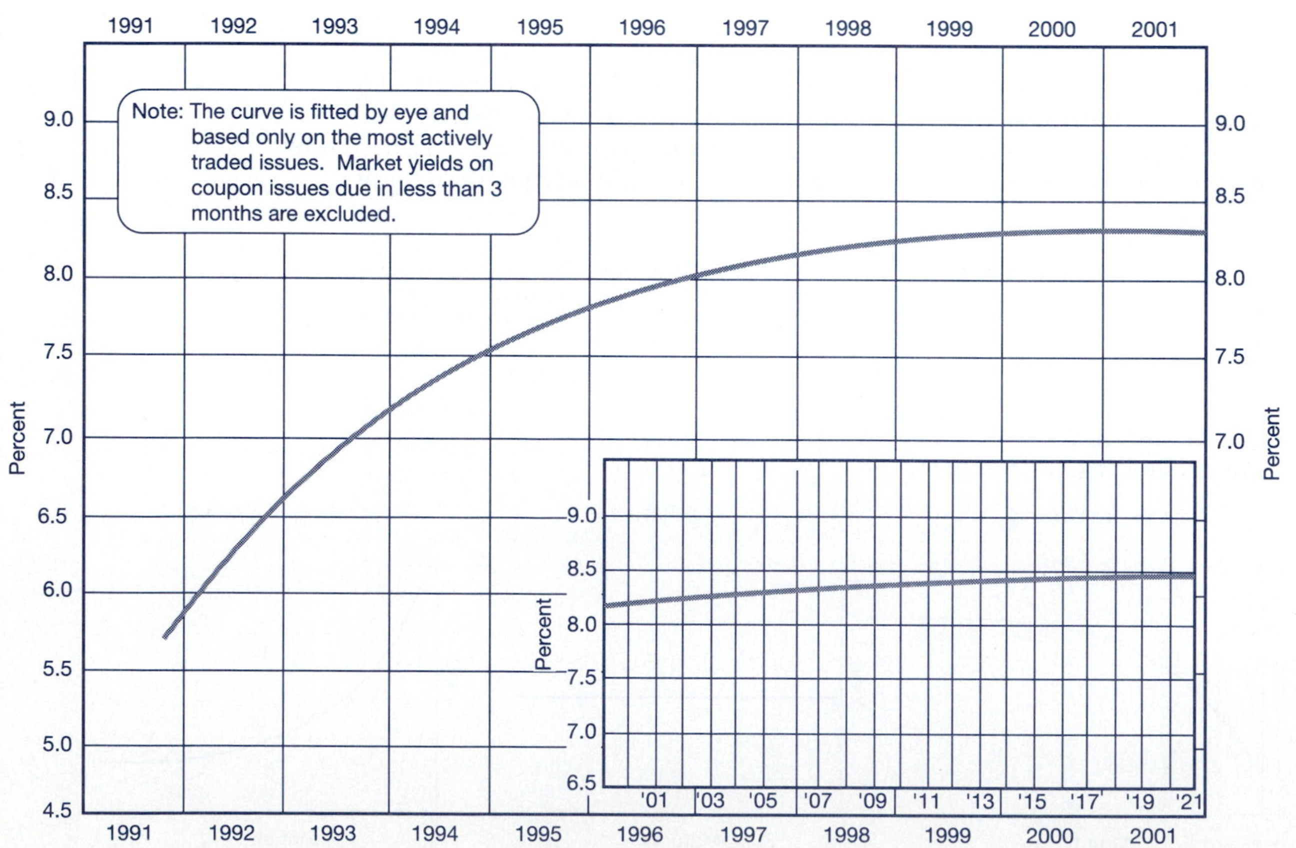

the spot rates of different magnitudes? And why do the differences in these rates change over time, where sometimes long-term spot rates are greater than short-term spot rates and sometimes the opposite occurs? Attempts to answer such questions can be found in various term structure theories.

TERM STRUCTURE THEORIES

Three theories have been generally used to explain the term structure of interest rates. In discussing them, the focus will be on the term structure of spot rates, since it is these rates and not yields-to-maturity that are critically important in determining the price of any Treasury security.

The Unbiased Expectations Theory

unbiased expectations theory

The **unbiased expectations theory** (or pure expectations theory, as it is sometimes called) holds that the forward rate represents the average opinion of the expected future spot rate for the period in question. Thus, a set of spot rates that is rising can be explained by arguing that the marketplace (that is, the general opinion of investors) believes that spot rates will be rising in the future. Conversely, a set of decreasing spot rates is explained by arguing that the marketplace expects spot rates to be falling in the future.[5]

Why does the marketplace expect spot rates to change? Because either the real rate or the inflation rate is expected to change. For example, the reason the spot rates are expected to rise could be owing to a perception in the marketplace that inflation is going to accelerate in the future. Conversely, spot rates might be expected to decline because of a perception that inflation is going to slow down in the future.

Upward-Sloping Yield Curves In order to understand this theory more fully, consider the earlier example where the one-year spot rate was 7% and the two-year spot rate was 8%. The basic question is this: Why are these two spot rates different? Equivalently, why is the yield curve upward sloping?

Consider an investor with $1 to invest for two years (for ease of exposition, it will be assumed that any amount of money can be invested at the prevailing spot rates). This investor could follow a "maturity strategy," investing the money now for the full two years at the two-year spot rate of 8%. With this strategy, at the end of two years the dollar will have grown in value to $1(1.08)(1.08) = $1.1664. Alternatively, the investor could invest the dollar now for one year at the one-year spot rate of 7%, so that the investor knows that one year from now he or she will have $1.07 = $1 (1.07) to reinvest for one more year. While the investor does not know what the one-year spot rate will be one year from now, the investor has an *expectation* about what it will be (this expected future spot rate will hereafter be denoted $es_{1,2}$). If the investor thinks it will be 10%, then his or her $1 investment has an expected value two years from now of $1 (1.07)(1.10) = $1.177. In this case, the investor would choose a "rollover strategy," meaning that the investor would choose to invest in a one-year security at 7% rather than in the two-year security, since

[5]Recently a "modern" expectations theory has been developed that is economically more logical than the "unbiased" expectations theory. However, it provides approximately the same empirical implications and explanations of the term structure as those given by the unbiased expectations theory. Thus, given the similarities of the two theories, only the unbiased expectations theory will be presented.

he or she would expect to have more money at the end of two years by doing so (note that $1.177 > $1.1664).

However, an expected future spot rate of 10% cannot represent the general view in the marketplace. This is because if it did, people would not be willing to invest money at the two-year spot rate, since a higher return would be expected from investing money at the one-year rate and using the rollover strategy. Thus, the two-year spot rate would quickly rise as the supply of funds for two-year loans at 8% would be less than the demand. Conversely, the supply of funds for one year at 7% would be more than the demand, causing the one-year rate to quickly fall. Thus, a one-year spot rate of 7%, a two-year spot rate of 8%, and an expected future spot rate of 10% cannot represent an equilibrium situation.

What if the expected future spot rate is 6% instead of 10%? In this case, according to the rollover strategy the investor would expect $1 to be worth $1(1.07)(1.06) = $1.1342 at the end of two years. Since this is less than the value the dollar will have if the maturity strategy is followed ($1.1342 < $1.1664), the investor would choose the maturity strategy. Again, however, an expected future spot rate of 6% cannot represent the general view in the marketplace because if it did, people would not be willing to invest money at the one-year spot rate.

Earlier, it was shown that the forward rate in this example was 9.01%. What if the expected future spot rate was of this magnitude? At the end of two years the value of $1 with the rollover strategy would be $1(1.07)(1.0901) = $1.1664, the same as the value of $1 with the maturity strategy. In this case, equilibrium would exist in the marketplace because the general view would be that both strategies have the same expected return. Accordingly, investors with a two-year holding period would not have an incentive to choose one strategy over the other.

Note that an investor with a one-year holding period could follow a maturity strategy by investing $1 in the one-year security and receiving $1.07 after one year. Alternatively, a "naive strategy" could be followed, where a two-year security could be purchased now and sold after one year. If so, the expected selling price would be $1.1664/1.0901 = $1.07, for a return of 7% (the security would have a maturity value of $1.1664 = $1(1.08)(1.08), but since the spot rate is expected to be 9.01% in a year, its expected selling price is just the discounted value of its maturity value). Since the maturity and naive strategies have the same expected return, investors with a one-year holding period would not have an incentive to choose one strategy over the other.

Thus, the unbiased expectations theory asserts that the expected future spot rate is equal in magnitude to the forward rate. In the example, the current one-year spot rate is 7% and, according to this theory, the general opinion is that it will rise to a rate of 9.01% in one year. It is this expected rise in the one-year spot rate that is the reason behind the upward-sloping term structure where the two-year spot rate (8%) is greater than the one-year spot rate (7%).

Equilibrium In equation format, the unbiased expectations theory states that in equilibrium the expected future spot rate is equal to the forward rate:

$$es_{1,2} = f_{1,2}. \tag{20.22}$$

Thus, equation (20.14) can be restated with $es_{1,2}$ substituted for $f_{1,2}$ as follows:

$$(1 + s_2)(1 + s_2) = (1 + s_1)(1 + es_{1,2}) \tag{20.23}$$

which can be conveniently interpreted to mean that the expected return from a maturity strategy must equal the expected return on a rollover strategy.[6]

The previous example dealt with an upward-sloping term structure, where the longer the term, the higher the spot rate. It is a straightforward matter to deal with a downward-sloping term structure, where the longer the term, the lower the spot rate. While the explanation for an upward-sloping term structure was that investors expect spot rates to rise in the future, the reason for the downward-sloping curve is that investors expect spot rates to fall in the future.

Changing Spot Rates and Inflation An interesting follow-up question is this: Why do investors expect spot rates to change, either rising or falling, in the future? A possible answer to this question can be found by noting that the spot rates that are observed in the marketplace are nominal rates. That is, they are a reflection of the underlying real rate and the expected inflation rate.[7] If either (or both) of these rates is expected to change in the future, then the spot rate will be expected to change.

For example, assume a constant real rate of 3%. Since the current one-year spot rate is 7%, this means that the general opinion in the marketplace is that the expected rate of inflation over the next year is approximately 4% (the nominal rate is approximately equal to the sum of the real rate and expected inflation rate). Now, according to the unbiased expectations theory, the expected future spot rate is 9.01%, an increase of 2.01% from the current one-year spot rate of 7%. Why is the spot rate expected to rise by 2.01%? Because the inflation rate is expected to rise by 2.01%. That is, the expected inflation rate over the next twelve months is approximately 4%, and over the following twelve months it is expected to be higher, at approximately 6.01%.

To recapitulate, the two-year spot rate (8%) is greater than the one-year spot rate (7%) because investors expect the future one-year spot rate to be greater than the current one-year spot rate. They expect it to be greater because of an anticipated rise in the expected rate of inflation, from approximately 4% to approximately 6.01%.

In general, when current economic conditions make short-term spot rates abnormally high (owing, say, to a relatively high current rate of inflation), according to the unbiased expectations theory, the term structure should be downward sloping. This is because inflation would be expected to abate in the future. Conversely, when current conditions make short-term rates abnormally low (owing, say, to a relatively low current rate of inflation), the term structure should be upward sloping, as inflation would be expected to rise in the future. Examination of historical term structures suggest that this is what has actually happened, since the structure has been upward sloping in periods of lower interest rates and downward sloping in periods of higher interest rates.

However, examining historical term structures uncovers a problem. In particular, with this theory, it is logical to expect that over time there will be roughly as many occurrences of upward-sloping term structures as downward-sloping term structures. In reality, upward-sloping structures tend to be more frequent. The liquidity preference theory (also known as the liquidity premium theory) provides an explanation for this observation.

---

[6]Equation (20.22) can be expressed more generally as $es_{t-1,t} = f_{t-1,t}$. Thus, using equation (20.16), the unbiased expectations theory states that, in general, $(1 + s_t)^t = (1 + s_{t-1})^{t-1} \times (1 + es_{t-1,t})$.

[7]See Chapter 6 for a discussion of the nature of the relationship between nominal rates, real rates, and expected inflation rates.

liquidity preference theory

The Liquidity Preference Theory

The **liquidity preference theory** starts with the notion that investors are primarily interested in purchasing short-term securities. That is, even though some investors may have longer holding periods, there is a tendency for them to prefer short-term securities. This is because these investors realize that they may need their funds earlier than anticipated and recognize that they face less "price risk" (that is, "interest rate risk") if they invest in shorter-term securities.

Price Risk For example, an investor with a two-year holding period would tend to prefer the rollover strategy since he or she would be certain of having a given amount of cash at the end of one year when it may be needed. If a maturity strategy had been followed, then the investor would have to sell the two-year security after one year if cash was needed. However, it is not known now what price the investor would get if he or she were to sell the two-year security in one year. Thus, there is an extra element of risk associated with the maturity strategy that is absent from the rollover strategy.[8]

The upshot is that investors with a two-year holding period will not choose the maturity strategy if it has the same expected return as the rollover strategy, since it is riskier. The only way investors will follow the maturity strategy and buy the two-year securities is if the expected return is higher. That is, borrowers are going to have to pay the investors a risk premium in the form of a greater expected return in order to get them to purchase two-year securities.

Will borrowers be inclined to pay such a premium when issuing two-year securities? Yes, they will be so inclined. First, frequent refinancing may be costly in terms of registration, advertising, paperwork, and so on. These costs can be lessened by issuing relatively long-term securities. Second, some borrowers will realize that relatively long-term bonds are a less risky source of funds than relatively short-term bonds since they will not have to be as concerned about the possibility of refinancing in the future at higher interest rates. Thus, borrowers may be willing to pay more (via higher expected interest costs) for relatively long-term funds.

In the example, the one-year spot rate was 7% and the two-year spot rate was 8%. As mentioned earlier, according to the liquidity preference theory, the only way investors will agree to follow a maturity strategy is if the expected return from doing so is higher than the expected return from following the rollover strategy. This means that the expected future spot rate must be something *less* than the forward rate of 9.01%—perhaps it is 8.6%. If so, then the value of a \$1 investment in two years is expected to be \$1(1.07)(1.086) = \$1.1620, given that the rollover strategy is followed. Since the value of a \$1 investment with the maturity strategy is \$1(1.08)(1.08) = \$1.1664, it can be seen that this strategy has a higher expected return for the two-year period that can be attributed to its greater degree of price risk.

---

[8]Unfortunately, this risk is often referred to as "liquidity risk" when it more appropriately should be called "price risk," since it is the price volatility associated with longer-term securities that is of concern to investors. Partially offsetting this price risk is a risk that is present in the rollover strategy and absent from the maturity strategy—namely, the risk associated with having an uncertain reinvestment rate at the end of the first year when the rollover strategy is chosen. The liquidity preference theory assumes that this risk is of relatively little concern to investors.

Liquidity Premium The difference between the forward rate and the expected future spot rate is known as the **liquidity premium.**[9] It is the "extra" return given investors in order to entice them to purchase the more risky two-year security. In the example, it is equal to 9.01% − 8.6% = .41%. More generally,

liquidity premium

$$f_{1,2} = es_{1,2} + L_{1,2} \tag{20.24}$$

where $L_{1,2}$ is the liquidity premium for the period commencing one year from now and ending two years from now.[10]

How does the liquidity preference theory explain the slope of the term structure? In order to answer this question, note that with the rollover strategy the expected value of a dollar at the end of two years is $\$1(1 + s_1)(1 + es_{1,2})$. Alternatively, with the maturity strategy, the expected value of a dollar at the end of two years is $\$1(1 + s_2)(1 + s_2)$. As mentioned earlier, according to the liquidity preference theory, there is more risk with the maturity strategy, which in turn means that it must have a higher expected return. That is, the following inequality must hold:

$$\$1(1 + s_2)(1 + s_2) > \$1(1 + s_1)(1 + es_{1,2})$$

or:

$$(1 + s_2)(1 + s_2) > (1 + s_1)(1 + es_{1,2}). \tag{20.25}$$

This inequality is the key to understanding how the liquidity preference theory explains the term structure.[11]

Downward-Sloping Yield Curves Consider the downward-sloping case first, where $s_1 > s_2$. The above inequality will hold in this situation only if the expected future spot rate ($es_{1,2}$) is substantially smaller than the current one-year spot rate (s_1).[12] Thus, a downward-sloping yield curve will be observed only when the marketplace believes that interest rates are going to decline substantially.

As an example, assume that the one-year spot rate (s_1) is 7% and the two-year spot rate (s_2) is 6%. Since 7% is greater than 6%, this is a situation where the term structure is downward sloping. Now, according to the previously given inequality,

$$(1 + .06)(1 + .06) > (1 + .07)(1 + es_{1,2})$$

---

[9]Sometimes the difference is referred to as the term premium; see Bradford Cornell, "Measuring the Term Premium: An Empirical Note," *Journal of Economics and Business*, 42, no. 1 (February 1990): 89–92.

[10]It should be noted that while the forward rate can be determined, neither the expected future spot rate nor the liquidity premium can be observed. All that can be done is estimate their respective values.

[11]Equation (20.24) can be expressed more generally as $f_{t-1,t} = es_{t-1,t} + L_{t-1,t}$. Thus, using equation (20.16), the liquidity preference theory states that:

$$(1 + s_t)^t = (1 + s_{t-1})^{t-1} \times (1 + es_{t-1,t} + L_{t-1,t}).$$

Since $L_{t-1,t} > 0$, it follows that, in general:

$$(1 + s_t)^t > (1 + s_{t-1})^{t-1} \times (1 + es_{t-1,t}).$$

[12]If $es_{1,2}$ were equal to or greater than s_1, then the inequality would not hold in the correct direction since it was assumed that $s_1 > s_2$.

which can only hold if the expected future spot rate ($es_{1,2}$) is substantially less than 7%. Given the one-year and two-year spot rates, the forward rate ($f_{1,2}$) is equal to 5.01%. Assuming the liquidity premium ($L_{1,2}$) is .41%, then according to equation (20.24), $es_{1,2}$ must be 4.6% = 5.01% − .41%. Thus, the term structure is downward sloping because the current one-year spot rate of 7% is expected to decline to 4.6% in the future.

In comparison, the unbiased expectations theory would also explain the term structure by saying that the reason it was downward sloping was that the one-year spot rate was expected to decline in the future. However, the unbiased expectations theory would only expect the spot rate to decline to 5.01%, not 4.6%.

Flat Yield Curves Consider next the case of a flat yield curve, where $s_1 = s_2$. The above inequality will hold in this situation only if $es_{1,2}$ is less than s_1. Thus, a flat term structure will occur only when the marketplace expects interest rates to decline. Indeed, if $s_1 = s_2 = 7\%$ and $L_{1,2} = .41\%$, then $f_{1,2} = 7\%$, and according to equation (20.24), the expected future spot rate is 6.59% = 7% − .41%, a decline from the current one-year spot rate of 7%. This is in contrast to the unbiased expectations theory, where a flat term structure would be interpreted to mean that the marketplace expected interest rates to remain at the same level.

Upward-Sloping Yield Curves The last case of an upward-sloping yield curve is one where $s_1 < s_2$. If it is slightly upward sloping, this can be consistent with an expectation that interest rates are going to decline in the future. For example, if $s_1 = 7\%$ and $s_2 = 7.1\%$, then the forward rate is 7.2%. In turn, if the liquidity premium is .41%, then the expected future spot rate is 6.79% = 7.2% − .41%, a decline from the current one-year spot rate of 7%. Thus, the reason for the slight upward slope to the term structure is that the marketplace expects only a slight decline in the spot rate. In contrast, the unbiased expectations theory would argue that the reason for the slight upward slope was the expectation of a slight increase in the spot rate.

If the term structure is more steeply sloped, then it is more likely that the marketplace expects interest rates to rise in the future. For example, if $s_1 = 7\%$ and $s_2 = 7.3\%$, then the forward rate is 7.6%. Continuing to assume a liquidity premium of .41%, equation (20.24) indicates that the marketplace expects the one-year spot rate to rise from 7% to 7.19% = 7.6% − .41%. The unbiased expectations theory would also explain this steep slope by saying that the spot rate was expected to rise in the future, but by a larger amount. In particular, the unbiased expectations theory would state that the spot rate was expected to rise to 7.6%, not 7.19%.

In summary, with the liquidity preference theory, downward-sloping term structures are indicative of an expected decline in the spot rate, while upward-sloping term structures may indicate either an expected rise or decline, depending on how steep the slope is. Generally, the steeper the slope, the more likely it is that the marketplace expects spot rates to rise. If roughly half the time investors expect spot rates will rise and half the time investors expect spot rates will decline, then the liquidity preference theory suggests that there should be more occurrences of upward-sloping term structures than downward-sloping ones. As mentioned earlier, this is indeed what has happened.

The Market Segmentation Theory

market segmentation theory

A third explanation for the determination of the term structure rests on the assumption that there is **market segmentation.** Various investors and borrowers are asserted to be restricted by law, preference, or custom to certain maturities. Perhaps there is a market for short-term securities, another for intermediate-term securities, and a third for long-term securities. According to the market segmentation theory, spot rates are determined by supply and demand conditions in each market. Furthermore, in the theory's most restrictive form, investors and borrowers will not leave their market and enter a different one even when the current rates suggest to them that there is a substantially higher expected return available by making such a move.[13]

With this theory, an upward-sloping term structure exists when the intersection of the supply and demand curves for shorter-term funds is at a lower interest rate than the intersection for longer-term funds. Conversely, a downward-sloping term structure would exist when the intersection for shorter-term funds was at a higher interest rate than the intersection for longer-term funds.

Empirical Evidence on the Theories

Empirical evidence provides some insight into the determinants of the term structure, but it is difficult to assess the relative importance of these three theories with a high degree of precision.

The market segmentation theory receives relatively slight empirical validation. This is understandable when it is realized that the theory will not hold if there are some investors and borrowers who are flexible enough to be willing to move into whatever segment has the highest expected return. By their actions, these investors and borrowers will give the term structure a continuity that is linked to expectations of future interest rates.

There does appear to be some evidence that the term structure conveys information about expected future spot rates, as hypothesized by both the unbiased expectations and liquidity preference theories. However, the evidence tends to favor the latter theory, since liquidity premiums also appear to exist.[14] In particular, there appear to be liquidity premiums of increasing size associated with Treasury securities of up to roughly one year in maturity. However, there do not appear to be any additional premiums beyond one-year maturities. That is, investors seem to demand a premium in order to get them to purchase a one-year security instead of, say, a one-month security. How-

[13]A more moderate version is the *preferred habitat theory*, where borrowers and investors will leave their desired maturity segment if there are significant differences in the yields in the various segments.

[14]The empirical evidence is not without dispute. Fama has argued that the evidence is inconsistent with both the unbiased expectations and liquidity preference theories, while McCulloch refutes Fama's findings and argues in favor of the latter theory. See Eugene F. Fama, "Term Premiums in Bond Returns," *Journal of Financial Economics*, 13, no. 4 (December 1984): 529–46; and J. Huston McCulloch, "The Monotonicity of the Term Premium: A Closer Look," *Journal of Financial Economics*, 18, no. 1 (March 1987): 185–92, and "An Estimate of the Liquidity Premium," *Journal of Political Economy*, 83, no. 1 (February 1975): 95–119. McCulloch's findings are supported by Matthew Richardson, Paul Richardson, and Tom Smith in "The Monotonicity of the Term Premium: Another Look," *Journal of Financial Economics*, 31, no. 1 (February 1992): 97–105.

ever, no additional premiums are needed in order to get them to purchase two-year securities (even though the two-year security has more price risk than a one-year security).

In summary, it appears that expectations about future spot rates are important determinants of the term structure. Liquidity premiums appear to exist, but they do not increase in size beyond roughly a year, meaning that investment strategies involving securities with maturities of one year or more will have roughly the same expected return.

Examining the term structure of interest rates is important for determining the current set of spot rates, which can be used as a basis for valuing any fixed-income security. Such an examination is also important because it provides some information about what the marketplace expects regarding the level of future interest rates.

SUMMARY

1. In order to understand how bonds are valued in the marketplace, it is convenient to initially examine those fixed-income securities that are free from default risk—namely, Treasury securities.

2. The yield-to-maturity of a security is the discount rate that makes the present value of the security's promised future cash flows equal to the current market price of the security.

3. The spot rate is the yield-to-maturity on a pure discount security.

4. Once spot rates (each one associated with a different maturity) have been calculated, they can be used, for example, to value coupon-bearing Treasury securities.

5. A forward rate is the interest rate, established today, that will be paid on money that is to be borrowed at some specific time in the future, and is to be repaid at an even more distant time in the future.

6. The payment of interest on interest is known as compounding.

7. Increasing the number of compounding intervals within a year will increase the effective annual interest rate.

8. A yield curve shows the relationship between yield-to-maturity and maturity for Treasury securities. This relationship is also known as the term structure of interest rates.

9. Three theories have generally been used to explain the term structure of interest rates: the unbiased expectations theory; the liquidity preference theory; and the market segmentation theory.

10. The unbiased expectations theory states that forward rates represent the consensus opinion about what spot rates will be in the future.

11. The liquidity preference theory states that forward rates overstate the consensus opinion about future spot rates by an amount necessary to compensate investors for holding longer-maturity securities.

12. The market segmentation theory states that different spot rates have different values owing to the interaction of supply and demand for funds in markets that are separated from each other by maturity.

13. Evidence tends to favor the liquidity preference theory, at least over maturities up to roughly one year.

KEY TERMS

yield-to-maturity
spot rate
discount factors
market discount function
discounting
forward rate
compounding
annual percentage rate
yield curve
term structure
unbiased expectations theory
liquidity preference theory
liquidity premium
market segmentation

QUESTIONS AND PROBLEMS

1. Consider two bonds, each with a $1,000 face value and each with three years remaining to maturity.
   (a) The first bond is a pure-discount bond that currently sells for $816.30. What is its yield-to-maturity?
   (b) The second bond currently sells for $949.37 and makes annual coupon payments at a rate of 7% (that is, it pays $70 in interest per year). The first interest payment is due one year from today. What is this bond's yield-to-maturity?
2. Camp Douglas Dirigibles has a bond outstanding with four years to maturity, a face value of $1,000, and an annual coupon payment of $100. What is the price of the Camp Douglas bond if its yield-to-maturity is 12%? If its yield-to-maturity is 8%?
3. The concept of yield-to-maturity is based on two crucial assumptions. What are those assumptions? What will happen to the bondholder's return if those assumptions are violated?
4. Patsy Dougherty bought a $1,000-face-value bond with a 9% coupon rate. The bond has three years to maturity, pays interest annually, and makes its first interest payment one year from today. Patsy bought the bond for $975.13.
   (a) What is the bond's yield-to-maturity?
   (b) If Patsy is able to invest the bond's cash flows at only 7%, what is Patsy's actual annual compounded return on the bond investment, assuming that it is held to maturity? (Hint: Think in terms of the cash flows paid to Patsy, the bond's purchase price, and the term of the investment.)
5. Consider three pure-discount bonds with maturities of one, two, and three years and prices of $930.23, $923.79, and $919.54, respectively. Each bond has a $1,000 face value. Based on this information, what are the one-year, two-year, and three-year spot rates?
6. What are the discount factors associated with three-year, four-year, and five-year $1,000-face-value pure-discount bonds that sell for $810.60, $730.96, and $649.93, respectively?
7. Distinguish between spot rates and forward rates.
8. Given the following spot rates for various periods of time from today, calculate forward rates from years one to two, two to three, and three to four.

YEARS FROM TODAY	SPOT RATE
1	5.0%
2	5.5
3	6.5
4	7.0

9. Given the following forward rates, calculate the one-, two-, three-, and four-year spot rates.

FORWARD TIME PERIOD	FORWARD RATE
$f_{0,1}$	10.0%
$f_{1,2}$	9.5
$f_{2,3}$	9.0
$f_{3,4}$	8.5

10. Assume that the current one-year spot rate is 8% and that the forward rates for one year hence and two years hence, are, respectively,

$$f_{1,2} = 9\%$$
$$f_{2,3} = 10\%.$$

What should be the market price of an 8% coupon bond, with a $1,000 face value, maturing three years from today? The first interest payment is due one year from today. Interest is payble annually.

11. Assume that the government has issued three bonds. The first, which pays $1,000 one year from today, is now selling for $909.09. The second, which pays $100 one year from today and $1,100 one year later, is now selling for $991.81. The third, which pays $100 one year from today, $100 one year later, and $1,100 one year after that, is now selling for $997.18.
    (a) What are the current discount factors for dollars paid one, two, and three years from today?
    (b) What are the forward rates?
    (c) Gracie Pierce, a friend, offers to pay you $500 one year from today, $600 two years from today, and $700 three years from today in return for a loan today. Assuming that Gracie will not default on the loan, how much should you be willing to loan?

12. Mercury National Bank offers a passbook savings account that pays interest at a stated annual rate of 6.5%. Calculate the effective annual interest rate paid by Mercury National if it compounds interest:
    (a) semiannually
    (b) daily (365 days in a year)

13. Using *The Wall Street Journal* as a data source, turn to the table entitled "Treasury Bonds, Notes & Bills." Find the yield-to-maturity for Treasury securities maturing in one month, three months, one year, five years, ten years, and twenty years. With this information, construct the yield curve as of the paper's publication date.

14. Is it true that an observed downward-sloping yield curve is inconsistent with the liquidity preference theory of the term structure of interest rates? Explain.

15. Assume that the current structure of forward interest rates is upward sloping. Which will have a lower yield-to-maturity:
    (a) A fifteen-year zero-coupon bond or a ten-year zero-coupon bond?
    (b) A ten-year 5% coupon bond or a ten-year 6% coupon bond?

16. How would your answers to question 15 change if the forward interest rate structure were downward sloping?

17. Three theories explaining the term structure of interest rates are described in the chapter. Which theory do you believe best explains the relationship between spot rates and term-to-maturity? Provide supporting arguments for your answer.

18. (Appendix Question) Recalculate the answer to question 12 assuming that interest compounds continuously.

19. (Appendix Question) What is the intrinsic value of a pure-discount bond with a $1,000 face value maturing one year from today, assuming an 8% discount rate with continuous compounding?

CFA Exam Questions

20. The following are the average yields on U.S. Treasury bonds at two different points in time:

TERM TO MATURITY	YIELD-TO-MATURITY JANUARY 15, 19XX	MAY 15, 19XX
1 year	7.25%	8.05%
2 years	7.50	7.90
5 years	7.90	7.70
10 years	8.30	7.45
15 years	8.45	7.30
20 years	8.55	7.20
25 years	8.60	7.10

(a) Assuming a pure expectations hypothesis, define a forward rate. Describe how you would calculate the forward rate for a three-year U.S. Treasury bond two years from May 15, 19XX, using the actual term structure above.

(b) Discuss how each of the three major term structure hypotheses could explain the January 15, 19XX, term structure shown above.

(c) Discuss what happened to the term structure over the time period and the effect of this change on U.S. Treasury bonds of two years and ten years.

(d) Assume that you invest solely on the basis of yield spreads, and in January 19XX acted upon the expectation that the yield spread between one-year and twenty-five year U.S. Treasuries would return to a more typical spread of 170 basis points. Explain what you would have done on January 15, 19XX, and describe the result of this action based upon what happened between January 15, 19XX, and May 15, 19XX.

21. (a) Calculate the two-year spot rate implied by the U.S. Treasury yield curve data given below. Assume that interest is paid annually for purposes of this calculation. Show all calculations.

YEARS TO MATURITY	CURRENT COUPON (YIELD-TO-MATURITY)	SPOT RATE
1	7.5%	7.5%
2	8.0	—

(b) Explain why a spot rate curve can be derived entirely from the current coupon (yield-to-maturity) yield curve.

(c) Given a U.S. Treasury one-year spot rate of 9.0% and a U.S. Treasury two-year spot rate of 9.5%, calculate the implied one-year forward rate for the two-year U.S. Treasury security with one year remaining to maturity. Explain why a one-year forward rate of 9.6% would not be expected to prevail in a market given these spot rates.

(d) Describe one practical application of the spot rate concept and one practical application of the forward rate concept.

APPENDIX A

Continuous Compounding

When you are computing an investment's return, the compounding interval can make a difference. For example, regulations may limit a savings institution to paying a fixed rate of interest, but make no specifications about the compounding interval. This was the situation in early 1975, when the legal limit on interest paid by savings and loan companies on deposits committed from six to ten years was 7.75% per year. Initially, most savings and loans paid "simple interest"—thus, $1 deposited at the beginning of the year would grow to $1.0775 by the end of the year. Later, in an attempt to attract depositors, some enterprising savings and loans announced that they would pay 7.75% per year, compounded semiannually at a rate of 7.75%/2 = 3.3875%. This meant that $1 deposited at the beginning of the year would grow to $1.03875 at the end of six months, and this total would then grow to $1.03875 × 1.03875 = $1.079 by the end of the year, for an effective annual interest rate of 7.9%. This procedure was considered within the letter, if not the spirit, of the law.

Before long, other competitors offered 7.75% per year compounded quarterly (that is, 7.75%/4 = 1.938% per quarter), giving an effective annual interest rate of 7.978%. Then others offered to compound the 7.75% rate on a monthly basis (at 7.75%/12 = .646% per month), for an effective annual interest rate of 8.031%. The end was reached when one company offered continuous compounding of the 7.75% annual rate. This rather abstract procedure represents the limit as interest is compounded more and more frequently. If r represents the annual rate of interest (in this case, 7.75%) and n the number of times compounding takes place per year, the effective rate, r_e, is given by:

$$\left(1 + \frac{r}{n}\right)^n = 1 + r_e. \tag{20.26}$$

Thus, with semi-annual compounding of 7.75%,

$$\left(1 + \frac{.0775}{2}\right)^2 = (1 + .03875)^2 = 1.079$$

and with quarterly compounding,

$$\left(1 + \frac{.0775}{4}\right)^4 = (1 + .01938)^4 = 1.07978$$

and so on. As the compounding interval grows shorter, the number of times compounding takes place (n) grows larger, as does the effective interest rate, r_e.

Mathematicians can prove that as n grows larger, the quantity $[1 + (r/n)]^n$ becomes increasingly close to e^r, where e stands for the number 2.71828 (rounded to five-place accuracy). In this case, $e^{.0775} = 1.0806$, indicating an effective annual rate of 8.06%.[15]

A more general formula for continuous compounding can also be derived. At an annual rate of r, with continuous compounding, P dollars will grow to F_t dollars t years from now, where the relationship between P, r, and F_t is:

$$Pe^{rt} = F_t. \quad (20.27)$$

Similarly, the present value of F_t dollars received t years later at an annual rate of r that is continuously compounded will be:

$$P = \frac{F_t}{e^{rt}}. \quad (20.28)$$

Thus, if spot rates are expressed as annual rates with continuous compounding, then the discount factors d_t can be calculated as:

$$d_t = \frac{1}{e^{rt}}. \quad (20.29)$$

These last three formulas can be used for any value of t, including fractional amounts (for example, if F_t is to be received in 2½ years, then $t = 2.5$).

REFERENCES

1. Many of the fundamental concepts having to do with bonds are discussed in:

   Homer Sidney and Martin L. Leibowitz, *Inside the Yield Book: New Tools for Bond Market Strategy* (Englewood Cliffs, N.J.: Prentice Hall, 1972).

[15] Tables of natural logarithms may be used for such calculations. The natural logarithm of 1.0806 is .0775, and the antilogarithm of .0775 is 1.0806.

2. For a thorough review of term structure theories and the associated empirical evidence, see:

John H. Wood and Norma L. Wood, *Financial Markets* (San Diego, Calif.: Harcourt Brace Jovanovich, Inc., 1985), Chapter 19;

Frederic S. Mishkin, *The Economics of Money, Banking, and Financial Markets* (Glenview, Ill.: Scott, Foresman and Company, 1989), Chapter 7;

James C. Van Horne, *Financial Market Rates & Flows* (Englewood Cliffs, N.J.: Prentice Hall, 1990), Chapter 5;

Frank J. Fabozzi and Franco Modigliani, *Capital Markets: Institutions and Instruments* (Englewood Cliffs, N.J.: Prentice Hall, 1992), Chapter 12;

Steven Russell, "Understanding the Term Structure of Interest Rates: The Expectations Theory," Federal Reserve Bank of St. Louis, *Review*, 74, no. 4 (July/August 1992): 36–50.

3. For a comparison of the traditional unbiased expectations theory and the modern expectations theory of the term structure of interest rates, see:

John H. Wood and Norma L. Wood, *Financial Markets* (San Diego, Calif.: Harcourt Brace Jovanovich, Inc., 1985), pp.645–51.

4. For a discussion of the preferred habitat theory of the term structure of interest rates, see:

James C. Van Horne, *Financial Market Rates & Flows* (Englewood Cliffs, N.J.: Prentice Hall, 1990), pp. 116, 122–23;

Frank J. Fabozzi and Franco Modigliani, *Capital Markets: Institutions and Instruments* (Englewood Cliffs, N.J.: Prentice Hall, 1992), pp. 387–88.

5. For an intriguing tax-based explanation of why the yield curve has usually been upward sloping, see:

Richard Roll, "After-Tax Investment Results from Long-Term vs. Short-Term Discount Coupon Bonds," *Financial Analysts Journal*, 40, no. 1 (January/February 1984): 43–54;

Ricardo J. Rodriguez, "Investment Horizon, Taxes and Maturity Choice for Discount Coupon Bonds," *Financial Analysts Journal*, 44, no. 5 (September/October 1988): 67–69.

21 Bond Analysis

Consider an investor who believes that the bond market is not semistrong-form efficient. That is, the investor believes that there are situations where public information can be used to identify mispriced bonds. To translate that belief into action about which bonds to buy and sell, an analytical procedure is needed. One procedure involves comparing a bond's yield-to-maturity with a yield-to-maturity that the investor feels is appropriate, based on the characteristics of the bond as well as current market conditions. If the yield-to-maturity is higher than the appropriate yield-to-maturity, then the bond is said to be underpriced (or undervalued), and it is a candidate for buying. Conversely, if the yield-to-maturity is lower than the appropriate one, then the bond is said to be overpriced (or overvalued), and it is a candidate for selling (or even short selling).

Alternatively, the investor could estimate the bond's "true" or "intrinsic" value, and compare it with the bond's current market price. Specifically, if the current market price is less than the bond's intrinsic value, then the bond is underpriced, and if it is greater, then the bond is overpriced.

Both procedures for analyzing bonds are based on the capitalization of income method of valuation. Accordingly, they correspond to the procedures mentioned in Chapter 15 for valuing common stocks. More fundamentally, the first procedure involving yields is analogous to the internal rate of return method that is discussed in most introductory finance textbooks, whereas the second procedure involving intrinsic value is analogous to the net present value method that also appears in such books. While the focus in those books is on making an investment decision involving some type of real asset (such as whether or not a new piece of machinery should be purchased), the focus here is on making an investment decision involving a particular type of financial asset—bonds.

APPLYING THE CAPITALIZATION OF INCOME METHOD TO BONDS

capitalization of income method of valuation

An investor who believes the bond market is efficient would question the ability of other investors to identify mispriced situations. However, if an investor believes such situations exist, then an economically sensible and logical approach to valuation is needed to identify them. One such approach is the **capitalization of income method of valuation.**

This method of valuation states that the intrinsic value of any asset is based on the discounted value of the cash flows that the investor expects to receive in the future from owning the asset. As mentioned earlier, one way that this method has been applied to bond valuation is to compare the bond's yield-to-maturity (y) with the appropriate one (y^*). Specifically, if $y > y^*$, then the bond is underpriced, and if $y < y^*$, then the bond is overpriced. However, if $y = y^*$, then the bond is said to be fairly priced.

Promised Yield-to-Maturity

promised yield-to-maturity

Letting P denote the current market price of a bond with a remaining life of n years, and promising cash flows to the investor of C_1 in year one, C_2 in year two, and so on, the yield-to-maturity (more specifically, the **promised yield-to-maturity**) of the bond is the value of y that solves the following equation:

$$P = \frac{C_1}{(1+y)^1} + \frac{C_2}{(1+y)^2} + \frac{C_3}{(1+y)^3} + \dots + \frac{C_n}{(1+y)^n}.$$

Using summation notation, this equation can be rewritten as:

$$P = \sum_{t=1}^{n} \frac{C_t}{(1+y)^t}. \tag{21.1}$$

For example, consider a bond that is currently selling for $900 and has a remaining life of three years. For ease of exposition, assume that it makes annual coupon payments amounting to $60 per year and has a par value of $1,000. That is, $C_1 = \$60$, $C_2 = \$60$, and $C_3 = \$1{,}060 = \$1{,}000 + \$60$. Using equation (21.1), the yield-to-maturity on this bond is the value of y that solves the following equation:

$$\$900 = \frac{\$60}{(1+y)^1} + \frac{\$60}{(1+y)^2} + \frac{\$1{,}060}{(1+y)^3}$$

which is $y = 10.02\%$. If subsequent analysis indicates that the yield-to-maturity should be 9.00%, then this bond is underpriced, since $y = 10.02\% > y^* = 9.00\%$.

Intrinsic Value

Alternatively, the intrinsic value of a bond can be calculated using the following formula:

$$V = \frac{C_1}{(1 + y^*)^1} + \frac{C_2}{(1 + y^*)^2} + \frac{C_3}{(1 + y^*)^3} + \ldots + \frac{C_n}{(1 + y^*)^n}$$

or, using summation notation,

$$V = \sum_{t=1}^{n} \frac{C_t}{(1 + y^*)^t}. \tag{21.2}$$

Since the purchase price of the bond is its market price P, the **net present value** (NPV) to the investor is equal to the difference between the value of the bond and the purchase price:

net present value

$$NPV = V - P = \left[\sum_{t=1}^{n} \frac{C_t}{(1 + y^*)^t} \right] - P. \tag{21.3}$$

The NPV of the bond in the previous example is the solution to the following equation:

$$\begin{aligned} NPV &= \left[\frac{\$60}{(1 + .09)^1} + \frac{\$60}{(1 + .09)^2} + \frac{\$1{,}060}{(1 + .09)^3} \right] - \$900 \\ &= \$24.06. \end{aligned}$$

Since this bond has a positive NPV, it is underpriced. This will always be the case when a bond has a yield-to-maturity that is higher than the appropriate one (earlier, it was shown that this bond's yield-to-maturity was 10.02%, which is more than 9.00%, the appropriate yield-to-maturity). That is, in general, any bond with $y > y^*$ will always have a positive NPV and vice versa, so that under either method it would be underpriced.[1]

Alternatively, if the investor had determined that y^* was equal to 11.00%, then the bond's NPV would have been −$22.19. This would suggest that the bond was overpriced, just as would have been noted when the yield-to-maturity of 10.02% was compared with 11.00%. This will always be the case—a bond with $y < y^*$ will always have a negative NPV and vice versa, so that under either method it would be found to be overpriced.

It should also be pointed out that if the investor had determined that y^* had a value of approximately the same magnitude as the bond's yield-to-maturity of 10%, then the NPV of the bond would be approximately zero. In such a situation, the bond would be viewed as being fairly priced.

[1] A more accurate method of determining a bond's intrinsic value involves the use of spot rates. That is, in determining the NPV of this bond, the investor might have determined that the relevant spot rates for the one-year, two-year, and three-year cash flows are 8.24%, 8.69%, and 9.03%, respectively. Using these values, the bond's intrinsic value would be equal to $[\$60/(1.0824)] + [\$60/(1.0869)^2] + [\$1{,}060/1.0903)^3] = \$924.06$. Although V is the same in this example when either spot rates or y^* are used in the calculations, this need not always be the case.

Note that in order to use the capitalization of income method of valuation, the values of C_t, P, and y^* must be determined. It is generally quite easy to determine the values for C_t and P, since they are the bond's promised cash flows and current market price, respectively. However, determining the value of y^* is difficult, since the investor must estimate an appropriate value for the bond. Such a decision will depend on the characteristics of the bond, as well as on current market conditions. Given that the key ingredient in bond analysis is determining the appropriate value of y^*, the next section will discuss what attributes should be considered in making such a determination.

BOND ATTRIBUTES

Six primary attributes of a bond are of significant importance in bond valuation: (1) length of time until maturity; (2) coupon rate; (3) call provisions; (4) tax status; (5) marketability; and (6) likelihood of default. At any time, the structure of market prices for bonds differing in these dimensions can be examined and described in terms of yields-to-maturity. This overall structure is sometimes referred to as the **yield structure.** Often, attention is confined to differences along a single dimension, holding the other attributes constant. For example, the set of yields of bonds of different maturities constitutes the **term structure** (discussed in the previous chapter), and the set of yields of bonds of different default risk is referred to as the **risk structure.**

yield structure

term structure

risk structure

Most bond analysts consider the yields-to-maturity for default-free bonds to form the term structure; "risk differentials" are then added to obtain the relevant yields-to-maturity for bonds of lower quality. While subject to some criticism, this procedure makes it possible to think about a complicated set of relationships sequentially.

The differential between the yields of two bonds is usually called a **yield spread.** Most often, it involves a bond that is under analysis and a comparable default-free bond (that is, a Treasury security of similar maturity and coupon rate). Yield spreads are sometimes measured in **basis points,** where one basis point equals .01%. If the yield-to-maturity for one bond is 11.50% and that of another is 11.90%, the yield spread is 40 basis points.

yield spread

basis points

Coupon Rate and the Length of Time Until Maturity

These attributes of a bond are important because they determine the size and timing of the cash flows that are promised to the bondholder by the issuer. Given a bond's current market price, these attributes can be used to determine the bond's yield-to-maturity, which will subsequently be compared with what the investor thinks it should be. More specifically, if the market for Treasury securities is viewed as being efficient, then the yield-to-maturity on a Treasury security that is similar to the bond under evaluation can form a starting point in the analysis of the bond.

Consider the previously mentioned bond that is selling for $900 and has promised cash flows over the next three years of $60, $60, and $1,060, respectively. In this case, a Treasury security that has a similar cash flow would form the starting point of the analysis. Perhaps a Treasury security with a cash flow over the next three years of $50, $50, and $1,050 is currently selling for $910.61. Since the yield-to-maturity on this security is 8.5%, this forms the starting point in determining what the yield-to-maturity should be on the $900 bond. In this situation, the yield spread between the bond and Treasury security is 10.02% − 8.50% = 1.52%, or 152 basis points.

Call Provisions

There are times when, by historical standards, yields-to-maturity are relatively high. Bonds issued during such times may, at first glance, appear to be unusually attractive investments. However, deeper analysis indicates that this is not necessarily the case. Why? Because most corporate bonds have a **call provision** that enables the issuer to redeem the bonds prior to maturity, usually for a price somewhat above par.[2] This price is known as the **call price,** and the difference between it and the par value of the bond is known as the **call premium.** An issuer will often find it financially advantageous to call the existing bonds if yields drop substantially after the bonds were initially sold, since the issuer will be able to replace them with lower-yielding securities that are less costly.[3]

call provision

call price

call premium

For example, consider a ten-year bond issued at par ($1,000) that has a coupon rate of 12% and is callable at $1,050 any time after it has been outstanding for five years.[4] If, after five years, yields on similar five-year bonds were 8% (an amount that is substantially less than 12%), the bond would probably be called. This means that an investor who had planned on receiving annual coupon payments of $120 for ten years would instead actually receive five $120 annual coupon payments and the call price of $1,050 after five years. At this time, the investor could take the $1,050 and reinvest it in the 8% bonds, thereby receiving $84 per year in coupon payments over the last five years (it is assumed here that the investor can purchase a fraction of a bond, so that the full $1,050 can be invested in the 8% bonds) and $1,050 at the end of the tenth year as a return of principal. Given this pattern of cash flows, the actual yield-to-maturity (otherwise known as the realized return) over the ten years would be 10.96%.

This example suggests that the higher the coupon rate of a callable bond, the greater is the likely divergence between actual and promised yields. This is borne out by experience. Figure 21-1 plots the coupon rate, set at time of issue, on the horizontal axis. Since most bonds are initially sold at (or very close to) par, the coupon rate is also a measure of the yield-to-maturity that an investor may have thought was obtainable by purchasing one of the newly issued bonds.

The vertical axis in this figure plots the subsequent actual yield-to-maturity obtained up to the original maturity date by an investor, assuming that the payments received in the event of a call were reinvested in noncallable bonds with appropriate maturities. The curve is based on experience for

[2]Many corporate bonds have, in addition to a call provision, a provision for a sinking fund where each year the issuer retires a prespecified portion of the original bond issue.

[3]The investor generally can escape having his or her bonds called if either Treasury securities or discounted corporate bonds are purchased. However, since these securities have less "call risk," they are likely to have lower yields-to-maturity than similar bonds with higher levels of "call risk."

[4]In this example, the **yield-to-call** (or, to be more specific, the yield-to-first-call) is 12.78%. That is, 12.78% is the discount rate that makes the present value of $120 received after each of the first four years and $1,170 (= $1,050 + $120) at the end of five years equal to the issue price of the bond, $1,000. Note how the yield-to-call is greater than the bond's promised yield-to-maturity at the time of issue (12%).

yield-to-call

FIGURE 21-1
Promised and Actual Yields of Callable Aa Utility Bonds, 1956–1964

Source: Frank C. Jen and James E. Wert, "The Effect of Call Risk on Corporate Bond Yields," *Journal of Finance*, 22, no. 4 (December 1967):646.

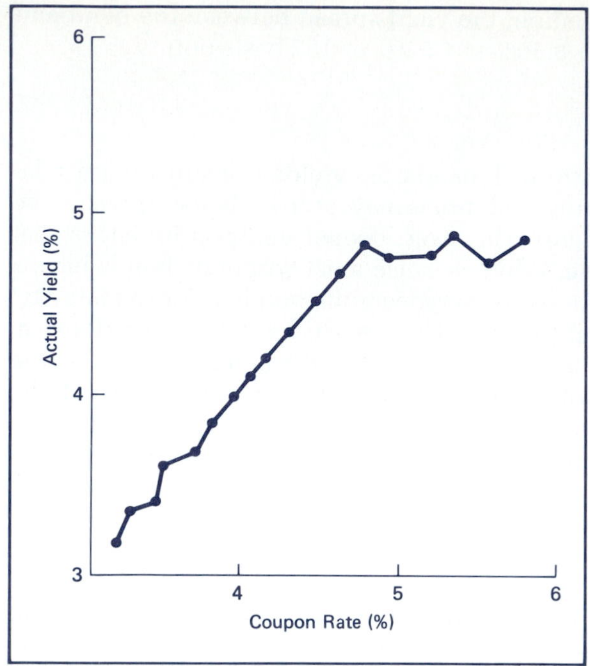

a group of callable bonds issued by utility companies during a period of fluctuating interest rates. As can be seen, the coupon rate and actual yield are quite similar in magnitude until the coupon rate gets near 5%. At this point, higher coupon rates are no longer associated with higher actual yields, since these coupon rates were relatively high during the time period examined; as a consequence, most of the bonds with coupon rates above 5% were ultimately called.

The upshot is that bonds with greater likelihood of being called should have a higher yield-to-maturity. That is, the higher the coupon rate or the lower the call premium, the higher the yield-to-maturity should be. Equivalently, bonds with higher coupon rates or lower call premiums will have lower intrinsic values, keeping everything else equal.

Tax Status

In Chapter 5, it was noted that tax-exempt municipal bonds have had yields-to-maturity that were approximately 20% to 40% lower than the yields-to-maturity on similar taxable bonds. Taxation affects bond prices and yields in other ways. For example, any low-coupon bond selling at a discount provides return in two forms: coupon payments and capital gains. In the United States, both are taxable as ordinary income, but taxes on the latter may be deferred until the bond either is sold or matures. This suggests that such **deep discount bonds** have a tax advantage because of this deferral. As a result, they should have slightly lower before-tax yields than high-coupon bonds, other things equal. That is, such low-coupon bonds will have a slightly higher intrinsic value than high-coupon bonds.

deep discount bonds

Marketability

marketability

Marketability (sometimes also referred to as *liquidity*) refers to the ability of an investor to sell an asset quickly without having to make a substantial price concession. An example of an illiquid asset would be a "collectible," such as a piece of artwork. An investor who owns a Van Gogh painting may have to settle for a relatively low price if he or she has to sell it within an hour. If the sale can be postponed for a length of time in order to set up a public auction, undoubtedly a much higher price could be obtained. Alternatively, an investor with $1,000,000 worth of IBM common stock who has to sell these shares within an hour will probably be able to receive a price close to the price that other sellers of IBM stock recently received. Furthermore, it is quite unlikely that waiting would increase the expected selling price of such a security.

Since most bonds are bought and sold in dealer markets, one measure of a bond's marketability is the bid-ask spread that the dealers are quoting on the bond. Bonds that are being actively traded will tend to have lower bid-ask spreads than bonds that are inactive. This is because the dealer is more exposed to risk when making a market in an inactive security than when making a market in an active security. The source of this risk is the inventory that the dealer holds, and the fact that interest rates in general may move in a way that causes the dealer to lose money on his or her inventory. Accordingly, bonds that are actively traded should have a lower yield-to-maturity and a higher intrinsic value than bonds that are inactive, keeping everything else equal.

Likelihood of Default

bond ratings

Currently a number of corporations—the two largest are Standard & Poor's Corporation and Moody's Investors Service, Inc.—provide ratings of the creditworthiness of thousands of corporate and municipal bonds. Such **bond ratings** are often interpreted as an indication of the likelihood of default by the issuer. Figure 21-2 provides details on the ratings assigned by Standard & Poor's, while Figure 21-3 provides similar details for Moody's.[5]

investment grade bonds
speculative grade bonds

A broader set of categories is often employed, with bonds classified as being of either **investment grade** or **speculative grade.** Typically, investment grade bonds are bonds that have been assigned to one of the top four ratings (AAA through BBB by Standard & Poor's; Aaa through Baa by Moody's). In contrast, speculative grade bonds are bonds that have been assigned to one of the lower ratings (BB and below by Standard & Poor's; Ba and below by Moody's). Sometimes these low-rated securities are called, derisively, **junk bonds.** Furthermore, if the junk bonds were of investment grade when originally issued, they are often called **fallen angels.**

junk bonds

fallen angels

At times, certain regulated financial institutions (such as banks, savings and loans, and insurance companies) have been prohibited from purchasing bonds that were not of investment grade. As a consequence, investment grade bonds are sometimes thought to command "superpremium" prices, and hence disproportionately low yields, since an important group of investors is

[5]Both rating agencies actually use finer gradations than those shown in the figures. Standard & Poor's sometimes places a + or − next to its letter rating if a bond is in a category ranging from AA to CCC. Similarly, Moody's may place a 1, 2, or 3 next to its letter rating if a bond is in a category ranging from Aa down to B. Both agencies also rate certain types of short-term debt instruments.

FIGURE 21-2
Standard & Poor's Debt Rating Definitions

A Standard & Poor's corporate or municipal debt rating is a current assessment of the creditworthiness of an obligor with respect to a specific obligation. This assessment may take into consideration obligors such as guarantors, insurers, or lessees.

The debt rating is not a recommendation to purchase, sell, or hold a security, inasmuch as it does not comment as to market price or suitability for a particular investor.

The ratings are based on current information furnished by the issuer or obtained by Standard & Poor's from other sources it considers reliable. Standard & Poor's does not perform any audit in connection with any rating and may, on occasion, rely on unaudited financial information. The ratings may be changed, suspended or withdrawn as a result of changes in, or unavailability of, such information, or based on other circumstances.

The ratings are based, in varying degrees, on the following considerations:

I. Likelihood of default-capacity and willingness of the obligor as to the timely payment of interest and repayment of principal in accordance with the terms of the obligation;
II. Nature of and provisions of the obligation;
III. Protection afforded by, and relative position of, the obligation in the event of bankruptcy, reorganization or other arrangement under the laws of bankruptcy and other laws affecting creditors' rights.

AAA Debt rated 'AAA' has the highest rating assigned by Standard & Poor's. Capacity to pay interest and repay principal is extremely strong.

AA Debt rated 'AA' has a very strong capacity to pay interest and repay principal and differs from the higher-rated issues only in small degree.

A Debt rated 'A' has a strong capacity to pay interest and repay principal although it is somewhat more susceptible to the adverse effects of changes in curcumstances and economic conditions than debt in higher-rated categories.

BBB Debt rated 'BBB' is regarded as having an adequate capacity to pay interest and repay principal. Whereas it normally exhibits adequate protection parameters, adverse economic conditions or changing circumstances are more likely to lead to a weakened capacity to pay interest and repay principal for debt in this category than in higher rated categories.

BB, B, CCC, CC, C Debt rated 'BB', 'B', 'CCC', 'CC', and 'C' is regarded, on balance, as predominantly speculative with respect to capacity to pay interest and repay principal in accordance with the terms of the obligation. 'BB' indicates the lowest degree of speculation and 'C' the highest degree of speculation. While such debt will likely have some quality and protective characteristics, these are outweighed by large uncertainties or major risk exposures to adverse conditions.

CI The rating CI is reserved for income bonds on which no interest is being paid.

D Debt rated D is in payment default.

Source: Standard & Poor's Bond Guide, June 1992, p. 10.

encouraged or forced to purchase them. However, a major disparity in yields could attract a great many new issuers who would increase the supply of such bonds, thereby causing bond prices to fall and yields to rise. For a significant superpremium to persist, rather substantial market segmentation on both the buying and the selling side would be required. Since there is no clear evidence that such segmentation exists, it seems more likely that the differences in yields between investment grade bonds and speculative grade bonds are roughly proportional to differences in default risk.

According to Moody's, ratings are designed to provide "investors with a simple system of gradation by which the relative investment qualities of bonds may be noted."[6] Moreover:

> Since ratings involve judgments about the future, on the one hand, and since they are used by investors as a means of protection, on the other, the effort is

[6]*Moody's Bond Record* (New York: Moody's Investors Service, June 1992), p. 3.

FIGURE 21-3
Moody's Corporate Bond Ratings

Aaa

Bonds which are rated **Aaa** are judged to be of the best quality. They carry the smallest degree of investment risk and are generally referred to as "gilt edge." Interest payments are protected by a large or by an exceptionally stable margin and principal is secure. While the various protective elements are likely to change, such changes as can be visualized are most unlikely to impair the fundamentally strong position of such issues.

Aa

Bonds which are rated **Aa** are judged to be of high quality by all standards. Together with the **Aaa** group they comprise what are generally known as high grade bonds. They are rated lower than the best bonds because margins of protection may not be as large as in **Aaa** securities or fluctuation of protective elements may be of greater amplitude or there may be other elements present which make the long term risks appear somewhat larger than in **Aaa** securities.

A

Bonds which are rated **A** possess many favorable investment attributes and are to be considered as upper medium grade obligations. Factors giving security to principal and interest are considered adequate but elements may be present which suggest a susceptibility to impairment sometime in the future.

Baa

Bonds which are rated **Baa** are considered as medium grade obligations, i.e., they are neither highly protected nor poorly secured. Interest payments and principal security appear adequate for the present but certain protective elements may be lacking or may be characteristically unreliable over any great length of time. Such bonds lack outstanding investment characteristics and in fact have speculative characteristics as well.

Ba

Bonds which are rated **Ba** are judged to have speculative elements; their future cannot be considered as well assured. Often the protection of interest and principal payments may be very moderate and thereby not well safeguarded during other good and bad times over the future. Uncertainty of position characterizes bonds in this class.

B

Bonds which are rated **B** generally lack characteristics of the desired investment. Assurance of interest and principal payments or of maintenance of other terms of the contract over any long period of time may be small.

Caa

Bonds which are rated **Caa** are of poor standing. Such issues may be in default or there may be present elements of danger with respect to principal or interest.

Ca

Bonds which are rated **Ca** represent obligations which are speculative in a high degree. Such issues are often in default or have other marked shortcomings.

C

Bonds which are rated **C** are the lowest rated class of bonds and issues so rated can be regarded as having extremely poor prospects of ever attaining any real investment standing.

Source: *Moody's Bond Record*, June 1992, p. 3.

made when assigning ratings to look at "worst" potentialities in the "visible" future, rather than solely at the past record and the status of the present. Therefore, investors using the ratings should not expect to find in them a reflection of statistical factors alone, since they are an appraisal of long-term risks, including the recognition of many non-statistical factors.[7]

[7]*Moody's Bond Record*, p. 3.

MONEY MATTERS
Taking Advantage of the Bond Rating Process

"Your bond rating: don't try to issue debt without it," might read the motto of U.S. bond rating agencies. Receiving an investment-grade bond rating has long been a prerequisite for any U.S. debt issuer desiring easy access to the domestic bond market. Without such a rating, debt issuers are forced to seek financing from more expensive sources: banks, the market for privately placed debt, or the high-yield (junk) bond market.

Once they have acquired an investment-grade bond rating, debt issuers strive to maintain that rating or even improve it. The benefits of an improved rating (and the costs of a lower rating) can be substantial. As Figure 21-6 illustrates, the difference in yields between the highest- and lowest-rated investment-grade bonds fluctuates over time, but is often well over a full percentage point. Yield differences between investment-grade and non-investment-grade bonds are often even greater. As U.S. corporations have increased the amount of debt on their balance sheets in recent decades, the financial ramifications of bond rating changes have increased commensurately.

Most bond portfolio managers focus their efforts on forecasting changes in interest rates and structuring their portfolios to benefit from those expected movements. However, the emphasis placed by the bond market on both a debt issue's initial rating and subsequent changes in that rating present insightful investors with another approach to bond management: anticipating bond rating changes. In exploring those opportunities, we first consider some additional background information on the bond rating process.

Two companies dominate the bond rating business: Standard & Poor's and Moody's. At least one of these organizations rates virtually every corporate debt security that comes to the public market. Over 2,000 debt issuers submit financial data to these organizations. For all practical purposes, no bond can be considered an investment-grade security without the acquiescence of S&P's or Moody's.

Additionally, a relatively small market exists for "third opinions." Three other firms—Fitch Investors; Duff & Phelps; and McCarthy, Crisanti & Maffel—produce ratings on a portion of the bonds rated by the two big firms. Although their ratings rarely differ significantly from S&P's and Moody's, in some situations investors and issuers are comforted by a confirmation of the two big firms' ratings or believe that the smaller rating agencies may uncover aspects of the debt issuers' financial conditions overlooked by S&P's and Moody's.

The text describes many of the financial factors that ratings agencies use in assigning bond ratings, including the issuers' leverage, earnings variability, and profitability. Research has shown that such factors systematically "explain" a large portion of bond rating differences among debt issues, implying that there is a significant "mechanical" aspect to the ratings process.

Despite this dominant formulistic element of bond ratings, qualitative judgments by the rating agencies still appear to play an important role in rating assignments. Interestingly, as corporations have increased the leverage on their balance sheets, a firm's ability to generate future cash flow to meet its interest expenses has come to play a major role in setting bond ratings. However, evaluating the prospective, rather than contemporaneous, cash flow strength of an issuer is an uncertain process and requires more subjective interpretations of the financial data on the part of the rating agencies.

Some bond portfolio managers attempt to take advantage of the uncertainty surrounding a bond's rating. They recognize that the bond market bids up the prices of bonds that have had their ratings upgraded and drives down the prices of bonds experiencing rating downgrades. If they can consistently purchase bonds before rating upgrades or sell bonds before rating downgrades, they can outperform a passive portfolio of similar risk.

Why do such bond managers expect to beat the ratings game? They believe that with intensive security analysis they can understand a debt issuer's financial condition more accurately and on a more timely basis than can the rating agencies. Essentially, these managers make their moves and wait for the rating agencies (and the market) to catch up to them.

Security analysis of this type is similar to fundamental stock analysis (see Chapter 14). It involves an emphasis on correctly interpreting the "true" financial condition of the debt issuer based on a wide range of disparate variables, from the quality of the debt issuer's management to the market for its products.

These bond managers also play a numbers game with the rating agencies. Both S&P and Moody's employ fewer than 100 analysts (the smaller rating agencies employ far fewer). Thus the rating agencies cannot cover all debt issuers at all times. Significant positive or negative news about an issuer often causes the rating agencies to reevaluate their bond ratings. The bond managers attempt to identify those issuers who are under review and anticipate the outcomes of those reviews.

Of course, as with successful common stock analysis, consistently and accurately forecasting bond rating changes requires rare skills available to few investors in an efficient market. But also as with common stock analysis, the potential profits to bond investors who correctly diverge from the current consensus can be large.

Despite this disclaimer, the influence of "statistical factors" on the ratings is apparently significant. Several studies have investigated the relationship between historical measures of a firm's performance and the ratings assigned its bonds. Many of the differences in the ratings accorded various bonds can in fact be attributed to differences in the issuers' situations, measured in traditional ways. For corporate bonds, better ratings are generally associated with lower financial leverage (that is, debt to total assets); smaller past variation in earnings over time; larger asset base (firm size); more profitable operations; and lack of subordination to other debt issues. One use of these findings is in the development of models for predicting the initial ratings that will be given to forthcoming bond issues as well as for predicting changes in the ratings of outstanding bonds.

Default Premiums Since common stocks do not "promise" any cash flows to the investor, they are not subject to default. To assess the investment prospects for a common stock, all possible holding-period returns might be considered. By multiplying each return by its perceived probability of occurrence and then adding up the products, an estimate of the expected holding-period return can be determined.

A similar procedure can be employed with bonds, with the analysis usually focusing on yield-to-maturity. Formally, all possible yields are considered, along with their respective probabilities, and a weighted average computed to determine the **expected yield-to-maturity.** As long as there is any possibility of default or late payment, the expected yield will fall below the promised yield. In general, the greater the risk of default and the greater the amount of loss in the event of default, the greater will be this disparity in yields.

expected yield-to-maturity

This is illustrated in Figure 21-4 for a hypothetical risky bond. Its promised yield-to-maturity is 12% but, owing to a high default risk, the expected yield is only 9%. The 3% difference between the promised and expected yields is the **default premium.** Any bond that has some probability of default should offer such a premium, and it should be greater, the greater the probability of default.

default premium

Just how large should a bond's default premium be? According to one model, the answer depends on both the probability of default and the likely

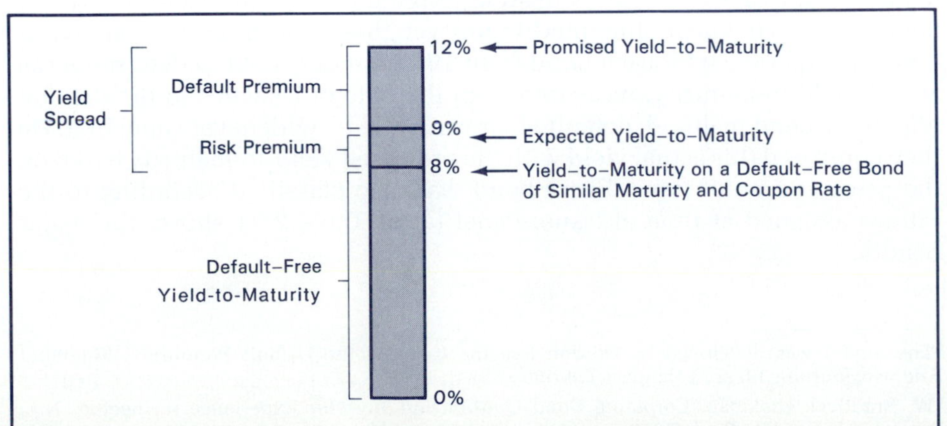

FIGURE 21-4
Yield-to-Maturity for a Risky Bond

financial loss to the bondholder in the event of default.[8] Also important in this model is the level of the bond's expected yield-to-maturity.

Consider a bond that is perceived to be equally likely to default in each year (given it did not default in the previous year), with the probability that it will default in any given year denoted by p_d. Assume that if the bond does default, a payment equal to $(1 - \lambda)$ times its market price a year earlier will be made to the owner of each bond. According to this model, a bond will be fairly priced if its promised yield-to-maturity (y) is:

$$y = \frac{\bar{y} + \lambda p_d}{1 - p_d} \tag{21.4}$$

where $\bar{y}$ denotes the bond's expected yield-to-maturity. The difference (d) between a bond's promised yield-to-maturity (y) and its expected yield-to-maturity ($\bar{y}$) was referred to earlier as the bond's default premium. Using equation (21.4), this difference for a fairly priced bond will be equal to:

$$\begin{aligned} d &= y - \bar{y} \\ &= \left[\frac{\bar{y} + \lambda p_d}{1 - p_d}\right] - \bar{y}. \end{aligned} \tag{21.5}$$

As an example, consider the bond illustrated in Figure 21-4. Assume that this bond has a 6% annual default probability, and that it is estimated that if the bond does default, each bondholder will receive an amount equal to 60% of the bond's market price a year earlier (meaning that $1 - \lambda = .60$, which in turn means that $\lambda = .40$). Using equation (21.5), this bond would be fairly priced if its default premium were equal to:

$$\begin{aligned} d &= \left[\frac{.09 + (.40 \times .06)}{1 - .06}\right] - .09 \\ &= .0313 \end{aligned}$$

or 3.13%. Since the actual default premium earlier was estimated to be 3%, it can be seen that the two figures are similar. This suggests that the actual default premium is appropriate, according to this model.

What sort of default experience might the long-run bond investor anticipate? And, how is this experience likely to be related to the ratings of the bonds held? In a massive study of all large bond issues and a sample of small bond issues, Hickman attempted to answer these questions.[9] He analyzed investor experience for each bond from 1900 through 1943 to determine the actual yield-to-maturity, measured from the date of issuance to the date on which the bond matured, defaulted, or was called—whichever came first. He then compared this actual yield with the promised yield-to-maturity based on the price at time of issue. Every bond was also classified according to the ratings assigned at time of issue. Panel (a) of Table 21-1 shows the major results.

---

[8]The model was developed by Gordon Pye in "Gauging the Default Premium," *Financial Analysts Journal*, 30, no. 1 (January/February 1974): 49–52.

[9]W. Braddock Hickman, *Corporate Bond Quality and Investor Experience* (Princeton, N.J.: Princeton University Press, 1958).

TABLE 21-1
Actual and Realized Bond Yields-to-Maturity, 1900–1943

(a) ALL LARGE AND A SAMPLE OF SMALL ISSUES

Composite Rating	Comparable Moody's Rating	Promised Yield-to-Maturity at Issue	Percent Defaulting Prior to Maturity	Actual Yield-to-Maturity
I	Aaa	4.5%	5.9%	5.1%
II	Aa	4.6	6.0	5.0
III	A	4.9	13.4	5.0
IV	Baa	5.4	19.1	5.7
V-IX	below Baa	9.5	42.4	8.6

(b) ALL LARGE ISSUES

Composite Rating	Comparable Moody's Rating	Promised Yield-to-Maturity	Actual Yield-to-Maturity	Modified Actual Yield-to-Maturity
I	Aaa	4.5%	5.1%	4.3%
II	Aa	4.5	5.1	4.3
III	A	4.9	5.0	4.3
IV	Baa	5.4	5.8	4.5

Source: (a) W. Braddock Hickman, *Corporate Bond Quality and Investor Experience* (Princeton, NJ: Princeton University Press, 1958), p. 10. (b) Harold G. Fraine and Robert H. Mills, "The Effect of Defaults and Credit Deterioration on Yields of Corporate Bonds," *Journal of Finance*, 16, no. 3 (September 1961): 433.

As might be expected, Hickman found that, in general, the riskier the bond, the higher the promised yield at time of issue and the higher the percentage of bonds that subsequently defaulted. However, a surprise was uncovered when the actual yields-to-maturity were compared with promised yields-to-maturity. As the last column on the right of the table shows, in four out of five rating classifications, the actual yield was found to *exceed* the promised yield. Fortunately, a convenient explanation exists for this finding—the period studied by Hickman was one where a substantial drop in interest rates occurred. This is important because the drop made it attractive for issuers to call their outstanding bonds, paying the bondholders a call premium in the process and resulting in an actual yield above the promised yield.

To see what might have happened had this not been the case, Fraine and Mills reanalyzed the data for large investment-grade issues.[10] Their results are shown in panel (b) of Table 21-1. The initial columns differ from those in panel (a) because smaller issues were excluded. The major difference between the panels appears in the right-hand column, where Fraine and Mills substituted a bond's promised yield for its actual yield whenever the latter was larger, thereby removing the effects of most calls. Unlike Hickman's, their results suggest that there was little difference in actual yields within the highest rating classifications.

More recently, Edward Altman examined the default experience of corporate bonds over the period from 1971 through 1990.[11] His methodology was somewhat different from Hickman's in that for each bond he noted its

[10]Harold G. Fraine and Robert H. Mills, "The Effect of Defaults and Credit Deterioration on Yields of Corporate Bonds," *Journal of Finance*, 16, no. 3 (September 1961): 423–34.

[11]Edward I. Altman, "Defaults and Returns on High-Yield Bonds Through the First Half of 1991," *Financial Analysts Journal*, 47, no. 6 (November/December 1991): 67–77.

rating when it was originally issued and then noted how many years later it went into default (if at all). From this he compiled "mortality tables," such as Table 21-2, which show the percentage of bond issues that went into default within various numbers of years after issuance.

There are several interesting observations that can be made upon inspection of this table. First, in looking down any particular column, it can be seen that the cumulative rate of default increases as one moves further from the date of issuance. Second, with the exception of those bonds originally rated AA, by looking across any row it can be seen that lower-rated bonds had higher default rates. Third, the default rates for the speculative grades of bonds are strikingly high. Indeed, it raises a question of whether or not such bonds make good investments, as their higher yields might not make up for their higher default rates. This question will be addressed shortly.

Risk Premiums It is useful to compare the expected return of a risky security with the certain return of a default-free security. In an efficient market, the difference in these returns will be related to the relevant systematic (or nondiversifiable) risk of the security. Consider common stocks, where the investor has a holding period of one year or less. In this situation, the expected return on a share is typically compared with the yield of a Treasury bill having a maturity date corresponding with the end of the holding period (note that the yield on such a Treasury bill is equal to its holding period return).

risk premium

Traditionally, a risky bond's expected yield-to-maturity is compared with that of a default-free bond of similar maturity and coupon rate. The difference between these yields is known as the bond's **risk premium.** In the example shown in Figure 21-4, default-free bonds of similar maturity and coupon rate offer a certain 8% yield-to-maturity. Since the risky bond's expected yield-to-maturity is 9%, its risk premium is 1% (that is, 100 basis points).

Every bond that might default should offer a default premium. But the risk premium is another matter. Any security's expected return should be related only to its systematic risk, for it is this risk that measures its contribution to the risk of a well-diversified portfolio; its total risk is not directly relevant.

For example, if a group of companies all faced the possibility of bankruptcy, but from totally unrelated causes, a portfolio that included all of

TABLE 21-2
Default Rates of U.S. Bonds, 1971–1990

YEARS AFTER ISSUANCE	ORIGINAL RATING						
	AAA	AA	A	BBB	BB	B	CCC
1	.00%	.00%	.00%	.03%	.00%	.87%	1.31%
2	.00	.00	.30	.57	.93	3.22	4.00
3	.00	1.11	.60	.85	1.36	9.41	19.72
4	.00	1.42	.65	1.34	3.98	16.37	36.67
5	.00	1.70	.65	1.54	5.93	20.87	38.08
6	.14	1.70	.73	1.81	7.38	26.48	40.58
7	.19	1.91	.87	2.70	10.91	29.62	NA
8	.19	1.93	.94	2.83	10.91	31.74	NA
9	.19	2.01	1.28	2.99	10.91	39.38	NA
10	.19	2.11	1.28	3.85	13.86	40.86	NA

Source: Edward I. Altman, "Defaults and Returns on High-Yield Bonds Through the First Half of 1991," *Financial Analysts Journal*, 47, no. 6 (November/December 1991): Table X, pp. 74–75.

their bonds would subsequently provide an actual return very close to its expected return. This is because the default premiums earned on the bonds that did not default would offset the losses incurred from those bonds that did default. Consequently, there should be little reason for this expected return to differ significantly from that of a default-free bond, since there is little doubt concerning what its actual return will be. Accordingly, each bond should be priced to offer little or no risk premium (but each bond should have a substantive default premium).

However, the risks associated with bonds are not unrelated. Figure 21-5 shows the ratio of the par value of corporate bonds defaulting during the year to the par value outstanding at the beginning of the year for each year from 1900 to 1965. Not surprisingly, the peaks coincide with periods of economic distress.[12] When business is bad, most firms are affected. The market value of a firm's common stock will decline when an economic downturn is anticipated. If the likelihood of default on its debt also increases, the market value of its outstanding bonds will follow suit. Thus, the holding-period return on a bond may be correlated with the returns of other bonds and with those of stocks. Most important, a risky bond's holding-period return is likely to be correlated, at least to some extent, with the return on a widely diversified "market portfolio" that includes both corporate bonds and stocks. It is this part of the risk of a bond that is known as systematic risk and causes a bond to have a risk premium in the form of an expected return that is greater than the default-free rate, since it is not diversifiable.

Bonds with greater likelihood of default will have greater potential sensitivity to market declines, which, in turn, represent lowered assessments of prospects for the economy as a whole. This is illustrated in Table 21-3,

[12]See Marshall E. Blume and Donald B. Keim, "Realized Returns and Defaults on Low-Grade Bonds: The Cohort of 1977 and 1978," *Financial Analysts Journal*, 47, no. 2 (March/April 1991): 63–72; and Marshall E. Blume, Donald B. Keim, and Sandeep A. Patel, "Returns and Volatility of Low-Grade Bonds, 1977–1989," *Journal of Finance*, 46, no. 1 (March 1991): 49–74; and Marshall E. Blume and Donald B. Keim, "The Risk and Return of Low-Grade Bonds: An Update," *Financial Analysts Journal*, 47, no. 5 (September/October 1991). A similar observation has been made for municipal bonds; see George H. Hempel, *The Postwar Quality of State and Local Debt* (New York: Columbia University Press, 1971).

FIGURE 21-5
Default Rates, 1900–1965
Source: Adapted from Thomas R. Atkinson and Elizabeth T. Simpson, *Trends in Corporate Bond Quality* (New York: Columbia University Press, 1967), p. 5.

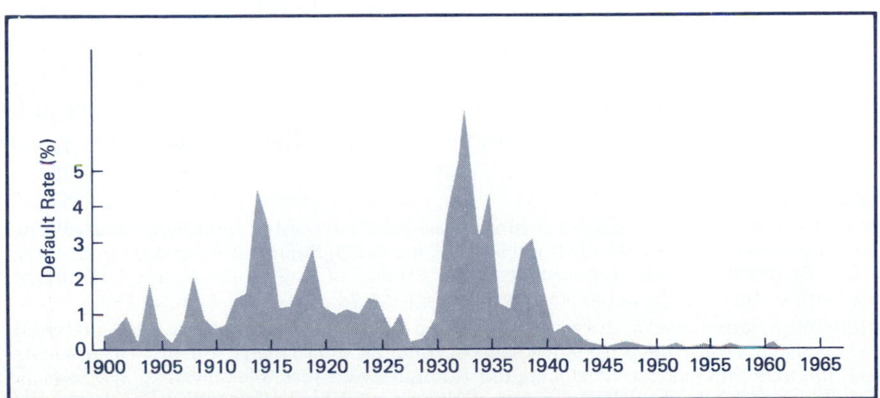

TABLE 21-3
Risk and Return, Keystone Bond Funds, 1968–1991

	FUND B1	FUND B2	FUND B4
	Conservative Bonds	Investment Grade Bonds	Discount Bonds
Average return (% per year)	7.84	8.53	8.64
Standard deviation of return (% per year)	8.27	9.35	13.68
Beta value, relative to S&P 500	.26	.38	.54
Proportion of variance explained by S&P 500	.28	.45	.42

which summarizes the investment performance of three portfolios of bonds, known as bond funds, in the Keystone group.[13] All values shown in the table are based on annual returns earned over a 24-year period by each portfolio. As might be anticipated, the bond portfolio with the lowest-rated bonds (fund B4) had the highest average return and highest standard deviation, while the bond portfolio with the highest-rated bonds (fund B1) had the lowest average return and lowest standard deviation.

To estimate each portfolio's sensitivity to changes in stock prices, each portfolio's returns were compared with those of Standard & Poor's 500. Specifically, a beta was calculated for each portfolio in order to measure the sensitivity of each portfolio to swings in the stock market. As can be seen in the table, the lower the bond rating of the portfolio, the higher the estimated beta, indicating that lower-rated bonds moved more with stocks and thus should have had higher average returns.

The final row in the table shows the proportion of the year-to-year variation in bond portfolio returns that was associated with stock market swings. As indicated, relatively more of the B2 and B4 portfolios' variation was associated with the stock market than was the case with the B1 portfolio. Thus, for higher-rated bonds, interest-rate risk appears to have been more important than stock market risk.[14]

THE RISK STRUCTURE OF INTEREST RATES

The greater a bond's risk of default, the greater its default premium. This alone will cause a bond with a higher default risk to offer a higher promised yield-to-maturity. If it is also true that the greater a bond's risk of default, the greater its risk premium, then the promised yield-to-maturity will have to be even higher. As a result, bonds given lower agency ratings should have higher promised yields-to-maturity if such ratings really do reflect the risk of default.

Figure 21-6 shows that this is indeed the case. Each of the curves plots

[13]For an in-depth analysis of such bond portfolios, see Bradford Cornell and Kevin Greene, "The Investment Performance of Low-Grade Bond Funds," *Journal of Finance*, 46, no. 1 (March 1991): 29–48, and Bradford Cornell, "Liquidity and the Pricing of Low-Grade Bonds," *Financial Analysts Journal*, 48, no. 1 (January/February 1992): 63–67, 74.

[14]In a study of preferred stocks, it was found that the price movements of low-rated preferred stocks were related more to the price movements of common stocks than to the price movements of bonds; for high-rated preferred stocks, the findings were just the opposite. See John S. Bildersee, "Some Aspects of the Performance of Non-Convertible Preferred Stocks," *Journal of Finance*, 28, no. 5 (December 1973): 1187–1201.

FIGURE 21-6
Corporate Bond Yields by Ratings
Source: *Moody's Bond Record,* June 1992, p. 574.

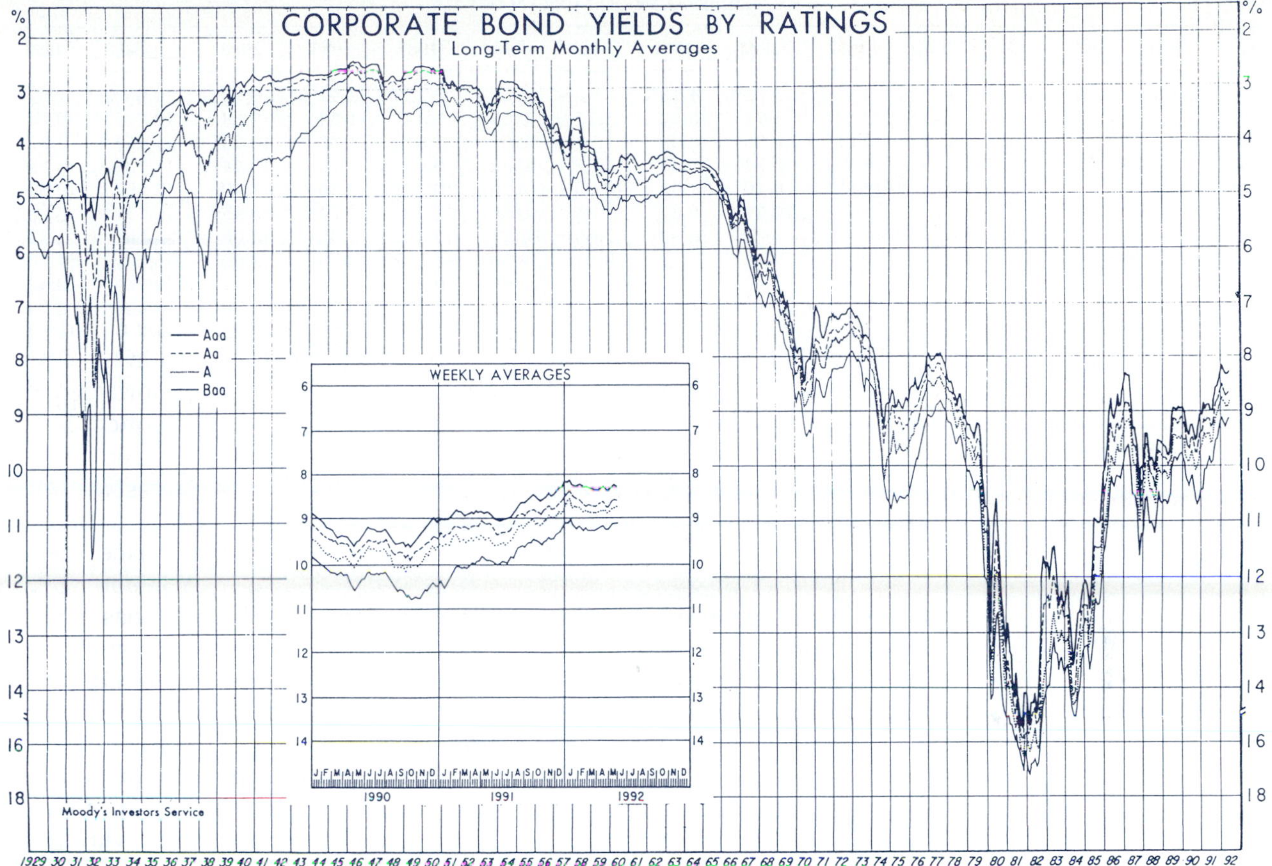

the promised yield-to-maturity for a group of corporate bonds assigned the same ratings by Moody's. Note that the scale is "upside down," so that higher promised yields plot at lower positions on the diagram (such a procedure is often employed for bonds).

While Figure 21-6 shows that bonds are priced so that higher promised yields go with lower ratings, it also shows that the differences between the yields in the rating categories vary considerably over time. This suggests that agency ratings indicate *relative* levels of risk instead of *absolute* levels of risk.

If an absolute level of risk were indicated by a rating classification, then each classification would be associated with a particular probability of default (or, more accurately, a range of probabilities of default). Consequently, as the economy became more uncertain in terms of things like the near-term level of GNP, bonds would be reclassified as necessary, with most moving to lower ratings. In this situation, yield spreads between classifications would change only slightly, since each classification would still reflect bonds having the same probability of default. However, Figure 21-6 shows that these spreads change greatly over time, an observation that can be interpreted as evidence that the bond market does not believe that the ratings reflect absolute levels of risk. Further evidence is provided in Table 21-4, which shows the historical difference in the returns on junk bonds and U.S. Treasuries for

TABLE 21-4 Historical Return Differences Between Junk Bonds and U.S. Treasuries

BASE PERIOD (JAN. 1)	TERMINAL PERIOD (DECEMBER 31)													
	1978	1979	1980	1981	1982	1983	1984	1985	1986	1987	1988	1989	1990	1991
1978	8.68%	6.60%	5.01%	5.51%	3.17%	5.82%	4.13%	2.70%	1.59%	2.22%	2.41%	0.98%	(0.04%)	1.37%
1979		4.55	3.23	4.48	1.71	5.22	3.32	1.77	0.62	1.44	1.73	0.23	(0.82)	0.74
1980			1.96	4.45	0.67	5.39	3.05	1.24	(0.02)	1.01	1.38	(0.25)	(1.35)	0.37
1981				7.08	(0.13)	6.74	3.36	1.07	(0.42)	0.85	1.29	(0.54)	(1.73)	0.19
1982					(9.63)	6.49	1.93	(0.69)	(2.16)	(0.33)	0.36	(1.60)	(2.80)	(0.60)
1983						19.57	6.62	1.84	(0.56)	1.22	1.74	(0.65)	(2.11)	0.26
1984							(6.32)	(7.60)	(7.73)	(3.48)	(1.89)	(4.06)	(5.19)	(2.31)
1985								(9.03)	(8.50)	(2.50)	(0.76)	(3.60)	(5.00)	(1.70)
1986									(7.99)	0.34	1.64	(2.41)	(4.30)	(0.54)
1987										7.34	5.89	(0.76)	(3.49)	0.93
1988											4.27	(5.16)	(7.31)	(1.04)
1989												(14.37)	(12.76)	(3.11)
1990													(11.24)	4.34
1991*														19.01

*First six months of 1991.

Source: Edward I. Altman, "Defaults and Returns on High-Yield Bonds Through the First Half of 1991," *Financial Analysts Journal*, 47, no. 6 (November/December 1991): Table XIV, p. 77.

various holding periods. As shown in the table, at times these differences are positive and at other times they are negative (for example, the average annual difference for 1978–1991 and 1984–1991 are +1.37% and −2.31%, respectively).

It is known that rating agencies prefer to avoid making a large number of rating changes as the economy becomes more uncertain. Instead, they prefer to use the classifications to indicate relative levels of risk. This means that an overall increase in economic uncertainty would not result in a significant number of reclassifications. Thus, the probability of default associated with bonds in a given rating classification would be greater at such a time. In turn, the yield spreads between classifications of corporate bonds and the yield spreads between corporate and government bonds would increase. Indeed, there is evidence that the spread between the promised yields of bonds of different rating classifications increases when the degree of uncertainty about the economy increases.

Some models have attempted to take advantage of this observation in order to predict the amount of economic uncertainty. In particular, these models use the size of the yield spread between, say, bonds rated AAA and those rated BBB by Standard & Poor's as an indication of the degree of economic uncertainty. For example, if this spread is widening, then that might be taken as an indication that the near-term future of the economy was becoming more uncertain. It should be noted that there are other models that look not at yield spreads but at differences in the holding-period returns of AAA and BBB bonds.

DETERMINANTS OF YIELD SPREADS

As mentioned previously, when bond analysts refer to a corporate bond's yield spread, they are typically referring to the difference between the corporate bond's promised yield-to-maturity and that of another bond (often a

Treasury security) having a similar maturity and coupon rate. The greater the risk of default, the greater this spread should be. Moreover, bonds that have more marketability might command an additional "premium" in price, and hence offer a lower yield-to-maturity with a corresponding lower spread. Given a large enough sample of bonds, it should be possible to see if these relationships really do exist.

One study of corporate bond prices did just this.[15] Three measures were used to assess the probability of default:

1. the extent to which the firm's net income had varied over the preceding nine years (measured by the coefficient of variation of earnings—that is, the ratio of standard deviation of earnings to average earnings);
2. the length of time that the firm had operated without forcing any of its creditors to take a loss;
3. the ratio of the market value of the firm's equity to the par value of its debt.

The fourth measure was used to provide an indication of marketability:

4. the market value of the firm's outstanding debt.

First, these measures were calculated, along with the yield spread, for each of 366 bonds. Second, the logarithm of every yield spread and measure was calculated. Third, statistical methods were used to analyze the relationship between a bond's yield spread and these measures. The one that was found to describe this relationship most accurately was:

$$\begin{aligned}\text{yield spread} = {} & .987 + .307\,(\text{earnings variability}) \\ & -.253\,(\text{time without default}) - .537\,(\text{equity/debt ratio}) \\ & -.275\,(\text{market value of debt}).\end{aligned} \tag{21.6}$$

This form of the relationship accounted for roughly 75% of the variation in the bonds' yield spreads.

The advantage of an equation such as this is that the coefficients can be easily interpreted. Since all yield spreads and values had been converted to logarithms, the effect is similar to that of using ratio scales on all axes of a diagram. This means that a 1% increase in a bond's earnings variability can be expected to bring about an increase of .307% in the bond's yield spread, other things being equal. Similarly, a 1% increase in a bond's time without default can be expected to cause a decrease of approximately .253% in the bond's yield spread, and so on. Each coefficient is an elasticity, indicating the percentage change in a bond's yield spread likely to accompany a 1% change in the associated measure. Since every measure was found to be related in the expected direction to the yield spread, the study provides substantial support for the notion that bonds with higher default risk and less marketability have higher yield spreads.

---

[15] Lawrence Fisher, "Determinants of Risk Premiums on Corporate Bonds," *Journal of Political Economy*, 67, no. 3 (June 1959): 217–37.

FINANCIAL RATIOS AS PREDICTORS OF DEFAULT

For years, security analysts have used accounting ratios to indicate the probability that a firm will fail to meet its financial obligations. Specific procedures have been developed to predict default with such ratios. Univariate analysis attempts to find the best single predictor for the purpose, while multivariate analysis searches for the best combination of two or more predictors.

Univariate Methods

Cash inflows can be viewed as contributions to the firm's cash balance, while cash outflows can be viewed as drains on this balance. When the balance falls below zero, default is likely to occur. This means that the probability of default will be greater for the firm when (1) the existing cash balance is smaller; (2) the expected net cash flow (measured before payments to creditors and stockholders) is smaller; and (3) the net cash flow is more variable.

In an examination of various measures used to assess these factors, it was found that the ratio of net cash flow (income before depreciation, depletion, and amortization charges) to total debt was particularly useful.[16] Panel (a) of Figure 21-7 shows the mean value of this ratio for a group of firms that defaulted on a promised payment and for a companion group that did not. As early as five years before default the two groups' ratios diverged, and the spread widened as the year of default approached.

This changing spread suggests that the probability of default may not be constant through time. Instead, warning signals may indicate an increase in the probability, which should, in turn, cause a fall in the market price of the firm's bonds along with a fall in the market price of its common stock. Panel (b) of Figure 21-7 shows that such signals are indeed recognized in the marketplace. The median market value of common stock in the firms that did not default went up, while that of the firms that subsequently defaulted went down as the date of default approached.

Multivariate Methods

Combinations of certain financial ratios and cash flow variables have been considered as possible predictors of default. In one of the first studies, statistical analysis indicated that the most accurate method of predicting default involved calculating a firm's default-risk rating, known as its *Z-score*, from some of its financial ratios as follows:

$$Z = 1.2X_1 + 1.4X_2 + 3.3X_3 + .6X_4 + .99X_5 \tag{21.7}$$

where the following ratios were calculated from information contained in the firm's most recent income statement and balance sheet:

X_1 = (current assets − current liabilities)/total assets

X_2 = retained earnings/total assets

[16]William H. Beaver, "Market Prices, Financial Ratios and the Prediction of Failure," *Journal of Accounting Research*, 6, no. 2 (Autumn 1968): 179–92.

FIGURE 21-7
Financial Ratios and Market Prices for Firms that Defaulted and Those That Did Not
Source: William H. Beavers, "Market Prices, Financial Ratios and the Prediction of Failure," *Journal of Accounting Research*, 6, No. 2 (Autumn 1968): 182, 185.

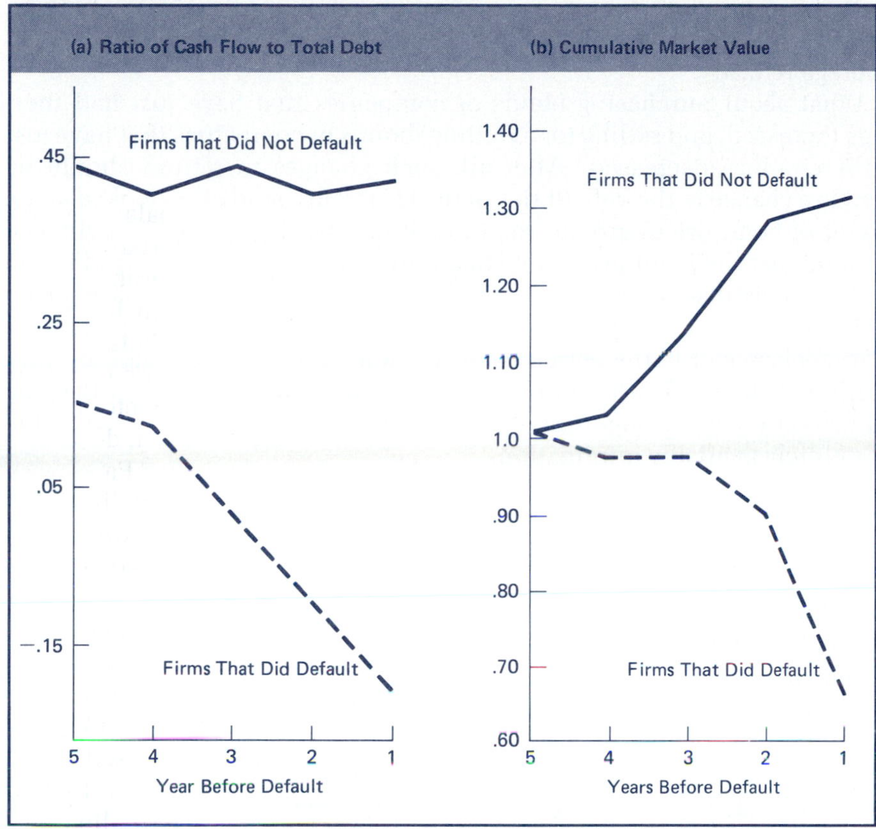

X_3 = earnings before interest and taxes/total assets

X_4 = market value of equity/book value of total debt

X_5 = sales/total assets.

Any firm with a Z-score below 1.8 was considered a likely candidate for default, and the lower the score, the greater the likelihood.[17]

Investment Implications

Does this mean that securities of firms whose cash-flow-to-total-debt ratio or Z-score had declined should have been avoided? Hardly. It should be remembered that the firms represented by the dashed lines in Figure 21-7 were chosen because they eventually defaulted. Had all firms with declining

[17]Edward I. Altman, "Financial Ratios, Discriminant Analysis and the Prediction of Corporate Bankruptcy," *Journal of Finance*, 23, no. 4 (September 1968): 589–609.

ratios been selected, corresponding decreases in their market price would undoubtedly have been observed, reflecting the increased probability of future default. However, only some of these firms would have ultimately defaulted, while the others would have recovered. Consequently, the gains on the firms that recovered might well have offset the losses on the firms that defaulted. In summary, the net result from purchasing a portfolio of stocks that had declining ratios or Z-scores is that the investor would have received an average return.

What about purchasing bonds of companies that have just had their ratings increased, and selling (or avoiding) bonds of companies that have just had their ratings decreased? After all, such changes in ratings should be related to a change in the default risk of the issuer. In a study that looked at the behavior of bond prices around the time of ratings changes, some evidence was found that the bond price adjustment to a rating change occurred in the period from eighteen to seven months *before* the rating change. Little or no evidence of a substantive price change was found either during the month of the rating change or in the period from six months before to six months after the rating change.[18] These findings are consistent with the notion that the bond market is semistrong-form efficient, since bond ratings are predictable from publicly available information.

SUMMARY

1. The capitalization of income method of valuation is a commonly used approach to identify mispriced bonds. It is based on the discounted value of the cash flows that the investor expects to receive from owning a bond.

2. Given the bond's current market price and promised cash flows, the investor can calculate the bond's yield-to-maturity and compare it to an appropriate discount rate.

3. Alternatively, the investor can use an appropriate discount rate to discount the bond's promised cash flows. The sum of the present value of these cash flows is compared to the bond's market price.

4. Six primary attributes are of significance in bond valuation: length of time to maturity; coupon rate; call provisions; tax status; marketability; and likelihood of default.

5. Time to maturity, call provisions, tax status, and likelihood of default tend to be directly related to promised yield-to-maturity. Coupon rate and marketability tend to be inversely related to promised yield-to-maturity.

6. Several corporations provide ratings of the credit-worthiness of thousands of corporate and municipal bonds. These ratings are often interpreted as an indication of the issuer's likelihood of default.

7. Bond ratings indicate relative levels of risk instead of absolute levels of risk.

8. A bond's promised yield-to-maturity can be decomposed into a default-free yield-to-maturity and a yield spread. Further, the yield spread can be decomposed into a risk premium and a default premium.

9. Various statistical models have been developed to predict the probability that a bond issuer will default. These models typically use financial ratios derived from the issuer's balance sheet and income statement.

[18]Mark I. Weinstein, "The Effect of a Rating Change Announcement on Bond Price," *Journal of Financial Economics*, 5, No. 3 (December 1977): 329–50. Another study that examined rating change announcements that were "noncontaminated by other news releases found a small but statistically significant upward movement in daily bond prices around upgrades; downgrades produced no significant movements." See John R.M. Hand, Robert W. Holthausen, and Richard W. Leftwich, "The Effect of Bond Rating Agency Announcements on Bond and Stock Prices," *Journal of Finance*, 47, no. 2 (June 1992): 733–52.

KEY TERMS

capitalization of income method of valuation
promised yield-to-maturity
net present value
yield structure
term structure
risk structure
yield spread
basis points
call provision
call price
call premium
yield-to-call
deep discount bonds
marketability
bond ratings
investment grade bonds
speculative grade bonds
junk bonds
fallen angels
expected yield-to-maturity
default premium
risk premium

QUESTIONS AND PROBLEMS

1. Bones Ely owns a $1,000-face-value bond with three years to maturity. The bond makes annual interest payments of $75, the first to be made one year from today. The bond is currently priced at $975.48. Given an appropriate discount rate of 10%, should Bones hold or sell the bond?
2. A broker has advised Jewel Ens to purchase a ten-year $10,000-face-value bond that makes 8% annual coupon payments. The appropriate discount rate is 9%. The first interest payment is due one year from today. If the bond currently sells for $8,560, should Jewel follow the broker's advice? (*Hint:* Remember how to calculate the present value of an annuity.)
3. Patsy Tebeau is considering investing in a bond currently selling for $8,785.07. The bond has four years to maturity, a $10,000 face value, and an 8% coupon rate. The next interest payment is due one year from today. The appropriate discount rate for investments of similar risk is 10%.
   (a) Calculate the intrinsic or fair value of the bond. Based on this calculation, should Patsy purchase the bond?
   (b) Calculate the yield-to-maturity of the bond. Based on this information, should Patsy purchase the bond?
4. Why is it convenient to use Treasury securities as a starting point for analyzing bond yields?
5. Bond A's yield-to-maturity is 9.80%. Bond B's yield-to-maturity is 8.73%. What is the difference in yields stated in basis points?
6. Bibb Falk recently purchased a bond with a $1,000 face value, a 10% coupon rate, and four years to maturity. The bond makes annual interest payments, the first to be received one year from today. Bibb paid $1,032.40 for the bond.
   (a) What is the bond's yield-to-maturity?
   (b) If the bond can be called two years from now at a price of $1,100, what is its yield-to-call?
7. Distinguish between yield-to-call and yield-to-maturity.
8. Burleigh Grimes purchased at par a bond with a face value of $1,000. The bond had five years to maturity and a 10% coupon rate. The bond was called two years later for a price of $1,200, after making its second annual interest payment. Burleigh then reinvested the proceeds in a bond selling at its face value of $1,000, with three years to maturity and a 7% coupon rate. What was Burleigh's actual yield-to-maturity over the five-year period?

9. What is the effect of a call provision on the price appreciation potential of a bond?
10. What is the purpose of bond ratings? Given the importance attached to bond ratings by bond investors, why don't common stock investors focus on quality ratings of entire companies in making their investment decisions?
11. According to Lave Cross, "Agency ratings indicate relative levels of risk instead of absolute levels of risk." Explain the meaning of Lave's statement.
12. Based on the default premium model presented in the text, what is the fair-value default premium for a bond with an expected yield-to-maturity of 8.5%, a 10% annual default probability, and an expected loss as a percent of market value of 60%?
13. Corporate default appears to be an event specific to an individual company. Yet despite the apparent diversifiable nature of corporate default (meaning that relatively few bonds would default in a well-diversified portfolio), the bond market systematically adds default premiums when valuing corporate bonds. Explain why.
14. Junk bonds are often viewed by investors as having financial characteristics much more akin to common stocks than to high-grade corporate bonds. Why?
15. Examining equation (21.6), explain the rationale underlying the observed relationship (positive or negative) between each of the variables and the yield spread.
16. How would you expect yield spreads to respond to the following macroeconomic events: recession, high inflation, tax cuts, stock market decline, improved trade balance? Explain the reasoning behind each of your answers.
17. Urban Shocker has noted that the spread between the yield-to-maturity on BBB-rated bonds and that on AAA-rated bonds has recently widened considerably. Explain to Urban what this might indicate.

CFA Exam Question

18. Barney Gray, CFA, is Director of Fixed-Income Securities at Piedmont Security Advisors. In a recent meeting, one of his major endowment clients suggested investing in corporate bonds yielding 9%, rather than U.S. government bonds yielding 8%. Two bond issues—one U.S. Treasury and one corporate—were compared to illustrate the point.

U.S. Treasury bond	8% due 6/15/2010	Priced at 100
AJAX Manufacturing	9.5% due 6/15/2015	Priced at 105
Rated AAA		
Callable @ 107.5 on 6/15/1995		

Gray wants to prepare a response based upon his expectation that long-term U.S. Treasury interest rates will fall sharply (at least 100 basis points) over the next three months.

Evaluate the return expectations for each bond under this scenario, and support an evaluation of which bond would be the superior performer. Discuss the price-yield measures that affect your conclusion.

REFERENCES

1. For a detailed discussion of the attributes of bonds that are important in their pricing, see:

   James C. Van Horne, *Financial Market Rates and Flows* (Englewood Cliffs, N.J.: Prentice Hall 1990).

   Karlyn Mitchell, "The Call, Sinking Fund, and Term-To-Maturity Features of Corporate Bonds: An Empirical Investigation," *Journal of Financial and Quantitative Analysis,* 26, no. 2 (June 1991): 201–22.

2. Some of the many studies that have investigated the relationship between historical measures of a firm's performance and its bond ratings are:

   Thomas F. Pogue and Robert M. Soldofsky, "What's in a Bond Rating?" *Journal of Financial and Quantitative Analysis,* 4, no. 2 (June 1969): 201–28;

   R. R. West, "An Alternate Approach to Predicting Corporate Bond Ratings," *Journal of Accounting Research,* 8, no. 1 (Spring 1970): 118–25;

   George E. Pinches and Kent A. Mingo, "A Multivariate Analysis of Industrial Bond Ratings," *Journal of Finance,* 30, no. 1 (March 1975): 201–6;

   Robert S. Kaplan and Gabriel Urwitz, "Statistical Models of Bond Ratings: A Methodological Inquiry," *Journal of Business,* 52, no. 2 (April 1979): 231–61;

   Ahmed Belkaoui, *Industrial Bonds and the Rating Process* (Westport, Conn.: Quorum Books, 1983).

3. Changes in bond ratings have been studied in:

   Steven Katz, "The Price Adjustment Process of Bonds to Rating Reclassifications: A Test of Bond Market Efficiency," *Journal of Finance,* 29, no. 2 (May 1974): 551–59;

   Paul Grier and Steven Katz, "The Differential Effects of Bond Rating Changes Among Industrial and Public Utility Bonds by Maturity," *Journal of Business,* 49, no. 2 (April 1976): 226–39;

   Mark I. Weinstein, "The Effect of a Rating Change Announcement on Bond Price," *Journal of Financial Economics,* 5, no. 3 (December 1977): 329–50;

   Douglas J. Lucas and John G. Lonski, "Changes in Corporate Credit Quality 1970–1990," *Journal of Fixed Income,* 1, no. 4 (March 1992): 7–14;

   Edward I. Altman and Duen Li Kao, "Rating Drift in High-Yield Bonds," *Journal of Fixed Income,* 1, no. 4 (March 1992): 15–20;

   Edward I. Altman, "The Implications of Bond Ratings Drift," *Financial Analysts Journal,* 48, no. 3 (May/June 1992): 64–75;

   John R. M. Hand, Robert W. Holthausen, and Richard W. Leftwich, "The Effect of Bond Rating Agency Announcements on Bond and Stock Prices," *Journal of Finance,* 47, no. 2 (June 1992): 733–52.

4. Municipal bond ratings are discussed in:

   John E. Petersen, *The Rating Game* (New York: The Twentieth Century Fund, 1974);

Robert W. Ingram, Leroy D. Brooks, and Ronald M. Copeland, "The Information Content of Municipal Bond Rating Changes: A Note," *Journal of Finance*, 38, no. 3 (June 1983): 997–1003;

George Foster, *Financial Statement Analysis* (Englewood Cliffs, N.J.: Prentice Hall, 1986), Chapter 14.

5. Default premiums and risks are discussed in:

Gordon Pye, "Gauging the Default Premium," *Financial Analysts Journal*, 30, no. 1 (January/February 1974): 49–52;

W. Braddock Hickman, *Corporate Bond Quality and Investor Experience* (Princeton, N.J.: Princeton University Press, 1958);

Harold G. Fraine and Robert H. Mills, "The Effect of Defaults and Credit Deterioration on Yields of Corporate Bonds," *Journal of Finance*, 16, no. 3 (September 1961): 423–34;

Thomas R. Atkinson and Elizabeth T. Simpson, *Trends in Corporate Bond Quality* (New York: Columbia University Press, 1967);

Ricardo J. Rodriguez, "Default Risk, Yield Spreads, and Time to Maturity," *Journal of Financial and Quantitative Analysis*, 23, no. 1 (March 1988): 111–17;

Edward I. Altman, "Measuring Corporate Bond Mortality and Performance," *Journal of Finance*, 44, no. 4 (September 1989): 909–22;

Paul Asquith, David W. Mullins, Jr., and Eric D. Wolff, "Original Issue High Yield Bonds; Aging Analysis of Defaults, Exchanges, and Calls," *Journal of Finance*, 44, no. 4 (September 1989): 923–52;

Marshall E. Blume and Donald B. Keim, "Realized Returns and Defaults on Low-Grade Bonds: The Cohort of 1977 and 1978," *Financial Analysts Journal*, 47, no. 2 (March/April 1991): 63–72;

Marshall E. Blume, Donald B. Keim, and Sandeep A. Patel, "Returns and Volatility of Low-Grade Bonds, 1977–1989," *Journal of Finance*, 46, no. 1 (March 1991): 49–74;

Bradford Cornell and Kevin Greene, "The Investment Performance of Low-Grade Bond Funds," *Journal of Finance*, 46, no. 1 (March 1991): 29–48;

Jerome S. Fons and Andrew E. Kimball, "Corporate Bond Defaults and Default Rates 1970–1990," *Journal of Fixed Income*, 1, no. 1 (June 1991): 36–47;

Marshall E. Blume and Donald B. Keim, "The Risk and Return of Low-Grade Bonds: An Update," *Financial Analysts Journal*, 47, no. 5 (September/October 1991): 85–89;

Edward I. Altman, "Defaults and Returns on High-Yield Bonds Through the First Half of 1991," *Financial Analysts Journal*, 47, no. 6 (November/December 1991): 67–77;

Bradford Cornell, "Liquidity and the Pricing of Low-Grade Bonds," *Financial Analysts Journal*, 48, no. 1 (January/February 1992): 63–67, 74.

6. The classic study on yield spreads is:

Lawrence Fisher, "Determinants of Risk Premiums on Corporate Bonds," *Journal of Political Economy*, 67, no. 3 (June 1959): 217–37.

7. Yield spreads for municipal bonds is discussed in:

   George Foster, *Financial Statement Analysis* (Englewood Cliffs, N.J.: Prentice Hall, 1986), pp. 510–11.

8. Predicting bankruptcy has been a subject of much research; see the following papers and their citations:

   William H. Beaver, "Financial Ratios as Predictors of Failure," *Empirical Research in Accounting: Selected Studies, 1966,* supplement to *Journal of Accounting Research*: 71–111;

   William H. Beaver, "Market Prices, Financial Ratios and the Prediction of Failure," *Journal of Accounting Research,* 6, no. 2 (Autumn 1968): 179–92;

   Edward I. Altman, "Financial Ratios, Discriminant Analysis and the Prediction of Corporate Bankruptcy," *Journal of Finance,* 23, no. 4 (September 1968): 589–609;

   Edward B. Deakin, "A Discriminant Analysis of Predictors of Business Failure," *Journal of Accounting Research,* 10, no. 1 (Spring 1972): 167–79;

   R. Charles Moyer, "Forecasting Financial Failure: A Re-examination," *Financial Management,* 6, no. 1 (Spring 1977): 11–17;

   Edward I. Altman, Robert G. Haldeman, and P. Narayanan, "Zeta Analysis: A New Model to Identify Bankruptcy Risk of Corporations," *Journal of Banking and Finance,* 1, no. 1 (June 1977): 29–54;

   James A. Ohlson, "Financial Ratios and the Probabilistic Prediction of Bankruptcy," *Journal of Accounting Research,* 18, no. 1 (Spring 1980): 109–31;

   Joseph Aharony, Charles P. Jones, and Itzhak Swary, "An Analysis of Risk and Return Characteristics of Corporate Bankruptcy Using Capital Market Data," *Journal of Finance,* 35, no. 4 (September 1980): 1001–16;

   Ismael G. Dambolena and Sarkis J. Khoury, "Ratio Stability and Corporate Failure," *Journal of Finance,* 35, no. 4 (September 1980): 1017–26;

   Edward I. Altman, "The Success of Business Failure Prediction Models: An International Survey," *Journal of Banking and Finance,* 8, no. 2 (June 1984): 171–98.

   Cornelius J. Casey and Norman J. Bartczak, "Cash Flow—It's Not the Bottom Line," *Harvard Business Review,* 62, no. 4 (July–August 1984): 61–66;

   Cornelius Casey and Norman Bartczak, "Using Operating Cash Flow Data to Predict Financial Distress: Some Extensions," *Journal of Accounting Research,* 23, no. 1 (Spring 1985): 384–401;

   James A. Gentry, Paul Newbold, and David T. Whitford, "Classifying Bankrupt Firms with Funds Flow Components," *Journal of Accounting Research,* 23, no. 1 (Spring 1985): 146–60;

   James A. Gentry, Paul Newbold, and David T. Whitford, "Predicting Bankruptcy: If Cash Flow's Not the Bottom Line, What Is?" *Financial Analysts Journal,* 41, no. 5 (September/October 1985): 47–56;

   Maggie Queen and Richard Roll, "Firm Mortality: Using Market Indicators to Predict Survival," *Financial Analysts Journal,* 43, no. 3 (May/June 1987): 9–26;

Ismael G. Dambolena and Joel M. Shulman, "A Primary Rule for Detecting Bankruptcy: Watch the Cash," *Financial Analysts Journal,* 44, no. 5 (September/October 1988): 74–78;

James M. Gahlon and Robert L. Vigeland, "Early Warning Signs of Bankruptcy Using Cash Flow Analysis," *Journal of Commercial Bank Lending,* 71, no. 4 (December 1988): 4–15;

Abdul Aziz and Gerald H. Lawson, "Cash Flow Reporting and Financial Distress Models: Testing of Hypothesis," *Financial Management,* 18, no. 1 (Spring 1989): 55–63.

22

Bond Portfolio Management

The methods currently in use for managing bond portfolios can be divided into two general categories—passive and active. Methods in the passive category rest on the basic assumption that bond markets are semistrong-form efficient. That is, current bond prices are viewed as accurately reflecting all publicly available information. Thus, bonds are felt to be priced fairly in the marketplace, providing a return that is commensurate with the risk involved. In addition to believing that individual bonds are not mispriced, passive investors also believe that attempting to predict interest rates is, in general, futile. In summary, passive management rests on the belief that attempts at both security selection (that is, identifying mispriced bonds) and market timing (for example, buying long-term bonds when interest rates are predicted to fall and replacing them with short-term bonds when interest rates are predicted to rise) will be unsuccessful in providing the investor with above-average returns.

Active methods of bond portfolio management are based on the assumption that the bond market is not so efficient, thereby giving some investors the opportunity to earn above-average returns. That is, active management is based on the ability of the portfolio manager either to identify mispriced bonds or to "time" the bond market by accurately predicting interest rates.

This chapter will discuss these two general approaches to bond portfolio management. It begins by reviewing some of the findings regarding the efficiency of the bond market.

BOND MARKET EFFICIENCY

In assessing the efficiency of the bond market, only a few of the major studies will be mentioned. The impression obtained from reading them is that bond markets appear to be highly, but not perfectly, semistrong-form efficient. That is, bond prices tend to reflect almost all publicly available information. Not surprisingly, this impression is similar to the one that is obtained from studies of the efficiency of stock markets.

Price Behavior of Treasury Bills

An early study of bond market efficiency focused on the price behavior of Treasury bills. In particular, the prices of Treasury bills were analyzed on a weekly basis from October 1946 through December 1964, a total of 796 weeks. The study found that knowledge of how Treasury bill prices changed in the past was of little use in trying to predict how they would change in the future. Consequently, the results from this study are consistent with the notion that the market for Treasury bills is weak-form efficient.[1]

Experts' Predictions of Interest Rates

Bond market efficiency has also been studied by examining the accuracy of interest rate predictions that have been made by experts. These people use a wide range of techniques and a number of different sources of information. Since it is reasonable to assume that their information is publicly available, such studies can be viewed as tests of semistrong-form efficiency.

One way these tests have been conducted involves the building of statistical models that are based on what the experts have said in regard to how interest rates should be predicted. Once these models have been constructed, their predictive accuracy can be evaluated. In one study, six different models were constructed and their one-month-ahead predictions were tested over the two-year period of 1973 to 1974. Consistent with the notion of efficient markets, it was found that a simple model of "no change" was more accurate in predicting interest rates than any of the six statistical models.[2]

---

[1]For details, see Richard Roll, *The Behavior of Interest Rates* (New York: Basic Books, Inc., 1970). Interestingly, this study also produced evidence rejecting the unbiased expectations theory of the term structure of interest rates (see Chapter 20 for a discussion of this theory). Surprisingly, U.S. Treasury bonds appear to have been mispriced in May and June of 1986; see Bradford Cornell and Alan C. Shapiro, "The Mispricing of U.S. Treasury Bonds: A Case Study," *Review of Financial Studies*, 2, no. 3 (1989): 297–310.

[2]J. Walter Elliott and Jerome R. Baier, "Econometric Models and Current Interest Rates: How Well Do They Predict Future Rates?" *Journal of Finance*, 34, no. 4 (September 1979): 975–86. It should be noted that the models used by major economic forecasting firms tend to have similar amounts of accuracy. See Stephen K. McNees, "Forecasting Accuracy of Alternative Techniques: A Comparison of U.S. Macroeconomic Forecasts," *Journal of Business & Economic Statistics*, 4, no. 1 (January 1986): 5–15, particularly Table 6, where ninety-day Treasury bill rate forecasts are evaluated.

Another way these tests have been conducted involves comparing a set of explicit predictions with what subsequently actually occurred. One source of such predictions is the quarterly survey of interest rate expectations that appears in the *Goldsmith-Nagan Bond and Money Market Newsletter*, published by Goldsmith-Nagan, Inc. Specifically, this survey reports the predictions made by a number (roughly fifty) of "money market professionals" regarding three-month-ahead and six-month-ahead levels of ten different interest rates. In one study, the predictions made from September 1969 through December 1972 (that is, fourteen sets of quarterly predictions) were compared with those of a "no-change" model—that is, a model that forecasts no change from the current level of interest rates.[3] Interestingly, the professionals seemed to forecast better than the "no-change" model for short-term interest rates (such as forecasting what the three-month Treasury bill rate will be three months in the future), but did worse than the no-change model for longer-term interest rates (such as forecasting what the intermediate-term Treasury note rate will be three months in the future).

A subsequent study examined the Goldsmith-Nagan predictions of three-month Treasury bill rates six months in the future during the time period from March 1970 through September 1979 (thirty-nine predictions).[4] These predictions were compared with those of three "simple" models, the first one being the no-change model. The second "simple" model was based on the liquidity preference theory of the term structure of interest rates (discussed in Chapter 20). According to this theory, the forward rate implicit in current market rates should be equal to the expected future interest rate plus a liquidity premium. Thus, a forecast of the expected future rate can be obtained by subtracting an estimate of the liquidity premium from the forward rate. The third "simple" model was what statisticians refer to as an autoregressive model. Basically, a forecast of the future T-bill rate was formed from the current T-bill rate as well as what the T-bill rate was one, two, three, and six quarters ago. The study found that the professionals were more accurate than both the no-change model and the liquidity premium model, but were less accurate than the autoregressive model.

Another study evaluated the six-month-ahead predictions of three-month Treasury bill rates that were made by nine economists and reported semiannually in *The Wall Street Journal*. Evaluating the forecasts published from December 1981 through June 1986, it was found that the no-change model was more accurate.[5]

In summary, it appears from this evidence that the no-change model sometimes provides the most accurate forecasts of future interest rates while at other times the experts are more accurate. On balance, a reasonable interpretation of these results is that the bond market is nearly semistrong-form efficient. While the bond market may not be perfectly efficient, the

---

[3]Michael J. Prell, "How Well Do the Experts Forecast Interest Rates?" Federal Reserve Bank of Kansas City *Monthly Review*, September–October 1973: 3–13.

[4]Adrian W. Throop, "Interest Rate Forecast and Market Efficiency," Federal Reserve Bank of San Francisco *Economic Review*, Spring 1981: 29–43. This article contains a useful reference list of other studies concerning the prediction of interest rates.

[5]Forecasts implicit in the futures market (to be discussed in Chapter 25) for Treasury bills were also found to be more accurate than those of the economists, but less accurate than those of the no-change model over this time period. For a longer time period, the futures market and no-change model forecasts were of comparable accuracy. See Michael T. Belognia, "Predicting Interest Rates: A Comparison of Professional and Market-Based Forecasts," Federal Reserve Bank of St. Louis *Review*, 69, no. 3 (March 1987): 9–15.

evidence clearly suggests that it is hard to consistently forecast interest rates with greater accuracy than a no-change model.[6]

Price Reaction to Bond Rating Changes

A different type of test of market efficiency concerned the reaction of bond prices to rating changes. If ratings are based on public information, then any rating change would follow the release of such information. This suggests that in a semistrong-form efficient market, a bond's price would react to the release of the public information rather than the subsequent announcement of the rating change. Thus, an announcement of a rating change should not trigger a subsequent adjustment in the associated bond's price.

In a study that examined 100 rating changes that took place during the period of 1962 through 1974, no significant changes in bond prices were detected in the period from six months before through six months after the announcement of the change. However, a significant change was observed in the period from eighteen months through seven months before the announcement. Specifically, rating increases were preceded by price increases, and rating decreases were preceded by price decreases.[7]

Money Supply Announcements

Every week, generally on Thursday, the Federal Reserve Board announces the current size of the money supply in the economy. Now, it is known that interest rates are related to, among other things, the availability of credit and that the money supply affects this availability. This means that if the money supply figures are surprisingly high or low, then the announcement should trigger adjustments in the levels of various interest rates.[8] Furthermore, such adjustments should take place rapidly in a semistrong-form efficient market.

---

[6]The reported accuracy of macroeconomic forecasters in regard to Treasury bill rates (see the Early Quarter results for a two-quarter horizon in Table 6 of McNees, "Forecast Accuracy") can be compared to the reported accuracy of the no-change model (see Table 1 of Belognia, "Predicting Interest Rates"). While such a comparison should be done with caution, it does suggest that the no-change model is of similar, and in some cases superior, accuracy. It appears that the record of the experts in predicting the level of the stock market is also of little value; see Werner F. De Bondt, "What Do Economists Know About the Stock Market?" *Journal of Portfolio Management*, 17, no. 2 (Winter 1991): 84–91.

[7]See Mark I. Weinstein, "The Effect of a Rating Change Announcement on Bond Price," *Journal of Financial Economics*, 5, no. 3 (December 1977): 329–50. A study of the prices of the common stocks associated with bonds that had rating changes reported similar results—stock prices tended to change several months prior to the announcement dates of the rating changes; see George E. Pinches and J. Clay Singleton, "The Adjustment of Stock Prices to Bond Rating Changes," *Journal of Finance*, 33, no. 1 (March 1978): 29–44.

Another study that examined rating change announcements that were "noncontaminated" by other news releases found a small but statistically significant upward movement in daily bond prices around upgrades; downgrades produced no significant movements. Oddly, these findings were reversed when stock prices were examined in that no significant movements were found around upgrades but marginally significant downward movements were observed around downgrades. See John R.M. Hand, Robert W. Holthausen, and Richard W. Leftwich, "The Effect of Bond Rating Agency Announcements on Bond and Stock Prices," *Journal of Finance*, 47, no. 2 (June 1992): 733–52.

[8]For an explanation and empirical investigation of this adjustment process, see Richard G. Sheehan, "Weekly Money Announcements: New Information and Its Effects," Federal Reserve Bank of St. Louis *Review*, 67, no. 7 (August/September 1985): 25–34, and Anthony M. Santomero, "Money Supply Announcements: A Retrospective," *Journal of Economics and Business*, 43, no. 1 (February 1991): 1–23.

Past studies indicate that such adjustments are indeed rapid, generally taking place within a day after the announcement.[9]

Summary

In summary, the evidence on the efficiency of the bond market is consistent with the notion that it is highly, but not perfectly, semistrong-form efficient.[10] Statistical tests of past prices of Treasury bills suggest that it is efficient. It appears that corporate bonds reflect the information leading to a rating change in a timely fashion and that interest rates change rapidly when there is a surprise in the announced size of the money supply, observations that are also consistent with the notion of efficiency.

However, there is some evidence that suggests that certain professionals are occasionally able to forecast interest rates in an accurate manner. With this in mind, it is not surprising that some bond managers have opted to follow a passive approach to investing, while others have decided to be more active in their approach. These two approaches will be presented next, beginning with a discussion of some bond pricing theorems. In turn, these theorems will be related to a concept known as duration, which is the basis for one method of passively managing a bond portfolio.

BOND PRICING THEOREMS

Bond pricing theorems deal with how bond prices move in response to changes in their yields-to-maturity. Before presenting the theorems, a brief review of some terms associated with bonds will be given.

The typical bond is characterized by a promise to pay the investor two types of cash flows. The first involves the payment of a fixed dollar amount periodically (usually every six months), with the last payment being on a stated date. The second type of cash flow involves the payment of a lump sum on this stated date. The periodic payments are known as **coupon payments,** and the lump-sum payment is known as the bond's principal (or par value or face value). A bond's **coupon rate** is calculated by taking the dollar amount of the coupon payments a bondholder would receive over the course of a year, and dividing this total by the par value of the bond. Finally, the amount of time left until the last promised payment is made is known as the bond's **term-to-maturity,** while the discount rate that makes the present value of all the cash flows equal to the market price of the bond is known as the bond's **yield-to-maturity** (or, simply, yield).

coupon payments

coupon rate

term-to-maturity

yield-to-maturity

Note that if a bond has a market price that is equal to its par value, then its yield-to-maturity will be equal to its coupon rate. However, if the market price is less than par value (a situation where the bond is said to be selling at a discount), then the bond will have a yield-to-maturity that is greater than the coupon rate. Conversely, if the market price is greater than par value (a

[9]See, for example, Thomas Urich and Paul Wachtel, "Market Response to Weekly Money Supply Announcements in the 1970s," *Journal of Finance,* 36, no. 5 (December 1981): 1063–72, and "The Effects of Inflation and Money Supply Announcements on Interest Rates," *Journal of Finance,* 39, no. 4 (September 1984): 1177–88; and Bradford Cornell, "Money Supply Announcements and Interest Rates: Another View," *Journal of Business,* 56, no. 1 (January 1983): 1–23.

[10]Like the stock market, the bond market has some anomalies. However, they are fewer in number and less pronounced. These anomalies are briefly discussed in the appendix.

situation where the bond is said to be selling at a premium), then the bond will have a yield-to-maturity that is less than the coupon rate.

With this in mind, five theorems that deal with bond pricing have been derived.[11] For ease of exposition, it is assumed that there is one coupon payment per year (that is, coupon payments are made every twelve months). The theorems are as follows:

1. *If a bond's market price increases, then its yield must decrease; conversely, if a bond's market price decreases, then its yield must increase.*

   As an example, consider bond A that has a life of five years, a par value of $1,000, and pays coupons annually of $80. Its yield is 8%, since it is currently selling for $1,000. However, if its price increases to $1,100, then its yield will fall to 5.76%. Conversely, if its price falls to $900, then its yield will rise to 10.68%.

2. *If a bond's yield does not change over its life, then the size of its discount or premium will decrease as its life gets shorter.*

   This can be seen by examining Figure 22-1. Note how the price of a bond that is selling at either a premium or discount today will converge overtime to its par value. Ultimately the premium or discount will completely disappear at the maturity date.

   As an example, consider bond B that has a life of five years, a par value of $1,000, and pays coupons annually of $60. Its current market price is $883.31, indicating that it has a yield of 9%. After one year, if it still has a yield of 9%, it will be selling for $902.81. Thus, its discount has

[11]Burton G. Malkiel, "Expectations, Bond Prices, and the Term Structure of Interest Rates," *Quarterly Journal of Economics*, 76, no. 2 (May 1962): 197–218.

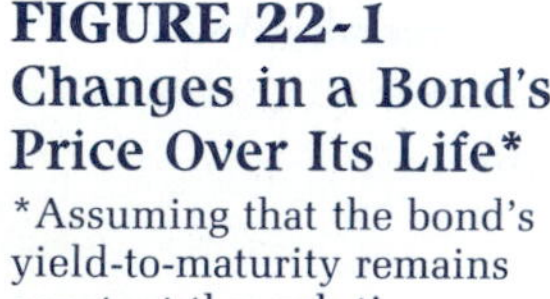

FIGURE 22-1
Changes in a Bond's Price Over Its Life*
*Assuming that the bond's yield-to-maturity remains constant through time.

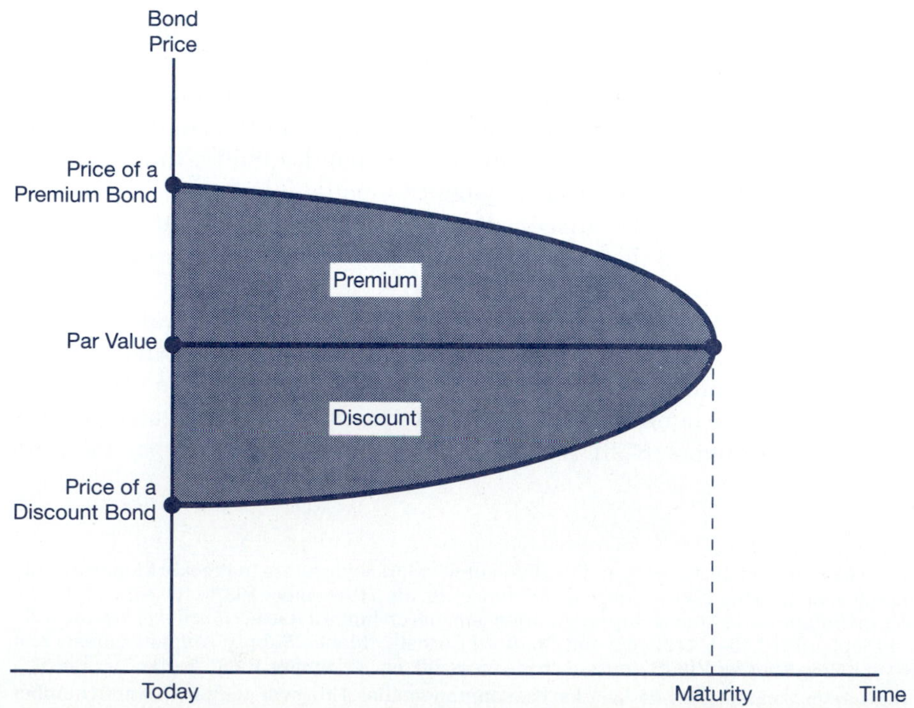

decreased from \$1,000 − \$883.31 = \$116.69 to \$1,000 − \$902.81 = \$97.19, for a change of \$116.69 − \$97.19 = \$19.50.

An equivalent interpretation of this theorem is that if two bonds have the same coupon rate, par value, and yield, then the one with the shorter life will sell for a smaller discount or premium. Consider two bonds, one with a life of five years and the other with a life of four years. Both bonds have a par value of \$1,000, pay annual coupons of \$60, and yield 9%. In this stiuation, the one with a five-year life has a discount of \$116.69, while the one with a four-year life has a smaller discount of \$97.19.

3. *If a bond's yield does not change over its life, then the size of its discount or premium will decrease at an increasing rate as its life gets shorter.*

   Figure 22-1 can also be used to illustrate this theorem. Note how the size of the premium or discount does not change much at first when time passes from today to tomorrow. In contrast, note how the size changes much more notably when time passes just before the maturity date.

   As an example, consider bond B again. After two years, if it still has a yield of 9%, it will be selling for \$924.06. Thus, its discount has decreased to \$1,000 − \$924.06 = \$75.94. Now, the amount of the change in the discount from five years to four years was \$116.90 − \$97.19 = \$19.50, for a percentage change from par of 1.950%. However, the amount of the change from four years to three years is larger, going from \$97.19 to \$75.94 for a dollar change of \$21.25 and a percentage change from par of 2.125%.

4. *A decrease in a bond's yield will raise the bond's price by an amount that is greater in size than the corresponding fall in the bond's price that would occur if there were an equal-sized increase in the bond's yield.*

   As an example, consider bond C that has a life of five years and a coupon rate of 7%. Since it is currently selling at its par value of \$1,000, its yield is 7%. If its yield rises by 1% to 8%, then it will be selling for \$960.07, a change of \$39.93. Alternatively, if its yield falls by 1% to 6%, then it will be selling for \$1,042.12, a change of \$42.12 that is of greater magnitude than the \$39.93 associated with the 1% rise in the bond's yield.

5. *The percentage change in a bond's price owing to a change in its yield will be smaller if its coupon rate is higher.* (Note: This theorem does not apply to bonds with a life of one year or to bonds that have no maturity date, known as consols or perpetuities.)

   As an example, compare bond D with bond C. Bond D has a coupon rate of 9%, which is 2% larger than C's. However, bond D has the same life (five years) and yield (7%) as C. Thus, D's current market price is \$1,082.00. Now, if the yield on both C and D increase to 8%, then their prices will be \$960.07 and \$1,039.93, respectively. This represents a decrease in the price of C equal to \$1,000 − \$960.07 = \$39.93, or 3.993% (note: 3.993% = \$39.93/\$1,000). For D, the decrease in price is equal to \$1,082 − \$1,039.93 = \$42.07, or 3.889% (note: 3.889% = \$42.07/\$1,082). Since D had the higher coupon rate, it has the smaller percentage change in price.

It is important for a bond analyst to thoroughly understand these properties of bond prices, since they are valuable in forecasting how bond prices will respond to changes in interest rates. In addition, there is another concept called duration that is valuable in understanding how the prices of bonds change in response to a change in interest rates. This concept forms the basis for one method of passively managing a bond portfolio, and will be discussed shortly.

CONVEXITY

convexity

The first and fourth bond pricing theorems have led to the concept in bond valuation known as **convexity.** Consider what happens to the price of a bond if its yield increases or decreases. According to Theorem 1, bond prices and yields are inversely related. However, this relationship is not linear, according to Theorem 4. The size of the rise in a bond's price associated with a given decrease in its yield is greater than the drop in the bond's price for a similar-sized increase in the bond's yield.

This can be seen by examining Figure 22-2. The current yield-to-maturity and price for the bond are denoted by P and y, respectively. Consider what would happen to the bond's price if the yield increased or decreased by a fixed amount (for example, 1%), denoted y^+ and y^-. The associated bond prices are denoted, respectively, P^- and P^+.

Two observations can be made by examining this figure. First, an increase in the yield to y^+ is associated with a drop in the bond's price to P^- and a decrease in the yield to y^- is associated with a rise in the bond's price to P^+. This is in accord with the first bond theorem (hence the symbols "+" and "−" are paired inversely so that, for example, y^+ is associated with P^-). Second, note that the size of the rise in the bond's price ($P^+ - P$) is greater than the size of the drop in the bond's price ($P - P^-$). This is in accord with the fourth bond theorem.

The curved line in the figure that shows the relationship between bond prices and yields is convex, since it opens upward. Accordingly, the relationship is frequently referred to as convexity. While this relationship is true for standard types of bonds, it should be mentioned that the degree of curvature

FIGURE 22-2
Bond Convexity

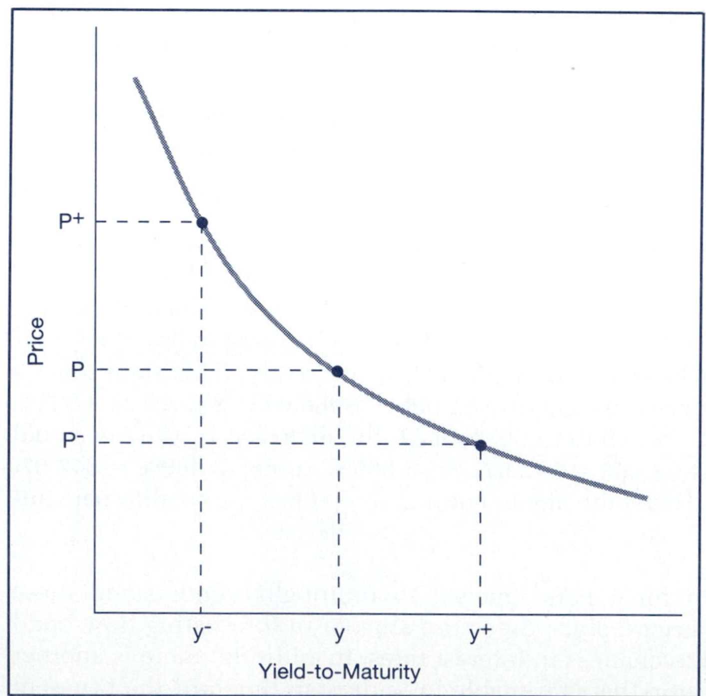

(or convexity) is not the same for all bonds. Instead, it depends on, among other things, the size of the coupon payments, the life of the bond, and its current market price.

DURATION

duration

Duration is a measure of the "average maturity" of the stream of payments associated with a bond. More specifically, it is a weighted average of the lengths of time until the remaining payments are made. Consider, for example, a bond with annual coupon payments of $80, a remaining life of three years, and a par value of $1,000. Since it has a current market price of $950.25, it has a yield-to-maturity of 10.00%. As shown in Table 22-1, its duration is 2.78 years. Note that this is calculated by taking the present value of each cash flow, multiplying each one by the respective amount of time until it is received, summing the resulting figures up, and then dividing this sum ($2,639.17) by the market price of the bond ($950.25).

The Formula

Specifically, the formula for a bond's duration (D) is:

$$D = \frac{\sum_{t=1}^{T} \text{PV}(C_t) \times t}{P_0} \tag{22.1}$$

where $\text{PV}(C_t)$ denotes the present value of the cash flow to be received at time t, calculated using a discount rate equal to the bond's yield-to-maturity; P_0 denotes the current market price of the bond; and T denotes the bond's remaining life.[12]

Why is duration thought of as the "average maturity of the stream of payments associated with a bond"? This can be seen by realizing that the current market price of the bond, P_0, is equal to the sum of the present values

[12]There are other methods of calculating a bond's duration. For example, instead of using the bond's yield to calculate $\text{PV}(C_t)$, the appropriate current spot rates could be used.

TABLE 22-1
Calculation of Duration

TIME UNTIL RECEIPT OF CASH FLOW	AMOUNT OF CASH FLOW	PRESENT VALUE FACTOR	PRESENT VALUE OF CASH FLOW	PRESENT VALUE OF CASH FLOW × TIME
1	$ 80	.9091	$ 72.73	$ 72.73
2	80	.8264	66.12	132.23
3	1,080	.7513	811.40	2,434.21
			$950.25	$2,639.17

$$\text{Duration} = \frac{\$2{,}639.17}{\$950.25} = 2.78 \text{ years}$$

of the cash flows, $PV(C_t)$, where the discount rate is the bond's yield-to-maturity:

$$P_0 = \sum_{t=1}^{T} PV(C_t). \tag{22.2}$$

Thus, there is an equivalent method for calculating a bond's duration that can be seen by rewriting equation (22.1) in a slightly different manner:

$$D = \sum_{t=1}^{T} \left[\frac{PV(C_t)}{P_0} \times t \right]. \tag{22.3}$$

First, the present value of each cash flow $[PV(C_t)]$ is expressed as a proportion of the market price (P_0). Second, these proportions are multiplied by the respective amount of time until the cash flows are received. Third, these figures are summed up, with the sum being equal to the bond's duration.

In the example shown in Table 22-1, note that .07653 = \$72.73/\$950.25 of the bond's market price is to be received in one year. Similarly, .06958 = \$66.12/\$950.25 is to be received in two years, and .85388 = \$811.40/\$950.25 is to be received in three years. Note how these proportions sum to one, which means that they can be interpreted as weights in calculating a weighted average. Thus, to calculate the average maturity of the payments associated with a bond, each weight needs to be multiplied by the respective amount of time until the corresponding cash flow is to be received, and then the products need to be summed up: (1 × .07653) + (2 × .06958) + (3 × .85388) = 2.78 years.

Note how a zero-coupon bond will have a duration equal to its remaining life, T, since there is only one cash flow associated with such a bond. That is, since $P_0 = PV(C_T)$ for such bonds, equation (22.3) reduces to:

$$\begin{aligned} D &= \frac{PV(C_T)}{P_0} \times T \\ &= 1 \times T \\ &= T. \end{aligned}$$

For any coupon-bearing bond, its duration will always be less than the amount of time to its maturity date, T. Again, examination of equation (22.3) indicates why this is so. Since the largest value that t can have is T, and each value of t is multiplied by a weight equal to $PV(C_t)/P_0$, it follows that D must be less than T.

Relationship to Bond Price Changes

One implication of Theorem 5 is that bonds having the same maturity date but different coupon sizes may react to a given change in interest rates in a dissimilar manner. That is, the prices of these bonds may adjust by notably different amounts when there is a given change in interest rates. However, bonds with the same *duration* will react quite similarly. Specifically, the percentage change in a bond's price is related to its duration in the following fashion:

$$\text{percentage change in price} \approx -D \times \text{percentage change in (one plus the bond's yield)} \quad (22.4a)$$

where the symbol ≈ means "is approximately equal to." This formula implies that when the yields of two bonds having the same duration change by the same percentage, then the prices of the two bonds will change by approximately equal percentages. Equivalently, equation (22.4a) is written as:

$$\frac{\Delta P}{P} \approx -D\left[\frac{\Delta y}{1+y}\right] \quad (22.4b)$$

where ΔP denotes the change in the bond's price, P is the bond's initial price, Δy is the change in the bond's yield-to-maturity, and y is the bond's initial yield-to-maturity.

As an example, consider a bond that is currently selling for $1,000 with a yield-to-maturity of 8%. Given that the bond has a duration of ten years, by how much will the bond's price change if its yield increases to 9%? Using equation (22.4b), it can be seen that $\Delta y = 9\% - 8\% = 1\% = .01$, so that $\Delta y/(1 + y) = .01/1.08 = .00926 = .926\%$ and $-D[\Delta y/(1 + y)] = -10[.926\%] = -9.26\%$. Hence the one percentage point rise in the yield will cause approximately a 9.26% drop in the bond's price to $926 = $1,000 − (.0926 × $1,000).

Relationship Between Convexity and Duration

At this point it is useful to consider just what kind of relationship the concepts of convexity and duration have to each other. After all, both have something to do with measuring the association of the change in a bond's price with a change in the bond's yield-to-maturity. Figure 22-3 shows the nature of the

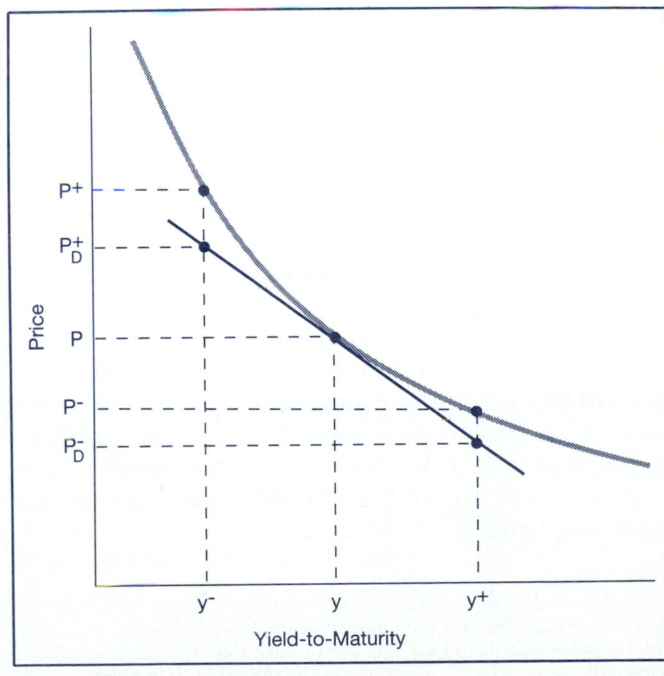

FIGURE 22-3
Bond Convexity and Duration

relationship. Like Figure 22-2, this figure represents a bond that is currently selling for P and has a yield-to-maturity of y. Note the straight line that is tangent to the curve at the point associated with the current price and yield.

If the bond's yield increases to y^+, then the associated price of the bond will fall to P^-. Conversely, if the bond's yield decreases to y^-, then the associated price of the bond will rise to P^+. However, by using equation (22.4b), the estimated prices will be P^-_D and P^+_D, respectively. This is because the equation, as mentioned earlier, is not exact. Instead, it is an approximation that states that the percentage change in the bond's price is a linear function of its duration. Hence, the equation approximates the new price in a linear fashion represented by the straight line and leading to an error that is a consequence of convexity (in the example, the size of the respective errors are $(P^- - P^-_D)$ and $P^+ - P^+_D)$. That is, since the relationship between yield changes and bond price changes is convex, not linear, the use of equation (22.4b) will underestimate the new price associated with either an increase or a decrease in the bond's yield.[13] However, for small changes in yields, the error is relatively small, and thus, as an approximation, equation (22.4b) works reasonably well. This can be seen by observing in Figure 22-3 that the size of the pricing error becomes smaller as the size of the yield change gets smaller (note that the distance between the linear approximating line and the convex curve will be smaller for smaller changes in yields from y).

Changes in the Term Structure

As mentioned earlier, when yields change, most bond prices also change, but some react more than others. Even bonds with the same maturity date can react quite differently to a given change in yields. However, it was shown in equations (22.4a) and (22.4b) that the percentage change in a bond's price is related to its duration. Hence the prices of two bonds that have the same duration will react similarly to a given change in yields.

For example, the bond shown in Table 22-1 had a duration of 2.78 and a yield of 10%. If its yield changes to 11%, then the percentage change in (one plus the bond's yield) is $(1.11 - 1.10)/(1.10) = .91\%$. Thus, its price should change by approximately $-2.78 \times .91\% = -2.53\%$. Using a discount rate of 11%, its price can be calculated to equal \$926.69, for an actual price change of $-\$23.56 = \$926.69 - \$950.25$ and a percentage change of $-2.48\% = -\$23.56/\$950.25$. Any other bond having a duration of 2.78 years will experience a similar price change if it has a similar percentage change in its yield.

Consider a bond with a maturity of four years that also has a duration of 2.78 years. When there is a shift in interest rates, and the yields on the three-year and four-year bonds change by the same amount, then their prices will change similarly. For example, if the yield on the four-year bond goes from 10.8% to 11.81% at the same time the yield on the three-year bond is going from 10% to 11%, then the percentage change in the present value of the four-year bond will be approximately $-2.78 \times [(1.1181 - 1.108)/(1.108)] = -2.78 \times .91\% = -2.53\%$, which is the same percentage as the three-year bond.

---

[13]It follows that if there are two bonds that are identical in all aspects except that one has "more convexity," then the one with more convexity would be more desirable. This is because if yields rise, its price will drop by a smaller amount than the other bond. Conversely, if yields drop, its price will rise by a larger amount than the other bond. In either case, the investor is better off with the bond having more convexity.

What if the "percentage change in (one plus the bond's yield)" is different? That is, what happens if the term structure shifts in a manner so that "the percentage change in (one plus the bond's yield)" is not the same for all bonds? Perhaps when the three-year bond goes from a yield of 10% to a yield of 11% [a percentage change of .91% = (1.11 − 1.10)/1.10], the four-year bond will go from a yield of 10.8% to a yield of 11.5% [a percentage change of .63% = (1.115 − 1.108)/1.108]. In this case, the percentage change in price for the four-year bond will be approximately −1.75% = −2.78 × [(1.115 − 1.108)/1.108], which is a smaller change than the −2.53% associated with the three-year bond. Accordingly, even though the two bonds have the same duration, it does not automatically follow that their prices will react identically to *any* change in yields, since these yield changes can be different for two bonds having the same duration.

IMMUNIZATION

The introduction of the concept of duration led to the development of the technique of bond portfolio management known as **immunization.** Specifically, this technique allegedly allows a bond portfolio manager to be relatively certain of being able to meet a given promised stream of cash outflows. Thus, once the portfolio has been formed, it is "immunized" from any adverse effects associated with future changes in interest rates.

immunization

How Immunization Is Accomplished

Immunization is accomplished simply by calculating the duration of the promised outflows and then investing in a portfolio of bonds that has an identical duration. In doing so, this technique takes advantage of the observation that the *duration of a portfolio of bonds is equal to the weighted average of the durations of the individual bonds in the portfolio.* For example, if a portfolio has ⅓ of its funds invested in bonds having a duration of six years and ⅔ of its funds in bonds having a duration of three years, then the portfolio itself has a duration of [(⅓) × 6] + [(⅔) × 3] = four years.

Consider a simple situation where a portfolio manager has one and only one cash outflow to make from his or her portfolio—an amount equal to $1,000,000, which is to be paid in two years. Since there is only one cash outflow, its duration is simply two years. Now, the bond portfolio manager is considering investing in two different bond issues. The first bond issue is the one shown in Table 22-1, where the bonds have a maturity of three years. The second bond issue involves a set of bonds that mature in one year, providing the holder of each bond with a single payment of $1,070 (consisting of a single coupon payment of $70 and a par value of $1,000). Since these bonds are currently selling for $972.73, their yield-to-maturity is 10%.

Consider the choices open to the portfolio manager. All of the portfolio's funds could be invested in the one-year bonds, with the notion of reinvesting the proceeds from the maturing bonds one year from now in another one-year issue. However, doing so would entail risks. In particular, if interest rates were to decline over the next year, then the funds from the maturing one-year bonds must be reinvested at a lower rate than the currently available 10%. Thus, the portfolio manager faces reinvestment-rate risk owing to the possibility that the funds one year from now can only be reinvested at a lower rate.[14]

A second alternative would be for the portfolio manager to invest all of the funds in the three-year issue. However, this also entails risks. In particular, the three-year bonds will have to be sold after two years in order to come up with the $1,000,000. The risk is that interest rates will have risen before then, meaning that bond prices, in general, will have fallen and the bonds will not have a selling price that is equal to or greater than $1,000,000. Thus, the portfolio manager faces interest-rate risk with this strategy.

One proposed solution is to invest part of the portfolio's funds in the one-year bonds and the rest in the three-year bonds. How much should be placed in each issue? If immunization is to be used, the solution can be found by solving simultaneously a set of two equations involving two unknowns:

$$W_1 + W_3 = 1 \tag{22.5}$$

$$(W_1 \times 1) + (W_3 \times 2.78) = 2. \tag{22.6}$$

Here, W_1 and W_3 denote the weights (or proportions) of the portfolio's funds that are to be invested in the bonds with maturities of one and three years, respectively. Note how equation (22.5) states that the sum of the weights must equal one, while equation (22.6) states that the weighted average of the durations of the bonds in the portfolio must equal the duration of the cash outflow, which is two years.

The solution to these two equations is easily found. First, equation (22.5) is rewritten as:

$$W_1 = 1 - W_3. \tag{22.7}$$

Then, $1 - W_3$ is substituted for W_1 in equation (22.6), resulting in:

$$[(1 - W_3) \times 1] + (W_3 \times 2.78) = 2. \tag{22.8}$$

Since this is one equation with one unknown, W_3, it can be easily solved. Doing so results in $W_3 = .5618$. Inserting this value into equation (22.7) indicates that $W_1 = .4382$. Thus, the portfolio manager should put 43.82% of the portfolio's funds in the one-year bonds and 56.18% in the three-year bonds.

In this case, the portfolio manager would need $826,446 = $1,000,000/(1.10²) in order to purchase bonds that would create a fully immunized portfolio. With this money, $362,149 = .4382 × $826,446 would be used to buy one-year bonds and $464,297 = .5618 × $826,446 would be used to buy three-year bonds. Since the current market prices of the one-year and three-year bonds are $972.73 and $950.25, respectively, this means that 372 one-year bonds (= $362,149/$972.73) and 489 three-year bonds (= $464,297/$950.25) would be purchased.

What does immunization accomplish? According to theory, if yields rise, then the portfolio's losses owing to the selling of the three-year bonds at

---

[14] If there were two-year coupon-bearing bonds available for investment, then there would be no reinvestment-rate risk associated with the principal. However, the investor would still face reinvestment-rate risk in terms of the coupon payments received after one year. While such risk appears to be relatively minor in this example, such risk becomes much more substantial in situations involving promised cash outflows that are more than two years into the future.

a discount after two years will be exactly offset by the gains from reinvesting the maturing one-year bonds (and first-year coupons on the three-year bonds) at the higher rate. Alternatively, if yields fall, then the loss from being able to reinvest the maturing one-year bonds (and first-year coupons on the three-year bonds) at a lower rate will be exactly offset by being able to sell the three-year bonds after two years at a premium. Thus, the portfolio is *immunized* from the effect of any movements in interest rates in the future.

Table 22-2 shows more explicitly what would happen to the portfolio. The second column shows what the portfolio would be worth at the end of two years if yields remained at 10% over the next two years. As can be seen, the value of the portfolio of one-year and three-year bonds would be approximately equal to the promised cash outflow of $1,000,000. Alternatively, if yields fell to 9% or rose to 11% before one year had passed and remained at the new level, then the value of the portfolio would be slightly more than the needed $1,000,000.[15]

Problems with Immunization

The previous paragraph described what immunization accomplishes in theory. This leaves open the possibility that it might not work quite as well in practice. What can cause it to work less than perfectly? Underlying this issue is this question: Why might duration fail to accurately measure the interest rate risk of a bond? In terms of the example, what can cause the value of the portfolio to be less than $1,000,000 at the end of two years?

Default and Call Risk To begin with, immunization (and duration) are based on the belief that all of the bonds' promised cash flows will subsequently be paid in full and on time. This means that immunization is based on the assumption that the bond will not default and will not be called before maturity—that is, the bonds are assumed to be free from both call risk and default risk. Consequently, if a bond in the portfolio either enters into default or is called, the portfolio will not be immunized.

[15]The reason that the value is more than $1,000,000 is because of the convexity property of bonds, discussed earlier.

TABLE 22-2
An Example of an Immunized Portfolio

	YIELD-TO-MATURITY AT THE END OF ONE YEAR		
	9%	10%	11%
Value at $t = 2$ from reinvesting one-year bond proceeds: $[\$1{,}070 \times 372.3 \times (1 + y)] =$	$ 434,213	$438,197	$ 442,181
Value at $t = 2$ of three-year bonds:			
Value from reinvesting coupons received at $t = 1$: $[\$80 \times 488.6 \times (1 + y)] =$	42,606	42,997	43,388
Coupons received at $t = 2$: $[\$80 \times 488.6] =$	39,088	39,088	39,088
Selling price at $t = 2$: $[\$1{,}080 \times 488.6/(1 + y)] =$	484,117	479,716	475,395
Aggregate portfolio value at $t = 2$:	$1,000,024	$999,998	$1,000,052

Multiple Nonparallel Shifts in a Nonhorizontal Yield Curve Immunization (and duration) are also based on the assumption that the yield curve is horizontal and that any shifts in it will be parallel and will occur before any payments are received from the bonds that were purchased. In the example, both the one-year and three-year bonds had the same 10% yield-to-maturity at the start, and the shift of 1% in yields was assumed to be the same for both bond issues. Furthermore, this shift was assumed to occur sometime before one year had passed.

In reality, the yield curve will not be horizontal at the start, and shifts in it are not likely to be either parallel or restricted in when they occur. Perhaps the one-year and three-year bonds will have initial yields of 10% and 10.5%, respectively, with the yields on the one-year and three-year bonds falling by 1% and .8%, respectively, after one year. Indeed, there is evidence of greater volatility in yields of shorter-term securities. If these kinds of shifts were to occur, then it is possible that the portfolio will not be immunized.[16]

cash matching

If the bond portfolio manager followed a special kind of immunization known as **cash matching,** then frequent nonparallel shifts in a nonhorizontal yield curve would have no adverse effect on the portfolio. This is because cash matching involves the purchase of bonds so that the cash received each period from the bonds is identical in size to the promised cash outflow for that period.

dedicated portfolio

Such a cash-matched portfolio of bonds is often referred to as a **dedicated portfolio.** Note that there is no need to reinvest any cash inflows in the future with a dedicated portfolio, so there is no reinvestment-rate risk. Furthermore, since bonds do not have to be sold prior to maturity, there is no interest-rate risk either.

In the simplest situation, where there is one promised cash outflow, the dedicated portfolio would consist of zero-coupon bonds where each bond has a life corresponding to the date of the promised cash outflow. In the previous example, where there was a promised cash outflow of $1,000,000 after two years, this would be accomplished by purchasing the requisite number of zero-coupon bonds having a maturity of two years.

However, cash matching is often not so easily accomplished. This is because the promised cash outflows may involve an uneven stream of payments for which no zero-coupon bonds exist. Indeed, it can be difficult (if not impossible) and expensive to exactly match cash inflows with promised outflows.

Another potential way around the problem of nonhorizontal yield curves that experience nonparallel shifts is to use one of a variety of more complicated immunization models. These models involve various other assumptions about the current shape of the yield curve and how it will shift in the future. Consequently, the bond portfolio manager must choose the one that he or she personally views as being most accurate. Interestingly, various studies have found that the best performer was the version of immunization that has been described in this chapter, and not the more complicated models.

---

[16]See the articles by Jeffrey Nelson and Stephen Schaefer, "The Dynamics of the Term Structure and Alternative Portfolio Immunization Strategies," pp. 61–101; and Jonathan E. Ingersoll, Jr., "Is Immunization Feasible? Evidence from the CRSP Data," pp. 163–82 in the book by George G. Kaufman, G. O. Bierwag, and Alden Toevs, eds., entitled *Innovations in Bond Portfolio Management: Duration Analysis and Immunization* (Greenwich, Conn.: JAI Press Inc., 1983) and Robert R. Reitano, "Non-Parallel Yield Curve Shifts and Spread Leverage," *Journal of Portfolio Management*, 17, no. 3 (Spring 1991): 82–87.

Thus, some researchers argue that the portfolio manager interested in immunization would be well advised to use this version.[17]

An implication is that regardless of the model being used, the bond portfolio manager must recognize that there is a risk being incurred—the risk that the yield curve will shift in a way that does not correspond with the way assumed by the model. For example, if the model presented here is used, then the bond portfolio is facing risk in that the yield curve will not shift in a parallel manner. Consequently, some people have argued that none of the immunization models are useful.[18] Others have argued that there are ways to use immunization in the presence of such risk, which has been called **stochastic process risk.**[19]

stochastic process risk

Rebalancing Another problem with the use of immunization is the effect of the passage of time on the duration of the bonds held and on the duration of the promised cash outflows. As time passes and yields change, these durations can change at different rates so that the portfolio is no longer immunized. This means that the portfolio may need to be rebalanced fairly often.

Here, rebalancing refers to selling some bonds currently held and replacing them with others so that afterwards, the duration of the portfolio matches the duration of the promised cash outflows. However, since rebalancing causes the portfolio manager to incur transaction costs, the manager might not want to rebalance whenever the durations do not match, since the costs might outweigh the perceived gains from rebalancing. Ultimately, the bond portfolio manager will have to decide how frequently to rebalance the portfolio, taking into consideration the risk of being unbalanced along with the transaction costs associated with rebalancing.

Many Candidates Finally, there are usually many portfolios that have a duration of the requisite length. Which one is the bond portfolio manager to choose? In the example, imagine that in addition to the one-year and three-year bonds, there is a zero-coupon bond having a life of four years (thus, its duration is also four years) that the manager is considering. Now the manager faces a choice of which portfolio to hold, since there are many that have the requisite duration of two years. In addition to the one previously

---

[17]For a summary and set of references, see G. O. Bierwag, George G. Kaufman, Robert Schweitzer, and Alden Toevs, "The Art of Risk Management in Bond Portfolios," *Journal of Portfolio Management*, 7, no. 3 (Spring 1981): 27–36; G. O. Bierwag, George G. Kaufman, and Alden Toevs, "Duration: Its Development and Use in Bond Portfolio Management," *Financial Analysts Journal*, 39, no. 4 (July–August 1983): 15–35; and Stephen M. Schaefer, "Immunisation and Duration: A Review of Theory, Performance and Applications," *Midland Corporate Finance Journal*, 2, no. 3 (Fall 1984): 41–58.

[18]See N. Bulent Gultekin and Richard J. Rogalski, "Alternative Duration Specifications and the Measurement of Basis Risk," *Journal of Business*, 57, no. 2 (April 1984): 241–64; for rebuttals and responses, see G. O. Bierwag, George G. Kaufman, Cynthia M. Latta, and Gordon S. Roberts, "Duration: Response to Critics," *Journal of Portfolio Management*, 13, no. 2 (Winter 1987): 48–52. N. Bulent Gultekin and Richard J. Rogalski, "Duration: Response to Critics: Comment," *Journal of Portfolio Management*, 15, no. 3 (Spring 1989): 83–87; G. O. Bierwag, George G. Kaufman, Cynthia M. Latta, and Gordon S. Roberts, "Duration as a Measure of Basis Risk: The Wrong Answer at Low Cost—Rejoinder," *Journal of Portfolio Management*, 15, no. 4 (Summer 1989): 82–85; and N. Bulent Gultekin and Richard J. Rogalski, "Duration as a Measure of Basis Risk: The Wrong Answer at Low Cost—Answer to Rejoinder," *Journal of Portfolio Management*, 15, no. 4 (Summer 1989): 86–87.

[19]G. O. Bierwag, George G. Kaufman, and Alden Toevs, "Bond Portfolio Immunization and Stochastic Process Risk," *Journal of Bank Research*, 13 (Winter 1983), 282–91; also see G. O. Bierwag, George G. Kaufman, and Cynthia M. Latta, "Duration Models: A Taxonomy," *Journal of Portfolio Management*, 15, no. 1 (Fall 1988): 50–54.

MONEY MATTERS
Surplus Management

Corporate pension funds are established to secure the funding of retirement benefits promised to corporate employees. Therefore, the primary investment objective of these funds is to accumulate sufficient assets, through contributions and investment income, to satisfy all pension obligations on a timely basis.

The management of corporate pension funds has traditionally focused solely on the asset side of the pension fund asset-liability equation. Those organizations charged with the oversight of pension funds (often referred to as "plan sponsors") have typically defined their investment policies in terms of seeking maximum returns subject to their tolerance for volatility of returns (see Chapter 17). This philosophy has led many plan sponsors to invest heavily in equity assets, particularly common stocks, based on perceived superior long-run risk-return characteristics of such assets.

The foundations of this investment approach received a jolt in 1986 when the Financial Accounting Standards Board issued FASB 87, a directive requiring corporations to report pension obligations on their financial statements beginning in 1989. Prior to FASB 87, corporate reporting on pension obligations was consigned to annual report footnotes. This level of disclosure seemed inadequate given that pension assets and liabilities would represent the largest items on many corporations' balance sheets and that annual pension expenses can represent a large portion of a corporation's earnings. FASB 87 was designed to remedy this deficiency.

FASB 87 requires that companies report any negative difference between their pension assets and their pension liabilities on their balance sheets as liabilities. (There is no corresponding balance sheet asset if pension assets exceed pension liabilities.) Moreover, the way in which companies report pension expenses on their income statements was redefined. The expense includes the costs associated with pension benefits earned in the current year, plus interest on past obligations, plus the amortization of any unfunded liabilities (that is, liabilities not offset by pension assets) less the expected earnings on the pension fund's assets.

As a result of FASB 87, a corporation's earnings become sensitive to changes in its pension fund's surplus, which is the difference in value between the fund's assets and liabilities. A significant decrease in pension surplus will result in an earnings reduction, while a significant increase can boost earnings. Thus FASB 87 created for the first time a source of reported earnings variability directly attributable to changes in a pension fund's assets and liabilities.

This new source of earnings variability has caused some companies to emphasize control of pension surplus volatility through a process known as *surplus management*. How does a plan sponsor manage pension surplus? By developing an investment strategy that causes the value of the pension fund's assets to move more closely with the pension fund's liabilities. That is, the plan sponsor wishes to "immunize" the pension fund's liabilities by creating an appropriately structured portfolio of assets. In this way, the variability of changes in pension surplus will be reduced, thereby lowering the pension fund's impact on the variability of the corporation's earnings.

In order to specify the appropriate composition of the pension fund's asset portfolio that will immunize the fund's pension liabilities, the plan sponsor must determine what factors can cause the value of those liabilities to change. In the short run, when promised pension benefits can be viewed as fixed, only movements in interest rates cause the value of pension liabilities to change. FASB 87 mandates that the value of pension liabilities be calculated as the discounted value of pension benefits earned to date by the company's employees (plus in some cases projected salary increases for current employees). The discount rate applied to these earned pension benefits is related to current market interest rates. Therefore, as those interest rates fluctuate so does the value of a company's pension liabilities. Interest rate increases reduce the value of pension liabilities, while interest rate declines increase pension liabilities.

As described in the text, a simple means of at least partially immunizing a set of interest-sensitive liabilities is to create a portfolio of bonds whose duration equals that of the liabilities. As interest rates change, the value of the assets will rise and fall more or less in line with the value of the liabilities, maintaining a relatively constant pension surplus.

FASB 87 has given rise to numerous sophisticated strategies designed to reduce pension surplus volatility. To implement these strategies, some plan sponsors have significantly reduced their pension funds' allocations to equity assets and purchased fixed-income securities.

Such shifts in asset allocation have led critics of surplus management to argue that by maintaining large fixed-income investments, pension plans are sacrificing the superior returns available from equity assets.

These critics further contend that surplus management is shortsighted. If one views pension liabilities on a longer-term basis, they are not fixed. Rather, they grow with inflation and worker productivity (which translate into pay raises and higher benefits). Thus, in the long run, equity assets may be more effective in hedging against these changes in pension liabilities than fixed-income investments.

described that consisted of just one-year and three-year bonds, there is also one where ⅔ and ⅓ of the portfolio's funds are invested in one-year bonds and four-year bonds, respectively [note how the duration of this portfolio is also two years: $(2/3 \times 1) + (1/3 \times 4) = 2$]. Furthermore, there are many other candidate portfolios.

One possible solution is to choose the portfolio having the highest average yield-to-maturity. Here, the yield of each issue is multiplied by the percentage of the portfolio's funds that are invested in that issue. Another possible solution is to choose the portfolio that most closely resembles a "bullet" or "focused" portfolio, since it has been argued that such a portfolio has less stochastic process risk than any other. Such a portfolio is one where the bonds in it have durations (or, alternatively, terms-to-maturity) most closely matching the duration of the promised outflows. In the example, the portfolio consisting of just one-year and three-year bonds would be more "focused" than the one consisting of the one-year and four-year bonds.

ACTIVE MANAGEMENT

As mentioned earlier, active management of a bond portfolio is based on the belief that the bond market is not perfectly efficient. Such management can involve security selection, where attempts are made at identifying mispriced bonds. Alternatively, it can involve market timing, where attempts are made at forecasting general movements in interest rates. It is also possible for an active portfolio manager to be involved in both security selection and market timing. While there are a large number of methods of actively managing a bond portfolio, some general types of active management can be described.

Horizon Analysis

The return on a bond over any given holding period, sometimes referred to as the bond's realized return, depends on its price at the beginning of the period and its price at the end of the period, as well as its coupon rate. Thus, the return on a bond over a one-year period will depend on the yield structure at the beginning of the year and the yield structure at the end of the year, since the price of the bond at these two points in time will depend on these structures. It follows that possible subsequent changes to the beginning-of-period yield structure must be analyzed in order to estimate possible bond returns over a given holding period. Bond portfolio managers who believe they are able to identify such changes will want to translate their beliefs into action.

horizon analysis

One way of doing this is known as **horizon analysis,** where a single holding period is selected for analysis and possible yield structures at the end of the period (that is, at the "horizon") are considered. The possible returns for two bonds—one currently held and one candidate to replace it—are then analyzed. In doing so, neither bond is assumed to default up to the horizon date. In the process of the analysis, the sensitivities of the returns to changes in key assumptions regarding yields are estimated, allowing at least a rough assessment of some of the relevant risks.

Horizon analysis can be viewed as another way of implementing the capitalization of income method of valuation that was discussed in Chapter 21. By focusing on the estimated end-of-period price of a bond, it seeks to determine if the current market price is relatively high or low. That is, for a given estimated end-of-period price, a bond will have a relatively high expected return if its current price is relatively low. Conversely, a bond will have a relatively low expected return if its current price is relatively high.

Figure 22-4 represents a page from a standard yield book for bonds with a 4% coupon. As indicated, a 4% bond with ten years remaining to maturity that is currently priced at $67.48 (for ease of exposition, a par of $100 is used here) will have a 9% promised annual yield-to-maturity (or 4.5% semiannually). Five years into the future, such a bond's term-to-maturity will have decreased and the relevant promised yield-to-maturity will probably have changed. Thus, as time passes, the bond might follow a path "through the table" such as that shown by the dashed line. If so, it would end up at a price of $83.78 at the *horizon* (five years hence) with an 8% promised annual yield-to-maturity (or 4% semiannually).

Over any holding period, a bond's return will typically be affected by both the passage of time and a change in yields. Horizon analysis breaks this into two parts: one owing solely to the passage of time whereby the bond's price moves toward the par value to be paid at maturity (assuming no change in yields), and the other owing solely to a change in yield (assuming no passage of time). This is illustrated in Figure 22–4. The total price change from $67.48 to $83.78 (or $16.30) is broken into a change from $67.48 to $80.22 (or $12.74) followed by an instantaneous change from $80.22 to $83.78 (or $3.56).

FIGURE 22-4

The Effect of Time and Yield Change on a 4% Coupon Bond

Note: y_0 and P_0 denote the bond's annual yield-to-maturity and price at the beginning of the period; y_H and P_H denote the bonds' annual yield-to-maturity and price at the horizon (that is, the end of the period); P_A denotes the bond's price at the horizon if its annual yield had remained at y_0 = 9%; yields are compounded semiannually.

Source: Martin L. Leibowitz, "Horizon Analysis for Managed Bond Portfolio," *Journal of Portfolio Management*, 1, no. 3 (Spring 1975): 26.

Yield to Maturity (%)	YEARS TO MATURITY						
	10 Yrs	9 Yrs	. . .	5 Yrs	. . .	1 Yrs	0 Yrs
7.00	78.68	80.22		87.53		97.15	100.00
7.50	75.68	77.39		85.63		96.69	100.00
y_H 8.00	72.82	74.68		83.78 P_H		96.23	100.00
8.50	70.09	72.09		81.98		95.77	100.00
y_0 9.00	P_0 67.48	69.60		80.22 P_A		95.32	100.00
9.50	64.99	67.22		78.51		94.87	100.00
10.00	62.61	64.92	. . .	76.83	. . .	94.42	100.00
10.50	60.34	62.74		75.21		93.98	100.00
11.00	58.17	60.64		73.62		93.54	100.00

Actual Price Pattern Over Time; Yield Change Effect; Time Effect

The intermediate value is the price the bond would command at the horizon if its promised yield-to-maturity had remained unchanged at its initial level of 9%. The actual price is that which it commands at its actual yield-to-maturity of 8%. In summary, the total price change can be broken into two parts, representing the two effects:

$$\text{price change} = \text{time effect} + \text{yield change effect.} \qquad (22.9)$$

Thus far, no account has been taken of the coupon payments to be received before the horizon date. In principle, one should consider all possible uses of such cash flows or at least analyze possible alternative yield structures during the period to determine likely reinvestment opportunities. In practice, this is rarely done. Instead, a single reinvestment rate is assumed and the future value of all coupon payments at the horizon date is determined by compounding each one using this rate.[20] This takes care of both interest (coupons) and "interest on interest" (that is, interest earned from reinvesting coupon payments), with only the former being accurately predictable at the beginning of the period.

For example, if $2 is received every six months (as in Figure 22-4), with the first payment occurring six months from now and the last payment occurring five years from now, and if each payment is reinvested at 4.25% per six months, then the value at the end of five years will be approximately $24.29. Of this amount, $20 can be considered interest (coupon payments of $2 for ten six-month periods) with the remaining $4.29 being "interest on interest."

In summary, a bond's overall dollar return has four components—the time effect, the yield change effect, the coupons, and the interest from reinvesting the coupons. In the example, the overall dollar return is:

$$\begin{aligned}\begin{matrix}\text{overall}\\ \text{dollar}\\ \text{return}\end{matrix} &= \begin{matrix}\text{time}\\ \text{effect}\end{matrix} + \begin{matrix}\text{yield}\\ \text{change}\\ \text{effect}\end{matrix} + \text{coupons} + \begin{matrix}\text{interest}\\ \text{on}\\ \text{coupons}\end{matrix}\\ &= (\$80.22 - \$67.48) + (\$83.78 - \$80.22) + \$20.00 + \$4.29\\ &= \$12.74 + \$3.56 + \$20.00 + \$4.29\\ &= \$40.59.\end{aligned}$$

This overall dollar return can be converted into an overall rate of return by dividing it by the market price of the bond at the beginning of the period, $67.48. In doing so, it can be seen that a bond's overall rate of return consists of four components:

$$\begin{aligned}\begin{matrix}\text{overall}\\ \text{rate of}\\ \text{return}\end{matrix} &= \frac{\$12.74}{\$67.48} + \frac{\$3.56}{\$67.48} + \frac{\$20.00}{\$67.48} + \frac{\$4.29}{\$67.48}\\ &= .1888 + .0528 + .2964 + .0635\\ &= .6015\end{aligned}$$

[20]The longer the horizon, the greater the importance of the size of the reinvestment rate in determining a bond's return. This means that if the investor's horizon is greater than, say, ten years, then alternative reinvestment rates should be considered.

or 60.15%. The first term is the return owing to the passage of time, the second term is the return owing to yield change, the third term is coupon return, and the fourth term is the return owing to the reinvestment of the coupon payments.

Since the second term is uncertain, it is important to analyze it further. In the example, a change in yield from 9.0% to 8.0% will result in a change in the market price from $80.22 to $83.78. Given that 8.0% was the expected yield at the horizon, an expected overall rate of return of 60.15% was computed. By using different end-of-period yields, different overall rates of return can be calculated. Then, with estimates of the probabilities of these yields occurring, a feel for the bond's risk can be obtained. Indeed, it can now be seen why bond portfolio managers devote a great deal of attention to making predictions of future yields.

Bond Swaps

bond swapping

Given a set of predictions about future bond yields, holding-period returns over one or more horizons for one or more bonds can be estimated. The goal of **bond swapping** is to actively manage a portfolio by exchanging bonds to take advantage of any superior ability to predict such yields.[21] In making a swap, the portfolio manager believes that an overpriced bond is being exchanged for an underpriced bond. Some swaps are based on the belief that the market will correct for its mispricing in a short period of time, while other types of swaps are based on a belief that corrections either will never take place or will take place, but over a long period of time.

There are several categories for classifying swaps, and the distinctions between the categories are often blurry. Nevertheless, many bond swaps can be placed in one of four general categories:

substitution swap

The **substitution swap** is ideally an exchange of a bond for a perfect substitute or "twin" bond. The motivation here is temporary price advantage, presumably resulting from a monetary imbalance in the relative supply/demand conditions in the marketplace.

intermarket spread swap

The **intermarket spread swap** is a more general movement out of one market component and into another with the intention of exploiting a currently advantageous yield relationship. The idea here is to benefit from a forecasted changing relationship between the two market components. While such swaps will almost always have some sensitivity to the direction of the overall market, the idealized focus of this type of swap is the spread relationship itself.

rate anticipation swap

On the other hand, the **rate anticipation swap** is frankly geared toward profiting from an anticipated movement in overall market rates.

pure yield pickup swap

The **pure yield pickup swap** is oriented toward yield improvements over the long term with little heed being paid to interim price movements in either the respective market components or the market as a whole.[22]

---

[21]Bond swaps should not be confused with interest-rate swaps, where two issuers of debt keep the respective amounts raised but exchange interest payments. See, for example, Stuart M. Turnbull, "Swaps: A Zero Sum Game?" *Financial Management*, 16, no. 1 (Spring 1987): 15–21, and Clifford W. Smith, Jr., Charles W. Smithson, and D. Sykes Wilford, *Managing Financial Risk* (New York: Harper & Row, 1990), Chapters 9–12.

[22]Martin L. Leibowitz, "Horizon Analysis for Managed Bond Portfolios," *Journal of Portfolio Management*, 1, no. 3 (Spring 1975): 32–33.

Consider a hypothetical portfolio manager who holds some of a 30-year, AA utility bond issue that has a 7% coupon rate. Since these bonds are currently selling at par, their yield-to-maturity is 7%. Now, imagine that there is another 30-year, AA utility bond issue with a 7% coupon rate that is being made available to the manager at a price so that its yield-to-maturity is 7.10%. An example of a substitution swap is where the manager exchanges a given dollar amount of the currently held bonds for an equivalent dollar amount of the second bond issue, thereby picking up 10 basis points in yield.

Alternatively, the manager might note that there is a 10-year AA utility bond issue outstanding that carries a 6% coupon and is priced at par; thus, its yield is 6%. In this case, there is a 100-basis-point yield spread between the currently held 30-year bonds and the 10-year bonds. If the manager feels that this spread is too low, then an intermarket spread swap might be used, where some of the 30-year bonds are exchanged for an equivalent dollar amount of the 10-year bonds. Since the manager expects the spread to increase in the future, the yield on the 10-year bonds is expected to fall. This means that the price on these bonds is expected to rise by an abnormal amount, resulting in an abnormally high holding-period return.

Another possibility is that the manager feels that yields in general are going to rise. In such a situation, the manager will recognize that the currently held portfolio is in a very risky position. This is because longer-term bonds generally move downward further in price for a given rise in yields than do shorter-term bonds, since they generally have a longer duration. Accordingly, the manager might use a rate anticipation swap to exchange a given dollar amount of the 30-year bonds for an equivalent amount of some short-term bonds.

Finally, the manager might not want to make any predictions about future yields or yield spreads. Instead, it might simply be noted that some 30-year, AA industrial bonds are currently priced to yield 8%. In this case, the manager might want to enter a pure yield pickup swap where some of the 7% utility bonds are exchanged for an equivalent dollar amount of the 8% industrial bonds, the motivation being to earn the extra 100 basis points in yield from the industrials.

Contingent Immunization

contingent immunization

One method of bond portfolio management that has both passive and active elements is **contingent immunization.** In the simplest form of contingent immunization, the portfolio will be actively managed as long as favorable results are obtained. However, if unfavorable results occur, then the portfolio will be immunized immediately.

As an illustration, consider the earlier example where the portfolio manager had to come up with $1,000,000 at the end of two years, and the current yield curve was horizontal at 10%. In this situation, it was mentioned that the portfolio manager could immunize the portfolio by investing $826,446 in one-year and three-year bonds. However, it may be that the portfolio manager convinces the client that the portfolio should be *contingently* immunized with $841,680. This means that the portfolio manager must be certain that the portfolio will be worth at least $1,000,000 at the end of the two years, with any excess going to the client and the manager being compensated accordingly. Equivalently, the portfolio manager must earn a minimum average return of 9% (note that $\$841,680 \times 1.09^2 = \$1,000,000$) over the two years. Here, the client is willing to settle for as low a return as 9%, but hopes that the portfolio manager will be able to exceed the 10% return that could have been locked in with an immunized portfolio.

In this situation, the manager would proceed to actively manage the portfolio by engaging in either selectivity or timing (or both). Perhaps the arrangement with the client is that the status of the portfolio will be reviewed weekly, and yields that are currently available will be determined.

Consider how the review would be conducted after one year has elapsed and the yield curve is still horizontal but at 11%. First, it is noted that \$900,901 = \$1,000,000/1.11 would be needed to immunize the portfolio at that point in time. Second, the market value of the current portfolio is determined to be \$930,000. Now, in this example, the arrangement between the client and portfolio manager is that the manager can continue to actively manage the portfolio as long as it is worth at least \$10,000 more than the amount needed for immunization. Since it is worth \$930,000, an amount greater than \$910,901 = \$900,901 + \$10,000, the portfolio manager can continue being active. However, if the portfolio had been worth less than \$910,901, then, according to the agreement, the manager would immediately immunize the portfolio.

Riding the Yield Curve

This method of bond portfolio management is sometimes used by people who, having liquidity as a primary objective, invest in short-term fixed-income securities. One way of investing is to simply purchase these securities and hold them until they mature, and then reinvest them. An alternative way is to ride the yield curve, provided that certain conditions exist.

One condition is that the yield curve be upward sloping, indicating that longer-term securities have higher yields. Another condition is that the investor believe that the yield curve will remain upward sloping. Given these two conditions, the investor who is riding the yield curve will purchase securities that have a somewhat longer term-to-maturity than desired, and then sell them before they mature, thereby capturing some capital gains.

For example, consider an investor who prefers investing in 90-day Treasury bills. Currently, such bills are selling for \$98.25 per \$100 of face value, indicating that they have a yield of 7.00% [note that \$98.25 = \$100 − (7.00 × 90/360)]. However, 180-day Treasury bills are currently selling for \$96.00, indicating that they have a higher yield of 8.00% [note that \$96 = \$100 − (8.00 × 180/360)]. Given that this investor believes that the yield curve will remain upward sloping over the next three months, it can be shown that riding the yield curve will result in a higher return than simply buying and holding the 90-day Treasury bills.

If the investor buys and holds the 90-day Treasury bills, then the resulting annualized rate of return will be:

$$\frac{\$100 - \$98.25}{\$98.25} \times \frac{365}{90}$$

which is 7.22%. Alternatively, if the investor buys the 180-day Treasury bills and subsequently sells them after 90 days, then the expected selling price will be \$98.25 (note that this is the same as the current price of 90-day bills, since it is assumed that the yield curve will not have changed after 90 days have elapsed). This means that the expected return is:

$$\frac{\$98.25 - \$96.00}{\$96.00} \times \frac{365}{90}$$

which is 9.50%. In comparison, the expected return from riding the yield curve is higher. This is because the investor expects to benefit from a decline in yield, a decline that does not result from a shift in the yield curve but is attributable to the shortening of the maturity of the 180-day Treasury bills that were initially purchased.

It should be kept in mind that if the yield curve does change, then "riding it" can be detrimental to the investor's return.[23] That is, riding the yield curve has more risk than simply buying securities that mature at the appropriate time. Similarly, there are two transactions necessary (buying and then selling the security) when riding the yield curve, whereas a maturity strategy has only one transaction (buying the security). Thus, there are going to be larger transaction costs associated with riding the yield curve.

PORTFOLIO PERFORMANCE EVALUATION

Chapter 18 discussed portfolio performance evaluation when the portfolio consisted of common stocks and short-term fixed-income securities such as Treasury bills. However, these methods are not as appropriate for a portfolio that invests primarily (or in large part) in fixed-income securities. What is frequently done in evaluating the performance of such portfolios is that their total returns (consisting of coupon payments plus capital gains or losses) are compared with those of an index representing a comparable class of fixed-income securities over some evaluation interval.

Bond indices typically represent either the average yield-to-maturity or the average price on a portfolio of bonds that have certain similar characteristics. Figure 22-5 presents various bond indices that are published regularly in *The Wall Street Journal*. The indices that are computed by Merrill Lynch are based on both value-weighted average prices and the associated average yields, while those computed by Dow Jones are based on equal-weighted average bond prices. Perhaps the most prominent bond index that is published in *The Wall Street Journal* is the Lehman Brothers Treasury Index, which is based on the value-weighted prices of long-term Treasury bonds. Other frequently used bond indices are calculated by Salomon Brothers (particularly their Broad Investment Grade and high-yield junk bond indices); *The Bond Buyer* (particularly their municipal bond indices); Lipper Analytical Services; and Standard & Poor's.[24]

Figure 22-6 illustrates two ways of comparing the returns on a bond portfolio with those on a benchmark bond index over an evaluation interval. In panel (a), a time-series comparison is made, where the bond portfolio's quarterly returns over time during the evaluation interval are graphed along with those of a benchmark bond index. In panel (b), a cross-sectional

---

[23]According to the unbiased expectations theory (discussed in Chapter 20), the yield curve would be expected to shift in such a manner that the expected return of both strategies (in the example, buy and hold the 90-day T-bills versus buy and sell 90 days later the 180-day T-bills) would be the same.

[24]Many of these indices are published weekly in *Barron's*; a discussion of the various methods of preparing market indices is contained in Chapter 14.

FIGURE 22-5

Bond Indices Published in The Wall Street Journal on Friday, June 19, 1992

Source: Reprinted by permission of *The Wall Street Journal*, Dow Jones & Company, Inc., June 19, 1991, pp. C5, C13–C15. All rights reserved worldwide.

YIELD COMPARISONS

Based on Merrill Lynch Bond Indexes, priced as of midafternoon Eastern time.

	6/18	6/17	–52 Week– High	Low
Corp.-Govt. Master	6.73%	6.76%	8.22%	6.53%
Treasury 1-10yr	5.71	5.76	7.57	5.44
10+ yr	7.82	7.84	8.68	7.43
Agencies 1-10yr	6.36	6.37	7.90	6.12
10+ yr	8.28	8.30	8.90	7.80
Corporate				
1-10 yr High Qlty	7.16	7.21	8.66	7.10
Med Qlty	7.62	7.67	9.26	7.62
10+yr High Qlty	8.39	8.42	9.43	8.30
Med Qlty	8.80	8.82	9.82	8.79
Yankee bonds(1)	8.03	8.07	9.21	7.79
Current-coupon mortgages (2)				
GNMA 7.50%	7.88	7.92	9.32	7.40
FNMA 7.50%	7.96	8.00	9.34	7.51
FHLMC8.00%	7.76	7.81	9.27	7.38
High-yield corporates	11.35	11.36	14.38	11.35
New tax-exempts				
10-yr G.O. (AA)	5.75	5.75	6.50	5.60
20-yr G.O. (AA)	6.35	6.35	7.05	6.25
30-yr revenue (A)	6.65	6.65	7.55	6.52

Note: High quality rated AAA-AA; medium quality A-BBB/Baa; high yield, BB/Ba-C.

(1) Dollar-denominated, SEC-registered bonds of foreign issuers sold in the U.S. (2) Reflects the 52-week high and low of mortgage-backed securities indexes rather than the individual securities shown.

HIGH YIELD BONDS

Thursday June 18, 1992

	Total Daily Return	Index Value	Average Price Change	Vol.
Flash Index	– 0.01%	133.68	– 0.03	L
Cash Pay	+ 0.00	130.36	– 0.03	L
Deferred Int	+ 0.00	144.03	unch	L
Distressed	– 0.03	141.83	– 0.04	L
Bankrupt	– 0.13	120.62	– 0.06	L

Volume Key: H = Heavy, M = Moderate, L = Light

Index value = 100 on July 1, 1990

Source: Salomon Brothers

Dow Jones Bond Averages

–1991– High	Low	–1992– High	Low		–––1992––– Close	Chg.	%Yld	––1991–– Close	Chg.
98.93	91.30	100.17	98.41	20 Bonds	100.01	+ 0.02	8.08	94.40	+ 0.29
100.81	93.44	101.17	98.45	10 Utilities	99.81	+ 0.13	8.20	95.50	+ 0.54
97.15	89.06	100.55	97.26	10 Industrials	100.21	– 0.09	7.96	93.30	+ 0.04

Municipal Bond Index

Merrill Lynch 500

Week ended Tuesday, June 16, 1992

The following index is based on yields that about 500 major issuers, mainly of investment grade, would pay on new long-term tax-exempt securities. The securities are presumed to be issued at par; general obligation bonds have a 20-year maturity and revenue bonds a 30-year maturity. The index, prepared by Merrill Lynch, Pierce, Fenner & Smith Inc., is calculated using yields on major outstanding bonds in the market. Yields are obtained from an internal source.

–500 MUNICIPAL BOND INDEX–

6.56 –0.05

–REVENUE BONDS–

Sub-Index 6.66 –0.07

	6-16	Change In Week
–25-YEAR REVENUE BONDS–		
AAA-Guaranteed ...	6.55	– 0.03
Airport	7.00	– 0.07
Power	6.45	– 0.07
Hospital	6.68	– 0.07
Housing-Single Family	6.89	– 0.05
Housing-Multi Family	6.72	– 0.07
Miscellaneous	6.75	– 0.07
Pollution Control/Ind. Dev.	6.69	– 0.07
Transportation	6.52	– 0.08
Water	6.63	– 0.06
Advance Refunded .	5.67	– 0.07
–20-YEAR GENERAL OBLIGATIONS–		
Sub-Index	**6.54**	**–0.09**
Cities	6.82	– 0.06
Counties	6.62	– 0.06
States	6.49	– 0.07
Other Districts	6.57	– 0.10

The transportation category excludes airports; other districts include school and special districts.

comparison is made where the bond portfolio's average return and standard deviation are graphed and compared with a line that goes through the average riskfree rate and the average return and standard deviation on the benchmark bond index, based on quarterly returns during the evaluation interval.[25]

[25]This method is similar to the method presented in Chapter 18 that was based on the ex post Capital Market Line and applied primarily to equity portfolios.

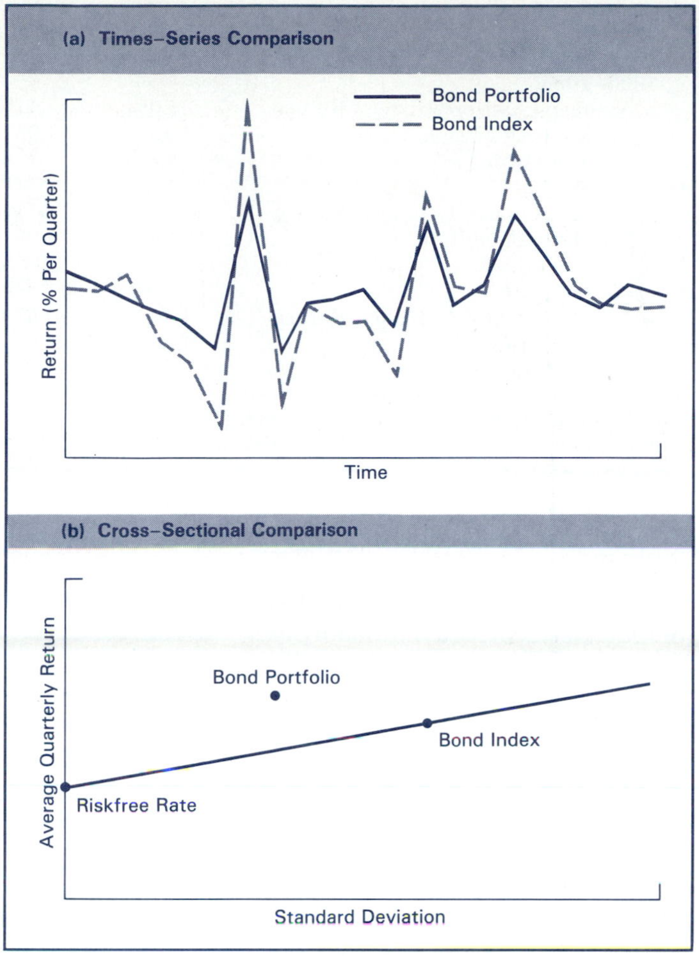

FIGURE 22-6
Bond Portfolio Performance Evaluation

BONDS VERSUS STOCKS

Bonds and stocks are different kinds of securities, with quite different characteristics. Making an investment decision between them should not be based on some simple one-dimensional comparison. In many cases this decision, known as **asset allocation**, will involve investing in both bonds and stocks.[26]

asset allocation

While historical relationships may not be useful for accurately predicting future relationships, it is instructive to examine the average values, standard deviations, and correlations of past stock and bond returns. These statistics are presented in Table 22-3, based on quarterly excess returns during one time period, 1926–1985, and two subperiods, 1926–1945 and 1946–1985.

[26]Chapter 17 presented a discussion of some methods for making the asset allocation decision. For a model on how to measure the interest-rate sensitivity of a portfolio consisting of both stocks and bonds, see Martin L. Leibowitz, "Total Portfolio Duration: A New Perspective on Asset Allocation," *Financial Analysts Journal*, 42, no. 5 (September/October 1986): 18–29.

TABLE 22-3
Historical Relationships Between Bonds and Stocks

	STOCKS	BONDS	CORRELATION
A. 1926–1985:			
Average Quarterly Excess Return	2.20%	.41%	
Standard Deviation	12.39	3.98	
Correlation			.30
B. 1926–1945:			
Average Quarterly Excess Return	2.94%	1.11%	
Standard Deviation	18.68	1.99	
Correlation			.45
C. 1946–1985:			
Average Quarterly Excess Return	1.83%	0.06%	
Standard Deviation	7.54	4.65	
Correlation			.40

Source: Adapted from Meir Statman and Neal L. Ushman, "Bonds Versus Stocks: Another Look," *Journal of Portfolio Management*, 13, no. 2 (Winter 1987): 33–38.

(The returns were published by Ibbotson Associates; see Figure 1-1 and Table 1-1 in Chapter 1.)

Based on average returns, stocks appear to have a substantial advantage for the investor with a reasonably long horizon. However, there is good reason to believe that the average returns on long-term bonds are not representative of investors' expectations for future returns. The returns show the results obtained by purchasing a long-term bond, holding it for a period of time, then replacing it with another long-term bond. The total returns include both income and capital gains or losses. During this period, bond price changes were negative more often than positive, averaging roughly −1% per year. A better estimate of investors' expectations might be obtained by assuming that the expected price would be as likely to increase as decrease. Expected future returns on bonds might then have been roughly 1% per year (.25% per quarter) greater than shown in the table.

For an investor concerned with month-to-month variation (such as an investor with a possible need for liquidity or with a known short horizon), bonds look relatively more attractive than stocks. This can be seen by examining the standard deviation of returns. In this sense, stocks were riskier than bonds during the period and both subperiods. Note that the increased uncertainty concerning the rate of inflation during the postwar subperiod has increased the variability of bond returns.

The correlation between stock and bond returns has been low, and during various twenty-six-year periods it has even had negative values. This indicates that portfolios combining both stocks and bonds could benefit considerably from the resulting diversification. More recently, however, correlations have been positive (and substantially so), owing in part to common reactions to changes in inflationary expectations. Consequently, the gains from diversification have recently been substantially reduced. Nevertheless, from the historical record, it would be reasonable to expect that in the future, bonds will still offer diversification benefits.

SUMMARY

1. Similar to the U.S. common stock market, the U.S. bond market appears to be highly, but not perfectly, semistrong-form efficient.

2. For a typical bond making periodic interest payments and a final principal repayment on a stated date, five bond pricing theorems apply:

(a) If a bond's market price increases, then its yield must decrease; conversely, if a bond's market price decreases, then its yield must increase.

(b) If a bond's yield does not change over its life, then the size of its discount or premium will decrease as its life gets shorter.

(c) If a bond's yield does not change over its life, then the size of its discount or premium will decrease at an increasing rate as its life gets shorter.

(d) A decrease in a bond's yield will raise the bond's price by an amount that is greater in size than the corresponding fall in the bond's price that would occur if there were an equal-sized increase in the bond's yield. (That is, the price-yield relationship is convex.)

(e) The percentage change in a bond's price owing to a change in its yield will be smaller if its coupon rate is higher.

3. Duration is a measure of the "average maturity" of the stream of payments associated with a bond. It is a weighted average of the length of time until the bond's remaining payments are made, with the weights equal to the present value of each cash flow relative to the price of the bond.

4. The duration of a portfolio of bonds is equal to the weighted average of the durations of the individual bonds in the portfolio.

5. A bond portfolio manager can be relatively certain of being able to meet a given promised stream of cash outflows by creating a bond portfolio with a duration equal to the liabilities. This procedure is known as immunization.

6. Problems with immunization include default and call risk, multiple nonparallel shifts in a nonhorizontal yield curve, costly rebalancings, and a wide range of candidate bond portfolios.

7. Active bond management may involve security selection, market timing (where attempts are made to forecast general movements in interest rates), or combinations of the two.

8. Active management strategies include horizon analysis, bond swaps, contingent immunization, and riding the yield curve.

KEY TERMS

coupon payments
coupon rate
term-to-maturity
yield-to-maturity
convexity
duration
immunization
cash matching
dedicated portfolio
stochastic process risk
horizon analysis
bond swapping
substitution swap
intermarket spread swap
rate anticipation swap
pure yield pickup swap
contingent immunization
asset allocation

QUESTIONS AND PROBLEMS

1. A $10,000-face-value pure-discount bond with a ten-year term-to-maturity currently sells so as to produce an 8% yield-to-maturity. What is the bond's price? Calculate the bond's price if its yield rises to 10%; if its yield falls to 5%.
2. Both bonds A and B have $10,000 face values, 10% coupon rates, and sell with yields-to-maturities of 9%. However, bond A has a twenty-year term-to-maturity while bond B has a five-year term-to-maturity. Calculate the prices of the two bonds. Despite having the same yields, why is one bond's price different from the other's?
3. Consider three pure-discount bonds, each with $1,000 face values; 7% yields-to-maturity; and terms-to-maturity of five, ten, and twenty years, respectively. Calculate each bond's price. Graph the bond's discounts (price divided by face value) versus their terms-to-maturity. Is the relationship linear? Why or why not?
4. Consider two bonds with 10% coupon rates and $1,000 face values. One

of the bonds has a term-to-maturity of four years, while the other has a term-to-maturity of fifteen years. Both make annual interest payments. Assuming that yields on the two bonds rise from 10% to 14%, calculate the intrinsic values of the two bonds before and after the change in interest rates. Explain the difference in percentage price changes.

5. Consider a five-year term-to-maturity bond with a $1,000 face value and $100 annual coupon interest payments. The bond sells at par. What is the bond's percentage price change if its yield-to-maturity rises to 12%? Falls to 8%?
6. Consider two bonds, one with five years to maturity and the other with twenty years to maturity. Both have $1,000 face values and 8% coupon rates (with annual interest payments), and both sell at par. Assume that the yields of both bonds fall to 6%. Calculate the dollar increases in the bonds' prices. What percentage of this increase in each case comes from a change in the present value of the bonds' principals and what percentage comes from a change in the present value of the bonds' interest payments?
7. Both bonds A and B have $10,000 face values, 8% yields-to-maturity, and ten-year terms-to-maturity. However, bond A has a 10% coupon rate while bond B sells at par. (Both make annual interest payments.) If the yields on both bonds decline to 6%, calculate the percentage price changes of the two bonds.
8. Consider a bond selling at its par value of $1,000, with three years to maturity and a 7% coupon interest rate (with annual interest payments). Calculate the bond's duration.
9. Why must the duration of a coupon-bearing bond always be less than the time to its maturity date?
10. Does a coupon-bearing bond's duration change if its yield-to-maturity changes at a point in time? Why?
11. Liz Funk owns a portfolio of four bonds with the following durations and proportions:

BOND	DURATION	PROPORTION
A	4.5 years	.20
B	3.0	.25
C	3.5	.25
D	2.8	.30

What is the duration of Liz's bond portfolio?

12. Rank order the following bonds in terms of duration. Explain the rationale behind your rankings. (You do not have to actually calculate the bonds' durations. Simple logical reasoning will suffice.)

BOND	TERM-TO-MATURITY	COUPON RATE	YIELD-TO-MATURITY
1	30 years	10.0%	10.0%
2	30	0.0	10.0
3	30	10.0	7.0
4	5	10.0	10.0

13. What impact would you expect the option features of callable bonds and mortgage participation certificates to have on the expected durations of such bonds as opposed to the durations calculated based on the bonds' stated maturity dates?
14. Consider a bond with a 3.5-year duration. If its yield-to-maturity increases from 8.0% to 8.3%, what is the expected percentage change in the price of the bond?
15. The price-yield relationship for a typical bond is convex (opens upward), as shown in Figure 22-2. Investment professionals often describe the price-yield relationship of mortgage pass-through securities as being "negatively convex." That is, a graph of the relationship opens downward. What features of these securities could produce such a relationship?
16. Explain why immunization permits a bond investor to be confident of meeting a given liability on a predetermined future date.
17. What are the advantages and disadvantages of meeting promised cash outflows through cash matching as opposed to duration matching?
18. Why can nonparallel shifts in the yield curve cause problems for an investor seeking to construct an immunized bond portfolio?
19. Describe the four components of return on a bond investment over a given holding period.
20. Consider a bond with a $1,000 face value, ten years to maturity, and $80 annual coupon interest payments. The bond sells so as to produce a 10% yield-to-maturity. That yield is expected to decline to 9% at the end of four years. Interest income is assumed to be invested at 9.5%. Calculate the bond's four-year holding period return and the four components of that return.
21. Distinguish between a substitution swap and an intermarket swap.

CFA Exam Question

22. Bill Peters is the investment officer of a $60 million pension fund. He has become concerned about the big price swings that have occurred lately in the fund's fixed-income securities. Peters has been told that such price behavior is only natural given the recent behavior of market yields. To deal with the problem, the pension fund's fixed-income money manager keeps track of exposure to price volatility by closely monitoring bond duration. The money manager believes that price volatility can be kept to a reasonable level as long as portfolio duration is maintained at approximately seven to eight years.

    Discuss the concepts of duration and convexity and explain how each fits into the price/yield relationship. In the situation described above, explain why the money manager should have used both duration and convexity to monitor the bond portfolio's exposure to price volatility.

APPENDIX

A Empirical Regularities in the Bond Market

The appendix to Chapter 13 discussed certain empirical regularities that have been observed in the stock market. Such regularities cannot be explained by any of the currently known asset pricing models, and hence are referred to as "anomalies." An interesting question to ponder is this: do such regularities also exist in the bond market? One study looked at this question by examining the daily performance from January 1963 through December 1986 of the Dow Jones Composite Bond Average (this bond index consists of twenty investment-grade U.S. corporate bonds, divided evenly between industrials and utilities).[27]

THE JANUARY EFFECT

Panel (a) of Table 22-A presents evidence that, as with common stocks, there is a January effect in bonds. That is, on average, corporate bonds have a notably higher return during the month of January than during the other eleven months of the year. Furthermore, as shown in panel (b), another study found that this observation was true across all investment-grade and two speculative-grade risk classes. Interestingly, the effect is extremely pronounced for the speculative classes.

THE DAY-OF-THE-WEEK EFFECT

Table 22-B presents the average daily returns for each business day of the week over the period from 1963 to 1986. As with common stocks, the average return on Monday is negative. However, it is also negative for every day except

[27]Susan D. Jordan and Bradford D. Jordan, "Seasonality in Daily Bond Returns," *Journal of Financial and Quantitative Analysis*, 26, no. 2 (June 1991): 269–85. Note that this study did not examine the bond market in order to see if the size effect (observed for common stocks) was present; hence, only two of the anomalies discussed in the appendix to Chapter 13 are discussed here.

TABLE 22-A
Seasonality in Bond Returns

	AVERAGE RETURN IN JANUARY	AVERAGE MONTHLY RETURN IN OTHER MONTHS
(a) 1963–1986[1]	4.34%	−.56%
(b) 1963–1979[2]		
Aaa	1.15%	.22%
Aa	1.21	.29
A	1.18	.30
Baa	1.55	.30
Ba	3.32	.27
B	5.09	.36

[1]*Source:* Susan D. Jordan and Bradford D. Jordan, "Seasonality in Daily Bond Returns," *Journal of Financial and Quantitative Analysis*, 26, no. 2 (June 1991): Table 5, p. 281.

[2]*Source:* Eric C. Chang and Roger D. Huang, "Time-Varying Return and Risk in the Corporate Bond Market," *Journal of Financial and Quantitative Analysis*, 25, no. 3 (September 1990): Table 1, p. 331.

TABLE 22-B
Analysis of Daily Returns

DAY OF WEEK	AVERAGE DAILY RETURN
Monday	−.20%
Tuesday	.93
Wednesday	−.00
Thursday	.44
Friday	−.00

Source: Susan D. Jordon and Bradford D. Jordan, "Seasonality in Daily Bond Returns," *Journal of Financial and Quantitative Analysis*, 26, no. 2 (June 1991): Table 5, p. 281.

Thursday, and the average returns for all five days are not statistically significantly different from each other.[28] Hence, in contrast to common stocks, the day-to-the-week effect does not appear to exist for corporate bonds.

REFERENCES

1. There have been many tests of efficiency in the bond market; text footnotes 1 through 9 contain citations of several of them, while some of the others are cited in:

   Frank J. Fabozzi and T. Dessa Fabozzi, *Bond Markets, Analysis and Strategies* (Englewood Cliffs, N.J.: Prentice Hall, 1989), pp. 300–303. This book also contains an extensive discussion of the concepts of convexity and duration in Chapter 4.

2. A book that discusses convexity, duration, and many related investment strategies is:

   Gerald O. Bierwag, *Duration Analysis* (Cambridge, Mass.: Ballinger Publishing Company, 1987).

3. A method for measuring convexity is given by:

   Robert Brooks and Miles Livingston, "A Closed-Form Equation for Bond Convexity," *Financial Analysts Journal*, 45, no. 6 (November/December 1989): 78–79.

[28]The returns on Wednesday and Friday are shown to be zero, but this is only because of rounding, as they are slightly negative.

4. The concept of duration and its use to measure interest rate risk was initially developed by:

   Frederick R. Macauley, *Some Theoretical Problems Suggested by the Movement of Interest Rates, Bond Yields, and Stock Prices in the United States Since 1856* (New York: National Bureau of Economic Research, 1938);

   J. R. Hicks, *Value and Capital*, 2nd ed. (Oxford, England: Clarendon Press, 1946; the first edition was published in 1939);

   Michael H. Hopewell and George G. Kaufman, "Bond Price Volatility and Term to Maturity: A Generalized Respecification," *American Economic Review*, 63, no. 4 (September 1973): 4749–53.

5. For interesting articles describing the development of the concept of duration (as well as immunization), see:

   Roman L. Weil, "Macauley's Duration: An Appreciation," *Journal of Business*, 46, no. 4 (October 1973): 589–92;

   Frank K. Reilly and Rupinder S. Sidhu, "The Many Uses of Bond Duration," *Financial Analysts Journal*, 36, no. 4 (July/August 1980): 58–72;

   G. O. Bierwag, George G. Kaufman, and Alden Toevs, "Duration: Its Development and Use in Bond Portfolio Management," *Financial Analysts Journal*, 39, no. 4 (July/August 1983): 15–35.

6. For alternative methods of calculating duration, see:

   Jess H. Chua, "A Generalized Formula for Calculating Bond Duration," *Financial Analysts Journal*, 44, no. 5 (September/October 1988): 65–67;

   Sanjay K. Nawalkha and Nelson J. Lacey, "Closed-Form Solutions of Higher-Order Duration Measures," *Financial Analysts Journal*, 44, no. 6 (November/December 1988): 82–84.

7. For the initial development and subsequent supportive tests of immunization, see:

   F. M. Redington, "Review of the Principles of Life-Office Valuations," *Journal of the Institute of Actuaries*, 78, no. 3 (1952): 286–315;

   Lawrence Fisher and Roman L. Weil, "Coping with the Risk of Interest-Rate Fluctuations: Returns to Bondholders from Naive and Optimal Strategies," *Journal of Business*, 44, no. 4 (October 1971): 408–31;

   G. O. Bierwag and George G. Kaufman, "Coping with the Risk of Interest-Rate Fluctuations: A Note," *Journal of Business*, 50, no. 3 (July 1977): 364–70;

   G. O. Bierwag, George G. Kaufman, Robert Schweitzer, and Alden Toevs, "The Art of Risk Management in Bond Portfolios," *Journal of Portfolio Management*, 7, no. 2 (Spring 1981): 27–36;

   Gerald O. Bierwag, *Duration Analysis* (Cambridge, Mass.: Ballinger Publishing Company, 1987), Chapter 12;

   Donald R. Chambers, Willard T. Carleton, and Richard W. McEnally, "Immunizing Default-Free Bond Portfolios with a Duration Vector," *Journal of Financial and Quantitative Analysis*, 23, no. 1 (March 1988): 89–104;

   Iraj Fooladi and Gordon S. Roberts, "Bond Portfolio Immunization," *Journal of Economics and Business*, 44, no. 1 (February 1992): 3–17.

8. For some interesting articles on the relationship of duration and convexity, see:

Mark L. Dunetz and James M. Mahoney, "Using Duration and Convexity in the Analysis of Callable Bonds," *Financial Analysts Journal,* 44, no. 3 (May/June 1988): 53–72;

Bruce J. Grantier, "Convexity and Bond Portfolio Performance: The Benter the Better," *Financial Analysts Journal,* 44, no. 6 (November/December 1988): 79–81;

Jacques A. Schnabel, "Is Benter Better: A Cautionary Note on Maximizing Convexity," *Financial Analysts Journal,* 46, no. 1 (January/February 1990): 78–79.

9. Some of the research that is critical of the use of duration, convexity, and immunization is mentioned in footnote 18; other critical research includes:

Jonathan E. Ingersoll, Jr., Jeffrey Skelton, and Roman L. Weil, "Duration Forty Years Later," *Journal of Financial and Quantitative Analysis,* 13, no. 4 (November 1977): 627–50;

Ronald N. Kahn and Roland Lochoff, "Convexity and Exceptional Return," *Journal of Portfolio Management,* 16, no. 2 (Winter 1990): 43–47;

Antti Ilmanen, "How Well Does Duration Measure Interest Rate Risk?" *Journal of Fixed Income,* 1, no. 4 (March 1992): 43–51.

10. For a discussion of how to use nondefault-free bonds in an immunized portfolio, see:

Gordon J. Alexander and Bruce G. Resnick, "Using Linear and Goal Programming to Immunize Bond Portfolios," *Journal of Banking and Finance,* 9, no. 1 (March 1985): 35–54;

G. O. Bierwag and George G. Kaufman, "Durations of Nondefault-Free Securities," *Financial Analysts Journal,* 44, no. 4 (July/August 1988): 39–46, 62;

Gerald O. Bierwag, Charles J. Corrado, and George G. Kaufman, "Computing Durations for Bond Portfolios," *Journal of Portfolio Management,* 17, no. 1 (Fall 1990): 51–55.

11. For a discussion of the effect of call risk on duration (and immunization), see:

Kurt Winkelmann, "Uses and Abuses of Duration and Convexity," *Financial Analysts Journal,* 45, no. 5 (September/October 1989): 72–75.

12. For a discussion of how to use duration to measure the risk of foreign bonds, see:

Steven I. Dym, "Measuring the Risk of Foreign Bonds," *Journal of Portfolio Management,* 17, no. 2 (Winter 1991): 56–61;

Steven Dym, "Global and Local Components of Foreign Bond Risk," *Financial Analysts Journal,* 48, no. 2 (March/April 1992): 83–91.

13. Dedicated bond portfolios and contingent immunization are discussed in:

Martin L. Leibowitz and Alfred Weinberger, "Contingent Immunization—Part I: Risk Control Procedures," *Financial Analysts Journal,* 38, no. 6 (November/December 1982): 17–31;

Martin L. Leibowitz and Alfred Weinberger, "Contingent Immunization—Part II: Problem Areas," *Financial Analysts Journal,* 39, no. 1 (January/February 1983): 39–50;

Martin L. Leibowitz, "The Dedicated Bond Portfolio in Pension Funds—Part I: Motivations and Basics," *Financial Analysts Journal,* 42, no. 1 (January/February 1986): 69–75;

Martin L. Leibowitz, "The Dedicated Bond Portfolio in Pension Funds—Part II: Immunization, Horizon Matching, and Contingent Procedures," *Financial Analysts Journal,* 42, no. 2 (March/April 1986): 47–57.

14. For a discussion of horizon analysis and bond swaps, see:

Sidney Homer and Martin L. Leibowitz, *Inside the Yield Book* (Englewood Cliffs, N.J.: Prentice Hall, 1972), Chapters 6–7;

Martin L. Leibowitz, "Horizon Analysis for Managed Bond Portfolios," *Journal of Portfolio Management,* 1, no. 3 (Spring 1975): 23–34;

Martin L. Leibowitz, "An Analytic Approach to the Bond Market," in *Financial Analyst's Handbook,* ed. Sumner N. Levine (Homewood, Ill.: Dow Jones–Irwin, Inc., 1975), pp. 226–77;

Marcia Stigum and Frank J. Fabozzi, *The Dow Jones–Irwin Guide to Bond and Money Market Investments* (Homewood, Ill.: Dow Jones–Irwin, Inc., 1987), Chapter 16.

15. For a discussion of various yield curve strategies, see:

Marcia Stigum and Frank J. Fabozzi, *The Dow Jones–Irwin Guide to Bond and Money Market Investments* (Homewood, Ill.: Dow Jones–Irwin, Inc., 1987), pp. 270–72;

Jerome S. Osteryoung, Gordon S. Roberts, and Daniel E. McCarty, "Ride the Yield Curve When Investing Idle Funds in Treasury Bills?" *Financial Executive,* 47, no. 4 (April 1979): 10–15;

Edward A. Dyl and Michael D. Joehnk, "Riding the Yield Curve: Does It Work?" *Journal of Portfolio Management,* 7, no. 3 (Spring 1981): 13–17;

Frank J. Jones, "Yield Curve Strategies," *Journal of Fixed Income,* 1, no. 2 (September 1991): 43–51;

Robin Grieves and Alan J. Marcus, "Riding the Yield Curve: Reprise," *Journal of Portfolio Management,* 18, no. 4 (Summer 1992): 67–76.

16. Bond indices are discussed and analyzed in:

Frank K. Reilly, G. Wenchi Kao, and David J. Wright, "Alternative Bond Market Indexes," *Financial Analysts Journal,* 48, no. 3 (May/June 1992): 44–58.

17. More on bond investment strategies is contained in:

Frank J. Fabozzi and T. Dessa Fabozzi, *Bond Markets, Analysis and Strategies* (Englewood Cliffs, N.J.: Prentice Hall, 1989), particularly Chapters 12–14;

Ehud I. Ronn, "A New Linear Programming Approach to Bond Portfolio Management," *Journal of Financial and Quantitative Analysis,* 22, no. 4 (December 1987): 439–66;

Michael C. Ehrhardt, "A New Linear Programming Approach to Bond Portfolio Management: A Comment," *Journal of Financial and Quantitative Analysis,* 24, no. 4 (December 1989): 533–37;

Randall S. Hiller and Christian Schaack, "A Classification of Structured Bond Portfolio Modeling Techniques," *Journal of Portfolio Management,* 17, no. 1 (Fall 1990): 37–48.

18. The evaluation of the performance of bond portfolio managers has been discussed by:

Mark Kritzman, "Can Bond Managers Perform Consistently?" *Journal of Portfolio Management*, 9, no. 4 (Summer 1983): 54–56;

Robert N. Anthony, "How to Measure Fixed-Income Performance Correctly," *Journal of Portfolio Management*, 11, no. 2 (Winter 1985): 61–65;

Arthur Gudikunst and Joseph McCarthy, "Determinants of Bond Mutual Fund Performance," *Journal of Fixed Income*, 2, no. 1 (June 1992): 95–101.

19. For an interesting discussion of what mix of bonds and stocks is appropriate for investors, see:

Martin L. Leibowitz and William S. Krasker, "The Persistence of Risk: Stocks Versus Bonds Over the Long Term," *Financial Analysts Journal*, 44, no. 6 (November/December 1988): 40–47;

Paul A. Samuelson, "The Judgment of Economic Science on Rational Portfolio Management: Indexing, Timing and Long-Horizon Effects," *Journal of Portfolio Management*, 16, no. 1 (Fall 1989): 4–12;

Martin L. Leibowitz and Terence C. Langetieg, "Shortfall Risk and the Asset Allocation Decision: A Simulation Analysis of Stock and Bond Profiles," *Journal of Portfolio Management*, 16, no. 1 (Fall 1989): 61–68;

Keith P. Ambachtscheer, "The Persistence of Investment Risk," *Journal of Portfolio Management*, 16, no. 1 (Fall 1989): 69–71;

Kirt C. Butler and Dale L. Domian, "Risk, Diversification, and the Investment Horizon," *Journal of Portfolio Management*, 17, no. 3 (Spring 1991): 41–47.

20. Pension fund management is discussed in:

Martin L. Liebowitz, "Total Portfolio Duration: A New Perspective on Asset Allocation," *Financial Analysts Journal*, 42, no. 5 (September/October 1986): 18–29, 77;

Martin L. Liebowitz and Roy D. Henriksson, "Portfolio Optimization Within a Surplus Framework," *Financial Analysts Journal*, 44, no. 2 (March/April 1988): 43–51;

William F. Sharpe, "Liabilities—A New Approach," *Journal of Portfolio Management*, 16, no. 2 (Winter 1990): 4–10.

21. Empirical regularities in the bond market have been investigated by:

Eric C. Chang and J. Michael Pinegar, "Return Seasonality and Tax-Loss Selling in the Market for Long-Term Government and Corporate Bonds," *Journal of Financial Economics*, 17, no. 2 (December 1986): 391–415;

Eric C. Chang and Roger D. Huang, "Time-Varying Return and Risk in the Corporate Bond Market," *Journal of Financial and Quantitative Analysis*, 25, no. 3 (September 1990): 323–40;

Susan D. Jordan and Bradford D. Jordan, "Seasonality in Daily Bond Returns," *Journal of Financial and Quantitative Analysis*, 26, no. 2 (June 1991): 269–85.

PART VI
ALTERNATIVE INVESTMENTS

23

Investment Companies

investment companies

Investment companies are a type of financial intermediary. They obtain money from investors and use it to purchase financial assets such as stocks and bonds. In return, the investors receive certain rights regarding the financial assets the investment company has bought and any earnings that it may make. In the simplest and most common situation, the investment company has only one type of investor—stockholders. These stockholders directly own the investment company, and thus indirectly own the financial assets that the company itself owns.

For an individual, there are two advantages to investing in such companies instead of investing directly in the financial assets these companies own. Specifically, the advantages arise from (1) economies of scale and (2) professional management. In describing these benefits, consider an individual with moderate financial resources who wishes to invest in the stock market.

In terms of economies of scale, the individual could buy stocks in odd lots and thus have a diversified portfolio. However, the brokerage commissions on odd lot transactions are relatively high. Alternatively, the individual could purchase round lots, but would only be able to afford a few different securities. Unfortunately, the individual would then be giving up the benefits of owning a well-diversified portfolio, in which declines in some securities would more likely be offset by gains in others. In order to receive the benefits of diversification and substantially reduced brokerage commissions, the individual could invest in the shares of an investment company. That is, economies of scale make it possible for an investment company to provide diversification at a lower cost per dollar of investment than would be incurred by a small individual investor.

In terms of professional management, the individual investing directly in the stock market would have to go through all the details of investing, including such things as making all buying and selling decisions as well as keeping records of all transactions for tax purposes. In doing so, the individual would have to continually be on the lookout for mispriced securities in an attempt to find undervalued ones for purchase, while selling any that were found to be overvalued. Simultaneously, the individual would have to keep track of the overall risk level of the portfolio so that it did not deviate from some desired level. However, by purchasing shares of an investment company, the individual can turn over all of these details to a professional money manager.

Many of these managers hope to identify areas of mispricing in the market, exploit them, and share the resultant abnormal gains with investors by charging them for a portion of the gains. However, it appears that they typically cannot find enough mispriced situations so as to recoup more than the additional costs they have incurred, costs that take the form of increased management fees and transaction costs owing to the continual buying and selling of securities. Nevertheless, other potential advantages to be gained from investing in an investment company may still outweigh any disadvantages.

Investment companies differ in many ways, and classification is difficult. Common practice will be followed here, where the term will be restricted to those financial intermediaries that do not obtain money from "depositors." Thus, the traditional operations of savings and loan companies and banks, for example, will be excluded. However, the process of deregulation is rapidly breaking down previous barriers, so the future may very well bring even more competition for traditional investment companies.

NET ASSET VALUE

net asset value

An important concept in understanding how investment companies operate is **net asset value.** Given that an investment company has assets consisting of various securities, it is generally quite easy to determine the market value of all the assets held by the investment company at the end of each business day. For example, an investment company that holds various common stocks traded on the New York Stock Exchange could easily find out what the closing prices were at the end of the day and then simply multiply these prices by the number of shares that they own. After adding up these figures, any liabilities that the investment company had outstanding would be subtracted; dividing the resulting difference by the number of outstanding shares of the investment company produces the net asset value for the investment company.

Equivalently, an investment company's net asset value at the end of day t (NAV_t) can be determined by using the following equation:

$$NAV_t = \frac{MVA_t - LIAB_t}{NSO_t} \tag{23.1}$$

where MVA_t, $LIAB_t$, and NSO_t denote the market value of the investment company's assets, the dollar amount of the investment company's liabilities, and the number of shares the investment company has outstanding, respectively, as of the end of day *t*. Thus, an investment company with 4,000,000 shares outstanding whose assets consisted of common stocks with an aggregate market value of $102,000,000 and whose liabilities amounted to $2,000,000 as of November 15, 1992, would report a net asset value on that date of ($102,000,000 − $2,000,000)/4,000,000 = $25 per share.

It should be noted that an investment company's net asset value will change every day, since the values of either MVA_t, $LIAB_t$, or NSO_t (or all three) will change.

MAJOR TYPES OF INVESTMENT COMPANIES

The Investment Company Act of 1940 classifies investment companies as follows:[1]

- unit unvestment trusts
- managed investment companies
  - closed-end investment companies
  - open-end investment companies

Unit Investment Trusts

unit investment trust

A **unit investment trust** is an investment company that owns a fixed set of securities for the life of the company.[2] That is, the investment company rarely alters the composition of its portfolio over the life of the company.

Formation To form a unit investment trust, a sponsor (often a brokerage firm) purchases a specific set of securities and deposits them with a trustee (such as a bank). Then, a number of shares known as redeemable trust certificates are sold to the public. These certificates provide their owners with a proportional interest in the securities that were previously deposited with the trustee. All income received by the trustee on these securities is subsequently paid out to the certificate holders, as are any repayments of principal. Changes in the original set of securities (that is, selling some of them and buying different ones) are made only under exceptional circumstances. Since there is no active management of a unit investment trust, the annual fees charged by the sponsor are correspondingly low (perhaps equal to .15% of NAV per year).

Most unit investment trusts hold fixed-income securuties and expire after the last one has been paid off (or, possibly, sold). Lifespans range from six months for unit investment trusts of money market instruments to over twenty years for trusts of bond market instruments. Some trusts include only federal government bonds, others only corporate bonds, others only municipal bonds, and so on.

Not surprisingly, the sponsor of a unit investment trust will seek compensation for the effort and risk involved in setting up the trust. This is accomplished by setting a selling price for the shares that exceeds the cost of

[1] Another classification covers certain companies that issue "face-amount certificates" promising specific payments. This type of company is rare and will not be discussed here.

[2] In the United Kingdom, a "unit trust" is an open-end investment company (described in a later section).

the underlying assets. For example, a brokerage firm might purchase $10,000,000 worth of bonds, place them in a unit investment trust, and issue 10,000 shares. Each share might be offered to the public for $1,035. When all the shares have been sold, the sponsor would have received $1,035 × 10,000 = $10,350,000. This is enough to cover the $10,000,000 cost of the bonds, leaving $350,000 for selling expenses and profit. Markups (or load charges) of this sort range from less than 1% for short-term trusts to 3.5% for long-term trusts.

Secondary Market Typically, an investor who purchases shares of a unit investment trust is not required to hold the shares for the entire life of the trust. Instead, the shares usually may be sold back to the trust at net asset value, calculated on the basis of bid prices for the assets in the portfolio.[3] That is, the market value of the securities in the portfolio is determined, using dealers' bid quotations. Since unit investment trusts do not have any liabilities, this amount is divided by the number of shares outstanding to obtain the net asset value per share. Having determined the per share price, the trustee may sell one or more securities to raise the required cash for the repurchase.

Alternatively, it is possible that a secondary market is maintained by the sponsor of the trust. In this situation, investors can sell their shares back to the sponsor. Afterwards, other investors who did not participate in the initial sale can subsequently purchase these shares; typically, the sponsor's selling price in the secondary market is equal to the net asset value of the securities in the portfolio (based on the dealers' asked prices) plus a load charge equal to that in effect at the time the trust was created.

Managed Companies

managed investment companies

While a unit investment trust has no board of directors and no portfolio manager, **managed investment companies** have both. Since they are organized as corporations (a few are limited partnerships), a managed investment company will have a board of directors that is elected by its shareholders. In turn, the board will commonly hire a firm—the "management company"—to manage the company's assets for an annual fee that is typically based (at least in part) on the total market value of the assets. These management companies may be independent firms, investment advisors, firms associated with brokers, or insurance companies. Often the management company is the business entity (for example, a subsidiary of a brokerage firm) that started and promoted the investment company. A management company may have contracts to manage a number of investment companies, each of which is a separate corporation with its own board of directors.

Annual management fees average about .60% (they can range from less than .25% to over 1%) of the market value of the investment company's total assets, with the percentage sliding downward as the assets increase. Some funds provide "incentive compensation," where the better the fund's investment performance, the higher the fee paid to the management company.

In addition to the fee paid by an investment company to its management company, there are administrative and custodial expenses. These services are usually provided by the management company, but the costs are charged to

[3]Dealers in fixed-income securities generally quote both bid and asked prices. The bid price is the amount the dealer will pay for a security; the asked price is the amount an investor must pay to purchase the security.

the investment company. For the typical investment company, such annual expenses are roughly .50% of the market value of its total assets. Many investment companies require their management company to cover all expenses over a specified amount, effectively limiting total expenses.[4]

closed-end investment companies

Closed-End Investment Companies Unlike unit investment trusts, **closed-end investment companies** (or closed-end funds) do not stand ready to purchase their own shares whenever one of their owners decides to sell them. Instead, their shares are traded either on an organized exchange or in the over-the-counter market. Thus, an investor who wants to buy or sell shares of a closed-end fund would simply place an order with a broker, just as if the investor wanted to buy or sell shares of IBM.

Most closed-end funds have unlimited lives. Dividends and interest received by a closed-end fund from the securities in its portfolio are paid out to its shareholders, as are any net realized capital gains. However, most funds allow (and encourage) the reinvestment of such payments. The fund keeps the money and sends the investor additional shares based on the net asset value per share at that time. For example, consider a closed-end fund that has just declared a dividend of $1 per share. If its net asset value were $15 per share, a holder of thirty shares would have a choice of receiving either $30 (= 30 × $1) or two shares (= $30/$15).

Being a corporation, a closed-end fund can issue new shares not only through reinvestment plans but also with public stock offerings. However, this is done infrequently, and the fund's capitalization is "closed" most of the time.[5]

Most closed-end funds can repurchase their own shares in the open market, although this is seldom done. Whenever a fund's market price falls substantially below net asset value, a repurchase will increase the fund's net asset value per share. For example, if net asset value were $20 per share at a time when the fund's shares could be purchased in the open market (say, on the New York Stock Exchange) for $16 per share, the managers of the fund could sell $20 worth of securities from the fund's portfolio, buy back one of the fund's outstanding shares, and have $4 left over. If the $4 was used to buy securities for the fund, the net asset value per share would increase, with the size of the increase depending on, in addition to the number of shares repurchased and their repurchase price, the number of remaining shares.

The market prices of the shares of closed-end funds are published daily in the financial press, provided that the funds are listed on an exchange or traded actively in the over-the-counter market. However, their net asset values are only published weekly, based on closing market prices for securities in their portfolios as of the previous Friday for stock funds, and two preceding Fridays for bond funds. Figure 23-1 provides an example. Both the net asset value and the last price at which the fund's shares traded on the day in question are shown (if no trade price is available, the last dealer's asked

[4]Owing to a 1980 ruling (Rule 12b-1) by the Securities and Exchange Commission, open-end funds may choose to pay a *distribution fee* annually. This fee, sometimes as much as 2% of the market value of total assets, goes for advertising and promoting the fund to prospective purchasers. The alleged benefit to the current owners of the fund is that the subsequent increased size of the portfolio will bring with it certain economies of scale; indications are that such a benefit is not being realized.

[5]Owing to restrictions in the Investment Company Act of 1940, few closed-end investment companies have any interest-bearing liabilities outstanding (that is, they typically have only a small amount of current liabilities outstanding).

FIGURE 23-1
Listing of Closed-End Funds

Source: Reprinted by permission of *Barron's*, © Dow Jones & Company, Inc., July 20, 1992, pp. 116–17. All rights reserved worldwide.

(a) CLOSED-END BOND FUNDS

Fund Name	Stock Exch.	N.A. Value	Share Price	% Diff.
Bond Funds				
1838 Bond-Deb Trading	NYSE	21.62	23⅝	+ 9.27
ACM Govt Inco Fund	NYSE	10.53	11⅜	+ 8.02
ACM Govt Oppor Fd	NYSE	9.45	9¾	+ 3.17
ACM Govt Securities	NYSE	10.55	10⅞	+ 3.08
ACM Govt Spectrum	NYSE	8.92	9¼	+ 3.70
ACM Mgd Inco Fd	NYSE	9.06	9¾	+ 7.62
AIM Strategic Inco	AMEX	9.27	9	− 2.91
AMEV Securities	NYSE	10.22	11¼	+10.08
American Adj Rate '95	NYSE	c10.01	10¼	+ 2.40
American Adj Rate '96	NYSE	c9.73	10⅛	+ 4.06
American Adj Rate '97	NYSE	c9.66	10	+ 3.52
American Adj Rate '98	NYSE	c9.66	9⅞	+ 2.23
American Capital Bond	NYSE	b20.06	19¾	− 1.55
American Capital Inco	NYSE	a7.95	8	+ 0.63
American Gov't Portf	NYSE	c10.73	11	+ 2.52
American Govt Income	NYSE	c8.22	8⅞	+ 7.97
American Govt Term	NYSE	c9.91	10¾	+ 8.48
American Opp Inco Fund	NYSE	c10.85	11⅛	+ 2.53
American Strat Inc	NYSE	c14.07	15¼	+ 8.39
Bunker Hill Income	NYSE	15.82	16¼	+ 2.72
CIGNA High Income Shs	NYSE	7.22	8	+10.80
Colonial Int High Inco	NYSE	6.57	7	+ 6.54
Colonial Intrmkt Inco I	NYSE	11.51	11½	− 0.09
Convertible Bond Funds				
Lincoln Natl Convert	NYSE	c18.43	17½	− 5.05
Putnam Hi Inco Conv	NYSE	a8.44	9⅛	+ 8.12
International Bond Funds				
ACM Mgd Multi-Market	NYSE	10.68	11⅛	+ 4.17
First Australia Prime	AMEX	10.98	11¾	+ 7.01
First Commonwealth	NYSE	14.95	14¾	− 1.34
Global Government	NYSE	8.20	7⅞	− 3.96
Global Income Plus	NYSE	a9.81	10⅜	+ 5.76
Global Yield Fund	NYSE	8.94	8¾	− 2.13
Kleinwort Benson Aust	NYSE	11.64	11⅜	− 2.28
Strat Global Income	NYSE	a14.24	14½	+ 1.83
Templeton Glbl Gov Inco	NYSE	9.24	10	+ 8.23
Templeton Global Inco	NYSE	a8.99	9½	+ 5.67
Municipal Bond Funds				
Allstate Mun Inc	NYSE	10.72	11	+ 2.61
Allstate Mun Inc II	NYSE	10.48	10¾	+ 2.58
Allstate Mun Inc III	NYSE	9.84	9¾	− 0.91
Allstate Mun Inc Op	NYSE	8.99	9¾	+ 8.45
Allstate Mun Inc Op II	NYSE	9.18	9¾	+ 6.21
Allstate Mun Inc Op III	NYSE	9.57	10	+ 4.49
Allstate Muni Pr Inco	NYSE	10.39	10⅝	+ 2.26
Amer Muni Term Tr	NYSE	c10.50	10¾	+ 2.38
Amer Muni Term Tr II	NYSE	c10.22	10⅛	− 0.93
Apex Muni Fund	NYSE	a10.30	10⅞	+ 5.58
Blackrock Insured Muni	NYSE	9.96	10	+ 0.40
Blackrock Muni Tar Trm	NYSE	9.99	9⅞	− 1.15
Colonial Hi Inco Muni	NYSE	8.87	9	+ 1.47
Colonial Inv Gr Muni	NYSE	11.00	11⅞	+ 7.95
Colonial Muni Inco Tr	NYSE	7.98	8⅛	+ 1.82
Dreyfus Cal Muni Inco	AMEX	9.43	9½	+ 0.74
Dreyfus Muni Inco	AMEX	10.01	10¾	+ 7.39
Dreyfus NY Muni Inco	AMEX	10.04	10⅛	+ 0.85
Dreyfus Strat Muni Bd	NYSE	9.90	10⅜	+ 4.80
Dreyfus Strat Munis	NYSE	10.13	11⅛	+ 9.82
Duff & Phelps Util T-F	NYSE	14.94	15⅜	+ 2.91
Intercap Ins Muni Bd	NYSE	15.42	16⅞	+ 9.44
Intercap Ins Muni Tr	NYSE	15.03	15⅝	+ 3.96
Intercap Qual Muni	NYSE	15.12	15½	+ 2.51
Kemper Muni Inco Tr	NYSE	12.56	13	+ 3.50
Kemper Strategic Inco	NYSE	11.95	12¾	+ 6.69
MFS Muni Inco Tr	NYSE	8.85	9¾	+10.17
Managed Municipals	NYSE	12.34	11⅞	− 3.77
Merrill High Inc Muni	N/A	10.75	N/A	N/A
Minnesota Mun Term II	AMEX	c9.74	10⅛	+ 3.95
Minnesota Muni Term Tr	NYSE	c10.09	10⅛	+ 0.35
MuniEnhanced Fund	NYSE	a12.58	13⅛	+ 4.33
MuniInsured Fd Inc	NYSE	a10.33	10¼	− 0.77
MuniVest Fund Inc	NYSE	a10.28	11¼	+ 9.44
MuniYield CA	NYSE	a14.89	15⅜	+ 3.26
MuniYield CA Ins	NYSE	14.27	N/A	N/A
MuniYield FL	NYSE	a14.92	15½	+ 3.89
MuniYield Fund	NYSE	a15.39	15½	+ 0.71
MuniYield Insured	NYSE	a15.08	15	− 0.53
MuniYield MI	NYSE	a14.96	15⅜	+ 2.77
MuniYield NY Ins	NYSE	a15.06	15½	+ 2.92
MuniYield NY Ins II	NYSE	14.22	N/A	N/A
MuniYield New Jersey	NYSE	a14.55	15⅜	+ 5.67
MuniYield Quality	NYSE	14.28	13½	− 5.46
Municipal High Income	NYSE	9.62	9⅞	+ 2.65
New York Tax-Exempt	AMEX	10.50	11	+ 4.76
Nuveen CA Inv Qual Muni	NYSE	15.52	15¾	+ 1.48
Nuveen CA Muni Inco	NYSE	12.14	13	+ 7.08
Nuveen CA Muni Mkt Opp	NYSE	15.75	15⅞	+ 0.79
Nuveen CA Muni Val	NYSE	10.52	11⅛	+ 5.75
Nuveen CA Perf Plus	NYSE	15.72	16	+ 1.78
Nuveen CA Qual Inc Muni	NYSE	14.64	14½	− 0.96
Nuveen NY Perf Plus	NYSE	15.78	16½	+ 4.56
Nuveen NY Qual Inc Mun	NYSE	14.74	14⅝	− 0.78
Nuveen NY Sel Qual Mun	NYSE	15.46	15½	+ 0.26
Nuveen OH Qual Inc Mun	NYSE	14.69	15	+ 2.11
Nuveen PA Inv Qual Muni	NYSE	15.44	16⅜	+ 6.06
Nuveen PA Qual Inc Mun	NYSE	14.94	15¼	+ 2.07
Nuveen Perf Plus	NYSE	15.39	15½	+ 0.71
Nuveen Prem Inco	NYSE	16.12	16⅝	+ 3.13
Nuveen Prem Ins Muni	NYSE	14.52	14¾	+ 1.58
Nuveen Prem Muni Inc	NYSE	14.46	14⅝	+ 1.14
Nuveen Qual Inco Muni	NYSE	15.22	15⅛	− 0.62
Nuveen Sel Qual Muni	NYSE	15.46	15⅛	− 2.17
Nuveen Sel Tx-Fr Inc	NYSE	14.72	14¾	+ 0.20
Nuveen Sel Tx-Fr Inc 2	NYSE	14.48	14⅞	+ 2.73
Nuveen TX Qual Inc Mun	NYSE	14.80	15	+ 1.35
Putnam Hi Yld Muni	NYSE	a9.24	10½	+13.64
Putnam Inv Grade Muni	NYSE	a12.48	12⅞	+ 3.17
Putnam Mgd Mun Inco	NYSE	a10.02	10½	+ 4.79
Putnam Tx-Fr Hlth Care	NYSE	14.20	15	+ 5.63
Seligman Quality Muni	NYSE	a14.77	14⅜	− 2.67
Seligman Select Muni	NYSE	a12.48	12¾	+ 2.16
Smith Barney Int Mun	AMEX	a10.34	10	− 3.29
Taurus Muni CA Hldgs	NYSE	a12.01	13⅜	+11.37
Taurus Muni NY Hldgs	NYSE	a12.24	13¾	+12.34
VanKamp CA Muni Tr	NYSE	10.44	10½	+ 0.57
VanKamp CA Qual Muni	NYSE	15.70	14⅞	− 5.25
VanKamp FL Qual Muni	NYSE	15.89	15½	− 2.45
VanKamp Inv Gr CA	NYSE	15.55	14¾	− 5.14
VanKamp Inv Gr FL	NYSE	15.71	15⅛	− 3.72
VanKamp Inv Gr Muni	NYSE	11.67	13¼	+13.54
VanKamp Inv Gr NJ	NYSE	15.63	15¼	− 2.43
VanKamp Inv Gr NY	NYSE	15.58	15⅜	− 1.32
VanKamp Inv Gr PA	NYSE	15.66	15⅝	− 0.22
VanKamp Muni Inc Tr	NYSE	10.88	11¾	+ 8.00
VanKamp Muni Oppty Tr	NYSE	16.01	15¼	− 4.75
VanKamp Muni Trust	NYSE	16.29	15¾	− 3.31
VanKamp NY Qual Muni	NYSE	16.29	15¾	− 3.31
VanKamp OH Qual Muni	NYSE	15.81	15⅞	+ 0.41
VanKamp PA Qual Muni	NYSE	16.15	16	− 0.93
VanKamp Tr For Ins Mun	NYSE	16.11	15⅛	− 6.11
VanKamp Tr Inv Gr Muni	NYSE	16.23	15½	− 4.50
Voyageur Minn Muni Inc	AMEX	14.29	15¾	+10.22

a - Ex-dividend. b - Fully diluted. N/A Not applicable. c - As of Thursday's Close. d - NAV on 3/27 was 11.03.

FIGURE 23-1 *(Continued)*

(b) CLOSED-END STOCK FUNDS

Friday, July 17, 1992

Following is a weekly listing of unaudited net asset values of publicly traded investment fund shares, reported by the companies as of Friday's close. Also shown is the closing listed market price or a dealer-to-dealer asked price of each fund's shares, with the percentage of difference.

Fund Name	Stock Exch.	N.A. Value	Stock Price	% Diff.
Diversified Common Stock Funds				
Adams Express	NYSE	19.88	18 3/4	− 5.68
Allmon Trust	NYSE	10.39	9 5/8	− 7.36
Baker Fentress	NYSE	21.95	18 1/4	− 16.85
Blue Chip Value	NYSE	7.50	7 7/8	+ 5.00
Clemente Global Gro	NYSE	b10.76	9 3/8	− 12.87
Gemini II Capital	NYSE	9.69	12 3/4	+ 31.58
Gemini II Income	NYSE	17.90	14 5/8	− 18.30
General Amer Invest	NYSE	27.47	27 3/4	+ 1.02
Jundt Growth Fd	NYSE	14.04	13 5/8	− 2.96
Liberty All-Star Eqty	NYSE	10.43	10 3/8	− 0.53
Niagara Share Corp.	NYSE	15.33	14 7/8	− 2.97
Quest For Value Cap	NYSE	26.13	21 5/8	− 17.24
Quest For Value Inco	NYSE	11.56	13 3/8	+ 15.70
Royce Value Trust	NYSE	11.90	11 1/8	− 6.51
Salomon Fd	NYSE	15.22	13 7/8	− 8.84
Source Capital	NYSE	41.76	45 1/8	+ 8.06
Tri-Continental Corp.	NYSE	27.87	27 1/4	− 2.22
Worldwide Value	NYSE	16.42	14 1/8	− 13.98
Zweig Fund	NYSE	11.12	12 7/8	+ 15.78
Specialized Equity and Convertible Funds				
Alliance Global Env Fd	NYSE	11.80	10 1/4	− 13.14
American Capital Conv	NYSE	22.20	19 1/8	− 13.85
Argentina Fd	NYSE	11.70	12 1/8	+ 3.63
ASA Ltd	NYSE	bc42.90	41 1/2	− 3.26
Asia Pacific	NYSE	13.71	16 1/4	+ 18.53
Austria Fund	NYSE	9.40	8 3/8	− 10.90
Bancroft Convertible	AMEX	22.39	19 3/4	− 11.79
Bergstrom Capital	AMEX	96.74	109 1/2	+ 13.19
BGR Precious Metals	TOR	be8.58	7 3/8	− 14.04
Brazil	NYSE	b17.57	18 1/2	+ 5.29
Brazilian Equity Fd	NYSE	b11.44	11 3/4	+ 2.71
CNV Holdings Capital	NYSE	11.55	7 1/2	− 35.06
CNV Holdings Income	NYSE	9.32	12 3/8	+ 32.78
Castle Convertible	AMEX	24.66	21 5/8	− 12.31
Central Fund Canada	AMEX	b4.28	4	− 6.54
Central Securities	AMEX	12.40	10 1/8	− 18.35
Chile Fund	NYSE	39.79	37 1/2	− 5.76
Couns Tandem Secs	NYSE	15.89	13 1/2	− 15.04
Duff&Phelps Utils Inc.	NYSE	9.64	10 1/4	+ 6.33
Ellsw Conv Gr&Inc	AMEX	9.16	8	− 12.66
Emerging Ger Fd	NYSE	9.53	8	− 16.05
Emerging Mark Tele Fd	NYSE	14.49	14 7/8	+ 2.66
Emerging Mexico Fd	NYSE	b21.01	20 1/4	− 3.62
Engex	AMEX	10.85	8 5/16	− 23.39
Europe Fund	NYSE	13.09	12 3/8	− 5.46
1stAustralia	AMEX	10.33	9 1/8	− 11.67
First Financial Fund	NYSE	12.98	11 3/8	− 12.37
First Iberian	AMEX	8.81	7 5/8	− 13.45
First Philippine Fund	NYSE	14.17	11 1/2	− 18.84
France Growth Fund	NYSE	11.95	9 3/4	− 18.41
Future Germany Fund	NYSE	16.18	13 1/2	− 16.56
Gabelli Equity Trust	NYSE	10.67	11	+ 3.09
Germany Fund	NYSE	12.25	11 1/8	− 9.18
Global Health Science Fd	NYSE	12.81	11 7/8	− 7.30
Growth Fund Spain	NYSE	10.59	9 5/8	− 9.11
GT Greater Europe Fd	NYSE	11.55	9 3/4	− 15.58
H&Q Healthcare Inv	NYSE	19.69	21 3/8	+ 8.56
H&Q Life Sciences Inv Fd	NYSE	14.15	14 5/8	+ 3.36
Hampton Utils Tr Cap	AMEX	b15.42	13 7/8	− 10.02
Hampton Utils Tr Pref	AMEX	b49.63	51	+ 2.76
India Growth Fund	NYSE	f19.56	15 7/8	− 18.84
Indonesia Fund	NYSE	8.90	9 3/4	+ 9.55
Inefficient Market Fund	AMEX	10.67	9 1/2	− 10.97
Irish Investment Fd	NYSE	9.71	8	− 17.61
Italy Fund	NYSE	9.71	9 1/8	− 6.02
Jakarta Growth Fd	NYSE	7.28	8 3/8	+ 15.04
Japan OTC Equity Fund	NYSE	7.85	10	+ 27.39
Korea Fund	NYSE	9.66	10 7/8	+ 12.58
Korean Investment Fd	NYSE	8.72	10 1/2	+ 20.41
Latin America Disc Fd	NYSE	14.81	14 1/4	− 3.78
Latin America Equity Fd	NYSE	18.14	16 1/4	− 10.42
Latin America Inv Fd	NYSE	31.64	27 7/8	− 11.90
Malaysia Fund	NYSE	15.49	14	− 9.62
Mexico Equity Inc Fd	NYSE	b16.52	15 5/8	− 5.42
Mexico Fund	NYSE	b26.39	26	− 1.48
Morgan Grenf SmCap	NYSE	10.81	11 1/4	+ 4.07
Morgan Stan Em Mks Fd	NYSE	17.66	17 1/4	− 2.32
New Germany Fund	NYSE	13.95	11 1/2	− 17.56
Pacific Eur Growth Fd	NYSE	b10.75	10 1/2	− 2.33
Patriot Prem Div Fd	NYSE	10.25	10 1/4	+ 0.00
Patriot Prem Div Fd II	NYSE	12.37	11 7/8	− 4.00
Patriot Select Div Trust	NYSE	16.17	17	+ 5.13
Petrol & Resources	NYSE	28.45	26 5/8	− 6.41
Pilgrim Regional	NYSE	11.65	11 1/8	− 4.51
Portugal Fund	NYSE	12.06	10 3/4	− 10.86
Preferred Income Fd	NYSE	18.33	19 3/8	+ 5.70
Preferred Inc Opport Fd	NYSE	12.50	13 1/2	+ 8.00
Putnam Dividend Inc Fd	NYSE	11.56	12 1/2	+ 8.13
Rl Estate Sec Inco Fd	AMEX	7.54	7 5/8	+ 1.13
ROC Taiwan Fund	NYSE	9.23	9	− 2.49
Scudder New Asia	NYSE	15.30	15 1/2	+ 1.31
Scudder New Europe	NYSE	10.59	9 1/4	− 12.65
SE Thrift & Bank Fd	OTC	b13.79	11 3/4	− 14.79
Singapore Fd	NYSE	b11.67	11 3/8	− 2.53
Spain Fund	NYSE	11.02	10	− 9.26
Swiss Helvetia Fd	NYSE	15.09	14 5/8	− 3.08
Taiwan Fund	NYSE	b21.15	19 3/8	− 8.39
TCW Convertible Secs	NYSE	8.04	9 3/8	+ 16.60
Templeton Em Mkts	NYSE	b19.90	23 7/8	+ 19.97
Templeton Global Util	AMEX	b13.51	13 3/4	+ 1.78
Thai Capital Fund	NYSE	9.51	8 1/4	− 13.25
Thai Fund	NYSE	16.04	15 1/4	− 4.93
Turkish Inv Fund	NYSE	6.06	6 5/8	+ 9.32
United Kingdom Fund	NYSE	11.59	10 1/4	− 11.56
Z-Seven	OTC	w14.90	16 7/8	+ 13.26

b-As of Thursday's close. c-Translated at Commercial Rand exchange rate. e-In Canadian Dollars. f-As of Wednesday's close, using the Free — Market Spot Rate. w-last price on the Pacific Stck Exch.

price is indicated). The final column indicates the difference between each fund's stock price and its net asset value. If this difference is positive (meaning that the stock price is greater than the NAV), the fund's shares are said to be selling at a premium. Conversely, if this difference is negative (meaning that the stock price is less than the NAV), the fund's shares are said to be selling at a discount. For example, Figure 23-1(b) indicates that the France Growth Fund was selling at a discount while the Korea Fund was selling for a premium (these two investment companies are known as "country funds," specializing in French and Korean stocks, respectively). Most closed-end funds (other than a few country funds) sell at a discount.[6]

open-end investment company

mutual funds

Open-End Investment Companies An investment company that stands ready at all times to purchase its own shares at or near their net asset value is termed an **open-end investment company** (or open-end fund). Most of these companies, commonly known as **mutual funds,** also continuously offer new shares to the public for a price at or near their net asset values. Hence their capitalization is "open," with the number of shares outstanding changing on a daily basis.

no-load funds
load funds
load charge

Some open-end companies, known as **no-load funds,** sell their shares at a price equal to net asset value. Others, known as **load funds,** offer shares through brokers or other selling organizations, which add a percentage **load charge** to the net asset value. The percentage charged is usually smaller, the greater the amount invested, and by law cannot exceed 8.5% of the amount invested. For example, a selling organization receiving $1,000 to be invested in a fund might retain as much as $85, leaving $915 to be used to purchase the fund's shares at the current net asset value per share. While this is usually described as a load charge of 8.5%, it is actually equal to 9.3% = $85/$915 of the amount ultimately invested. Load charges of this magnitude are levied by many funds for small purchases but typically are reduced for larger purchases.[7]

redemption fee

When mutual fund shareholders want to sell their shares, they usually receive an amount equal to the fund's net asset value times the number of shares sold. However, a few funds charge a **redemption fee** (also known as a back-end load or exit fee or contingent deferred sales charge), which may run as high as 6% of the fund's net asset value. Typically, those funds that do charge such a fee will lower the percentage charged the longer the shareholder owns the shares. Thus, investors selling their shares within six months of purchase might have to pay a 6% fee, while investors selling their shares after owning them for five or more years might not have to pay any fee; for those investors selling between six months and five years, a sliding-scale fee may be applicable.

As will be discussed later, the investment performance of no-load funds as a whole does not differ in any notable way from that of load funds. This is not surprising. The load charge (roughly 30% to 50% of which goes to the individual who sold the shares, with the selling organization keeping the rest) represents the cost of education and persuasion. Mail-order firms often sell items for less than what stores charge. Salespersons who work in stores and those who sell mutual funds provide a service and require compensation.

real estate investment trusts

low-load funds

[6]**Real estate investment trusts** (REITs), although not classified as investment companies for legal purposes, are similar to closed-end funds in that they serve as a conduit for earnings on investments in real estate or loans secured by real estate, passing earnings on to their shareholders and avoiding corporate taxation.

[7]Funds that have a load charge of 3.5% or less are often referred to as **low-load funds.**

Buyers who consider such services worth less than their cost can and should avoid paying for them.

Figure 23-2 shows a portion of the quotations for mutual funds provided in the financial press following each business day.[8] The net asset value, based on closing prices for the fund's securities on the day in question, is shown first. This is followed by the "offer" price—the net asset value plus the load charge applicable to the smallest possible purchase; for no-load funds, this column contains the letters "NL." The final column indicates the difference

[8]Funds that are listed under a name in boldface type have a common management company that is associated with that name; for example, note all the funds listed under Calvert Group in Figure 23-2.

MUTUAL FUND QUOTATIONS

Wednesday, July 15, 1992

Price ranges for investment companies, as quoted by the National Association of Securities Dealers. The NASD requires a mutual fund to have at least 1,000 shareholders or $25 million in net assets before being listed. NAV stands for net asset value per share; the offering includes net asset value plus maximum sales charge, if any.

	NAV	Offer Price	NAV Chg.
AAL Mutual:			
CaGr p	14.11	14.81	-.02
Inco p	10.40	10.92	+.03
MuBd p	10.71	11.24	+.01
AARP Invst:			
CaGr	30.98	NL	+.06
GinIM	16.08	NL	+.04
GthInc	28.92	NL	-.08
HQ Bd	16.20	NL	+.05
TxFBd	17.97	NL	+.02
ABT Funds:			
Emrg p	10.31	10.82	+.02
FL TF	10.93	11.48	...
GthIn p	10.11	10.61	-.03
Utilln p	12.61	13.24	+.02
AEGON USA:			
CapApp	4.47	4.69	-.01
Gwth	7.10	7.45	-.02
HIYld	10.51	11.03	+.01
TaxEx	11.80	12.39	...
AHA Funds:			
Balan	12.23	NL	-.01
Full	10.66	NL	+.02
Lim	10.54	NL	+.01
AIM Funds:			
AdjGv p	9.91	10.22	...
Chart p	8.33	8.81	...
Const p	12.11	12.81	+.03
CvYld p	12.85	13.49	+.05
HIYld p	....	....	...
IntlE p	9.54	10.10	+.04
LimM p	10.24	10.34	+.02
Sumit	9.49	....	-.01
TF Int	10.54	10.87	+.02
Weing p	16.13	17.07	-.01
AIM Funds C:			
AgrsvC p	14.32	15.15	+.08
GoScC px	10.33	10.85	-.04
GrthC p	13.61	14.40	...
HYldC p x	9.39	9.86	-.08
IncoC p x	8.04	8.44	-.01
MuBC p x	8.34	8.76	-.04
TeCtC p	10.71	11.24	+.01
UtilC p x	13.81	14.61	-.04
ValuC p	17.71	18.74	-.03
AMF Funds:			
AdjMtg	10.01	NL	...
IntMtg	9.95	NL	+.04
IntlLiq	10.94	NL	+.03
MtgSc	11.39	NL	+.03
ASO Funds:			
Balance	10.97	11.49	...
Bond	11.22	11.75	+.04
Equity	13.14	13.76	-.04
LtdMat	10.80	11.08	+.01
AcornF	49.22	49.22	+.10
AdsnCa p	19.43	20.03	-.03
Advest Advant:			
Govt p	8.96	8.96	+.04
Gwth p	16.20	16.20	+.03
HY Bd p	8.80	8.80	+.01
Inco p	11.72	11.72	+.02
Spcl p	14.68	14.68	+.09
AetnaBd	10.10	NL	+.06
AetnaFd	10.20	NL	...
Afuture	9.07	9.84	-.06

	NAV	Offer Price	NAV Chg.
DivMu	13.36	NL	+.01
NYMu	13.45	NL	+.02
BerwynFd	15.02	NL	-.01
Blanchard Funds:			
GlGr p	9.99	NL	...
PrcM p	5.96	NL	+.14
ST Gl	1.89	NL	...
BdEndw	19.17	NL	+.10
Boston Co:			
AAloc p	14.73	NL	...
AMEF	....	....	...
CaAp p	27.12	NL	...
Intl	10.89	NL	+.05
IntGv p	12.84	NL	+.04
Mgdl p	11.64	NL	+.02
SpGth p	14.33	NL	-.02
TF Bd	12.37	NL	...
Brndyw	18.34	NL	-.02
Bruce	92.03	NL	+.07
Bull & Bear Gp:			
FNCI p	17.90	NL	-.08
Gold p	11.94	NL	+.16
GovtSc p	14.95	NL	+.04
HIYld p	8.70	NL	+.04
SpEq p	20.02	NL	-.09
TxFr p	17.55	NL	+.02
USOvs p	8.37	NL	+.03
Burnhm	20.87	21.97	-.02
C&SRlty n	26.99	NL	...
CGM Funds:			
CapDv	24.75	NL	-.35
Mutl	26.32	NL	-.06
Calmos	12.77	13.37	+.01
CalTrst	12.50	NL	...
CalUS	10.38	NL	+.03
Calvert Group:			
Ariel	29.30	30.76	-.05
ArielA	19.01	19.96	-.01
Capitl p	....	....	...
Inco	17.20	18.06	+.03
Social p	28.66	30.09	+.06
SocBd	16.76	17.60	+.04
SocEq	19.50	20.47	+.01
TxF Lt	10.69	10.91	+.01
TxF Lg	16.45	17.27	+.01
TxF VT	15.92	16.54	+.01
US Gov	15.67	16.45	+.03
Cambridge Fds:			
CapGrA	14.17	14.99	+.01
CapGrB t	14.17	14.17	+.01
GvInB t	14.46	14.46	+.03
GwthB t	13.90	13.90	-.01
CapitolEq	10.02	NL	-.01
CapitolFI	10.57	NL	+.04
Capstone Group:			
CshFr	10.33	10.85	...
Fd SW	16.51	17.33	+.05
GvtInc	4.78	4.78	...
MedRs	18.19	19.10	+.21
PBHG	9.16	9.62	+.03
Ray EI	7.01	7.36	...
Trend	13.90	14.59	-.01
Cardnl	12.69	13.87	-.06
CrdnlGv	8.97	9.39	+.01
CarilCa	12.54	13.20	-.01
CrnOHTE	9.61	10.06	...

FIGURE 23-2
Listing of Mutual Funds (Excerpt)

Source: Reprinted by permission of *The Wall St. Journal*, © Dow Jones & Company, Inc., July 16, 1992, p. C18.

(in dollars) between the day's net asset value per share and that computed at the close of the previous trading day.

Figure 23-3 shows the weekly quotations that appear for a special type of mutual fund known as a money market fund. Such funds invest in short-term, fixed-income securities such as Treasury bills, commercial paper, and bank certificates of deposit. A special type of money market fund that invests primarily in short-term municipals is also shown in the lower right-hand part of the figure. Next to the name of such a fund is shown the average maturity of its holdings, the annual yield based on what was earned over the last seven days, the compounded annual yield based on what was earned over the last seven days, and the aggregate market value of its assets. Not shown, but an important factor in deciding on what money market fund to invest in, is the degree of safety (that is, default risk) associated with the assets held by each fund.

An Example In order to highlight the differences in purchasing shares of closed-end funds, no-load funds, and load funds, consider the following example. An investor has $1,000 to use in purchasing shares of a fund, and is

FIGURE 23-3
Listing of Money Market Mutual Funds (Excerpt)

Source: Reprinted by permission of *The Wall St. Journal*, © Dow Jones & Company, Inc., July 16, 1992, p. C9. All rights reserved worldwide.

MONEY MARKET MUTUAL FUNDS

The following quotations, collected by the National Association of Securities Dealers Inc., represent the average of annualized yields and dollar-weighted portfolio maturities ending Wednesday, July 15, 1992. Yields don't include capital gains or losses.

Fund	Avg. Mat.	7Day Yld.	e7Day Yld.	Assets
AALMny	64	2.40	2.43	125
AARP HQ	54	2.54	2.57	338
AIMCshC	52	3.02	3.07	79
AIM MM	27	2.70	2.74	111
AIMMMC	56	3.03	3.08	98
ASO Pr	74	3.25	3.30	458
ASO US	57	3.10	3.15	324
ActAsGv	66	3.19	3.24	545
ActAsMny	72	3.37	3.43	3773
Aetna MM	62	4.02	4.02	28
AlexBwn	49	3.21	3.26	1137
AlxBTr	51	3.18	3.23	654
AlgerMM	77	3.82	3.89	144
AlliaCpRs	79	3.27	3.32	1977
AllaGvR	79	3.10	3.15	1601
AlliMny	85	3.26	3.31	1438
AmAAdTr	58	3.44	3.50	60
AmAAdMM	80	3.89	3.97	2275
AmCRes	60	2.70	2.74	322
AmExDDiv	89	3.31	3.36	17137
AmExGv	86	3.26	3.31	3918
AmPerCsh	86	3.33	3.39	155
AmPerTrs	58	2.83	2.87	203
AmbMM	41	3.35	3.40	306
AmbTreas	54	3.30	3.35	62
ArchUSTr	49	3.20	3.25	156
ArchFd	44	3.01	3.05	550
AMF St Lq	10	3.11	3.12	126
AutCsh	56	3.41	3.47	1219
AutGvt	51	3.15	3.20	3272
AuGvSvc	40	3.17	3.22	362
AutTreasC	40	3.05	3.10	36
Babson	50	2.99	3.04	60
BartCsR	78	3.52	3.59	69
BayFdMM	66	3.31	3.36	275
BaysCsh	57	3.30	3.35	435
BaysUS	58	3.14	3.19	246
BedfdGv	39	2.86	2.91	251
BdfdMM	64	2.99	3.04	753
BenhGvAg	52	3.30	3.35	811
WmBlrRdy	41	3.19	3.24	435
BlnchGv	81	3.75	3.82	70
BostCo	83	3.24	3.29	276
BostGvt	49	3.28	3.33	88
BradGovObl	39	2.86	2.91	45
Bradfd	42	3.01	3.05	655
BullBDlr	80	2.97	3.01	64
CBC Cn Pr	84	3.21	3.26	332
CBC Cn Tr	39	2.95	2.99	945
CIMCO	25	2.82	2.86	9
CalvSoc f	55	3.10	3.15	179
CapCash	22	3.46	3.52	2
CapPre II	1	2.64	2.67	361
CapPrsv	52	3.21	3.26	3092

Fund	Avg. Mat.	7Day Yld.	e7Day Yld.	Assets
USAA Mutl	84	3.60	3.67	931
USAA Treas	76	3.46	3.52	22
USFG Cs	35	3.08	3.13	28
UST Gvt	53	3.16	3.21	1111
UST Mny	44	3.35	3.41	789
UST Treas	67	3.13	3.18	198
USTrCshIns	43	3.39	3.45	98
US TreCs	38	2.95	2.99	52
UnionInst	86	3.51	3.57	355
UnionInv	86	3.26	3.31	155
UtdCshM	66	3.03	3.08	443
UtdGvt	59	5.15	5.29	135
VIMMP	59	3.77	3.84	228
ValLin	59	4.34	4.43	468
VnEckUS a	33	1.69	1.71	22
VanKmpMM	54	2.53	2.56	25
VangFdl f	58	3.59	3.65	1923
VangPr f	59	3.63	3.70	12747
VangUST	59	3.56	3.63	2249
VisnMM	44	3.47	3.52	164
VisnTr	60	3.32	3.37	103
VistaUS	50	2.94	2.98	336
Voyager	48	3.28	3.33	79
WPG GovMM	60	2.84	2.88	90
WestcrCs	30	3.26	3.22	190
WestcrGv	40	3.17	3.16	92
WestcrPr	39	3.30	3.23	88
WestcrTr	53	3.02	3.04	119
WoodGv	65	3.39	3.45	306
WoodMM	73	3.46	3.52	982
WorkAsets	63	2.97	3.05	219
WrightMgd	36	3.15	3.19	21
ZweigGvt	58	3.34	3.40	101

TAX EXEMPTS

Fund	Avg. Mat.	7Day Yld.	e7Day Yld.	Assets
AARPHTe	51	1.59	1.60	129
AIMTeCtC	51	1.69	1.71	18
AIMTxC	58	1.77	1.78	31
ASO TxEx	82	2.43	2.45	40
AT OhioTx	42	2.12	2.15	270
ActAsCal	69	1.66	1.67	180
ActAstTx	59	2.01	2.03	1387
AlxB TF	44	1.94	1.96	271
AllMuNY	65	1.99	2.01	106
AlliaMun	78	2.05	2.07	952
AllTxCal	71	2.13	2.15	133
AmExCal	61	1.89	1.91	708
AmExTxDD	78	2.09	2.11	3504
AmExNY	87	2.01	2.03	563
AmbTxFr	86	2.21	2.24	101
ArchFd	58	1.67	1.68	158
AtlasCA	68	2.45	2.48	61
BayshrTF	73	2.39	2.42	140
BdfdTxFr	57	1.96	1.97	177
BedfordNY	56	2.30	2.33	52
BenCAMu	49	2.51	2.54	254
BenCaTF	45	2.00	2.02	310
BenNaTF	48	1.94	1.96	107
BostonCo	48	2.06	2.08	156
BradfordTF	57	1.96	1.97	77

considering the following funds, all of which have the same net asset value (NAV) of $10 per share.

Closed-end fund E is selling for a market price that equals its NAV, while closed-end fund D is selling at a 20% discount, or $8 (= $10 × .80); the broker charges a commission equal to 2% of the market price for each share purchased. Mutual fund N is a no-load fund, while mutual fund L charges an 8½% load. How many shares does the investor end up with in each case?

Closed-end fund E:	cost per share = $10 + $.20 commission = $10.20
	number of shares = $1,000/$10.20 = 98.04
Closed-end fund D:	cost per share = $8 + $.16 commission = $8.16
	number of shares = $1,000/$8.16 = 122.55
Mutual fund N:	cost per share = $10
	number of shares = $1,000/$10 = 100
Mutual fund L:	cost per share = $10 + $.93 load = $10.93
	(note: 8.5% × $10.93 = $.93)
	number of shares = 91.50

Thus, the largest number of shares would be received when buying the shares of discounted closed-end fund D, while the fewest shares would be received when buying the shares of load fund L.

INVESTMENT POLICIES

Different investment companies follow different investment policies (also termed investment styles). Some companies are designed as substitutes for their shareholders' entire portfolio; others expect their shareholders to own other securities. Some restrict their domain or selection methods severely; others give their managers wide latitude. Many engage in highly active management, with substantial portfolio changes designed to exploit perceived superior investment predictions. However, others are more passive, concentrating instead on tailoring a portfolio to serve the interests of a particular clientele.

While categorization is difficult, broad classes can be identified. As mentioned earlier, money market funds hold short-term (typically less than one year) fixed-income instruments such as bank certificates of deposit, commercial paper, and Treasury bills. These open-end funds make it possible for small investors to move in and out of the short-term market. The fund manager will extract an annual fee for this service, usually between .25% and 1% of the average value of total assets. There are usually no load charges, and investors may add or remove money from their accounts at almost any time. Dividends are usually declared daily. Arrangements with a cooperating bank often make it possible to write a check on an account, where the bank obtains the amount involved by redeeming "shares" in the fund when the check clears.

Bond funds invest in fixed-income securities. Some go further, specifying that only particular types will be purchased. There are corporate bond funds, U.S. government bond funds, GNMA (or "Ginnie Mae") funds, convertible bond funds, and so on. Some are organized as open-end investment companies, others as closed-end investment companies.

As indicated earlier, the predominant type of unit investment trust in the United States is the bond unit investment trust. Some are based on government issues, others on corporate issues, and still others on specialized types. Municipal bond unit investment trusts, like open-end municipal bond funds, often make it easier for those in high tax brackets to obtain diversification and liquidity while taking advantage of the exemption of such securities from personal income taxation. Bond unit investment trusts typically hold securities with different coupon payment schedules and pay roughly equal-size dividends every month.

A few open-end investment companies and some unit investment trusts are restricted to holdings of preferred stocks. Others include both bonds and preferred stocks in their portfolios.

Many open-end companies consider themselves managers for the bulk of the investment assets of their clients. Those that hold both equity and fixed-income securities particularly fit this description. Wiesenberger Investment Companies Services' annual *Investment Companies* manual refers to such companies as balanced funds. These funds seek to "minimize investment risks without unduly sacrificing possibilities for long-term growth and current income."[9] Somewhat similar to balanced funds are flexible income funds. These funds seek to "provide a liberal current income."[10] Some of these funds hold relatively constant mixes of bonds, preferred stock, convertible bonds, and equities; others alter the proportions periodically in attempts to "time the market."

A diversified common stock fund invests most of its assets in common stocks, although some short-term money market instruments are often held to accommodate irregular cash flows or to engage in market timing. In 1991, Wiesenberger's manual classified the majority of diversified common stock funds as having one of three types of objectives: (1) capital gain; (2) growth; and (3) growth-income.[11] Two factors appear to be involved in this classification: the relative importance of dividend income versus capital gains and the overall level of risk to be taken. The classifications "are arranged in descending order of emphasis on capital appreciation and, consequently, in ascending order of the importance placed on current income and relative price stability."[12] Since high-dividend portfolios are generally less risky than those with low dividends, relatively few major conflicts arise, although two rather different criteria are involved.

Borderline cases remain: "The difference between a capital gain fund and a growth fund is a matter of degree, and in some cases there is little distinction. Similarly, there is no sharp line of demarcation between a growth

[9]Wiesenberger Investment Companies Services, *Investment Companies 1991* (New York: Warren, Gorham & Lamont, Inc., 1991), p. 21.

[10]Wiesenberger, *Investment Companies 1991*, p. 21. Option-income funds are a type of income fund that invests primarily in high-dividend-paying common stocks while also writing call options on these stocks. (Call options will be discussed in the next chapter.) Equity income and fixed-income funds are other types of income funds that invest in, respectively, common stocks and fixed-income securuties.

[11]Sometimes the capital gain category is referred to as "maximum capital gain" or "aggressive growth." A fourth category ("specialized") consists of funds that, by design, are not highly diversified. One interesting kind of fund (sometimes organized as a limited partnership) is a hedge fund, where the manager will often engage in short selling and margin purchasing of common stocks.

[12]Wiesenberger, *Investment Companies 1991*, p. 20.

fund and a growth-income fund."[13] Classification is difficult because the official statement of investment objectives in a fund's prospectus is often fuzzy.

The Investment Company Act of 1940 defines a diversified investment company as one that invests at least 75% of its funds in a diversified manner, meaning that within this portion of the portfolio, no single issuer's securities may account for more than 5% of the fund's assets. Furthermore, within this 75% portion, the fund may not own more than 10% of the voting shares of any single issuer (the 25% exemption is designed to encourage funds to invest in small companies). Those not meeting this standard are classified as nondiversified investment companies. Some choose the latter classification simply to maintain flexibility, while others do so to specialize in certain types of securities.

A few specialized investment companies concentrate on the securities of firms in a particular *industry* or *sector*. For example, there are chemical funds, aerospace funds, technology funds, and gold funds. Others deal in securities of a particular type; examples include funds that hold restricted (that is, "letter") stock, and funds that invest in over-the-counter stocks. Still others provide a convenient means for holding the securities of firms in a particular *country*, such as the previously mentioned France and Korea funds. There are also investment companies that, by design, invest more widely internationally, purchasing stocks and bonds from a variety of different countries (from a U.S. viewpoint, international funds are those investing in non-U.S. securities, while global funds invest in both U.S. and non-U.S. securities).

While municipal bond unit investment trusts have been available for many years, open-end municipal bond funds were first offered in 1976. Some municipal bond funds hold long-term issues from many states. Others specialize in the long-term issues of governmental units in one state ("single-state" funds) in order to provide an investment vehicle for residents of that state who wish to avoid paying state taxes (as well as federal taxes) on the income. Still others buy short-term municipal securities (as noted in Figure 23-3), with some specializing in the short-term issues of governmental units in one state.

An index fund attempts to provide results similar or identical to those computed for a specified market index. For example, the *Vanguard Index Trust*, a no-load open-end investment company, provides a vehicle for small investors who wish to obtain results similar to those of Standard & Poor's 500-stock index. Similarly, a number of banks have established commingled index funds, and corporations and other organizations have set up index funds for their own employee retirement trust funds.

Table 23-1 provides an indication of the number of mutual funds having various kinds of investment objectives, along with the amount of assets under their control.

MUTUAL FUND ACCOUNTS

The U.S. Internal Revenue Code allows an investment company to avoid corporate income taxation. A unit investment trust or a closed-end investment company or an open-end investment company can qualify under Subchapter M of the code as a regulated investment company by meeting

[13]Wiesenberger, *Investment Companies 1991*, p. 20.

TABLE 23-1
Mutual Fund Classifications as of Year-end 1991

	NUMBER OF FUNDS	TOTAL ASSETS (IN BILLIONS)
A. Classifications by Assets:		
Equity	1,216	$ 367.7
Bond & Income	1,387	439.4
Taxable Money Market	553	449.7
Tax-exempt Money Market	267	89.9
Total	3,423	$1,346.7
B. Classifications by Investment Objectives:		
Aggressive Growth	209	$ 63.3
Growth	395	105.0
Growth & Income	308	129.5
Precious Metals	35	2.9
International	128	19.1
Global—Equity	65	17.3
Income—Equity	72	29.3
Option Income	4	1.4
Flexible Portfolio	60	10.0
Balanced	77	20.2
Income—Mixed	95	25.6
Income—Bond	139	27.5
U.S. Government Income	223	96.9
Ginnie Mae	54	36.6
Global Bond	59	26.8
Corporate Bond	61	15.5
High-yield Bond	95	26.1
Long-term Municipal	193	88.3
State Municipal Bond—Long-term	331	65.8
Tax-exempt Money Market	267	89.9
Taxable Money Market	553	449.7
Total	3,423	$1,346.7

Source: Adapted from *1992 Mutual Fund Fact Book*, pp. 22, 28, 48, 86, 87. Used with permission of the Investment Company Institute, Washington, D.C.

certain standards concerning diversification and by paying out at least 90% of its net income, exclusive of capital gains, each year.[14] Net realized capital gains may be distributed or retained. If the company chooses to retain these gains, it must pay a tax calculated at the maximum rate applied to capital gains for personal income taxes. Shareholders are then given credit for having paid tax at this rate on the gains on their shares. However, most companies choose to distribute the gains, making cash payments to the shareholders for their respective portions. Thus, most mutual funds make two kinds of payments to their shareholders—one for income (from dividends and interest that the fund has received) and one for net realized capital gains. However, the shareholders must subsequently pay personal income taxes on these distributions.

Accumulation Plans

While an investor can purchase shares in a fund and receive all distributions in cash, this is only one of many possible arrangements. Mutual funds offer

[14]At least 50% of the company's assets must be diversified, meaning that within this portion (1) no more than 5% of the fund's assets can be invested in the securities of any one issuer; and (2) no more than 10% of the voting shares of any one issuer can be held. Moreover, of the remaining portion, no more than 25% of total assets may be invested in the securities of any one company.

plans of several types to satisfy investors' desires for different patterns of contributions and withdrawals over time. Accumulation plans are designed for those who do not want to receive any income or capital gains distributions over some period of time. The simplest procedure involves automatic reinvestment of these distributions, where the shareholder elects to receive additional shares in the fund instead of cash. As with other plans, this often involves fractional shares, but since most accounts are maintained via computerized records, this poses no problem.

Voluntary accumulation plans allow an investor to add to an account as desired, subject only to some minimum amount that must be invested each time. Alternatively, a fixed dollar amount may be invested at periodic intervals—in some cases via automatic bank transfers.

Contractual accumulation plans call for a fixed amount to be contributed at regular intervals (usually monthly) over a relatively long period (often five or more years). Sales charges may or may not be lower than those applicable to a voluntary accumulation plan. The investor is not legally bound to make all the payments, but since a large proportion of early contributions typically goes toward sales charges, commitment to a contractual plan should not be considered if cancellation is at all likely.

The Investment Company Amendments Act of 1970 placed limits on the load charges for contractual plans. Specifically, no more than 50% of the first year's contribution may be allocated to sales charges (that is, at least half must be invested in fund shares). Moreover, if a 50% "front-end" load charge is assessed in the first year, cancellation of the plan within eighteen months entitles the investor to a refund, reducing the effective charge to 15% of the amount paid in.

A few funds offer insurance with their contractual accumulation plans. This insurance provides the remaining contributions if the investor dies or is disabled before all the contracted payments have been made. The premium for such insurance is, in effect, added to the sales charge.

Retirement Plans

Accumulation of funds for retirement may be accomplished via an individual retirement account (IRA) or a Keogh plan.[15] In 1991 anyone could contribute up to $2,000 of his or her earned income to an IRA, and if the income earner's spouse has no earned income, a total of $2,250 could be contributed to two IRAs. No taxes would be paid on the earnings of such funds until the investor began making withdrawals. Furthermore, under certain circumstances the investor can deduct the amount contributed from gross income when personal income taxes are being calculated.[16]

Self-employed individuals can contribute 25% of their net earnings from self-employment (up to a maximum of $30,000 in 1991) to a Keogh plan account, with such contributions also deductible from gross income for tax purposes. Either type of account is maintained by a custodian, often a bank. Contributions and any cash received from investments are invested in

[15]IRAs and Keogh plans are discussed more fully in Chapter 5. Also see Richard R. Simonds, "Mutual Fund Strategies for IRA Investors," *Journal of Portfolio Management*, 12, no. 2 (Winter 1986): 40–43.

[16]For example, the contribution will be deductible provided (1) the investor is not covered by an employer-sponsored retirement plan and does not have a Keogh plan; or (2) the investor is single and earns less than $25,000; or (3) the investor is married and the combined incomes are less than $40,000.

accordance with the investor's desires. Funds may be withdrawn beginning at age 59½ and withdrawals must begin by age 70½.

Exchange Privileges

It is increasingly common to find several investment companies operating as a "family of funds." An investor may purchase shares in more than one of the funds under common management and also may exchange shares of one fund for another. Sales charges for such exchanges are typically lower than those applicable to similar transactions involving funds managed by different companies; in some cases, exchanges within a family may be made without charge.

In this situation, the investor is given the opportunity to make timing decisions, switching shares from one fund to another one that is believed to be underpriced at that time. For example, consider an investor who owns shares of a gold fund that is in a family that includes a technology fund. If the investor feels that technology stocks are, in general, quite underpriced, then the investor could exchange the gold fund shares for technology fund shares.

Withdrawal Plans

Many mutual funds offer voluntary withdrawal plans. The investor instructs the fund to pay out either a fixed amount or a specified percentage of the account's value periodically (for example, monthly), decreasing the number of shares that the investor owns in the process.

MUTUAL FUND PERFORMANCE

Mutual funds need to compute and publicize their net asset values daily. Since their income and capital gain distributions are also publicized, they are ideal candidates for studies of the performance of professionally managed portfolios. Thus, it is hardly surprising that mutual funds have frequently been the subject of extensive study.

Calculating Returns

In studies of performance, the rate of return on a mutual fund for period t is calculated by adding the change in net asset value to the amount of income and capital gains distributions made during the period, denoted I_t and G_t, respectively, and dividing this total by the net asset value at the beginning of the period:

$$r_t = \frac{(\text{NAV}_t - \text{NAV}_{t-1}) + I_t + G_t}{\text{NAV}_{t-1}}. \tag{23.2}$$

For example, a mutual fund that had a net asset value of \$10 at the beginning of month t and made income and capital gain distributions of, respectively, \$.05 and \$.04 per share during the month, and then ended the month with a net asset value of \$10.03 would have a monthly return of:

$$r_t = \frac{(\$10.03 - \$10.00) + \$.05 + \$.04}{\$10.00}$$

$$= 1.20\%.$$

It should be noted that returns calculated in this manner can be used to evaluate the performance of the portfolio manager of a mutual fund, since this indicates the results of the manager's investment decisions. However, it does not necessarily indicate the return earned by the shareholders in the fund, since there may have been a load charge involved. In the example, perhaps the investor paid $10.50 at the beginning of the month for one share of this fund, with $.50 being a front-end load. If this were the case, the investor's return for this month could be calculated using equation (23.2), where NAV_{t-1} would be $10.50, not $10.00:

$$r_t = \frac{(\$10.03 - \$10.50) + \$.05 + \$.04}{\$10.50}$$

$$= -3.62\%.$$

Thus, the return for the investor who bought one share at the beginning of the month and paid a $.50 per share load charge at that time would be −3.62%. However, the portfolio manager was only given $10.00 per share to invest, since the load charge was given to certain people who were responsible for getting the investor to buy the share. Accordingly, the portfolio manager should be evaluated on the basis of the return provided on the $10.00, which in this example was 1.20%.

Recently, data on professionally managed pension funds and bank commingled funds have become available. The performance of the managers of such funds appears to be similar to that of mutual fund managers: They do reasonably well tailoring portfolios to meet clients' objectives, but few seem to be able to consistently "beat the market." While the following sections deal only with U.S. mutual funds, many of the results apply to other investment companies, both in the United States and in other countries.

Risk Control

One of the functions that a mutual fund can perform for its investors is the maintenance of a particular risk posture. Formal statements of objectives provide some idea of a fund's intended posture, but often the wording is vague. Nevertheless, there appears to be a general relationship between portfolio risk and stated objectives.

Figure 23-4 summarizes information on the standard deviations of monthly excess returns over a ten-year period for funds with similar objectives, using classifications assigned by Wiesenberger at the beginning of the period. In particular, the monthly returns for each one of 123 mutual funds were calculated using equation (23.2). Then, using these 120 monthly returns, the standard deviation was calculated for each one of the funds. Each bar in the figure plots the range of values of the standard deviations for funds having the same objective, with the average standard deviation being shown by a square near the middle of the bar. It can be seen that generally, the lower the amount of promised risk, the lower the amount of actual risk (a similar-looking figure resulted when beta was used). However, the overlapping of some of the bars indicates that some funds with conservative objectives took on more risk than others with less conservative objectives.

It is quite possible that past risk exposure may be a better guide to future risk exposure than the rather general statements found in a fund's prospectus. Figure 23-5 shows that this is often the case. Each point plots the beta for a fund in two different periods (based on daily returns). While the points do not

FIGURE 23-4
Risk versus Fund Objectives: 123 Mutual Funds, 1960–1969
Source: John G. McDonald, "Objectives and Performance of Mutual Funds, 1960–1969," *Journal of Financial and Quantitative Analysis*, 9, no. 3 (June 1974): 316.

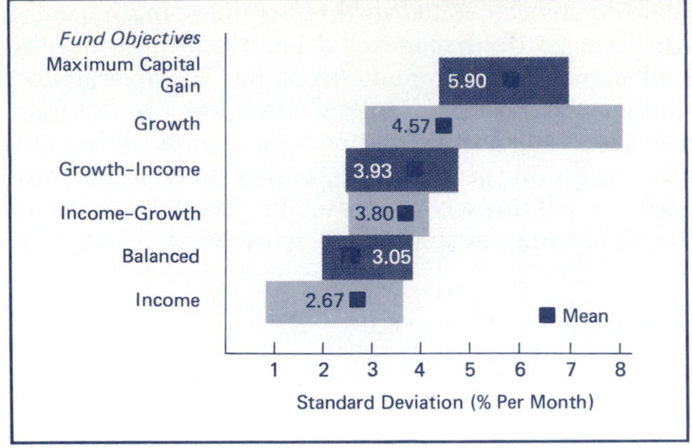

plot neatly along a 45-degree line from the origin that represents equal betas in both periods, there is a clear relationship between "past beta" and "future beta." This suggests that the typical mutual fund keeps its risk level at roughly the same value over time.

Diversification

An important task for any investment manager is the provision of an appropriate degree of portfolio diversification. The correct amount depends on the

FIGURE 23-5
Past versus Future Beta Values: 90 Mutual Funds, January 1969–May 1970 versus June 1970–October 1971
Source: Gerald A. Pogue and Walter Conway, "On the Stability of Mutual Fund Beta Values," (unpublished working paper, MIT Sloan School of Management, June 1972).

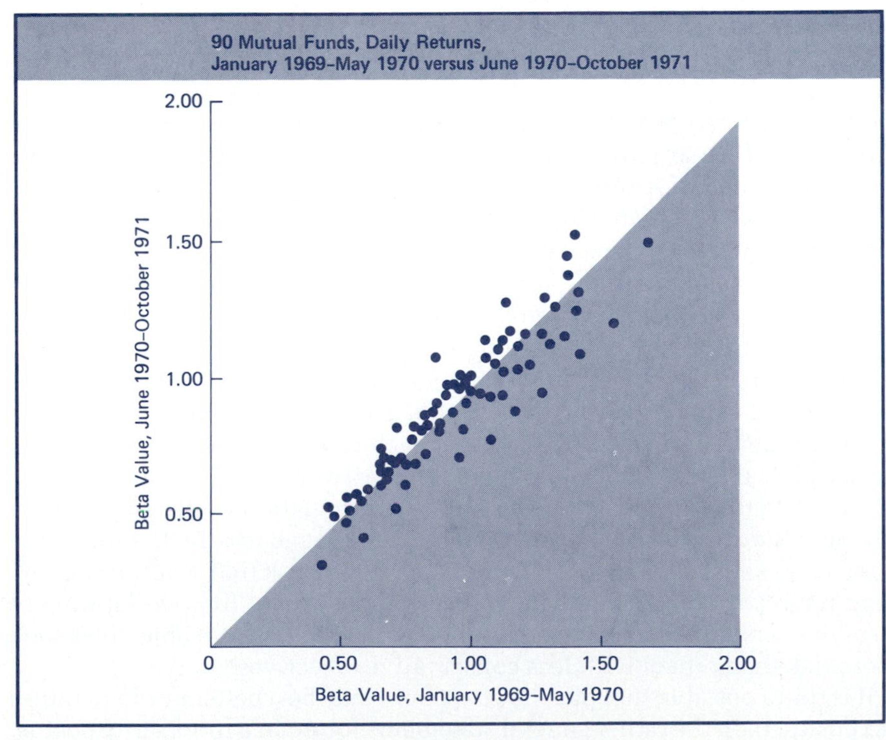

proportion of clients' funds managed and on the likelihood that superior abnormal returns can be obtained by sacrificing diversification. Since most mutual funds are intended to be a major component of a shareholder's portfolio, it is reasonable to expect them to be substantially diversified.

Figure 23-6 shows that many are. Quarterly excess returns over a five-year period were computed for 100 common stock funds and compared with corresponding values for Standard & Poor's 500-stock index. For each fund a value of R^2, the coefficient of determination, was computed. This indicates the proportion of the variation in a fund's excess returns that can be attributed to variations in excess returns on the index. As the figure shows, approximately 90% of the quarter-by-quarter variation in a typical fund's excess return was associated with swings in the value of the S&P 500 during this period, with values ranging from 66% to 98%.

Average Return

Some organizations have established two kinds of indices based on the net asset values of mutual funds that have similar investment objectives. One kind of index is based on nearly all of the U.S.-based mutual funds, while the second kind is based on a much smaller sample. As shown in Figure 23-7, this comparison is done every week (and, more extensively, every quarter) in *Barron's*, where mutual fund indices that have been prepared by Lipper Analytical Services are published. Note that the first three parts of the figure (General Equity Funds, Other Equity Funds, and Other Funds) present indices of the first kind, while the fourth part (Value Lipper Indexes) presents indices of the second kind. Last are a set of stock market indices made up of U.S. and foreign stocks. It can be seen in the figure that, with the exception of the American Stock Exchange (ASE) Index, all of the U.S. indices are presented

FIGURE 23-6
Proportion of Variation in Quarterly Returns Attributable to Market Fluctuations: 100 Mutual Funds, 1970–1974
Source: Merrill Lynch, Pierce, Fenner, & Smith, Inc., *Investment Performance Analysis, Comparative Survey, 1970–1974*. Reprinted by permission.

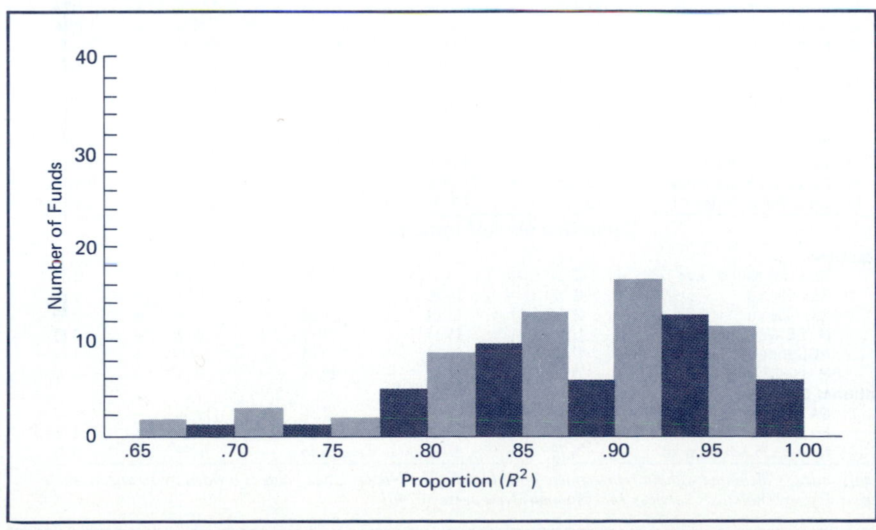

FIGURE 23-7
Mutual Fund Indices

Source: Reprinted by permission of *Barron's*, © Dow Jones & Company, Inc., July 20, 1992, p. 116. All rights reserved worldwide.

LIPPER MUTUAL FUND PERFORMANCE AVERAGES

Weekly Summary Report: July 17, 1992
Cumulative Performances With Dividends Reinvested

NAV Mil. $	No. Funds		10/11/90-07/16/92	07/12/90-07/16/92	07/18/91-07/16/92	12/31/91-07/16/92	07/09/92-07/16/92
General Equity Funds:							
1,081.9	131	Capital Appreciation	+ 52.01%	+ 17.51%	+ 10.27%	− 2.09%	+ 1.41%
111,956.3	321	Growth Funds	+ 49.62%	+ 17.75%	+ 9.35%	− 2.14%	+ 1.25%
21,766.7	135	Small Company Growth	+ 64.10%	+ 18.80%	+ 9.80 %	− 4.66%	+ 1.96%
113,211.6	264	Growth and Income	+ 45.55%	+ 19.95%	+ 10.97%	+ 1.59%	+ 0.88%
31,025.7	72	Equity Income	+ 43.50%	+ 22.15%	+ 13.30%	+ 3.84%	+ 0.79%
309,042.2	923	Gen. Equity Funds Avg.	+ 50.16%	+ 18.81%	+ 10.36%	− 0.90%	+ 1.23%
Other Equity Funds:							
5,234.2	14	Health/Biotechnology	+ 77.91%	+ 49.66%	+ 10.89%	− 12.01%	+ 3.05%
1,675.3	23	Natural Resources	+ 4.58%	− 3.32%	− 1.47%	+ 2.30%	+ 2.14%
238.6	7	Environmental	+ 9.11%	− 19.73%	− 11.70%	− 10.48%	+ 1.34%
2,741.0	21	Science & Technol.	+ 69.93%	+ 16.12%	+ 11.08%	− 5.25%	+ 2.93%
1,964.0	28	Specialty/Misc.	+ 55.04%	+ 19.14%	+ 12.18%	+ 3.72%	+ 1.27%
10,939.0	33	Utility Funds	+ 36.56%	+ 29.93%	+ 19.72%	+ 4.77%	+ 1.02%
646.5	12	Financial Services	+ 115.43%	+ 60.74%	+ 34.69%	+ 15.09%	− 0.36%
236.4	6	Real Estate	+ 42.80%	+ 14.99%	+ 12.09%	+ 2.50%	+ 0.49%
799.6	5	Option Income	+ 35.31%	+ 15.18%	+ 9.23%	+ 5.51%	+ 0.97%
2,538.1	34	Gold Oriented Funds	− 3.15%	− 8.65%	− 6.47%	+ 1.53%	+ 4.09%
17,364.1	62	Global Funds	+ 24.19%	+ 2.66%	+ 8.55%	+ 0.93%	+ 1.35%
13,797.3	97	International Funds	+ 15.47%	− 2.04%	+ 7.92%	+ 2.14%	+ 1.39%
3,368.1	28	European Region Fds	+ 8.92%	− 6.33%	+ 11.08%	+ 4.45%	+ 1.46%
1,539.5	20	Pacific Region Funds	+ 17.43%	− .95%	+ 4.34%	+ 3.13%	+ 0.82%
479.0	5	Japanese Funds	− 22.44%	− 37.49%	− 22.32%	− 17.08%	+ 0.10%
303.5	3	Latin American Funds	N/A%	N/A%	N/A%	+ 8.72%	+ 4.69%
50.8	3	Canadian Funds	+ 3.05%	− 7.15%	− 7.99%	− 1.89%	+ 1.11%
372,957.2	1324	All Equity Funds Avg.	+ 43.61%	+ 15.24%	+ 9.59%	− 0.13%	+ 1.36%
Other Funds:							
7,468.7	64	Flexible Portfolio	+ 36.49%	+ 20.76%	+ 12.07%	+ 1.65%	+ 0.76%
1,477.7	15	Global Flex Port.	+ 20.80%	+ 12.12%	+ 9.03%	+ 2.04%	+ 0.78%
21,291.7	76	Balanced Funds	+ 39.05%	+ 23.55%	+ 12.40%	+ 1.45%	+ 0.74%
825.9	8	Balanced Target	+ 42.39%	+ 27.06%	+ 16.11%	− 0.55%	+ 0.85%
2,310.8	28	Conv. Securities	+ 43.82%	+ 22.54%	+ 15.33%	+ 4.49%	+ 0.87%
6,322.3	18	Income Funds	+ 36.93%	+ 27.13%	+ 15.84%	+ 4.77%	+ 0.51%
30,395.4	96	World Income Funds	+ 18.27%	+ 26.32%	+ 13.36%	+ 3.60%	+ 0.40%
227,536.9	688	Fixed Income Funds	+ 29.36%	+ 27.00%	+ 15.45%	+ 4.76%	+ 0.23%
670,586.6	2317	Long-Term Average	+ 38.31%	+ 19.57%	+ 11.71%	+ 1.66%	+ 0.93%
		Long-Term Median	+ 36.30%	+ 22.20%	+ 12.50%	+ 2.90%	+ 0.70%
		Funds with % Change	1727	1679	1972	2114	2277
Value Lipper Indexes:							
338.23	30	Capital Apprec Index	+ 49.05%	+ 18.28%	+ 9.44%	− 4.58%	+ 1.60%
616.05	30	Growth Fund Index	+ 50.37%	+ 18.56%	+ 10.52%	− 1.30%	+ 1.03%
324.12	30	Small Co Growth Index	+ 60.65%	+ 17.48%	+ 9.93%	− 5.83%	+ 2.11%
945.90	30	Growth & Income Index	+ 45.54%	+ 21.18%	+ 12.08%	+ 3.88%	+ 0.87%
615.79	30	Equity Income Index	+ 42.78%	+ 24.31%	+ 13.81%	+ 3.67%	+ 0.71%
224.29	10	Sci & Tech Index	+ 63.00%	+ 13.36%	+ 10.90%	− 7.11%	+ 2.72%
320.02	30	Global Fund Index	+ 20.40%	+ 0.36%	+ 7.62%	+ 0.93%	+ 1.46%
365.16	30	International Index	+ 15.54%	− 1.19%	+ 10.14%	+ 4.03%	+ 1.52%
143.70	10	Gold Fund Index	+ 1.40%	− 4.70%	− 6.45%	+ 2.13%	+ 4.43%
734.93	30	Balanced Fund Index	+ 40.26%	+ 23.69%	+ 12.59%	+ 2.07%	+ 0.61%
159.02	10	Conv Secur Index	+ 40.90%	+ 22.15%	+ 15.22%	+ 5.77%	+ 0.93%

Securities Market Indexes

Value		10/11/90-07/16/92	07/12/90-07/16/92	07/18/91-07/16/92	12/31/91-07/16/92	07/09/92-07/16/92
U.S. Equities:						
3,361.63	Dow Jones Ind. Avg. xd	+ 42.14	+ 13.19	+ 11.45	+ 6.08	+ 1.13
417.54	S&P 500 xd	+ 41.32	+ 14.26	+ 8.35	+ 0.11	+ 0.80
490.83	S&P 400 xd	+ 41.51	+ 13.26	+ 6.80	− 0.38	+ 0.99
229.49	NYSE Composite xd	+ 41.49	+ 15.14	+ 8.72	+ 0.02	+ 0.85
338.34	ASE Index	+ 32.22	+ 7.21	+ 5.05	− 1.70	+ 1.70
191.23	Russell 2000 Index xd	+ 59.33	+ 12.87	+ 10.99	+ 0.70	+ 1.90
International Equities:						
1,740.53	DAX Index	+ 21.85	− 9.17	+ 7.55	+ 10.30	− 0.97
2,486.40	FT S-E 100 Index	+ 18.28	+ 4.89	− 2.39	− 0.27	+ 0.56
1,698.76	Nikkei 225 Average xd	− 24.79	− 47.85	− 25.85	− 26.09	+ 0.83

xd-Price only index. Calculated without reinvestment of dividends. The Nikkei index value is divided by 10 due to space limitation. Source: Lipper Analytical Services Inc., Summit, New Jersey 07901

without giving any consideration to the dividends paid on the underlying stocks. Since the mutual fund indices do consider dividends, the two sets of indices are not directly comparable.

Many studies have compared the performance of investment companies that have invested primarily in common stocks with the performance of a **benchmark portfolio** that consisted of a combination of (1) a market index, such as Standard & Poor's 500-stock index; and (2) a riskfree asset, such as Treasury bills.[17] Each particular combination was chosen so that the benchmark portfolio had a risk level that was equal to that of the investment company. Thus, an investment company that had a beta of .80 would be compared with a benchmark portfolio that had 80% invested in the market index and 20% invested in the riskfree asset.[18]

benchmark portfolio

One way of determining whether or not a mutual fund has "beaten the market" is to subtract the average return on the benchmark portfolio from the average return of the mutual fund. This amount, when risk is measured by beta, is known as the fund's **ex post alpha.** Figure 23-8(a) shows the distribution of ex post alpha values for seventy mutual funds, based on monthly returns beginning in 1955 and going through 1964. The average value was .09% per year, suggesting that the typical fund provided approximately the same return as a market-based passive fund with a constant beta equal to the fund's average beta. Of the seventy funds, forty had positive ex post alphas and thirty had negative ex post alphas.

ex post alpha

Different time periods give slightly different results. Figure 23-8(b) shows the distribution of ex post alphas based on monthly returns for 125 funds beginning in 1960 and going through 1969. The average alpha was .05% per month, or about .60% per year. During this period, the typical fund outperformed a passive fund of similar risk by slightly more than .50% per year, and slightly over half (53%) of the funds had positive ex post alphas.

Figure 23-8(c) provides a third example. It shows returns for 100 funds based on quarterly returns beginning in 1970 and going through 1974. The average ex post alpha was −.50% per quarter, or approximately −2.00% per year, and only twenty of the funds had positive alphas.

These results suggest that the average mutual fund has not significantly outperformed an equal-risk passive alternative over any extended period. This is not too surprising. After all, the market's performance is itself an average of the performance of all investors. If, on average, mutual funds had "beaten" the market, then some other group of investors would have "lost" to the market. With the substantial amount of professional management in today's stock market, it is difficult to think of a likely group of victims.

Expenses

Funds typically incur two kinds of expenses. Management fees and administrative expenses are direct and generally reported. Transaction costs are only

[17]Performance evaluation for common stock and bond portfolios is discussed in detail in Chapters 18 and 22, respectively.

[18]Alternatively, the benchmark portfolio may be based on the investment company's standard deviation relative to that of a market index, such as the S&P 500. For example, if the investment company's standard deviation has been 60% of the index's standard deviation, then the mix should consist of 60% invested in the market index and 40% invested in the riskfree asset. The results from evaluating mutual fund performance when using beta as the measure of risk seems to be very similar to the results when standard deviation is used. See, for example, Hany A. Shawky, "An Update on Mutual Funds: Better Grades," *Journal of Portfolio Management*, 8, no. 2 (Winter 1982): 29–34.

MONEY MATTERS
Past Performance Versus Future Performance

Like the swallows returning to Capistrano, the publication of mutual fund performance surveys by prominent business magazines is an eagerly awaited annual event. These surveys provide a cornucopia of information for small investors seeking to select from the hundreds of available mutual funds. Through these surveys investors can conveniently access valuable basic information regarding the funds' investment objectives, fees and expenses, addresses and phone numbers, and so on.

However, the primary attraction of these surveys is the historical performance data displayed for each fund. Performance results are sliced and diced in a wide (and some would say confusing) assortment of calculations. What has been a particular fund's returns over various time periods? How well has the fund performed relative to the broad market? Where does the fund stand relative to other funds? What has been the recent trend in the fund's relative performance?

The implication behind all of this energy expended in compiling and comparing past performance is that there is a strong positive correlation between past success and future success. Certainly, the surveys do not attempt to disabuse their readers of this notion. Further, many investors appear to believe that such a correlation exists, as money typically cascades into the latest "hot" mutual funds.

Despite all the hoopla surrounding the mutual fund performance surveys, empirical evidence casts strong doubt on the naive application of past performance to the selection of investment managers. We sample some of that evidence below.

John Bogle investigated the performance of previously successful equity mutual funds (*Journal of Portfolio Management*, Winter 1992). Over a twenty-year period he ranked the members of a large group of funds by annual return. He found that funds ranked in the top twenty in one year had an average ranking of 249 (out of 554) in the next year. Over longer periods the results were no different. A fund ranked in the top twenty in one ten-year period had an average rank of 137 (out of 309) in the next ten years.

Patricia Dunn and Rolf Thiesen examined the performance of a group of institutional portfolios over a ten-year period (*Journal of Portfolio Management*, Summer 1983). They split the time period in half and divided the portfolios into quartiles on the basis of returns over the first five years. They then placed the portfolios into quartiles on the basis of returns over the next five years. If past performance is a useful indicator of future performance, the portfolios should remain on average in the same quartile over the two periods—a top-quartile performer in one period should remain a top-quartile performer in the next period. Surprisingly, the results indicated just the opposite relationship—top-quartile

FIGURE 23-8
Mutual Fund Performance: Ex Post Alpha Values

Source: (a) Adapted from Norman E. Mains, "Risk, the Pricing of Capital Assets, and the Evaluation of Investment Portfolios: Comment," *Journal of Business*, 50, no. 3 (July 1977): 378–80 © The University of Chicago, 1977. (b) United States Securities and Exchange Commission, *Institutional Investor Study Report*, March 10, 1971 (Washington, D.C.: U.S. Government Printing Office). (c) Merrill Lynch, Pierce, Fenner & Smith, Inc., *Investment Performance Analysis, Comparative Survey*, 1970–1974.

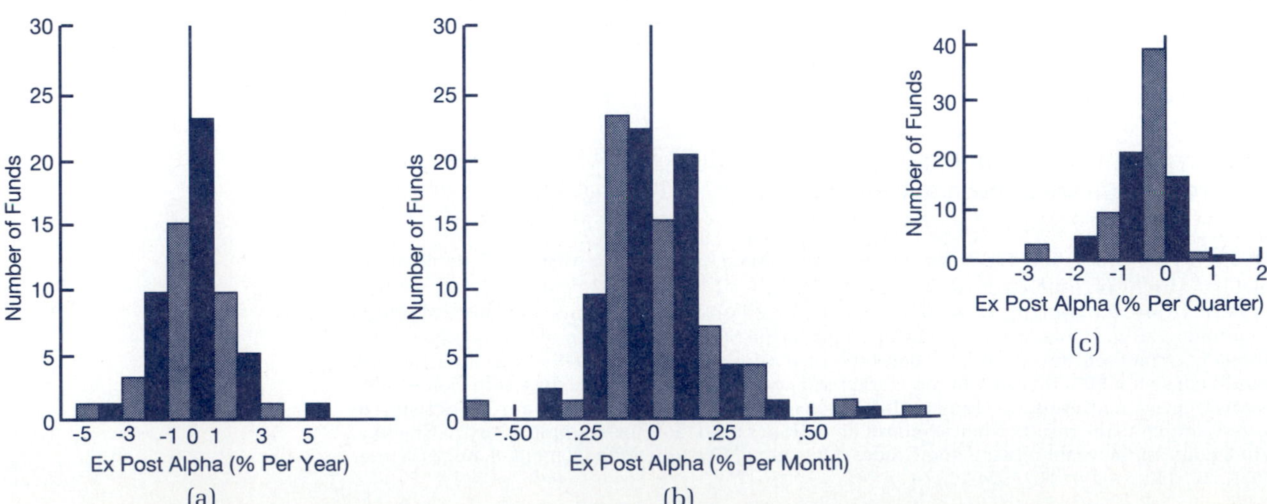

performers tended to move to the bottom quartile and vice versa.

How should we interpret such studies? First, the studies do not rule out the possibility that superior managers exist. They simply indicate that investors relying solely on past performance data to select investment managers are likely to be disappointed.

Second, these studies lend support to the proposition that the capital markets are highly efficient. For the most part, it appears that past performance is dominated by luck rather than skill.

Finally, the lack of an observed relationship between past and future performance points out the need for better benchmarks in evaluating manager performance. As Chapter 18 discussed, the areas of the market in which managers choose to specialize (investment styles) can strongly affect performance. Small growth stocks did relatively well in the late 1970s and early 1980s. They performed in just the opposite fashion in the mid-1980s. A manager specializing in small growth stocks could be ranked highly relative to his or her peers in the former period and ranked poorly in the latter period, regardless of the manager's true investment skill in selecting among small growth stocks.

Where does all this leave the small investor seeking to select from among the wide range of mutual funds available? Many factors will determine an investor's final decision, some of them unique to the investor's individual situation. Nevertheless, several basic considerations apply to all mutual fund investors:

1. Identify your level of risk tolerance. (This process does not necessarily have to be quantitative in nature.) Select a combination of funds consistent with that risk tolerance.
2. Give preference to mutual fund organizations that offer a "family of funds." These organizations can provide you with a variety of investment options and allow you to more conveniently control your mix of funds through low-cost exchange privileges.
3. Seriously consider passive management. An increasing variety of index funds are being offered, particularly by larger mutual fund organizations.
4. If you choose to invest in actively managed mutual funds, diversify across funds with different investment policies.
5. Request and read the prospectuses that mutual funds are required to provide you. At first glance these documents seem intimidating, but with a bit of effort you will be able to compare and contrast funds. Be certain that you are comfortable with a fund's investment approach, as described in the prospectus, before buying.
6. Pay attention to *all* fees and expenses charged by the funds as well as their portfolio turnover. Differences in operating costs among mutual funds can be substantial. There is no reason to believe that high costs are anything more than a drag on performance.
7. Do not rely on past performance as an indicator of future performance.

partly measurable in that brokerage commissions are reported, but implicit costs such as bid-ask spreads and the price impacts of trading are usually not even estimated.

By adding management and administrative expenses and explicit transaction costs to a fund's rate of return, it is possible to obtain an estimate of its gross performance (that is, its performance based on the assumption that such expenses were nonexistent). This is done by adding to the numerator of equation (23.2) the per-share values of such expenses. In the example shown earlier, perhaps the fund had paid expenses of this nature totaling $.02 per share during month t. In such a situation, the net return of 1.20% = $.12/$10.00 corresponds to a gross return of 1.40% = ($.12 + $.02)/$10.00

Figure 23-9 shows the distribution of ex post alphas based on this measure of gross performance for the funds covered in the analysis previously summarized in Figure 23-8(a). While ex post alphas based on *net* performance averaged .09% per year, the ex post alphas based on *gross* performance averaged 1.07% per year. Moreover, fifty of the seventy funds had positive ex post alphas based on gross performance. This suggests that portfolio managers might have some skill, but not enough to recoup the transaction costs that are incurred in hiring them and carrying out their buy and sell orders.

A study by the Securities and Exchange Commission attempted to estimate the relationship between several factors and portfolio perfor-

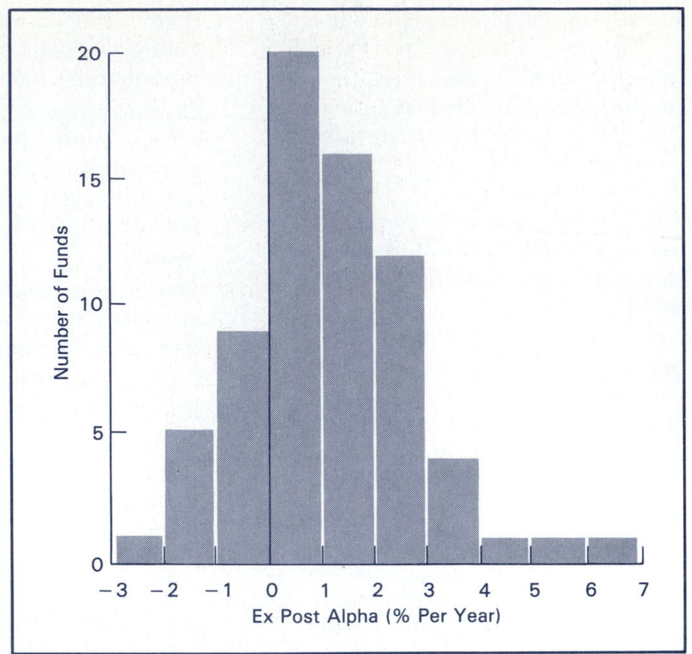

FIGURE 23-9
Mutual Fund Performance: Ex Post Alpha Values Based on Gross Returns
Source: Adapted from Norman E. Mains, "Risk, the Pricing of Capital Assets, and the Evaluation of Investment Portfolios: Comment," *Journal of Business*, 50, no. 3 (July 1977): 378–80 © The University of Chicago, 1977.

mance.[19] Ex post alphas were computed and analyzed for 132 mutual funds using monthly returns from 1965 through 1969. The following observations were made:

1. Larger funds performed no better, other things being equal, than smaller funds, where size is measured by the fund's total assets.
2. Funds with load charges performed no better, other things being equal, than those with no load charges (consequently, investors in load funds did worse than those in no-load funds).
3. Funds associated with management companies having larger amounts of assets under their control performed no better, other things being equal, than those with smaller amounts under their control.

portfolio turnover

However, fund performance was found to be *negatively* related to **portfolio turnover,** which is a periodic measure of how much buying and selling of securities was incurred (technically, it is the ratio of the smaller of purchases or sales during a time period divided by the average total asset value during the period). This suggests that, on average, the more frequently a mutual fund's portfolio was revised, the lower its subsequent performance.

One possible explanation for this observation is that in an efficient market, more frequent revisions will cause a fund to incur more transaction costs, but without being able to consistently receive gains from the purchase of underpriced securities as an offset. While revisions in a fund's portfolio may be desirable so as to maintain a desired risk level or dividend yield, revisions intended to exploit supposed market inefficiencies will generally prove undesirable because of the associated transaction costs.

[19] *Institutional Investor Study Report of the Securities and Exchange Commission* (Washington, D.C.: U.S. Government Printing Office, 1971), vol. 2, pp. 328–32.

Market Timing

To achieve superior portfolio performance, an investor must either select securities that outperform others of comparable risk or switch from risk class to risk class at appropriate times. The latter strategy is often called market timing. The idea is to hold a high-beta portfolio prior to market rises and a low-beta portfolio prior to market declines. An all-equity fund can change its beta by switching among stocks that have different betas. That is, a high-beta portfolio can be achieved by holding high-beta securities, and a low-beta portfolio can be achieved by holding low-beta securities. While a balanced fund can also do this, it can change its beta in another manner—namely, by altering the relative proportions it has invested in stocks and bonds. Typically, the more a balanced fund has invested in stocks, the higher its beta.

Successful market timing will eventually be reflected in a positive ex post alpha that is based on long-term performance. Overall performance may also be separated into one part attributed to security selection and another part attributed to market timing.

In a study of the performance of fifty-seven mutual funds over the period from 1953 through 1962, only one was found with a record suggesting any significant ability to time the market.[20] A later study of the performance of 116 funds from February 1968 through June 1980 found that only three funds had significant timing ability over the entire period, with only one fund having a record indicating significant market timing ability in both the first and the second half of the period.[21]

Such results are not surprising. If many funds were consistently successful at market timing, they would have shown up in the previously mentioned tests for superior overall performance unless they were consistently engaging in inferior security selection that offset their superior timing ability. However, such a situation seems highly improbable. More likely, investment managers find it as difficult to time the market as to select underpriced securities. Such is the lot of an investor in a highly efficient market.

Relative Performance

Some organizations rate a mutual fund's performance relative to those having a similar objective. One of the most prominent of these organizations is Morningstar, Inc., located in Chicago. Besides providing a wealth of information on a given fund, it also provides a performance/risk analysis of past returns. An example for the Fidelity Magellan Fund is shown in Figure 23-10.

Return Analysis In the upper left-hand corner of the figure are average returns earned by the fund over various time periods ending March 31, 1992, and ranging from the past three months to the past fifteen years. Next to each average return is an indication of how that average compares with the average return on the S&P 500 (different indices are used for bond funds, international funds, and small stock funds) over the same time period. In the third and

---

[20]Jack L. Treynor and Kay Mazuy, "Can Mutual Funds Outguess the Market?" *Harvard Business Review*, 44, no. 4 (July–August 1966): 131–36.

[21]Roy D. Henriksson, "Market Timing and Mutual Fund Performance: An Empirical Investigation," *Journal of Business*, 57, no. 1, pt. 1 (January 1984): 73–96. Similar results suggesting that mutual fund managers have no special ability to time the market is provided by Stanley J. Kon, "The Market-Timing Performance of Mutual Fund Managers," *Journal of Business*, 56, no. 3 (July 1983): 323–47; and Eric C. Chang and Wilbur G. Lewellen, "Market Timing and Mutual Fund Investment Performance," *Journal of Business*, 57, no. 1, pt. 1 (January 1984): 57–72.

FIGURE 23-10
Performance Analysis of the Magellan Fund
Source: Morningstar Mutual Funds, May 1, 1992, p. 179 (Chicago: Morningstar, Inc.).

PERFORMANCE/RISK 03/31/92	TOTAL RETURN %	+/- S&P 500	PERCENTILE RANK ALL	PERCENTILE RANK OBJ.
3 MONTH	-0.70	1.79	56	45
6 MONTH	6.95	1.28	27	57
1 YEAR	16.48	5.51	19	35
3 YEAR AVG.	18.01	3.17	9	22
5 YEAR AVG.	12.66	2.28	7	13
10 YEAR AVG.	24.19	6.07	1	2
15 YEAR AVG.	27.32	12.69	1	1

	ALPHA	BETA	R^2	STD. DEV.
	2.4	1.08	95	4.89
PERCENTILE RANK ALL	14	17	7	21
PERCENTILE RANK OBJ.	24	36	10	46

RETURN	RISK
High	Average
RATING	
★★★★★	
Highest	

	M-STAR RISK % RANK ALL	M-STAR RISK % RANK OBJ.	MORNINGSTAR RETURN (1.00 = EQUITY AVG)	MORNINGSTAR RISK (1.00 = EQUITY AVG)	MORNINGSTAR RISK-ADJUSTED RATING
3 YEAR	69	33	1.47	0.86 →	★★★★
5 YEAR	73	45	1.56	0.92 →	★★★★
10 YEAR	61	27	1.59	0.89 →	★★★★★
WEIGHTED AVG.			1.55	0.89	★★★★★

Percentile Ranks: 1 = Highest, 100 = Lowest, Except M-STAR Risk: 1 = Lowest, 100 = Highest

fourth columns from the left are the percentile ranks of the fund's average return relative to all mutual funds and those categorized as having a similar stated investment objective. Here a rank of "1" places a fund at the top and a rank of "100" places a fund at the bottom.

Over the recent three months Magellan had a return of −.70%, which was 1.79% better than the S&P 500. This return caused the fund to be ranked slightly below the middle (56th percentile) against all funds and slightly above the middle (45th percentile) against those funds having a similar objective. However, over the past fifteen years it can be seen that the Magellan fund did substantially better than the S&P 500, placing it in the first percentile overall and in its category.

Ex Post Characteristic Line Analysis Below this section is a section with headings ALPHA, BETA, R^2, and STD. DEV. These statistics correspond to the statistics related to a portfolio's ex post characteristic line, which was discussed in Chapter 18. Here the previous thirty-six monthly rates of return on the portfolio (less the corresponding three-month Treasury bill rates) are regressed on the previous thirty-six monthly rates of return on the S&P 500 (less the corresponding three-month Treasury bill rates). The intercept and slope of the regression are the portfolio's ex post ALPHA and BETA, respectively. Similarly, R^2 is the coefficient of determination of the regression (multiplied by 100), while STD. DEV. is the standard deviation associated with the portfolio's past thirty-six monthly returns. Percentile ranks are again presented for these four statistics relative to all mutual funds and those having a similar investment objective.

It can be seen that Magellan had a beta of 1.08, making it slightly riskier than the S&P 500. Its ex post alpha of 2.4% indicates that it did better than the market on a risk-adjusted basis over the last thirty-six months. The R^2 of 95 means that roughly 95% of the variation in the excess returns of the fund could be attributed to variations in the excess returns on the S&P 500. Finally, its monthly variation in returns is measured by its standard deviation of 4.89%. Percentile ranks reveal that the Magellan fund performed relatively well and had a moderate amount of risk over the past thirty-six months. Note how the percentile ranks of the fund's three-year average return (9 and 22) correspond to its risk-adjusted return percentile ranks based on alpha for the same period (14 and 24).

Ratings In the lower right-hand side are M-STAR RISK % RANK, MORNINGSTAR RETURN RISK, and MORNINGSTAR RISK-ADJUSTED RATING. In order to understand these columns the two columns labeled RETURN and RISK need to be explained first. Here it is easiest to focus on the 3 YEAR row, as the other two rows are straightforward extensions of it. First, the average return for Magellan and all other portfolios having similar objectives are determined for the past three years. Second, the average three-year returns for all of the similar funds are averaged. Third, Magellan's average return is divided by this overall average. Hence a return measure of greater than 1 means that the fund did better than average, while a return measure of less than 1 indicates that the fund did worse than average. In Magellan's case, the return measure of 1.47 indicates that its average return was 47% better than the overall average.

For the RISK entry, the three-month Treasury bill rate is subtracted from each of the previous thirty-six monthly rates of return to calculate the fund's excess returns. Then only the negative excess returns are summed and divided by 36 to provide a measure of the fund's downside risk. Comparable figures are calculated for all similar funds, and then an overall average is determined. Finally, the fund's downside risk measure is divided by this overall measure; the resulting number is Morningstar's measure of the risk of the fund. In the case of Magellan, it is .86, indicating that it had 14% less downside risk than the average similar fund.

Under the heading M-STAR RISK % RANK will be found the percentile ranking of the fund's downside risk measure against all funds and the set of similar funds. Here a percentile rank of "1" indicates that the fund had the least risk, while a rank of "100" indicates that the fund had the most risk. In the case of Magellan, its ranks of 69 and 33 over three years indicate that it had more risk than 69% of all the other funds and 33% of the other funds having a comparable objective.

Morningstar's rating system has five categories, as follows:

Stars	Percentile	Return Category	Risk Category
*****	1–10	Highest	Lowest
****	11–32.5	Above Average	Below Average
***	33.5–67.5	Average	Average
**	68.5–90	Below Average	Above Average
*	91–100	Lowest	Highest

Hence the percentile rank, based on the set of funds with similar objectives, determines how many stars the fund gets and the category in which it is placed.[22]

The MORNINGSTAR RISK-ADJUSTED RATING is determined by subtracting the fund's downside risk measure from its return measure; in the case of Magellan, its three-year risk-adjusted measure is $1.47 - .86 = .61$. This measure is also determined for all the other funds having similar objectives, and then percentile ranks are determined. In the case of Magellan, it ranked somewhere between 11 and 32.5, resulting in a four-star rating.

These measures are used to fill in the RETURN, RISK, and RATING boxes in the top right-hand corner of the figure. Consider the return measure

[22]Similar ratings are provided in *The Individual Investor's Guide to No-Load Mutual Funds* (Chicago: International Publishing Company, 1992).

first. Here the previously described return measures for three, five, and ten years are averaged using weights of 20%, 30%, and 50% to arrive at a weighted-average return. After doing this for each of the other funds that have similar objectives, the fund is given a percentile rank and then a rating as indicated above. In the case of Magellan, its percentile rank was somewhere between 1 and 10, giving it a High ranking. Similar weighted-average calculations are done for the fund's downside risk measure and risk-adjusted measures, resulting in Magellan receiving an Average risk rating and a five-star Highest risk-adjusted rating.

Caveats Morningstar's performance measures are useful in giving an investor a quick reading of how a mutual fund has performed in the past relative to other funds. However, three things should be kept in mind. First, the measures do not provide an indication of the difference between the fund's performance and that of a specific benchmark. Second, past performance in most cases is not a reliable indicator of future performance, as discussed in this chapter's "Money Matters." Third, the use of peer group comparisons to evaluate performance has several serious conceptual and practical shortcomings. For example, the set of similar funds may not be entirely appropriate (even though they may be the best match that Morningstar can provide), causing the ratings to be misleading. (For example, one fund may be restricted to buying just NYSE-listed common stock while another is free to purchase stocks that are listed on the NYSE, AMEX, or NASDAQ.)

CLOSED-END FUND PREMIUMS AND DISCOUNTS

Several studies have shown that the performance of diversified closed-end investment company managers in the United States is similar to that of open-end investment company managers.[23] When returns are measured by changes in net asset values (plus all distributions), closed-end investment companies appear to be neither better nor worse than open-end ones. Again, there is little evidence that portfolio managers can either select underpriced securities or time the market successfully.

Pricing of Shares

However, there is more to be said about closed-end funds. An investor can purchase an open-end fund's shares for their net asset value (plus any required load charge) and sell them later at the subsequent net asset value. Except for any load charges, the performance of the *management* of such a fund, based on net asset values, corresponds exactly to the returns provided to the *shareholders*. This is not the case for closed-end investment companies, since investors buy and sell shares of investment companies at prices

[23]See, for example, William F. Sharpe and Howard B. Sosin, "Closed-End Investment Companies in the United States: Risk and Return," *Proceedings, 1974 Meeting of the European Finance Association*, ed. B. Jacquillat (Amsterdam: North-Holland Publishing Co., 1975): 37–63; Antonio Vives, "Analysis of Forecasting Ability of Closed-End Fund's Management" (unpublished working paper, Carnegie-Mellon University, September 1975) and "Discounts and Premiums on Closed-End Funds: A Theoretical and Empirical Analysis" (unpublished Ph.D. thesis, Carnegie-Mellon University, 1975).

determined on the open (secondary) market. While some companies have share prices that are above their net asset values (such shares are said to sell at a premium), many have share prices below their net asset values (such shares are said to sell at a discount).

This has resulted in three "puzzles" concerning the typical pricing of closed-end fund shares. First, the shares sell at a premium of roughly 10% of NAV when initially sold. Second, the shares fall to a discount of roughly 10% of NAV within 120 days of the initial offering. Third, the size of this discount fluctuates widely over time.[24] Figure 23-11 shows the price behavior of a sample of eighteen closed-end funds. Note how the average fund sells at a discount that ranged from roughly 1.5% to 9% over the previous four quarters.

Investing in Fund Shares

The fact that the price of a closed-end investment company differs from its net asset value, with the magnitude of the difference varying from time to time, introduces an added source of risk and potential return to investors. By purchasing shares at a discount, an investor may be able to earn more than just the change in the company's net asset value. Even if the company's discount remains constant, the effective dividend yield will be greater than that of an otherwise similar no-load, open-end investment company, since the purchase price will be less. If the discount is substantial when the shares are purchased, it may subsequently narrow and the return will be even greater.[25] On the other hand, if the discount increases, the investor's overall return may be less than that of an otherwise comparable open-end investment company.

---

[24]These puzzles are presented and investigated in Charles M. C. Lee, Andrei Shleifer, and Richard H. Thaler, "Investor Sentiment and the Closed-End Fund Puzzle," *Journal of Finance*, 46, no. 1 (March 1991): 75–109.

[25]There is some evidence that discounts narrow during "down markets" and widen during "up markets." See R. Malcolm Richards, Donald R. Fraser, and John C. Groth, "Premiums, Discounts, and the Volatility of Closed-End Mutual Funds," *Financial Review*, (Fall 1979): 26–33 and "The Attractions of Closed-End Bond Funds," *Journal of Portfolio Management*, 8, no. 2 (Winter 1982): 56–61.

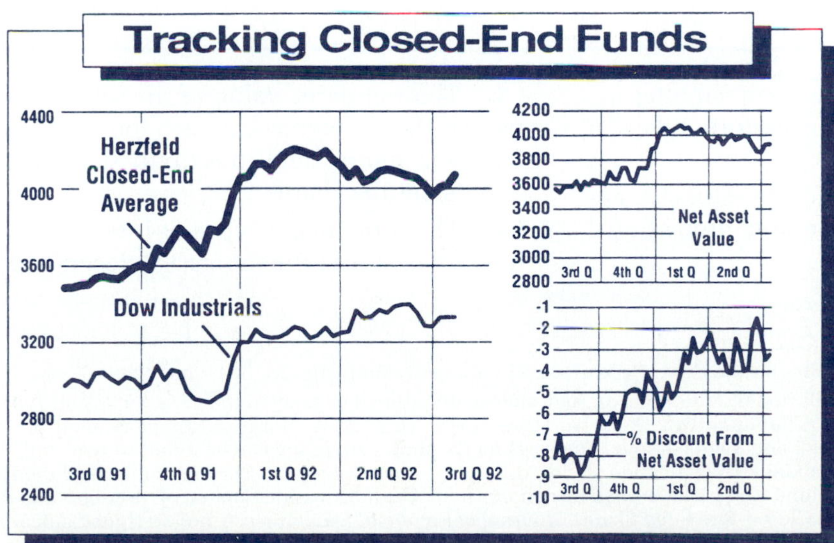

FIGURE 23-11
Closed-End Fund Performance

Source: Reprinted by permission of *Barron's*, © Dow Jones & Company, Inc., July 20, 1992, p. 116. All rights reserved worldwide.

Consider a fund that at the beginning of the year has a net asset value of $10 per share but is selling at a 10% discount for $9 per share. Over the year it receives cash dividends amounting to $.50 per share that it distributes to its shareholders. Hence its dividend yield is 5.6% (= $.50/$9.50), which is larger than the 5% yield (= $.50/$10) that it would pay if it were open-ended. Furthermore, if its net asset value at year-end remains at $10 per share but its discount shrinks to 4% so that it is selling at $9.60 per share, then the annual return would be 12.2% [= ($.60 + $.50)/$9] instead of 5% if it were open-ended. Of course, if its discount widened to 20% so that it was selling at $8 per share, then the annual return would be −5.6% [=(−$1 + $.50)/$9], which is worse than the 5% it would return if open-ended.

Some of the risk associated with varying discounts can be reduced by holding a portfolio of shares in several closed-end investment companies. Discounts on different companies move together, but not perfectly. For example, past data suggest that the standard deviation of the percentage change in the ratio of market price to net asset value for a *portfolio* of ten to twelve closed-end investment companies is likely to be approximately half that of a typical investment in the shares of a *single* closed-end investment company.[26]

Open-Ending of Closed-End Funds

Explaining the puzzling behavior of prices of closed-end investment companies is a challenge for anyone who believes that capital markets are perfectly efficient. For anyone not firmly committed to such a view, the purchase of shares of closed-end investment companies at prices sufficiently below net asset values may provide an opportunity for superior returns.[27] One way of realizing superior returns is for the closed-end investment company to convert to an open-end one.[28] By doing so, the discount on the shares would have to disappear, since conversion would result in the investment company offering its shareholders the right to redeem their shares for net asset value.

SUMMARY

1. Investment companies are financial intermediaries that obtain money from investors and use it to purchase financial assets.

2. Investment companies offer investors the advantages of economies of scale and professional management.

3. The net asset value of an investment company is the difference between the market value of its assets and its liabilities divided by the number of outstanding shares.

4. The three major types of investment companies are unit investment trusts, closed-end invest-

[26]Sharpe and Sosin, "Closed-End Investment Companies in the United States."

[27]Burton G. Malkiel advocated such an investment strategy in the 1973, 1975, and 1981 editions of *A Random Walk Down Wall Street* (New York: W. W. Norton & Company, Inc.), but not in the 1985 and 1990 editions. The basis for his initial advocacy can be found in two studies: Burton Malkiel, "The Valuation of Closed-End Investment Company Shares," *Journal of Finance*, 32, no. 3 (June 1977): 847–59; and Rex Thompson, "The Information Content of Discounts and Premiums on Closed-End Fund Shares," *Journal of Financial Economics*, 6, no. 2/3 (June/September 1978): 151–86.

[28]For an analysis of the "open-ending" of closed-end investment companies, see Greggory A. Brauer, " 'Open-Ending' Closed-End Funds," *Journal of Financial Economics*, 13, no. 4 (December 1984): 491–507.

ment companies, and open-end investment companies.

5. Unit investment trusts typically make a set of initial investments in fixed-income securities, and then hold those securities until they mature.

6. Closed-end investment companies issue an initial number of shares to capitalize the fund. After that, new shares are rarely issued (or repurchased). Closed-end investment company shares trade on organized exchanges or on the over-the-counter market at prices determined by the market.

7. Open-end investment companies have a variable capitalization, standing ready to issue new shares or repurchase existing shares at prices based on their net asset values.

8. Different investment companies follow different investment policies. These policies determine such characteristics as the asset classes in which the investment companies invest, the degree of active management (if any), and the emphasis on income as opposed to capital appreciation.

9. Owing to data availability, mutual funds have been the subject of many performance studies. The results show that, on average, mutual funds consistently maintain risk postures in line with their stated investment policies. However, the typical fund has not been able to consistently produce superior rates of return.

10. Closed-end investment companies typically sell at premiums to their net asset values at their initial funding. Later they typically sell at discounts to their net asset values. Explaining this price behavior is a puzzle for efficient market proponents.

KEY TERMS

investment companies
net asset value
unit investment trust
managed investment companies
closed-end investment companies
open-end investment company
mutual funds
no-load funds
load funds
load charge
redemption fee
real estate investment trusts
low-load funds
benchmark portfolio
portfolio turnover

QUESTIONS AND PROBLEMS

1. The Neptune Value Fund has sold 150,000 shares to investors. Currently, the fund has accrued investment management fee obligations of $50,000. The fund's portfolio is shown below. Calculate the fund's net asset value.

STOCK	SHARES	PRICE/SHARE
A	50,000	$ 10
B	20,000	7
C	35,000	30
D	10,000	100

2. Using a recent *Wall Street Journal*, find the NAV for the following funds:
(a) The Magellan Fund (Fidelity Investments)
(b) The Wellington Fund (Vanguard Group)
(c) The Quasar Fund (Alliance Capital)
What is the percentage change in each fund's NAV over the previous day? Calculate each fund's load as a percentage of its NAV.

3. Wildfire Schulter, a veteran mutual fund investor, argued, "I can compute the monthly time-weighted rate of return on a mutual fund by calculating the percentage change in the fund's NAV from the beginning to the end of the month (assuming no distributions to shareholders)." Is Wildfire correct? Why or why not?

4. Discuss the advantages and disadvantages of unit investment trusts compared with managed investment companies.
5. Distinguish between closed-end and open-end investment companies.
6. Why do some mutual funds have load charges while others do not? Why are investors willing to pay load charges?
7. Assume that you placed a $1,000 investment with a mutual fund that charged an 8.5% load. Management and other fees charged by the fund total 1.10% per annum. Ignoring other costs, over five years, what annual return would the fund have to produce to equal the value that your initial investment would have earned in a savings account paying 5% interest? (Assume annual compounding of income and no taxes.)
8. In recent years so-called "families of funds" that offer a wide range of investment policies through narrowly focused mutual funds have become popular. Discuss why these funds have achieved such popularity.
9. There are literally hundreds of mutual funds available for purchase. Describe what criteria you might use in selecting from among these many funds.
10. At the end of 1991, the Saturn Fund's NAV was $18.50. At the beginning of the year its NAV was $16.90. At year-end the fund paid out $1.25 in income and capital gains. What was the return to an investor in the Saturn Fund during 1991?
11. Over the last three years, the Pluto Fund produced the following per-share financial results. Calculate the annual returns on an investment in the Pluto Fund from 1989 to 1991.

	1989	1990	1991
NAV-Beginning of Year	$13.89	$14.40	$15.95
NAV-End of Year	14.40	15.95	15.20
Income Distribution	0.29	0.33	0.36
Capital Gains Distribution	0.12	0.25	0.05

12. Analysis of mutual fund performance has been extensive. What does the evidence indicate about the ability of mutual fund managers, as a group, to consistently produce positive abnormal returns?
13. Lip Pike is attempting to select a superior-performing mutual fund. Based on the evidence presented in the text, discuss how much importance Lip should attach to the past performance of mutual funds in making a decision.
14. If most investment managers appear unable to "beat the market" on a risk-adjusted basis, should an investor still consider investing in investment companies? Why or why not?
15. Consider three individuals: a young, well-educated woman just beginning a career with high expected future earnings; a middle-aged man with a young family who has a secure job but modest expected future earnings growth; a widow in her seventies, living comfortably but not richly off a pension. Referring to Table 23-1, prescribe and explain an investment strategy for these persons involving investments in the

various funds listed. (Feel free to introduce other assumptions regarding the individuals' risk tolerance, consumption preferences, etc.)

16. Assuming that certain conditions are satisfied, the income earned by investment companies is exempt from federal taxes. Why?

17. Why do the market prices of closed-end investment company shares represent a "mystery" to proponents of market efficiency?

REFERENCES

1. Good reference sources for information on investment companies are:

1992 Mutual Fund Fact Book (to order, write: Investment Company Institute, P.O. Box 66140, Washington, DC 20035–6140);

Investment Companies 1992 (to order, write: Wiesenberger Financial Services, Warren, Gorham & Lamont, Inc., One Penn Plaza, New York, NY 10119);

The Individual Investor's Guide to No-Load Mutual Funds (to order, write: American Association of Individual Investors, 625 North Michigan Avenue, Department NLG, Chicago, IL 60611);

Morningstar Mutual Funds (to order this biweekly publication, write: Morningstar, Inc., 53 West Jackson Boulevard, Chicago, IL 60604).

2. While annual management fees of investment companies are usually a given percentage of the market value of the assets under management, performance-based fees are allowed; in addition to the January/February 1987 issue of the *Financial Analysts Journal*, which is devoted to this topic, see:

Laura T. Starks, "Performance Incentive Fees: An Agency Theoretic Approach," *Journal of Financial and Quantitative Analysis*, 22, no. 1 (March 1987): 17–32;

Mark Grinblatt and Sheridan Titman, "How Clients Can Win the Gaming Game," *Journal of Portfolio Management*, 13, no. 4 (Summer 1987): 14–23;

Joseph H. Golec, "Do Mutual Fund Managers Who Use Incentive Compensation Outperform Those Who Don't?" *Financial Analysts Journal*, 44, no. 6 (November/December 1988): 75–78;

Mark Grinblatt and Sheridan Titman, "Adverse Risk Incentives and the Design of Performance-Based Contracts," *Management Science*, 35, no. 7 (July 1989): 807–22;

Jeffery V. Bailey, "Some Thoughts on Performance-Based Fees," *Financial Analysts Journal*, 46, no. 4 (July/August 1990): 31–40;

Philip Halpern and Isabelle I. Fowler, "Investment Management Fees and Determinants of Pricing Structure in the Industry," *Journal of Portfolio Management*, 17, no. 2 (Winter 1991): 74–79.

3. The imposition of 12b-1 distribution fees by mutual funds has been contentious: see:

Stephen P. Ferris and Don M. Chance, "The Effect of 12b-1 Plans on Mutual Fund Expense Ratios: A Note," *Journal of Finance*, 42, no. 4 (September 1987): 1077–82;

Charles Trzcinka and Robert Zweig, *An Economic Analysis of the Cost and Benefits of S.E.C. Rule 12b-1*, Monograph Series in Finance and

Economics #1990-1, New York University Salomon Center, Leonard N. Stern School of Business.

4. Closed-end investment companies known as "country funds" have been examined by:

   Catherine Bonser-Neal, Greggory Brauer, Robert Neal, and Simon Wheatley, "International Investment Restrictions and Closed-End Country Fund Prices," *Journal of Finance,* 45, no. 2 (June 1990): 523–47.

5. Real estate investment trusts (REITS) are discussed in:

   William L. Burns and Donald R. Epley, "The Performance of Portfolios of REITS + Stocks," *Journal of Portfolio Management,* 8, no. 3 (Spring 1982): 37–42;

   Robert H. Zerbst and Barbara R. Cambon, "Real Estate: Historical Returns and Risks," *Journal of Portfolio Management,* 10, no. 3 (Spring 1984): 5–20;

   Paul M. Firstenburg, Stephen A. Ross, and Randall C. Zisler, "Real Estate: The Whole Story," *Journal of Portfolio Management,* 14, no. 3 (Spring 1988): 22–34;

   Stephen E. Roulac, "How to Value Real Estate Securities," *Journal of Portfolio Management,* 14, no. 3 (Spring 1988): 35–39.

6. For evidence on the performance of funds outside the United States, see:

   John G. McDonald, "French Mutual Fund Performance: Evaluation of Internationally Diversified Portfolios," *Journal of Finance,* 28, no. 5 (December 1973): 1161–80;

   Juan A. Palacios, "The Stock Market in Spain: Tests of Efficiency and Capital Market Theory," in *International Capital Markets,* eds. Edwin J. Elton and Martin J. Gruber (Amsterdam: North-Holland Publishing Company, 1975): 114–49;

   Andre L. Farber, "Performance of Internationally Diversified Mutual Funds," in *International Capital Markets,* eds. Edwin J. Elton and Martin J. Gruber (Amsterdam: North-Holland Publishing Company, 1975): 298–309;

   Michael A. Firth, "The Investment Performance of Unit Trusts in the Period 1965–75," *Journal of Money, Credit and Banking,* 9, no. 4 (November 1977): 597–604;

   James R. F. Guy, "The Performance of the British Investment Trust Industry," *Journal of Finance,* 33, no. 2 (May 1978): 443–55;

   James R. F. Guy, "An Examination of the Effects of International Diversification from the British Viewpoint on Both Hypothetical and Real Portfolios," *Journal of Finance,* 33, no. 5 (December 1978): 1425–38;

   R. S. Woodward, "The Performance of U.K. Investment Trusts as Internationally Diversified Portfolios Over the Period 1968 to 1977," *Journal of Banking and Finance,* 7, no. 3 (September 1983): 417–26;

   Jess H. Chua and Richard S. Woodward, "Gains from Market Timing," Monograph Series in Finance and Economics #1986-2, New York University Salomon Center, Leonard N. Stern School of Business;

   Robert E. Cumby and Jack D. Glen, "Evaluating the Performance of International Mutual Funds," *Journal of Finance,* 45, no. 2 (June 1990): 497–521;

   Cheol S. Eun, Richard Kolodny, and Bruce G. Resnick, "U.S.-Based

International Mutual Funds: A Performance Evaluation," *Journal of Portfolio Management*, 17, no. 3 (Spring 1991): 88–94.

7. Studies of common stock mutual fund performance are discussed and cited in:

Gordon J. Alexander, *Portfolio Analysis* (Englewood Cliffs, N.J.: Prentice Hall, 1986), Chapter 13;

Mark Grinblatt and Sheridan Titman, "Mutual Fund Performance: An Analysis of Quarterly Portfolio Holdings," *Journal of Business*, 62, no. 3 (July 1989): 393–416;

Edwin J. Elton and Martin J. Gruber, *Modern Portfolio Theory and Investment Analysis* (New York: John Wiley & Sons, Inc., 1991), Chapter 22.

John C. Bogle, "Selecting Equity Mutual Funds," *Journal of Portfolio Management*, 18, no. 2 (Winter 1992): 94–100;

8. The finding of inferior performance by mutual funds is contested in:

Bruce N. Lehmann and David M. Modest, "Mutual Fund Performance Evaluation: A Comparison of Benchmarks and Benchmark Comparisons," *Journal of Finance*, 42, no. 2 (June 1987): 233–65;

Cheng-few Lee and Shafiqur Rahman, "Market Timing, Selectivity, and Mutual Fund Performance: An Empirical Investigation," *Journal of Business*, 63, no. 2 (April 1990): 261–78.

9. For a discussion and extensive set of references regarding closed-end funds, see, along with the citations given in the chapter, the following papers:

Rex Thompson, "The Information Content of Discounts and Premiums on Closed-End Fund Shares," *Journal of Financial Economics*, 6, no. 2/3 (June/September 1978): 151–86;

Greggory A. Brauer, "Closed-End Fund Shares' Abnormal Returns and the Information Content of Discounts and Premiums," *Journal of Finance*, 43, no. 1 (March 1988): 113–27;

Kathleen Weiss, "The Post-Offering Price Performance of Closed-End Funds," *Financial Management*, 18, no. 3 (Autumn 1989): 57–67;

Charles M. C. Lee, Andrei Shleifer, and Richard H. Thaler, "Anomalies: Closed-End Mutual Funds," *Journal of Economic Perspectives*, 4, no. 4 (Fall 1990): 153–64;

Charles M. C. Lee, Andrei Shleifer, and Richard H. Thaler, "Investor Sentiment and the Closed-End Fund Puzzle," *Journal of Finance*, 46, no. 1 (March 1991): 75–109;

James Brickley, Steven Manaster, and James Schallheim, "The Tax-Timing Option and Discounts on Closed-End Investment Companies," *Journal of Business*, 64, no. 3 (July 1991): 287–312;

J. Bradford DeLong and Andrei Shleifer, "Closed-End Fund Discounts," *Journal of Portfolio Management*, 18, no. 2 (Winter, 1992): 46–53.

10. Open-ending of closed-end investment companies is discussed in:

Greggory A. Brauer, " 'Open-Ending' Closed-End Funds," *Journal of Financial Economics*, 13, no. 4 (December 1984): 491–507;

James A. Brickley and James S. Schallheim, "Lifting the Lid on Closed-End Investment Companies: A Case of Abnormal Returns," *Journal of Financial and Quantitative Analysis*, 20, no. 1 (March 1985): 107–17.

24

Options

---

option

In the world of investments, an **option** is a type of contract between two people where one person grants the other person the right to buy a specific asset at a specific price within a specific time period. Alternatively, the contract may grant the other person the right to sell a specific asset at a specific price within a specific time period. The person who has received the right and thus has a decision to make is known as the option buyer, since he or she must pay for this right. The person who has sold the right and thus must respond to the buyer's decision is known as the option writer.

The variety of contracts containing an option feature is enormous. Even within the domain of publicly traded securities, many types can be found. Traditionally, only certain instruments are referred to as options; the others, though similar in nature, are designated in other ways. This chapter will present an introduction to the institutional features of such contracts, along with some basics regarding how they are valued in the marketplace.

TYPES OF OPTION CONTRACTS

Call Options

call option

The most prominent type of option contract is the **call option** for stocks. It gives the buyer the right to buy ("call away") a specific number of shares of a specific company from the option writer at a specific purchase price at any time up to and including a specific date. Note how the contract specifies four items:

1. the company whose shares can be bought,
2. the number of shares that can be bought,
3. the purchase price for those shares, known as the **exercise price** (or striking price), and
4. the date when the right to buy expires, known as the **expiration date.**

exercise price

expiration date

An Example Consider a simple hypothetical example where investors *B* and *W* are thinking about signing a call option contract. This contract will allow *B* to buy from *W* 100 shares of Widget for $50 per share at any time during the next six months. Currently, Widget is selling for $45 per share on an organized exchange. Investor *B*, the potential option buyer, believes that the price of Widget's common stock will rise substantially over the next six months; investor *W*, the potential option writer, has a different opinion about Widget, believing that its stock price will not rise above $50 over this time period.

Will investor *W* be willing to sign this contract without receiving something in return from investor *B*? No. *W* is running a risk by signing the contract, and would demand compensation for doing so. The risk is that Widget's stock price will subsequently rise above $50 per share, in which case *W* will have to buy the shares at that price and then turn them over to *B* for only $50 per share. Perhaps the stock will rise to $60, costing *W* $6,000 (= $60 × 100 shares) to buy the stock. Then *W* will give the 100 shares to *B* and receive in return $5,000 (= $50 × 100 shares). Consequently, *W* will have lost $1,000 (= $6,000 − $5,000).

premium

The point is that the buyer of a call option will have to pay the writer something in order to get the writer to sign the contract. The amount paid is known as the **premium,** although *option price* is a more appropriate term. In the example, perhaps the premium is $3 per share, meaning that investor *B* will pay $300 (= $3 × 100 shares) to investor *W* in order to induce *W* to sign the contract. Since investor *B* expects Widget's stock price to rise in the future, he or she would expect to make money by purchasing shares of Widget at $45 per share. The attraction of purchasing call options instead of shares is that investor *B* can apply a high degree of leverage, since only $3 per share needs to be spent in order to purchase the option.

At some point in time after investors *B* and *W* have signed the call option contract, investor *W* might like to get out of the contract. Since breaching the contract is illegal, how can this be done? Investor *W* could buy the contract back from investor *B* for a negotiated amount of money, and then destroy the document. If Widget rises in one month to $55 per share, perhaps the amount will be \$7 per share (or, in total, \$700 = \$7 × 100 shares). In this case, *W* will have lost \$400 (= \$300 − \$700) and *B* will have made \$400. Alternatively, if Widget falls to \$40 per share, perhaps the amount will be \$.50 per share (or, in total, \$50 = \$.50 × 100 shares), in which case *W* will have made \$250 (= \$300 − \$50) and *B* will have lost \$250.

Another way that *W* can get out of the contract is to find someone else to take his or her position in the contract (assume that the contract has a provision that allows this to be done). For example, if Widget has risen to \$55 per share after one month, perhaps investor *W* will find an investor, denoted *WW*, who is willing to become the option writer if *W* will pay him or her \$7 per share (or \$700 in total) to do so. Assuming that they both agree, the contract will be amended so that *WW* is now the option writer, with *W* no longer being a party in the contract.

What if investor *B* wants to subsequently get out of the contract? In this case, *B* could look and see if someone is willing to pay an agreeable sum of money in order to possess the right to buy Widget stock under the terms of the contract. That is, *B* could attempt to sell the contract to someone else. In this situation, perhaps investor *B* will find another investor, denoted *BB*, who is willing to pay *B* \$7 per share (or \$700 in total) in return for the right to buy Widget under the terms of the call option contract. Provided that *B* is agreeable, the call option contract will be sold to *BB* and amended, making *BB* the option buyer.

In this example, both of the original parties, *W* and *B*, have "closed out" their positions and are no longer involved in the call option contract. However, the example suggests that the original writer and buyer must meet face to face in order to draw up the terms of the contract. It also suggests that if either the original writer or buyer wants to get out of the contract, then he or she must reach an agreeable price with the other original party or, alternatively, find a third investor to whom he or she can transfer the position in the contract. Thus, it would appear that there is a great amount of effort involved if an investor wants to deal in options.

Role of Exchanges Fortunately, this is not the case in the United States because of the introduction of *standardized contracts* and the maintenance of a relatively liquid marketplace by organized exchanges for listed options.[1] The Options Clearing Corporation (OCC), a company that is jointly owned by several exchanges, greatly facilitates trading in these options. It does so by maintaining a computer system that keeps track of all of these options by recording the position of each investor in each one. Although the mechanics are rather complex, the principles are simple enough. As soon as a buyer and a writer decide to trade a particular option contract and the buyer pays the agreed-upon premium, the OCC steps in, becoming the effective writer as far as the buyer is concerned and the effective buyer as far as the writer is concerned. Thus, at this time all direct links between original buyer and writer are severed. If a buyer chooses to exercise an option, the OCC will randomly choose a writer who has not closed his or her position and assign

[1]Prior to 1973, options were traded over the counter through the efforts of dealers and brokers in a relatively illiquid market. These dealers and brokers brought buyers and writers together, arranged terms, helped with the paperwork, and charged fees for their efforts. Despite the introduction of exchanged-traded options, the over-the-counter market for options has thrived. Most of the options traded in the OTC market are customized to the particular needs of the parties involved.

the exercise notice accordingly. The OCC also guarantees delivery of stock if the writer is unable to come up with the shares.

The OCC makes it possible for buyers and writers to "close out" (or "unwind") their positions at any time. If a buyer subsequently becomes a writer of the same contract, meaning that the buyer later "sells" the contract to someone else, the OCC computer will note the offsetting positions in this investor's account and will simply cancel both entries. Consider an investor who buys a contract on Monday and then sells it on Tuesday. The computer will note that the investor's net position is zero, and will remove both entries. The second trade is a **closing sale,** since it serves to "close out" the investor's position from the earlier trade. Closing sales thus allow buyers to sell options rather than exercise them.

closing sale

A similar procedure allows a writer to pay to be relieved of the potential obligation to deliver stock. Consider an investor who writes a contract on Wednesday and buys an identical one on Thursday. The latter is a **closing purchase** and, analogous to a closing sale, serves to close out the investor's position from the earlier trade.

closing purchase

Stock Split and Dividend Protection Call options are protected against stock splits and stock dividends on the underlying stock. In the example where the option was on 100 shares of Widget stock with an exercise price of $50, a two-for-one stock split would cause the contract to be altered so that it was for 200 shares at $25 per share. The reason for this protection has to do with the effect that stock splits and stock dividends have on the share price of the firm. Since either of these events will cause the share price to fall below what it otherwise would have been, they work to the disadvantage of the call option buyer and to the advantage of the call option writer.

In terms of cash dividends, there is no protection for listed call options.[2] That is, the exercise price and number of shares are unaffected by the payment of cash dividends. For example, the terms of the Widget call option would remain the same if Widget declared and paid a $4 per share cash dividend.

Put Options

put option

A second type of option contract for stocks is the **put option.** It gives the buyer the right to sell ("put away") a specific number of shares of a specific company to the option writer at a specific selling price at any time up to and including a specific date. Note how the contract specifies four items that are analogous to those for call options:

1. the company whose shares can be sold,
2. the number of shares that can be sold,
3. the selling price for those shares, known as the **exercise price** (or striking price), and
4. the date when the right to sell expires, known as the **expiration date.**

exercise price

expiration date

An Example Consider an example where investors *B* and *W* are thinking about signing a put option contract. This contract will allow *B* to sell to *W* 100

[2]However, there is protection for any cash dividend that is formally designated a "return of capital." Furthermore, options that are traded over the counter typically are protected from any type of cash dividend. In both cases, the protection is in the form of a reduction in the exercise price.

shares of XYZ Company for \$30 per share at any time during the next six months. Currently, XYZ is selling for \$35 per share on an organized exchange. Investor *B*, the potential option buyer, believes that the price of XYZ's common stock will fall substantially over the next six months; investor *W*, the potential option writer, has a different opinion about XYZ, believing that its stock price will not fall below \$30 over this time period.

As with the call option on Widget, investor *W* would be running a risk by signing the contract, and would demand compensation for doing so. The risk is that XYZ's stock price will subsequently fall below \$30 per share, in which case *W* will have to buy the shares at \$30 per share from *B* when they are not worth that much in the marketplace. Perhaps XYZ will fall to \$20, costing *W* \$3,000 (= \$30 × 100 shares) to buy stock that is only worth \$2,000 (= \$20 × 100 shares). Consequently, *W* would have lost \$1,000 (= \$3,000 − \$2,000). In this case, *B* would make \$1,000, purchasing XYZ in the marketplace for \$2,000 and then selling the shares to *W* for \$3,000.

As with a call option, the buyer of a put option will have to pay the writer an amount of money known as a premium in order to get the writer to sign the contract and assume this risk. Also as with call options, the buyer and writer may "close out" (or "unwind") their positions at any time by simply entering an offsetting transaction. As with calls, this is easily done for listed put options in the United States, since these contracts are standardized.

Again, the Options Clearing Corporation facilitates trading in listed puts, since these options exist only in the memory of its computer system. As with calls, as soon as a buyer and a writer decide to trade a particular put option contract and the buyer pays the agreed-upon premium, the OCC steps in, becoming the effective writer as far as the buyer is concerned and the effective buyer as far as the writer is concerned. If a buyer chooses to exercise an option, the OCC will randomly choose a writer who has not closed his or her position and assign the exercise notice accordingly. The OCC also guarantees delivery of the exercise price if the writer is unable to come up with the necessary cash.

Like calls, puts are protected against stock splits and stock dividends on the underlying stock. In the example where the option was on 100 shares of XYZ stock with an exercise price of \$30, a two-for-one stock split would cause the contract to be altered so that it was for 200 shares at \$15 per share. In terms of cash dividends, there is no protection for listed puts.

OPTION TRADING

Exchanges begin trading in a new set of options on a given stock every three months, where the options have roughly nine months before they expire.[3] For example, options on Widget might be introduced in January, April, July, and October, with expiration dates in, respectively, September, December, March, and June. Furthermore, the exchange might decide to introduce long-term options on Widget (dubbed LEAPS by the exchanges for Long-term Equity Anticipation Securities) that expire as far into the future as two to three years.

Generally, two call options on a stock are introduced at the same time, the two being identical in all respects except for the exercise price. In terms of the exercise price, if the stock is selling for \$200 or less at the time the options

---

[3]For some active stocks, options may be introduced that have only one or two months to expiration.

are to be introduced, then the two exercise prices will be set at $5 intervals bracketing the stock price.[4] Furthermore, a pair of put option contracts may also be introduced at the same time. For example, if Widget is selling for $43 in January, then two September call options may be introduced that have exercise prices of $40 and $45; similarly, two September put options with exercise prices of $40 and $45 may also be introduced.

After an option has been introduced, new options having the same terms as the existing ones but with different exercise prices may be introduced when the stock price of the company moves up or down so much that it is substantially outside of the initial bracket. In terms of Widget, if its stock price rises in the next month to $49, perhaps September put and call options having a $50 exercise price will be introduced.

Once listed, an option remains listed until its expiration date. Specifically, listed options on common stocks generally expire at 10:59 P.M. Central Time on the Saturday after the third Friday of the specified month.

In recent years, common stock options have been traded on the Chicago Board Options Exchange (CBOE) and on the American, Pacific, Philadelphia,

[4]If the stock sells for less than $25, then the interval may be $2.50 (for example, at $15 and $17.50 for a stock selling at $16); if the stock sells for more than $200 the interval will be for $10 (or perhaps even $20). It should be noted that exchange officials have a reasonable amount of latitude in setting the terms of the options.

FIGURE 24-1
Listed Options Quotations (Excerpt)
Source: Reprinted by permission of *The Wall Street Journal*, © Dow Jones & Company, Inc., July 16, 1992, p. C14. All rights reserved worldwide.

LISTED OPTIONS QUOTATIONS

Wednesday, July 15, 1992

Options closing prices. Sales unit usually is 100 shares. Stock close is New York or American exchange final price.

CHICAGO BOARD

Option & NY Close	Strike Price	Calls-Last			Puts-Last		
		Jul	Aug	Nov	Jul	Aug	Nov
AlexAl	20	r	3	r	r	r	r
AllanP	17½	r	3⅞	r	r	⅝	r
20⅝	20	15/16	2 1/16	r	r	1¼	2¾
20⅝	22½	⅛	1⅛	r	1⅞	r	r
20⅝	25	r	½	1⅞	r	r	r
Amdahl	15	r	2¾	r	r	r	¾
17⅝	17½	r	1	r	⅜	r	r
17⅝	20	1/16	⅛	r	r	r	r
AlnGrp	80	12⅜	r	r	r	r	r
92⅞	85	r	8¼	r	r	⅝	r
92⅞	90	2¾	4¼	r	¼	r	r
92⅞	95	r	1⅝	4¼	r	r	r
92⅞	100	s	r	s	s	7¾	s
Amoco	45	r	r	5½	r	⅛	¾
50⅛	50	¼	1¼	2⅜	r	r	r
50⅛	55	r	r	½	r	5⅝	r
A M P	55	r	1 13/16	r	⅝	1⅝	3
54⅝	60	r	r	r	r	5¾	r
Anadrk	22½	r	4¼	r	r	r	r
27	25	r	3	r	r	r	r
27	30	r	r	1⅛	r	r	r
BMC Sft	40	6¾	7¾	r	r	¾	r
46	45	1 13/16	4½	r	9/16	2½	r
46	50	⅛	2¼	r	r	5	7¼
Baxter	30	r	7⅜	r	r	r	r
37½	35	r	r	r	r	⅜	1⅛
37½	40	r	7/16	1⅛	r	r	r
BioTcG	7½	r	¼	¾	¾	r	r
7	10	r	r	r	3¼	3¼	r
Blk Dk	17½	r	r	4⅜	r	r	r
20⅞	20	⅞	r	r	⅛	r	1⅜
20⅞	22½	r	½	r	1¼	1⅞	2½
20⅞	25	r	3/16	r	4	4	r
Boeing	35	r	r	5½	r	¼	⅞
39⅞	40	⅜	1⅜	2 7/16	9/16	1½	2⅝
39⅞	45	r	¼	⅞	5⅝	5½	6⅛
39⅞	50	r	⅛	⅜	r	r	r
39⅞	55	s	1/16	s	s	15½	s
Bois C	17½	r	⅞	r	r	r	1½
17⅜	20	r	r	r	r	2½	r
Brunos	10	r	r	4	r	r	r
14⅛	15	r	r	9/16	r	r	1 7/16
C B S	185	r	r	r	r	2	r
199⅞	190	r	12⅜	r	¼	r	r
199⅞	195	5¾	r	r	r	r	r
199⅞	200	1 5/16	r	r	1⅝	r	r

and New York stock exchanges. Figure 24-1 shows a portion of the daily listing of the trading activity on the CBOE. The first column shows the name of the company and, indented below it, the closing price on its common stock. The next column shows the exercise price for the option contracts on the company. The next three columns show the premiums on the last trades for call options having expiration dates on the three specified months, and the final three columns show the corresponding premiums for put options.

For example, Boeing common stock closed at $39.875 on July 15, 1992. At the end of that day, Boeing call options with an exercise price of $40 per share that expire on the third Friday of July, August, and November of 1992 were traded at $.375, $1.375, and $2.4375, respectively. Similarly, Boeing put options with an exercise price of $40 that expire on the third Friday of July, August, and November of 1992 were traded at $.5625, $1.50, and $2.625, respectively.

Some options are not traded during a day, and are indicated by the letter "r" (see, for example, "Boeing July 35 puts" in Figure 24-1). Others, while included because of the format of the report, have not been introduced and are therefore unavailable for trading. These contracts are indicated by the letter "s" (in Figure 24-1, see, for example, "Boeing July 55 calls").

At the bottom of all of an exchange's listings, the total volume (that is, the number of contracts traded) and open interest (the number of contracts outstanding) for calls and puts are displayed.

Quotations

Quotations for options are reported in the format shown in Figure 24-1. Additional information is provided every day for the "most active" options on each of several exchanges. Figure 24-2 provides an example of the most active options on the Philadelphia Exchange. After the name of the company and the contract specifications comes the sales volume on the contract on that day, the closing price on the contract, the change this represents from the previous day's closing price, and the closing price on the underlying stock.

For example, Abbott Labs August 30 calls were traded on the Philadelphia Exchange and were one of the most active issues there on July 15, 1992.

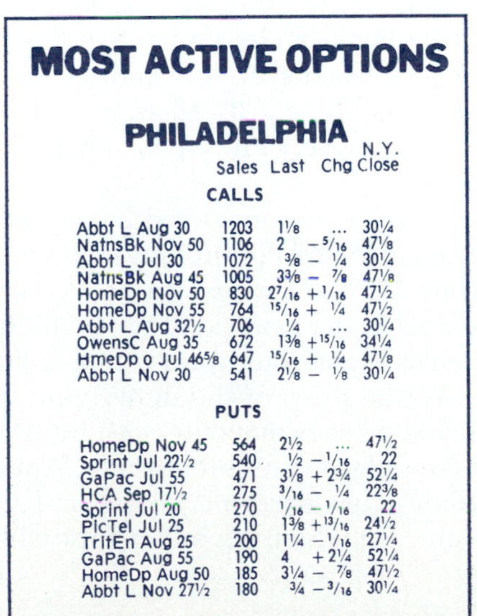

MOST ACTIVE OPTIONS

PHILADELPHIA

	Sales	Last	Chg	N.Y. Close
CALLS				
Abbt L Aug 30	1203	1⅛	...	30¼
NatnsBk Nov 50	1106	2	−5/16	47⅛
Abbt L Jul 30	1072	⅜	− ¼	30¼
NatnsBk Aug 45	1005	3⅜	− ⅞	47⅛
HomeDp Nov 50	830	2 7/16	+1/16	47½
HomeDp Nov 55	764	15/16	+ ¼	47½
Abbt L Aug 32½	706	¼	...	30¼
OwensC Aug 35	672	1⅜	+15/16	34¼
HmeDp o Jul 46⅝	647	15/16	+ ¼	47⅛
Abbt L Nov 30	541	2⅛	− ⅛	30¼
PUTS				
HomeDp Nov 45	564	2½	...	47½
Sprint Jul 22½	540	½	−1/16	22
GaPac Jul 55	471	3⅛	+ 2¾	52¼
HCA Sep 17½	275	3/16	− ¼	22⅜
Sprint Jul 20	270	1/16	−1/16	22
PicTel Jul 25	210	1⅜	+13/16	24½
TritEn Aug 25	200	1¼	−1/16	27¼
GaPac Aug 55	190	4	+ 2¼	52¼
HomeDp Aug 50	185	3¼	− ⅞	47½
Abbt L Nov 27½	180	¾	−3/16	30¼

FIGURE 24-2
Most Active Options Quotations

Source: Reprinted by permission of *The Wall Street Journal*, © Dow Jones & Company, Inc., July 16, 1992, p. C14.

On that day, 1,203 of these contracts were traded. The premium on the last trade was $1.125 per share (or $112.50 per contract, since a contract is for 100 shares). This represents no change from the premium on the previous day. At this time, the closing price on the common stock of Abbott Labs was $30.25 per share.

Investors may place the same kinds of orders for options as for stocks—market, limit, stop, and stop limit orders (these were discussed in Chapter 2). However, the way the orders for options are executed on the exchanges is, in some cases, different from the way that orders for stocks are executed.

Trading on Exchanges

As was mentioned in Chapter 3, trading on stock exchanges centers around specialists. These people serve two functions, acting as both dealers and brokers. As dealers, they keep an inventory of the stocks that are assigned to them, and buy and sell from that inventory at bid and ask prices, respectively. As brokers, they keep the limit order book and execute the orders in it as market prices move up and down. Some option markets, such as the American Stock Exchange, function in a similar manner. These markets have specialists who are assigned specific option contracts, and these specialists act as dealers and brokers in their assigned options. As with the stock exchanges, there may also be **floor traders,** who trade solely for themselves, hoping to buy low and sell high, and **floor brokers,** who handle orders from the public.

floor traders
floor brokers

Other option markets, such as the Chicago Board Options Exchange, do not involve specialists. Instead, they involve **market-makers,** who act solely as dealers, and **order book officials** (previously known as board brokers), who keep the limit order book. The market-makers must trade with floor brokers, who are members of the exchange that handle orders from the public. In doing so, the market-makers have an inventory of options and quote bid and ask prices. While there is one and only one specialist typically assigned to a stock, there usually is more than one market-maker assigned to the options on a given stock. Furthermore, a market-maker is prohibited from handling public orders in his or her assigned options, but may handle public orders in other options. That is, market-makers can also act as floor brokers, but only in unassigned options.

market-makers
order book officials

The order book official, in keeping the limit order book, is not allowed to engage in any trading. Unlike the specialist, the order book official's limit order book can be shown to other members of the exchange. The order book official stands at the trading post for those options that are his or her responsibility. All orders must be executed by means of an auction at the trading post with "open outcry," meaning that the auction is conducted orally.

Like the organized stock exchanges in the United States, all option exchanges are continuous markets, meaning that orders can be executed any time the exchanges are open. However, actual trading in options is, on occasion, far from continuous. In the financial press, it is not unusual to find prices for various options that appear to be "out of line" with one another or with the price of the underlying stock. It should be remembered that each listed price is that of the last trade of the day, and that these trades may have taken place at different times. Apparent price disparities may simply reflect trades that occurred before and after major news, rather than concurrent values at which obviously profitable trades could have been made.

MONEY MATTERS
Open Outcry

Is it a scene from a Fellini movie? Or perhaps the crowd at a 90%-off sale at Bloomingdale's? No, it is simply the members of the Chicago Board Options Exchange (CBOE) participating in the time-honored tradition of open outcry.

As the text describes, at the CBOE and other option exchanges (as well as at futures exchanges—see Chapter 25), members come together in various trading pits to conduct transactions in specific option contracts. Like the trading posts of the New York Stock Exchange (NYSE) (see Chapter 3), the CBOE trading pits serve as central locations where market-clearing prices for option contracts are continuously determined through an auction process. Unlike the NYSE trading posts, however, the CBOE and most other option exchanges do not use a specialist system; no one individual acts as a monopolistic dealer and auctioneer, ensuring the setting of market-clearing prices. Instead, those prices are established through open outcry, a public auction method involving verbal bids and offers initiated by the exchange members in the pit.

Open outcry is a raucous and colorful trading mechanism that combines the mental gymnastics of rapid-fire decision making with a set of physical skills ranging from strategic positioning in the trading pit to shouted instructions to frenetic hand signaling.

To describe the open outcry system as "the pits" is no exaggeration. The process begins in the trading pits, large depressions in the exchange floor surrounded by several levels of stairs on which the members stand. Although no formal rules are involved, traders generally behave very territorially in the pit. Floor traders usually have certain market-makers with whom they prefer to trade, and these individuals position themselves to make convenient contact with each other. Further, the most senior and important traders take positions in the pit where they have most efficient access to their counterparts. Junior members must stand in less desirable positions where they are less likely to catch the attention of other traders.

The trading pits are often crowded, noisy, and uncomfortable. Members may jostle each other for position. Hence, attributes such as voice strength and physical endurance are important. The pits are dominated by men, and the disadvantages endured by women in this physical environment are not lost on critics of the open outcry system.

Members deliver their trading intentions through a system of verbal orders and hand signals. For example, a floor broker may enter the IBM trading pit and verbally announce his or her intention to purchase June IBM call option contracts at a specified price. At the same time, he or she will typically repeat the buy order and desired price through hand signals. If a market-maker wishes to sell at that price, he or she will signal the desired quantity by hand.

To the uninitiated, the hand gestures used by members appear wild and unintelligible. In actuality, the signals are simple and highly efficient. Buy and sell orders are indicated by the position of the trader's palm(s). If the trader's palms are facing him or her, a buy is signaled. The trader signals a sell by keeping his or her palms pointed outward.

The trader indicates the bid or asked price by holding his or her hand in a vertical position and using fingers to indicate the fraction of a dollar involved. For example, one finger indicates an eighth of a dollar, while a closed fist indicates a full dollar.

Traders likewise display their quantity intentions with their hands. In this case, however, fingers pointed vertically indicate one through five contracts, while fingers pointed horizontally indicate six through nine contracts. One finger to the forehead indicates ten contracts.

At any given time, members in the pit may be trading in different option contracts, shouting in an attempt to make their voices heard above the din, and flailing their arms about to signal their trading intentions. Add to this scene runners milling about the edge of the pit, time and sale clerks, price reporters, order book officials keeping track of transactions, and persons situated away from the pit signaling in orders to the floor brokers, and pandemonium hardly seems an adequate description of the trading process.

Open outcry is a controversial trading mechanism. It has been criticized as an archaic method designed primarily to perpetuate control over lucrative option trading by the exchanges' members. In an age of advanced electronics, there are readily available computer systems that could facilitate electronic auctions and permit wider access to the auction process. (For example, in mid-1992 the Chicago Board of Trade and Chicago Mercantile Exchange initiated a trading system known as Globex. This system involves electronic trading in various futures contracts traded on the two exchanges during times when those exchanges are closed. When these exchanges are open, they use an open outcry system that is essentially the same as that used on the CBOE.) The benefits of such electronic auction systems would appear to be lower trading costs and greater liquidity.

Defenders of the open outcry system claim that it is the most efficient system of price discovery. They believe that the system's face-to-face contact permits traders to better ascertain the "true" intentions of buyers and sellers. Moreover, the defenders contend that price manipulation is less likely in an open environment.

Commissions

While a commission must be paid to a stockbroker whenever an option is either written, bought, or sold, the size of the commission has been reduced substantially since options began to be traded on organized exchanges in 1973. Furthermore, this commission is typically smaller than the commission that would be paid if the underlying stock had been purchased instead of the option. However, the investor should be aware that exercising an option will typically result in the buyer having to pay a commission equivalent to the commission that would be incurred if the stock itself were being bought or sold.

MARGIN

Any buyer of an option would like some assurance that the writer can deliver as required if the option is exercised. Specifically, the buyer of a call option would like some assurance that the writer is capable of delivering the requisite shares, and the buyer of a put option would like some assurance that the writer is capable of delivering the necessary cash. Since all option contracts are with the Option Clearing Corporation, the OCC is actually the one concerned with the ability of the writer to fulfill the terms of the contract.

To relieve the OCC of this concern, margin requirements have been set by the exchanges where the options are traded. However, brokerage firms are allowed to impose even stricter requirements if they so desire, since they are ultimately liable to the OCC for the actions of their investors.

In the case of a call, shares are to be delivered by the writer in return for the exercise price. In the case of a put, cash is to be delivered in return for shares. In either case, the net cost to the option writer will be the absolute difference between the exercise price and the stock's market value at the time of exercise. Since the OCC is at risk if the writer is unable to bear this cost, it is not surprising that the OCC would have a system in place that protects itself from the actions of the writers. This system is known as margin, and it is similar in some ways to the notion of margin associated with stock purchases and short sales that was discussed in Chapter 2.[5]

Calls

covered call writing

In a situation known as **covered call writing,** where the writer of a call owns the underlying stock, the writer does not need to come up with any cash. Instead, the premium paid by the buyer is given to the writer but the writer's stock is kept in escrow by the brokerage firm. Thus, if the buyer chooses to exercise the option, the requisite shares are at hand for delivery. If the option expires or if the writer enters a closing purchase, then the writer will have access to the shares.

naked call writing

In a situation known as **naked call writing,** where the writer of a call does not own the underlying stock, the margin requirements are more complicated. Specifically, it involves determining the higher of two figures. The first figure is equal to the option premium plus 20% of the market value of

[5]It should be noted that a call or put buyer is not allowed to use margin. Instead, the option buyer is required to pay 100% of the option's purchase price. In contrast, the stock buyer could use margin, where part of the cost of purchasing the stock is borrowed.

the underlying stock, less an amount equal to the call's exercise price less the stock's market price (provided that the exercise price is larger than the stock's market price). The second figure is equal to the sum of the option premium and 10% of the market price of the underlying stock.

As an example of the margin required for naked call writing, consider an investor who writes a December 60 call and receives a premium of $3 per share. If the underlying stock is selling for $58, then the margin is the higher of two figures calculated as follows:

Method 1:	Option premium	
	= $3 × 100 shares	$300
	20% of market value of stock	
	= .20 × $58 × 100 shares	1160
	Less amount by which call's exercise price exceeds stock's market price	
	= ($60 − $58) × 100 shares	−200
	Total	$1,260
Method 2:	Option premium	
	= $3 × 100 shares	$300
	10% of market value of stock	
	= .10 × $58 × 100 shares	580
	Total	$880

Since the first method results in a higher figure, it is applicable. Thus, in this example the amount of margin required is equal to $1,260, meaning that the writer must deposit $1,260 in cash with his or her broker. Since the premium can be used for this purpose, the writer only needs to come up with $960 = $1,260 − $300.

Puts

For puts, the margin requirements are similar. If the brokerage account of the writer of a put contains cash (or other securities) amounting to the exercise price of the put, then no margin is required. Furthermore, the writer can remove from the account an amount of cash that is equal to the premium received from the buyer. The reason for this is that the account will still have collateral that is equal in value to the exercise price.

naked put writing

If the brokerage account of a put writer does not contain cash (or securities), then the situation is known as **naked put writing.** The amount of margin required for such a writer is calculated in a manner similar to that for the writer of a naked call option. That is, the put writer must come up with margin equal to the larger of two figures. The first figure is equal to the option premium plus 20% of the market value of the underlying stock, less an amount equal to the stock's market price less the put's exercise price (note that this is the reverse of the amount for a call, and is subtracted only if the stock's market price is larger than the exercise price). The second figure is calculated exactly as previously described for calls, being equal to the sum of the option premium and 10% of the market price of the underlying security.

As an example of the margin required for naked put writing, consider an investor who writes a March 40 put and receives a premium of $4 per share. If the underlying stock is selling for $41, then the margin is the higher of two figures calculated as follows:

Method 1:	Option premium	
	= $4 × 100 shares	$400
	20% of market value of stock	
	= .20 × $41 × 100 shares	820
	Less amount by which stock's market price exceeds put's exercise price	
	= ($41 − $40) × 100 shares	−100
	Total	$1,120
Method 2:	Option premium	
	= $4 × 100 shares	$400
	10% of market value of stock	
	= .10 × $41 × 100 shares	410
	Total	$810

Since the first method results in a higher figure, it is applicable. Thus, in this example the amount of margin required is equal to $1,120, meaning that the writer must deposit $1,120 in cash with his or her broker. Since the premium can be used for this purpose, the writer only needs to come up with $720 = $1,120 − $400.

It should be noted that maintenance margin requirements for options are the same as initial margin requirements. Furthermore, the calculation of margin requirements becomes much more complex when the individual is engaged in various investment activities (such as simultaneously buying and writing different put and call options as well as buying some common stocks on margin while short selling others). Finally, when index options are involved, the margin requirements are reduced (specifically, the 20% figure is reduced to 15%) owing to the fact that index options tend to be less volatile than individual stock options. (Index options are discussed later in the chapter.)

TAXATION OF OPTION PROFITS AND LOSSES

While income tax regulations can be quite complex, the general approach to the taxation of profits and losses from option trading is reasonably easy to understand. Usually short-term capital gains and losses are involved, since the buying and selling transactions are usually within one year of each other. Hence the net amount is usually treated as ordinary income if it is a gain and is fully deductible (subject to a $3,000 cap) from ordinary income if it is a loss. Commissions paid are added to purchase prices and subtracted from selling prices in determining the amount of the capital gains and losses.

Consider a call option buyer first. If the call is exercised, the buyer is considered to have bought the stock for a total cost equal to the exercise price plus the premium paid for the option itself. When the stock is subsequently sold, the difference between this cost and the selling price will be the buyer's capital gain or loss.

If the call buyer later sells the option instead of exercising it, the difference between the buying and selling prices is the amount of the capital gain or loss. However, if the call expires unexercised, the buyer will have a capital loss equal to the premium paid on the option.

Consider the writer of a call option next. If the call is exercised, the writer is considered to have sold the stock for a total value equal to the exercise price plus the premium received for the option. The difference between this value and the price paid when the stock was purchased is the amount of the capital gain or loss incurred by the writer.

If the call writer later buys the option, thereby closing out his or her position, the difference between the premium that was received when the option was written and the premium that was paid to close out the position is the amount of the capital gain or loss. However, if the option expires unexercised, then the writer will have a capital gain equal to the amount of the premium received.

The treatment of puts is quite similar. If the put expires unexercised, then the buyer has a capital loss and the writer has a capital gain that are both equal to the premium on the put. If a closing transaction is entered, then the difference between the buying and selling prices is the amount of the capital gain or loss. If the put is exercised, then the buyer has a capital gain equal to the exercise price less the amount paid for both the stock and the put. The writer who receives the stock in this situation is treated as having made a stock purchase for an amount equal to the exercise price less the premium received on the put.

These and other rules give rise to a number of strategies that take tax consequences into account. For example, consider an investor who previously bought a stock and has seen its market price rise dramatically. If the investor sells it now, a capital gain will be incurred. However, the investor could buy a January put and hold off selling the stock until the turn of the year. By doing so, the capital gain will not be realized this year, so no taxes will need to be paid on the stock this year. However, the gain on the stock will have been protected by the use of the put. Once January comes around, the investor can decide to either exercise the put or sell the stock, realizing the gain at that time and thus deferring tax payments for a year.

VALUATION OF OPTIONS

Valuation at Expiration

The value of an option is related to the value of the underlying security in a manner that is most easily seen just prior to expiration (which for simplicity will be referred to as "at expiration"). Figure 24-3(a) relates the value of a call option with an exercise price of $100 to the price of the underlying stock at expiration. If the stock price is below $100, the option will be worthless when it expires. If the price is above $100, the option can be exercised for $100 to obtain a security with a greater value, resulting in a net gain to the option buyer that will equal the difference between the security's market price and the exercise price. However, there is no need for the option buyer to actually exercise the option. Instead, the option writer can simply pay the buyer the difference between the security price and the exercise price, thereby allowing both parties to avoid the inconvenience of exercise. This is commonly done for listed options (by using the services of the Options Clearing Corporation), although a minority of investors choose to exercise their options, possibly for tax purposes.

FIGURE 24-3
Values of Options at Expiration

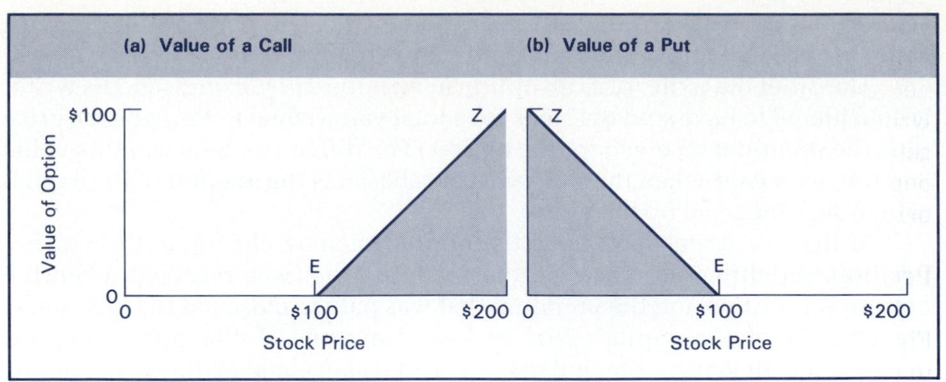

Figure 24-3(b) shows the value at expiration of a put option with an exercise price of $100. If the stock price is above $100, the option will be worthless when it expires. If the price is below $100, the option can be exercised to obtain $100 for stock having a lower value, resulting in a net gain to the option buyer that will equal the difference between the exercise price and the stock's market price. As with a call option, neither the put option buyer nor the writer need actually deal in the stock. Instead, the writer of any put option that is worth exercising at expiration can simply pay the buyer of the option the difference between the stock price and the exercise price.

In both panels of Figure 24-3, the lines indicating the value of a call and a put at expiration can also be interpreted to be the value of a call or put *at the moment the option is exercised*, no matter when that occurs during the life of the option. In particular, for calls the kinked line connecting points 0, E, and Z is known as the **intrinsic value** of the call. Similarly, for puts the kinked line connecting points Z, E, and $200 is known as the intrinsic value of the put.

intrinsic value

The kinked lines representing the *intrinsic values* of calls and puts such as those that are shown in Figure 24-3 can be expressed as IV_c and IV_p, respectively, as follows:

$$IV_c = \text{MAX}\,\{0, P_s - E\} \quad (24.1a)$$

$$IV_p = \text{MAX}\,\{0, E - P_s\} \quad (24.1b)$$

where P_s denotes the market price of the underlying stock and E denotes the exercise price of the option. (Here MAX means to use the larger of the two values in brackets.)

Consider the call option in Figure 24-3(a). Its intrinsic value, according to equation (24.1a), is MAX $\{0, P_s - \$100\}$ since its exercise price is $100. Note that for any market price of the stock that is below $100, such as $50, its intrinsic value is MAX $\{0, \$50 - \$100\} = 0$. Hence $IV_c = 0$ in such situations. Next, imagine that the market price of the stock is above $100, for example $150. In this situation its intrinsic value is MAX $\{0, \$150 - \$100\} = \$50$. Hence $IV_c = P_s - E$. Thus the kinked intrinsic value line has its kink at E, as it has two components that meet there: a horizontal line going through the origin out to the value E, and then a 45-degree line (and therefore having a slope of one) going northeast from E. Similar analysis reveals that the kinked intrinsic value line for the put also has its kink at E, as shown in Figure 24-3(b).

Calls and puts will not sell for less than their intrinsic values, owing to the actions of shrewd investors. If an option sold for less than its intrinsic value, then such investors could instantaneously make riskless profits. For example, if the stock price was \$150 and the call was selling for \$40, which is \$10 less than its intrinsic value of \$50, then these investors would simultaneously buy these calls, exercise them, and sell the shares received from the writers. In doing so they would spend \$140 on each call and exercise price and get \$150 in return for each share sold, resulting in a net riskless profit of \$10 per call. As a consequence, the call will not sell for less than \$50 if the stock price is \$150.

Profits and Losses at Expiration

Figure 24-3 shows the values of call and put options at expiration. However, in order to determine profits and losses from buying or writing these options, the premiums involved must be taken into consideration.[6] Figure 24-4 does this for investors who engage in some of the more complicated option strategies. Each strategy assumes that the underlying stock is selling for \$100 at the time an option is initially bought or written. It is also assumed that closing transactions are made just prior to the expiration date for the option being considered. Outcomes are shown for each of ten strategies. Since the profit obtained by a buyer is the writer's loss and vice versa, each diagram in the figure has a corresponding mirror image.

Panels (a) and (b) in Figure 24-4 show the profits and losses associated with buying and writing a call, respectively. Similarly, panels (c) and (d) show the profits and losses associated with buying and writing a put, respectively.

Consider panels (a) and (c) first. The kinked lines representing profits and losses in these two panels are simply graphs of the intrinsic value equations given in equations (24-1a) and (24-1b) and shown in Figure 24-3, less the premiums on the options. Thus, they are graphs of the following equations:

$$\begin{aligned}\pi_c &= IV_c - P_c \\ &= \text{MAX}\,\{0, P_s - E\} - P_c \\ &= \text{MAX}\,\{-P_c, P_s - E - P_c\} \qquad (24.2a)\end{aligned}$$

$$\begin{aligned}\pi_p &= IV_p - P_p \\ &= \text{MAX}\,\{0, E - P_s\} - P_p \\ &= \text{MAX}\,\{-P_p, E - P_s - P_p\} \qquad (24.2b)\end{aligned}$$

where π_c and π_p denote the profits associated with buying a call and put, and P_c and P_p denote the premiums on the call and put, respectively. This means that the kinked profit line for the call is simply the same kinked line for the intrinsic value but lowered by an amount equal to the call premium, P_c. Similarly, the kinked profit line for the put is simply the kinked intrinsic value line for the put, lowered by an amount equal to the put premium, P_p.

If the premium on the call and put options shown in Figure 23-3 were \$5, then their profit lines would be graphs of the following two equations:

$$\pi_c = \text{MAX}\,\{-\$5, P_s - \$100 - \$5\}$$

[6]Since the premium is paid by the buyer to the writer at the time the option is created, it should be compounded to an equivalent value at expiration using an appropriate rate of interest when calculating profits and losses.

FIGURE 24-4
Profits and Losses from Various Strategies

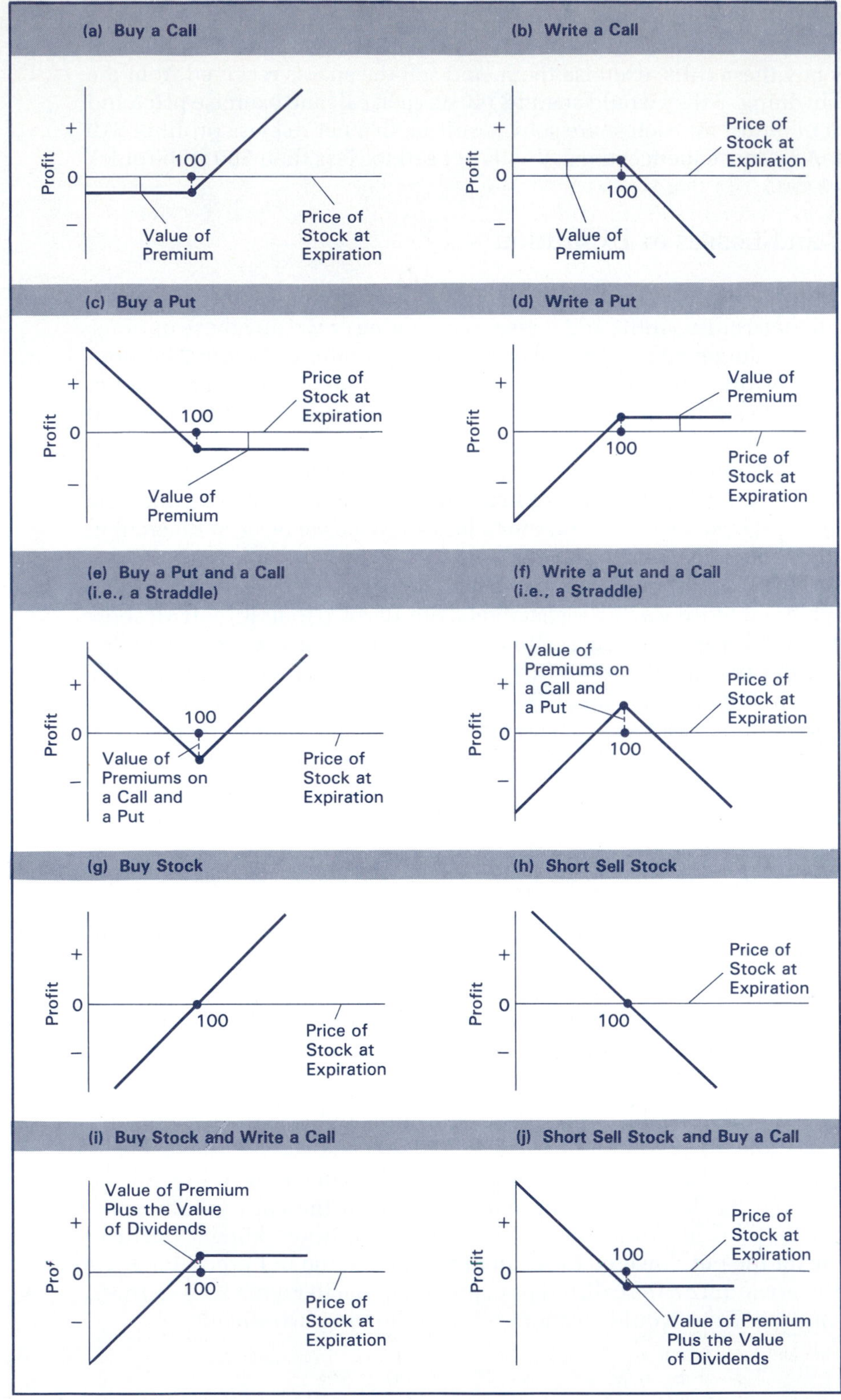

$$= \text{MAX}\,\{-\$5,\ P_s - \$105\}$$

$$\pi_p = \text{MAX}\,\{-\$5,\ \$100 - P_s - \$5\}$$

$$= \text{MAX}\,\{-\$5,\ \$95 - P_s\}$$

Hence, the kinked line for the call would be a horizontal line intersecting the vertical axis at −$5 that would have a kink at a stock price of $100, where it would turn upward to intersect the horizontal axis at $105. This indicates that the call buyer would not make a profit unless the stock price was above $105 at expiration, since $105 is the breakeven point. Each dollar that the stock price is above $105 represents an additional dollar of profit (hence a price of $108 would represent a profit of $3, since the call buyer pays a premium of $5 and an exercise price of $100 to procure a share of stock that is worth $108).

Similarly, the kinked line for the put would be a downward-sloping line that would have a kink at a stock price of $100 after intersecting the horizontal axis at $95; at the kink the line would become horizontal so that if this part of the line were extended to the vertical axis, it would intersect it at −$5. This indicates that the put buyer would not make a profit unless the stock price was below $95 at expiration, since $95 is the breakeven point. Each dollar that the stock price is below $95 represents an additional dollar of profit (hence a price of $92 would represent a profit of $3, since the put buyer pays a premium of $5 and gives up a share of stock worth $92 in order to receive $100 in return).

Panels (b) and (d) are mirror images of panels (a) and (c), respectively. This is because options are zero-sum games, where the profits to one party are at the expense of the other party. Hence, if the stock price is at $108 so that the call buyer has a $3 profit, then the call writer has a $3 loss (since the writer receives the $5 premium and $100 exercise price but must give up a share of stock worth $108). Similarly, if the put buyer has a $3 profit, then the put writer has a loss of $3.

Panels (e) and (f) in Figure 24-4 illustrate a more complicated options strategy known as a **straddle.** This strategy involves buying (or writing) both a call and a put on the same stock, with the options having the same exercise price and expiration date.[7] Note how panel (e) can be derived by adding the profits and losses shown in panels (a) and (c), while panel (f) can be derived by adding the profits and losses shown in panels (b) and (d). It can also be seen that panels (e) and (f) are mirror images of each other, again reflecting the fact that the profits to buyers equal the losses to writers and vice versa.

straddle

Panel (g) of Figure 24-4 shows the profit or loss made by an investor who avoids options entirely, but buys a share of the underlying stock (at $100) at the same time that others buy or write options, and sells the stock when the options expire. Assuming that no dividends are paid in the interim, the relationship is that shown by the solid line.[8] Similarly, panel (h) shows the profit or loss obtained by an investor who short sells the stock at the initial date and then buys it back at the expiration date.

---

[7]Strips and straps are option strategies similar to a straddle; the former involves combining two puts with one call and the latter involves combining two calls with one put. Another kind of strategy is known as a spread, where one call is bought while another is written on the same underlying security. Specifically, a price spread involves two calls having the same expiration date but different exercise prices; a time spread involves two calls having the same exercise price but different expiration dates.

[8]If there are dividends, they should be expressed as a compounded value at the expiration date associated with the options (since they would have been previously received) and added to the line, thereby shifting it upward.

Panel (i) of Figure 24-4 shows the results obtained by an investor who buys one share of stock and simultaneously writes a call on it; these results can be derived by adding the profits and losses shown in panels (b) and (g). As mentioned earlier, such an investor is said to have written a fully covered option. In contrast, the writer who does not hold the underlying stock, depicted in panel (b), is said to have written a naked option.

Panel (j) of Figure 24-4 shows the results obtained by an investor who short sells one share of stock and simultaneously buys a call option, and can be derived by adding the profits and losses in panels (a) and (h). Note that this panel is the mirror image of panel (i).

Comparison of the diagrams in Figure 24-4 suggests that similar results can be obtained via alternative strategies. Panels (c) and (j) are similar, as are (d) and (i). Neither the premiums involved nor the initial investments required need be equal in every case. Nonetheless, the similarity of the results obtained with different "packages" of securities suggests that the total market values of the packages will be similar.

Having discussed the value of options (and option-based strategies) when they expire, it is appropriate to discuss next the value of options before they expire. Specifically, what is the fair (or true) value of an option today if it expires at some future date? A method utilizing the binomial option pricing model can be used to answer such a question; it is presented next.

THE BINOMIAL OPTION PRICING MODEL

European options

American options

As was just mentioned, the binomial option pricing model (or BOPM) can be used to estimate the fair value of a call or put option; it will be presented by use of an example. It will be assumed that the options are **European options,** meaning that they can be exercised only on their expiration dates. In addition, it will be assumed that the underlying stock does not pay any dividends during the life of the option. It should be noted that the model can be modified to value **American options,** which are options that can be exercised any time during their lifetime, and can also be used to value options on stocks that pay dividends during the life of the option.

Call Options

Assume that the price of Widget stock today ($t = 0$) is \$100, and that after one year ($t = T$) its stock will be selling for either \$125 or \$80, meaning that the stock will either rise by 25% or fall by 20% over the year. In addition, the annual riskfree rate is 8% compounded continuously; investors are assumed to be able to either *lend* (by purchasing these 8% bonds) or *borrow* (by shorting the bonds) at this rate.

Now consider a call option on Widget that has an exercise price of \$100 and an expiration date of one year from now. This means that on the expiration date the call will have a value of either \$25 (if Widget is at \$125) or \$0 (if Widget is at \$80). Panel (a) of Figure 24-5 illustrates the situation by use of a "price tree." It can be seen from this tree why this is called a binomial model, since there are only two branches that represent prices at the expiration date.

Valuation The question that arises is this: What is a fair value for the call at time 0? The binomial option pricing model is designed to answer this question.

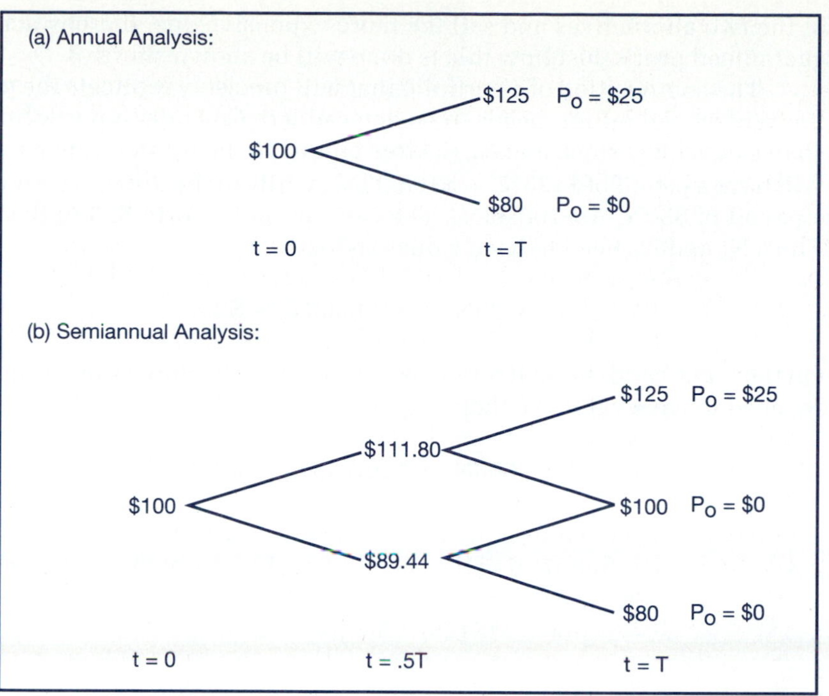

FIGURE 24-5
Binomial Model of Prices for Widget

There are three investments that are of interest here: The stock, the option, and a riskfree bond. The prices and payoffs for the stock are known. It is also known that $100 invested in a riskfree bond will grow to approximately $108.33 if interest is continuously compounded at an annual rate of 8%.[9] Finally, the end-of-period payoffs associated with the option are known. What is to be determined is a fair price that the option should sell for now.

The key to understanding the situation is the observation that there are two possible future *states* of the world. The stock's price may go *up* or *down*. For simplicity, these two states are called the "up state" and the "down state," respectively. This essential information is summarized as follows:

SECURITY	PAYOFF IN UP STATE	PAYOFF IN DOWN STATE	CURRENT PRICE
Stock	$125.00	$80.00	$100.00
Bond	$108.33	$108.33	$100.00
Call	$25.00	$0.00	???

Note that at this juncture the current price of the call is unknown.

Replicating Portfolios While the Widget call option may seem exotic, its characteristics can in fact be replicated with an appropriate combination of the Widget stock and the riskfree bond. Moreover, the cost of this *replicating portfolio* constitutes the fair value of the option. Why? Because otherwise there would be an *arbitrage* opportunity—an investor could buy the cheaper

[9]In general, $1 will grow to $\$1e^{RT}$ at the end of T periods if it is continuously compounded at a rate of R. Here, e represents the base of the natural logarithms, which is equal to approximately 2.71828. For a more detailed discussion, see the Appendix to Chapter 20.

of the two alternatives and sell the more expensive one, thereby achieving a guaranteed profit (just how this is done will be shown shortly).

The composition of a portfolio that will precisely replicate the payoffs of the Widget call option needs to be determined. Consider a portfolio with N_s shares of Widget stock and N_b riskfree bonds. In the up state, such a portfolio will have a payoff of $\$125N_s + \$108.33N_b$, while in the down state it will have a payoff of $\$80N_s + \$108.33N_b$. The call option is worth \$25 in the up state. Thus, N_s and N_b need to have values so that:

$$\$125N_s + \$108.33N_b = \$25. \tag{24.3a}$$

On the other hand, the call option is worthless in the down state. Thus, N_s and N_b need to have values so that:

$$\$80N_s + \$108.33N_b = \$0. \tag{24.3b}$$

These two linear equations, (24.3a) and (24.3b), have two unknowns and can easily be solved. Subtracting the second equation from the first gives:

$$(\$125 - \$80)N_s = \$25 \tag{24.3c}$$

so that N_s equals .5556. Substituting this value in either equation (24.3a) or (24.3b) gives the remainder of the solution, $N_b = -.4103$.

What does this mean in financial terms? That an investor can replicate the payoffs from the call by *shorting* \$41.03 of the riskfree bonds (note that investing −.4103 in \$100 bonds is equivalent to shorting \$41.03 of the bonds or borrowing \$41.03 at the riskfree rate) and *purchasing* .5556 shares of Widget stock. This is indeed the case, as can be seen here:

PORTFOLIO COMPONENT	PAYOFF IN UP STATE	PAYOFF IN DOWN STATE
Stock investment	\$.5556 × \$125 = \$69.45	.5556 × \$80 = \$44.45
Loan repayment	−\$41.03 × 1.0833 = −\$44.45	−\$41.03 × 1.0833 = −\$44.45
Net payoff	\$25.00	\$0.00

Since the replicating portfolio provides the same payoffs as the call, only its cost needs to be calculated in order to find the fair value of the option. To obtain the portfolio, \$55.56 must be spent to purchase .5556 shares of Widget stock (at \$100 per share). However, \$41.03 of this amount is provided by the proceeds from the short sale of the bond. Thus, only \$14.53 = \$55.56 − \$41.03 of the investor's own funds must be spent. Accordingly, this is the fair value of the call option.

More generally, the value of the call option will be:

$$V_o = N_sP_s + N_bP_b \tag{24.4}$$

where V_o represents the value of the option, P_s is the price of the stock, P_b is the price of a riskfree bond, and N_s and N_b are the number of shares and riskfree bonds required to replicate the option's payoffs.

Overpricing To show that equilibrium will be attained if the call if selling for \$14.53, consider what a shrewd investor would do if the call were selling for either more or less than this amount. Imagine that the call is selling for \$20, so it is overpriced. In this case the investor would consider writing one call, buying .5556 shares, and borrowing \$41.03. The net cash flow when this is done (that is, at $t = 0$) would be $\$20 - (.5556 \times \$100) + \$41.03 = \$5.47$, indicating that the investor has a net cash inflow. At the end of the year (that is, at $t = T$) the investor's net cash flow will be as follows:

PORTFOLIO COMPONENT	PAYOFF IN UP STATE	PAYOFF IN DOWN STATE
Written call	= −\$25.00	= \$0.00
Stock investment	.5556 × \$125	.5556 × \$80
	= \$69.45	= \$44.45
Loan repayment	−\$41.03 × 1.0833	−\$41.03 × 1.0833
	= −\$44.45	= −\$44.45
Net payoff	\$0.00	\$0.00

Since the net aggregate value is zero regardless of the ending stock price, the investor has no risk of loss from this strategy. Thus, the investor currently has a means for generating free cash as long as the call is priced at \$20, since the investment strategy does not require any cash from the investor later on. This cannot represent equilibrium, as anyone can get free cash by investing similarly.

Underpricing Next, imagine that the call is selling for \$10 instead of \$20, so it is underpriced. In this case the investor would consider buying one call, short selling .5556 shares, and investing \$41.03 at the riskfree rate. The net cash flow when this is done (that is, at $t = 0$) would be $-\$10 + (.5556 \times \$100) - \$41.03 = \$4.53$, indicating that the investor has a net cash inflow. At the end of the year (that is, at $t = T$) the investor's net cash flow will be as follows:

PORTFOLIO COMPONENT	PAYOFF IN UP STATE	PAYOFF IN DOWN STATE
Call investment	= \$25.00	= \$0.00
Repay shorted stock	−.5556 × \$125	−.5556 × \$80
	= −\$69.45	= −\$44.45
Riskfree investment	\$41.03 × 1.0833	\$41.03 × 1.0833
	= \$44.45	= \$44.45
Net payoff	\$0.00	\$0.00

Once again, the net aggregate value is zero regardless of the ending stock price, indicating that the investor has no risk of loss from this strategy. Hence the investor currently has a means for generating free cash as long as the call is priced at \$10, but this cannot represent equilibrium, as anyone can get free cash by investing similarly.

The Hedge Ratio To replicate the Widget call option, imagine borrowing \$41.03 and purchasing shares of Widget stock. Now, consider the effect of a change in the price of the stock tomorrow (not a year from now) on the value of the replicating portfolio. Since .5556 shares of stock are included in the portfolio, the value of the portfolio will change by \$.5556 for every \$1 change in the price of Widget stock. But, since the call option and the portfolio should sell for the same price, it follows that the price of the call should also change by \$.5556 for every \$1 change in the price of the stock. This relationship is defined as the option's **hedge ratio**. It is equal to the value of N_s that was determined in equation (24.3c).

hedge ratio

In the case of the Widget call option, the hedge ratio was equal to .5556, which equals the value of (\$25 − \$0)/(\$125 − \$80). Note that the numerator equals the difference between the option's payoffs in the up and down states and the denominator equals the difference between the stock's payoffs in the two states. More generally, in the binomial model:

$$h = \frac{P_{ou} - P_{od}}{P_{su} - P_{sd}} \tag{24.5}$$

where P represents the end-of-period price and the subscripts indicate the instrument (o for option, s for stock) and the state of the world (u for up, d for down).

To replicate a call option in a binomial world, *h* shares of stock [where *h* represents the hedge ratio determined by using equation (24.5)] must be purchased while simultaneously an amount must be risklessly borrowed by shorting bonds; this amout is equal to:

$$B = PV(hP_{sd} - P_{od}) \tag{24.6}$$

where PV indicates to take the present value of the figure calculated in the following parentheses since the figure in parentheses is the value of the bond at the end of the period.[10]

To summarize, the value of a call option is given to be:

$$V_o = hP_s - B \tag{24.7}$$

where h and B are the hedge ratio and current value of a short bond position in a portfolio that replicates the payoffs of the call, and are calculated by using equations (24.5) and (24.6).

More Than Two Prices At this juncture it is reasonable to wonder about the accuracy of the BOPM if it is based on an assumption that the price of Widget stock can assume only one of two values at the end of a year. Realistically, Widget stock can assume any one of a great number of prices at year-end. It turns out that this is not a problem, as the model can be extended in a straightforward manner.

In the case of Widget, divide the year into two six-month periods. In the first period, assume that Widget can go up to \$111.80 (an 11.80% increase) or down to \$89.44 (a 10.56% decrease). For the second six-month period, the price of Widget can again go either up by 11.80% or down by 10.56%. Hence

[10]Equations (24.5) and (24.6) can be derived by solving the set of equations (24.3a) and (24.3b) using symbols instead of numbers.

the price of Widget will follow one of the paths of the price tree shown in panel (b) of Figure 24-5 over the forthcoming year. Note how Widget can now assume one of three prices at year-end: \$125, \$100, or \$80. The associated value of the call option is also given in the figure for each of these stock prices.

How can the value of the Widget call option at time 0 be calculated from the information given in the figure? The answer is remarkably simple. All that is done is that the problem is broken down into three parts, each of which is solved in a manner similar to that shown earlier when panel (a) was discussed. The three parts must be approached sequentially by working backwards in time.

First, imagine that six months have passed and the price of Widget stock is \$111.80. What is the value of the call option at this node in the price tree? The hedge ratio h is calculated to be (\$25 − \$0)/(\$125 − \$100) = 1.0, and the amount of the borrowing B is calculated to be [(1 × \$100) − \$0]/1.0408 = \$96.08 (the 8% riskfree rate compounded continuously corresponds to a discrete discount rate of 4.08%). Using equation (24.7), the value of the call is determined to be (1 × \$111.80) − \$96.08 = \$15.72.

Second, again imagine that six months have passed but the price of Widget is \$89.44. While equations (24.5), (24.6), and (24.7) could be used to determine the value of the call at this node in the price tree, intuition gives the answer more quickly: The call has to be selling for \$0. This is because in six months the price of Widget will be either \$100 or \$80, and regardless of which it is, the call will still be worthless. That is, investors will realize that the call will be worthless at the end of the year if the stock price is at \$89.44 after six months, and hence will be unwilling to pay anything for the call option.

Third, imagine that no time has elapsed so it is time 0. In this case the price tree can be simplified to:

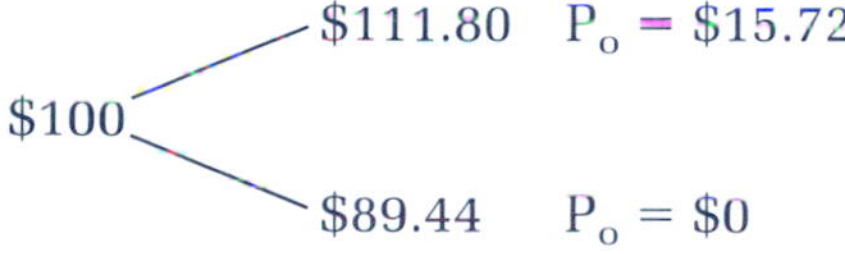

Applying equations (24.5) and (24.6), indicate that the hedge ratio h is equal to (\$15.72 − \$0)/(\$111.80 − \$89.44) = .7030 and the amount of borrowing B is equal to [(.7030 × \$89.44) − \$0]/1.0408 = \$60.41. Applying equation (24.7) results in a value for the call at $t = 0$ of \$9.89 = (.7030 × \$100) − \$60.41.

There is no need to stop here. Instead of analyzing 2 six-month periods, 4 quarterly periods can be analyzed, or 12 monthly periods. Note that the number of year-end stock prices for Widget is equal to one more than the number of periods in a year. Hence when annual periods were used in panel (a) of Figure 24-5, there were 2 year-end prices, and when semiannual prices were used there were 3 year-end prices. It follows that if quarterly or monthly periods were used, there would have been 5 or 13 year-end prices, respectively.

Put Options

Can the BOPM be used to value puts? Since the formulas cover any set of payoffs, they can be applied directly. Consider Widget once again from an annual perspective, where the put option has an exercise price of \$100 and an expiration date of one year. Its price tree will be:

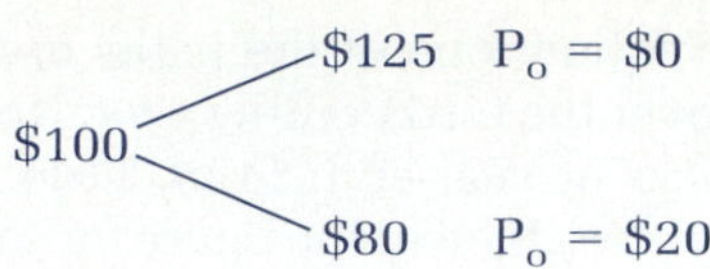

Applying equation (24.5) gives the hedge ratio for the put option of −.4444 [= ($0 − $20)/($125 − $80)]. Note that this is a negative number, indicating that a rise in the price of the stock will lower the price of the put.

Applying equation (24.6) shows that B equals −$51.28, which is the present value of the year-end value of the bond of −$55.55. Since these are negative numbers, they denote the amount of bonds to be purchased (that is, the negative value of a short position should be interpreted as the value of a long position).

To replicate the put option, then, one *sells short* .4444 shares of Widget and *lends* (that is, invests in the riskfree bond) $51.28. Since the short sale will generate on $44.44 while the bond purchase will cost $51.28, the net cost of the replicating portfolio will be $6.84 (= $51.28 − $44.44). Accordingly, this is the fair value of the put.

This is the same value that is obtained when equation (24.7) is used: $6.84 = (.4444 × $100) − (−$51.28), where h = .4444, B = −$51.28, and P_s = $100. Hence, equations (24.5), (24.6), and (24.7) can be used to value not only calls but also puts. Furthermore, the procedure for extending the valuation of puts to the situation where there is more than one period between now and the expiration date is analogous to the one that was given for calls.

Put-Call Parity

Earlier it was shown that the call on Widget had a hedge ratio of .5556. Note than 1 − .5556 = .4444, the hedge ratio for the put. This is not a coincidence. The hedge ratios of a European put and call having the same exercise price and expiration date are related in the following manner:

$$1 - h_c = h_p \tag{24.8}$$

where h_c and h_p denote the hedge ratios for the call and put, respectively.

Of even greater interest is the relationship between the market prices of a call and a put on a given stock that have the same exercise price and expiration date. Again, consider the example involving Widget options that have an exercise price of $100 and an expiration date of one year. Two investment strategies need to be compared. Strategy A involves buying a put and a share of stock; strategy B involves buying a call and investing an amount of money in the riskfree asset that is equal to the present value of the exercise price.

At the expiration date the values of these two investment strategies can be calculated under two scenarios: the price of Widget being below its exercise price of $100, and the price of Widget being above its exercise price (the case where it is exactly equal to its exercise price can be added to either scenario without affecting the results). Table 24-1 does this. Note that if the stock of Widget is selling for less than the $100 exercise price on the expiration date, both strategies have a payoff of $100 in cash. Alternatively, if the price of Widget stock is above $100, both strategies result in the investor's having possession of a share of stock that is worth more than $100. Hence,

TABLE 24-1 Put-Call Parity Involving Widget

STRATEGY	INITIAL COST	VALUE AT EXPIRATION DATE	
		$P_s < E = \$100$	$E = \$100 > P_s$
A: Buy put Buy share of stock	$P_p + P_s$ $= \$6.84 + \$100$ $= \$106.84$	Exercise put, get $100	Throw away put, have stock worth P_s
B: Buy call Invest present value of E in riskfree asset	$P_c + E/e^{RT}$ $= \$14.53 + \$92.31$ $= \$106.84$	Throw away call, get $100 from riskfree asset	Exercise call, get stock worth P_s

since both strategies have the same payoffs, they must cost the same amount in equilibrium:

$$P_p + P_s = P_c + E/e_{RT} \tag{24.9}$$

where P_p and P_c denote the current market price of the put and call, respectively.

put-call parity

This equation represents what is known as **put-call parity.** In Table 24-1 it can be seen that the cost of each strategy is $106.84, just as was suggested previously by the calculations using equations (24.5), (24.6), and (24.7).

THE BLACK-SCHOLES MODEL FOR CALL OPTIONS

Consider what would happen with the binomial option pricing model if you allow the number of periods before the expiration date to increase. For example, with Widget's option for which the expiration date was a year in the future, there could be a price tree with periods for each one of the approximately 250 trading days in a year. Needless to say, the fair value of any call associated with such a tree is found by using a computer to quickly perform calculations such as those shown earlier for Widget. If the number of periods was even larger, with each one representing a specific hour of each trading day, then there would be about $7 \times 250 = 1{,}750$ hourly periods. Note that the number of periods in a year gets larger as the length of each period gets shorter. In the limit, there will be an infinite number of infinitely small periods. In this situation the BOPM given in equation (24.7) reduces to the Black-Scholes model, so named in honor of its originators.[11]

Limitations on Its Use

At first, this model might seem to have limited use, since almost all options in the United States are American options which can be exercised at any time up to their expiration date. Furthermore, strictly speaking, the model is only

[11]Fischer Black and Myron Scholes, "The Pricing of Options and Corporate Liabilities," *Journal of Political Economy*, 81, no. 3 (May/June 1973): 637–54. Also see Fischer Black, "How We Came Up with the Option Formula," *Journal of Portfolio Management*, 15, no. 2 (Winter 1989): 4–8, and "How to Use the Holes in Black-Scholes," *Journal of Applied Corporate Finance*, 1, no. 4 (Winter 1989): 67–73.

applicable to options on stocks that will not pay any dividends over the life of the option. However, most of the common stocks on which options are written do in fact pay dividends.

The first drawback of the Black-Scholes model—that it is only applicable to European options—can be dispensed with rather easily when the option is a call and the underlying stock does not pay dividends. This is because it can be shown that it is unwise for an investor holding an American call option on a non-dividend-paying stock to exercise it prior to maturity.[12] Since there is no reason for exercising such an option prior to maturity, the opportunity to do so is worthless. Consequently, there will be no difference in the values of an American and European call option. In turn, this means that the Black-Scholes model can be used to estimate the fair value of American call options on non-dividend-paying stocks.

at the money

out of the money

in the money

The reason for this can be seen in Figure 24-6, but first some terminology must be introduced. A call option is said to be **at the money** if the underlying stock has a market price roughly equal to the call's exercise price. If the stock's market price is below the exercise price, the call is said to be **out of the money,** and if the market price is above the exercise price, the call is said to be **in the money.** Occasionally finer gradations are invoked, and one hears of "near the money," "deep in the money," "far out of the money," and so on.

time value

As mentioned earlier, the value of an option if it were exercised immediately is known as its intrinsic value. This value is equal to zero if the option is out of the money. However, it is equal to the difference between the stock price and the exercise price if the option is in the money. The excess of the price of the option over its intrinsic value is the option's **time value** (or time premium). As shown in Figure 24-3(a) for call options, at expiration the time value is zero. However, before then the time value is positive. Note that a call option's premium is simply the sum of its intrinsic and time values.

[12]See Robert C. Merton, "Theory of Rational Option Pricing," *Bell Journal of Economics and Management Science*, 4, no. 1 (Spring 1973): 141–83.

FIGURE 24-6
Option Terminology for Calls

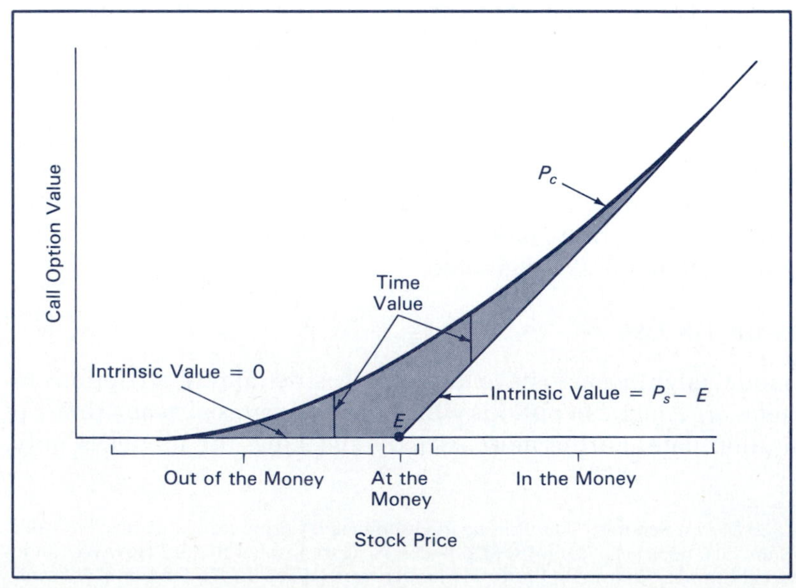

An investor considering exercising a call option on a non-dividend-paying stock prior to its expiration date will always find it cheaper to sell the call option and purchase the stock in the marketplace. This is because exercising the call will result in the investor's losing the time value of the option (hence the expression that call options are "worth more alive than dead").

For example, consider a stock that has a current price of $110. If this stock has a call option with an exercise price of $100 that is selling for $14, then the intrinsic and time values of this option are $10 (= $110 − $100) and $4 (= $14 − $10), respectively. An investor who owns one of these calls could exercise it by spending an additional $100. However, it would be cheaper for the investor to get the share of stock by selling the call option and buying the share of stock in the marketplace, since the additional cost would be only $96 (= $110 − $14).

The second drawback of the Black-Scholes model—that it is only applicable to non-dividend-paying stocks—cannot be easily dismissed, since many call options are written on stocks that will pay dividends over the life of the option. In this situation, some procedures have been suggested on how this formula can be amended in order to value call options on such stocks.[13]

The Formula

In a world not bothered by taxes and transaction costs, the fair value of a call option can be estimated by using the valuation formula developed by Black and Scholes. It has been widely used by those who deal with options to search for situations where the market price of an option differs substantially from its fair value. A call option that is found to be selling for substantially less than its Black-Scholes value is a candidate for purchase, while one that is found to be selling for substantially more is a candidate for writing. The Black-Scholes formula for estimating the fair value of a call option (V_c) is:

$$V_c = N(d_1)\,P_s - \frac{E}{e^{RT}}\,N(d_2) \quad , \tag{24.10}$$

where:

$$d_1 = \frac{\ln(P_s/E) + (R + .5\sigma^2)T}{\sigma\sqrt{T}} \tag{24.11}$$

$$d_2 = \frac{\ln(P_s/E) + (R - .5\sigma^2)T}{\sigma\sqrt{T}} \tag{24.12a}$$

$$= d_1 - \sigma\sqrt{T}. \tag{24.12b}$$

and where: P_s is the current market price of the underlying stock,
E is the exercise price of the option,
R is the continuously compounded riskfree rate of return expressed on an annual basis,

[13]A number of these procedures are reviewed in William F. Sharpe and Gordon J. Alexander, *Investments* (Englewood Cliffs, N.J.: Prentice Hall, 1990), Chapter 18.

T is time remaining before expiration, expressed as a fraction of a year, and

σ is the risk of the underlying common stock, measured by the standard deviation of the continuously compounded annual rate of return on the stock.

Note that E/e^{RT} is the present value of the exercise price where a continuous discount rate is used. The quantity $\ln(P_s/E)$ is the natural logarithm of P_s/E. Finally, $N(d_1)$ and $N(d_2)$ denote the probabilities that outcomes of less than d_1 and d_2, respectively, will occur in a normal distribution that has a mean of zero and a standard deviation of one.

Table 24-2 provides values of $N(d)$ for various levels of d.[14] This table and a pocket calculator are all that is needed in order to use the Black-Scholes formula for valuing a call option.

For example, consider a call option that expires in three months and has an exercise price of \$40 (thus, $T = .25$ and $E = 40$). Furthermore, the current price and risk of the underlying common stock are \$36 and 50%, respectively, while the riskfree rate is 5% (thus, $P_s = 36$, $R = .05$, and $\sigma = .50$). Solving equations (24.11) and (24.12b) provides the following values for d_1 and d_2:

$$d_1 = \frac{\ln(36/40) + [.05 + .5(.50)^2].25}{.50\sqrt{.25}} = -.25$$

$$d_2 = -.25 - .50\sqrt{.25} = -.50.$$

Now, Table 24-2 can be used to find the corresponding values of $N(d_1)$ and $N(d_2)$:

$$N(d_1) = N(-.25) = .4013$$

$$N(d_2) = N(-.50) = .3085.$$

Finally, equation (24.10) can be used to estimate the fair value of this call option:

$$V_c = (.4013 \times \$36) - \left(\frac{\$40}{e^{.05 \times .25}} \times .3085\right)$$

$$= \$14.45 - \$12.19 = \$2.26.$$

If this call option is currently selling for \$5, the investor should consider writing some of them. This is because they are overpriced (according to the Black-Scholes model), suggesting that their price will fall in the near future. Thus, the writer would receive a premium of \$5 and would expect to be able to enter a closing buy order later for a lower price, making a profit on the difference. Conversely, if the call option were selling for \$1, the investor should consider buying some of them. This is because they are underpriced and can be expected to rise in value in the future.

[14]Table 24-2 is an abbreviated version of a standard cumulative normal distribution table. More detailed versions can be found in most statistics textbooks.

TABLE 24-2
Values of $N(d)$ for Selected Values of d

d	$N(d)$	d	$N(d)$	d	$N(d)$
		−1.00	.1587	1.00	.8413
−2.95	.0016	−.95	.1711	1.05	.8531
−2.90	.0019	−.90	.1841	1.10	.8643
−2.85	.0022	−.85	.1977	1.15	.8749
−2.80	.0026	−.80	.2119	1.20	.8849
−2.75	.0030	−.75	.2266	1.25	.8944
−2.70	.0035	−.70	.2420	1.30	.9032
−2.65	.0040	−.65	.2578	1.35	.9115
−2.60	.0047	−.60	.2743	1.40	.9192
−2.55	.0054	−.55	.2912	1.45	.9265
−2.50	.0062	−.50	.3085	1.50	.9332
−2.45	.0071	−.45	.3264	1.55	.9394
−2.40	.0082	−.40	.3446	1.60	.9452
−2.35	.0094	−.35	.3632	1.65	.9505
−2.30	.0107	−.30	.3821	1.70	.9554
−2.25	.0122	−.25	.4013	1.75	.9599
−2.20	.0139	−.20	.4207	1.80	.9641
−2.15	.0158	−.15	.4404	1.85	.9678
−2.10	.0179	−.10	.4602	1.90	.9713
−2.05	.0202	−.05	.4801	1.95	.9744
−2.00	.0228	.00	.5000	2.00	.9773
−1.95	.0256	.05	.5199	2.05	.9798
−1.90	.0287	.10	.5398	2.10	.9821
−1.85	.0322	.15	.5596	2.15	.9842
−1.80	.0359	.20	.5793	2.20	.9861
−1.75	.0401	.25	.5987	2.25	.9878
−1.70	.0446	.30	.6179	2.30	.9893
−1.65	.0495	.35	.6368	2.35	.9906
−1.60	.0548	.40	.6554	2.40	.9918
−1.55	.0606	.45	.6736	2.45	.9929
−1.50	.0668	.50	.6915	2.50	.9938
−1.45	.0735	.55	.7088	2.55	.9946
−1.40	.0808	.60	.7257	2.60	.9953
−1.35	.0885	.65	.7422	2.65	.9960
−1.30	.0968	.70	.7580	2.70	.9965
−1.25	.1057	.75	.7734	2.75	.9970
−1.20	.1151	.80	.7881	2.80	.9974
−1.15	.1251	.85	.8023	2.85	.9978
−1.10	.1357	.90	.8159	2.90	.9981
−1.05	.1469	.95	.8289	2.95	.9984

Comparison to BOPM

At this juncture the binomial option pricing model formula [given in equation (24.7)] can be compared with the Black-Scholes option pricing formula [given in equation (24.10)]:

$$V_c = hP_s - B \tag{24.7}$$

$$V_c = N(d_1)P_s - \frac{E}{e^{RT}} N(d_2). \tag{24.10}$$

In comparing the two equations, the quantity $N(d_1)$ in equation (24.10) can be seen to correspond to h in equation (24.7). Remembering that h is the hedge ratio, the quantity $N(d_1)$ in the Black-Scholes formula can be interpreted in a similar manner. That is, it corresponds to the number of shares that an investor would need to purchase in executing an investment strategy that was designed to have the same payoffs as a call option. Similarly, the quantity $EN(d_2)/e^{RT}$ corresponds to B, the amount of money that the investor borrows as the other part of the strategy. This means that the quantity $EN(d_2)$ corresponds to the face amount of the loan, since it is the amount that must be paid back to the lender at time T, the expiration date. Hence e^{RT} is the present value (or discount) factor, indicating that the interest rate on the loan is R and that the loan is for T periods. Thus, the seemingly complex Black-Scholes formula can be seen to have an intuitive interpretation. It simply involves calculating the cost of a buy-stock-and-borrow-money investment strategy that has the same payoffs at T as a call option.

In the example, $N(d_1)$ was equal to .4013 and $EN(d_2)/e^{RT}$ was equal to \$12.19. Hence, an investment strategy that involves buying .4013 shares and borrowing \$12.19 at time 0 will have payoffs exactly equal to those associated with buying the call.[15] Since this strategy costs \$2.26, it follows that the cost of the call must also be \$2.26 in equilibrium.

Static Analysis

Close scrutiny of the Black-Scholes formula reveals some interesting features of European call option pricing. In particular, it can be noticed that the fair value of a call option is dependent on five inputs—the market price of the common stock (P_s), the exercise price of the option (E), the length of time until the expiration date (T), the riskfree rate (R), and the risk of the common stock (σ). What happens to the fair value of a call option when one of these inputs is changed while the other four remain the same?

1. The higher the price of the underlying stock (P_s), the higher the value of the call option.
2. The higher the exercise price (E), the lower the value of the call option.
3. The longer the time to the expiration date (T), the higher the value of the call option.
4. The higher the riskfree rate (R), the higher the value of the call option.
5. The greater the risk (σ) of the common stock, the higher the value of the call option.

Of these five factors, the first three (P_s, E, and T) are readily determined. The fourth factor, the riskfree rate, is often estimated by using the yield-to-maturity on a Treasury bill having a maturity date close to the expiration date of the option. The fifth factor, the risk of the underlying stock, is not readily observed; consequently, various methods for estimating it have been proposed. Two of these methods will be presented next.

---

[15]It should be pointed out that the investment strategy is more complicated than it might appear, since the number of shares that are to be held will change over time as the stock price changes and the expiration date gets closer. Similarly, the amount of the loan will change over time.

Estimating a Stock's Risk from Historical Prices

One method for estimating the risk of the underlying common stock associated with a call option involves analyzing historical prices on the stock. Initially, a set of $n + 1$ market prices on the underlying stock must be obtained from either financial publications like *The Wall Street Journal* or a computer database. These prices are then used to calculate a set of n continuously compounded returns as follows:

$$r_t = \ln(P_{s_t}/P_{s_{t-1}}) \tag{24.13}$$

where P_{s_t} and $P_{s_{t-1}}$ denote the market price of the underlying stock at time t and $t-1$, respectively. Here, "ln" denotes taking the natural logarithm of the quantity $P_{s_t}/P_{s_{t-1}}$, thereby resulting in a continuously compounded return.

For example, the set of market prices for the stock might consist of the closing price at the end of each of fifty-three weeks. If the price at the end of one week was \$105 and the price at the end of the next week was \$107, then the return r_t will be equal to $1.886\% = \ln(107/105)$. Similar calculations will result in a set of fifty-two returns.

Having calculated a set of n returns on the stock, the next step involves using them to estimate the stock's average return:

$$ar = \frac{1}{n}\sum_{t=1}^{n} r_t. \tag{24.14}$$

The average return is then used in estimating the per-period variance (that is, the square of the per-period standard deviation):

$$s^2 = \frac{1}{n-1}\sum_{t=1}^{n} (r_t - ar)^2. \tag{24.15}$$

This is called the per-period variance because its size is dependent on the length of time over which each return is measured. In the example, weekly returns were calculated and would lead to the estimation of a weekly variance. Alternatively, daily returns could have been used, leading to a daily variance that would be of smaller magnitude than the weekly variance. However, what is needed is not a weekly or daily variance, but an annual variance. This is obtained by multiplying the per-period variance by the number of periods in a year. Thus, an estimated weekly variance would be multiplied by 52 in order to estimate the annual variance, σ^2 (that is, $\sigma^2 = 52s^2$).[16]

Alternative methods of estimating a stock's total risk exist. One such method involves subjectively estimating the probabilities of possible future stock prices. Another method involves combining the historical and subjective risk estimates.

For any estimate of future uncertainty, historical data are likely to prove more helpful than definitive. And since recent data may prove more helpful

---

[16]If daily data are used, it is best to multiply the daily variance by 250 instead of 365 since there are about 250 trading days in a year. See Mark Kritzman, "About Estimating Volatility: Part I," *Financial Analysts Journal*, 47, no. 4 (July/August 1991): 22–25, and "About Estimating Volatility: Part II," *Financial Analysts Journal*, 47, no. 5 (September/October 1991): 10–11.

than older data, some analysts study daily price changes over the most recent six to twelve months, sometimes giving more weight to later days than to earlier ones. Others take into account the price histories of related stocks and the possibility that a stock whose price has recently decreased may be more risky in the future than it was in the past. Still others make explicit subjective estimates of the future, taking into account changes in uncertainty concerning the economy in general as well as uncertainty in specific industries and in stocks.

In some cases, an analyst's estimate of a stock's risk over the next three months may differ from that for the following three months, leading to the use of different values of σ for call options on the same stock that have different expiration dates.

The Market Consensus of a Stock's Risk

Another way to estimate a stock's risk is based on the assumption that a currently outstanding call option is fairly priced in the marketplace. Since this means that $P_c = V_c$, the current market price of the call (P_c) can be entered in place of the fair value of the call (V_c) on the left-hand side of equation (24.10). Next, all the other factors except for σ are entered on the right-hand side, and a value for σ, the only unknown variable, is found that satisfies the equation. The solution for σ can be interpreted as representing a consensus opinion in the marketplace on the size of the stock's risk, and is sometimes known as the stock's **implicit volatility.**

implicit volatility

For example, assume that the riskfree rate is 6%, and that a six-month call option with an exercise price of \$40 sells for \$4 when the price of the underlying stock is \$36. Different estimates of σ can be "plugged into" the right-hand side of equation (24.10) until a value of \$4 for this side of the equation is obtained. In this example, an estimated value of .40 (that is, 40%) for σ will result in a number for the right-hand side of equation (24.10) that is equal to \$4, the current market price of the call option that is on the left-hand side.

The procedure can be modified by applying it to several call options on the same stock. For example, σ can be estimated for each of several call options on the same stock that have different exercise prices but the same expiration date. Then, the resulting estimates for σ can be averaged and, in turn, used to determine the fair value of another call option on the same stock having yet another exercise price but a similar expiration date.

In the example, σ can be estimated not only for a six-month option having an exercise price of \$40, but also for six-month options having exercise prices of \$35 and \$45. Then, the three estimates of σ can be averaged to produce a "best estimate" of σ that is used to value a six-month \$50 option on the same stock.

Alternatively, the procedure can be modified by averaging the estimates for σ associated with each of several expiration dates. In the example, σ can be estimated not only for a six-month option having an exercise price of \$40 but also for a three-month and a nine-month option that each have an exercise price of \$40. The three estimates of σ can be averaged to produce a "best estimate" of σ that will subsequently be used to determine the fair value of a one-month \$40 option on the same stock.

There are other ways of using a set of estimates of σ that correspond to different call options on the same stock. Perhaps σ will be estimated for a set of calls having different expiration prices and different exercise prices, and then averaged. Perhaps σ will be estimated from historical returns using equation (24.15), with the resulting figure averaged with one or more estimates of the stock's implicit volatility. While it is still too early to tell, it appears that methods based on calculating implicit volatilities are better than methods based on historical returns.[17]

More on Hedge Ratios

The slope of the Black-Scholes value curve at any point represents the expected change in the value of the option per dollar change in the price of the underlying common stock. This amount corresponds to the hedge ratio of the call option, and is equal to $N(d_1)$ in equation (24.10). As can be seen in Figure 24.6 (assuming that the market price of the call is equal to its Black-Scholes value), the slope (that is, the hedge ratio) of the curve is always positive. Note that if the stock has a relatively low market price the slope will be near zero; for higher stock prices the slope increases and ultimately approaches a value of one for relatively high prices.

Because the hedge ratio is typically less than one, a \$1 increase in the stock price will typically result in an increase in a call option's value of less than \$1. However, the percentage change in the value of the call option will generally be greater than the percentage change in the price of the stock. It is this relationship that leads people to say that options offer high leverage.

The reason for referring to the slope of the Black-Scholes value curve as the hedge ratio is that a "hedge" portfolio, meaning a nearly riskfree portfolio, can be formed by simultaneously writing one call option and purchasing a number of shares equal to the hedge ratio, $N(d_1)$. For example, assume that the hedge ratio is .5, indicating that the hedge portfolio consists of writing one call and buying .5 shares of stock. Now, if the stock price rises by \$1, the value of the call option will rise by approximately \$.50. This means that the hedge portfolio would lose approximately \$.50 on the written call option but gain \$.50 from the rise in the stock's price. Conversely, a \$1 decrease in the stock's price would result in a \$.50 gain on the written call option but a loss of \$.50 on the half-share of stock. Overall, it can be seen that the hedge portfolio will neither gain nor lose value when the price of the underlying common stock changes by a relatively small amount.[18]

Even if the Black-Scholes model is valid and all the inputs have been correctly specified, it should be noted that risk is not permanently eliminated in the hedge portfolio when the portfolio is first formed (or, for that matter, at any time). This is because the hedge ratio will change as the stock price changes and as the life of the option decreases with the passage of time. In order to eliminate risk from the hedge portfolio, the investor will have to continuously alter its composition. Altering it less often will reduce but not completely eliminate risk.

---

[17]For a further discussion of these methods, see Chapter 10 of Peter Ritchken, *Options* (Glenview, Ill.: Scott, Foresman and Company, 1987), or any of the other options books cited at the end of the chapter. Also see Menachem Brenner and Marti Subrahmanyam, "A Simple Formula to Compute the Implied Standard Deviation," *Financial Analysts Journal*, 44, no. 5 (September/October 1988): 80–83.

[18]This explanation of a hedge ratio follows from the BOPM-based interpretation of the Black-Scholes formula that was given earlier. That is, if a call's payoffs can be duplicated by buying stock and borrowing at the riskfree rate, it follows that buying stock and writing a call will duplicate investing in the riskfree asset.

Adjustments for Dividends

Thus far, the issue of dividend payments on the underlying stock during the life of an option has been avoided. Other things being equal, the greater the amount of the dividends to be paid during the life of a call option, the lower the value of the call option. This is because the greater the dividend that a firm declares, the lower its stock price will be. Since options are not "dividend protected," this lower stock price will result in a lower value for the call option.

Moreover, it may pay to exercise an American call option just prior to an ex-dividend date. Earlier, it was mentioned that in the absence of dividends, an American call option would be worth at least as much "alive" (not exercised) as "dead" (exercised). When dividends are involved, however, the situation may be different. This is shown in Figure 24-7.

The call option's value if exercised immediately, referred to in Figure 24-6 as the option's "intrinsic value," lies along the lower boundary 0*EZ*. If

FIGURE 24-7
Option Values Before and After an Ex-Dividend Date

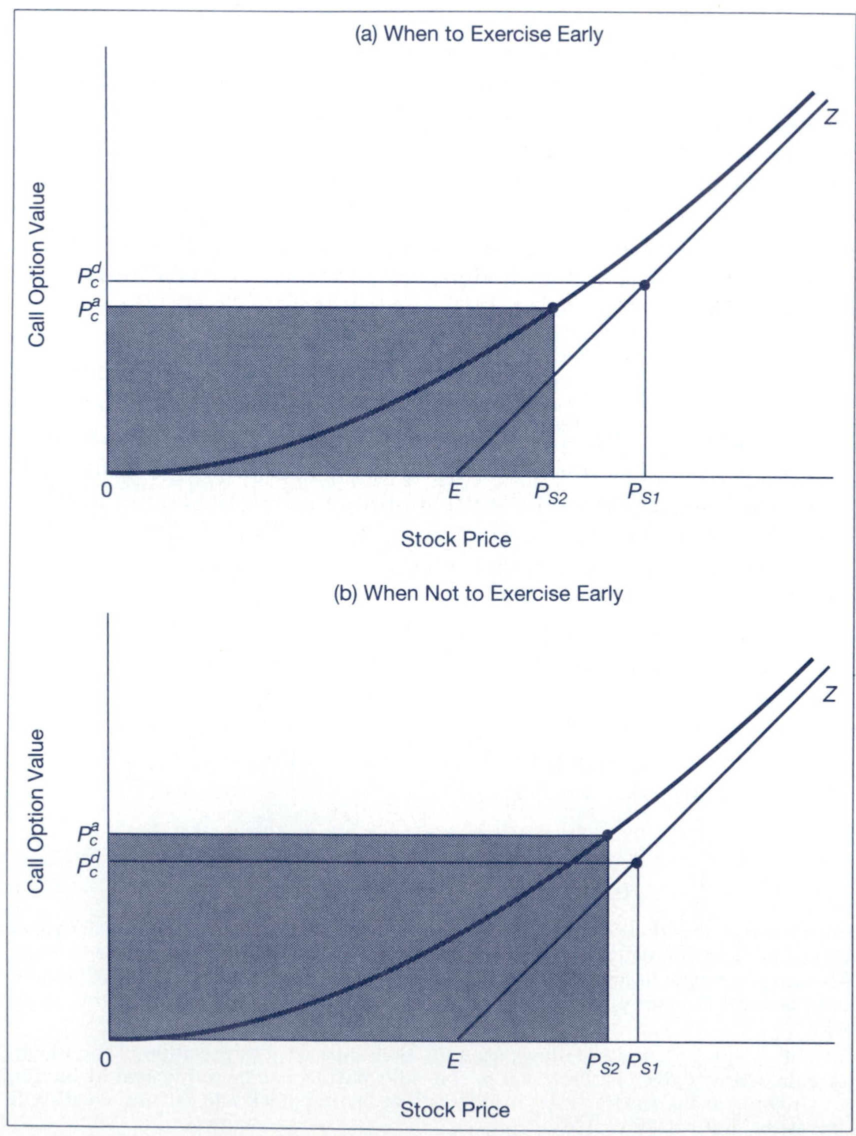

allowed to live, the option's value will lie along the higher Black-Scholes curve as shown in the figure. Imagine that the stock is currently priced at P_{s1} and is about to go ex-dividend for the last time prior to the option's expiration. Afterward, it can be expected to sell for a lower price, P_{s2}. The Black-Scholes formula can be used to estimate the option's value if it remains "alive" just after the ex-dividend date. In Figure 24-7, this "alive" value is P_c^a. If instead the option is exercised just before the ex-dividend date while the stock price is still P_{s1}, the investor will obtain the "dead" value (that is, the "intrinsic value") of P_c^d. If P_c^d is greater than P_c^a [as is the case in panel (a)], the option should be exercised now, just before the ex-dividend date; if P_c^d is less than P_c^a [as is the case in panel (b)], the option should not be exercised. Hence, for a call option on a dividend-paying stock, the possibility of early exercise must be taken into consideration.[19]

THE VALUATION OF PUT OPTIONS

Similar to a call option, a put option is said to be at the money if the underlying stock has a market price roughly equal to the put's exercise price. However, the terms out of the money and in the money have, in one sense, *opposite meanings* for puts and calls. In particular, a put option is out of the money if the underlying stock has a market price above the exercise price, and is in the money if the market price is below the exercise price. Figure 24-8 provides an illustration of how these terms apply to a put option.

As mentioned earlier, the value of either a call or a put, if it were exercised immediately, is known as its intrinsic value. This value is equal to zero if the option is out of the money; and equal to the difference between the stock price and exercise price if the stock is in the money. Thus, in another

[19]See footnote 13.

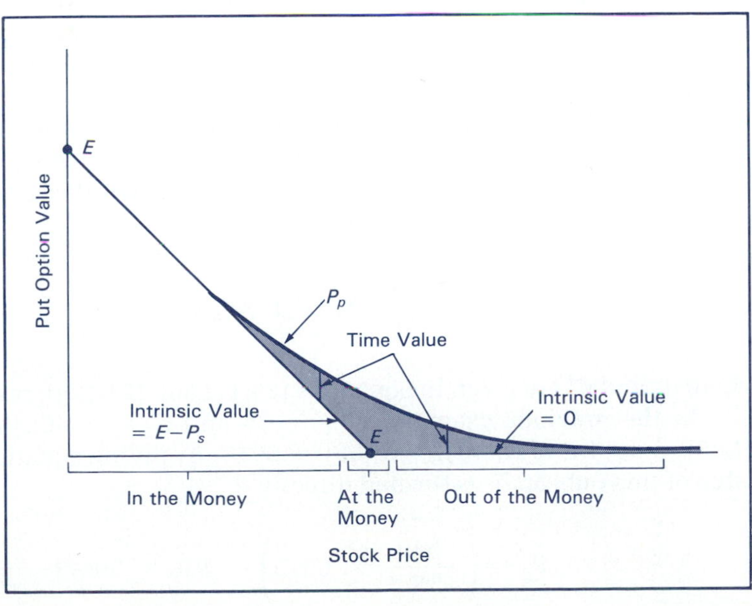

FIGURE 24-8
Option Terminology for Puts

sense, the terms "out of the money" and "in the money" have *similar meanings* for puts and calls.

The excess of the price of a call or a put over this intrinsic value is the option's time value (or time premium). As shown for calls and puts in panels (a) and (b) of Figure 24-3, respectively, the time value is zero at expiration. However, Figures 24-6 and 24-8 show that the time value is generally positive before expiration. Note that an option's premium is simply the sum of its intrinsic value and time value.

Put-Call Parity

Consider a put and a call on the same underlying stock that have the same exercise price and expiration date. Earlier it was shown in equation (24.9) that their market prices should be related, with the nature of the relationship known as *put-call parity*. However, it should be noted that this relationship is valid only for European options on non-dividend-paying stocks.

Equation (24.9) can be rearranged in the following manner so that it can be used to estimate the value of European put options:

$$P_p = P_c + E/e^{RT} - P_s. \tag{24.16}$$

Thus, the value of a put can be estimated by using either the BOPM or the Black-Scholes formula to estimate the value of a matching call option, then adding an amount equal to the present value of the exercise price to this estimate, and finally subtracting from this sum an amount that is equal to the current market price of the underlying common stock.

For example, consider a put option that expires in three months and has an exercise price of \$40, while the current market price and risk of the underlying common stock are \$36 and 50%, respectively. Assuming that the riskfree rate is 5%, it was shown earlier that the Black-Scholes estimate of the value for a matching call option was \$2.26. Since the 5% riskfree rate is a continuously compounded rate, the present value of the exercise price is equal to $\$39.50 = \$40/(e^{.05 \times .25})$. At this point, since it has been determined that $P_c = \$2.26$, $E/e^{RT} = \$39.50$, and $P_s = \$36$, equation (24.16) can be used to estimate the value of the put option as being equal to $\$5.76 = \$2.26 + \$39.50 - \$36$.

Alternatively, the Black-Scholes formula for estimating the value of a call given in equation (24.10) can be substituted for P_c in equation (24.16). After doing so and simplifying, an equation that can be used directly for estimating the value of a put is obtained:

$$P_p = \frac{E}{e^{RT}} N(-d_2) - P_s N(-d_1) \tag{24.17}$$

where d_1 and d_2 are given in equations (24.11) and (24.12a), respectively.

In the previous example, $d_1 = -.25$ and $d_2 = -.50$; thus $N(-d_1) = N(.25) = .5987$ and $N(-d_2) = N(.50) = .6915$. Applying equation (24.17) the value of this put can be estimated directly:

$$P_p = \left(\frac{\$40}{e^{.05 \times .25}} \times .6915\right) - (\$36 \times .5987)$$
$$= \$27.31 - \$21.55 = \$5.76$$

which is the same estimated value as indicated earlier when equation (24.16) was used.

Static Analysis

Close scrutiny of the put-call parity equation reveals some interesting features of European put option pricing. In particular, the value of a put option is dependent on the values of the same five inputs used for call valuation—the market price of the common stock (P_s), the exercise price of the option (E), the length of time until the expiration date (T), the riskfree rate (R), and the risk of the common stock (σ). What happens to the value of a put option when one of these inputs is changed while the other four remain the same?

1. The higher the price of the underlying stock (P_s), the lower the value of the put option.
2. The higher the exercise price (E), the higher the value of the put option.
3. Generally, the longer the time to the expiration date (T), the higher the value of the put option.
4. The higher the riskfree rate (R), the lower the value of the put option.
5. The greater the risk (σ) of the common stock, the higher the value of the put option.

The relationships for the underlying stock price (P_s), exercise price (E), and riskfree rate (R) are in the opposite direction from those shown earlier for call options, while the relationships for the time to the expiration date (T) and risk (σ) are in the same direction. It should be noted that exceptions can occur with T when the put is deep in the money. In such a situation a longer time to expiration could actually decrease the value of the put.

Early Exercise and Dividends

Equations (24.16) and (24.17) apply to a European put on a stock that will not pay dividends prior to the option's expiration. As with call options, complications arise when it is recognized that most put options are American, meaning that they can be exercised before expiration, and that often dividends on the underlying common stock will be paid before the expiration date.

Consider first the ability to exercise a put option at any time up to its expiration date. Earlier, it was shown that if there were no dividends on the underlying stock, then a call option was worth more "alive" than "dead," meaning that call options should not be exercised prior to expiration. Such an argument does *not* hold for put options.

Specifically, if a put option is in the money, meaning that the market price of the stock is less than the exercise price, then the investor may want to exercise the put option. In doing so, the investor will receive an additional amount of cash equal to $E - P_s$. In turn, this cash can be invested at the riskfree rate to earn money over the remaining life of the option. Since these earnings may be greater than any additional profits received by the investor if the put option were held, it may be advantageous to exercise the put early and thereby receive the earnings.

An example can be used to illustrate the point. Consider a put option on Widget that has a year left until its expiration date. The exercise price on the put is $100 and the annual riskfree rate is 10%. Imagine that the stock price of Widget is now at $5 per share, having recently plunged in value. If an investor owned such a deep-in-the-money option it would be in his or her best interest to immediately exercise it. The logic is as follows.

The intrinsic value of the put is currently $95 = $100 − $5, indicating that if the put is immediately exercised, the buyer will receive $95. That is, the buyer will spend $5 to buy a share of Widget and then turn the share and the put over to the writer in return for the exercise price of $100. The net cash inflow to the put buyer of $95 could be invested in the riskfree asset so that in one year it is worth $104.50 = $95 × 1.10. Alternatively, if the put is held, what is the best that the buyer can hope to earn at year-end? If the stock price of Widget drops to $0, the buyer will receive $100 at expiration from the put writer. Clearly the buyer would be better off exercising the put now instead of holding onto it. Hence, early exercise is merited in such a situation.

What will happen to the market price of the put in such a situation? In equilibrium it will be equal to the put's intrinsic value, $E - P_s$. Hence the put's time premium would be zero. This is because nobody would pay more than the intrinsic value for the put, knowing that they could get a better return by investing in the riskfree asset. In addition, nobody would be willing to sell a put for less than its intrinsic value since this would open up the opportunity for immediately earning riskfree profits by purchasing the put and exercising it right away. Hence the only price that the put could sell for would be its intrinsic value.

In the case of Widget, the put would sell for $95. Nobody would be willing to pay more for it, since buying it would be inferior to investing the $95 in the riskfree asset. Conversely, nobody would be willing to sell the put for less, say at $94, since investors would immediately buy it at that price and then exercise it in order to receive $95 for a riskless profit of $1 per put.

Consider next the impact of dividends on put valuation. Previously, it was shown that the owner of a call may find it optimal to exercise just *before* an ex-dividend date, since doing so allowed the investor to receive the forthcoming dividends on the stock. With respect to a put, the owner may find it optimal to exercise just *after* the ex-dividend date, since the corresponding drop in the stock price will cause the value of the put to rise.[20]

OPTIONS ON OTHER KINDS OF ASSETS

Not all options are written on individual issues of common stock. In recent years, many new and somewhat exotic options have been created that have as an underlying asset something other than the stock of a particular company. Some of them are discussed here, the appendix discusses others, while the next chapter discusses what are known as futures options.

Index Options

A call option on General Motors stock is a relatively simple instrument. Upon exercise, the call buyer literally calls away 100 shares of GM stock. The call writer is expected to physically deliver the shares. In practice, both the buyer

[20]See Robert Geske and Kuldeep Shastri, "The Early Exercise of American Puts," *Journal of Banking and Finance*, 9, no. 2 (June 1985): 207–19, and footnote 13.

and the writer may find it advantageous to close their positions in order to avoid the costs associated with the physical transfer of shares. In this event, the buyer may expect a gain (and the seller a loss) approximately equal to the difference between the current market price of the security and the option's exercise price.

Cash Settlement It would be entirely feasible to use only a "cash settlement" procedure upon expiration. Here, the writer would be required to pay the buyer an amount equal to the difference between the current price of the security and the call option's exercise price (provided that the current price is larger than the exercise price). Similarly for puts, the writer could be expected to pay the buyer an amount equal to the difference between the option's exercise price and the current market price (provided that the exercise price is larger than the current price).

While listed options on individual securities retain the obligation to "deliver," the realization that "cash settlement" can serve as a substitute has allowed the creation of index options.

The Contract An index option is based on the level of an index of stock prices and thus allows investors to take positions in the market that the index represents. Some indices are designed to reflect movements in the stock market, broadly construed. Other "specialized" indices are intended to capture changes in the fortunes of particular industries or sectors. Figure 24-9 shows some of the major indices on which options were offered in 1992, along with their quotations. Some of the indices are highly specialized, consisting of only a few stocks. Others are broadly representative of major portions of the stock market. Roughly one-half are European and the other half are American.

Generally, the options expire within a few months, but a few (the LEAPs) expire in over a year. While most of the indices are based on U.S. stocks, one is based on Japanese stocks, thereby giving American investors a chance to indirectly take various positions in the Japanese stock market.

Contracts for index options are not stated in terms of numbers of shares. Instead, the size of a contract is determined by multiplying the level of the index by a multiplier specified by the exchange on which the option is traded. The premium (price) of an index option times the applicable multiplier indicates the total amount paid.

Consider, for example, the S&P 100 index option that is traded on the Chicago Board Options Exchange with an exercise price of 385 and expiring in September 1992. Note that it has an indicated premium of 10 on July 15, 1992. Since the multiplier for S&P 100 option contracts is 100, this means that an investor would have to pay \$1,000 (= 10 × 100) for this contract (plus a commission).

After purchasing this contract, the investor could later sell it or exercise it for its cash settlement value. Perhaps in August 1992, the S&P 100 will be at 400. In this case, the investor could exercise the call, receiving its intrinsic value of \$1,500 [=(400 − 385) × 100] for doing so. Alternatively, the investor could simply sell the call on the exchange; in doing so, the amount received would almost certainly be greater than \$1,500 since it would sell for an amount equal to the sum of its intrinsic and time values (see Figure 24-6).

Warrants A rather unusual kind of index option that has appeared recently is actively traded on the American Stock Exchange. These options, referred to as "warrants," are issued by entities that run the gamut from the Kingdom of

FIGURE 24-9
Index Options Quotations

Source: Reprinted by permission of *The Wall Street Journal,* © Dow Jones & Company, Inc., July 16, 1992, p. C15.

INDEX TRADING

Wednesday, July 15, 1992

OPTIONS

CHICAGO BOARD

S&P 100 INDEX-$100 times index

Strike Price	Calls—Last Jul	Aug	Sep	Puts—Last Jul	Aug	Sep
350	....	....	....	1/16	....	....
360	30 3/8	30 1/2	....	1/16	7/8	1 7/8
365	24	24 3/4	....	1/16	1	2 3/8
370	19	21	....	1/16	1 3/8	3 1/8
375	14 1/8	15 5/8	18 1/4	1/8	1 7/8	3 5/8
380	9 1/2	11 1/2	14 3/8	3/16	2 13/16	4 3/4
385	5	8	10	1/2	4 1/8	6 5/8
390	1 1/4	5 1/8	7 3/8	2 1/16	6 1/4	8 3/4
395	1/8	2 7/8	4 3/4	6 1/8	9 1/2	....
400	1/16	1 7/16	3 1/8	10 1/2	12 1/2	....
405	1/16	11/16	1 3/4	....	....	....
410	....	5/16	15/16	....	....	....

Total call volume 122,351 Total call open int. 395,493
Total put volume 102,682 Total put open int. 437,198
The index: High 390.23; Low 388.13; Close 389.08, −1.11

S&P 500 INDEX-$100 times index

Strike Price	Calls—Last Jul	Aug	Sep	Puts—Last Jul	Aug	Sep
325	....	....	....	....	1/16	3/16
350	....	....	....	....	....	7/16
365	....	....	....	....	1/4	....
370	....	....	....	....	....	1
375	....	....	....	....	1/2	1 1/4
380	37 7/8	....	....	....	9/16	1 9/16
385	....	....	....	1/16	3/4	1 15/16
390	26 3/4	28 3/4	....	1/16	1	2 7/16
395	22 7/8	....	....	1/16	1 1/4	....
400	....	17 3/4	21 1/4	1/16	1 7/8	4
405	12	15	16 1/8	3/16	2 1/2	4 7/8
410	7	10 1/4	12 5/8	3/8	2 1/2	4 7/8
415	7	10 1/4	12 5/8	3/8	3 5/8	6 1/4
420	3	6 7/8	9 1/4	1 1/4	5 1/4	7 3/4
425	1/16	2 5/8	5 1/4	8	10 3/8	12 1/2
430	....	1 1/8	2 7/8	12 3/4	14 3/8	15 3/4
435	....	5/8	1 3/4	....	....	....
440	....	1/4	1	....	....	....
450	....	....	3/16	....	....	32 1/2

Total call volume 38,622 Total call open int. 454,152
Total put volume 36,071 Total put open int. 610,398
The index: High 417.81; Low 416.29; Close 417.10, −0.58

LEAPS-S&P 100 INDEX

Strike Price	Calls—Last Dec 92	Dec 93	Dec 94	Puts—Last Dec 92	Dec 93	Dec 94
35	....	5 1/2	....	1/2	1 5/8	....
37 1/2	....	....	....	1 1/16	2 1/2	....
40	....	....	....	2 1/16	3 1/2	....

Total call volume 10 Total call open int. 33,096
Total put volume 205 Total put open int. 160,566
The index: High 39.02; Low 38.81; Close 38.91, −0.11

LEAPS-S&P 500 INDEX

Strike Price	Calls—Last Dec 92	Dec 93	Puts—Last Dec 92	Dec 93
35	7	7 1/8	....	....
40	....	....	1	....
45	....	....	....	4 1/2

Total call volume 40 Total call open int. 30,942
Total put volume 104 Total put open int. 137,322
The index: High 41.78; Low 41.63; Close 41.71, −0.06

JAPAN INDEX

Strike Price	Calls—Last Jul	Aug	Sep	Puts—Last Jul	Aug	Sep
155	17 3/8	....	....	1/16	....	2 3/8
160	12 3/4	....	....	1/8	2	....
165	7 3/8	10 1/2	....	5/16	3	4 3/4
170	2 13/16	7 1/4	9 1/4	15/16	4 7/8	6 3/8
175	11/16	4 7/8	6 3/8	3 3/4	7	....
180	1/8	2 3/4	4 1/4	....	10	11 1/2
185	1/16	....	2 7/8	13	13 3/4	....
190	....	3/4	1 3/4	....	....	....
195	....	5/16	....	....	....	....

Total call volume 1,327 Total call open int. 18,268
Total put volume 1,235 Total put open int. 22,867
The index: Close 172.41, +0.55

PHILADELPHIA

GOLD/SILVER INDEX

Strike Price	Calls—Last Jul	Aug	Sep	Puts—Last Jul	Aug	Sep
80	5 1/8	4 5/8	5 5/8	3/16	1 5/8	1 3/8
85	1 1/8	3 1/2	4 3/8	3/8	2 9/16	3 7/8
90	....	....	2 1/8	4 5/8	7 1/8	....
95	....	....	1	....	....	....

Total call volume 361 Total call open int. 2,438
Total put volume 218 Total put open int. 1,500
The index: High 85.76; Low 82.92; Close 85.76, +2.49

VALUE LINE INDEX OPTIONS

Strike Price	Calls—Last Jul	Aug	Sep	Puts—Last Jul	Aug	Sep
310	....	....	....	....	....	9/16
320	....	....	....	....	1/8	....
345	5 1/8	....	....	....	2 5/8	....
350	1 5/16	....	7 3/4	15/16	4 1/4	....

Total call volume 332 Total call open int. 3,894
Total put volume 67 Total put open int. 1,361
The index: High 350.71; Low 349.99; Close 350.39, +0.38

PACIFIC

FINANCIAL NEWS COMPOSITE INDEX

Strike Price	Calls—Last Jul	Aug	Sep	Puts—Last Jul	Aug	Sep
260	....	....	27 1/8	....	....	....
280	6 1/4	....	....	....	....	....
290	....	....	....	4 5/8	....	....

Total call volume 88 Total call open int. 2,834
Total put volume 5 Total put open int. 1,593
The index: High 286.64; Low 284.69; Close 285.20, −1.18

NEW YORK

NYSE INDEX OPTIONS

Strike Price	Calls—Last Jul	Aug	Sep	Puts—Last Jul	Aug	Sep
220	....	....	....	....	1 1/16	....
225	4 1/2	....	....	....	....	....
230	1/2	....	4	1 1/8	4	....
235	....	7/8	....	....	....	....

Total call volume 357 Total call open int. 4,186
Total put volume 417 Total put open int. 5,165
The index: High 229.57; Low 228.83; Close 229.20, −0.31

Denmark to Salomon Brothers to Bankers Trust. These issuers act as writers, doing so in order to raise money. Usually the underlying asset is a foreign stock market index such as the Nikkei 225, which is an index based on the stocks traded on the Tokyo Stock Exchange. Daily trading activity in these warrants is reported in the AMEX's stock tables, listed in the appropriate alphabetical place under the name of the issuer (such as under S for Salomon Brothers).

Put warrants give the owner the right to "sell the index" at a stated exercise price, while call warrants give the owner the right to "buy the index" at a stated exercise price. Consider Nikkei 225 put and call warrants with an exercise price of 20,000 and an expiration date in six months. If the index at expiration is at 25,000, the put is out of the money but the call is in the money. Conversely, if the index is at 15,000, then the put is in the money but the call is out of the money. Hence calls let investors take bullish positions in the Tokyo Stock Exchange if they believe that that market is going to move up, and puts let investors take bearish positions if they believe a move downward is forthcoming.

These contracts involve two forms of cash settlement. Consider the simplest case first, where the exchange rate for the warrant is given in the contract itself. Say, for ease of exposition, that it is fixed at 100 yen per dollar, and the Nikkei 225 ends at 25,000. Then the payoff to the call owner would be determined by (1) calculating the difference between the index level and the exercise price, which in this example is 5,000; (2) multiplying this difference by a stated multiplier, such as .5, in order to get 2,500; and (3) converting the resulting figure to dollars, producing a payoff in this example of $25 = 2,500/$100. Hence the owner of one of these calls would receive $25; whether or not a profit was made would depend on the purchase price of the warrant.

In the second case, the exchange rate is not fixed in the warrant. Instead it is based on the current exchange rate at the expiration date. Hence the payoff is subject to two sources of uncertainty: the level of the index and the yen-dollar exchange rate. In the previous example, if the exchange rate was 50 the buyer would receive $50 = 2,500/$50 but if the exchange rate was 200 the buyer would receive $12.50 = 2,500/$200. Thus, if the dollar appreciates the owner gets a higher payoff, but if it depreciates the payoff is lower.

As time passes some of the warrants expire and new ones are created. Investors need to pay close attention to the terms of the contracts, since new contracts may differ from recently expired ones. Note that the warrants are only as good as the credit quality of the issuer, and the warrant owner might be left with an option that cannot be exercised if the issuer goes bankrupt. Needless to say, issuers have taken steps to allay these worries by, for example, undertaking various transactions in order to hedge themselves from the risk involved in writing the warrants.[21]

Interest Rate Options

Call and put options are also traded on debt instruments such as U.S. Treasury bills, bonds, and notes. Options on these securities are based on specific issues, with a given dollar amount of face value to be delivered upon exercise. Figure 24-10 shows two of these options that were offered in 1992, along with their quotations.

The "options on short-term interest rates," dubbed the IRX options, are based on the yield-to-maturity of the most recently issued 13-week Treasury bills. They have an exercise price equal to ten times this yield. Hence the exercise price of 37½ shown in Figure 24-10 can be interpreted to mean a yield of 3.75%. Hence if an investor buys one of these IRX calls and the T-bill yield rises above 3.75%, the investor will make a profit (assuming that the call's premium is recovered). For example, if the yield rises to 4%, then the

[21]For a discussion of how the possibility of default by the writer affects the prices of such options, see Herb Johnson and Rene Stulz, "The Pricing of Options with Default Risk," *Journal of Finance*, 42, no. 2 (June 1987): 267–80.

FIGURE 24-10
Interest Rate Options Quotations

Source: Reprinted by permission of *The Wall Street Journal*, © Dow Jones & Company, Inc., July 16, 1992, p. C13.

INTEREST RATE INSTRUMENTS

Wednesday, July 15, 1992

CHICAGO BOARD

OPTIONS ON SHORT-TERM INTEREST RATES

Strike Price	Calls—Last Jul	Aug	Sep	Puts—Last Jul	Aug	Sep
37½	....	....	⅛	....	....	....

Total call volume 30 Total call open int. 974
Total put volume 0 Total put open int. 310
IRX levels: High 32.00; Low 31.60; Close 31.80, −0.30

OPTIONS ON LONG-TERM INTEREST RATES

Strike Price	Calls—Last Jul	Aug	Sep	Puts—Last Jul	Aug	Sep
70	¼	....	....	....	....	....

Total call volume 5 Total call open int. 819
Total put volume 0 Total put open int. 390
LTX levels: High 70.26; Low 69.73; Close 69.73, −0.67

investor's profit will be $250 = (40 − 37.5) × $100, less the premium paid to buy the call. Note that the multiplier for these contracts is $100.

The "options on long-term interest rates," dubbed the LTX options, are based on the average yield-to-maturity of the two most recently auctioned 7-year, 10-year, and 30-year Treasury issues. As with the IRX options, their exercise price is equal to ten times this average yield. Hence an exercise price of 70 as shown in the figure means a yield of 7%. Thus, if the average yield on these Treasury securities rises to 8%, then the investor's profit will be $1,000 = (80 − 70) × $100.

On July 15, 1992, the calls for both of these interest rate options were out of the money while the puts were in the money. This is because the IRX and LTX levels on that date were 31.80 and 69.73, respectively, as shown in the figure. Note that both of these options are European, so they are settled in cash on the expiration date.

While these contracts allow investors to take positions based on their forecasts of changes in both short-term and long-term interest rates, their future is not clear as long as the amount of trading in them remains relatively small. This can be seen by noting the low volume figures in Figure 24-10. Traditionally, if volume remains low for too long a period of time, the exchange will drop the contract.

Foreign Currency Options

Call and put options are also traded on foreign currencies such as Swiss francs. These are similar to stock options—when exercised, the underlying asset must be delivered. Since each option involves units of a "foreign" (non–United States) currency, delivery is made in a bank account in the country of origin of the currency in question (typically, brokers can readily assist an investor in arranging for this to be done). Figure 24-11 shows some of these options that were offered in 1992, along with their quotations. Both American and European types exist; unless otherwise indicated, the option is American.

For example, the Philadelphia Exchange (PHLX) maintains an option market in foreign currencies, one of which is Swiss francs. Specifically, these options involve the delivery of 62,500 Swiss francs. On July 15, 1992, one of the call options on this currency had an exercise price of 72 and an expiration date of September 1992. That is, the dollar amount involved in the exercise of this option was $45,000 (= 62,500 × $.72). The market price (that is, the

FIGURE 24-11
Foreign Currency Options Quotations

Source: Reprinted by permission of *The Wall Street Journal*, © Dow Jones & Company, Inc., July 16, 1992, p. C13. All rights reserved worldwide.

OPTIONS PHILADELPHIA

Wednesday, July 15, 1992

Option & Underlying	Strike Price	Calls—Last Aug	Calls—Last Sep	Calls—Last Dec	Puts—Last Aug	Puts—Last Sep	Puts—Last Dec
50,000 Australian Dollars-cents per unit.							
ADollr.....	74	r	r	r	0.44	r	r
74.81	75	0.26	r	r	r	r	r
31,250 British Pounds-European Style.							
BPound ..	185	r	r	r	0.76	r	r
31,250 British Pounds-cents per unit.							
BPound ..	180	r	r	r	0.20	r	r
192.22 ..	182½	r	r	r	0.31	0.96	r
192.22 ..	185	r	r	r	0.70	r	4.55
192.22 ..	187½	r	5.20	r	1.50	r	r
192.22 ..	190	r	r	4.99	r	r	7.10
192.22 ..	192½	r	r	3.89	r	r	8.65
192.22 ..	195	1.40	r	r	4.94	r	r
192.22 ..	197½	r	r	r	6.82	r	r
192.22 ..	200	r	r	r	9.12	10.47	r
50,000 Canadian Dollars-cents per unit.							
CDollr.....	82	r	r	r	r	r	0.64
83.89	82½	r	r	r	r	0.23	r
83.89	84½	r	0.22	r	r	r	r
62,500 European Currency Units-cents per unit.							
ECU......	132	r	r	r	r	1.14	r
62,500 German Mark-Japanese Yen cross.							
GMk-YJn	86	0.25	r	r	r	r	r
62,500 German Marks-cents per unit.							
DMark	57	r	r	r	r	r	0.11
67.47	59	r	r	r	r	r	0.23
67.47	61	r	r	r	r	0.07	r
67.47	61½	r	r	s	r	0.10	s
67.47	63	r	r	r	r	0.21	r
67.47	63½	r	r	s	r	0.28	s
67.47	64	r	r	r	0.16	r	1.28
67.47	64½	r	r	s	r	0.48	s
67.47	65	r	r	r	0.36	1.26	1.62
67.47	65½	r	r	s	r	0.78	s
67.47	66	1.81	r	r	0.54	0.92	2.13
67.47	67	1.05	1.36	1.80	1.04	1.35	2.70
67.47	67½	0.92	1.06	s	1.22	r	s
67.47	68	0.75	0.95	r	1.42	r	r
67.47	68½	0.58	0.64	s	r	r	s
67.47	69	0.42	0.62	1.00	r	r	r
67.47	70	0.18	r	0.77	r	r	r
67.47	70½	r	0.24	s	r	r	s
67.47	71½	r	0.19	s	r	r	s
6,250,000 Japanese Yen-100ths of a cent per unit.							
JYen......	78½	r	r	s	0.29	r	s
79.96	79½	r	1.27	s	r	1.01	s
79.96	80	r	1.07	1.70	r	1.20	r
79.96	81	0.36	r	r	r	r	r
62,500 Swiss Francs-cents per unit.							
SFranc....	65	r	r	r	r	r	0.21
74.60	70	r	r	r	r	0.30	1.11
74.60	70½	r	r	s	0.14	r	s
74.60	71½	r	r	s	r	0.58	s
74.60	72	r	3.00	r	0.34	r	1.85
74.60	72½	2.13	s	s	0.52	s	s
74.60	73	r	r	r	0.68	1.04	r
74.60	74	1.48	r	r	r	r	r
74.60	74½	1.14	r	s	r	r	s
74.60	75	1.00	r	r	r	r	r
74.60	75½	r	0.93	s	r	r	s
74.60	76	0.48	r	r	r	r	r
Total Call Vol	84,548			Call Open Int			232,498
Total Put Vol	21,744			Put Open Int			454,918

premium) for this call was "3.00" on that day, meaning that the cost of purchasing the call was $1,875 (= $.0300 × 62,500). Note that the exchange rate at that time was "74.06" or $.7406 per Swiss franc. Hence the 72 September call option was "in the money" (since 74.06 > 72).[22]

[22]For another example, see Mark Kritzman, "About Option Replication," *Financial Analysts Journal*, 48, no. 1 (January/February 1992): 21–23.

portfolio insurance

Recently one of the more popular uses of options is in procuring **portfolio insurance.** Consider an investor who holds a highly diversified portfolio. This investor would like to be able to benefit from any upward movements that may subsequently occur in the stock market, but would also like to be protected from any downward movements.[23] There are, in principle, at least three ways this might be accomplished.[24]

Purchase an Insurance Policy

One alternative would be to sign a contract with an insurance company. For example, assume that the portfolio is currently worth $100,000. The insurance company might agree to cover any loss in value over some specified period, such as over the forthcoming year. At the end of the year, if the portfolio value were $95,000, the insurance company would pay the investor $5,000. On the other hand, if the value were $105,000, the insurance company would pay nothing.

Figure 24-12(a) illustrates this situation. The horizontal axis measures the value of the portfolio at year-end. The 45-degree line 0*BC* shows the value of the uninsured portfolio, while curve *ABC* shows the value of the insured portfolio. As the figure shows, if the portfolio value at the end of the year is more than $100,000, then the insured portfolio will be worth the same amount as the uninsured portfolio. However, if the portfolio value is less than $100,000, then the insured portfolio is worth more, with the vertical difference between 0*B* and *AB* representing the size of the payment made to the investor by the insurance company.

Unfortunately, insurance companies rarely sign contracts of this sort. However, this is not the only alternative. Instead of dealing with an insurance company, the investor could consider purchasing a put option.

Purchase a Protective Put

Assume that a put option is available on a stock market index that closely resembles the investor's portfolio. Curve *ADE* in Figure 24-12(b) shows the value to a *buyer* of such a put at the expiration date, where the put has an exercise price of $100,000 [note how it corresponds to Figure 24-3(b)]. Curve 0*BC* is the value of the portfolio on the expiration date, assuming that the put was not purchased.

What would happen to an investor who (1) held the portfolio and (2) purchased this put? Figure 24-12(c) shows the answer. The value of the portfolio (*ABC*) is simply the combination of the values *OBC* and *ADE* that are shown in Figure 24-12(b). Not surprisingly, it is precisely the same as curve *ABC* in Figure 24-12(a).

In this case, the purchase of a put provides protection against declines in portfolio value. In this role, it is termed a protective put. In practice, stock

[23]In an efficient market, investors with "average" attitudes toward risk should not purchase portfolio insurance. Those who are especially averse to "downside risk" (relative to "upside potential") may find it useful to buy insurance. The key is the nature of the investor's attitudes toward risk and return. See Hayne E. Leland, "Who Should Buy Portfolio Insurance?" *Journal of Finance*, 35, no. 2 (May 1980): 581–94.

[24]Some people would argue that the use of stop orders represents a fourth way.

FIGURE 24-12
Portfolio Insurance

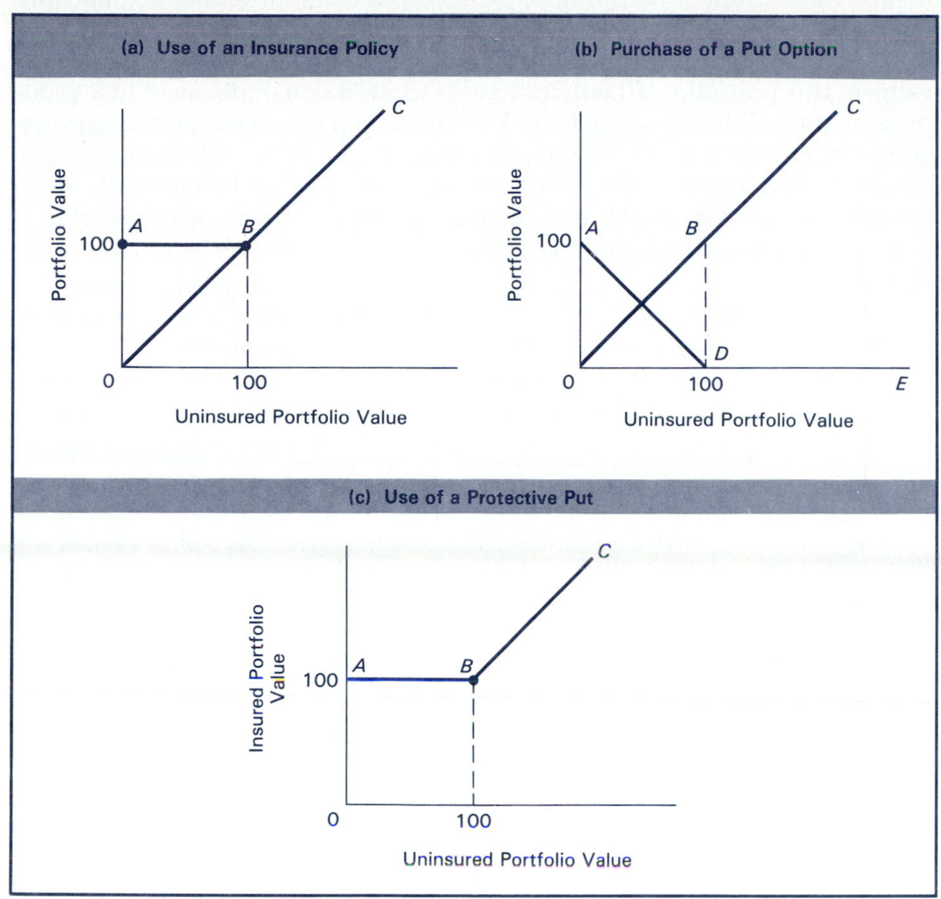

indices may not closely correspond with an investor's portfolio. Thus, purchase of a put on a stock index may provide only imperfect insurance. In a graph such as that shown in Figure 24-12(c), the resulting curve would be somewhat fuzzy owing to the possible divergence of values of the portfolio and index. For example, the portfolio may decline in value by $25,000 while the index is declining only by $10,000. In this case, the portfolio would only be insured for 40% of its decline in value (40% = $10,000/$25,000).

What if neither explicit insurance nor an appropriate put were available? Can something still be done to insure the portfolio's value against market declines? Yes, if the allocation of funds between the portfolio and a riskless security can be altered frequently enough (and at reasonable cost). This type of portfolio insurance involves the creation of a **synthetic put,** and its application involves the use of a dynamic strategy for asset allocation which will be discussed next.

synthetic put

Create a Synthetic Put

Insuring a portfolio by creating a synthetic put can most easily be described with an example.[25] Assume that the investor has $100,000 and is considering the purchase of a portfolio of common stocks. It is believed that the market value of this portfolio will either increase to $125,000 or decrease to $80,000 in six months. If it does increase to $125,000, then it will end up being worth either $156,250 or $100,000 after another six months. Alternatively, if it decreases to $80,000, then it will subsequently end up being worth either $100,000 or $64,000. Each one of these possible "states of the world" is indicated by a letter in Figure 24-13(a), with the current state being denoted as state *A*.

Figure 24-13(a) also shows two sets of terminal portfolio values (that is, portfolio values after twelve months) on the assumption that the common stock portfolio is purchased. The first set gives the values of the portfolio if it is uninsured. The second shows the desired portfolio values—that is, the values of an insured portfolio. In this example, the investor wants to be certain

[25]For an exposition, see Mark Rubinstein and Hayne E. Leland, "Replicating Options with Positions in Stock and Cash," *Financial Analysts Journal*, 37, no. 4 (July/August 1981): 63–72; Mark Rubinstein, "Alternative Paths to Portfolio Insurance," *Financial Analysts Journal*, 41, no. 4 (July/August 1985): 42–52; Robert Ferguson, "How to Beat the S&P 500 (Without Losing Sleep)," *Financial Analysts Journal*, 42, no. 2 (March/April 1986): 37–46; and Thomas J. O'Brien, "The Mechanics of Portfolio Insurance," *Journal of Portfolio Management*, 14, no. 3 (Spring 1988): 40–47.

FIGURE 24-13
Creation of a Synthetic Put

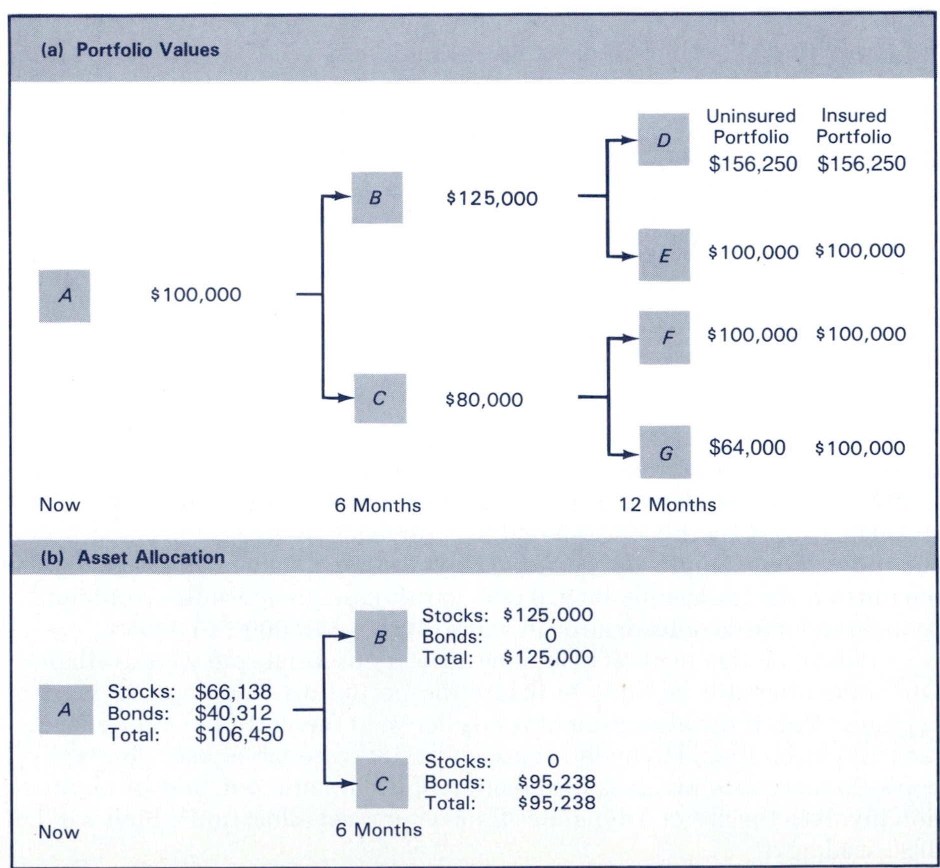

that the ending portfolio is worth at least \$100,000, while also being able to earn the returns associated with state D, should that state occur.[26]

What should the investor do initially in order to be certain of this? Clearly, the investor cannot simply purchase the portfolio of stocks, since then the portfolio will only be worth \$64,000 if state G occurs. However, the investor could consider purchasing portfolio insurance—that is, creating a synthetic put—by investing in both the stock portfolio and riskfree bonds.

The way this is done is to imagine that six months have passed and that state B has occurred. In this situation, how might one be certain to have \$156,250 if the final state is D and \$100,000 if the state is E? The answer is simple—if state B occurs, make sure that the portfolio at that point is worth \$125,000. Thus, an initial investment strategy is required that will provide \$125,000 if the six-month state turns out to be state B.

It is also possible that after the first six months, state C will occur. In this situation, how might one be certain to have \$100,000 regardless of the final state? Assuming that riskfree bonds return 5% (compounded discretely) per six months, the investor should purchase \$95,238 (= \$100,000/1.05) of these bonds if state C occurs. This means that an initial investment strategy is required that will provide \$95,238 if the six-month state turns out to be state C.

Figure 24-13(b) shows the investments and the amounts required in situations B and C. It remains only to determine an appropriate initial set of investments (at point A).

An amount of \$1 invested in the common stock portfolio at A will grow to \$1.25 after six months if the state at that time is B. More generally, s invested in the common stock portfolio at A will grow to $1.25s$ if the six-month state is B. Similarly, b invested in bonds at A will grow to $1.05b$ after six months. Thus, a set of initial investments that will provide \$125,000 if state B occurs can be found by solving the following equation for s and b:

$$1.25s + 1.05b = \$125{,}000. \tag{24.18}$$

If the six-month state is C, s invested in the common stock portfolio will be worth $.8s$, while b invested in bonds will be worth $1.05b$. Thus, a set of initial investments that will provide \$95,238 if state C occurs can be found by solving the following equation for s and b:

$$.8s + 1.05b = \$95{,}238. \tag{24.19}$$

Solutions for s and b that meet *both* equations can now be found, since there are two equations and two unknowns. The solution, shown in Figure 24-13(b), is that the investor should initially put \$66,138 in common stocks and \$40,312 in bonds (that is, s = \$66,138 and b = \$40,312), for a total initial investment of \$106,450.

Making this initial investment is equivalent to investing \$100,000 in the common stock portfolio and buying a protective put option (or an insurance policy) for \$6,450. Indeed, this analysis could be used to determine the

---

[26]In this example, portfolio insurance is sought for a one-year horizon with a floor of 0% (meaning that the investor does not want to lose any of the initial investment over the next twelve months). Other horizons and floors, such as a two-year horizon with a floor of −5% (meaning that the investor does not want to lose more than 5% of the initial investment over the next twenty-four months), are possible. Note the parallel to the discussion of the BOPM, which provides a theoretical basis for the development of portfolio insurance.

appropriate price for such an option or insurance policy. Equivalently, the actions of the investor have resulted in the creation of a synthetic put where the stocks being held are the underlying asset.

By design, this initial investment will provide precisely the desired ending values, but only if the "mix" is altered as values change. The goal is achieved by using a *dynamic strategy* in which investments are bought and sold at intermediate points, depending on the returns of the underlying assets.

In the example, if state *B* occurs, the stocks will be worth $82,672 (= $66,138 × 1.25) and the bonds will be worth $42,328 (= $40,312 × 1.05), for an aggregate value of $125,000. In this situation, the $42,328 of bonds would be sold and the proceeds used to make an additional investment in the common stock portfolio so that the investor is entirely invested in common stocks for the last six months.

However, if state *C* occurs, the stocks will be worth $52,910 (= $66,138 × .8) and the bonds will be worth $42,328 (= $40,312 × 1.05), for an aggregate value of $95,238. In this situation, the $52,910 of stocks would be sold and the proceeds used to make an additional investment in the riskfree bonds for the last six months.

Thus, more money is invested in common stocks if the initial portfolio rises in value, with the money obtained by selling bonds. However, if the initial portfolio falls in value, more money is invested in bonds, with the money obtained by selling stocks. In this example, the percentage invested in stocks is initially 62.13% (= $66,138/$106,450) and subsequently goes to either 100% (if stocks go up) or 0% (if stocks go down).

More realistic applications involve many time intervals within the one-year period, with smaller stock price movements in each interval. Consequently, there would be more changes in the mix of stocks and bonds after each interval, but the changes would be of smaller magnitude. Nevertheless, the essential nature of the strategy would be the same:

When stock prices rise, sell some bonds and buy more stocks.
When stock prices fall, sell some stocks and buy more bonds.

Often computers are used to monitor stock price movements of investors who have obtained portfolio insurance in this manner. When these movements are of sufficient magnitude, the computer is used to electronically place the requisite buy and sell orders. Since much of this monitoring and ordering is programmed into a computer, portfolio insurance is often referred to as a form of **program trading**.[27]

program trading

If there are only two states of the world in each interval, and reallocation is possible after every interval, and there are no transaction costs, then the values associated with any desired "insured portfolio" can be replicated exactly with a dynamic strategy. In practice, however, the results are likely to be only approximately equal. First, there are transaction costs associated with buying and selling securities for the dynamic strategy.[28] Second, if an interval is defined as a length of time over which only two alternative states may occur,

---

[27]The next chapter discusses another form of program trading that is known as index arbitrage.

[28]There is another dynamic strategy for insuring the portfolio that is often preferred because it has smaller transaction costs. The use of it involves index futures, which are a type of financial contract that is discussed in the next chapter.

then the amount of time to an interval may be so short that reallocation is impossible after each interval.

In practice, arbitrary rules are applied to avoid frequent revisions and the associated high level of transaction costs while being reasonably certain of providing the portfolio with the desired level of insurance.[29] Unfortunately, these arbitrary rules did not work very well on Black Monday and Terrible Tuesday (October 19–20, 1987). During these two days, stock prices moved downward so fast that reallocation could not be performed in a timely fashion, resulting in a situation where portfolio insurance did not provide the protection that had been anticipated. As a result, some people believe that dynamic strategies will be used less frequently in the future, and that puts will be used more often.[30]

SUMMARY

1. An option is a contract between two investors that grants one investor the right (but not the obligation) to sell to or buy from the other investor a specific asset at a specific price within a specific time period.

2. A call option for a stock gives the buyer the right to buy a specific number of shares of a specific company from the option writer at a specific purchase price at any time up to and including a specific date.

3. A put option for a stock gives the buyer the right to sell a specific number of shares of a specific company to the option writer at a specific selling price at any time up to and including a specific date.

4. Option trading is facilitated by standardized contracts traded on organized exchanges. These exchanges employ the services of a clearing corporation, which maintains records of all trades and acts as a buyer from all option writers and a writer to all option buyers.

5. Option writers are required to deposit margin to ensure performance of their obligations. The amount and form of the margin will depend on the particular option strategy involved.

6. The intrinsic value of a call option equals the difference between the stock's price and the option's exercise price, if this difference is positive. Otherwise, the option's intrinsic value is zero.

7. The intrinsic value of a put option equals the difference between its exercise price and the stock's price, if this difference is positive. Otherwise, the option's intrinsic value is zero.

8. Calls and puts will not sell for less than their intrinsic values. However, they may sell for more than their intrinsic values owing to their time values.

9. An option's hedge ratio indicates the change in the option's value resulting from a one-dollar change in the value of the underlying asset.

10. The Black-Scholes option valuation model shows that the fair value of an option is determined by five factors: the market price of the stock, the exercise price, the life of the option, the riskfree rate, and the risk of the common stock.

---

[29]For a discussion of transaction costs, see John E. Gilster, Jr., and William Lee, "The Effects of Transactions Costs and Different Borrowing and Lending Rates on the Option Pricing Model: A Note," *Journal of Finance*, 39, no. 4 (September 1984): 1215–22; Hayne E. Leland, "Option Pricing and Replication with Transactions Costs," *Journal of Finance*, 40, no. 5 (December 1985): 1283–1301; Fischer Black and Robert Jones, "Simplifying Portfolio Insurance," *Journal of Portfolio Management*, 14, no. 1 (Fall 1987): 48–51; and Phelim P. Boyle and Ton Yorst, "Option Replication in Discrete Time with Transactions Costs," *Journal of Finance*, 47, no. 1 (March 1992): 271–93.

[30]See Mark Rubinstein, "Portfolio Insurance and the Market Crash," *Financial Analysts Journal*, 44, no. 1 (January/February 1988): 38–47. For a discussion of various types of dynamic strategies, see Andre F. Perold and William F. Sharpe, "Dynamic Strategies for Asset Allocation," *Financial Analysts Journal*, 44, no. 1 (January/February 1988): 16–27, and Philip H. Dybrig, "Inefficient Dynamic Portfolio Strategies or How to Throw Away a Million Dollars in the Stock Market," *Review of Financial Studies*, 1, no. 1 (Spring 1988): 67–88.

11. Put-call parity states that buying both a put option on a stock and a share of the stock will produce the same payoff as buying both a call option on the stock and a riskfree bond (assuming that both options have the same exercise price and expiration date).

12. In addition to put and call options on individual common stocks, options on other assets are traded, such as options on stock indices, debt instruments, and foreign currency.

13. Synthetic options can be created by holding the underlying asset and a riskfree asset in relative amounts that vary with the market price of the underlying asset.

KEY TERMS

option
call option
exercise price
expiration date
premium
closing sale
closing purchase
put option
floor traders
floor brokers
market-makers
order book officials
covered call writing
naked call writing
naked put writing
intrinsic value
straddle
European options
American options
hedge ratio
put-call parity
at the money
out of the money
in the money
time value
implicit volatility
portfolio insurance
synthetic put
program trading

QUESTIONS AND PROBLEMS

1. Why have organized option exchanges been so important to the growth in options trading?
2. How do organized option exchanges permit option buyers and writers to open and close positions without having to directly contact one another?
3. Consider the following stocks selling for the prices listed below:

STOCK	CURRENT PRICE
A	$26
B	73
C	215

   Specify the likely exercise prices that will be set for newly created options on these stocks.
4. From the latest two consecutive issues of *The Wall Street Journal*, find the prices of the General Motors call option with the nearest expiration date and exercise price closest to the current price of GM stock. What is the premium on the call option? What has been the percentage change in the option's price from the previous day? From another part of the *Journal*, calculate the percentage change in the price of GM stock from the previous day. Compare this number to the option's percentage price change.
5. Polly Wolfe has written a September 45 naked call option on Albion Software stock. When the option was written, the stock sold for $42 per share. The option premium was $2.75. Calculate how much margin Polly had to deposit upon writing the call.

6. Dasher Troy wrote a March 75 naked put option on Lodi Mines stock. When the option was written, the stock sold for $80 per share. The option premium was $0.30. How much margin did Dasher have to deposit?
7. Draw a profit-loss graph for the following option strategies.
   (a) Buy a put, $2 premium, $70 exercise price.
   (b) Write a call, $3 premium, $40 exercise price.
   (c) Buy a stock for $80 and buy a put on the same stock, $1 premium, $70 exercise price.
8. Elizabeth Stroud has only a few hours left to decide whether to exercise a call option on Carson Company stock. The call option has an exercise price of $54. Elizabeth originally purchased the call six months ago for $400 (or $4 per share).
   (a) For what range of stock prices should Elizabeth exercise the call on the last day of the call's life?
   (b) For what range of stock prices would Elizabeth realize a net loss (including the premium paid for the call)?
   (c) If Elizabeth had purchased a put instead of a call, how would your answers to parts a and b change?
9. On November 18, 1992, three call options on Lodi Associates stock, all expiring in December 1992, sold for the following prices:

EXERCISE PRICE	OPTION PRICE
$50	$7½
60	3
70	1½

   Firpo Marberry is considering a "butterfly spread" that involves the following positions:
   Buy one call at $50 exercise price.
   Sell (write) two calls at $60 exercise price.
   Buy one call at $70 exercise price.
   (a) What would be the values at expiration of Firpo's spread if Lodi Associates' stock price is below $50? Between $50 and $60? Between $60 and $70? Above $70?
   (b) What dollar investment would be required of Firpo to establish the spread?
10. What is the time value of an option? Why does an option's time value decline as the option approaches expiration?
11. Given the following information, calculate the three-month call option price that is consistent with the Black-Scholes model: $P_s = \$47$, $E = \$45$, $R = .05$, $\sigma = .40$.
12. If the premium on a call option has recently declined, does this indicate that the option is a better buy than it was previously? Why or why not?
13. List the variables needed to estimate the value of a call option. Describe how changes in the values of these variables affect the value of the call option.
14. Calculate the hedge ratio of a call option for a stock with a current price of $40, an exercise price of $45, a standard deviation of 34%, and a time to expiration of six months, given a riskfree return of 7% per annum.

15. Blondy Ryan owns 20,000 shares of Merrimac Monitoring Equipment stock. This stock makes up the bulk of Blondy's wealth. Concerned about the stock's near-term prospects, Blondy wishes to fully hedge the risk of the stock. Given a hedge ratio of .37 and a premium of $2.50 for the near Merrimac put option, how many put options should Blondy buy?

16. A six-month call option with an exercise price of $40 is selling for $5. The current price of the stock is $41.25. The hedge ratio of the option is .65.
    (a) What percentage change in the option's price is likely to accompany a 1% change in the stock's price?
    (b) If the beta of the stock is 1.10, what is the beta of the option? (Hint: Recall what the beta of a stock implies about the relationship between the stock's price and that of the market.)

17. Given the following information, calculate the three-month put option price that is consistent with the Black-Scholes model: $P_s = \$32$, $E = \$45$, $R = .06$, $\sigma = .35$.

18. Explain why call options on non-dividend-paying stocks are "worth more alive than dead."

19. Why does a stock index option sell at a lower price than the cost of a portfolio of options on the constituent stocks (assuming that the index call option and portfolio of call options control the same dollar value of stocks)?

20. Distinguish between portfolio insurance implemented through a protective put and through dynamic asset allocation.

21. (Appendix Question) What is the primary advantage to an investor of a warrant compared with a call option?

22. (Appendix Question) Wheeling Corp. has a 10% subordinated convertible debenture outstanding, maturing in eight years. The bond's face value is $1,000. It currently sells for 99 and is convertible into fifteen shares of common stock. The company's common stock currently sells for $50 per share. Nonconvertible bonds of similar risk have a yield of 12%.
    (a) What is the bond's conversion value?
    (b) What is the bond's conversion premium?
    (c) What is the bond's investment value?

APPENDIX A

Securities With Optionlike Features

Many securities have features that are similar to stock options, particularly call options. In some cases, the optionlike features are explicit. In other cases, more subtle optionlike features are involved. This appendix discusses some of these securities.

Warrants

A stock purchase warrant (or, more simply, a warrant) is a call option issued by the firm whose stock serves as the underlying security.[31] At the time of issue, a warrant usually has a longer time to expiration (for example, five or more years) than a typical call option. Some perpetual warrants, with no expiration date, have also been issued. Generally, warrants may be exercised before expiration—that is, they are like American call options—but some require an initial waiting period.

The exercise price may be fixed or it may change during the life of the warrant, usually increasing in steps. The initial exercise price is typically set to exceed the market price of the underlying security at the time the warrant is issued, often by a substantial amount.

At time of issue, one warrant typically entitles the holder to purchase one share of stock for the appropriate exercise price. However, most warrants are protected against stock splits and stock dividends. This means that any warrant with such protection will enable the investor to buy more or less than one share at an altered exercise price if a stock dividend or stock split is declared. For example, a two-for-one stock split would allow the warrant-holder to purchase two shares at one-half the original exercise price, whereas a one-for-two reverse stock split would allow the warrantholder to purchase one-half share at twice the original exercise price.

[31]These warrants should not be confused with the put warrants and call warrants on foreign stock market indices that were discussed earlier in the chapter. Those warrants are issued by some entity like a brokerage firm; these warrants are issued by the firm whose shares can be purchased by the owner of the warrant.

Warrants may be distributed to stockholders in lieu of a stock or cash dividend or sold directly as a new security issue. Alternatively, warrants may be issued in order to "sweeten" an offering of some other kind of security. For example, a bond may be sold by the firm with warrants attached to it. In some cases, the warrants are nondetachable, except upon exercise. This means that if an investor wants to sell one of the bonds, the warrants must be either exercised or sold with the bond. In other cases, the warrants are detachable, meaning that after the initial sale of the bonds an investor may sell either the bonds or the warrants (or both).

Terms associated with a warrant are contained in a warrant agreement, which serves the same function as an indenture for a bond issue. In this agreement, the scope of the warrantholder's protection is defined (for example, the treatment of warrants in the event of a merger); it may also specify certain restrictions on corporate behavior.

Some warrants that are issued with bonds have an additional attribute. Although they may be detached and exercised by paying cash to the corporation, an alternative method of payment is provided. This alternative allows bonds from the initial issue to be used in lieu of cash to pay the exercise price, with the bonds being valued at par for this purpose.

One difference between warrants and call options is the limitation on the amount of warrants that are outstanding. A specific number of warrants of a particular type will be issued; the total generally cannot be increased, and typically will be reduced as the warrants are exercised. In contrast, a call option can be created whenever two people wish to create one; thus, the number oustanding is not fixed. Exercise of a call option on its stock has no more effect on a corporation than a transaction in its stock on the secondary market. However, the exercise of a warrant does have an effect. In particular, it leaves the corporation with more cash, fewer warrants outstanding, and more stock outstanding.

Warrants are traded on major stock exchanges and on the over-the-counter market. Quotations for those with active markets are provided in the financial press in the sections devoted primarily to stocks.

Rights

A right is similar to a warrant in that it also is like a call option issued by the firm whose stock serves as the underlying security. Rights, also known as subscription warrants, are issued to give existing stockholders their preemptive right to subscribe to a new issue of common stock before the general public is given an opportunity. Each share of stock receives one right. A stated number of rights plus cash equal to a specified subscription price are required in order to obtain one new share. To insure the sale of the new stock, the subscription price is usually set below the stock's market price at the time the rights are issued. This does not mean that new subscribers get a bargain, since they must pay old stockholders for the required number of rights, which become valuable as a result.

Rights generally have short lives (from two to ten weeks when issued) and may be freely traded prior to exercise. Up to a specified date, old shares of the stock trade *cum rights*, meaning that the buyer of the stock is entitled to receive the rights when issued. Afterward, the stock trades *ex rights* at a correspondingly lower price. Rights for popular issues of stock are sometimes traded on exchanges; others are available in the over-the-counter market.

Often trading begins prior to actual availability, with the rights sold for delivery on a *when-issued* basis.

A right is, in effect, a warrant, although one with a rather short time before expiration. It also differs with regard to exercise price, which is typically set above the stock's market price at issuance for a warrant and below it for a right. Because of their short lives, rights need not be protected against stock splits and stock dividends. Otherwise, they have all the attributes of a warrant and can be valued in a similar manner.[32]

Bond Call Provisions

Many firms issue bonds with call provisions that allow the firm to repurchase the bonds before maturity, usually at a price above par value. This amounts to the sale of a straight bond and the simultaneous purchase by the corporation of a call option sold by the purchaser of the bond that is paid by the corporation in the form of a relatively lower selling price for the bond. The writer of the option is the bond purchaser.

Bond call provisions usually can be exercised only after some specified date (for example, five years after issue). Moreover, the exercise price, known as the call premium, may be different for different exercise dates (typically shrinking in size the longer the bond is outstanding). The implicit call option associated with such a bond is thus both longer-lived and more complex than those traded on the listed option markets.[33]

Convertible Securities

A particularly popular financial instrument is a security that can be converted into a different security of the same firm under certain conditions. The typical case involves a bond or preferred stock convertible into shares of the firm's common stock, with a stated number of shares received for each bond or share of preferred stock. Usually, no cash is involved: The old security is simply traded in, and the appropriate number of new securities are issued in return. Convertible preferred stocks are issued from time to time, but tax effects make them, like other preferred stock, attractive primarily to corporate investors. For other investors, many issues of convertible bonds are more attractive.

If a $1,000 par value bond can be converted into twenty shares of common stock, the conversion ratio is 20. Alternatively, the conversion price may be said to be $50 (= $1,000/20), since $50 of the bond's par value must be given up to obtain one common share. Neither the conversion ratio nor the conversion price is affected by changes in a bond's market value.

Conversion ratios are typically set so that conversion will not prove attractive unless the stock price increases substantially from its value at the time the convertible security was first issued. This is similar to the general practice used in setting exercise prices for warrants.

A convertible bond's conversion value, obtained by multiplying the conversion ratio by the stock's current market price, is the value that would be obtained by conversion; it is the bond's current "value as stock." The conversion premium is the amount by which the bond's current market price

---

[32]Rights are also discussed in Chapter 13. Valuation of rights is relatively simple if it is assumed that there is no chance that they will end up being out of the money on the expiration date and the time value of money is ignored (meaning that the riskfree rate is assumed to be zero).

[33]Bond call provisions are also discussed in Chapters 19 and 21.

exceeds its conversion value, expressed as a percent of the latter. A related amount is the convertible's investment value. This value is an estimate, based on the convertible's maturity date, coupon rate, and rating, of the amount for which the bond might sell if it were not convertible. Equivalently, it is the convertible's "value as a straight bond."

Consider a $1,000 par value bond convertible into twenty shares of stock. If the market price of the stock is $60 per share, then the conversion value of the bond is $1,200 (= $60 × 20). If the current market price of the convertible bond is $1,300, then its conversion premium is $100 (= $1,300 − $1,200). Its investment value might be estimated to be, say, $950, meaning that the bond would sell for this much if it did not provide the investor with the option of convertibility.

Convertible securities of great complexity can be found in the marketplace. Some may be converted only after an initial waiting period. Some may be converted up to the bond's maturity date; others only for a stated, shorter period. Some have different conversion ratios for different years. A few can be converted into packages of two or more different securities; others require the additional payment of cash upon conversion.

Convertible bonds are usually protected against stock splits and stock dividends via adjustment in the conversion ratio. For example, a bond with an initial conversion ratio of 20 could be adjusted to have a ratio of 22 following a 10% stock dividend. Protection against cash dividends is not generally provided, but some indentures require that the holders of convertible bonds be notified prior to payment of cash dividends so that they may convert before the resultant fall in the stock's market price.

Convertible securities often contain a call provision, which may be used by the corporation to force conversion when the stock's market price is sufficiently high to make the value of the stock obtained on conversion exceed the call price of the bond. For example, if the conversion value of the bond is $1,200 (the bond is convertible into twenty shares of stock that are currently selling for $60 per share) and the call price is $1,100, the firm can force conversion by calling the bond. This is because a bondholder faces two choices when the call is received—either convert and receive twenty shares collectively worth $1,200 or receive cash of $1,100—and should choose the shares since they have a higher value.

A convertible bond is, for practical purposes, a bond with nondetachable warrants plus the restriction that *only* the bond is usable (at par) to pay the exercise price. If the bond were not callable, the value of this package would equal the value of a straight noncallable bond (that is, the estimated investment value) plus that of the warrants. However, most convertible bonds are callable and thus involve a double option: The holder has an option to convert the bond to stock, and the issuing corporation has an option to buy the bond back from the investors.

REFERENCES

1. Investment strategies involving options are discussed in many papers; here are three of the most notable ones:

Robert C. Merton, Myron S. Scholes, and Mathew L. Gladstein, "The Returns and Risk of Alternative Call Option Portfolio Investment Strategies," *Journal of Business*, 51, no. 1 (April 1978): 183–242;

Robert C. Merton, Myron S. Scholes, and Mathew L. Gladstein, "The

Returns and Risk of Alternative Put-Option Portfolio Investment Strategies," *Journal of Business*, 55, no. 1 (January 1982): 1–55;

Aimee Gerberg Ronn and Ehud I. Ronn, "The Box Spread Arbitrage Conditions: Theory, Tests, and Investment Strategies," *Review of Financial Studies*, 2, no. 1 (1989): 91–107.

2. A description and comparison of the specialist and market-maker systems for trading options is presented by:

   Robert Neal, "A Comparison of Transaction Costs Between Competitive Market-Maker and Specialist Structures," *Journal of Business*, 65, no. 2 (July 1992): 317–34.

3. The binomial option pricing model was initially developed in:

   William F. Sharpe, *Investments* (Englewood Cliffs, N.J.: Prentice Hall, 1978), Chapter 14.

4. A short while later the following two papers expanded upon Sharpe's model:

   John C. Cox, Stephen A. Ross, and Mark Rubinstein, "Option Pricing: A Simplified Approach," *Journal of Financial Economics*, 7, no. 3 (September 1979): 229–63;

   Richard J. Rendleman, Jr., and Brit J. Bartter, "Two-State Option Pricing," *Journal of Finance*, 34, no. 5 (December 1979): 1093–1110.

5. Two seminal papers on option pricing are:

   Robert C. Merton, "Theory of Rational Option Pricing," *Bell Journal of Economics and Management Science*, 4, no. 1 (Spring 1973): 141–83;

   Fischer Black and Myron Scholes, "The Pricing of Options and Corporate Liabilities," *Journal of Political Economy*, 81, no. 3 (May/June 1973): 637–54.

6. Both the Black-Scholes and binomial option pricing models assume that the riskfree rate is constant over the life of the option. For two interesting papers that relax this assumption, see:

   Ramon Rabinovitch, "Pricing Stock and Bond Options When the Default-Free Rate Is Stochastic," *Journal of Financial and Quantitative Analysis*, 24, no. 4 (December 1989): 447–57;

   Stuart M. Turnbull and Frank Milne, "A Simple Approach to Interest-Rate Option Pricing," *Review of Financial Studies*, 4, no. 1 (1991): 87–121.

7. The Black-Scholes model also assumes that the volatility of the underlying asset is constant over the life of the option. For papers that relax this assumption, see:

   Herb Johnson and David Shanno, "Option Pricing When the Variance Is Changing," *Journal of Financial and Quantitative Analysis*, 22, no. 2 (June 1987): 143–51;

   John Hill and Alan White, "The Pricing of Options on Assets with Stochastic Volatilities," *Journal of Finance*, 42, no. 2 (June 1987): 281–300;

   Louis O. Scott, "Option Pricing When the Variance Changes Randomly: Theory, Estimation, and an Application," *Journal of Financial and Quantitative Analysis*, 22, no. 4 (December 1987): 419–38;

   James B. Wiggins, "Option Values Under Stochastic Volatility: Theory and Empirical Estimates," *Journal of Financial Economics*, 19, no. 2 (December 1987): 351–72;

Marc Chesney and Louis Scott, "Pricing European Currency Options: A Comparison of the Modified Black-Scholes Model and a Random Variance Model," *Journal of Financial and Quantitative Analysis*, 24, no. 3 (September 1989): 267–84;

Thomas J. Finucane, "Black-Scholes Approximations of Call Option Prices with Stochastic Volatilities: A Note," *Journal of Financial and Quantitative Analysis*, 24, no. 4 (December 1989): 527–32.

8. Portfolio insurance has received much attention; in addition to the citations given in the chapter, see:

M. J. Brennan and R. Solanki, "Optimal Portfolio Insurance," *Journal of Financial and Quantitative Analysis*, 16, no. 3 (September 1981): 279–300;

Ethan S. Etzioni, "Rebalance Disciplines for Portfolio Insurance," *Journal of Portfolio Management*, 13, no. 1 (Fall 1986): 59–62;

Richard J. Rendelman, Jr., and Richard McEnally, "Assessing the Costs of Portfolio Insurance," *Financial Analysts Journal*, 43, no. 3 (May/June 1987): 27–37;

C. B. Garcia and F. J. Gould, "An Empirical Study of Portfolio Insurance," *Financial Analysts Journal*, 43, no. 4 (July/August 1987): 44–54;

Robert Ferguson, "A Comparison of the Mean-Variance and Long-Term Return Characteristics of Three Investment Strategies," *Financial Analysts Journal*, 43, no. 4 (July/August 1987): 55–66;

Fischer Black and Robert Jones, "Simplifying Portfolio Insurance for Corporate Pension Plans," *Journal of Portfolio Management*, 14, no. 4 (Summer 1988): 33–37;

Thomas J. O'Brien, *How Option Replicating Portfolio Insurance Works: Expanded Details*, Monograph Series in Finance and Economics #1988-4, New York University Salomon Center, Leonard N. Stern School of Business;

Yu Zhu and Robert C. Kavee, "Performance of Portfolio Insurance Strategies," *Journal of Portfolio Management*, 14, no. 3 (Spring 1988): 48–54;

Erol Hakanoglu, Robert Koppraseh, and Emmanuel Roman, "Constant Proportion Portfolio Insurance for Fixed-Income Investment," *Journal of Portfolio Management*, 15, no. 4 (Summer 1989): 58–66;

Michael J. Brennan and Eduardo Schwartz, "Portfolio Insurance and Financial Market Equilibrium," *Journal of Business*, 62, no. 4 (October 1989): 455–72;

Sanford J. Grossman and Jean-Luc Vila, "Portfolio Insurance in Complete Markets: A Note," *Journal of Business*, 62, no. 4 (October 1989): 473–76;

Charles J. Jacklin, Allan W. Kleidon, and Paul Pfleiderer,"Underestimation of Portfolio Insurance and the Crash of October 1987," *Review of Financial Studies*, 5, no. 1 (1992): 35–63.

9. A great deal has been written on warrants and convertibles; for an introduction to this literature, see:

Richard A. Brealey and Stewart C. Myers, *Principles of Corporate Finance* (New York: McGraw-Hill, 1991), Chapter 22.

10. A number of books are devoted exclusively to options or have options as one of their primary subjects. Most cover everything discussed in this chapter but in more detail and with a more complete list of citations. Here are a few:

Robert A. Jarrow and Andrew Rudd, *Option Pricing* (Homewood, Ill.: Richard D. Irwin, 1983);

John C. Cox and Mark Rubinstein, *Options Markets* (Englewood Cliffs, N.J.: Prentice Hall, 1985);

Peter Ritchken, *Options: Theory, Strategy, and Applications* (Glenview, Ill.: Scott, Foresman, 1987);

Richard M. Bookstaber, *Option Pricing & Investment Strategies* (Chicago: Probus Publishing, 1987);

Don M. Chance, *An Introduction to Options & Futures* (Fort Worth, Texas: The Dryden Press, 1991);

John Hull, *Introduction to Futures and Options Markets* (Englewood Cliffs, N.J.: Prentice Hall, 1991);

Robert W. Kolb, *Options: An Introduction* (Miami: Kolb Publishing, 1991);

Alan L. Tucker, *Financial Futures, Options, & Swaps* (St. Paul: West Publishing, 1991);

David A. Dubofsky, *Options and Financial Futures* (New York: McGraw-Hill, 1992);

Hans R. Stoll and Robert E. Whaley, *Futures and Options* (Cincinnati: South-Western Publishing, 1993).

11. A useful software package and manual for valuing options is:

Stuart M. Turnbull, *Option Valuation* (Toronto: Holt, Rinehart and Winston of Canada, 1987).

25

Futures

Consider a contract that involves the delivery of some specific asset by a seller to a buyer at an agreed-upon future date. While such a contract also specifies the purchase price, the asset is not to be paid for until the delivery date. However, the buyer and the seller will both be requested to make a security deposit at the time the contract is signed. The reason for this deposit is to protect each person from experiencing any losses, should the other person renege on the contract. Hence, the size of the deposit is checked daily to see that it provides sufficient protection. If it is insufficient, it will have to be increased; if it is more than sufficient, the excess can be withdrawn.

futures

These contracts are often referred to as **futures** (short for futures contract), and in the United States they involve assets such as agricultural goods (for example, wheat), natural resources (for example, copper), foreign currencies (for example, Swiss francs), fixed-income securities (for example, Treasury bonds), and market indices (for example, the Standard & Poor's 500).[1] As with options, standardization of the terms in these contracts makes it relatively easy for anyone to create and subsequently trade the contracts.

[1]The term *commodity futures* is often used to refer to futures on agricultural goods and natural resources.

speculators
hedgers

There are two types of people who deal in futures—speculators and hedgers. **Speculators** buy and sell futures for the sole purpose of making a profit by selling them at a price that is higher than their buying price (or so they hope); such people neither produce nor use the asset in the ordinary course of business. In contrast, **hedgers** buy and sell futures to offset an otherwise risky position in the spot market; in the ordinary course of business, they either produce or use the asset.

Hedgers

For example, consider wheat futures. A farmer might note today that the market price for a wheat futures contract with delivery around harvest time is $4 per bushel, a price that is high enough to ensure a profitable year. While the farmer could sell wheat futures today, alternatively the farmer could wait until harvest and sell the wheat on the spot market at that time.[2] However, waiting until harvest entails risk because the spot price of wheat could fall by then, perhaps to $3 per bushel, which would bring personal ruin to the farmer. In contrast, selling wheat futures today will allow the farmer to "lock-in" a $4 per bushel selling price. Doing so would remove an element of risk from the primary business of the farmer of growing wheat. Thus, a farmer who sells futures is known as a hedger or, more specifically, a **short hedger.**

short hedger

Perhaps the buyer of the farmer's futures contract is a baker who uses wheat in making bread. Currently, the baker has enough wheat in inventory to last until harvest season. In anticipation of the need to replenish the inventory at that time, the baker could buy a wheat futures contract today at $4 per bushel. Alternatively, the baker could simply wait until the inventory runs low, and then buy wheat in the spot market. However, there is a chance that the spot price will be $5 per bushel at that time. Should this happen, the baker would have to raise the selling price of bread and perhaps lose sales in doing so. Alternatively, by purchasing wheat futures, the baker can "lock-in" a $4 per bushel purchase price, thereby removing an element of risk from the bread business. Thus, a baker who buys futures is also known as a hedger or, more specifically, a **long hedger.**

long hedger

Speculators

The farmer and the baker can be compared with a speculator—a person who buys and sells wheat futures, based on the forecasted price of wheat, in the pursuit of relatively short-term profits. As mentioned earlier, such a person neither produces nor uses the asset in the ordinary course of business.

A speculator who thinks that the price of wheat is going to rise substantially will buy wheat futures. Later, this person will enter a **reversing trade** by selling wheat futures; if the forecast was accurate, a profit will have been made on an increase in the wheat futures price.

reversing trade

For example, consider a speculator expecting at least a $1 per bushel rise in the spot price of wheat. While this person could buy wheat, store it, and hope to sell it later at the anticipated higher price, it would be easier and more profitable to buy a wheat futures contract today at $4 per bushel. Later, assuming that the spot price of wheat rises by $1, the speculator would enter a reversing trade by selling the wheat futures contract for perhaps $5 per

spot market
spot price

[2]The **spot market** involves the immediate exchange of an asset for cash; the purchase price of the asset is known as its **spot price.**

bushel (a $1 rise in the spot price of wheat will cause the futures price to rise by about $1). Thus, the speculator will make a profit of $1 per bushel or $5,000 in total, since these contracts are for 5,000 bushels. As will be shown later, the speculator might need to make a security deposit of $1,000 at the time the wheat futures contract was bought. Since this is returned when the reversing trade is made, the speculator's rate of return is quite high (500%) relative to the percentage rise in the price of wheat (25%).

Alternatively, if a speculator forecasts a substantial price decline, then initially wheat futures would be sold. Later, the person would enter a reversing trade by purchasing wheat futures; assuming that the forecast was accurate, a profit will have been made on the decrease in the wheat futures price.

THE FUTURES CONTRACT

Futures contracts are standardized in terms of delivery as well as the type of asset that is permissible for delivery. For example, the Chicago Board of Trade specifies the following requirements for its July wheat contract:

1. The seller agrees to deliver 5,000 bushels of either No. 2 soft red wheat, No. 2 hard red winter wheat, No. 2 dark northern spring wheat, or No. 1 northern spring wheat at the agreed-upon price. Alternatively, a number of other grades can be delivered at specified premiums or discounts from the agreed-upon price. In any case, the seller is allowed to decide which grade shall be delivered.
2. The grain will be delivered by registered warehouse receipts issued by approved warehouses in Chicago or Toledo, Ohio (Toledo deliveries are discounted $.02 per bushel).
3. Delivery will take place during the month of July, with the seller allowed to decide the actual date.
4. Upon delivery of the warehouse receipt from the seller to the buyer, the latter will pay the former the agreed-upon price in cash.

After an organized exchange has set all the terms of a futures contract except for its price, the exchange will authorize trading in the contract.[3] Buyers and sellers (or their representatives) meet at a specific place on the floor of the exchange and try to agree on a price at which to trade. If they succeed, one or more contracts will be created, with all the standard terms plus an additional one—the price involved. Prices are normally stated on a per-unit basis. Thus, if a buyer and seller agree to a price of $4 per bushel for a contract of 5,000 bushels of wheat, the amount of money involved is $20,000.

Figure 25-1 shows a set of daily quotations giving the prices at which some popular futures contracts were traded and the total volume of sales for each type of contract. Such listings of active futures markets are published regularly in the financial press, with each item for delivery (such as corn)

---

[3]For a relatively complete description of the terms for many exchange-traded futures contracts, see the *Commodity Trading Manual* (Chicago Board of Trade, 1989); and Malcolm J. Robertson, *Directory of World Futures and Options* (Englewood Cliffs, N.J.: Prentice Hall, 1990). These two books also contain descriptions of various futures exchanges.

FIGURE 25-1
Quotations for Futures Prices (Excerpt)

Source: Reprinted by permission of *The Wall Street Journal,* © Dow Jones & Company, Inc., July 16, 1992, p. C12. All rights reserved worldwide.

Wednesday, July 15, 1992.

Open Interest Reflects Previous Trading Day.

GRAINS AND OILSEEDS

CORN (CBT) 5,000 bu.; cents per bu.

	Open	High	Low	Settle	Change	Lifetime High	Lifetime Low	Open Interest
July	232¾	232¾	230½	231	− 3¼	285	230½	2,152
Sept	233	233¼	231½	232¼	− 1¾	279½	231½	54,599
Dec	235½	237	235¼	235½	− 1¼	275¾	235¼	123,489
Mr93	244	245	243¾	244	− 1	281¼	243¾	18,925
May	249½	250½	249	249½	− ¾	284¾	249	5,378
July	253¾	254	252¾	253¼	− ¾	286	252¾	4,106
Sept	252	252¾	251½	252	− 1	271½	251½	316
Dec	251	252¼	250½	251½	+ ¼	268½	250½	2,407

Est vol 38,000; vol Tues 41,567; open int 211,372, +935.

OATS (CBT) 5,000 bu.; cents per bu.

	Open	High	Low	Settle	Change	Lifetime High	Lifetime Low	Open Interest
July	131½	133½	131½	132½	+ 1½	191½	122¼	33
Sept	132¾	135¾	132¾	135	+ 2½	194	127¼	6,871
Dec	138½	142	138½	140¾	+ 2½	198½	135	5,331
Mr93	145½	145½	144½	145¼	+ 3	195¼	140½	506

Est vol 1,000; vol Tues 866; open int 12,816, −136.

SOYBEANS (CBT) 5,000 bu.; cents per bu.

	Open	High	Low	Settle	Change	Lifetime High	Lifetime Low	Open Interest
July	568	569	566¼	566¾	− 3	668	554	1,863
Aug	568½	571½	568½	569	− 2½	660	565	26,819
Sept	571½	573½	570¾	571¼	− 2	645	557	15,650
Nov	574	578	574	575¾	− 1½	651	552	55,963
Ja93	582½	585	581½	583¾	− 1½	659	578½	7,294
Mar	591½	593¼	591	591¼	− 1¾	664	590½	5,084
May	599½	600	598½	598¾	− 1½	668½	598½	2,659
July	604	604½	602½	602¾	− 1	671	602½	2,746
Nov	592	593	589	591¼	− 1	620	589	1,406

Est vol 32,000; vol Tues 34,942; open int 119,508, +793.

METALS AND PETROLEUM

GOLD (CMX) – 100 troy oz.; $ per troy oz.

	Open	High	Low	Settle	Change	Lifetime High	Lifetime Low	Open Interest
July		....	....	354.00	+ 2.90	347.30	347.30	0
Aug	351.90	354.80	351.40	354.70	+ 2.90	426.50	336.60	48,403
Oct	353.90	356.60	353.20	356.40	+ 2.90	410.80	338.50	3,910
Dec	355.50	358.50	355.00	358.30	+ 2.90	431.00	340.40	20,376
Fb93	357.50	360.40	357.40	360.20	+ 2.90	404.20	343.00	10,594
Apr	359.20	362.30	359.20	362.00	+ 2.80	410.00	346.00	8,802
June	361.50	363.00	361.30	363.90	+ 2.70	418.50	347.70	5,771
Aug	363.50	364.40	363.50	366.00	+ 2.60	395.50	353.80	2,675
Oct		....	....	368.20	+ 2.50	395.00	365.60	644
Dec		....	....	370.40	+ 2.40	402.80	356.40	4,388
Fb94	372.10	372.10	372.10	372.90	+ 2.40	372.10	364.50	442
Apr		....	....	375.50	+ 2.40	....	....	220
June		....	....	378.20	+ 2.40	379.00	367.00	206
Dec		....	....	388.70	+ 2.40	383.00	383.00	2
Ju95		....	....	399.10	+ 2.40	....	....	100
Dec		....	....	409.40	+ 2.40	....	....	100

Est vol 33,000; vol Tues 24,595; open int 106,663, +506.

CRUDE OIL, Light Sweet (NYM) 1,000 bbls.; $ per bbl.

	Open	High	Low	Settle	Change	Lifetime High	Lifetime Low	Open Interest
Aug	21.38	21.73	21.38	21.71	+ .25	22.95	17.75	54,498
Sept	21.29	21.63	21.28	21.60	+ .24	24.00	17.78	69,567
Oct	21.25	21.55	21.22	21.54	+ .24	22.75	18.42	35,001
Nov	21.23	21.48	21.23	21.48	+ .21	22.60	18.50	24,575
Dec	21.19	21.40	21.19	21.41	+ .19	24.00	18.25	29,611
Ja93	21.14	21.32	21.11	21.32	+ .18	22.30	18.62	27,737
Feb	21.05	21.22	21.03	21.22	+ .17	22.10	18.67	12,393
Mar	20.96	21.07	20.93	21.10	+ .16	21.91	18.51	9,254
Apr	20.87	20.95	20.87	20.99	+ .15	21.75	18.75	4,757
May	20.81	20.87	20.81	20.90	+ .15	21.59	18.93	3,331
June		....	....	20.81	+ .15	23.00	18.63	11,942
July	20.65	20.68	20.65	20.72	+ .15	22.58	18.97	8,673
Aug		....	....	20.63	+ .15	21.22	18.99	3,610
Sept		....	....	20.57	+ .15	21.18	18.90	9,719
Oct		....	....	20.54	+ .15	21.15	19.05	1,843
Nov		....	....	20.52	+ .15	21.15	20.24	607
Dec		....	....	20.51	+ .15	23.00	18.70	11,477
Ja94		....	....	20.50	+ .15	21.15	20.66	521
Mar		....	....	20.47	+ .14	21.10	19.14	998
June		....	....	20.47	+ .14	21.35	19.25	11,961
Dec		....	....	20.47	+ .14	21.26	19.40	6,322
Ju95		....	....	20.53	+ .14	21.21	20.55	7,777

Est vol 91,716; vol Tues 67,930; open int 346,174, −611.

CURRENCY

JAPAN YEN (IMM) – 12.5 million yen; $ per yen (.00)

	Open	High	Low	Settle	Change	Lifetime High	Lifetime Low	Open Interest
Sept	.7850	.7865	.7849	.7851	− .0009	.8080	.7265	48,053
Dec	.7852	.7856	.7852	.7849	− .0009	.8045	.7410	2,083
Mr93	....	....	....	.7857	− .0009	.8005	.7445	2,508

Est vol 7,377; vol Fri 8,204; open int 52,644, −92.

DEUTSCHEMARK (IMM) – 125,000 marks; $ per mark

	Open	High	Low	Settle	Change	Lifetime High	Lifetime Low	Open Interest
Sept	.6276	.6306	.6276	.6292	+ .0024	.6400	.5685	50,507
Dec	.6198	.6219	.6197	.6209	+ .0024	.6220	.5645	5,556
Mr93	....	....	....	.6140	+ .0024	.6155	.5724	660

Est vol 30,020; vol Fri 32,737; open int 56,726, +1,022.

INTEREST RATE

TREASURY BONDS (CBT) – $100,000; pts. 32nds of 100%

	Open	High	Low	Settle	Chg	Yield Settle	Yield Chg	Open Interest
Sept	101-29	102-20	101-28	102-17	+ 18	7.749	− .055	318,428
Dec	100-22	101-13	100-22	101-10	+ 18	7.869	− .056	16,815
Mr93	99-25	100-07	99-22	100-05	+ 17	7.984	− .054	13,539
June	98-21	99-03	98-18	99-00	+ 16	8.102	− .051	10,859
Sp93	97-20	97-31	97-16	97-30	+ 16	8.212	− .052	792
Dec	....	....	....	96-31	+ 16	8.313	− .054	154
Sp94	94-13	94-20	94-13	94-20	+ 16	8.566	− .055	100

Est vol 270,000; vol Tues 239,186; op int 360,795, −2,663.

TREASURY BILLS (IMM) – $1 mil.; pts. of 100%

	Open	High	Low	Settle	Chg	Discount Settle	Discount Chg	Open Interest
Sept	96.80	96.86	96.80	96.84	+ .05	3.16	− .05	28,207
Dec	96.57	96.62	96.56	96.61	+ .07	3.39	− .07	7,424
Mr93	96.45	96.54	96.45	96.54	+ .11	3.46	− .11	2,684
June	96.27	96.28	96.27	96.28	+ .13	3.72	− .13	231

Est vol 3,141; vol Tues 2,596; open int 38,548, −716.

EURODOLLAR (IMM) – $1 million; pts of 100%

	Open	High	Low	Settle	Chg	Yield Settle	Yield Chg	Open Interest
Sept	96.49	96.55	96.49	96.54	+ .06	3.46	− .06	294,505
Dec	96.08	96.14	96.07	96.12	+ .06	3.88	− .06	280,255
Mr93	96.06	96.12	96.04	96.10	+ .07	3.90	− .07	214,766
June	95.73	95.80	95.73	95.79	+ .10	4.21	− .10	146,503
Sept	95.26	95.38	95.26	95.37	+ .14	4.63	− .14	101,855
Dec	94.67	94.78	94.67	94.77	+ .14	5.23	− .14	65,136
Mr94	94.43	94.55	94.43	94.54	+ .14	5.46	− .14	65,517
June	94.02	94.14	94.02	94.12	+ .13	5.88	− .13	45,106
Sept	93.66	93.76	93.66	93.75	+ .12	6.25	− .12	34,997
Dec	93.21	93.31	93.21	93.29	+ .11	6.71	− .11	31,377
Mr95	93.14	93.24	93.14	93.21	+ .10	6.79	− .10	27,633
June	92.88	92.97	92.88	92.94	+ .09	6.06	− .09	20,482
Sept	92.67	92.75	92.67	92.73	+ .08	6.27	− .08	16,884
Dec	92.39	92.46	92.38	92.43	+ .07	6.57	− .07	17,719
Mr96	92.38	92.43	92.38	92.42	+ .06	6.58	− .06	15,155
June	92.28	92.31	92.26	92.29	+ .05	6.71	− .05	7,304
Sept	92.11	92.14	92.11	92.14	+ .04	6.86	− .04	2,346
Dec	91.89	91.89	91.86	91.88	+ .03	7.12	− .03	1,921
Mr97	91.89	91.89	91.86	91.87	+ .02	7.13	− .02	1,752
June	91.81	91.81	91.78	91.79	+ .02	7.21	− .02	1,336

Est vol 235,163; vol Tues 204,975; open int 1,392,548, −5,157.

INDEX

S&P 500 INDEX (CME) 500 times index

	Open	High	Low	Settle	Chg	High	Low	Open Interest
Sept	417.40	418.10	415.90	417.20	− .50	425.50	376.25	146,457
Dec	418.20	418.45	416.40	417.75	− .45	427.25	391.40	4,014
Mr93		....	....	418.55	− .40	423.80	397.50	740

Est vol 41,019; vol Tues 38,708; open int 151,307, +1,701.
Indx prelim High 417.81; Low 416.29; Close 417.10 −.58

NIKKEI 225 Stock Average (CME) – $5 times NSA

	Open	High	Low	Settle	Chg	High	Low	Open Interest
Sept	17190.	17225.	17160.	17170.	− 45.0	25300.	15775.	21,207
Dec		....	....	17295.	− 50.0	21100.	15950.	103

Est vol 767; vol Tues 686; open int 21,310, −150.
The index: High 17274.49; Low 17092.13; Close 17116.92 +52.29

EXCHANGE ABBREVIATIONS
(for commodity futures and futures options)

CBT-Chicago Board of Trade; CME-Chicago Mercantile Exchange; CMX-Commodity Exchange, New York; CRCE-Chicago Rice & Cotton Exchange; CTN-New York Cotton Exchange; CSCE-Coffee, Sugar & Cocoa Exchange, New York; FOX-London Futures and Options Exchange; IPE-International Petroleum Exchange; KC-Kansas City Board of Trade; MCE-MidAmerica Commodity Exchange; MPLS-Minneapolis Grain Exchange; NYM-New York Mercantile Exchange; PBOT-Philadelphia Board of Trade; WPG-Winnipeg Commodity Exchange.

having a heading that indicates the number of units per contract (5,000 bushels) and the terms on which prices are stated (cents per bushel).

Below the heading for the asset are certain details for each type of contract. Moving from left to right in Figure 25-1, the first column shows the delivery dates for the contracts. For example, there are seven different futures contracts for corn, each one involving the same item but having different delivery dates. Next comes the *open*, denoting the price at which the first transaction was made; the *high* and *low*, representing the highest and lowest prices during the day; and the **settle** (short for settlement price), a price that is a representative price (for example, the average of the high and low prices) during the "closing period" designated by the exchange in question (for example, the last two minutes of trading). After the *change* from the previous day's settlement price comes the highest and lowest prices recorded during the lifetime of the contract. The last column on the right shows the **open interest** (the number of outstanding contracts) on the previous day.

settle

open interest

For each futures contract, summary figures are given below the figures for the last delivery date (in the case of corn, these summary figures are below the December 1992 delivery date figures), and indicate the total volume (that is, the number of contracts) traded on that day and on the previous trading day as well as the total open interest in such contracts on that day and the change in total open interest from the previous day.

Futures Markets

The futures contracts shown in Figure 25-1 are traded on various organized exchanges. The Chicago Board of Trade (CBT) was the earliest one, founded in 1848, and currently is the largest futures exchange in the world. Other futures exchanges are listed in the lower left-hand corner of Figure 25-1.

The method of trading futures on organized exchanges is similar in some ways to and different in other ways from the way stocks and options are traded. As with stocks and options, customers can place market, limit, and stop orders. Furthermore, once an order is transmitted to an exchange floor, it must be taken to a designated spot for execution by a member of the exchange, just as is done for stocks and options. This spot is known as a "pit" because of its shape, which is circular with a set of interior descending steps on which members stand. What transpires in the pit is what distinguishes trading in futures from trading in stocks and options.

First, there are no specialists or market-makers on futures exchanges. Instead, members can be floor brokers, meaning that they execute customers' orders. In doing so, they (or their phone clerks) each keep a file of any stop or limit orders that cannot be immediately executed. Alternatively, members can be floor traders (those with very short holding periods, of less than a day, are known as **locals** or scalpers), meaning that they execute orders for their own personal accounts in an attempt to make profits by "buying low and selling high." Floor traders are in some ways similar to market-makers, since a floor trader may have an inventory of futures contracts and may act as a dealer. However, unlike a market-maker, a floor trader is not required to do so.

locals

Second, all futures orders must be announced by "open outcry," meaning that any member wishing to buy or sell any futures contract must verbally announce the order and a price at which the member is willing to trade. This way, the order is exposed to everyone in the pit, thereby enabling an auction to take place that will lead to the order being filled at the best possible price.

The Clearinghouse

Each futures exchange has an associated clearinghouse that becomes the "seller's buyer" and the "buyer's seller" as soon as a trade is concluded. The procedure is similar to that used for options. This is not surprising, since the first market in listed options was organized by people associated with a futures exchange (specifically, the Chicago Board Options Exchange was set up by the Chicago Board of Trade).

In order to understand how a clearinghouse operates, consider the futures market for wheat. Assume that on the first day of trading in July wheat, buyer *B* agrees to purchase 5,000 bushels (one contract) from seller *S* for $4 per bushel or $20,000 in total (actually, what happens is that a floor broker working for *B*'s brokerage firm and a floor broker working for *S*'s brokerage firm meet in the wheat pit and agree on a price). In this situation, *B* might believe that the price of wheat is going to rise while *S* might believe it is going to fall.

After *B* and *S* reach their agreement, the clearinghouse will immediately step in and break the transaction apart. That is, *B* and *S* no longer deal directly with each other. Now it is the obligation of the clearinghouse to deliver the wheat to *B* and to accept delivery from *S*. At this point, there is an open interest of one contract (5,000 bushels) in July wheat, since only one contract exists at this time (technically there are two, since the clearinghouse has separate contracts with *B* and *S*). Figure 25-2 summarizes the creation of this contract.

It is important to realize that if nothing else is done at this point, the clearinghouse is in a potentially risky position. For example, if the price of wheat rises to $5 per bushel by July, what happens if *S* does not deliver the wheat? The clearinghouse would have to buy the wheat on the spot market for $25,000 (= 5,000 × $5), and then deliver it to *B*. Because the clearinghouse will receive the selling price of $20,000 (= 5,000 × $4) from *B* in return, it will have lost $5,000. While the clearinghouse has a claim on *S* for the $5,000, it faces protracted legal battles in trying to recover this amount, and may end up with little or nothing from *S*.

Alternatively, if the price of wheat falls to $3 per bushel by July, then *B* will be paying $20,000 for delivery of wheat that is only worth $15,000 (= 5,000 × $3) on the spot market. What happens if *B* refuses to make payment? In this case, the clearinghouse will not deliver the wheat that it received from *S*. Instead, it will have to sell the wheat for $15,000 on the spot

FIGURE 25-2
Creating a Futures Contract

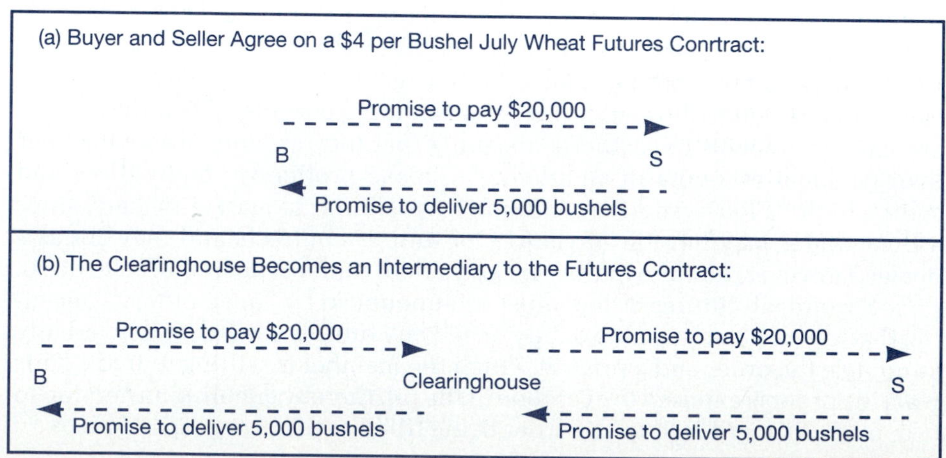

market. Since the clearinghouse paid S $20,000 for the wheat, it has lost $5,000. Again, while the clearinghouse has a claim on *B* for the $5,000, it may end up with little or nothing from *B*.

The procedures that protect the clearinghouse from such potential losses involve having brokers (1) impose initial margin requirements on both buyers and sellers; (2) mark to market the accounts of buyers and sellers every day; and (3) impose daily maintenance margin requirements on both buyers and sellers.

Initial Margin In order to buy and sell futures, an investor must open a commodity account with a brokerage firm. This type of account must be kept separate from other accounts (such as a cash account or a margin account) that the investor might have. Whenever a futures contract is signed, both buyer and seller are required to post initial margin. That is, both buyer and seller are required to make security deposits that are intended to guarantee that they will in fact be able to fulfill their obligations; accordingly, initial margin is often referred to as **performance margin.** The amount of this margin is roughly 5% to 15% of the total purchase price of the futures contract. However, it is often stated as a given dollar amount regardless of the purchase price.[4]

performance margin

For example, a July wheat futures contract for 5,000 bushels at $4 per bushel would have a total purchase price of $20,000 (= 5,000 × $4). With a 5% initial margin requirement, buyer *B* and seller *S* would each have to make a deposit of $1,000 (= .05 × $20,000). This deposit can be made in the form of either cash, cash equivalents (such as Treasury bills), or a bank line of credit, and forms the equity in the account on the first day.

While initial margin provides some protection to the clearinghouse, it does not provide complete protection. As indicated earlier, if the futures price of wheat rises to $5 per bushel by July, the clearinghouse faces a potential loss of $5,000, only $1,000 of which can be quickly recovered owing to the margin deposit. This is where the use of marking to market, coupled with a maintenance margin requirement, provides the requisite amount of additional protection.

Marking to Market In order to understand marking to market, the previous example, where *B* and *S* were, respectively, a buyer and a seller of a 5,000-bushel wheat futures contract at $4 per bushel, will be continued. Assume now that on the second day of trading the settlement price of July wheat is $4.10 per bushel. In this situation, *S* has "lost" $500 owing to the rise in the price of wheat from $4 to $4.10 per bushel, while *B* has "made" $500. Thus, the equity in the account of *S* is reduced by $500 and the equity in the account of *B* is increased by $500. Since the initial equity was equal to the initial margin requirement of $1,000, this means that *S* has equity of $500 while *B* has equity of $1,500. This process of adjusting the equity in an investor's commodity account in order to reflect the change in the settlement price of the futures contract is known as **marking to market.** It should also be noted that as part of the marking-to-market process, the clearinghouse every day replaces each existing futures contract with a new one that has the

marking to market

[4]Since Black Monday and Terrible Tuesday (October 19–20, 1987), a number of people have advocated an increase in the size of the initial margin deposit for certain futures contracts (particularly stock index futures, which will be discussed later). The levels of initial and maintenance margins are set by each exchange, with brokers being allowed to set them higher. Typically higher amounts of margin are required on futures contracts that have greater price volatility since the clearinghouse faces larger potential losses on such contracts.

settlement price as reported in the financial press as the purchase price in the new contract.

In general, the equity in either a buyer or seller's commodity account is (1) the sum of the initial margin deposit, and (2) the sum of all daily gains, less losses, on open positions in futures. Since the amount of the gains (less losses) changes every day, the amount of equity changes every day.

In the example, if the settlement price of the July wheat futures contract had fallen to $3.95 per bushel the third day (that is, the day after rising to $4.10), then *B* would have "lost" $750 [= 5,000 × ($4.10 − $3.95)] while *S* would have "made" $750 on that day. When their accounts are marked to market at the end of the day, the equity in *B*'s account would have dropped from $1,500 to $750, while *S*'s equity would have risen from $500 to $1,250.

Maintenance Margin Another key concept is the requirement of maintenance margin. According to this requirement, the investor must keep the commodity account's equity equal to or greater than a certain percentage of the amount deposited as initial margin. Since this percentage is roughly 65%, the investor must have equity equal to or greater than 65% of the initial margin. If this requirement is not met, the investor will receive a margin call from his or her broker. This call is a request for an additional deposit of cash (nothing else can be deposited for this purpose) known as **variation margin** to bring the equity up to the initial margin level. If the investor does not (or cannot) respond, then the broker will close out the investor's position by entering a reversing trade in the investor's account.

variation margin

For example, reconsider investors *B* and *S*, who had, respectively, bought and sold a July wheat futures contract at $4 per bushel; each investor had made a deposit of $1,000 in order to meet the initial margin requirement. The next day, the price of the wheat futures contract rose to $4.10 per bushel, or $20,500. Thus, the equity of *B* had increased to $1,500 while the equity of *S* had decreased to $500. If the maintenance margin requirement is 65% of initial margin, both *B* and *S* are required to have equity of at least $650 (= .65 × $1,000) in their accounts every day. Since the actual level of equity for *B* clearly exceeds this amount, *B* does not need to do anything. Indeed, *B* may withdraw an amount of cash equal to the amount by which the equity exceeds the initial margin; in this example, *B* can withdraw cash of $500.

However, *S* is undermargined, and will be asked to make a cash deposit of at least $500, since this would increase the equity from $500 to $1,000, the level of the initial margin. In the event that *S* refuses to make this deposit, the broker will enter a reversing trade for *S* by purchasing a July wheat futures contract. The result is that *S* will simply receive an amount of money approximately equal to the account's equity, $500, and the account will be closed. Since *S* initially deposited $1,000, this represents a personal loss of $500.

On the third day the price of the July wheat futures contract is assumed to settle at $3.95 per bushel, representing a $750 loss for *B* and a $750 gain for *S* (see Figure 25-3). As a consequence, *B* is now undermargined, and will be asked to deposit $750 so that the equity in *B*'s account is $1,000. Conversely, *S* can withdraw $750, as the equity in *S*'s account is over the $1,000 initial margin requirement by this amount.

Reversing Trades Suppose that on the next day, *B* finds that people are paying $4.15 per bushel for July wheat. This represents daily profit to *B* of $.20 per bushel, since the price was $3.95 the previous day. If *B* believes that the

FIGURE 25-3
Margin Requirements for a Futures Contract

			Buyer *B*		Seller *S*	
DAY	PRICE OF WHEAT	EVENT	AMOUNT	EQUITY IN ACCOUNT	AMOUNT	EQUITY IN ACCOUNT
(a) If Maintenance Margin Were Not Required:						
1	$4	Deposit initial margin	$ 1,000	$1,000	$ 1,000	$1,000
2	$4.10	Mark to market	+500	1,500	−500	500
3	$3.95	Mark to market	−750	750	+750	1,250
4	$4.15	Mark to market	1,000	1,750	−1,000	250
(b) With Required Maintenance Margin:						
1	$4	Deposit initial margin	$ 1,000	$1,000	$ 1,000	$1,000
2	$4.10	Mark to market:	+500	1,500	−500	500
		Buyer withdraws cash	−500	1,000	—	—
		Seller deposits cash	—	—	+500	1,000
3	$3.95	Mark to market:	−750	250	+750	1,750
		Buyer deposits cash	+750	1,000		
		Seller withdraws cash	—	—	−750	1,000
4	$4.15	Mark to market:	+1,000	2,000	−1,000	0
		Reversing trade and withdrawal of cash	−2,000	0	—	—

price of July wheat will not go any higher, then *B* might sell a July wheat futures contract for $4.15 to someone else. (Conversely, *S* might buy a July wheat futures contract, since S's equity has been reduced to zero.) In this situation, *B* has made a reversing trade, since *B* now has offsetting positions with respect to July wheat (equivalently, *B* is said to have unwound or closed out his or her position in July wheat).

At this point, the benefit to *B* of having a clearinghouse involved can be seen. Nominally, *B* is obligated to deliver 5,000 bushels of wheat to the clearinghouse in July, which is in turn obligated to deliver it back to *B*. Why? Because *B* is involved in two July wheat contracts, one as a seller and one as a buyer. However, the clearinghouse will note that *B* has offsetting positions in July wheat, and will immediately cancel both of them. Furthermore, once the reversing trade has been made, *B* will be able to withdraw $2,000, consisting of (1) the initial margin of $1,000; (2) a variation margin deposit owing to the daily marking to market of $250; and (3) the $750 [= 5,000 × ($4.15 − $4)] profit that has been made. Figure 25-3 illustrates the effect these events have had on the equity in the account of *B* (and S).

In effect, a futures contract is replaced every day by (1) adjusting the equity in the investor's commodity account, and (2) drawing up a new contract that has a purchase price equal to the current settlement price. This daily marking-to-market procedure, coupled with margin requirements, results in the clearinghouse always having a security deposit of sufficient size to protect it from losses owing to the actions of the individual investors.[5]

These rather complex arrangements make it possible for futures traders

[5]Actually, only brokerage firms belong to a clearinghouse, and it is *their* accounts that are settled by the clearinghouse at the end of every day. Each brokerage firm acts in turn as a clearinghouse for its own clients. For more information on clearing procedures, see Chapter 6 of the *Commodity Trading Manual.*

to think in very simple terms. In the example, *B* bought a contract of July wheat at $4 and sold it on day four for $4.15, making a profit of $.15 per bushel. If S, having initially sold a contract of July wheat at $4, later made a reversing trade for $4.25, then S's position can also be thought of in simple terms—specifically, S sold July wheat for $4 and later bought it back for $4.25, suffering a loss of $.25 per bushel in the process.

Futures Positions

In the previous example, *B* was the person who initially bought a July wheat futures contract. Accordingly, *B* now has a long position and is said to be *long* one contract of July wheat. In contrast, S, having initially sold a July wheat futures contract, has a short position, and is said to be *short* one contract of July wheat.

The process of marking to market every day means that changes in the settlement price are realized as soon as they occur. When the settlement price *rises*, those with long positions realize *profits* equal to the change and those who are short realize *losses*. When the settlement price *falls*, those with long positions realize *losses*, while those with short positions realize *profits*. In either event, total profits always equal total losses. Thus, either the buyer gains and the seller loses, or the seller gains and the buyer loses, since both parties are involved in a "zero-sum game" (as was also the case with buyers and writers of options, discussed in Chapter 24).

Taxation

Earlier, it was mentioned that there are two types of people who deal in futures—speculators and hedgers. These two types of investors are treated differently by the Internal Revenue Service.

A speculator in futures is considered to have a capital asset for tax purposes, whether he or she is long or short. When the position is closed out, the resultant profit or loss is treated as a capital gain or loss, and is taxed accordingly. In comparison, since a hedger has dealt in futures as part of normal business activities, the resulting profit or loss is generally viewed as ordinary income or loss for the business, and is taxed accordingly.

Open Interest

When trading is first allowed in a contract, there is no open interest since no contracts are outstanding. Subsequently, as people begin to make transactions, the open interest grows. At any time, open interest equals the amount that those with short positions (the sellers) are currently obligated to deliver. It also equals the amount that those with long positions (the buyers) are obligated to receive.

Open interest figures are typically shown with futures prices in the financial press. For example, Figure 25-1 indicates that on July 15, 1992, a total of 123,489 contracts in December 1992 corn were outstanding on the Chicago Board of Trade (CBT). Note the substantial differences in the open interest figures for the other corn contracts on the Chicago Board of Trade on that day. This is quite typical. Figure 25-4 shows why. Open interest in a wheat contract is shown for every month from the preceding January until the contract expired at the end of the delivery month, December. From January until the end of September, more trades were generally made to open new positions than to reverse old ones, and open interest continued to increase. As

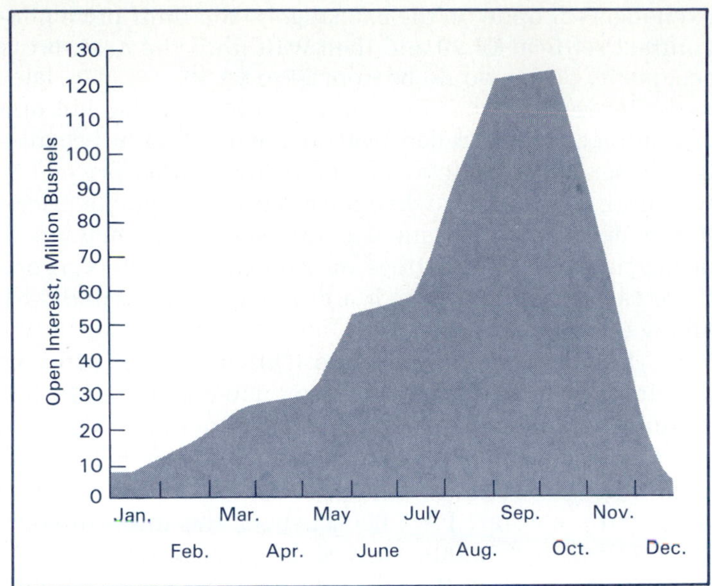

FIGURE 25-4
Open Interest, December 1978, Chicago Board of Trade Wheat Contract: January 3, 1978 Through December 28, 1978

the delivery month came closer, reversing trades began to outnumber those intended to open new positions, and the open interest began to decline. The amount remaining at the beginning of December was the maximum number of bushels of wheat that could have been delivered against futures contracts at that time, but most of these contracts were also settled by reversing trades instead of delivery.

Relatively few futures positions—less than 3% of the total—end in actual delivery of the asset involved.[6] However, the fact that delivery is a possibility makes a contract's value in the delivery month differ only slightly, if at all, from the spot price (that is, the current market price) of the asset.

If not reversed, most futures contracts require delivery of the corresponding asset. Notable exceptions are market index futures, since they do not require delivery of the set of securities comprising the corresponding index. Instead, an amount equal to the difference between the level of the index and the purchase price must be paid *in cash* on the delivery date. Nevertheless, similar to other types of futures, most positions in market index futures are closed out with reversing trades prior to the date at which delivery (in cash) is required.

Price Limits

Commodity Futures Trading Commission

The futures exchanges, subject to approval by the **Commodity Futures Trading Commission** (CFTC), place dollar limits on the extent to which futures prices are allowed to vary from day to day. For example, if July wheat closed at $4 on the previous day and the daily price limit is $.20, then on the following day contracts at prices outside the range from $3.80 to $4.20 would not be allowed to be traded on the exchange. If a major piece of news during the day led traders to consider $4.25 a reasonable price for the contract, they would have to either (1) trade privately, forgoing the advantages offered by the

[6]Merrill Lynch, Pierce, Fenner & Smith, Inc., *Speculating on Inflation: Futures Trading in Interest Rates, Foreign Currencies and Precious Metals*, July 1979.

exchange; (2) trade on the exchange at the limit price of \$4.20; or (3) let the contract settle at \$4.20 and then wait until the next day, when the range of acceptable prices would be from \$4 to \$4.40.

One result of the "limit move" to \$4.20 is that it is entirely possible that no contracts will be traded at all on that day. This is because nobody will want to sell these wheat contracts for a below-market price of \$4.20, preferring to wait until the next day when the range of acceptable prices is raised. Indeed, if the news is important enough (such as a massive freeze in Florida, destroying many orange trees and dramatically affecting orange juice futures), there can be limit moves for a number of successive days, with no trading taking place for several days.

The futures exchanges impose price limits on futures because of a belief that traders may overract to major news and should be "protected" from voluntarily entering into agreements under such conditions. Interestingly, initial margins are usually set at an amount that is roughly equal to the price limit times the size of the contract. In the case of wheat having a \$.20 price limit and a contract for 5,000 bushels, the initial margin is usually about \$1,000 (= \$.20 × 5,000). Thus, if the price of wheat moves the limit against the investor, no more than the initial margin of \$1,000 will be lost on the day of the adverse limit move. In a sense, the price limit has "protected" the investor (and the clearinghouse) from losing more than \$1,000 on that day. However, it is possible that the investor cannot enter a reversing trade as soon as prices have moved the limit, meaning that much larger losses can be incurred later (as in the case of the Florida freeze and orange juice futures).

BASIS

basis

The difference between the current spot price on an asset (that is, the price of the asset for immediate delivery) and the corresponding futures price (that is, the purchase price stated in the futures contract) is known as the **basis** for the futures:

$$\text{basis} = \text{current spot price} - \text{futures price}. \tag{25.1}$$

A person with a short position in a futures contract and a long position in the deliverable asset (meaning that he or she owns the asset) will profit if the basis is positive and widens (or is negative and narrows). This is because the futures price will be falling or the spot price will be rising (or both); a falling futures price benefits those who are short futures and a rising spot price benefits those who own the asset. Using the same type of reasoning, it can be shown that this person will lose if the basis is positive and narrows (or is negative and widens).

As an example, consider the situation previously discussed where the July futures price of wheat was \$4 per bushel and the contract was for 5,000 bushels. Assuming that the current spot price of wheat is \$4.30 per bushel, the basis is +\$.30 = \$4.30 − \$4.00. Now imagine that the basis widens by \$.10 to \$.40 owing to the futures price falling to \$3.95 and the spot price rising to \$4.35 (note that other combinations of price movements could cause the \$.10 widening of the basis). A person who has a short position in one futures contract and a long position of 5,000 bushels of wheat will make a profit of \$500 = \$.10 × 5,000 bushels. This is because he or she gains on both the short position in the futures contract owing to the \$.05 fall in the futures price and the long position in the asset itself owing to the \$.05 rise in its spot price.

However, if the basis narrows by $.10 to $.20, then the person will have a loss of $500 = $.10 × 5,000 bushels. Perhaps the narrowing resulted from a $.05 rise in the futures price, causing a $250 loss on the person's short position, and a $.05 fall in the spot price, which caused a $250 loss on his or her long position.

Note that if the $.30 basis was negative because of the spot price being $3.70 and it subsequently widened by $.10 to −$.40, then the person would have a loss of $500 = $.10 × 5,000 bushels. However, if it narrowed by $.10 to −$.20, then he or she would have a gain of $500. Hence, the person gains if the basis is positive and widens or is negative and narrows, but loses if the basis is positive and narrows or is negative and widens:

	LONG IN SPOT MARKET, SHORT IN FUTURES MARKET	
	POSITIVE BASIS	NEGATIVE BASIS
Basis Widens	Gain	Loss
Basis Narrows	Loss	Gain

Conversely, a person with a long position in a futures contract and a short position in the deliverable asset (meaning that he or she has borrowed the asset and sold it, and now has an obligation to buy the asset in order to repay the loan or has contracted to purchase it at a fixed price) will profit if the basis is positive and narrows (or is negative and widens). However, a loss would be incurred if a positive basis widened (or a negative basis narrowed):

	SHORT IN SPOT MARKET, LONG IN FUTURES MARKET	
	POSITIVE BASIS	NEGATIVE BASIS
Basis Widens	Loss	Gain
Basis Narrows	Gain	Loss

The risk of the basis narrowing or widening, causing gains or losses to these people, is known as **basis risk.** The only type of uncertainty they face concerns the difference between the spot price of the deliverable asset and the price of the futures contract. Such a person is said to be *speculating on the basis.*[7]

basis risk

SPREADS

It is quite possible to take a long position in a futures contract and a short position in another futures contract in the same asset, but with a different delivery date. The person who does this is speculating on changes in the difference between the prices of the two contracts, a difference that constitutes the "basis" for this particular hedge.

Others attempt to profit from temporary imbalances among the prices of

[7]Typically, the basis narrows over time until it equals zero on the delivery date. For more on the relationship between spot and futures prices as reflected in the basis, see the *Commodity Trading Manual*, Chapter 8. It should be noted that sometimes basis is defined as the futures price less the current spot price—the reverse of what is shown in equation (25.1).

futures contracts on different but related assets. For example, one might take a long position in soybeans along with a short position in an item produced from soybeans, such as soybean meal. Another possibility involves a position in wheat with an offsetting position in corn, which serves as a substitute for wheat in many applications.

Such people are known as *spreaders* and, like those who speculate on the basis, they reduce or eliminate the risk associated with general price moves. Instead, they take on the risk associated with changes in price *differences* in the hope that their alleged superior knowledge will enable them to consistently make profits from such changes.

RETURNS ON FUTURES

During the period from 1950 through 1976, a portfolio made up of unlevered positions in twenty-three different futures contracts was compared with a diversified portfolio of common stocks.[8] The average rate of return and risk level of the two portfolios were found to be of similar magnitude:

PORTFOLIO	AVERAGE ANNUAL RETURN	STANDARD DEVIATION
Futures	13.83%	22.43%
Common stocks	13.05	18.95

Given these results, an investor might view the two alternatives as equally desirable. Better yet, during the period from 1950 to 1976, a combination of the two portfolios was found to be more desirable than either portfolio by itself. This resulted from the fact that the returns of futures and stock portfolios were negatively correlated, suggesting that the return on a combined portfolio would have had considerably less variation than either one separately. Specifically, the correlation coefficient was found to equal −.24, resulting in the following standard deviations for portfolios with different combinations:

PERCENT IN STOCKS	PERCENT IN FUTURES	STANDARD DEVIATION	AVERAGE ANNUAL RETURN
0%	100%	22.43%	13.83%
20	80	17.43	13.67
40	60	13.77	13.52
60	40	12.68	13.36
80	20	14.74	13.21
100	0	18.95	13.05

[8]The futures contracts consisted of agricultural goods and natural resources; see Zvi Bodie and Victor Rosansky, "Risk and Return in Commodity Futures," *Financial Analysts Journal*, 36, no. 3 (May/June 1980): 27–39. Similar conclusions were reached when the period from 1978 to 1981 was examined. See Cheng F. Lee, Raymond M. Leuthold, and Jean E. Cordier, "The Stock Market and the Commodity Futures Market: Diversification and Arbitrage Potential," *Financial Analysts Journal*, 41, no. 4 (July/August 1985): 53–60.

While there was little difference in the level of the average return for the various portfolios, there was a noticeable change in the level of risk. In particular, the portfolio with 60% in stocks and 40% in futures seems to have had much less risk than the others.

Also of interest was the observation that futures have been found to be at least a partial hedge against inflation. During the period from 1950 to 1976, the returns on the portfolio of twenty-three futures were positively correlated with changes in the Consumer Price Index, having a correlation coefficient of .58. In contrast, the returns on the portfolio of common stocks were negatively correlated with changes in the Consumer Price Index, having a correlation coefficient of −.43.

At this point it is appropriate to discuss the pricing of futures contracts. Specifically, what is the relationship between the futures price and investors' expectations of what the spot price will be on the delivery date? And what is the relationship between the futures price and the current spot price of the deliverable asset? The next two sections explore these relationships and provide some answers to the questions.

FUTURES PRICES AND EXPECTED SPOT PRICES

Certainty

If future spot prices could be predicted with certainty, there would be no reason for anyone to be either a buyer or a seller of a futures contract. To understand why, imagine what a futures contract would look like in a world of certainty. First, the purchase price of the futures contract would simply equal the (perfectly predictable) expected spot price on the delivery date. This means that neither buyers nor sellers would be able to make profits from the existence of futures. Second, the purchase price would not change as the delivery date got closer.[9] Finally, no margin would be necessary because there would not be any unexpected "adverse" price movements.

Uncertainty

While it is useful to know something about the way in which futures prices and expected spot prices are related to each other in a world of certainty where forecasting is done with complete accuracy, the real world is uncertain. Given this, how are futures prices related to expected spot prices? While there are several possible explanations, no definitive answer has been provided.

expectations hypothesis

Expectations Hypothesis One possible explanation is given by the **expectations hypothesis:** The current purchase price of a futures contract equals the market consensus expectation of the spot price on the delivery date. In symbols:

$$P_f = \overline{P}_s$$

[9]These first two points do not mean that the current spot price will not change as time passes. For futures involving a seasonal commodity (like wheat), the spot price will sometimes be greater than and sometimes be less than the futures price during the life of the contract. Furthermore, sometimes a futures contract involving a more distant delivery date will sell for more than one with a nearer delivery date, while at other times it will sell for less.

where P_f is the current purchase price of the futures contract and $\overline{P}_s$ is the expected spot price of the asset on the delivery date. Thus, if a July wheat futures contract is currently selling for \$4 per bushel, then it can be inferred that the consensus opinion is that in July the spot price of wheat will be \$4.

If the expectations hypothesis is correct, a speculator should not expect to either win or lose from a position in the futures market, be it long or short. Neglecting margin requirements, a speculator who takes a long position in futures agrees to pay P_f at the delivery date for an asset that is expected to be worth $\overline{P}_s$ at that time. Thus, the long speculator's expected profit is $\overline{P}_s - P_f$, which is equal to zero. Conversely, a speculator with a short position will have sold an asset at a price of P_f and will expect to enter a reversing trade at $\overline{P}_s$ on the delivery date. Thus, the short speculator's expected profit is $P_f - \overline{P}_s$, which is equal to zero.

The expectations hypothesis is often defended on the grounds that speculators are indifferent to risk and are thus happy to accommodate hedgers without any compensation in the form of the risk premium. The reason for their indifference has to do with the belief that the impact of a specific futures position on the risk of a diversified portfolio that includes many types of assets will be very small. Thus, speculators holding diversified portfolios may be willing to take over some risk from hedgers with little (if any) compensation in the form of a risk premium.

Figure 25-5 shows the pattern of futures prices implied by the expectations hypothesis, given that the expected spot price $\overline{P}_s$ does not change during the life of the contract.

Normal Backwardation John Maynard Keynes felt that the expectations hypothesis did not correctly explain futures prices.[10] He argued that, on balance, hedgers will want to be short in futures, and therefore they will have to entice the speculators to be long in futures. Since there are risks associated with being long, Keynes hypothesized that the hedgers would have to entice

[10]J. M. Keynes, *Treatise on Money*, vol. 2 (London: Macmillan, 1930), 142–44.

FIGURE 25-5
Price of a Futures Contract Through Time When the Spot Price Expected at the Time of Delivery Does Not Change

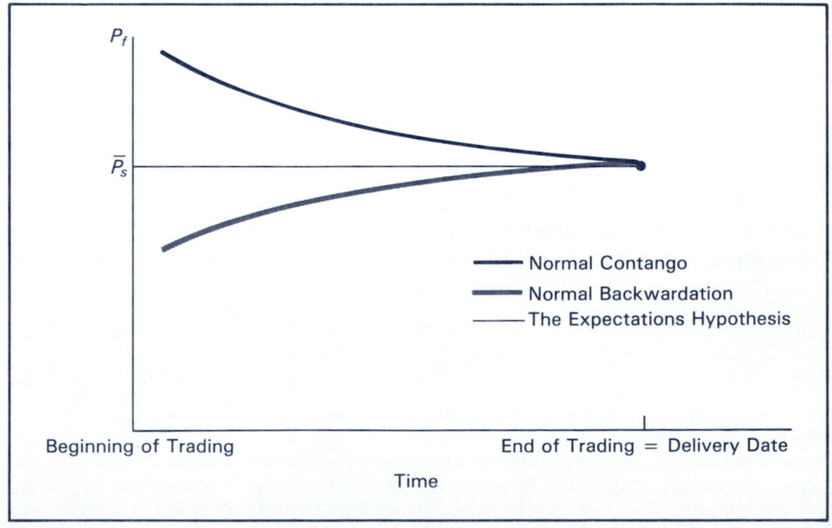

the speculators by making the expected return from a long position greater than the riskfree rate. This requires the futures price to be less than the expected spot price:

$$P_f < \overline{P}_s.$$

Thus, a speculator who bought a futures contract at a price of P_f would expect to be able to sell it on (or near) the delivery date at a higher price, $\overline{P}_s$. This relationship between the futures price and expected spot price has been referred to as **normal backwardation,** and implies that the price of a futures contract can be expected to rise during its life, as shown in Figure 25-5.

normal backwardation

Normal Contango A contrary hypothesis holds that, on balance, hedgers will want to be long in futures and therefore they will have to entice speculators to be short in futures. Since there are risks associated with being short, it can be hypothesized that the hedgers will have to entice the speculators by making the expected return from a short position greater than the riskfree rate. This requires the futures price to be greater than the expected spot price:

$$P_f > \overline{P}_s.$$

Thus, a speculator who short sold a futures contract at a price of P_f would expect to be able to buy it back on (or near) the delivery date at a lower price, $\overline{P}_s$. This relationship between the futures price and expected spot price has been referred to as **normal contango,** and implies that the price of a futures contract can be expected to fall during its life, as shown in Figure 25-5.[11]

normal contango

FUTURES PRICES AND CURRENT SPOT PRICES

The previous section discussed the relationship between the futures price associated with an asset and the expected spot price of the asset on the delivery date given in the futures contract. What about the relationship between the futures price and the current spot price of the asset? In general, they will be different, but is there some explanation for why these prices are different? Is there some model that can be used to forecast how the size of the difference will change over time? This section attempts to answer these questions.[12]

The General Model

Consider the owner of a circa-1910 Honus Wagner baseball card who is getting ready to sell the card. The owner knows that the current market price of the card is $100,000, since there are very few (reputedly fewer than five) of these cards available (one actually sold for $451,000 in 1990!). Furthermore, an investor has offered to buy it but wants to pay for it a year from now. The buyer

[11]There are other hypotheses regarding the relationship between futures prices and expected spot prices. See, for example, Paul H. Cootner, "Speculation and Hedging," Stanford University, *Food Research Institute Studies*, Supplement, 1967.

[12]This section and the next one borrow from Kenneth R. French, "Pricing Financial Futures Contracts: An Introduction," *Journal of Applied Corporate Finance*, 1, no. 4 (Winter 1989): 59–66. It ignores the apparently minor effect that daily marking to market has on the futures price that is stated in futures contracts (see p. 65 and footnotes 5 and 6 in French's paper).

is willing to take delivery of the card then, and wants to sign the contract for sale today. More specifically, he or she would like to sign a futures contract with the owner in which the delivery date is one year from now.

No Costs or Benefits of Ownership What price should the owner ask for in the futures contract? Assume that there is no risk that either party will default on the contract, and that there are no benefits (such as from showing the card) or costs (such as insurance) associated with owning the card. Given that the current one-year interest rate is 4%, the owner could sell the card today on the spot market for $100,000, put the proceeds in the bank to earn 4%, and have $104,000 in one year. Hence, the owner would not be willing to sign the futures contract for any futures price that is less than $104,000. The buyer, on the other hand, is unwilling to pay more than $104,000, since he or she could pay $100,000 now and get the card immediately but forgo $4,000 of interest that would have been earned had the $100,000 been left in the bank where it earned 4%. Since the seller wants to receive at least $104,000 and the buyer will pay no more than $104,000, they will settle at a futures price of $104,000.

To generalize, let P_s denote the current spot price of the asset (in this case, $100,000) and I denote the dollar amount of interest corresponding to the period of time from the present to the delivery date (in this case, $4,000). If P_f denotes the futures price, then:

$$P_f = P_s + I. \tag{25.2}$$

This equation shows that the futures price will be greater than the spot price by the amount of the interest that the owner forgoes by holding on to the asset, provided that there are no costs or benefits associated with ownership.

Benefits from Ownership To add a complication to the model, imagine that a baseball card exhibition will be held in twelve months, just before the delivery date. The exhibitor is willing to pay the card owner $1,000 in order to have the card displayed at the exhibition. How will this benefit of ownership affect the futures price?

As mentioned earlier, if the owner sells the card now, then he or she will receive $100,000 immediately, which could be invested right away and be worth $104,000 in twelve months. Alternatively, the owner could hold on to the card and receive the $1,000 exhibitor fee as well as the futures price. Hence the futures price must be at least $103,000 in order for the owner to be as well off financially by selling the card by means of a futures contract as by selling it immediately in the spot market. On the other side, the buyer will accept a futures price of no more than $103,000. This is because he or she could buy the card on the spot market for $100,000, thereby forgoing $4,000 of interest but receiving the $1,000 exhibitor fee. Consequently, the futures price will be $103,000, as this is the only price that is agreeable to both buyer and seller.

What if the exhibition were to be held in six months instead of one year? In that case, the owner of the card would receive the $1,000 exhibitor fee in six months and would be able to invest it risklessly at 2% for the remaining six months until the delivery date. Thus, the $1,000 in six months is equivalent to $1,020 in twelve months, and the futures price would be $102,980 = $100,000 + $4,000 − $1,020.

Let B denote the value of the benefits of ownership (sometimes known as the convenience yield of the asset) as of the delivery date (in this case, $1,020).

When such benefits are present, the futures price can be calculated as:

$$P_f = P_s + I - B. \tag{25.3}$$

This equation shows that the futures price can be greater or less than the spot price, depending upon whether the net amount of interest forgone less benefits received is positive or negative and provided that there are no costs associated with ownership of the asset.

Costs of Ownership What if the owner of the baseball card decides that it must be insured at an annual cost of $100? How will this affect the futures price? The easiest way to think of such costs of ownership as insurance and storage is to view them as the opposite of benefits of ownership. Since the benefits of ownership result in cash inflows to the owner, the costs of ownership result in cash outflows. Hence, the previously calculated futures price of $102,980 would have to be increased by the $100 cost of insurance to $103,080. If C denotes the costs of ownership (in this example, $100), then the futures price will be:

$$P_f = P_s + I - B + C. \tag{25.4}$$

The total value of interest less benefits received plus cost of ownership, $I - B + C$, is known as the **cost of carry** associated with the futures contract. Note that the futures price can be greater or less than the spot price, depending upon whether the cost of carry is positive or negative.

cost of carry

It has just been shown that the futures price will be related to the current spot price. But is this compatible with the earlier discussion of the relationship between the futures price and the expected future spot price? It is. By adjusting production and consumption over time, producers and consumers of a good can bring about an appropriate relationship between the current price and the price expected in the future. The price of a futures contract will reflect both this relationship and that implied by the current price plus the cost of carry.

FINANCIAL FUTURES

Until the 1970s, futures contracts were limited to those on agricultural goods and natural resources. Since then, financial futures, based on foreign currencies, fixed-income securities, and market indices, have been introduced on major exchanges. Indeed, in terms of trading volume, they are now far more important than both the underlying assets and traditional futures contracts. Unlike other types of futures that permit delivery any time during a given month, most financial futures have a specific delivery date (the exceptions involve some fixed-income futures).

Foreign Currency Futures

Anyone who has crossed a national border knows that there is an active spot market for foreign currency, and that the rate at which one currency can be exchanged for another varies over time. At any particular point in time, however, all such rates must be in conformance or else a riskless profit-making situation would arise. For example, it is usually possible to exchange

U.S. dollars for British pounds, then exchange the British pounds for French francs, and, finally, to exchange the French francs for dollars. If all three exchange rates were not in line, an investor might end up with more dollars at the end of this chain of transactions than at the beginning. Such an opportunity would attract large amounts of money, placing pressure on exchange rates and rapidly restoring balance. While transaction costs and certain exchange restrictions might limit the ability of people to exploit such imbalances among exchange rates, they would nevertheless force the rates into being closely lined up.

The familiar market in foreign currency, operated by banks, travel agents, and others, is in effect a spot market, since both the agreement on terms and the actual exchange of currencies occur at the same time. There are also markets for agreements involving the future delivery of foreign currency.

The largest such market is operated by banks and specialized brokers, who maintain close communications with each other throughout the world. Corporations, institutions, and some individuals deal in this market via large banks. Substantial amounts of money are involved, and every agreement is negotiated separately. Typical rates are quoted daily in the financial press, as shown in Figure 25-6. This network of large institutions is generally termed the *market for forward exchange,* since there is no marking to market. Furthermore, since the contracts are not standardized, no organized secondary market for them exists.

However, there is a market that deals in standardized futures contracts for foreign currency.[13] Procedures are similar to those used for commodity futures. For example, one of the currency futures contracts traded on the International Monetary Market (IMM) of the Chicago Mercantile Exchange requires the seller to deliver 12,500,000 Japanese yen to the buyer on a specific date for a number of U.S. dollars agreed upon in advance. Only the price of the transaction (expressed in both dollars per yen and yen per dollars) is negotiated by the parties involved; all other terms are standard. Clearing procedures allow positions to be covered by reversing trades, and few contracts result in the actual delivery of foreign currency. As shown in Figure 25-1, prices and volumes for such contracts are quoted daily in the financial press along with those for other futures.

Markets for foreign currency futures attract both hedgers and speculators. Hedgers wish to reduce or possibly eliminate the risk associated with planned future transfers of funds from one country to another.

An Example For example, an American importer might know on July 15, 1992, that he or she will have to make a payment of 50 million yen to a Japanese exporter in December of 1992. The current exchange rate is \$.007994 per yen (or, equivalently, 125.10 yen per dollar), so the anticipated dollar size of the payment is \$399,700 (= \$.007994 × 50,000,000). The risk the importer faces by simply waiting until December to make this payment is that the exchange rate will change in an unfavorable manner—perhaps rising to

[13]The prices of foreign currency forward and futures contracts appear to be quite similar. See Bradford Cornell and Marc Reinganum, "Forward and Futures Prices: Evidence from the Foreign Exchange Market," *Journal of Finance,* 36, no. 5 (December 1981): 1035–45. Their findings are challenged by Michael A. Polakoff and Paul C. Grier, "A Comparison of Foreign Exchange Forward and Futures Prices," *Journal of Banking and Finance,* 15, no. 6 (December 1991): 1057–79, but supported by Carolyn W. Chang and Jack S. K. Chang, "Forward and Futures Prices: Evidence From the Foreign Exchange Markets," *Journal of Finance,* 45, no. 4 (September 1990): 1333–36.

FIGURE 25-6
Quotations for Foreign Exchange

Source: Reprinted by permission of *The Wall Street Journal*, © Dow Jones & Company, Inc., July 16, 1992, p. C13. All rights reserved worldwide.

CURRENCY TRADING

EXCHANGE RATES

Wednesday, July 15, 1992

The New York foreign exchange selling rates below apply to trading among banks in amounts of $1 million and more, as quoted at 3 p.m. Eastern time by Bankers Trust Co., Telerate and other sources. Retail transactions provide fewer units of foreign currency per dollar.

	U.S. $ equiv.		Currency per U.S. $	
Country	Wed.	Tues.	Wed.	Tues.
Argentina (Peso)	1.01	1.01	.99	.99
Australia (Dollar)	.7439	.7482	1.3443	1.3365
Austria (Schilling)	.09587	.09577	10.43	10.44
Bahrain (Dinar)	2.6522	2.6522	.3771	.3771
Belgium (Franc)	.03273	.03271	30.55	30.57
Brazil (Cruzeiro)	.00027	.00028	3643.00	3613.00
Britain (Pound)	1.9220	1.9210	.5203	.5206
30-Day Forward	1.9110	1.9097	.5233	.5236
90-Day Forward	1.8894	1.8893	.5293	.5293
180-Day Forward	1.8600	1.8596	.5376	.5378
Canada (Dollar)	.8370	.8384	1.1948	1.1927
30-Day Forward	.8354	.8368	1.1970	1.1950
90-Day Forward	.8328	.8342	1.2007	1.1987
180-Day Forward	.8292	.8310	1.2060	1.2034
Czechoslovakia (Koruna)				
Commercial rate	.0372301	.0372578	26.8600	26.8400
Chile (Peso)	.002864	.002860	349.20	349.71
China (Renminbi)	.182815	.182815	5.4700	5.4700
Colombia (Peso)	.001722	.001722	580.64	580.64
Denmark (Krone)	.1752	.1750	5.7065	5.7135
Ecuador (Sucre)				
Floating rate	.000698	.000698	1433.01	1433.01
Finland (Markka)	.24643	.24606	4.0580	4.0640
France (Franc)	.19980	.19966	5.0050	5.0085
30-Day Forward	.19862	.19843	5.0347	5.0395
90-Day Forward	.19629	.19619	5.0944	5.0970
180-Day Forward	.19317	.19302	5.1767	5.1808
Germany (Mark)	.6752	.6741	1.4810	1.4835
30-Day Forward	.6715	.6703	1.4892	1.4919
90-Day Forward	.6641	.6633	1.5057	1.5076
180-Day Forward	.6542	.6531	1.5286	1.5311
Greece (Drachma)	.005491	.005485	182.10	182.30
Hong Kong (Dollar)	.12933	.12935	7.7323	7.7310
Hungary (Forint)	.0131700	.0131839	75.9300	75.8500
India (Rupee)	.03545	.03545	28.21	28.21
Indonesia (Rupiah)	.0004938	.0004938	2025.11	2025.11
Ireland (Punt)	1.7982	1.7958	.5561	.5569
Israel (Shekel)	.4180	.4202	2.3925	2.3799
Italy (Lira)	.0008870	.0008892	1127.34	1124.57
Japan (Yen)	.007994	.007987	125.10	125.20
30-Day Forward	.007985	.007979	125.23	125.33
90-Day Forward	.007973	.007969	125.43	125.49
180-Day Forward	.007964	.007961	125.56	125.61
Jordan (Dinar)	1.5298	1.5298	.6537	.6537
Kuwait (Dinar)	3.4662	3.4662	.2885	.2885
Lebanon (Pound)	.000570	.000570	1755.00	1755.00
Malaysia (Ringgit)	.4002	.4004	2.4985	2.4975
Malta (Lira)	3.3727	3.3727	.2965	.2965
Mexico (Peso)				
Floating rate	.0003210	.0003210	3115.00	3115.00
Netherland (Guilder)	.5986	.5978	1.6705	1.6728
New Zealand (Dollar)	.5457	.5480	1.8325	1.8248
Norway (Krone)	.1716	.1716	5.8280	5.8285
Pakistan (Rupee)	.0400	.0400	25.00	25.00
Peru (New Sol)	.8322	.8322	1.20	1.20
Philippines (Peso)	.04082	.04082	24.50	24.50
Poland (Zloty)	.00007769	.00007772	12871.01	12867.03
Portugal (Escudo)	.007913	.007917	126.37	126.31
Saudi Arabia (Riyal)	.26738	.26738	3.7400	3.7400
Singapore (Dollar)	.6207	.6202	1.6110	1.6125
South Africa (Rand)				
Commercial rate	.3639	.3640	2.7483	2.7473
Financial rate	.2591	.2551	3.8600	3.9200
South Korea (Won)	.0012705	.0012705	787.10	787.10
Spain (Peseta)	.010575	.010587	94.56	94.45
Sweden (Krona)	.1857	.1857	5.3840	5.3840
Switzerland (Franc)	.7471	.7457	1.3385	1.3410
30-Day Forward	.7437	.7422	1.3447	1.3474
90-Day Forward	.7367	.7357	1.3574	1.3593
180-Day Forward	.7271	.7258	1.3753	1.3778
Taiwan (Dollar)	.040900	.040750	24.45	24.54
Thailand (Baht)	.03957	.03957	25.27	25.27
Turkey (Lira)	.0001462	.0001473	6838.00	6788.00
United Arab (Dirham)	.2723	.2723	3.6725	3.6725
Uruguay (New Peso)				
Financial	.000314	.000314	3185.01	3185.01
Venezuela (Bolivar)				
Floating rate	.01512	.01512	66.14	66.14
SDR	1.44695	1.44753	.69111	.69083
ECU	1.37580	1.37510	....	....

Special Drawing Rights (SDR) are based on exchange rates for the U.S., German, British, French and Japanese currencies. Source: International Monetary Fund.

European Currency Unit (ECU) is based on a basket of community currencies.

$.0090 per yen, in which case the dollar cost to the importer will have risen to $450,000 (= $.0090 × 50,000,000). The importer can hedge this risk by purchasing four December futures contracts for yen. Figure 25-1 indicates that the settlement price on July 15, 1992, for these contracts was $.007966, meaning that the dollar cost of one contract is $398,300 (= $.007966 × 50,000,000). Thus, the importer can remove the risk of the yen appreciating against the dollar before the payment date and at the same time save $1,400 (= $399,700 − $398,300) by purchasing the four yen futures contracts.

Speculators are attracted to the foreign currency futures market when they believe that the current price of the futures contract is substantially different from what they expect the spot rate to be on the delivery date.

For example, a speculator might believe that the price of the December futures contract for Japanese yen is too high. Perhaps a speculator might believe that when December comes around, the exchange rate will be $.0075 per yen (or, equivalently, 133.33 yen per dollar). By selling (that is, shorting) a December futures contract for yen, the speculator will be selling yen for \$.007966, the settlement price on July 15, 1992. At the time delivery has to be made, the speculator believes that yen can be bought on the spot market for \$.0075, thereby allowing a profit to be made on the difference between the selling and buying prices.[14] Specifically, the speculator expects to be able to make a profit of \$5,825 [= (\$.007966 − \$.0075) × 12,500,000)] per futures contract.

interest rate parity

Pricing Futures contracts involving foreign currencies are priced according to the notion of **interest rate parity,** which is just a special application of the model of futures pricing given in equation (25.4).

Imagine that it is December 1992 and you are planning to invest some money for one year. You could simply invest in a one-year U.S. riskfree security and then receive the principal and interest a year later in the form of U.S. dollars. Alternatively, you could exchange the dollars for German marks and use the marks to buy a one-year German riskfree security. In addition, you would short the requisite number of one-year German mark futures contracts so that a year later, when you receive the principal and interest in the form of German marks, you would know exactly how many U.S. dollars you would receive for them.

Both of these strategies—invest in U.S. riskfree securities or invest in German riskfree securities—have no risk associated with them in that you know exactly how many U.S. dollars they will yield after one year. If the German strategy had a lower cost, Americans would not buy the U.S. riskfree securities since they could earn the same amount for a smaller investment by buying the German riskfree securities. Similarly, if the U.S. strategy had a lower cost, Germans would not buy the German riskfree securities since they could earn the same amount for a smaller investment by buying U.S. dollars in the spot market, purchasing U.S. riskfree securities, and buying a one-year German mark futures contract. As a consequence, in equilibrium the two strategies must have the same cost if they have the same dollar payoffs.

Consider what would happen per dollar invested. The strategy of investing \$1 in a U.S. riskfree security that has a return of R_{US} will provide a cash inflow of $\$1(1 + R_{US})$ after one year. The strategy of investing \$1 in a German riskfree security that has a return of R_G where the current spot rate of exchange is P_s and the futures price is P_f will provide a dollar cash inflow of $(\$1/P_s)(1 + R_G)P_f$ after one year. (Here both P_s and P_f are stated in dollars per mark.) Given that these two strategies cost the same (\$1), their payoffs must be equal:

$$\$1(1 + R_{US}) = (\$1/P_s)(1 + R_G)P_f. \tag{25.5}$$

Hence the futures price of the mark can be determined by rewriting equation (25.5) as the interest rate parity equation:

$$P_f = P_s\,(1 + R_{US})/(1 + R_G). \tag{25.6}$$

[14]Actually the typical speculator will plan to realize this profit by entering a reversing trade instead of buying yen on the spot market and then making delivery. Similarly, the previously mentioned hedging importer will typically plan to enter a reversing trade.

Thus, if the current spot rate of exchange for the German mark is \$.70, and the U.S. and German one-year riskfree rates are 4% and 5%, respectively, then the one-year futures price of the mark will be \$.6933 [= \$.70(1.04/1.05)].

In relation to equation (25.4), the cost of carry is −\$.0067 (= \$.6933 − \$.70). In the case of foreign currency, the costs of ownership (C) are zero. However, the net benefits of ownership ($I - B$) amount to the −\$.0067 cost of carry. More generally, the cost of carry, CARRY, will equal:

$$\text{CARRY} = P_S(R_{US} - R_G)/(1 + R_G) \tag{25.7}$$

for foreign currency futures where R_G now denotes the riskfree rate in the foreign currency under consideration. From equation (25.7) it can be seen that since CARRY $= I - B$, it follows that:

$$I = P_S R_{US}/(1 + R_G) \tag{25.8a}$$

$$B = P_S R_G/(1 + R_G). \tag{25.8b}$$

Hence, in the example the amount of interest forgone by the owner by selling marks in the futures market instead of the spot market (I) equals \$.0267, while the benefit of owning marks instead of selling them (B) equals \$.0333. Consequently, the cost of carry equals −\$.0067 (= \$.0267 − \$.0333), as shown earlier.

Equation (25.4) indicates that the futures price will be less than the current spot price when the cost of carry is negative. This will occur when the U.S. riskfree rate is less than the foreign riskfree rate, since the numerator on the right-hand side of equation (25.7) will be negative while the denominator is positive in such a situation. Conversely, the futures price will be greater than the current spot price when the cost of carry is positive, which will occur when the U.S. riskfree rate is greater than the foreign riskfree rate. Hence the reason why futures prices are different from spot prices is that riskfree interest rates between countries are different.

Interest Rate Futures

Futures involving fixed-income securities are often referred to as interest rate futures since their prices are greatly influenced by the current and forecasted interest rates. More specifically, their pricing can be related to the term structure of interest rates, which in turn is related to the concept of forward rates.[15]

An Example Just how the pricing of interest rate futures is related to the concept of forward rates can be illustrated with an example. Consider the futures market for 90-day Treasury bills (T-bills). As Figure 25-1 indicates, on July 15, 1992, any purchaser of a futures contract calling for delivery in March 1993 of \$1,000,000 face value of 90-day T-bills (maturing in June 1993) would have paid a settlement price of 96.54. More precisely, the seller of the contract was obligated to deliver T-bills to the buyer in March 1993 for an amount that would make the interest rate on the T-bills, stated on an annualized discount

[15]See Chapter 20 for a discussion of term structure and forward rates.

basis, equal to 3.46% per year.[16] Thus, on July 15, 1992, the forward rate on 90-day T-bills to be delivered in March 1993 was 3.46%.

As with commodity futures, neither the buyers nor the sellers of such contracts must maintain their positions until the delivery date. Reversing trades can be made at any time, and relatively few contracts result in actual delivery.

Figure 25-1 shows that on July 15, 1992, the structure of 90-day forward rates was upward sloping, ranging from 3.16% for September 1992 delivery to 3.72% for September 1993 delivery. Under the unbiased expectations hypothesis (discussed in Chapter 20), these forward rates can be interpreted to represent what investors, on average, think that spot rates will be in the future. Specifically, the 3.46% forward rate on 90-day T-bills to be delivered in March 1993 can be taken as an indication that on July 15, 1992, investors, on average, expect the interest rate on 90-day T-bills to be equal to 3.46% in March 1993. Since the interest rate that is available on July 15, 1992, on 90-day T-bills for immediate delivery is approximately 3.22%, it can be seen that investors, on average, expect interest rates to rise in the near future.

Actively traded interest rate futures involve underlying securities ranging from short term (such as 90-day Treasury bills) to intermediate term (such as 10-year Treasury notes) to long term (such as 20-year Treasury bonds). Prices are generally stated in terms of percentages of par values for the corresponding securities; yields-to-maturity (or discounts) associated with the settlement prices are also given.[17]

Pricing In general, pricing of interest rate futures contracts involves applying the cost of carry model given in equation (25.4). As an example, consider a 90-day T-bill futures contract that calls for delivery in six months. Note that nine-month T-bills will be equivalent to 90-day T-bills after six months have passed. Hence they could be delivered as the underlying assets in 90-day T-bill futures contracts where the delivery date is six months from now. What futures price is fair for these contracts?

Assume that the current market price of a nine-month T-bill is $95.24, providing a yield of 5% over the nine months (this yield and those that follow are not annualized). If the owner sold the security now, he or she would be able to risklessly earn 3% over the next six months on the proceeds. Thus, the owner should not sign a six-month futures contract where the price is less than $98.10 (= $95.24 × 1.03).

Conversely, the buyer should not agree to a price that is more than $98.10. This is because the buyer could buy the nine-month T-bill in the spot market today for $95.24 and receive $100 in nine months, or the buyer could risklessly invest the $95.24 for six months at 3% and then use the $98.10 proceeds to pay the futures price for a 90-day T-bill that pays $100 at maturity. If the futures price were greater than $98.10 (for example, $99), then the buyer would have to invest more than $95.24 today (for example, $96.12 = $99/1.03 would have to be invested today) so that the principal plus 3% interest for six

[16]The use of annualized discount-based yields introduces some errors into the analysis that are ignored here. See French, "Pricing Financial Futures Contracts," p. 62.

[17]For some interest rate futures, there is flexibility in just what the seller has to deliver, known as the *quality option*. Sometimes there is also some flexibility regarding when an intention to deliver must be announced, known as the *wild card option*.

months would be sufficient to pay the futures price after six months. In such a situation, nobody would choose to be long in the futures contract, since he or she would be better off buying a nine-month T-bill in the spot market for \$95.24 instead of investing more at 3% for six months in order to be able to pay the futures price upon delivery of the T-bill. Consequently, the futures price must be \$98.10, since this is the only price that is acceptable to both parties to the futures contract.

Generalizing, the futures price P_f must equal the spot price P_s plus the forgone interest I, just as shown in equation (25.2), since the benefits (B) and costs (C) of ownership are zero with such assets. Equivalently, letting R denote the riskfree interest rate that exists on Treasuries that mature on the delivery date, the futures price is:

$$P_f = P_s\,(1 + R). \qquad (25.9)$$

Notice that the futures price will be greater than the spot price as long as the riskfree rate R is positive. Similarly, note that the cost of carry equals:

$$\text{CARRY} = P_s R \qquad (25.10)$$

since both B and C are equal to zero. In this example, CARRY = \$2.86 (= \$95.24 × .03); note that the difference between the futures price of \$98.10 and spot price of \$95.24 equals \$2.86.

Market Index Futures

Figure 25-1 shows a set of quotations for futures contracts on two market indices. Each of these contracts involves the payment of *cash* on the delivery date of an amount equal to a *multiplier* times the difference between (1) the value of the index at the close of the last trading day of the contract and (2) the purchase price of the futures contract. If the index is above the futures price, those with short positions pay those with long positions. If the index is below the futures price, those with long positions pay those with short positions.

In practice, a clearinghouse is used, and all contracts are marked to market every day. In a sense, the delivery day differs from other days in only one respect—all open positions are marked to market for the last time and then closed.

Cash settlement provides results similar to those associated with delivery of all the securities in the index. It avoids the effort and transaction costs associated with (1) the purchase of securities by people who have taken short futures positions; (2) the delivery of these securities to people who have taken long futures positions; and (3) the subsequent sale of the securities by those who receive them.

Major Contracts Four major stock market index futures were available in 1992, with the most popular one in terms of both trading volume and open interest based on the Standard & Poor's 500 (S&P 500). This contract, along with one on the Nikkei 225 (a major Japanese index), are traded on the Index and Option Market Division of the Chicago Mercantile Exchange (CME). The two other stock index futures involve the New York Stock Exchange Composite Stock Index [traded at the New York Futures Exchange (NYFE)] and the Major Market Index (this index, when multiplied by five, closely resembles

MONEY MATTERS
Derivatives

The investment management industry is entering the brave new world of "derivative" investment instruments. Investment strategies involving these securities offer sophisticated investors the opportunity to control the risk-return characteristics of their portfolios in ways that could barely be imagined just a few years ago. However, in the hands of naive investors, derivative investments also carry the threat of expensive disappointments.

The term *derivatives* generically refers to securities such as options and futures contracts that have no intrinsic value without reference to an underlying asset or portfolio. For example, an S&P 500 index futures contract "derives" its value from its relationship with the aggregate of the 500 securities that constitute the S&P 500.

Through the use of derivatives an investor can adjust the payoff pattern of his or her portfolio. Imagine that you own a broadly diversified stock portfolio and are fearful of a stock market decline, but you do not wish to forgo the benefits of a market rise. Purchasing put options on the S&P 500 stock index with a strike price near the current market level will protect you against market declines (for a price, of course) but allow you to participate fully if the market should rise in value.

In a more complex strategy, suppose you want your derivatives investment to be self-financing. You could also sell call options on the S&P 500 with a strike price above the current market level. Properly implemented, the proceeds from the call options would pay for the cost of the put option. You are now protected against market declines and will participate in market rallies up to a point. Beyond that point you can gain no further; but remember, you were initially more concerned about a bear market than a bull market. For obvious reasons, this strategy is referred to as a "collar," as both potential losses and gains are constrained.

The two examples cited above are relatively simple derivatives strategies. Many other strategies exist, some equally simple, others much more complex. Some are created using exchange-traded derivatives; others are created virtually out of thin air using custom-designed derivatives traded over the counter, usually by large institutional investors. The critical common element behind all these strategies is that they permit an investor to take a portfolio invested in various securities and modify the level of profits and losses that the portfolio might earn and the conditions under which those profits and losses will be earned.

In essence these derivatives strategies manipulate the distribution of returns on a portfolio. For example, consider the simple purchase of a put option on the S&P 500 mentioned earlier. Assume that prior to the purchase of the put option the distribution of returns for the investor's portfolio was normal (bell-shaped), with a particular expected value and a standard deviation around that expected value. With the purchase of the put

---

the Dow Jones Industrial Average; it is traded on the Chicago Board of Trade).[18]

For all contracts but the Nikkei 225 Futures, the multiplier is $500; for the Nikkei 225, it is $5. Thus, the purchase of an S&P 500 contract when the index is 400 would cost $200,000 (= $500 × 400); the subsequent sale of this contract when the index is 420 would result in proceeds of $210,000 (= $500 × 420) and a profit of $10,000 (= $210,000 − $200,000).

A bond index futures contract has been introduced on the Chicago Board of Trade. It is based on the Municipal Bond Index (MBI), which is an index compiled by *The Bond Buyer* that consists of forty actively traded tax-exempt bonds.

Trading Volume The volume of trading in futures contracts is very large. To assess its relative size, the number of contracts can be multiplied by the total dollar value represented by one contract. As shown in Figure 25-1, the estimated volume on July 15, 1992 for S&P 500 futures was 41,019 contracts.

[18]The NYFE is a subsidiary of the New York Stock Exchange. There are other market index futures available besides these four, such as the Value Line Average Stock Index (traded on the Kansas City Board of Trade).

option, the investor has effectively truncated the portion of the portfolio's returns distributed to the left of (below) the exercise price of the put. The investor faces a distribution of returns that contains primarily "good news." Of course, the return on the portfolio is reduced by the cost of the put option. Nevertheless, by using this derivatives strategy, the investor has exercised control over the portfolio's payoff pattern.

While the many derivatives strategies applied by investors are far too numerous and diverse to describe here, we will touch on several of the most popular ones.

Covered Call Writing (Overwriting) This is one of the oldest and most popular derivatives strategies. An investor sells calls against individual stocks in his or her portfolio (or even against his or her entire portfolio). The premium obtained from this call writing provides extra income, enhancing portfolio returns if the market remains steady or declines. If stocks appreciate significantly, however, the stocks on which calls were written will be called away, limiting upside portfolio returns.

Market Exposure Adjustments Futures may be used to quickly reduce or increase market exposure without generating significant transaction costs or disturbing the composition of the investor's underlying portfolio. For example, an investor may fear a general market decline, but be satisfied with the individual stock or bond holdings in his or her portfolio. By selling futures, the investor reduces the portfolio's sensitivity to stock or bond market movements, yet will benefit if the individual security holdings perform relatively well. Further, the investor avoids the costs of selling the securities, an important consideration if they represent illiquid holdings.

Portfolio Insurance As discussed in Chapter 24, this strategy is designed to replicate a put option purchased on the investor's portfolio by appropriately increasing market exposure (by buying index futures contracts) as the portfolio rises in value and reducing exposure (by selling index futures contracts) as the portfolio declines in value. At the cost of reduced expected return, the investor protects against declines in the portfolio's value yet participates in market rallies.

Low-Risk Enhanced Equity Strategies By appropriately buying and selling options and futures contracts in different markets, investors can take advantage of small mispricings while exposing themselves to limited risk. For example, in a reasonably efficient market, the prices of an index futures contract and the underlying stocks should be linked in a specific way. To the extent that prices deviate from this linkage, arbitrage opportunities exist. One such strategy involves buying (or selling) futures contracts on a broad market index such as the S&P 500 and at the same time selling (or buying) the underlying securities in the equivalent effective dollar amounts. These "basket" trades have become quite popular in recent years, eliminating most arbitrage opportunities (as should be expected). Other, more complicated but conceptually similar low-risk strategies have taken their place as investors have moved to exploit other mispricings.

At a value of 417.20 for the lowest-priced S&P 500 contract, the total dollar value is in excess of $41{,}019 \times 417.20 \times \$500 = \$8.5$ billion! In comparison, the average daily dollar value of all trades of shares on the New York Stock Exchange during 1991 was $6.0 billion per day—a figure that is much less than the dollar size of the S&P futures on July 15, 1992. This is not unusual. On many days, the dollar value involved in trades of S&P 500 futures exceeds that of trades of individual stocks.

Hedging What accounts for the popularity of market index futures in general and the S&P 500 in particular? Simply stated, they provide relatively inexpensive and highly liquid positions similar to those obtained with diversified stock portfolios.

For example, instead of purchasing 500 stocks in anticipation of a market advance, one can invest an equivalent amount of money in Treasury bills and take a long position in S&P 500 futures. Alternatively, instead of trying to take short positions in 500 stocks in anticipation of a market decline, one can take a short position in S&P 500 futures, using Treasury bills as margin.

Another important use of market index futures involves allowing broker-dealers to hedge the market risk that is associated with the temporary positions they often take in the course of their business.[19] This hedging ultimately benefits investors by providing them with greater liquidity than they would have otherwise.

For example, consider an investor who wants to sell a large block of stock. In this situation, a broker-dealer might agree to purchase the stock immediately at an agreed-upon price, and then spend time "lining up" buyers. In the interim, however, economic news might cause the market to fall, and with it the price of the stock. This would cause the broker-dealer to experience a loss, since the broker-dealer owns the stock during the period between purchasing it from the investor and lining up the ultimate buyers. One traditional way that broker-dealers protect themselves (at least partially) from this risk is to pay the investor a relatively low price for the stock. However, the broker-dealer can now hedge this risk (at least partially) by shorting S&P 500 futures at the time the stock is bought from the investor, and reversing this position when the ultimate buyers are found.

Conversely, when an investor wants to buy a large block of stock, a broker-dealer might agree to provide it at a certain price, and then go about the task of "lining up" sellers. In the interim, however, economic news might cause the market to rise, and with it the price of the stock. This would cause the broker-dealer to experience a loss, since the price that will have to be paid to the sellers might end up being greater than the price agreed to with the investor. Traditionally, broker-dealers protect themselves from such risk by charging the investor a relatively high price for the stock. However, a broker-dealer can now hedge this risk (at least partially) by going long in S&P 500 futures at the time the investor agrees to buy the stock, and then reversing this position when the stock is ultimately bought.

Given competition among broker-dealers, the existence of S&P 500 futures will lead broker-dealers to provide higher bid prices and lower asked prices. This reduced bid-ask spread means that the existence of S&P 500 futures has provided the associated spot market for stocks with greater liquidity.

It should be pointed out that the use of S&P 500 futures in such situations does not remove all risk from the position of the broker-dealer. All it removes is market risk, since these futures contracts involve a broad market index, not an individual stock. Thus, it is possible for the broker-dealer to experience a loss even if an appropriate position has been taken in futures. Specifically, the individual stock with which the broker-dealer is involved may move up or down in price while the S&P 500 is stable, or the S&P 500 may move up or down while the individual stock is stable. In either case, the broker-dealer who has hedged with S&P 500 futures may still experience a loss. The possibility of this happening will be substantial when the broker-dealer has little diversification, with the greatest possibility associated with a one-stock portfolio.

Index Arbitrage When stock index futures were first proposed, a number of people predicted that at long last there would be an indicator of investors' expectations about the future course of the stock market. It was said that the market price of such a futures contract would indicate the consensus opinion of investors concerning the future level of the associated index. In times of optimism, the futures price might be much higher than the current level of the market, while in times of pessimism, the futures price might be much lower.

---

[19]Similarly, interest rate futures are often used by financial institutions to hedge interest rate risk to which they may be exposed. That is, when a large movement in interest rates would cause a large loss, these institutions will seek protection by either buying or selling interest rate futures.

Such predictions have since been found to be quite off the mark. This is because the price of a futures contract on an asset will not diverge too much from the spot price of the asset. Should a relatively large divergence occur, clever investors known as "arbitrageurs" can be expected to make trades designed to capture riskless (that is, "arbitrage") profits.

What effect does the presence of these arbitrageurs have on the pricing of stock index futures? Their actions will force the price of a stock index futures contract to stay close to an "appropriate" relationship with the current level of the associated index. To find out just what is meant by "appropriate," consider a hypothetical example. Today is a day in June when the Standard & Poor's 500 is at 100 and a December Standard & Poor's 500 futures contract is selling for 110. The following investment strategies will be compared:

1. Purchase the stocks in the S&P 500, hold them until December, and then sell them on the delivery date of the December S&P 500 contract.
2. Purchase a December S&P 500 futures contract along with Treasury bills that mature in December. Hold the futures contract until the delivery date in December.

Strategy 1 would cost \$100 (in "index terms") at the outset. In return, it would provide the investor with (1) an amount of money equal to the value of the S&P 500 on the delivery date, and (2) dividends on those stocks that "went ex-dividend" prior to the delivery date. That is, by denoting the level the S&P 500 will have on the delivery date as P_d and assuming that the dividend yield over the six-month time period from June to December is 3%, the investor following strategy 1 will receive in December an amount that is equal to $P_d + \$3$ [that is, $P_d + (.03 \times \$100)$].[20]

Assume that \$100 is invested in Treasury bills in strategy 2. Since Treasury bills can be used as margin on futures, the total cost of strategy 2 is \$100, which is the same as the cost of strategy 1. In return, strategy 2 would provide the investor with (1) an amount of money equal to the difference between the value of the S&P 500 and \$110 on the delivery date, and (2) the face value of the Treasury bills on the delivery date. That is, by assuming that the six-month yield on the Treasury bills is 5%, the investor following strategy 2 will receive in December an amount that is equal to $P_d - \$5$ [that is, $(P_d - \$110) + (1.05 \times \$100)$].

By design, both strategies require the same initial outlay. Furthermore, both strategies are subject to precisely the same uncertainty: the unknown level of the S&P 500 on the future delivery date, denoted P_d. However, the inflows are not equal, indicating that an opportunity exists for **index arbitrage.**[21]

index arbitrage

In this example, the way index arbitrage would work is for an investor to

[20]The 3% dividend yield is actually the accumulated December value of the dividends divided by the purchase price of the stocks. Hence the dividends might be received in three months and amount to 2.93% of the purchase price of the index. Putting them in a riskfree asset that returns 2.47% for the last three months results in a yield of 3%, or \$3 in December.

[21]Index arbitrage is one of two major forms of program trading; the other form, known as portfolio insurance, was discussed in the previous chapter. For a discussion and example of how futures can be used to procure portfolio insurance, see Stephen R. King and Eli M. Remolona, "The Pricing and Hedging of Market Index Deposits," Federal Reserve Bank of New York *Quarterly Review*, 12, no. 2 (Summer 1987): 9–20 or Thomas J. O'Brien, *How Option Replicating Portfolio Insurance Works: Expanded Details*, Monograph Series in Finance and Economics #1988-4, New York University Salomon Center, Leonard N. Stern School of Business. It should be noted that after Black Monday and Terrible Tuesday (October 19–20, 1987), there has been less use of both portfolio insurance and index arbitrage.

go "long" strategy 1 and "short" strategy 2. Why? Because strategy 1 has a higher payoff than strategy 2 (note that $P_d + \$3 > P_d - \$5$). Going long strategy 1 means that the investor is to do exactly what was indicated earlier—purchase the stocks in the S&P 500 and hold them until the December delivery date. Going short strategy 2 means to do exactly opposite of what was indicated earlier. Specifically, the investor is to short (that is, sell) a December S&P 500 futures contract and sell Treasury bills that mature in December (it is assumed that the investor has these in his or her current portfolio). The net cash outflow of going long strategy 1 and short strategy 2 is zero—$100 is spent buying the stocks in going long strategy 1, which is obtained by selling $100 worth of December Treasury bills when the investor went short strategy 2. The margin necessary for being short the futures contract is met by having purchased the underlying stocks. Thus, no additional cash needs to be committed in order to engage in index arbitrage—all that is necessary is for the investor to own Treasury bills that mature in December.

Having gone long strategy 1 and short strategy 2, consider the investor's position on the delivery date in December. First of all, the investor "bought" the individual stocks in the S&P 500 at $100 and "sold" them at $110 by being short the S&P 500 futures contract. Thus, the investor has made $10 from being long the individual stocks and short the futures on the index. Second, the investor will have received dividends totaling $3 (= .03 × $100) from owning the stocks from June to December. Third, the investor will have given up $5 (= .05 × $100) in interest that would have been earned on the December Treasury bills. This is because the investor sold $100 of these T-bills in June in order to get the requisite cash to buy the individual stocks. Overall, the investor would have increased the dollar return that would have been made on the Treasury bills by $8 (= $10 + $3 − $5). Furthermore, this increase is certain, meaning that it will be received regardless of what happens to the level of the S&P 500. Thus, by going long strategy 1 and short strategy 2 the investor will not have increased the risk of his or her portfolio, but will have increased the dollar return.

Earlier, it was mentioned that an investor going long strategy 1 would receive cash of $P_d + \$3$ in December, while an investor going long strategy 2 would receive cash of $P_d - \$5$. It can now be seen that going long strategy 1 and short strategy 2 will provide a net dollar return of $8 [that is, $(P_d + \$3) - (P_d - \$5)$], just as was shown in the previous paragraph. However, if enough investors do this, the opportunity for making the $8 profit will disappear. This is because (1) going long the individual stocks will push the prices of these stocks up, thereby raising the current level of the S&P 500 from 100, and (2) going short the S&P 500 futures will push the price of the futures down from 110. These two adjustments will continue until it is no longer profitable to go long strategy 1 and short strategy 2.

What if the price of the S&P 500 December futures contract was $90 instead of $110? The dollar return from being long strategy 1 is still equal to $P_d + \$3$. However, the dollar return from being long strategy 2 will be different. In particular, purchasing Treasury bills and the futures contract will provide the investor with a dollar return in December that is equal to $P_d + \$15$ [that is, $(P_d - \$90) + (1.05 \times \$100)$]. Since these two inflows are not equal, again there is an opportunity for index arbitrage. However, it would involve the investor going short strategy 1 and long strategy 2. Why? Because strategy 1 now has a lower payoff than strategy 2 (note that $P_d + \$3 < P_d + \$15$). By doing this, the investor will, without risk, earn $12 [that is, $(P_d + \$15) - (P_d + \$3)$]. Furthermore, being short the individual stocks and long the futures will push the current level of the S&P 500 down from 100 and the price of the futures up from 90.

In equilibrium, since these two strategies cost the same to implement, prices will adjust so that their dollar returns are equal. Letting y denote the dividend yield on the stocks in the index, P_f denote the current price of the futures contract on the index, and P_s denote the current spot price of the index, the dollar return from strategy 1 is:

$$P_d + yP_s.$$

Letting R denote the interest rate on Treasury bills, the dollar return from strategy 2 is:

$$(P_d - P_f) + [(1 + R) \times P_s].$$

Setting these two dollar returns equal to each other results in:

$$P_d + yP_s = (P_d - P_f) + [(1 + R) \times P_s]. \tag{25.11}$$

Simplifying this equation results in:

$$P_f - P_s = (R - y)P_s \tag{25.12}$$

or

$$P_f = P_s + RP_s - yP_s. \tag{25.13}$$

Equation (25.12) indicates that the difference between the price of the futures contract and the current level of the index should depend only on (1) the current level of the index, P_s, and (2) the difference between the interest rate on Treasury bills and the dividend yield on the index, $(R - y)$. As the delivery date nears, the difference between the interest rate and dividend yield diminishes, converging to zero on the delivery date. Thus, as the delivery date approaches, the futures price (P_f) should converge to the current spot price (P_s).

Equation (25.13) shows that index futures are priced according to the cost of carry model given earlier in equation (25.4) where the costs of ownership C are zero. Here the interest forgone by ownership I is equal to RP_s, while the benefit of ownership B is the dividend yield, yP_s. Hence the cost of carry is:

$$\text{CARRY} = RP_s - yP_s \tag{25.14}$$

which will be positive as long as the riskfree interest rate (R) is greater than the dividend yield on the index (y)—a situation that exists nearly all the time.

In the example the interest rate was 5%, the dividend yield was 3%, and the current level of the S&P 500 was 100. This means that the difference between the S&P 500 December futures contract and the current level of the S&P 500 should be $(.05 - .03) \times 100 = 2$. Equivalently, the equilibrium price of the futures contract when the S&P 500 is 100 would be 102, since the cost of carry is 2. Note that when three of the six months have passed, the interest rate and dividend yield will be 2.5% (= 5%/2) and 1.5% (= 3%/2), respectively.

Thus, the difference should be about (.025 − .015) × 100 = 1, assuming that the S&P 500 is still at 100 at that time.

In practice, the situation is not this simple, for a number of reasons. Positions in futures, stocks, and Treasury bills involve transaction costs.[22] This means that arbitrage will not take place unless the difference diverges far enough from the amount shown in equation (25.12) to warrant incurring such costs. The futures price, and hence the difference, can be expected to move within a band around the "theoretical value," with the width of the band determined by the costs of those who can engage in transactions most efficiently.

To add to the complexity, both the dividend yield and the relevant interest rate on Treasury bills are subject to some uncertainty. Neither the amounts of dividends to be declared nor their timing can be specified completely in advance. And, since futures positions must be marked to market daily, the amount of cash required for strategy 2 may have to be varied via additional borrowing (if short this strategy) or lending (if long this strategy). Furthermore, on occasion market prices may be reported with a substantial time lag, making the current level and futures price of the index appear to be out of line when they actually are not. Thus, an investor may enter into the transactions necessary for index arbitrage when actual prices are in equilibrium, thereby resulting in useless transaction costs. Nevertheless, index arbitrage is still actively pursued, most notably by brokerage firms, as shown in Figure 25-7.

Stock index futures are also used extensively by other professional money managers. As a result, prices of such contracts are likely to track their underlying indices very closely, taking into account both dividends and current interest rates. It is unlikely that a private investor will be able to exploit "mispricing" of such a contract by engaging in index arbitrage. Nevertheless, stock index futures can provide inexpensive ways to take positions in the stock market or to hedge portions of the risk associated with other positions. Furthermore, their use can lower transaction costs by reducing the size of the bid-ask spread for investors who may never take direct positions in such contracts.

FUTURES VERSUS OPTIONS

People occasionally make the mistake of confusing a futures contract with an options contract.[23] With an options contract, there is the possibility that both of the parties involved will have nothing to do at the end of the life of the contract. In particular, if the option is "out of the money" on the expiration date, then the options contract will be worthless and can be thrown away. However, with a futures contract, both parties involved must do something at the end of the life of the contract. In particular, the parties are obligated to complete the transaction, either by a reversing trade or by actual delivery.

[22]People involved in index arbitrage need to be able to quickly make a large number of transactions in individual stocks. In order to do this, they often have their computers send in their orders through the SuperDOT system (this system was discussed in Chapter 3). For a discussion of some of the complications involved in successfully executing index arbitrage strategies, see David M. Modest, "On the Pricing of Stock Index Futures," *Journal of Portfolio Management*, 10, no. 4 (Summer 1984): 51–57.

[23]Adding to the confusion is the existence of a contract known as a *futures option*, which is an option that has a futures contract instead of a stock as its underlying asset. Futures options are discussed in more detail in the appendix.

PROGRAM TRADING

NEW YORK — Program trading in the week ended July 31 accounted for 10.4%, or an average 21.4 million daily shares, of New York Stock Exchange volume.

Brokerage firms executed an additional 1.6 million daily shares of program trading away from the Big Board, mostly on foreign markets. Program trading is the simultaneous purchase or sale of at least 15 different stocks with a total value of $1 million or more.

Of the program total on the Big Board, 46.6% involved stock-index arbitrage, up from 36.3% the prior week. In this strategy, traders dart between stocks and stock-index options and futures to capture fleeting price differences.

Some 44% of program trading reflected firms' trading for their own accounts, or principal trading, while 53.2% involved trading for customers. An additional 2.8% was executed by firms using principal positions to facilitate customer trades.

Of the five most-active firms, Nomura Securities and Kidder Peabody did most of their program trading for their own accounts. Morgan Stanley, Bear Stearns and W&D Securities did all or most of their program trading for customers.

NYSE PROGRAM TRADING

Volume (in millions of shares) for the week ending July 31, 1992

Top 15 Firms	Index Arbitrage	Other Strategies	Total
Nomura Securities	12.8	7.2	20.0
Morgan Stanley	0.3	12.6	12.9
Bear Stearns	.....	8.3	8.3
Kidder Peabody	7.0	0.7	7.7
W&D Securities	.....	7.3	7.3
PaineWebber	.....	5.9	5.9
Salomon Brothers	1.8	3.6	5.4
First Boston	3.9	1.5	5.4
Susquehanna	4.4	0.3	4.7
Daiwa Securities	4.1	0.2	4.3
Walsh Greenwood	4.0	0.1	4.1
Merrill Lynch	.....	3.8	3.8
UBS Securities	3.0	0.1	3.1
LIT America	2.9	0.2	3.1
Thomas Williams	2.2	.....	2.2
OVERALL TOTAL	49.8	57.1	106.9

Source: New York Stock Exchange

FIGURE 25-7
Index Arbitrage as a Form of Program Trading

Source: Reprinted by permission of *The Wall Street Journal*, © Dow Jones & Company, Inc., August 14, 1992, p. C10. All rights reserved worldwide.

Figure 25-8 contrasts the situation faced by the buyer and the seller of a call option with the situation faced by the buyer and the seller of a futures contract. Specifically, terminal values for buyers and sellers are shown at the last possible moment—the expiration date for the option, and the delivery date for the futures contract.

As shown in panel (a), no matter what the price of the underlying stock, an option buyer cannot lose and an option seller cannot gain on the expiration

FIGURE 25-8
Terminal Values of Positions in Calls and Futures

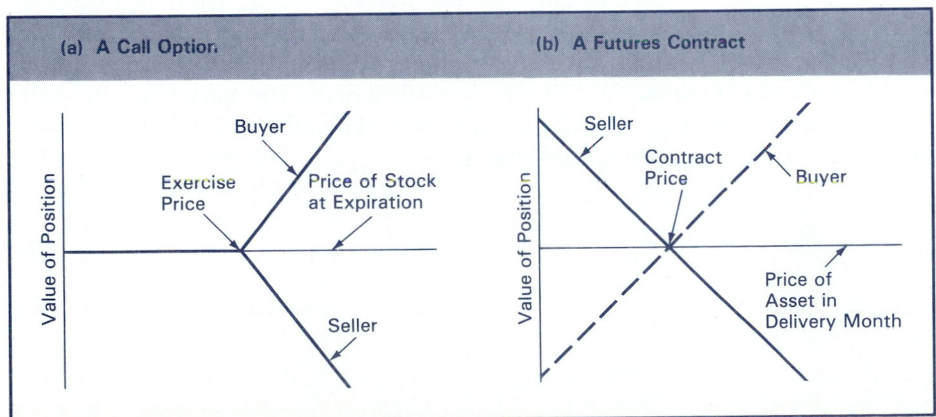

date. Option buyers compensate sellers for putting themselves in this position by paying them a premium when the contract is signed.

The situation is quite different with a futures contract. As shown in panel (b), the buyer may gain or lose, depending on the price of the asset in the delivery month. Whatever the buyer gains or loses, an exactly offsetting loss or gain will be registered by the seller. The higher the contract price (that is, the price of the futures contract when the buyer purchased it from the seller), the greater the likelihood that the buyer will lose and the seller will gain. The lower the contract price, the greater the likelihood that the seller will lose and the buyer will gain.

SYNTHETIC FUTURES

synthetic futures contract

For some assets, futures contracts are unavailable but both put and call options are available. In such cases, an investor can create a **synthetic futures contract.**

The clearest example involves European options on common stocks. As shown in the previous chapter, the *purchase* of a European call option and the *sale* of a European put option at the same exercise price and with the same expiration date will provide a value at expiration that will be related, dollar for dollar, to the stock price at that time. This is shown in Figure 25-9.

Panel (a) shows the payoff associated with the purchase of a call at an exercise price of E, while panel (b) shows the payoff associated with the sale of a put at the same exercise price. The results obtained by taking *both* positions are those shown by the solid line in panel (c).

Depending on the prices (that is, premiums) of the call and put, this strategy may initially either require a net outflow of cash or provide a net inflow. For comparability with the purchase of a futures contract, this cash flow may be offset with borrowing or lending as required to bring the net investment to zero. The dashed line in panel (c) shows a case in which the call option costs more than is provided by the sale of the put option. The difference is borrowed, requiring the loan repayment shown in the figure. The dashed line thus indicates the net end-of-period payoffs for a strategy requiring no initial outlay. Since these payoffs are equivalent to the payoffs from a futures contract with a contract price equal to F, a "synthetic" futures contract has been created.

In practice, the equivalence is not perfect. Most listed options are American, not European, raising the possibility that the buyer of the put will exercise it prior to maturity. Moreover, the synthetic future is not marked to market on a daily basis. Despite these differences, the existence of well-functioning markets for call and put options will enable investors to synthetically create futures on the underlying asset.

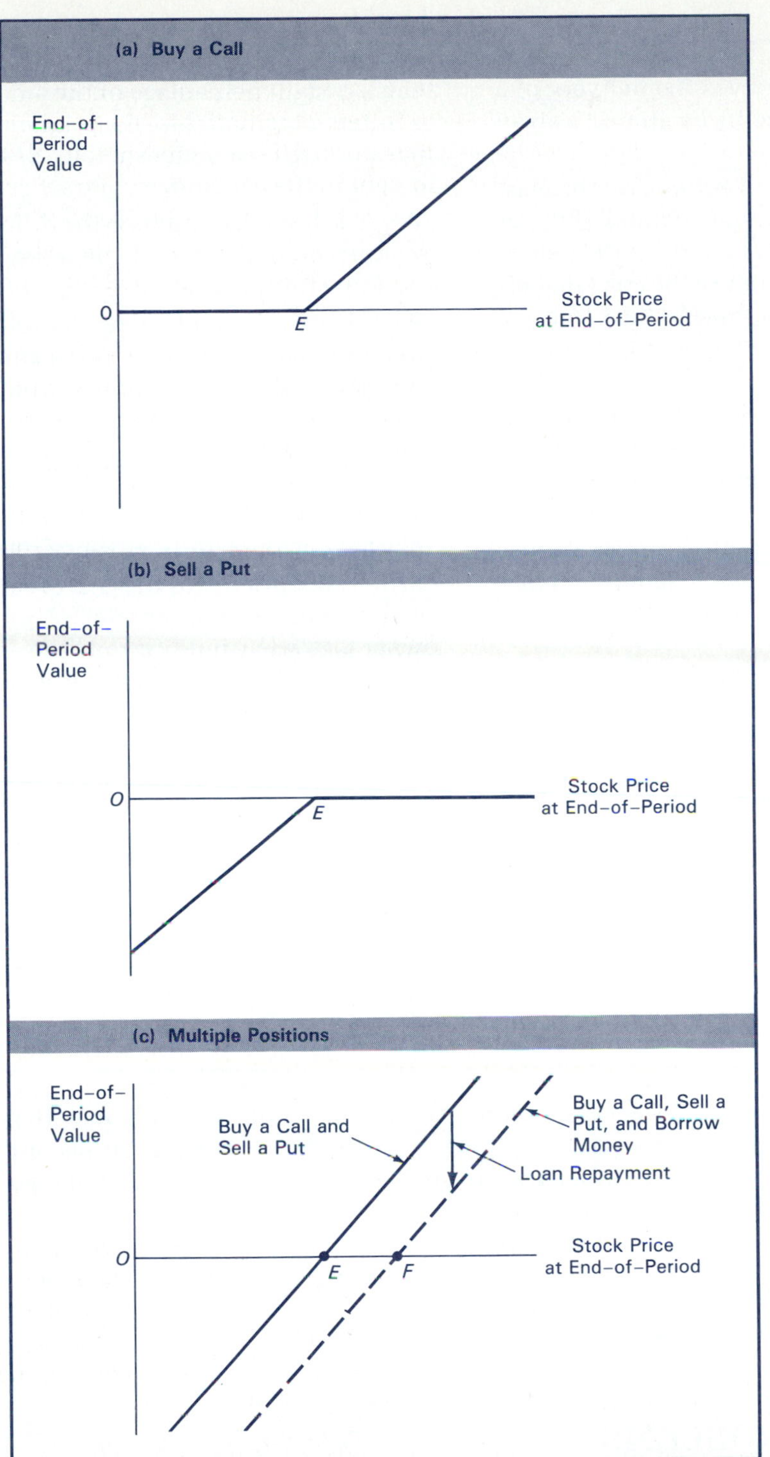

FIGURE 25-9
Creating a Synthetic Futures Contract

SUMMARY

1. A futures contract involves the delivery of a specific type of asset at a specific location at a given future time.

2. People who buy and sell futures can be classified as either hedgers or speculators. Hedgers transact in futures primarily to reduce risk, since these people either produce or use the asset in their ordinary course of business. Speculators transact in futures in pursuit of relatively short-term profits.

3. Futures are bought and sold on organized exchanges. Futures are standardized in terms of the type of asset, time of delivery, and place of delivery.

4. Each futures exchange has an associated clearinghouse that becomes the "seller's buyer" and the "buyer's seller" as soon as the trade is concluded.

5. A futures investor is required to deposit initial margin in order to guarantee fulfillment of his or her obligations.

6. A futures investor's account is marked to market daily, with the equity in the investor's account adjusted to reflect the change in the futures contract's settlement price.

7. A futures investor must maintain his or her commodity account's equity equal to or greater than a certain percentage of the amount deposited as initial margin. If this requirement is not met, the investor will be requested to deposit variation margin in the account.

8. The basis for futures is the difference between the current spot price of the asset and the corresponding futures price.

9. There are three possible relationships between the current futures price and the expected spot price: the expectations hypothesis (futures price equal to expected spot price), normal backwardation (futures price less than expected spot price), and normal contango (futures price greater than expected spot price).

10. The current futures price should equal the current spot price plus the cost of carry. The cost of carry equals (1) the amount of interest that the owner forgoes by holding onto the asset less (2) the benefits of owning the asset plus (3) the costs of owning the asset.

11. If the price of a futures contract becomes too far removed from the current spot price of the asset plus the cost of carry, arbitrageurs will enter into transactions that generate riskless profits from the perceived price discrepancy. Their actions will cause prices to adjust until the opportunity to make such profits disappears.

KEY TERMS

futures
speculators
hedgers
short hedger
long hedger
reversing trade
spot market
spot price
settle
open interest
locals
performance margin
marking to market
variation margin
Commodity Futures Trading Commission
basis
basis risk
expectations hypothesis
normal backwardation
normal contango
cost of carry
interest rate parity
index arbitrage
synthetic futures contract
futures options
triple witching hour

QUESTIONS AND PROBLEMS

1. Distinguish between a speculator and a hedger. Give an example of a short hedger and a long hedger.

2. Using the latest *Wall Street Journal*, for the near futures contracts in corn, orange juice, and gasoline, calculate the percentage change in the settlement price from the previous day. Find the open interest in these contracts. Into how many units of the commodities do these open interest figures translate?

3. How do organized futures exchanges ensure that the obligations incurred as various parties enter into futures contracts are ultimately satisfied?
4. What is the purpose of initial and maintenance margins? How does marking to market affect the amount of funds held in the futures investor's margin account?
5. Chicken Wolf sells ten June 5,000-bushel corn futures at $2 per bushel. Chicken deposits $5,000 in performance margin. If the price of corn rises to $2.20 per bushel, how much equity is in Chicken's margin account? What if corn fell to $1.80 per bushel?
6. Zack Wheat has just bought four September 5,000-bushel corn futures contracts at $1.75 per bushel. The initial margin requirement is 3%. The maintenance margin requirement is 80% of the initial margin requirement.
   (a) How many dollars in initial margin must Zack put up?
   (b) If the September price of corn rises to $1.85, how much equity is in Zack's commodity account
   (c) If the September price of corn falls to $1.70, how much equity is in Zack's commodity account? Will Zack receive a margin call?
7. Do exchange-imposed price limits protect futures traders from losses that would result in the absence of such limits? Explain.
8. Corky Withrow is long a stock market futures contract and short a diversified portfolio of stocks. Would Corky prefer the basis to widen or narrow? Why?
9. A publication used by farmers such as Mordecai Brown provides diagrams of the typical annual patterns of "cash prices" for a number of seasonal commodities. Should Mordecai expect that the price of a futures contract will follow the same pattern? Why?
10. In the market for a particular agricultural or natural resource commodity, what kind of market forces might lead to normal backwardation or normal contango?
11. Byrd Lynn owns a famous Renoir painting that has a current market value of $5,000,000. It costs Byrd $200,000 annually to insure the painting; This fee was recently paid for coverage over the forthcoming year. Byrd is able to loan the painting to a local art gallery for $300,000 per year, paid each year in advance. Byrd is considering selling the painting under a futures contract arrangement that calls for delivery one year from today. If the one-year riskfree rate is 5%, what is the fair value of the futures contract?
12. Tuck Turner is planning a trip in six months to Germany, where Tuck plans to purchase a BMW for 80,000 Deutsche Marks (DM). Using a recent *Wall Street Journal*, calculate how much the purchase would cost in U.S. dollars at the current exchange rate. Given the recent settlement price of a six-month DM futures contract, how much would Tuck have to pay to hedge the BMW purchase?
13. The exchange rate between British pounds and U.S. dollars is currently $1.80 per pound. If the six-month riskfree rate is 3% in the U.S. and 3.5% in Great Britain, what should the six-month futures price of U.S. dollars in British pounds be? Why is the futures exchange rate greater or less than the current spot exchange rate?
14. Estel Crabtree believes that the spread between long-term and short-term interest rates is going to narrow in the next few months, but does not

know in which direction interest rates in general will move. What financial futures positions would permit Estel to profit from this forecast if it is correct?

15. Sleeper Sullivan bought five S&P 500 December futures contracts at 310. If the S&P 500 index rises to 318, what is Sleeper's dollar profit?
16. Why does hedging a common stock portfolio using stock index futures work best if the portfolio being hedged is very similar to the underlying stock index of the futures contract?
17. Assume that the S&P 500 currently has a value of 200 (in "index" terms). The dividend yield on the underlying stocks in the index is expected to be 4% over the next six months. New issue six-month Treasury bills now sell for a six-month yield of 6%.
    (a) What is the theoretical value of a six-month futures contract on the S&P 500?
    (b) What potential problems are inherent in this calculation?
18. In each of the following situations, discuss how Hippo Vaughn might use stock index futures to protect a well-diversified stock portfolio.
    (a) Hippo expects to receive a sizable bonus check next month and would like to invest it in stocks, believing that current stock market prices are extremely attractive (but realizing that they may not remain so for long).
    (b) Hippo expects the stock market to decline dramatically very soon and realizes that quickly selling a stock portfolio would result in significant transaction costs.
    (c) Hippo has a large unrealized gain and for tax purposes would like to defer the gain until the next tax year, which is several weeks away.
19. Does the fair value of a stock index futures contract depend on investors' expectations about the future value of the underlying stock index? Why or why not?
20. How does a futures contract differ from a forward contract?
21. Swats Swacina, a futures investor who has lost considerable sums in futures investments, said, "Even though I don't directly borrow to invest in futures, the performance of my investments acts as if I were highly leveraged." Is Swats correct? Why or why not?
22. (Appendix Question) Pinky Swander buys a call option on a March 5,000-bushel soybean futures contract. The call cost $0.50 per bushel and had an exercise price of $5.25 per bushel. If Pinky exercises the option in February at a price of $5.55 per bushel, what is Pinky's return on investment in the option?

CFA Exam Question

23. Robert Chen, CFA, is reviewing the characteristics of derivative securities and their use in portfolios.
    (a) Chen is considering the addition of either a short position in stock index futures or a long position in stock index options to an existing well-diversified portfolio of equity securities. **Contrast** the way in which each of these two alternatives would affect the risk and return of the resulting combined portfolios.
    (b) Four factors affect the value of a futures contract on a stock index. Three of these factors are: the current price of the stock index, the time remaining until the contract maturity (delivery) date, and the

dividends on the stock index. **Identify** the fourth factor and **explain** how and why changes in this factor affect the value of the futures contract.

(c) Six factors affect the value of call options on stocks. Three of these factors are: the current price of the stock, the time remaining until the option expires, and the dividend on the stock. **Identify** the other three factors and **explain** how and why changes in each of these three factors affect the value of call options.

APPENDIX

A Futures Options

futures options

The previous chapter described options, while this chapter has described futures. Interestingly, there are contracts currently in existence that are known as **futures options** (or options on futures). As might be expected, these contracts are, in a sense, combinations of futures and options contracts. In particular, a futures option is an option where the underlying asset is a specific futures contract, with the expiration date on the option being about the same as the delivery date on the futures contract.[24] Figure 25-10 provides a set of quotations on some of the more frequently traded ones. As the figure shows, there are both put and call options on futures. Thus, an investor can be either a buyer or a writer of either a put or a call option on a futures contract.[25]

Call Options on Futures Contracts

If a call option on a futures contract is exercised, then the writer must deliver the appropriate futures contract to the buyer. That is, the writer must assume a short position in the futures contract while the buyer assumes the long position. For example, consider the buyer of a call option on December corn futures where the exercise price is 250 (that is, $2.50) per bushel. Since the futures contract is for 5,000 bushels, the total exercise price is $12,500 (= 5,000 × $2.50). If the buyer purchased this option at the settle price on July 15, 1992, that is given in Figure 25-10, then the buyer would have paid the

triple witching hour

[24]The near-simultaneous quarterly expiration of (1) options on individual stocks and market indices, (2) futures on market indices, and (3) options on market index futures has been referred to as the **triple witching hour.** When it occurs, the stock market is allegedly roiled, particularly in the latter part of the day. See Hans R. Stoll and Robert E. Whaley, "Program Trading and Expiration Day Effects," *Financial Analysts Journal*, 43, no. 2 (March/April 1987): 16–28; Arnold Kling, "How the Stock Market Can Learn to Live with Index Futures and Options," *Financial Analysts Journal*, 43, no. 5 (September/October 1987): 33–39; and G. J. Santoni, "Has Programmed Trading Made Stock Prices More Volatile?" Federal Reserve Bank of St. Louis, *Review*, 69, no. 5 (May 1987): 18–29.

[25]For more on futures options, see Chapter 12 of the *Commodity Trading Manual*. For a computer program that can be used to determine the "true" value of these complex contracts, see Chapter 8 of Stuart M. Turnbull, *Option Valuation* (Holt, Rinehart and Winston of Canada, Limited, 1987).

FIGURE 25-10

Quotations for Futures Options (Excerpt)

Source: Reprinted by permission of *The Wall Street Journal*, © Dow Jones & Company, Inc., July 16, 1992, p. C13. All rights reserved worldwide.

FUTURES OPTIONS PRICES

Wednesday, July 15, 1992.

AGRICULTURAL

CORN (CBT)
5,000 bu.; cents per bu.

Strike	Calls–Settle			Puts–Settle		
Price	Sep	Dec	Mar	Sep	Dec	Mar
210	....	26¼	....	....	⅞	1¼
220	13	18¼	....	1	3	2¾
230	6¼	12	18½	4⅝	6½	5
240	3	7½	14	11	11⅞	9½
250	1⅜	4¾	9¼	19¼	19	15½
260	¾	3⅛	6¾	28	27	21½

Est. vol. 11,000;
Tues vol. 7,387 calls; 2,664 puts
Op. int. Tues 93,385 calls; 47,644 puts

SOYBEANS (CBT)
5,000 bu.; cents per bu.

Strike	Calls–Settle			Puts–Settle		
Price	Aug	Sep	Nov	Aug	Sep	Nov
525	44	47	52	⅛	⅞	2
550	19¾	24¾	31	1	3½	6½
575	3	10	18½	8½	13½	18
600	¼	4½	11½	31	33	35¾
625	⅛	2½	8	56	56¼	56¾
650	cl	1½	5⅜	81	80½	78¾

Est. vol. 14,000;
Tues vol. 11,061 calls; 3,200 puts
Op. int. Tues 137,673 calls; 42,444 puts

OIL

CRUDE OIL (NYM)
1,000 bbls.; $ per bbl.

Strike	Calls–Settle			Puts–Settle		
Price	Sep	Oct	Nov	Sep	Oct	Nov
20	1.66	1.69	1.72	0.06	0.16	0.25
21	0.79	0.96	1.03	0.19	0.42	0.55
22	0.26	0.42	0.50	0.66	0.88	1.07
23	0.07	0.18	0.23	1.47	1.63	1.74
24	0.03	0.09	0.12	2.42	2.54	2.62
25	0.01	0.04	0.07	....	....	....

Est. vol. 36,931;
Tues vol. 12,184 calls; 13,835 puts
Op. int. Tues 167,679 calls; 149,960 puts

METALS

COPPER (CMX)
25,000 lbs.; cents per lb.

Strike	Calls–Settle			Puts–Settle		
Price	Sep	Dec	Mar	Sep	Dec	Mar
112	4.80	5.50	4.70	1.00	3.15	4.10
114	3.40	4.55	4.00	1.60	4.20	5.50
116	2.40	3.80	3.30	2.60	5.30	7.90
118	1.60	3.15	2.60	3.80	6.80	8.30
120	1.05	2.55	2.05	5.25	8.20	9.50
125	0.30	1.35	1.20	9.50	12.00	13.65

Est. vol. 1,250;
Tues vol. 462 calls; 266 puts
Op. int. Tues 6,259 calls; 3,599 puts

GOLD (CMX)
100 troy ounces; $ per troy ounce

Strike	Calls–Settle			Puts–Settle		
Price	Sep	Oct	Dec	Sep	Oct	Dec
340	16.70	16.90	19.60	0.30	0.60	1.60
350	7.60	8.60	11.80	1.20	2.30	3.80
360	2.30	3.70	6.80	5.90	7.40	8.40
370	0.70	1.70	3.60	14.30	15.20	15.30
380	0.40	0.90	2.30	23.90	24.40	23.70
390	0.20	0.50	1.30	33.80	34.00	32.50

Est. vol. 7,000;
Tues vol. 6,950 calls; 956 puts
Op. int. Tues 69,719 calls; 18,784 puts

SILVER (CMX)
5,000 troy ounces; cts per troy ounce

Strike	Calls–Settle			Puts–Settle		
Price	Sep	Oct	Dec	Sep	Oct	Dec
350	46.2	50.6	50.5	0.2	0.6	0.9
375	21.7	26.1	28.3	0.7	1.1	3.5
400	4.3	8.5	12.6	8.3	8.5	12.6
425	1.1	2.9	6.3	30.1	27.9	31.3
450	0.5	1.3	3.6	54.5	51.3	53.5
475	0.4	0.8	2.4	79.4	75.8	77.0

Est. vol. 1,900;
Tues vol. 1,331 calls; 218 puts
Op. int. Tues 39,421 calls; 14,380 puts

TREASURY BILLS (IMM)
$1 million; pts. of 100%

Strike	Calls–Settle			Puts–Settle		
Price	Sep	Dec	Mar	Sep	Dec	Mar
9625	0.59	0.42	....	.0004	0.06	....
9650	0.34	....	....	.0004	0.12	....
9675	0.13	....	....	0.04	....	....
9700	....	....	....	....	....	....
9725	....	....	....	....	....	....
9750	....	....	....	....	....	....

Est. vol. 34;
Tues vol. 24 calls; 5 puts
Op. int. Tues 1,107 calls; 3,036 puts

EURODOLLAR (IMM)
$ million; pts. of 100%

Strike	Calls–Settle			Puts–Settle		
Price	Sep	Dec	Mar	Sep	Dec	Mar
9600	0.55	0.31	0.39	0.01	0.19	0.29
9625	0.31	0.18	0.26	0.02	0.31	0.40
9650	0.12	0.09	0.16	0.08	0.47	....
9675	0.03	0.04	....	0.24	....	....
9700	.0004	....	....	0.46	....	....
9725	....	....	....	....	....	....

Est. vol. 43,890;
Tues vol. 14,818 calls; 9,105 puts
Op. int. Tues 345,053 calls; 393,637 puts

INDEX

S&P 500 STOCK INDEX (CME)
$500 times premium

Strike	Calls–Settle			Puts–Settle		
Price	Jly	Aug	Sep	Jly	Aug	Sep
405	12.30	14.60	16.60	0.10	2.45	4.50
410	7.45	10.60	12.95	0.25	3.45	5.80
415	3.15	7.25	9.70	0.95	5.05	7.50
420	0.55	4.50	6.95	3.35	7.30	9.75
425	.0000	2.50	4.70	7.80	10.25	12.40
430	.0000	1.20	2.90	12.80	13.95	15.60

Est. vol. 7,798;
Tues vol. 3,338 calls; 5,194 puts
Op. int. Tues 41,422 calls; 87,122 puts

INTEREST RATE

T-BONDS (CBT)
$100,000; points and 64ths of 100%

Strike	Calls–Settle			Puts–Settle		
Price	Aug	Sep	Dec	Aug	Sep	Dec
98	4-34	4-37	4-09	0-01	0-04	0-54
100	2-35	2-49	2-51	0-01	0-14	1-32
102	0-47	1-17	1-45	0-12	0-47	2-26
104	0-03	0-27	0-61	1-33	1-57	3-38
106	0-01	0-06	0-31	3-31	3-35	5-07
108	....	0-02	0-15	....	....	6-54

Est. vol. 105,000;
Tues vol. 41,482 calls; 26,397 puts
Op. int. Tues 297,693 calls; 251,105 puts

CURRENCY

JAPANESE YEN (IMM)
12,500,000 yen; cents per 100 yen

Strike	Calls–Settle			Puts–Settle		
Price	Aug	Sep	Oct	Aug	Sep	Oct
7900	1.20	1.50	....	0.39	0.69	....
7950	0.88	1.22	1.45	0.57	0.91	1.29
8000	0.62	0.97	1.20	0 81	1.16	1.54
8050	0.43	0.76	1.02	1.12	1.45	....
8100	0.29	0.60	....	1.47	1.79	....
8150	0.20	0.45	....	....	....	....

Est. vol. 1,957;
Tues vol. 1,734 calls; 1,832 puts
Op. int. Tues 24,694 calls; 30,914 puts

DEUTSCHEMARK (IMM)
125,000 marks; cents per mark

Strike	Calls–Settle			Puts–Settle		
Price	Aug	Sep	Oct	Aug	Sep	Oct
6600	1.39	1.72	1.47	0.57	0.90	....

Strike	Calls–Settle			Puts–Settle		
Price	Aug	Sep	Oct	Aug	Sep	Oct
6650	1.09	1.43	1.28	0.77	1.11	....
6700	0.84	1.18	1.09	1.02	1.36	....
6750	0.63	0.98	0.92	1.31	1.66	....
6800	0.47	0.79	....	1.65	1.97	....
6850	0.34	0.64	....	....	....	....

Est. vol. 88,361;
Tues vol. 8,102 calls; 49,472 puts
Op. int. Tues 140,543 calls; 215,975 puts

writer a premium of 3⅛ (that is, \$.03125) per bushel or \$156.25 (= 5,000 × \$.03125) in total.

Now if the buyer subsequently decides to exercise this option, then the writer of this option must deliver a December corn futures contract to the buyer. Furthermore, this futures contract will be fully marked to market at the time it is delivered. In the example, assume that the option is exercised in September when December corn futures are selling for \$3.00 per bushel. What happens in September is that the call writer must provide the call buyer with a December corn futures contract that has a delivery price of \$2.50 that has been marked to market. This can be accomplished in two steps. First, the writer must purchase a December corn futures contract and deliver it to the call buyer. Since the cost of the futures will be $3.00 per bushel (the current market price of December corn futures), this is costless to the call writer. Second, the futures contract that has been delivered must be marked to market, which is done by having the call writer pay the call buyer an amount of cash equal to $.50 (= $3.00 − $2.50) per bushel or $2,500 (= 5,000 × $.50) in aggregate. Thus, the call writer has lost $2,343.75 (= $2,500 − $156.25) while the call buyer has made an equivalent amount.

While this example has shown what happens when the call is exercised, it should be noted that most futures options are not exercised. Instead, just as with most options and futures, buyers and writers of futures options typically make reversing trades before the expiration date.

Put Options on Futures Contracts

If a put option on a futures contract is exercised, then the writer must accept delivery of the appropriate futures contract from the buyer. That is, the writer must assume a long position in the futures contract while the buyer assumes the short position. For example, consider the buyer of a put option on December corn where the exercise price is 250, meaning $2.50 per bushel or $12,500 in total since the futures contract is for 5,000 bushels. If the buyer purchased this put at the settlement price on July 15, 1992, that is given in Figure 25-10, then the buyer would have paid the writer a premium of 27 per bushel or $1,350 (= 5,000 × $.27) in total.

Now if the buyer subsequently decides to exercise this option, then the writer of this option must accept delivery of a December corn futures contract from the buyer. Furthermore, this futures contract must be fully marked to market at the time it is delivered. In the example, assume that the option is exercised in November when December corn futures are selling for $2.00 per bushel. What happens in November is that the put buyer will become the seller of a December corn futures contract where the purchase price is $2.00 per bushel. That is, when this contract is marked to market, the put writer must pay the put buyer an amount of cash equal to $.50 (= $2.50 − $2.00) per bushel or $2,500 (= 5,000 × $.50) in aggregate. Thus, the put writer has lost $1,150 (= $2,500 − $1,350) while the put buyer has made an equivalent amount.

Again, it should be kept in mind that most put options on futures are not exercised. Instead, these option buyers and writers typically enter reversing trades sometime before the expiration date.

In summary, the positions of futures options buyers and writers in the futures contracts upon exercise by the buyer are as follows:

	BUYER	WRITER
Call	Long	Short
Put	Short	Long

As mentioned earlier, neither a writer nor a buyer needs to maintain his or her position, as they are free to enter into offsetting trades after the buyer has exercised the option.

Comparison with Futures

At this point, it is worthwhile to think about the distinctions between futures and futures options. In doing so, consider an investor who is contemplating *buying* a futures contract. If this contract is purchased, the investor can potentially make or lose a great deal of money. In particular, if the price of the asset rises substantially, then so will the price of the futures and the investor will have made a sizable profit. In contrast, if the price of the asset drops substantially, then the investor will have lost a sizable amount of money.

In comparison, if the investor had bought a futures call option on the asset, then the investor would also make a sizable profit if the price of the asset rose substantially. Unlike futures, however, if the price of the asset dropped, then the investor need not worry about incurring a sizable loss. Instead, only the premium (the price paid to buy the futures option) would be lost. This does not mean that purchasing a futures call option is "better" than purchasing a futures contract. Why? Because the protection on the downside that an investor gets from buying a futures call option is paid for in the form of the premium. This premium would not be present if the investor had bought a futures contract instead.

Consider next an investor who is contemplating *selling* a futures contract. In doing so, the investor can potentially make a great deal of money if the price of the asset declines substantially. However, if the price of the asset rises substantially, then the investor will have lost a sizable amount of money.

In comparison, the investor could buy a futures put option on the asset. If this was done, the investor would make a sizable profit if the price of the asset declined substantially. Unlike futures, however, if the price of the asset rose, then the investor need not worry about incurring a sizable loss. Instead only the premium would be lost. Again, this does not mean that purchasing a futures put option is "better" than selling a futures contract.

Comparison with Options

Having established that futures options can exist if futures already exist, one may wonder why futures options exist if options already exist. For example, there are futures options and options on Japanese yen (as well as futures on Japanese yen). The commonly given reason why futures options exist in such a situation is that it is easier to make or take delivery of a futures contract on the asset as required by the futures options contract than to make or take delivery in the asset itself as required by the options contract. That is, the deliverable asset in the case of the Japanese yen futures option contract is a futures contract in Japanese yen, which is more easily delivered than Japanese yen as required for the options contract.

In addition, there is sometimes more timely price information on the deliverable asset for the futures option contract (namely, price information on the futures contract) than on the deliverable asset for the options contract (namely, price information in the spot market).

For these reasons (although they are not compelling for certain contracts), futures, futures options, and options can simultaneously exist with the same underlying asset.

REFERENCES

1. A number of books are devoted either exclusively to futures or have futures as one of their primary subjects. Most cover everything discussed in this chapter in more detail and with a more complete list of citations. Here are a few:

Stephen Figlewski, *Hedging with Financial Futures for Institutional Investors* (Cambridge, Mass.: Ballinger Publishing, 1986);

Edward W. Schwarz, Joanne M. Hill, and Thomas Schneeweis, *Financial Futures* (Homewood, Ill.: Richard D. Irwin, 1986);

Robert W. Kolb, *Understanding Futures Markets* (Glenview, Ill.: Scott, Foresman and Company, 1988);

Commodity Trading Manual (Chicago: Chicago Board of Trade, 1989);

Darrell Duffie, *Futures Markets* (Englewood Cliffs, N.J.: Prentice Hall, 1989);

Daniel R. Siegel and Diane F. Siegel, *Futures Markets* (Hinsdale, Ill.: The Dryden Press, 1990);

Don M. Chance, *An Introduction to Options & Futures* (Fort Worth, Texas: The Dryden Press, 1991);

John Hull, *Introduction to Futures and Options Markets* (Englewood Cliffs, N.J.: Prentice Hall, 1991);

Alan L. Tucker, *Financial Futures, Options, & Swaps* (St. Paul, Minn.: West Publishing, 1991);

David A. Dubofsky, *Options and Financial Futures* (New York: McGraw-Hill, 1992);

Hans R. Stoll and Robert E. Whaley, *Futures and Options* (Cincinnati: South-Western Publishing, 1993).

2. For a discussion of the market structure of futures exchanges, see:

Sanford J. Grossman and Merton H. Miller, "Liquidity and Market Structure," *Journal of Finance*, 43, no. 3 (July 1988): 617–33;

Michael J. Fishman and Francis A. Longstaff, "Dual Trading in Futures Markets," *Journal of Finance*, 47, no. 2 (June 1992): 643–71.

3. For a more complete discussion of margin and marking to market, see:

Robert W. Kolb, Gerald D. Gay, and William C. Hunter, "Liquidity Requirements for Financial Futures Investments," *Financial Analysts Journal*, 41, no. 3 (May/June 1985): 60–68;

Don M. Chance, *The Effect of Margins on the Volatility of Stock and Derivative Markets: A Review of the Evidence*, Monograph Series in Finance and Economics #1990-2, New York University Salomon Center, Leonard N. Stern School of Business;

Ann Kremer, "Clarifying Marking to Market," *Journal of Financial Education*, 20 (November 1991): 17–25.

4. The concepts of spreads and basis are discussed in:

Martin L. Leibowitz, *The Analysis of Value and Volatility in Financial Futures*, Monograph Series in Finance and Economics #1981-3, New York University Salomon Center, Leonard N. Stern School of Business.

5. Foreign exchange markets are discussed in:

J. Orlin Grabbe, *International Financial Markets* (New York: Elsevier Science, 1991), Part II.

6. Interest rate futures were shown to be useful in immunizing bond portfolios by:

   Robert W. Kolb and Gerald D. Gay, "Immunizing Bond Portfolios with Interest Rate Futures," *Financial Management*, 11, no. 2 (Summer 1982): 81–89.

7. Stock index futures and their relationship to the market crash in October 1987 have been heavily researched; some of the papers are:

   Paula A. Tosini, "Stock Index Futures and Stock Market Activity in October 1987," *Financial Analysts Journal*, 44, no. 1 (January/February 1988): 28–37;

   F. J. Gould, "Stock Index Futures: The Arbitrage Cycle and Portfolio Insurance," *Financial Analysts Journal*, 44, no. 1 (January/February 1988): 48–62;

   Lawrence Harris, "The October 1987 S&P 500 Stock-Futures Basis," *Journal of Finance*, 44, no. 1 (March 1989): 77–99;

   Marshall E. Blume, A. Craig MacKinlay, and Bruce Terker, "Order Imbalances and Stock Price Movements on October 19 and 20, 1987," *Journal of Finance*, 44, no. 4 (September 1989): 827–48;

   Lawrence Harris, "S&P 500 Cash Stock Price Volatilities," *Journal of Finance*, 44, no. 5 (December 1989): 1155–75;

   Hans R. Stoll and Robert E. Whaley, "The Dynamics of Stock Index and Stock Index Futures Returns," *Journal of Financial and Quantitative Analysis*, 25, no. 4 (December 1990): 441–68;

   Avanidhar Subrahmanyam, "A Theory of Trading in Stock Index Futures," *Review of Financial Studies*, 4, no. 1 (1991): 17–51;

   Kolak Chan, K. C. Chan, and G. Andrew Karolyi, "Intraday Volatility in the Stock Index and Stock Index Futures Markets," *Review of Financial Studies*, 4, no. 4 (1991): 657–84;

   Kolak Chan, "A Further Analysis of the Lead-Lag Relationship Between the Cash Market and Stock Index Futures Market," *Review of Financial Studies*, 5, no. 1 (1992): 123–52.

8. Papers on index arbitrage and program trading include:

   A. Craig MacKinlay and Krishna Ramaswamy, "Index-Futures Arbitrage and the Behavior of Stock Index Futures Prices," *Review of Financial Studies*, 1, no. 2 (Summer 1988): 137–58;

   Michael J. Brennan and Eduardo S. Schwartz, "Arbitrage in Stock Index Futures," *Journal of Business*, 63, no. 1, part 2 (January 1990): S7–S31;

   Hans R. Stoll and Robert E. Whaley, "Program Trading and Individual Stock Returns: Ingredients of the Triple-Witching Brew," *Journal of Business*, 63, no. 1, part 2 (January 1990): S165–S192;

   Gary L. Gastineau, "A Short History of Program Trading," *Financial Analysts Journal*, 47, no. 5 (September/October 1991): 4–7.

9. Forward and futures prices were shown to be equal when interest rates are constant over time in:

   John C. Cox, Jonathan E. Ingersoll, and Stephen A. Ross, "The Relation Between Forward Prices and Futures Prices," *Journal of Financial Economics*, 9, no. 4 (December 1981): 321–46.

10. The performance of commodity funds, which are investment companies that speculate in futures, has not been attractive, according to:

Edwin J. Elton, Martin J. Gruber, and Joel C. Rentzler, "Professionally Managed, Publicly Traded Commodity Funds," *Journal of Business*, 60, no. 2 (April 1987): 175–99.

11. The relationships among futures, options, and futures options are discussed in:

Clifford W. Smith, Jr., Charles W. Smithson, and D. Sykes Wilford, "Managing Financial Risk," *Journal of Applied Corporate Finance*, 1, no. 4 (Winter 1989): 27–48;

Clifford W. Smith, Jr., Charles W. Smithson, and D. Sykes Wilford, *Managing Financial Risk* (New York: Harper & Row, 1990).

12. The seminal paper on the pricing of futures options is:

Fischer Black, "The Pricing of Commodity Contracts," *Journal of Financial Economics*, 3, nos. 1/2 (January/March 1976): 167–79.

13. For a thought-provoking book that covers futures markets, among other things, see:

Merton H. Miller, *Financial Innovations & Market Volatility* (Cambridge, Mass.: Blackwell, 1991).

26

Extended Diversification

One of the major themes of modern portfolio theory concerns the merits of diversification: In an efficient capital market, sensible investment strategies will include holdings of many different assets. Previous chapters have considered traditional securities, such as stocks and bonds, and some less traditional ones, such as options and futures. However, an investor should also consider holding foreign securities and tangible assets.

This chapter will discuss these two aspects of diversification, and then turn to a less lofty subject: betting on sporting events. As indicated in previous chapters, active investment management can be considered a form of betting. Now, this rather subtle form of wagering that is handled by security brokers and dealers will be compared and contrasted with the more explicit form handled by people at racetracks and by "bookmakers."

INTERNATIONAL INVESTMENT

If the world were under one political jurisdiction, with one currency and complete freedom of trade, then "the market portfolio" could be thought of as including all securities in the world, each in proportion to its market value. In such a situation, limiting one's investments to securities representing firms located in only one part of the world would most likely result in a relatively low rate of return per unit of risk. After all, few people would advocate that Californians own only securities issued by California firms. And in a world without political boundaries, few people would advocate that Americans own only securities issued by American firms.

Unfortunately, there are political boundaries, different currencies, and restrictions on trade and currency exchange. Such irritants diminish, but do not destroy, the advantages to be gained from international investment.

The World Market Wealth Portfolio

Figure 26-1 provides a 1984 year-end estimate of the world market wealth portfolio, defined to include those "capital market securities that are most marketable and most readily identifiable. These are the securities that make up the opportunity set faced by most investors."[1]

[1]Roger G. Ibbotson, Laurence B. Siegel, and Kathryn S. Love, "World Wealth: Market Values and Returns," *Journal of Portfolio Management*, 12, no. 1 (Fall 1985): 5.

FIGURE 26-1
The World Market Wealth Portfolio, Year-end 1984
Source: Roger G. Ibbotson, Laurence B. Siegel, and Kathryn S. Love, "World Wealth: Market Values and Returns," *Journal of Portfolio Management*, 12, no. 1 (Fall 1985): 6.

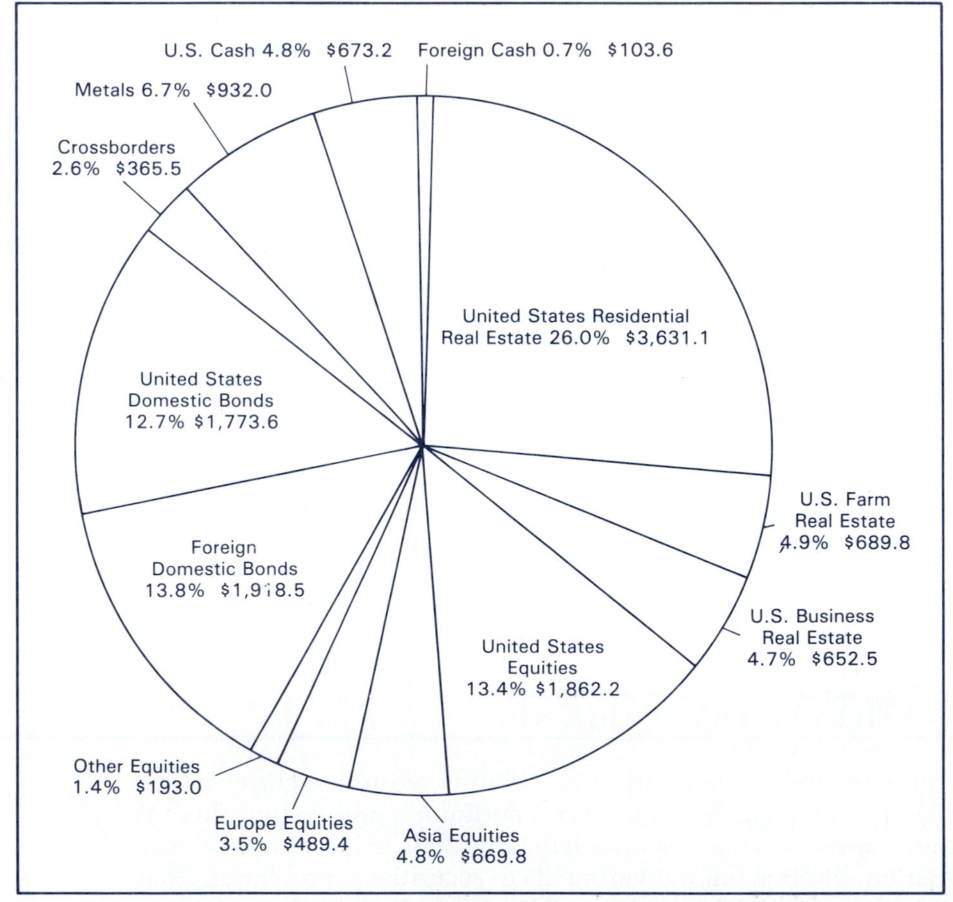

Many problems are encountered in the construction of a world market wealth portfolio. It is almost impossible to adequately represent *all* security markets, as indicated by the authors of the paper from which Figure 26-1 is taken:

> We have excluded huge categories of assets from the portfolio, while at the same time we have included categories that are not wealth at all.
>
> . . . The most important omission is human capital, which is probably the largest single component of world wealth. We have also excluded . . . foreign real estate . . . proprietorships and partnerships . . . many small corporations . . . [and] personal holdings such as automobiles, cash balances, and various consumer capital goods. We have not only omitted a large proportion of wealth, but we also have little idea as to how large the omitted proportion is.
>
> Our inclusions may misrepresent the market even more than our omissions. We have included U.S. and foreign government debt that is almost certainly not backed dollar-for-dollar by government-owned assets such as parks and bridges. More likely, it is backed by claims on a future tax base. Other inclusions in our portfolio also misrepresent wealth. For example, some corporations own parts of other corporations, causing double counting.[2]

Table 26-1 provides a breakdown of the values of equities and bonds that are shown in Figure 26-1.[3] As shown in panel (a) of the table, U.S. bonds and stocks made up $3,635.8 billion (= $1,862.2 + $1,773.6) of the $7,272.0 billion world equity and bond value at the end of 1984. In percentage terms, this is about half the value of the world total. Panel (b) indicates that most of the U.S. equity total is attributable to the equities listed on the New York Stock Exchange, while most of the foreign equity total is attributable to Asian equities. Panel (c) indicates that government debt is larger than corporate debt both inside and outside the United States.[4]

International Equity Indices

In most countries, there are indices of overall stock values and of the values of stocks within various industry or economic sectors. Such indices can be used for assessing "market moves" within the country and, more importantly, for comparative performance measurement. Important indices include the Financial Times–Stock Exchange 100 Index (often referred to as FT-SE, or the "footsie") for the London Stock Exchange; the Nikkei 225 Average for the Tokyo Stock Exchange; and the TSE 300 Composite Index for the Toronto Stock Exchange.[5] As shown in Figure 26-2(a), these and other indices are published daily in *The Wall Street Journal*.

---

[2]Ibbotson, Siegel, and Love, "World Wealth: Market Values and Returns," p. 5.

[3]In this table, preferred stocks are arbitrarily listed under corporate debt. Also, a bond is considered to be "crossborder" if the currency of the bond is not the currency of the borrower's home country or the bond is primarily bought by investors outside the borrower's home country.

[4]A more recent study of bonds estimated their global value to be $11 trillion at the end of 1989. Of this total, $6.3 trillion was government debt, $2.4 trillion was local corporate debt, $1 trillion was "crossborder" debt (that is, foreign bonds and Eurobonds), and $1.3 trillion was "other domestic" debt. See Roger G. Ibbotson and Laurence B. Siegel, "The World Bond Market: Market Values, Yields, and Returns," *Journal of Fixed Income*, 1, no. 1 (June 1991): 90–99.

[5]For a discussion of European stock markets, see Gabriel Hawawini, *European Equity Markets: Price Behavior and Efficiency*, Monograph Series in Finance and Economics 1984–4/5, Salomon Brothers Center for the Study of Financial Institutions, Graduate School of Business Administration, New York University.

TABLE 26-1
World Equity and Bond Values, Year-end 1984 (in billions of U.S. dollars)

(A) SUMMARY

United States Equities	$1,862.2	
Foreign Equities	1,352.4	
Total Equities		$3,214.4
United States Bonds	$1,773.6	
Foreign Bonds	2,284.0	
Total Bonds		$4,057.6
Total Equities and Bonds		$7,272.0

(B) MARKET VALUES OF EQUITIES

United States:			
New York Stock Exchange	$1,587.0		
American Stock Exchange	68.2		
Over-the-Counter	207.0		
Total United States		$1,862.2	
Foreign:			
Europe	$ 489.4		
Asia	669.8		
Other	193.0		
Total Foreign		$1,352.4	
Total Equities			$3,214.4

(C) MARKET VALUES OF BONDS

United States:				
Government				
Notes	$ 720.0			
Bonds	164.8			
Agencies	525.9			
Total Government		$1,410.7		
Corporate				
Medium-Term	$ 164.5			
Long-Term	152.9			
Preferred Stock	45.5			
Total Corporate		$ 362.9		
Total United States			$1,773.6	
Foreign:				
Domestic				
Government	$1,288.2			
Corporate	630.3			
Total Domestic		$1,918.5		
Crossborders		365.5		
Total Foreign			$2,284.0	
Total Bonds				$4,057.6

Source: Adapted from Roger G. Ibbotson, Laurence B. Siegel, and Kathryn S. Love, "World Wealth: Market Values and Returns," *Journal of Portfolio Management*, 12, no. 1 (Fall 1985): 7–9.

On the international level, the indices produced by *Morgan Stanley Capital International Perspective* are also widely used for such purposes. Each index represents the value of a market-weighted portfolio of stocks (using total shares outstanding). Values for each of twenty-two national indices are given in both the local currency and in U.S. dollars based on

FIGURE 26-2
International Equity Indices on July 15, 1992

Source: Reprinted from *The Wall Street Journal*, © Dow Jones & Company, Inc., July 16, 1992, p. C11. All rights reserved worldwide.

(a) Foreign Stock Market Indices

EXCHANGE	7/15/92 CLOSE	NET CHG	PCT CHG
Tokyo Nikkel Average	17116.92	+ 52.29	+ 0.31
Tokyo Topix Index	1298.84	+ 4.69	+ 0.36
London FT 30-share	1896.2	− 1.2	− 0.06
London 100-share	2486.4	+ 2.4	+ 0.10
London Gold Mines	88.2	+ 2.5	+ 2.92
Frankfurt DAX	1734.62	+ 0.52	+ 0.03
Zurich Swiss Market	1844.4	+ 9.3	+ 0.51
Paris CAC 40	1853.26	− 6.18	− 0.33
Milan Stock Index	875	− 5	− 0.57
Amsterdam ANP-CBS General	204.5	+ 0.6	+ 0.29
Stockholm Affarsvarlden	887.5	− 0.6	− 0.07
Brussels Bel-20 Index	1171.86	+ 6.67	+ 0.57
Australia All Ordinaries	1636.7	− 2.1	− 0.13
Hong Kong Hang Seng	6125.46	+ 28.27	+ 0.46
Singapore Straits Times	1481.15	− 2.63	− 0.18
Johannesburg J'burg Gold	1090	+ 30	+ 2.83
Madrid General Index	231.07	− 3.47	− 1.48
Mexico I.P.C.	1639.76	+ 3.76	+ 0.23
Toronto 300 Composite	3472.03	+ 8.86	+ 0.26
Euro, Aust, Far East MSCI-p	797.0	+ 2.4	+ 0.30

p-Preliminary
na-Not available

(b) Morgan Stanley Indices

	Jul 14	Jul 13	% This Year
U.S.	390.0	387.9	0.0
Britain	735.8	734.0	− 0.2
Canada	391.3	389.8	− 1.1
Japan	747.4	749.9	− 24.5
France	534.9	534.9	+ 6.9
Germany	261.0	261.3	+ 7.3
Hong Kong	4460.5	4438.1	+ 44.1
Switzerland	228.3	229.1	+ 11.3
Australia	350.6	350.4	− 0.2
World Index	507.1	506.6	− 5.3

exchange rates at the time. Values of the other indices are stated only in U.S. dollars. At last count, approximately 1,500 stocks were included, representing about 60% of the aggregate market value listed on the twenty-two covered stock exchanges.[6]

All the stocks are used to compute the "World" index. The "Europe" index includes companies representing the European countries. The "Europe, Australia, Far East" (EAFE) index is widely used by U.S. investors as a benchmark when evaluating the performance of international portfolio managers. Several of the Morgan Stanley indices are published daily in *The Wall Street Journal*, as shown in panel (b) of Figure 26-2; the EAFE index appears at the bottom of panel (a).

Risk and Return from Foreign Investing

Investing in a foreign security involves all the risks associated with investing in a domestic security plus additional risks. The investor expects to receive cash flows in the future from the foreign security. However, these cash flows will be in a foreign currency and thus will be of relatively little use to the investor if they cannot be converted into the investor's domestic currency. The additional risks associated with foreign investing result from uncertainties associated with converting these foreign cash flows into domestic currency. They are known as **political risk** and **exchange** (or currency) **risk.**[7]

political risk
exchange risk

[6]For more on these and other indices, see Chapter 5 in Bruno Solnik, *International Investments* (Reading, Mass.: Addison-Wesley Publishing Company, Inc., 1991).

[7]The effects these types of risk have on asset pricing has been considered by a number of people. For a discussion and list of references, see Chapters 1 and 5 in Solnik, *International Investments*.

MONEY MATTERS
Currency Risk: To Hedge or Not to Hedge

Investors in securities denominated in currencies other than those of their home country incur a risk not borne by their domestic investor counterparts: currency risk. For investors in foreign assets, currency risk is the variability in portfolio returns caused by fluctuations in the rate at which foreign currencies can be converted into their home currency. Whether investors in foreign securities should attempt to minimize currency risk in their portfolios has become a topic of considerable controversy in recent years. Among institutional investors, the issue has taken on increased importance as these investors have expanded their foreign investments.

As the text describes, the return on an investor's foreign portfolio can be divided into two components: a domestic (also called local) return and a currency (also called foreign exchange) return. Likewise, foreign portfolio risk can be decomposed into domestic risk, currency risk, and any possible interaction between the two. Most studies indicate that currency risk can increase total portfolio risk by anywhere from 15% to 100% of the underlying domestic risk.

Investors have a choice of whether to bear currency risk. Through a variety of techniques, currency risk can be "hedged" and almost eliminated. The most popular means of hedging currency risk is to purchase units of the investor's home currency in the forward market equivalent to the value of the foreign investment. For example, consider a U.S. investor holding 1,000 shares of a Japanese company selling for 4,000 yen per share. He or she can purchase dollars for delivery six months from today at a rate of 125 yen per dollar. (The forward market is quite similar to the futures market—see Chapter 25. Both forward and futures contracts involve a promise to deliver something of value on a specified future date at a currently agreed-upon price. The forward market, however, does not involve a standardized contract traded on an organized exchange with a third party clearinghouse that ensures that contracts are honored. Moreover, forward contracts, unlike futures contracts, are not marked to market daily.) By purchasing $32,000 for delivery six months from today to be paid for with 4,000,000 yen, the investor insulates himself or herself from changes in the exchange rate between the yen and the dollar over the next six months.

Despite the availability of effective hedging tools, why do many investors in foreign securities choose not to hedge their currency risks and instead remain exposed to exchange rate fluctuations? We consider the primary arguments presented in support of and in opposition to currency risk hedging.

Proponents of hedging currency risk contend that a no-hedge policy violates one of the basic laws of modern portfolio theory: Only accept risks for which adequate compensation is expected to be earned. They view currencies as having zero expected returns. That is, in a world in which capital is free to flow across borders,

Political risk refers to uncertainty about the *ability* of an investor to convert the foreign currency into domestic currency. Specifically, a foreign government might restrict, tax, or completely prohibit the exchange of one currency for another. Since such policies change from time to time, the ability of an investor to repatriate foreign cash flows may be subject to some uncertainty. There may even be a possibility of complete expropriation, making the political risk very large.

Exchange risk refers to uncertainty about the *rate* at which a foreign currency can be exchanged for the investor's domestic currency in the future. That is, at the time a foreign security is bought, the rate at which future foreign cash flows can be converted into domestic currency is uncertain, and it is this uncertainty that is known as exchange risk.

Hedging Exchange Risk To an extent, exchange risk can be reduced by hedging in the forward (or futures) market for foreign currency. In the case of default-free fixed-income securities, it may be possible to completely eliminate such risk in this way. For example, assume that a one-year pure discount bond paying 1,000 British pounds at maturity can be purchased for 850 British pounds. Furthermore, assume that a forward contract can be signed where the investor will receive $1,300 for delivering 1,000 British pounds a year from

there is no reason to expect the value of foreign currencies to move systematically in one direction relative to an investor's home currency. However, exchange rates definitely do fluctuate, thereby generating additional risk for an investor in foreign securities. As a result, hedging proponents view currency risk as uncompensated and believe that risk-averse investors should seek its minimization. Investors who do not hedge would seem to be passing up an opportunity to reduce portfolio risk while not diminishing portfolio returns. Proponents point out that the reduction in portfolio variability gained by hedging currency risk can be substantial.

Opponents of currency hedging generally concede that forgoing hedging means accepting additional uncompensated risks. (However, there is a school of thought that contends that currency risk should be systematically rewarded by the market.) Nevertheless, they believe that market "frictions" cause the costs of currency hedging to outweigh the risk reduction benefits. That is, significant expenses are likely to be incurred by an investor managing currency risk. Currency dealers must be compensated for facilitating hedging transactions. Custodian banks must be paid for recordkeeping. Investment managers charge fees for maintaining the hedge. Estimates of the total cost of hedging typically range from .25% to .50% per year of the value of the hedged assets, enough to convince opponents that currency risk hedging may not be cost-effective.

In addition, some hedging opponents have questioned the wisdom of hedging for an investor who spends a high percentage of his or her income on goods produced abroad. Suppose the value of foreign currencies declines relative to the investor's home currency (thereby negatively affecting the investor's foreign portfolio returns, other things equal). The declining relative value of the foreign currencies also reduces the effective cost of foreign-produced goods to the investor. In a sense the investor's consumption basket serves as a hedge against currency risk in his or her portfolio.

In the final analysis, an investor's optimal currency hedge will depend on a number of factors, including the following:

1. correlations between currencies,
2. correlations between domestic returns and currency returns within and across countries,
3. the cost of hedging,
4. the portions of the investor's portfolio allocated to foreign securities,
5. the variability of foreign asset returns,
6. the variability of currency returns,
7. the investor's consumption basket,
8. the investor's level of risk aversion, and
9. the premium earned (if any) for holding foreign currencies.

These factors are difficult to quantify, making it difficult to build a strong case for or against currency hedging. Moreover, since investors differ in both their circumstances and their beliefs about the characteristics of currencies and security markets, it is not surprising that we observe everything from zero hedges to fully hedged positions.

now. In this situation, the rate of return *in British pounds* on this security is 17.65% [= (1,000 − 850)/850].

If the current (that is, spot) exchange rate were $1.35 per pound, then the cost of this bond to an American investor would be $1,147.50 (= 850 × $1.35). Thus, the rate of return *in American dollars* on this British security would be 13.29% [= ($1,300 − $1,147.50)/$1,147.50]. Except for political risk, this is a certain return, since exchange risk has been completely removed by hedging with a forward contract.

Unfortunately, it is not possible to completely hedge the exchange risk associated with risky investments. Forward contracts can be made to cover expected cash flows, but if the actual cash flows are larger or smaller than expected, then some of the foreign currency may have to be exchanged at the spot rate prevailing at the time that the cash is received. Since future spot rates usually cannot be predicted with complete certainty, this will affect overall risk. As a practical matter, this "unhedgeable" risk is likely to be small. Nevertheless, the cost of hedging foreign investments may exceed the benefit—perhaps by a large amount (see the above "Money Matters").

Foreign and Domestic Returns Changes in exchange rates can cause major differences between the returns obtained by domestic investors and the returns obtained by unhedged foreign investors.

domestic return

Consider an American investor and a Swiss investor, both of whom purchase shares of a Swiss company whose stock is traded only in Switzerland. Let the price of the stock in Swiss francs be P_0 at the beginning of a period and P_1 at the end of the period. The **domestic return,** denoted r_d, is:

$$r_d = \frac{P_1 - P_0}{P_0}. \tag{26.1}$$

For example, if $P_0 = 10$ Swiss francs and $P_1 = 12$ Swiss francs, then $r_d = (12 - 10)/10 = 20\%$.

For the Swiss investor, r_d is the stock's return. Not so for the U.S. investor. Assume that at the beginning of the period the price (in dollars) of one Swiss franc is \$.50. Denoting this exchange rate (that is, the exchange rate at the beginning of the period) as X_0, the cost of a share to the American investor will be X_0P_0. In the example, this cost will be $\$.50 \times 10 = \$5$.

Now, assume that the exchange rate rises to \$.55 per Swiss franc at the end of the period. Denoting this by X_1, the ending value of the stock for the American investor will be X_1P_1. In the example, this value will be $\$.55 \times 12 = \$6.60$.

foreign return

The **foreign return** (that is, the return to a foreign investor), denoted r_f, is:

$$r_f = \frac{X_1P_1 - X_0P_0}{X_0P_0}. \tag{26.2}$$

In the example, the foreign investor (an American) would have earned a return of $r_f = (\$6.60 - \$5.00)/\$5.00 = 32\%$ on an investment in the Swiss firm's stock.

In effect, the American made *two* investments: (1) an investment in a Swiss stock, and (2) an investment in the Swiss franc. Accordingly, the overall return to the American can be decomposed into a return on the investment in the Swiss stock and a return on the investment in the Swiss franc. This can be illustrated by considering an American who had purchased a Swiss franc at the beginning of the period. If the American subsequently sold the franc at the end of the period, the return on foreign currency, denoted r_c, would be:

$$r_c = \frac{X_1 - X_0}{X_0}. \tag{26.3}$$

In the example, $r_c = (\$.55 - \$.50)/\$.50 = 10\%$.

From equations (26.1), (26.2), and (26.3), it can be shown that:

$$1 + r_f = (1 + r_d)(1 + r_c) \tag{26.4}$$

which can be rewritten as:

$$r_f = r_d + r_c + r_dr_c. \tag{26.5}$$

In the example, equation (26.5) reveals that $r_f = .20 + .10 + (.20 \times .10)$, which is equal to 32%.

The last term in this equation (r_dr_c) will generally be smaller than the two preceding ones, since it equals their product, and both are generally less than 1.0. Thus, equation (26.5) can be restated as an approximation:

$$r_f \approx r_d + r_c. \qquad (26.6)$$

It can now be seen that the return on a foreign security (r_f) can be decomposed into two parts, representing the domestic return on the security (r_d) and the return on foreign currency (r_c). In the example, the precise value for r_f was shown earlier to be 32%; use of the approximation indicates its value to be equal to .20 + .10, or 30%. Thus, the approximation is in error by 2%, a relatively small amount.

Expected Returns Equation (26.6) leads directly to the proposition that the expected return on a foreign security will approximately equal the expected domestic return plus the expected return on foreign currency:

$$\bar{r}_f \approx \bar{r}_d + \bar{r}_c. \qquad (26.7)$$

It might be tempting for an investor to purchase a foreign security that has a high expected return in its host country, $\bar{r}_d$, on the belief that this means that the security will have a high expected return to the investor, $\bar{r}_f$. However, equation (26.7) reveals this type of logic to be flawed. Just because a foreign security has a high value for $\bar{r}_d$ does not mean that it has a high value for $\bar{r}_f$, since $\bar{r}_c$ can be negative. This can be shown by considering the case of bonds.

The expected domestic returns of bonds in countries with high expected inflation rates will typically be high. However, a foreign investor in a country with a lower expected inflation rate should expect a *negative* return on foreign currency, as his or her currency can be expected to *appreciate* relative to that of the country with the higher expected inflation rate. In evaluating the expected return on the foreign security, there is thus good news (a high expected domestic return, $\bar{r}_d$) and bad news (a negative expected return on foreign currency, $\bar{r}_c$). On balance, the expected foreign return $\bar{r}_f$ might not be as exceptional as first thought when just $\bar{r}_d$ was considered. Indeed, if markets were completely integrated, it would be reasonable to expect the values of $\bar{r}_d$ and $\bar{r}_c$ to sum to an amount $\bar{r}_f$ that is equal to the expected return on an equivalent bond in the investor's own country.

Foreign and Domestic Risks Having seen in equation (26.7) that the expected return on a foreign security consists of two components, it is appropriate that the risk of the foreign security be evaluated next. As before, consider an American investor and a Swiss investor who have purchased shares of a Swiss company. The domestic variance, denoted σ_d^2, is the risk that the Swiss investor faces with respect to the Swiss stock. Correspondingly, the foreign variance, denoted σ_f^2, is the risk that the American investor faces with respect to the Swiss stock. Based on equation (26.6), it can be shown that the foreign variance consists of three components:

$$\sigma_f^2 = \sigma_d^2 + \sigma_c^2 + 2\rho_{dc}\sigma_d\sigma_c \qquad (26.8)$$

where σ_c^2 is the variance associated with the currency return to an American from investing in Swiss francs and later exchanging them for American dollars, and ρ_{dc} is the correlation coefficient between the return on the Swiss stock and the return on Swiss francs.

For example, assume that the domestic variance is 225 (meaning that the domestic standard deviation, σ_d, is $\sqrt{225} = 15\%$) and the currency variance is 25 (meaning that the currency standard deviation, σ_c, is $\sqrt{25} = 5\%$). If

$\rho_{dc} = 0$, then equation (26.8) indicates that the foreign variance is $225 + 25 = 250$. Accordingly, the foreign standard deviation is $\sqrt{250} = 15.8\%$, which is only slightly greater than the domestic standard deviation of 15%.

Equation (26.8) reveals that the smaller the correlation between returns on a foreign currency and returns on a foreign investment, the smaller will be the foreign variance. One study that used data from seventeen countries over the period from January 1971 through December 1980 found an average correlation of .034, which is effectively zero.[8] Thus, it appears that the correlation is sufficiently small that the foreign variance will typically be near, but not less than, the sum of the domestic and currency variances.[9]

Table 26-2 provides evidence on the relative magnitudes of the three types of risk. Standard deviations of monthly values over the period from December 1970 through December 1980 are shown for domestic risk (corresponding to σ_d), currency risk (corresponding to σ_c), and foreign risk (corre-

[8]Bruno Solnik and Eric Nemeth, "Asset Returns and Currency Fluctuations: A Time Series Analysis," paper presented at the second tagung, Geld Banken und Versicherungen, Universitat Karlsruhe, December 1982.

[9]Since standard deviation is the square root of variance, this means that the foreign standard deviation will typically be substantially less than the sum of the domestic and currency standard deviations.

TABLE 26-2
Risks for Domestic and U.S. Investors Based on Historic Values, December 1970–December 1980

	(1) DOMESTIC RISK	(2) CURRENCY RISK	(3) FOREIGN RISK	(4) FOREIGN/ DOMESTIC RISK
		Stocks		
Australia	24.62%	9.15%	27.15%	1.10
Belgium	13.28	11.02	18.76	1.41
Canada	18.92	4.16	20.29	1.07
Denmark	15.41	10.28	17.65	1.15
France	22.00	10.24	25.81	1.17
Germany	13.87	11.87	18.39	1.33
Hong Kong	47.95	5.63	45.80	.96
Italy	24.21	8.58	26.15	1.08
Japan	16.39	10.42	19.55	1.19
Netherlands	16.37	10.97	18.91	1.16
Norway	28.61	8.89	29.92	1.05
Singapore	35.82	6.52	36.03	1.01
Spain	16.71	9.10	20.26	1.21
Sweden	15.05	8.89	18.06	1.20
Switzerland	16.80	14.67	21.40	1.27
United Kingdom	28.94	8.84	31.61	1.09
United States	16.00	.00	16.00	1.00
		Bonds		
Canada	6.16	4.16	7.93	1.29
France	4.39	10.24	11.80	2.69
Germany	6.91	11.87	14.35	2.08
Japan	6.53	10.42	14.36	2.20
Netherlands	7.16	10.97	13.61	1.90
Switzerland	4.33	14.67	15.33	3.54
United Kingdom	12.30	8.84	16.29	1.32
United States	8.96	.00	8.96	1.00

Source: Adapted from Bruno Solnik and Bernard Noetzlin, "Optimal International Asset Allocation," *Journal of Portfolio Management*, 9, no. 1 (Fall 1982): 13.

sponding to σ_f), where the latter two types of risk have been measured from the perspective of an American investor. The last column represents the ratio of foreign risk to domestic risk. Thus, a ratio greater than one can be taken as an indication that the risk to an American investor is greater than the risk to a domestic investor. Indeed, with the exception of Hong Kong stocks, all the ratios are greater than one, suggesting that fluctuations in currency exchange rates increased the risk an American investor would have faced in buying foreign securities.

The importance of currency risk can easily be exaggerated. Calculations such as those in Table 26-2 assume that investors purchase only domestic goods and services and thus convert all proceeds from foreign investments into their own currency before engaging in any spending for consumption purposes. But most people buy foreign goods and many buy foreign services as well (for example, as tourists). The cheaper another country's currency relative to one's own, the more attractive purchases of its goods and services will be. Other things being equal, it may make sense to invest more in countries whose products and scenery are admired, for the effective currency risk is likely to be smaller there than elsewhere.

Multinational Firms

Firms operating in many countries provide international diversification at the corporate level. One might expect that investment in the stocks of such **multinational firms** could serve as a good substitute for investment in stocks of foreign ("national") firms.

multinational firms

A number of studies have shown that this may not be the case. In one, returns on portfolios of stocks of multinational firms headquartered in each of nine countries were calculated for the period from April 1966 through June 1974. Then each portfolio's returns were compared with the returns on the market index for the country of its headquarters. The middle column in Table 26-3 shows the proportion of each portfolio's variance that can be attributed to movements in its corresponding "domestic" market index. Finally, each portfolio's returns were compared with the returns on market indices in all nine countries. The final column in Table 26-3 shows the proportion of each portfolio's variance that can be attributed to movements in its domestic market index as well as the foreign market indices.

TABLE 26-3
Proportions of Returns on Stocks of Multinational Firms Explained by Stock Market Indices

	PROPORTION OF VARIANCE IN RETURNS EXPLAINED BY	
Headquarters Country of Multinational Firms	**Domestic Market Index**	**Domestic and Other Market Indices**
Belgium	45%	58%
France	45	62
Germany	65	74
Italy	47	51
Netherlands	50	63
Sweden	42	50
Switzerland	52	75
United Kingdom	44	49
United States	29	31

Source: Adapted from Bertrand Jacquillat and Bruno Solnik, "Multinationals Are Poor Tools for Diversification," *Journal of Portfolio Management*, 4, no. 2 (Winter 1978): 10.

During the period covered in Table 26-3, the returns on multinational firms based in the United States had only 2% (= 31% − 29%) of their variance that could be attributed to foreign market indices. This suggests that U.S.-headquartered multinationals were a poor substitute for direct investment in foreign stocks by U.S. investors. The situation was somewhat better for non-U.S. multinationals, since the differences in the percentages shown in the two columns were greater than 2%. One possible explanation for this is that non-U.S. multinationals have more extensive foreign operations than U.S. multinationals.

International Listings

The common stocks of many firms are traded not only on the major stock exchange in their home country but also on an exchange in a foreign country. For this reason foreign investors no longer have to engage in foreign currency transactions when buying and selling the firm's stock. It is also possible that foreign investors can escape certain taxes and regulations to which they would be subject if the security were to be bought in the firm's home country. As mentioned in Chapter 3, there are two ways that such internationally listed foreign securities can be traded in the United States.

American Depository Receipts

The first way foreign securities may be traded in the United States is with **American Depository Receipts** (ADRs). ADRs are financial assets that are issued by U.S. banks and represent indirect ownership of a certain number of shares of a specific foreign firm that are held on deposit in a bank in the firm's home country. The advantage of ADRs over direct ownership is that the investor need not worry about the delivery of the stock certificates or converting dividend payments from a foreign currency into U.S. dollars. The depository bank automatically does the converting for the investor and also forwards all financial reports from the firm; the investor pays the bank a relatively small fee for these services. At the end of 1990, sixty-two foreign firms had their common stock traded as ADRs on the New York Stock Exchange, while eighty-seven foreign firms were traded as ADRs on the NASDAQ system.[10]

The second way foreign securities may be traded in the United States is for the shares of the firm to be traded directly, just like the shares of a typical U.S. firm. At the end of 1990, thirty-four foreign firms had their common stock traded directly on the New York Stock Exchange, while the stocks of 170 foreign firms were traded directly on the NASDAQ system. Of these, twenty-eight and 132 were Canadian firms, respectively.

One study that examined the diversification implications of investing in ADRs found that such securities were of notable benefit to U.S. investors.[11] Specifically, a sample of forty-five ADRs was examined and compared with a sample of forty-five U.S. securities over the period from 1973 to 1983. Using an index based on all NYSE-listed stocks, the betas of the ADRs had an average value of .26, which was much lower than the average beta of 1.01 for the U.S. securities. Furthermore, the correlation of the ADRs' returns with those of the

---

[10]The London Stock Exchange began trading many of these ADRs in August 1987, with prices quoted in U.S. dollars. See National Association of Security Dealers *1991 NASDAQ Fact Book*, pp. 14–15; New York Stock Exchange *Fact Book 1991*, pp. 29–31.

[11]Dennis T. Officer and J. Ronald Hoffmeister, "ADRs: A Substitute for the Real Thing?" *Journal of Portfolio Management*, 13, no. 2 (Winter 1987): 61–65. See also Leonard Rosenthal, "An Empirical Test of the Efficiency of the ADR Market," *Journal of Banking and Finance*, 7, no. 1 (March 1983): 17–29.

NYSE market portfolio averaged .33, while U.S. securities had a notably higher average correlation of .53. Given these two observations, it is not surprising that portfolios formed from U.S. securities and ADRs had much lower standard deviations than portfolios consisting of just U.S. securities. For example, portfolios consisting of ten U.S. securities had an average standard deviation of 5.50%, while a ten-security portfolio split evenly between U.S. securities and ADRs had an average standard deviation of 4.41%. Thus, in contrast to investing in multinationals, it seems that investing in ADRs brings significant benefits in terms of risk reduction.

Correlations Between Equity Markets

If all economies were tied together completely, stock markets in different countries would move together, and little advantage could be gained through international diversification. But this is not the case. Table 26-4 shows the correlations of returns on diversified "market" portfolios of equities in various national stock markets with the returns on an index of equities in all the included countries (that is, the "world" portfolio). The value for the United States is large, owing primarily to the importance of the United States in the world index. However, the striking feature is that many of the figures are very small (and some are even negative), even though each of the national indices represents a well-diversified domestic equity portfolio. These low correlations suggest that there are sizable potential advantages, in terms of risk reduction, from international diversification.[12]

[12]Another study of 349 stocks in eleven countries revealed an average intercountry correlation coefficient of .234 for the period from January 1973 to December 1983. See D. Chinhyung Cho, Cheol S. Eun, and Lemma W. Senbet, "International Arbitrage Pricing Theory: An Empirical Investigation," *Journal of Finance*, 41, no. 2 (June 1986): 313–29. For a multiperiod approach that indicates the benefits from international diversification, particularly for highly risk-averse investors, see Robert R. Grauer and Nils H. Hakansson, "Gains from International Diversification: 1968–85 Returns on Portfolios of Stocks and Bonds," *Journal of Finance*, 42, no. 3 (July 1987): 721–39.

TABLE 26-4
Correlations of Annual U.S. Dollar-Adjusted Total Equity Returns with World Total Equities, 1960–1980

COUNTRY	CORRELATION
Australia	.753
Austria	−.042
Belgium	.483
Canada	.716
Denmark	.358
France	.384
Germany	.322
Hong Kong	.848
Italy	.281
Japan	.385
Netherlands	.804
Norway	−.045
Singapore	.700
Spain	−.015
Sweden	.470
Switzerland	.557
United Kingdom	.703
United States	.967

Source: Adapted from Roger G. Ibbotson, Richard C. Carr, and Anthony W. Robinson, "International Equity and Bond Returns," *Financial Analysts Journal*, 38, no. 4 (July/August 1982): 71.

MONEY MATTERS
Foreign Currencies

As the investment industry becomes increasingly international, the importance of understanding how foreign security markets operate will grow. The truly sophisticated international investor will have command of a broad range of institutional details, including a familiarity with foreign currencies. Just how skillful are you at recognizing the currencies of various nations? As a test, match the currencies listed below with the corresponding countries. (Answers are provided in the Questions and Problems section at the end of the chapter.)

COUNTRY	CURRENCY
1. Austria	1. Guilder
2. Brazil	2. Markka
3. Britain	3. Schilling
4. China	4. Renminbi
5. Denmark	5. Won
6. Finland	6. Shekel
7. France	7. Yen
8. Germany	8. Cruzeiro
9. Greece	9. Pound
10. Hungary	10. Drachma
11. Ireland	11. Krone
12. Israel	12. Forint
13. Italy	13. Lira
14. Japan	14. Zloty
15. Malaysia	15. Peseta
16. Mexico	16. Franc
17. Netherlands	17. Punt
18. Poland	18. Ringgit
19. Spain	19. Mark
20. South Korea	20. Peso

TANGIBLE ASSETS

In the first half of the 1970s, marketable securities such as stocks and bonds provided returns that were relatively disappointing, especially after adjusting for inflation. And, as shown in Chapter 6, neither bonds nor stocks have served as good hedges against unanticipated inflation in recent years. Overall, tangible assets have been better hedges against inflation. One example, real estate, was shown in Chapter 6 to have been an attractive inflation hedge in recent years.[13] Other examples, such as collectible assets and precious metals (like gold and silver), provide various degrees of protection against inflation.

Collectible Assets

Not surprisingly, periodic disenchantment with returns on marketable securities has led some investors to examine a host of tangible assets that are normally considered only by "collectors." Table 26-5 shows the average returns over three five-year periods for several different kinds of collectible assets (often referred to as simply "collectibles").

Some of the returns shown in the table are quite high. However, none of the collectible assets provided consistently high results over all three periods. This is not surprising because if one (or more) had provided consistently high returns, many investors would have been attracted to it and bid its price up to a level where high returns would no longer have been possible.

[13]While not a tangible asset, commodity futures were shown in Chapter 25 to have also been an attractive inflation hedge.

TABLE 26-5 Annual Returns on Collectible Assets, Five-Year Periods Ending June 1

	1969–1974	1974–1979	1979–1984
Chinese ceramics	31.1%	−3.1%	15.7%
Coins	9.5	32.4	11.3
Diamonds	11.6	13.6	6.1
Old masters	7.3	17.3	1.5
U.S. stamps	14.1	24.9	9.8

Source: Based on data in R. S. Salomon, Jr., and Mallory J. Lennox, "Financial Assets—A Temporary Setback," *Stock Research Investment Policy*, Salomon Brothers, Inc., June 8, 1984.

In a sense, a collectible asset often provides income to the owner in the form of consumption. For example, an investor can admire a Rembrandt painting, sit on a Chippendale chair, play a Stradivarius violin, and drive a Morgan car. Value received in this manner is not subject to income taxation and is thus likely to be especially attractive for those in high tax brackets. However, the value of such consumption depends strongly on one's preferences.

If markets are efficient, collectible assets will be priced so that those who enjoy them most will find it desirable to hold them in greater-than-market-value proportions, while those who enjoy them least will find it desirable to hold them in less-than-market-value proportions (and, in many cases, not at all).

Institutional funds and investment pools have been organized to hold paintings, stamps, coins, and other collectible assets. Such arrangements are subject to serious question if they involve locking such objects in vaults where they cannot be seen by those who derive pleasure from this sort of consumption. On the other hand, if the items are rented to others, the only loss may be that associated with the transfer of a portion of the consumption value to the government in the form of a tax on income.

Investors in collectibles should be aware of two types of risk that are especially notable. The first is that the bid-ask spread is often very large. Thus, an investor must see a large price increase just to recoup the spread and break even. The second is that collectibles are subject to "fads." For example, Chinese ceramics may be actively sought by many investors today, leading to high prices, and big returns for earlier purchasers. However, they may fall out of favor later on, and plunge in value. Unlike financial assets, there is no such thing as "fair" value for collectibles that can act as a kind of anchor for the market price.

Gold

In the United States, private holdings of gold bullion were illegal before the 1970s. In other countries, investment in gold has long been a tradition. According to one estimate, at the end of 1984 gold represented over 6% of the world market wealth portfolio.[14]

Table 26-6 contrasts a U.S. investor's returns from gold with the returns from U.S. equities over the period from 1960 through 1984. Gold is clearly a risky investment, but in this period, at least, it also provided high average returns.

[14] Ibbotson, Siegel, and Love, "World Wealth: Market Values and Returns," 9.

TABLE 26-6
Characteristics of Gold and U.S. Equity Returns, 1960–1984

	AVERAGE ANNUAL RETURN	STANDARD DEVIATION OF ANNUAL RETURNS
U.S. Equities	10.20%	16.89%
Gold	12.62	29.87
Correlation:		
Gold and U.S. Equities	−.09	
Gold and Inflation	.63	

Source: Adapted from Roger G. Ibbotson, Laurence B. Siegel, and Kathryn S. Love, "World Wealth: Market Values and Returns," *Journal of Portfolio Management*, 12, no. 1 (Fall 1985): 17, 21.

For any single investment, risk and return are only parts of the story: Correlations of an asset's return with the returns on other assets are also relevant. In the period covered in Table 26-6, gold price changes were slightly negatively correlated with stock returns. Similar results have been obtained for other periods. Gold thus appears to be an effective diversifying asset for an equity investor. Table 26-6 also shows that gold prices were highly correlated with the rate of inflation in the United States as measured by changes in the Consumer Price Index. This is consistent with gold's traditional role as a hedge against inflation, since higher inflation generally brings higher gold prices.

Investors interested in gold need not restrict themselves to bullion. Other possibilities range from stocks of gold mining companies to gold futures to gold coins and commemoratives. Furthermore, there are other types of precious metals, such as silver, that investors may want to consider.

SPORTS BETTING

Throughout the world, large amounts of money are wagered on the outcomes of sporting events. In the United States, betting on horse races is conducted legally at race tracks in many states and via legal off-track betting establishments in some states. In addition, illegal bookmakers in every state accept bets on horse races. Bets on other events—most notably professional football games—are made legally in Nevada and illegally with bookmakers almost everywhere.

There are some interesting parallels between betting and investing in securities. Both involve an initial outlay of cash and an outcome that, being uncertain, can be thought of as a random variable. For both betting and investing, an individual must have some sort of strategy in deciding where to put his or her money—after all, there are a large number of sporting events as well as securities. Furthermore, these strategies can be thought of as being either fundamental or technical in nature. In the case of fundamental strategies, an investor or bettor looks at the underlying strength of the firm or team or horse that is being evaluated, while in the case of a technical strategy, only past performance is of concern. Both of these strategies are typically based on publicly available information; thus, the historical performance of investors and bettors can be examined in order to see if the respective financial markets and "sports markets" are semistrong-form efficient. To begin the discussion, a parallel will be made between a security dealer and a bookmaker.

A security dealer typically wishes to operate with, on average, a small inventory of securities so as to have relatively little exposure to loss through security price fluctuations. To do this, the dealer usually sets a bid price and an asked price that will bring roughly an equal number of orders for purchases and sales in a given time period (say, a week's time). The bid-ask spread represents the dealer's profit margin and part of the investor's transaction costs.

Similarly, in sports betting the bookmaker acts as dealer and wishes to have relatively little "inventory" (exposure to loss). Two major methods are employed to achieve this: "spread betting" and "odds betting." The former is used for bets on games such as football and baseball and the latter for bets on contests such as horse races and presidential elections.

Spread Betting

In order to understand spread betting, consider a hypothetical professional football game between the San Francisco 49'ers and the Minnesota Vikings. It is widely felt that the 49'ers are likely to win. Thus, the bookmaker establishes a spread, perhaps deciding that the 49'ers are "favored by 7 points." This means that the final score will, in effect, be modified by subtracting 7 points from the 49'ers score and then paying those who bet on the "winner" using that adjusted score. People who bet on San Francisco believe that the S.F. team will "cover the spread"; those who bet on Minnesota believe that Minnesota will cover the spread. If the final score is 28–20 in favor of San Francisco, then after adjusting for the spread the score is 21–20 in favor of San Francisco, and those betting on San Francisco will have won. However, if the final score is 24–20 in favor of San Francisco, then the adjusted score will be 17–20 in favor of Minnesota, and those betting on Minnesota will have won.[15]

The point spread serves as an equilibrating mechanism. Other things being equal, the greater the spread, the smaller will be the amount bet on San Francisco and the larger the amount bet on Minnesota. At some level the "books will be balanced," meaning that an equal amount has been bet on both teams. Given local prejudices, this may be accomplished by San Francisco bookmakers "laying off" excess money bet on the 49'ers with Minnesota bookmakers who have excess money bet on the Vikings.

How does the bookmaker make a living? With a range that corresponds to the security dealer's bid-ask spread. Typically, the bettor puts up $11 for a $10 bet, meaning that a winner will receive $10 (plus his or her initial $11 bet, if paid in advance) while a loser is out the initial $11 bet. If the books are balanced, the bookmaker will pay out $21 for every $22 taken in. For example, if there is one $11 bet on San Francisco and one $11 bet on Minnesota, the books are balanced. Then, whichever team wins, the bookmaker will pay out $21 of the $22 that was bet.

While bookmakers generally set point spreads to balance their books, in an efficient market such spreads would provide good estimates of the expected differences in points scored (and, by and large, the evidence is consistent with market efficiency).

Odds Betting

A goal of many "dealers" in bets is to be reasonably certain that after the contest is over, less money will be paid out than is received. Hence, if they are

[15]In the event of a tie in the adjusted score, the money that was bet is returned to both sides.

successful, the average return to bettors will be negative. To do this, terms must be set so that bets on underdogs are attractive. Spreads are one way; odds are another.

An example from horse racing will illustrate the procedure. Assume that Black Socks is favored to win the sixth race at Golden Gate Fields, while the other seven horses are considered inferior but of roughly equal speed. If the payoff per dollar bet were the same for all eight horses, most of the bets would be placed on the favorite. To spread the betting over the contenders, a larger amount must be paid per dollar bet if a long shot is bet on and subsequently wins.

Assume that the odds are set at 7-to-1 for each of the seven slow horses. This means that if $1 is bet on one of them and the horse wins, the bettor will receive $8 (the original $1 that was bet plus $7 in winnings). Assume also that the odds on Black Socks are set at 5-to-3, so that every $3 bet on the favorite will return $8 (the original $3 that was bet plus $5 in winnings) if the horse wins. Now imagine that the amounts bet, given these odds, are as shown in Table 26-7. The total pool or "handle" (that is, the total amount bet) is $1,000, but no matter which horse wins the race, only $800 will be paid out. The remaining $200 is for the track, the government, and the bookmaker, and is known as the "take." Note that the average return to the bettors is −20% (= −$200/$1,000) because of the take.

The numbers in Table 26-7 may seem contrived, but they represent the kind of situation achieved automatically by parimutuel betting. In this form of wagering (used at most horse racetracks), the actual odds for a horse are determined *after all betting has finished* by subtracting the take (typically about 20%) and the amount bet on the horse from the handle, then dividing this amount by the amount bet on that horse.[16] For example, in the case of Black Socks (horse number 1), the odds are ($1,000 − $200 − $300)/$300 = $500/$300 = 5/3, as shown in the table. It should be noted that the "dealer" is always assured of receiving a fixed percentage (20%) for "transaction costs" with this procedure, and hence the average bettor loses money.

Thus, betting on horses is a negative-sum game: Owing to transaction costs, the amount paid out is less than the amount paid in. Consequently, the expected return on the average bet will be negative. Since it is difficult to justify such activity on the basis of hedging, a bettor either (1) believes that he or she is a superior predictor, or (2) is willing to pay in this manner for

[16]This applies only to bets that a horse will win the race. More complex procedures are used for "place" (second or better) and "show" (third or better) in bets. In addition, the actual payoff is usually rounded down to the nearest multiple of, say, $.10 per $2 bet.

TABLE 26-7
Odds, Amounts Bet, and Payouts for a Horse Race

HORSE	AMOUNT BET	ODDS	AMOUNT PAID OUT IF HORSE WINS
#1 (favorite)	$ 300	5-to-3	$800
2	100	7-to-1	800
3	100	7-to-1	800
4	100	7-to-1	800
5	100	7-to-1	800
6	100	7-to-1	800
7	100	7-to-1	800
8	100	7-to-1	800
Total amount bet =	$1,000		

entertainment, or (3) prefers risk. Undoubtedly, all three aspects play a role in the sports betting market. One attribute that makes betting on sports entertaining is the suspension of the bettor's usual mind set and the taking of risks with relatively small amounts of money. In such an environment and with limited exposure, even a conservative investor may take pleasure in acting like a riverboat gambler.

Evidence consistent with risk preference of this sort has been found in many analyses of the expected returns from bets on horses with different probabilities of winning races. Figure 26-3 summarizes a number of such studies. The horizontal axis indicates closing odds (on a logarithmic scale). Favorites plot at the left end of the scale and extreme long shots at the right end. The vertical axis indicates average returns. All are negative, but the returns on favorites are considerably better than those on long shots. "Investors" at the track are apparently willing to give up some expected return to get more risk—in this domain they appear to prefer risk.

The Efficiency of Horse Race Betting

Investors in stocks can avail themselves of the results of financial analysis, both fundamental and technical. However, the high degree of efficiency of the stock market diminishes the value of such information for a single investor, since much of it is already reflected in security prices.

A similar situation prevails in the market for horse race betting. Fundamental analyses of such factors as the abilities of horses and trainers and the effects of weather abound, as do technical analyses of trends, reversals, and other changes in "form." If the market is efficient, public information provided by such analysts ("handicappers") will be reflected in prices ("closing odds").

In one test that examined the bets placed at Belmont Race Track in New York State, the odds at the track appeared to reflect the information contained in published "picks" by fourteen handicappers. However, this did not seem to

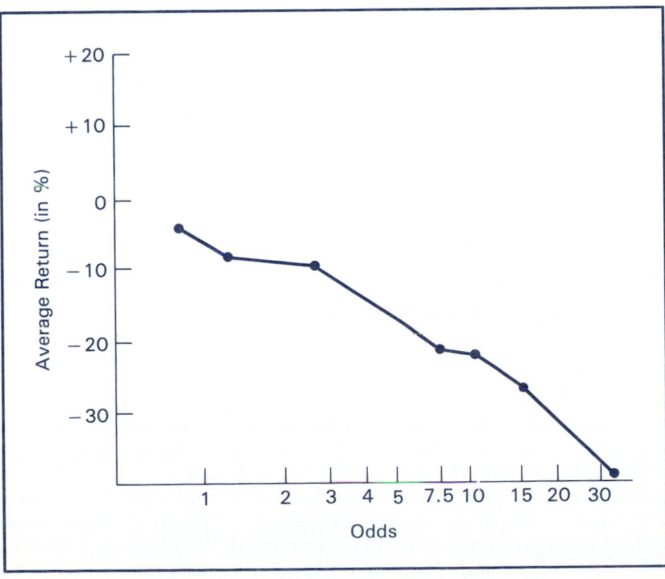

FIGURE 26-3
Average Return versus Odds in Horse Race Betting
Source: Wayne W. Snyder, "Horse Racing: Testing the Efficient Markets Model," *Journal of Finance*, 33, no. 4 (September 1978): 1113.

be the case in the less "professional" (and higher-transaction-cost) off-track betting market—a fact that may give some solace to those who invest in small and little-followed stocks.[17]

SUMMARY

1. Investing in a foreign security involves all the risks associated with investing in a domestic security, plus political and exchange (currency) risks associated with converting foreign cash flows into domestic currency.

2. The return on a foreign security can be decomposed into a domestic return and a return on the currency in which the security is denominated.

3. The standard deviation of return on a foreign security is a function of the security's domestic return standard deviation, the foreign currency return standard deviation, and the correlation between the two returns.

4. Exchange risk can be reduced by hedging in the forward or futures market for foreign currency.

5. Investments in U.S.-headquartered multinational firms offer U.S. investors only limited diversification benefits. ADRs, however, appear to bring investors significant risk reduction benefits.

6. Overall, tangible assets have been better hedges against unanticipated inflation than stocks or bonds.

7. Sports betting and security investing exhibit interesting parallels. For example, both involve an initial outlay of cash and generally uncertain outcomes. Further, publicly available information appears to be quickly impounded into both betting spreads and odds as well as security prices.

KEY TERMS

political risk
exchange risk
domestic return
foreign return
multinational firms
American Depository Receipts

QUESTIONS AND PROBLEMS

1. What types of political risks are relevant only for foreign investors? What types are relevant for both foreign and domestic investors? To what extent and in what manner would you expect the current prices of securities in a particular country to reflect these types of political risk?

2. Using a recent *Wall Street Journal*, find the exchange rate between German marks, British pounds, and U.S. dollars. Lyle Luttrell, a British citizen, is planning a trip to Germany and has budgeted expenses of 30 pounds per day. At current exchange rates, into how many dollars and marks does 30 pounds translate?

3. How might a U.S. citizen or company use currency futures to hedge against exchange-rate risk?

---

[17]Stephen Figlewski, "Subjective Information and Market Efficiency in a Betting Market," *Journal of Political Economy*, 87, no. 1 (February 1979): 75–88. It should be noted that there is some evidence that information is better reflected in the win pool than in the show and place pools. For details of a "system" designed to exploit such discrepancies, see Donald B. Hausch, William T. Ziemba, and Mark Rubenstein, "Efficiency of the Market for Racetrack Betting," *Management Science*, 27, no. 12 (December 1981): 1435–52; and Peter Asch, Burton G. Malkiel, and Richard E. Quandt, "Market Efficiency in Racetrack Betting," *Journal of Business*, 57, no. 2 (April 1984): 165–75, and "Market Efficiency in Racetrack Betting: Further Evidence and a Correction," *Journal of Business*, 59, no. 1 (January 1986): 157–60.

4. Wickey McAvoy, a U.S. citizen, holds a portfolio of French common stocks. Last year the portfolio produced an 8% return, denominated in French francs. Over that year the franc appreciated 20% against the U.S. dollar. What was Wickey's return measure in U.S. dollars?

5. Tris Speaker bought a Japanese stock one year ago when it sold for 280 yen per share and the exchange rate between U.S. dollars and Japanese yen was $0.008 per yen. The stock now sells for 350 yen, and the exchange rate is $0.010 per yen. The stock paid no dividends over the year. What was Tris's rate of return on this stock? What would be the rate of return on the stock to a Japanese investor?

6. Why is international diversification attractive to an investor already holding a well-diversified domestic portfolio?

7. Peek-A-Boo Veach, a U.S. citizen, estimates that a diversified portfolio of German common stocks has a standard deviation of 24%. Peek-A-Boo also estimates that the standard deviation of the U.S. and German currency return is 7%. Finally, Peek-A-Boo estimates the correlation between the dollar-mark currency return and the German stock market return to be 0.20. Given this information, what should Peek-A-Boo conclude is the standard deviation for a U.S. investor investing solely in the German stock market?

8. When a U.S. citizen, such as Smead Jolly, is attempting to estimate the expected return and standard deviation of return for a foreign security, what factors, in addition to those recognized in domestic security analysis, should be considered?

9. Lin Storti, a U.S. citizen, is considering investing in both U.S. and Zanistan common stock index funds. Lin estimates the following market characteristics:

U.S. market expected return	20%
U.S. market standard deviation	18%
Zanistan market expected return	30%
Zanistan market standard deviation	30%
U.S.-Zanistan expected currency return	0%
U.S.-Zanistan currency return standard deviation	10%
Zanistan domestic return and U.S.-Zanistan currency return correlation	0.15

Further, Lin estimates that the U.S. and Zanistan markets are uncorrelated as is the U.S. market return (or the Zanistan market return) and the U.S.-Zanistan currency exchange rate. Given that Lin is planning to hold a portfolio 60% invested in the U.S. index fund and 40% invested in the Zanistan index fund, what is the expected return and standard deviation of Lin's portfolio?

10. Eva Lange wants the diversification benefits of international investments, but does not want to own foreign securities directly. Would investing in domestically headquartered multinational corporations and ADRs be effective substitutes for Eva? Explain.

11. Is a low correlation between the price movements of two countries' market indices a sufficient condition to ensure that a portfolio containing securities of both countries dominates a portfolio containing only domestic securities?

12. Hal Chase, a neophyte sports gambler, was heard to remark to Joe Jackson, "The bookmakers took a terrible beating this week because 80% of the underdogs beat the point spread." Does this seem plausible? Why or why not?

13. Picks of handicappers such as Dolph Luque generally do not add directly to the information reflected in the odds given at the track. Does this mean that Dolph and the other handicappers cannot pick winners? Does it mean that their picks are of no value? What aspects of security markets are comparable to the position of track handicappers?

CFA Exam Questions

14. Robert Devlin and Neil Parish are portfolio managers at the Broward Investment Group. At their regular Monday strategy meeting, the topic of adding international bonds to one of their portfolios came up. The portfolio, an ERISA-qualified pension account for a U.S. client, was currently 90% invested in U.S. Treasury bonds, and 10% invested in 10-year Canadian government bonds. Devlin suggested buying a position in 10-year West German government bonds, while Parish argued for a position in 10-year Australian government bonds.

(a) Briefly discuss the three major issues that Devlin and Parish should address in their analysis of the return prospects for German and Australian bonds relative to those of U.S. bonds.

Having made no changes to the original portfolio, Devlin and Parish hold a subsequent strategy meeting and decide to add positions in the government bonds of Japan, United Kingdom, France, West Germany and Australia.

(b) Identify and discuss two reasons for adding a broader mix of international bonds to the pension portfolio.

15. Advisor 1: "A currency cannot consistently appreciate or depreciate relative to an investor's local currency, since some local or global economic adjustment must eventually redress the currency change. Therefore, having currency exposure in a portfolio increases risk but does not increase long-term expected returns. Since you are not compensated for taking currency risk, you should always hedge a portfolio's currency exposure back to your local currency."

Advisor 2: "I completely disagree, except as to the implication that economic changes are related to currency changes. Because economic changes affect international stocks, bonds, and currencies, as well as domestic stocks and bonds in ways that often offset each other, currency exposure improves diversification in a portfolio. Portfolios should never hedge their currency exposures; otherwise, they would be less diversified."

Advisor 1 Rebuttal: "I have evidence which would appear to refute your claim of improved diversification resulting from currency exposure. My studies of hedged and unhedged international bond portfolios show very little difference between either their risks or returns over the past ten years."

Evaluate the strengths and weaknesses of each of the two approaches presented above. Recommend and justify an alternative currency strategy that draws from the strengths of each approach and corrects their weaknesses.

The currencies associated with the countries listed in the Money Matters section of this chapter are:

Austria	Schilling
Brazil	Cruzeiro
Britain	Pound
China	Renminbi (also known as the Yuan)
Denmark	Krone
Finland	Markka
Germany	Mark
Greece	Drachma
Hungary	Forint
Ireland	Punt
Israel	Shekel
Italy	Lira
Japan	Yen
Malaysia	Ringgit
Mexico	Peso
Netherlands	Guilder
Poland	Zloty
Spain	Peseta
South Korea	Won

REFERENCES

1. Two books devoted to understanding international financial markets and investing are:

Bruno Solnik, *International Investments* (Reading, Mass.: Addison-Wesley Publishing, 1991);

J. Orlin Grabbe, *International Financial Markets* (New York: Elsevier Science, 1991).

2. Foreign stock market indices are studied in:

Richard Roll, "Industrial Structure and the Comparative Behavior of International Stock Market Indices," *Journal of Finance*, 47, no. 1 (March 1992): 3–41.

3. Investing internationally in bonds has been recently studied by:

Kenneth Cholerton, Pierre Pieraerts, and Bruno Solnik, "Why Invest in Foreign Currency Bonds?" *Journal of Portfolio Management*, 12, no. 4 (Summer 1986): 4–8;

Haim Levy and Zvi Lerman, "The Benefits of International Diversification of Bonds," *Financial Analysts Journal*, 44, no. 5 (September/October 1988): 56–64;

Paul Burik and Richard M. Ennis, "Foreign Bonds in Diversified Portfolios: A Limited Advantage," *Financial Analysts Journal*, 46, no. 2 (March/April 1990): 31–40;

Roger G. Ibbotson and Laurence B. Siegel, "The World Bond Market:

Market Values, Yields, and Returns," *Journal of Fixed Income,* 1, no. 1 (June 1991): 90–99;

Victor S. Filatov, Kevin M. Murphy, Peter M. Rappoport, and Russell Church, "Foreign Bonds in Diversified Portfolios: A Significant Advantage," *Financial Analysts Journal,* 47, no. 4 (July/August 1991): 26–32;

Mark Fox, "Different Ways to Slice the Optimization Cake," *Financial Analysts Journal,* 47, no. 4 (July/August 1991): 32–36;

Richard M. Ennis and Paul Burik, "A Response from Burik and Ennis," *Financial Analysts Journal,* 47, no. 4 (July/August 1991): 37;

Fischer Black and Robert Litterman, "Asset Allocation: Combining Investors Views with Market Equilibrium," *Journal of Fixed Income,* 1, no. 2 (September 1991): 7–19;

Mark R. Eaker and Dwight M. Grant, "Currency Risk Management in International Fixed-Income Portfolios," *Journal of Fixed Income,* 1, no. 3 (December 1991): 31–37;

Steven Dym, "Global and Local Components of Foreign Bond Risk," *Financial Analysts Journal,* 48, no. 2 (March/April 1992): 83–91.

4. Investing internationally in stocks has also been studied recently; here are some of the papers:

Jeff Madura and Wallace Reiff, "A Hedge Strategy for International Portfolios," *Journal of Portfolio Management,* 12, no. 1 (Fall 1985): 70–74;

Lee R. Thomas III, "Currency Risks in International Equity Portfolios," *Financial Analysts Journal,* 44, no. 2 (March/April 1988): 68–71;

Warren Bailey and Rene M. Stulz, "Benefits of International Diversification: The Case of Pacific Basin Stock Markets," *Journal of Portfolio Management,* 16, no. 4 (Summer 1990): 57–61;

John E. Hunter and T. Daniel Coggin, "An Analysis of the Diversification Benefit from International Equity Investment," *Journal of Portfolio Management,* 17, no. 1 (Fall 1990): 33–36;

Mark R. Eaker and Dwight Grant, "Currency Hedging Strategies for Internationally Diversified Equity Portfolios," *Journal of Portfolio Management,* 17, no. 1 (Fall 1990): 30–32;

Martin L. Leibowitz and Stanley Kogelman, "Return Enhancement from 'Foreign' Assets: A New Approach to the Risk Return Trade-off," *Journal of Portfolio Management,* 17, no. 4 (Summer 1991): 5–13.

5. Many of the previously cited papers include a discussion of hedging foreign exchange risk; for a description of how this can be done, see:

Stephen L. Nesbitt, "Currency Hedging Rules for Plan Sponsors," *Financial Analysts Journal,* 47, no. 2 (March/April 1991): 73–81;

Ira G. Kawaller, "Managing the Currency Risk of Non-Dollar Portfolios," *Financial Analysts Journal,* 47, no. 3 (May/June 1991): 62–64;

Mark Kritzman, "About Currencies," *Financial Analysts Journal,* 48, no. 2 (March/April 1992): 27–30.

6. International asset allocation has been studied by:

Philippe Jorion, "Asset Allocation with Hedged and Unhedged Foreign Stocks and Bonds," *Journal of Portfolio Management,* 15, no. 4 (Summer 1989): 49–54.

7. The evaluation of the performance of professionally managed portfolios that invest internationally has been the subject recently of:

Robert E. Cumby and Jack D. Glen, "Evaluating the Performance of International Mutual Funds," *Journal of Finance*, 45, no. 2 (June 1990): 497–521;

Cheol S. Eun, Richard Kolodny, and Bruce G. Resnick, "U.S.-Based International Mutual Funds: A Performance Evaluation," *Journal of Portfolio Management*, 17, no. 3 (Spring 1991): 88–94.

8. For an interesting paper that examines the market crash of October 1987 from a worldwide perspective, and three subsequent related papers, see:

Richard Roll, "The International Crash of October 1987," *Financial Analysts Journal*, 44, no. 5 (September/October 1988): 19–35;

Mervyn A. King and Sushil Wadhwani, "Transmission of Volatility Between Stock Markets," *Review of Financial Studies*, 3, no. 1 (1990): 5–33;

Yasushi Hamao, Ronald W. Masulis, and Victor Ng, "Correlations in Price Changes and Volatility Across International Stock Markets," *Review of Financial Studies*, 3, no. 2 (1990): 281–307;

C. Sherman Cheung and Clarence C. Y. Kwan, "A Note on the Transmission of Public Information Across International Stock Markets," *Journal of Banking and Finance*, 16, no. 4 (August 1992): 831–37.

9. For some general thoughts on investing in collectibles and a study of one type of collectible (stamps), see:

Burton G. Malkiel, *A Random Walk Down Wall Street* (New York: W. W. Norton, 1990), 304–9;

William M. Taylor, "The Estimation of Quality-Adjusted Auction Returns with Varying Transaction Intervals," *Journal of Financial and Quantitative Analysis*, 27, no. 1 (March 1992): 131–42.

10. In addition to the sports betting citations given in footnote 17 in this chapter, see:

Joseph Golec and Maurry Tamarkin, "The Degree of Inefficiency in the Football Betting Market," *Journal of Financial Economics*, 30, no. 2 (December 1991): 311–23.

Selected Solutions to End-of-Chapter Questions and Problems

Chapter 1

2. 18.2%

3. a. 30.0%
b. −13.3%
c. 4.0%

8. First period average return: 0.67%
First period standard deviation: 0.45%
Second period average return: 2.08%
Second period standard deviation: 0.72%

9. Small stock average return: 16.05%
Small stock standard deviation: 24.79%
Common stock average return: 12.48%
Common stock standard deviation: 17.05%

Chapter 2

2. Five round lots, one 11 share odd lot

6. a. 62.5%
b. 75.0%
c. 57.1%

8. 40.0%

9. $9.23

10. $40,000

12. 17.1%

13. 74.0%, −26.0%

14. a. 56.0%
b. −65.2%
c. 36.7%, −30.0%

15. Total assets: $18,750
Total liabilities: $12,500

16. a. 25.0%
b. 72.6%

17. Actual margin: 39.5%

18. $53.57

20. −20.0%

21. a. −27.6%
b. 43.6%

24. a. $5,400
b. $5,500

25. a. Total assets: $12,750
b. Total liabilities: $7.600

Chapter 3

17. Round trip transaction cost: 27.3%
Return before transaction costs: 12.5%

Chapter 4

3. $30 100 shares
$40 90 shares
$50 80 shares
$60 70 shares
$70 60 shares

Chapter 5

6. Preferred stock after-tax return: 6.2%
Corporate bond after-tax return: 6.5%

8. $7,154.50

10. a. 6.7%
b. 8.3%
c. 9.0%

11. Municipal bond tax-equivalent yield: 7.1%

14. Tax bill if:
Gain is long-term: $23,580.00
Gain is short-term: $24,115.50
Gain is half short-term, half long-term: $23,580.00

15. Tax bill if:
Gain is long-term: $23,580.00
Gain is short-term: $24,115.50
Gain is half short-term, half long-term: $23,815.50

17. 29.6%

Chapter 6

1. 8.8%

2. a. 20.0%
b. 13.4%
c. −7.4%

3. Arithmetic average inflation rate:
1926–1933 −3.7%
1934–1952 3.9%
1953–1965 1.4%
1966–1981 7.1%
1982–1990 4.0%

6. a. $0.78
b. $0.62
c. $0.50

7. $20,286.85

9. 3.2%

10. Nominal value triples in 12.75 years
Real value triples in 29.50 years

20. $525,000

Chapter 8

1. Expected return: 8.5%
Standard deviation: 10.1%

2. Covariance: −52.1
Correlation: −.98

3. Correlation (A,B): .53
Correlation (A,C): .71
Correlation (B,C): .21

4. 18.3%

5. 35.0%

7. 11.6%

8. Expected return: 5.3%
Standard deviation: 4.7%

11. a. 8.8%
b. 4.7%
c. Weight in security A: .556
Weight in security B: .444

17. Minimum standard deviation: 9.2%
Maximum standard deviation: 23.3%

23. 1.03%

25. 19.7%

26. Portfolio 1 standard deviation: 25.0%
Portfolio 2 standard deviation: 22.1%

28. a. 1325
b. 152

Chapter 9

4. a. 17.0%
b. 14.0%
c. 12.5%

5. Risky portfolio weight: 1.46

6. a. 26.0%
b. 18.0%
c. 14.0%

7. 11.0%

14. b. Expected return: 9.0%
Standard deviation: 10.2%
c. Expected return: 8.0%
Standard deviation: 7.7%

Chapter 10

10. $\bar{r}_p = 5\% + .39\sigma_p$

12. 15.8%

17. 1.03

18. 25.2

19. c. Security A expected return: 9.4%
Security B expected return: 10.8%

20. b. $\beta_1 = 1.50$
$\beta_2 = 0.60$

21. $\beta_A = 0.74$
$\beta_B = 1.17$

Chapter 11

6. 82% factor related, 18% non-factor related.

7. a. 490.5
b. 43.8
c. 23.1%

8. 22.4%

9. Standard deviation of security A: 28.9%
Standard deviation of security B: 26.3%

10. 22.5, 2.25, 0.225

12. 220, 20

14. Sensitivity to factor 1: 0.28
Sensitivity to factor 2: 4.60
Sensitivity to factor 3: 0.24

15. Expected return: 15.5%
Standard deviation: 15.8%

16. Security A standard deviation: 64.8%
Security B standard deviation: 30.2%
Covariance (A,B): 1936.5

Chapter 12

4. a. Weight of security B: −.10
b. Weight of security C: −.10

8. 26.0%

10. 13.6%

12. a. $\beta_A = 0.65$
$\beta_B = 1.02$

b. Security A expected return: 9.9%
Security B expected return: 12.1%

15. a. Weight of security A: −0.043
Weight of security C: −0.019
Weight of security D: 0.012
b. 0.3%

16. $\beta_A = 2.08$
$\beta_B = 1.56$

Chapter 13

2. a. 750,001
b. 500,001
c. 1

8. a. 1,380,000, $34.78
b. 1,600,000, $30.00
c. 400,000, $120.00

9. a. 0.05
b. $0.476
c. $74.00

10. a. $6.00
b. $35,310.00
c. $34,050.70
d. $34,050.70

13. 0.67

14. a. 1.18
b. −0.05
c. 1.45
d. 0.91

16. a. 1.07
b. 1.26

18. 0.69

Chapter 14

2. a. 1.967
b. 1.130
c. 1.478

4. a. $3,000,000
b. 8.0%
c. 0%

5. a. 15.00
b. 18.67
c. 18.67
d. 120.00

7. a. 3.5%
b. 4.5%

8. 207.6, 215.3

Chapter 15

1. $25.82

2. $1,978.10

3. 7.0%

4. a. $6.52
b. 8.0%

5. $80.00

6. $52.00

7. 12.0%

10. $106.83

11. $70.44

12. a. $35.00
b. $46.34
c. $3.13

13. $73.03

14. 10.60

15. 14.53

Chapter 16

2. a. Purchase $400,000 of new equity
b. Sell $400,000 of existing equity
c. No action

7. D_1 = $13.0 million
D_3 = $15.3 million
D_4 = $13.6 million
D_5 = $14.4 million

16. $SUE_6 = -0.03$
$SUE_7 = +1.14$
$SUE_8 = +0.77$
$SUE_9 = -0.91$

Chapter 17

9. 32.1

10. 8.7%

Chapter 18

1. 12.7%

3. −2.6%

4. 18.8%

5. 10.5%

6. 9.4%

7. a. 26.0%
b. 22.6%

9. 3.1%

10. Time-weighted return: 40.7%
Dollar-weighted return: 43.0%

13. 0.8%

14. Ex post alpha of portfolio: 0.05%
Reward-to-volatility ratio of portfolio: 0.55
Reward-to-variability ratio of portfolio: 0.06

19. a. 0.89%
d. −0.51%
e. 1.11%

20. Ex post alpha of portfolio: 3.50%
Reward-to-volatility ratio of portfolio: 8.24
Reward-to-variability ratio of portfolio: 0.35

21. Quadratic coefficient: −0.009
Dummy variable coefficient: −0.200

23. Performance difference due to sector/factor differences: 5.97 percentage points

Chapter 19

1. 16.9%

2. a. 13.0%
   b. 13.2%

Chapter 20

1. a. 7.0%
   b. 9.0%
2. $939.26, $1,066.23
4. a. 10.0%
   b. 9.2%
5. One-year spot rate: 7.5%
   Two-year spot rate: 4.0%
   Three-year spot rate: 2.8%
6. Three-year discount factor: 0.810
   Four-year discount factor: 0.731
   Five-year discount factor: 0.650
8. Forward rate from year one to two: 6.0%
   Forward rate from year two to three: 8.5%
   Forward rate from year three to four: 8.5%
9. One-year spot rate: 10.0%
   Two-year spot rate: 9.8%
   Three-year spot rate: 9.5%
   Four-year spot rate: 9.2%
10. $976.02
11. a. One-year discount factor: 0.909
       Two-year discount factor: 0.819
       Three-year discount factor: 0.731
    b. Forward rate from today to one year: 10.0%
       Forward rate from year one to two: 11.0%
       Forward rate from year two to three: 12.0%
    c. $1,457.60
12. a. 6.6%
    b. 6.7%
18. 6.7%
19. $923.36

Chapter 21

1. Bond's intrinsic value: $937.82
2. Bond's intrinsic value: $9,358.16
3. a. $9,366.03
   b. 12.0%
5. 107 basis points
6. a. 9.0%
   b. 12.5%
8. 10.6%
12. 7.6%

Chapter 22

1. $10,000.00, $8,770.68, $12,316.36
2. Price of Bond A: $10,912.50
   Price of Bond B: $10,388.70
3. Five-year bond's price: $713.00
   Ten-year bond's price: $508.30
   Twenty-year bond's price: $258.40
4. Four-year bond's price decline: −11.6%
   Fifteen-year bond's price decline: −24.6%
5. −7.2%, 8.0%
6. Proportion of five-year bond's price increase due to change in present value of principal: 79.1%
   Proportion of twenty-year bond's price increase due to change in present value of principal: 42.4%
7. 10% coupon bond's price increase: 14.1%
   8% coupon bond's price increase: 14.7%
8. 2.8 years
11. 3.4 years
14. −0.98
20. Overall rate of return: 50.9%

Chapter 23

1. $17.60
7. 8.0%
10. 16.9
11. 1989 return: 6.6%
    1990 return: 14.8%
    1991 return: −2.1%

Chapter 24

5. $815.00
6. $1,130.00
11. $5.08
14. .411
15 216
16. a. 5.4%
    b. 5.94
17. $11.48
21. a. $750.00
    b. $240.00
    c. $900.66

Chapter 25

5. $15,000.00, $0.00
6. a. $1,050.00
   b. $3,050.00
   c. $50.00
11. $5,150,000
13. $1.79
15. $20,000.00
17. a. 204
22. 60.0%

Chapter 26

4. 29.6%
5. 56.3%, 25.0%
7. 26.3%
9. Expected return: 24.0%
   Standard deviation: 16.1%

Glossary

Abnormal Return The return earned on a financial asset in excess of that required to compensate for the risk of the asset.

Account Executive A representative of a brokerage firm whose primary responsibility is servicing the accounts of individual investors.

Accounting Beta A relative measure of the sensitivity of a firm's accounting earnings to changes in the accounting earnings of the market portfolio.

Accounting Earnings (alternatively, Reported Earnings) A firm's revenues less its expenses. Equivalently, the change in the firm's book value of the equity plus dividends paid to shareholders.

Accrued Interest Interest earned, but not yet paid.

Active Management A form of investment management that involves buying and selling financial assets with the objective of earning positive risk-adjusted returns.

Active Position The difference between the percentage of an investor's portfolio invested in a particular financial asset and the percentage of a benchmark portfolio invested in that same asset.

Actual Margin The equity in an investor's margin account expressed as a percentage of the account's total market value (for margin purchases) or total debt (for short sales).

Adjusted Beta An estimate of a security's future beta, derived initially from historical data, but modified by the assumption that the security's "true" beta has a tendency over time to move toward the market average of 1.0.

Aggressive Stocks Stocks that have betas greater than one in magnitude.

Alpha The difference between a security's expected return and its equilibrium expected return.

American Depository Receipts (ADRs) Financial assets issued by U.S. banks that represent indirect ownership of a certain number of shares of a specific foreign firm. ADRs are held on deposit in a bank in the firm's home country.

American Option An option that can be exercised any time through its expiration date.

Annual Percentage Rate (APR) With respect to a loan, the APR is the yield-to-maturity of the loan, computed using the most frequent time between payments as the compounding interval.

Anomaly An empirical regularity that is not predicted by any known asset pricing model.

Approved List A list of securities that an investment organization deems worthy of accumulation in a given portfolio. For an organization that uses an approved list, typically any security on the list may be purchased by the organization's portfolio managers without additional authorization.

Arbitrage The simultaneous purchase and sale of the same, or essentially similar, security in two different markets for advantageously different prices.

Arbitrage Portfolio A portfolio that requires no investment, has no sensitivity to any factor, and has a positive expected return. More strictly, a portfolio that provides inflows in some circumstances and requires no outflows under any circumstances.

Arbitrage Pricing Theory An equilibrium model of asset pricing that states that the expected return on a security is a linear function of the security's sensitivity to various common factors.

Arbitrageur A person who engages in arbitrage.

Ask (or Asked) Price The price at which a market-maker is willing to sell a specified quantity of a particular security.

Asset Allocation The process of determining the optimal division of an investor's portfolio among available asset classes.

Asset Class A broadly defined generic group of financial assets, such as stocks or bonds.

Asymmetric Information A situation in which one party has more information than another party.

At the Money Option An option whose exercise price is roughly equal to the market price of its underlying asset.

Attribute See **Factor Loading.**

Automated Bond System (ABS) A computer system established by the New York Stock Exchange to facilitate the trading of inactive bonds.

Average Tax Rate The amount of taxes paid expressed as a percentage of the total income subject to tax.

Back-End Load See **Redemption Fee.**

Bank Discount Basis A method of calculating the interest rate on a fixed-income security that uses the principal of the security as the security's cost.

Bankers' Acceptance A type of money market instrument. It is a promissory note issued by a business debtor, with a stated maturity date, arising out of a business transaction. A bank, by endorsing the note, assumes the obligation. If this obligation becomes actively traded, it is referred to as a bankers' acceptance.

Basis The difference between the spot price of an asset and the futures price of the same asset.

Basis Point 1/100th of 1%.

Basis Risk The risk to a futures investor of the basis widening or narrowing.

Bearer Bond A bond that has attached coupons representing the right to receive interest payments. The owner submits each coupon on its specified date to receive payment. Ownership is transferred simply by the seller endorsing the bond over to the buyer.

Benchmark Portfolio A portfolio against which the investment performance of an investor can be compared for the purpose of determining investment skill. A benchmark portfolio represents a relevant and feasible alternative to the investor's actual portfolio, and in particular, is similar in terms of risk exposure.

Best-Efforts Underwriting A security underwriting in which the members of the investment banking group serve as agents instead of dealers, agreeing only to obtain for the issuer the best price that the market will pay for the security.

Beta Coefficient (alternatively, **Market Beta**) A relative measure of the sensitivity of an asset's return to changes in the return on the market portfolio. Mathematically, the beta coefficient of a security is the security's covariance with the market portfolio divided by the variance of the market portfolio.

Bid-Ask Spread The difference between the price that a market-maker is willing to pay for a security and the price at which the market-maker is willing to sell the same security.

Bidder In the context of a corporate takeover, the firm making a tender offer to the target firm.

Bid Price The price at which a market-maker is willing to purchase a specified quantity of a particular security.

Block House A brokerage firm with the financial capacity and the trading expertise to deal in block trades.

Block Trade A large order (usually 10,000 shares or more) to buy or sell a security.

Bond Ratings An indicator of the creditworthiness of specific bond issues. These ratings are often interpreted as an indication of the likelihood of default on the part of the respective bond issuers.

Bond Swap A form of active bond management that entails the replacement of bonds in a portfolio with other bonds so as to enhance the yield of the portfolio.

Book Value of the Equity The sum of the cumulative retained earnings and other balance sheet entries classified under stockholders' equity such as common stock and capital contributed in excess of par value.

Book Value Per Share A corporation's book value of the equity divided by the number of its common shares outstanding.

Bottom-Up Forecasting A sequential approach to security analysis that entails first making forecasts for individual companies, then for industries, and finally for the economy. Each level of forecasts is conditional on the previous level of forecasts made.

Broker An agent, or middleman, who facilitates the buying and selling of securities for investors.

Call Market A security market in which trading is allowed only at certain specified times. At those times, persons interested in trading a particular security are physically brought together and a market clearing price is established.

Call Money Rate The interest rate paid by brokerage firms to banks on loans used to finance margin purchases by the brokerage firm's customers.

Call Option A contract that gives the buyer the right to buy a specific number of shares of a company from the option writer at a specific purchase price during a specific time period.

Call Premium The difference between the call price of a bond and the par value of the bond.

Call Price The price that an issuer must pay bondholders when an issue is retired prior to its stated maturity date.

Call Provision A provision in some bond indentures that permits an issuer to retire some or all of the bonds in a particular bond issue prior to the bonds' stated maturity date.

Capital Asset Pricing Model (CAPM) An equilibrium model of asset pricing that states that the expected return on a security is a positive linear function of the security's sensitivity to changes in the market portfolio's return.

Capital Consumption Adjustment As calculated by the U.S. Department of Commerce, a measure of the portion of corporate earnings attributable to understated depreciation owing to inflation. It is the estimated difference between aggregate depreciation of corporate fixed assets based on historic cost and aggregate depreciation based on replacement cost.

Capital Gain (or Loss) The difference between the current market value of an asset and the original cost of the asset, with the cost adjusted for any improvement or depreciation in the asset.

Capital Market Line The set of portfolios obtainable by combining the market portfolio with risk-free borrowing or lending. Assuming homogeneous expectations and perfect markets, the Capital Market Line represents the efficient set.

Capital Markets Financial markets in which financial assets with a term-to-maturity of typically more than one year are traded.

Capitalization of Income Method of Valuation An approach to valuing financial assets. It is based on the concept that the "true" or intrinsic value of a financial asset is equal to the discounted value of future cash flows generated by that asset.

Capitalization-Weighted Market Index See **Value-Weighted Market Index.**

Cash Account An account maintained by an investor with a brokerage firm in which deposits (cash and the proceeds from security sales) must fully cover withdrawals (cash and the costs of security purchases).

Cash Matching A form of immunization that involves the purchase of bonds that generate a stream of cash inflows identical in amount and timing to a set of expected cash outflows over a given period of time.

Certainty Equivalent Return For a particularly risky investment, the return on a riskfree investment that makes the investor indifferent between the risky and riskfree investments.

Certificate of Deposit A form of time deposit issued by banks and other financial institutions.

Certificate of Incorporation See **Charter.**

Characteristic Line (alternatively, **Market Model**) A simple linear regression model expressing the relationship between the excess return on a security and the excess return on the market portfolio.

Charter (alternatively, **Certificate of Incorporation**) A document issued by a state to a corporation that specifies the rights and obligations of the corporation's stockholders.

Chartist A technical analyst who primarily relies on stock price and volume charts when evaluating securities.

Clearinghouse A cooperative venture between banks, brokerage firms, and other financial intermediaries that maintains records of transactions made by member firms during a trading day. At the end of the trading day, the clearinghouse calculates net amounts of securities and cash to be delivered among the members, permitting each member to settle once with the clearinghouse.

Close See **Closing Price.**

Closed-End Investment Company A managed investment company, with an unlimited life, that does not stand ready to purchase its own shares from its owners and rarely issues new shares beyond its initial offering.

Closing Price (alternatively, **Close**) The price at which the last trade of the day took place in a particular stock.

Closing Purchase The purchase of an option contract by an investor that is designed to offset, and thereby cancel, the previous sale of the same option contract by the investor.

Closing Sale The sale of an option contract by an investor that is designed to offset, and thereby cancel, the previous purchase of the same option contract by the investor.

Coefficient of Determination (alternatively, **R-Squared**) In the context of a simple linear regression, the proportion of the variation in the dependent variable that is related to variation in (that is, "explained by") the independent variable.

Coefficient of Nondetermination In the context of a simple linear regression, the proportion of the variation in the dependent variable that is not related to variation in (that is, not "explained by") the independent variable. Equivalently, one minus the coefficient of determination.

Coincident Indicators Economic variables that have been found to change at the same time that the economy is changing.

Collateral Trust Bond A bond that is backed by other financial assets.

Commercial Paper A type of money market instrument. It represents unsecured promissory notes of large, financially sound corporations.

Commission The fee an investor pays to a brokerage firm for services rendered in the trading of securities.

Commission Broker A member of an organized security exchange who takes orders that the public has placed with brokerage firms and sees that these orders are executed on the exchange.

Commodity Fund An investment company that speculates in futures.

Commodity Futures Trading Commission (CFTC) A federal agency established by the Commodity Futures Trading Commission Act of 1974 that approves (or disapproves) the creation of new futures contracts and regulates the trading of existing futures contracts.

Common Factor A factor that affects the return on virtually all securities to a certain extent.

Common Stock Legal representation of an equity (or ownership) position in a corporation.

Comparative Performance Attribution Comparing the performance of a portfolio with that of one or more other portfolios (or market indices) in order to determine the sources of the differences in their returns.

Competitive Bidding With respect to selecting an underwriter, the process of an issuer soliciting bids on the underwriting and choosing the underwriter offering the best overall terms.

Competitive Trader See **Floor Trader.**

Composite Stock Price Tables Price information provided on all stocks traded on the national exchanges, the regional stock exchanges, the NASDAQ system, and the Instinet system.

Compounding The payment of interest on interest.

Computer-Assisted Order Routing and Execution System (CORES) A computer system for trading all but the 150 most active stocks on the Tokyo Stock Exchange.

Consolidated Quotations System A system that lists current bid-ask prices of specialists on the national and regional stock exchanges and of certain over-the-counter dealers.

Consolidated Tape A system that reports trades that occur on the national stock exchanges, the regional stock exchanges, the NASDAQ system, and the Instinet system.

Constant Growth Model A type of dividend discount model in which dividends are assumed to exhibit a constant growth rate.

Consumer Price Index A cost-of-living index that is representative of the goods and services purchased by U.S. consumers.

Contingent Deferred Sales Charge See **Redemption Fee.**

Contingent Immunization A form of bond management that entails both passive and active elements. Under contingent immunization, as long as "favorable" results are obtained, the bond portfolio is actively managed. However, if "unfavorable" results occur, then the portfolio is immediately immunized.

Continuous Market A security market in which trades may occur at any time during business hours.

Contrarian An investor who has opinions opposite to those of most other investors, leading to actions such as buying recent losers and selling recent winners.

Convertible Bond A bond that may, at the holder's option, be exchanged for other securities, often common stock.

Corner Portfolio An efficient portfolio possessing the property that, if combined with any adjacent corner portfolio, the combination will produce another efficient portfolio.

Correlation Coefficient A statistical measure similar to covariance, in that it measures the degree of mutual variation between two random variables. The correlation coefficient rescales covariance to facilitate comparison among pairs of random variables. The correlation coefficient is bounded by the values −1 and +1.

Cost of Carry The differential between the futures and spot prices of a particular asset; it equals the interest forgone less the benefits plus the costs of ownership.

Cost-of-Living Index A collection of goods and services, and their associated prices, designed to reflect changes over time in the cost of making normal consumption expenditures.

Coupon Payments The periodic payment of interest on a bond.

Coupon Rate The annual dollar amount of coupon payments made by a bond expressed as a percentage of the bond's par value.

Coupon Stripping The process of separating and selling the individual cash flows of Treasury notes or bonds.

Covariance A statistical measure of the relationship between two random variables. It measures the extent of mutual variation between two random variables.

Covered Call Writing The process of writing a call option on an asset owned by the option writer.

Cross-Deductibility An arrangement among federal and state tax authorities that permits state taxes to be deductible expenses for federal tax purposes, and federal taxes to be deductible expenses for state tax purposes.

Crown Jewel Defense A strategy used by corporations to ward off hostile takeovers. The strategy entails the target company selling off its most attractive assets to make itself less attractive to the acquiring firm.

Cumulative Dividends A common feature of preferred

stock that requires that the issuing corporation pay all previously unpaid preferred stock dividends before any common stock dividends may be paid.

Cumulative Voting System In the context of a corporation, a method of voting in which a stockholder is permitted to give any one candidate for the board of directors a maximum number of votes equal to the number of shares owned by that shareholder times the number of directors being elected.

Currency Risk See **Exchange Risk.**

Current Yield The annual dollar amount of coupon payments made by a bond expressed as a percentage of the bond's current market price.

Customer's Agreement See **Hypothecation Agreement.**

Date of Record The date, established quarterly by a corporation's board of directors, on which the stockholders of record are determined for the purpose of paying a cash or stock dividend.

Day Order A trading order for which the broker will attempt to fill the order only during the day in which it was entered.

Day-of-the-Week Effect (alternatively, **Weekend Effect**) An empirical regularity whereby stock returns appear to be lower on Mondays as opposed to other days of the week.

Dealer (alternatively, **Market-Maker**) A person who facilitates the trading of financial assets by maintaining an inventory in particular securities. The dealer buys for and sells from this inventory, profiting from the difference in the buying and selling prices.

Dealer's Spread The bid-asked spread quoted by a security dealer.

Debenture A bond that is not secured by specific property.

Debit Balance The dollar amount borrowed from a broker as the result of a margin purchase.

Debt Refunding The issuance of new debt for the purpose of paying off currently maturing debt.

Dedicated Portfolio The portfolio of bonds that provides its owner with cash inflows that are matched against a specific stream of cash outflows.

Deep Discount Bond A bond whose coupon interest rate is considerably below those of other bonds that otherwise possess similar attributes. Hence, these bonds sell at prices significantly below those of the other bonds.

Default Premium The difference between the promised and expected yield-to-maturity on a bond arising from the possibility that the bond issuer might default on the bond.

Defensive Stocks Stocks that have betas less than one in magnitude.

Delisting The process of removing a security's eligibility for trading on an organized security exchange.

Delta See **Hedge Ratio.**

Demand Deposit A checking account at a financial institution.

Demand-to-Buy Schedule A description of the quantities of a security that an investor is prepared to purchase at alternative prices.

Demand-to-Hold Schedule A description of the quantities of a security that an investor desires to maintain in his or her portfolio at alternative prices.

Depository Trust Company A central computerized depository for securities registered in the names of member firms. Members' security certificates are immobilized and computerized records of ownership are maintained. This permits electronic transfer of the securities from one member to another as trades are conducted between the members' clients.

Differential Return See **Ex Post Alpha.**

Discount Broker An organization that offers a limited range of brokerage services and charges fees substantially below those of brokerage firms that provide a full range of services.

Discount Factor The present value of one dollar to be received from a security in specified number of years.

Discount Rate The interest rate used in calculating the present value of future cash flows. The discount rate reflects not only the time value of money, but also the riskiness of the cash flows.

Discounting The process of calculating the present value of a given stream of cash flows.

Discretionary Order A trading order that permits the broker to set the specifications for the order.

Disintermediation A pattern of funds flow whereby investors withdraw funds from financial intermediaries, such as banks and savings and loans, because market interest rates exceed the maximum interest rates that these organizations are permitted to pay. The investors reinvest their funds in financial assets that pay interest rates not subject to ceilings.

Diversification The process of adding securities to a portfolio in order to reduce the portfolio's unique risk and, thereby, the portfolio's total risk.

Dividend Decision The process of determining the amount of dividends that a corporation will pay its shareholders.

Dividend Discount Model The term used for the capitalization of income method of valuation as applied to common stocks. All variants of dividend discount models assume that the intrinsic value of a share of common stock is equal to the discounted value of the dividends forecast to be paid on the stock.

Dividend Yield The current annualized dividend paid

on a share of common stock, expressed as a percentage of the current market price of the corporation's common stock.

Dividends Cash payments made to stockholders by the corporation.

Dollar-Weighted Return A method of measuring the performance of a portfolio over a particular period of time. It is the discount rate that makes the present value of cash flows into and out of the portfolio, as well as the portfolio's ending value, equal to the portfolio's beginning value.

Domestic Return The return on an investment in a foreign financial asset, excluding the impact of exchange rate changes.

Double Auction Bidding among both buyers and sellers for a security that may occur when the specialist's bid-ask spread is large enough to permit sales at one or more prices within the spread.

Duration A measure of the average maturity of the stream of payments generated by a financial asset. Mathematically, duration is the weighted average of the lengths of time until the asset's remaining payments are made. The weights in this calculation are the proportion of the asset's total present value represented by the present value of the respective cash flows.

Earnings Per Share A corporation's accounting earnings divided by the number of its common shares outstanding.

Earnings-Price Ratio The reciprocal of the price-earnings ratio.

Econometric Model A statistical model designed to explain and forecast certain economic phenomena.

Economic Earnings The change in the economic value of the firm plus dividends paid to shareholders.

Economic Value of the Firm The aggregate market value of all securities issued by the firm.

Efficient Market A market for securities in which every security's price equals its investment value at all times, implying that a set of information is fully and immediately reflected in market prices.

Efficient Portfolio A portfolio within the feasible set that offers investors both maximum expected return for varying levels of risk and minimum risk for varying levels of expected return.

Efficient Set (Frontier) The set of efficient portfolios.

Efficient Set Theorem The proposition that investors will choose their portfolios only from the set of efficient portfolios.

Empirical Regularities Differences in returns on securities that occur with regularity from period to period. Of particular interest are empirical regularities not consistent with the Capital Asset Pricing Model.

Endogenous Variable In the context of an econometric model, an economic variable that represents the economic phenomena explained by the model.

Equal-Weighted Market Index A market index in which all the component securities contribute equally to the value of the index, regardless of the various attributes of those securities.

Equilibrium Expected Return The expected return on a security assuming that the security is correctly priced by the market. This "fair" return is determined by an appropriate asset pricing model.

Equipment Obligation (alternatively, **Equipment Trust Certificate**) A bond that is backed by specific pieces of equipment that, if necessary, can be readily sold and delivered to a new owner.

Equipment Trust Certificate See **Equipment Obligation.**

Equity Premium The difference between the expected rate of return on common stocks and the rate of return on Treasury bills.

Equivalent Yield The annualized yield-to-maturity on a fixed-income security sold on a discount basis.

Eurobond A bond that is offered outside of the country of the borrower and usually outside of the country in whose currency the security is denominated.

Eurodollar Certificate of Deposit A certificate of deposit denominated in U.S. dollars and issued by banks domiciled outside of the United States.

Eurodollar Deposit A U.S. dollar-denominated time deposit held at a bank domiciled outside of the United States.

European Option An option that can only be exercised on its expiration date.

Ex Ante Before the fact; future.

Ex-Dividend Date The date on which ownership of stock is determined for purposes of paying dividends. Owners purchasing shares before the ex-dividend date receive the dividend in question. Owners purchasing shares on or after the ex-dividend date are not entitled to the dividend.

Ex Post After the fact; historical.

Ex Post Alpha (alternatively, **Differential Return**) A portfolio's alpha calculated on an *ex post* basis. Mathematically, over an evaluation interval, it is the difference between the average return on the portfolio and the equilibrium average return on a portfolio of equal market risk.

Ex Post Selection Bias In the context of constructing a security valuation model, the use of securities that have performed well and the avoidance of securities that have performed poorly, thus making the model appear more effective than it truly is.

Ex-Rights Date The date on which ownership of stock is determined for purposes of granting rights to purchase new stock in a rights offering. Owners purchasing shares before the ex-rights date receive the rights in question. Owners purchasing shares on or after the ex-rights date are not entitled to the rights.

Excess Return The difference between the return on a security and the return on a riskfree asset.

Exchange Distribution or Acquisition A trade involving a large block of stock on an organized security exchange whereby a brokerage firm attempts to execute the order by finding enough offsetting orders from its customers.

Exchange Risk (alternatively, **Currency Risk**) The uncertainty in the return on a foreign financial asset owing to unpredictability regarding the rate at which the foreign currency can be exchanged into the investor's own currency.

Exercise Price (alternatively, **Striking Price**) In the case of a call option, the price at which an option buyer may purchase the underlying asset from the option writer. In the case of a put option, the price at which an option buyer may sell the underlying asset to the option writer.

Exit Fee See **Redemption Fee.**

Exogenous Variables In the context of an econometric model, an economic variable taken as given and used in the model to explain the model's endogenous variables.

Expectations Hypothesis A hypothesis that the futures price of an asset is equal to the expected spot price of the asset on the delivery date of the futures contract.

Expected Rate of Inflation That portion of inflation experienced over a given period of time that was anticipated by investors.

Expected Return The return on a security (or portfolio) over a holding period that an investor anticipates receiving.

Expected Return Vector A column of numbers that correspond to the expected returns for a set of securities.

Expected Value A measure of central tendency of the probability distribution of a random variable. Equivalently, the mean of the random variable.

Expected Yield-to-Maturity The yield-to-maturity on a bond calculated as a weighted average of all possible yields that the bond might produce under different scenarios of default or late payments, where the weights are the probabilities of each scenario occurring.

Expiration Date The date on which the right to buy or sell a security under an option contract ceases.

Face Value See **Principal.**

Factor (alternatively, **Index**) An aspect of the investment environment that influences the returns of financial assets. To the extent that a factor influences a significant number of financial assets, it is termed common or pervasive.

Factor Beta A relative measure of the mutual variation of a particular common factor with the return on the market portfolio. Mathematically, a factor beta is the covariance of the factor with the market portfolio, divided by the variance of the market portfolio.

Factor Loading (alternatively, **Attribute** or **Sensitivity**) A measure of the responsiveness of a security's returns to a particular common factor.

Factor Model (alternatively, **Index Model**) A return generating process that attributes the return on a security to the security's sensitivity to the movements of various common factors.

Factor Risk That part of a security's total risk that is related to moves in various common factors and, hence, cannot be diversified away.

Factor Risk Premium The expected return over and above the riskfree rate on a portfolio that has unit sensitivity to a particular factor and zero sensitivity to all other factors.

Fail to Deliver A situation in which a seller's broker is unable to deliver the traded security to the buyer's broker on or before the required settlement date.

Fallen Angel A junk bond that was of investment grade when originally issued.

Feasible Set (alternatively, **Opportunity Set**) The set of all portfolios that can be formed from the group of securities being considered by an investor.

Federally Sponsored Agency A privately owned federal agency that issues securities and uses the proceeds to support the granting of various types of special purpose loans.

Fill-or-Kill Order A trading order that is cancelled if the broker is unable to execute it immediately.

Financial Analyst (alternatively, **Security Analyst** or **Investment Analyst**) An individual who analyzes financial assets in order to determine the investment characteristics of those assets and to identify mispricings among those assets.

Financial Asset See **Security.**

Financial Institution See **Financial Intermediary.**

Financial Intermediary (alternatively, **Financial Institution**) An organization that issues financial claims against itself and uses the proceeds of the issuance primarily to purchase financial assets issued by corporations, government entities, and other financial intermediaries.

Financial Investment An investment in financial assets.

Financial Leverage The use of debt to fund a portion of an investment.

Financial Market (alternatively, **Security Market**) A mechanism designed to facilitate the exchange of financial assets by bringing buyers and sellers of securities together.

Firm Commitment An arrangement between underwriters and a security issuer whereby the underwriters agree to purchase, at the offering price, all of the issue not bought by the public.

Floating Rate (alternatively, **Variable Rate**) A rate of interest on a financial asset that may vary over the life of the asset, depending on changes in a specified indicator of current market interest rates.

Floor Broker A member of an organized security exchange who assists commission brokers when there are too many orders flowing into the market for the commission brokers to handle alone.

Floor Order Routing and Execution System (FORES) A computer system for trading the 150 most active stocks on the Tokyo Stock Exchange.

Floor Trader (alternatively, **Competitive Trader** or **Registered Competitive Market Maker** or **Registered Trader**) A member of an organized security exchange who trades solely for his or her own account and is prohibited by exchange rules from handling public orders.

Foreign Return The return on an investment in a foreign financial asset, including the impact of exchange rate changes.

Forward Rate The interest rate that links the current spot interest rate over one holding period to the current spot interest rate over a longer holding period. Equivalently, the interest rate agreed to at a point in time where the loan will be made at a future date.

Fourth Market A secondary security market in which investors (typically, financial institutions) trade securities directly with each other, bypassing the brokers and dealers on organized security exchanges and the over-the-counter market.

Fundamental Analysis A form of security analysis that seeks to determine the intrinsic value of securities based on underlying economic factors. These intrinsic values are compared to current market prices to estimate current levels of mispricing.

Futures (Futures Contract) An agreement between two people under which the seller promises to deliver a specific asset on a specific future date to the buyer for a predetermined price to be paid on the delivery date.

Futures Option (alternatively, **Options on Futures**) An option contract for which the deliverable asset is a specific futures contract.

General Obligation Bond A municipal bond that is backed by the full faith and credit of the issuing agency.

Generally Accepted Accounting Principles (GAAP) Accounting rules established by recognized authorities, such as the Financial Accounting Standards Board (FASB).

Geometric Mean Return The compounded per-period average rate of return on a financial asset over a specified time interval.

Good-Till-Cancelled Order See **Open Order.**

Greenmail An offer by the management of a corporation that is the target of a hostile takeover to repurchase its shares from the hostile bidder at an above-market price.

Group In the context of a specific asset class, a collection of financial assets that have common distinguishing financial characteristics.

Group Selection A component of the security selection process involving the identification of desirable combinations of groups within an asset class.

Guaranteed Bond A bond issued by one corporation but backed by another corporation.

Hedge Ratio (alternatively, **Delta**) The expected change in the value of an option per dollar change in the market price of the underlying asset.

Hedger An investor in futures contracts whose primary objective is to offset an otherwise risky position.

Historical Beta An estimate of a security's beta, derived solely from historical returns. Equivalently, the slope of the ex post characteristic line.

Holding Period The length of time over which an investor is assumed to invest a given sum of money.

Holdout Sample See **Out-of-Sample Data.**

Holiday Effect The observation that average stock returns have been abnormally high on the trading day immediately before a federal holiday.

Homogeneous Expectations A situation in which all investors possess the same perceptions with regard to the expected returns, standard deviations, and covariances of securities.

Horizon Analysis A form of active bond management where a single holding period is selected for analysis and possible yield structures at the end of the period are considered. Bonds with the most attractive expected returns under the alternative yield structures are selected for the portfolio.

Hypothecation Agreement (alternatively, **Customer's Agreement**) A legal arrangement between a brokerage firm and an investor that permits the brokerage firm to pledge the investor's securities as collateral for bank loans, provided that the securities were purchased through the investor's margin account.

Idiosyncratic Risk See **Nonfactor Risk.**

Immunization A bond portfolio management technique that permits an investor to meet a promised stream of cash outflows with a high degree of certainty.

Implicit Volatility The risk of an asset derived from an options valuation model, assuming that an option on the asset is fairly priced by the market.

Implied Return See **Internal Rate of Return.**

In the Money Option In the case of a call (put) option, an option whose exercise price is less than (greater than) the market price of its underlying asset.

Income Bond A bond for which the size of the interest payments varies, based on the income of the issuer.

Indenture A legal document formally describing the terms of the legal relationship between a bond issuer and bondholders.

Index See **Factor.**

Index Arbitrage An investment strategy that involves buying a stock index futures contract and selling the individual stocks in the index or selling a stock index futures contract and buying the individual stocks in the index. The strategy is designed to take advantage of a mispricing between the stock index futures contract and the underlying stocks.

Index Fund A passively managed investment in a diversified portfolio of financial assets designed to mimic the investment performance of a specific market index.

Index Model See **Factor Model.**

Indifference Curve All combinations of portfolios, considered in terms of expected returns and risk, that provide an investor with an equal amount of satisfaction.

Industrial Development Bond (IDB) A form of revenue bond used to finance the purchase or construction of industrial facilities that are leased by the issuing municipality to firms on a favorable basis.

Inefficient Portfolio A portfolio that does not satisfy the criteria of an efficient portfolio and, hence, does not lie on the efficient set.

Inflation The rate of change in a price index over a certain period of time. Equivalently, the percentage change in the purchasing power of a unit of currency over a certain period of time.

Inflation Hedge An asset that preserves the value of its purchasing power over time despite changes in the price level.

Information Coefficient The correlation coefficient between a security analyst's predicted returns and subsequent actual returns that is used to measure the accuracy of the analyst's predictions.

Information Content of Dividends Hypothesis The proposition that dividend announcements contain inside information about a corporation's future prospects.

Initial Margin Requirement The minimum percentage of a margin purchase (or short sale) price that must come from the investor's own funds.

Initial Public Offering (IPO) (alternatively, **Unseasoned Offering**) The first offering of the shares of a company to the public.

Initial Wealth The value of an investor's portfolio at the beginning of a holding period.

Inside Quotes The highest bid price and the lowest ask price for a given stock in the over-the-counter market.

Insider Narrowly defined, stockholders, officers, and directors of a corporation who own a "significant" proportion of a corporation's stock. More broadly defined, anyone who has access to information that is both "materially" related to the value of a corporation's securities and unavailable to the general public.

Instinet Acronym for **Institutional Network.** A computerized communications system that provides price quotations and order execution for fourth market participants.

Interest Rate Parity An explanation for why spot and futures exchange rates differ; it asserts that such differences result from different interest rates in the two countries.

Interest Rate Risk The uncertainty in the return on a fixed-income security caused by unanticipated fluctuations in value of the asset owing to changes in interest rates.

Intermarket Spread Swap A type of bond swap where an investor moves out of one market segment and into another because the investor believes that one segment is significantly underpriced relative to the other.

Intermarket Trading System An electronic communications network that links the national and regional organized security exchanges and certain over-the-counter dealers. The network provides market-maker price quotes and allows participating brokers and dealers to route orders to market-makers offering the best prices.

Internal Rate of Return (alternatively, **Implied Return**) The discount rate that equates the present value of future cash flows expected to be received from a particular investment to the cost of that investment.

Intrinsic Value of an Option The value of an option if it were exercised immediately. Equivalently, the market price of the asset upon which a call option is written less the exercise price of the option (or the exercise price less the market price of the asset, in the case of a put option).

Inventory Valuation Adjustment As calculated by the U.S. Department of Commerce, a measure of the portion of corporate earnings attributable to changes in the value of inventories owing to inflation.

Investment The sacrifice of certain present value for (possibly uncertain) future value.

Investment Advisor An individual or organization that provides investment advice to investors.

Investment Analyst See **Financial Analyst.**

Investment Banker (alternatively, **Underwriter**) An organization that acts as an intermediary between issuers and the ultimate purchasers of securities in the primary security market.

Investment Banking The process of analyzing and selecting a means of procuring financing on behalf of an issuer of securities.

Investment Committee With a traditional investment organization, a group of senior management responsible for establishing the organization's broad investment strategy.

Investment Company A type of financial intermediary that obtains money from investors and uses that money to purchase financial assets. In return, the investors receive shares in the investment company, and thus indirectly own a proportion of the financial assets that the company itself owns.

Investment Environment The financial structure in which investors operate, consisting of the kinds of marketable securities available for purchase or sale and the process by which these securities are bought and sold.

Investment Grade Bonds Bonds that possess bond ratings that permit them to be purchased by the vast majority of institutional investors, particularly regulated financial institutions. Usually, investment grade bonds have a BBB (Standard & Poor's) or Baa (Moody's) or higher bond rating.

Investment Policy A component of the investment process that involves determining an investor's objectives and the amount of the funds available to invest.

Investment Process The set of procedures by which an investor decides what marketable securities to invest in, how extensive those investments should be, and when the investments should be made.

Investment Style The method an investor uses to take active positions in certain types of securities.

Investment Value The present value of a security's future prospects as estimated by well-informed market participants.

January Effect An empirical regularity whereby stock returns appear to be higher in January as opposed to other months of the year.

Junk Bonds See **Speculative Bonds.**

Lagging Indicators Economic variables that have been found to follow movements in the economy.

Lambda The expected return premium (above the risk-free rate of interest) per unit of sensitivity to a particular common factor.

Leading Indicators Economic variables that have been found to signal future changes in the economy.

Letter Stock (alternatively, **Restricted Stock**) Stock that is unregistered and sold directly to the purchaser, rather than through a public offering. Such stock must be held at least two years and cannot be sold even at that time unless ample information on the company is available and the amount sold is a relatively small percentage of the total shares outstanding.

Leveraged Buyout See **Management Buyout.**

Limit Order A trading order that specifies a limit price at which the broker is to execute the order. The trade will be executed only if the broker can meet or better the limit price.

Limit Order Book (alternatively, **Specialist's Book**) The records kept by the specialist identifying the limit, stop, and stop limit orders that brokers want to execute in a particular security.

Limit Price The price specified when a limit order is placed with a broker, defining the maximum purchase price or minimum selling price at which the order can be executed.

Limited Liability An aspect of the corporate form of organization that prevents common stockholders from losing more than their investment if the corporation should default on its obligations.

Liquidity (alternatively, **Marketability**) The ability of investors to convert securities to cash at a price similar to the price of the previous trade in the security, assuming that no significant new information has arrived since the previous trade. Equivalently, the ability to sell an asset quickly without having to make a substantial price concession.

Liquidity Preference (Premium) Theory An explanation of the term structure of interest rates. It holds that the term structure is a result of the preference of investors for short-term securities. Investors can only be induced to hold longer-term securities if they expect to receive a higher return.

Liquidity Premium The expected incremental return of longer-term securities over shorter-term securities that compensates investors for the greater interest rate risk entailed in holding longer-term securities.

Listed Security A security that is traded on an organized security exchange.

Load Charge A sales charge levied by a mutual fund when an investor buys its shares.

Load Fund A mutual fund that has a load charge.

Local (alternatively, **Scalper**) A member of an organized futures exchange who trades for his or her own account and has a very short holding period.

Long Hedger A hedger who offsets risk by buying futures contracts.

Low-Load Fund A mutual fund that has a small load charge, usually 3.5% or less.

Maintenance Margin Requirement The minimum actual margin that a brokerage firm will permit investors to keep in their margin accounts.

Majority Voting System (alternatively, **Straight Voting System**) In the context of a corporation, a method of voting in which a stockholder is permitted to give any one candidate for the board of directors a maximum number of votes equal to the number of shares owned by that shareholder.

Managed Investment Company An investment company with a portfolio that may be altered at the discretion of the company's portfolio manager.

Management Buyout (alternatively, **Leveraged Buyout**) A situation in which the existing management of a publicly owned firm buys all the shares of the existing stockholders, thereby gaining complete control of the firm.

Margin Account An account maintained by an investor with a brokerage firm in which securities may be purchased by borrowing a portion of the purchase price from the brokerage firm, or may be sold short by borrowing the securities from the brokerage firm.

Margin Call A demand upon an investor by a brokerage firm to increase the equity in the investor's margin account. The margin call is initiated when the investor's actual margin falls below the maintenance margin requirement.

Margin Purchase The purchase of securities financed by borrowing a portion of the purchase price from a brokerage firm.

Marginal Tax Rate The amount of taxes, expressed as a percentage, paid on each additional dollar of taxable income received.

Markdown The difference in prices between what an investor's broker receives and what the investor receives for a security sold in the over-the-counter market.

Marked (or **Marking**) **to the Market** The process of calculating, on a daily basis, the actual margin in an investor's account. Equivalently, the daily process of adjusting the equity in an investor's account to reflect the daily changes in the market value of the account's assets and liabilities.

Market Beta See **Beta Coefficient.**

Market Capitalization The aggregate market value of a security, equal to the market price per unit of the security multiplied times the total number of outstanding units of the security.

Market Discount Function The set of discount factors on all default-free bonds across the spectrum of terms-to-maturity.

Market Index A collection of securities whose prices are averaged to reflect the overall investment performance of a particular market for financial assets.

Market-Maker See **Dealer.**

Market Model A simple linear model that expresses the relationship between the return on a security and the return on a market index.

Market Order A trading order that instructs the broker to buy or sell a security immediately at the best obtainable price.

Market Portfolio A portfolio consisting of an investment in all securities. The proportion invested in each security equals the percentage of the total market capitalization represented by the security.

Market Risk (alternatively, **Systematic Risk**) A part of a security's total risk that is related to moves in the market portfolio and, hence, cannot be diversified away.

Market Segmentation Theory An explanation of the term structure of interest rates. It holds that various investors and borrowers are restricted by law, preference, or custom to certain maturity ranges. Spot rates in each market segment are determined by supply and demand conditions there.

Market Timing A form of active management that entails shifting an investor's funds between a surrogate market portfolio and a riskfree asset, depending on the investor's perception of their near-term prospects.

Marketability See **Liquidity.**

Markup The difference in prices between what an investor pays and what the investor's broker pays for a security purchased in the over-the-counter market.

Maturity Date The date upon which a bond issuer promises to repay investors the principal of the bond.

May Day The date (May 1, 1975) that the New York Stock Exchange ended its fixed-commission rate requirement and permitted member firms to negotiate commission rates with customers.

Member Corporation See **Member Firm.**

Member Firm (alternatively, **Member Corporation** or **Member Organization**) A brokerage firm with one or more memberships in an organized security exchange.

Member Organization See **Member Firm.**

Merger A form of corporate takeover in which two firms combine their operations and become one firm. Mergers are usually negotiated by the management of the two merging corporations.

Mispriced Security A security that is trading at a price substantially different from its intrinsic value.

Money Market Deposit A short-term fixed income security.

Money Markets Financial markets in which financial assets with a term-to-maturity of typically one year or less are traded.

Mortgage Bond A bond that is secured by the pledge of specific property. In the event of default, bondholders are entitled to obtain the property in question and sell it to satisfy their claims on the issuer.

Multiple Growth Model A type of dividend discount model in which dividends are assumed to grow at different rates over specifically defined time periods.

Municipal Bond A bond issued by a state or local unit of government.

Mutual Fund See **Open-end Investment Company.**

Naked Call Writing The process of writing a call option on a stock that the option writer does not own.

Naked Put Writing The process of writing a put option on a stock when the writer does not have the sufficient cash (or securities) in his or her brokerage account to purchase the stock.

NASDAQ International An early morning system for trading NYSE, AMEX, and NASDAQ securities through the use of a dealer network.

National Association of Securities Dealers (NASD) A self-regulatory agency that establishes rules and regulations and monitors the activities of brokers and dealers in the over-the-counter market.

National Association of Securities Dealers Automated Quotations (NASDAQ) An automated nationwide communications network operated by the NASD that connects dealers and brokers in the over-the-counter market. NASDAQ provides current market-maker bid-ask price quotes to market participants.

National Market System (NASDAQ/NMS) A segment of the over-the-counter market comprised of issues with relatively large trading volumes. More detailed trading information is provided on stocks included in NASDAQ/NMS than on other over-the-counter stocks.

Neglected Firm Effect An empirical observation that firms followed by relatively few security analysts have had abnormally high returns.

Net Asset Value The market value of an investment company's assets, less any liabilities, divided by the number of shares outstanding.

Net Present Value The present value of future cash flows expected to be received from a particular investment less the cost of that investment.

No Growth Model See **Zero Growth Model.**

No-Load Fund A mutual fund that does not have a load charge.

Nominal Return The percentage change in the value of an investment in a financial asset, where the beginning and ending values of the asset are not adjusted for inflation over the time of the investment.

Nonfactor Risk (alternatively, **Idiosyncratic Risk**) That part of a security's total risk which is not related to moves in various common factors and, hence, can be diversified away.

Nonmarket Risk See **Unique Risk.**

Nonsatiation A condition whereby investors are assumed to always prefer higher levels of terminal wealth to lower levels of terminal wealth.

Normal Backwardation An expected relationship between the futures price of an asset and the expected spot price of the asset on the delivery date of the contract. Normal backwardation states that the futures price will be less than the expected spot price.

Normal Contango An expected relationship between the futures price of an asset and the expected spot price of the asset on the delivery date of the contract. Normal contango states that the futures price will be greater than the expected spot price.

Normal Probability Distribution A symmetrical bell-shaped probability distribution, completely described by its mean and standard deviation.

Normative Economics A form of economic analysis that is prescriptive in nature, dealing with what "ought to be."

Odd Lot An amount of stock, generally from 1 to 99 shares.

Open See **Opening Price.**

Open-End Investment Company (alternatively, **Mutual Fund**) A managed investment company, with an unlimited life, that stands ready at all times to purchase its shares from its owners and usually will continuously offer new shares to the public.

Open Interest The number of a particular futures contract that are outstanding at a particular point in time.

Open Order (alternatively, **Good-Till-Cancelled Order**) A trading order that remains in effect until it is either filled or cancelled by the investor.

Opening Price (alternatively, **Open**) The price at which the first trade of the day took place in a particular stock.

Opportunity Set See **Feasible Set.**

Optimal Portfolio The feasible portfolio that offers an investor the maximum level of satisfaction. This portfolio represents the tangency between the efficient set and an indifference curve of the investor.

Option A contract between two investors in which one investor grants the other the right to buy (or sell) a specific asset at a specific price within a specific time period.

Options on Futures See **Futures Option.**

Order Book Officials The people who keep the limit order book in those option markets that involve market-makers instead of specialists.

Order Specification The investor's instructions to a broker regarding the particular characteristics of a trading order, including the name of the security's issuing firm, whether to buy or sell, order size, maximum time the order is to be outstanding, and the type of order to be used.

Ordinary Least Squares See **Simple Linear Regression.**

Organized Exchange A central physical location where trading of securities is done under a set of rules and regulations.

Original Issue Discount (OID) Security A security that is issued with a coupon interest rate below prevailing market interest rates on similar securities and, thus, is originally sold at a discount from par value.

Out of the Money Option In the case of a call (put) option, an option whose exercise price is greater than (less than) the market price of its underlying asset.

Out-of-Sample Data (alternatively, **Holdout Sample**) In the context of constructing a security valuation model, information that is obtained from periods different from those used to estimate the valuation model.

Over-the-Counter Market (OTC Market) A secondary market for securities distinct from an organized security exchange.

Overmargined Account (alternatively, **Unrestricted Account**) A margin account in which the actual margin has risen above the initial margin requirement.

Overpriced Security (alternatively, **Overvalued Security**) A security whose expected return is less than its equilibrium expected return. Equivalently, a security with a negative alpha.

Oversubscription Privilege The opportunity given shareholders who have exercised their rights in a rights offering to buy shares that were not purchased in the offering.

Overvalued Security See **Overpriced Security.**

Pac-Man Defense A strategy used by corporations to ward off hostile takeovers. The targeted company reverses the takeover effort and seeks to acquire the firm making the initial takeover attempt.

Par Value of Bond See **Principal.**

Par Value of Common Stock The nominal value of shares of common stock as legally carried on the books of a corporation.

Participating Bond A bond that promises to pay a stated rate of interest to its owner, but may also pay additional interest if the issuer's earnings exceed a specified level.

Participation Certificate A bond that represents an ownership interest in a pool of fixed-income securities. The holders of the certificates receive the interest and principal payments on the pooled securities in proportion to their ownership of the pool.

Passive Investment System (alternatively, **Passive Management**) The process of buying and holding a well-diversified portfolio.

Passive Management See **Passive Investment System.**

Payout Ratio The percentage of a firm's earnings paid to shareholders in the form of cash dividends.

Pegging The process by which investment bankers attempt to stabilize the price of an underwritten security in the secondary market for a period of time after the initial offering date.

Perfect Markets Security markets in which no impediments to investing exist. These impediments include such things as finite divisibility of securities, taxes, transaction costs, and costly information.

Performance Attribution The identification of sources of returns for a portfolio or security over a particular evaluation interval of time.

Performance Margin The initial margin that must be posted by a futures buyer or seller.

Pink Sheets Written published quotations on over-the-counter stocks that are not listed on NASDAQ.

Poison Pill Defense A strategy used by corporations to ward off hostile takeovers. The targeted company gives its shareholders certain rights that can be exercised only in the event of a hostile takeover, and that, once exercised, will be extremely onerous to the acquirer.

Political Risk The uncertainty in the return on a foreign financial asset owing to the possibility that the foreign government might take actions that are detrimental to the investor's financial interests.

Portfolio Construction (alternatively, **Security Selection**) A component of the investment process that involves identifying which assets to invest in and determining the proportion of funds to invest in each of the assets.

Portfolio Insurance An investment strategy designed to guarantee a minimum rate of return while allowing the investor to benefit substantially from the positive returns generated by an investment in a risky portfolio.

Portfolio Manager An individual who utilizes the information provided by financial analysts to construct a portfolio of financial assets.

Portfolio Performance Evaluation A component of the investment process involving periodic analysis of how a portfolio performed in terms of both returns earned and risk incurred.

Portfolio Revision A component of the investment process, involving periodically repeating the process of setting investment policy, conducting security analysis, and constructing a portfolio.

Portfolio Turnover A measure of how much buying and selling occurs in a portfolio over a given period of time.

Positive Economics A form of economic analysis that is descriptive in nature, dealing with "what is."

Preemptive Rights When a corporation plans an issuance of new common shares, the right of existing shareholders to purchase the new shares in proportion to the number of shares that they currently own.

Preferred Stock A hybrid form of security that has characteristics of both common stocks and bonds.

Premium The price of an option contract.

Price-Earnings Ratio A corporation's current stock price divided by its earnings per share.

Price Impact The effect on the price of a security

resulting from a trade in that security. Price impact is the result of several factors: size of the trade, demand for immediate liquidity, and presumed information of the individual or organization placing the order.

Price Relative The price of a security in one period divided by the price of that same security in a previous period.

Price-Weighted Market Index A market index in which the contribution of a security to the value of the index is a function of the security's current market price.

Primary Security Market The market in which securities are sold at the time of their initial issuance.

Principal (alternatively, **Face Value** or **Par Value of Bond**) The nominal value of a bond that is repaid to bondholders at the maturity date.

Private Placement The direct sale of a newly issued security to a small number of large institutional investors.

Probabilistic Forecasting A form of security analysis that begins with a series of economic scenarios, along with their respective probabilities of occurrence. Under each of these scenarios, accompanying projections are made as to the prospects for various industries, companies, and stock prices.

Probability Distribution A model describing the relative frequency of possible values that a random variable can assume.

Professional Money Manager An individual or organization that invests funds on behalf of others.

Program Trading The purchase or sale of a collection of securities as if the collection were one security. Program trades are prominently employed in portfolio insurance and index arbitrage strategies.

Promised Yield-to-Maturity The yield-to-maturity on a bond calculated assuming that all promised cash flows are received on a full and timely basis.

Prospectus The official selling circular that must be given to purchasers of new securities registered with the SEC. The prospectus provides various information about the issuer's business, its financial condition, and the nature of the security being offered.

Proxy The signing by a shareholder of a power of attorney, thereby authorizing a designated party to cast all of the shareholder's votes on any matter brought up at the corporation's annual meeting.

Proxy Fight An attempt by dissident shareholders to solicit proxies to vote against corporate incumbents.

Purchase Group See **Syndicate.**

Purchasing-Power Risk The risk experienced by investors in financial assets owing to uncertainty concerning the impact of inflation on the real returns produced by those financial assets.

Pure-Discount Security A fixed-income security that promises to make only one payment to its owner.

Pure Factor Play See **Pure Factor Portfolio.**

Pure Factor Portfolio (alternatively, **Pure Factor Play**) A portfolio that possesses a unit sensitivity to one factor, no sensitivity to any other factor, and has zero nonfactor risk.

Pure Yield Pickup Swap A type of bond swap where an investor exchanges one bond for another to obtain a higher yield over the long term, with little attention paid to the near-term outlook for the bond's respective market segments or the market as a whole.

Put-Call Parity The relationship between the market price on a put and a call that have the same exercise price, expiration date, and underlying stock.

Put Option A contract that gives the buyer the right to sell a specific number of shares of a company to the writer at a specific price within a specific time period.

R-Squared See **Coefficient of Determination.**

Random Error Term The difference between the actual value of a random variable and the predicted value based on some model.

Random Variable A variable that takes on alternative values according to chance.

Random Walk (or **Random Walk Model**) In general, it refers to a situation in which changes in the value of a random variable are independent and identically distributed. When applied to common stocks, it refers to a situation in which security price changes are independent and identically distributed, meaning that the size of a security's price change from one period to the next can be viewed as being determined by the spin of a roulette wheel.

Rate Anticipation Swap A type of bond swap where an investor exchanges bonds that are expected to perform relatively poorly for those that are expected to perform relatively well, given an anticipated movement in interest rates.

Rate of Return The percentage change in the value of an investment in a financial asset (or portfolio of financial assets) over a specified time period.

Real Estate Investment Trust (REIT) An investment fund, similar to an investment company, whose investment objective is to hold primarily real-estate-related assets, either through mortgages, construction and development loans, or equity interests.

Real Investment An investment involving some kind of tangible asset, such as land, equipment, or buildings.

Real Return The percentage change in the value of an investment in a financial asset, where the beginning and ending values of the asset are adjusted for inflation over the time of the investment.

Realized Capital Gain (or Loss) A capital gain (or loss) on an asset that is recognized, for tax purposes, through the sale or exchange of the asset.

Red Herring A preliminary prospectus that provides much of the information in the final prospectus, but is not an offer to sell the security, nor does it display an actual offering price.

Redemption Fee (alternatively, **Back-End Load** or **Contingent Deferred Sales Charge** or **Exit Fee**) A fee levied by an investment company when an investor sells shares back to the investment company.

Regional Brokerage Firm An organization offering brokerage services that specializes in trading the securities of companies located in a particular region of the country.

Regional Exchange An organized exchange that specializes in trading the securities of companies located in a particular region of the country.

Registered Bond A bond for which the owner is registered with the issuer. The bondholder receives coupon payments directly from the issuer. Ownership changes require notification of the issuer.

Registered Competitive Market Maker See **Floor Trader.**

Registered Representative See **Account Executive.**

Registered Trader See **Floor Trader.**

Registrar A designated agent of a corporation responsible for canceling and issuing shares of stock in the corporation as these shares are issued or traded.

Registration Statement A document filed with the Securities and Exchange Commission prior to initiating a public security offering.

Reinvestment-Rate Risk The uncertainty in the return on a fixed-income asset caused by unanticipated changes in the interest rate at which cash flows from the asset can be reinvested.

Replacement Cost Accounting The use of estimated replacement costs instead of historical book-value costs when calculating corporate earnings.

Repo Rate The rate of interest involved in a repurchase agreement.

Reported Earnings See **Accounting Earnings.**

Repurchase Agreement A type of money market instrument. It involves the sale of a financial asset from one investor to another. The investor selling the asset simultaneously agrees to repurchase it from the purchaser on a stated future date at a predetermined price, which is higher than the original transaction price.

Repurchase Offer An offer by the management of a corporation to buy back some of its own stock.

Residual Standard Deviation See **Standard Deviation of the Random Error Term.**

Restricted Account A margin account in which the actual margin has fallen below the initial margin requirement, but remains above the maintenance margin requirement.

Restricted Stock See **Letter Stock.**

Retention Ratio The percentage of a firm's earnings that are not paid to shareholders, but instead are retained by the firm. Equivalently, one minus the payout ratio.

Return Generating Process A statistical model that describes how the returns on a security are produced.

Return on Equity The earnings per share of a firm divided by the firm's book value per share.

Revenue Bond A municipal bond that is backed solely by the revenues from a designated project, authority, or agency, or by the proceeds from a specific tax.

Reverse Stock Split A form of stock split whereby the number of shares is reduced and the par value per share is increased.

Reversing Trade The purchase or sale of a futures (or options) contract designed to offset, and thereby cancel, the previous sale or purchase of the same contract.

Reward-to-Variability Ratio An ex post risk-adjusted measure of portfolio performance where risk is defined as the standard deviation of the portfolio's returns. Mathematically, over an evaluation interval, it is the excess return of a portfolio divided by the standard deviation of the portfolio's returns.

Reward-to-Volatility Ratio An ex post risk-adjusted measure of portfolio performance where risk is defined as the market risk of the portfolio. Mathematically, over an evaluation interval it is the excess return of a portfolio divided by the beta of the portfolio.

Right An option issued to existing shareholders that permits them to buy a specified number of new shares at a designated subscription price. For each shareholder, this number is proportional to the number of existing shares currently owned by the shareholder.

Rights Offering The sale of new stock conducted by first offering the stock to existing shareholders in proportion to the number of shares owned by each shareholder.

Risk The uncertainty associated with the end-of-period value of an investment in an asset or portfolio of assets.

Risk-Adjusted Return The return on an asset or portfolio, modified to explicitly account for the risk to which the asset or portfolio is exposed.

Risk-Averse Investor An investor who prefers an investment with less risk over one with more risk, assuming that both investments offer the same expected return.

Risk-Neutral Investor An investor who has no preference between investments with varying levels of risk, assuming that the investments offer the same expected return.

Risk Premium The difference between the expected

yield-to-maturity of a risky bond and the expected yield-to-maturity of a similar default-free bond.

Risk-Seeking Investor An investor who prefers an investment with more risk over one with less risk, assuming that both investments offer the same expected return.

Risk Structure The set of yields-to-maturity across bonds that possess different degrees of default risk, but are similar with respect to other attributes.

Risk Tolerance The trade-off between risk and expected return demanded by a particular investor.

Riskfree Asset An asset whose return over a given holding period is certain and known at the beginning of the holding period.

Riskfree Borrowing The act of borrowing funds that are to be repaid with a known rate of interest.

Riskfree Lending (Investing) The act of investing in a riskfree asset.

Round Lot An amount of stock generally equal to 100 shares or a multiple of 100 shares.

Savings Forgone consumption. The difference between current income and current consumption.

Scalper See **Local.**

SEAQ Automated Execution Facility (SEAF) A small-order execution system, similar to SOES, that is used on the London Stock Exchange.

Seat The designation of membership in an organized exchange. By holding a seat, the member has the privilege of being able to execute trades using the facilites provided by the exchange.

Secondary Distribution A means of selling a block of stock where the shares are sold away from an organized exchange after the close of trading in a manner similar to the sale of new issues of common stock.

Secondary Security Market The market in which securities are traded that have been issued at some previous point in time.

Sector Factor A factor that affects the return on securities within a particular economic sector.

Securities and Exchange Commission (SEC) A federal agency established by the Securities Exchange Act of 1934 that regulates the issuance of securities in the primary market and the trading of securities in the secondary market.

Securities Investor Protection Corporation (SIPC) A quasi-governmental agency that insures the accounts of brokers against loss owing to the brokerage firm's failure.

Security (alternatively, **Financial Asset**) A legal representation of the right to receive prospective future benefits under stated conditions.

Security Analysis A component of the investment process that involves determining the prospective future benefits of a security, the conditions under which such benefits will be received, and the likelihood of such conditions occurring.

Security Analyst See **Financial Analyst.**

Security Market See **Financial Market.**

Security Market Line Derived from the CAPM, a linear relationship between the expected returns on securities and the risk of those securities, with risk expressed as the security's beta (or equivalently, the security's covariance with the market portfolio).

Security Selection See **Portfolio Construction.**

Selectivity An aspect of security analysis that entails forecasting the price movements of individual securities.

Self-Regulation A method of governmental regulation where the rules and standards of conduct in security markets are set by firms that operate in these markets, subject to the oversight of various federal agencies such as the SEC and CFTC.

Selling Group A group of investment banking organizations that, as part of a security underwriting, are responsible for selling the security.

Semistrong-Form Market Efficiency A level of market efficiency in which all relevant publicly available information is fully and immediately reflected in security prices.

Sensitivity See **Factor Loading.**

Separation Theorem A feature of the Capital Asset Pricing Model that states that the optimal combination of risky assets for an investor can be determined without any knowledge about the investor's preferences toward risk and return.

Serial Bond A bond issue with different portions of the issue maturing at different dates.

Settle (or **Settlement**) **Price** The representative price for a futures contract determined during the closing period of the futures exchange.

Settlement Date The date after a security has been traded, on which the buyer must deliver cash to the seller and the seller must deliver the security to the buyer.

Shelf Registration Under SEC Rule 415, issuers may register securities in advance of their issuance and sell these securities up to a year later.

Short Hedger A hedger who offsets risk by selling futures contracts.

Short Interest Position The number of shares of a given company that have been sold short and, as of a given date, the loans remain outstanding.

Short Sale The sale of a security thus is not owned by an investor, but rather is borrowed from a broker. The investor eventually repays the broker in kind by purchasing the same security in a subsequent transaction.

Simple Linear Regression (alternatively, **Ordinary**

Least Squares) A statistical model of the relationship between two random variables in which one variable is hypothesized to be linearly related to the other. This relationship is depicted by a regression line which is a straight line, "fitted" to pairs of values of the two variables, so that the sum of the squared random error terms is minimized.

Sinking Fund Periodic payments made by a bond issuer to reduce, in an orderly manner, the amount of outstanding principal on a bond issue over the life of the bond.

Size Effect (alternatively, **Small Firm Effect**) An empirical regularity whereby stock returns appear to differ consistently across the spectrum of market capitalization. Over extended periods of time, smaller capitalization stocks have outperformed larger capitalization stocks on a risk-adjusted basis.

Small Firm Effect See **Size Effect.**

Small Order Execution System (SOES) A computer system associated with NASDAQ that provides for automatic order execution of as many as 1,000 shares.

Soft Dollars Brokerage commissions ostensibly paid for having a brokerage firm execute a trade and indirectly designated, in part, as payment for non-trade-related services rendered.

Special Offering A trade involving a large block of stock on an organized security exchange whereby a number of brokerage firms attempt to execute the order by soliciting offsetting orders from their customers.

Specialist A member of an organized exchange who has two primary functions. First, the specialist maintains an orderly market in assigned securities by acting as a dealer: buying and selling from his or her inventory of securities to offset temporary imbalances in the number of buy and sell orders. Second, the specialist facilitates the execution of limit, stop, and stop limit orders by acting as a broker. This is done by maintaining a limit order book and executing these orders as they are triggered.

Specialist Block Purchase or **Sale** The accommodation of a relatively small block trade by a specialist who buys or sells from his or her inventory at a price negotiated with the seller or buyer.

Specialist's Book See **Limit Order Book.**

Speculative Grade Bonds (alternatively, **Junk Bonds**) Bonds that are not investment grade bonds. Usually, speculative bonds have a BB (Standard & Poor's) or Ba (Moody's) or lower rating.

Speculator An investor in futures contracts whose primary objective is to make a profit from buying and selling these contracts.

Split-Funding A situation in which an institutional investory divides its funds among two or more professional money managers.

Spot Market The market for an asset that involves the immediate exchange of the asset for cash.

Spot Price The purchase price of an asset in the spot market.

Spot Rate The annual yield-to-maturity on a pure-discount security.

Standard Deviation A measure of the dispersion of possible outcomes around the expected outcome of a random variable.

Standard Deviation of the Random Error Term (alternatively, **Residual Standard Deviation**) In the context of simple linear regression, a measure of the dispersion of possible outcomes of the random error term.

Standard Error of Alpha The standard deviation of a security's estimated alpha, as derived from the ex post characteristic line.

Standard Error of Beta The standard deviation of a security's estimated beta, as derived from the ex post characteristic line.

Standardized Unexpected Earnings The difference between a firm's actual earnings over a given period less an estimate of the firm's expected earnings, with this quantity divided by the standard deviation of the firm's previous earnings forecast errors.

Standby Agreement An arrangement between a security issuer and an underwriter as part of a rights offering. The underwriter agrees to purchase at a fixed price all securities not purchased by current stockholders.

Stochastic Process Risk In the context of immunization, the risk that the yield curve will shift in a way that prevents an immunized bond portfolio from producing its expected cash inflows.

Stock Dividend An accounting transaction that distributes stock to existing shareholders in proportion to the number of shares currently owned by the shareholders. A stock dividend entails a transfer from retained earnings to the capital stock account of a dollar amount that is equal to the market value of the distributed stock.

Stock Exchange Automated Quotations (SEAQ) A computer system, similar to NASDAQ, that is used to trade stocks on the London Stock Exchange.

Stock Split Similar to a stock dividend, an accounting transaction that increases the amount of stock held by existing shareholders in proportion to the number of shares currently owned by the shareholders. A stock split entails a reduction in the par value of the corporation's stock and the simultaneous exchange of a multiple number of new shares for each existing share.

Stop Limit Order A trading order that specifies both a stop price and a limit price. If the security's price reaches or passes the stop price, then a limit order is created at the limit price.

Stop Loss Order See **Stop Order.**

Stop Order (alternatively, **Stop Loss Order**) A trading order that specifies a stop price. If the security's price reaches or passes the stop price, then a market order is created.

Stop Price The price specified by an investor when a stop order or a stop limit order is placed that defines the price at which the market order or limit order for the security is to become effective.

Straddle An options strategy that involves buying (or writing) both a call and a put on the same asset, with the options having the same exercise price and expiration date.

Straight Voting System See **Majority Voting System.**

Street Name An arrangement between an investor and a brokerage firm where the investor maintains an account in which the investor's securities are registered in the name of the brokerage firm.

Striking Price See **Exercise Price.**

Strong-Form Market Efficiency A level of market efficiency in which all relevant information, both public and private, is fully and immediately reflected in security prices.

Subordinated Debenture A debenture whose claims, in the event of bankruptcy, are junior to other bonds issued by the firm.

Subscription Price The price at which holders of rights are permitted to purchase shares of stock in a rights offering.

Substitution Swap A type of bond swap where an investor exchanges one bond with a lower yield for another with a higher yield, yet both bonds have essentially the same financial characteristics.

Super Designated Order Turnaround (SuperDot) A set of special procedures established by the New York Stock Exchange to handle routine small trading orders. Through these procedures, participating member firms can route orders directly to the specialist for immediate execution.

Supply-to-Sell Schedule A description of the quantities of a security that an investor is prepared to sell at alternative prices.

Sustainable Earnings The amount of earnings that a firm could pay out each year, with the result that the firm's future earnings neither increase nor decrease.

Syndicate (alternatively, **Purchasing Group**) A group of investment banking organizations that, as part of a security underwriting, are responsible for purchasing the security from the issuer and reselling it to the public.

Synthetic Futures (Synthetic Futures Contract) The creation of a position equivalent to either the purchase of a futures contract by buying a call option and writing a put option on the asset or to the sale of a futures contract by buying a put option and writing a call option on the asset.

Synthetic Put A form of portfolio insurance that emulates the investment outcomes of a put option through the use of a dynamic asset allocation strategy.

Systematic Risk See **Market Risk.**

Takeover An action by an individual or firm to acquire controlling interest in a corporation.

Target Firm A firm that is the subject of a takeover attempt.

Taxable Municipal Bond A municipal bond whose income is fully taxable by the federal government.

Tax-Exempt Bond A security whose income is not taxable by the federal government.

Technical Analysis A form of security analysis that attempts to forecast the movement in the prices of securities based primarily on historical price and volume trends in those securities.

Tender Offer A form of corporate takeover in which a firm or individual offers to buy some or all of the shares of a target firm at a stated price. This offer is publicly advertised and material describing the bid is mailed to the target's stockholders.

Term Bond A bond issue where all of the bonds mature on the same date.

Term Structure The set of yields-to-maturity across bonds that possess different terms-to-maturity, but are similar with respect to other attributes.

Term-to-Maturity The time remaining until a bond's maturity date.

Terminal Wealth The value of an investor's portfolio at the end of a holding period. Equivalently, the investor's initial wealth multiplied times one plus the rate of return earned on the investor's portfolio over the holding period.

Third Market A secondary security market where exchange-listed securities are traded over the counter.

Time Deposit A savings account at a financial institution.

Time Value (Premium) The excess of the market price of an option over its intrinsic value.

Time-Weighted Return A method of measuring the performance of a portfolio over a particular period of time. It is the cumulative compounded rate of return of the portfolio, calculated on each date that a cash flow moves into or out of the portfolio over the performance measurement period.

Timing An aspect of security analysis that entails forecasting the price movements of asset classes relative to one another.

Top-Down Forecasting A sequential approach to security analysis that entails first making forecasts for the economy, then for industries, and finally for individual companies. Each level of forecasts is conditional on the previous level of forecasts made.

Total Risk The standard deviation of the return on a security or portfolio.

Trading Halt A temporary suspension in the trading of a security on an organized exchange.

Trading Post The physical location on the floor of an organized exchange where a specialist in a particular stock is located and where all orders involving the stock must be taken for execution.

Transfer Agent A designated agent of a corporation, usually a bank, which administers the transfer of shares of a corporation's stock between old and new owners.

Treasury Bill A security issued by the U.S. Treasury with a maximum term-to-maturity of one year. Interest and principal are paid only at maturity.

Treasury Bond A security issued by the U.S. Treasury with a term-to-maturity of over seven years. Interest is paid semiannually and principal is returned at maturity.

Treasury Note A security issued by the U.S. Treasury with a term-to-maturity between one and seven years. Interest is paid semiannually and principal is returned at maturity.

Treasury Stock Common stock that has been issued by a corporation and then later purchased by the corporation in the open market or through a tender offer. This stock does not include voting rights or rights to receive dividends and is equivalent economically to unissued stock.

Triple Witching Hour The date when options on individual stocks and market indices, futures on market indices, and options on market index futures expire simultaneously.

Trustee An organization, usually a bank, that serves as the representative of bondholders. The trustee acts to protect the interests of bondholders and facilitates communication between them and the issuer.

Turn-of-the-Month Effect The observation that average stock returns have been abnormally high during a four-day period beginning on the last trading day of the month.

Two-Dollar Broker See **Floor Broker.**

Unbiased Expectations Theory An explanation of the term structure of interest rates. It holds that a forward rate represents the average opinion of the expected future spot rate for the time period in question.

Undermargined Account A margin account in which the actual margin has fallen below the maintenance margin requirement.

Underpriced Security (alternatively, **Undervalued Security**) A security whose expected return is greater than its equilibrium expected return. Equivalently, a security with a positive alpha.

Undervalued Security See **Underpriced Security.**

Underwriter See **Investment Banker.**

Underwriting The process by which investment bankers bring new securities to the primary security market.

Unexpected Rate of Inflation That portion of inflation experienced over a given period of time that was not anticipated by investors.

Unique Risk (alternatively, **Unsystematic Risk**) That part of a security's total risk which is not related to moves in the market portfolio and, hence, can be diversified away.

Unit Investment Trust An unmanaged investment company with a finite life that raises an initial sum of capital from investors and uses the proceeds to purchase a fixed portfolio of securities (typically bonds).

Unrealized Capital Gain (or **Loss**) A capital gain (or loss) on an asset that has not yet been recognized for tax purposes through the sale or exchange of the asset.

Unrestricted Account See **Overmargined Account.**

Unseasoned Offering See **Initial Public Offering.**

Unsystematic Risk See **Unique Risk.**

Upstairs Dealer Market An adjunct to organized exchanges, where block houses that are member firms handle large block trades. The block houses act as both agents and principals, lining up trading partners to take the other side of the block orders.

Up-Tick A trade in a security made at a price higher than the price of the previous trade in that same security.

Value-Weighted Market Index (alternatively, **Capitalization-Weighted Market Index**) A market index in which the contribution of a security to the value of the index is a function of the security's market capitalization.

Variable Rate See **Floating Rate.**

Variance The squared value of the standard deviation.

Variance-Covariance Matrix A table that symmetrically arrays the covariances between a number of random variables. Variances of the random variables lie on the diagonal of the matrix, while covariances between the random variables lie above and below the diagonal.

Variation Margin The amount of cash that an investor must put up to meet a margin call on a futures contract.

Voting Bond A bond that gives its holder a voice in the management of the issuer.

Wash Sale The sale and subsequent purchase of a "substantially identical" security solely for the purpose of generating a tax deductible capital loss.

Weak-Form Market Efficiency A level of market efficiency in which all previous security price data are fully and immediately reflected in current security prices.

Weekend Effect See **Day-of-the-Week Effect.**

White Knight Another firm, favorably inclined toward a target firm's current management, that during the process of a hostile takeover of that corporation agrees to make a better offer to the corporation's stockholders.

Yield The yield-to-maturity of a bond.

Yield Curve A visual representation of the term structure of interest rate.

Yield Spread The difference in the promised yields-to-maturity of two bonds.

Yield Structure The set of yields-to-maturity across bonds differing in terms of a number of attributes. These attributes include term-to-maturity, coupon rate, call provisions, tax status, marketability, and likelihood of default.

Yield-to-Call The yield-to-maturity of a callable bond calculated assuming that the bond is called at the earliest possible time.

Yield-to-Maturity For a particular fixed-income security, the single interest rate (with interest compounded at some specified interval) that, if paid by a bank on the amount invested in the security, would enable the investor to obtain all the payments made by that security. Equivalently, the discount rate that equates the present value of future cash flows from the security to the current market price of the security.

Zero Coupon Bond See **Pure-Discount Security.**

Zero Growth Model (alternatively, **No Growth Model**) A type of dividend discount model in which dividends are assumed to maintain a constant value in perpetuity.

Zero-Plus Tick A trade in a security made at a price equal to that of the previous trade in that security but higher than that of the last trade made in the security at a different price.

Index

A

B

C

D

E

G

H

J

K

L

M

N

O

P

Q

R

S

U

V

W

Y

Z